Taxation, Valuation & Investment Strategies in Volatile Markets

EDITED BY

David W. Chodikoff & James L. Horvath

CARSWELL®

A cataloguing record for this publication is available from Library and Archives Canada.

ISBN 978-0-7798-2797-8

Composition: Computer Composition of Canada Inc.

Printed in the United States by Thomson Reuters.

THOMSON REUTERS

CARSWELL, A DIVISION OF THOMSON REUTERS CANADA LIMITED

One Corporate Plaza
2075 Kennedy Road
Toronto, Ontario
M1T 3V4

Customer Relations
Toronto 1-416-609-3800
Elsewhere in Canada/U.S. 1-800-387-5164
Fax: 1-416-298-5082
www.carswell.com
Online www.carswell.com/email

Table of Contents

Acknowledgements

Since coming to the world of the private practice of law five years ago, David has been fortunate to have the exceptional assistance of Filomena Mendonca. Filomena, or "Fil" as she prefers to be called, has already endured the pressures of captaining the administrative work involved in bringing a major book to publication. As our "Chief of Staff", Fil played a pivotal role in bringing about the publication of our previous work, *Taxation and Valuation of Technology* (2008). Once again, Fil has played a key role in the administration and co-ordination of bringing about this publication. We are truly indebted to Fil for her sense of humour and outstanding level of professionalism. We also thank Pat Barnes and Savio Dias of Deloitte & Touche LLP for their many hours of assistance on this and past book projects.

In a book of this complexity and size, there are lots of people to thank. Many work in different departments at Miller Thomson LLP. For the constant support of research and verification, we are sincerely grateful to our entire Miller Thomson library staff: Ines Freeman, Arlene Mazur, Erin Murphy, Dian Galita, Julia Luke, Jennifer Bonomo, Elizabeth Szmit, and Fernanda Leite.

We are equally indebted to an unrivalled, dedicated group of readers who assisted us in our editorial functions. We would have stumbled far worse, without the outstanding and able assistance of Brittany Benning. The commentary and input from Sabina Mexis of Torkin Manes LLP, Andrew Valentine, Tarsem Basraon and Patrick Déziel, all of Miller Thomson LLP, and Kimberly Horvath of Deloitte & Touche LLP were always insightful and of great value. To all of our drafts and proofs readers, our sincere gratitude for your contributions.

Speaking of contributions, this book would not have been possible without the unselfish efforts of our many contributors. We thank them for the quality of their individual efforts and the patience that they have demonstrated throughout the production process.

As some of our readers would know from our previous works, and this book is no exception, all proceeds from the contributors' portion of this book will be donated to the Canadian Cancer Society.

We also want to thank the staff at Thomson Reuters and, in particular, the editorial assistance of Emma Dobell, the leadership of Fred Glady, and the technical support of Heather Cant.

To our many business colleagues and friends, we also give our thanks for your unwavering support.

David W. Chodikoff
James L. Horvath
June, 2010

Foreword

A year ago, the Oracle of Omaha, Warren Buffett, told us that the economy had fallen off a cliff. Real estate in some regions of the United States and stock markets around the world were in free fall. The Dow Jones Industrial Average and the S&P/TSX Composite hit their lows in March of 2009, falling some 50 per cent from their highs of a year earlier. But the Oracle is also reputed to have said, "Be fearful when others are greedy and greedy when others are fearful". As of the time that I write this foreword, the same indexes have since rebounded by about 50 per cent (albeit from a lower base). We live in a time of volatile markets.

It is hard to think of a work that could be more timely than *Taxation, Valuation & Investment Strategies in Volatile Markets*. This has been an enormous project covering a vast array of topics. The articles are contributed from Canadian experts and those from a number of other countries and continents. Insights are provided from a global perspective, which again is timely in today's globalized economy.

After the Introduction, the Taxation section of the work consists of 12 chapters commencing with a judicial perspective of tax litigation in current times. The section then goes on to deal with tax planning. Estate freezes assume asset values will continuously increase. How can you preserve losses within affiliated companies? What are the tax implications of debt forgiveness? These are a few of the issues outlined in this section that arise in an economic downturn and that have tax implications.

The Valuation section of the volume consists of 27 chapters. Market based approaches to valuation are canvassed. The difficult questions of valuing intellectual property and technology are explored. Canadian, American, European, South American, Chinese and other experiences and approaches to valuations are then undertaken. The thorny issue of transfer pricing is examined. And coming back to today's economy, valuation difficulties in falling and volatile markets are addressed. It is difficult to conceive that anything has been left out.

The third section of the book is entitled, "Investment Strategies" and consists of 14 chapters. The importance of understanding and assessing risk and developing investment strategies commensurate with the investor's tolerance for risk is all the more important in turbulent financial times. Relying on portfolio theory, asset allocation strategies, and approaches to investment tax planning, the chapters in this section offer a sober assessment of the current state of markets and a number of basic investment strategies.

The last section deals with Corporate Fraud. International business is vulnerable to corruption in certain parts of the world. Evaluating this risk is considered in the first chapter of this section, while fraud detection for business valuators is addressed in the second. These are vitally important matters in a globalized economy.

Taxation, Valuation & Investment Strategies in Volatile Markets will make a most important and up-to-date contribution to the existing literature in these transformative economic times.

The authors who have participated in this effort are a jurist, practitioners, and academics with expertise and experience in their respective fields and their work will be of great value to all who have an interest in these subjects.

I want to express my thanks to those who have contributed to this important work for sharing their insights with us. I commend the co-editors for once again producing a work of immense value. The time and effort expended by the authors and co-editors is obvious and all readers owe them a debt of gratitude.

Justice Marshall Rothstein
Ottawa
January, 2010

Preface

In today's global marketplace, the opportunity for price volatility has increased exponentially. Sometimes financial or other crises affect a specific industry, country, or region and sometimes have an impact that is global in scope. The volatile markets of today result from a variety of factors, including increased financial market integration, rapid transaction execution, designer investments, and complicated models designed to measure, mitigate, manage, and make "mainstreet" all forms of risks. The current situation is exacerbated by a massive U.S. consumer debt burden and rapidly increasing government deficits and debt designed to shore up the demand side of the price equation and provide market order in an environment of inconsistent liquidity. The current volatility and the crisis of confidence spread quickly around the world.

For years, market pundits have been warning of a day of reckoning when the credit bubble would pop and there would be both financial chaos and ruin. Now into the second year of the worst financial crisis of our generation (and somewhat similar to the Great Depression), some see hope on the horizon as the billions of dollars pumped into the global economy by governments around the world over the past year seems to have temporarily, if not permanently, stopped the spiral into the economic abyss. The fact remains that no one knows whether we are in the midst of a "V", "W", or "" shaped recovery or something else. There is only one truth: the markets are volatile and serious damage that will take years to recover from has been inflicted upon us all.

The markets are hoping for a recovery in 2010-2011 but it is more likely that the world will experience at least several years of slow, grinding, sporadic, and uncertain growth. As in earlier financial crises, the stock markets have been extremely unpredictable, with violent price swings (the worst to date being the US$1-trillion May 6, 2010 "flash crash" when the Dow Jones Industrial Average dropped almost 1000 points (approximately a 10% drop) intraday, the majority of which occurred over a five-minute period) challenging the conventional methodologies used in business valuations of both publicly-traded and private companies. The importance of liquidity in establishing "fair value" has been laid bare. For many companies, projections are made with limited visibility and certainty. When the ability to identify, measure, and effectively forecast revenue and earnings is combined with fluid and difficult to quantify risks, and taking place in an environment of sporadic and unreliable liquidity, the presence of significant volatility should be of no real surprise.

Market volatility and economic declines and rebounds can be times of significant opportunity. Faced with declining and unpredictable revenues, many firms survive by becoming lean and efficient. Such markets often present significant wealth-building opportunities, especially for those who see the value inherent in underpriced and sometimes distressed assets and are in a position to select the best opportunities to add value as they arise. This is also a time of heightened need for due diligence because of the risk that dead or damaged assets will linger on the books longer than is justifiable.

We want to thank the various experts gathered in this book for their willingness to share their thoughts about issues, opportunities, and possible solutions to business valuation challenges faced during times of volatile markets, and for providing their professional insights and advice as applied to the current financial market scenarios or to some as-yet-unforeseen volatile market.

This is our third book project as co-editors. We are proud of the talent that we have amassed to give the reader something to think about. What impresses us about all of our contributors is their willingness to share some thoughts about what you can do, or at least think about, during these volatile times. This book reflects the personal views of the authors and not necessarily the opinion of the firms they work for. The authors are not liable for any damage arising from any viewpoint, application of theory, or any other material presented in this book.

The subjects of the chapters are divided into four primary categories: substantive tax issues, valuation topics of interest in a global economy experiencing a downturn, investment ideas or strategies in volatile markets, and two chapters on the important and growing problem of corporate fraud. We are certain that you will find some valuable information contained in the pages of this book.

Finally, we are indeed indebted to all of our contributors because, as with our previous works *Taxation and Valuation of Technology* (Irwin Law, 2008) and *Advocacy and Taxation in Canada* (Irwin Law, 2004), they have each graciously agreed to donate their share of the royalties to the Canadian Cancer Society.

As we continue to work on publications, we welcome any comments, suggestions, and observations you might have. You can contact us either by email or phone at:

David Chodikoff: DChodikoff@MillerThomson.com +1 (416) 595-8626

Jim Horvath: JimHorvath@ValuQuest.ca +1 (416) 844-4422

David W. Chodikoff
James L. Horvath
June 2010

DEDICATION

To my best friend and wife, Tanya, and my son, Daniel, the loves of my life.

David W. Chodikoff

In loving memory of Dad, Eugene Horvath.

To my mother, Jeanette, and my family – Natalie, Michael, Jeffrey, Kimberly, Edward, Janet, and Doug.

Many thanks to my colleauges John Anderson and Mark Keuleman, who for the past 20 years have provided me with their thoughtful insights and perspectives on valuation issues.

James L. Horvath

*****

To the many who have been afflicted with cancer and survived, thank you for showing the rest of us the true meaning of bravery.

To the many who have lost their lives to cancer, your families and friends have not forgotten you. You are always remembered.

To the future, we are working, each in our own way, to bring an end to this disease.

All net royalties from the sale of this book will be donated to cancer education and research.

David & Jim
June 2010

Volatile Times: Challenges and Opportunities

James L. Horvath

Past Lessons

Every now and then the world is visited by one of these delusive seasons, when the credit system, as it is called, expands to full luxuriance, everybody trusts everybody; a bad debt is a thing unheard of; the broad way to certain and sudden wealth lies plain and open; and men are tempted to dash forward boldly, from the facility of borrowing.

Washington Irving
"The Great Mississippi Bubble [of 1719–1720]:
'A Time of Unexampled Prosperity'" in *The Crayon Papers*
(New York: John B. Alden, 1886), p. 41.

Volatile markets pose significant challenges for businesses, accountants, business valuators, investors and many others. Periods of extreme volatility are not unusual. They often begin with a bursting bubble: a bubble being a time when many investors buy at knowingly high prices in the hopes of selling at yet even higher prices, followed by a fear-driven stock market price drop, the quick move from certainty to uncertainty, a recessionary period, numerous economic shocks, periods of uncertainty containing hopes of an imminent revival, revival of investor confidence, overreaction to signs of improvement, periods of stagnation, stock prices at times retrenching or treading water, complacent attitudes, conflicting economic reports deflating some of the optimism, and the fear of another calamity. Sometimes they are isolated to a certain industry, country or region. Unlike many volatile markets or times, the current financial crisis, which began in mid- to late-

2008 and continues to date (May 2010), has had a significant global impact, affecting almost all industries and the lives of billions of people.

In mid-April 2010, the Dow closed above 11,000, this being a significant comeback. From a high of 14,164 on Oct. 9, 2007, the Dow declined about 54 per cent before hitting a low of 6,547 on March 9, 2009. But the volatility continued with the Dow closing below 10,000 in May and noodling around in June 2010. The global financial crisis has witnessed the lightning speed at which fear and volatility spread through the global stock markets, and the subsequent market turmoil created. This has been a period of significant volatility which is expected to continue for years to come, albeit hopefully at subsiding levels. However, investors are easily rattled and there are always many events unfolding which create fear and volatility such as fraud charges brought against Goldman Sachs, Dubai's debt meltdown, Greece's mushrooming budget deficit, the risk of nation states defaulting, the increase in the unemployment rate, oil prices and inventory levels, changes in industrial production, changes in housing starts, changes in retail sales, political intervention, speculation, whispered earnings expectations, short selling, changes in company earnings and expectations, and market-influencing unexpected events.

The global financial crisis and dramatic decline in the trading value of stocks and residential and commercial real estate in the United States have provided a challenge to the new fair value accounting rules. In late 2008 and 2009, securities regulators, accountants, and business valuators struggled to gain consensus on the appropriate impairment tests and valuation methods to apply. Many questioned whether they should be fair-valuing assets at market prices in a non-market, when fear has driven transaction prices to seemingly unrealistically low values.

This book is part of a two-book project put together largely to address a number of taxation, valuation, investment and other financial-related issues faced in volatile markets. The valuation related chapters of this book were published by Thomson Carswell in 2010 in *Valuing a Business in Volatile Markets* (edited by me [James L. Horvath]), which is the third book in a series that also includes *Taxation & Valuation of Technology* (Chodikoff & Horvath, eds., Irwin Law, 2008) and *Advocacy and Taxation in Canada* (Chodikoff & Horvath, eds., Irwin Law, 2004).

The book is divided into four sections. The first group of chapters, being chapters 2 through 13, covers a wide spectrum of tax issues, opportunities, and possible strategies during turbulent times. The second covers a number of valuation methods and issues typically faced by business valuators and businesses requiring valuations. This section has a global reach, with a multidisciplinary group of contributors from Asia, Asia-Pacific, Europe, North America, and South America addressing country-specific, regional, and global valuation issues and challenges encountered in volatile markets. The third group of chapters (41 to 54) looks at investment strategies. Certainly, volatile markets often deliver significant wealth building opportunities. Finally, the last section (chapters 55 and 56) discusses the importance of fraud awareness in our increasingly complex business world. During volatile and economically depressed times, the risk and incidence of fraud are heightened.

In Chapter 2, the Hon. Justice Gerald Rip presents an overview of tax litigation, particularly towards streamlining the practices and procedures to reflect the restrictions of today's economy. He outlines how the Tax Court has recently amended many of its Rules and the challenges faced to continue simplifying its methods towards affordability and efficiency.

Chapter 3 provides the reader with an overview of the Federal debt collection regime under the *Income Tax Act*. David Chodikoff and Andrew Valentine examine the steps that the CRA may take to collect on tax debts, as well as the restrictions of their powers. They outline the fundamental options available to tax debtors in response to the enforcement actions by the CRA. Each debt collection situation is unique. But, the authors show that with creativity and the will to persevere, a taxpayer can survive the onslaught of the CRA's collection activities.

In Chapter 4, the issue of estate freezing is discussed. The authors, Martin Rochwerg and Krystle Ng-A-Mann, explore the concept of estate freezing and the ways in which to modify an estate freeze, such as re-freezing, melting, and thawing. This chapter concludes with a discussion of the CRA administrative policy with respect to estate re-freezing, and an overview of the case law affecting estate freezing.

As the economic cycles of the country move from bust to boom, tax planners will be able to capitalize on unrealized losses within the corporate group. The utilization and preservation of tax losses will continue to be an area that, while fraught with many pitfalls, can yield great opportunities. Chapter 5 outlines the main loss utilization techniques and provides an overview of strategies and challenges of how to make use of the losses within the corporate group, while avoiding inefficiency and underutilization.

Chapter 6 addresses the issue of how to reduce the cost of innovation during times of economic turbulence such as we are facing today. The chapter covers the eligibility rules and the benefits available from various federal and provincial incentive programs for performing research and development in Canada. These incentives come in a variety of forms including grants, tax credits, and tax credits refundable in cash. Also discussed is the impact of corporate structuring initiatives such as acquisitions of control, amalgamations, and windups. These transactions are reviewed to explain the impact they may have on the value and utilization of the credits. Finally, the international environment for research and development incentives is reviewed. In this section, the reader is provided factors to consider when comparing incentive programs available in many countries.

Dalton Albrecht outlines in chapter 7 the implications of GST for a company and its partners, and how the continued collecting and remitting of GST is crucial to a company's financial viability in a difficult economic environment, while in Chapter 8, David Chodikoff presents a discussion of banking secrecy laws and the financial challenges faced by Canadian taxpayers holding overseas accounts.

Chapter 9 outlines the recognition of life insurance as an asset. George Goldsmith explains this important tool for financial planners and how it is an essential element for consideration in any investment portfolio. Chapter 10 continues the theme of strategic financial planning, with a summary of recommended tax strategies for owners/managers of small- to medium-sized enterprises, which can improve cash flow and result in immediate and significant cash flow savings to the enterprise.

Chapters 11 and 12 discuss the topic of debt forgiveness. With the current economic downturn in the global economy, this topic is back in the forefront. The authors in each chapter explain how familiarity with and a full understanding of the debt forgiveness regime under the *Income Tax Act* can provide planning opportunities and help financially troubled companies minimize tax burdens and maintain valuable tax attributes necessary for survival.

In chapter 13, Nick Sauro and Dominic Belley provide a summary of the *Valiant Cleaning Technology* case, a landmark case in jurisprudence which now provides the circumstances where it is appropriate to claim loan losses to a subsidiary as non-capital expenditures. Given the globalization of the Canadian economy, this is a precedent setting case which redefines the previously held presumption that advances to a subsidiary would only be held on the account of capital.

Chapters 14 through Chapter 21 give an overview of general valuation methods and issues, a discussion of intellectual property valuation issues by Robert Reilly (in chapter 16) and specific technology valuation methods. In chapter 18, Péter Harbula discusses the equity risk premium and how the economy's volatility should be reflected in the determination. This determination is particularly complicated in volatile markets where the emotions of greed (*e.g.*, investors buying shares because they believe or hope the share price will continue to rise) and fear (investors selling in the fear that the downward slide in share prices will continue) often cause stock prices to fluctuate dramatically and to trade at prices significantly in excess or below *pro rata* intrinsic value. For example, in late February to early March 2009, the shares of many publicly-traded companies were trading at fear-motivated lows. Volatile market valuation issues and critical changes affecting valuations are discussed further by John Barton (in chapter 19) and Richard Wise (chapter 20).

Economic downturns and volatile markets often create invaluable opportunities for astute investors to capitalize on the inherent intrinsic value and reorganization potential of some distressed companies. Chapter 21 looks at many of the issues and value drivers that should be taken into account when valuing a financially distressed business.

In chapters 22 through chapter 27, we take a spin around the globe: International Financial Reporting Standards (IFRS) valuation issues being faced in Australia; the valuation of businesses in the emerging, changing, and volatile markets in central and eastern Europe; valuation issues faced during Argentina's 2002 financial crisis; business valuation practices and challenges in China; the trend toward developing international valuation standards; and valuation considerations, issues, and methods when valuing businesses in emerging markets.

In many cases, tomorrow's products and services start with today's ideas. Business valuators are often presented with an idea that the prospective client says is worth millions and sometimes hundreds of millions of dollars. In my own case, I generally conclude that the idea itself has minimal fair market value, if any. In a recessionary, volatile environment, such as in late 2008 through 2009, many investors were reverting to placing more weight on the value of tangible assets; thus ideas were of little value *per se*. In chapter 28, we look at many of the major considerations valuators and businesses face when trying to place a value on an idea and, more importantly, the ability to create value.

In chapter 29, Richard De Rose comments on a number of appraisal cases decided under s. 262 of the Delaware *General Corporation Law*. These cases provide valuable insights as to the Delaware judiciary's perspective on issues of valuation methodology. De Rose offers suggestions on how the approaches to valuation employed by the Delaware courts might apply in other contexts (*e.g.*, the "fair price" component of the "entire fairness" standard).

As previously noted, when valuing business interests in volatile times, asset-based approaches are used more often. From a Canadian perspective in chapter 30, Steve Z. Ranot discusses the methods of valuing lost tax shields and the importance of using the expertise of tax professionals.

Chapters 31 through chapter 33 are devoted to transfer-pricing issues. Transfer pricing is one of the most rapidly expanding areas of valuation analysis. The increase in globalization that has occurred over the past several decades has resulted in an ever-increasing number of multinational entities that maintain operations in multiple jurisdictions. The various operations or functions of the larger corporate entity are often segregated and assigned to a specific country. Intra-company transfers between various functions of a larger corporate entity, and the non-arm's length "value" assigned to these goods and services, are classified as transfer pricing. Fundamentally, such transfer pricing is a valuation issue. The process of measuring the appropriate risk/return profile of an individual tangible or intangible asset, a grouping of assets in the form of a specialized business function or the entire corporate entity is essentially the same; namely, determining what cash flow is attributable to that specific investment and how much risk is associated with its realization.

Transfer pricing is by definition a non-arm's length transaction that assigns value to the goods and/or services being transferred within the same corporation. The measurement of this transfer value and what is considered a market rate are a subset of the broader exercise of valuing an entire company. Normalizations or market value adjustments are central to any valuation exercise, be it transfer pricing, the allocation of corporate costs or goodwill across subsidiary operations, or adjusting related-party financings. A business valuation will seek to adjust the entity's operations to reflect an arm's length perspective from each individual transaction through to the overall value of the corporate entity.

Fundamentally, valuations are an exercise in measuring the market value of an asset or group of assets to reflect what they can return in the form of production when optimally operated in an arm's length fashion. As transfer pricing deals with the pricing assigned to assets transferred between related parties, it is critical that any adjustments or opinions relating to appropriate "pricing" or "returns" *vis-à-vis* transfer pricing are consistent with a broader valuation analysis of the entire corporate entity. Inconsistent measurement of risks and value creates questions for a variety of third-party interests, such as tax regimes from any of the company's governing jurisdictions, current bond holders and investors with claims to specific operations or assets or arm's length parties considering a possible acquisition of all or part of the operations. Any analysis of the variables that drive the value of business must be internally consistent if they are to be considered well-reasoned and accurate.

In chapter 34, David Chodikoff and Tarsem Basraon give us the benefit of their years of practising law, preparing experts for trial, and testing their credibility through cross-examinations. Although the comments are given from a Canadian court perspective, much of the advice is applicable to those about to give evidence at a trial in any country. Chapters 35 and 36 cover a broad range of valuation topics and issues through practice tips and essays. Chapter 36 also has a global reach, with contributing authors from six countries.

During recessionary times, governments often try to stimulate their economies through infrastructure spending. Shortly after the start of the current global financial crisis, many governments implemented infrastructure spending measures to boost their economies. Such spending generally has a medium- to long-term impact, since the typical infrastructure project has a three- to five-year life. In chapter 37, Rick Ellsworth discusses the investment characteristics of infrastructure assets and provides guidance on appropriate valuation methods.

Chapters 38 and 39 address the valuation of real estate and machinery and equipment. Purchase-price allocations and the adoption by most nations of IFRS have increased the need for valuing interests in land, buildings, and machinery and equipment. With chapter 40, the valuation section concludes with a comprehensive business valuation questionnaire. It is designed to assist in collecting information for analysis and upon which a value judgment can be based. Since no two businesses are identical, it is impossible to develop a single questionnaire or checklist that will apply in every case. It is, however, possible to produce a general guide to the valuation process. The questionnaire included in chapter 40 is intended as a guide and not meant to be exhaustive. It is applicable to businesses of various sizes and operating in a variety of industries.

Chapter 41 looks at exit strategies in volatile markets. Since it is generally difficult to get top dollar in a recessionary climate, it is important to have a well-developed exit strategy. Valuation analysis of transactions occurring in recessionary markets should take into account that the transaction prices are not necessarily indicative of fair market value but, in many cases, are only valid in a non-market.

The focus of chapter 42 is to provide a simple strategy illustrating how an investment may be structured to minimize losses and maximize potential profits. The authors provide a quick overview of the origins of money, fundamental investment vehicles, and various funds, before discussing portfolio structuring, protection, and value at risk.

In chapter 43, Ronald Rodgers and John Kimpton focus on two investment strategies, guaranteed insured annuity (GRA) and guranteed estate multiplier (GEM), that are vehicles for providing low risk and reasonable return alternatives in these uncertain times. They discuss the benefits of and strategies for preserving capital for the investor.

In chapter 44, Peter Jarman reviews the recent approach to real estate investment, and the advantages and risks of including real estate in an investment portfolio.

In recent years restructuring has become even more complex due to globalization, increased capital structure sophistication (including creative, and often opaque, financial instruments), and organizational evolution. In chapter 45, Ryan Brain and Huey Lee explore these factors to explain how they contribute to the growing complexity of both formal and informal restructuring proceedings.

When Shaun Darchiville first entered the investment industry during the summer of 1987, he didn't realize how much would change in the following three months and how much would continue to change over the following 22 years. In the midst of these changes, people lost sight of the core fundamentals that, to him, had never changed. In this chapter, Shaun notes that the themes of market volatility, unscrupulous activity, geopolitical influences, and limited market oversight are recurring rather than one-off isolated events. As part of the valuation process, the valuator looks at general economic and industry conditions. This is especially important during volatile times, when there tends to be a greater number of business-world changes taking place – many of them previously unexpected–and a heightened risk of yet unimagined changes. In chapter 47 Maneesh Mehta summarizes the 2008–2009 financial crisis. He provides an historical context and understanding of this crisis and looks to our learning from past crises and fundamental principles to provide some useful guidelines. Of particular interest, to anyone estimating the value of a business, is the understanding of the impact of changes on the value of a business. This value change results largely from changes in the key value drivers, the impact on projected future earnings, and changes in the ability to finance a business. Then, in chapter 48, Maneesh teams up with Jacob Hirsh (of the Department of Psychology, University of Toronto) to give a perspective on how the health of a human economy is directly linked to the diversity of roles within it. Thus, a loss of diversity over the past 30 years has constrained our thinking and damaged the health of the economy.

Chapter 49 outlines the numerous and relatively straightforward tax strategies that an individual investor can use to navigate the complex investment world and to help generate pre-tax returns to be able to meet financial goals.

Eli Swirsky and Sam Cohen (chapter 50) provide valuable insight into the use of commercial real estate as an investment tool. They show that a disciplined approach to real estate investment, coupled with realistic and achievable goals, can reap continued benefits for the astute investor.

In chapter 51, William Zinger presents a personal account of his experience in the business sector. He explains how entrepreneurial spirit and a passion for success, along with a healthy dose of optimism, can benefit any business and enable it to profit during good times and face the challenges of an unpredictable marketplace.

Greg Knudsen presents an in-depth analysis of the hedge fund industry in chapter 52, and explains the strategic benefits of hedge fund investing.

In chapter 53, Jordan Waldman outlines some of the methods available for corporate asset transfer. He explains the advantages in offsetting or eliminating tax obligations on both business income and capital gains to provide business owners with long-term, stable, and tax-deferred investment growth.

Chapter 54 explores the recent shift back to attracting and reinforcing the human assets of a firm or business. Jon Cooper explains the importance of strategic development initiatives with respect to human resource strategies, in order to improve, grow, and meet the challenges ahead.

Finally, as pointed out in chapters 55 and 56, business valuators should be alert to the possibility of fraud and that someone may be "cooking the books". The risk of financial statement fraud is especially high during a slowing economy, with increased pressures on companies to meet, and even exceed, short-term performance goals or to demonstrate that shareholder value is improving. As pointed out by Gary Moulton and Peter Dent, despite the stringent *Sarbanes-Oxley Act* ("SOX"), enacted to ensure publicly traded companies have robust fraud prevention and detection protocols, fraud and other business crimes continue to be a major problem and the number of instances generally increases in a deteriorating economic environment. Business valuators and, in particular, those also skilled in forensic accounting, should also do their part by being able to identify the common fraud schemes.

Tax Litigation in Today's Economy

The Honourable Chief Justice Gerald L. Rip*

Courts cannot ignore what is taking place outside the courtroom. Today we are experiencing an economic recession, if not a depression, that is affecting the economic well-being of most Canadians.

Compounded to our current economic situation is the fact that during the past 20 years, at least, the cost of appearing in court has skyrocketed. While wealthier Canadians can afford the costs of a lawyer and lower income Canadians are supported, to some extent, by their provincial aid programs, members of the large middle class often have to forego enforcing their rights because they simply cannot afford a lawyer.

I have been told that no one should even consider engaging the services of experienced counsel to fight a tax appeal from the objection level to court unless the amount of tax in dispute is in six figures. As a result, we are seeing more and more taxpayers representing themselves or represented by family friends and laymen. In some appeals, these people are successful; in most they are not. They are usually successful when they produce evidence no one thought of considering before trial, either in the assessment or appeal stages. Frequently, this type of information was thought not important by the taxpayer and often comes to light as an afterthought by the taxpayer or the representative or because the judge may have asked a rather obvious question to the taxpayer that the latter never thought of. In some cases, the taxpayer and the Canada Revenue Agency auditor may have had a personality conflict and the taxpayer does not want to give any information to anyone until he or she is in court.

---

* Editor's note: We are truly grateful for the Chief Justice's work. It is an important contribution to the literature on the subject.

As Tax Court judges, we want to make sure that each taxpayer has been assessed tax in accordance with the law. When a taxpayer who, from the pleadings, appears to have a good case does not show up at trial because he or she cannot afford the cost of a lawyer or who, in a complicated case, appears without benefit of counsel because he or she cannot afford a lawyer, there is obviously something wrong with the system.

Also, when the appeal from the assessment takes place, we want it to proceed effectively without any delay. Delay means money. It appears to me that trials are getting longer. While I may have heard, perhaps, four informal trials in one day 20 years ago, today I would probably hear two and, if lucky, three appeals in a day. The number of cases and the complexity of cases all influence the delay in a taxpayer having his or her appeal heard, as well as the overall cost of the litigation.

Statistics

It may help to note the number of appeals to the Tax Court that were filed in 2008 and were still active (as of January 1, 2009):

Income Tax	*Filed*	*Still Active*
General Procedure	1188	1135
Informal Procedure	1446	1117
GST		
General Procedure	185	176
Informal Procedure	286	236
Employment Insurance	429	313
Canada Pension Plan	218	176
Miscellaneous	4	2

From the time an appeal (Income Tax and GST) is filed to the time it is heard, it takes, on the average, eight months in an Informal Procedure appeal and 20 months for a General Procedure appeal.

In 2008, 53 General Procedure income tax appeals filed were closed by the end of the year. Twenty-four appeals were consented to prior to hearing, seven appeals were quashed or dismissed, and 22 appeals were withdrawn. For the same reasons, 329 income tax appeals under the Informal Procedure and other statutes filed in 2008 were closed before year end.

During 2008, the Tax Court scheduled for hearing 902 General Procedure appeals and 2,276 Informal Procedure appeals from income tax assessments. Of those appeals, 452 were not heard either because they were settled before hearing or were adjourned. Some parties in General Procedure appeals requested pre-trial settlement conferences which delayed trial.

A new challenge to the Court is groups of appeals, that is, appeals by 10 or more taxpayers concerning a single issue. For example, multiple parties may have "invested" in a tax avoidance transaction and the fisc has disallowed any deduction of income arising from the investment. There are approximately 44 groups of appeals currently filed. We have, for example, one group of 466 appellants and another group of approximately 1,200 appellants. Rather than hear the appeal of each taxpayer separately, the Court would prefer to hear only one appeal and all the investors be bound by the decision of the Court for that one trial.

The Court, the Bench and Bar, and the Rules Committee of the Court are reviewing whether these types of cases can be heard more efficiently as class actions. We are considering whether section 174 of the *Income Tax Act* can apply to such cases.[1] This review is still in its initial stage.

We are attempting to improve our services in both the Informal and General Procedures in order to bring the Canadian public more efficient, and ideally a less costly, court experience.

Informal Procedure

The Tax Court will be testing pre-trial conferences in Informal Procedure appeals. The participants will include the taxpayer and his representative, if he or she has one, and a lawyer from the Department of Justice as well as a judge. These conferences will be in person or by conference call. Hopefully, this will solve three immediate problems.

Problem one is that trials often take too long. It is hoped that a pre-trial conference could help shorten a trial. The next two problems are related to the time it takes to hold a trial.

---

1 Section 174 reads as follows:

Where the Minister is of the opinion that a question of law, fact or mixed law and fact arising out of one and the same transaction or occurrence or series of transactions or occurrences is common to assessments or proposed assessments in respect of two or more taxpayers, the Minister may apply to the Tax Court of Canada for a determination of the question.

The second problem is that a self-represented taxpayer frequently appears in Court without a clue of what he or she has to prove to win the appeal. Often the taxpayer relies on court procedure that he or she sees on television lawyer programs. A pre-trial conference, which may be held by telephone, will first of all permit the judge – who, of course, will not hear the particular appeal – to determine what satisfaction the taxpayer wants from the court and make sure that the Tax Court is the right forum for the taxpayer. Next, the judge can explain to the taxpayer what the taxpayer must do if he or she wants to succeed. The judge can also indicate to both parties their chances of success and if the appeal has potential to settle. The parties then can discuss any settlement proposals. If the case goes to trial, the judge could inform the taxpayer what evidence may be required.

In Informal Procedure appeals, it is not infrequent for the appellant to appear in court without documents and without the knowledge that he or she can subpoena reluctant witnesses. Sometimes a taxpayer appeals because he or she believes – and the taxpayer may often be right – that nobody at the Canada Revenue Agency really considered his or her position prior to assessment or at the objection level. The taxpayer simply wants someone – in this case a judge – to hear his or her complaint. It is not uncommon for a taxpayer to tell a judge after a trial that even though the taxpayer lost, at least he or she finally got a fair hearing.

A third problem it is hoped a pre-trial will solve is the late date the Canada Revenue Agency sends the scheduled appeal files to the Department of Justice. I understand that not infrequently the files arrive as little as two weeks before trial. And then the file must be assigned to a lawyer to attend at the appeal. This does not give much time to the lawyer to review the file, determine the merits of the Minister's position, and get in touch with the appellant. Indeed, there is often no time to get in touch with the taxpayer and discuss settlement. What is happening is that settlements, if they are made, are often made at the eleventh hour. As a result of late settlements, the settled appeals are struck from the Court docket and the judge and the court staff are left with an empty courtroom and no appeals to hear for a half day or longer. If the appeals were settled earlier, other appeals could be put in their place on the docket, thus expediting appeals and saving costs of administering justice.

A pre-trial conference in the Informal Procedure will force the Canada Revenue Agency to forward files to the Department of Justice at a much earlier date and permit the lawyers to deal with the files in advance of the hearing.

There is at least one other thing that can be done to improve Informal Procedure Appeals: Crown pleadings, the reply to the notice of appeal, ought to be drafted by lawyers and not laymen. I have seen a notice of appeal of six or seven lines met by a reply of 10 to 15 pages. Often, these 15 pages are full of irrelevant facts and allegations that do nothing to help the Court, nothing to advance the case, but probably intimidate the poor unsophisticated taxpayer. A competent experienced draftsman would keep the reply simple and understandable. This is not being done now. As a result, time is taken at trial with the judge explaining to the self-represented appellant what the Minister's position is, notwithstanding the verbiage of the reply; again, a costly waste of time for the administration of justice.

General Procedure

General Procedure appeals can be made more efficient if counsel put their minds to it. This has to do with pleadings, discovery, motions, and the trial itself.

Pleadings

With respect to pleadings, as in the Informal Procedure, they are frequently too long, containing a pillowcase full of facts, both relevant and irrelevant, as well as a mixture of facts and law. This is particularly the case in replies to notices of appeals where the assumptions contain material and immaterial facts and then, at trial, as my colleague Bowie J. declared in *Foss v. The Queen*,[2] respondent's counsel takes the position that every fact that is pleaded to has been assumed by the Minister in assessing or confirming the assessment and every conclusion of mixed fact and law included in the pleadings as an assumption becomes a fact for purposes of trial, unless the appellant can disprove the particular fact. This is a distortion of what was decided in *R. v. Anderson Logging Co.*[3] and *Johnston v. M.N.R.*[4]

Tax litigation is not unlike ordinary civil litigation. In both it is the person who prosecutes the litigation, the appellant or the plaintiff, who, in most circumstances, has the burden of proof. The respondent or the defendant should recognize this and not pursue relentlessly the mantra in pleadings and at trial that the taxpayer has the onus.

---

2 2007 TCC 201, 2007 CarswellNat 797, [2007] 4 C.T.C. 2024, 2007 D.T.C. 650.

3 (1924), 1924 CarswellBC 105, [1917-27] C.T.C. 198, 52 D.T.C. 1209 (S.C.C.), appeal dismissed (1925), 1925 CarswellBC 104, 52 D.T.C. 1215, [1917-27] C.T.C. 210 (B.C. P.C.).

4 [1948] S.C.R. 486, 3 D.T.C. 1182, [1948] C.T.C. 195, 1948 CarswellNat 26.

Lawyers ought not to forget the purpose of pleadings. As my confrère Bowie J. wrote in *Foss*,

> the purpose of pleadings is to define the issues between the parties for the purposes of discovery, both documentary and testamentary, and trial. That requires no more than a statement of the precise findings of fact that underpin the assessment. It is potentially prejudicial to the appellant to plead more – certainly to plead more by way of assumptions of fact. The appellant is, of course, entitled to particulars of the evidence that the Crown intends to lead at trial, but these are properly obtained on discovery, not disguised as material facts as to which the Crown at trial may claim a presumption of truth.

Motions

Litigants are making more and more motions before they get to trial. Those include motions to strike, motions for particulars, *etc.* Counsel should think before making these motions: these motions should be made only when it is obvious that a certain allegation of fact is uncalled for and truly prejudices one's case. Courts are reluctant to strike pleadings or order particulars early in the appeal process so counsel may be wasting their time and their client's money by acting prematurely.

Appellants, for example, may want to swallow carelessly drafted assumptions rather than make application to strike. These assumptions may contain a small mine of facts that, at the end of the day, help the appellant. In *Gould v. Canada*,[5] former Chief Justice Bowman observed:

> ... that the complaint that is usually made is that the Crown has not pleaded all of the material assumptions or has not pleaded assumptions that assist the appellant. Here the reverse is true. The appellant is complaining that too many assumptions are pleaded. It would seem to me that if an assessment is based on assumptions that are irrelevant, contradictory or illogical, as the appellant alleges, this could arguably form a cogent basis for attacking the assessment. If those assumptions are removed from the Reply the appellant has deprived himself of one of the weapons in his arsenal. Why he would wish to do so escapes me. There is a danger that one can, in getting too engrossed in technical minutiae, lose sight of the substantial tactical advantage of forcing the Crown to live with its own pleadings. There is much to be said for the venerable rule about not educating your opponent.

In General Procedure cases the parties have the benefit of discovery through which the party examining his or her opponent may obtain particulars of the evidence the opponent may lead a trial to prove the material facts

---

5 [2005] T.C.J. No. 403 (QL), 2005 CarswellNat 2707, 2005 D.T.C. 1311, [2005] 5 C.T.C. 2044, at para. 22 [T.C.J.].

pleaded.[6] Frequently, it might be better for counsel to wait until discovery before making a motion for particulars and, if he or she does make such a motion, make sure it refers to material facts raised by their opponent. And counsel should base the motion on one of the Court's rules.

Applications to Amend Timetable

The Tax Court is getting more and more applications to amend timetables agreed to by the parties at a status hearing or in a letter to the Court. The timetable is confirmed by an Order of the Court. If the discovery, for example, is not held at the date fixed by the Order, the parties have violated the Order and, it has been suggested by some people, may be in contempt. If for good and unanticipated reasons the Order has to be amended, an application to amend should be made *before*, not after, the fixed date for the procedure has expired.

An amendment extending time is not a litigant's right. Why counsel agree to dates in an Order that they cannot observe amazes me. A convincing submission should support any extension to change times. It may be that discovery is taking longer than anticipated or that there are more undertakings than anticipated. If the extension is sought because one of the counsel was slow or not cooperative, for example, costs may be awarded regardless of who is eventually successful and may be payable within days. Where an extension is sought after the times in the order have expired, the application for extension, contrary to past practice, may be denied, again with costs. The moral is: counsel should agree to a timetable they can live with.

Experts

Over the years I have had the experience of hearing good and mediocre (not so good) expert evidence. Sometimes it is a delight to hear such evidence. I have heard Wayne Gretzkys, as well as those to whom Mario Lemieux once referred as garage league players. At times it is quite obvious that the expert witness is a hired gun for the person paying his bill and was engaged for no other purpose than to advance the client's case. It is sometimes simply annoying and offensive that two experts for opposing parties can look at the same property, for example, and come to valuations that bear no resemblance to each other. The comparables are different, the highest and best use of the property is sometimes different. And a few expert witnesses' demeanor on the stand is based on the assumption that they know

---

6 *Foss*, para. 12.

everything worth knowing about the subject and that the judge is either an idiot or extremely naïve. It is true that the judge may have absolutely no knowledge of the area of the witness's expertise. An expert should be called to testify only if his or her evidence is necessary and will assist the Court. Otherwise it is a waste of time and money. The expert witness is a teacher and, when testifying, should avoid any condescending tone or attitude. There have to be some improvements in the presentation of expert evidence. Experts should write their reports and testify using ordinary English or French. They should avoid professional jargon. One need not use polysyllables to make an impression with the judge. Indeed, the opposite is true.

In the 1990's, Lord Woolf, a future Lord Chief Justice of England – equivalent to the Chief Justice of Canada – reviewed the civil justice system in England. Among the subjects of his report was that of expert evidence.

In his report, Lord Woolf stated that experts sometimes take on the role of partisan advocates instead of neutral fact-finders or opinion givers. They are, he said, being paid for a reason. There is no rule requiring an expert witness not to be biased. Ideally, they should be neutral and objective. But trials do take place in the real world.

Lord Woolf was concerned with access to justice, and hence with reductions in costs, delay, and complexity. He wanted to move away from the adversarial tradition.

He stated that the traditional English way of deciding a contentious expert issue is for a judge to decide between two contrary views. He believed that this is not necessarily the best way of achieving a just result. He explained that the judge may not be sure that either side is right, especially if the issues are very technical or fall within an area in which the judge has no expertise. Nevertheless, the judge hopes to arrive at the right answer. Whether consciously or not, his decision may be influenced by factors such as the apparently greater authority of one side's expert or the experts' relative fluency and persuasiveness in putting across their arguments. In other words, the B.S. factor can be influential. Experience in our court is not substantially different from England.

The expert's function here in Canada and in the U.K., believe it or not, is to assist the Court. As Lord Woolf states, there should be no expert evidence at all unless it will help the Court. And the expert's evidence should be evidence that only an expert can give. I have presided at appeals where after 30 minutes or so a person is finally qualified as an expert in a particular field of expertise but the person's testimony could have been provided by a layman or, at the end of the day, the evidence is wholly useless because it is irrelevant to the issue before the Court.

Lord Woolf wanted to foster an approach to expert evidence which emphasizes the expert's duty to help the court impartially on matters within his expertise and encourage, in his words, "a more focused use of expert evidence by a variety of means".

Several recommendations[7] made by Lord Wolf are already present in the *Canada Evidence Act*, for example, limiting the number of experts. There is at least one recommendation that he makes that Canadian practitioners should consider: that the parties' experts meet so as to identify and reduce areas of difference. They could meet either before or after they have exchanged reports. (I question whether lawyers should be present at this meeting.) This, I believe, will reduce the time each person testifies and might even serve to open settlement discussions.

One other thing concerning experts: a lawyer's engagement letter to an expert should be more specific than general. "Please provide your usual report" is not a good request for an expert opinion. The request should be more detailed and explicit, requiring the expert to opine on specific questions directly related to the issue in appeal. The expert witness should know what the issue before the Court is and be confident that his or her opinion will assist the Court in its consideration of the matter for which the opinion has been requested.

Experts are expensive. Parties should get the best experts possible. But, as in hiring any professional, the parties and their counsel should consider the amount of tax in issue and what the party can afford in the circumstances. A litigant may not want to hire the lowest bidder who may not be that experienced in the area he or she requires expert evidence or a person who may have a reputation or be identified as a friend of the client or the client's industry. One might waste time and money on a witness who may not survive cross-examination.

Discovery

Like trials, discoveries are taking too long, sometimes longer than the trial itself.[8] It is trite to say that discoveries are not fishing expeditions. Discovery

---

7 For Lord Woolf's report go to www.dca.gouv.uk/civil/reporter. Not all of Lord Woolf's recommendations were accepted.

8 I understand discoveries in *GlaxoSmithKline Inc. v. The Queen*, 2008 TCC 324, 2008

is what it says it is: an effort by a litigant to discover his or her opponent's case, it should be added, within the confines of the pleadings and relevancy, to narrow issues and consider the strength of one's case for possible settlement.

Discovery is often the first time opposing parties, the taxpayer, and the auditor, meet face-to-face in the appeal process to see what the other side really has for ammunition. Indeed, it is usually the first time the taxpayer is in a position to ask the questions of the fisc's representative that raised the assessment in appeal. Discovery thus offers the opportunity to clear up misunderstandings and litigants should not ignore this opportunity.

Pre-trial Conference

Pre-trial conferences are important. They can lead to settlement or even abandonment of a party's position. At the very least, they can help clarify material facts and law and have the parties agree as to how many facts are in dispute. But, here too, the lawyers and their clients must come to the conference well-prepared and with an open mind, willing to cooperate. It is a waste of time when one party – usually the fisc – refuses to compromise, insisting any compromise goes against its own policy even if there is case law contrary to its policy. The parties and the judge must often be creative in trying to formulate a possible settlement.

Witnesses

Counsel should think long before he or she calls a person as a witness. Does one really need this person? Sometimes a party's own witness can ruin the party's case. This sometimes happens when the Crown calls an auditor to testify for no good reason. Witnesses serve, or should serve, to describe to the judge first-hand knowledge of facts in support of a party's position. The witness should know what he or she is testifying about and if the potential witness is not sure of the facts, that person should not be called. For a witness to testify that an auditor or taxpayer was uncooperative during an audit does not bring the relevant facts to life; such a witness's evidence is a waste of time, unless credibility is in issue.

CarswellNat 1666, 2008 D.T.C. 3957 took 92 days; the trial took 46 days, interlocutory motions took 12 days.

Trials

At trial, lawyers should discriminate as to facts one wants to get from one's own witnesses and then, in argument, the law counsel wants the judge not only to consider but also to adopt in his reasons. Witnesses should not be asked the same question over and over. This wastes time, it grates on the judge, and could end up being the Achilles heel of a case. Needless to say, cases should be prepared carefully. Counsel must know what he or she has to prove. One should not fly by the seat of one's pants: opposing counsel and the judge will usually see through this.

As far as case law is concerned, counsel should cite the leading cases, not cases that have a distant relationship to one's case or have since been distinguished by a respected trial judge or overturned by an appellate court. Consider the comments of Scollin J. in a Manitoba case *Unicity Taxi Ltd. v. Manitoba Taxicab Board*[9]:

> Before closing these reasons, I must state two concerns. The first is that Unicity has perceived that the elucidation of its case requires well over 100 pages of written argument and some 65 case citations (as well as some texts). Given that initial momentum, it is not surprising that the natural or fabricated complexities of the case generated a total of nearly 230 pages of written argument, well over 100 case citations and an arm-numbing weight of more than 33 kilograms of material. Irrespective of the merits, a review of all the circumstances and a careful reading of all the cases has satisfied me that Unicity has sought to relieve poverty of fact by wealth of law. Unicity's counsel have showered a confetti of cases on a few frail facts. Advocacy is the mastery of cogency and a measure of good advocacy is the ability of counsel to distinguish volume from weight and length from depth. Too often the errant knight-at-law mistakes caterpillars for dragons: something of that sort has happened here, with little issues being dragged out and savaged by citation. However, despite the length of Unicity's argument and its profligate strewing of precedent, I found no need on the facts of this case to refer to more than half-dozen or so authorities which bear reasonably on the real issues.

Justice Scollin continued,

> My second concern is related to my first. Inadequacy or frailty of fact is one thing. Absence of fact is another. In litigation, law without fact is lunch without food. In several instances, which I have referred to, propositions of law have been invoked and discussed in detail without there being any real foundation in fact to warrant any citation or analysis of cases. As a result, the application has at times taken on the air of an academic moot court and much time, energy and money has been squandered that could have been better used in a more worthy cause.

---

9 (1992), 80 Man. R. (2d) 241, 1992 CarswellMan 129, appeal dismissed (1992), 1992 CarswellMan 421, 83 Man. R. (2d) 305 (C.A.).

Lawyers

There is one more thing that can help in reducing the costs of litigation – lawyers' fees. Is it still an appropriate law firm business model to bill for each hour worked?[10] Does hourly billing prolong litigation? It is arguably time for new billing practices such as a negotiated fixed fee for services or some other more creative pay structure. If lawyers are creative in designing tax avoidance plans, surely they can create new billing practices that are more mutually satisfactory to themselves and their clients. Lawyers better start tackling this problem before their provincial governments do.

Conclusion

Many lawyers, in particular younger lawyers, have never experienced an economic recession that may well affect their egos and income. When an economic downfall affects professionals, they should avoid the temptation of spending more time on a file than is required. Clients are also suffering from the recession. A court must also recognize the economic problems facing the litigants and their advisors.

In the meantime, taxpayers, for example, want to contest what they see as unfair assessments. They may not have the money to do so. Everyone in the judicial process - lawyers, litigants, court officials - has to search out means to make litigation less expensive and more efficient for Canadians.

Courts may have to amend their rules and practices to accommodate the new situation. The Tax Court has recently amended many of its Rules and continues to study ways of simplifying its procedures and practices toward affordability and efficiency.[11] It is hoped that perhaps one or two of the proposals expressed in this chapter will contribute to this goal.

---

10 Changes in billing practices have been discussed widely. See, for example, an article in *The New York Times*, "Billable Hours Giving Ground at Law Firms", by J.D. Glater, January 30, 2009, p. A-1, New York ed.

11 Published in *Canada Gazette* Part II on December 10, 2008: the Rules can be found at http://www.tcc-cci.gc.ca/rules_e.htm.

Debt Collection

David W. Chodikoff & Andrew D. Valentine

Introduction

Economic and stock market pundits alike have, for the most part, concluded that we are working our collective way out of the "Great Recession". But, are we? For example, the net charge-offs by U.S. banks rose to 3.04 per cent of loans. This is the worst level since 1934, which was in the midst of the Great Depression. In the U.S., there continue to be record foreclosures. In 2009, Realty Trac reported that there was a record 2.8 million homes with at least one foreclosure filing and it says that the number may be as high as 3 to 3.5 million in 2010.[1] Coupled with the U.S. housing problem, there is also weak loan growth. Further, if the U.S. banks are not healthy enough to lend more, or the U.S. banks are still seeing weak loan demand, then this is bad news for the U.S. economy. Why should we care in Canada? The answer is simple. If the U.S. economy is unpredictable and slow to recover, so too is the Canadian economy, as our economy is so heavily dependent on American fortunes. Given this situation, it is no wonder that businesses and individuals alike must consider all options for the future including worst case scenarios, such as going into debt and/or owing money to the Crown. It is therefore prudent in such volatile times that average Canadians and businesses possess some basic understanding of the subjects of tax, debt, and collection.

In this chapter, we provide the reader with an overview of the Federal debt collection regime under the *Income Tax Act*.[2] We also examine the steps that the Canada Revenue Agency ("CRA") may take to collect on tax debts, as well as the restrictions of their powers. Finally, we outline the fundamental

---

1 A. Barr, "Bank Stocks Beyond the Abyss", *Market Watch*, March 5, 2010, p. 2.

2 *Income Tax Act*, R.S.C. 1985, c. 1 (5th Supp.) [*ITA* or the "Act"].

options available to tax debtors in response to enforcement actions by the CRA.

Payments, Interest & Penalties

The term "tax debt" is defined in the *ITA* as "any amount payable by a taxpayer under this Act."[3] As a consequence, the collections regime applies not only to the principal amounts owing, but also to any penalties and interest which may accrue pursuant to the *ITA*.[4] It is therefore important to review how and when amounts become payable, as well as how and when penalties and interest accumulate on unpaid taxes.

When Are Taxes Due?

The *ITA* provides a deadline by which balances owing must be paid, which varies according to the type of taxpayer: this deadline is referred to as the "balance-due day".[5] The balance-due day for different taxpayers is as follows:

- For individual taxpayers (including individuals who have died on or before October 31st in the previous taxation year), April 30 in the following taxation year;[6]
- For individuals who have died after October 31st in the previous year, but before May of the next year, six months after the day of death;[7]
- For trusts, 90 days after the end of the year;[8]
- For corporations, two months after the fiscal year end of the corporation,[9] unless the corporation meets certain conditions, in which case the balance-due day is three months after the corporation's fiscal year end.[10]

---

3 *ITA*, ss. 222(1) "tax debt".

4 As discussed below, "tax debt" also includes any costs incurred by the CRA in taking collection action which must also be borne by the tax debtor and which are subject to the same collections regime: *ITA*, s. 222.1.

5 *ITA*, ss. 248(1) "balance-due day".

6 *ITA*, ss. 248(1)(c) "balance-due day".

7 *ITA*, ss. 248(1)(b) "balance-due day".

8 *ITA*, ss. 248(1)(a) "balance-due day".

9 *ITA*, ss. 248(1)(d)(ii) "balance-due day".

10 *ITA*, ss. 248(1)(d)(i) "balance-due day". The corporation must meet three conditions to qualify for the 3-month balance-due day. The corporation must have claimed a small business deduction pursuant to s. 125, the corporation must qualify as a Canadian-controlled private corporation, and its taxable income (either alone or in combination with any associated corporations) must not exceed its business limit for the preceding taxation year.

Most corporations[11] and individuals[12] are required to make instalment payments throughout the year. Interest and other penalties accrue on late payments of instalments, as well as late payments of tax owing on the balance-due day.

For individuals, taxes are deemed paid on the date that they are mailed by first class mail.[13] In the case of corporations, the *ITA* deems taxes to have been paid on the day they are received by the Receiver General.[14] This latter requirement also applies to remittances of amounts deducted or withheld. Therefore, it is essential that the taxpayer ensure that the payment is received by the CRA to ensure that no penalties or interest accrue on the payments.

Interest

Section 161 of the *ITA* provides for interest on all unpaid instalment payments,[15] as well as all amounts due but unpaid on the balance-due day.[16] This applies to both full and partial non-payment. Interest will be charged on any portion of unpaid tax until it is paid.

Interest is charged at a rate equal to the average equivalent yield (rounded to the nearest whole percent) on Government of Canada Treasury Bills maturing three months after issue, plus 4 per cent.[17] Rates of interest are determined on a quarterly basis – interest on any non-payment will be charged at the rate determined for the quarter in which the payment was

---

11 Under ss. 157(1), corporations whose income exceeds $3,000 must pay monthly instalments of tax (according to one of the formulae provided in the section), unless the corporation qualifies as an eligible Canadian-controlled private corporation, in which case it may make quarterly instalments (ss. 157(1.1) and (1.2)). On corporate instalment payments generally, see CRA Guide T7B Corp. (E), *Corporate Instalment Guide 2009* (released November 19, 2008).

12 Most individuals whose net tax owing for the year will exceed $3,000 ($1,800 for residents of Quebec) must make quarterly instalments of tax throughout the year. The instalment payment requirements for individuals are set out in s. 156. Note that a different instalment payment system is used for individuals whose main source of income is farming or fishing: s. 155. On payment of tax by instalments for individuals, see CRA Pamphlet P110, *Paying Your Income Tax by Instalments* (released November 4, 2008).

13 *ITA*, ss. 248(7)(a).

14 *ITA*, ss. 248(7)(b).

15 *ITA*, ss. 161(2). Interest under this section is computed only until the balance-due date, at which point the interest is computed under ss. 161(1).

16 *ITA*, ss. 161(1).

17 Regulation 4301(a).

outstanding. The interest is compounded daily, including on any unpaid interest.[18]

Certain provisions in s. 161 provide some means by which the taxpayer may reduce interest owing on unpaid taxes. Section 161(2.2), sometimes referred to as "contra" interest, reduces the accumulated interest for a year on any late instalment payments to the extent that any other instalment payments for the year were made prior to the month-end deadline.[19] Section 161(7) provides rules permitting some reduction of interest on late or unpaid taxes to the extent that the taxpayer carries back any deductions or exclusions in subsequent taxation years.

Courts have held that interest accrues from the date on which the debt becomes payable, rather than the date on which the CRA sends (or the taxpayer receives) a Notice of Assessment or Reassessment.[20] Interest also accrues on any penalties imposed under the Act, from the date the penalty becomes payable until the date on which it is paid.[21]

Penalties

In addition to interest on late or deficient payments of income tax, which accumulates daily from the date the payment was due, the *ITA* provides for additional penalties on certain late or deficient payments.

Section 162(1) provides a general penalty for failure to file a return of income pursuant to ss. 150(1). The amount of the penalty is 5 per cent of any unpaid tax payable on the filing deadline, plus an additional 1 per cent of such unpaid tax for each complete month (not exceeding twelve) that elapses after the return was required to be filed. For repeat failures to file within three years of a previous failure to file, the amount of the penalty is increased to 10 per cent of any unpaid tax owed on the filing deadline, plus 2 per cent of the unpaid tax for each complete month between the filing

---

18 *ITA*, ss. 248(11); in the 1st quarter of 2010, the CRA charges 5% on unpaid amounts.

19 In other words, although the Minister will not pay interest outright on instalment payments made prior to the deadline, it will allow the taxpayer to deduct from the interest owing the value of such interest that would accrue on any pre-payment or overpayment of instalments in the year: ss. 161(2.2).

20 *Whent v. The Queen* (1999), [2000] 1 C.T.C. 329 (Fed. C.A.), leave to appeal refused (2000), 2000 CarswellNat 2397 (S.C.C.).

21 *ITA*, ss. 161(11).

deadline and the actual filing of the return by the taxpayer.[22] The maximum number of months on which the additional 2 per cent will be charged is increased to 20 for repeat failures to file.[23] The penalty is assessed on tax payable as of the date on which the filing was due; thus, it applies notwithstanding that a subsequent loss carry-back reduces or eliminates the tax owing for that year.[24]

A penalty is also imposed on late or deficient instalment payments.[25] The penalty is 50 per cent of the amount by which the interest payable on instalments under s. 161 exceeds the greater of $1,000 and 25 per cent of the interest that would have been payable had no instalment been made for the year.

Additional penalties are also imposed for various other forms of late or deficient payments, or failure to file returns, under the Act. These include:

- an additional penalty for non-resident corporations that fail to file returns;[26]
- small penalties for trustees who fail to file a return as required under ss. 150(3);[27]
- penalties for failure to make partnership information returns;[28]
- penalties for failure to collect and remit withholding taxes.[29]

---

22 *ITA*, ss. 162(2). For the increased penalties to apply under this provision, it is necessary that the taxpayer fail to file a return as required by ss. 150(1), that the Minister have served a demand for a return for the year under ss. 150(2), and that the taxpayer have incurred penalties for failure to file a return under ss. 162(1) in respect of any of the previous three years' returns.

23 *ITA*, ss. 162(2)(e).

24 *ITA*, ss. 162(11). See also *Reemark Chelsea Terraces Project Ltd. v. The Queen* (1993), 93 D.T.C. 469 (T.C.C.); *Yang v. R.*, [2004] 3 C.T.C. 2408 (T.C.C. [Informal Procedure]).

25 *ITA*, s. 163.1.

26 *ITA*, ss. 162(2.1). The additional penalty for non-resident corporations that fail to file is $25 per day (up to a maximum of 100 days) for each day that passes after the return was required to be filed. This penalty is in addition to the penalty for failure to file imposed by ss. 162(1) or (2).

27 *ITA*, ss. 162(3). The penalty is $10 for each day of default, but not exceeding $50.

28 *ITA*, ss. 162(7.1).

29 *ITA*, ss. 227(8). This section provides that a failure to deduct or withhold any amount as required by ss. 153(1) or s. 215 of the Act results in a penalty in the amount of 10% of the amount that should have been deducted or withheld, or 20% of the amount if the failure to deduct or withhold was made knowingly or in circumstances amounting to gross negligence. Ss. 227(8.3) imposes interest on such amounts. Ss. 227(9) imposes a penalty for failure to *remit* any amounts required to be deducted or withheld. The amount of this penalty is calculated as a percentage of the unpaid remittance, and depends on how late the Receiver General receives payment. Where the failure to remit was made knowingly or under circumstances amounting to gross negligence, the penalty is 20% of the unremitted deductions or withholdings.

Where a taxpayer fails to include income in an information return that is required to be included under the Act, and has similarly failed to include all income in one of the previous three years' returns, ss. 163(1) imposes a penalty of 10 per cent of the amount of the omission.[30]

A penalty is imposed where a person knowingly, or under circumstances amounting to gross negligence, makes, participates in making, or acquiesces in the making of a false statement or omission in a return, form, certificate, statement or answer that is filed or made under the Act.[31] The amount of the penalty is the greater of $100 and 50 per cent of the total of several amounts.[32]

As this overview suggests, the failure to make all necessary payments of tax when payable can result in substantial additional financial penalties. These penalties are in addition to the interest that accrues on late or deficient payments, and are themselves a source of additional interest obligations if not paid immediately. Once such penalties and interest have been incurred, they, along with the principal tax debts outstanding, can become the subject of a wide variety of collections action by the CRA.

Collection and Enforcement Powers: What Can CRA Do to You?

The CRA has statutory powers that enable it to collect any tax debts outstanding, as well as any interest or additional penalties payable in respect of those debts. These powers are best described as the CRA power to take "actions" to enforce the payment of tax debts.[33] These actions can potentially apply to any amount payable under the Act.[34]

---

30 However, where the person liable under this section would also be liable for making a false statement or omission under ss. 163(2), the penalties under the latter provision will prevail: ss. 163(1).

31 *ITA*, ss. 163(2). This penalty is coupled with a parallel provision imposing civil penalties on third parties who participate in the making of such false statements and omissions: s. 163.2.

32 For greater detail on penalties imposed on taxpayers for making false statements or omissions, see C. Campbell, *Administration of Income Tax 2009* (Thomson, Carswell, 2009) at section 11.2.

33 *ITA*, ss. 222(1) defines "action" as "an action to collect a tax debt of a taxpayer and includes a proceeding in a court anything done by the Minister under subsection 129(2), 131(3), 132(2) or 164(2), section 203 or any provision of [Part XV of the Act]."

34 *ITA*, ss. 222(1) defines "tax debt" (*i.e.*, that to which collections action by the CRA may apply) to mean "any amount payable by a taxpayer under this Act".

In the section that follows, we review the more commonly used forms of collection action by the CRA.

Timing Issues

Tax debts come into existence under the Act on the date that the taxpayer earns the income giving rise to the tax.[35] They become payable either on the balance-due day or other date set out in the Act. However, before the CRA can take legal action to *enforce* payment of such tax debts, it is required to observe certain procedural steps designed to ensure administrative fairness to the taxpayer in collecting on the debt.

Collection Restrictions

Section 225.1 of the Act provides for certain restrictions on collections action by the CRA. In most cases, the CRA is prevented from commencing action to collect on a tax debt until 90 days after the mailing of a notice of assessment or reassessment.[36] This 90-day wait period applies to most forms of collections action by the CRA, including commencing legal proceedings in court, certifying the amount payable under s. 223, garnisheeing amounts owing to the taxpayer, or issuing a certificate of non-payment and directing that the taxpayer's goods and chattels be seized and sold.

The Minister of National Revenue ("Minister") is required under ss. 152(1) to examine, with all due dispatch, each taxpayer's return of income and assess the amount of tax payable. It is required to send a notice of assessment to the taxpayer upon completing this review.[37] Section 152(4) provides the time limits within which the Minister may issue an assessment, reassessment, or additional assessment of tax for a taxation year. Generally, the normal reassessment period within which the Minister may reassess is three years (four years in the case of mutual fund trusts and non-CCPC corporations) from the mailing of the original Notice of Assessment.[38] However, this period is extended in certain circumstances under ss. 152(4). Section 158

---

[35] In other words, tax debts do not depend for their existence on an assessment or reassessment by the CRA. See *R. v. Simard-Beaudry Inc.* (1971), 71 D.T.C. 5511 (Fed. T.D.); *Garland v. Minister of National Revenue* (1988), 88 D.T.C. 1271 (T.C.C.). This principle has been affirmed in the GST context in *Beaupré c. R.* (2005), 2005 G.T.C. 1420 (F.C.A.).

[36] *ITA*, ss. 225.1(1) restricts the CRA from commencing most types of collection action prior to the "collection commencement date". Ss. 225.1(1.1) provides that in most cases, the collection-commencement period is 90 days from the mailing of a notice of assessment.

[37] *ITA*, ss. 152(2).

[38] *ITA*, ss. 152(3.1).

requires taxpayers to pay any tax owing forthwith upon the mailing of a notice of assessment.

The CRA has set out its policies with respect to collection and enforcement of tax debts in Information Circular IC 98-1R3.[39] The CRA states, consistent with the collections restrictions in the Act, that subject to certain exceptions it will not generally start legal action under 90 days after the CRA mails a notice of assessment or notice of reassessment.[40] However, in certain cases, the CRA may begin collections action immediately following the mailing of a notice of assessment.[41] The CRA may begin collections action immediately in respect of assessments of the following items:

- Certain amounts deemed to be held in trust for the purpose of payment to the Receiver General;[42]
- Any amounts payable pursuant to Part VIII of the Act (scientific research and experimental development tax credits);
- Non-resident tax;[43]
- Any penalties for failure to remit funds held pursuant to a deemed trust;
- Interest payable on any of the amounts above;
- 50 per cent of the amounts assessed as payable by certain large corporations;[44]
- Reassessments with the taxpayer's consent under ss. 152(4.2);
- Reassessments after the disposition of an appeal with the consent or writing of the taxpayer under ss. 169(3); and
- A reassessment after the waiver of penalty and/or interest under ss. 220(3.1).

---

39 CRA, Information Circular IC 98-1R3, "Collections Policies" (February 12, 2008) [IC 98-1R3].

40 IC 98-1R3 at 3.

41 *ITA*, ss. 225.1(6).

42 The Act deems certain amounts to be held in trust for the purpose of payment to the Receiver General. These include any amounts deducted from employees and other individuals for income tax, Canada Pension Plan contributions, and Employment Insurance Premiums. Also included are GST/HST collected as or on account of tax under the *Excise Tax Act*, R.S.C. 1985, c. E-15 and charges collected under the *Air Travellers Security Charge Act*.

43 This includes unpaid amounts payable under s. 116 of the Act, and under any regulation made under ss. 215(4).

44 Under ss. 225.1(7), where a large corporation as defined in ss. 225.1(8) of the Act has been assessed, the CRA may take action to collect half of the amount assessed at any time during the first 90 days after the amount is assessed, regardless of whether an objection or appeal has been filed. After this 90-day period, the CRA states, if there is no objection or appeal, it may collect the outstanding balance. After the 90-day period, where an objection or appeal has been filed, the CRA may collect on 50% of the balance under dispute and any balance not in dispute.

Taxpayers should take advantage of the 90-day period following receipt of a notice of assessment to file any notice of objection or appeal disputing the assessment. Section 225.1 provides that in most cases, the filing of an objection or appeal prevents further collections action by the CRA until a decision on the assessment has been issued by the adjudicative body.[45] Provided that the taxpayer commences the objection or appeal process within 90 days of the mailing of the notice of assessment, most taxpayers will not face collection action. That process will commence after the taxpayer has exhausted both the objection and appeal rights.

Jeopardy Orders (or "You Can't Delay")

Section 225.2 provides an exception to the general rule in situations where the CRA persuades a judge[46] on *ex parte* application that there are reasonable grounds to believe that its ability to collect on tax assessed would be jeopardized by a delay in collection. In these circumstances, the court may authorize the CRA to immediately commence collections action.[47] The CRA may apply for a jeopardy order even before sending a notice of assessment or reassessment to the taxpayer.[48]

These orders involve an *ex parte* application made by the CRA. Accordingly, the CRA is required to make full and frank disclosure of all relevant facts. Where the CRA fails to do this, the authorization may be set aside by the court.[49]

---

45 In most cases, where a taxpayer has served a notice of objection to an assessment, the CRA cannot begin collections action until 90 days after the Appeals Division of the CRA has either confirmed or varied the assessment: ss. 225.1(2). Where a taxpayer has appealed from an assessment to the Tax Court of Canada, the CRA cannot begin collections action until a copy of the court's decision has been mailed to the taxpayer or the day the taxpayer discontinues the appeal: ss. 225.1(3). Where a taxpayer has agreed under ss. 173(1) to refer a question for determination to the Tax Court of Canada (or where the taxpayer is served with an application for the determination of a question), the CRA cannot collect on the portion of the tax debt that will be affected by the decision until the day on which the decision is determined in court: ss. 225.1(4).

46 *ITA*, ss. 225.2(1). The judge must be a local judge of either the Federal Court or a provincial superior court.

47 *ITA*, ss. 225.2(2). Where authorized under this subsection, the CRA may immediately initiate any of the collections actions set out in ss. 225.1(a) to (g) – that is, the collections actions which are normally restricted until the collection commencement date.

48 *ITA*, ss. 225.2(3). Where a judge is satisfied that receipt of a notice of assessment would jeopardize the collection of an amount, the judge may authorize immediate collection and the subsection deems the tax debts to be amounts payable, notwithstanding the absence of a notice of assessment.

49 *Tran v. The Queen*, [2008] 3 C.T.C. 209, 2008 D.T.C. 6584 (Eng.) (F.C.) [*Tran*].

The CRA is required to serve taxpayers with a copy of the authorization within 72 hours of the Order being granted.[50] Taxpayers may review jeopardy orders on six days' notice to the CRA within 30 days of being served with an authorization,[51] though the Act provides that this limitation period can be extended by the court where the court is satisfied that the application for review of the authorization was made as soon as practicable.[52] It can also be extended pursuant to the court's inherent power, provided that the common law test for an extension of time is met.[53] The limitation period does not continue to run during settlement negotiations with the CRA.[54]

On applications for review of an authorization, the taxpayer first bears the onus of establishing the following: the taxpayer must demonstrate that there are reasonable grounds to doubt that the test required by ss. 225.2(2) has been met – that is, the collection of all or any or any part of the amounts assessed would be jeopardized by delay in the collection.[55] If the taxpayer succeeds, the onus shifts to the CRA, and the court must examine the evidence upon which the jeopardy order was obtained as well as any other evidence that would show on a balance of probabilities that the collection would be jeopardized by delay.[56]

Courts have set out the principles that apply in evaluating whether a jeopardy order was properly issued. In 2003, in *M.N.R. v. Services M.L. Marengère Inc.*,[57] Lemieux J. summarized the basis on which the Minister may justify a jeopardy order:

> The evidence must show, on a balance of probability, that it is more likely than not that collection would be jeopardized by delay. The test is not whether the

---

50 *ITA*, ss. 225.2(5). Service must be effected by personal service on the taxpayer, or by other method authorized by the Court: ss. 225.2(6).

51 *ITA*, ss. 225.2(8).

52 *ITA*, ss. 225.2(8)(b). See, for example, *Tran, supra*, which denied an application by a taxpayer for an extension of time on the basis that that taxpayer's counsel has waited over a month to file the application even after knowing that they were already outside the limitation period.

53 See *Tran, supra*, citing *Canada (Attorney General) v. Hennelly* (1999), 244 N.R. 399 (Fed. C.A.), which set out the test for an extension of time. The applicant must establish the following:

1. there is a continuing intention to pursue his or her application;
2. the application has some merit;
3. there would be no prejudice arising from the delay on the not moving party; and
4. there exists a reasonable explanation for the delay.

54 *Minister of National Revenue v. Rudyk* (1995), 96 D.T.C. 6192 (Fed. T.D.).

55 *M.N.R. v. Services M.L. Marengère Inc.*, [2003] 1 C.T.C. 229 [*Marengère*].

56 *144945 Canada Inc., Re*, [2003] F.C.J. No. 937, [2003] 4 C.T.C. 112, (*sub nom. 144945 Canada Inc. v. Minister of National Revenue*) 2003 D.T.C. 5409 (Fed. T.D.).

57 Above, note 55.

> evidence shows beyond all reasonable doubt that the time allowed to the taxpayer would jeopardize the Minister's debt.

The Minister may certainly act not only in cases of fraud or situations amounting to fraud, but also in cases where the taxpayer may waste, liquidate or otherwise transfer his property to escape the tax authorities: in short, to meet any situation in which the taxpayer's assets may vanish into thin air because of the passage of time. However, the mere suspicion or concern that delay may jeopardize collection is not sufficient *per se*. As Rouleau J. put it in *1853-9049 Québec Inc., supra*, the question is whether the Minister had reasonable grounds for believing that the taxpayer would waste, liquidate or otherwise transfer its assets, so jeopardizing the Minister's debt. The Minister has to show that the taxpayer's assets can be liquidated in the meantime or be seized by other creditors, making them unavailable to the Minister.[58]

Thus, CRA must establish that there are reasonable grounds to conclude that the taxpayer will waste, liquidate, or otherwise transfer assets so as to jeopardize the Minister's collection of the debt. In *M.N.R. v. Thériault-Sabourin*,[59] Layden-Stevenson J. set out three additional principles:

- The sale of assets alone does not justify a jeopardy order;[60]
- The taxpayer's inability to pay the amount assessed at the time of the direction is not by itself conclusive or determinative;[61] and
- The nature of the assessment itself may raise a reasonable apprehension that the taxpayer had not been conducting [her] affairs in what might be called an orthodox fashion and can therefore contribute to the reasonable grounds to believe that the collection of the amount assessed would be jeopardized by delay.[62]

Judges must determine the issue summarily and may confirm, set aside, or vary the authorization and make any other order the judge considers appropriate.[63] The judge's determination cannot be appealed.[64]

---

58 *Ibid.* at para. 63.

59 *Minister of National Revenue v. Thériault-Sabourin*, [2003] 2 C.T.C. 296, 2003 D.T.C. 5151 (Fed. T.D.).

60 *Minister of National Revenue v. Landru* (1992), [1993] 1 C.T.C. 93 (Sask. Q.B.).

61 *Danielson v. Canada (Deputy Attorney General)* (1986), [1987] 1 F.C. 335 (Fed. T.D.).

62 *Laframboise v. R.*, [1986] 3 F.C. 521 (Fed. T.D.); *Minister of National Revenue v. Rouleau*, [1995] 2 C.T.C. 442, 95 D.T.C. 5597 (Fed. T.D.).

63 *ITA*, ss. 225.2(11).

64 *ITA*, ss. 225.2(13).

Limitations

Assuming that the Minister has issued a notice of assessment or reassessment within the time permitted by the Act, it must also be determined whether the CRA is within the relevant limitation period for collections action.

The limitation period within which the CRA may take action to collect on a tax debt is set out under s. 222 of the Act. In 2004, s. 222 was substantially amended to effectively overrule a 2003 decision of the Supreme Court of Canada which had held that actions by the CRA to collect on tax debts were subject to a general six-year limitation period. In *Markevich v. Canada*,[65] the court considered whether the CRA was permitted to take collections action in 1998 to collect on federal and provincial tax debts that were assessed in 1986. From 1987 to 1998, CRA had made no effort to collect the debt and statements issued to the taxpayer during that period did not reflect the 1986 balance.

The court in *Markevich* held that collections action by the CRA was subject to s. 32 of the *Crown Liability and Proceedings Act* ["*CLPA*"], which applied to all "proceedings ... in respect of a cause of action". Because the *ITA* at the time did not provide for a limitation period in respect of collections action, the court held that the general provisions of the *CLPA* prevailed and imposed a general six-year limitation on collections action.

Parliament responded to *Markevich* with s. 222, which was introduced with the 2004 Federal Budget. Section 222 applies to all actions to enforce on tax debts.[66] Subsection 222(3) provides that the Minister may not commence action to collect a tax debt after the end of the relevant limitation period, which is provided for by ss. 222(4). The basic limitation period is 10 years, the beginning of which depends on the date of mailing or service of the notice of assessment. If the notice of assessment[67] was mailed or served after March 3, 2004, the limitation period begins 90 days after the mailing of the notice.[68] If the notice was served earlier and the tax was payable on March 3, 2004 (or would have been but for an otherwise applicable limitation period), then the limitation period began on March 4, 2004.[69] Thus, the new rules not only resurrect collections actions whose limitation periods have expired but also restart the limitation period as of March 4, 2004.

---

65 [2003] 1 S.C.R. 94, [2003] 2 C.T.C. 83, 2003 D.T.C. 5185 [*Markevich*].

66 *ITA*, ss. 222(1).

67 Or notice referred to in ss. 226(1), which applies when the Minister suspects that a taxpayer has left or is about to leave Canada. In these circumstances, the Minister may issue a notice of assessment before the date otherwise fixed for payment.

68 *ITA*, ss. 222(4)(a)(i).

69 *ITA*, ss. 222(4)(a)(ii).

Subsection 222(5) provides that the limitation period restarts on the occurrence of any of the following events:

- The taxpayer acknowledges the debt.
- The Minister commences action to collect on the debt.
- The Minister assesses any person in respect of the tax debt under certain sections of the Act.[70]

The most important of these factors from the taxpayer's perspective is the first, acknowledgement of the debt, because this factor is under the taxpayer's control. The actions which constitute "acknowledging the debt" are defined widely – they include any written statements promising to pay or otherwise acknowledging the debt and any payment on account of the debt.[71] It is critical that taxpayers consult legal counsel before communicating with the CRA in any way with regard to debts outstanding.

Subsection 222(8) provides for certain extensions of the limitation period. This subsection provides that limitation periods under ss. 222(4) will be extended by as many days as the following circumstances apply:

- The Minister is prevented from taking action by ss. 225.1(1), which, as discussed above, imposes the 90-day wait period following the mailing of a notice of assessment;
- The Minister has accepted and holds security in lieu of payment, as discussed below;
- The taxpayer is non-resident;
- The Minister is prevented from taking action under the *Bankruptcy and Insolvency Act*, the *Companies' Creditors Arrangement Act* or the *Farm Debt Management Act*.

In general, the limitations provisions in s. 222 are very favourable to the CRA. The retrospective application of the provisions, and the ease with which the Minister may restart the limitation period, will allow the CRA to take collections actions in a large number of cases where it would otherwise be prevented through the expiry of limitations periods. Subsection 222(10) provides that any court judgments made after March 3, 2004 holding that tax debts were not payable due to the expiry of a limitation period are effectively overturned and that the tax debt is deemed payable.

---

70 These sections are ss. 159(3), 160(2), or para. 227(10)(a).

71 *ITA*, ss. 222(5)(a). Ss. 222(6) provides that in order to constitute "acknowledgement of a tax debt", the taxpayer must either (a) promise, in writing, to pay the tax debts; (b) make a written acknowledgement of the tax debt, whether or not a promise to pay can be inferred; or (c) make a payment (including a dishonoured payment) on account of the tax debt. Acknowledgements by an agent or legal representative will also constitute acknowledgment for the purposes of ss. 222(5): *ITA*, ss. 222(7).

Certificate

Section 223 of the Act allows the Minister register a certificate of certain debts owing[72] with the Federal Court, and upon registration to have the same status as a judgment creditor in respect of the debt. The Act provides that where such a certificate is registered, it is deemed to be a judgment of the Federal Court against the debtor for the amount certified plus interest accruing until the date of payment.[73] All costs incurred by the Minister in registering the certificate are also recoverable in the same way.[74]

Registration of the certificate allows the Minister to pursue the available collections remedies under the Act, including garnishee proceedings and the seizure of the taxpayer's property. It also enables the Minister to register the certificate provincially to obtain a charge, lien, or other security interest on the taxpayer's property pursuant to the laws of the province in question.[75] This effectively allows the Minister to act as judgment creditor of the relevant provincial superior court and to pursue provincial collections remedies available to the provincial Minister of Revenue in respect of provincial tax debts.[76]

In *Re Piccott*,[77] the Federal Court of Appeal considered the extent to which the Minister was bound to follow the enforcement procedures that normally apply to judgment creditors of the Federal Court. The Minister had registered a certificate of tax debt owing under s. 223 of the Act (as well as the equivalent section of the *Excise Tax Act*), and had delivered this certificate to the Sheriff of Newfoundland & Labrador pursuant to the *Judgment Enforcement Act* (Nfld. & Labrador) with instructions to seize and sell as much of the debtor's property as was necessary to satisfy the tax debt. The Sheriff

---

72 Ss. 223(1) defines "amount payable" as including any amount owing under the Act, the *Employment Insurance Act*, the *Unemployment Insurance Act*, the *Canada Pension Plan* and any amount payable under a provincial Act where the federal Minister of Finance has entered into an agreement for the collection of taxes.

73 *ITA*, ss. 223(3).

74 *ITA*, ss. 223(4).

75 *ITA*, ss. 223(5). Ss. 223(6) provides that any charge, lien, or priority created on property in the province shall be subordinate to any other security interest duly registered against the property prior to the creation of the security interest under ss. 223(5).

76 The Act provides that once the certificate has been registered provincially under ss. 223(5), the Minister may commence proceedings in respect of the certificate, including proceedings to enforce payment of the amount certified, proceedings to renew or otherwise prolong the effectiveness of the certificate, proceedings to cancel or withdraw the certificate, or to postpone the effectiveness of the registration in favor of other security interests filed or intended to be filed in respect of any property or interest affected by the certificate: ss. 223(7).

77 2004 D.T.C. 6642 (F.C.A.).

did as instructed and the taxpayer challenged the propriety of the seizure on the basis that the procedure used was not compliant with the *Federal Courts Act* and *Federal Courts Rules*, which normally apply to judgment creditors of the Federal Court. Specifically, the Minister had not obtained a writ of execution and provided it to the Sheriff, which is normally required by the Rules before execution can be levied.

The motions judge hearing the application to have the seized assets returned concluded that because the certificate is deemed to be a judgment of the Federal Court, the Minister is therefore required to observe the procedure that applies to judgment creditors of that Court. Accordingly, because the Minister had failed to follow this procedure, the motions judge ordered the return of the seized assets. On appeal, Pelletier J.A. reversed this decision and upheld the seizure of property. Pelletier J.A. held that because the Act provided a specific enforcement procedure in s. 223, the Minister may simply follow this process, even though it may conflict with the normal rules that apply to execution by judgment creditors of the Federal Court.[78] Pelletier J.A. stated:

> Parliament has enacted comprehensive provisions for the enforcement of tax liabilities, and has provided for modalities of enforcement which differ from the normal scheme. It is clear that Parliament is competent to legislate specific enforcement provisions for the collection of tax payable, even if those provisions deal with what would otherwise be questions of property and civil rights in a province (see *TransGas Ltd. v. Mid-Plains Contractors Ltd.*, [1994] 3 S.C.R. 753 (S.C.C.), aff'g (1993), 105 Sask. R. 211 (Sask. C.A.)). As a result, the Minister can rely upon those specific provisions as they appear in the *Income Tax Act*, even if they differ from the enforcement provisions of the *Federal Court Act*.[79]

The narrow effect of the decision in *Re Piccott* is that it is sufficient for the Minister to provide provincial Sheriffs with a copy of the federal certificate, without needing to obtain a writ of execution as normally required by the *Federal Courts Rules*. The broader effect of the decision, however, is that the CRA appears to be required only to follow the execution procedures set out in the Act, even where they conflict with the normal execution procedures in the *Federal Courts Act* or *Rules*. The effect of this may be to remove certain procedural bases for an appeal by the taxpayer of collections actions by the CRA.

---

78 *Ibid.* at para. 31.

79 *Ibid.* at para. 32.

Set-off and Seizure of Property

Certain provisions in the Act allow the Minister to set off any tax debts owing against refunds or other payments owed by the federal Crown to the taxpayer. Subsection 164(2) provides that the Minister may apply any tax debt owing to reduce the amount of any repayment or refund. Section 224.1 provides that the Minister may set off tax debt against any amounts owed by the federal government.[80]

Section 225 authorizes the seizure and sale of a taxpayer's goods and chattels to satisfy tax debts. Under section 225, the CRA may give 30 days' notice of its intention to seize the assets of a taxpayer and, if the taxpayer fails to pay all taxes outstanding within those 30 days, the CRA may order the seizure of taxpayer property.[81] If after 10 days the owner has still failed to pay all tax debts, the CRA may direct that the property be sold by public auction.[82]

Garnishment

The CRA also has the power to garnishee payments to a taxpayer by third parties in satisfaction of tax debts owing. Subsection 224(1) provides that where the Minister knows or suspects that a third party will be required to make a payment to the taxpayer within one year, the Minister may order that third party to make payments to the Minister as they come due, until the taxpayer's tax debt has been paid.[83] This includes loans to the taxpayer

---

80 The Federal Court of Appeal has held that the Crown may not avail itself set-off under s. 224.1 unless the taxpayer was *at that time* indebted to the Crown, even if the debt would not become payable until some time in the future: *Aero Trades (Western) Ltd. (Receiver of) v. Canada* (1988), (*sub nom. Clarkson Co. v. R.*) 89 D.T.C. 5050, (*sub nom. Clarkson Co. v. Canada*) [1989] 1 C.T.C. 142 (Fed. C.A.); *Deputy Minister of National Revenue (Customs, Excise & Taxation) v. Millar*, [2006] 4 C.T.C. 40 (B.C. S.C.), appeal dismissed (2007) 2007 CarswellBC 1734 (C.A.), leave to appeal refused (2008), 2008 CarswellBC 130 (S.C.C.).

81 Ss. 224.3(1) permits the CRA to seize monies of the tax debtor which have been seized by police in the course of criminal law administration or enforcement. The CRA may direct the person holding the money to remit the seized funds to the Receiver General. This includes property taken illegally by police: *Deputy Minister of National Revenue (Customs, Excise & Taxation) v. Millar*, [2006] 4 C.T.C. 40 (B.C. S.C.), appeal dismissed (2007) 2007 CarswellBC 1734 (C.A.), leave to appeal refused (2008), 2008 CarswellBC 130 (S.C.C.).

82 *ITA*, ss. 225(2). The costs associated with the holding of the property pending sale at public auction, or return of the property to the owner, are borne by the owner. Ss. 225(3) provides details of the notice requirement for a sale of goods and chattels at a public auction. The subsection provides that except in the case of perishable goods, notice of the sale setting out the time and place, together with a general description of the property, must be published in one or more local newspapers a reasonable period of time before the auction.

83 *ITA*, ss. 224(2) provides that a receipt from the Minister for amounts paid as required will discharge the third party's original liability to the taxpayer to the extent of the payment.

by banks, credit unions and trust companies which are to be made to the taxpayer within 90 days.[84] Also, any payments by employers or non-arm's length corporations can be garnisheed by the CRA on account of tax debts.[85] The CRA may require any third party liable to make periodic payments to the tax debtor to continually remit them to the CRA until the tax debtor's tax liabilities have been paid.[86]

Generally, a garnishment order under s. 224 does not give CRA priority over other secured creditors.[87] However, ss. 224(1.2) deals with garnishment priority in respect of withholdings and creates an exception to the general rule that the Minister does not obtain priority over other creditors through the operation of s. 224. Subsection 224(1.2) provides that notwithstanding any relevant provisions of the *Bankruptcy and Insolvency Act*[88] or the *Companies' Creditors Arrangement Act*, the Minister may garnishee payments from a third party on account of unremitted withholdings of a taxpayer under federal or provincial tax law,[89] and will become the owner of these monies notwithstanding the security interests of any prior secured creditors.[90] It also allows the Minister to garnishee payments intended for secured creditors of the tax debtor.[91]

Subsections 224(4) and (4.1) impose penalties on third parties who fail to make payments to the Receiver General when ordered to do so by the CRA.[92]

---

84 *ITA*, ss. 224(1.1)(a). The subsection provides that the loans must be secured.

85 *ITA*, ss. 224(1.1)(b).

86 *ITA*, ss. 224(3).

87 *Royal Bank v. The Queen*, [1984] C.T.C. 573, 84 D.T.C. 6439 (Fed. T.D.), appeal dismissed [1986] 2 C.T.C. 211, 86 D.T.C. 6390 (Fed. C.A.).

88 With the exception of ss. 69 and 69.1 which deal with the availability of stays of proceedings by creditors.

89 *ITA*, ss. 224(1.2)(a). The provision applies where the tax debtor is liable to pay an amount under ss. 227(10.1) of the *ITA* or any other similar provision. "Similar provision" is defined in ss. 224(1.3) as a provision similar to ss. 227(10.1) of any Act of a province that imposes a withholding tax, and where the province has entered into an agreement with the Minister for the collection of taxes payable under that Act.

90 The Minister's priority over other secured creditors was confirmed in *Canada Trustco Mortgage Corp. v. Port O'Call Hotel Inc.* (1996), (*sub nom. R. v. Alberta Treasury Branches*) 96 D.T.C. 6245, (*sub nom. Pigott Project Management Ltd. v. Land-Rock Resources Ltd.*) [1996] 1 C.T.C. 395 (S.C.C.). "Secured creditor" and "security interest" are defined broadly in ss. 224(1.3), but do not include absolute ownership of property. Thus, the Minister does not have priority over owners of property.

91 *ITA*, ss. 224(1.2)(b). See, for example, *Royal Bank v. Saskatchewan Power Corp* (1990), 90 D.T.C. 6330, (*sub nom. Royal Bank v. Canada*) [1990] 2 C.T.C. 285 (Sask. Q.B.), appeal dismissed (1990), [1991] 1 W.W.R. 1 (Sask. C.A.), in which the CRA's third party demand under ss. 224(1.2) was held to have priority over a bank in its capacity as secured creditor.

92 Where a third party has failed to pay monies owed to a tax debtor when ordered to do so by the CRA under ss. 224(1), (1.2) or (3), the third party is liable for an amount equal to the amount that the third party was required to pay under the garnishment order: ss.

Joint and Several Liability

Section 160 allows the CRA to impose joint and several liability for tax debts where a taxpayer has transferred property to certain related persons. This provision is intended to prevent taxpayers from escaping their liability for taxes by transferring their assets to persons with whom they do not deal at arm's length for inadequate consideration.[93] The CRA makes reference to this provision in IC 98-1R3.

The provision applies to transfers of property by a taxpayer to one of three categories of recipient:[94]

- The transferor's spouse or common law partner;
- A person under 18 years of age; and
- A person with whom the transferor does not deal at arm's length.

Where such a person has acquired property from a taxpayer, both the taxpayer and the transferee become jointly and severally liable for two amounts:

- the amount by which transferor's tax owing for the year exceeds the income or capital gains tax that would result from the transfer of property if the attribution rules in sections 74.1 to 75.1 did not apply;[95]
- the lesser of the amount by which the fair market value of the transferred property exceeds the consideration given on the transfer and the transferor's tax owing for the year.[96]

224(4). Where a third party has failed to comply with a garnishment order under ss. 224(1.1), the penalty is equal to the lesser of the total monies lent, advanced, or paid to the taxpayer, and the amount the institution was required to pay under the garnishment order: ss. 224(4.1).

93 *Darte v. The Queen*, [2008] 5 C.T.C. 2178, 2008 D.T.C. 2567 (T.C.C. [General Procedure] at para. 24 [C.T.C.].

94 *ITA*, ss. 160(1).

95 *ITA*, ss. 160(1)(d).

96 *ITA*, ss. 160(1)(e). The Tax Court of Canada held in *Darte, supra* that the value of constructive trusts held by the transferor in the transferred property may be taken into account in determining whether consideration was given on the transfer. If on the transfer the transferor relinquishes his or her beneficial interest in the property pursuant to the constructive trust, this will constitute consideration. This is so even if a Court of Equity has not yet determined whether a constructive trust exists. The Court in *Darte* held that fair market value of the transferor's right to apply to court of equity for declaration of constructive trust was equal to one half of fair market value of property.

There is no limitation period beyond which the CRA may not reassess; reassessments for amounts owing under s. 160 may be made at any time.[97]

Powers Under the Canada-U.S. Tax Treaty

Article XXVIA of the *Canada-U.S. Income Tax Convention*[98] provides that Canada and the United States will lend each other assistance in the collection of income taxes, including any interest and penalties.[99] Thus, notwithstanding the general common law principle that states will not assist each other in the collection of each other's taxes, the CRA may apply to the United States for assistance in collecting tax payable under the Act, and the Internal Revenue Service may likewise request assistance in collecting on U.S. tax debts.

Where the United States accepts a request from CRA for assistance in collection, the amount owing under the Act is deemed to be an assessment under U.S. law against the taxpayer.[100] Thus, the taxpayer will be subject to the U.S. collections regime in respect of the tax debt. All amounts collected are forwarded to the Receiver General of Canada, and the normal costs of collection are borne by the U.S.[101] The mirror of this applies to applications from the IRS that are accepted in Canada.

The mutual collections regime applies only to tax debts that have been "finally determined" in the state seeking collection assistance.[102] Paragraph 2 of Article XXVIA provides that a debt has been finally determined when the applicant state has the right under its internal law to collect the revenue claim and all administrative and judicial rights of the taxpayer to restrain collection in the applicant state have lapsed or been exhausted. Thus, the same timing considerations that apply to collections action by the CRA will apply to collections by the U.S. under the Tax Treaty. Only when the CRA is authorized to take collections action in Canada will the taxpayer be subject to collections action in the U.S.

---

97 *Addison & Leyen Ltd. v. Canada*, 2007 SCC 33, [2008] 2 C.T.C. 129, 2007 D.T.C. 5365 (Eng.).

98 *Convention Between Canada and The United States with Respect to Taxes on Income and on Capital*, Canada and United States, September 26, 1980, S.C. 1984, c. 20, as amended. For more information, see generally D. Kerzner, V. Timokhov & D. Chodikoff, *The Tax Advisor's Guide to the Canada-U.S. Tax Treaty*, (looseleaf) (Thomson, Carswell, 2008).

99 Para. 1.

100 Para. 4(a).

101 Para. 6.

102 Para. 2.

Article XXVIA confirms that the taxpayer has no right of administrative or judicial review of the amount deemed owing in the requested state.[103] Thus, the taxpayer cannot appeal the substance of the Canadian tax debt in U.S. courts. If, while execution in the United States is pending, the right of the CRA to collect on the tax debt lapses or ceases, the CRA must promptly withdraw its request for collection assistance.

The mutual collections regime does not apply to tax debts owing by a person who was a citizen of the requested state during the taxable period to which the tax debt relates.[104] Thus, the U.S. will not aid enforcement of a Canadian tax debt incurred by a person who was a U.S. citizen in the relevant taxation period.

Responses: What Can You Do About It?

In Canada, we have a variety of protective actions that taxpayers can take in response to the CRA enforcement and/or collections actions. Some measures are aimed at reducing the tax debt owing – these include seeking relief from interest and penalties, and seeking reassessments or refunds outside the normal reassessment period.[105] Other measures are simply aimed at negotiating payment arrangements with the CRA. In all circumstances involving CRA collections action, it is vital that a taxpayer faced with a tax debt consult legal counsel immediately to determine options going forward, as time is of the essence.

Taxpayer Relief

Waiver of Penalties and Interest

Subsection 220(3.1) of the Act provides that the Minister has discretion to waive or cancel all or part of any interest and penalties.[106] Subsection 220(3.1) applies only to penalties and interest – it does not apply to principal amounts owing. The CRA has said in a policy statement that its ability to waive or cancel penalties and interest is not intended to allow taxpayers to

---

103 Para. 5.

104 Para. 8.

105 CRA, Information Circular IC 07-1, "Taxpayer Relief Provisions" (May 31, 2007).

106 A "waiver" of penalties refers to penalties and interest otherwise payable for which relief has been granted before these amounts were assessed or charged to the taxpayer. A "cancellation" refers to penalties and interest amounts that were assessed or charged to a taxpayer for which relief is granted by the CRA: IC 07-1 at ¶22.

arbitrarily reduce or settle their tax debts.[107] The CRA has set out three bases on which it will consider waiving or cancelling penalties and interest:

- Extraordinary circumstances;
- Actions by the CRA; and
- Inability to pay or financial hardship.

"Extraordinary circumstances" refer to circumstances beyond the taxpayer's control that prevented the taxpayer from making a payment when due, filing a return on time, or otherwise complying with an obligation under the Act.[108] Courts have held that this is the primary factor to be considered by the CRA when deciding whether to grant relief.[109] Such extraordinary circumstances might include natural or man-made disasters such as flood or fire, civil disturbances or disruptions in services such as a postal strike, serious illness or accident, or serious emotional or mental distress. Generally, this will not include errors made by third parties (*e.g.*, lawyers, accountants, *etc.*) acting on the taxpayer's behalf, although the CRA has stated that it may consider waiving penalties and/or interest on the basis of third party error where extraordinary circumstances beyond the control of the taxpayer's representative prevented the taxpayer from complying with the Act.[110]

Penalties and interest can also be waived or cancelled if the penalty or interest arose primarily because of the actions of CRA. In its policy statement, the CRA has provided some examples, which include:[111]

- processing delays that result in the taxpayer not being informed, within a reasonable time, that an amount is owing;
- errors in material available to the public, which led taxpayers to file returns or make payments based on incorrect information;
- incorrect information provided to a taxpayer, such as in the case where the CRA wrongly advises a taxpayer that no instalment payments will be required for the current year;
- errors in processing;
- delays in providing information, such as when a taxpayer could not make the appropriate instalment or arrears payments because the necessary information was not available; or

---

107 IC 07-1 at ¶21.

108 IC 07-1 at ¶25.

109 *3500772 Canada Inc. v. Minister of National Revenue*, [2008] 4 C.T.C. 1, 2008 D.T.C. 6396 (F.C.) at para. 40 [C.T.C.]; *Gandy v. Canada (Customs & Revenue Agency)*, [2006] 5 C.T.C. 109, 2006 D.T.C. 6510 (F.C.) at para. 21 [C.T.C.].

110 IC 07-1 at ¶35-36.

111 IC 07-1 at ¶26.

- undue delays in resolving an objection or an appeal, or in completing an audit.

The CRA will also consider financial hardship on the taxpayer of any penalties or interest. The CRA recognizes that in some circumstances where there is a confirmed inability to pay all amounts owing, it may be appropriate to consider waiving or cancelling interest to enable taxpayers to pay their account. This applies only to interest; the CRA will not generally consider reducing or cancelling penalties unless extraordinary circumstances have prevented compliance.[112] Circumstances which may justify waiver or cancellation of interest due to financial hardship include:[113]

- when collection has been suspended due to an inability to pay and substantial interest has accumulated or will accumulate;
- when a taxpayer's demonstrated ability to pay requires an extended payment arrangement, consideration may be given to waiving all or part of the interest for the period from when payments start until the amounts owing are paid, as long as the agreed payments are made on time and compliance with the Act is maintained; or
- when payment of the accumulated interest would cause a prolonged inability to provide basic necessities such as food, medical help, transportation, or shelter, consideration may be given to cancelling all or part of the total accumulated interest.

In reviewing a request for relief due to any of the circumstances set out above, the CRA has indicated that it will consider the following factors in deciding whether to grant relief:[114]

- whether the taxpayer has a history of compliance with tax obligations;
- whether the taxpayer has knowingly allowed a balance to exist on which arrears interest has accrued;
- whether the taxpayer has exercised reasonable care and has not been negligent or careless in conducting their affairs under the self-assessment system; and
- whether the taxpayer has acted quickly to remedy any delay or omission.

---

112 IC 07-1 at ¶28. The CRA recognizes that such exceptional circumstances may exist which will give rise to a cancellation of penalties. For example, where a business is experiencing extreme financial difficulty, and enforcement of a penalty would jeopardize the continuity of its operations, the jobs of employees, and the welfare of the community as a whole, consideration may be given to providing relief of the penalties.

113 IC 07-1 at ¶27.

114 IC 07-1 at ¶33.

Late, Amended, or Revoked Elections

The Act provides for numerous elections which permit taxpayers to select alternative forms of tax treatment. Such elections may reduce a taxpayer's tax payable under the Act. Subsection 220(3.2) allows the CRA to extend the time for making an election, or to permit a taxpayer to amend or revoke an election beyond the normal period within which such elections must normally be made. Taxpayers may apply to take advantage of this discretion and may accordingly reduce their tax debt.

Subsection 220(3.2) applies only to certain prescribed elections set out in Regulation 600 to the Act. These are set out in Schedule "A" to IC 07-1. Where the CRA accepts a late election, the election is deemed to have been made at the time it was required to have been made.[115] Where the CRA accepts a late revocation of an election, the election is deemed never to have been made.[116] In order to be accepted, the late, amended, or revoked election must be legal under the relevant legislation in place for the applicable year to which the election applies.[117] Taxpayers will not be permitted to make requests seeking to take advantage of changes in the law enacted after the due date of the election.[118]

The CRA has set out circumstances in which it may accept a request to make, amend, or revoke an election under ss. 220(3.2).[119] These include situations where:

- there have been tax consequences not intended by the taxpayer, and there is evidence that the taxpayer took reasonable steps to comply with the law. This could include, for example, the situation where the taxpayer obtained a *bona fide* valuation for a property, but after the CRA's review the valuation was found not to be correct.
- the request arises from circumstances beyond the taxpayer's control. These include the same sorts of circumstances set out above regarding waiver or cancellation of penalties or interest.
- it is evident that the taxpayer acted on incorrect information given by the CRA. This could include incorrect written replies to queries and errors in the CRA publications.
- the request results from a mechanical error. This could include using the net book value amount when obviously the taxpayer

115 *ITA*, para. 220(3.3)(a).
116 *ITA*, para. 220(3.3)(b).
117 IC 07-1 at ¶48.
118 IC 07-1 at ¶57(a).
119 IC 07-1 at ¶56.

intended to use the undepreciated capital cost or using an incorrect cost.

- the later accounting of the transactions by all parties is as if the election had been made, or had been made in a particular manner.
- the taxpayer can demonstrate that they were unaware of the election provision, even though they took reasonable care to comply with the law, and took remedial action as soon as possible.

Where the CRA accepts a late, amended, or revoked election, a penalty applies under ss. 220(3.5). The penalty is the lesser of $8,000 or $100 for each month passing between the date on which the election was required to have been made and the date on which the taxpayer applied for relief. This penalty is subject to rules regarding waiver or cancellation of penalties under ss. 220(3.1).[120]

Refunds or Reduction in Amount Payable

Normally, individuals and testamentary trusts seeking to file an income tax return to claim a refund must do so within three years of the end of the taxation year to which the refund relates.[121] Similarly, a three-year limitation period applies to requests for adjustments to an assessment by the CRA.[122] However, the Act provides that the CRA has discretion to refund any overpayment of tax or to make a reassessment outside the normal three-year limitation period.[123]

The ability to make a late claim for a refund or reassessment applies only to individuals and testamentary trusts. With respect to reassessments, the relief provision applies only to reassessments in respect of certain amounts set out in ss. 152(4.2).

The CRA states that it may issue a refund or reduce an amount owed if it is satisfied that such a refund or reduction would have been made if the return or request had been filed or made on time, and provided that the necessary assessment is correct in law and has not already been allowed.[124] Late requests for refunds may be granted where the taxpayer was unaware of or

---

120 IC 07-1 at ¶54.

121 *ITA*, ss. 164(1).

122 *ITA*, ss. 152(4). The limitation period runs from the date of the original notice of assessment.

123 *ITA*, ss. 164(1.5) and 152(4.2).

124 IC 07-1 at ¶71.

missed claiming a deduction, a non-refundable credit, unclaimed provincial tax credits,[125] or payroll deductions.[126]

The CRA states that a request for an adjustment is not a basis on which to dispute the correctness of an assessment, nor to have issues reconsidered when the taxpayer chose not to challenge the issues through the normal objection and appeals process.[127] The CRA will also not permit reassessments of statute-barred returns if the request is made as the result of a court decision.[128]

Where a refund cancels all or part of penalties or interest previously paid, or reduces the amount of tax previously paid as a result of the CRA accepting an adjustment or a late, amended, or revoked election, ss. 164(3.2) provides for interest payable to the taxpayer. Compound daily interest accrues on the 31st day after the written request for relief was received by the CRA.[129] However, the CRA states that where the taxpayer has provided inadequate documentation accompanying a request for relief, the calculation of interest may be delayed until such time as CRA received all necessary documentation.

Limitations

All requests for relief that we have outlined are subject to a 10-year limitation period. The CRA is only authorized to grant relief for tax years ending within 10 years before the calendar year in which the request or income tax return is filed.[130] Thus, taxpayers have 10 years from the end of the calendar year in which the relevant taxation year or fiscal period ended to make a request to the CRA for relief. The CRA has provided examples of how the limitation period is to be calculated:

- an initial request or income tax return filed during the 2007 calendar year must deal with an issue related to a taxpayer's 1997 or later taxation year (or fiscal period) to be eligible for relief;
- An initial request or income tax return, filed on or after January 1, 2008 related to a taxpayer's 1997 and previous taxation years (or fiscal periods), is not eligible for relief since those years are beyond the 10-year period.

---

125 Note that the relief provision in ss. 164(1.5) does not override provincial limitation periods, unless provincial law allows for it: IC 07-1 at ¶84.

126 IC 07-1 at ¶72.

127 IC 07-1 at ¶73.

128 IC 07-1 at ¶87.

129 Interest on refunds and repayment is set at a prescribed rate in Reg. 4301(b).

130 IC 07-1 at ¶12.

- CRA has no authority to grant relief for the 1998 taxation year (or fiscal period) unless the taxpayer has filed an initial request or income tax return for that year before January 1, 2009.[131]

If an assessment or reassessment is issued by the CRA in a later year, or if an objection or appeal is initiated by the taxpayer that may take considerable time to resolve, taxpayers should immediately submit requests for relief to ensure that they will come within the 10-year limitation period. Where an objection or appeal is in process, CRA will informally indicate its opinion as to whether the relief will be granted, but will reserve its final decision until the objection or appeal is resolved or until all rights of appeal have expired.

Procedure

All applications for relief are made using Form RC4288 *Request for Taxpayer Relief*. The Form requires the taxpayer to set out, in detail, all forms of relief sought along with the circumstances supporting the request, and any relevant documentation in support of the request.[132]

There is no right of objection if the CRA denies a request for relief. However, taxpayers are permitted to request a second review of the original request for relief from the CRA, during which the taxpayer will have the opportunity to make additional submissions.[133] The second review is carried out by the officials of the CRA not involved in the first administrative review, who make recommendations to the director of the relevant tax services office. The ultimate decision is made by the director. If the taxpayer on second review believes that the CRA's discretion was not properly exercised, the taxpayer may seek judicial review in the Federal Court within 30 days of the date the decision was first received. Although the Federal Court cannot substitute its own decision for a decision of the CRA, it can refer the decision back to the CRA to be considered by another delegated official.

Payment Arrangements and Security for Payment

The *ITA* provides CRA with some discretion to enter into payment arrangements with taxpayers, or to accept security interests in taxpayer property as

---

131 IC 07-1 at ¶109.

132 Details regarding appropriate information and documentation to include in respect of different bases for relief are set out in IC 07-1.

133 IC 07-1 at ¶103-104.

security for the tax debt, as a means of lessening the burden on the tax debtor.

The CRA has stated that where a taxpayer cannot pay a total amount owing, it may accept a mutually satisfactory short-term payment arrangement based on the taxpayer's ability to pay.[134] The CRA indicates that it will consider such arrangements when the taxpayer has tried all reasonable ways of obtaining the necessary funds, either by borrowing or the rearrangement of the taxpayer's financial affairs, and still cannot pay. The taxpayer will be required to make full financial disclosure, including evidence of income, expenses, assets and liabilities, which will be verified by collections officers before any payment arrangement is accepted.

Subsection 220(4) allows the CRA to accept security for payment of any amount owing under the *ITA*, if the CRA considers it advisable. The CRA is required to accept security for payment where the taxpayer has objected to or appealed from an assessment and the objection or appeal remains outstanding.[135] The CRA must surrender any security taken that exceeds the total tax payable by the taxpayer.[136]

There are other conditions and terms related to payment arrangements and the security for payment. Because no two situations are the same, it is critical for a taxpayer to obtain legal advice and guidance. After all, this type of assistance will likely result in the best possible outcome in negotiations with the CRA.

Objections and Appeals

In the section of this chapter entitled "Timing Issues", we indicated that the filing of a Notice of Objection or Notice of Appeal can prevent, in most circumstances, the CRA from commencing a collection action. Resolving tax disputes with particular reference to the objection and/or appeals process is outside the scope of this chapter. Taxpayers are advised that the navigation of the objection and appeals process is best served by retaining the services and expertise of an experienced tax professional.

---

134 IC 98-1R3 at 3.

135 *ITA*, ss. 220(4.1).

136 *ITA*, ss. 220(4.2).

Conclusion

The debt collection regime found within the *Income Tax Act* is complex. It is full of qualifications and exceptions. However, it is also clear that the CRA has extraordinary powers to collect on tax debts. Taxpayers do have a variety of rights and options. These options and rights give the taxpayer a fighting chance when dealing with the powers of the CRA. Sometimes, it is a battle of attrition and, in other instances, it is the art of the possible and compromise. Each debt collection situation is unique. But, with creativity and the will to persevere, a taxpayer can survive the onslaught of the CRA's collection activities.

Estate Freezing and Re-Freezing in an Economic Downturn

Martin J. Rochwerg & Krystle A. Ng-A-Mann

Introduction

Estate freezing has been a very popular mechanism used in estate and succession planning for an owner-manager of a privately held corporation or an investor with an asset portfolio. To be effective to defer tax liability upon death, however, an estate freeze at a particular point in time assumes an increase in value of the frozen holdings in future years. Given the current economic climate, this presupposition has proven to be a premature miscalculation for some estate freezes that have been implemented in recent years. As such, it is a prudent course of action for a taxpayer to look for ways to offset the negative impact of a previously undertaken estate freeze, or to consider conducting an estate freeze for the first time now, while values are low.

In this chapter, the authors first canvass the concept of estate freezing. Next, the authors explore ways in which to modify an estate freeze, such as re-freezing, melting, and thawing. Finally, this chapter concludes with a discussion of the Canada Revenue Agency ("CRA") administrative policy with respect to estate re-freezing, and an overview of the case law affecting estate freezing.

Estate Freezing Basics: The Tip of the Iceberg

The topic of estate freezing is extremely broad. No attempt is made in this chapter to provide a comprehensive analysis with respect to estate freezing, as this has previously been the subject of a number of articles, papers, and books.[1] Instead, a high level overview of the mechanics of estate freezing is provided herein to afford the reader a general understanding of the subject matter.

What is an "Estate Freeze"?

"Estate freeze" is a term used to describe a basic reorganization in which the value of an enterprise is "frozen" in fixed-value preferred shares equal to the fair market value ("FMV") of the business or holdings at the date of the freeze, allowing the future growth to be attributed to common shares held by others, such as children or a family trust. A variety of procedures may be employed to accomplish an estate freeze for an individual, ranging in complexity from a simple exchange of assets to more complicated corporate reorganizations. An estate freeze achieves a number of goals, both tax-related and otherwise, such as the minimization of capital gains tax upon death.

The minimization or deferral of capital gains tax upon death is possible because an estate freeze enables the freezor to avoid paying capital gains tax on the entire amount of the future increase in a corporation's value, which would otherwise occur as a result of the deemed disposition rule in ss. 70(5) of the *Income Tax Act* (Canada) (the "ITA").[2] Subsection 70(5) of the ITA provides that when a taxpayer dies, he or she is deemed to have disposed of his or her property immediately before his or her death for proceeds equal to the FMV of such property immediately before death. This subsection effectively creates a deemed disposition of certain types of property of the taxpayer immediately before his or her death and consequently triggers the realization of any capital gains that have accrued to date.

Assume, for example, that in Year 1 an individual (the "freezor") subscribes for 100 common shares in a corporation for $100 and leverages its undertakings. The adjusted cost base ("ACB") and paid-up capital ("PUC") of the freezor's 100 common shares are each $100. If in Year 10, the value of the corporation has grown to $5,000,000, and it is anticipated that the value of the corporation will continue to increase, it would be advisable for the freezor to lock-in or fix the value of the freezor's shareholding in the corporation in order, among other things, to minimize the amount of capital gains tax triggered on death. The freezor could exchange the freezor's

---

1 See *e.g.*, M.J. Rochwerg & M.Y. Berry, "The Art of Estate Freezing", *Current Trends in Estate Planning* (Toronto: The Canadian Institute, 1990); M.J. Rochwerg & M.Y. Berry, "Unfreezing an Estate", *Estate Planning New Developments, New Tax Strategies* (Toronto: Insight Press, 1993).

2 R.S.C. 1985, c. 1 (5th Supp.), as amended.

common shares in the corporation for fixed-value preferred shares with a value equal to the FMV of the corporation in Year 10. The common shares, to which the future increase in value of the corporation would accrue, could then be acquired by others for a nominal cost. In this way, the capital gain that would be realized by the freezor upon death would be limited to the difference between the value of the corporation at the date of the freeze ($5,000,000) and the ACB of the freezor's shares ($100) (*i.e.*, $5,000,000 - $100 = $4,999,900), one half of which would be included in computing the freezor's income for the taxation year (*i.e.*, $2,499,950).

If, on the other hand, an estate freeze had not been implemented in Year 10, and the value of the corporation would have risen to $10,000,000 by the date of the freezor's death, then the capital gain realized upon death would be equal to the difference between the FMV of the shares at the date of death ($10,000,000) and the freezor's original ACB in the shares ($100) (*i.e.*, $10,000,000 - $100 = $9,999,900), one half of which would be included in the freezor's income for the taxation year (*i.e.*, $4,999,950).

As a corollary to limiting the amount of the capital gain triggered upon death to the difference between the value of the corporation at the date of the freeze and the ACB of the freezor's common shares, there is a capital gains deferral equal to the difference between the value of the corporation at the freezor's death and the value of the corporation at the date of the estate freeze. The tax deferral is not permanent, but will be effective until such time as the common shares are disposed of by the common shareholders, whether by death or otherwise (discussed below).

Tax Considerations

Aside from the minimization and deferral of capital gains tax, there are other valuable tax benefits to conducting an estate freeze, such as:

- minimizing probate fees;
- enabling family members to become shareholders and to contribute to the future growth of the corporation at a minimal cost to them;
- income-splitting opportunities through taking advantage of other family members' lower marginal income tax rates;
- multiplying the use of the lifetime capital gains exemption ("LCGE"); and
- providing access to/crystallizing the LCGE for the original shareholder.

Certain of these benefits will be discussed in turn.

Enabling Participation in Future Growth

An estate freeze is a beneficial mechanism for enabling family members to participate and share value in a family business. Since the common/growth shares are normally issued for nominal value, family members can acquire and hold equity in the family business for little consideration. This is intuitive, since one of the primary intentions behind executing an estate freeze is to have as much future growth attributable to the common shares as possible and to thereby maximize the amount of the capital gains deferral at the instigation of the freezor.

Income-Splitting

An estate freeze also presents income-splitting opportunities for family members, causing income and capital gains to be taxed at a potentially lower marginal income tax rate of the common shareholder(s). Corporate distributions, such as dividends, and capital gains may arise from the freeze corporation and shareholdings and be taxed in the hands of lower tax bracket shareholders following the establishment of the estate freeze.

Although the benefits of distributing dividends has fluctuated over time and is contingent upon the disparity between the effective corporate and personal tax rate, as will be explored below, changes to the eligible dividend regime in Canada have made the distribution of eligible dividends an even more attractive option in recent times. Distributing dividends can also achieve the outcome of reducing the corporation's assets and maintaining a lower value in the corporation, where desirable.

The attribution rules in the ITA become an exceedingly important consideration when contemplating income-splitting opportunities. Where applicable, they operate to require the transferor of certain types of property, rather than the transferee, to report the value of a distribution or income for taxation purposes. The personal attribution rules, "kiddie tax" and corporate attribution rules will be discussed immediately below, while the attribution rules relevant to trusts will be examined in the section entitled "21-Year Deemed Disposition Rule" in this chapter.

Personal Attribution Rules

Property that is loaned or transferred (either directly or indirectly through a trust) to a spouse, child, niece or nephew, or any other individual that does not deal at arm's length with the transferor and who is under the age of 18 (a "non-arm's length minor") may fall within the ambit of the personal attribution rules in ss. 74.1 and 74.2 of the ITA, respectively. If the attribution rules apply, then income or capital gains transferred to or for the benefit of a spouse will be attributable to the transferor, while income only (*e.g.*, dividends) transferred to or for the benefit of a non-arm's length minor will be attributed to the transferor.

In the context of an estate freeze, this could occur, for example, where the growth shares of the freeze corporation are acquired by the spouse or minor child from the freezor, or money is lent by the freezor to the spouse or child for the purpose of acquiring the growth shares. However, if the loan to acquire the growth shares is made for value, then ss. 74.5(1) and 74.5(2) of the ITA provide exceptions to the personal attribution rules. The interest on the loan for value must be charged at a prescribed rate,[3] or at a rate to which arm's length parties would have agreed. In the alternative, a spouse or minor child may use his or her or their own independent funds to finance the share subscription.[4] In the further alternative, if the transfer of property is made for proceeds of disposition equal to the property's FMV, then ss. 74.5(1) will also shield the transaction from the attribution rules.[5]

"Kiddie Tax"

In terms of income-splitting with minor children, a freezor should be aware of the "kiddie tax" rules, another form of attribution rule, in s. 120.4 of the ITA. According to ss. 120.4(2) of the ITA, effective for the year 2000 and later, 29 per cent of the "split income"[6] of a child (*i.e.*, a minor)[7] will be

---

3 The prescribed rate dropped to 1% in April, 2009 and continues to be 1% for the first quarter of 2010.

4 In Canada Revenue Agency ("CRA") CRA Document Technical Interpretation No. 2001-0072705, dated May 8, 2001, CRA confirmed that if the shares held by a trust for minor children were acquired for an amount equal to their FMV and are paid for with funds that are not supplied by the freezor, then dividends paid on such shares held by the trust will not be subject to the attribution rule in ss. 74.1(2). See also *Romkey v. The Queen*, 2000 D.T.C. 6047, [2000] 1 C.T.C. 390 (F.C.A.), leave to appeal refused (2000), 2000 CarswellNat 2423 (S.C.C.) where the Court found that dividends paid on shares issued to a trust as part of an estate freeze for an amount other than their FMV were attributed back to the original shareholders.

5 See CRA Interpretation Bulletin IT-510, "Transfers and loans of property made after May 22, 1985 to a related minor", dated December 30, 1987, and CRA Interpretation Bulletin IT-511, "Interspousal and Certain Other Transfers and Loans of Property", dated February 21, 1994, for a comprehensive discussion of the personal attribution rules as they relate to spouses and minors.

6 See ss. 120.4(1) of the ITA for a definition of "split income".

7 The "kiddie tax" rules apply to attribute the percentage of income tax to a "specified individual", which is also defined in ss. 120.4(1) of the ITA, and includes an individual who: (a) had not attained the age of 17 years before the year; (b) at no time in the year was non-resident; and (c) has a parent who is resident in Canada at any time in the year.

added to such child's income tax payable for the year. The minor's income tax will be calculated in accordance with ss. 120.4(3) of the ITA. The "kiddie tax" rules apply to the income of a minor child attributable to dividends or shareholder appropriations from a privately held business, or income earned through a trust or partnership stemming from goods or services provided to a related person's business, but does not apply to capital gains. Effectively, the rules apply the top marginal income tax rate to such income in the hands of a minor.

Corporate Attribution

Where, for example, property is transferred or loaned to a corporation (as in an estate freeze), whether directly or indirectly through a trust, and one of the main purposes for doing so may reasonably be considered to have been to reduce the income of the transferor and to confer a benefit on a "designated person", ss. 74.4(2) may apply to attribute to the transferor an amount of interest based on a prescribed rate. As mentioned above, a "designated person" is defined in ss. 74.5(5), and includes a spouse or common law partner of the individual, or the child, niece or nephew, or other individual under the age of 18 that does not deal at arm's length with the individual.

In an estate freeze, it is not difficult to demonstrate that the main purposes may reasonably be considered to be the reduction of the income of the transferor (*e.g.*, the reduction of the capital gains tax liability on death) and the conferral of a benefit on a designated person (*e.g.*, the conferral of the benefit of the future growth of the freeze corporation). In this way, ss. 74.4(2) may result in adverse tax consequences to the freezor.

For ss. 74.4(2) to apply, the following conditions must be satisfied:

- one of the main purposes for the transfer or the loan may reasonably be considered to be to reduce the income of the transferor and to directly or indirectly benefit a designated person (called the "main purpose test");
- the designated person must be a "specified shareholder"[8] of the corporation;
- the transferor was a resident of Canada during the relevant period; and
- the corporation is not a "small business corporation".[9]

---

8 "Specified shareholder" is defined in ss. 248(1) of the ITA to include a person owning at least 10% of the shares of a "related corporation" other than a small business corporation.

9 See ss. 248(1) for the definition of "small business corporation".

It should be noted that if any of the above conditions cease to apply, the corporate attribution rule will also cease to apply. To the extent that the corporation is a small business corporation, or certain other requirements are met where there is trust ownership, ss. 74.4(4) of the ITA may apply so as to preclude attribution.

It can never be stressed enough that, while there certainly are ways to structure affairs to avoid invoking the various attribution rules and negative tax consequences ensuing therefrom, it is always recommended that professional tax advice be solicited in the context of planning in general, and estate freezing in particular.

The Lifetime Capital Gains Exemption ("LCGE")

To the extent that the freezor's shares are considered "qualified small business corporation shares", a term defined in ss. 110.6(1) of the ITA, a significant portion of a capital gain realized on the disposition of such shares, including disposition on death, may be tax-exempt under the LCGE.

The LCGE enables individuals (not corporations) to shelter up to $750,000 of capital gains ($375,000 of taxable capital gains) arising out of the disposition of shares in a qualified small business corporation ("QSBC"), subject to certain restrictions. To be eligible to claim the LCGE, the corporation whose shares are disposed of must be a Canadian-controlled private corporation ("CCPC"), which is a Canadian corporation that is not controlled (usually ownership of more than 50 per cent of the voting rights) directly or indirectly by one or more non-residents, public corporations, or a corporation whose class of shares of its capital stock is listed on a designated stock exchange.[10] In addition, to qualify for the LCGE, at least 90 per cent of the assets of the corporation must have been used to carry on an active business in Canada; and, in the 24 months preceding the sale of shares, the individual must have owned the shares personally and more than 50 per cent of the corporation's assets must have been used in an active business in Canada.

Concerns have been expressed that access to the LCGE in future will be restricted, or that the exemption will be repealed altogether. There may also be a concern that the freeze corporation will not continue to meet the definition of a QSBC, or the shares will not continue to be characterized as "qualified small business corporation shares". Therefore, it is advisable to "crystallize" the freezor's right to claim the LCGE, where possible, through

---

10 See ss. 125(7) of the ITA for the definition of "Canadian-controlled private corporation".

an estate freeze.[11] Estate freezing also facilitates the multiplying of the LCGE in favor of those holding growth shares in the freeze corporation, and could potentially extend separate LCGE claims to all of the freeze beneficiaries. In a case where children of the freezor are the freeze beneficiaries, there is no concern that the personal attribution rules in s. 74.1 of the ITA will attribute the capital gain back to the freezor, since ss. 74.1(2) does not apply to capital gains. Thus, the growth shares can be given to children, either directly or by means of a trust, for the purpose of multiplying the LCGE. On the other hand, the spousal attribution rule contained in ss. 74.1(1) will apply to income and capital gains, so particular attention must be paid in structuring the estate freeze to circumvent the application of the spousal attribution rule.[12]

If available, the LCGE is of considerable benefit to the freezor and other shareholders. However, it should be noted that the rules under the ITA governing eligibility for the LCGE are extremely complicated, and there are many pitfalls to be aware of that are associated with claiming the exemption.

Non-Tax Considerations

Aside from the attractive tax-related opportunities discussed above, non-tax concerns are often a driving force in contemplating an estate freeze and deciding upon the method by which an estate freeze will be structured, and are therefore worthy of comment.

Control

One of the most fundamental of these non-tax considerations is control of the corporation. The timing of an estate freeze is imperative, not only because of volatile market conditions, but also in ensuring the continued success of a business through the proper exercise of control, often at the hands of the freezor. Depending on the age of the freezor's successors who acquire the common shares of the freezor's corporation, the freezor may not wish for total control of the business to pass to his or her successors. In such a case, it may be desirable for a freezor to retain partial control of the business through a partial freeze, where only some of the freezor's common shares are converted, or the freezor takes back consideration on the transfer

---

11 For example, this could be done in an estate freeze by electing into a capital gain in respect of the freeze shares.

12 This could be achieved, for example, by requiring the spouse to acquire the growth shares with independent capital. Since growth shares are usually acquired for a nominal amount, this will not be cost-prohibitive for such a freeze beneficiary.

that will allow him or her to participate in future growth. However, this may subvert some of the income tax objectives of estate freezing, since there is greater exposure to capital gains tax upon death under a partial freeze than there is under a full estate freeze.

In the alternative, it may be possible for the freezor to exchange his or her common shares for shares with specific control attributes attached to them. However, in subsequently exercising control, regard must be had for the rights of all of the shareholders not to be unduly prejudiced in the management of the corporation.

Generally, under Canadian corporate legislation, directors are required to act "honestly and in good faith with a view to the best interests of the corporation" and are required to "exercise the care, diligence and skill that a reasonably prudent person would exercise in comparable circumstances."[13] Where, for example, control is exercised to the detriment of some or all of the shareholders, directors, or officers, s. 248 of the OBCA[14] may provide relief to the shareholder(s), director(s), or officer(s) so prejudiced. Section 248 of the OBCA, the "oppression remedy", grants a court extensive powers to rectify situations in which a complainant[15] applies to the court, and the court is satisfied that the acts, omissions, or affairs of the corporation or any of its affiliates, or the powers of the directors of the corporation or any of its affiliates have been or are threatened to be exercised in a manner that is oppressive, unfairly prejudicial, or that unfairly disregards the interests of any security holder, creditor, director, or officer of the corporation.[16] Section 241 of the CBCA[17] is the federal counterpart to s. 248 of the OBCA, and contains nearly identical language to the OBCA provisions.

---

13 See *e.g.*, ss. 122(1) of the *Canada Business Corporations Act*, R.S.C. 1985, c. C-44 (the "CBCA"); ss. 134(1) of the *Business Corporations Act* (Ontario), R.S.O. 1990, c. B.16 (the "OBCA").

14 OBCA, *ibid.*

15 "Complainant" is broadly defined in s. 245 of the OBCA to include a registered or beneficial security holder of a corporation, a former registered or beneficial security holder of a corporation, a director, officer, former director, former officer of the corporation or any of its affiliates, or any other person, within the discretion of the court, who is a proper person to make an application to the court.

16 See *e.g.*, *Naneff v. Con-Crete Holdings Ltd.* (1995), 1995 CarswellOnt 1207, [1995] O.J. No. 1377 (C.A.), an oppression remedy case where a son was successful in alleging that his father had acted in an oppressive manner in terminating his employment in the corporation subsequent to an estate freeze in which the father received a class of control shares in the corporation. The remaining shareholders were therefore required by the Court to purchase the son's shares for an amount equal to their fair market value.

17 CBCA, above note 13.

Section 207 of the OBCA also affords a court discretion to order the winding-up of a corporation in circumstances where, as in s. 248 of the OBCA, the court is satisfied that the affairs of the corporation are conducted in an oppressive or unfairly prejudicial manner, or where the court believes it is "just and equitable" for some other reason. Moreover, ss. 190(3) of the CBCA empowers a minority shareholder to dissent and force the corporation to purchase his or her shares for an amount equal to their "fair value" in instances where he or she disagrees with a proposed fundamental change. These are but a few of the corporate law provisions that may affect the validity of an estate freeze or subsequent modification that a freezor (owner-manager) should bear in mind.

Hence, while a freezor's main objective in implementing an estate freeze is to assign the growth value of the corporation to others (the "freeze beneficiaries"), the freezor should be aware that, in doing so, he or she is enabling the freeze beneficiaries to acquire shares, which are comprised of a bundle of rights and privileges in respect of the corporation, including participation in the decision-making therein. To the extent that a shareholder's "reasonable expectations" with respect to the administration of the corporation are offended, the freezor's original intentions in carrying out the estate freeze may be thwarted.[18]

Another method of preserving control is for the freezor to effect an estate freeze on a post-mortem basis, whereby the freezor's Will sets out the terms by which the freezor's assets in the corporation will be restructured and future growth allocated. However, insofar as the freezor is concerned, post-mortem estate freezing does not provide a reduction and deferral of capital gains tax, and may therefore postpone the primary benefit of instituting an estate freeze.

Sufficiency of Assets

In addition to control, other non-tax considerations are the sufficiency of assets retained by the freezor and the financial consequences of an estate freeze. Due to inflation, changing market conditions, and longer life expectancy, a freezor may come to realize that there is inadequate value in his or

---

18 See *e.g.*, *Animal House Investments Inc. v. Lisgar Development Ltd.* (2008), 2008 CarswellOnt 3306, [2008] O.J. No. 2240 (Div. Ct.), affirming (2007), 87 O.R. (3d) 529 (S.C.J.), where the Court refused to order the purchase of a son's shares by his mother and sister (the remaining shareholders) under s. 207 of the OBCA because the son failed to demonstrate that he had a reasonable expectation that the corporation would be wound up or his shares would be purchased in circumstances where there were irreconcilable differences between the parties involved.

her retained shareholdings to ensure an adequate lifestyle during retirement, and freezing prematurely may have a significant impact on the freezor's needs. The freezor may thus have to adjust to a different standard of living, or approach the freeze beneficiaries to ask for help or discuss other options. This may be challenging for the freezor if the relationship between the freezor and the freeze beneficiaries has deteriorated.

Estate freezing can become a challenging foray as a result of the interplay of the above-mentioned factors; and that can be compounded where family breakdowns occur following the execution of an estate freeze. In all cases, elucidating and managing the reasonable expectations of all parties involved is crucial. As much as possible, these ought to be sufficiently documented (*e.g.*, in the form of a shareholder's agreement[19]) in advance of the estate freeze in order to avoid any misapprehensions, and in the event a court is compelled to make a determination with respect to the reasonable expectations of the parties.

Ultimately, estate freezing is done on a case-by-case basis, and a careful examination of the particular circumstances of the prospective freezor should be carefully undertaken before an estate freeze is executed.

Effecting an Estate Freeze

As mentioned, there are many variations for implementing an estate freeze, which can range considerably in degree of complexity. In this section, estate freezing through the rollover provisions in ss. 85 and 86 of the ITA will be addressed as well as the option of utilizing an *inter vivos* trust. The particular method selected by the prospective freezor will depend on his or her circumstances, and the circumstances of the others involved, such as the prospective freeze beneficiaries.

Section 85 Rollover

Section 85 of the ITA facilitates the transfer of certain types of property, including shares, to a corporation on a rollover basis, such that no immediate income tax liability is incurred by the transferor on the transfer, but is instead shifted to the transferee corporation. In CRA Interpretation Bulletin

---

19 Note, however, that a court's arsenal of remedies in a s. 248 oppression action includes "creating or amending" a unanimous shareholder agreement pursuant to para. 248(3)(c) of the OBCA.

IT-291R3 ("IT-291R3"),[20] CRA sets out the criteria that must be satisfied in order to be eligible for the ss. 85(1) rollover:[21]

- the transferee corporation must be a "taxable Canadian corporation";
- the property transferred must be "eligible property";
- a joint election must be filed by the transferor and the transferee corporation; and
- the consideration received by the transferor must include at least one share of the capital stock of the transferee.[22]

The transferor can be an individual or a corporation. On the other hand, the transferee must be a "taxable Canadian corporation", which is defined in ss. 89(1) of the ITA to mean a corporation that was resident at the relevant time of the transfer, that was either incorporated or resident in Canada between June 18, 1971 and the date of the transfer, and that is not exempt from Part I tax. "Eligible property" is defined in ss. 89(1.1) of the ITA to include, *inter alia,* shares of the capital stock of a corporation. The joint election by the transferor and transferee must be filed within the requisite time,[23] on the prescribed form (T2057), and must specify the agreed amount for which the transfer will have occurred.[24]

Assuming the conditions in ss. 85(1) are met, the freezor can transfer his or her common shares to the freeze corporation in exchange for preferred shares by filing a joint election with the freeze corporation; or the freezor can transfer his or her common shares to a holding corporation in exchange for preferred shares of the holding corporation on a tax-deferred basis under ss. 85(1). Both variations are commonly used.

The effect of the election is to deem the transferor's proceeds of disposition, and the freeze (or holding) corporation's cost of the common shares, to be

---

20 CRA Interpretation Bulletin IT-291R3, "Transfer of Property to a Corporation under Subsection 85(1)", dated January 12, 2004 [*IT-291R3*].

21 See also CRA Information Circular IC 76-19R3, "Transfer of Property to a Corporation under Section 85", dated June 17, 1996 [*IC 76-19R3*].

22 *IT-291R3,* above note 20 at para. 1; *IC 76-19R3, ibid.* at para. 8.

23 See ss. 85(6) of the ITA.

24 In particular, pursuant to para. 85(1)(c), the agreed amount cannot be greater than the FMV of the property disposed of, and cannot be less than the FMV of the non-share consideration received in exchange under para. 85(1)(b) of the ITA. If the FMV of the transferred property exceeds the value of the consideration received by the transferor and the agreed amount, and it is reasonable to regard any part of the excess as a benefit that the transferor wished to confer on a related person, then ss. 85(1)(e.2) may apply to increase the agreed amount: *IT-291R3* at paras. 10 and 18. Note, however, that ss. 85(1)(e.2) does not apply in a case where the transferee is a wholly-owned corporation of the transferor.

the agreed amount. At the same time, para. 85(1)(g) of the ITA provides that the cost of the preferred shares to the transferor that are received as consideration for the common shares disposed of will be deemed to be the lesser of: (a) the FMV of the shares immediately after the transfer; and (b) the elected proceeds of disposition minus any non-share consideration. If preferred shares of more than one class are received by the freezor, then the amount assigned to each class will be determined on a *pro rata* basis.

In allowing an "agreed amount" to be selected under ss. 85(1), this rollover provision permits a freezor to select the amount of capital gain that he or she would like to trigger at the time of the rollover, if any, perhaps making use of the LCGE or offsetting the gains with capital losses.

Section 86 Share Reorganization

Section 86 involves an internal reorganization of share capital where a freezor's common shares in the freeze corporation are exchanged for preferred shares. Under s. 86, the freezor must dispose of all of his or her shares of any particular class of the capital stock of a corporation in the course of the reorganization to be eligible for the rollover. Sections 86 and 85 are mutually exclusive, since ss. 86(3) of the ITA states that s. 86 does not apply where ss. 85(1) applies.

As in a s. 85 rollover, there may be non-share consideration received as part of the proceeds of disposition of the common shares. However, under s. 86, there will not be a complete rollover insofar as the value of the non-share consideration exceeds the ACB of the common shares exchanged; and where the non-share consideration exceeds the PUC of the common shares, there will be a deemed dividend under ss. 84(3) of the ITA which will be excluded from the proceeds of disposition of the common shares.

Where non-share consideration is received by the freezor as all or part of the consideration for the disposition of the common shares, then the ACB of the non-share consideration is deemed to be the FMV of the non-share consideration at the date of the disposition under para. 86(1)(a) of the ITA. Pursuant to para. 86(1)(b), the amount by which the original ACB of the common shares disposed of exceeds the FMV of the non-share consideration is deemed to be the freezor's ACB of the freeze shares.

In effecting a s. 86 rollover, ss. 86(2) and 15(1) of the ITA must be observed. Subsection 86(2) may apply to the rollover where the freezor has disposed of his or her common shares in the freeze corporation and the value of the shares and any non-share consideration is less than the FMV of the exchanged common shares, and it is reasonable to regard any portion of the difference as a benefit that the freezor desired to confer on a related person. The effect of ss. 86(2) is to limit the rollover and reduce the cost of the new freeze shares. If, on the other hand, the value of the shares plus non-share consideration received in exchange for the common shares is greater than the FMV of the common shares, then there may be a shareholder benefit under ss. 15(1). If the freezor only receives shares in return for the common shares, then the ACB of the freeze shares received by the freezor will be the same as the ACB of the exchanged shares.

As mentioned, to avail himself or herself of the s. 86 rollover the freezor must dispose of all of the shares of a particular class of shares of the capital stock of the corporation, and must receive property from the freeze corporation that includes other shares of the corporation's capital stock (but not necessarily of the same class of the shares exchanged). In addition, the common shares exchanged in the rollover must be held by the freezor as capital property, not inventory.

One of the disadvantages in using a rollover provision to execute an estate freeze is that the freezor will be unable to crystallize his or her LCGE unless an appropriate election is jointly filed by the freezor and the freeze corporation under the s. 85 rollover to deem the proceeds of disposition of the common shares to be the amount of the LCGE plus the original ACB of the shares.

Without the rollover provisions in ss. 85 and 86 of the ITA, the disposition of shares that occurs on the reorganization of share capital under an estate freeze could be considered a taxable event. It must be remembered that in all cases, the constating documents (*e.g.*, Articles of Incorporation) of the freeze corporation will generally need to be amended in order to provide for a new class of preference shares to be issued as part of the consideration.

Section 51 Share Conversion

Yet another common method of implementing an estate freeze is through the use of a s. 51 share conversion. A s. 51 share conversion is substantially the same as a s. 86 share reorganization in that a freezor exchanges his or her old shares for new shares in the freeze corporation without causing an immediate disposition giving rise to a taxable capital gain. Unlike a s. 86 share reorganization, however, under s. 51 the freezor is not required to dispose of *all* of the shares of a particular class of the freeze corporation.

Section 51 allows convertible securities,[25] such as shares, bonds, debentures, or promissory notes to be exchanged.

It should be noted that ss. 51(2) of the ITA might be invoked to limit the rollover in situations where a taxpayer gifted a portion of the value of the convertible property to a related person. This may force the recognition of a capital gain and alter the ACB of the shares received on the conversion. Subsection 51(2) will apply where:

- ss. 51(1) would otherwise have applied to the conversion of shares;
- the FMV of the convertible property before the conversion is greater than the FMV of the shares received in exchange; and
- such excess can reasonably be considered to be a benefit that the taxpayer wished to confer on a related person.

Typically, s. 51 will not apply in circumstances where there is a triggering event creating an automatic conversion of the common shares, or the shares automatically convert on a specific date.[26] Section 51 will also not apply where s. 85 or 86 applies.

Utilizing a Discretionary Family Trust

The common shares to which the growth of the corporation accrues can be held in various ways, such as by individuals alone, a holding corporation, or through a discretionary *inter vivos* trust. The method of using a discretionary trust in estate freezing is also sometimes referred to as a "flexible freeze". Not surprisingly then, holding the common shares through a discretionary trust provides a great measure of flexibility to the freezor, and affords the beneficiaries of the trust only possible access to the income from the shares. The freezor, as settlor, can appoint the beneficiaries of his or her choice, including himself or herself as potential income beneficiary. If the freezor is established as the trustee of the trust, then the freezor can play a role in determining the amount and manner in which distributions are to be

---

25 See CRA Interpretation Bulletin IT-96R6, "Options Granted by Corporations to Acquire Shares, Bonds, or Debentures and by Trusts to Acquire Trust Units", dated October 23, 1996 [*IT-96R6*] for a discussion about several aspects of convertible securities.

26 See "Revenue Canada Round Table", in *Report of the Proceedings of the Thirty-Ninth Tax Conference*, 1987 Conference Report (Toronto: Canadian Tax Foundation, 1988), 47: 51-103, question 67.

made.[27] As will be seen where the freezor is not the settlor, the use of a discretionary trust can also be a means of altering an estate freeze previously implemented, where the freezor, as beneficiary, can retain some of the benefit of the growth shares through receipts of income or capital out of the trust.

It is also possible for a testamentary trust to succeed to the freeze shares of the freezor, while an *inter vivos* trust holds the growth shares. This could enable the benefits flowing from the freeze shares to be provided to the freezor's spouse after he or she is deceased. The spousal trust is not subject to the same 21-year deemed disposition rule (discussed below) as an *inter vivos* trust.[28]

21-Year Deemed Disposition Rule

The efficacy of using a discretionary trust is limited by the 21-year deemed disposition rule in ss. 104(4) of the ITA, which is designed to compel trusts to recognize and pay tax on their accrued capital gains every 21 years, and prevents trusts from avoiding taxation on an indefinite basis. Subsection 104(4) states that a trust is deemed to have disposed of its capital property for proceeds equal to their FMV on the 21st anniversary of the trust's establishment, forcing the realization of capital gains accrued to date. There are, however, ways to limit the application of this rule.[29]

Trust Attribution Rules

When using an *inter vivos* trust in estate planning, the attribution rule in ss. 75(2) of the ITA must be observed. In certain circumstances, the income of

---

27 See CRA Interpretation Bulletin IT-381R3, "Trusts – Capital Gains and Losses and the Flow-Through of Taxable Capital Gains to Beneficiaries", dated February 14, 1997 [*IT-381R3*] for a complete discussion, among other things, of the tax treatment of capital gains and losses to a trust and its beneficiaries.

28 Note that there are different rules for pre-1972 spousal trusts and post-1972 spousal trusts. For instance, a post-1972 spousal trust is not subject to the deemed disposition rule until the date of death of the spouse. See ss. 108(1) of the ITA for a definition of a "pre-1972 spousal trust". There are also different deemed disposition rules that apply to new trusts introduced into the ITA after 1991, which may permit a trust to later defer the deemed disposition. These should be consulted when using trusts in estate planning.

29 One way in which the 21-year deemed disposition rule may be circumvented is by conducting a re-freeze (discussed earlier in this chapter), where the common shares of the freeze corporation are frozen in advance of anticipated growth, and a new family trust subscribes for the new growth shares therein. If the common shares are retained at the 21st anniversary, then the deemed disposition and corresponding capital gain realized by the first trust under ss. 104(4) would then be limited to the difference between the FMV of the growth shares at the date of the re-freeze and their ACB.

the beneficiary of the trust will be attributed back to the transferor. Where a person (including a corporation) transfers property to a trust and retains control of the transferred property as if the property was his, hers, or its own, then it may be possible for the income to be attributed back to the transferor. This could apply, for instance, where the freezor establishes a discretionary trust as settlor, and there is a reversionary right to the property in the trust.

Under ss. 75(2) there will be attribution of certain amounts derived from property held by a trust to the person from whom the property was received (whether directly or indirectly). In Interpretation Bulletin IT-369R ("IT-369R"),[30] CRA states that any income or loss from the property, and any taxable capital gain or allowable capital loss from the disposition thereof will be attributed to the transferor where the terms of the trust provide that the property:

- may revert to the transferor;[31]
- may be distributed to the beneficiaries as determined by the transferor after the trust's creation; or
- may only be disposed of with the consent or at the direction of the transferor, while alive.[32]

Note that there does not have to be an actual transfer of property to the trust by the person to whom income or gain is attributed under the terms of ss. 75(2), so long as the income is derived from property "held" by the trust.[33] Subsection 75(2) does not apply to income or loss from a business, and therefore does not attribute business income back to the transferor.[34]

Perhaps even more significantly, the interaction between ss. 75(2) and ss. 107(4.1) of the ITA must be considered. Pursuant to ss. 107(4.1) of the ITA, where ss. 75(2) applies, or ever applied to a particular trust, the rollout of

---

30 CRA Interpretation Bulletin IT-369R, "Attribution of Trust Income to Settlor", dated March 12, 1990 [*IT-369R*].

31 CRA has previously expressed that even if there is a remote possibility that the property of the trust will be returned to the person who contributed the property to the trust in the first place, ss. 75(2) may apply: CRA Document No. 2006-0185571C6, dated September 11, 2006. In the context of a loan to a trust, it has been held that a *bona fide* loan, on its face, is not subject to ss. 75(2), since reversion occurs by operation of the terms of the loan, not the terms of the trust: *Howson v. The Queen*, 2007 DTC 141 (T.C.C.) [*Howson*]. As such, CRA later acknowledged *Howson* and retracted its previous position: CRA Document No. 2007-0240421C6, dated June 08, 2007.

32 *IT-369R*, above note 30 at para. 3; see also ss. 75(2)(a)(i), (ii) and 75(2)(b) of the ITA.

33 CRA Interpretation Bulletin IT-369RSR, "Attribution of Trust Income to Settlor" (Revised), dated June 24, 1994 [*IT-369RSR*] at para. 1.

34 *Ibid.* at para. 5.

property of such trust to the capital beneficiaries will be estopped. Normally, under ss. 107(2) of the ITA, a "personal trust",[35] which includes either an *inter vivos* or testamentary trust, is able to roll out its capital property on a tax-deferred basis to a beneficiary resident in Canada. One of the reasons for using a ss. 107(2) rollout is to avoid the 21-year deemed disposition rule. Therefore, where the freezor is the settlor of a discretionary trust that, as part of an estate freeze, holds the growth shares in the freeze corporation, and the freezor retains a reversionary right such that ss. 75(2) applies, ss. 107(4.1) will inhibit a distribution in satisfaction of a capital beneficiary's interest by nullifying a rollout.

Where possible, an *inter vivos* trust used in such estate planning should be irrevocable. Alternatively, the property of a reversionary trust may be transferred to a new trust that does not carry a reversionary right.[36] Another suggestion is for a person other than the freezor to be the settlor of the trust, where the freezor is going to be a trustee. However, CRA has opined that it might be possible for ss. 75(2) to apply to a person other than the settlor, where such person transfers property to a trust with such terms as have been enumerated above.[37]

Another important trust attribution rule is found in s. 74.3 of the ITA. Much like the personal attribution rules found in ss. 74.1 and 74.2 of the Act, where an individual has lent or transferred property to a trust (whether directly or indirectly by means of a trust) in which a "designated person" is beneficially interested, then income and capital gains recognized by such a designated person will be attributed back to the transferor. "Designated person" is defined in ss. 74.5(5) to include a spouse, or person under the age of 18 who does not deal at arm's length with, or is a niece or nephew of, the transferor.

Accordingly, there are a number of attribution rules to be cognizant of when utilizing a trust in estate freezing or estate planning, in general. Aside from the income tax consequences that may arise, there are common law considerations applicable to trusts.

Trustee Duties and Obligations

There are certain common law duties and obligations that trustees must observe. Specifically, a trustee is obliged to act in the best interests of the beneficiaries, and has a duty to act even-handedly and solely for the benefit

---

35 See ss. 248(1) for a definition of "personal trust".

36 CRA Document No. 2001-0067955, dated January 3, 2002.

37 *IT-369R*, above note 30 at para. 11.

of the beneficiaries in the performance of the trustee's duties. The trustee may not act irresponsibly or capriciously.

The trustees are usually permitted, unless prohibited by the terms of the trust, to exercise the rights attached to any shares the trust owns, including voting rights, and may also dispose of such shares. Often times, a freezor has been appointed as the trustee under the discretionary trust, and will therefore be in a position to consent to a transaction, such as one of those discussed below, which modifies the initial freeze. The freezor will, however, be governed by the overarching common law duties to which trustees are normally subject in his or her capacity as trustee. As such, the freezor will be precluded from acting contrary to the best interests of the beneficiaries, and cannot engage in activities solely to satisfy the freezor's needs otherwise he or she will be in breach of his or her fiduciary duties. To that end, there are certain remedies available to beneficiaries so prejudiced, such as applying to a court for an order removing the trustee.[38]

Freeze Share Attributes

A consideration of the freeze share attributes is extremely important in planning an estate freeze. Generally, freeze shares should have the same FMV as the common frozen shares at the date of the freeze so as not to attract adverse income tax consequences. The attributes of the freeze shares must sufficiently capture the FMV as at the date of the freeze, and this can be difficult to accomplish. This is important because it will militate against an argument that a shareholder benefit has been conferred on the freeze beneficiaries, for example.[39]

A usual feature of freeze shares is a redemption right which provides that the freeze shares may be redeemed by the freeze corporation for proceeds equal to the FMV of the assets exchanged for the freeze shares at the date of the freeze. Similarly, the freeze shares may carry a retraction right whereby the freezor can cause the freeze corporation to reacquire the freeze shares for proceeds equal to their FMV.[40] CRA has also opined that freeze shares should have a preferential dividend entitlement, should entitle the holder of such shares to vote on fundamental changes to share capital, and

---

38 See *e.g.*, *Re Lithwick* (1975), 9 O.R. (2d) 643 (H.C.).

39 See CRA Interpretation Bulletin IT-432R2, "Benefits Conferred on Shareholders", dated February 10, 1995 [*IT-432R2*] for a complete discussion of shareholder benefits.

40 In CRA Document No. 9639985, dated May 1, 1997, CRA stated that the removal of a retraction feature from preferred shares suggests that the preferred shares do not have a value equal to their redemption amount.

should afford the holder priority in a distribution on the dissolution, winding-up, or liquidation of the corporation.[41]

It should also be noted that in terms of share characterization, the freeze shares resulting from an estate freeze are normally considered "taxable preferred shares" for taxation purposes. "Taxable preferred share" is defined in ss. 248(1) of the ITA, and includes, *inter alia*, most shares conventionally described as preferred shares. Normally, a dividend paid on a taxable preferred share would be subject to certain rules under the ITA. However, these rules are not invoked in a classic estate freeze scenario where dividends are paid to the freezor, by virtue of the shareholder (freezor)'s control over the freeze corporation paying the dividends. If a freezor has a "substantial interest"[42] in the freeze corporation, then dividends on preferred shares held by the freezor (*i.e.*, the freeze shares) will be considered to be excluded dividends, not exposed to certain tax liability.

Altering an Estate Freeze: "Re-Freezing" and Other Options

As the quote saying goes: "What goes down must come up". As can be seen from the recent moderate increase in values, exploring re-freezing options can prove to be a good strategy To maximize the amount of tax savings, it makes sense to fix the freezor's interest in a corporation when the corporation's value is at its lowest. However, the utmost amount of care and attention must be paid when altering or unfreezing an estate freeze, as any attempts to unwind an estate freeze may cause a realization of capital gains or other income.

In this next section, in addition to the basic estate "re-freeze", other modifications, such as thaws, melts, and reverse freezes will be examined.

---

41 See *e.g.*, "Revenue Canada Round Table," in *Report of Proceedings of the Thirty-Second Tax Conference*, 1980 Conference Report (Toronto: Canadian Tax Foundation, 1981), 591-628, question 13, at 602; "Revenue Canada Round Table," in *Report of Proceedings of the Thirty-Third Tax Conference*, 1981 Conference Report (Toronto: Canadian Tax Foundation, 1982), 726-66, question 45, at 759; CRA Document No. 9229105, dated January 13, 1993; and CRA Document No. AC59387, dated February 26, 1990.

42 See ss. 191(2) of the ITA for a discussion of when a shareholder has a "substantial interest" in a corporation. One way of having a "substantial interest" is by being "related" to such corporation, which is defined in ss. 251(2) of the ITA.

The Basic "Re-Freeze" in Challenging Economic Times

A "re-freeze" is a transaction whereby an existing freeze is altered, but not reversed. Essentially, a basic "re-freeze" involves converting, once again, the freezor's existing shares into a new class of shares valued at the current FMV of the corporation, or converting the freeze beneficiaries' growth shares into preferred shares with a redemption amount equal to the FMV of the growth shares at the date of the re-freeze. Typically, a re-freeze ascribes any growth up to the date of the re-freeze to the freeze beneficiaries, and growth beyond that point to either the freezor and/or new freeze beneficiaries ("re-freeze beneficiaries").

Using the same example outlined at the "What is an 'Estate Freeze'?" section of this chapter, assume the ACB and PUC of the freezor's 100 common shares is $100. As in the previous example, in Year 10, the value of the freezor's corporation has risen to $5,000,000, an estate freeze is implemented, and the freezor now owns freeze shares valued at $5,000,000. Assume this time, however, that in Year 15, the value the freezor's corporation has declined to $100,000, but the value will hopefully rise again by the date of the freezor's death. At this point in time, it would be fruitful for the freezor to implement an estate re-freeze to further minimize the capital gain that would otherwise be triggered upon death as a result of ss. 70(5) of the ITA.

Under a basic re-freeze, the freezor could exchange his or her freeze shares with a FMV of $5,000,000 for new fixed-value preferred shares with a redemption amount equal to the freeze shares, being $100,000 ("new freeze shares"). As such, the capital gain triggered upon death will be limited to the difference between the FMV of the new freeze shares ($100,000) and the original ACB of the common shares ($100) (*i.e.*, $100,000 - $100 = $99,900), one half of which is included in computing the freezor's income for the taxation year ($49,950), as opposed to the difference between the FMV of the freeze shares ($5,000,000) and the original ACB of the common shares ($100) (*i.e.*, $5,000,000 - $100 = $4,999,900).

In other words, whereas the capital gain that would otherwise be realized following an estate freeze in Year 10 without a re-freeze in Year 15 would be $4,999,900 (with a taxable capital gain equal to $2,499,950), the capital gain upon death following a re-freeze in Year 15 will be $99,900 (with a taxable capital gain of only $49,950)–a substantial reduction of $4,900,000, and $2,450,000 of taxable capital gain. Simply put, a re-freeze precludes any future growth in value of the freeze shares, and attributes such future growth to new freeze shares.

An economy such as in early 2009 can constitute a catalyst for a re-freeze. An obvious benefit to an estate re-freeze is locking in a minimized tax liability upon death for the freezor, resulting from the decrease in the amount of the deemed capital gain arising on death. Again, as a corollary, this produces an even larger capital gains deferral for the freezor, as the example above illustrates.

Another possible reason to re-freeze an estate is that as part of an estate freeze, the common shares will have been limited in the payment of dividends where the value of the company has been reduced below the freeze value. As such, a reduction in value of the corporation beyond that of the original freeze may hinder income-splitting opportunities going forward. In this way, re-freezing at the lower value of the corporation will advance the opportunity for the issuance of dividends on the common shares, and the reduction of tax liability by shifting the burden to potentially lower income earning spouses and children. This basically allows income-splitting to re-commence sooner.

Implementing an Estate Re-Freeze

Since an estate re-freeze may be viewed simply as another estate freeze subsequent to the original, it should come as no surprise that the techniques to implement an estate re-freeze bear many of the same characteristics and utilize the same provisions of the ITA as those used to implement an initial estate freeze.

Reverse Freeze (Section 85 Rollover)

As indicated at "Section 85 Rollover" of this chapter, a s. 85 rollover can facilitate the transfer of assets to a corporation in exchange for shares on a tax-free basis. Where an estate re-freeze is involved, the freeze corporation could transfer its assets to a new freeze corporation in exchange for preferred shares having a redemption amount equal to the FMV of the assets transferred.

"Reverse freeze" is another term used to describe a type of re-freeze arrangement where the assets of the freeze corporation are transferred to a new transferee corporation. The rollover provisions in ss. 85(1) of the ITA could be used to transfer the assets to the transferee corporation. As consideration for the assets transferred, the transferee corporation issues freeze shares to the transferor (*i.e.*, preferred shares having a redemption amount equal to the FMV of the transferred assets). Others parties, such as loved ones, could then subscribe for common growth shares in the new freeze corporation.

Alternatively, the freeze corporation could subscribe for common shares in the new freeze corporation for a nominal amount.

The advantage of using this method of re-freezing is that it allows the freezor to choose which of the assets of the freeze corporation will be subject to the reverse freeze. In addition, the corporate attribution rule in ss. 74.4(2) (as discussed in the "Corporate Attribution" section of this chapter) will not apply to a reverse freeze because the transferor will be the freeze corporation, not an individual freezor. The courts have interpreted the actions of a corporation and its shareholder to be independent of one another; and hence, the freezor will not be seen to have transferred or loan property to a corporation indirectly through the freeze corporation, for the purposes of ss. 74.4(2).[43]

Normally, a s. 85 rollover affords the transferor corporation a great degree of latitude to select the specific assets transferred. Where the s. 85 rollover is in respect of all of the assets of the freeze corporation, then the approval of the shareholders of the freeze corporation will need to be obtained by special resolution otherwise shareholders may be entitled to a right of dissent. There may also be other tax considerations to keep in mind, such as whether provincial sales tax ("PST") and/or harmonized sales tax ("HST") is payable.

Section 86 Share Reorganization

To execute a s. 86 share reorganization, there must be a reorganization of share capital in which all of the shares of a particular class of the freeze corporation are disposed of, and other shares of the freeze corporation's capital stock (but not necessarily of the same class) must be received as at least part of the consideration for the conversion. Where available, the conversion of the freeze beneficiaries' growth shares to preferred shares with a fixed value (*i.e.*, redemption amount equal to the FMV of the exchanged growth shares at the date of the conversion, which is typically nominal) will occur on a tax-deferred basis. In addition, the freezor can convert all of his or her freeze shares to new freeze shares with a redemption amount equal to the FMV of the freeze shares at the date of the conversion. Of course, the downside to utilizing a s. 86 share reorganization versus a

---

[43] In the landmark Supreme Court of Canada decision in *Army & Navy Department Store v. Minister of National Revenue*, [1953] 2 S.C.R. 496, it was held that the independent actions of a corporation are not considered to be the indirect actions of its shareholders. As a longstanding principle of corporate law affirms, a corporation has a separate legal existence from its shareholder(s).

s. 85 rollover is that a capital gain cannot be elected into where the FMV still exceeds ACB, and the LCGE may not be crystallized.

Section 51 Share Conversion

As with the s. 85 rollover and s. 86 share reorganization, the basic mechanics of a s. 51 share conversion have already been dealt with in the "Section 51 Share Conversion" section of this chapter. In the context of an estate re-freeze, the common (growth) shares held by the freeze beneficiaries may be converted into non-participating, non-voting (*i.e.*, fixed-value preferred) shares with a redemption amount equal to the FMV of the common shares at the date of the re-freeze; or the freeze shares held by the freezor may be converted into new freeze (participating) shares with a redemption amount equal to the FMV of the freeze shares at the date of the re-freeze. If a re-freeze was envisioned at the outset, then the shares so converted would likely already carry a conversion right pursuant to which the conversion could take place. A characterization of the conversion as a "disposition" should be avoided, unless the transaction is planned to take advantage of the LCGE.[44] A characterization of a shareholder benefit under ss. 15(1) of the ITA must also be avoided.

Other Means of Reversing or Altering an Estate Freeze

Depending on the particular circumstances of the freezor and having regard for a host of other factors, a re-freeze may not always be the best option with respect to addressing a freeze previously executed. As such, there are a number of other permutations and combinations to estate freezes with similar nomenclature, such as melts, thaws, gels, and reverse freezes. Each will be discussed in turn.

Melt

A "melt" is a term used to describe an arrangement where the freezor is able to access some of the appreciation of the corporation, not necessarily through growth shares, but by other means. Essentially, a melt allows some future value of the corporation to accrue to the freezor while leaving the legal structure of the initial freeze intact. There are various ways in which a

[44] In this context, special consideration should be given to the anti-avoidance provision in ss. 110.6(8) of the ITA, which will deny the LCGE if it is reasonable to conclude that a significant part of the gain is attributable to the fact that dividends were not paid on a share (other than a prescribed share as set out in Reg. 6205 of the ITA) of any class, or that dividends paid on such shares were insufficient.

freezor can retain the benefit of some of the future appreciation of the freeze corporation, namely by: increasing the salary or bonus paid to the freezor, the amount of dividends declared in favor of the freezor, management fees, or interest on any notes the freezor took back as part of the initial estate freeze; or through a share redemption.

Salaries and Bonuses

In a typical estate freeze, the freezor, in addition to being a shareholder, will usually be a director, officer, or employee of the freeze corporation; hence the "owner-manager" reference. The freeze corporation can pay the freezor a salary or bonus (or an increase thereof) for his or her services to the corporation, which must be included in computing the freezor's income for a taxation year in accordance with ss. 5(1) of the ITA, insofar as the freezor is considered an "employee" of the freeze corporation. In a corresponding manner, the freeze corporation will be able to deduct such a payment as an expense of the business, subject to certain provisions of the ITA.[45] Paragraph 18(1)(a) and s. 67 of the ITA will affect the ability of the freeze corporation to deduct the remuneration that is so paid or increased under a melt. Pursuant to para. 18(1)(a), in computing the income of a taxpayer from a business or property, no deduction shall be made in respect of an outlay or expense except to the extent that it was made or incurred for the purpose of gaining or producing income from the business or property. According to s. 67 of the ITA, no deduction shall be made in respect of an outlay or expense in computing income except to the extent that the outlay or expense was "reasonable in the circumstances".

Under current Canadian law, a corporation can deduct an unlimited amount of salary or bonus paid to an owner-manager on the basis that the corporation's profits are attributable to the owner-manager's work.[46] CRA admin-

---

[45] For example, ss. 78(4) of the ITA provides that a bonus declared by an employer corporation must be paid no later than 180 days after the taxation year in which the bonus was declared in order to be deductible by such corporation.

[46] See *e.g.*, *Safety Boss Ltd. v. The Queen*, [2000] 3 C.T.C. 2497, 2000 D.T.C. 1767 (T.C.C. [General Procedure]) [*Safety Boss*]. Interestingly, remuneration in the form of bonuses paid to children might be warranted depending on the services rendered by the children, to the extent that they are reasonable: *Mépalex Inc. c. R.*, 2004 D.T.C. 2232 (Eng.), [2004] 2 C.T.C. 2681 (T.C.C.) [*Mépalex*]. It has recently been held that directors' fees paid to children are also deductible regardless of how little work is done, but they are subject to the reasonableness test in s. 67 of the ITA: *Manchester Chivers & Associates Insurance Brokers Inc. v. The Queen*, [2005] 5 C.T.C. 2180, 2005 D.T.C. 1429 (T.C.C. [General Procedure]) [*Manchester*]. On the other hand, whether CRA considers a bonus or management fee paid to a family trust as reasonable having regard for s. 67 of the ITA is a "question of fact": CRA Document No. 2002-0141115, dated June 12, 2002 [*Doc No. 2002-0141115*].

istrative policy[47] with respect to the payment of bonuses and salaries is that it will not challenge the reasonableness of salaries and bonuses paid to *principal shareholder/managers* of a corporation when:

> ... the general practice of the corporation is to distribute the profits of the company to its shareholder/managers in the form of bonuses or additional salaries; or the company has adopted a policy of declaring bonuses to the shareholders to remunerate them for the profits the company has earned that are attributable to special know-how, connections or entrepreneurial skills of the shareholders.[48]

CRA has also opined that such salaries and bonuses may go unchallenged where they are paid to managers who are shareholders of CCPCs (either directly or through a holding corporation), are Canadian residents, and are "actively involved in the day-to-day operations of the company."[49]

In the context of s. 67, the courts have held that a deduction in respect of a bonus or salary will not be denied to the freeze corporation unless "no reasonable business person" would pay such amount.[50]

The concept of owner-manager remuneration is not new, and does not only arise in the context of an estate freeze or melt. For example, CCPCs have followed a traditional practice of paying salaries and bonuses to owner-managers in order to reduce their taxable income to or below the amount of the small business deduction ("SBD"). However, in view of the recent amendments to the dividend tax credit ("DTC") regime in Canada and the concept of "eligible dividends",[51] "bonusing down" to the SBD is no longer as commonplace as it previously was.

---

47 It should be noted that while persuasive in nature and indicative of the way CRA will likely assess a taxpayer's circumstances, CRA administrative policies, such as Interpretation Bulletins, Information Circulars, and Technical Interpretations, do not have the force of law, and must yield to the ITA and a court of law's interpretation of the ITA.

48 Adapted from "Revenue Canada Round Table", in *Report of the Proceedings of the Thirty-Third Tax Conference*, 1981 Conference Report (Toronto: Canadian Tax Foundation, 1982); CRA *Income Tax Technical News No. 22*, dated January 11, 2002 [*IT Technical News No. 22*].

49 Doc No. 2002-0141115, above note 46; see also "CCRA Round Table", in *Report of the Proceedings of the Fifty-Fifth Tax Conference*, 2003 Conference Report (Toronto: Canadian Tax Foundation, 2004).

50 *Safety Boss*, above note 46; *Manchester*, above note 46 at ¶ 15; *Welton v. The Queen*, [2005] T.C.J. No. 251, [2005] 3 C.T.C. 2406, 2005 D.T.C. 869 (T.C.C. [General Procedure]) at ¶ 18 [T.C.J.].

51 "Eligible dividends" received by Canadian resident taxpayers enjoy preferential tax treatment. "Eligible dividends" are defined in ss. 89(1) of the ITA. Income that is available to be paid as "eligible dividends" is tracked in a notional account referred to as the General Rate Income Pool ("GRIP"). The GRIP tracks the corporation's income that was taxed at the general corporate rate (as opposed to the small business tax rate) at the end of the year, and will also include eligible dividend income received by the corporation. The

Ultimately, care must be taken to ensure that the salary or bonus paid, or increase thereof, is reasonable in the circumstances and is paid for the purpose of earning income from a business (*i.e.*, in respect of services provided by the owner-manager to the freeze corporation or for expertise). If viewed as merely a way of distributing the profits of the freeze corporation, then the entire characterization of the bonus or salary may be affected.

Dividends

Another way to cause a melt is through the issuance of additional dividends to the freezor. Preferred shares (*i.e.*, the freeze shares) in a freeze transaction will often have terms attached providing for the declaration of dividends up to a certain limit (*e.g.*, as a percentage of the redemption amount of the freeze shares), or at the discretion of the director(s). Melting can have the effect of increasing the amount that is paid out to the freezor in the form of dividends. Note that, according to s. 42 of the CBCA, a corporation will be restricted in its ability to declare and pay dividends if there are reasonable grounds for believing the corporation is or will be unable to pay its liabilities, or the realizable value of the corporation's assets would be less than the aggregate of its liabilities and stated capital. The same is provided by ss. 38(3) of the OBCA.

If improperly structured, a melt can result in adverse tax consequences for the freezor. For example, the freeze shares may provide for cumulative or non-cumulative dividends, or may be retractable non-dividend-bearing shares or shares with a fixed dividend entitlement; the freezor may thus want to alter the attributes of the freeze shares by causing a reorganization of share capital pursuant to a s. 86 rollover. However, as discussed below, a minor alteration of the share conditions that falls short of a reorganization may still be considered to be a "disposition" within the meaning of the ITA[52] and a reacquisition, thereby triggering immediate tax consequences to the freezor.

In CRA Interpretation Bulletin IT-448 ("IT-448"),[53] CRA generally discusses factors that are considered in determining whether a "disposition" has taken

---

amount included in the taxpayer's income is "grossed up" and the individual then receives a credit to offset the tax the corporation is presumed to have paid, resulting in less tax in an individual's hands. A CCPC can pay an eligible dividend only to the extent that it has GRIP at year-end, and a non-CCPC can pay an eligible dividend as long as it has no Low Rate Income Pool ("LRIP") at the time the dividend is paid. An eligible dividend received by a trust can be flowed out as such pursuant to ss. 104(19) of the ITA to a beneficiary.

52 See ss. 248(1) of the ITA for the definition of "disposition" for income tax purposes.

53 CRA Interpretation Bulletin IT-448, "Dispositions ? Changes in Terms of Securities", dated June 6, 1980 [*IT-448*].

place for the purposes of the ITA. In particular, CRA examines situations in which alterations of share conditions may be considered to be a disposition. In IT-448, CRA acknowledges that there are no "hard and fast" rules of universal application, and that it will examine the *effect* a particular set of changes seeks to achieve rather than the *method* used to accomplish those changes.[54] However, among those types of share changes that CRA regards as dispositions, it lists:

> (a) a change in voting rights attached to shares that effects a change in the voting control of the corporation;
>
> (b) a change in a defined entitlement (e.g. a change in par value) to share in the assets of a corporation upon dissolution (preferred shares only);
>
> (c) the giving up or the addition of a priority right to share in the distribution of assets of the corporation upon dissolution;
>
> *(d) the addition or deletion of a right attaching to a class of share that provides for participation in dividend entitlements beyond a fixed preferential rate or amount;*
>
> *(e) a change from a cumulative to a non-cumulative right to dividends or vice versa.* [Emphasis added.][55]

Curiously, among those changes that CRA enumerates as *not* being considered dispositions is: "... (i) an increase or decrease in the amount or rate of a fixed dividend entitlement."[56] It should be noted at this point that there have been several opposing views expressed in this regard; and it is, therefore, difficult to derive any sort of clear guidance as to what will or will not constitute a disposition in the eyes of the CRA.

Another possibility is to modify the provisions of the freeze shares by adding a conversion privilege so that the freeze shares could later be converted into shares bearing a higher dividend rate. This change, in and of itself, should not attract negative tax consequences as outlined above.[57] If the addition of a share conversion feature is viewed as increasing the value of the freeze shares, there is some speculation as to whether a shareholder benefit[58] will have been conferred on the freezor, or another anti-avoidance provision might apply to the freezor.

---

54 *Ibid.*, at paras. 2 and 3.

55 *Ibid.*, at para. 14.

56 *Ibid.*, at para. 15.

57 *Ibid.*, at paras. 5 and 14.

58 See *e.g.*, ss. 15(1) of the ITA.

If there is a holding company structure in place, such dividends may be issued to the holding corporation on a tax-free basis.[59] As alluded to above, recent changes to the dividend regime in Canada have made the payment of certain types of dividends, called "eligible dividends", more tax-efficient than paying an owner-manager a salary or bonus in some circumstances.

Share Redemption

Often, in exchange for his or her common shares in the corporation during the initial freeze, the freezor will have received preferred shares that are redeemable at the option of the freezor for an amount equal to the FMV of the shares at the date of the freeze, less any amount of debt and cash proceeds received on the transfer of assets to the freeze corporation.

The redemption of all or part of the shares will, however, cause a deemed dividend under ss. 84(3) of the ITA equal to the amount by which the redemption amount exceeds PUC, and a capital gain equal to the amount by which the redemption amount, minus the amount of any deemed dividends, exceeds the ACB of the shares. As is the case with dividends, the freeze corporation will be required to meet solvency tests, under ss. 36(2) of the CBCA and ss. 32(2) of the OBCA.

There are other possible ways to accomplish a melt, such as increasing the interest rate on promissory notes that the freezor has received in addition to the freeze shares as part of the consideration received during the estate freeze. Alternatively, the freezor may earn supplementary profits for providing management services to the freeze corporation through a management corporation owned by him or her. As is the case with any type of estate planning, melting involves nuances and complexities that are situation-specific.

The need for a melt during a recession may be questionable when the corporation's common shares may have depreciated, and as such, there may

---

[59] This is insofar as the dividend does not exceed the "safe income" (income earned or realized after 1971) attributable to the shares owned by the corporate shareholder, the dividend will retain its tax-free character. Pursuant to the anti-avoidance provision in ss. 55(2) of the ITA, where a corporation has received a tax-free inter-corporate dividend as part of a transaction or series of transactions or events, one of the purposes of which was to cause a reduction in the capital gain that would have resulted from a disposition of the shares at fair market value, the dividend will not be received on a tax-free basis and will be deemed to be part of the proceeds of disposition, to the extent that the dividend cannot be attributable to income earned or realized by the corporation after 1971. Exceeding "safe income" by any amount will cause a re-characterization of the entire amount of the dividend.

be reduced cash flow in the freeze corporation for a freezor to access. However, in conjunction with an estate re-freeze at a lower corporate value, a melt becomes a more sensible approach in future years when values regain momentum and are, once again, on the rise. In the alternative, a melt may now make sense in circumstances where the freezor has incurred unexpected losses and therefore requires the assets of the freeze corporation for his own purposes.

In any event, a melt is a convenient approach to temporarily soften an estate freeze while still maintaining the corporate structure put in place and respecting the freezor's intent in freezing the corporation in the first place.

Thaw

As its name so aptly suggests, a thaw is utilized to dissolve the effects of an estate freeze. In a thaw transaction, it is intended that the estate freeze is retroactively unwound, such that the freezor is put in virtually the same position that he or she was in before the estate freeze. Three methods of thawing an estate freeze will be canvassed: (a) reacquisition of growth shares by the freezor; (b) conversion of freeze shares into common shares; and (c) the use of a trust vehicle.

Reacquisition of Growth Shares

In one method of using a thaw, the freeze beneficiaries could transfer the common (growth) shares of the freeze corporation acquired during the estate freeze back to the freezor. However, this may result in immediate capital gains being realized, to the extent that the proceeds of disposition of the common shares exceed their ACB. Eligibility for the LCGE (as discussed in detail above) will have to be considered.

The proceeds resulting from such a disposition between non-arm's length related parties[60] will have to occur for the FMV of the shares at the date of the disposition, since in accordance with ss. 69(1) of the ITA, where a taxpayer has disposed of anything to a person with whom the taxpayer is not dealing at arm's length for proceeds less than FMV, the taxpayer will be deemed to have received proceeds of disposition equal to the FMV of the property, and the transferee will be deemed to have received the property at its FMV. It has been widely acknowledged that valuing shares of a privately-held corporation can be exceptionally difficult. It is therefore strongly sug-

---

60 See ss. 251(1) of the ITA for a definition of "arm's length" and ss. 251(2) for a definition of "related persons".

gested that a freezor obtain a valuation from a qualified expert, such as an independent valuator, in connection with thawing and estate freezing, in general. Improper or inaccurate valuation can leave such transactions vulnerable to scrutiny by CRA.

In this regard, a price adjustment clause can be a useful tool in an agreement pertaining to the purchase of the shares to avoid the application of the anti-avoidance rule in s. 69 of the ITA. It is a mechanism whereby the price agreed upon may subsequently be readjusted in the event that CRA has contested the value specified by the parties. CRA's Interpretation Bulletin IT-169 ("IT-169")[61] sets out the criteria that must be met in order for a price adjustment clause to be accepted. Among other things, the price adjustment clause must reflect a "*bona fide* intention of the parties to transfer the property at fair market value and arrives at that value for purposes of agreement by a fair and reasonable method."[62] To the extent that a price falls short of the FMV, as later determined, the shortfall must be accounted for.[63]

To the freezor, a thaw executed via a repurchase of the common growth shares may be ideal in a depressed economy where the value of the corporation has not risen substantially between the date of the initial freeze and the contemplated thaw, as the freezor would be able to reacquire the growth shares for a minor cost. At the same time, this will not be a unilateral event; the consent of the freeze beneficiaries would have to be acquired, and a consensus with respect to the purchase price for the growth shares will have to be reached. Preferably, there will have been a shareholder's agreement in place from the outset, which could provide the manner in which the shares could be reacquired by the freezor (*e.g.*, shotgun clause). In Information Circular IC 89-3 ("IC 89-3"),[64] CRA has stated that an agreement, such as a buy-sell agreement, will be accepted as determinative of value between non-arm's length parties as long as: (1) the agreement is a *bona fide* business arrangement; (2) the purchase price in the agreement provides "full and adequate consideration, and represents the fair market value of the shares determined without reference to the agreement at the time it is executed"; and (3) it is a legal and binding agreement.[65]

---

61 CRA Interpretation Bulletin IT-169, "Price Adjustment Clauses", dated August 6, 1974 [*IT-169*].

62 *Ibid.*, at para. 1; see also CRA Document No. 2005-0112321E5, dated April 11, 2005.

63 *IT-169, ibid.*, at para. 1.

64 CRA Information Circular IC 89-3, "Policy Statement on Business Equity Valuations", dated August 25, 1989 [*IC 89-3*].

65 *Ibid.*, at para. 29.

Conversion of Freeze Shares into Common Shares

Another way to effect a thaw is the conversion of convertible freeze shares into common shares of the freeze corporation. If a thaw was not envisaged at the date of the initial freeze, then the preferred shares obtained by the freezor during the freeze may have to be amended to attach a conversion right to such shares. Again, the issue of whether there has been a "disposition" in CRA's view will become relevant. If so, the arrangement may be regarded as having conferred a shareholder benefit on the freezor equal to the value of the conversion right so attached; pursuant to ss. 15(1) of the ITA, the freezor will be required to include such an amount (except to the extent that it is deemed by s. 84 to be a dividend) in his or her income for the year.

If, on the other hand, a thaw was contemplated from the outset, then the freeze shares obtained by the freezor will have had a conversion right attached, and they can be converted into common shares. Such conversions often provide for a notice period and require the shareholder to be alive at the end of the notice period. It is generally accepted that no disposition is considered to have occurred where the conversion took place under s. 51 of the ITA. There may be a triggering event creating an automatic conversion of the freeze shares. Another option is to have the conversion right and/or triggering event expressly provided for in a shareholder's agreement.

The Use of a Trust

A further way of completing a thaw is through the use of a discretionary family trust (already discussed in detail previously in this chapter) on which the growth shares are settled. This method of thawing is also sometimes referred to as a "gel". Again, care must be taken to ensure that the attribution rules in s. 74.3 and ss. 75(2) and 107(4.1) do not apply to the arrangement.

It has been suggested that, by virtue of the freezor's interest in the discretionary trust and possible position as trustee, the freezor has an interest worth more than a nominal amount, as may have been purported. This concern might be mitigated, however, by prescribing a nominal value only for the freezor in the discretionary trust. The freezor may also act as trustee with other independent trustees, and the freezor's discretionary interest should not have a more significant value than the other discretionary beneficiaries.

There is a bit of comfort in the fact that CRA has affirmed that the use of a discretionary trust for flexible estate freezing purposes will not necessarily trigger the application of the general anti-avoidance rule ("GAAR") in s. 245 of the ITA (discussed below).[66] Nonetheless, this does not mean that other avoidance rules, such as those found in ss. 56(2) and 86(2) of the ITA, are not applicable.

Key CRA Administrative Policies

CRA's administrative statements in respect of certain fact situations, where non-taxpayer-friendly, have been known to produce a chilling effect on estate and succession planning in those affected areas in the past. Estate re-freezing was one such area. As will be discussed below, it now appears that CRA's overall position with respect to re-freezing and the application of GAAR to such arrangements no longer leaves taxpayers contemplating these transactions out in the cold.

Estate Re-Freezing

CRA's longstanding policy with respect to estate re-freezing was that it conferred a shareholder benefit in circumstances where the freezor's freeze shares were exchanged for shares with a lower redemption or retraction value.[67] However in 1997, CRA warmed up to estate re-freezing and revised its former position.

Notably, in CRA Technical Interpretation 9607635, dated May 28, 1997, and Technical Interpretation 9229905, dated June 3, 1997, CRA indicated that as long as the decrease in the value of the shares causing the need for a re-freeze is not attributable to the "stripping of corporate assets", it will not ordinarily consider a benefit to have been conferred on the common shareholders or the freezor on the exchange of the freeze shares for new freeze shares having a FMV equal to the current FMV of the freeze shares. Of note however, CRA did not elaborate on the issue of what "stripping of corporate assets" meant.

More recently, in CRA Technical Interpretation 2000-0029115, dated November 17, 2000, CRA confirmed its statements in Technical Interpretations

---

66 See "Revenue Canada Round Table", in *Report of Proceedings of the Forty-Second Tax Conference*, 1990 Conference Report (Toronto: Canadian Tax Foundation, 1991).

67 See *e.g.*, "Revenue Canada Round Table", in *Report of Proceedings of the Thirty-Seventh Tax Conference*, 1985 Conference Report (Toronto: Canadian Tax Foundation, 1986), 49:1-32, question 53; CRA Document No. 9M19020, dated October 10, 1997, "Federal Round Table on Taxation," 1997 APFF Conference, question 2.5.

9607635 and 9229905; namely, that there is no benefit conferred on the common shareholders in a re-freeze transaction provided the reduction in FMV of the preferred shares has not been caused by a stripping of the assets of the corporation and the FMV of the new preferred shares corresponds to the FMV of the preferred shares that would be covered by the re-freeze. This Ruling also gives taxpayers more guidance on what constitutes "stripping of corporate assets", since CRA viewed a payment of a dividend on another class of shares as being tantamount to "stripping" the corporate assets. CRA also reaffirmed its position in Technical Interpretation 2003-0046823, dated January 28, 2003, in the context of a reverse estate freeze.

General Anti-Avoidance Rule ("GAAR")

For the most part, it is acknowledged that estate freezing is a form of legitimate tax planning insulated from the effects of GAAR. In Information Circular IC 88-2 ("IC 88-2"),[68] CRA offers guidance with respect to the general applicability of GAAR. In particular, at paragraph 10 of IC 88-2, CRA states that estate freezes "would not ordinarily result in misuse or abuse given the scheme of the Act" and having regard for the specific attribution rules found in s. 74.4 of the ITA. Shortly thereafter, in the context of an estate freeze in favor of a discretionary trust where the freezor was also a discretionary beneficiary, while CRA declined to state definitively whether this would always be acceptable, it found that the facts, in and of themselves, would not generally result in the application of the GAAR.[69] Subsequently, in 2002, in response to the question of whether there were any business transactions that were "really safe" from GAAR, the CRA listed estate freezing as an area where GAAR has been found not to apply.[70] This, of course, must not be taken to be a blanket endorsement of all estate freezing transactions.

On the other hand, consideration by CRA of the application of GAAR to re-freezing transactions has been sparse. Technical Interpretation 2000-0050983, dated in 2001, considers the application of GAAR in a re-freeze transaction. This Technical Interpretation involves a convoluted set of facts; however, CRA ultimately found that GAAR did not apply to the re-freeze in question. Because there has been so little examination of GAAR in respect of estate re-freezing, it is doubtful that any meaningful principles can be

---

68 CRA Information Circular IC 88-2, "General Anti-Avoidance Rule - Section 245 of the I.T.", dated October 21, 1988.

69 "Revenue Canada Round Table", in *Report of the Proceedings of the Forty-Second Tax Conference*, 1990 Conference Report (Toronto: Canadian Tax Foundation, 1991) 50:1-68, question 20.

70 *IT Technical News No. 22*, above note 48 at question 7.

derived and applied to estate planning going forward. Nonetheless, given the anticipated increase in popularity of re-freezing in today's challenging times, we will likely hear a lot more from the taxing authorities on the issue of whether GAAR will apply to estate re-freezing as taxpayers attempt to obtain CRA's blessing on such transactions.

Case Law Affecting Estate Freezing and Re-Freezing

No chapter on estate freezing and re-freezing would be complete without a discussion of the recent jurisprudence that has developed in the area, as this inevitably shapes the manner in which estate planning is conducted going forward. Many of the cases that will be discussed below, examine the issue of what happens when an estate freeze goes wrong, and the solutions that may be employed to remedy them, such as rectification. There are also several family law cases which consider whether shares owned following an estate freeze should form part of net family property ("NFP") for the purposes of dividing property upon marital breakdown.

Given that a freezor's pool of wealth may have shrunk considerably as a result of the recession, it would be ill-advised to ignore the current case law in the area of estate freezing and re-freezing.

Family Law Cases

As a general principle, any assets gained during marriage are equally divided between spouses on the dissolution of the marriage. However, there are some exceptions to this rule. For instance, a gift or inheritance received after the date of marriage is excluded from the calculation of NFP, but the income from such a gift may be included if not specifically excluded by the donor. Whether assets received as a part of an estate freeze are included in a calculation of NFP under family law is an issue that has not been heavily considered by the courts. However, a few decisions have provided some guidance.

An important case in this area was *Black v. Black* ("*Black*").[71] In that case, the husband had received shares in a business as part of an estate freeze by his father. The transaction had been carefully structured as a purchase to avoid gift tax under the *Gift Tax Act*. On the breakdown of his marriage, when calculating the division of property, the husband argued that the shares should be excluded from the calculation since they were a gift. The court

71 (1988), 66 O.R. (2d) 643 (H.C.) [*Black*].

rejected this position, holding that the husband could not consider the shares a purchase for tax purposes and a gift for family law purposes. Therefore, they were included in the assets to the divided.

In *Armstrong v. Armstrong*,[72] the husband had acquired during the marriage a contingent interest in a family trust. The trust was created as a part of an estate freeze. The husband had given no consideration for his inclusion in the trust, which had a provision specifically excluding any gift or benefit in favor of any beneficiary of the trust from NFP property of the beneficiary for the purposes of the *Family Law Act*. Therefore, the interest in the trust was considered to be a gift from the father and was not included in the calculation of NFP.

Dalgleish v. Dalgleish[73] also involved a husband who had received assets during the marriage as a result of his father's estate freeze. In this case, as in *Black*, the estate freeze had been structured such that that husband had given consideration for the shares. However, the husband's father testified to the effect that he had in fact paid his son's subscription price for the shares and, accordingly, there was no actual consideration and the shares were a gift. The court rejected this reasoning, citing the precedent in *Black* that since they were structured to be a purchase, they were considered so for family law purposes. Therefore his shares were included in the calculation of the NFP.

This decision has been the subject of some criticism. It has been pointed out that since the *Gift Tax Act* is no longer in force, there is no longer the same rationale for considering the transfer of stocks to not be a gift. Nevertheless, given the courts' perspective on this matter, if an estate freeze can be structured as a gift, it would be to the benefit of the children or other recipients of the property that it be done so. Perhaps even more importantly, marital contracts should be considered where important corporate assets or shares are owned or likely to be owned in the future by one of the spouses, in order to ensure that they will not be included in the division of family assets should the marriage fail.

Rectification: What to Do When the Execution of an Estate Freeze Does Not Reflect the True Intention of the Parties

Rectification is an equitable doctrine that allows a court to amend an agreement that does not reflect the actual intentions of the parties. It is meant to

[72] [1997] O.J. No. 4137, 1997 CarswellOnt 4268 (Gen. Div.) [*Armstrong*].

[73] 2003 CarswellOnt 2758 (S.C.J.) [*Dalgeish*].

apply to a situation in which there was a genuine meeting of the minds of the parties involved, but there was an error in the legal instruments which has the effect of altering the original intention of the parties. When an order for rectification is granted, a court will allow for the correction of the impugned agreement and enforce the agreement as amended.

In the tax context, rectification is usually sought as a remedy where a mistake in legal instruments gives rise to adverse tax consequences. However, caution must be used when seeking this remedy, as parties will not be successful where it is regarded as an invitation for the court to engage in retroactive tax planning to enable parties to obtain more favorable tax treatment.

Rectification becomes an important device in the context of estate planning where there has been an improperly executed estate freeze. *Juliar v. Canada (Attorney General) ("Juliar")*[74] is a landmark Ontario Court of Appeal decision considering the doctrine of rectification in the context of an estate freeze. It involved a s. 85 rollover where the disposition of shares that would otherwise occur on a tax-free basis was viewed as a disposition of property giving rise to immediate tax liability under s. 84.1 of the ITA, and resulting in a deemed dividend. On the rollover, the parties took back promissory notes instead of shares based on incorrect information from their advisors. The Minister of National Revenue (the "Minister") reassessed, resulting in additional tax liability for the parties of over $100,000.

The Ontario Court of Appeal, per Austin J.A., upheld the trial decision and allowed the rectification. The Court of Appeal agreed with the trial judge that the true intention of the parties was to execute an estate freeze without attracting immediate tax liability, and that the only reason that this had not been done was because of a misapprehension. The Court also found that there was evidence that the transaction would never have been entered into if it could not have been done on a tax-deferred basis. *Juliar* is significant because it is said to represent the high-water mark with respect to intention, or embody the "modern principle of intention" whereby parties may have intended to arrange their affairs "on a basis which would not attract immediate liability for income tax on the transaction."[75]

Di Battista v. 874687 Ontario Inc. ("*Di Battista*")[76] is a recent Ontario Superior Court of Justice case that also considered the rectification of three share purchase agreements in the context of an estate freeze. The freeze was

---

74 (2000), 2000 CarswellOnt 3518, [2000] O.J. No. 3706 (C.A.), leave to appeal refused (2001), 2001 CarswellOnt 1805 (S.C.C.) [*Juliar*].

75 *Ibid.*, at ¶ 19 [O.J.].

76 [2006] 5 C.T.C. 152 (Ont. S.C.J.) [*Di Battista*].

executed improperly such that it frustrated the intentions of the parties and gave rise to unintended immediate tax liability. The facts in *Di Battista* are not set out in detail in the decision. However, *Di Battista* is significant because it affirms the principle expounded in *Juliar*, namely that if the Court is satisfied that the true agreement between the parties, which can be based on not attracting or minimizing tax liability, is frustrated, rectification may be permitted to reflect the transaction as intended.

In sum, an important principle that can be drawn from these cases is that, assuming the other criteria for rectification are met, the intention of the parties to avoid immediate tax liability is a valid intention that may justify the equitable doctrine of rectification. It is not unusual that many of the rectification cases involve estate freezing, since reorganization in the estate planning area can be extremely cumbersome and complicated. It is, however, a bit of a reassurance to know that there is a remedy available to counteract the negative tax implications of an improperly executed estate freeze or subsequent modification. Where a rectification order is sought, CRA must be informed[77] and the Department of Justice's Rectification Committee, established after the *Juliar* decision, will review the rectification application. Where CRA does not oppose the rectification application, it will often issue a comfort letter to an applicant, which has informally been suggested to be required by courts in cases where a tax issue is raised.

Conclusion

The authors trust that this chapter has given the reader a good overview of the relevant rules, concepts, and issues involved in estate freezing, re-freezing, or otherwise modifying an existing estate freeze. It should be noted that this chapter is not intended, in any way, to be a substitution for proper and sound legal advice with respect to estate and succession planning. It is therefore recommended that professional tax advice be sought when considering an estate freeze, re-freeze, reverse freeze, melt, thaw, *etc.*

Overall, the authors have hoped to convey the idea that a depressed economy need not cause the reader's spirits to dip below zero as well. This is especially true in light of the myriad tax opportunities available to take advantage of a recession and weather the storm. For many individuals, the legal costs associated with estate planning may seem like an additional strain, particularly in challenging markets. But these initial costs may be far out-

---

77 *Re Columbia North Realty Co.* (2005), [2006] 2 C.T.C. 158, 60 D.T.C. 6124 (N.S. S.C. [In Chambers]).

weighed by the ensuing savings, and should not, therefore, put estate and succession planning “on ice”.

Utilization and Preservation of Losses Within an Affiliated Group

Gerald D. Courage, James A. Hutchinson & James A. Fraser

Introduction

It is not uncommon for some members within a corporate group to be in a taxable position, while others are incurring or have incurred losses. The challenge is how to make use of the losses within the group and avoid the inefficiency of some members paying taxes as loss carryforwards lie unutilized within the group.

With some exceptions, loss consolidation involves transactions amongst and between "affiliated persons", which refers to a narrower set of entities than those considered "related persons" for the purposes of the *Income Tax Act* (Canada) (the "*ITA*"). The most significant difference between the affiliated persons' rules and the related persons' rules is that children are related, but not affiliated, with their parents, and siblings are related, but not affiliated, with each other. The implications of these categories of persons must be kept in mind when effecting loss consolidation transactions within a closely-held group of companies where estate freezing arrangements have been put in place to introduce children as shareholders.

The Canada Revenue Agency (the "CRA") considers attempts to transfer the benefit of losses between non-affiliated corporations to be subject to the general anti-avoidance rule set out in s. 245 of the *ITA* ("GAAR").[1] In applying this administrative position, the CRA relies on a modified definition of affiliation based on ss. 69(11) of the *ITA* so that *de jure* control is the relevant

[1] The CRA's position is set forth in "Income Tax Technical News No. 9" dated February 10, 1997.

standard, as opposed to *de facto* control, which would otherwise be the basis for determining affiliation pursuant to ss. 251.1(3) of the *ITA*.[2]

Loss Utilization Techniques

Loss utilization techniques can be broken down into four broad categories:

1. Reorganizations of the affiliated corporate group.
2. Transactions within an affiliated corporate group.
3. Self-help by a loss corporation ("Lossco").
4. Transactions involving non-affiliated persons.

Reorganizations of the Affiliated Corporate Group

Reorganizing an affiliated group by (1) amalgamations pursuant to s. 87 of the *ITA* or (2) winding-up pursuant to s. 88 of the *ITA* are two effective means of utilizing losses within the group.

Amalgamations[3]

Amalgamations are a useful technique for loss utilization within an affiliated corporate group because the *ITA* generally provides for rollover treatment at both the corporate level and the shareholder level and an amalgamation is a relatively straightforward corporate proceeding.

The rules regarding loss carryovers are set out in ss. 87(2.1) of the *ITA*. Subsection 87(2.1) deems an amalgamated corporation to be the same corporation as, and a continuation of, each predecessor corporation for purposes of determining the amalgamated corporation's non-capital loss, net

---

[2] See Sinclair, "High Cost of Leaving, Loss Utilization: A Review of Recent Positions of the Department of National Revenue", 1996 Conference Report, Canadian Tax Foundation, 1997, 7:1 at 7:20.

[3] Much has been written about the tax issues involved in amalgamations and the reader is referred to that body of literature. This chapter focuses solely on the aspects of amalgamations which are relevant for purposes of loss utilization within an affiliated corporate group. See, for instance, Kakkar, "An Overview of the Technical Aspects of the New Legislative and Administrative Issues involving Wind-ups and Amalgamations", 2005 Ontario Conference Report, Canadian Tax Foundation 2005 at 4B:1; Crowe & Senyk, "Amalgamation and Wind-up: What's the Difference?", 2003 Prairie Provinces Conference Report, Canadian Tax Foundation, 2003 at 10:1; Schwartz, "Statutory Amalgamations, Arrangements, and Continuations: Tax and Corporate Law Considerations", 1991 Conference Report, Canadian Tax Foundation, 1992 at 9:1; and Dunn, *op. cit.*

capital loss, restricted farm loss, farm loss, and limited partnership loss and in determining the application of the acquisition of control rules in ss. 111(4) to (5.4), which might otherwise apply to restrict the deductibility of such losses by the amalgamated corporation. Thus, the amalgamated corporation may utilize the loss carryforwards of the predecessors, subject to the usual timing and acquisition of control restrictions; however, subject to the discussion regarding ss. 87(2.11) below, losses of the amalgamated corporation may not be carried back to reduce the taxable income or tax payable of the predecessor corporations.

Subsection 87(2.11) of the *ITA* provides an exception to the general restriction on the carrying back of losses to the predecessor corporation where there is an amalgamation of a parent corporation ("Parentco") and one or more of its wholly-owned subsidiary corporations, in which case the amalgamated corporation is deemed, for a variety of provisions, including the loss carryover rules, to be the same corporation as, and a continuation of, the Parentco. The effect of this rule is that post-amalgamation losses may be carried back against the taxable income of the Parentco, subject to the usual three-year carryback restriction. This rule was enacted to bring the rules on amalgamations more closely into line with those for the winding-up of a wholly-owned subsidiary under ss. 88(1) of the *ITA*.[4]

The opportunity to carry back losses should not be overlooked and steps should be taken to come within the application of ss. 87(2.11) prior to implementing an amalgamation. For example, where a Parentco has two wholly-owned subsidiary corporations, a profitable corporation ("Profitco") and Lossco, and wishes to amalgamate the two corporations, it would make sense to transfer the shares of the Lossco to the Profitco on a tax-deferred basis pursuant to s. 85 of the *ITA* ("s. 85 rollover") so that the Lossco becomes a wholly-owned subsidiary of the Profitco before amalgamating the two corporations. In turn, the amalgamation would proceed and ss. 87(2.11) should be applicable. The risk of review based on anti-avoidance issues is mitigated by the fact the same result could be achieved by the otherwise legitimate transferring of shares of the Lossco to the Profitco and then

---

[4] Prior to the enactment of this rule, the safer route for amalgamating a loss subsidiary with a profitable parent was to wind up the subsidiary utilizing the provisions of ss. 88(1) discussed further below. Specifically, prior to the enactment of ss. 87(2.11), if the profitable parent and loss subsidiary had been amalgamated and the amalgamated corporation incurred losses, the losses would not be available for carryback against the predecessor parent's income. In contrast, on a wind-up under ss. 88(1), the Parentco is the surviving entity and losses of the parent incurred subsequent to the winding up of the subsidiary can be carried back to be offset against income of the parent in prior years subject to the usual temporal restrictions.

winding-up the Lossco under ss. 88(1).[5] Nonetheless, care must be taken in applying ss. 87(2.11) to specific circumstances so that the application of the provision is not foregone. Two fact scenarios that were the subject of a 1998 technical interpretation issued by the CRA illustrate how the carrying back of losses may be prohibited or restricted in the context of an amalgamation:[6]

Scenario 1

The first scenario involved the amalgamation of three corporations: Aco, Bco, and Cco. Bco was wholly-owned by Aco and Cco was wholly-owned by Bco. For the taxation year ending on the amalgamation, Aco and Bco had taxable incomes and, in the first taxation year of the amalgamated corporation, a non-capital loss of $125 was incurred. The CRA took the view that the non-capital loss of Amalco was available to reduce the taxable income of Aco, as the parent corporation of the group, but was not available to reduce the taxable income of Bco notwithstanding that it was in a sense the parent of Cco. The CRA's position was that under ss. 87(2.11), both Bco and Cco were wholly-owned subsidiary corporations of Aco and therefore the amalgamated corporation was deemed to be a continuation of Aco only for purposes of applying s. 111 of the *ITA*.

Scenario 2

The second scenario considered was one where two sister corporations, Xco and Yco, and their respective wholly-owned subsidiaries, Subco 1 and Subco 2, were amalgamated. The CRA's view was that ss. 87(2.11) would not apply as the amalgamation involved two sister corporations and their respective wholly-owned corporations.

These examples are instructive because in either case the desired result could have been achieved by multiple amalgamations or windings-up, although the resulting number of deemed year ends might in certain circumstances defeat the objective.[7]

When amalgamating corporations, the date of amalgamation is an important issue to consider. Corporations within an affiliated corporate group tend to have the same taxation and financial year to facilitate financial statement consolidation. Paragraph 87(2)(a) of the *ITA* deems the fiscal

---

5 See Strother, "Creative Corporate Tax Planning", 1994 Conference Report, Canadian Tax Foundation, 1995, 11:1 at 11:4.

6 CRA Letter No. 9802725 dated November 20, 1998.

7 For another variation dealing with the interplay between ss. 87(2.1) and ss. 87(2.11), see CRA Letter No. 2006-0170341E5 dated October 26, 2006.

years of the predecessor corporations to end immediately before the amalgamation which, according to the CRA[8] in the absence of specific time being outlined in the certificate of amalgamation (which neither the *Canada Business Corporations Act* nor the *Business Corporations Act* (Ontario) contemplates), is the earliest point on the day on which the articles of amalgamation become effective. Thus, on the amalgamation of two corporations with October 31 year-ends and a short fiscal year is not sought, the effective date of the amalgamation should be November 1. A short fiscal year will shorten the carryforward period for non-capital losses since the short year will constitute a full taxation year for those purposes. Nevertheless, there are some situations in which an immediate amalgamation may be considered useful notwithstanding that a short fiscal period may result.[9]

Subsection 87(11) of the *ITA* presents another planning consideration when amalgamating a Parentco and one or more of its wholly-owned subsidiaries. One effect of the provision is to "bump" the adjusted cost base of certain non-depreciable capital property of the subsidiary in the hands of the amalgamated corporation, similar to the bump available on the wind-up of a subsidiary. Parallel to the wind-up rules, ss. 87(11) may also in certain circumstances[10] deem a capital gain to be realized on, similar to that which may occur on a wind-up. As a matter of due diligence, an investigation should be made to ensure that no capital gain will result on the amalgamation.[11]

---

8 CRA Interpretation Bulletin IT-474R, para. 9.

9 For instance, if it is intended to amalgamate an unprofitable subsidiary with a profitable one, it must be remembered that, subject to ss. 87(2.11) (which only applies in limited circumstances), losses of the new corporation cannot be carried back to predecessor corporations (*i.e.*, tax paid by the profitable predecessor corporation prior to amalgamation can never be recovered) and accordingly, it may be prudent to amalgamate the corporations as quickly as possible in order that the ongoing profits of the business of the profitable corporation may be sheltered from tax by the carryforward of losses from the unprofitable predecessor corporation to the new corporation. However, where a presently profitable corporation has non-capital losses of prior years which are in danger of becoming staledated by virtue of the (7-, 10- or) 20-year carryforward limitation, it will be necessary to make some projections as to the ongoing profits of the new corporation in order to determine the risk that these losses may be staledated before they can be effectively utilized by the new corporation by virtue of there being a short fiscal period on an amalgamation.

10 For instance, where the paid-up capital exceeds the parent's adjusted cost base of the shares of the subsidiary because the parent acquired the subsidiary from a third party.

11 For examples of rulings dealing with the "bump" under ss. 87(11), see CRA Letter No. 2007-0231331R3 dated November 7, 2007, CRA Letter No. 2007-0237482R3 dated November 7, 2007, CRA Letter No. 2006-0194321R3 dated May 30, 2007, CRA Letter No. 2006-0198211R3 dated March 7, 2007, CRA Letter No. 2007-0231331R3 and CRA Letter No. 2007-0237481R3.

Another issue that is relevant on an amalgamation or a ss. 88(1) wind-up is whether property, such as depreciable property, will retain its character on the merger, particularly property with an accrued loss. While the Supreme Court of Canada decisions in *Mara Properties* and *Hickman Motors*[12] were both decided in favor of the taxpayer, those decisions are arguably confined to their own facts and leave open the question of which property retains its character on such a merger. More unequivocal assistance to taxpayers may be found in the Supreme Court of Canada decisions in the *Continental Bank* cases.[13]

When amalgamating affiliated corporations, capital tax issues should not be overlooked. While the federal large corporations tax has now been repealed, provincial capital taxes rely on financial statement values and an amalgamation can, in some cases, result in an alteration of those values and may result in a substantially greater liability for provincial capital tax.[14] In Ontario, capital tax was eliminated for certain manufacturing and resource corporations. For all other corporations, capital tax will be eliminated on July 1, 2010. Generally, no sales tax issues arise on an amalgamation.

Winding-up Under Subsection 88(1) of the ITA

Generally, a wind-up to which ss. 88(1) of the *ITA* applies (*i.e.*, wind up of a wholly-owned subsidiary into its parent) provides a rollover at both the corporate level and, in most cases, at the shareholder level.[15] Also, as mentioned above, an increase (bump) in the tax cost of certain non-depreciable capital property may be available on a winding-up.

With respect to loss utilization, ss. 88(1.1) deems any non-capital losses, restricted farm losses, farm losses, or limited partnership losses of the former subsidiary to be those of the parent for the taxation year in which the subsidiary's loss year ended, but limits the availability of such losses to

---

12 *Mara Properties Ltd. v. The Queen*, [1996] 2 C.T.C. 54, 96 D.T.C. 6309 (S.C.C.) and *Hickman Motors Ltd. v. The Queen*, 1997 D.T.C. 5363, [1998] 1 C.T.C. 213 (S.C.C.).

13 *Continental Bank of Canada v. The Queen*, (*sub nom. Continental Bank Leasing Corp. v. R.*) [1998] 4 C.T.C. 119, 98 D.T.C. 6505 (S.C.C.) and *Continental Bank of Canada v. The Queen*, [1998] 4 C.T.C. 77, 98 D.T.C. 6501 (S.C.C.). For very worthwhile commentaries on these cases, see Bauer, "Partnerships: A Matter of Substance", Current Cases (1998) 46 Can. Tax Journal at 1067 and Monaghan & Raizenne, "Recent Cases of Interest to Corporate Financing Transactions", 1998 Conference Report, Canadian Tax Foundation, 1998, 13:1 at 13:12ff.

14 See Desloges & Marley, "Group Taxation – Canada", 2004 Cahiers de Droit Fiscal International, International Fiscal Association, 2004, 197 at 206.

15 It is possible for the parent to have a capital gain on the disposition of the shares of subsidiary. This is obviously a matter which should be investigated prior to undertaking the winding-up.

taxation years commencing after the winding-up provided that such losses were not previously deducted by the former subsidiary and would have otherwise been deductible by the former subsidiary after the winding-up. Such losses of the former cannot be carried back to the parent's taxation years that commenced before the commencement of the winding-up (*i.e.*, the passing of the requisite shareholders' resolution authorizing the wind-up). Subsection 88(1.2) provides essentially the same rules for net capital losses of the subsidiary.

As a general planning note, where the parent and subsidiary have the same year-end, and the subsidiary is wound up at or near the year-end, the results on a winding up in terms of the timing and utilization of loss carryforwards are identical to those on amalgamations. However, where the parent and the subsidiary have different year-ends, the utilization of losses may be somewhat delayed because any of the former subsidiary's losses are only available to the parent for taxation years commencing after the commencement of the winding-up.[16] However, para. 88(1.1)(f) enables the parent to elect that the former subsidiary's losses be treated as a loss of the parent for its immediately preceding taxation year for the purposes computing the parent's taxable income for taxation years beginning after the commencement of the winding-up. This provision can accelerate the utilization of the former subsidiary's loss by one year.

As with amalgamations, the capital tax (where applicable) as well as the sales tax implications of winding-up must be kept in mind and carefully considered.[17]

Transactions Within an Affiliated Corporate Group

Reorganizing an affiliated corporate group is not the only way to effectively utilize losses. There are a number of other techniques that can be implemented to use and preserve loss amongst and between affiliated corporations. The following techniques are discussed in more detail below:

1. transfer profitable business to Lossco;
2. rollover of appreciated assets to Lossco and subsequent taxable sale by Lossco;
3. techniques to reduce Lossco's interest expense or to generate interest income for Lossco;

---

16 To take an extreme example, if a parent has a calendar year-end, the subsidiary a January 31 year-end, and the winding up commences January 1, 2006, the losses may only be utilized by the parent in its taxation year ending December 31, 2007.

17 See above note 6.

4. sale of assets by Lossco in exchange for interest-bearing debt;
5. inter-company charges;
6. lease assets to affiliated corporations;
7. taxable preferred share financing; and
8. use of partnerships.

It is important to bear in mind that the implementation of any of these techniques must be undertaken with caution because this is an area where taxpayers may be relying on administrative concessions from the CRA,[18] which means an update of the CRA's position on these issues is advisable. Moreover, the CRA's more aggressive use of GAAR and the impact of recent case law should also be considered.

At the Canadian Tax Foundation's Annual Conference in September, 2003, during the CRA/Practitioner Round Table, CRA officials confirmed that transferring losses within an affiliated corporate group remains acceptable and that rulings on such matters will continue to be available. If a ruling from the CRA is sought with respect to loss transfers, the following information should accompany the ruling request:

- a summary of losses and incomes of members of the affiliated group for each year in question;
- the period of time the members had been affiliated; and
- a summary of the planned application of the losses to specific years.

As a cautionary note, transactions implementing a loss consolidation should make some commercial sense and rulings will not be given if the amounts or timeframes are blatantly artificial. To demonstrate commercial reality, the CRA has mentioned that the quickest route is to obtain a commitment letter from a financial institution.[19]

---

18 See, for instance, the comments of the Court in *Mark Resources Inc. v. The Queen*, [1993] 2 C.T.C. 2259, 93 D.T.C. 1004 (T.C.C.), at 1017 [D.T.C.]. See also *C.R.B. Logging Co. v. The Queen*, [2000] 4 C.T.C. 157, 2000 D.T.C. 6547 (Fed. C.A.), affirming [1999] 2 C.T.C. 2279, 99 D.T.C. 840 (T.C.C.) and the CRA's comments on that case in Income Tax Technical News No. 18 dated June 6, 2000.

19 See Lynch, *et al.*, "CCRA Round Table", 2003 Conference Report, Canadian Tax Foundation, 2004 at 8A:1 to 8A:10ff and CCH Canadian Tax Topics Report No. 1648 dated October 9, 2003.

Transfer Profitable Business to Lossco

A common loss utilization technique is simply to transfer the assets of a profitable business on a tax-deferred basis to an affiliated Lossco by way of a s. 85 rollover. Thereafter, Lossco will carry on the business with the resulting profits being sheltered by any available loss carryforwards in Lossco.[20, 21]

For such transactions, it is critical that the transfer of the business to the subsidiary be legally effective and properly documented in order to avoid any suggestion that the transaction is ineffective or that the Lossco is merely a trustee or agent for the transferor corporation. The commercial aspects of such a transaction should also be considered, particularly where the loss corporation has significant actual or contingent liabilities.[22]

Rollover of Appreciated Assets to Loss Corporation and Subsequent Taxable Sale by Loss Corporation

Another technique for utilizing loss carryforwards is to transfer an asset with appreciated value on a s. 85 rollover to a Lossco in exchange for shares of the Lossco. The resulting capital gain realized on a sale of the asset by the Lossco to an arm's length third party could then be sheltered by the non-capital or net capital losses of the Lossco. (In all these types of transactions, the GST (HST as applicable), retail sales tax, and land transfer tax issues should be considered carefully.)

In Information Circular IC 88-2, which deals with GAAR,[23] the CRA considers this type of transaction and points out that there are specific anti-avoidance rules (ss. 69(11) to (13) of the *ITA*) that restrict this type of transaction between unrelated corporations. The CRA's historic view has been that since those specific provisions are confined to unrelated corporations, GAAR should not be applied in the context of a transaction involving related corporations and hence the transaction would be permissible. In light of

---

20 This type of arrangement was expressly approved of by the Supreme Court of Canada in *Stubart Investments Ltd. v. The Queen*, [1984] C.T.C. 294, 84 D.T.C. 6305 (S.C.C.). The CRA has also commented positively on such an arrangement in para. 8 of Information Circular 88-2 entitled [General Anti-Avoidance Rule – Section 245 of the Income Tax Act" dated October 31, 1988.

21 See CRA Letter Nos. 2004-0098561R3 dated January 26, 2005 and 2005-0155451R3 January 11, 2006.

22 See Stadtegger, "*Corporate Loss Utilization: Where Are We Now and What Can Be Done?*" 2003 Conference Report, Canadian Tax Foundation, 2004, 30:1 at 30:9 for a more detailed commentary.

23 IC 88-2 above note 20.

the 1995 amendment to ss. 69(11), this historic position is continued but modified to apply to affiliated corporations rather than related corporations.[24]

Something that should be kept in mind where capital property of the transferor is sold by a Lossco shortly after its acquisition is whether the CRA might seek to recharacterize the property as inventory rather than capital property in the hands of the Lossco. The CRA has indicated administratively that it would not do so.[25] This position does not seem to have been affected by the Supreme Court of Canada decisions in *Mara Properties* and *Hickman Motors* which, while decided in favor of the taxpayers, still leave open the possibility of recharacterization in certain cases.[26] Moreover, the *Continental Bank Leasing* decision of the Supreme Court of Canada provides further strong support for the continuation of the CRA's administrative position.[27]

It is worth noting that these types of transactions do not necessarily require that the asset be sold outside the group. For instance, in CRA documents 2004-0098561R3 dated January 26, 2005 and 2005-0155451R3 dated January 11, 2006, Parentco transferred depreciable industrial property to its loss subsidiary on a tax-deferred basis to enable the subsidiary to earn income from the sale of the output of those assets and, approximately one year later, Parentco repurchased the same assets at fair market value creating income from recapture which would be sheltered by non-capital losses and expiring tax credits of the subsidiary.

---

24 On the other hand, the CRA is apparently of the view that ss. 69(11) would apply to a deemed disposition of property under para. 111(4)(e). The CRA in 1996 considered a situation similar to that described above, except that the transferee corporation did not resell the property but, in an unrelated transaction within three years after the transfer of the property, there was an acquisition of control of the transferee and the transferee elected under para. 111(4)(e) to revalue its property including that contributed by the transferor. The CRA concluded that ss. 69(11) was applicable in the circumstances. See CRA File No. 9639150 (Round Table response at Tax Executives Institute) December 5, 1996.

25 See para. 9 of IC 88-2.

26 In the CRA review at the 1995 Canadian Tax Foundation Conference, Michael Hiltz indicated that the CRA would maintain its position notwithstanding the Federal Court of Appeal decision in *Mara Properties* which went against the taxpayer. Since *Mara Properties* was reversed on appeal to the Supreme Court of Canada and the Supreme Court of Canada similarly found in favor of the taxpayer in *Hickman Motors*, *a fortiori*, this position appears to continue.

27 See above note 5.

Techniques to Reduce Lossco's Interest Expense or to Generate Interest Income for Lossco

The use of certain financing arrangements provides a variety of techniques to utilize losses within an affiliated corporate group. Some simple examples include:

> *Example 1*
>
> Where a subsidiary Lossco is carrying on a business which needs additional capital and additional borrowing by Lossco would exacerbate its loss position, profitable Parentco could borrow from the bank and subscribe for additional common shares of Lossco. The resulting interest charges would reduce Parentco's income and the cash infusion would hopefully generate profits in Lossco.[28]
>
> *Example 2*
>
> Profitable Parentco has a wholly-owned subsidiary with non-capital losses. Parentco borrows from the bank and uses the money to subscribe for common shares of the subsidiary. The subsidiary lends these monies to the parent at a commercial rate of interest. The parent uses the funds to repay the bank. As a result, Parentco has deductible interest charges to reduce its taxable income and the subsidiary has interest income which will enable it to utilize its non-capital loss carryforwards.[29, 30]
>
> *Example 3*
>
> Profitable Parentco has a loss subsidiary with existing borrowings. Parentco borrows from the bank and subscribes for shares of the Lossco which uses the funds to pay its bank debt thereby reducing its interest expense and increasing the interest expense of the Parentco.

Where Lossco is the parent in the group, for instance, similar arrangements can be undertaken in effect to transfer the parent's losses to a newly-formed subsidiary in the group and subsequently merge the subsidiary with a another profitable subsidiary in the group. To take a simple example, Parentco has non-capital losses and a profitable subsidiary. Parentco incorporates two new subsidiaries, Lossco and Shareco. Parentco borrows money on a daylight loan basis within its borrowing capacity at an arm's length commercial rate from a financial institution. Parentco lends the proceeds to Lossco, with the loan being payable on demand and bearing interest at a commercial market rate applicable to loans to the parent. Lossco uses the proceeds to subscribe for preferred shares in Shareco, which will carry a

---

28 See para. 19 of IC 88-2.

29 For a variation on this theme, see CRA Letter No. 2002-0177363 dated February 12, 2003.

30 See para. 5 of the Supplement to IC 88-2 dated July 13, 1990.

cumulative dividend rate and will enable Lossco to realize a profit on these investment activities. Shareco uses the proceeds received to make a demand interest-free loan to Parentco, which then uses the proceeds to repay the daylight loan. Lossco will accumulate losses since it will have interest expense and tax-free dividend income. Parentco will make contributions of capital to Shareco from time to time to fund the dividends payable by Shareco. After an appropriate passage of time, the process will be reversed and Lossco will then be merged with the profitable subsidiary in the group so that the losses "manufactured" in Lossco and siphoned off from Parentco may be utilized by the profitable subsidiary.[31] [32]

Generally, the CRA is comfortable with these types of transactions from an anti-avoidance perspective, although it does require that the share subscription not exceed the amount that an arm's length borrower would have been prepared to lend to the loss subsidiary.[33] In the *CRB Logging case*,[34] the CRA was not prepared to sanction interest deductibility where the funds were borrowed to subscribe for preferred shares on the basis that there was no realistic expectation of dividend income on the preferred shares. With arrangements of this sort, it is always wise to confirm that the proposed transaction is within the scope of the CRA's administrative policy. The Supreme Court of Canada decisions in *Singleton*[35] and *Ludco*[36] should generally be of assistance to taxpayers in justifying interest deductibility in this and other areas. However, in a *Singleton*-like situation, the Tax Court of

---

[31] See, for example, CRA Letter Nos. 2003-0181283 dated September 3, 2003 and 2003-0013723 dated June 18, 2003. For an interesting variation, see CRA Letter Nos. 2003-0020553 dated August 14, 2003, 2005-0118061R3 dated August 24, 2005, 2005-0132891R3 dated November 9, 2005 2005-0160471R3 dated March 8, 2006. See also the discussion of the foregoing in Welch & Borgman, "Recent CRA Views of Interest", Canadian Life and Health Insurance Association, Tax Officers Conference, 2006.

[32] For further examples of these types of transactions, see CRA Letter Nos. 2005-0118061R3 dated August 24, 2005, 2005-0143711R3 dated September 14, 2005, 2004-0109481R3 dated October 5, 2005, 2005-0118951R3 dated October 5, 2005, 2005-0139621R3 dated October 5, 2005, 2005-0132891R3 dated November 9, 2005, 2006-0185221R3, 2006-0171291R3 dated July 19, 2006 and 2006-0180261R3 dated August 23, 2006. For a somewhat different variant see CRA Letter No. 2005-0160471R3 dated March 8, 2006. See also CRA Letter Nos. 2007-0226151R3 dated October 10, 2007, 2007-0226931R3 dated September 12, 2007, 2007-022921R3 dated May 16, 2007, 2006-0219051R3 dated May 9, 2007 and 2007-0220051R3 dated March 14, 2007.

[33] See IC 88-2, Advance Tax Ruling ATR-44 and CRA Letters Nos. 9728683 dated April 17, 1998 and 9727343 dated April 17, 1998, for examples. See also Kellough & McQuillan, "Taxation of Private Corporations and Their Shareholders", Canadian Tax Foundation, 1999 at 13:31 to 13:33.

[34] Above note 11.

[35] *Singleton v. The Queen* (2001), [2002] 1 C.T.C. 121, 2001 D.T.C. 5533 (S.C.C.).

[36] *Ludco Enterprises Ltd. v. The Queen*, [2002] 1 C.T.C. 95, 2001 D.T.C. 5505 (S.C.C.).

Canada decided against the taxpayer with respect to interest deductibility in *Lipson*,[37] on the basis of the application of the GAAR.[38]

Lipson was appealed to the Supreme Court of Canada. In January, 2009, on a 4-3 split, the Supreme Court of Canada dismissed the taxpayer's appeal based on the application of GAAR.[39] The taxpayer entered into a series of transactions in order to deduct interest payments on a loan used to purchase a home (ss. 20(1)(c) and 20(3) of the *ITA*) and attribute the interest deductions to the higher income-earning spouse (ss. 73(1) and 74.1 of the *ITA*). The majority concluded that the automatic operation of ss. 74.1(1) did not matter and allowing ss. 74.1(1) to reduce the taxpayer's income tax frustrated the purpose of the attribution rules. The result of this decision is that the automatic operation of a particular section may subject an otherwise legitimate transaction to GAAR. In addition, taking advantage of non-arm's length relationships may subject otherwise legitimate transactions to GAAR.

R v. John MacKay[40] is another example of how GAAR may apply. In *MacKay*, the taxpayers agreed to purchase with the National Bank of Canada a shopping centre, which was the subject of foreclosure proceedings. The bank, together with its newly-formed subsidiary, formed a limited partnership and transferred its interest in the mortgage on the shopping centre to the partnership. The taxpayers purchased units in the partnership, and the property was subsequently transferred to the partnership on completion of the foreclosure proceedings. The partnership wrote down the value of the shopping centre under ss. 10(1) of the *ITA* generating $6 million in losses allocated to the taxpayers. The Minister reassessed the taxpayers under GAAR and the loss deductions and carryforwards were denied.

The Tax Court of Canada allowed the taxpayer's appeal, concluding that GAAR did not apply. The Federal Court of Appeal allowed the Minister's appeal and found that GAAR did apply.

The finding that a series of transactions had a *bona fide* business purpose does not preclude a finding that the primary purpose of one or more steps within the series was to obtain a tax benefit. If at least one transaction in a series of transactions is an "avoidance transaction", then the benefit that

---

37 *Lipson v. The Queen*, [2006] 3 C.T.C. 2494, 2006 D.T.C. 2687 (T.C.C. [General Procedure]), affirmed [2007] 3 C.T.C. 110, 2007 D.T.C. 5172 (F.C.A.).

38 See also *Overs v. The Queen*, [2006] 3 C.T.C. 2255, 2006 D.T.C. 2192 (T.C.C. [General Procedure]) for a similar situation in which the taxpayer was unsuccessful based on GAAR at the Tax Court of Canada level.

39 [2009] 1 C.T.C. 314, 2009 D.T.C. 5528 (S.C.C.).

40 *MacKay v. The Queen*, [2008] 4 C.T.C. 161, 2008 D.T.C. 6238 (F.C.A.), leave to appeal refused (2009), 2009 CarswellNat 19 (S.C.C.).

results from the series may be denied under GAAR. Conversely, if each transaction in a series was carried out primarily for a *bona fide* non-tax purpose, then GAAR cannot be applied to deny a tax benefit.[41]

The CRA had indicated in an advance income tax ruling that while tax loss consolidation within an affiliated group is generally permissible, the refreshing of a Lossco's loss through a mechanism which resulted in a profitable affiliated company incurring interest expense which exceeded the profitable company's taxable income, hence creating a non-capital loss in the profitable corporation, was not permissible. The reason for this position was that such a transaction would effectively allow the losses of the Lossco to be refreshed in a manner which extends the original 7- (now 20-) year loss carryforward period. The CRA considered this to be an abuse of the temporal restrictions on loss carryforwards in s. 111 of the *ITA*. For further comments by the CRA in this regard, see Income Tax Technical News No. 25 dated October 30, 2002 and Income Tax Technical News No. 30 dated May 21, 2004.

Sale of Assets by Loss Corporation in Exchange for Interest Bearing Debt

Another way for a Lossco to generate income is to sell assets (even if the assets have not appreciated) to a Profitco within the affiliated group and take back interest-bearing debt as consideration. The interest payments (and capital cost allowance if the asset is depreciable property) should generally be deductible to Profitco and would be included as income for Lossco, which could then be offset by any available loss carryforwards.[42]

It should be noted, however, that where depreciable property, which has appreciated in value, is transferred and a capital gain is realized, the transferee (*i.e.*, Profitco) will not enjoy a full write-up of the asset to fair market value, but the cost will, in general terms, be the cost to the loss corporation plus one-half of the loss corporation's capital gain by virtue of para. 13(7)(e) of the *ITA*. Nevertheless, the gain on the sale (in addition to the interest income) will utilize losses of Lossco.

Inter-Company Charges

Reviewing inter-company charges to determine whether those charged to a Lossco may be legitimately reduced or charges by a Lossco may be legiti-

---

41 *Ibid.* at para. 21.

42 For an example of this type of planning, see CRA Letter No. 9615073 dated March 7, 1997.

mately increased is always useful when dealing with a Lossco within an affiliated group. The group may wish to consider transferring management personnel to the Lossco, which would then provide management services to the other corporations in the group for a reasonable management fee. Again, it is important to properly document these transactions and ensure that they have appropriate substance.[43]

Lease Assets to Affiliated Corporations

Provided that projected rental income will exceed the capital cost allowance and other operating expenses, having a Lossco acquire assets to lease to the other corporations in the group may be worth considering.[44]

Taxable Preferred Share Financing

Where third party financing is available, a Lossco could raise funds by issuing taxable preferred shares and using the funds to generate income in some fashion (*e.g.*, lending the funds to other corporations in the group). While the Lossco would potentially be subject to tax under Part VI.1 of the *ITA*, generally, the first $500,000 of dividends on taxable preferred shares would not be subject to the tax; not to mention that the tax liability could be shifted to a related corporation pursuant to s. 191.3 of the *ITA*. If the related corporation is sufficiently profitable, the liability for Part VI.1 tax will generate a corresponding deduction in computing taxable income for Part I purposes pursuant to para. 110(1)(k) of the *ITA* with the effect of potentially offsetting the effect of Part VI.1 tax for the group.

Use of Partnerships

As an alternative to transferring a business to a Lossco, a partnership could be entered into between the Profitco currently carrying on the business and the Lossco. For a variety of commercial reasons, such an arrangement might be preferable to having the Lossco acquire the business. For the Lossco to share in an appropriate amount of the profits of the partnership, Lossco must make an adequate contribution to the partnership, which means corresponding financing would be required. To achieve such financing, for example, a dividend from an affiliated corporation could be provided as the proceeds for Lossco's investment in the partnership.

---

43 See Vukets, "Structural Issues in Utilization of Domestic Loss Carryforward Pools", 1993 Conference Report, Canadian Tax Foundation, 1994, 23:1 at 23:17.

44 See Bernstein, "Loss Utilization by Individuals and Private Corporations", 1996 Conference Report, Canadian Tax Foundation, 1997, 58:1 at 58:18? 58:19.

When entertaining this type of arrangement, there are three principal considerations that should be kept in mind:

> First, Lossco will only obtain the benefit of its proportionate share of the partnership's income, in contrast to the benefit it might otherwise have received if the business had been transferred to Lossco directly.
>
> Second, the arrangement must be adequately documented and legally effective so that the transaction is effective for tax purposes.[45]
>
> Third, the profit-sharing ratio should be justifiable to avoid the risk of a reallocation by the CRA pursuant to ss. 103(1.1) of the Act.[46]

A further alternative to transferring appreciated property to a Lossco on a s. 85 rollover basis with a mind to reselling it would be to establish a partnership between the owner of the property and the Lossco. However, this type of arrangement runs the risk, in addition to those listed above, of not meeting the definition of partnership (*i.e.*, two or more persons carrying on business in common with a view to profit). The arrangement is also vulnerable if the partnership is set up for only a short period of time,[47] although the *Continental Bank* decisions are of considerable assistance in this regard.

A case which addressed some of these issues is *West Topaz Property Ltd.*, a 2005 decision of the Tax Court of Canada, which was later affirmed by the Federal Court of Appeal.[48, 49] In *West Topaz,* there was a partnership consisting of two corporations one of whom was West Topaz as to a 99 per cent interest. The partnership was in the business of selling and managing real estate assets. It was anticipated that the partnership would sell a partnership asset (an apartment building) and realize a significant gain on the disposition.

Prior to the sale of the apartment building, Woodwards, which had significant non-capital losses, became a member of the partnership. The partnership agreement was amended so that Woodwards' interest was tied to the sale of the apartment building in that 80 per cent of the profit from the sale of the apartment building would be attributable to Woodwards, with the intention that Woodwards would use its non-capital loss to shelter the gain

---

45 See above note 5.

46 See Strother above note 5 at 11:6ff.

47 See Strother *ibid.* at 11:10. See also Vukets above note 43 at 23:11ff. Also noteworthy with respect to the topic of partnerships are the more recent Supreme Court of Canada decisions in *Backman v. The Queen*, [2001] 2 C.T.C. 11, 2001 D.T.C. 5149 (S.C.C.) and *Spire Freezers Ltd. v. The Queen*, [2001] 2 C.T.C. 40, 2001 D.T.C. 5158 (S.C.C.).

48 (*sub nom. XCO Investments Ltd. v. The Queen*) [2006] 1 C.T.C. 2220, 2005 D.T.C. 1731 (T.C.C.).

49 [2007] 2 C.T.C. 243, 2007 D.T.C. 5146 (F.C.A.).

attributable to the sale of the apartment building. Shortly after the sale of the apartment building, Woodwards withdrew from the partnership by transferring its partnership to West Topaz for nominal consideration.

Woodwards received approximately $550,000 to participate in this transaction and the two original corporate partners saved an excess of $2,000,000 in tax. The Tax Court applied s. 103 to reallocate the income received by the partnership.

In the course of the Court's decision, GAAR was also considered. The Court noted that GAAR was a provision of last resort and however far reaching s. 245 may be, it does not confer discretionary powers on the Minister either in the decision to apply it or in the determination of its consequences. As to the interrelation between s. 103 and the GAAR, the Court observed that where a specific anti-avoidance provision (*i.e.*, s. 103) covers the transaction but does not in the Minister's view provide a remedy that the Minister considers sufficient, s. 245 is not to be used to top up the more specific remedy the Minister believes to be inadequate. In other words, GAAR is ousted by specific anti-avoidance provisions in the Act.

Self-Help

In addition to transactions with other corporations in the affiliated group, there are a number of ways that a Lossco may improve its own tax position, including:

1. sell assets to third parties;
2. capitalize interest under s. 21 of the *ITA*;
3. apply losses against Part IV of tax; and
4. non-use of discretionary deductions.

Sell Assets to Third Parties

An obvious technique for loss utilization is to sell assets that have appreciated in value to an arm's length third party, realize the accrued gain, and generate either income or taxable capital gains to offset losses which may be on the verge of expiring.

Capitalize Interest under Section 21 of the ITA

Rather than deduct interest expense which will then be subject to the 20-year non-capital loss carryforward limitation, a Lossco could capitalize such interest under s. 21 of the *ITA* as much as possible. This may be relevant where, for instance, Lossco has borrowed money to acquire depreciable property.[50]

Apply Losses Against Tax under Part IV of the ITA

As a last resort, if non-capital losses are on the verge of expiring, non-capital losses may be applied to reduce Part IV tax. In computing the base on which Part IV tax is levied, a corporation is entitled to deduct non-capital losses if it chooses in accordance with the usual carryover rules. Generally, one would not choose to use non-capital losses in this manner since they will be reducing a tax which is refundable in any event.

Non-Use of Discretionary Deductions

Discretionary deductions should only be taken if it makes senses to do so. Generally, a Lossco should avoid claiming for capital cost allowance, eligible capital property, and scientific research, particularly in the case of capital cost allowance classes with rapidly accelerated write-offs. Similarly, choosing not to claim reserves under para. 40(1)(a)(iii) of the *ITA* (*i.e.*, five-year reserve on the disposition of capital property) and para. 20(1)(n) of the *ITA* (*i.e.*, three-year reserve in respect of property sold in the course of a business which generates ordinary income), where a taxpayer has had non-capital losses in danger of expiring, may recognize a sufficient amount of income to utilize the potentially expiring losses.

As well, a taxpayer could decline any applicable so-called "rolling reserves" in the *ITA* (*i.e.*, where the taxpayer claims a reserve in year 1, the taxpayer is required to include in year 2 the amount of the reserve claimed in year 1 and may then proceed to claim a fresh reserve for year 2) as these reserves are generally discretionary. If losses are in danger of expiring, declining such reserves in a particular year, so that the prior year's reserves come into income to offset non-capital losses that are about to expire may make sense. Assuming a constant claim for reserves over the relevant period, declining such reserves would have the effect of increasing in the taxpayer's income in the year in which the reserve was not taken and decreasing the taxpayer's income in the year in which the reserve was reinstated.

The CRA's administrative position dealing with revision of capital cost allowance claims and other permissive deductions is set out in Information Circular 84-1. Generally, a revision requested for a loss will be allowed

---

[50] *Ibid.*

provided there is no change in the tax payable for that year or any other year filed, including statute-barred years, for which the time has expired for filing a notice of objection. Thus, if losses are about to expire, refilling prior years' tax returns to reverse claims for capital cost allowance and other permissive deductions may be advantageous.

Transactions Involving Non-affiliated Persons

The foregoing techniques for loss utilization assumed that the composition of the corporate group remained the same; however, it is possible to introduce new shareholders into a Lossco without necessarily triggering an acquisition of control. For instance, a Parentco may have a wholly-owned subsidiary Lossco carrying on a particular business. An arm's length corporation which carries on a profitable business within the same industry may see the advantages of transferring its business on a s. 85 rollover basis to the Lossco in exchange for a minority interest on the rationale that the synergies produced by combining the two businesses may generate greater profits overall and utilize the existing losses in the Lossco. There should not be change of control, particularly if there is no shareholders' agreement which gives extraordinary rights to the minority shareholder.

The risk in this type of arrangement is that the minority shareholder's rollover treatment of its business may be denied pursuant to ss. 69(11) of the *ITA*. Subsection 69(11) denies rollover treatment where:

(i) the minority shareholder in the above example disposes of property for proceeds of disposition of less than fair market value (*e.g.*, on a s. 85 rollover);

(ii) it can reasonably be considered that one of the main purposes of the series of transactions is to utilize the tax losses of the Lossco, which was unaffiliated with the minority shareholder immediately before the series of transactions began; and

(iii) arrangements for the subsequent disposition of any property so transferred to the Lossco are made within three years of the acquisition by the Lossco.

This is a particularly significant issue with respect to inventory transferred for less than fair market value. When dealing with the service industry, the risk of offending this provision is diminished.

Paragraphs 7 and 8 of Interpretation Bulletin IT-302R3[51] are informative of CRA considerations when assessing the utilization of losses when a majority

[51] Interpretation Bulletin IT-302R3 Losses of a corporation – The effect that acquisitions of

interest shareholder is brought into the fold, and looks at some of the factors that the CRA may consider to determine whether an acquisition of control has effectively taken place. Generally, however, a person seeking access to another person's tax losses will tend to only accept a minority position provided that meaningful protections, particularly where the Lossco is dormant, and a substantial business are being infused into the corporation by the third party.[52]

Obviously, attempts to "disguise" an acquisition of control is fraught with peril, which is only emphasized by the CRA's concern and vigilance for "improper" utilization of tax losses and the acknowledgement in the first appellate GAAR decision (*OSFC Holdings*) that there is a general policy in the *ITA* against the transferring of losses between arm's length parties. The most significant case in this area is *Duha Printers*,[53] where a complicated tax loss utilization scheme in which the taxpayers sought to avoid a technical acquisition of control of a corporation, having previously been struck down by the Federal Court of Appeal, on a review of all of the relevant documentation, was upheld by the Supreme Court of Canada. While the *Duha Printers* case is perhaps of some encouragement to tax planners, it must be borne in mind that it is a pre-GAAR case and therefore of limited definitive assistance for current tax planning. Taxpayers who embark into this murky area must exercise extreme caution. As one writer puts it:

> Given the CRA's hostile approach to extra group tax planning, prudent advisers should take pains to think through all potential technical weaknesses in a proposal and encourage the parties to add significant non-tax business substance to the transactions to assist in defending an assessment based on GAAR. All of the technical requirements inherent in each provision of the Act that is being relied upon to support the plan must be carefully followed. All specific anti-avoidance provisions must be identified and dealt with. The transactions must be carefully documented and the commercial relationships established by the documents must be consistently followed by the parties in actual practice ...
>
> Taxpayers contemplating extra group transactions to access losses and other tax shield[s] of unrelated corporations should expect audit scrutiny from the CRA and should guide themselves accordingly. Planning and implementation must be thoughtful and meticulous. The audit trail should be limited to the transaction documents and there should be limited, if any, retention of planning memoranda, meeting notes, and like materials. Taxpayers' document retention should be kept to a minimum, and advisers should conduct themselves so as to protect the

---

control, amalgamations, and winding-up have on their deductibility – After January 15, 1987.

52 See Stadtegger above note 22 at 30:16 for an interesting example of such a transaction.

53 *Duha Printers (Western) Ltd. v. The Queen*, [1998] 3 C.T.C. 303, 98 D.T.C. 6334 (S.C.C.).

> solicitor-client privilege and generally to expect the likelihood of audit and possible litigation.[54]

Among the particular statutory provisions which should be considered would be ss. 69(11), the collateralized preferred share rules in ss. 112(2.4), ss. 256(8) and, most importantly, the general anti-avoidance rule itself.

In 2002, a CRA official stated:

> Finance policy and CRA policy has always been to accept in-house loss utilizations. The qualifications are that the loss utilization transactions must be legally effective and they must meet the specific provisions of the Act. ... One point that I would like to make on loss utilizations in general is that in-house loss utilizations are fine. Selling losses outside the corporate group is not acceptable *and we will use all the tools available to us to not allow loss utilization outside the corporate group. We're pretty serious about that.*"[55] [Emphasis added.]

At the CRA Round Table at the 2005 Canadian Tax Foundation Annual Conference, the CRA was asked whether restrictions in the Act regarding the use of losses applied to the sale of tax losses where *de facto* and not *de jure* control is acquired (*e.g.*, 45 per cent of votes) but substantially all the value of the loss company is acquired by a profitable company. The CRA's response was that matters to be considered included, as per *Duha Printers*, were "effective control" acquired; was the acquiror acting in concert with other shareholders so that a group or the acquirer itself acquired *de jure* control?; and finally, do any of the various specific anti-avoidance provisions referred to above (ss. 256(8), 69(11), 112(2.4), *etc.*) apply? In addition, the CRA commented that the general anti-avoidance rule could apply consistent with the policy against trading in non-capital losses established in *OSFC Holdings* by the Federal Court of Appeal.[56] At a 2008 CRA Round Table, the CRA addressed artificial losses and stated that it had assessed about 75 cases with capital losses of $2.3 billion. Several different methods were utilized and taxpayers are currently manufacturing high ACB shares with little value for future use. There are also several cases currently before the courts.

The CRA's Views on Provincial Loss Consolidation Issues

At the 2005 CRA Round Table referred to above, the CRA was also asked if it was concerned about provincial taxation implications of loss consoli-

---

54 Strother above note 5 at 11:15.

55 Jack, *et al.*, "Interest Deductibility: Where From, Where To, Where Now?", 2002 Conference Report, Canadian Tax Foundation, 2003, 11:1 at 11:10.

56 See Income Tax Technical News No. 34, dated April 27, 2006.

dation. The CRA responded that loss consolidation may affect provincial revenues and, accordingly, ruling requests on loss consolidation proposals must contain an analysis of the provincial tax implications of the proposed transactions. Further, issued loss consolidation rulings will provide no comfort as to the application of the GAAR of the affected provinces, although the CRA indicated that it was not aware of any instances where a province sought to apply a provincial GAAR to loss consolidation transactions on which the CRA had ruled favorably. The CRA indicated that it does consult with provincial tax authorities before issuing loss consolidation rulings where the loss consolidation materially affects a province with which it has a tax collection agreement. If the impact on a province with which the federal government has a tax collection agreement is minimal or if the ruling affects the province with which the federal government has not entered into a tax collection agreement, the CRA will normally not consult prior to issuing the ruling but will forward a copy of the issued ruling to the affected province. The CRA cautioned that when a loss consolidation transaction affects a province with which the federal government does not have a tax collection agreement, it may be advisable for the taxpayers to obtain a provincial ruling. The CRA further indicated that a working group is being created to review transactions that affect provincial tax bases, including loss consolidation. The CRA did not directly respond to a question as to whether it has taken steps to cause provinces with which it has tax collection agreements not to apply provincial GAAR provisions where the CRA has issued a favor loss consolidation ruling.[57]

As part of the tax on income distributions by specified investment flow-through (SIFT) trusts and partnerships introduced in 2006, the ITA was amended to provide for the tax-deferred conversion of SIFTs into corporate entities. Since 2006, the SIFT conversion rules have been used to facilitate loss trading transactions that corporations were not otherwise able to implement. In reaction to the inappropriate use of these rules, the 2010 Federal Budget proposes changes to the acquisition of control rules in the ITA to restrict certain types of loss consolidation on conversions from SIFT to corporate form. Addressing this issue is a high priority for both the CRA and the Department of Finance and it is anticipated that enforcement will be aggressively pursued.

As the economic cycles of the country move from bust to boom, tax planners will be able to capitalize on unrealized losses within the corporate group. The utilization of tax losses will continue to be an area with great opportunities yet fraught with many pitfalls.

---

57 *Ibid.*

R&D Credits: Reducing the Cost of Innovation in Volatile Times

Anil Chawla & David Douglas

We are in the midst of a once-in-a-generation economic crisis that is testing the strategic and managerial capabilities of CEOs across Canada. As innovative Canadian companies face increasing competition from Asia and tightened credit terms and conditions from Canadian banks, the need for reducing costs and managing cash flow becomes essential. The cost of innovation is particularly vulnerable in these economic times. In these volatile times, incentives for conducting R&D can significantly reduce the cost of innovation to allow Canadian companies to be competitive with the world.

In Canada, incentives for performing research and development (R&D)[1] come in a variety of forms, grants, tax credits (which reduce a taxpayer's taxes payable directly), and additional deductions in computing a taxpayer's taxable income. These incentives may be refundable in cash to the R&D performer even if the taxpayer has no corporate taxes payable.

R&D remains a high priority for management during volatile times. A recent McKinsey survey indicates that management tends to cut operating costs before making significant cuts to R&D departments. To preserve the long term while maintaining accountability and control, R&D projects may become shorter term, modified to reflect a tighter scope, and be more incremental to the previous technology rather than a comprehensive redesign.[2] This may require some subtle changes to claiming strategies in the technical write-ups for claiming SR&ED, but should not impact the ability to claim SR&ED credits in the first instance.

---

1 In Canada the incentive regime is known as the scientific research and experimental development program (SR&ED).

2 R&D in the downturn: McKinsey Global Survey Results, April 2009.

In this chapter, we examine the incentives in Canada at the federal and provincial levels as well as the global environment for these incentives. We will pay particular attention to regimes providing refundable cash payments as refundable incentives are of immediate benefit to companies experiencing these tough economic times.

Another aspect of claiming SR&ED in volatile times is that strategic or tactical opportunities may present themselves to, or be may even be forced on companies. Changes in the control, going private transactions, or insolvency may occur. This chapter also examines how to preserve and maximize these credits in such circumstances.

Rationale for Government Support

The rationale for these incentives is that technological innovation is a major driver of economic growth.[3] In order to attract firms that drive technology innovation, governments provide support as, otherwise, companies will not spend the optimal amount on R&D as their economic returns will not justify that level of spending. However, the social benefits of R&D spending, including the spin-off benefits, exceed those accruing to the firm that is investing in R&D. Therefore, government investment targeted to increasing private sector R&D is likely to generate external benefits to the economy as a whole that are well in excess of the tax revenue foregone.

Through the various incentive programs, governments are trying to influence R&D performers to either locate their R&D activities in the country, or to at least stop research jobs from leaving the country. This occurs as sophisticated R&D performers have systems in place to capture eligible activities and the related expenditures and to allocate the incentives back to the group that actually performs the work. These groups build the incentives into the future planning and budgeting process. During these volatile times, the availability of R&D incentives becomes a significant factor in ranking investment decisions or the location of future development activities. During these times, the availability of refundable incentives is increasingly important to the budget and planning process.

---

3 For a more complete explanation, see the publication published by the Department of Finance, Canada, *Why and How Governments Support Research and Development*, December, 1997, available on the government of Canada's website at http://www.fin.gc.ca.

The Canadian System

For the rationale noted above, the Canadian government has put in place tax incentives to encourage companies to undertake R&D or, in the Canadian terminology, scientific research and experimental development ("SR&ED"). In addition, many Canadian provinces offer additional incentives for SR&ED carried out within their borders. In most provinces, recent amendments have increased the refundable status of these incentives.

The Canadian system rewards taxpayers through a system of deductions for SR&ED expenditures which reduce a taxpayer's taxable income, and investment tax credits (ITCs) which reduce taxes payable on a dollar for dollar basis or, in certain cases, are refundable in cash even if the taxpayer has no taxable income. The Canadian system is volume-based which means that the incentives are available on every dollar of SR&ED spending. Other regimes, like the United States, only provide incentives on incremental R&D spending over and above a calculated base amount.

SR&ED expenditures generate a favorable tax treatment since current and capital SR&ED expenditures can be deducted in the year incurred or can be carried forward indefinitely as is deemed necessary to minimize a taxpayer's tax liability. This flexibility is particularly important during volatile times. The ability to carry forward SR&ED expenditures operates similarly to the ability to carry forward losses. These deductions may be carried forward indefinitely and applied on a discretionary basis.

In addition to the flexibility regarding the timing of the deduction of the SR&ED expenditures, a taxpayer may also obtain the benefit of the ITCs. ITCs are earned on qualifying SR&ED expenditures.[4]

ITC Rates and Utilization

In Canada there is a two-tier system in place. Qualifying Canadian-controlled private corporations[5] ("CCPCs") can generally claim a higher rate of ITCs on their qualifying expenditures as well as both refundable and non-refundable ITCs.

---

4 There may be differences between expenditures that are deductible for tax purposes as SR&ED and the expenditures that earn ITCs. For example, salary expenditure for time outside of the country in excess of 10% of the labor dollars claimed may be deducted for tax purposes, but are not eligible for the ITC.

5 A CCPC is a private corporation in Canada that is *not* controlled by non-residents. Control of a corporation means either *de jure* control or *de facto* control for purposes of making this determination.

Qualifying Corporations and Refundable ITCs

During volatile times earnings may decline to the point where there are no taxes payable. Non-refundable credits are of little immediate use in these circumstances. Accordingly, provisions in the Act allow for refundable treatment for qualifying CCPCs. The ITCs earned in a taxation year are eligible for refund under certain circumstances. A "qualifying" corporation for purposes of the refundable ITC is a CCPC which, together with any corporations associated with it, has a taxable income not exceeding the prior year business limit of the corporation and its associated corporations after the application of the grind for capital tax. A qualifying CCPC throughout the year with $500,000 or less of taxable income[6] in the previous taxation year may receive a refundable ITC equal to 35 per cent of its qualifying SR&ED expenditures for ITC purposes. Although income and business limits are determined for the preceding year as discussed above, association is determined for the current year.

The 35 per cent rate and refund are calculated on the first $3 million of eligible expenditures ("expenditure limit"). However, this expenditure limit is reduced by $10 for every $1 of taxable income between $500,000 and $800,000 in the preceding taxation year.[7] It is also reduced as taxable capital exceeds $10 million and is eliminated when taxable capital reaches $50 million.[8]

ITCs earned on expenditures exceeding the limit are calculated at a rate of 20 per cent and may, under certain conditions, be partially refundable to qualifying corporations. Any non-refundable portion of the ITCs can be carried back three years and forward 20 years and applied against taxes payable.

For claimants other than qualifying CCPCs, ITCs are earned at a rate of 20 per cent on both current and capital SR&ED expenditures and are not refundable. The ITCs can be applied to reduce taxes payable in the current year or carried back or forward on the same basis as noted above.

---

6 The taxable income threshold includes the taxable income of all associated corporations: $400,000 for 2008 and earlier taxation years. The $500,000 essentially tracks the corporation's business limit for small business deduction purposes.

7 The taxable income for this purpose includes the taxable income of all Canadian associated corporations: $700,000 for 2008 taxation year.

8 The taxable capital for this purpose includes the taxable capital of all Canadian associated corporations. Taxable capital is essentially the liability side of a company's balance sheet including all loans, retained earnings and share capital.

Refund Rates

There are two refund rates available to a qualifying corporation with respect to its qualified expenditures. First, a qualifying corporation may earn a 100 per cent cash refund on its share of any ITC earned at the 35 per cent rate up to $3 million of current SR&ED expenditures. Second, the capital SR&ED expenditures eligible for the 35 per cent credit rate are eligible for only the 40 per cent refund and not the 100 per cent refund. This 40 per cent refund rate is also available to a qualifying corporation to the extent of any SR&ED expenditures in excess of its expenditure limit.

Offsetting Refund Against Other Taxes

Currently, a valid refundable tax credit claim is deemed to have been paid on account of tax at the time a final balance of instalments of tax is due two or three months after year-end. The purpose of this change is to allow the deemed payment of tax to offset interest on taxes which may be owing under other parts of the *Income Tax Act*.

The following table summarizes recent changes to certain federal thresholds for the purpose of calculating refundable ITCs.

	Taxation years ending after January 1, 2009	Taxation years ending after February 25, 2008	Taxation years ending before February 25, 2008	Straddle year
Maximum expenditure limit	$3 million	$3 million	$2 million	Prorate $1 million increase based on number of days in tax year after February 25, 2008
Prior year taxable income limit	$800,000	$700,000	$600,000	Prorate $100,000 increase based on number of days in tax year after February 25, 2008
Taxable income phase-out range	$500,000 to $800,000	$400,000 to $700,000	$400,000 to http://en.wikipedia.org/wiki/Ted_Levine$600,000	The 2009 change applies where the previous taxation year ends after 2008
Prior year taxable capital limit	$50 million	$50 million	$15 million	Prorate $35 million increase based on number of days in tax year after February 25, 2008
Taxable capital phase-out range	$10 - $50 million	$10 - $50 million	$10 - $15 million	

Anti-Avoidance Provisions

Anti-avoidance rules are intended to apply where two or more corporations are not otherwise associated but one of the main reasons for their separate existences may reasonably be considered to be to duplicate the small business deduction, or to increase their refundable investment tax credits. In such a case, where it is reasonable to conclude that the separate existence of the corporations was mainly tax motivated, the corporations will be treated as associated with each other. Accordingly, when planning for the separate existence of corporations it is necessary to have distinct business purposes for their existence.

Qualifying Activities

The federal *Income Tax Act* ("*ITA*")[9] considers SR&ED activities for income tax purposes to be a systematic investigation or search that is carried out in a field of science or technology by means of experiment or analysis and that falls into one of the following categories:

Basic research - work undertaken to advance scientific or technological knowledge without a practical application in view;

Applied research - work undertaken to advance scientific or technological knowledge with a practical application in view;

Experimental development - work undertaken to achieve a technological advancement in order to create, or improve even slightly, materials, products, or processes (many SR&ED claims involve experimental development); and

Support work - work that directly supports and is commensurate with the needs of basic or applied research, or experimental development. Such work includes the following:

- engineering;
- design;
- operations research;
- mathematical analysis;
- computer programming;
- data collection;
- testing; and
- psychological research.

Even if a project and its activities fall within one of the above-mentioned categories, the project and related activities will qualify for the SR&ED tax incentives only if all of the following three criteria are met.

Scientific or technological advancement - The project advances the taxpayer's understanding of scientific or technological relations and increases

---

[9] R.S.C. 1985, c. 1 (5th Supp.) as amended (herein referred to as "the Act").

its technology base or level. The following diagram illustrates the concept of advancement: developing the know-how to overcome a technological uncertainty or obstacle in order to achieve the technological objective.

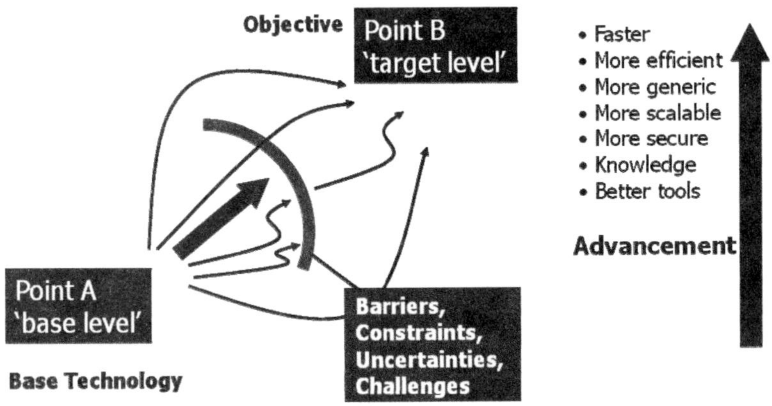

Scientific or technological obstacle/uncertainty - The possibility of attaining a given objective or result, and/or how to attain it, are unknown based on current or generally available scientific or technological knowledge.

Scientific and technical content - There is evidence that a systematic investigation through experiment or analysis was carried out by qualified personnel having relevant experience in science, technology, or engineering. In this regard, the eligible work may be performed either by the taxpayer directly, or on its behalf by another party.

Generally, only SR&ED activities carried out in Canada will qualify although recent amendments now allow up to 10 per cent of the total of SR&ED salaries or wages claimed for SR&ED performed in Canada. The work done outside of Canada must be performed directly by employees of the taxpayer and who are resident of Canada at the time the expenditure is incurred. The work must also form part of the SR&ED carried on by the taxpayer in Canada. The amount of eligible expenditures for work done outside of Canada is limited to 10 per cent of the total of SR&ED salaries or wages claimed for SR&ED performed in Canada.

It is important to note that the Act excludes certain activities from the SR&ED program:

- market research or sales promotion;
- quality control or routine testing of materials, devices, products, or processes;

- research in the social sciences or the humanities;
- prospecting, exploring, or drilling for or producing minerals, petroleum, or natural gas;
- commercial production of a new or improved material, device, or product, or the commercial use of a new or improved process;
- style changes; and
- routine data collection.

The CRA has published extensive guidance in the form of Information Circulars, Sector Specific Guidance and Application Policy & Guides to assist taxpayers in understanding the meaning of SR&ED within their context.[10]

Qualifying Expenditures

Generally, qualifying expenditures deductible for SR&ED purposes conducted in Canada will include:

- salaries and wages of employees performing the SR&ED work;[11]
- arm's length contract payments;
- third party payments (universities, approved organizations, *etc.*);
- materials (consumed or transformed);
- equipment rentals;
- equipment purchases;[12]
- related overheads (see below)

Interpretation Bulletin IT-151-R5 provides an excellent overview of all the rules on qualifying expenditures.[13]

Salaries or Wages of Employees

"Salaries or wages" is defined by the Act to mean income from an office or employment including vacation pay, statutory holiday pay, sick leave, and

---

[10] This material is available on the government of Canada's website at http://www.cra-arc.gc.ca/txcrdt/sred-rsde/menu-eng.html.

[11] For ITC purposes there are restrictions on salaries paid to shareholders working in the company who own more than 10% of the shares of the company.

[12] For SR&ED purposes, equipment and other capital asset purchases will qualify to the extent that it was intended that the equipment would be used during all or substantially all (greater than 90%) of its operation time throughout its expected useful life for SR&ED in Canada, or that all or substantially all (greater than 90%) of its value would be consumed in SR&ED in Canada.

[13] Above note 10.

taxable benefits. Salaries or wages does not include the employer's share of Canada Pension Plan or Quebec Pension Plan payments, employment insurance or worker's compensation contributions, nor payments to an approved employee pension plan and employee medical, dental, or optical insurance plans. Salaries or wages does not include expenditures for extended vacation or sick leave. CRA considers extended leave to be longer than the normal annual vacation or sick leave provided to an employee. These expenditures not included in salaries or wages may be deductible as overhead expenditures if the traditional method of computing overheads is elected (see below where traditional versus proxy is discussed in further detail).

Arm's Length Contract Payments

In the Canadian system, the basic premise is that funding for SR&ED received from outside of Canada will not reduce a taxpayer's qualifying SR&ED expenditures for ITC purposes. The funding related to current SR&ED expenditures will be included in the calculation of taxable income unless it is in the form of a loan. However, if one Canadian taxpayer funds another Canadian taxpayer the premise is that only one taxpayer will be entitled to the assistance.[14]

There is a complex series of rules dealing with situations where one company dealing at non-arm's length with another company in the group either performs SR&ED on behalf of the second company or provides services or goods to it which are used in its SR&ED activities. The purpose of these rules is to ensure that no inter-company profits are included in the calculation of a company's qualifying SR&ED expenditures.

Third Party Payments

Payments to an approved association, university, college, research institute, or similar organization may be eligible SR&ED expenditures provided the payments are made for SR&ED carried on in Canada which relates to the taxpayer's business, and where the taxpayer is entitled to exploit the results of the SR&ED. An "approved" entity means it has obtained approval from the CRA. All Canadian universities and their affiliated colleges are considered to be approved. Typically, the person making a third party payment

---

14 The rules which determine whether the payor or the recipient of the funding are entitled to the credits are known as the contract payment rules. These rules are highly complex and are dealt with in CRA's Application Paper 94-04.

does not control the SR&ED work being performed or own exclusive rights to the SR&ED.[15]

The following table emphasizes the distinguishing characteristics of contracts and third-party payments.

SR&ED contract or third-party payment?		
Characteristic	**SR&ED Contract**	**Third-party payment**
Control of SR&ED	Payer	Performer
Rights	Exclusive	Non-exclusive (generally published)
Number of funders	Usually limited to one payer	Multiple funders
Type of SR&ED	Commercially focused	Often basic or applied research

From *Guide to Form T661, CRA T4088(E) Rev. 08*

Materials

The cost of materials consumed or transformed in the course of carrying on SR&ED may be deducted as an SR&ED expenditure. Materials consumed refers to materials destroyed or rendered valueless in the SR&ED process. Materials transformed refers to materials that have been incorporated into other materials or products. CRA's Application Policy 2000-01 provides further discussion and examples of materials consumed. Note that where expenditures for materials transformed claimed for ITC purposes are later sold as part of the product that they are incorporated into, the law has provisions to essentially recapture the ITCs previously earned.

Leases

Where equipment is leased rather than purchased, the full amount of the lease cost may be claimed if the equipment is used all or substantially all for SR&ED based on total operating time. If claiming under the proxy method, eligible equipment does not include general purpose office equipment and furniture. Also, under the proxy method (as discussed below), one half of the lease costs of equipment that is used less than 90 per cent and more than 50 per cent of the time for SR&ED may be claimed. Under the traditional method, the lease costs for equipment used less than 90 per cent may be claimed as overhead expenditures.

---

15 Application Policy 96-04.

Overhead and Proxy Amount

Companies may claim overheads associated with their qualifying SR&ED activities provided they are directly related and attributable to the R&D. However, in an environment where SR&ED activities and routine production are carried on, it may be difficult to determine eligible overhead for SR&ED purposes. In order to facilitate this exercise, the Act provides that taxpayers may elect an alternative method of calculating the overhead called the "proxy method".

This alternative method basically allows taxpayers to compute a notional overhead based on 65 per cent of salaries and wages of employees directly engaged in SR&ED, instead of the actual overhead incurred,[16] for purposes of calculating the SR&ED investment tax credits.

As noted earlier in this chapter, it is often the case that operating costs are reduced before SR&ED budgets are cut. In some cases, this may impact the best choice of overhead claiming methodology. Accordingly, this should be revisited in situations where the company's business model has been significantly impacted by the economic situation.

Supporting the Claim

In order to access the benefits of the SR&ED program, taxpayers must file a complete Form T661 and Schedule 31 along with all of the attachments. *These forms must be filed no later than 18 months following the end of the taxation year in which the SR&ED expenditures were incurred or all rights to the benefits are lost.*

In addition to these forms, taxpayers must include with Form T661 a technical description of the SR&ED projects undertaken in order to demonstrate that the SR&ED program's criteria are respected. This description will cover the project's scientific or technological objectives, the scientific or technological knowledge base of the taxpayer at the beginning of the project, and the scientific or technological advancements sought. It will also describe the activities undertaken in the year and list the information supporting the claim.

A typical management response to volatile times is to narrow the scope of development projects in R&D departments. These projects may be more "incremental" in nature and less comprehensive in the scope of the devel-

---

16 The proxy overhead is not an allowable expenditure for deduction purposes.

opment initiatives. It is important to note that the *ITA* definition of SR&ED, goes out of its way to make clear that "*incremental*" improvements to products and processes qualify so long as the eligibility criteria are met. In the current environment it is all the more important to ensure that projects are not discounted for eligibility simply because of their incremental nature.

Recent Changes to Form T661

A new Form T661 was released in the fall of 2008 by the CRA. It applies to all fiscal years ending on or after January 1, 2009. The new Form T661 implementation follows the CRA's Small & Medium Size Enterprises ("SME") related consultations and strategies involving, amongst others, the simplification of SR&ED filing requirements for SMEs. The June 2008 Update on the SR&ED Small Business Action Plan is available on the CRA's website and describes this strategy more fully.

The declared objective is to simplify the filing requirements for all SR&ED claimants. This objective is expected to be achieved through the following:

- access to E-filing for technical descriptions;
- limited number of words prescribed by Form T661;
- changes to the format and wording of Form T661 simplifying the instructional content.

E-filing is Simpler but all Projects Must be Filed

Taxpayers who file their tax returns electronically currently need to file technical descriptions separately, which renders the filing process somewhat inefficient. New Form T661 should eventually provide for electronic formatting of the required technical descriptions such that no separate manual submission is required.

This is clearly an advantage for those taxpayers who do file electronically. On the other hand, taxpayers will need to file Form T661 for all projects as compared to the current requirement to only file the top 20 project descriptions. This will require some adjustment since companies may not capture technical and financial information in the required format.

Limited Number of Words

Whereas technical descriptions are now typically written in free-form style, the new prescribed form will require that each section have a limited number of words. The prescribed form will not allow more than 350 words for each of the technological advancement and technological uncertainty sections, whereas the description of work section will be limited to 700 words. Furthermore, it appears that no distinction will be made for size of projects. It will be interesting to see how reducing the number of words will impact clarity, particularly in cases of large, complex projects.

New Format and Instructions

Over the history of this program, the industry, the CRA and tax courts have developed an understanding of terms such as "advancement", "uncertainty", and "objective". A number of new terms are being introduced which will require further clarification. For example, "obstacle" is used, most likely instead of "uncertainty". The form will be accompanied by a new guide, which will help in this process.

Furthermore, a checklist of prescribed information will be enclosed to ensure the company understands the CRA requirements such as for documentation. For example, it appears that the company will need to indicate whether a development plan existed in anticipation of the SR&ED project claimed.

Considering that this is a prescribed Form, taxpayers will want to ensure their claim is complete to avoid being rejected. If this rejection occurs beyond the 18-month filing period, it could jeopardize the claim altogether.

Provincial Incentives

Summary of Provincial/Territorial R&D Tax Incentives

Province	Rate	Refundable
British Columbia	10%	Yes
Alberta	10%	Yes
Saskatchewan	15%	Yes
Manitoba	20%	Yes
Ontario Innovation Tax Credit (OITC)	10%	Yes
Ontario Business-Research Institute Tax Credit (OBRITC)	20%	Yes
Ontario Research and Development Tax Credit (ORDTC)	4.5%	No
Quebec R&D Wage Tax Credit	Canadian-controlled corporations – 37.5% Others – 17.5%	Yes
Quebec Credit for contract payments to/for R&D entities and projects	35%	Yes
New Brunswick	15%	Yes
Nova Scotia	15%	Yes
Newfoundland	15%	Yes
Yukon	15%	Yes

All provincial government programs utilize the federal government's definition of what qualifies as SR&ED and, in most cases, mirror the federal government's expenditure rules with some exception. The major differences are with the Quebec system, and are discussed below.

Newfoundland and Labrador

Generally, a corporation carrying out SR&ED activities in Newfoundland and Labrador is eligible for a 15 per cent refundable tax credit on eligible expenditures. Eligible expenditures are those made by a corporation with a permanent establishment in Newfoundland and Labrador for SR&ED carried out in that province.

Nova Scotia

A corporation having a permanent establishment in Nova Scotia and making eligible expenditures in respect of SR&ED carried out in that province may receive a tax credit on eligible expenditures.

For eligible expenditures made in a taxation year, a corporation may receive a tax credit equal to 15 per cent of those expenditures. Any amount in excess of Nova Scotia income tax payable is refunded to the corporation.

New Brunswick

A corporation having a permanent establishment in New Brunswick and making eligible expenditures in respect of SR&ED carried out in that province may receive a tax credit on eligible expenditures.

For eligible expenditures incurred after January 1, 2003, the credit is calculated at a rate of 15 per cent and is fully refundable.

Quebec

Tax Credit for SR&ED Salaries and Wages

A corporation carrying on business in Canada and performing SR&ED activities in Quebec, or having such activities performed on its behalf in Quebec, may claim a refundable tax credit on salaries and wages paid in Quebec (see below for the meaning of "salaries and wages" for this purpose).

For a CCPC corporation with assets below $25 million for its preceding taxation year, the tax credit rate is 37.5 per cent[17] on the first $3 million[18] of eligible salaries and wages. If, however, the corporation's assets exceed $25 million, the tax credit rate drops progressively and reaches 17.5 per cent when assets reach $50 million. It should be noted that for this purpose, assets of associated corporations on a worldwide basis must be included.

The tax credit rate is also 17.5 per cent on eligible salaries and wages in excess of the annual $3 million limit and for corporations controlled by non-residents of Canada.

The salaries and wages giving rise to the tax credit are generally those paid to the corporation's Quebec employees and, where the corporation has contracted out the SR&ED to an arm's length subcontractor, 50 per cent of the amount paid to the subcontractor that can reasonably be attributed to the work carried out by the subcontractor's employees in Quebec.

---

17 As per the 2005-2006 Quebec Budget tabled April 21, 2005.

18 $2 million for fiscal periods ending before March 13, 2008.

Tax Credit for SR&ED Under a University Research Contract

A corporation carrying on business in Canada and entering into a research contract with an eligible Quebec university may claim a refundable tax credit equal to 35 per cent of 80 per cent of the payment made to the university for SR&ED.

To be entitled to this tax credit, the corporation must first obtain a favorable ruling from the Quebec Ministry of Revenue.

Ontario

Ontario Innovation Tax Credit

Ontario offers a 10 per cent refundable tax credit, the Ontario innovation tax credit ("OITC"), to corporations having a permanent establishment in Ontario, which is calculated on the first $3 million[19] of expenditures related to SR&ED activities carried out in the province. The OITC applies to qualifying current expenditures and 40 per cent of qualifying capital expenditures.

A corporation is eligible to claim the full OITC where it has up to $25 million of taxable paid-up capital. The annual expenditure limit of $3 million of qualifying expenditures is phased out as the corporation's taxable paid-up capital for its preceding taxation year exceeds $25 million and is eliminated where it reaches $50 million. The expenditure limit is also phased out where the corporation's taxable income for its preceding taxation year is over $300,000 but does not exceed $500,000.[20]

Ontario Business Research Institute Tax Credit

An Ontario corporation is entitled to claim the 20 per cent refundable Ontario business research institute tax credit ("OBRI"), in addition to any OITC, for SR&ED expenditures incurred in Ontario as part of an eligible business research institute contract. This tax credit is limited to $20 million in expenditures per year per associated group of corporations.

---

19 $3 million per the 2009 Ontario Budget to be implemented as per the timing of the parallel federal provisions.

20 In establishing a corporation's eligibility to the OITC, it is necessary to consider the taxable capital of all associated corporations on a worldwide basis.

Manitoba

A corporation having a permanent establishment in Manitoba is entitled to an SR&ED tax credit equal to 20 per cent of eligible expenditures made by it in respect of SR&ED carried out in the province.[21]

The SR&ED tax credit is non-refundable, but it may be carried over to any of the three preceding or ten subsequent taxation years to reduce Manitoba income taxes payable. The March 2009 Manitoba budget announced that the credit will become refundable for expenditures incurred after 2009.

Saskatchewan

The province of Saskatchewan provides for a 15 per cent non-refundable income tax credit for qualifying SR&ED expenditures incurred in Saskatchewan, by a corporation having a permanent establishment in that province. Unused tax credits can be carried back up to three years and carried forward up to 10 years and applied against Saskatchewan income taxes payable. Following the national trend toward refundability, the March 18, 2009 Saskatchewan budget announced that expenditures after that date will result in a refundable credit.

British Columbia

A corporation with a permanent establishment in British Columbia and carrying out SR&ED activities in British Columbia is entitled to tax credits, refundable or non-refundable, on eligible SR&ED expenditures incurred in that province.

In order to qualify for the credit, a qualified expenditure must be made in respect of SR&ED carried out in British Columbia before September 1, 2009 by a corporation at a time when the corporation has a permanent establishment in British Columbia.

The tax credit is refundable for CCPCs. The amount of the refundable credit for a taxation year is 10 per cent of the lesser of the corporation's SR&ED qualified expenditures for the taxation year and its expenditure limit, as determined for federal purposes.

The tax credit is non-refundable for other qualifying corporations, and CCPCs whose SR&ED qualifying expenditures exceed their expenditure

---

21 This rate is in effect since March 9, 2005. Prior to that date, the rate was 15%.

limit. The non-refundable tax credit is equal to 10 per cent of the corporation's SR&ED qualified expenditures for the year. Non-refundable tax credits may be carried back three years or carried forward 10 years to reduce British Columbia income taxes payable.

Corporate Restructuring

Restructuring initiatives during volatile times are often accompanied by an increase in transactions, either strategic or forced, which may impact the treatment of ITCs or the ability of the companies to maintain the value of the ITCs as a future tax asset. The following are some issues to consider.

Carryover of ITCs

Reorganization of Corporations through Amalgamation and Wind-up

The Act provides that, for the computation of ITC of a newly amalgamated corporation, the new entity is deemed to be the same corporation as, and a continuation of, any predecessor corporation. This provision allows the amalgamated corporation to claim any unused ITCs of the predecessor corporation. It does not follow, however, that the ITC of an amalgamated company can be carried back to a predecessor unless the amalgamation is a vertical amalgamation (a short-form amalgamation of the parent and its wholly-owned subsidiary).

For a wind-up of a 90 per cent controlled subsidiary, the Act provides for the flow-through of ITCs from a subsidiary corporation to its parent corporation.

Acquisition of Control

The unused ITC earned prior to the acquisition of control may be carried forward, subject to certain restrictions. These restrictions are similar to those for loss carryforwards. In general, the restrictions limit the application of the unused ITC prior to the acquisition of control to the income earned from a particular business carried on prior to the acquisition of control.

Assignment of Investment Tax Credits to Third Parties

Corporations sometimes assign expected investment tax credit refunds to creditors. This is especially true for the 100 per cent refund of SR&ED tax credits, which are assigned to lenders for bridge financing. A Supreme Court of Canada case decided in 1994, *Marzetti v. Marzetti*,[22] involving bankruptcy issues highlighted the fact that under the *Financial Administration Act*,[23] income tax refunds are not legally assignable unless specifically allowed by statute (such as the *Tax Rebate Discounting Act*[24]). The Federal Budget of March 6, 1996 proposed that the assignment of that part of an income tax refund attributable to an investment tax credit would become assignable after March 5, 1996, subject to the limitations that the assignment is not binding against the government, creates no liability to the assignee as against the government, and leaves the CRA the right to set off the refund against any debts of the taxpayer under the *ITA*. The absence of liability of the government seems to mean that while it would undertake to deliver the refund to the assignee, it would not be liable if misdelivered or if the refund differed from the amount assigned. Consequences of the right of set-off are self-evident.

The Budget addressed this issue in the context of SR&ED and film production credits only, but the legislation provides that a taxpayer may assign any amount payable to it under the *ITA*, subject to the conditions above. Accordingly, the right of assignment would apply to any investment tax credit component of a refund, or indeed to any amount refundable, however created.

Those provinces for which the federal government collects corporate tax would automatically adopt the federal position with respect to provincial tax refunds, since their statutes typically adopt the federal section containing this rule.

Quebec added an identical rule for assignments made after March 9, 1999. Ontario and Alberta have no such parallel rule.

International Environment

Currently, approximately 40 countries offer various tax incentives to R&D performers. Over the past few years, a number of countries such as Ireland and the United Kingdom have introduced tax incentives for R&D and a number of other countries such as Austria and Australia have recently enhanced their systems.

---

22 [1994] 2 S.C.R. 765.

23 R.S.C. 1985, c. F-11, s. 67.

24 R.S.C. 1985, c. T-3.

One interesting feature of these various tax incentives regimes is that the definition of what activities qualify as R&D are remarkable similar. Many countries use the definition contained in the Frascati[25] Manual as a basis for their legislation. Even regimes such as the United States that do not use the definition contained in the Frascati Manual as a basis for their criteria have similar regimes. However, differences in the regimes arise in a number of areas including: the rates of the incentives, types of expenditures that qualify, refundability of the incentives, territorial restrictions, calculation of the credit (volume or incrementally based), *etc.*

During volatile times, all levels of government are examining their R&D models and are increasingly converting non-refundable credits into refundable credits as a stimulus measure during times when many companies are not paying tax. Notably, France and Ireland have recently enhanced the refundable nature of their credits.[26]

International Comparisons

In order to rank the various incentives, a number of factors must be considered:

1. Is the system volume based or incremental? In other words are the incentives available on every dollar of R&D spending or just on R&D spending in excess of a base amount. Incrementally-based incentives such as the United States credit are less attractive.
2. What is the rate of the credit on an after-tax basis? This will be impacted by the size of the additional deduction or tax credit and, where additional deductions are offered, the effective tax rate of the country.
3. Is all or a portion of the credit refundable? For example, in France, unused credits have recently been made fully refundable from the government.
4. What types of activities qualify? Is it just the "R" portion of research and development or is it both R&D? The original definition of R&D in the United Kingdom was heavily biased towards just research by using words such as novelty and innovation. The current definition recognizes that both R&D does qualify.

---

25 Organization for Economic Development and Co-operation and Development (2002), ch. 2, pp. 29-45.

26 Deloitte & Touche, Recent changes in France and Ireland, R&D Tax Update, March 2009 (09-1).

5. What types of expenditures qualify? For example, in the United Kingdom, the base only includes salaries, materials consumed and transformed, and limited subcontract expenditures. Although, the recent budget expanded the range of costs to include utility costs and software tools. However, in Canada, not only salaries and materials are included but also 100 per cent of R&D subcontractor costs, R&D capital equipment and overheads.
6. How certain is one of obtaining the credits? There is no point in investing time and effort in preparing claims for the credit only to lose them in the audit process or having to spend an unreasonable amount of time and effort in defending the claim. In order for the incentives to be considered in the business planning model, companies must have confidence in the stability of the rules as well as in the efficiency of the audit process.
7. Are there opportunities to claim incentives in more than one jurisdiction on the same project?

Canada's regime for CCPCs is still one of the best in the world. However, for non-CCPCs and public corporations other countries are catching up. Refundable regimes in other countries include Austria, Belgium, France, New Zealand, United Kingdom and, most recently, Australia. In volatile times, multinational companies may increasingly plan for R&D centers to gravitate towards countries having refundable regimes.

Conclusion

It is important to consider the impact of decreases in taxable income on the rates, provincial credit availability, and the claiming structure for more focused development initiatives. Planning during these volatile times may allow for the ability to access immediate cash refunds which may not otherwise be available. It is also important to consider the impact that certain transactions may have on the refundable status of the company, as well as the impact a transaction may have on the future value of the ITCs.

Appendix 1 – Case Study: R&D Co.

Many companies may overlook opportunities for immediate cash refunds in situations where they were not previously eligible for high rate treatment, and refundable status during better times. This case study will examine how changes in taxable income from year to year may dramatically alter the rate and refundable status of a company during an economic downturn.

R&D Co. operates a manufacturing plant and produces chemical products for the pulp and paper industry. Consistent with the volatile times in the pulp and paper industry, the plant was highly profitable until the past year when the bottom fell out of forest products exports due to the housing collapse recession south of the border. This volatility resulted in yearly taxable income as follows:

2008 Taxable Income	$ 1,000,000
2009 Non-Capital Loss	$ (500,000)

In order to illustrate the tax advantages related to SRED, and to illustrate the differences in refundable status during volatile times, we will present a scenario covering a two-year period of 2009 and 2010. In addition, the R&D will take place partially in the province of Quebec, and partially in the province of Ontario to demonstrate the significant impact of provincial credits.

In the 2009 year, R&D Co. is a CCPC whose taxable income for the preceding year exceeds $700,000. Recall that qualifying corporations must have taxable income less than the business limit of $400,000. Accordingly, in 2009 the corporation is subject to the low federal rate, as well as the low rate on Quebec labor, and is not eligible for the OITC in Ontario. This outcome will be substantially different in 2010 despite identical qualifying expenditures due the loss being incurred for 2009.

R&D Initiatives

To remain competitive in the downturn, R&D Co. undertook to improve its process efficiency by developing a continuous manufacturing process instead of manufacturing its products in batch mode. The process sought is an innovative concept that would allow more process flexibility and improved product quality and would be more cost effective.

As for ingredients to be used, their amounts are known and well-controlled for the manufacturing process in batch mode. With a fully automated and continuous manufacturing process, however, it is uncertain if the same ingredients can be used and in what quantities thy can be used. The engineering team of R&D Co., assisted by operation personnel, made efforts to implement the continuous process and was required to run experiments and trials. A subcontractor was also hired for some engineering tasks. This subcontractor is located and conducted the work in the province of Quebec.

Equipment was acquired for commercial use but a temporary installation had to be put in place to trial purposes. This installation was removed and scrapped at the end of the trials. Trials also involved the use of chemical agents, which were destroyed through the trial process. Minutes of meetings were kept in a logbook, as well as timesheets and invoices for the equipment, material, and subcontractor. Trial reports were drafted every time a trial was performed.

The allocation of employees to the SR&ED project for 2009. For planning purposes, the project and expenditures are expected to be similar for 2010. The annual expenditures to be incurred are as follows:

Number of engineers spending *all or substantially all* of their time on eligible SR&ED activities:	5
Average annual salary per engineer:	$ 80,000
Operating employees involved in the project (*all or substantially all of the time*):	2
Average annual salary of operating employees:	$ 50,000
Amount paid to subcontractor for detailed engineering:	$ 25,000
Cost of equipment used for SR&ED only:	$100,000
Cost of chemical agents destroyed during the trials:	$ 50,000
Overhead costs related to SR&ED:	$400,000

The traditional method has been elected for federal ITC purposes.

2009

Case Study R&D Co. – (CCPC non-qualifying corporation)

	2009 **Federal**	**Quebec**	**Ontario**
SR&ED Tax Credits			
Salaries (eligible employees)	$ 500,000	$ 250,000	$ 250,000
Subcontractors	25,000	25,000	
Materials consumed	50,000	-	50,000
Capital expenditures (used all or substantially all in SR&ED)	100,000	-	100,000
Overheads (traditional method)	400,000	-	400,000
OITC			-
		-	-
ORDTC	(36,000)	-	
Quebec R&D credit	(45,938)		
Eligible expenditures tor tax credit purposes[27]	$ 993,062	$ 262,500	$ 800,000
Federal SR&ED credit (20% on eligible expenditures)	198,612		
Provincial SR&ED credits (Quebec - 17.5% on eligible expenditures)		45,938	
(OITC – 10.0% on eligible expenditures)			-
(ORDTC – 4.5% on eligible Expenditures)			36,000
Summary			
Tax credits for the current year	$ 198,612	$ 45,938	$ 36,000
Total savings	$ 198,612	$ 45,938	$ 36,000
Combined savings	$280,550		
Refundable Credits		$ 45,938	
Carried back to prior 3 years taxes payable.	$ 198,612		$ 36,000
Combined savings	$280,550		

27 For Quebec tax credit purposes, in addition to the eligible salaries, only 50 per cent of the amount paid to a non-related subcontractor is eligible.

2010

Case Study R&D Co. – (CCPC qualifying corporation)

	2010 Federal	 Quebec	 Ontario
SR&ED Tax Credits			
Salaries (eligible employees)	$ 500,000	$ 250,000	$ 250,000
Subcontractors	25,000	25,000	
Materials consumed	50,000	-	50,000
Capital expenditures (used all or substantially all in SR&ED)	100,000	-	100,000
Overheads (traditional method)	400,000	-	400,000
OITC	(74,000)		-
ORDTC	(32,670)	-	-
Quebec R&D credit	(98,438)	-	
Eligible expenditures tor tax credit purposes[28]	$ 869,892	$ 262,500	$ 800,000
Federal SR&ED credit (35% on eligible expenditures)	304,462		
Provincial SR&ED credits (Quebec – 37.5% on eligible expenditures)		98,438	
(OITC – 10.0% on eligible expenditures)			74,000
(ORDTC – 4.5% on eligible Expenditures)			32,670
Summary			
Tax credits for the current year	$ 304,462	$ 98,438	$ 106,670
Total savings	$ 304,462	$ 98,438	$ 106,670
Combined savings	$509,570		
Refundable Credits	$ 284,302	$ 98,438	$ 74,000
Carried back or carry forward to reduce taxes payable.			$ 32,670
Combined savings	$ 509,570		

28 For Quebec tax credit purposes, in addition to the eligible salaries, only 50% of the amount paid to a non-related subcontractor is eligible.

Summary of Case Study

In the 2009 year, R&D Co. is unable to generate refundable credits at the high rate despite having incurred a loss in the year. Accordingly, the corporation is subject to the low federal ITC rate of 20 per cent, as well as the 17.5 per cent rate on Quebec labor. Further, the company is not eligible for the OITC in Ontario. In cases where there was insufficient taxable income in the prior three years to apply the credits, the credits would go unutilized at a time they are required most. Although the non-refundable credits may be carried forward for up to 20 years, this is of little benefit for a company facing more immediate financial challenges.

As is evident in the table above, the outcome is significantly different in 2010 despite identical qualifying expenditures. The corporation was able to obtain the high rates both federally and in Quebec as well as to qualify for the OITC. The impact of this is an increase in the available credits for a total savings of $513,294.

GST in Hard Times: What To Do

Dalton J. Albrecht

Introduction

The Goods and Services Tax ("GST") enacted in Part IX of the *Excise Tax Act*[1] (the "Act") is applied on a transaction by transaction basis. Every transaction or event must be analyzed for GST purposes, not just the net result as in income tax. Accordingly, all parties are impacted, positively or negatively, by the GST issues arising on an insolvency or in situations where good debt has gone bad. Debtors and creditors, as well as trustees/receivers, must be aware of the GST implications of their actions (or inactions). This will become even more important as the Harmonized Sales Tax ("HST") comes into force in Ontario and British Columbia in July, 2010 (and potentially across the country in the next few years) as the combined federal-provincial HST rate will be as much as 15 per cent.

This chapter outlines the relevant provisions in the Act that arise in the context of good businesses gone bad. It is not intended to provide specific advice in particular circumstances, nor to serve as a substitute for the advice of experienced counsel.

Creditors

Seizure or Repossession of Property by a Creditor in a Receivership – Section 183

If a creditor plans on seizing or repossessing the property of a debtor, there are specific GST implications, with the exception of when leased property is seized or repossessed by a lessor (which is deemed not to be a "transaction" for GST purposes).

---

[1] R.S.C. 1985, c. E-15.

While s. 183 of the Act (all statutory references are to the *Excise Tax Act* unless otherwise noted) provides that where a creditor seizes or repossesses property there is no GST on the seizure, the creditor who seizes the property is deemed to have acquired the property for no consideration (subject to special rules for certain exempt real property where self-assessment rules may be triggered where the property has not been previously subjected to tax). In the case of real property, the debtor (who owned the property) may be able to claim an Input Tax Credit ("ITC") or rebate under paras. 183(1)(c) or (d) to recover embedded GST (GST paid by the debtor that was not recovered through an ITC).

When the creditor then *sells* the property in satisfaction of a debt, the sale is normally taxable under ss. 183(2) (as it is deemed to be made in the course of a commercial activity, other than when made by an Officer of the Court under a Court Order or judgment). The sale is deemed to have been made by the creditor (who is deemed to have acquired the property from the debtor for no consideration). The creditor is then responsible for collecting and remitting GST on the sale and is eligible to take ITCs for GST incurred in connection with the sale of the property, although not in connection with other activities such as the repossession (that is, there are ITCs for the delivery but not for the cost of the repo man or the tow truck to seize the property). There may also be an ITC available to the creditor on the sale of personal property under ss. 183(7) where there is embedded tax that the debtor would have been entitled to reclaim (that is, the debtor paid tax but did not take full ITCs) had there been a supply to the creditor by the debtor on an exempt basis.

If the creditor *uses* the property for its own use instead of selling it, a deemed supply occurs and the creditor is deemed to have paid tax calculated on the fair market value. The tax must be remitted by the creditor, although an ITC may be available depending on the use of the property. Subsection 183(4) governs this deemed "self supply" by use of real property and ss. (6) governs the "self supply" of personal property.

To round out these provisions, ss. 183(10) provides that a creditor exercising a right of sale of another person's property is deemed to have seized the property immediately before that supply and that supply will be deemed to have been made by the creditor and not by the person.

Finally, ss. 183(9) provides that in a situation where property is voluntarily transferred by a debtor to the creditor for the purpose of satisfying a debt (a quitclaim), it will be treated in a manner similar to a seizure or repossession of property by a creditor from a debtor.

Breach of Contract/Termination/Modifications Trigger Tax – Section 182

When economic times are bad, there are many occasions where there is a breach of contract or negotiated changes to agreements. It is important to realize that there are significant GST implications. If as a consequence of a breach, modification, or cancellation of an agreement, an amount is paid (that is, damages) or forfeited (a deposit) by the purchaser to the supplier, the amount of the payment or deposit is deemed to be GST included. For example, if an amount is paid by a purchaser to a vendor as damages for a breach of contract, the tax fraction (currently 5/105ths, but soon to be 13/113ths in Ontario) by the recipient creditor must be remitted (as there is a deemed taxable supply). The payer debtor may be able to claim ITCs depending on its prior use of the property or service. However, payments by a supplier to a recipient or by a lessor to a lessee are excluded from this section.

This section also applies if as a consequence of a breach, modification, or cancellation, a debt or other obligation of the supplier is reduced or extinguished.

Section 182 does not apply where the original agreement was for the making of an exempt or zero-rated supply. Many court ordered payments are also not within the scope of s. 182, and, unless there is a specific supply involved, there is no taxable transaction (for example, on court awarded damages for a tort). A detailed discussion of this concept is beyond the scope of this chapter but can be found as outlined in the CRA Policy Statement P-218R.

Creditor Interference with Remittance – Section 323.1

Secured creditors must be careful in interfering with a payment or remittance of GST because there could be consequences.

Proposed s. 323.1[2] will parallel the joint and several liability rules in the new ss. 227(5.2) to (5.4) of the *Income Tax Act*[3] ("*ITA*"). While this proposed addition is still on ice, it was intended to apply where the secured creditor exercises "influence" for the purpose of interfering with a payment or remittance of GST either by way of postponing it, subordinating it in favor of

2 Proposed but not enacted as part of S.C. 1996, c. 21. The Department of Finance's position is that these "proposed rules" are still pending. They seem to exist as a threat to large financial institutions, if they do not voluntarily comply with the clearly stated policy of the proposed rules, which could be enacted retroactively to the date first proposed.

3 R.S.C. 1985, c. 1 (5th Supp.).

another payment, or simply by causing the payment or remittance to not be made. The proposals are that the secured creditor would become jointly and severally liable with the debtor to pay or remit the amount in respect of which the creditor exercised influence and all other amounts payable because of the failure to make the payment or remittance when required. If applicable, there is a specific secured creditor subrogation right to recover from the debtor any amounts paid by the secured creditor on account of this liability (ss. 323.1(1)(e)).

Joint and several liability would not arise in certain circumstances such as where the exercise of this "influence" is pursuant to a court action such as a decree, order, or judgment (ss. 323.1(3)(c)). In addition, joint and several liability would not arise where the influence was exercised after the day the person became a bankrupt and the amounts relate solely to activities in which the person began to engage on or after the day the person became a bankrupt and that are unrelated to the bankruptcy (this follows from the "Insolvency Code" discussed below).

"Fighting the Taxman" – Creditors and Priorities

As a result of bankruptcy law reform, the Crown is now normally in the position of an unsecured creditor. There are, however, two important exceptions to this position that creditors must keep in mind:

1. s. 222, which deems the moneys collected by registrants on account of GST to be held in trust for the taxman (the Crown), although the effectiveness of this provision is muted in bankruptcy situations; and
2. third party demand or garnishment rules in ss. 317(3) of the Act that give the taxman a property interest in or a "super priority" over amounts owed by third parties (receivables) to tax debtors, which are intended to provide the Crown with a process to claim amounts owing to a tax debtor by a third party in priority to all secured creditors if the Crown acts in a timely manner (in effect, amounting to a seizure of the creditor's property rights in the receivables).

Further, while preferred Crown claims have been abolished such that all provable Crown claims will only rank as ordinary unsecured claims in a bankruptcy or proposal, the Crown will still be able to register a claim pursuant to federal or provincial legislation against the property of the bankrupt (for example, a memorial under s. 316 of the Act can still be registered). This does not, however, give the Crown any priority as it ranks as an unsecured creditor, although it is a simple way to establish the liability.

CRA Deemed Trust Takes Priority – Section 222

Subsections 222(1) and (1.1) provide for a deemed trust in favor of the Crown for any amounts collected on account of GST for all purposes, other than on a bankruptcy where it ceases to apply, despite any security interest (other than "prescribed security interests"). Thus, a lien arises by the operation of a law that has some of the attributes of a trust at common law, including the trust tracing mechanism, and the beneficiary (the Crown) has the right to enforce the trust by appropriate court proceedings. Subsection 222(1) provides that the amount deemed to be held in trust shall for all purposes be deemed to have been held separate and form no component of the debtor's property, whether or not the moneys were actually held separate and apart. This provision recognizes the practical reality that such funds are invariably commingled with the tax debtor's other funds and, therefore, eliminates the need for complying with the cumbersome equitable tracing rules (which provide that the amounts remain subject to the trust even if converted into other property, but only provided they can be directly traced into or identified with that other property and only apply to real trusts at law in any event).

The provision, therefore, has the effect of taking equivalent moneys out of the property of the debtor (or the estate in bankruptcy) and making those moneys the property of the Crown. Subsection 222(3) was added in 2000 to override certain court decisions (see for example, *Royal Bank v. Sparrow Electric Corp.*[4]) to make it clear that the deemed trust takes priority over security interests such as a general assignment of book debts and inventory (other than certain "prescribed security interests" apparently intended to cover fixed charges, such as mortgages, where there are pre-existing property rights not benefited by the failure to remit the tax).

Subsequently, the Alberta Court of Queen's Bench in *Re Gauntlet Energy Corp.*[5] concluded that ss. 222(3) took priority over the *Companies' Creditors Arrangement Act*[6] (the "*CCAA*"). In *Re Ottawa Senators Hockey Club Corp*,[7] the CRA asserted a statutory deemed trust over a portion of the hockey club's assets. The team was insolvent and was operating under the *CCAA*. Two of the secured creditors argued that the deemed trust in ss. 222(3) was of no application due to ss. 18.3(1) of the *CCAA*. The Trial Court, however, concluded that the *CCAA* trumps ss. 222(3). However, the Ontario Court of

---

4 [1997] S.C.R. 411, 97 D.T.C. 5089.

5 2003 ABQB 894.

6 R.S.C. 1985, c. C-36.

7 2005 G.T.C. 1327, 2005 D.T.C. 5233 (Ont. C.A.).

Appeal agreed with the *Gauntlet* decision and ruled that ss. 222(3) *in fact trumps* the *CCAA*.

Nevertheless, as the *Bankruptcy and Insolvency Act*[8] (the "*BIA*") amendments removed the traditional Crown preferences and priorities formerly provided to the Crown prior to the bankruptcy law reform, deemed trusts or, more accurately, statutory liens are not effective in a bankruptcy. Further, the preferred status of the Crown was abolished by these amendments and the Crown simply ranks as another unsecured creditor. Property will not be considered as being held in trust unless it would have been so regarded in the absence of such a statutory provision. Thus, only actual trusts arising under the law of equity will be recognized. Therefore, the Crown will have rights only as an unsecured creditor unless it obtains property rights under the enhanced garnishment or "super priority" provisions of ss. 317(3) prior to bankruptcy discussed below. This was confirmed very recently by the Supreme Court of Canada in *Re Alternative granite & marbre inc.*[9]

The abolition of statutory deemed trusts does not apply in respect of the deemed trusts for source deductions established pursuant to the *ITA*, *Canada Pension Plan*, *Quebec Pension Plan*, and employment insurance legislation or any provincial legislation imposing taxes similar to those imposed under the *ITA*. However, an exception is not provided for the GST deemed trust arising under s. 222 of the Act. Similarly, any provincial retail sales tax deemed trusts/liens are also abolished. Therefore, for all practical purposes, the deemed trust under s. 222 (and all provincial deemed trusts) are relevant only in insolvency situations outside of bankruptcy.

Thus, subject to the above exceptions, the deemed trust is not effective for all amounts collected before the time of bankruptcy. However, ss. 222(1), when read in conjunction with ss. 222(1.1), purports to resurrect the deemed trust for any amounts collected post-bankruptcy by a person. The "bankruptcy" of the tax debtor will be included as one of the events during which the moneys collected as tax are deemed to have been kept separate and apart. Thus, the intention is quite clear that the "new" deemed trust applies only to amounts collected during the course of the bankruptcy.

One question is whether this re-instatement of the deemed trust is effective in light of the wording of ss. 67(2) of the *BIA*, which states that all statutory deemed trusts are of no effect upon bankruptcy. The only trusts that survive bankruptcy are those that meet the test for a trust under the law of equity (namely, where there is certainty of intention, of subject matter and of the

---

8 R.S.C. 1985, c. B-3.

9 2009 SCC 49.

objects of the trust), and those outlined in the *BIA*, (the above-noted exceptions for some deductions, *etc.*). It is noted, however, that para. 265(1)(d) of the Act makes the trustee personally responsible for post-bankruptcy GST collections, so the issue appears to be moot.

The deemed trust does not apply to any ITCs or other amounts deducted from net tax on a debtor's GST return and applies only to property equal in or up to the value of the amount deemed to be held in trust.

GST Super Priority-Garnishments – Subsection 317(3)

The provisions found in s. 317 of the GST legislation enable the Crown to intercept amounts owing by a third party to the tax debtor and demand that the third party pay them directly to the Crown. These provisions, known as the "garnishment rules" because they were derived from the rules providing for the garnishment of wages to pay income tax arrears, are controversial and have been the subject of much jurisprudence. The general provision pursuant to ss. 317(1) creates a purely statutory right and not an equitable charge. It is clear that the wording is too imprecise to deprive secured creditors of their pre-existing security interest in the property of the tax debtor. The demand does not convey the indebtedness to the Crown and the Crown does not acquire an equitable or any other interest in the indebtedness, nor does it become a holder of a security.

To avoid the narrow ambit of this general garnishment provision, enhanced garnishment rules were added to the GST legislation as ss. 317(3). This provision is substantially the same as in the *ITA* for source deductions. In effect, it gives a "super priority" to the Crown ahead of all other security interests, *whether prior to or subsequent* to the interest of the Crown. Thus, the taxman may, by letter or personal service, require that any moneys owing to a tax debtor by a third party (the debtor's debtor) be paid to the Crown, and on receipt of the letter (or on its mailing pursuant to the deemed receipt rules), the amounts *become the property of the Crown*. The provision explicitly states that it overrides all other Acts of Parliament or of a province or, indeed, any other law, with the exception of the *BIA*.

However, there is a potential conflict with the *CCAA*, which provides for stays of all government claims to facilitate the reorganization as s. 21 thereof states that the *CCAA* applies to federal and provincial Crowns. The *CCAA* also provides that statutory deemed trusts are not effective (subject to source deduction exclusions) and the Crown's claims rank as unsecured claims (s. 18).

Query, the ambit of this ss. 317(3); for example, does it apply to "true factor" situations where there is an outright sale of the receivables without recourse to the seller (see *Alberta (Treasury Branches) v. Minister of National Revenue*[10])? Further, does the provision extend to an unpaid purchase price or other situations where someone must pay money to a tax debtor (for example, a solicitor holding money in trust; see *Re San Diego Catering Ltd.*[11]) other than pursuant to a trade account receivable? These cases suggest ss. 317(3) has its limits.

The provisions at the end of ss. 317(3) that the moneys "shall, despite any security interest in those moneys, become the property of Her Majesty", and that the Receiver General is entitled to the moneys "in priority to any such security interest" were added to respond to the deficiencies identified in such cases and it is generally accepted that the Crown's priority over every prior secured creditor has been made clear as a matter of statutory interpretation. This is the conclusion that was reached in *Berg v. Parker Pacific Equipment Sales*[12] and confirmed in the *Alberta (Treasury Branches)*[13] case. Thus, in simple terms, the Crown gets a win if it gets its letter in – that is, if the glove fits... .

Subsection 462(2.1) of the *Bank Act*[14] (and parallel provisions of other financial legislation for other financial institutions), as added in 2004, provide that the CRA can issue a garnishment notice to the "designated office" of a bank, so as to seize a tax debtor's accounts at any branch of that bank. This procedure is routinely used by the CRA.

GST Bad Debt Input Tax Credit – Section 231

With many companies fighting to stay afloat in this economic climate, it is no surprise that the incidences of bad debt rise significantly. Section 231 allows a remedy for recovering GST that has been billed and, therefore remitted to the CRA, but is subsequently uncollectable. After all, the supplier is merely an "agent" of the Crown to collect the tax. If a bad debt arises and the supplier writes off the bad debt on its books of account in accordance with GAAP, the supplier may (in determining the reporting entity's net tax for the reporting period in which it is written off) deduct the amount determined by a formula in ss. 231(1). The "reporting entity" is usually the

10 (*sub nom. Canada Trustco Mortgage Corp. v. Port O'Call Hotel Inc.*), [1996] 1 S.C.R. 963, (*sub nom. Pigott Project Management Ltd. v. Land-Rock Resources Ltd.*) [1996] 1 C.T.C. 395.

11 [1996] G.S.T.C. 78 (B.C. C.A.).

12 [1991] 1 C.T.C. 442 (B.C. S.C.).

13 Above note 10.

14 S.C. 1991, c. 46.

supplier but may be an agent elected under ss. 177(1.1). In order to deduct the amount under ss. 231(1), the supply must be taxable and not zero-rated, there must have been consideration and the recipient and the supplier must be dealing at arm's length. Generally, an allowance for doubtful accounts or amounts stolen from the supplier will not constitute bad debt for the purposes of ss. 231(1).

Technically, the operation of the subsection is by means of a deduction from the "net tax" under s. 225. The reporting entity may only deduct the amount if the tax collectable in respect of the supply is included in determining the amount of net tax reported in the reporting entity's return for the reporting period in which the tax became collectable (the GST on the supply was actually remitted). In addition, all net tax remittable as reported in that return must have been remitted and a person may not claim a deduction unless the deduction is claimed in a return filed within four years of writing off the bad debt.

If any or all of a bad debt is recovered at any time in the future, the supplier must add an amount for tax collectable on the recovered amount in determining the supplier's net tax for the reporting period. The amount recovered is deemed to be tax included (that is 5/105ths or 13/113ths is the tax portion). The supplier cannot deem it is just collecting the debt owing to it.

The GST/HST "Insolvency Code" For Receivers and Trustees

Introduction

This transaction-specific nature of the tax caused significant interpretative difficulty when applied to receiverships and bankruptcies prior to significant amendments to create a "Code" that effectively legislated out the application of the common law or law of equity. The reason for the confusion is that there are multiple transactions occurring in an insolvency that all have different GST consequences. For example, a receiver can be supplying a service to secured creditors (a "private receiver" who is making sales on their behalf or otherwise looking after their property) or to creditors generally (such as in the case of a court-appointed receiver or "court receiver"). On the other hand, a trustee in bankruptcy (the "trustee") is supplying a service to creditors under a statutory duty and may also be selling property on behalf of itself as the property is vested or transferred to the trustee on bankruptcy. In addition, there are supplies of property or services made from the debtor's business assets made either on an ongoing basis or the disposal of the assets, for which tax must be accounted.

The basic premise of this self-contained "Insolvency Code" in ss. 265 and 266 of the Act is to deem that there is no transfer of property from the debtor as a result of the appointment of the trustee and that the receiver or trustee is the agent of the debtor for the purposes of the Act. Because this is contrary to the general common law or statutory regimes governing debtor creditor relations, the Act attempts to provide a separate, all-encompassing GST Code to deal with the resulting artificial regime. The general legal principles and the customary practice in receiverships or bankruptcies must, therefore, be disregarded when determining the GST consequences of the receivership or bankruptcy and any transactions connected with the debtor's business or property.

Under this Code there is no transfer of property to the trustee on the bankruptcy, nor is there a transfer on repossession by a secured creditor. This Code must be continually consulted in all transactions and, moreover, must be rigidly adhered to, to avoid potentially significant personal GST liability for receivers and trustees.

There are some significant differences at law between a trustee and a receiver. The most important one is that secured creditors generally are able to carry out their realizations outside of the bankruptcy provisions. The *BIA* does not affect the priority scheme for secured creditors. While it does regulate "receivers" to the extent that they are required to file notice before they take certain steps, and also requires receivers to make various reports to the trustee throughout the steps of their realization process, the general position that receivers operate outside the bankruptcy has not changed for GST purposes.

The other matter of note is the broad definition of a "receiver". An agent selling property for a bank under the *Bank Act* will be a "receiver", as well as a person administering an estate involving a business along with liquidators, *etc.* This is significant because of the rules applicable to and the liability involved for a "receiver". Accordingly, the "receivership" rules take priority over the s. 183 seizure rules and over the trustee rules under s. 265 where they conflict.

GST and Receiverships and Bankruptcies: General Rules

Sections 265 and 266 of the Act form a Code that is intended to apply to all situations of receiverships and bankruptcies to the exclusion of other provisions. The receiver or trustee is deemed to be the agent of the debtor GST registrant for all purposes of the Act. Sections 265 and 266 are not merely procedural in nature. The most important result of these rules is that the property of a bankrupt registrant remains vested in the debtor for all purposes of the GST legislation. Thus, it is deemed that there is no transfer of property to the trustee on the bankruptcy, nor is there a transfer on repossession by a secured creditor. This has significant impact for GST collection and ITC purposes. This is a fundamental concept and the key to understanding the GST treatment of receiverships and bankruptcies under the artificial regime created by the GST Code.

The receiver or the trustee in effect steps into the shoes of the debtor for GST purposes. That is, receivers or trustees do not act in their normal capacity but rather function as the debtor for purposes of the GST. In effect, they become the debtor. Accordingly, all Elections and Notices under the Act as well as all rights under the legislation to input tax credits and the filing of credit returns, subject to certain specific provisions in respect of the denial of certain credit returns and rebates, are available as if the debtor had never entered into a bankruptcy or receivership. The only significant change in status for GST purposes is that the appointment of the receiver or trustee results in the termination of the current GST reporting period of the debtor for those activities of the debtor which relate to the bankruptcy or insolvency (as post-bankruptcy business or activities unconnected to the receivership continue to be the responsibility of the debtor under the same reporting periods as before). The Rules are deemed to take effect beginning on the day of the appointment of the trustee or receiver. This is a logical provision as trustees and receivers can only be expected to have GST responsibility for the debtor's business commencing with their appointment.

GST Remittance and Registration

The deeming of the receiver or trustee as agent brings the responsibility to collect GST on behalf of ongoing supplies made in connection with the debtor's business or property. Paragraphs 265(1)(c) and 266(1)(d) provide for personal liability on the part of the trustee or receiver jointly with the debtor for tax that is or should be collected on behalf of the debtor. The Act also provides for liability on the part of the receiver for GST arrears of the debtor and also for the trustee in limited circumstances.

A new GST registration number is not required for the activities of the bankrupt's estate or in respect of the assets under a receiver's administration. The trustee or receiver is deemed to be the agent and, in effect, the continuation of the debtor. There is, accordingly, no need for a new registration for the estate or insolvent person, although a new account number (the last four digits *e.g.*, RT-0002) can be issued if the receiver requests one (this is useful where the debtor has other activities or where there are multiple receivers or trustees involved).

Liability for Current Tax

If there is a receiver, the receiver will operate the business on an ongoing basis in the course of realizing on the creditors' security unless the receiver decides to liquidate the assets immediately (which is itself a management decision). Also, pursuant to the usual deemed agency clause found in most security agreements, the receiver will be acting as agent of the debtor in most situations. Where a receiver or trustee sells the property or services of the business in the ordinary course of that business, GST must be collected and remitted. This is consistent with the deeming of the receiver or trustee to be an agent of the debtor for all purposes of the GST.

The Act specifically deals with the issues of the liability of a receiver or trustee for current GST remittances and for liability for GST remittances in connection with unrelated post-appointment business by making the receiver and trustee liable for tax collected subsequent to the appointment. Paragraphs 265(1)(d) and 266(2)(c) and (d) then exclude liability for payment or remittance of amounts that do not relate solely to activities of the debtor or property of the debtor to which the appointment relates. In other words, the GST remittances must arise exclusively in connection with the assets under administration or control of the trustee or receiver before they are responsible for the tax. Activities independent of the receiver or trustee or unrelated to the assets subject to the appointment are the debtor's responsibility alone.

Multiple Roles

The potential for multiple receivers is dealt with by the "relevant assets" concept in ss. 266(2). As it is certainly possible that more than one receiver can be appointed, each with responsibility to manage a particular property or asset group, para. 266(2)(c) is important as it restricts liability for collection and remittance of GST to assets under control. There is nothing preventing the same person from being both the receiver and trustee-in-bankruptcy. Just as the receiver and trustee are not liable for GST arising out of the debtor's activities in carrying on an unrelated business after the appointment, the trustee will not have liability to the extent a receiver is approved who has liability under s. 266. Subparagraph 265(1)(d)(ii) provides that the trustee "is not liable for the payment or remittance of any amount for which a receiver" within the meaning assigned by ss. 266(1) "is liable under section 266". Thus, a trustee will have liability only to the extent that it has actual control over the assets of the debtor and is acting on the debtor's behalf in making supplies using those assets or disposing of the assets. In most cases, this will remove any liability from the trustee just as the trustee is normally removed from any knowledge of or making any decisions with respect to the operation of the debtor's business where there is a receiver in place.

There is no definition of "liquidation" or "liquidator" in the Act. However, it is generally accepted that a liquidator is a person who is appointed to wind up a company under the federal winding-up and restructuring legislation.[15] This person can be appointed by the shareholders of a corporation, but is usually appointed by a court. As a result, as an officer of the court, a liquidator has a duty to the whole body of those affected by its actions (*e.g.*, shareholders, creditors, court), and must maintain "an even and impartial hand". Such a liquidator is, however, also a "receiver" within the meaning of ss. 266(1). Therefore, the liquidator is an agent of the person under liquidation for all purposes of the GST and is subject to all of the obligations and responsibility of a receiver under s. 266.

GST Clearance Certificates Mandatory – Section 270

Section 270 of the Act provides that all legal representatives, when disposing of assets pursuant to the administering or winding-up of a business or estate of the person, must apply for a certificate from the taxman certifying that the other person's GST obligations have been or will be fulfilled. This must be done before distributing to one or more persons any property or money under the control of the representative in its capacity as representative. Failure to obtain the certificate renders the representative liable for payment of the amounts payable under the Act by the person to the extent of the value of the property or money so "distributed". Trustees in bankruptcy are specifically excluded from the requirement, presumably because they are subject to strict monitoring under the bankruptcy regime.

Receivers and "other representatives" are specifically subjected to the provision. The section formerly referred only to the "distributing" of "property". It now refers to the distribution of "money" as well. The words "distribute" or "distribution" cannot be defined in a precise manner, but connote the delivery or handing over to a beneficiary or other person legally entitled to property of their entitlement in the property in which they have an interest. A receiver would not usually deliver or hand over the particular property to the secured creditor or other person entitled to it under bankruptcy provisions. The receiver would distribute any surplus money to the

---

15 *Winding-up and Restructuring Act*, R.S.C. 1985, c. W-11.

trustee or other persons entitled to it, but it would be rare to actually "distribute" property to any person with an interest therein.

The addition of the words "or money" to the "distribution of property" phrase means the section has relevance for a receiver (and for other representatives) because there is liability for the distribution of proceeds realized from dispositions of property. The liability of receivers is only for funds that become payable, or could be reasonably expected to have become payable or remittable by the receiver in its capacity as receiver in the reporting period in which the distribution is made (thus, the need for the words "are, or can reasonably be expected to become, payable or remittable") or in any previous reporting period. The concluding words "or any previous reporting period" are significant and must be read in the context of the entire subsection. These words relate to the GST "payable or remittable under this Part by the receiver in that capacity" wording of the subsection. Therefore, the Clearance Certificate requirement pertains to GST arrears of the debtor (apart from any surplus arising from a disposition of assets). This amendment then removed the conflict between ss. 266 and 270 that previously existed, as the Clearance Certificate and the receiver's liability are dependent upon the receiver complying with its obligations to remit GST arising while it was receiver (that is, post-appointment collections rather than arrears).

This imposition of personal liability under s. 270 for post-appointment GST is, in a sense, redundant as the receiver already has that liability under s. 266. The obtaining of a Clearance Certificate is, therefore, a safe harbor mechanism for the receiver to enable it to ensure that it has complied with all of its obligations as receiver.

Administratively, the taxman provides Clearance Certificates if there is substantial compliance with ss. 265 and 266. The taxman expects to receive funds only to the extent that there is money or property available after all secured parties have been satisfied. The taxman accepts that it ranks behind all secured creditors and *pro rata* with unsecured creditors for purposes of GST arrears. Therefore, the CRA collection officers do not require that certificates be obtained where the only assets available do not satisfy the secured creditor(s) in full; that is, where there is no surplus realization by the receiver. Similarly, if there is a concurrent bankruptcy and any surplus realization is turned over to the trustee, a certificate is not required according to administrative practice. However, the obtaining of a certificate has the advantage of removing any uncertainty about personal liability during the period for reassessment as the certificate may estop the Crown from later claiming that there were any outstanding tax amounts in respect of the debtor's property or business. Certificates are obtained through the local

District Tax Office of the debtor and the procedure is similar to the obtaining of distribution certificates for income tax purposes.

Seizure or Repossession of Property by a Creditor in a Receivership – Section 183

Sections 183 (seizure or repossession of property by a creditor, as discussed above) and 266 are intended to have exclusive application. A receiver operates under s. 266, and the creditor and its agent under s. 183. Where the agent is not a "receiver" as defined in ss. 266(1), there is no overlap or conflict between the sections. It is simply necessary to analyze the functions the person in question is carrying out in respect of the transactions under consideration. This requirement is no different than any other careful reading of the provisions of the Act. However, where a person acting as agent on behalf of a secured creditor when disposing of the assets of the debtor is also a "receiver" as defined, the seizure and repossession rules in s. 183 lead to the exact opposite result of that under s. 266, as the secured creditor would be the supplier for GST purposes and not the receiver acting as an agent of the debtor pursuant to under s. 266.

Subsection 183(11) was amended to deal with the problem of the potential overlapping jurisdiction of ss. 183 and 266 by proclaiming the paramountcy of s. 266. Where a creditor exercises a power to seize or repossess property or appoints an agent to do so and the creditor or the agent falls within the definition of a "receiver" under s. 266, such a person shall be deemed to be acting as a receiver for all purposes of the Act and not under s. 183. This provision, of course, only applies to the extent of the debtor's property interest at the time of appointment of the receiver.

It would, however, be desirable if the possibility of the overlap between ss. 183 and 182 (forfeitures) was also dealt with, perhaps, by proclaiming the paramountcy of s. 183 over 182. However, this is an unresolved conflict.

Impact of Subsection 317(3) on Bankruptcies and Receiverships

As discussed above, the wording of ss. 317(3) is clear. It actually transfers the property interest of the tax debtor in the payment to the Crown. Accordingly, there would be no property interest that could vest in the trustee upon the bankruptcy of the tax debtor. A bankruptcy occurs on a voluntary assignment to the official receiver by a debtor or when a receiving order is made in response to a petition of a creditor. As a result, it appears that if the notice is mailed prior to that time, the Crown's property interest defeats the vesting of the property in the trustee and any secured creditor's claims.

Canada Trustco Mortgage Corp. v. Port O'Call Hotel Inc.[16] illustrates the principle that where the taxman sends the notice by registered mail prior to the bankruptcy occurring, it will obtain any monies owed by a third party at that time in priority to secured creditors, notwithstanding the amounts are not paid until after the petition for the receiving order is filed by the secured creditors. This case also confirms that any amounts that become owing after the date of the petition are excluded from application of ss. 317(3).

In *Port O'Call*, the CRA served by registered mail a requirement to pay under ss. 317(3) to various debtors of two tax debtors. Subsequently, in the case of one of the companies in question, the creditors filed a petition for a receiving order. In the case of the other company, a voluntary assignment in bankruptcy was made subsequent to the serving of the ss. 317(3) requirement. In both cases, the court held that the Crown was entitled to all amounts owing and payable to the tax debtor prior to the day that the petition was filed (because the bankruptcy is deemed to have occurred on the date of the petition) and on the day the assignment in bankruptcy was made, respectively. At the time the requirements to pay were served, neither company possessed the status of a "bankrupt". The court held that bankruptcy legislation establishes a priority regime only for purposes of the distribution of the property of the bankrupt, it could not affect the distribution of property that was not the property of the bankrupt at the time of bankruptcy. At the time of bankruptcy, the entitlement of the secured creditor to the money in question had been severed by the operation of ss. 317(3). The new *BIA* provisions make substantial changes to the priority regime but these changes do not purport to affect the nature of the property that is available for distribution.

The Supreme Court of Canada upheld the trial judge in *Alberta (Treasury Branches)*.[17] As a result, it is clear that ss. 317(3) applies to a general assignment of bank debts, and the Crown can "scoop" secured creditors, but it does not apply to an absolute assignment or outright disposition (that is, sale) that is not subject to equity of redemption, as there is no property interest to "assign".

---

16 [1992] G.S.T.C. 14 (Alta. Q.B.), reversed (1994), (*sub nom. Country Inns Inc., Re*) 94 D.T.C. 6650, (*sub nom. Country Inns Inc., Re*) [1995] 1 C.T.C. 75, 2 G.T.C. 7065 (Alta. C.A.), leave to appeal allowed [1994] 9 W.W.R. lxxiii (S.C.C.), reversed (*sub nom. R. v. Alberta Treasury Branches*) 96 D.T.C. 6245, (*sub nom. Pigott Project Management Ltd. v. Land-Rock Resources Ltd.*) [1996] 1 C.T.C. 395 (S.C.C.). (Alberta Court of Queen's Bench, In Bankruptcy).

17 Above note 10.

As noted above, these draconian garnishment powers are not effective once a bankruptcy proceeding pursuant to the *BIA* is underway. Further, the filing of a notice of intention or a proposal by an insolvent person under the *BIA* will stay the garnishment powers of Her Majesty in Right of Canada under s. 317 of the Act until the proposal is rejected or the debtor does not meet the other requirements under the *BIA* "stay" provisions. These stay provisions operate to stay any proceedings, including the sending of a ss. 317(3) requirement but, again, they do not operate to affect the debtor's property interest prior to bankruptcy.

There may be an argument that ss. 317(3) can operate retroactively to attach to amounts paid before the appointment of the trustee, even though the letter may be delivered after the assignment or the petitioning of the tax debtor into bankruptcy. This argument does not appear to be a strong one given the "stay" provisions of the *BIA*. However, if the Crown actually receives payment under a valid garnishment requirement (that is, if it is satisfied) served in the period intervening between the petition and receiving order, it will be entitled to keep the amount in priority to the trustee even though the bankruptcy relates back to the date of filing of the petition.

The impact of ss. 317(3) on a receivership is not entirely clear. In general, secured creditors operate outside of the bankruptcy law provisions. Therefore one could argue that, as ss. 317(3) is the only governing statutory provision concerning receiverships, the provision is otherwise effective. However, under the *BIA*, prior to bankruptcy an insolvent person or a receiver may file a "proposal" or notice of a "proposal" with the Official Receiver which has the effect of staying all rights and remedies of creditors for 30 days (which can be extended). Since ss. 317(3) cannot have application during the stay period, the CRA is precluded from sending the requirement. However, outside of these "proposal" proceedings there appears to be nothing preventing ss. 317(3) from being effective if initiated (that is, similar to a judgment, the remedy is "executed") prior to the bankruptcy of the debtor. Further, if the proposal is not accepted or is annulled, ss. 317(3) can have application (see *San Diego Catering*[18]) as long as it is issued before the resulting bankruptcy.

---

18 Above note 11.

Struggling Debtors

Director's Liability – Section 323

The need to remit GST may seem immaterial compared to the other financial difficulties that a company faces in an economic downtown. However, the consequences for failing to remit GST can be very significant and detrimental to directors (or "partners").

Directors of corporations (or partners) should be wary of the temptation to not remit the s. 225 net tax under s. 228 in order to conserve cash and pay trade creditors in tough economic times due to s. 323 of the Act. Section 323 parallels the rule for unremitted source deductions in s. 227.1 of the *ITA*. Directors for corporations are liable for unremitted net tax whether or not the GST was collected. The directors of the corporation at the time the corporation was required to remit the GST are jointly and severally liable with the corporation for the amount and, as well, any interest or penalties that may arise. The directors are also liable for overpaid net tax refunds for which the corporation is not entitled and for unremitted retail sales taxes in some provinces such as Ontario. A director who satisfies the claim is entitled to contribution from other directors who were liable for the claim (ss. 323(8)).

A director of a corporation is not liable unless one of the following scenarios applies:

- a certificate for the amount of the corporation's liability has been registered in the Federal Court under s. 316 and execution for that amount has been returned unsatisfied in whole or in part (unsuccessful collection proceedings);
- the corporation has commenced liquidation or dissolution proceedings or has been dissolved and a claim for the amount of the corporation's liability has been proved within six months after the earlier of the date of commencement of the proceedings and the date of dissolution (upon liquidation or dissolution); or
- the corporation has made an assignment or a bankruptcy order has been made against it and a claim for the amount of the corporation's liability has been proved within six months after the date of the assignment or bankruptcy order (bankruptcy of the corporation).

The only exemption to s. 323 liability, apart from the defences discussed below, is for tax not remittable under s. 228 (for example, *liability* of the corporations for repayable ITCs).

There are various defences available for directors against a s. 323 assessment. For example, the director could provide evidence that he or she never agreed to become a director and never signed a legally sufficient consent or that he or she legally resigned (there are certain steps that must be taken to achieve such a resignation).

The most prevalent defence is that of "due diligence" under ss. 323(3). The director will not be liable where the director exercised the degree of care, diligence, and skill to prevent the failure that a reasonably prudent person would have exercised in comparable circumstances. A director's background and experience in business is given great weight in determining whether the director acted with due diligence. The director must act responsibly and take active steps to ensure that the corporation makes its GST remittances. Directors must take reasonable steps to prevent the failure and not wait to act until after the failure has already occurred. Directors should ensure that there are open lines of communication in the organization so that they are aware of a potential lack of GST remittances.

There is also a limitation period under ss. 323(5) whereby an action or proceeding against a director to recover any amount payable must be made within two years after the person last ceased to be a director of the corporation.

Liability of Partners – Subsection 272.1(5)

Members of a partnership must be aware of GST obligations as well. According to ss. 272.1(1), anything done by a person as a member of a partnership is deemed to have been done by the partnership in the course of the partnership's activities and not to have been done by the person. However, according to ss. 272.1(5), each member or former member of the partnership is jointly and severally liable for the payment or remittance of all amounts that become payable or remittable before or during the period that the member was a member of the partnership.

Criminal Penalties – Sections 326, 327, 329, and 330

The Act also provides for criminal offences for certain avoidance actions. Prosecutions under ss. 326, 327, 329, and 330 require criminal prosecution in a provincial court and must be proved beyond a reasonable doubt.

A director who is involved with a corporation that *wilfully* fails to pay, collect, or remit tax or net tax may have more worries than "simply" being jointly and severally liable for the unremitted tax under ss. 323(1) as ss. 330(1) creates the potential to be charged for a criminal offence. Under ss. 330(1), every officer, director, or agent of a corporation who directed, authorized, assented, acquiesced in, or participated in wilfully failing to pay, collect, or remit tax or net tax as and when required is guilty of the offence and liable on conviction to the punishment provided for the offence.

Under ss. 329(1), every person who *wilfully* fails to pay, collect, or remit tax or net tax as and when required is guilty of an offence punishable on summary conviction and liable to a fine not exceeding the aggregate of $1,000 and an amount equal to 20 per cent of the amount of tax or net tax that should have been paid, collected, or remitted or both a fine and imprisonment for up to six months.

In addition, s. 326 creates a criminal offence for failing to file a return and s. 327 creates a criminal offence for making a false statement on a GST return or for participating in similar acts of evasion.

It is the position of the taxman that criminal penalties will be imposed where a person is convicted of knowingly neglecting to file a return or withholding payment to the Crown. Therefore, individuals, including directors, should never undertake a decision which will result in the wilful avoidance of remitting tax or net tax. The taxman will not be sympathetic to a corporation's financial difficulties. The decision to avoid remitting tax or to make a false statement on a GST return has serious consequences. Experienced counsel should be consulted immediately when the taxman starts talking about "charges".

For example, in *R. v. Nagel*,[19] the accused was issued a requirement to provide documents to the Minister with respect to a partnership in which he was a partner. The accused did not comply with the request for information and the accused was convicted. The court upheld the conviction and noted that the offence of failing to comply with a requirement is a "strict liability" offence (subject to a defence of due diligence).

Accurate and correct records must be maintained at all times. In *R. v. J.I.L.M. Enterprises & Investments Ltd.*,[20] the accused acted in his personal capacity for a gasoline business and misstated amounts owed for GST. The court found that the accused as an individual was liable but the corporation was

---

19 [2008] G.S.T.C. 173 (Sask. Prov. Ct.), affirmed 2009 SKQB 502.

20 [2005] G.S.T.C. 117 (Ont. S.C.J.).

not. The corporation did not have any liability to remit GST from the gasoline business, which was operated by the accused personally. The accused was sentenced to six months of imprisonment and a fine. Similarly, in *R. v. Onkar Travels Inc.*,[21] the accused failed to remit $756,527 in GST and made false entries in books and records filed with the CRA. The court found that the accused had to pay $105,000 in restitution, $200,000 as a fine, and was subject to imprisonment for two years less one day.

In *R. v. Bannon*,[22] the accused reported certain sales to be tax-exempt when they were in fact not exempt. The court found that the accused had the requisite criminal intent to commit the offence and imposed a four-month "conditional" custody sentence, 50 hours of community service, restitution, and a fine.

Wind-up or Amalgamation – Sections 271 and 272

Under s. 271, if two or more corporations merge or amalgamate to form one corporation (other than the result of the acquisition of property of one corporation by another corporation pursuant to the purchase of the property by the other corporation or as a result of a winding-up), the new corporation will be deemed to be a separate person from each of the predecessors. However, where there is a transfer of any property by a predecessor to the new corporation as a consequence of the merger or amalgamation, the transfer is deemed to not be a supply. An assessment can still be issued to an amalgamated corporation in respect of GST liability of the predecessor corporation.

Under s. 272, where a subsidiary corporation (at least 90 per cent owned) is wound up, the transfer of any property to the parent corporation as a consequence of the winding-up is deemed to not be a supply.

Voluntary Disclosures

A voluntary disclosure to the CRA of any violations of the Act can prevent penalties or hard time in prison if done on a timely basis. The stated objective of the Voluntary Disclosures Program (VDP) as set out in the current CRA Publication IC00-1R2 *Voluntary Disclosures Program* is to promote voluntary compliance:

---

21 [2005] G.S.T.C. 93 (Ont. C.A.).

22 [2000] G.S.T.C. 66 (Ont. S.C.J.).

> The VDP promotes compliance with Canada's tax laws by encouraging taxpayers to voluntarily come forward and correct previous omissions in their dealings with the CRA.[23]

The Circular currently provides that a disclosure must meet four conditions to qualify as a valid disclosure:

1. The disclosure must be voluntary.
2. The disclosure must be complete.
3. The disclosure must involve the application, or potential application, of a penalty.
4. The disclosure must include information that is:
   (a) at least one year past due, or
   (b) less than one year past due where the disclosure is to correct a previously filed return or where the disclosure contains information that also meets the condition of subparagraph 4 a) above.

Effective April 1, 2007, the federal government introduced harmonized accounting rules with a view to implementing the common methodology for the application of interest and penalties to the various taxes administered by the CRA. The harmonized accounting rules selected were based upon those that had existed prior to April 2007 for income tax purposes and, as a result, have highlighted significant and key differences between income tax (a tax imposed upon annual profits) and the GST (a consumption tax imposed on a transactional basis).

For example, income tax is reported annually whereas GST is reported monthly (primarily), quarterly, or annually, based on transactions within that period. Income tax is reported and paid directly by the taxpayer to the government whereas GST is reported and remitted indirectly through registrants who act as the government's agent in charging and collecting the tax. In income tax, the taxpayer bears the burden of the tax. Under the GST, the "taxpayer" is often just a collector on behalf of the government.

In the voluntary disclosure context, errors made by a taxpayer in filing its income tax return inherently involve the loss of tax revenues to the government (due to the nature of the income tax); however, errors made by a GST registrant in filing its GST returns frequently do not result in any net revenue loss to the government due to the cash flow aspect of the GST. Yet, the collector/agent is liable for an interest penalty on this "virtual" tax revenue

---

23 Income Tax Information Circular No. IC00-1R2 *Voluntary Disclosures Program*, at 8.

loss (it is not a real loss as the recipient would have recovered the tax it should have paid with its ITC), provided the recipient was engaged in commercial activities (that is, had ITCs available). This situation is called a "wash transaction".

Accordingly, the current Information Circular does not address GST properly in a voluntary disclosure process. This process is currently under review and submissions have been made by the author as Chair of the CICA GST Leaders' Forum. It is understood that changes are being made to make the voluntary disclosure process more "user friendly" in a GST context. Nevertheless, it is far better to consider a voluntary disclosure enabled by the existence of solicitor-client privilege in situations where GST returns have not been filed or GST has not been remitted, as opposed to sitting tight and burying your head in the sand. A voluntary disclosure will eliminate penalties and prison and should result in elimination of interest penalty in so called "wash" transactions (where the recipient of the supply would be entitled to ITCs).[24]

Conclusion

A company and its directors (or partners) can be exposed to significant GST liability if they do not carefully consider the implications of GST on the company's day-to-day activities and major transactions. Every party affected by an insolvency situation (including debtors, creditors, trustees, and receivers) must be aware of the possible impact of the Act and its Insolvency Code on their liabilities. The GST issues are heightened and problems accelerate when things start going bad. The failure to understand the GST priority rules by a creditor could lead to the potential for a loss of funds to the taxman. The creditor could recover less or even nothing under its security. Creditors can suddenly become liable for collecting and remitting the GST in the place of the debtor and face penalties for failing to do so. In addition, even though it may seem that the company's financial viability is the most important objective in a difficult economic environment, the continued collecting *and remitting* of GST is crucial. The failure to do so can lead to joint and several liability for the directors of the corporation (or for

---

24 The author has been informed that the thrust of the CICA GST Leaders Forum Recommendations to the CRA have been adopted so that the interest "penalty" will be waived. However, unlike under the Quebec tax authorities (M.R.Q.) QST Voluntary Disclosure Rules, the tax must still be collected and remitted (or paid by the agent if the tax debtor cannot be found or if it refuses to pay and the requirements in s. 223 have not been met to let the agent sue under s. 224). The CRA will also consider accepting voluntary disclosures even where the program has been accessed before (as long as it is not the same issue in question).

receivers and trustees or partners) for the unremitted amount or, even worse, time in prison. Voluntary disclosures to the CRA, if done on a timely basis, can prevent penalties and hard time.

The UBS Scandal, The LGT Affair, and The Unfolding HSBC Story: Hard Times Ahead For Canadian Taxpayers Who Hold Secret Bank Accounts

David W. Chodikoff*

The *Income Tax Act*, R.S.C. 1985, c. 1 (5th Supp.), as amended (the "Act"), contains civil penalty provisions that deal with a variety of situations including circumstances where a taxpayer has been careless, grossly negligent, or wilfully blind.[1] Since the Act is administered by officials of the Canada Revenue Agency (the "CRA" or "Agency"), it is initially up to these bureaucrats to determine if a taxpayer is grossly negligent, careless, or wilfully blind. The Act further contains criminal sanctions for offences including misrepresentation and fraud.[2] In this chapter, I examine the recent global banking scandals and the potential consequences that a taxpayer could encounter if he/she fails to disclose unreported income and/or unpaid

* I am grateful for the assistance of Lisa Csele, Crown Counsel, Office of the Director of Public Prosecutions (Canada) and Julia Luke of the Miller Thomson library for proofing the chapter. Any errors or omissions are mine.

1 There are a variety of penalties in the Act. Some of these other provisions include: the failure by an individual to file his/her tax return on time (ss. 162(1) and 162(2)); the failure by large corporations to file a return on time (s. 235); the failure to provide information on a prescribed form (subs. 162(5)); the failure to provide a social insurance number on request (subs. 162(6)); the failure to comply with the *Income Tax Act* or Regulations (ss. 162(7) and 162(7.1)); the failure to file a corporate tax return electronically (subs. 162(7.2)); and the late or inadequate amount of payment for income tax instalments (s. 163.1).

2 The failure to file a tax return or comply with specific sections of the Act (s. 238 of the Act). Ss. 239(1) deals with tax evasion: ranging from false and deceptive statements (para. 239(1)(a)) to tax evasion (para. 239(1)(d)).

taxes. As one would expect, depending upon the particular circumstances, CRA officials take a very dim view of just about any taxpayer who fails to report the amount of his/her income in his/her yearly filed tax return. The global banking scandals remind those Canadians who maintain secret offshore bank accounts that the world has indeed changed and that global banking secrecy laws are under attack and could, within time, crumble.

One of the most interesting bank scandals to unravel in the last three years involves the Internal Revenue Service of the United States, the giant Swiss financial company, UBS, and a whistleblower by the name of Bradley Birkenfeld.

Mr. Birkenfeld, who was born in the United States, lived and worked in Switzerland for many years. He was a banker and worked for UBS. In the spring of 2007, Mr. Birkenfeld went to the U.S. Justice Department.[3] His reasons for going to see these U.S. officials remain somewhat of a mystery although he claims his motive was primarily altruistic.[4] He spoke to U.S. government officials and provided them with documentation that plainly revealed that UBS was actively involved in assisting American clients evade the payment of taxes on billions of dollars. Birkenfeld's information touched off a major investigation by IRS agents, the Justice Department, and the U.S. Securities and Exchange Commission. In a television interview on the CBS news program "60 Minutes", Birkenfeld explained that UBS would sponsor major events in the U.S. such as yacht races or art festivals that would attract very wealthy Americans. UBS would send its bankers to these events in order to service existing clients but also in order to develop new client relationships.[5] The fact of the matter was that these Swiss bankers were not licensed to carry out business in the U.S. They were in clear violation of U.S. banking laws. Birkenfeld provided the Justice Department with internal UBS documents that implicated UBS executives in their efforts to protect their fellow bankers and to avoid detention by the U.S. authorities.

According to Thomas Perrelli, the associate attorney general of the United States, "[UBS executives] were going out of their way to cover their tracks."[6] Perrelli also noted that "the [UBS bankers] would bring checks [sic] or sometimes they would actually carry money from one client to the next, all with the purpose of disguising and avoiding detection of large transfers of

---

3 Interview Transcript, CBS News – 60 Minutes "Banking: A Crack In The Swiss Vault", Steve Kroft, correspondent, January 3, 2009.

4 T. Brown, P. Fletcher & M. Lewis, "UBS Whistleblower Asks Why He Is Going To Prison", Thomson Reuters, Reuters News, December 30, 2009.

5 *Ibid.*

6 *Ibid.*

money."[7] Perrelli further stated that "it was certainly surprising that there would be a unit within a major bank that would be behaving in that way."[8] Perrelli indicated that "the Justice Department later learned that senior UBS executives knew about all of this; they knew it was wrong; but, it was profitable and [UBS] did not stop doing it."[9]

Acting on the information supplied by Birkenfeld and apparently other informants, the IRS and U.S. Justice Department sought a court order forcing UBS to turn over the banking records of some 52,000 account holders.[10] These "John Doe" summons were issued in Florida. By February 2009, UBS initially agreed to hand over the identities of 250 U.S. account holders that it believed were set up as sham accounts. In order to avoid criminal prosecution, UBS admitted to setting up these accounts that helped wealthy Americans hide nearly $20 billion overseas and agreed to pay the staggering sum of $780 million (USD) in penalties.

The Justice Department vigorously pursued these American UBS clients. By the summer of 2009, Americans were starting to turn up in U.S. courts pleading guilty to tax fraud. In June 2009, it was reported that Steven Rubinstein, an accountant in the yacht business, avoided an indictment by pleading guilty to a single count of filing a false tax return for the 2004 tax year.[11] He was accused of failing to disclose his offshore UBS accounts. According to published newspaper accounts, Rubinstein agreed to cooperate with the U.S. government in its ongoing investigation into the secret bank accounts of American clients of UBS. Rubinstein was specifically accused of keeping a secret UBS private bank account through a British Virgin Islands company. He was alleged to have used this account to transfer $7 million back to the U.S. without paying taxes to purchase property and build a huge home in Florida. He also was alleged to have sold more than $2 million in Krugerrand gold coins through his UBS bank account.

In July 2009, Jeffrey Chernick from New York pled guilty to using his UBS Swiss bank account to hide more than $8 million from the IRS.[12]

---

7 *Ibid.*

8 *Ibid.*; also see: L. Browning "U.S. Is Said To Consider Easing Informant's Term", *The New York Times*, January 4, 2010.

9 Above note 5.

10 C. Mollenkamp, "UBS, U.S. Talk On Tax Case", *The Wall Street Journal*, July 13, 2009; A. Dale, "UBS Tax Case Unsettles Account Holders", *The Wall Street Journal*, July 14, 2009; and C. Mollenkamp, S. Fidler & L. Saunders, "UBS, Swiss Reach Pact On U.S. Tax Probe – The IRS Could Get Thousands Of Client Names As Part Of A Compromise On Bank Secrecy Laws", *The Wall Street Journal*, August 1, 2009.

11 L. Browning "U.S. Tax Inquiry Of UBS Clients Gets Conviction", *The New York Times*, International Herald Tribune, June 27, 2009.

12 T. Brown, "American UBS Client Admits Tax Dodge", *National Post*, July 29, 2009.

By August 2009, the continuing and growing global embarrassment of the UBS scandal forced both UBS and the Swiss government to finally come to terms and settle with the U.S. government on the tax evasion probe. The agreement called for UBS to disclose the identities of some 4,450 account holders to the U.S. authorities.[13] The criteria for the release of these accounts have remained secret. However, the Swiss Minister of Justice, Eveline Widner-Schlumpf, said that "the U.S.-Swiss agreement fully complied with the laws of Switzerland and that with this agreement, we have managed to avoid a conflict between sovereignty of two states."[14] Essentially, the two governments agreed to amend the Article on Exchange of Information in their treaty. Currently, there is a public policy clause that would allow Switzerland to deny any requests for information that contravene its laws such as bank secrecy rules. A similar Article exists in the Canada-Switzerland tax treaty. However, the provision does not even consider situations involving tax fraud and it is therefore considered of limited value.

By the fall of 2009, the CRA was making an effort to obtain information regarding the UBS accounts in order to enforce the provisions of the Act. Undoubtedly, the international and national press coverage encouraged dozens of Canadians to come forward and use the Voluntary Disclosures Program to disclose their UBS accounts and specifically any unreported income and unpaid taxes. Simply put, some Canadians with secret accounts became very concerned that they could face a tax prosecution with the prospects of public humiliation, fines, and possible jail time.

Another wrecking ball to the global wall of banking secrecy came with the break of the LGT scandal. The story dates back to the late 1990s when Heindrich Kieber ("Kieber") joined an information technology company in Vaduz, Liechtenstein.[15] The company did some work for LGT, a bank with approximately 77,000 international clients and owned by Liechtenstein's royal family. In 2001, Kieber was employed by the Trust Unit of LGT to transfer account information to an electronic archive. It was only after Kieber was hired that the bank learned of his pending charges against him

---

13 L. Browning, "Judge Refuses To Delay Prison For UBS Informant", *The New York Times*, January 5, 2010.

14 *Wall Street Journal*, p. C.1, August 20, 2009; more recently, the Swiss Federal Council, the Government's Cabinet, said that it would seek to override recent Swiss court decisions in order to hand over the names of the 4,450 UBS clients to the IRS. See: L. Browning, "Release of Client Names Is a Step Closer For UBS", *The New York Times*, March 31, 2010; C. Seib, "Switzerland Seeks Law Change to Hand Details of UBS 'tax evaders' to United States", *The Times* (U.K.), April 1, 2010.

15 P. Waldie & T. Perkins, "Tax Evasion Probe Spreads To Canada: Authorities Are Reviewing Client Data Allegedly Stolen From LGT, A Liechtenstein Bank, To See Who Owes Money", *The Globe and Mail*, February 27, 2008, p. B4.

for fraud in Spain over a real estate deal. In 2002, Kieber fled from Vaduz but, before leaving, he copied four CDs worth of LGT client information. Later, it was learned that Kieber had taken the specifics of 1,400 different account holders. Kieber sought the help of Prince Hans-Adam, Liechtenstein's head of state but no help was given. Kieber was criminally charged in Liechtenstein and he did return to face the consequences of his actions. In 2003, he was convicted, received probation, and returned the stolen CDs to the bank. However, unknown to the Bank, Kieber made a copy of the returned CDs and he initiated efforts to sell the information to various countries. In 2006, German authorities commenced negotiations to purchase the data. Finally, in 2008, the German foreign intelligence service was reported to have paid approximately 4.2 million euros for the data from Kieber. The account files were stolen from LGT Treuhand AG, a subsidiary of Liechtenstein's LGT group.

The information disclosure had an almost immediate impact in Europe. In February 2008, Klaus Zumwinkel, the then CEO of Deutsche Post AG, was arrested on tax evasion charges. He was subsequently convicted and given a two-year suspended sentence and fined 1 million euros.[16] The German authorities shared the purchased information with other countries including the U.S. and Canada. Ultimately, the CRA obtained a list of over a hundred names from the German officials who shared the information with other members of the Organization for Economic Co-operation and Development's Forum on Tax Administration. As a spokeswoman for the CRA stated in early 2008, "if [the CRA] get to [the account holders] before they get to us, then [the CRA] would take appropriate measures, unless [the account holders] want to go through the voluntary disclosure program before [the CRA] actually can identify them."[17] It was therefore not a surprise to many tax specialists, like myself, that Canadian taxpayers holding secret Swiss bank accounts came forward in order to avoid the possibility of a tax prosecution. These Canadian taxpayers sought the protection of the Voluntary Disclosures Program. In fact, in December 2009, the then Minister responsible for the CRA, Jean-Pierre Blackburn, promised a broadening of an investigation of the LGT scandal so that it would include all Canadian banks. The Minister stated that "we will go after every other bank to obtain the list of their clients who do business abroad and to see if these clients

---

16 D. Crawford, "Big Liechtenstein Bank Sells Its Trust Operations; Principality Is The Latest European Tax Haven To Bend To A Global Outcry Over Tax Evasion", *The Globe and Mail*, March 11, 2009, p. B10.

17 Above note 15.

declare their income."[18] This broadening of the CRA enforcement activity was largely due to the Agency's work related to Project Jade. As a result of the information the government obtained in relation to LGT, CRA was able to identify three investment advisors that the Agency maintained were involved in helping Canadian taxpayers set up Liechtenstein entities for the purpose of hiding investments and other income.[19] The LGT matter is still unfolding.

The most recent banking scandal involves HSBC Holdings PLC ("HSBC"). In 2010, HSBC admitted that a former employee stole data on a number of accounts. At first, HSBC claimed that less than a dozen accounts were compromised.[20] However, in late February, officials at HSBC admitted that information on approximately 24,000 accounts was stolen. According to press reports, Hervé Falciani, a former information technology employee of HSBC, stole the data between 2006 and 2007.[21] Initially, he is alleged to have attempted a "sale" of the data to a number of governments without success. At some early point in the unfolding of this story, HSBC executives confronted Falciani with allegations of theft. Falciani was a dual citizen of Italy and France. So, faced with these allegations, Falciani fled to France. Within a month's time, French authorities raided Falciani's home and confiscated the stolen data. The French authorities held the data for some time before returning it to Switzerland. Upon its return, the French informed the Swiss that they reserved the right to use the data to chase after tax evaders in France.[22] They further indicated that it might give the information

---

18 J. Greenwood, "This Is Not The End, Blackburn Declares", National Post, December 15, 2009, p. FP1; see also: D. Crawford & D. Ball, "World News: Swiss Bank Data Offered To Germany - Berlin Considers Paying For Stolen Information Detailing Alleged Tax Evasion, As Pressure Rises About Secret Accounts", *The Wall Street Journal*, February 1, 2010; see also: G. McArthur, "Ghost In The Machine Appears In Liechtenstein Bank Scandal", *The Globe and Mail*, July 17, 2008; J. Greenwood, "Ottawa Takes Flak Over Tax Scandal; No Action Taken On Stolen Account", *National Post*, September 2, 2008, p. FP1; T. Perkins & P. Waldie "Tax Havens Feeling Pressure From Global Community", *The Globe and Mail*, B.17.

19 G. McArthur, "Canada's Largest Brokerage Firm Linked To Alleged Tax Haven Scheme - RBC Dominion Staff Accused Of Helping Clients Hide Wealth In Liechtenstein", *The Globe and Mail*, December 14, 2009, p. A1.

20 R. Fletcher & S. Farrell "HSBC Reveals Swiss Data Theft Affects 24,000 Clients", *The Daily Telegraph*, March 12, 2010, p. 1.

21 D. Ball &d D. Gauthier-Villars, "Data Theft Hits 24,000 HSBC Clients", from *The Wall Street Journal* reprinted in *The Globe and Mail*, March 12, 2010, p. B12.

22 R. Fletcher & S. Farrell, "HSBC Gives Data Theft Warning To Thousands", *The Daily Telegraph*, March 2, 2010, p. 2; D. Jolly, "Bank Revises Number Affected By Data Theft", *The New York Times*, March 12, 2010, p. 2; and "Details Of 24,000 HSBC Accounts Stolen", *Daily Mail* (London, U.K.), March 12, 2010, p. 82; and also see: L. Browning, "Case Is Said To Link HSBC To U.S. Tax Evasion Inquiry", *The New York Times*, February 17, 2010, Late Edition.

to other governments so they, too, could pursue tax evaders. Once again, Canadians that hold offshore HSBC accounts are weighing the options and consequences of disclosing unreported income and unpaid taxes.

These three separate banking incidents – I more commonly refer to them as the UBS scandal, LGT affair, and the unfolding HSBC story – plainly demonstrate that the attack on foreign banking secrecy laws will continue whether it is state instigated or perpetrated by those persons seeking economic gain by selling secret banking information to state hungry revenue authorities.

Canadian taxpayers that presently hold secret offshore bank accounts are best advised to at least rethink the status quo, or the "just do nothing" position. If detection occurs, a taxpayer's options may be exceptionally limited. The alternative course is to disclose the existence of the secret account before detection under the protection afforded by the Voluntary Disclosures Program ("VDP").

The purpose of the VDP is to encourage taxpayers to come forward to the CRA and voluntarily disclose inaccurate or incomplete information or to disclose previously unreported information without civil or criminal penalties or tax prosecution.[23] The statutory authority for the relief of penalties and interest is found in ss. 220(3.1) of the Act. It states that: the "Minister may, on or before the day that is ten calendar years after the end of a taxation year of a taxpayer ... or on application by the taxpayer ... on or before that day, waive or cancel all or any portion of any penalty or interest otherwise payable under this Act by the taxpayer ... in respect of that taxation year or fiscal period ..."[24]

In order for the voluntary disclosure to be valid, the taxpayer must comply with four basic and fairly rigid requirements.[25] First, the disclosure must be voluntary. If, for any reason, the CRA can conclude that the disclosure was somehow prompted by either some early warning to the taxpayer or because of some sort of audit investigation, then the disclosure will not be considered voluntary. In practice, this means a taxpayer should be proactive and the earlier a voluntary disclosure is made, the better for the taxpayer. Second, the disclosure must be complete. The CRA Interpretation Bulletin states that the taxpayer must provide not only all of the facts and documentation for all of the previously inaccurate, incomplete, or unreported information

---

23 Income Tax Information Circular – IC00-1R2 at paragraphs 4-9.

24 Ss. 220(3.1) of the Act.

25 IC00-1R2 at paras. 31–42.

for all taxation years but this information must also be accurate.[26] Third, the disclosure must involve the application or the potential application of a penalty. Penalties vary and can include such types as an instalment penalty, a late filing penalty, a failure to remit penalty, a discretionary penalty, or a gross negligence penalty. Fourth, the disclosure must include information that is at least a year past due or if less than a year to correct information from a previously filed tax return. The Interpretation Bulletin explains that the intent of this later requirement is to permit the timely correction of previously filed returns and to allow the inclusion of unfiled tax returns only when they form part of a voluntary disclosure submission.[27]

There are two methods by which a taxpayer can make a disclosure: one is the "named" method and the second is called the "no-name" option.[28] The named disclosure method requires the taxpayer to identify him or herself on the initial disclosure submission. The "no name" disclosure method gives the taxpayer the opportunity to engage in preliminary discussions with the CRA about their situation on a "no name" basis. Although these discussions with the VDP officer are informal, non-binding, and general in nature, these exchanges are designed to give comfort to the taxpayer and, more precisely, to encourage the taxpayer to complete the disclosure process. As stated in the CRA Interpretation Bulletin, "these discussions are for the benefit of the taxpayer" and to give "a better understanding of the risks involved in remaining non-compliant".[29] Even though disclosure can be commenced on a no-name basis, a taxpayer cannot complete the disclosure process without eventually revealing his/her identity.

The Minister of National Revenue (the "Minister") also has limits on his ability to grant relief. In respect of income tax submissions made on or after January 1, 2005, the Minister can only grant relief to any taxation year that ended within the previous 10 years before the calendar year in which the submission is filed. As an example, if a taxpayer made an income tax submission on May 1, 2010, the limitation would apply so that relief would only be available for the 2000 and subsequent taxation years.[30] In practical terms, even where the disclosure may involve more than seven years, the CRA has a tendency to limit the assessing period to six taxation years. However, this is not to say that in some cases, where the voluntary disclosure concerns ten or more years, the assigned VDP officer requires that the taxpayer file all returns for those years and further, the taxpayer is assessed for all of those

---

26 IC00-1R2 at para. 37.

27 IC00-1R2 at para. 40.

28 IC00-1R2 at paras. 25 and 26.

29 *Ibid.*, para. 26.

30 *Ibid.*, para. 13.

years. As pointed out in the Interpretation Bulletin, the CRA cannot waive all penalties in relation to a voluntary disclosure that exceed the 10-year limitation period.

The Interpretation Bulletin sets out the method by which a taxpayer can make a voluntary disclosure. There is no specific requirement to use a CRA form. However, if a taxpayer does not use Form RC199, the review process could be delayed. Put simply, a taxpayer should send in his/her written submission using as the initial basis of submission the RC199 form. This form contains a number of pieces of information that must be submitted by the taxpayer before the CRA considers the taxpayer's request valid. The information is detailed and includes the following:

(a) the name, address, telephone number, social insurance number, partnership number, trust account number, business number, license number, GST/HST registration number or any other identification tax number assigned by the CRA to the taxpayer;

(b) the taxpayer's postal code;

(c) the address, telephone, and fax numbers of the taxpayer's authorized representative;

(d) the taxation year(s), reporting period(s), or fiscal period(s) involved in the disclosure;

(e) the amount of income (be it, business, investment, pension, capital gain) being disclosed;

(f) the type of return involved (such as a taxpayer's personal return of income, a corporate return, GST/HST, *etc.*);

(g) the type of omission;

(h) the reason for the omission;

(i) the primary business activity; and

(j) a complete explanation of how the taxpayer believes that he or she has complied with the four basic requirements of a voluntary disclosure.[31]

It is expected that either the taxpayer or his/her representative will make available to the CRA VDP officer all documents, records, and any other information in order to verify the facts of the disclosure.

---

[31] *Ibid.*, para. 44.

The effective date of the voluntary disclosure is the date that the CRA receives the completed and signed RC199 taxpayer agreement. Where the RC199 form is not used, a letter signed by either the taxpayer or the taxpayer's authorized representative must be received by the CRA.

Once the submission is made, it could take some months before the CRA VDP officer completes his/her review. If the submission is rejected, the VDP officer will advise the taxpayer or the taxpayer's representative that the disclosure is simply being denied. It is possible that the disclosure may qualify for some alternative CRA program and the matter may be referred to any section of the CRA for handling and resolution. The information contained in the disclosure may simply result in either an assessment or reassessment. In some cases, the VDP officer may recommend and impose penalties and interest costs. Finally, it is possible that the VDP officer will refer the file for further investigation and prosecution could be the outcome.

Even though a taxpayer has no right to object to a discretionary decision that denies him/her relief, he/she is permitted to challenge the Minister in circumstances where the taxpayer believes that the Minister has not exercised discretion in a fair and reasonable manner. The taxpayer can have a second level review conducted by the Director of the District Taxation Office by making the request in writing. In some instances, the second level internal CRA administrative review may still be unsatisfactory and the taxpayer may still conclude that the Minister did not exercise his discretion in a fair and reasonable manner. A final recourse lies with the Federal Court of Canada. Pursuant to s. 18.1 of the *Federal Courts Act*, a taxpayer can make an application to the Federal Court for a judicial review of the Minister's discretionary decision. Where the Federal Court finds that the Minister failed to properly exercise his discretion, the Federal Court will generally refer the request back to the CRA for reconsideration.

The alternative to the proactive disclosure approach is to remain silent and cling to the hope that the account will never be discovered by the tax authorities. Depending upon the taxpayer's particular circumstances and, more precisely, the level and nature of the activity in the account, state detection could result in the requirement that the taxpayer pay any outstanding taxes with the addition of fines to the prospect of a full-blown tax prosecution for tax evasion.

Generally, the civil penalties under the Act are found in a number of different sections including ss. 162, 163, 163.1, 163.2, 188.1, 227(8), 227(9), 227(9.1), and 237.1 of the Act. All of these penalty provisions involve the payment of fines and there is no prospect of jail. The penalties are also determined on the basis of the balance of probabilities test as opposed to the criminal standard of beyond a reasonable doubt.

S. 150 of the Act provides the authority under which taxpayers are required to file tax returns.[32] Specifically, the section requires that each taxpayer shall file a return of income, in a prescribed form, containing prescribed information with the Minister of National Revenue, for each taxation year. In other words, this section creates the obligation on Canadian citizens to comply with the tax system.

While our system is voluntary, the government is well aware that some taxpayers will try to avoid the payment of their share of tax. Therefore, the Minister is empowered by s. 152 of the Act to examine all income tax returns and make assessments of tax, interest, and penalties.

If the Minister determines that there was an omission as a result of circumstances amounting to gross negligence, the Minister can impose a substantial penalty in accordance with ss. 163(2) of the Act. Subsection 163(2) requires there to be a particular state of mind, or *mens rea*, on the part of the taxpayer. In accordance with ss. 163(3) of the Act, the burden of proving that the "guilty mind" exists in order to support a finding of gross negligence falls upon the Minister. The burden of proving that a person failed to take reasonable care is a particularly high standard to meet.[33]

Taxpayers can fight the imposition of the penalty. The courts have tended to favor taxpayers so that a high degree of negligence is required in order to establish that there is justification for the levying of a penalty.[34] In the circumstances that I describe in this chapter, it is my view that the courts would likely find it proper to levy ss. 163(2) penalties. However, each case will turn on its specific facts. There are defences that a taxpayer can raise against the imposition of penalties.[35]

The CRA will issue ss. 163(2) assessments before commencing a tax prosecution. Pursuant to ss. 239(4) of the Act, the civil assessments will be held in abeyance pending the completion of any criminal actions taken against the taxpayer.[36]

---

32 S. 150 of the Act.

33 See: *The Queen v. Taylor*, 84 D.T.C. 6459 (F.C.T.D.).

34 *Shair v. R.*, 2006 D.T.C. 2869 (T.C.C.).

35 See for example: *Udell v. M.N.R.*, 70 D.T.C. 6019 (Ex. Ct.) and *Howell v. M.N.R.*, 81 D.T.C. 1523 (T.C.C.).

36 Ss. 239(4) of the Act.

The same acts and omissions that are subject to civil penalties can also be the subject of criminal sanctions in accordance with s. 238 and s. 239 of the Act. As you would expect, penalties imposed under ss. 238 and 239 carry heavier fines than the civil ones and there is the distinct possibility of a prosecution and jail. Furthermore, a criminal conviction would result in a criminal record.

Section 238 imposes liability on summary conviction for the failure to file returns or to comply with other obligations imposed by the Act. Section 239 of the Act makes it a criminal offence to purposely evade or to attempt or conspire to evade tax by wilful deceit. Subsection 239(1) of the Act states as follows:

> Every person who has
>
> (a) made, or participated in, assented to or acquiesced in the making of, false or deceptive statements in a return, certificate, statement or answer filed or made as required by or under this Act or a regulation,
>
> (b) evaded payment of a tax imposed by this Act, destroyed, altered, mutilated, secreted or otherwise disposed of the records or books of account of a taxpayer,
>
> (c) made, or assented to or acquiesced in the making of, fake or deceptive entries, or omitted, or assented to or acquiesced in the omission to enter a material particular, in records or books of account of a taxpayer,
>
> (d) wilfully, in any manner, evaded or attempted to evade compliance with this Act or payment of taxes imposed by this Act, or
>
> (e) conspired with any person to commit an offence described in paragraphs 239(1)(a) to 239(1)(d),
>
> is guilty of an offence and, in addition to any penalty otherwise provided, is liable on summary conviction to
>
> (f) a fine of not less than 50%, and not more than 200%, of the amount of the tax that was sought to be evaded, or
>
> (g) both the fine described in paragraph 239(1)(f) and imprisonment for a term of not exceeding 2 years.[37]

The Attorney General of Canada can elect to prosecute upon indictment of the offences listed under ss. 239(1). Of course, indictable offences carry

---

[37] Ss. 239(1) of the Act.

much heavier fines and lengthy terms of imprisonment. Generally, the Crown does not elect to proceed by way of indictment. Proceeding by indictment is reserved for the most serious of cases.

Before the decision is made to prosecute, the Special Investigations Division ("SI") of each CRA District Taxation Office carries out a full investigation. SI's function is to obtain evidence of any criminal offence, and, where the evidence is found, to prepare the case for prosecution. Once SI determines that there is sufficient evidence to lay a criminal charge, the case is handed over to the Department of Justice for prosecution. Criminal charges under the Act are heard by the regular criminal courts rather than the Tax Court of Canada.

When a case proceeds by summary conviction, the hearing is held before a justice or provincial court judge in a court having jurisdiction where the taxpayer is a resident, conducts a business, or is found, apprehended, or in custody.

In criminal matters, the burden of proof rests with the Crown. The taxpayer is presumed innocent and need not prove a thing. The onus is on the Crown to prove both the *actus reus* and the *mens rea*. Pursuant to para. 239(1)(d) of the Act, a person who evades or attempts to evade the payment of taxes is guilty of an offence. In order to prove the *actus reus* component of the offence, the Crown must prove that taxes were payable by the accused. The Crown must also prove that the taxpayer either attempted to evade the payment of taxes owing or, in fact, evaded taxes owing to the Fisc.

Legitimate tax planning and what is really tax evasion has been well-defined by the courts. In *R. v. Klundert*, the Ontario Court of Appeal stated the following:

> The authorities that require that the evasion be deceitful or underhanded confuse the conduct component of the crime of tax evasion with the fault component of that crime ... It is the culpable state of mind that distinguishes the legitimate planner from the dishonest tax evader. Both may engage in the same course of conduct that can aptly be described as a deliberate attempt to avoid the payment of tax. The difference lies in their respective states of mind. Unlike the tax evader, the tax planner does not intend to avoid the payment of a tax that he or she knows is owed under the Act, but rather intends to avoid owing tax under the Act.[38]

The Court further described the elements of the offence of tax evasion as follows:

---

38 *R. v. Klundert*, 2004 D.T.C. 6609 at 6614 [*Klundert*].

In most cases of tax evasion, the trial judge will adequately describe the elements of the offence by instructing the jury that they must be satisfied beyond a reasonable doubt that the accused:

> did something or engaged in a course of conduct that avoided or attempted to avoid the payment of tax imposed by the Act;
>
> knew there was tax imposed by the Act; and
>
> engaged in the conduct for the purpose of avoiding or attempting to avoid payment of tax imposed by the Act or knowing that avoiding payment of tax imposed by the Act was a virtual certain consequence of his actions.[39]

The definition in *Klundert* has gained widespread support throughout the Canadian court system.

Taxpayers should also be aware of the possibility for the imposition of both civil penalties and criminal penalties for the same offence. The concept and practice of double penalties applies when the civil penalty is imposed before the criminal charges are laid. The Minister will typically impose civil penalties during the civil audit stage resulting in a notice of assessment that contains the civil penalty. Thus, the taxpayer has already been assessed for civil penalties before a charge is laid under s. 238 or 239 of the Act. Generally, double penalties are only avoided where a taxpayer has not been penalized under s. 162 or 163 when the criminal charge is laid. In these exceptional instances, the taxpayer is solely faced with punishment imposed on conviction for the criminal offence.

Banking secrecy laws are under global state attack. There should be little doubt that more financial institutions in more tax haven nations will be forced by collective, international nation-state pressure to disclose, in some manner, possible accounts that hold monies representing either unreported income and/or unpaid taxes. Any Canadian taxpayer maintaining an offshore account should review the basis for the creation of the account and the utility of maintaining it. It is possible that, after a careful review of the pros and cons, it may be in the taxpayer's best interests to disclose the existence and activities of the account. Fortunately, Canadian taxpayers are provided with a high degree of financial protection and the elimination of potential criminal charges by resorting to the VDP. The alternative to disclosure is to remain in silence and hope to avoid detection. If the overseas account is discovered by the tax authorities, the Canadian taxpayer faces all sorts of financial challenges that could include civil and criminal penalties and the cost of a defence if charged with tax evasion.

---

39 *Ibid.*, p. 6615.

Life Insurance Viewed as a Financial Derivative

George H.R. Goldsmith

Introduction

Not long ago, a senior executive in the financial investment community asserted that life insurance is a waste of money. At about the same time, in a meeting of senior executives of a major life insurance company about a concept I was developing, one declared, "My goodness, George has a radical approach here ... he's attempting to sell pure life insurance!" Too much insurance is sold for what it is not, and not enough for what it is – a mortality-based financial derivative. Without bells and whistles, the basic life insurance contract is simple; pay a premium, receive a basic death benefit. No side accounts, policyholder dividends, reinvestment options, or cash surrender value due. Viewed solely as a mortality-based financial derivative, life insurance offers unique attributes that qualify it for consideration in many investment portfolios; to manage risk and for real return. "Self-completion", non-taxable status, non-correlation to other investments, definable risk, inherent leverage, and contractual liquidity are examples of its unique features.

Defining life insurance as a form of financial derivative means that it should be considered in asset allocation strategies, compete with, and be assessed against, other portfolio assets. It also means that insurance "assets" ought to be reviewed on a regular basis, as part of asset allocation and performance reviews. Financial advisors and portfolio managers need to understand the product in order to properly execute these tasks and considerations. Advisors must work collegially to maximize portfolio performance, as mandated by consensus needs analysis, where client needs are placed ahead of sales quotas, commissions, or defensive posturing.

Life insurance premiums are typically accounted for as an expense and, thus, never find themselves onto any balance sheet, to any extent, beyond cash surrender value. Furthermore, the contract may cease to exist with failure to pay those premiums. These two factors have reinforced the view that a life insurance contract is not an asset, *per se*. Now, under certain circumstances, U.S. accounting recognizes life insurance as a bookable asset and even offers choices on how to account for it.[1] Regardless of how it is handled for accounting purposes, life insurance has intrinsic value.

Why a Derivative?

The basic financial derivative is a contract where, for current consideration from the owner, the counterparty agrees to pay an agreed sum upon a triggering event. The triggering event, or underlying[2] can be a real asset,

---

1 In the United States, pursuant to the Financial Accounting Standards Board ("FASB"), third party investors in life insurance policies (referred to as "Life Settlement Contracts" in such circumstances) can account for them on one of two bases:

- The Investment Method in which all outlays (initial purchase price and premiums) are capitalized with no income recognition until "maturity" (death).
- The Fair Value Method in which the investor books the original transaction, and then adjusts for changes in fair market value, based on actual and prospective cash flows, adjusted for the time value of money and probabilistics.

From a practical point of view, it seems that what is good for the goose ought to be good for the gander; if it is appropriate for a holder in due course to book premiums and outlays relating to a life insurance policy as an asset, then it should be appropriate for the owner/beneficiary to do so (when they are the same person or entity). Regardless, the FASB position establishes intrinsic value, and, since their position paper also amends FASB Statement No. 133 (Accounting for Derivative Instruments and Hedging Activities) to reflect FTB 85-4-1 (Accounting for Life Settlement Contracts by Third-Party Investors) they have buttressed my argument that life insurance be evaluated as a financial derivative.

2 I took this definition from Wikipedia, the free Internet encyclopedia located at http://en.wikipedia.org/wiki/Derivative_(finance). Their precise definition is set out below.

Derivatives are financial contracts, or financial instruments, whose values are derived from the value of something else (known as the underlying). The underlying on which a derivative is based can be an asset (e.g., commodities, equities (stocks), residential mortgages, commercial real estate, loans, bonds), an index (e.g., interest rates, exchange rates, stock market indices, consumer price index (CPI) – see inflation derivatives), or other items (e.g., weather conditions, or other derivatives). Credit derivatives are based on loans, bonds or other forms of credit.

The main types of derivatives are: forwards (which if traded on an exchange are known as futures); options; and swaps.

Derivatives can be used to mitigate the risk of economic loss arising from changes in the value of the underlying. This activity is known as hedging. Alternatively, derivatives can be used by investors to increase the profit arising if the value of the underlying moves in the direction they expect. This activity is known as speculation.

another financial instrument like a share, an index, weather, or, in this case, mortality. Many derivatives facilitate the buying and selling of risk (*e.g.*, currency swaps, credit derivatives, puts) for both defensive reasons (risk management) and for yield (speculation, investment). Life insurance is a derivative in which the traded risk is mortality (either the event or the timing). Just like other risk management derivatives, life insurance can be used purely for risk management, or proactively employed for yield. The premium is, arguably, a form of purchase finance, meaning that life insurance is a financial derivative with a high degree of inherent leverage.

Mortality-based derivatives can be of a purely risk mitigating type (term insurance), or a mixed use vehicle (permanent life insurance). Term insurance can be assessed in the same sorts of ways as puts and calls; there is an amount of money paid to obtain rights in the event of an underlying (death) within a fixed time frame. By contrast, permanent insurance involves payment for an entitlement for when death occurs. The investment return on such a derivative (permanent life insurance contract) is based upon the amount of premium, the amount of the death benefit, and the term that elapses from the start of the contract to its "maturity". The premium, which permits payment over time, may be viewed as vendor finance, or inherent leverage to the buyer.

The difference between "if" and "when" is the difference, first between term and permanent insurance and, second, between pure risk management and an alternative investment vehicle held for investment returns. This discussion concerns itself primarily with permanent insurance which can best be understood, compared, and analyzed by reference to investment return, risk, tax efficiency, and liquidity.

Investment Return

Wrapped up in any return on mortality-based instruments is the mathematics of probabilistics, as expressed in mortality tables issued by the Canadian Institute of Actuaries. These are the tables that form the basis for life insurance premium calculations (although the Life Insurance Companies ("Lifecos")[3] alter them for certain assumptions including longevity increases). Probabilistics is, perhaps obviously, about probabilities. A reasonable point

---

Because the value of a derivative is contingent on the value of the underlying, the notional value of derivatives is recorded off the Balance Sheet of an institution, although the market value of derivatives is recorded on the Balance Sheet.

3 For greater certainty, the term "Lifeco" is intended to be generic. It does not refer to any specific company. This chapter reflects my opinions only. There are many highly professional people and organizations who might disagree in whole or in part with them.

of departure for the discussion of investment returns is internal rate of return on premium outlays that the death benefit produces, weighted by the probability of death (maturity of the contract) in each year from policy issue to insured age 104, at which point the actuaries have us all dead and buried.

A summary of probabilistic investment returns and timing risks associated with policies issued at different ages is set out below.

VARIOUS STATISTICS BASED ON PEOPLE WHO HAVE JUST QUALIFIED TO BUY LIFE INSURANCE AT STANDARD PRICING (1)

	Age of Median Deaths	# Years Before Median	# Years After Median	Probabilistic Investment Return(2)	Equivalent Investment Return (3)
Non-Smokers:					
Male age 40	80	40	24	8.04%	13.40%
Female age 40	84	44	20	7.91%	13.18%
Male age 50	82	32	22	7.74%	12.90%
Female age 50	85	35	19	7.76%	12.93%
Male age 60	82	22	22	7.66%	12.77%
Female age 60	86	26	18	7.54%	12.57%
Male age 70	85	15	19	5.97%	9.95%
Female age 70	87	17	17	5.80%	9.67%
Smokers:					
Male age 40	72	32	32	8.16%	13.60%
Female age 40	80	40	24	7.76%	12.93%
Male age 50	74	24	30	7.89%	13.15%
Female age 50	81	31	23	7.68%	12.80%
Male age 60	76	16	28	7.99%	13.32%
Female age 60	83	23	21	7.63%	12.72%
Male age 70	82	12	22	7.00%	11.67%
Female age 70	85	15	19	5.70%	9.50%

(1) Using "middle-of-the-road" pricing on T-100 (permanent insurance product) taken from the industry quote device LifeGuide©.
(2) Calculated by applying mortality table "Canadian Institute of Actuaries 1986-92 Table" without increased life expectancy adjustments, and life expectancy adjustments, and then determining Internal Rate of Return (I.R.R.) assuming all premiums are annual and paid on the first day of the year, while all deaths occur on the final day of the year.
(3) The yield on an equivalent taxable instrument assuming a marginal tax rate of 40%.

This chart tells us:

- Probabilistic returns on life insurance are attractive.[4]
- Tax-affected returns are quite compelling. Since life insurance proceeds flow tax-free, it is necessary to recalculate the investment return as the pre-tax equivalent that another investment would need to earn in order to produce equal returns to the life insurance policy. The column entitled "Equivalent Investment Return" on the extreme right side of the chart makes the point.
- Policies issued relatively early in life appear to offer a better investment return than those purchased relatively late.
- The slope of the graph of the number of years after the median death age tends to be steeper than that for deaths before it.
- Investment returns on policies issued to smokers are also good, the median term to "maturity" is shorter, but timing risk is relatively unattractive (in investment terms the left-hand tail is fatter).
- The investment return is an after-tax compound rate of return. Many investment alternatives show compound returns, and disclose reinvestment assumptions that are hard to implement in the real world; the compounding and tax effectiveness of life insurance are two valuable attributes.

Probabilistic return is interesting from an analytical point of view, but not something one actually earns. The "underlying" either "matures" or it doesn't. You either have, effectively, an infinite return (the insured person dies a month after the policy is issued), or they live to be 104, or something in between. I worked out static returns on various groups, assuming the life insured dies at the median age for his or her group. These are set out immediately below.

---

[4] An often-asked question is "How can returns on a life insurance contract exceed long-term interest rates?" There are two primary reasons: a portion of mortality profit in policy pricing, and "lapse support". "Lapse support" is the money paid by policy holders who subsequently lapse their policy. Expected lapse support is built into policy pricing.

STATIC INVESTMENT RETURNS TO MEDIAN AGE AT DEATH (1) ON NEW POLICIES ISSUED AT VARIOUS AGES

Group Return Basis	Issue Age 40			Issue Age 50			Issue Age 60			Issue Age 70		
	Raw	@35% (2)	@42% (2)	Raw	@35% (2)	@42% (2)	Raw	@35% (2)	@42% (2)	Raw	@35% (2)	@42% (2)
Male Non-Smoker	6.44	9.91	11.11	5.77	8.87	9.94	6.37	9.80	10.98	5.51	8.47	9.49
Male Smoker	6.58	10.12	11.34	6.23	9.58	10.74	7.70	11.85	13.28	6.55	10.08	11.29
Female Non-Smoker	6.41	9.86	11.05	6.11	9.39	10.53	5.80	8.92	9.99	5.33	8.19	9.18
Female Smoker	5.65	8.69	9.74	5.52	8.50	9.52	5.44	8.36	9.37	5.52	8.50	9.52
Joint-and-Last to Die (3) (Male/Female Non-Smoker)	6.23	9.58	11.98	6.66	10.24	11.48	6.75	10.38	11.63	8.56	13.17	14.76

(1) Median age of death for the various groupings and issue ages may be found in the first column of the prior chart.
(2) pre-tax equivalent tax yield necessary to do as well as the disclosed marginal tax rates.
(3) rarely bought before age 50

The first thing to note is that while the Static Investment Returns to median age of death are lower than the probabilistic, they, and the equivalent returns, render a new issue – minimum funded permanent life insurance policy – a competitive investment alternative.

Directing the reader's attention to the bottom row in the "Static Yields" chart, some attention should be paid to the Joint-and-Last-to-Die policy ("JLTD"). A JLTD is a single policy on two (or more) lives. It pays off on the second death, or in the case of more than two lives the last death of the lives insured. Premiums may be payable until the first or the last death. The one shown above, and the most common in practice, has premiums paid until the second death of two lives insured. JLTD policies are less expensive because there is a significantly reduced risk to the insurance company of early payout due to a cataclysmic event. As a result, the median age for payout is shifted right on a time grid.

To give an example, set out below is a chart of expected mortality by attained age for each of a male and female non-smoker aged 65, and the mortality expected on a policy on those two lives, issued on a JLTD basis, with premiums payable until the second death. Note that the projected mortality for males peaks at somewhere between age 80 and 85, while that for females peaks somewhere between 85 and age 90, while that for the joint-and-last-to-die peaks just south of 90 years of age. Also note that the curve of each graph is not symmetrical, in that the run up to the median mortality age is less steep than the decline thereafter. Variability of the investment is skewed in favor of an extremely high one more than an extremely low one.

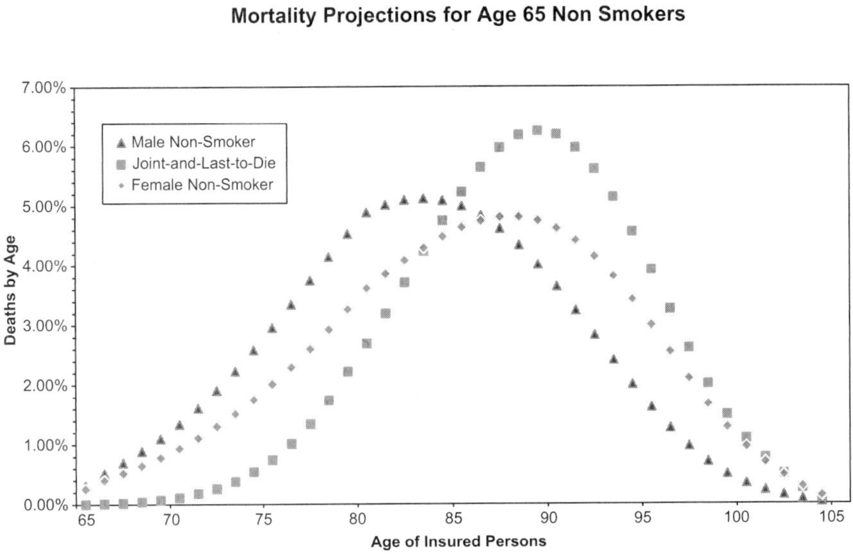

The Static Investment Return to median death age 90 of a JLTD policy is attractive, and even more so when assessed on a "tax equivalent basis".

If one compares mortality projections for a group of policyholders of the same age, gender, and smoking status, one will discover a difference between what the industry refers to as "Select" and "Ultimate" risks. "Select" means a person who has just been approved for life insurance, while "Ultimate" refers to a person who has been insured for 15 or more years. The industry presumes that projected mortality is different for the "Selects", but that the gap comes to zero by year 15. A schedule to show that difference is set out below:

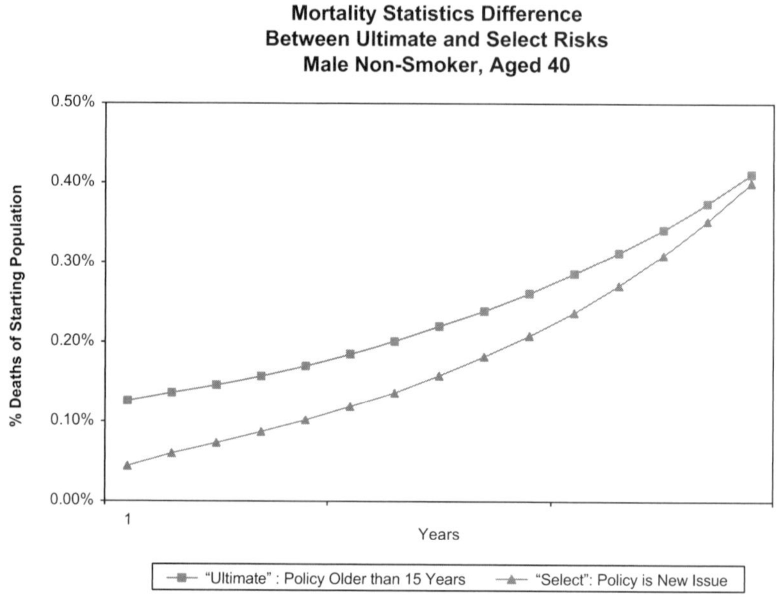

The point is that from a pure investment point of view, policies that have been around for a while are more likely to mature earlier than policies that have recently been purchased even though the two insureds are the same age, but that the difference in term to expected mortality closes relatively quickly and is gone after 15 years of policy existence.

The four charts viewed as a group indicate life insurance is a highly competitive investment yield vehicle if acquired on a minimum premium basis, with reliance solely upon the contractual right to a death benefit. This analysis is based on a new life insurance policy. Yields increase substantially if an owner assumes ownership of a policy on an insured life, where that insured life is significantly older than issue ages as indicated above. For example, a 75-year-old who has acquired a life insurance policy in his or her 30s, should always offer ownership of the policy to at least a family member, rather than simply letting the policy lapse. There is significant inherent value in a life insurance policy as the person insured becomes older.

Risk

The concept of Beta ("systemic" or "market") risk, common to portfolio assessments, is irrelevant with a mortality-based investment because mortality is uncorrelated to markets. Alpha risk (the value a fund manager adds or subtracts to/from fund return) is replaced by the probabilistics of mortality. However, a number of other specific risks come into play:

Failure to complete. It is perhaps obvious that a life insurance policy won't pay off if the premium commitment falls short. Beyond the grace period of one month, the insurer can declare the policy void, or ask for new evidence of insurability and, in any case, will restart the statutory period [5] without any savings in premium cost. No permanent insurance works as a pure mortality-based derivative unless its cost is fixed. Policies with guaranteed level cost of insurance fall into this category. Many policies have increasing or variable costs of insurance. These are fundamentally unstable. They are wolves in sheep's clothing. They can eat up the policyholder's money and then consume themselves. Unless a permanent policy has a guaranteed level cost structure, it is likely to fail the owner. Many programmes sold on the basis of "cash surrender build up" and "tax-sheltered investments accounts" have a rising insurance cost base; these programmes frequently fail to perform with the result being an unhappy consumer left with poor investment yields and the empty husk of an insurance policy that has become too costly because of increasing insurance costs.

Longevity. Means, medians, slopes and tails are interesting, but the actual investment return on a specific policy is determined by lifespan of one or more (JLTD) people. For example, a new policy on a 40-year-old non-smoker male will generate a probabilistic yield of 8.04 per cent and a static yield of 6.44 per cent to age 80 (median age of death). However, if the life insured lives to be 100 years old, the yield drops to 3.24 per cent (5.59 per cent pre-tax equivalent at a marginal tax rate of 42 per cent).

Inflation. A problem common to any financial instrument, the potential for a real rate of return is higher with a life insurance instrument over similar terms in part because its tax exempt status means the entire pre-tax yield accrues for the benefit of the entitled person.

Tax status. At this point in time, life insurance death benefits are tax exempt.[6] This is not expected to change, but the planning period is long and the appetite of government is nothing if not voracious.

---

5 Statutory provisions are so called because they are law, although most insurance contracts offer terms better than required by law. The provisions provide for suicide and fraudulent declarations. In these cases, the insurer has the right to cancel the contract within two years (statutory), usually reduced to one year by contract. Mis-statement relating to age, gender, and smoker status survive this "statutory period"; but are remediated by adjustment of the death benefit rather than outright cancellation.

6 Taxation of life insurance is not specifically covered in this chapter, but the tax implications of the transactions discussed here are assumed to be minimal. If an individual begins an

Counterparty is, in most cases, a significant risk, but in the case of life insurance, this risk is low because of regulation, and the industry protection arrangement called "Assuris".

In Canada there is one federal institution (the Office of the Superintendent of Financial Institutions ("OSFI")) that monitors solvency of federally licensed life insurance companies. OSFI provides continual monitoring of Lifecos on a risk management basis, to attempt to ensure solvency on the one hand and to deal with emerging problems, proactively, on the other. The OSFI website reports they have a four-stage program ranging from "early warning", "risk to financial viability or solvency", "future financial viability in serious doubt", through to "non-viable/insolvency imminent" stages. Regulator tools range from monitoring to seizing of temporary control and government-controlled wind-ups.

Apart from OSFI, there is "Assuris" (formerly CompCorp). This is an industry-sponsored, federally incorporated company that backstops benefits obligations of failed member companies (all non-fraternal life insurance companies licensed in Canada are required to become members). The present value of Assuris' assessment capacity exceeds $4.5 billion, which is more than 15 times the cost of any insolvency to date. Assuris operates its own funds, but the Assuris *modus operandi* is to arrange an orderly transfer of policyholder rights and obligations from insolvent insurance companies to those of solvent ones, and to write cheques for deficiencies, studies, and necessary agreements to cause an orderly transfer of rights and obligations to solvent companies. There are limits on coverage, but for practical purposes, not as it relates to pure death benefit coverage.

The 2007 Assuris Annual Report reports that three life insurance company insolvencies occurred during the 90s: Les Coopérants, Sovereign Life, and Confederation Life. All were resolved by a transfer of policyholder rights and obligations to solvent life insurance companies. When Les Coopérants went down (in 1992), there were individual insurance contracts with 222,000 policyholders and another 600,000 people covered by group insurance.

---

investment program through the acquisition of numerous life insurance policies, then, arguably, they have entered into an adventure in the nature of trade and there may be issues relating to the taxability of the death benefit. However, at this point in time, the CRA treats death benefits as tax free receipts, but imposes taxation potential as "other income" on the gain of the disposition of a life insurance policy by a Canadian resident owner. In any transaction involving the change in ownership of life insurance policy, issues relating to inclusions as "other income" should be reviewed with appropriate advisors.

Those interested in a complete look at taxation issues are referred to editors: Joel T. Cuperfain & Florence Marino, *Canadian Taxation of Life Insurance*, Tax and Estate Planning Group, Manulife Financial (Toronto: Thomson–Carswell, 2008), p. 585.

Assuris paid out $180 million in support, but no policyholder lost any benefit whatsoever. In the case of Sovereign Life (1993) there were 249,000 policyholders, 96 per cent of whom were 100 per cent covered by Assuris. Assuris developed the concept of proportional reinsurance and actually established a reinsurance subsidiary of its own, spending approximately $20 million to facilitate a rollover of rights and obligations to solvent insurers. The 96 per cent of policyholders that were fully covered received 100 per cent of their benefits, while the 4 per cent who were not, retained at least 90 per cent of benefits. In the case of Confederation Life (1994), 260,000 individuals and 1.5 million under group plans in Canada, obtained full recovery of all benefits at a final cost to Assuris of some $5 million. To quote from the Assuris Annual Report "by all measures, Assuris has had an enviable record protecting Canadian policyholders' benefits. Through the three insolvencies, Assuris coverage has protected almost three million people representing over 10% of Canadians".

More recently, AIG ran into serious trouble in 2008. On January 13, 2009, the Bank of Montreal announced that it was acquiring AIG Life of Canada for $375 million in cash, thereby resolving potential issues for some 400,000 policyholders (as well as 300 employees). These examples indicate that counterparty risk is well-managed in Canada, on a consistently proven basis.

Role in Portfolio

In his recent book *When Markets Collide*, author Mohamed El-Erian[7] indicates that a significant change in portfolio management is mandated to manage risk. He proposes that individual investment portfolios that used to be appropriately managed as 60 per cent equity and 40 per cent bonds might now be more appropriately 10 per cent in real assets and 18 to 50 per cent in alternative investments (that includes derivatives), with the balance allocated to stocks and bonds. It may be that given the unique risk averse characteristics, return potential, and tax efficiency of mortality-based derivatives, that an allocation to these instruments is an appropriate addition under the "alternatives" section recommended by one of the world's most celebrated investors.

Responsible financial and estate planning clearly involve considerations of life (and other) insurance products. Even the most grizzled anti-insurance proponent must acknowledge the need of young families for large amounts of term life insurance! Asset allocation strategies and portfolio management tactics ought to consider life insurance because:

---

7 M. El-Erian, *When Markets Collide* (New York: McGraw Hill, 2008), p. 298.

- In its stripped down form, the product is a cost-effective risk management tool. Managed risks can include:

  a) Premature death resulting in an incomplete asset accumulation program. This is easily mitigated by the use of term insurance.
  b) Excess exposure to market correlated products. Since life expectancy is not correlated to stocks, commodities, interest rates, or financial indices, it can be used to provide asset allocation balance.
  c) Portfolios can be immunized against encroachment, erosion, or other diminution on a competitive return basis through the use of permanent life insurance.
  d) The vicissitudes of market timing can be guarded against by a life insurance investment that provides liquidity regardless of market values, thus avoiding forced liquidations to fund expenses and taxes. For obvious but different reasons this is also true where other portfolio assets are illiquid.

- Viewed exclusively on a return basis, life insurance can be competitive with instruments already in many portfolios. For example:

  a) On a probabilistic return basis, it is competitive with many alternatives.
  b) It is one of only a very few products in which compounding (often shown in examples), actually works in practice. An interesting discussion is held in the article "Understanding Risk" by Shawn Brayman in the September, 2008 *CA Magazine*. In that article, Mr. Brayman suggests that about 91 per cent of portfolio yield is dictated by the choice of asset classes as opposed to yield on any given asset within the category. More importantly, the article suggests that clients do about 400 per cent better than the average investor if they just leave their money at work and eschew trading; a huge flow of money in and out of investments at non-optimal times results in significant portions of otherwise available return being lost by peripatetic investors. Life insurance doesn't permit such activity and, as a result, may lead to higher returns over longer periods for "erstwhile equity flippers".
  c) Its exempt tax status may make life insurance a better inflationary hedge than many other long-term instruments.

- Risks are manageable:

  a) Counterparty risk is so low that it can be dismissed from consideration in any circumstance other than Armageddon. In such a case, it is likely that other portfolio assets (perhaps excepting gold), would also have come a cropper.

b) If risk is defined as variability of return, then there is a greater chance of higher than average yield than there is of the reverse (in industry lingo, the right tail is fatter).

c) (Assuming premium continuance) there is no capital risk.

- MERs are non-existent, on a directly charged basis, on the basic policy, although issue and management costs are taken into account in pricing.
- Life insurance policies are illiquid until maturity, so care needs to be taken in establishing an ongoing commitment to the premium outlay.

Uses

Mortality-based derivatives can be used in any portfolio to facilitate a number of different investment strategies including;

- ensure investment strategy "completion" in the event of mortality;
- establish an inherent, low-cost principal protection strategy; and,
- long-, medium-, or short-term investment for yield.

There are numerous applications for life insurance, which I categorize as "the good", "the bad", and "the ugly".

"The good" involve a pure insurance "play". A basic death benefit is acquired for a minimum premium, and the arrangement is structured around the simplest arithmetic, made even more attractive by its tax exempt status. Within this context, a number of opportunities exist to utilize life insurance as a classic financial derivative for risk management, hedging, and speculative investing. Risk management could, for example, involve the purchase of term insurance to protect the income potential of an individual (consistent with references to "human capital"), or to complete an investment strategy, in both corporate and individual situations. Another risk mitigated by life insurance is liquidity risk, due to the nature of assets (*e.g.*, homes, art, real estate, shares of private companies). Related but different is market timing risk. Insurance obviates the need to sell other financial assets at inopportune points to fund essential cash flow requirements. Within the corporate environment, permanent mortality-based derivative product has been used to fund disclosed and undisclosed sinking funds to provide capital for shareholder buyouts, immunize against contingent liabilities such as environmental cleanup, and to provide for generational capital payouts by family-owned illiquid companies and as part of an effective capital recovery program in the case of tax loss sale circumstances. In one case, I utilized term insurance to protect a public company searching for new product because patent protection on existing products was drawing to an end, and loss of the intellectual capital of the research team needed to be guarded against. Permanent insurance is frequently used to help executives pay off loans to employees when stock purchase plans end up "underwater". The purchase (or assumption) of permanent insurance policies on one's own life or the lives of others (*e.g.*, parents, partners) represents an interesting response to classic investor needs ranging from pure risk management to pure speculation.

To this point, the discussion has been about insurance newly-issued on an insured. Yields are as demonstrated. The term on a mortality-based derivative investment can be significantly shortened and the yield increased through acquisition of an in-force life insurance policy. Obviously, the older the policy with lower fixed premium costs, the larger the potential for return, from that point in time. In fact, in the United States, an active market has emerged in which owners of life insurance policies can actually sell their policies to investors on a negotiated basis that brings together internal rate of return and expected mortality estimates. At this point, such a market does not exist in Canada.

Consideration should be given by parents to acquire life insurance on their own lives for acquisition by their children at a point in the future when the children are able to pay premiums. The effluxion of time renders the transaction unusually attractive for the children and many of the macabre discussions are eliminated if the parent is pro-active. In these situations, the policy serves as a defensive derivative in the hands of the parent and as a return-based investment for the children after they take it over.

Another application that I have shown is a version of the Principle Protected Note ("PPN") approach. In this case, Mr. or Mrs. "Big" can ensure intact estates to grandchildren regardless of profligacy, misfortune, or other vicissitudes which may be visited upon the Big children. In this arrangement, insurance on the lives of the children is acquired in insurance trusts, with funding guaranteed from the net worth of Mr. Big and, later, his or her estate. If all goes well, the grandchildren inherit significantly more than they might otherwise have done but if all does not go well with the second generation then the third generation does not become disenfranchised. This strategy makes sense for both the defensive and investment return characteristics of insurance.

"Bad" applications are those where the policy is utilized to accumulate cash in investments that could be accumulated outside of the life insurance policy on a more competitive basis; that is to say that the insurance policy is functioning as more than a mortality-based derivative. The minute a life insurance policy is utilized to accumulate cash resources that could be otherwise managed, MERs, liquidity, beta risk, and even tax efficiency issues means "life insurance" needs to be assessed by parts . . . the basic chassis as a mortality-based derivative, and the rest as something else that ought to compete with traditional savings/investment alternatives. "Life insurance" is in quotes because, any element of a life insurance policy beyond the pure mortality "play" is a mixed-use and requires severance of its elements for separate analysis of each component. The problem that prudent investment managers have with life insurance tends to begin and end with the latter. In preparing to write this chapter, I requested a number of sample insurance contracts from a variety of insurance companies. In general, I found that a straightforward term life insurance policy requires 14 pages. By contrast, the "king of the hill" Universal Life policy can contain as many as 45 pages. What is my point? The basic life insurance mortality risk management tool is straightforward. All of the extra "stuff" is not about life insurance; it is about money management and classic investment choices and fees relating to extra money in the policy. If a policy permits policyholder money, otherwise for his or her account, to accumulate on any basis inside the life insurance policy then, to that extent, the policy is a traditional investment vehicle and should be assessed as such.

"Ugly" involves structures involving linkage to complex structures utilized for tax and related reasons, or for purely tax-driven incentives. For example, reputable members of the life insurance industry are marketing a strategy called the "10-8". This involves locking in a "tax effective" spread inside the life insurance policy and creating tax deductibility resources to fund it outside the policy. The recent *Lipson* case aside, significant debate has risen within the industry regarding both actual and tax effectiveness of the "10-8".[8] Triple-back annuities are another structure where aggressive tax planning has driven complex structures that may be non-optimal and risky from a tax point of view. The most common of the "ugly" set is, in my mind, what has been marketed as the "leveraged retirement plan". In this case, a taxpayer is sold a plan where he or she maximum funds a Universal Life policy, with the intention to borrow against cash surrender value in the policy during their twilight years, with that loan accumulating interest on a compound basis, all to be repaid at death. These plans may not survive critical analysis when fees, liquidity, reasonable expectations of returns on cash

---

[8] In 2009, the Supreme Court of Canada issued a split decision that has created uncertainty for financial planners and tax advisors: *Lipson v. Canada*, 2009 SCC 1, [2009] 1 S.C.R. 3.

surrender value, potential tax exposures, reliance on banks to do lending in the future, and susceptibility to program collapse are taken into account. In another "ugly", some people have availed themselves of life insurance policies written by nominee Lifecos in off-shore jurisdictions, with the sole intent being self-management of investment funds inside a life insurance policy to obtain tax cover.

Role of Advisors

Portfolio management is designed around required returns limited by acceptable risk. However, a portfolio management plan should not be undertaken in isolation from an analysis of the total client financial and estate planning. Those deal with retirement, estate planning, charitable, and other financial and non-financial issues. Both term and whole life insurance product can provide elements of the retirement and succession plan which alternative investments considered for a portfolio cannot do, on the basis of competitive return, acceptable risk, and using inherent leverage (premium). Moreover, within the portfolio itself, there are specific investment goals much more amenable to life insurance product. Return plays can involve insurance on the client (efficient sinking funds) or on others (for risk amelioration or for return).

In addition to thinking of its inclusion in portfolios, life insurance demands advisors' periodic and event-driven review for several reasons as highlighted below.

Contractual exposures need to be watched. Solid planning and appropriate review of policies in advance should mitigate any significant contractual risk, and the following need to be looked at:

- Beneficiary designation. Life insurance policies carry "default" or "fall back" provisos to cover a number of unique situations. It is possible to have unintended results where the wrong estate becomes the beneficiary, or a contingent beneficiary is either overlooked or inappropriately paid because of invocation of the "default" designation. Attention should therefore be paid to the beneficiary designation declaration at the time the policy is issued and, subsequently, upon review.
- Inappropriate results upon the death of the owner of the life insurance policy can also result because of "default" provisos. It is important in estate and business planning to denote clearly through agreement and/or Will the transfer of ownership of a life insurance policy because it is an asset and, with time, becomes an increasingly important one.

- The incontestability clause provisions in life insurance policies tend to lapse after one or two years (the later is the law). What frequently is not known is that the incontestability period can reopen if a policy lapses and then is reinstated. That means that, upon reinstatement, an insured person and the validity of the policy may be governed by the invocation of a new incontestability period.
- Also dealing with the incontestability period, fraudulent declarations, and incorrect age declarations can survive the incontestability period. Many people may be reluctant to make maximum disclosure at the time of purchase of a life insurance policy. That is absolutely the time to make complete, plain, and true disclosure in the most absolute sense.
- Corporate-owned life insurance can become a significant asset of the business and when it is either sold or, more interestingly, when one shareholder buys out the other, the issue comes up of how to "split" the policy. Obtaining an appropriate and fair result in this circumstance can require significant negotiation with the underwriting company, but it has been done.
- Often, ownership, beneficiary, and premium payment arrangements violate prudent tax, insolvency, and family law planning.
- Each policy must be reviewed to ensure it has a guaranteed premium cost structure.
- Excess cash surrender can build up in the policy itself and/or paid-up additions. I have "found" a great deal of money for a large number of clients by cashing in paid-up additions because the ratio of cash surrender value to death benefit may be so high that it makes more sense to take the cash out.

Conclusion

While life insurance is not a panacea, it is an important tool for financial planners and an essential element for consideration in any investment portfolio. It has attributes that permit portfolio managers significant new scope for optimizing portfolio performance, eliminating or reducing risk, altering the market correlation dependence in the portfolio, reducing MERs, and eliminating significant risks. Inclusion in periodic review of mortality-based derivative products is an important part of the portfolio manager's responsibility because relevance, cash flow optimization, and concurrence with contractual terms are all essential elements that require periodic review.

Tax Strategies for the Owner Manager

John Doma

Introduction – Current Realities

In this chapter, I set out tax strategies that an owner of a Small-to-Medium Enterprise (SME) should consider during these current, difficult economic times. I do suggest, however, that, before applying any of the strategies contained in this chapter, a discussion occur with your business/tax adviser as to what approach would better address your particular enterprise.

This past year, many small- and medium-sized enterprises have been severely impacted by the economic downturn. This is particularly true due to the rapidity of the deterioration as Canada's Gross Domestic Product (GDP) went from a positive reading for 10 consecutive years to a negative reading in 2008 of 5.4 in the fourth quarter. Unemployment rates increased from 5.8 per cent in January 2007 to 8.7 per cent in July 2009.[1] Most of the increase was incurred in the first quarter of 2009.

Over the past decade, companies have been accustomed to what appeared to be unlimited growth of their business. In addition, the banking industry approved what appeared to be an unlimited supply of credit at low borrowing rates. Interest rates, on January 1, 2001 were 5.75 per cent since April 1 in 2009 to April 2010 but the bank rate has declined to .5 per cent.[2] Financial institutions further reduced the rates to below bank prime rate in order to compete for SME business. This resulted in businesses expanding in anticipation of continued growth. Consumers also had access to financing, which allowed for unrepentant demand for product and services. However, the

[1] Online: www.tradingeconomics.com.

[2] Online: www.bankofcanada.ca.

end came very abruptly and with a swift vengeance as access to credit decreased, unemployment rates increased, and the GDP sustained negative growth.

The past expansion, which was financed with the expectation of continued growth, ended with the reduction in business and consumer activity. However, the commitments on cash flow required to repay the debt continues and the cash demands on the SME have further burdened the working capital deficiencies. If the government stimulus program does not result in a sustainable economic recovery, many SMEs will undoubtedly run out of working capital that will result in their demise. Many economists believe a recovery from this down turn will be a slow and prolonged process. Small- and medium-sized businesses do not have access to the public markets nor do they generally maintain a significant amount of cash. Bank economists forecast that SMEs will find it difficult financing sustained losses during a prolonged economic downturn.

SMEs will play an integral part in the economic recovery and therefore will require the implementation of the outlined recommendations to ensure their survival (CFIB SME are the engine drivers). SMEs generally do not have available funds to employ professional staff and are less inclined to consult with external advisers, especially during these difficult times.

Recommended Strategies

As SME businesses work to streamline their expenses on an operational basis, there are tax strategies that should be considered to improve cash flow and also ensure their survival until the economic recovery allows the owners to once again enjoy their profits and the returns on their invested capital.

The following list of strategies should be considered when advising clients during these difficult times. It is important to note that this list is not comprehensive but merely suggestions to begin dialogues with SME owners:

- shareholder remuneration;
- shareholder loans;
- refundable dividend tax on hand (RDTOH);
- others:
  - capital dividends
  - general rate income pool (GRIP)
  - RRSP
  - vehicle

Shareholder Remuneration

Generally speaking, most SME owners have the ability to determine the type of compensation that they receive, namely wages versus dividends. Wages require that the employer withhold Canada Pension Plan (CPP) (2010 employer and employee limit is $2,163) and income tax contributions that are then remitted to the Canada Revenue Agency (CRA) on a monthly basis. Owners who have shareholdings in excess of 40 per cent are exempt from employment insurance withholding requirements. Dividends, on the other hand, are not subject to CPP and income tax withholdings for Canadian residents. Restrictions may at times be imposed by bank covenants and shareholder agreements in regards to management compensation. The SME owner should consider converting their remuneration from a wage to a dividend as there will be an immediate reduction of source deduction payments for the company.

The benefit to the SME will be twofold:

- The company will improve cash flow with an immediate reduction of the required withholdings to CRA.
- The profitability will improve by reducing the wage expense and statutory benefit payments to CRA.

With dividend payments, personal income taxes owing on the dividends would not be due until the following year on April 30th. Instalments for the ensuing year would not be due until September 15th and December 15th, should the owner decide to continue with dividend payments as compensation. The additional benefit of paying a dividend to the owner would be to take advantage of the corporate taxes paid in the past, thereby resulting in lower overall personal taxes in the current year. This is further enhanced if the dividends are eligible dividends explained below under the heading of Dividends under GRIP. The reduced personal income tax payments will also improve cash flow since the owner manager will be able to reduce the cash drawn from the business due to lower personal taxes on dividend income, as illustrated below.

Remuneration of $100,000 at the top tax rate:

Personal Income Tax (2009)

Wages	$ 46,400	46,400
Non-eligible dividends	31,340	
Eligible dividends		23,060
Personal Tax Savings	15,060	23,340

The savings illustrated are short-term in nature and are not to be considered a comprehensive evaluation of the overall after-tax cash retained, as all funds are extracted from the corporation either through wages or dividends. The integration analysis of dividends versus wages must also be performed provincially. For example, for Ontario corporate taxpayers with taxation years ending in 2009, the imposition of the Ontario surtax can result in an overall tax cost associated with the dividend strategy. However, this tax cost is deferred until funds are extracted from the company.

As previously mentioned, the SME owner should review the bank covenants since most bank agreements have included in their term sheets that dividends are not allowed without the permission of the bank. In order to maintain a strong relationship with the bank, the owner manager should review their bank loan covenants and should discuss and obtain written permission on this form of compensation from lenders. I have found bankers to be amenable to the change in compensation with an explanation. Thus, prior approval is recommended. A breach of covenants may result in the bank requesting immediate payment of the loan, which would not be a desirable result of altering the compensation arrangement.

One of the drawbacks to receiving all compensation in the form of a dividend is that it will not give rise to earned income for the calculation of available room for Registered Retirement Savings Plans (RRSP) in the future. Also of lesser concern, the SME owner would not be earning pensionable income allowing for the contribution to the CPP. Therefore, the SME owner could consider taking a hybrid form of compensation to maximize registered retirement savings plan contributions by paying themselves a wage for 2010 of $124,722 thereby allowing for the $22,450 (18% of $124,722) in maximum contributions in the following year (2011). Based on the new limits allowed with the current budget, the owner should actually pay the following:

	Earned Income Previous year	**Maximum RRSP contribution**
2010	122,223	22,000
2011	124,722	22,450

Compensation in the form of wages for the above amounts will allow the owner to maintain the maximum RRSP contribution limits in the future and, of lesser importance, contribute towards their own CPP.

A further benefit of the reduced wages will be a decrease in the amount paid for Ontario Employer Health Tax (EHT). EHT is applicable on Ontario remuneration in excess of $400,000. Employers must pay EHT in the amount of 1.95 per cent of any Ontario remuneration in excess of this threshold.

Shareholder Loans

Historically, SME owners have, under the guidance of their tax advisers, reinvested their management bonuses back into the company in order to reduce corporate tax to the small business limit. This practice of reinvesting the bonuses was due to the company requiring the after-tax funds to finance working capital requirements. If the company incurs losses, the SME owner should consider compensating themselves by repaying the tax paid loans rather than paying a wage to themselves.

If the SME owner does not have shareholder advances invested in the business and allowing for the shareholder to receive personal cash flow without the requirement to pay source deductions, the *Income Tax Act* ("the Act") allows the owner to take financial advances from the corporation subject to repayment within one year. A review of ss. 15(1) and 15(2) of the Act is necessary prior to withdrawing funds from the corporation. However, we can use these rules to our advantage during these difficult times by not having to pay source deduction remittances on wages or personal income tax instalments on dividend income.

The downside to this approach is that CRA requires the owner to assess him/herself a deemed interest benefit. Given the low prescribed interest rates as provided by CRA, this is an inexpensive method to help improve personal and corporate cash flow even though the owner will incur a cost personally for the deemed interest benefit.

Prescribed rates in the past two quarters were:

January to March 2010:	1%
April to June 2010:	1%

The personal income tax effect is significantly lower if one utilizes this strategy since no tax will be due on April 30th in the following year in comparison to a dividend payment. This can provide further short-term cash savings for the company and shareholder if straddled over a calendar year-end. However, the owner will be required to pay back the loan or be subject to ss. 15(1) income inclusion IT432 R2 without the corporation receiving a deduction for the payment, therefore, careful attention should be given to repaying the loan within the following year-end. From a practical point of view, the owner could prepare a resolution before the year-end declaring all draws to date be declared a dividend. A more conservative approach would be to have the owner pay a dividend evidenced with a cheque from the company and redeposit back to the company. This is a one-time consideration and should not be considered year after year. This type of deferral is short-term; it can assist in improving the cash flow and provide the owner with personal cash flow with minimal tax implications.

Refundable Dividend Tax on Hand ("RDTOH")

Keeping in mind my previous discussion along the line of the type of compensation the SME owner should consider, a dividend may give rise to a dividend refund through the refundable dividend tax on hand account, also known as the RDTOH, to the company. The tax adviser should review the corporate tax returns of the various entities to determine if a RDTOH amount exists and trigger the refund with dividend payments generating a refund from the government.

Generally speaking, refundable taxes are generated under Part I, II, and IV of the Act:

- Part I refundable tax generally applies to Canadian Controlled Private Companies (CCPC) which represent approximately 26.66 per cent tax paid on investment income.
- The following dividends are subject to Part IV tax:

  Taxable dividends received from a taxable Canadian corporation which are not connected company or taxable dividends received from a taxable Canadian corporation to the extent that the payer corporation received a dividend refund as a result of payment of the dividend.

A refund is generated based on taxable dividends paid (not payable). Therefore, ensure you have paid the dividend prior to the companys' year-end. This discussion is similar to the one above given that the owner should consider the source of the dividends when compensation by means of a dividend is the strategy followed. A proper review can be structured to generate the refund of the RDTOH that had been built up over the years in an investment company account. SME that set up holding/investment companies in the prior years, investing surplus funds taxed at lower corporate rates, which were planned to be taken out during retirement years, may be looked at sooner due to the current difficult times. The refunds generated in the paying corporation could be used to replace the cash paid to the shareholder. Choosing to take your compensation from the holding/investment company in the form of a dividend could let you have your cake and eat it!

Other Considerations

Capital Dividend Account ("CDA")

A corporation's CDA represents one of the few opportunities for the SME owner manager to extract cash from a private corporation tax-free. Very briefly, the corporation's CDA represent the non-taxable portion of a capital gain and of cumulative eligible expenditures at the inclusion rate prevailing in the year they occurred. In addition, there are certain amounts of life insurance proceeds the company receives as a policy's beneficiary. Amounts can be paid from a corporation's CDA to shareholders tax-free. The CDA is optimized when paid to shareholders in the highest marginal tax rate. The appropriate tax election must be filed along with director's resolutions at the time the CDA is paid. Although most tax preparers are diligent at paying out non-taxable capital dividends, one should review previously filed corporate income tax returns to ensure the accuracy of the CDA. Furthermore, if there is any doubt as to the accuracy of the CDA, consideration can be given to preparing and sending CRA a draft CDA calculation and they will confirm the company's CDA based on data in their records. A capital dividend benefits the owner's personal tax position providing tax-free funds requiring less cash from the corporation.

General Rate Income Pool ("GRIP")

Although not as favorable as the CDA, the GRIP represents another tax-effective method for SME owners to extract cash from their corporation in the form of a dividend. In Ontario, the top marginal tax rate applicable to "regular dividends" is approximately 31 per cent. Dividends paid from a company's GRIP (known as "eligible dividends") received by an individual taxpayer in Ontario attracts a top marginal tax rate of approximately 23 per cent. At an overview level, a company's GRIP represents its income that has been taxed at the general corporate tax rate (*i.e.*, income that has not taken advantage of the small business deduction) and eligible dividends the CCPC has received from other companies' GRIP. The actual GRIP calculation is complicated and should involve a tax professional. If the corporation wants to pay dividends subject to the general tax rates, it must designate the dividend as such by notifying CRA in writing at that time. Payment of excessive dividends over and above GRIP are subject to onerous tax penalties. If the corporation pays "other" dividends, no designation is required.

Once GRIP has been calculated, eligible dividends can be a valuable tool in funding the dividend remuneration strategy previously discussed. Finally, eligible dividends need to be designated as such to maintain their favorable tax treatment.

Registered Retirement Savings Plan (RRSP) Contributions

Many SME owners consider RRSP contributions an important part of their overall personal financial planning. They diversify their investments by making investments aside from their business. If you decide to take the strategy of taking remuneration in the form of a dividend, it would not make sense to contribute for the current year when the tax rate is low due to the dividend tax credit. If, however, you receive a portion of your compensation with wage then you should have the company pay for the contribution directly. This is a wonderful (and I believe not well-known) strategy that many do not take advantage of: allowing the company to make contributions on behalf of the employee without deductions subject to payroll withholdings. This strategy allows the owner to use corporate funds before tax to contribute to the RRSP. Many individuals like to generate personal tax refunds; however, these are difficult times and we should stop worrying about the interest-free loans we have provided the government in the past. The earned income required to maximize the RRSP contributions are as follows:

	Earned income Previous year	**RRSP contribution limit**
2009	$116,667	$21,000
2010	122,223	22,000
2011	124,722	22,450

Simply having the corporation pay the RRSP on behalf of the owner once again allows for reduced amount of cash taken from the company .

Vehicle Expenses

SME owners can become preoccupied with seeking professional advice regarding a better way of dealing with vehicle expenses than the options provided by CRA. The tax guidelines for company-owned vehicles are complex and discourage most owner managers from purchasing their vehicle through the company. Generally speaking, the rules restrict the deduction of the capital cost of the vehicle as well as the amount of interest a company may deduct. If the vehicle is leased, the lease payments are also restricted. However, the taxable benefit calculation is based on the original cost of the vehicle. The onerous task of maintaining a mileage log has, with the last Budget, been simplified, effective for years subsequent to 2008. The logs may be maintained for a single month and could be extrapolated for the balance of the year. Even with the complex rules set out by CRA, here are a couple of planning techniques a SME owner should consider:

- finance the vehicle through working capital thereby not being restricted to the monthly maximum of $300;
- consider a longer term lease reducing the monthly payments and thereby not being affected by the monthly maximum of $800 plus taxes;
- reduce the availability of the vehicle (somewhat unrealistic as it would require you to leave the vehicle on company premises thereby reducing the standby charge);
- visit supplier, customers, and spheres of influence on the way home or to business which decreases the kilometres driven for personal purposes.

The taxable benefits are based on the original cost of the car regardless of age or depreciated value yet the company is restricted on the CCA base taken on the vehicle at rates that have not changed since 2001 ($30,000 plus GST and PST). In these times of expense containment, the owner of a SME may consider buying the used company vehicle from the company and charge back the company based on the prescribed mileage rate that has not changed since the reduction in gas prices from the highs in 2008 of $1.20 per litre. 52 cents/kilometre for the first 5,000 km and 46 cents/kilometre thereafter would place some non-taxable income in the hands of the owner. A 325 BMW three years old with less than 100,000 km goes for less than $30,000. Based on 30,000 kilometres a year of business driving, an owner would receive $14,100. The company could also claim a GST refund of approx $670. The cost of operating the vehicle based on 29.6 cents/litre would be less than 52 cents/km, based on putting over 30,000 business kilometres on a car.[3]

Conclusion

Based on the outline above, I believe SMEs can improve both corporate and personal cash flow by taking into account the above tax strategies. In particular, consideration to take dividend income as compensation by the SME owner will result in immediate and significant cash flow savings. A review of the various tax accounts such as the RDTOH and CDA should be confirmed with CRA.

---

[3] The above figures can be found online at www.cra.gc.ca.

Forgiveness of Debt in Financially Troubled Companies

Claudio R. Saverino & Mustafa Nazarali

During times of economic prosperity, corporations rarely have to address forgiveness of debt. This was likely the case over the past decade, since the global economy was strong and credit was readily available. However, the current downturn in the global economy has brought this topic of debt forgiveness back to the forefront. When financial conditions are tight, companies focus on cash flow. Companies that are financially unstable will search for alternatives to improve cash flow while they attempt to meet debt obligations. Some struggling companies may attempt to restructure their debt obligations; others may try to have their debts forgiven. This chapter highlights the debt restructuring options that are available to companies that are financially unsound. In particular, this chapter focuses on the debt forgiveness rules that are available to any corporation under the Canadian income tax system. When any company undergoes debt restructuring, it must be cognizant that different restructuring alternatives could give rise to different tax implications. Accordingly, this chapter includes a discussion on the tax implications that arise from the debt forgiveness. Finally, this chapter considers some tax planning opportunities available while working within the debt forgiveness rules.

Corporate Borrowing and the Recession

All shareholders have a vision of running a highly successful and profitable company. Corporate spending is usually limited when a corporation is first created, since the company will attempt to keep costs low in order to boost the bottom line. However, as a company becomes profitable, this initial focus on cost management may be disregarded. This is particularly true during periods of economic prosperity. When the economy is strong, companies either have excess cash or can easily obtain funding from lenders. In these good times, companies are more willing to borrow. Accordingly, a corporation may take on substantial debts, believing that it will be able to generate corporate profits to repay these obligations. Some companies are successful in paying back these loans; however, many run into financial difficulty. The reality is that as a company becomes highly leveraged, it is more likely to be financially troubled at some point. Moreover, if an economic recession occurs, any company that is highly leveraged will be hugely impacted by the credit crunch, since the market is tightened and credit in is not as easily available.

Any corporation that hopes to be successful should analyze and project the appropriate amount of debt that it will undertake. A company's amount of debt should be decided upon based on the company's overall business risk. Moreover, it is imperative that a corporation constantly manage the risks associated with these debts. Companies should regularly consider strategies that could be implemented if profitability begins to sour. It is always easier to remedy problems before a company becomes financially troubled; therefore, these alternative strategies should be contemplated before signs of financial hardship appear.

The Alternative to Debt Restructuring

Should a company fail to implement these strategies for managing business risk, the corporation may begin to show signs of financial weakness. Some signs which may indicate that a company is at risk of financial troubles include: 1) a company struggling with cash flow, 2) a corporation having difficulty satisfying existing debt obligations, 3) a company not recording profits over a number of years, or 4) a company being highly leveraged. Once a company is considered financially troubled, it brings into question its ability to remain a going concern. This has a negative impact on all aspects of a company and its goodwill. Nonetheless, a financially troubled company can be seen as an opportunity for the eager and savvy purchaser. Often, these companies will have attractive assets or valuable business models except that they carry burdensome debt. An interested purchaser may view this as an opportunity for expansion, joining of synergies, or utilization of losses that are otherwise trapped in the company.

Once the company is no longer a going concern, the individuals managing that company may only have a few options available. They can either sell the business through a sale of shares or sale of assets, or they can attempt to restructure the company's debt. Should the company choose to restructure its debt, it would likely attempt to obtain more favorable terms with its creditors. For example, the company may seek an extension in the timing of scheduled repayments; alternatively, the corporation may want a reduction in its interest rates. A restructuring of this kind will typically result in the replacement of an old debt by a new debt. The new debt will reflect the more "debtor-friendly" terms. Alternatively, during the restructuring process a corporation may request that some or all of the debt be forgiven.

The Tax Implications of Debt Restructuring

While the commercial benefits of debt restructuring are attractive, debt restructuring does have tax implications. Most importantly, debt restructuring may seriously jeopardize the corporation's ability to access its losses.[1] As a result, it is necessary to carefully analyze the debt restructuring rules in the Canadian *Income Tax Act* ("the Act") in order to avoid any unexpected tax obligations.

The debt forgiveness rules were first introduced into the Canadian income tax system in the early 1970s, when s. 80 of the Act was passed. The basic assumption underlying these rules is that when a debt is cancelled the debtor has gained an economic advantage. This cancellation of liabilities increases a person's net assets; therefore, the cancelled debt should be acknowledged in the taxation process. When this section was first drafted, it only consisted of one provision that required taxpayers to reduce their tax attributes by the cancelled amount of a debt obligation. The section was subsequently expanded to four subsections in the mid-1980s. Additionally, in the 1994 federal Budget, substantial changes were made to this section.

The debt forgiveness rules apply where a commercial debt obligation has been settled or extinguished for an amount that is less than the principal amount. A commercial debt obligation is defined as: a debt obligation issued by the debtor in respect of which interest was deductible or would have been deductible if interest had been paid or payable on the debt by the debtor pursuant to a legal obligation. In other words, a commercial debt obligation is a debt which has been acquired to earn income from a business or property (as interest on this debt would normally be deductible pursuant to para. 20(1)(c) of the Act). Based on this definition, most debts incurred by corporations are commercial debt obligations, including interest-free obligations where interest would have been deductible. It should be noted that interest payable by a debtor is a separate obligation issued by the debtor. However, the interest payable is only a separate obligation to the extent that

---

1 Courage, "Utilization of Tax Losses and Debt Restructuring", 2006 Conference Report, Canadian Tax Foundation.

the interest is deductible in computing the debtor's income for a taxation year. This rule would not apply to compound interest, since compound interest is only deductible once it is paid.

If a debt is a commercial debt obligation, it must be determined when the commercial debt obligation has been forgiven. In the Canadian income tax system, debt is only forgiven at the time that it is settled or extinguished. Since there is no definition in the Act as to when a debt is actually settled or extinguished, the Canada Revenue Agency ("CRA") has stated in Interpretation Bulletin IT-293R that a debt is settled or extinguished when, "all liability for payment is terminated. Payment, cancellation, set-off, substitution of debtors and releases are examples of some possible means of settlement."

The definition of a forgiven amount in s. 80 of the Act does not include certain debts in the application of the debt-forgiveness rules. The definition excludes: (1) an amount that was already included in the debtor's income as an employee or shareholder benefit or business income; (2) an amount such as government assistance that reduced the debtor's undeducted expenses or the cost of the debtor's property; (3) capital gains resulting from the application of ss. 39(3) in respect of an open market purchase of certain debt obligations that the debtor previously issued; and (4) any portion of the principal amount of the obligation that was included in the debtor's proceeds of disposition under the foreclosure rules in s. 79 of the Act. The forgiven amount also excludes the principal amount of a debt obligation issued by a debtor who is bankrupt.[2]

When it has been determined that the debt forgiveness rules apply, s. 80 of the Act requires the debtor to reduce reported tax attributes in accordance with the amount that has been forgiven. Where there are insufficient tax attributes available, one-half of the excess forgiven amount is included in income. The forgiven amount must be applied to reduce the debtor's tax attributes in accordance with ss. 80(3)-(5) and (7)-(12) of the Act. The forgiven amount must also be included in income under ss. 80(13) of the Act.

In general terms, the order in reducing the debtor's tax attributes is as follows:

1) unapplied non-capital losses of preceding years, excluding allowable business investment losses (ABILs), starting with the oldest losses;

2) farm losses of preceding years (oldest first);

---

[2] Baek, "Tax Planning For Recessionary Times", 2003 Tax Conference.

3) restricted farm losses of preceding years (oldest first);

4) ABILs of preceding years (oldest first);

5) net capital losses;

6) capital cost of depreciable property and undepreciated capital cost of depreciable property of a prescribed class;

7) cumulative eligible capital, and resource pools;

8) adjusted cost base of non-depreciable property, excluding shares and debt of corporations of which the debtor is a specified shareholder (generally a 10 per cent shareholder, counting in related person's shares);

9) adjusted cost base of shares and debt of corporations of which the debtor is a specified shareholder at the time that the debt is settled;

10) adjusted cost base of shares and debt of corporations related to the debtor at the time the debt is settled;

11) current year net capital losses, including those arising on wind-up of a 90 per cent-owned subsidiary;

The rules for applying the forgiven amount to the above tax attributes are complex. The forgiven amount *must* be applied first to the loss carryovers, outlined in items 1 to 5 above. It is then at the discretion of the corporation whether the forgiven amount should be applied to items 6 to 8. If the forgiven amount is applied to items 6 to 8, the application of the forgiven amount between items 6 and 7 can be done in any order; however, the maximum of the forgiven amount must be applied for all items in 6 and 7 before the remaining balance of the forgiven amount can be applied to 8. The forgiven amount must be applied to items 6 to 8 before any application to items 9 and 10 can be made. The forgiven amount may be applied to item 11 as long as the debtor has designated the maximum amounts for items 6 to 8, and the maximum amounts have been applied to items 9 and 10, if applicable. As can be seen, the ordering is complex and therefore any tax planning made with respect to debt forgiveness should include consultation with a professional.

As stated earlier, if the debtor chooses not utilize all of these reductions or where a forgiven amount remains after all possible reductions have been made, 50 per cent of the remaining unapplied portion of the forgiven amount is included in the debtor's income. For some debtors, some relief from the 50 per cent income inclusion under ss. 80(13) of the Act is available. Individuals, corporations and insolvent corporations can claim a reserve under ss. 61.2, 61.3, and 61.4 of the Act. These reserves allow an individual to spread out the required income inclusion over a number of years if the individual's yearly income exceeds $40,000. It also allows a corporation to spread out the income inclusion over a maximum of five years. Where a corporation is insolvent, these sections limit the corporation's income inclusion from the debt forgiveness rules to twice the corporation's net assets.

Obligations Which May be Caught by the Debt Forgiveness Rules

Despite the attempt by finance to clearly outline the ordering of the tax consequences when a forgiveness of debt occurs, the application of the debt forgiveness rules is still challenging. Perhaps even more difficult is recognizing when an amount is caught by the debt forgiveness rules. Many situations where these rules apply may be overlooked by the untrained professional. It is therefore necessary to examine some examples of obligations which may be caught by the debt forgiveness rules.

The debt forgiveness rules will apply when the debtor is considered to have "parked" an obligation. Section 80.01 of the Act outlines the debt-parking rules. Basically, the debt-parking rules may apply where a commercial debt obligation is transferred to an arm's length party for a cost that is less than 80 per cent of the principal amount of the obligation. If, following the transfer, the new holder of the obligation does not deal at arm's length with the debtor, then the debt will be considered "parked" for the purposes of s. 80.01. The forgiven amount under these rules is equal to the difference between the specified cost and principal amount of the obligation. In other words, the discount of more than 20 per cent on the debt will become a forgiven amount. The debtor will be required to apply it in the manner outlined against the reduction of various tax attributes previously noted. There is some relief available for taxpayers who ultimately pay off the forgiven or parked debt, in whole or in part, since they will be entitled to deduct from income a portion of that payment in the year in which it is made.

In past recessions, different forms of financing instruments were created to assist companies in financial difficulty. One such instrument was distress preferred shares. A company in financial difficulty could issue preferred shares to existing creditors of its debt obligations as a replacement for those obligations. The creditor would receive dividends rather than interest – these dividends, in turn, would receive favorable tax treatment for the creditor. However, with the changes to the Act in 1994, where distress preferred shares are issued in substitution for a company's debt obligation, that obligation is deemed to have been settled for the lesser of its principal amount and the increase in the paid-up capital of shares of that class attributable to the issuance of the distress preferred shares. Any difference between the principal amount and the deemed settlement amount is treated as forgiveness of debt.

As noted earlier, under ss. 80.01(3) of the Act, the debt forgiveness rules may also apply to a corporate amalgamation. Similarly, ss. 80.01(4) applies the debt forgiveness rules to the winding-up of a corporation. Both of these subsections deem an obligation of the debtor to be settled for the creditor's cost amount of the obligation. However, in a winding-up, both the debtor and the creditor must elect to settle the obligation for the creditor's cost amount. On the positive side, both situations generally do not give rise to a forgiven amount since the debt is deemed to be settled for the creditor's cost. The exception to this is an amalgamation where the creditor's cost amount is less than the principal amount of the debt and this difference will give rise to a forgiven amount.

Most provincial legislation prohibits the enforcement of collection against a debtor after a certain period of time. When collection is prohibited, ss. 80.01(9) of the Act deems the debt to be settled for purposes of the debt forgiveness rules. As a result, the amount will be considered forgiven and subject to the debt forgiveness rules.

A common occurrence in debt restructuring is to issue new debt in consideration for old debt. When a debt-for-debt exchange occurs, para. 80(2)(h) of the Act deems that the amount paid in satisfaction of the old debt is to be the principal amount of the new debt. This deeming provision avoids the result of a forgiven amount. However, when a debt-for-share exchange occurs, and the fair market value of the shares issued does not equal the principal amount of the debt, the remainder may be considered a forgiven amount. If there is a concern that the fair market value of the shares issued to satisfy a debt obligation does not equal the principal amount of the obligation, the inclusion of a price adjustment clause in the share rights should be considered. Pursuant to para. 80(2)(g) of the Act, the CRA has confirmed that they will utilize such a clause when determining the fair market value of the shares.[3]

Alternatives Within the Debt Forgiveness Rules

Financially troubled companies may find it difficult to escape the debt forgiveness rules since most commercial debt obligations are caught within these provisions of the Act. It is therefore important to plan for the appli-

---

[3] J. Glass, "Section 80: An Update", 2002 B.C. Tax Conference.

cation of the debt forgiveness rules and find ways to work within this regime. The ability to claim a reserve under ss. 61.2, 61.3, or 61.4 of the Act may not suffice since this may only provide temporary relief. However, there are a number of ways that debt can be settled without full payment of the debt and without the creation of a forgiven amount.

Two techniques that are commonly used to avoid triggering a forgiven amount are: (1) the replacement of debt with new debt, and (2) the replacement of debt with shares. As mentioned earlier, when issuing new debt to replace old debt, the amount of the new debt must equal the principal amount of the old debt in order to avoid triggering a forgiven amount. The debtor is then provided with the opportunity to issue new debt with more favorable terms. Alternatively, if issuing shares to replace old debt, the debtor can avoid triggering a forgiven amount if the fair market value of the shares equals either the lesser of the issued amount of the debt or the principal amount. However, this could pose a problem where the debtor is a loss company.

As addressed earlier, a debtor may also use an amalgamation or winding-up as a method to avoid triggering a forgiven amount based on ss. 80.01(3) and (4) of the Act. These subsections are particularly useful in a related party situation where inter-corporate debt exists. For example, in a situation where the parent company has financed the losses of its subsidiary through debt, two steps can be taken to avoid triggering a forgiven amount. First, the parent can set up a new subsidiary which would acquire the debt for fair market value. Next, the new subsidiary can amalgamate with the debtor company. This amalgamation would result in a deemed settlement of the debt. This deemed settlement would not trigger in a forgiven amount.

In the situation where a debtor is facing the application of the debt parking rules, one possible way of getting out of these rules is to bifurcate the debt. The debt forgiveness rules would only apply to one of the debts. For example, a debtor is willing to pay $600,000 of a $1,000,000 debt obligation. Under the debt parking rules, this will result in a forgiven amount of $400,000. However, if we bifurcate the debt obligation into two separate obligations of $750,000 and $250,000, the $750,000 would not be subject to the debt forgiveness rules. The $750,000 would not be subject to the debt forgiveness rules since the obligation has not been sold for less than 80 per cent of the principal amount. Only the $250,000 debt obligation would be subject to the debt forgiveness rules resulting in forgiven amount of $250,000. The application of the general anti-avoidance rule ("GAAR"), however, must still be considered.[4]

---

4 L. Glass, "Section 80: An Update", 2002 BCC.

Where the application of the debt forgiveness rules will be inevitable, it may be advantageous to use s. 80.04 of the Act, since this section allows for tax planning within the debt forgiveness rules. Under this section, once the maximum forgiven amount has been applied to the tax attributes of the debtor through the eleven steps outlined earlier, the unapplied portion of the forgiven amount may be transferred to and applied against the tax attributes of eligible transferees. Any taxable Canadian corporation or eligible Canadian partnership related to the debtor is an "eligible transferee" of a debtor. The debtor and eligible transferee must file an election to transfer the unapplied portion of the forgiven amount. Furthermore, to obtain the most effective tax outcome using this section, it may be necessary to reorganize prior to the debt settlement. Depreciable property or capital property should be transferred out of the debtor company before the debt is settled to allow the forgiveness to be redirected to the eligible transferee. For example, if a corporation is going to undergo a debt forgiveness of $3,000,000 and its only assets are land worth $3,000,000, a building with an undepreciated capital cost of $3,000,000, and shares of a subsidiary with net capital losses of $3,000,000, the transfer of the land and building to a new subsidiary prior to the application of the debt forgiveness rules would yield the most advantageous outcome. After the reorganization, the corporation's only assets would be the shares of the two subsidiaries. The parent corporation must enter into agreement with the subsidiary that has the net capital losses to transfer the forgiven amount to that subsidiary. Should the corporations make this agreement, the result is that the net capital losses will be reduced while the cost of the land and building held by the other subsidiary are preserved. Therefore, the loss corporation's more valuable tax attributes are preserved.[5] Note there is anti-avoidance rule in ss. 80.04(8). This section applies to corporations that become related solely for the purpose of applying s. 80.04. In order to avoid being caught under the anti-avoidance rules, the subsidiary should be established and the transfer should take place well in advance of any forgiven amount. The potential application of GAAR by the CRA should also be considered when such reorganization is carried out.

Undergoing an amalgamation or winding-up prior to debt forgiveness may also be advantageous if the result of an amalgamation or winding-up is that the tax attributes are mixed in such a way that the more valuable tax attributes are preserved. For instance, a corporation may be about to undergo a forgiveness of debt and that corporation only has fast depreciating capital assets. A related corporation has non-capital losses that are about to expire. By amalgamating with a related corporation prior to undergoing the debt forgiveness, the corporation will be able to utilize the otherwise expiring

---

5 Tunney, "Update on Debt Forgiveness", at 9:13-14, 2003 OC.

non-capital losses and preserve the undepreciated capital cost of its fast depreciating capital assets.[6]

On the other hand, a corporation may be in a situation that may warrant the application of the debt forgiveness rules. For example, if a debtor has loss carryforward balances that would otherwise expire, the debtor should create a forgiven amount in order to apply it to the expiring loss carryforwards. The creditor would obviously have to agree with the restructuring.

Conclusion

Not understanding the debt forgiveness rules and when they may apply may result in unintended tax consequences to the debtor. For financially troubled companies, these unexpected tax consequences could contribute to their demise. However, those that are familiar with the rules may be able to plan around them. Alternatively, corporations familiar with the debt forgiveness regime could work within it. Working within the rules can provide planning opportunities as well as allow a financially troubled company to maintain the valuable tax attributes often needed for survival. At the very least, working within the debt forgiveness rules can minimize the company's tax burden. However, it cannot be overemphasized that professional advice is warranted, especially given the complexity of the debt forgiveness provisions.

---

6 *Ibid.*

An Unforgivable Proposal: Insolvent Debtors Caught in the Complex Web of Debt Forgiveness Under the *Income Tax Act*

Craig Mills

"Without forgiveness, there's no future."

– Archbishop Desmond Tutu

Introduction

With the current economic climate, many Canadians are being forced to carefully examine their financial situation. Debts that may have been serviceable prior to the economic downturn are now a bigger burden than some can afford to carry. In some cases, many professionals may be considering what was once thought to be unthinkable - filing for bankruptcy as an exit strategy.

Current statistics compiled by the Office of the Superintendent of Bankruptcy Canada[1] show that bankruptcies are, not surprisingly, on the rise. According to the Superintendent in Bankruptcy, the total number of bankruptcies in Canada in the 12-month period ending December 31, 2009, increased by 25.9 per cent compared with the 12-month period ending

[1] The Office of the Superintendent of Bankruptcy ("Superintendent in Bankruptcy") is a special operating agency associated with Industry Canada. Its role is to protect the integrity of the bankruptcy and insolvency system in Canada. It licenses and regulates trustees in bankruptcy and sets and enforces professional standards for the administration of bankruptcy estates.

December 31, 2008.[2] Consumer bankruptcies alone increased by 28.4 per cent, with over 116,000 individuals filing for bankruptcy in all of 2009.[3]

However, as these statistics show, bankruptcy is not always the only option. More than 35,000 Canadians opted to file a consumer proposal under the *Bankruptcy and Insolvency Act*[4] in 2009, an increase of 40.3 per cent over 2008.[5] Proposals generally result in a greater return to creditors while allowing individuals to reduce their debt load and continue to function without destroying their credit and having to declare bankruptcy.

While the prospect of reducing debt through a process other than bankruptcy should be attractive to any overburdened professional, a proposal could create an unexpected tax liability. Under the debt forgiveness rules of the *Income Tax Act*,[6] commercial debts that are "forgiven" under a proposal will be attributed to the individual as income. By comparison, where the individual has filed for bankruptcy, there is no such income inclusion.

The purpose of this chapter is to examine the paradox created by the interplay between the *Bankruptcy and Insolvency Act* ("*BIA*") and the *Income Tax Act* ("*ITA*"). Although the structure of the *BIA* clearly demonstrates Parliament's clear preference for proposals, the debt forgiveness rules under the *ITA* appear to "reward" bankrupts and yet penalize individuals who make a proposal.

We begin with an overview of the proposal provisions in the *BIA* and the forgiveness of debt provisions in the *ITA*. We then examine the attempts that have been made through judicial intervention and legislative efforts to resolve, and sometimes circumvent, the unfair results of this unnecessary clash.

The *Bankruptcy and Insolvency Act* (Canada)

Bankruptcy legislation has been part of the Canadian economic landscape since 1869, starting with *An Act Respecting Insolvency*. However, it was the not until the *Bankruptcy Act*[7] was first enacted by Parliament in 1919 that

---

2 *Insolvency Statistics in Canada – December 2009*, Office of the Superintendent of Bankruptcy Canada. For more details, insolvency statistics in Canada are maintained by the Office of the Superintendent of Bankruptcy and can be located at www.ic.gc.ca.

3 *Ibid.*

4 R.S.C. 1985, c. B-3, as amended.

5 Above note 3.

6 R.S.C. 1985, c. 1 (5th Supp.), s. 80.

7 9-10 Geo. V, c. 36.

Canada had bankruptcy legislation that was uniformly applied across the nation.[8] The underlying philosophy of its current incarnation, the *BIA*, is the concept of a "fresh start" – allowing an honest, but unfortunate, debtor to discharge a crippling burden of debt and consequently resume his or her place as a productive member of the business community.[9] At the same time, its purpose is to ensure fair treatment for all creditors by appointing a trustee in bankruptcy to oversee the process of realization and distribution.

For individuals, the *BIA* contains two options to allow for the financial rehabilitation[10] of an insolvent person. The first is the process of filing for personal bankruptcy. Bankruptcy allows a debtor to stop creditor collection efforts and discharge most debts. It is intended to be a rehabilitative process that allows a debtor to start his or her financial life afresh. This is usually the path taken where there is no hope of restoring an insolvent person to financial viability without the vehicle of a bankruptcy.

By contrast, where restoration is possible, individuals may be able to take advantage of a second option under the *BIA*: filing a proposal. With a proposal, the debtor is able to restructure his or her debt by offering to pay creditors a percentage of what is owed to them over a specified period of time. It can be a powerful alternative to bankruptcy as it allows a debtor to solve his or her money problems without going bankrupt.

Both of these options are explored in more detail below.

Bankruptcy

The term "filing for bankruptcy" is familiar in modern parlance. The mechanics of filing for bankruptcy are relatively straightforward. An individual can either voluntarily make an assignment into bankruptcy[11] or be forced into bankruptcy by way of a creditor applying for a bankruptcy order against the individual.[12] This chapter focuses on the voluntary procedure.

---

8 Report of the Standing Senate Committee on Banking, Trade and Commerce, "Debtors and Creditors Sharing the Burden: A Review of the *Bankruptcy and Insolvency Act* and the *Companies' Creditors Arrangement Act*" (November 2003) at 1, online: Parliament of Canada http://www.parl.gc.ca/37/2/parlbus/commbus/senate/com-e/bank-e/rep-e/bankruptcy-e.pdf.

9 *Re Irwin* (1994), 24 C.B.R. (3d) 211, 112 D.L.R. (4th) 164 (B.C. C.A.) at para. 69; *Moody v. Ashton* (1997), 47 C.B.R. (3d) 91 (Sask. C.A.) at para. 5.

10 *Ramgotra (Trustee of) v. North American Life Assurance Co.*, [1996] 1 S.C.R. 325, 37 C.B.R. (3d) 141, (*sub nom. Royal Bank v. North American Life Assurance Co.*) 96 D.T.C. 6157, [1996] 1 C.T.C. 356 at para. 17.

11 *BIA*, ss. 49(1).

12 *Ibid.*, s. 43.

Under the voluntary route, the individual must demonstrate that he or she is insolvent in order to file for bankruptcy. In other words, the individual must establish that his or her liabilities to creditors total at least $1,000 and that he or she is unable to make payments to creditors. To initiate the process, an individual consults with a trustee in bankruptcy who assesses the debtor's assets, liabilities, income, and expenses. Assuming that insolvency can be established, the individual executes an assignment that is filed with the Official Receiver.[13] Upon the filing of the assignment, all of the debtor's assets and property automatically vest in the trustee in bankruptcy.[14] The trustee then embarks on the process of liquidating the bankrupt's assets and distributing the proceeds to creditors in accordance with the priority schemes contained in the *BIA*.

Where the individual has never previously been bankrupt, in most cases, he or she can expect to be automatically discharged nine months from the date of bankruptcy. Upon discharge, all of the individual's pre-existing debts are discharged,[15] giving the individual a clean financial slate to begin again.

The Impact of Filing for Bankruptcy

Although the effect of filing for bankruptcy is well-known, the impact of a bankruptcy filing is not always clear to the uninitiated. Not only does bankruptcy affect the debtor directly, but it also affects relatives and all who have business dealings with the now bankrupt individual. Even after the bankrupt has been discharged from bankruptcy, it has residual effects that last for many years.

For instance, the act of declaring bankruptcy will immediately reduce one's credit rating to the lowest possible rating score. In addition, a notation that the individual has filed for bankruptcy will remain on a credit report for approximately six to seven years, depending on the jurisdiction in which the debtor files for bankruptcy.[16] Every time the debtor seeks to obtain credit, this fact will come to the creditors' attention. As a result, it will be difficult during this period for an individual to obtain any sort of bank loan, mortgage, or credit card until he or she has been able to repair his or her credit

---

13 An official receiver is a court officer appointed for each bankruptcy district under ss. 12(2) of the *BIA*. The official receiver is required to report every bankruptcy in its division to the Superintendent in Bankruptcy.

14 *BIA*, s. 71.

15 *Ibid.*, ss. 178(2).

16 *Consumer Reporting Act*, R.S.O. 1990, c. C.33, s. 9(3); *Consumer Reporting Act*, R.S.N.S. 1989, c. 93, s. 10(3)(e); *Consumer Reporting Act*, R.S.P.E.I. 1988, c. C-20, s. 9(3)(e); *Consumer Reporting Agencies Act*, R.S.N.L. 1990, c. C-32, s. 20(1)(c).

rating. To begin this process, a discharged bankrupt may be forced to apply for a secured credit card – a credit card that has been secured by funds deposited by the individual with his or her financial institution.

Bankruptcy will also have an impact on the individual's business dealings. Where the individual is a director of a corporation, his or her bankruptcy will disqualify him or her from serving as a director.[17] A person appointed as a trustee under a trust agreement or a will may be replaced as a result of being declared bankrupt.[18] Further, until the debtor has been discharged, he or she is required to disclose the fact of his or her bankruptcy to anyone with whom he or she enters into a business transaction.[19]

Certain professionals may also risk losing a licence to practice as a result of a bankruptcy filing. For instance, lawyers and accountants in Ontario are required to notify their licensing bodies immediately upon becoming bankrupt under the *BIA*.[20] In some cases, lawyers who are undischarged from bankruptcy cannot operate a trust account.[21] Further, a bankruptcy may effect the individual's status as a partner at a law firm or accounting practice under the partnership agreement.

Real estate, mortgage, and insurance professionals are also required to disclose the fact of a bankruptcy in an application for registration in most provinces.[22] In some provinces, bankruptcy may lead to the loss of one's status as a registered lender,[23] or the forfeit of a surety bond posted by a mortgage dealer.[24] Similarly, securities dealers who become bankrupt can no longer practice.[25]

This chapter is not intended to be an exhaustive survey of the impact of bankruptcy on a professional designation. It is recommended that the debtor consult the applicable provincial legislation and regulations or speak to the appropriate governing body or association for further information.

---

17 *Canada Business Corporations Act*, R.S.C. 1985, c. C-44, s. 105(1)(d); *Business Corporations Act*, R.S.O. 1990, c. B.16, s. 118(1).

18 *Trustee Act*, R.S.O. 1990, c. T.23, s. 3(1).

19 *BIA*, para. 199(a).

20 See By-Law 8 made pursuant to the *Law Society Act*, R.S.O. 1990, c. L.8 and Bylaw 358 of the Bylaws of the Institute of Chartered Accountants of Ontario, respectively.

21 By-Law 9 made pursuant to the *Law Society Act*, R.S.O. 1990, c. L.8.

22 For instance, under the *Mortgage Brokerages, Lenders and Administrators Act, 2006*, S.O. 2006, c. 29, one of the circumstances to be considered in assessing whether an applicant is suitable for a mortgage broker or agent licence is bankruptcy.

23 *Cost of Credit Disclosure Act*, S.N.B. 2002, c. C-28.3, s. 13.

24 *Mortgage Dealers Act*, S.M. 1985-86, c. 16, C.C.S.M. c. M210, s. 38(2).

25 *Manis v. Manis* (2001), 55 O.R. (3d) 758, 29 C.B.R. (4th) 215 (C.A.).

Proposals

In light of the long-term impact that a bankruptcy filing may have, many high income earners and professionals are advised to consider making a proposal under the *BIA*. A proposal is a contract between a debtor and his or her creditors to repay all or part of the debtor's liabilities over a specified period of time. It is an alternate means by which an insolvent debtor can avoid bankruptcy and yet discharge outstanding liabilities in an organized fashion.

The rationale for making a proposal is that it benefits both the debtor, in terms of not having the stigma of bankruptcy, and creditors, in terms of receiving a better recovery than would have been available by an assignment into bankruptcy. In addition, a proposal can be completed in much less time than a bankruptcy, depending on its structure. In contrast, a discharge from bankruptcy can be delayed significantly where there is opposition from creditors, particularly where the debtor is a professional with a high income. A more detailed review of the benefits of a proposal is set out below.

Types of Proposals

Under ss. 50(1) of the *BIA*, a proposal may be made by an "insolvent person". To be insolvent, an individual must owe at least $1,000 in unsecured debt to his creditors and:

(a) be unable to meet his or her obligations as they generally become due,

(b) has ceased paying his or her current obligations and the ordinary course of business as they become due, or

(c) have property, the aggregate of which is not, on a fair evaluation, sufficient to enable payment of all obligations.

There are two types of proposals that can be made under the *BIA*. The first is known as a "consumer proposal" and the second is called a "commercial" proposal.

Consumer Proposal (Division II proposal)

In order to make a consumer proposal, the individual's debts cannot exceed $250,0000 (excluding a mortgage on the principal residence).[26] The process

---

[26] *BIA*, s. 66.11.

is initiated by the filing of a Notice of Intention to File a Proposal,[27] which provides a stay of proceedings of 30 days, protecting the individual from the enforcement of debts. Within 30 days (or as extended by court order), the debtor must file a proposal with the Official Receiver which is sent to all creditors for consideration.[28] The creditors then have 45 days to consider the proposal and to decide to accept or reject it.[29] The proposal is deemed to have been accepted after 45 days unless creditors having 25 per cent in value of the claims request a meeting of creditors.[30]

If deemed to have been accepted, the consumer proposal is deemed to be approved by the court 15 days later.[31] This forms a binding contract between the insolvent debtor and all of his or her creditors. If the proposal is rejected by the majority of creditors, the stay of proceedings is dissolved and creditors are then able to take steps to recover their debts against the debtor.

Commercial Proposal (Division I proposal)

A commercial proposal is similar in structure to a consumer proposal although there is no restriction on the amount of the indebtedness. The major difference between a commercial and a consumer proposal is that if a commercial proposal fails, the individual is automatically deemed to be bankrupt.[32] In contrast, there is no deemed bankruptcy upon the failure of a consumer proposal; however, creditors would then be free to continue collection efforts against the debtor.

Another difference is that for a commercial proposal to be accepted by creditors, a vote is taken at a meeting of creditors called within 21 days after the proposal is filed. If the majority of creditors in number and two-thirds in value accept the proposal, the proposal has been approved.[33] The trustee is then required to seek court approval of the proposal.[34] It is only after court approval is granted that the proposal becomes a binding contract upon all creditors.

---

27 *Ibid.*, ss. 50.4(1).
28 *Ibid.*, ss. 50.4(8) to (9).
29 *Ibid.*, ss. 66.17(1).
30 *Ibid.*, ss. 66.15(2) and 66.18(1).
31 *Ibid.*, ss. 66.22(2).
32 *Ibid.*, para. 57(a).
33 *Ibid.*, para. 54(2)(d).
34 *Ibid.*, para. 58(a).

The Benefits of Filing a Proposal

The benefits to an individual making a proposal are numerous. They include:

(a) an automatic stay of proceedings protects the debtor from creditor pursuit and provides the debtor with time to formulate a proposal;

(b) a proposal can be made to both unsecured *and* secured creditors;

(c) the debtor retains possession and control of his or her assets during the proposal process. This ensures that he or she has ongoing cash flow, maintains possession of his or her house or investments or retains control of leased equipment necessary to the debtor's business operations;

(d) a proposal provides a better credit rating than a bankruptcy;[35]

(e) if the proposal is accepted by the majority of creditors and receives court approval, it has the effect of a contract that binds all creditors, including those who may have opposed the proposal;

(f) if the proposal is approved, the debtor will then only be required to pay off a portion of his or her debts or be able to extend the time in which the debt has to be paid or some combination of the two;

(g) it generally affords creditors a greater dividend and/or a quicker dividend than they would receive in bankruptcy;

(h) in a bankruptcy, assets that are transferred or disposed of by the debtor for less than fair market value in the five years prior to bankruptcy can be challenged by the trustee in bankruptcy.[36] The proposal mechanism may be the more favorable route in order to shelter the assets from attack (although careful creditors will wish to have that issue investigated so that they can make an "apples to apples" comparison when deciding on the proposal versus a bankruptcy);

(i) upon the successful completion of the terms of the proposal, the debtor will receive a certificate of completion from the proposal

---

35 In Ontario, once a consumer files a consumer proposal, his or her credit rating becomes an R7, meaning that he or she is in a consumer proposal, consolidation order, or debt management plan. A consumer proposal remains on a credit report for three years after the proposal is completed.

36 *BIA*, ss. 91(2).

trustee which has the effect of a discharge order in bankruptcy;[37] and

(j) most importantly, provided the proposal is accepted by the majority of creditors and is approved by the court, the debtor never goes bankrupt.

By pursuing a proposal, the debtor inherently has more control over the end result and the timing of payment. This may be a key consideration where the individual wishes to protect certain transactions, such as a transfer of property to a spouse for nominal consideration, which could potentially be unwound by a trustee or creditors in a bankruptcy.

Another key consideration is *timing*. In a bankruptcy, although first time bankrupts are generally entitled to a discharge from bankruptcy within nine months, there may be factors which could lead to the imposition of conditions on the individual by the court or worse yet, a suspension of the discharge. For instance, an individual's prior bankruptcy may be a stumbling block to a speedy discharge or lead to particularly onerous conditions being imposed. By comparison, the individual has input as to the terms and the timing of the completion of the proposal. In addition, as bankruptcy is avoided altogether, the debtor can continue with his or her business dealings without the stigma of being declared a bankrupt.

In light of these benefits, where at all possible, a debtor should generally consider making a proposal to his or her creditors if his or her income exceeds living expenses. Alternatively, if the individual can borrow sufficient funds from relatives or friends willing to assist, a proposal may also be an option.

Clearly, when facing a mounting debt load, it makes sense in most cases for professionals to file a proposal under the *BIA*. However, this must be carefully considered, taking into account the totality of the debtor's financial arrangements.

Parliament's Preference for Proposals

Generally speaking, in light of the impact to the individual and the general public, bankruptcy should be a last resort for insolvent debtors. A strong economy is premised on a backbone of Canadians contributing to the col-

---

37 *Ibid.*, s. 65.3; *Flint v. Bernard* (1888), 22 Q.B.D. 90 (C.A.); L.W. Houlden & G.B. Morawetz, *Bankruptcy and Insolvency Law of Canada*, looseleaf, 3rd ed. (Toronto: Thomson Carswell, 1989) at E28.2.

lective effort through individual labors. Clearly, it is in the best interests of the Canadian government to foster an individual's productive contribution to society and the reduction of insolvencies.

Evidence of Parliament's preference for proposals is found throughout the *BIA*. For example, Parliament attempted to contain the steady increase in the number of consumer insolvencies by way of the 1992 amendments to the *BIA*.[38] Under these amendments, consumer proposals were introduced in order to give consumer debtors an alternative to bankruptcy.[39]

The 1997 amendments to the *BIA* also saw the introduction of the surplus income payment obligations in which bankrupt individuals with income in excess of their basic needs were required to make payments to their estates for the benefit of their creditors. It was thought that the threat of having to pay one's surplus income to a trustee while bankrupt would push individuals to consider making a proposal.[40] The goal of these provisions was to address public concerns that some debtors were taking advantage of bankruptcy too quickly and using it to rid themselves of debt when they could afford to pay at least some of those debts, either through consumer proposals or outside of bankruptcy altogether.

Other provisions designed with this goal in mind include the requirement imposed on trustees to consider whether the bankrupt could have made a viable proposal in reporting to the court as to their recommendations on a bankrupt's discharge hearing.[41] This is also one of the enumerated factors to be considered by a court in considering whether a bankrupt should be discharged: could the bankrupt have made a viable proposal and instead chose bankruptcy as a means to resolve the indebtedness?[42] If the court determines that the debtor could have made a proposal, the bankruptcy court will suspend the debtor's discharge for a fixed period of time or impose conditions on discharge.[43] In plain terms, the *BIA* provides that a person should try to make a proposal before he or she goes bankrupt.

---

38 *Re Bernier*, [2000] R.D.F.Q. 7 (Que. C.A.).

39 Industry Canada, Marketplace Framework Policy Branch, Policy Sector, *Report on the Operation and Administration of the Bankruptcy and Insolvency Act and the Companies' Creditors Arrangement Act*, (September 2002) at 15, online: Industry Canada http://www.ic.gc.ca/eic/site/cilp-pdci.nsf/vwapj/3040-Bankruptcies.pdf/$FILE/3040-Bankruptcies.pdf.

40 *Ibid.*

41 *BIA*, ss. 170.1(2).

42 *Ibid.*, para. 173(1)(n). See also *Re Drummie* (2002), 37 C.B.R. (4th) 241 (N.B. Q.B.); *Re Rosenfeld* (2002), 38 C.B.R. (4th) 73 (Ont. S.C.J.), affirmed (2004), 4 C.B.R. (5th) 70 (Ont. C.A.); *Re Morrison*, (2007), 34 C.B.R. (5th) 21 (B.C. S.C.).

43 *BIA*, ss. 172 to 173.

Based on the increased number of individuals filing a proposal as noted earlier, it appears that Parliament's efforts are having the desired effect.

Income Tax Act (Canada)

As previously indicated, despite all of the favorable aspects of a proposal under the *BIA* (and the fact that the *BIA* essentially mandates that a person should try to make a proposal before going bankrupt), restructuring one's debt by way of a proposal may have some unforeseen consequences. The reason for this is that the discharge or reduction of a debt for less than the principal amount through a proposal will cause a reduction in the debtor's various tax accounts or tax attributes, or worse, create an income inclusion under the debt forgiveness rules of the *ITA*. In other words, the very process of discharging a debt through a proposal may create a tax liability.

The debt forgiveness rules are outlined in s. 80 of the *ITA*. The current rules were introduced as part of the 1994 federal Budget following a period of economic downturn with a significant number of court-ordered restructurings.[44] They were designed to tax a debtor on the economic benefit gained as a result of the debts being compromised. The concern with debt forgiveness was that a debtor, having used borrowed money for activities which generate tax deductions, would have received something for nothing.[45] However, a necessary component to the debt forgiveness rules was fairness such that taxpayers were not burdened by crushing amounts of income tax activated due to debt forgiveness.[46] Unfortunately, the emphasis on fairness resulted in the sacrifice of simplicity. The result is an extremely complex and cumbersome set of rules.

Forgiveness of Debt Rules

The debt forgiveness rules contained in s. 80 of the *ITA* apply where a taxpayer has a "commercial debt obligation" and that debt is settled for an amount less than the principal amount owed. Where the commercial debt is forgiven, the amount of debt forgiven will be added to the individual's future income.

---

44 The Certified General Accountants Association of Canada, *Submission to the Advisory Panel on Canada's System of International Taxation* (July 11, 2008) at 5, online: Advisory Panel on Canada's System of International Taxationhttp://www.apcsit-gcrcfi.ca/05/sbrmms/12%20-%20Certified%20General%20Accountants%20Association%20of%20Canada. pdf.

45 S. Suarez, "Debt Forgiveness" *CMA – The Management Accounting Magazine* 69:6, (July-August 1995) 28(1).

46 Above note 44 at 5.

The debt forgiveness rules are activated when the following elements are present:

(a) there must be a "commercial obligation";

(b) there must be a debtor;

(c) the "commercial obligation" must be settled; and

(d) there must be a "forgiven amount"

Commercial Debt Obligation

A "commercial debt obligation" is a debt obligation in which the interest is or may have been deductible in computing income, taxable income, or "taxable income earned in Canada".[47] As an example, a debt incurred in order to earn income from a business or property is classified as a "commercial debt obligation". In contrast, the settlement of a consumer debt or the compromise of income tax obligations would not activate these rules.

Settlement

Although not defined in the *ITA*, "settlement" has generally been interpreted by the courts to mean a final resolution between a debtor and creditor in which the debtor's obligation is reduced or brought to an end. It must be a final and legally binding termination or reduction of the debtor's obligations.[48]

Forgiven Amount

Generally speaking, under ss. 80(1), the "forgiven amount" is the result of the difference between the principal amount of the obligation and the amount paid pursuant to a settlement in satisfaction of the principal amount of the obligation.

Treatment of the Forgiven Amount

Once the forgiven amount has been calculated, s. 80 provides a framework for determining the amount to be included in the individual's income. To

---

47 *ITA*, ss. 80(1).

48 *Carma Developers Ltd. v. The Queen*, [1996] 3 C.T.C. 2029, 96 D.T.C. 1798 (T.C.C.), appeal dismissed [1997] 2 C.T.C. 150, 96 D.T.C. 6569 (Fed. C.A.).

begin, the "forgiven amount" is reduced by applying it to the individual's tax attributes in the following order:

(a) the debtor's loss carryforwards relating to various types of unused losses from prior taxation years such as non-capital losses, farm losses, restricted farm losses, allowable business losses and net capital losses;[49]

(b) at the option of the debtor, the capital cost and undepreciated capital cost of depreciable property, cumulative eligible capital and/or resource expenditure pools; [50]

(c) the adjusted cost base of the debtor's capital properties;[51] and

(d) the debtor's current year net capital losses.[52]

Once the debtor has applied the forgiven amount to the categories of tax attributes set out above, if a balance still remains, then 50 per cent of the remaining unapplied balance is added to the taxpayer's income.[53]

Fortunately, depending on the debtor's annual income, he or she may then be eligible for relief from this "hardship" using a special reserve. Under s. 61.2 of the *ITA*, a taxpayer is able to defer the inclusion of the forgiven amount until the individual's annual income exceeds $40,000. At this point, the taxpayer would begin paying tax on the forgiven amount to a maximum of 20 per cent of annual income over $40,000. This, in effect, enables the debtor to defer the inclusion of the forgiven amount into his or her income over a five-year period.

As this is intended to be an overview of the debt forgiveness rules only, seeking out the advice of a tax professional is strongly recommended.

An Example

The following simple example will illustrate the impact of the application of the debt forgiveness rules. The rules are much more complicated than the following example and the debtor's specific circumstances should be considered.

---

49 *ITA*, ss. 80(3) and 80(4).

50 *Ibid.*, ss. 80(5)-80(8).

51 *Ibid.*, ss. 80(9)-80(11).

52 *Ibid.*, ss. 80(12).

53 *Ibid.*, ss. 80(13).

Consider the situation where Patrick owes $100,000 to a third party creditor. Patrick enters into discussions with the creditor and after some deft negotiations is able to convince the creditor to agree to accept a payment of $20,000 and the loan would be retired. Therefore, the "forgiven amount" in this case would be $80,000. This amount must then be applied to the tax attributes set out above.

After applying the forgiven amount to Patrick's tax attributes, the remaining balance of the forgiven amount is $60,000. Under ss. 80(13) of the *ITA*, 50 per cent of the balance, or $30,000, is added to Patrick's income as debt forgiveness income.

If Patrick's income is $40,000 or less, the debt forgiveness income would not be added to his income. However, if Patrick has an income of $100,000 in the following year, he would be entitled to take advantage of the reserve noted above. Using the reserve calculation, the following amount would need to be included into his taxable income:

> Debt Forgiveness Income - 20% x (Current Year Income - $40,000) = Reserve Amount
>
> $30,000 - 20% x ($100,000 - $40,000) = $18,000

Under this formula, Patrick's income for the year would be $118,000 (consisting of his annual income of $100,000 plus $18,000, being the difference between the debt forgiveness income and the eligible reserve).

Conclusion

With the threat of such an income inclusion, a debtor must tread carefully in his or her negotiations and seek appropriate advice before any compromise is reached. Depending on the individual's income levels in the years following the debt being forgiven, the resulting income inclusion can have drastic and significant effects upon the debtor's tax liability.

The Conflict – The Treatment of Bankruptcy Under the Debt Forgiveness Rules

Not every settlement or compromise of debt will lead to a higher tax liability. Where debts have been discharged or extinguished as a result of bankruptcy proceedings, the forgiveness of debt rules are not triggered.[54] In cases where a debtor is bankrupt, the definition for "forgiven amount" in ss. 80(1) pro-

---

54 *Ibid.*, ss. 80(1), para. (i) in variable B of the definition "forgiven amount".

vides that the "forgiven amount" is calculated as the difference between the principal amount of the debt obligation and the principal amount of the debt obligation. As this will lead to a nil result, there is no "forgiven amount" to be applied by the bankrupt debtor to reduce his or her tax accounts or the tax attributes or to include in income.

One would expect the same exemption to be applied to debtors making a proposal, particularly with Parliament's emphasis on this method of dealing with debt. However, this is not the case. The Canada Revenue Agency ("CRA") has taken the position that debts forgiven under a proposal made under the *BIA* are not afforded the treatment as would be the case in a bankruptcy. For instance, the CRA, in a Technical Interpretation dated April 30, 2004[55] responding to a query on the application of the debt forgiveness rules in s. 80 had the following to say:

> [A] person who is at law an insolvent person, but who does not have the legal status of a "bankrupt" ("A debtor whose estate is vested in a trustee for division amongst his creditors, pursuant to an order of the court adjudicating him bankrupt" ...) would not fall within the ambit of paragraph (i) in variable B of the definition "forgiven amount" in subsection 80(1) of the Act.[56]

This difference in treatment highlights the inequity faced by debtors making a proposal. Although proposal debtors have the benefit of many of the features of bankruptcy as outlined above, the debt forgiveness rules are structured to exempt only bankrupts from their application. Why would Parliament promote the making of a proposal in one federal statute and yet encourage bankruptcy under another? The conflict is extremely perplexing and inexplicable.

As a consequence, the tax liability arising from debt being forgiven by way of a proposal will likely outweigh any benefit gained as a result. Faced with these options, an insolvent professional will most likely opt for bankruptcy.

Treatment in the Case Law

Unfortunately, there have been no cases considering the issue of whether the use of the word "bankruptcy" in ss. 80(1) of the *ITA* can be expansively interpreted to include proposals. However, some guidance is provided by

---

55 Canada Revenue Agency, "Forgiveness of Debt; Bankruptcy," April 30, 2004, CRA Document No. 2004-00575531E5.

56 Similarly, the Canada Revenue Agency has noted that a debtor or a bankrupt making an approved proposal under Part III of the *Bankruptcy Act* would not come within the exclusion for bankrupts: Canada Revenue Agency, *Interpretation Bulletin* IT-293R, "Debtor's Gain on Settlement of Debt," July 16, 1979, para. 16.

cases that have considered other sections of the *ITA* which also use the phrase "bankrupt" or "bankruptcy".

For instance, in *Marchessault v. R.*,[57] the Federal Court of Appeal was asked to determine whether para. 128(2)(d) of the *ITA*, which provides that a current tax year is deemed to end on the day before the individual became bankrupt, also applied to circumstances in which a proposal has been filed under the *BIA*.

Not surprisingly, the Crown argued in *Marchessault* that this section should be strictly interpreted. Its position was that based on the wording of the provision, unless the debtor was bankrupt, he was not entitled to use his proposal to divide his tax year under para. 128(2)(d). The debtor countered with the argument that the very definition of bankruptcy in the *ITA* refers to the *BIA*.[58] Therefore, as s. 66 of the *BIA* states that all provisions of the Act apply to bankruptcies and proposals (to the extent they are applicable), he argued that he was entitled to the benefit of the deemed year end under ss. 128(2) under the *ITA*.

At trial, Marchessault's arguments prevailed. The Tax Court of Canada concluded that although ss. 128(2) of the *ITA* only used the word "bankruptcy", its provisions were also applicable to proposals. Although ss. 128(2) did not specifically refer to a proposal, the court concluded it should be interpreted as if it did so based on the provisions of the *BIA* and the general scheme of the *ITA*.

On appeal, the Federal Court of Appeal rejected this conclusion. Writing for the court, Trudel J.A. concluded that:

> Once again, the purposes of the BIA are praiseworthy, but it is not the courts' function to add to the wording of other statutes in order to carry them out, especially when Parliament has spoken clearly and unambiguously, as it has here...[59]
>
> Bankruptcy and a proposal are different vehicles which are available to an insolvent person. The choice of one or the other depends on several factors and also carries with it different consequences...[60]
>
> Parliament is aware of the differences in principles and policy existing between bankruptcy and proposals. It chose not to amend the Act in response *inter alia* to the request of the CAIRP.[61] Moreover, it dealt with proposals in other provi-

57 (2007), 291 D.L.R. (4th) 750 (F.C.A.) ("*Marchessault*").

58 *ITA*, R.S.C. 1985, c. 1 (5th Supp.), s. 2.

59 Above note 57 at para. 73.

60 *Ibid.* at para. 75.

61 The Canadian Association of Insolvency and Restructuring Professionals.

> sions of the Act (for example, 15.1(3)(d) and 15.2(3)(d) under "qualifying debt obligation"; 212(3)(a)(i) under "replacement obligations").[62]
>
> I conclude that Parliament incorporated in the Act only the definition of "bankrupt" found in section 2 of the BIA, not the scheme of law applicable to a person who makes an assignment or against whom a receiving order has been made.[63]

On the basis of this conclusion, it seems likely that, absent intervention by Parliament, a court would conclude that Parliament's intent in using the word "bankrupt" was deliberate and intentional and that the term "proposal" was excluded on purpose. This is consistent with the principles of statutory interpretation which state that when the statute is silent with respect to the thing in question, the legal presumption is that Parliament intended to exclude it.[64] As the *ITA* is said to be the most detailed, complex, and comprehensive statute in Canada, courts will be reluctant to modify the statute to address a perceived deficiency.[65]

Efforts to Address the Conflict

Bankruptcy legislation has been an ever-evolving creature. The *BIA* has been amended at various times, including major amendments in 1992, 1997, and 2005 (not in force).

As the 1997 amendments to the *BIA* provided for a five-year review period,[66] Parliament created a committee to report on the effects of these amendments and specifically review bankruptcy and insolvency legislation. In anticipation of this review, both Industry Canada and the Superintendent of Bankruptcy[67] (through the Personal Insolvency Task Force) prepared reports designed to assist the parliamentary committee on the operation and administration of the *BIA*. Interestingly, these reports contain some commentary on the interaction between bankruptcy legislation and the debt forgiveness rules.

---

62 Above note 57 at para. 79.

63 *Ibid.* at para. 80.

64 Based on the maxim of interpretation, *expressio unius est exclusio alterius*: to express one thing is to exclude another: R. Sullivan, *Sullivan on the Construction of Statutes*, 5th ed (Markham: LexisNexis Canada Inc., 2008) at p. 227.

65 *65302 British Columbia Ltd. v. The Queen*, [1999] 3 S.C.R. 804, [2000] 1 C.T.C. 57, 99 D.T.C. 5799 at para. 51 [S.C.R.].

66 *BIA*, s. 216.

67 The Office of the Superintendent of Bankruptcy is a special operating agency associated with Industry Canada. Its role is to protect the integrity of the bankruptcy and insolvency system in Canada. It licenses and regulates trustees in bankruptcy and sets and enforces professional standards for the administration of bankruptcy estates.

Report of the Personal Insolvency Task Force

The Final Report of the Personal Insolvency Task Force (the "Task Force")[68] was released on August 7, 2002 (the "PITF Report"). The purpose of the PITF Report was to allow the insolvency community to suggest ways of reforming the personal insolvency provisions of the *BIA*.

As indicated by the Task Force, the single most important event giving rise to its creation was the rapid escalation in the number of consumer bankruptcies.[69] As such, the PITF Report made several recommendations as to proposed reforms of the personal insolvency provisions of the *BIA* designed to address this.

In that regard, it specifically examined the disparate treatment of debt forgiveness in a bankruptcy context versus under a proposal. As the current structure of s. 80 of the *ITA* did not afford the same protection to individuals filing a proposal, the Task Force opined that more professionals and small business owners would likely opt for bankruptcy for the obvious advantage gained as a result. In the view of the Task Force, this is inconsistent with the underlying philosophy of the *BIA*. In its words "[l]ogic would dictate that the provisions of the *Income Tax Act* should not encourage bankruptcies over proposals".[70]

To rectify this imbalance, it recommended that the "debt forgiveness" provisions found in s. 80 of the *ITA* should not be applicable to individuals who file proposals under the *BIA*.

Industry Canada Report

Industry Canada also consulted with various stakeholders in preparing a report for Parliament's consideration.[71] Its purpose was simply to present issues and potential policy options to the parliamentary committee to be established under the legislation for deliberation and recommendations. Although Industry Canada's report summarized various issues of concern

---

68 The Personal Insolvency Task Force is an advisory group set up by the Office of the Superintendent of Bankruptcy in the fall of 2000. The membership of the Task Force consisted of a wide cross-section of judges, lawyers, bankruptcy trustees, and academics.

69 Personal Insolvency Task Force, *Final Report*, (August 2002) at 77, online: Industry Canada http://strategis.ic.gc.ca/eic/site/bsf-osb.nsf/vwapj/pitf.pdf/$FILE/pitf.pdf.

70 *Ibid*. at 47.

71 Industry Canada, Marketplace Framework Policy Branch, Policy Sector, *Report on the Operation and Administration of the Bankruptcy and Insolvency Act and the Companies' Creditors Arrangement Act*, (September 2002), online: Industry Canada http://www.ic.gc.ca/eic/site/cilp-pdci.nsf/vwapj/3040-Bankruptcies.pdf/$FILE/3040-Bankruptcies.pdf.

for the Committee, it did not contain any recommendations relating to the issues arising from the debt forgiveness rules. However, it did note that, "[i]n many cases it is preferable to avoid bankruptcies through the use of business reorganizations or consumer proposals."[72]

Report of the Standing Senate Committee on Banking, Trade and Commerce

Following the amendments to the *BIA* in 1997, Parliament established the Standing Senate Committee on Banking, Trade and Commerce to consider and review bankruptcy and insolvency law in Canada. In November 2003, the Standing Committee submitted a report outlining its review of various provisions in the *BIA*.[73]

At the outset, the Standing Committee stated that the prerequisites for a well-functioning insolvency system are: fairness, accessibility, predictability, responsibility, cooperation, efficiency, and effectiveness.[74] It emphasized that the system must not only be fair to debtors and creditors alike, but it must ensure that they act cooperatively.[75]

To that end, the Standing Committee considered the concerns expressed in the PITF Report that the debt forgiveness provisions of the *ITA* motivated business owners to file for bankruptcy rather than attempting a reorganization.[76] It noted similar frustrations voiced by the Canadian Bar Association[77] that the discrepancy had no apparent foundation in policy and that it prevented well-intentioned debtors from addressing their obligations through a proposal despite the clear policy goals of the *BIA*.[78]

The Standing Committee agreed with these perspectives, stating that the insolvency system should not be structured in a manner that gives debtors

---

72 *Ibid.* at 10.

73 Report of the Standing Senate Committee on Banking, Trade and Commerce, "Debtors and Creditors Sharing the Burden: A Review of the *Bankruptcy and Insolvency Act* and the *Companies' Creditors Arrangement Act*" (November 2003), online: Parliament of Canada http://www.parl.gc.ca/37/2/parlbus/commbus/senate/com-e/bank-e/rep-e/bankruptcy-e.pdf.

74 *Ibid.* at 5.

75 *Ibid.* at 7.

76 *Ibid.* at 71.

77 Canadian Bar Association, National Bankruptcy and Insolvency Law Section, *Submission on the Five-Year Review of the Bankruptcy and Insolvency Act and the Companies' Creditors Arrangement Act* (May 2003) at 26, online: Canadian Bar Association http://www.cba.org/CBA/sections%5FBI/pdf/review.pdf.

78 Above note 73 at 72.

an incentive to pursue a filing for bankruptcy rather than a consumer proposal. This incentive did not serve debtors well, given the social and economic costs of bankruptcy. Furthermore, it did not serve the interest of creditors in light of the fact that a creditor facing an individual bankruptcy is likely to recover much less than it would under a consumer proposal.[79]

On this basis, the Standing Committee made the following recommendation:

> The Bankruptcy and Insolvency Act be amended to provide that ... the Income Tax Act should be amended to ensure that the debt forgiveness provisions in Section 80 of the Act are not applicable to individuals who file proposals under the Bankruptcy and Insolvency Act.[80]

Legislative Changes Since the Reports

Although many of the recommendations of the Standing Committee in its report were adopted in Bill C-55, none of the proposed amendments responded to the Standing Committee's recommendations concerning debt forgiveness under the *ITA*.[81] Similarly, further amendments to the *BIA* proposed in 2007 under Bill C-52, the *Budget Implementation Act, 2007*,[82] and Bill C-12, *An Act to amend the Bankruptcy and Insolvency Act and the Companies' Creditors Arrangement Act, the Wage Earner Protection Program Act and chapter 47 of the Statutes of Canada, 2005*,[83] did not address the Standing Committee's recommendations.

Therefore, despite the hard work of many industry groups and the clear recommendation of the Standing Committee for the equal treatment for bankrupts and proposal debtors under the debt forgiveness rules of s. 80 of the *ITA*, Parliament has not taken any steps to address the current discrepancy.

---

79 *Ibid.*

80 Above note 73 at 73.

81 Although Bill C-55 was passed by both the House and the Senate in November 2005, thereby becoming *An Act to Establish the Wage Earner Protection Program Act, to amend the Bankruptcy and Insolvency Act and the Companies' Creditors Arrangement Act and to make consequential amendments to other Acts*, this legislation has not yet been proclaimed in force on the premise that the Senate would hold further hearings and make amendments.

82 *Budget Implementation Act, 2007*, S.C. 2007, c. 29.

83 *An Act to amend the Bankruptcy and Insolvency Act, the Companies' Creditors Arrangement Act, the Wage Earner Protection Program Act and chapter 47 of the Statutes of Canada, 2005*, S.C. 2007, c. 36. A similar bill was introduced in the previous session of Parliament. C-62 did not proceed past First Reading in the Senate.

Case Law

Despite the fact that there have been no legislative efforts made to resolve this statutory conflict, individuals have attempted to address it through other means. For instance, in *H.M.T.Q. v. Beach*,[84] an individual attempted to seek court approval for a proposal crafted to extinguish the application of the debt forgiveness provisions of the *ITA*.

In November 1998, Beach formulated a proposal to his creditors in which third parties agreed to pay $500,000 on his behalf for the benefit of his creditors. Beach's financial supporters also agreed to waive their debt claims against him (which amounted to approximately $3 million) in order to increase the funds available for his creditors. Under the terms of the proposal, the remaining creditors, including the CRA, were to receive approximately four cents on the dollar. By comparison, as Beach's liabilities amounted to more than $12 million and he had insignificant assets, his creditors would have received nothing in a bankruptcy.

The majority of Beach's creditors voted in favor of the proposal. The only creditor that voted against the proposal was the CRA, which was owed about 10.5 per cent of outstanding claims. The principal reason for the CRA's opposition was due to Beach's attempt to oust the application of the forgiveness of debt rules.

The impugned provision in the proposal was clause 7(b) which read as follows:

> 7. THAT it is a condition of this Proposal that the claims provable under this Proposal by Her Majesty the Queen in Right of Canada and in Right of any Province shall include all taxes, interest and penalties that are payable:[85]
>
> (a) in respect of income earned by the debtor to and including the date of filing of the Notice of Intention to Make this Proposal; and
>
> (b) in respect of debts forgiven as a result of acceptance and full performance of this Proposal regardless of the date of actual assessment or imposition of such taxes, interest and penalties...

Clearly, clause 7(b) was an attempt to extinguish all federal and provincial tax liabilities that would arise from Beach's debts being forgiven under the proposal. It was a work-around the harsh effects of s. 80 of the *ITA*. The CRA vigorously objected to this attempt to skirt around the impact of s. 80 on the basis that it was unlawful.

---

84 *R. v. Beach* (2001), 196 D.L.R. (4th) 512, 84 B.C.L.R. (3d) 254 (C.A.).

85 *Ibid.* at para. 9.

As the proposal had the support of the requisite majority of creditors, the proposal trustee applied for court approval of the proposal under para. 58(a) of the *BIA*. The Chambers Judge found the terms of the proposal to be reasonable. However, in coming to this conclusion, he declined to make any ruling on the efficacy of clause 7(b) of the proposal. In his view, until the CRA assessed Beach, the issue was not squarely before the court. On that basis, he declined to make any ruling regarding clause 7 of the Proposal and, instead, conditionally approved the proposal.

Despite the Chambers Judge's obvious attempt to forestall making a conclusive ruling, the CRA appealed the decision of the Chambers Judge on the basis that the terms of a proposal could not be left for later interpretation. Otherwise, the Minister of National Revenue would be bound by the clause. The Court of Appeal agreed with this position, holding that the Chambers Judge erred in leaving the question of the meaning and effect of clause 7(b) for subsequent proceedings. In its view, a court must consider the proposal's legal effect at the time of the approval hearing in order to decide if it is reasonable.

In examining the impugned clause, the Court of Appeal acknowledged that its obvious purpose was to exempt Beach from the provisions of s. 80 of the *ITA*. In considering whether a court could approve a bankruptcy proposal that attempted to do so, the Court of Appeal held that such a clause was illegal. As a result, clause 7(b) rendered the proposal illegal and therefore, not reasonable.

The Court of Appeal further held that as a matter of law, such a provision falls outside the powers of the Minister of National Revenue. As stated by Mr. Justice Low for the court:

> A completed proposal is a contract between the debtor and his creditors ... As a matter of law, the Minister of National Revenue lacks the power to contract out of his statutory duty to assess tax in accordance with the law: see *Cohen v. The Queen*, [1980] C.T.C. 318 (F.C.A.). It follows that the court cannot sanction a proposal that exempts the debtor from s. 80 and imposes that exemption on Revenue Canada. This is so whether or not Revenue Canada is a creditor involved in the proposal process under the *Bankruptcy and Insolvency Act*.[86]

By allowing the appeal, the Court of Appeal was effectively refusing to approve Beach's proposal. As the defeat of the proposal would automatically force Beach into bankruptcy under ss. 61(2) of the *BIA*, thereby depriving Beach's creditors of the proposal funds, the British Columbia Court of

---

86 *Ibid.* at para. 18.

Appeal referred the matter back to the Chambers Judge with the direction that the proposal could not be approved with clause 7(b) included.

Therefore, in *Beach*, the British Columbia Court of Appeal sent a clear message that a court could not approve a proposal under the *BIA* that purported to exempt a debtor from the operation of s. 80 of the *ITA*. Although a decision of the British Columbia Court of Appeal is only binding on the lower courts in British Columbia,[87] this appellate court decision will certainly have persuasive value for other courts in Canada and will mostly likely be followed.[88] Although there is no certainty that a court in another province will follow *Beach*, the fact that there have been no other reported cases with a fact pattern similar to *Beach* gives some indication of how bankruptcy professionals view the *Beach* decision.

Therefore, until Parliament clarifies the different treatment of debts forgiven in the context of a bankruptcy proceeding versus under a proposal under the *BIA*, the *Beach* decision stands for the proposition that courts cannot address this apparent imbalance by approving a proposal that attempted to do so.

Conclusion

When faced with an overwhelming debt load, the natural inclination for an individual is to negotiate a reduction in the amount owed with his or her creditors. This is a logical and reasonable path, particularly when done under the umbrella of the *BIA*. The fact that consumer proposals are more advantageous for both debtors and creditors is obvious. Not only is the debtor provided with a creative mechanism by which he or she can restructure debt, it also allows a superior recovery to creditors. The positive impact of making a successful proposal goes beyond a financial benefit; it addresses an individual's desire to continue to be a contributing member of Canadian society. It is for this reason that the grand design of the *BIA* is a structure that encourages the proposal route where possible.

The fact that this rehabilitative pathway also leads to an unexpected land mine in the form of the debt forgiveness rules under the *ITA* is a true

---

87 Under the common law doctrine of *stare decisis,* every court is bound to follow any case decided by a court above it in hierarchy.

88 The decisions of courts in one province are not binding on courts in other provinces. As stated by the Supreme Court of Canada in *Wolf v. R.*, [1975] 2 S.C.R. 107 at 109, a provincial appellate court is not obliged, as a matter of either law or practice, to follow a decision of the appellate court of another province unless it is persuaded that it should do so on its merits or for other independent reasons.

paradox. The exclusion reserved for bankrupts under these rules completely negates the policy objectives established by Parliament in the *BIA*. One statute mandates that a debtor pursue a proposal (and penalizes those who do not); while the other inextricably mandates that one file for bankruptcy. The result is a tangled web of contradictions in that a high income earning individual may be better off making an assignment into bankruptcy in order to avoid the income inclusion.

Why a bankrupt should have an enhanced protection in such circumstances is inexplicable. As aptly noted by the Canadian Bar Association, the discrepancy in the tax treatment of proposal debtor as opposed to a bankrupt has no foundation in policy.[89] While industry professionals have called upon Parliament to correct this imbalance as there appears to be no merit to the conflict created by these two federal statutes, it remains to be seen whether anything will be done.

This means that until Parliament implements any corrective measures, only bankrupts will be able to evade the debt forgiveness rules. Professionals and business owners faced with mounting commercial debt obligations are well-advised to seek the advice of legal and tax professionals before committing to debt forgiveness under a proposal. The sheer complexity of the forgiveness of debt rules necessitates a careful review with a tax professional. However, if the conclusion is that the individual will be left with a substantial income inclusion, no doubt most will be forced to file for bankruptcy rather than considering a proposal. Surely, this is to the detriment of the Canadian economy.

---

89 Canadian Bar Association, National Bankruptcy and Insolvency Law Section, *Submission on the Five-Year Review of the Bankruptcy and Insolvency Act and the Companies' Creditors Arrangement Act* (May 2003) at 26, online: Canadian Bar Association http://www.cba.org/CBA/sections%5FBI/pdf/review.pdf.

Loan Losses to Foreign Affiliates Previously Considered Capital Losses now Re-characterized as Deductible Expenses

Nick Sauro & Dominic C. Belley

Introduction

The Tax Court of Canada recently presided over a landmark case in which a Canadian parent company advanced money to a European subsidiary which eventually filed bankruptcy and ruled that the losses as a result of the non-repayment of the loans could be treated as non-capital losses for the Canadian parent company.

In *Valiant Cleaning Technology Inc. v. The Queen*,[1] deductibility resulted from the finding of the Honourable Diane Campbell that advances made by Valiant to its European subsidiary became deductible when they ceased to capitalize the subsidiary and became payments made to protect the Canadian income stream of Valiant by preserving its business reputation and future revenues. Valiant was allowed to re-characterize its losses that were originally filed as capital losses to become non-capital losses

The importance of the case resides in the fact that Justice Campbell looked beyond the form of how the advances where made, some by way of shares and the remainder by way of advances, to take into consideration the substance of what was occurring and the intention of the principals. After a certain point in time, the cash injections were no longer intended to capitalize the subsidiary's operations and became payments made to continue

[1] 2008 TCC 637, [2009] 1 C.T.C. 2454, 2008 D.T.C. 5112.

the operations of the European subsidiary so that existing contracts could be completed in order to preserve Valiant's business reputation and future orders from its North American customers for Valiant's operations located in Canada. The case takes into consideration the globalization of the Canadian marketplace by considering the fact that global customers do not look kindly on vendors that do not comply with their delivery commitments irrespective of whether the failure occurs in a European subsidiary or at the Canadian parent; in such a case, future business will be at risk.

Summary of Facts

Business Considerations

Valiant was in the business of designing and supplying industrial pressure washers to the automotive industry. As a Tier 1 equipment supplier to the automotive industry, it directly filled contracts for customers such as the Ford Motor Company as compared to the less profitable businesses of Tier 2 and Tier 3 suppliers, which only supplied the Tier 1 suppliers.

In the 1990s, the major automotive companies implemented globalization plans in order to both reduce the number of Tier 1 suppliers as well as to have global uniformity of equipment being produced. Tier 1 suppliers were thus required to have a global footprint by having locations not only in North America but also in Europe.

Some Tier 1 suppliers were unable or unwilling to meet these requirements. In contrast, Valiant was eager to maintain its Tier 1 status in order to keep Ford as a customer. Thus Valiant acquired companies in both Belgium and England in 1996 with an existing European customer base. The business in England was incorporated as Valiant Elan Systems Limited (UK) (Elan), a UK subsidiary of Valiant. This fulfilled Valiant's global footprint requirements to Ford in order to maintain its Tier 1 status.

In 1997 and 1998, Valiant made various cash advances to Elan which were made to initially capitalize the recently acquired UK subsidiary and never repaid (these losses would remain as capital losses for tax purposes). By 1999, Elan was in serious financial difficulty and clearly headed towards bankruptcy arising from its inability to complete its projects to its global customers. These projects needed to be completed to preserve Valiant's reputation within the automotive industry and, particularly, with Ford; otherwise it risked losing its Tier 1 status.

Tax Considerations

During the period from 1999 to 2001, Valiant made additional cash advances to enable Elan to complete the projects it had undertaken even though Valiant knew that these advances would do nothing more than delay Elan's impending bankruptcy which ultimately occurred in March 2001. These advances were used to buy materials and to pay for labor and overhead costs so that the projects would not be abandoned and were completed as scheduled. These later advances formed the subject matter of this tax case.

Valiant had originally claimed these losses as capital losses in its 2000 and 2002 income tax returns. During a 2004 tax audit, the recently hired Chief Financial Officer of Valiant decided that the advances made to Elan would be more appropriately classified as current expenses and, to that effect, submitted a request for a Determination of Losses to the Canada Revenue Agency ("CRA"). The CRA refused the request, confirming that the losses were capital in nature, consistent with Valiant's previously filed tax returns. Valiant objected to CRA's determination and eventually appealed before the Tax Court of Canada.

Analysis

Position of the Parties

At trial, Valiant argued that advances made between 1999 and 2001 should be characterized as being on account of income because the purpose of those advances was to protect Valiant's Canadian income stream in order to protect its Tier 1 status. Justice Campbell found as a fact, after hearing testimony from a parade of witnesses (more than 10), that the only motivation of continuing the advances after it was absolutely clear that they would never be recovered was to ensure that the foreign subsidiary would have the funding to complete the projects it had undertaken which were essential to preserving Valiant's reputation within the automotive industry and to maintain Valiant's Tier 1 status.

CRA's position, not surprisingly, was that form does matter in income tax law and that Valiant held interest bearing notes and shares in its foreign subsidiary which are capital in nature and thus the nature of those losses cannot be altered. Valiant's past treatment of the advances as capital outlays in both its accounting records and tax returns were also indicative of its capital intent. In addition, Valiant choose to establish a separate legal entity by creating Elan as a subsidiary when it could have set up a European branch operation thus enabling it to include the income/loss from that branch operation in its Canadian income.

Decision and Reasons

Valiant's initial treatment of the advances in its accounting records and tax returns as capital outlays was, to say the least, a "hurdle" that Valiant had to overcome. Justice Campbell noted that the Crown had to concede that financial statements and tax returns are not necessarily indicative of taxpayer intent. Justice Campbell was satisfied that the recently hired Chief Financial Officer's fresh review of the facts provided the necessary support for the re-characterization of the losses as non-capital. Finally, she quoted a passage from *Berman & Co. v. Minister of National Revenue*,[2] stating that the question in determining deductibility was "not how the transactions ... were recorded but what the true nature of the payments in question was and what purpose they served in the appellant's business."

Determining whether an expenditure will be as a result of capital or income is based on the facts both objective and subjective. Key to the subjective factor was Valiant's intent, clearly supported by evidence, in making the advances, with objective factors confirming that intent. For this purpose, Canadian courts have often relied on the statement of Lord Pearce in *B.P. Australia Ltd. v. Commissioner of Taxation of Australia*,[3] that the solution to the problem is not solved by any specific test but based on the whole set of facts, some of which may point in different directions.

In jurisprudence, there is a rebuttable presumption that payments made by a parent company to its subsidiary to help finance the subsidiary's operations are considered capital in nature. However, this presumption is subject to two exceptions. The first exception applies where the parent is not only in the business of loaning money but, as a result of the case of *Berman*, also to a situation where it can be established that a payment is made for the benefit of the income-producing process related to the taxpayer's own business. The second exception applies where the shares in the subsidiary are held by the taxpayer as trading assets. Justice Campbell correctly stated that for the amounts advanced to be characterized as current expenses, she would have to find that the advances, although filtered through the subsidiary, were in reality for the benefit of Valiant's business.

Justice Campbell also explained that deductibility does not mean that the advances must have resulted in a direct source of income for Valiant. The

2 [1961] C.T.C. 237, 61 D.T.C. 1150 (Can. Ex. Ct.).

3 [1966] A.C. 224, [1965] 3 All E.R. 209 (P.C.).

case of *Minister of National Revenue v. Algoma Central Railway*,[4] is an example of how indirect such an income source may be. In that case, the taxpayer, a railway operator, was able to deduct expenses for surveying mining possibilities on the basis that they might lead to increased business activity and therefore to increased revenue for the railway.

Justice Campbell concluded that the evidence established that Valiant fell within the first exception to the normal rule that advances to a subsidiary are presumptively on capital account. Despite Valiant's past treatment of the advances as capital outlays in both its accounting records and tax returns, and despite the fact that the advances were made to a separate and distinct legal entity in which Valiant held shares and notes, the advances made from 1999 onward were held to be on current account. From both a business and a practical perspective, the advances were made to ensure that the projects in progress were completed by Elan to protect Valiant's reputation, future revenue, and future as a Tier 1 supplier. The advances were not for the benefit of the financially bankrupt subsidiary but, rather, for the protection of future revenue for Valiant's Canadian business.

In reaching her conclusion, Justice Campbell considered the case of *Stewart & Morrison Ltd. v. Minister of National Revenue.*[5] In that case, the Supreme Court of Canada held that advances to a U.S. subsidiary that were found to provide working capital to enable the subsidiary to get started and to continue to operate were considered to be on account of capital. However, Elan, unlike the U.S. subsidiary in *Stewart*, was already established with its own customers and contracts, and the advances were to ensure that the projects would be completed so that the Valiant group's reputation was preserved and its revenue and Tier 1 status protected. Further, Elan had no hope of being successful when the advances were made, whereas in *Stewart* the advances were supplied to the U.S. subsidiary with exactly such an expectation.

Similarly, Justice Campbell considered the cases of *Cathelle Inc. v. The Queen*[6] and *Morflot Freightliners Ltd. v. The Queen*, in which the Tax Court of Canada and the Federal Court Trial Division, respectively, found the advances made to a subsidiary to provide it with working capital were capital expenditures, on the basis that those advances were made with the expectation that the relevant subsidiary would be profitable. In contrast, there was no expectation that Elan would be profitable or that the advances would even be repaid.

---

4 [1968] C.T.C. 161, 68 D.T.C. 5096 (S.C.C.).

5 [1974] S.C.R 477, [1972] C.T.C. 73, 72 D.T.C. 6049.

6 [2005] 3 C.T.C. 2436, 2005 D.T.C. 858 [*Cathelle*] and [1989] 1 C.T.C. 413, 89 D.T.C. 5182 [*Morflot*].

On the other hand, Justice Campbell found that there were striking factual similarities between the facts in the Valiant case and those in *Berman.* In the *Berman* case, the taxpayer made payments to the suppliers of its subsidiary for the purpose of protecting its own goodwill since the subsidiary had defaulted on its obligations to those suppliers. The Exchequer Court held that although the subsidiary remained a separate legal entity, the subsidiary was for all practical purposes operating as a branch of the taxpayer. The Court held that the payments were current expenses and deductible on the account of income. Justice Campbell attached no significance to the fact that the advances in *Berman* were made directly to the suppliers, whereas in Valiant's case the advances were made directly to the subsidiary Elan to complete its projects. The distinction was insignificant and the end result was the same in that the payments were made for the protection of the parent company's reputation and future revenue. The distinction that is notable was that the subsidiary in *Berman* was a Canadian company and that Valiant's subsidiary was foreign, thus allowing expenditures from the global marketplace to be deducted against domestic revenues.

Reference was also made to *The Queen v. F.H. Jones Tobacco Sales Co.*[7] In that case, the taxpayer, a tobacco seller, honored a guarantee that it had provided for a cigarette-manufacturing company on its purchase of shares of the taxpayer's financially troubled customer. The guarantee had been provided in exchange for the purchaser's undertaking to buy tobacco from the taxpayer. The Federal Court Trial Division held that the payment was on current account because the taxpayer made the payment for the purpose of gaining or producing income from its business. Justice Campbell observed that in *Jones Tobacco*, as in *Valiant*, the survival of the customer base was absolutely linked to the income stream of the taxpayer.

Finally, Justice Campbell noted that in her prior decision in *Excell Duct Cleaning Inc. v. The Queen*,[8] she had clarified that expenses incurred to protect existing goodwill and to increase profitability were for a purpose that was income in nature, whereas expenses incurred to increase goodwill were for a purpose that was capital in nature. Valiant's purpose in providing the advances was to protect its existing reputation, existing Tier 1 status and thus its future income stream.

---

7 [1973] C.T.C. 784, 73 D.T.C. 5577.

8 [2006] 1 C.T.C. 2432, 2006 D.T.C. 2040.

Conclusion

The reasons for judgment provide further support for the role of common sense and business reality in the determination of whether an expense is on income or capital account. Justice Campbell relied on common sense and commercial realities to conclude that there could be only one business purpose for which the advances were made to a subsidiary heading toward bankruptcy, and that was to ensure that the subsidiary's contracts were completed so that the parent company's existing reputation, existing Tier 1 status, and future economic viability were protected. Justice Campbell drew on the testimony of Valiant's CFO in that the contracts to be completed by Elan were with American clients of the Canadian operations. The non-performance of those contracts would therefore have a direct impact on Valiant's operations in Canada.

The advances from Valiant to Elan changed over time from advances on account of capital to expenditures made solely for the purpose of protecting Valiant's future revenue stream. Justice Campbell was careful to point out that the case was unique on its particular facts and that she was in no way suggesting that the decision be used to allow a window of opportunity for the deductibility of financing activities between a parent company and its subsidiary.

Given the globalization of the Canadian economy, this will become a landmark case in jurisprudence, redefining the previously held presumption that advances to a subsidiary would only be held on the account of capital. This case now provides the circumstances where it is appropriate to claim loan losses to a subsidiary as non-capital expenditures. Just as Valiant followed the automotive manufacturers into the global marketplace, CRA is now following its Canadian clients "the taxpayers" in those very same footsteps.

Conventional Valuation Methodologies in Unconventional Markets

James L. Horvath & Vince Conte[1]

Introduction

The valuation of a business, investment, or asset is a complex exercise involving the in-depth analysis of numerous qualitative and quantitative factors that is even more complex in volatile economic times. No matter how the markets are acting – whether good or bad, stable or volatile – valuations will always be required. During boom times, valuations are often required for mergers and acquisitions; during tough economic times, they are frequently required in restructurings. Financial reporting, corporate tax, transfer pricing, re-balancing of investment portfolios, strategic planning, raising capital, estate planning, employee stock ownership plans, damages, among others, always require valuation analysis. The global economic crisis in late 2008 and 2009, which is considered by many financial experts to be the worst crisis since the Great Depression, has created many unique valuation issues. For instance, both accounting regulatory boards and security regulators, such as the International Accounting Standards Board (IASB), the Canadian Accounting Standards Board (AcSB), the Financial Accounting Standards Board (FASB) and the U.S. Securities and Exchange Commission (SEC), have developed guidance relative to the fair value measurement of assets recently, some directly in connection with the current volatile market. For example, in April 2008, FASB issued three staff position documents related to fair value dealing with illiquid markets, interim disclosures, and impairment losses on securities. The IASB, in May 2009, pub-

[1] The authors would like to recognize the research, editing, and suggestions provided by their colleague Tim Dunham.

lished an exposure draft on fair value measurement in general to replace fair value discussed in all other standards similar to the FASB-issued FAS 157. Even as these new valuation issues arise or are often magnified, the basic principles of valuation remain the same. Our goal in this chapter is to describe fundamental aspects of the valuation process and to lay a theoretical foundation for other chapters in the book that are focused on specific valuation areas. The body of valuation knowledge, tools, and techniques continues to develop and expand, as does the number of information sources available for assistance in performing valuation analysis.

The valuation of companies in volatile times, especially in the early stages of a recession, can become increasingly difficult for numerous reasons:

- Information can be less reliable.
- Market views may become more divergent.
- Access to funding and normal leverage can be constrained.
- The market value of assets of private equity investment funds and pension plans can swing wildly due to the asset mix and current fair value accounting standards.
- Capital investments that previously might have been funded through internally generated cash flows may now seem more like liabilities than assets.
- Capital markets funding may be constrained or not available at all, resulting in cash becoming "king" due to scarcity.
- Investors require higher rates of return.
- Preparing and evaluating forecasts becomes difficult due to elevated levels of uncertainty.

Even good companies with strong underlying operations, potentially even with growing earnings, may see their market values decline as a result of a large number of competing alternative investments selling for distressed prices. The result is a trickle-down effect that means nearly all companies are affected, positively or negatively, by volatile markets. The graph below shows how quickly asset values can decline at the onset of a recession.

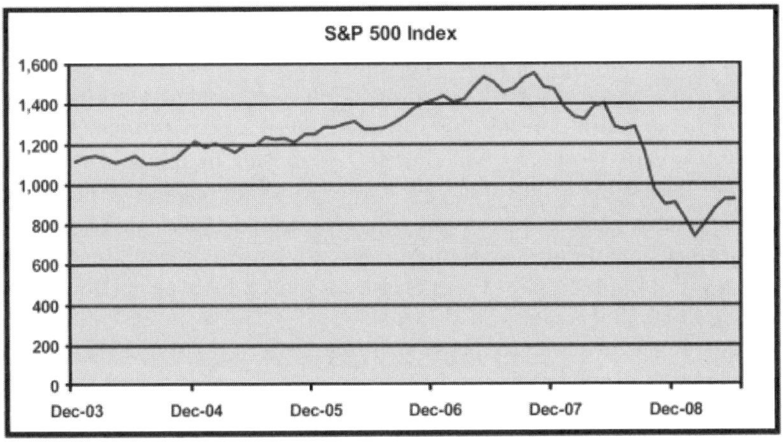

The drop in the S&P 500 from the peak in October 2007 to the trough in March 2009, approximated 50 per cent and the drop during just the last three months of 2008 was 22 per cent. More importantly, all of the gains accumulated in the five-year period since 2003 were reversed in 2008.

There are many valuation methodologies available to use in valuing an asset or business, but it is critical to select the appropriate method and understand how to use it to arrive at an accurate and useful conclusion. In volatile times, the basic methodologies do not change, but the inputs will. In terms of methodologies, however, it is possible that what previously might have been a clear primary valuation method may change or that alternative methods may be considered and/or weighed differently. For instance, a comparable public company multiple approach may be used as the primary valuation method for certain assets; however, given the volatile movements in the comparables' asset-to-share prices and/or illiquidity in certain markets, the application of such an approach may not yield fair market value. As a result, a discounted cash flow (DCF) methodology or another valuation approach would need to be used. In terms of inputs, these are likely to change as a result of increased uncertainty. Subjectivity will increase, but it is a challenge for the valuator to provide evidence that objectively supports the valuation method(s) chosen, its implementation, and its conclusions. The value derived from any valuation model is affected by both firm-specific details and broader industry and economic information. The value conclusion may only be relevant for a short period of time due to new and/or unexpected developments relating to the subject company and/or the industry.

Considering that a significant portion of the enterprise value (EV) of many corporations today relates to intangible assets (*e.g.*, patented products and services, trademarks, and customer relationships), it is important to understand their value and how the intangible assets are being valued. In particular, in a volatile market and economic downturn, the sustainability of the company's operations is affected by the "stickiness" of the customers with the company. Hence, a significant portion of the company's value may relate to the value of customer relationships and/or patented products or services. This chapter also contains two detailed examples of formats commonly applied to intangible asset valuations – the dual excess earnings method and the relief-from-royalty method. These methodologies provide the business valuator with considerable guidance in allocating value among various forms of business intangible assets via exercises such as fair value accounting and purchase price allocation.

Core Concepts

Valuation First Principles

When conducting a valuation, the valuator must consider several fundamental principles:

1. A valuation applies to a specific point in time. The valuator must consider information in existence only on or before the specific valuation date. The valuator cannot use hindsight to conduct a valuation. This does not mean that the valuator should ignore all subsequent events. Instead, the valuator should consider the event's proximity to the valuation date, any evidence of a material change in the nature or underlying fundamentals of the business, and whether the event could have been reasonably foreseen. Furthermore, although managers and investors can take long-term views in terms of running the business, creating a forecast, and choosing when to dispose of an investment, a valuation needs to look at value assuming the investment was sold at the valuation date, not the value of what the business could sell it for at some future, more "reasonable" time. We raise this point because a common refrain of some investors is "Who would we sell at these current very low prices, anyway?"

2. In determining the value of a business, one should assess the following:

    a. The present value of all future cash flows expected to be generated; and
    b. The fair market value of the net tangible assets of the enterprise.

The higher of these two values will generally represent the fair market value of the business.

When considering the present value of all future cash flows, it is important to consider how much of the resulting value is transferable from a commercial standpoint. Cash flows generated by the specific traits, contacts, and personality unique to the owner are generally considered to be non-transferable.

3. In determining the value of an intangible asset, one should assess the following:

    a. The present value of all future cash flows that the asset will generate; and
    b. The cost to reproduce or replace the asset with similar functionality.

    The lower of these two values will generally represent the fair market value of the intangible asset.

    If the cost to reproduce or replace the asset is higher than the associated present value of cash flows, a purchaser would reasonably expect to pay an amount equal to the present value of future cash flows. Paying more would mean that the price was higher than the expected benefits. If the cost to reproduce or replace the asset is lower than the associated present value of future cash flows, a purchaser would expect to pay an amount up to the replacement cost of the asset. Why pay a higher price if you could obtain the same benefit by simply reproducing or replacing the asset?

4. The present values mentioned earlier should be based on market rates of return at the valuation date.

5. In general, the higher the fair market value of a business's net tangible assets, the higher the overall value of the business and the lower the required rate of return, holding all other factors constant for the following reasons:

    a. Downside risk is relatively lower, since the sale of tangible assets would generate more of the assessed value on liquidation; and
    b. The business cash flows depend less on intangible assets, which typically require a higher rate of return to compensate for their higher risk.

6. Risk is reduced as the amount of market liquidity available to the investment or asset increases. When liquidity is limited or restricted, a liquidity discount may be appropriate.

7. There are special considerations when valuing individual interests in a business. Controlling interests may attract a higher value than minority interests because minority shareholders have less influence on operational and strategic decisions about the company.

Given these prevailing first principles, the following topics merit further consideration in the majority of valuation assignments.

Price versus Value

The discussion in this chapter revolves primarily around the fair market value of a business, investment, or asset. Often this will differ from price – the amount that prospective buyers and sellers will pay in the open market. Fair market value (as the standard of value) and price (a market-based concept of value and historic fact) may differ. In a perfect notional market, however, they would be equal. The valuator constructs a hypothetical notional market to establish the most likely transaction price without actually exposing the asset or business for sale.

Fair market value is the most widely used and widely discussed term related to value. It is defined as "the price, expressed in terms of cash equivalents, at which property would change hands between a hypothetical willing and able buyer and a hypothetical willing and able seller, acting at arm's length in an open and unrestricted market, when neither is under compulsion to buy or sell and when both have reasonable knowledge of the relevant facts. [NOTE: In Canada, the term 'price' should be replaced with the term 'highest price']."[2]

Any deviations in the open market from the attributes of this definition will lead to potential variances between the fair market value and the actual price. Common reasons for variances are shown in the table below, with some notes as to how these change during volatile times.

---

2 From the International Glossary of Business Valuation Terms (IGBVT), June 2001, https://www.cicbv.ca/?page=Glossary.

Variances between Fair Market Value and Price	
Reasons for Variances	**In volatile times . . .**
Differences in negotiating abilities of buyer and seller	Difference may widen due to forced sales, need, or lack of liquidity.
Variances in the level of information and knowledge among the parties involved	Outside investors are at a disadvantage in fast-moving markets and may discount forecasts simply on the basis of uncertainty.
Non-arm's-length relationships between parties	Their fairness may be further questioned as parties seek to maximize cash.
Number of prospective purchasers and/or sellers	This will increase in a rising market and decrease in a declining market as some buyers retrench to protect core assets.
Motivation and transaction timeline of the parties	This is dependent on the strategy of the acquirer, but generally more due diligence is advisable, offset by price considerations.
Unique value to acquirer	There is no direct relationship.
Strategic or special-interest buyers	The difference may widen as strategic value remains more constant, while in a declining market, fair market value plummets.
Existing legal and contractual obligations	There is no direct relationship.
Nature of any non-cash consideration	Non-cash consideration may not be worth what it is purported to be worth.

In volatile markets, there are also wider spreads between buyer and seller expectations. For example, in a normal market, the seller might expect to sell at 6.0 times EDITDA and the buyer to pay 4.0 times. Whereas in a volatile market, the seller might expect to transact at 7.0 times (albeit to a lower level of earnings due to the seller's view that current EBITDA is not representative of the future) and the buyer at 3.0 times. Thus, in volatile markets, we tend to see significantly fewer transactions and greater variances of fair market value determinations and implied transaction multiples.

The Standard of Value Estimated

The standard of value and the level of value must be clearly defined in any valuation analysis. Although valuation terms are widely recognized, their meanings may vary with the circumstances and jurisdiction in question. The valuator should consider several questions raised by the following common valuation terms:

Fair Market Value – as defined above.

- Are special purchasers included in the calculation? How many are required to influence the valuation conclusion?
- The vendor and purchaser would have very different and biased views on the value of the subject asset/business. In a volatile market environment, such differences in the value opinion between the two parties would be even larger. However, the concept of fair market value assumes prevailing economic and market conditions at the date of the valuation. Thus, the valuator needs to properly address this question: At what price would the transaction be expected to take place under the conditions existing at the valuation date?[3]

Fair Value – This term is employed in a number of contexts and often with different meanings. Today, the term is most commonly associated with fair value accounting. In this connection, fair value is defined by the Canadian Institute of Chartered Accountants (CICA) Handbook Section 1581 as "the amount of the consideration that would be agreed upon in an arm's-length transaction between knowledgeable, willing parties who are under no compulsion to act."

Under Canadian Generally Accepted Accounting Principles (GAAP), the fair value of an asset is the amount at which the asset could be bought or sold in a current transaction between willing parties, other than in liquidation.[4] On the other side of the balance sheet, the fair value of a liability is the amount at which that liability could be incurred or settled in a current transaction between willing parties, other than in liquidation.

---

3. S.P. Pratt & A.V. Niculita (collaborator), *Valuing a Business: The Analysis of Appraisal of Closely Held Companies, Fifth Edition* (New York: The McGraw Hill Companies, Inc., 2008), p. 42.

4. Fair value has a similar definition under the U.S. GAAP, in which it is defined as "the price that would be received to sell an asset or paid to transfer a liability in an orderly transaction between market participants at the measurement date" (FASB Financial Accounting Standard (FAS) 157, para. 5).

Practice Tip

> In today's dynamic and volatile markets, whether it is to buy or sell, what people want to know is what an asset is worth today.
>
> **Jackson M. Day, Former Deputy Chief Accountant, Office of the Chief Accountant, U.S. Securities and Exchange Commission**

In Canada, in the application of appraisal and oppression remedies available to minority shareholders in squeeze-outs, fair value generally equals *pro rata* fair market value, with no minority discount. Under certain circumstances, it can include a premium for forcibly taking shares.

- How instructive is the relevant jurisprudence for the jurisdiction governing the subject company?

Fair value is also the base used for publicly regulated utility rates. In this context, it normally means a fair and reasonable rate of return on the investment in net tangible assets employed in the operations.

Investment Value – The value to a particular investor based on individual investment requirements and expectations.

- Will the determination of value change based on the identity of the potential purchaser?

Intrinsic Value[5] – The fair market value, excluding synergies (*i.e.*, the value of an asset on a stand-alone basis).

- Is an optimal utilization of the assets assumed or status quo?

Going-concern Value – The value of a business that is expected to operate into the future. The intangible elements of going-concern value include having in place a trained work force, an operational plant, and the necessary licences, systems, and procedures.

- Is this analogous to fair market value?

Market Value – Market value is used in a number of contexts and has many different meanings. For marketable securities, market value is normally the actual trading price. The trading price of a minority shareholding is not

---

5 The official definition from the IGBVT is the following: "The value that an investor considers, on the basis of an evaluation or available facts, to be the 'true' or 'real' value that will become the market value when other investors reach the same conclusion. When the term applies to options, it is the difference between the exercise price or strike price of an option and the market value of the underlying security."

necessarily the same as the *pro rata* fair market value of all the issued and outstanding shares considered together. The open market trading prices are based in part on transactions between parties with unequal negotiating abilities and unequal knowledge of all the factors influencing value. They represent a price equilibrium between buyers and sellers at a specific time. Market value is therefore distinct from fair market value, which, among other differences, assumes that the seller and the buyer have equal negotiating skills and that both are apprised of all factors influencing value.

In real-estate appraisal, market value is usually defined as "the most probable price at which property would sell at the date of appraisal allowing a reasonable time to find a purchaser." Until 1986, the term "highest price," rather than the current term, "most probable price," was generally used. The change in definition was made by many mortgage lenders to reflect the fact that the market value of a property usually falls within a range and should not automatically be at the high end of the range.

Speculative Value – Speculative value is generally based on conjecture rather than measurable economic considerations.

Value in Use/Utility Value – The value in use of an asset is its value in an operating situation. Such a value, also defined as the utility or usefulness of the asset, may be considerably higher than the property's market or exchange value.

Value to Owner – The value of a business to its owner is often greater than its fair market value. The larger value may arise from the additional earnings the business can generate by capitalizing on the owner's personal goodwill. The business's value to the owner may also include its sentimental value.

Hindsight

Hindsight raises concerns in valuation assignments that are not conducted in real time. In any valuation assignment that is not conducted in real time as of the current date, the valuator will have to contend with the issue of hindsight. This is because the valuator will know with certainty about events whose occurrence and outcome were uncertain at the valuation date.

Fundamental valuation principles require the determination of value as of a specific time. The valuator must step into the shoes of the buyer and seller at that past date and attempt to establish the market reality that existed at that time. The valuator should consider only information based on a reasonable knowledge of the relevant facts. In volatile times, the valuator should be careful how much emphasis is placed on stock market valuations as what was a drop one day, week, or month could be a spike the following day, week, or month.

What constitutes reasonable hindsight based on allowable post-valuation date information? The answer to this question depends on the distinction between the following two points:

- *Subsequent Events That Are Restricted*:

The valuator must consider only information that a reasonably informed person would know on the valuation date. Information unknown or unavailable at that time and events occurring because of that information should not influence the valuation analysis.

Parties restrict the use of subsequent information based on the following points:

- It is not possible to establish the exact point in the future when information or events become unknowable at the valuation date.
- External information relating to the industry environment and general economy requires adjustment.
- Were the subsequent transactions valued at fair market value or some other valuation standard?

- *Subsequent Events That Are Not Restricted*:

The valuator should consider information that existed at the valuation date or was discoverable through reasonable investigation at that time, even if it was not actually known. The valuator may appropriately consider subsequent events or transactions if they constitute evidence of value on the valuation date and the price was set at or around the valuation date.

The valuator should not reject any unexpected external events that occurred subsequent to the valuation date and must reflect on the following points:

- the event's proximity to the valuation date and whether there was any evidence of a material change in the nature of the business or the underlying fundamentals of the company before the event occurred;
- the likelihood that a valuator could reasonably have foreseen subsequent events or information under the terms of an enhanced valuation engagement encompassing greater scrutiny and a more comprehensive scope; and
- adjustments for general economic and industry factors that have changed in the interim.

In volatile times, it becomes more difficult to determine allowable hindsight information and allowable events that occur subsequent to the valuation date. The more rapid the change in the risk/return profile of the economy, the company's industry sector, and the subject company itself, the greater the difficulty. If the environment and operational risks have fundamentally changed, then subsequent transactions will not reflect appropriately the conditions prevailing at the valuation date, and adjusting for the changing environment will be difficult.

Special Purchasers

Most calculations of fair market value do not identify potential special purchasers and rarely quantify the additional value attributable to them. This usually occurs because of limitations on the overall valuation engagement and on the scope of the review. It often becomes expensive to identify and difficult to measure the impact of a company's potential special purchasers, even though they do exist.

Some valuators argue that, unless multiple special purchasers can be identified, a single special purchaser should pay no more than a nominal amount, such as $1, above the intrinsic value of a business.

Special purchasers are considered as special because they have identified additional return-based benefits in excess of the intrinsic value of the company. These returns motivate a special purchaser to pay a premium. If both the buyer and seller understand the components of these synergistic returns, they should reasonably become negotiable in determining the value of the business. The agreed price will reflect the proportion of these incremental returns payable to the seller as part of the transaction price and the proportion that the buyer will earn upon assuming operation of the target company or asset.

The valuator should keep in mind that a prudent and rational buyer will negotiate a price based on the risk/return profile of the investment. Such a buyer will not walk away from a significant additional return simply because the identified synergies cannot be acquired for a nominal amount.

Still, the valuator may have difficulty in identifying synergistic benefits and determining the price that a special purchaser might pay for them. We once acted for a company with a large processing plant that needed to estimate the price that it would reasonably pay for a similar plant. The two plants had slightly different processing equipment, which affected the relative mix of finished products. Our client engaged two of the world's top engineering and financial consultants who had substantial experience with these types of processing plants to identify and assess the synergistic benefits that would likely arise from combining the operations of the two plants, each worth hundreds of millions of dollars. After considerable analysis, the engineering consultants concluded that there would be very little, if any, synergistic benefit. Another team, however, concluded that our client could increase its gross margins by partially processing raw material through the target plant, then completing the processing at its existing plant. This dual-plant procedure would generate a higher percentage of higher-grade and higher-value finished product. According to this analysis, the synergistic benefits to the purchaser exceeded $100 million. Our client concluded that it could pay up to 30 per cent more than the asking price for the target business.

In volatile times, depending on the industry, special purchasers may all but disappear such that it would be unreasonable to include any special purchaser premium. A good example of this would be certain non-prized financial services companies in the late-2008, early-2009 period. Due to the credit crisis and the need for banks to focus on the health of their own balance sheets, there was little appetite for acquisitions. In this way, one could make a clear argument that the value of companies at best would be their intrinsic value or carve-out value as opposed to a premium value due to the existence of a market of buyers, some being special purchasers. However, in other industries such as gold and even copper mining, the existence of special purchasers and special purchaser premiums were more evident. For example, on December 11, 2008, Iamgold Corporation announced a takeover of Orezone Resources Inc. at a 91 per cent premium to the 30-day weighted-average trading price, with the premium likely due to the healthy fundamentals and favorable investor views of the gold industry. Also, on October 1, 2008, Mitsubishi Materials Corporation agreed to make a $29 million equity investment in a near-term (2011) producer of copper. The investment was for a 25 per cent interest when the company had a market capitalization in the order of $40 million, implying a valuation of $116 million and 200 per cent premium to the recent trading prices. The likely cause of the premium was the long-term price assumptions assumed in the negotiation as opposed to current pricing and current market sentiment and the need for Mitsubishi Materials to replace copper supply from a mine that was due to close in 2011, thus critically affecting its upstream copper businesses.

The Valuation Process

The valuation process comprises the following general stages:

Qualitative Analysis – Understanding and quantifying the specific qualitative aspects of the company that influence its overall risk/return profile.

Quantitative Analysis – Analyzing the historic, current, and prospective financial statements and forecasts and selecting the most suitable valuation methodologies.

Assessing Reasonableness – Assessing the range of values that emerges and ensuring that it makes sense in light of the qualitative and quantitative considerations, industry norms, and past experience.

Qualitative Analysis

A meaningful qualitative analysis provides the context from which to make sound and supportable quantitative assumptions. Qualitative analysis includes an assessment of the following:

- general context;
- value drivers; and
- technical considerations.

The extent to which these factors are analyzed depends on the specific circumstances of the valuation: certain situations require deeper analysis. As such, not all of the analyses described below will be necessary for all valuations. It is up to the valuator to determine the degree of analysis required to gain the necessary insight into the subject of the valuation.

General Context

In the case of a business valuation, this includes industry, economic, and company-specific research. Valuations of intangible assets require research into the attributes of the intangible asset in question.

Company

By first understanding the company, the valuator can then focus the analysis more deeply and precisely on the industry and economy in which it operates. The valuator should understand high-level company issues as well as specific company details. In general, the valuator needs to understand how the company has generated its revenues historically and how it will do so in the future, as well as any other factors influencing the company's generation of net cash flows.

High-level aspects to consider include the following:

- Strategic considerations:

  i. vision, mission, values, corporate culture; and
  ii. core competencies, value proposition, product or service offering, short- and long-term goals.

- Management:

  i. management's historic impact on earnings and ability to meet future earnings projections;
  ii. details of track record and experience of key management: does the company administer a knowledge-management program to ensure these individuals make use of best practices? Is intellectual capital documented or does it primarily reside in employees' heads?
  iii. the quality of relationships with customers, suppliers, and the company's work force;
  iv. the accuracy of past operational forecasts;
  v. remuneration and performance-incentive structure relative to competitors; and
  vi. any non-arm's-length relationships between management and company shareholders.

- Strengths and weaknesses;
- Sources of competitive advantage;
- Customer information:

  i. customer composition, concentration issues, key customers, length of relationships;
  ii. key-person issues: do customers attach to certain employees or to the company's products and services?
  iii. historic and anticipated customer attrition;
  iv. source of new customers; and
  v. key criteria influencing customer purchasing decisions.

- Current, pending, and anticipated litigation;
- Degree of reliance on owner or a few employees to generate business or sustain competitive advantages;
- Key employees;
- Key suppliers;
- Nature of information systems;
- Critical business processes;
- Growth potential;
- Pipeline of new products and services;
- Direct competition;
- Market positioning; and
- Distribution channels.

Industry

Several critical aspects of a business are related to industry-wide factors and conditions, but a valuator can easily get overwhelmed with the volume of information available with respect to a given industry. The valuator should focus on the most relevant aspects of the industry from a valuation perspective. The following key industry aspects warrant investigation:

- general industry overview and mechanics;
- key industry economics;
- critical industry measures and metrics;
- key players;
- current trends in the industry;
- industry-wide regulatory controls;
- anticipated changes in cost and pricing structures; and
- industry outlook, opportunities, and threats.

Useful frameworks for industry analysis include the following:

Porter's Five Forces: Analyzes the threat of new entrants, bargaining power of suppliers, bargaining power of buyers, threat of substitutes, and competitive rivalry.

PEST Analysis: Analyzes an industry's political, economic, social, and technological aspects.

Economy

In addition to industry-wide influences, a business is also affected by the general economic environment. To perform a meaningful economic analysis, the valuator must identify the key economic variables affecting the operations of the subject business and the industry overall. These key variables will become apparent as the valuator gains an understanding of the overall industry and the specific company. Once these variables have been identified, the valuator can obtain their historic, current, and forecast values. By analyzing the movement in these variables compared with the historic, current, and forecast results of the business, the valuator can measure the relative importance of the variables identified. The valuator should strive to establish points of strong correlation between the variables and performance and whether they can assist in projecting the company's future operating performance.

Forecast variables should not be analyzed in isolation. Prices of commodities, exchange rates, interest rates, *etc.*, are correlated to an extent. For example, when we recently valued a copper mine, we worked closely with an economist who, when creating scenarios, was careful to select an oil price forecast that was consistent with each of his three (base, high, and low) copper price forecasts. In volatile times, forecasting becomes more difficult; however, reliance is often placed on long-run prices and the assumption that prices will revert to a long-run average and that value beyond the initial years of the forecast drive a majority of the subject-company's value.

Value Drivers

After the valuator understands a business's general context and completes the financial analysis, these findings can be synthesized into insights regarding the key drivers of value. Many factors affect the value of an investment or business, and the valuator needs to understand all of them to some degree and should identify and concentrate primarily on the factors that influence the value of the subject company to the greatest extent. By analyzing these variables, the valuator also gains a basis of comparison for considering company-specific risk and market comparables.

Key drivers of value can often be broken down into sub-drivers of value. It is up to the valuator to determine the level of detail needed about a particular driver that will allow important assumptions to be made during the valuation.

Technical Considerations

Industry Specialist

Depending on the subject, a valuator may seek the help of specialists in the specific industry to help understand the most relevant factors in the valuation and to assess the company's relative positioning in its industry. Without an appreciation of the complexities involved and the position of the subject relative to key industry factors and competitors, the valuator may not have adequate information to make appropriate assumptions or assess the reasonableness of management's assumptions. Examples of such specialists include actuaries, geologists, engineers, environmental specialists, economists, and software consultants.

Relative Qualitative Strength

In general, the value drivers of the subject company or assets can be better appreciated if the valuator understands how similar companies or assets are positioned relative to the same value drivers. By assessing the qualitative strength of the subject relative to comparable companies or assets, the valuator can obtain other useful insights. Using a market approach, these insights can assist the valuator in comparing firms or understanding the company's relative qualitative strengths to determine the company-specific risk premium applied to the discount rate.

The valuator must also decide whether to prioritize the value drivers by assigning weightings or creating tiers. An overall ranking allows for comparability among similar companies or assets.

When analyzing qualitative strength, the valuator should consider factors that, if not sufficiently strong, will significantly affect value. This is accomplished in part through prioritization of value drivers. The valuator should also pay special attention to potential deal breakers in making a qualitative assessment.

Qualitative Analysis

To determine the appropriate valuation methodology, the valuator generally conducts a financial analysis of the subject business or asset and assesses its profitability, liquidity, efficiency, and solvency historically, currently, and prospectively. The valuator often uses common-size financial statements to conduct this analysis. This will allow a comparison of figures across companies of different absolute sizes. Likewise, ratio analysis will enable the valuator to gain financial insights relative to chosen benchmarks.

Valuation Methodologies Overview

The graphic below outlines available valuation approaches and methodologies. We will discuss several of them at greater length.

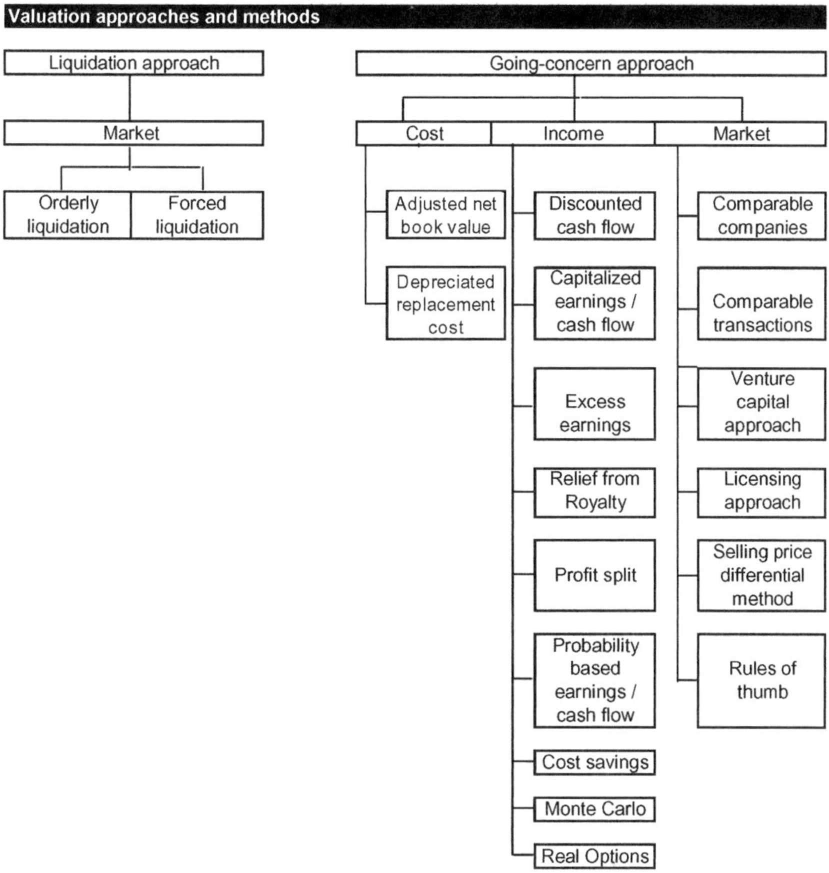

The valuator initially determines whether the subject business is a going concern by asking the following questions:

- Does the company have a history of consistent positive operating cash flow?
- Is the company expected to have positive net cash flow in the future?
- Is the future industry outlook positive?

If the valuator concludes that the business will continue for the foreseeable future, the valuator will take a going-concern approach to valuation; otherwise, a liquidation approach is suitable.

In valuing intangible assets, a liquidation approach will not necessarily be applicable. However, a liquidation of a business will often include marketable assets, some of which could be intangible. For example, a licence may have value to a competitor to prevent competition.

If the valuator adopts a going-concern methodology, one of three traditional approaches to valuation can be taken:

- cost;
- income; or
- market.

The valuator's choice depends on the specific situation and professional judgment. The following sections describe situations in which one of these three approaches is most suitable.

Layers of Value

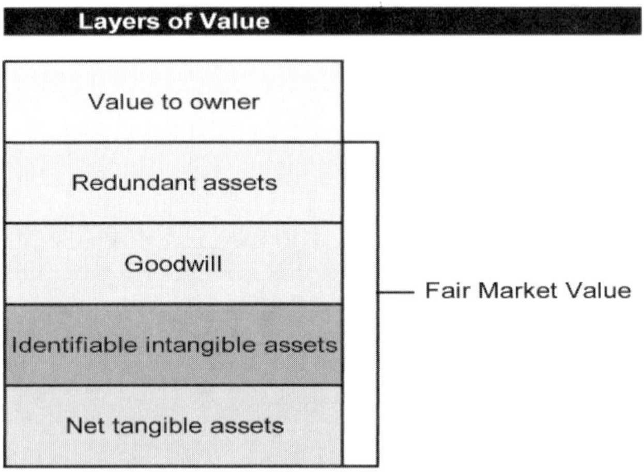

Before assessing these approaches in detail, the valuator should understand the high-level components of the value of a business. The valuator can conceptualize these components by viewing them as layers of value.

At the base lie the net tangible assets of the business. These can be valued relatively objectively. Consequently, they are less risky from a realization perspective, since they can usually be sold with comparatively little effort, with the exception of special-purpose tangible assets, which may be difficult to sell even at a distressed price.

The next layer of value includes identifiable intangible assets,[6] which can be transferred from the entity that controls them. Their benefits and value can

[6] Non-physical assets such as franchises, trademarks, patents, copyrights, goodwill, equities,

be isolated and quantified separately. Goodwill, on the other hand, relates to intangible value that cannot be transferred separately or whose benefits cannot be segregated. A business may also own redundant assets, which are not necessary for its ongoing core operations. Common redundant assets include excess working capital, underutilized capital equipment, vacant land, and assets purchased by owners for personal use such as artwork and luxury vehicles. In down markets, there is a greater likelihood of businesses or assets that once contributed to earnings no longer doing so; these would currently be classified as discontinued operations. The assets of these businesses would be clear candidates for redundant assets unless market participants thought they could be used in normal operations once markets return to normal. It is also possible that upon some restructuring or discontinuation of unprofitable business lines, businesses that were thought to be redundant or discontinued could actually return to a reasonable profit level.

Liquidation Approaches

When a valuator does not expect an investment or business to generate an adequate risk-adjusted return on capital, it is no longer a viable going concern. As a result, the valuator will take a liquidation approach so that capital can be returned to the investors and subsequently reinvested.

Liquidation of a company's business operations occurs through either an orderly process or a forced process.

Orderly Liquidation

An orderly liquidation will result in the highest net proceeds. Given the time value of money and the risk of deteriorating market conditions for the assets being sold, orderly is often perceived as an immediate liquidation. However, the duration of a liquidation depends on several factors, including the following:

- condition of business's books and records;
- nature and condition of the underlying assets;
- ability to salvage a viable operating segment;
- the party initiating the liquidation process; and
- the level of cooperation from owners and management.

The liquidation value typically depends on two primary calculations:

---

mineral rights, securities, and contracts (as distinguished from physical assets) that grant rights and privileges and have value for the owner.

1. The available net cash proceeds after all liquidation costs and corporate liabilities – including interim liabilities and corporate income tax – have been identified.

2. The remaining net cash amount after all or part of the related tax and any costs associated with distributing the net proceeds to creditors and shareholders have been deducted.

Forced Liquidation

When a forced liquidation occurs, the company's assets are sold as quickly as possible, at an auction, for example. Such circumstances do not allow adequate time to solicit all prospective bids or expose the assets to the marketplace for an extended period.

Going-concern Approaches

The valuator should use a going-concern approach if a business or investment is considered to be prospectively viable on a risk-return basis. A company needs more than a positive cash flow or return on investment. It must also earn a return commensurate with its level of risk. With an adequate risk-adjusted return, the resulting going-concern approach will assume that the company will remain viable for an indefinite period. The valuator calculates fair market value using one of the previously identified approaches: cost, income, or market.

Cost Approach

To apply the cost approach to a business, the valuator determines its adjusted book value. This is the difference between the value in use[7] of its assets and the value in use of its liabilities. This method is most appropriate when a business has nominal goodwill or identifiable intangible value or, when its cash flows, although positive, reflect returns below its cost of capital. Examples include real-estate holding companies and underperforming businesses, although with the latter, the valuator needs to assess carefully the long-term viability of the subject business.

The valuator often appraises tangible assets such as real estate, machinery, and equipment. In reviewing an asset's remaining productive capacity and

---

7 Value in use refers to the value of an asset or liability in the context of being used as part of a going concern (*e.g.*, the value in use of an asset may be greater than its liquidation value).

estimating its current market replacement cost, the valuator must consider several factors, including the degree of physical usage, the remaining useful life, and the technological change resulting in functional obsolescence.

The three most common cost approaches to valuing assets or businesses are the following:

- reproduction cost;
- replacement cost; and
- cost plus rate of return.

Valuators may use one of these approaches to analyze companies that are early stage, that have little prospect of current earnings, or that currently have negative cash flows. Approaches such as a DCF approach, whose value conclusion is very sensitive to minor changes of input variables, do not generate meaningful results because of the highly uncertain prospects of early-stage or bankrupt companies.

Likewise, if market data is unavailable, a market-based approach will not generate meaningful results either. In such cases, valuators again turn to a cost approach as the primary method for calculating value.

Despite its usefulness, a cost approach suffers from significant limitations. Many companies invest large sums of money and generate no value, for example, while others invest small sums of money and generate significant value. In many cases, the sunk costs bear little or no relation to the business's value. Still, the valuator can sometimes rely on cost data. If nothing else, the information will indicate the amount of money that a purchaser has to invest to achieve the same status as the current owner.

Reproduction Cost

Using the reproduction cost approach, the valuator considers the cost to create an exact copy of the asset. Often the valuator estimates these costs by studying the actual costs incurred historically and applies a reasonable inflation factor to estimate the equivalent costs at the valuation date. Sometimes, however, historical records are not maintained on a project-by-project basis. Historical records that are incomplete, inaccurate, or missing will inhibit the accuracy of this approach.

Replacement Cost

Using the replacement cost approach, the valuator tries to determine the cost, at the valuation date, not of reproducing the asset itself but of re-creating its functionality or benefits. The valuator must first determine whether the asset's functionality can be achieved more effectively using current knowledge, by replacing it rather than reproducing it, often at lower cost. This requires a highly technical and subjective assessment and the valuator may need to consult with an expert in the pertinent discipline.

Consider, for example, a banking software package developed seven years ago at a cost of $120 million. With improvements since then to software development tools, the current cost of developing software with the same functionality might be only $25 million to $50 million.

Cost Plus Rate of Return

A biotech company may spend $2 million over the course of a year to develop a therapeutic medication. A purchaser may be willing to pay $2 million plus a 20 per cent return, a total of $2.4 million, for the work. If the purchaser wants to enter the marketplace for the medication, it gains a head start, for which it will pay a premium over direct costs, while effectively eliminating a likely competitor. The vendor, meanwhile, gains a return on its investment.

Example of banking software under various approaches:

1. Reproduction cost – original cost of $120 million, adjusted upward for inflation: $150 million.

2. Replacement cost – original cost of $120 million, adjusted upward for inflation, but adjusted downward for recent software tools and applets that allow for increased efficiency in building the software: $25 million to $50 million.

3. Cost plus rate of return – a software consulting firm may be able to build the software at reduced risk and faster than the company itself and may charge $25 million to $50 million, plus a 20 per cent markup, for a total of $30 million to $60 million.

   The valuator then considers the three approaches. The reproduction cost approach would likely be disregarded because of its high cost relative to the more realistic replacement cost. The decision between the replacement cost approach and the cost plus rate of return approach may depend on the likely action of market participants (*i.e.*, Can the software be built in-house by the sponsoring company or by the typical market participant? Can the type of company that would buy the software wait 12 to 18 months for it to be built or is it needed sooner?). An alternative method, one using an income or relief-from-royalty approach, would value the software based on the licensing fees saved by owning versus renting the software from a software vendor or application service provider.

Income Approaches

Asset valuation depends fundamentally on economic principles rather than accounting or tax-reporting measurements. Broadly speaking, the key drivers of any income-based valuation analysis are the following:

- growth rate (revenues);
- cash flows (profitability); and
- discount rate (risk).

Using an income approach, the valuator applies these factors as part of a direct fundamental analysis of the subject company's operations and underlying value. Using a market approach, on the other hand, the valuator considers these factors indirectly. Instead, past transactions that contribute to a company's fundamental valuation analysis are reviewed. Income and market-comparable approaches both provide evidence of the value of a company's intangible assets, which does not usually appear on the balance sheet.

The intrinsic value of any business, asset, or investment is the present value of all future cash flows generated by its ongoing operations. The present value of these future cash flows is affected by their magnitude, degree of certainty, and timing. These are the fundamental drivers of any valuation effort: the return generated by the assets and the degree of risk – or certainty – attached to those returns. The valuator uses them to calculate the total present value of each individual year's projected future return. Taken together, they represent the fair market value of the investment.

In general, the value of an investment or business is represented by the following formula:

$$V_0 = \frac{CF_1}{1+r} + \frac{CF_2}{(1+r)^2} + \frac{CF_3}{(1+r)^3} + \ldots \qquad = \qquad V_0 = \sum_{t=1}^{\infty} \frac{CF_t}{(1+r)^t}$$

where

V_0 = Value on the present date
CF = Cash flow per period
'r' = Risk to cash flow (required return)

Valuators may modify this formula to reflect different measures of cash flow, calculations of terminal value, or rates of growth. However, the fundamental premise supporting the equation remains: the value of any business, asset, or investment is the present value of all future cash flows that it will generate.

DCF Approach

Practice Tip

> While scenario-based discounted cash flow techniques can help bound and quantify uncertainty, they will not make it disappear. High-growth companies have volatile stock prices for sound and logical reasons.
>
> ***Valuation: Measuring and Managing the Value of Companies*, 4th ed., by Tim Koller, Marc Goedhart, and David Wessels**

Several basic valuation models use the DCF approach. Each differs depending on the cash flow input used in the formula, and each represents a different level of return generated by the business. The valuator may use dividends in the calculation; for example, free cash flow-to-equity or operating cash flow. Depending on the proxy selected, the resulting value represents either the value of the shareholders' equity or the EV, which represents the value of all capital invested (shareholders' equity plus debt less cash).

The projection and discounting of a series of annual future cash flows is a complex undertaking, and it becomes increasingly difficult in industries that experience rapid technological, regulatory, and competitive changes. Until the 1990s, valuators seldom used DCFs unless a business or industry had certain attributes, such as the following:

- a stable (although some would argue an unstable) operating environment;
- limited or finite operational life;
- significant capital expenditure requirements; and
- irregular, high-growth, or declining cash flows from operations.

In the past, valuators applied a DCF approach most frequently to companies in resource-based or extractive industries, such as mining and minerals, oil and gas, or forestry. They also applied the approach to projects with a limited time horizon.

More recently, the DCF approach has become the primary valuation methodology used in a wide variety of industries and at various stages of the corporate growth cycle. The appropriate valuation method still depends on the circumstances, but we have found a DCF approach to valuation is now used about 75 per cent to 80 per cent of the time. Likewise, we have found that valuators use a capitalization approach, such as capitalization of earnings, cash flow, EBIT, or EBITDA, in 50 per cent to 60 per cent of their valuations. In volatile times, one would expect use of the DCF approach to increase because of the need to model earnings that may decline at first, followed by an upswing a few years later as the economy stabilizes. It should be noted that earnings are driven by both operating and financial leverage; thus, a drop in revenues would have an outsized impact on net income due to fixed operating costs and fixed financing costs that do not fluctuate with revenues.

In unique situations, valuators may use a hybrid approach that includes DCFs to estimate value. They will base their valuation conclusion mainly on the best benchmarks of value.

To value a business as a going concern, the valuator will use the general DCF formula (as presented above), which requires estimates of a significant number of terms. This becomes unwieldy since reliability diminishes with the forecast of each additional annual cash flow.

The valuator can address the problem of forecasting to infinity by using certain simplifying assumptions about cash flow growth and projections. At some point in the future, the projection period ceases and the cash flows generated by the business become maintainable for the purposes of the valuation. Typically, this occurs at a point between five and 10 years. At this point, the valuator assumes that fluctuations in revenue growth and operating cash flow level off or cannot be forecast with any confidence. When cash flows reach this maintainable level, they can be capitalized. This capitalized cash flow calculation represents the residual, or terminal, value. It captures the future benefits from the post-cash flow projection period at the point when future cash flow growth is assumed to be constant.

The terminal value in year "n" of the forecast is present-valued with the cash flows projected for the final year of the forecast period. The present-value formula is amended as follows:

$$V_0 = \frac{CF_1}{1+r} + \frac{CF_2}{(1+r)^2} + \frac{CF_3}{(1+r)^3} + \ldots + \frac{CF_n + V_{n(Terminal)}}{(1+r)^n}$$

where

V_n = Terminal value at year "n"

$$V_n = \frac{CF_{(n+1)}}{r - g_{Constant}}$$

$'g'_{Constant}$ = Constant growth rate

As part of the discounting process, the valuator computes a terminal value at the point when growth slows to its expected long-term sustainable rate. Since a valuator derives a significant portion of a business valuation from cash flows attributable to the terminal value, the firm's potential long-term growth must be accurately reflected. The longer the period from the present valuation date to the date of terminal valuation, the more difficult it becomes to accurately estimate the required numeric inputs. This makes it challenging to estimate a terminal value.

The mechanics of the terminal value calculation are identical to those of the capitalized cash flow valuation approach. The valuator must make assumptions about the rate at which growth will stabilize, as well as net capital expenditures, working capital requirements, and all other variables needed to ensure that the business earns a constant return on its invested capital. By capitalizing an estimate of the maintainable discretionary cash flow, the valuator determines the terminal value at period "n" in the future.

Example:

Company A is expected to generate annual free cash flows for the next five years as follows:

(In $ millions)	Year 1	Year 2	Year 3	Year 4	Year 5
Free cash flow	$ 90	$ 120	$ 150	$ 130	$ 100

It is expected that the company's business will reach a mature stage after Year 5 and generate a stable annual free cash flow of $100 million at the expected long-term industry annual growth rate of approximately two per cent. The required rate of return is 12 per cent. The company currently has net debt of $300 million. Based on the foregoing, the EV and equity value of Company A is as estimated as follows:

(In $ millions)			Year 1	Year 2	Year 3	Year 4	Year 5	Terminal
Free cash flows (FCF)			$ 90	$ 120	$ 150	$ 130	$ 100	$ 102
Terminal value at terminal growth of	2%	*(Note 1)*						$ 1,020
Present value factor at	12%	*(Note 2)*	0.945	0.844	0.753	0.673	0.601	0.601
Present value of FCFs			$ 85	$ 101	$ 113	$ 87	$ 60	$ 613
Enterprise Value (=sum of present value of FCFs)			**$ 1,059**					
Less: Net Debt			$ 300					
Equity Value			**$ 759**					

Notes

1 Terminal value is calculated as follows:

$$\frac{FCF_{Year\ 5} * (1 + \text{Terminal Growth})}{\text{Discount rate - Terminal Growth}} = \frac{100*(1+2\%)}{(12\% - 2\%)}$$

2 Present value factor is calculated as follows: (assumes mid-period discounting - i.e. Year 1 uses 0.5 instead of 1)

Year 1	Year 2	Year 3	Year 4	Year 5
$(1.12)^{-0.5}$	$(1.12)^{-1.5}$	$(1.12)^{-2.5}$	$(1.12)^{-3.5}$	$(1.12)^{-4.5}$

The valuator often discounts the terminal value using the same risk rate applied to the annual cash flow projections. Alternatively, the valuator may present the terminal value component distinctly from the annual cash flow forecasts because the greater uncertainty of the distant time horizon and timing of the moderated growth expectations may warrant a higher risk rate in calculating the present value.

Practice Tip

Valuators tend to overvalue the terminal value either by not extending the finite period to where growth is expected to level off, not adjusting maintenance capital expenditures to replace plant assets when they wear out or become inefficient, not reducing revenue/margins for competitive response as horizon is further out, *etc.*

Mark Keuleman, CA, CBV

Constant Growth Dividend Discount Model

A constant growth dividend discount model (DDM) is a form of DCF analysis. Valuators typically use constant growth DDMs to value common shares of mature companies – often publicly traded – which can be assumed to grow at a constant average annual growth rate over time. The appropriateness of DDMs varies depending on the nature of the company, its dividend history, and, more broadly, whether it is publicly or privately held. Dividends are usually less volatile than earnings or other return measures, at least for publicly traded companies. Public companies tend to maintain more consistent dividend policies than private companies.

$$V_{C/S} = \frac{Div_1}{r_{C/S} - g_{Div}}$$

where

$V_{C/S}$ = Current value of common shares
Div_1 = Next year's dividend
'g'$_{\text{Div}}$ = Dividend growth rate

Example:

Company B is a mature manufacturing company that pays an annual dividend to its common shareholders. The current year's dividend is $1.50 per share. It is expected that the future annual dividend growth rate will be two per cent, which is consistent with the historical growth rate. The required rate of return is 10 per cent. Thus, the value of one common share of Company B is estimated as follows:

$$V_{c/s} = \frac{\$1.50^{*}(1+2\%)}{10\% - 2\%}$$

$$= \frac{1.53}{0.08}$$

$$= \underline{\mathbf{\$\ 19.13}}$$

where

Div_1 = Next year's dividend = $1.50 per share * (1 + growth rate of 2%)
'g'$_{\text{Div}}$ = Dividend growth rate = 2%

No-Growth Dividend Discount Model

Valuators typically use a no-growth DDM to value most preferred share investments. Preferred shares function as perpetuities, since the dividend cash flow is predetermined, indefinite, and typically without growth potential; however, one should carefully look at the terms and conditions attached to the preferred shares as these can vary as a result of such features as a terminal value or retraction rights.

$$V_{P/S} = \frac{Div_1}{r_{P/S}}$$

where

$V_{P/S}$ = Current value of preferred shares
Div_1 = Next year's dividend
'r'$_{P/S}$ = Risk to preferred share cash flow

Example:

Company C pays preferred share dividends every year to its preferred shareholders. The annual dividend is $1.50 per share. There are no special terms and conditions attached to the preferred shares. The required rate of return is 10%. Thus, the value of one preferred share of Company C is estimated as follows:

$$V_{p/s} = \frac{\$1.50}{10\%}$$

$$= \underline{\$\ 15.00}$$

where

Div_1 = Next year's dividend = $1.50 per share

Functionally, preferred shares combine characteristics of both debt and equity. To allocate a portion of a business's overall EV to a class of preferred shares, the valuator has to analyze all additional factors that could potentially influence both the absolute cash flow to the investor and the risk associated with that cash flow. To value a preferred share investment, the valuator must understand the preferred shareholder's rights relating to the company's assets, discretionary cash flows, and ability to exercise control.

Preferred share value typically includes the following key elements:

- dividends may be cumulative or non-cumulative;
- liquidation preference may be participating or non-participating;
- conversion features may be at a fixed or variable ratio;
- redemption by the issuer may or may not be mandatory;

- the shares may include anti-dilution, participation, or first-refusal features; and
- the shares may include voting, veto, and board composition rights.

Because of the unique features and flexibility of many preferred share investments, the valuator must clearly identify the various rights and quantify their value independently when allocating overall enterprise value.

Capitalized Cash Flow Approach

The valuator uses the same mechanics for the capitalized cash flow and the constant-growth DDMs. Both approaches assume a level of maintainable cash flow and a constant growth rate in perpetuity. Since the capitalized cash flow approach captures more than dividend-paying common shares in its calculation, the valuator can use it to determine either EV or equity value, depending on the specific cash flow used in the numerator.

$$V_n = \frac{CF_1}{r - g_{Constant}}$$

where

V_n = Value at period "n"
CF_1 = Next year's cash flow
'g' $_{Constant}$ = Constant growth rate

In fact, the capitalized cash flow technique is a simplification of the DCF technique, but with several key distinctions:

1. Future cash flow growth is accounted for in the capitalization rate ($r - g_{Constant}$) rather than by a specific annual forecast. The valuator assumes that after-tax discretionary cash flows have an infinite duration and are less susceptible to year-over-year variations than investments customarily valued using a DCF approach.

2. Under the capitalized cash flow approach, the valuator estimates the sustaining capital reinvestment and working capital investment required to maintain existing operations based on the future estimated sustaining level or an average of the recent periods. In estimating the sustaining capital reinvestment, the valuator deducts tax savings in the form of future capital cost allowance deductions against the gross amount to determine net sustaining capital reinvestment. By com-

parison, the DCF approach calculates required net sustaining capital investment and working capital in each year of the forecast period, then selects a sustaining level in the terminal year.[8]

The valuator deducts the amounts of net sustaining capital reinvestment and working capital investment, as described above, from the after-tax discretionary operating cash flows to arrive at the maintainable level of the total discretionary cash flow (or free cash flow) of the business. The valuator then determines the applicable capitalization rate ($r - g_{Constant}$) with reference to risk (r) and maintainable growth ($g_{Constant}$) to arrive at the present value of the business. The valuator then adds the present value of the tax shield of the existing capital assets' undepreciated capital cost balance to this amount, which now represents the estimate value of the business.

Some valuators, when applying the capitalized cash flow approach, will also include a deduction for sustaining working capital investment. The rationale for doing so is to ensure completeness so that material cash outlays have not been ignored and a true free cash flow figure can be determined. On the other hand, some valuators will argue that sustaining working capital requirements are mostly inflationary in nature and have already been taken into account elsewhere and do not need to be taken into consideration when applying the capitalized cash flow approach.

When capitalizing the capital cost allowance at the valuation date to determine the present value of the existing tax shield, the valuator sometimes uses a lower risk rate than that used to capitalize after-tax operating cash flows. The valuator uses different risk rates because the risk of the business earning enough to use its available capital cost allowance is significantly lower than the risk associated with the overall business operation. However, there is divergence in practice, with some business valuators using one discount rate and others preferring to use an alternative rate.

Capitalization of Earnings

Valuators calculate capitalization of net earnings using a similar approach to capitalization of cash flows. Both require the valuator to adjust or normalize earnings reported in financial statements for non-recurring and unusual items. The valuator then multiplies normalized after-tax earnings from operations by the appropriate capitalization rate to produce the overall value of the business.

---

8 It is a common shortcut in the discounted cash flow approach to calculate the tax savings as described above with respect to the capitalized cash flow approach instead of forecasting tax depreciation, taxable income, and income taxes in each future period.

The earnings approach is appropriate when after-tax cash flow reasonably approximates accounting net income. Under these conditions, no further adjustments are required to reflect the difference between accounting and economic reality. This typically occurs in service-oriented businesses in which accounting depreciation approximates cash outflows for capital acquisitions and working capital requirements remain relatively constant.

As a proxy for cash flow from operations, valuators also measure EBITDA which, when normalized for non-recurring items, is an approximation of a company's future sustainable cash flow from ongoing operations. It ignores other non-cash items beyond depreciation and amortization. Furthermore, it ignores changes in working capital accounts such as accounts receivable, inventory, and accounts payable.

Capitalization of Excess Earnings

In this hybrid residual-income method, valuators capitalize excess earnings above a threshold rate of return, then add the amount to the adjusted book value of the company's tangible assets.

Sometimes called abnormal earnings or dual capitalization, as well as excess earnings or residual income, the model's fundamentals begin with the adjusted book value of the company, to which the valuator adds the present value of future excess earnings. The valuator must adjust the book value, which forms a large part of the calculated value, for off-balance-sheet items and aggressive accounting practices. Accelerating revenue, deferring or capitalizing expenses, and charge-offs will affect both earnings and book value and must be normalized to arrive at the adjusted book value. This makes it possible to establish the threshold return accruing to the capital invested in assets and the excess or residual return generated beyond this base amount.

Excess earnings or residual income methods explicitly recognize the economic cost of equity capital. A company may have a positive net income, but if earnings do not exceed the threshold cost of equity capital, the business is not economically profitable.

The valuator can construct an excess earnings model in a fashion similar to a capitalized maintainable return. The valuator uses the growth rate to adjust the required return and determine the appropriate capitalization rate. Alternatively, the valuator can project annual residual earnings and book values for each year in the future, then discount them to arrive at a present value.

$$V_0 = B_0 + \sum_{t=1}^{\infty} \frac{RI}{(1+r_{CE})^t}$$

where

Residual Income $= RI = (ROE_t - r_{CE})\,B_{t-1}$
B_0 = Current adjusted book value
ROE_t = Return on equity
'r'$_{C/E}$ = Required return on common equity

The excess earnings or residual income model requires clean surplus accounting. Ending equity book value must equal beginning book value plus earnings less dividends. Any changes to book value that do not relate to earnings and dividends will affect the return on equity and must be adjusted.

The most appropriate application of the excess earnings approach is for the purpose of allocating the total value of the company's assets between tangible and intangible assets since the method was originally developed for the purpose of valuing the intangible value of a business.[9] Nevertheless, the excess earnings approach is most often used for valuations of small- and medium-sized businesses or for the following businesses:

- that do not pay dividends or that pay unpredictable dividends;
- that do not expect positive cash flows in the near term or through the forecast period or that have unpredictable cash flows; and
- that derive a significant portion of total value from terminal value or whose terminal value is difficult to forecast.

Other Considerations

Monte Carlo Simulation

Valuation approaches such as a DCF analysis typically require inputs from a number of variables. The resulting value can fluctuate significantly given the variance among the inputs, creating a high level of prediction risk. To address this risk, valuators can use a Monte Carlo simulation.

Computer-run Monte Carlo simulations incorporate a wide range of input values into the relevant valuation model. The model then iterates thousands

9 Pratt & Niculita, above note 3, at pp. 332-333. This valuation method originally appeared in a 1920 publication by the U.S. Treasury entitled *Appeals and Review Memorandum Number 34* (ARM 34). It was adopted in order to estimate the intangible value of goodwill that breweries and distilleries lost because of the legal imposition of prohibition in the U.S. Treasury laws.

of times and generates random results for the given range of input variables to produce a distribution of outcomes.

Real-Option Pricing Models

Using a traditional DCF analysis, the valuator will often consider only the most likely values for any input variables in a specific valuation model. The valuator does not usually include possible but improbable variables such as natural disasters, regulatory changes, and sovereign risk. The valuator can best capture the impact of such variables on a business or investment valuation using alternative forms of analysis such as real-option pricing models.

A DCF analysis reflects the value at the current date of all options and their cash flow consequences. In applying a DCF technique to development-stage companies, however, the valuator does not fully capture all potential growth or risk-mitigating opportunities inherent in the development process. These may include, for example, the option to pause or abandon a project or strategic partnership.

Real-option valuation approaches assign values to contingent decisions. They capture value most effectively in smaller firms whose potential value resembles an option-type outcome. These approaches depend on the application of fundamental financial option-pricing theory to real assets.

When using option-pricing models, the valuator should consider several general propositions:

- Selective Use: use option models only if they make a difference in the valuation.
- Exclusivity: before they qualify as options, possible opportunities must legally restrict competition, confer a competitive advantage, or provide some other form of advantage to the business.
- Double Counting: the valuator should disregard the effect of options on cash flow fundamentals and avoid applying additional premiums to reflect the same option outcomes.

Evidence indicates that both real-option and net-present-value approaches such as DCF decision trees all lead to similar conclusions, and one approach generates no better results than another. In practice, DCF approaches usually serve well because they are based on fundamental principles of finance, whereas option pricing is premised on more abstract principles.[10]

In volatile bear markets, some stocks will trade like call options and others will trade on a basis not recognizable as anything other than overreactive

---

[10] K.M. Bode-Greuel & J.M. Greuel, "Determining the Value of Drug Development Candidates and Technology Platforms" (2005) 11 *Journal of Commercial Biotechnology* 170.

emotion. From a DCF perspective, value may be nil to nominal, but investors may buy the shares because of the option to be invested if value increases significantly due to an unlikely future event. An example would be companies that are cash flow positive from an operational perspective, but whose debt approximately equates to the value of the company's assets. In this scenario, the DCF value of the company's share might be nil, nominal, or even negative, but investors may still ascribe value to the shares because of the possibility that the company returns from the brink. In essence, the shares represent a call option on the company's assets, with the strike price equal to the fair market value of the company's debt.

Measuring Return

To determine a company's return, represented by maintainable earnings, maintainable cash flows, or annual cash flow projections, the valuator begins by reviewing the most recent years' financial statements and analyzing the company's future prospects. The valuator must use professional judgment to determine the periods that contain reliable and relevant data. Generally, the valuator will refer to industry norms to determine the projection period and to forecast maintainable future returns. These norms should best reflect anticipated changes in the operations of the business and the natural course of the business cycle. The company's historical returns and performance are relevant to forecasting future returns only if they indicate probable prospective operating cash flows.

Whether a valuator uses earnings or cash flows to measure return, several adjustments must first be made to the reported financial statements.

Financial Statement Adjustments

There are many infrequent or one-time occurrences in normal business operations, and the significant ones generally require a normalization adjustment, as do any irregular or outsized amount, non-arm's length transaction, and amount unrelated to core operations. The one-time occurrences typically include the following:

- start-up or expansion costs;
- moving costs;
- merger-related activity;
- restructuring costs;
- strike-related or settlement costs;
- litigation settlements or proceeds;
- insurance proceeds;
- outsized inventory increases;

- outsized pension contributions;
- shareholder financing at non-market rates;
- shareholder remuneration at non-market rates;
- gains/losses from asset sales; and
- unusual income tax refunds.

Normalized earnings should reflect the core operations of the business, but they should not be adjusted so radically that they become unrealistic. Occasional unusual or infrequent items are a normal function of any business operation. In fact, it may make sense to calculate a multi-year average of these items and include them as the expected annual amount for unusual items.

Valuation approaches based on earnings figures such as net income or EBITDA, selected from the financial statements, may also reflect accounting misclassifications, manipulations, or smoothing techniques used by company management. Whether they result from GAAP flexibility or overstep the boundaries of GAAP, the impact is the same: the utility of earnings-based measures is diminished and becomes less likely to reflect the economic reality of the business.

The following accounting choices can affect both the comparability between companies and the analytical value of the financial statements:

- product research and development costs expensed as incurred versus capitalized and amortized over several subsequent accounting periods;
- distortions based on fixed asset financing using an operating lease versus capital lease structure or an outright acquisition;
- customer acquisition costs related to increasing the subscriber base in certain industries, such as telecommunications, that are capitalized and recorded as long-term assets;
- misclassification of investment proceeds as cash flow from operations;
- increased accounts receivable through premature revenue recognition that increases net earnings but does not affect operating cash flow;
- extending depreciation or amortization periods based on management's estimate of an asset's useful life, which increases reported earnings;
- write-offs (*e.g.*, those taken by technology firms for large portions of acquisition costs such as in-process research and development (IPR&D)) allowing earnings increases in subsequent periods; and
- reserves for bad debts, losses, or product returns that exceed economic reality in good earnings years and can be used in poorer years to smooth out earnings.

Companies may try to manage their earnings, especially in the notoriously volatile technology sector, so they can meet their forecast revenue and earnings per share numbers. The lower a company's earnings volatility, the lower its presumed risk.

In addition, historical financial information is in nominal dollars. The valuator should be careful to compare earnings from five years ago with current earnings when inflation is not immaterial. For example, to compare average earnings from five years ago with current earnings, the historical earnings should be increased by inflation over that five-year period.

Influencing Factors

When a valuator uses the income approach to measure the value of a business, its earnings or cash flow must reflect the core operating returns accruing from the continuation of the business as a going concern. The valuator can determine maintainable earnings or cash flows, along with elements of company-specific risk, with reference to several influencing factors:

- Qualitative Considerations (as discussed in section 1): The intention is to take into account several key factors influencing value, such as the following:

  i. General Economic Conditions: an assessment of the factors affecting the economy as a whole and a determination of the general economic conditions that will affect the business. The valuator should strive to identify strong correlations between the variables and the company's performance and whether they can assist in projecting the company's future operating returns. During volatile times, valuators need to make a supported call on where markets will be going (*e.g.*, if and when prices will come off recent highs or when a recession may end). Significant incremental research may be required. Analyst and economic forecasts are useful as are the market's own forecast such as futures curves and inflation rates implied by long-term inflation-protected bonds.

  ii. Industry and Market Position: the valuator must understand the industry and its outlook. The participants and the company's market position must be analyzed relative to its competitors. The valuator must also understand the company's specific market positioning. In down markets, additional value may be ascribed to companies that are likely to be survivors and come out on top as a result of the difficulties of companies that are under significant stress; likewise, companies that are weak may have more of a discount applied to them compared to when the market is normal.

iii. Management Strength: the valuator must assess the effectiveness of the company's management to review its impact on historic earnings and assess its ability to meet future earnings projections. In volatile times, the valuator should spend more time questioning and analyzing management's forecasts. Forecast sales that are solid should be differentiated from those that are less likely to occur. Has management been through a recession or extreme bullish market before? Does management understand what is truly driving sales and whether an uptick in sales is sustainable, such as sales of homes and automobiles prior to the credit crisis of 2008, which were driven by access to easy credit?

- Financial Framework Considerations: The valuator must determine future operating earnings or cash flows in light of several factors, including the following:

  i. Capital Structure: financing changes and costs assumed to occur during the projection period must be incorporated into the cash flows or discount rate where possible. During volatile times, access to corporate credit may be easily available or may be constrained, affecting both the level of debt available and its cost. Equity returns requirements, especially in down markets, may also be elevated, mirroring investors' higher required returns on debt instruments.

  ii. Inflation: if an inflation component is not incorporated into the cash flow projections, then the discount rate (r – g) will have to reflect this underlying growth. If a DCF approach is used and the explicit forecast captures the expected horizon of volatile times, then the "g" will relate to a long-term growth forecast. In other cases such as when a capitalized cash flow or earnings approach is used, the "g" may have to represent a combined growth rate relating to both the current volatile period and a long-term period, which is a less-transparent approach.

  iii. Working Capital: changes in working capital requirements over the projection period should be quantified and included in the cash flow analysis. During down markets, customers may seek to extend payables and inventory may build up, causing the investment in working capital to increase compared with historical norms.

iv. Deferred Tax: timing differences between the marginal tax rate for accounting purposes and the effective tax paid as a cash outflow will give rise to deferred tax. The valuator should consider if and when deferred tax balances will likely become payable. Typically, the accelerated deductions allowed for tax purposes will begin to reverse themselves when future sales growth moderates and capital investment declines.

v. Infrastructure: the valuator should consider projected future cash flows in light of the company's infrastructure and capacity and the impact of any future upgrades.

vi. Sustaining Capital Expenditure: the valuator must assess the expected annual investment in assets that a business must make to meet its estimated cash flow projections. The investment must adequately ensure the maintenance of current operating capacity to support projected cash flows. The investment should also provide adequate capital expenditures to support future growth in operating capacity. This requires consideration of several factors, including the following:

- remaining useful life;
- replacement and maintenance costs;
- industry technology trends; and
- anticipated growth requirements.

These factors will drive the estimate of future returns and assist the valuator in determining cash flow projections or maintainable return and growth levels. In down markets, it may be difficult to obtain financing for significant capital projects. In up markets, greenfield expansion options may have value; in down markets, the value of these options may be significantly impaired. The value of brownfield expansion options are more likely to maintain their value and so should be given increased emphasis in down markets.

Financial statements often classify income and expenses differently than valuations. For valuation purposes, projected cash flows often have greater utility when grouped by the following factors:

- operating revenue and expenses;
- non-operating income and expenses;
- capital expenses, and
- financial expenses.

Free Cash Flow Measurement

Free Cash Flow-to-Firm

Free cash flow (FCF)-to-firm or net cash flow-to-firm represents the after-tax cash flow available to all providers of invested capital, including debt and equity. The valuator calculates it either by adjusting cash flow from operations or by beginning with the net income available to common shareholders. To calculate the specific value of the company to equity shareholders, the valuator then deducts the market value of the debt from the firm's total value.

To arrive at the FCF-to-firm, the valuator makes several adjustments to the normalized net income. The valuator then capitalizes the return measure to arrive at the total firm value.

FCF–to-Firm = Net Income
+ Non-cash Expenses
+ Interest Expense × (1 − tax rate)
− Fixed Asset Investment
− Working Capital Investment
FCF-to-Firm

- Net Income: the firm's income available to common shareholders after interest expense, taxes, depreciation, amortization, and preferred dividends normalized for unusual, non-recurring, and non-arm's length items.
- Non-cash Expenses: non-cash charges affect net income but do not involve a cash outflow. They include depreciation, amortization, restructuring charges, asset gains/losses, and deferred taxes.
- Interest Expense: interest cost is a cash outflow to providers of debt capital. In determining the overall EV, the valuator adds after-tax interest back to net income (in effect excluding it from the earnings level) consistent with the after-tax weighted-average cost of capital (WACC) used to capitalize the FCF-to-firm. Calculating earnings without interest expense is done so as to be consistent with the goal of calculating EV, which is a "pre-debt" value.
- Fixed Asset Investment: investments in assets such as property, plants, and equipment represent cash outflows required to maintain and grow operations. An asset sale would result in a cash inflow.
- Working Capital Investment: additional working capital re-

quired to maintain ongoing operations must be reflected in the cash flow forecast.

The valuator must calculate the appropriate discount rate used to establish the capitalized value of the firm's cash flow with respect to all providers of capital. The valuator uses the WACC to calculate the required rate of return for all debtholders, preferred shareholders, and common shareholders.

Free Cash Flow-to-Equity

FCF-to-equity or net cash flow-to-equity represents post-debt free cash flow. It takes into account the superior claim of debtholders on the firm's free cash flow. Unlike the FCF-to-firm approach, in which the valuator deducts debt financing from the overall firm value, FCF-to-equity captures the cost of debt in the measure of return as an interest expense.

Matching the risk measure and the return measure is important. As such, the cost of equity is used in valuation models when the return is defined as earnings, dividends, or FCF-to-equity.

Free Cash Flow-to-Equity versus Free Cash Flow-to-Firm

Theoretically, either approach will result in the same answer and any difference in value between the two is due to inconstant assumptions. During the last 10 years, FCF-to-firm (an EV approach) has gained more notoriety than FCF-to-equity. However, today, FCF-to-equity is used when capital structure (*i.e.*, debt) is being paid down over the life of the investment. For example, when valuing leveraged buyouts (LBOs); infrastructure assets such as airports, power and water utilities, roads, and mining projects at the financing stage; and banks and insurance companies, the FCF-to-equity approach is generally used. The FCF-to-firm approach works best when the capital structure is expected to stay fairly constant, such as in mature businesses in the manufacturing or consumer business sectors.

To show that either approach results in the same value conclusion, take the following example:

- Annual after-tax cash flow before interest expenses of $100;
- Normal debt of $300 and pre-tax cost of debt of 5%;
- Required after-tax equity rate of return: 12.8%; and
- Assume nil to nominal growth.

The value of equity under the FCF-to-equity approach can be calculated by subtracting the after-tax interest expense from the pre-interest cash flow as follows:

Free cash flow to equity = \$100 – \$300 × 5% × (1 – 30%) = \$89.5

Then, the free cash flow-to-equity is capitalized using the equity rate of return as follows:

Value of equity = \$89.5 / 12.8% = \$699

Given that the equity is approximately \$700 and debt is \$300, the above implies a debt-to-equity split of 30-to-70, which becomes an input into the FCF-to-firm approach.

Under the FCF-to-firm approach, the value of equity is also calculated, but it is done by first calculating a weighted-average required return to both debt and equity holders as follows:

Weighted-average return =
70% × 12.8% + 30% × 5% × (1 – 30%) = 10.0%

Then the firm-wide cash flow is capitalized as follows:

Value of firm = \$100 / 10% = \$1,000

Finally, the debt is subtracted to arrive at the value of equity:

\$1,000 – \$300 = \$700

Note how the value-to-equity ratio is identical under either approach. The weighted-average return concept is discussed in further detail below.

Other Considerations

Redundant Assets

The capitalization or discounting of cash flows relates only to the risk and return of cash flows generated by the operations of the business. Only the company's operating assets can generate these returns. In assessing the business's risk/return profile, the valuator should disregard assets that do not contribute to the generation of operational cash flows. Examples of redundant assets may include excess cash that is not required for working capital, short-term investments (term deposits, marketable securities), excess land, non-operating assets (plants and machinery), and investments in other companies that are not related to the operations.

However, the valuator should add the net realizable value of redundant assets to the business's going-concern value if these non-core assets can be liquidated and distributed. Issues such as disposal costs, taxes, portfolio discounts, and portfolio premiums should be considered.

Measuring Risk

The valuator can measure a company's risk through direct and comparative means. In establishing firm risk, the valuator determines the rate of return that an investor would require from a firm's operations and the current or present value that the valuator should give to anticipated future cash flow generated from the business's ongoing operations. Whether the valuator uses the term risk rate, discount rate, cost of capital, or required rate of return, all refer to a measure of risk that quantifies the present value of a company's future return from operations.

However, the capitalization rate and the discount rate are not synonymous. In capitalized earnings or cash flow approaches, as we discussed earlier, the company's cash flow projections do not reflect the growth in future operations. So the valuator adjusts the discount rate (r) for growth (g) (*i.e.*, "r – g") before capitalizing maintainable returns. The valuator then uses this adjusted amount to capitalize the firm's earnings.

The valuator can use one of several established methods to determine the measure of risk applicable to a company's operational returns. These include the following:

Capital Asset Pricing Model

Under the capital asset pricing model (CAPM), the expected return on an asset should equal the risk-free rate plus a risk premium related to the volatility of the excess return on an individual security to the market (beta), multiplied by the market-risk premium.

$R = R_F + B \times E(RP_{Market})$

where

R_F = Rate of return at the valuation date for a risk-free security, typically government-issued securities with durations matching the period of the firm's projected cash flows being discounted.

$E(RP_{Market})$ = Equity risk premium for the market benchmark, representing the expected future stock returns in excess of the return from bonds.

B = The risk or volatility of the subject security compared with the general market benchmark. The valuator uses the beta or volatility of the company compared with the market average to establish the company's specific risk.

In determining the cost of equity via CAPM, the valuator must consider the possibility of irregular or irrational values that without deeper reflection could be used for each of the risk-free rate, the equity risk premium and beta.

In terms of the risk-free rate, it is possible that market movements may temporarily cause the observed yield on government bonds to show anomalous results. In the case of the equity risk premium based on formulaic derivations, it, too, can yield illogical results. For these reasons, care should be taken when selecting these inputs and a well-measured amount of judgment should be included at times. In the next paragraph, we discuss this issue in connection with the determination of beta.

In volatile markets, it may be challenging to determine a reliable measure of a company's beta. This is especially challenging in the valuation of relatively small companies, since a company's volatility compared with the market benchmark is often unreliable for small publicly traded companies[11] and, for illiquid private companies, often immeasurable. Nevertheless, for larger companies, the research by Louis K. Chan and Josef Lakonsihok (1993) indicates that betas are a useful guide in extreme market conditions, based on the observation of the ten worst months for the market between 1926 and 1991.[12]

In volatile markets, where each company's returns are affected differently relative to the market, the valuator should select and apply a proper beta estimation method. For instance, during the economic crisis in late 2008 and 2009, the market was overly affected by financial stocks and stocks of highly leveraged companies. The relative volatility of returns for a company with no debt or with a low level of debt has decreased relative to the market, whose returns are overweighted by financial companies. In situations like this, it is suggested that the valuator do the following:[13]

1. Consider using other beta estimation methods such as sum beta and Miles-Ezzell formulas since the typical textbook methods are based on more stable markets.

---

11 Pratt & Niculita, above note 3, at 187. The primary reason for this is that small companies trade less frequently than the large companies in the market index, and this leads to an apparent covariance between the company and the market that is lower than the reality. Academics have proposed various ways of correcting for this problem, the simplest being the sum beta measure, which incorporates lagged market effects in the beta statistic. The details of methodology are described in Morningstar's *Ibbotson SBBI Valuation Yearbook.*

12 A. Damodaran, *Investment Valuation: Tools and Techniques for Determining the Value of Any Asset, Investment Valuation: Tools and Techniques for Determining the Value of Any Asset* (New York: John Wiley & Sons, Inc., 2002), p. 77. Original reference: L.K. Chan & J. Lakonsihok, "Are the Reports of Beta's Death Premature?" (1993) 19 *Journal of Portfolio Management* 51–62.

13 S.P. Pratt & R.J. Grabowski, "Cost of Capital in Valuation of Stock by the Income Approach: Updated for an Economy in Crisis" (2009) *The Value Examiner* 8.

2. Observe if and when there were any changes in the underlying relationship between returns for the subject/guideline company and returns for the market by graphing the monthly returns for the subject/guideline company and the market (*e.g.*, S&P 500 and TSX).

3. Consider basing the beta on the average of the month-end beta estimates over a 12-month period under "normal" market conditions, where the relationship of returns for the subject/guideline company and returns for the market appear to be more "normal."

Regardless of the methodology used for the beta estimates, the valuator must be cautious that the estimates reflect the underlying risk of the company.

In determining the cost of equity, the valuator should bear in mind that the cost of equity should be higher than the cost of debt. The absolute level of market yield for the appropriate debt rating, based on the actual or synthetic debt rating of the subject company, should be used as a benchmark for reference because the yield reflects the leverage and the company-specific risks that are imbedded in the credit rating. As an alternative method, the cost of capital could be estimated based on the current market yield of the company's debt plus an equity risk premium of four to seven per cent, depending on the rating of the debt (*i.e.*, the lower the rating, the higher the premium).[14]

Build-up Method

An alternative to CAPM is the build-up method. The rate of return for a risk-free security (R_F) is increased for the following factors:

- The market equity risk premium (RP_{Market});
- The risk premium for small size (RP_{Size});
- The industry risk premium; and
- The specific company's risk premium ($RP_{Specific}$).

$$r_{CE} = R_F + RP_{Market} + RP_{Size} + RP_{Industry} + RP_{Specific}$$

where

R_F = Rate of return for a risk-free security as of the valuation date.

---

14 *Ibid.*, pp. 11–12.

RP_{Market} = Equity risk premium as set by the determined market benchmark viewed over the appropriate period.

RP_{Size} = Size-risk premium, added in cases involving small, closely held companies to attract capital. Size may be measured by several variables, including market or book value of equity, market or book value of invested capital, revenue, and net income.

$RP_{Industry}$ = An additional industry-specific risk premium. The valuator must ensure that the equity risk premium and the company-specific risk premium have not already been captured.

$RP_{Specific}$ = The operational and financial risk of the subject company, quantified via the company-specific risk premium. An alternative to adjusting the discount rate is to quantify the cost to remedy (in cases of environmental risk). The probability is reflected in the cash flow projections as a cost.

In volatile markets, all the above variables should be reconsidered. For example, R_F may fall to a level outside of long-term norms due to investor risk aversion and RP_{Market} may not represent current expectation for returns requirements. During the economic crisis in late 2008 and 2009, the demand for risk-free assets soared significantly due to flight to quality and caused the U.S. 20-year bond yields to significantly drop by 18 per cent to 33 per cent in November (3.72 per cent) and December 2008 (3.03 per cent) from the average level of approximately 4.5 per cent in the first eight months of 2008. As the significant decline in the treasury bond yields are not related to the expected declines in the long-term inflation, the decline is expected to be temporary given the state of the economy and market at that time, and bond yields are expected to increase or return to the normal levels that existed before November 2008 as long-term inflation is expected to increase given the projected U.S. budget deficit and increase in the money supply. Unrelated to volatile markets, the appropriate RP_{Size} may be that related to the company on a stand-alone basis or that related to the potential set of acquirers. In down markets, smaller companies that are less diversified tend to suffer more and so an argument could be made for higher RP_{Size} or additional $RP_{Specific}$. Even betas may become less reliable due to historical correlations that no longer exist, with a potential solution being to favor long-term betas over short-term betas.

Weighted-Average Cost of Capital

If the return measure used is FCF-to-firm, as discussed earlier, then the value of the company must be calculated using the WACC. The value of equity is equal to the value of the entire firm less the value of the outstanding debt (and preferred shares, if applicable).

Inherent in the WACC calculation is the assumption that the current risk of the company's operation represents the future risk. If the current capital structure is significantly different from the company's future capital structure or if it does not represent the optimal capital structure for the industry, the valuator may have to make an adjustment. Target debt-to-equity weightings will be preferable in the WACC calculation.

$$WACC = \left(\frac{MV_{Debt}}{MV_{Total}} \right) r_D (1-t) + \left(\frac{MV_{CE}}{MV_{Total}} \right) r_{CE}$$

where

MV_{Debt} = Total market value of the company's outstanding debt. If the company is privately held, the valuator must use professional judgment in determining its fair market value.

r_D = Pre-tax cost of debt financing available to the company as of the valuation date.

(1-t) = After-tax cost of debt given the income-tax rate applicable to the company.

MV_{CE} = Total market value of the company's common equity.

R_{CE} = The cost of common equity as determined by CAPM, build-up, or alternative methods.

MV_{Total} = Total market value of all sources of capital (both debt and equity).

In calculating a company's cost of capital, the valuator should consider the following factors:

- All sources of capital must be reflected in the WACC calculation, including off-balance-sheet financing and preferred shares.
- Market values rather than book values must be used when determining the current weighting. This best reflects the required return on these forms of capital at the time of valuation.
- A target weighting for the capital structure is sometimes appropriate if the current capital structure is not the company's optimal financing structure or if it does not reflect the anticipated future cost of capital to the firm.

In volatile markets, it may be difficult to obtain financing or financing may be abundant. Availability of financing in the short term should be balanced with long-term expectations and the debt weighting should be adjusted accordingly.

Optimal Capital Structure

An optimal capital structure reduces a company's overall risk. With lower risk, investors require a lower rate of return. Future cash flows from operations translate into a greater present value, and the company acquires a higher overall EV. The valuator should keep in mind that an optimal capital structure is established by referencing the subject company's industry average. The valuator needs to examine reasons why the subject company's capital structure would be similar or different. Altering a firm's proportion of debt and equity is not a cost-free proposition, and the valuator should view an optimization from the perspective of what is not only possible but also what is practical. An industry-average capital structure does not require all companies to revert to the mean. However, in a volatile market downturn, where credit conditions are tight and economic uncertainties exist, such as the post-2008 global financial crisis, many companies, both public and private, are required to de-lever. Furthermore, significant higher equity investment is required by the financial lenders for corporate acquisitions. Thus, a valuator is required to understand and take into consideration the current market's financing conditions and requirements in determining a reasonable capital structure for the subject company.

The valuator should consider the following factors before adjusting a company's capital structure to lower its overall cost of capital:

- Private companies typically have less access to debt and less liquid equity instruments than public companies.
- Measuring the cost of debt financing can be difficult for companies at the venture-capital stage or in technology industries where equity-participation features and embedded convertible options are common.
- If the company's existing management has not opted for a lower cost of capital, is it limited in its options or limited in its abilities? If you use a lower risk rate through an alternative capital structure, you may be acknowledging higher risk from weak management. However, one should be cognizant of the fact that an optimal capital structure is often improbable for many private companies, which are more often driven by the owner's risk tolerances.
- In valuing a minority interest that has minimal control over operations and little influence over management, lowering a firm's overall risk is not always possible.

Company-Specific Risk

A company-specific risk premium is a component of each cost-of-capital model and is based on company-specific external and internal risk factors that have not been considered by other means in the valuation. It reflects the specific risk of the subject company's future cash flows as a result of its overall operational structure and competitive positioning.

Company-specific risk is generally difficult to identify and imprecise to measure. Valuators must consider it, however, in valuing an investment that is not completely liquid and diversified. Company-specific risk must also be quantified for any business that is not structured as a limited liability entity.

Valuators use models such as CAPM and arbitrage-pricing theory to assess the required return of publicly traded securities within a larger diversified portfolio. They use a company-specific risk premium to calculate the return required by investors for risks that cannot be tempered by diversification. There are no generally accepted models, formulas, equations, or methods to measure company-specific risk premiums. Either directly, in determining the cost of equity capital, or indirectly, in deriving pricing multiples from comparable company transactions, the valuator must use professional judgment to measure and quantify the financial, operational, and strategic factors of the subject company.

Risk factors typical to company-specific analysis include the following:

- historic volatility of revenue and earnings;
- management depth and ability;
- key-person dependency;
- technology reliance and obsolescence risk;
- access to capital resources;
- geographical diversification;
- purchasing power and economies of scale;
- customer diversification;
- reliance on key suppliers;
- key contracts;
- owning patents;
- forecast risk;
- unique product, proprietary products, or market niche; and
- quality of financial reporting and controls.

When reviewing and quantifying the risk factors specific to the valuation of an individual company, the valuator must guard against double counting. Company-specific risk factors are difficult to segregate from the overall analysis of the subject company's return projections and its required return.

In calculating company-specific risk and incorporating it into the valuation exercise, valuators most commonly make errors such as the following:

- adjusting for the same company-specific risk factors in both the discount rate and the projection of future cash flows;
- making a company-specific risk adjustment that is already captured in the industry analysis and small-company risk premium; and
- making en bloc adjustments for company-specific risk for key-person dependency, supplier dependency, and customer concentration that are already included in the discount rate to capitalize cash flows.

Common Cost-of-Capital Errors

Small changes to the estimated required rate of return are magnified when earnings or cash flows are capitalized. Confusion or misunderstanding arises most frequently in determining a firm's cost of capital when the following occurs:

- The cost of capital is based on the risk of the business operations or the investment, independent of the specific investor.
- The valuator does not distinguish between a firm's historic required rate of return and the expected required rate of return in the future.
- The cost of a company's capital is based on current market value returns and not historic book value returns.
- The valuator confuses discount rate with capitalization rate.
- The valuator uses the firm's historic cost of capital to evaluate projects or future business operations that are expected to be more or less risky.
- The valuator inconsistently matches risk and return measures, such as pre-tax versus after-tax and real versus nominal.
- The valuator continues to project revenue growth beyond the capital structure's sustainable limit.

Residual Growth Rate

Whether it is used to project future cash flows or to determine constant growth to establish the terminal capitalization rate and residual value, a company's rate of growth is a critical component of all valuations. In fact, for a technology firm, anticipated future growth will often account for most of its total value, especially if the firm is privately held.

The valuator should consider several points to calculate a reasonable residual growth rate or growth rate in perpetuity (GRIP), including the following:

- evidence used to establish the GRIP;
- underlying financial forecast for the company;
- adjustments made to the forecast in the terminal period; and
- reasonableness of terminal value given business environment and overall value conclusion.

Supporting Evidence

Valuators frequently determine a company's GRIP with reference to the growth of the economic sector in which it operates and the growth in gross domestic product (GDP). Most companies experience rapid growth during their development and expansion phases, but eventually they reach a mature phase when their expansion becomes slow but steady. In most cases, in the long run a company will seldom grow faster than the economy. However, a valuator needs more than the forecast growth rate of the GDP to determine an appropriate GRIP. Other factors should be considered as well, such as the growth rate of the industry in which the business operates. The valuator should also critically ask and examine where the growth is coming from and the likelihood of its persistence. In some cases, such as in auto parts, revenue growth may not grow in line with expenses, as automobile manufacturers often contract for a reduced price over time, whereas employee salary costs may increase over time, unless productivity increases are significant.

If inflation affects the pricing of the company's products or services, the valuator should incorporate into the GRIP the expected rate of inflation. Since inflation adjustments are usually based on the Consumer Price Index (CPI), the valuator should carefully evaluate the goods and services included in the CPI. The CPI represents a basket of average goods and services, but it may not indicate accurately the pricing pressures applicable to more specialized products or services. In some industries, the Producer Price Index (PPI) may be more applicable or the GDP deflator, which combines both CPI and PPI. A good measure of long-term inflation is the excess return on long-term Treasury bills compared with real-return or inflation-protected bonds.

The valuator may also review analysts' research reports on comparable public companies to determine a reasonable GRIP. Research analysts clearly understand the companies they cover and their related industries and often include a GRIP in their research, which can be used to support the valuator's own conclusions.

Underlying Financial Forecasts

The length and accuracy of a financial forecast will influence the selection of the appropriate GRIP. The longer the period covered by the financial forecast, the more uncertain the company's ability to meet it. The valuator also has to assess carefully a company's ability to meet a high-growth forecast over an extended period, especially in the terminal period. The valuator may even incorporate excess forecast risk into the company's WACC, especially in volatile times. If management's forecast, however, has been revised appropriately to consider market uncertainties and down markets and fewer sales to marginal customers, then this would decrease forecast risk and the WACC.

Terminal Period Adjustments

The valuator should make appropriate adjustments to ensure that the GRIP is consistent with the company's financial forecast in the terminal period. Valuators most commonly adjust standard charges such as working capital and sustaining capital expenditures for the terminal period, since these factors must be included to support a company's growth forecast.

In volatile times, the forecast should capture enough years such that there is ample time for the revenue and earnings to revert to historical norms or trends. In this way, the terminal value only captures steady-state earnings, instead of doing double duty where it must capture growth during volatile times and steady-state earnings, a combination that would decrease transparency in the valuation.

Overall Reasonability

After determining a GRIP, valuators should assess its impact on their value conclusion and ensure, for example, that the WACC captures any additional risk generated by the selected GRIP. They can assess the GRIP by calculating the exit multiple (such as EBITDA multiple) implied by the terminal value. They should also examine the proportion of total enterprise value that relates solely to the terminal value. A longer-term forecast with terminal value comprising a significant portion of the overall value is inherently more risky.

Market-Based Approaches

Using a market-based approach, the valuator compares a company directly with other companies to estimate the fair market value of its common shares.

Also called relative or comparable valuation, it involves the comparison of several key ratios. These comparable multiples are determined using traditional valuation methodologies such as earnings and cash flow analysis. The most commonly used ratios or price multiples include price-to-earnings, price-to-cash flow, price-to-book value, enterprise value-to-sales and enterprise value-to-EBITDA.

Valuators cannot use a comparable price multiple approach in all situations. They must first analyze prior transactions to determine if they meet several criteria:

- Arm's Length: transactions based on related-party transactions have little evidentiary value;
- Size of Transaction: comparable transactions must be sufficiently similar in size to be useful;
- Time Proximity: the valuator should make adjustments to account for differences in company specifics or market conditions that arise between the valuation date and the dates of comparable transactions; and
- Contractual Agreements: the valuator should consider contractual commitments specific to other transactions to determine if constraints or requirements reduce the utility of the comparables.

Comparative or relative valuation techniques are intuitive, easy to compute, and quickly understood. They show how investments are currently valued in the broader marketplace. Unlike DCF models, they do not require the valuator to estimate multiple input variables.

However, the relevance and reliability of a comparable analysis depends on certain factors such as the following:

- The comparison must be appropriate in terms of industry, company size, historical growth rates, profitability margins, total assets, and risk characteristics. Public companies will often have multiple business segments, whereas the company being valued may only operate in one segment.
- Open-market transactions may contain a synergistic component. The valuator will have difficulty segregating these perceived transaction-specific strategic advantages from the overall price.
- The valuator should understand how price multiples relate to the company's underlying fundamentals.
- The valuator should confirm that the industry group from which the multiples are derived is not in the midst of extreme, broad-based fluctuations in valuation.

- A company's accounting choices will affect price multiples to varying degrees. The valuator may have to make normalization adjustments to improve comparability.
- Many open-market transactions include non-cash components such as share exchanges, vendor take-back notes at non-market interest rates, earn-outs, management contracts, and non-competition payments. The valuator must convert these alternative forms of payment into a cash-equivalent value.

Price-to-Earnings

Relative price-to-earnings (P/E) ratios are used most frequently in the valuation of large public companies whose shares are traded on liquid public exchanges. Their valuation incorporates adjustments for management discretion in applying allowable accounting practices and for items of a transitory, non-recurring, or cyclical nature.

Privately held companies are more likely to use P/E ratios indirectly in determining a fundamental valuation that reflects the market's required rate of return appropriate for the business's projected future cash flows. To determine the return required for capital invested in a company, the valuator may consider P/E multiples of comparable private companies at the time of their acquisition or current P/E multiples of publicly traded companies and industry indexes. The P/E is inversely related to the required rate of return.

For example, a comparable transaction at a per-share value of \$44, with earnings per share of \$5.50, implies a P/E ratio of 8.0 times. The implied required return is the inverse of this calculation: \$5.50 of annual earnings per \$44 of capital invested, or 12.5 per cent. This 12.5 per cent return is the risk multiple that the valuator uses to determine the appropriate discount rate. This rate is applied to a company's projected future earnings.

$$\text{P/E} = \mathbf{8x} = \frac{\$44.00}{\$5.50} \qquad \text{Required Return} = \mathbf{12.5\%} = \frac{\$5.50}{\$44.00}$$

To the extent there is growth, P/E multiples are higher.

Price-to-Cash Flow

A price-to-cash flow (P/CF) ratio is often used in relative valuation models. It is generally considered more stable and less vulnerable to manipulation than reported earnings. However, the method of estimating cash flow can influence the P/CF ratio. Free cash flow-to-equity is often considered the appropriate comparable cash flow measure.

The P/CF ratio presents potential drawbacks, including the following:

- Measures such as free cash flow-to-equity may be negative and are frequently volatile. For instance, companies in the start-up and early stages may have negative free cash flow due to the initial investments in machinery and equipment (*e.g.*, technology companies).
- Items such as non-cash revenue or net change in working capital are poorly accounted for in some cash flow measures such as cash flow from operations.

Enterprise Value-to-Sales

Privately held businesses such as investment management companies, partnerships, and professional practices have long been valued using a multiple of their annual maintainable revenues or expected sales. Like cash flow, sales figures are considered more resistant to manipulation than earnings.

Enterprise value-to-sales (EV/S) ratios are now used increasingly as a reliable valuation indicator for both public and private companies. Specifically, EV/S ratios are often used to value companies that are mature, cyclical, or not yet or not currently profitable.

There are several advantages to using a EV/S ratio in a valuation analysis:

- Sales are positive even when earnings are negative. A meaningful EV/S ratio is possible even when a P/E analysis is not viable and may be more appropriate for mature, zero-income, and/or cyclical businesses.
- Top-line sales are usually less subject to distortion than book values or earnings per share. However, during the dot-com bubble between 1995 and 2001, some high-tech companies applied abusive and questionable revenue-boosting and revenue-recognition policies, such as recognizing intercompany and instalment sales, booking barter transactions at highly inflated prices, and, in the case of some dot-com auction sites, booking the gross selling price of goods rather than a commission, often overstating their true revenue level by more than 20 times.
- EV/S ratios do not reflect operating or financial leverage. They are generally more stable than earnings, book value, or cash flow ratios.

- EV/S ratios eliminate cost structure differences. A vivid example would be the acquisition of a small growth-oriented investment management company by a larger competitor. The acquirer, being much bigger, would have economies of scale and would likely downsize certain management and administrative positions as the target's operations are folded into its own. In this way, valuing the target based on earnings, which may have been depressed by expenses used to build the business, may be less useful than an EV/S valuation. This is especially true in a market context where there would be multiple bidders for the company who would bid the value of the company up to a market-participant fair market value as opposed to a base intrinsic value.

Nevertheless, EV/S ratios have some drawbacks. To have value as a going concern, for example, a business must ultimately generate a positive cash flow. Ultimately, all businesses depend on cash flow for their value. The further removed the valuation metric or ratio is from this primary consideration, the less reliable the analysis.

Further drawbacks of using the EV/S ratio include the following:

- A company's cost structure influences its value and risk and often requires analysis that the EV/S ratio cannot capture.
- Revenue-recognition accounting practices may bias sales numbers. However, most companies in the same industry sector follow similar generally accepted accounting standards, accessible to the valuator.

Price-to-Book Value

A company's price-to-book value (P/BV) per share represents the price paid for a share divided by the book value per share. The book value per share represents the history of the investment made in the company by common shareholders plus retained earnings since inception. Book value can also be calculated through a rearranging of the standard accounting equation such that it is the book value of assets less the book value of liabilities. It is derived from historic accounting book values as opposed to market values.

Recently, it has become a less useful indicator of value for U.S. banks. Historically, P/BV multiples for Citigroup Inc. were mostly in the order of 2.0 times to 2.5 times. However, in 2008, as book values remained elevated and were written down at most quarterly compared with market values that were based on current share prices, the multiple became less useful as a measure of value. An investor may have a view as to what the "correct" multiple ought to be, but to what book value should this be applied? To make the application of the P/BV multiple approach more challenging, investors had to consider to what extent Citigroup had already taken massive writedowns to book values, mostly mortgages, such that applying a low multiple to a low book value may be double counting. At the time of writing, Citigroup's book value was in the range of 0.2 times to 0.3 times, suggesting that significant writedowns of assets were imminent and that applying traditional measures of price-to-book value would be quite meaningless to determine value due to the potential divergence in inputs and outputs in connection with the P/BV approach.

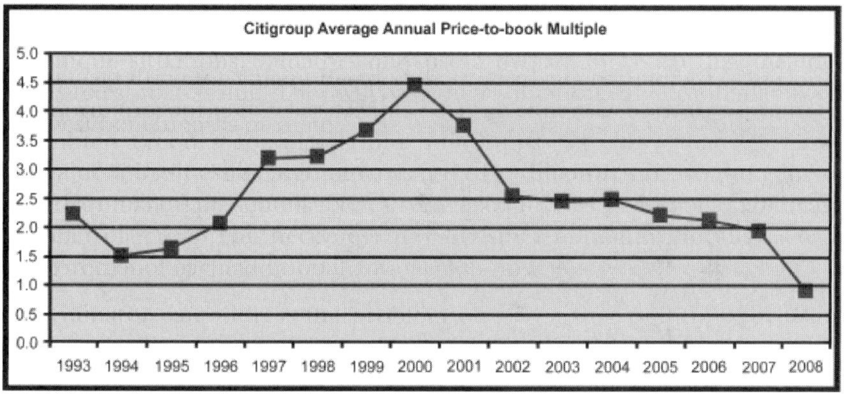

Price-to-earnings, price-to-cash flow, and EV-to-sales ratios all contain measures of value in the denominator relating to the income statement. The measure of value in a P/BV ratio is derived from the balance sheet.

A P/BV ratio is more relevant when market value is close to book value or can be derived from it. This is often the case in finance, investment, and insurance companies and in manufacturing companies, whose value depends primarily on hard or tangible assets such as pulp and paper plants, steel mills, or power plants or businesses that have yet to begin generating operating cash flows. P/BV can also be employed in valuing companies that are expected to cease operations. However, in volatile times, such as in late 2008 and 2009, when both mortgages and the overall credit worthiness of numerous banks, other corporations, and individuals were called into question, historic book values may overstate or not correspond well to fair market value as shown in the Citigroup example above.

On the other hand, most high-tech and dot-com businesses have a large portion of value for intellectual property such as patents, trademarks, trade secrets, and human capital brainpower, which is usually not reflected in historical book values of these companies.

Book value is more stable than earnings. However, valuators use it most frequently as a relative risk measure when making income-based value assessments.

In many cases, however, using a P/BV metric may not reflect all elements of a business's value, for reasons such as the following:

- Service companies, for example, depend heavily for their value on human capital, the skills and knowledge possessed by their work forces.
- The balance sheet often does not reflect the value of identifiable intangible assets such as trademarks, formulas, and business processes.
- Accounting treatments for inventory costing, depreciation, and research and development expenditures may compromise book values. Uncertainties may also arise around book values as a result of capitalization policies of certain costs such as interest, application of fair value accounting for acquisitions but not for the company's previously owned assets, and impairment write-downs in down markets.
- Factors such as inflation and technological change will cause a significant divergence between book and market values.

Book values also reflect poorly the value of a common equity investment. This in turn impairs the comparability of P/BV between different companies in the same industry. As previously stated, the primary driver of an investment's value is future cash flow, not historic book value, income for reporting purposes, or taxable income.

Non-Financial Metrics

Non-financial metrics are mathematical formulas or ratios developed from relationships between historic prices and certain variables derived from past comparable transactions. They frequently incorporate significant industry knowledge, tend to represent the mean or median average, and are typically not traceable to a specific transaction.

Valuators occasionally use industry-specific metrics in valuing companies when useful rules regarding acquisition and value have become well-established as generally accepted practice. Valuators refer to price-per-bed metrics, for example, when valuing companies in the health-care industry or price-per-subscriber for companies operating in the cable or mobile communications industries. Valuation measurement tools often become established in industries in which regulations restrict or mandate returns.

Alternatively, valuators use non-financial metrics to check the reasonableness of values based on more conventional income-based methods.

Assessing Reasonableness

Determination of the Valuation Range

Since valuations involve judgment and assumptions, valuators generally express their conclusions as a range of value. The range must be wide enough to capture the valuator's key assumptions while narrow enough to be meaningful to the end user. The range itself requires good judgment from the valuator. Typically, it extends five per cent to 10 per cent in both directions from the midpoint value, but the range can be wider in volatile markets.

Due to the significant economic uncertainty in volatile markets, some valuators have expanded the qualifications and limitations attached to their reports. The reason for this is because of the extraordinary times in which we live at the time of writing. Many consider the events of late-2008 to mid-2009 to be a "black swan" event, and significant uncertainty is expected to permeate the markets into late-2009 and beyond.

Primary and Secondary Approaches

The valuator generally chooses one method as the primary approach to valuation but will often use several methods to confirm that the valuation conclusion is reasonable. The valuator will analyze differences in value reached through the primary and secondary methods and may adjust the assumptions if the differences don't make sense. In the end, the major qualitative and quantitative considerations and the valuator's experience should be reconciled with the value conclusion. In fact, the valuator's experience strongly influences the ability to assess the value conclusion. Based on this experience, the valuator can assess whether an informed party would pay the price implied by the valuation. The valuator can also determine if the range of value corresponds consistently to similar situations encountered in the past.

In volatile times, secondary approaches could become more or less useful depending on the circumstances. For example, trading multiples of minority interests may become less useful as a value indicator for control interest. Forecasts used for DCF analyses may become increasingly less reliable – when will we come out of the recession or inflated bull market? How bad or overinflated will it get? The valuator, in order to produce an opinion on value, will need to answer these questions and, in the case of a DCF approach to value, answer them explicitly. In a recessionary market, the cost approach may become prevalent either due to the possibility of liquidation or lack of earnings.

Goodwill Reasonableness

The value of a business often consists of tangible value and goodwill (including identifiable intangible assets). A valuator can measure tangible value with relative objectivity. To assess the value of goodwill, the valuator must choose one of several measures, including the following:

- Level of Implied Goodwill: the value of the business, excluding redundant assets and tangible asset backing,[15] usually expressed as a percentage of the business's overall value. The valuator compares this figure with similar businesses to assess its reasonableness.
- Goodwill/Maintainable Cash Flow: the number of years of maintainable cash flow represented by goodwill. The valuator reaches a reasonable conclusion by considering the length of time it would take to re-create existing goodwill if the same business were started from scratch.
- Goodwill/Other Bases: goodwill divided by sales, EBITDA, or other industry-specific measures. The valuator compares this figure with multiples in similar businesses based on prior experience and comparables.
- Dual Capitalization: the discount rate used in valuing a business represents a blended weighted-average rate encompassing the rates of return required on all the asset classes of the business. Using the dual capitalization approach, the valuator applies a charge to the net tangible assets and subtracts this amount from the overall maintainable cash flow to determine the implied cash flows related to goodwill/intangible assets. The valuator divides this figure by the implied level of goodwill to determine the implied return on goodwill. The valuator then uses past experience and comparables to assess this return. For example:

Value of the business excluding redundant assets:	$1,000,000
Value of net tangible assets:	$200,000
Maintainable cash flow:	$150,000
Assessed required return on tangible assets:	10%
Implied goodwill ($1,000,000 – $200,000)	$800,000

---

15 Tangible asset backing is calculated the same way as adjusted book value, mentioned earlier. The term tangible asset backing, however, is used when assessing risk, while the term adjusted book value relates to the value of a business under the cost approach.

Maintainable cash flow (above)	$150,000
Less: return on tangible assets: $200,000 * 10%	$20,000
Implied cash flow related to intangible assets:	$130,000
Implied goodwill (above)	$800,000
Implied return on goodwill:	
$130,000/$800,000 =	16.25%

Overall Reasonableness Checks

In addition to assessing goodwill, the valuator assesses total firm value, also referred to as EV, excluding redundant assets. To do this, the valuator calculates such multiples as EV-to-EBITDA, EV-to-EBIT, EV-to-book value of EV (typically employed to a lesser extent than the other multiples), and EV-to-sales and compares them with previously valued companies and comparable companies.

Valuators often use EV instead of equity value to eliminate the impact of differing leverage among companies in making comparisons. In assessing EV, the valuator must use comparable multiples, determined appropriately (*i.e.*, redundant assets are not included in the numerator).

Communication of the Value Conclusion

The valuator commonly communicates the conclusion in a formal valuation report that ranges from 30 to 150 pages or more. A portion of the document may consist of schedules and appendices.

At a minimum, the valuation report should disclose enough information to allow a reader to understand how the valuator has arrived at a value or value range. Valuators must abide by generally accepted standards that ensure quality and consistency of valuation assignments and communications. To this end, organizations such as the Canadian Institute of Chartered Business Valuators (CICBV) and the American Society of Appraisers (ASA) guide valuators in producing valuation reports. For example, the CICBV suggests three types of reports:

- comprehensive valuation;
- estimate valuation; and
- calculation valuation.

Each type of report requires a different degree of information disclosure, depending on the complexity, purpose, and level of assurance required.

Depending on the context, the valuator may present the results of a valuation in presentation form or as an advisory, expert, or limited-critique report.

Intangible Asset Valuations

As we stated in the previous chapter, an ever-increasing percentage of overall corporate value is attributable to assets with no tangible presence. These intangible assets typically include patents, trademarks, copyrights, formulas, processes, and licences.

To assign value to these assets, valuators often use a variation of the income approach, which includes elements of a market-based comparable analysis. It is called the relief-from-royalty method.

> ***Practice Tip***
>
> A company that does not possess intangible assets is not likely ever to be very valuable.
>
> **Russell L. Parr,**
> ***Investing in Intangible Assets: Finding and Profiting from Hidden Corporate Value***

Relief-from-Royalty Method

In the relief-from-royalty method, the valuator assumes that property such as a trademark, know-how, or technology is owned by a third party; the true owner pays a royalty for the right to use it and reaps the associated economic benefits. Since the true owner actually owns the asset, there is a cost saving equivalent to the calculated royalty.

The valuator begins with an analysis of business operations to estimate future revenue associated with ownership of the property. After projecting revenue, the valuator determines an appropriate royalty rate[16] to calculate annual royalty savings. To this end, the valuator discounts annual royalty savings at a rate commensurate with the risk of the future benefit stream. Finally, the sum of the resulting present values is calculated to estimate the overall value of the asset.

Using the royalty savings method, the valuator performs the following steps:

- compares margins of industry competitors;
- reviews market evidence of arm's length royalty rates;
- establishes a reasonable range based on expected profitability;

[16] A royalty typically provides for periodic payments that are proportionate to the degree of use of the licensed property and is most often expressed as a percentage of the revenue.

- forecasts sales for subject trademarked goods or services;
- calculates royalty savings based on sales, royalty rate, and tax rate; and
- establishes the discount rate and present value of the royalty stream.

Using this method, the valuator assumes exclusive use of the asset by one party. Alternatively, the valuator could assume licensing of the asset to several parties and consider the present value of cash flows to all of them.

Royalty Rate Analysis

The valuator must structure the notional licence agreement and the means of payment to reach a royalty scheme reasonable to all parties. This is done by considering the method of royalty calculation and economic factors that have emerged through the valuator's licensing experience.

Intellectual property licences most commonly involve a running royalty, which provides for periodic royalty payments in proportion to the degree of use of the licensed property. The royalty rate is typically applied to a base such as revenue associated with the licensed product. Less commonly, royalty rates are expressed as a charge per unit of goods produced or some other degree of use.

Running royalties have become popular because they link payments to actual usage. The licensee's payment obligation to the licensor increases or decreases in proportion to the benefit derived from the asset. For the licensor, the running royalty provides a rational basis for negotiation and ensures that remuneration corresponds to the actual value of the transferred asset.

A running royalty payment depends on the royalty base and the royalty rate. A desirable royalty base should vary directly with the degree of asset use while minimizing associated accounting issues.

In many instances, particular industries license technology at a prevailing range of royalty rates. Since royalty rates vary among industries, the valuator must identify the characteristics of the market served and select transactions from the same market or similar markets when analyzing royalty rate data.

Companies often enter into licensing agreements after protracted negotiations with unrelated third parties whose economic interests differ from their own. The valuator can usefully apply the royalty rate specified in these arm's length transactions to the property in question, establishing a basis from which to estimate value. However, the valuator must select only market royalty-rate transactions involving assets and industries similar to the ones under consideration.

Royalty Rate

The royalty rate represents the rate that owners of the intangible asset would charge for licensing it to a third party. To estimate the appropriate royalty rate for valuing an intangible asset, the valuator must obtain data involving the licensing of intellectual property. Arm's length consideration for a controlled transfer of an intangible asset generally equals the consideration charged or incurred in a comparable uncontrolled transaction. When reasonable information is available, the comparison of uncontrolled transactions provides the most accurate measure of an arm's length charge for the transfer of intangible property.

In applying this method, valuators should consider access to relevant pricing and other financial information and the existence of an active market in which contemporaneous transactions involving comparable assets occur between uncontrolled parties. Since royalty rates vary among industries, valuators should compare market transactions from the same or similar industries.

The table below shows royalty rates applied to developed technologies licensed in arm's length agreements:

Guideline Transactions for Technology Licenses

Technology Comparable	Royalty Rate
Technology A	3%
Technology B	5%
Technology C	4%
Technology D	5%
Technology E	5%
Technology F	3%
Technology G	5%
Technology H	4%

The royalty rates in the above table range between three per cent and five per cent of revenues. This provides an initial range of royalty rates for valuing a developed technology. The valuator applies the royalty rate to revenue projections to calculate the relief from royalty associated with the asset over its estimated remaining useful life. The valuator calculates the annual royalty savings by multiplying projected revenue for each year by the royalty rate.

To conduct a valid royalty-rate analysis, the valuator needs sufficient and meaningful comparative data. This can be obtained from the following sources:

- the transfer-pricing groups of major accounting firms, which often maintain data on tens of thousands of royalty-rate transactions;
- firms that specialize in the valuation of intellectual property;
- industry associations; and
- financial information services that collect and sell royalty information (*e.g.*, RoyaltySource.com, Royaltystat.com).

Discount Rate

The valuator can also assess the economic benefits of an intangible asset using future cash flows for each year of expected use. The valuator converts these figures to a present value using the cost-of-capital or discount rate. This addresses the risks inherent in the asset and compensates an investor for assuming them. The capital structure for the asset can be established by considering the capital structure for similar assets.

The valuator calculates the present value of the after-tax projected cash flows using the midpoint convention, which assumes that cash flows are distributed throughout each reporting period and are appropriately discounted using the midpoint.

Amortization Tax Benefit

All the cash flows associated with an asset's ownership contribute to its value. When an asset's future cash flow includes the benefits associated with shielding income from tax through amortization, the valuation must capture that benefit. The valuator must include the incremental value associated with the amortization tax benefits in the DCF analysis to estimate the fair value of the intangible asset.

The valuator incorporates tax benefits from amortization of the intangible asset value according to the governing tax regulations. For instance, under the U.S. Internal Revenue Code, amortization is recognized if the asset is acquired and held in connection with a trade or business or used in an activity for the production of income. The amortization deduction reduces the taxes payable on the pre-tax income associated with the intangible asset. The tax savings from amortization represents an additional economic benefit associated with the intangible asset. Consequently, intangible asset value equals the sum of the incremental after-tax cash flows directly attributable to the intangible asset plus the tax benefits accruing from amortization.

Intangible asset value can be expressed mathematically as the sum of the pre-amortization value and the amortization tax benefit. The valuator establishes the relationship between the value exclusive of amortization and the value inclusive of amortization benefits with the following calculation:

$$AV = PAV + ((AV)(t) / TL)(ADF)$$

where

AV = Asset value
PAV = Pre-amortization asset value
t = Tax rate
ADF = Annuity discount factor (present value factor sum for the tax life)
TL = Tax life of the intangible asset

PAV represents the pre-amortization value of the intangible asset, considering the incremental after-tax cash flows attributable to the asset, but before inclusion of the asset's amortization. AV (t(ADF)/TL) represents the benefit from amortizing the asset value over its tax life. The intangible asset value equals the sum of these two values.

The annuity discount factor (ADF) represents the present value of a constant annuity over the tax life of the intangible asset. In many instances, the valuator considers a mid-period discounting convention when analyzing an intangible asset valuation. The valuator modifies the calculation to reflect a mid-period convention, applying the following adjustment to the annuity discount factor:

$$ADF = \frac{((1 - (1 + r)^{-TL})(1 + r)^{0.5})}{r}$$

To calculate the value of the amortization tax benefit, the valuator first calculates the value without considering the tax benefit obtained from the purchase of the intangible asset. The valuator then modifies the pre-amortization asset value to reflect amortization tax benefits from the acquired intangible asset by incorporating the present value of the tax benefit achieved from amortizing the intangible asset over its tax life. The valuator then combines the tax amortization benefit associated with the amortization of the intangible asset with the present value of the cash flows to calculate the intangible asset value.

Technology Valuations

A valuator can assess a going-concern technology business using one or more of the approaches described previously. The dual excess earnings method, however, has become increasingly common as a technology valuation model. Valuators frequently use the dual excess earnings approach for fair value accounting purposes to estimate the contributory value of various assets.

Dual Excess Earnings

In technology-based businesses, the combination of technology and customer relationships often produces a measurable economic benefit. Technology in such businesses generates value through the sale of a proprietary technology to a recurring customer base, in contrast to the sale of a product or service in which the technology is embedded. As a result, the valuator may have to use an income approach to value the technology rather than a relief-from-royalty or cost approach. If the valuator relies on an excess earnings approach as the primary methodology for valuing technology and customer relationships, complications can arise in the derivation of contributory asset charges needed to separate earnings from excess earnings.

In these circumstances, valuators may face the challenge of circularity if they use an excess earnings approach to value a saleable technology or intellectual property asset that also leverages intangible customer relationship assets to drive value.

Since technology contributes to the value of customer relationships and customer relationships contribute to the value of technology, the determination of an appropriate contributory asset charge for each appears iterative. A technology charge is needed to value customer relationships and vice versa. For example:

ABC Company is a mature software provider, selling one product suite, AlphaSuite 3.0. Long-term projections for ABC are as follows:

	%	Year 1	Year 2	Year 3	Year 4	Year 5	Year 6	Year 7	Year 8	Year 9	Year 10
Revenue	*5.0%*	1,000	1,050	1,103	1,158	1,216	1,276	1,340	1,407	1,477	1,551
COGS	*15.0%*	150	158	165	174	182	191	201	211	222	233
R&D	*35.0%*	350	368	386	405	425	447	469	492	517	543
S&M	*20.0%*	200	210	221	232	243	255	268	281	295	310
G&A	*10.0%*	100	105	110	116	122	128	134	141	148	155
EBIT		**200**	**210**	**221**	**232**	**243**	**255**	**268**	**281**	**295**	**310**

Based on historical experience and norms for the industry, the estimated life of the technology is five years, assuming 25 per cent of research and development spending is directed toward maintenance of the technology. ABC Company has an established customer base with an estimated life of eight years, assuming 50 per cent of sales and marketing expenditures are directed toward the existing customer base. We assume the following characteristics apply to the expected operating results of ABC Company.

Assumptions

Revenue Growth	5.0%
COGS – % of Revenues	15%
R&D – % of Revenues	30.0%
S&M – % of Revenues	20.0%
G&A – % of Revenues	12.5%
Technology Annual Migration Factor	20.0%
Customer Relationship Annual Migration Factor	12.5%
Working Capital CAC	1.0%
Fixed Asset CAC	2.0%
Technology R&D Maintenance – % of R&D	25.0%
Customer S&M Maintenance – % of S&M	50.0%

Based on these assumptions and characteristics, valuing both ABC Company's technology and customer relationship assets under an excess earnings approach with dual contributory asset cross-charges (CAC) would produce the following results:

Technology	Rate	Year 1	Year 2	Year 3	Year 4	Year 5	Year 6
Revenue		1,000	1,050	1,103	1,158	1,216	1,276
Technology Migration Factor		100%	80%	60%	40%	20%	0%
Adjusted Technology Revenues		1,000	840	662	463	243	-
COGS	15.0%	150	126	99	69	36	-
R&D	8.8%	88	74	58	41	21	-
S&M	10.0%	100	84	66	46	24	-
G&A	10.0%	100	84	66	46	24	-
Working Capital CAC	1.0%	10	8	7	5	2	-
Fixed Asset CAC	2.0%	20	17	13	9	5	-
Customer CAC	34.2%	342	288	226	159	83	-
Excess Earnings		190	160	126	88	46	-
Present Value Factor	20%	0.83	0.69	0.58	0.48	0.40	0.33
Present Value		158.43	110.90	72.78	42.45	18.57	0.00
	403						
Required Rate of Return	20%						
Annual Return On (constant dollars)	81						
Annual Return Of (constant dollars)	81						
Implied CAC - Technology	**16.1%**						

Customer Relationship Valuation	Rate	Year 1	Year 2	Year 3	Year 4	Year 5	Year 6	Year 7	Year 8	Year 9
Revenue		1,000	1,050	1,103	1,158	1,216	1,276	1,340	1,407	1,477
Customer Migration Factor		100%	88%	75%	63%	50%	38%	25%	13%	0%
Adjusted Technology Revenues		1,000	919	827	724	608	479	335	176	-
COGS	15.0%	150	138	124	109	91	72	50	26	-
R&D	8.8%	88	80	72	63	53	42	29	15	-
S&M	10.0%	100	92	83	72	61	48	34	18	-
G&A	10.0%	100	92	83	72	61	48	34	18	-
Working Capital CAC	1.0%	10	9	8	7	6	5	3	2	-
Fixed Asset CAC	2.0%	20	18	17	14	12	10	7	4	-
Technology CAC	16.1%	161	148	133	117	98	77	54	28	-
Excess Earnings		371	341	307	269	226	178	124	65	-
Present Value	20%	0.83	0.69	0.58	0.48	0.40	0.33	0.28	0.23	0.19
Present Value		309	237	178	130	91	60	35	15	0.00
	1,053									
Required Rate of Return	20%									
Annual Return On (constant dollars)	211									
Annual Return Of (constant dollars)	132									
Implied CAC - Customer Relationships	**34.2%**									

As the table above shows, the calculation of ABC Company's technology and customer relationships is circular via their respective contributory asset charges. Although we can force spreadsheet programs to solve the circularity of this approach, we still have to address questions about the bases of our results:

- Are earnings from the sale of existing technology to a new customer being burdened with a charge for existing customer relationships?
- Are earnings from the sale of new technology to existing customers being burdened with a charge for existing technology?
- Does the technology contributory asset charge provide adequate returns for new technology yet to be developed?
- To what degree are excess earnings attributed to existing customer relationships generated from the sale of new technology or existing technology?
- Does the customer contributory asset charge provide adequate returns for new customer relationships yet to be developed?
- To what degree are excess earnings attributed to existing technology generated from sales to new customers versus existing customers?

Quadrant Approach

To address some of the above questions and avoid the circularity of the excess earnings approach, the valuator can directly partition the future cash flows (sometimes referred to as a profit-split approach). This isolates the individual future economic benefits attributable to each intangible asset. As a starting point for the approach, the valuator must allocate the total forecast earnings between existing and future technology and existing and new customers. That is, earnings should be delineated between the following:

- sale of existing technology to existing customers;
- sale of existing technology to new customers;
- sale of new technology to existing customers; and
- sale of new technology to new customers.

In this way, the valuator can attribute excess earnings of the business to excess earnings from the technology or customer assets or both as illustrated in the matrix below.

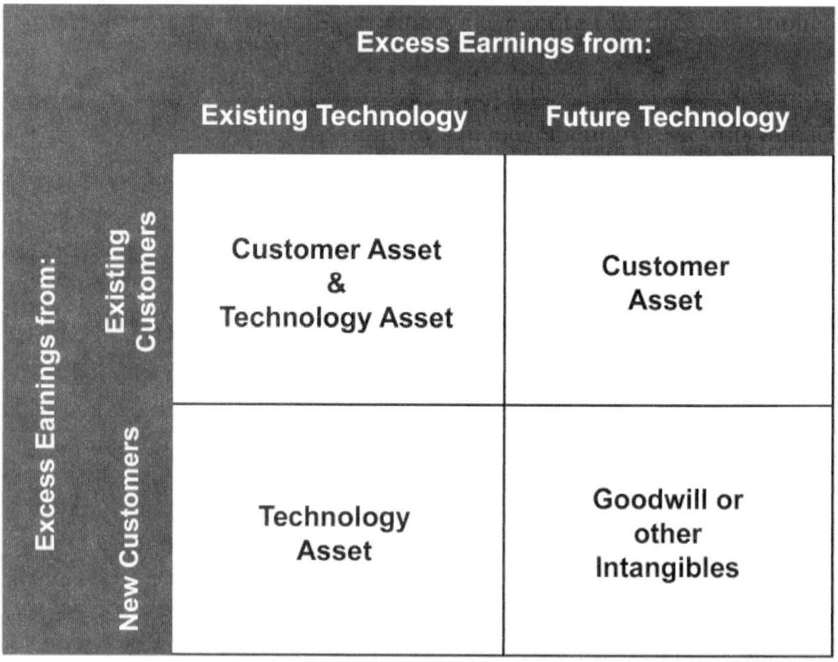

- Excess earnings from the sale of existing technology through existing customer relationships can be attributed to both an existing customer asset and an existing technology asset, in some proportion (Quadrant I);
- Excess earnings from the sale of new technologies through existing customer relationships can be attributed to a customer relationship asset, but not to an existing technology asset (Quadrant II);
- Excess earnings from the sale of existing technology to new customers can be attributed to the technology asset, but not to existing customer relationships (Quadrant III); and
- Excess earnings from the sale of new technologies to new customers can not be attributed to an existing customer asset or technology asset and reflects goodwill or another intangible asset (Quadrant IV).

This matrix also highlights the risk profile attributable to each stream of excess earnings. Quadrant I is supported by two existing intangible assets. Quadrant IV is not supported by any assets that are considered separable or contractual. As a result, the risk profile of Quadrant I is lower than Quadrant IV. Likewise, the risk profile of the excess earnings from Quadrant I, supported by two separable or contractual assets, should be lower than Quadrants II or III, which are supported by only one asset.

Practice Tip

The excess earnings in Quadrant IV may be attributable to intangible assets such as technology, a brand, or an uncommercialized patent. Investigate prior to assigning to general business goodwill.

Richard Ginsberg, CA, CBV

Continuing with our previous example of ABC Company, such an apportionment would appear as follows:

Technology Revenues		Year 1	Year 2	Year 3	Year 4	Year 5	Year 6	Year 7	Year 8	Year 9	Year 10
Existing Technology		1,000	840	662	463	243	-	-	-	-	-
	%ofRevenues	*100%*	*80%*	*60%*	*40%*	*20%*	*0%*	*0%*	*0%*	*0%*	*0%*
New Technology		-	210	441	695	972	1,276	1,340	1,407	1,477	1,551
	%ofRevenues	*0%*	*20%*	*40%*	*60%*	*80%*	*100%*	*100%*	*100%*	*100%*	*100%*
Total Revenue		1,000	1,050	1,103	1,158	1,216	1,276	1,340	1,407	1,477	1,551
Customer Relationship Revenues											
Existing Customer Relationships		1,000	919	827	724	608	479	335	176	-	-
	%ofRevenues	*100%*	*88%*	*75%*	*63%*	*50%*	*38%*	*25%*	*13%*	*0%*	*0%*
New Customer Relationships		-	131	276	434	608	798	1,005	1,231	1,477	1,551
	%ofRevenues	*0%*	*13%*	*25%*	*38%*	*50%*	*63%*	*75%*	*88%*	*100%*	*100%*
Total Revenues		1,000	1,050	1,103	1,158	1,216	1,276	1,340	1,407	1,477	1,551
Revenue Allocation											
Existing Technology Sold to Existing Customers		1,000	735	496	289	122	-	-	-	-	-
	%ofRevenues	*100%*	*70%*	*45%*	*25%*	*10%*	*0%*	*0%*	*0%*	*0%*	*0%*
Existing Technology Sold to New Customers		-	105	165	174	122	-	-	-	-	-
	%ofRevenues	*0%*	*10%*	*15%*	*15%*	*10%*	*0%*	*0%*	*0%*	*0%*	*0%*
New Technology Sold to Existing Customers		-	184	331	434	486	479	335	176	-	-
	%ofRevenues	*0%*	*18%*	*30%*	*38%*	*40%*	*38%*	*25%*	*13%*	*0%*	*0%*
New Technology Sold to New Customers		-	26	110	260	486	798	1,005	1,231	1,477	1,551
	%ofRevenues	*0%*	*3%*	*10%*	*23%*	*40%*	*63%*	*75%*	*88%*	*100%*	*100%*
Total Revenues		1,000	1,050	1,103	1,158	1,216	1,276	1,340	1,407	1,477	1,551

Once the valuator has compartmentalized the excess earnings of the business into quadrants, as discussed, excess earnings in Quadrant I must be attributed to either a technology or to customers, in some proportion. The valuator can avoid the circularity challenge in bifurcating excess earnings for both technology and customers through a cross-charge by using one of the following methods:

1. Implied Royalty: A royalty for the use of existing technology can be implied from Quadrant III (the sale of existing technology to new customers). This implied royalty can then be applied to Quadrant I revenues to attribute the quadrant's excess earnings to technology. The balance of excess earnings in Quadrant I after applying the notional technology royalty is then attributable to customer relationships. For ABC Company, such an approach would yield the following results:

Existing Technology Sold to New Customers - Quadrant III			**Year 1**	**Year 2**	**Year 3**	**Year 4**	**Year 5**	**Year 6**
Revenue			-	105	165	174	122	-
COGS	15.0%		-	15.8	24.8	26.0	18.2	-
R&D	8.8%		-	9.2	14.5	15.2	10.6	-
S&M	20.0%		-	21.0	33.1	34.7	24.3	-
G&A	10.0%		-	10.5	16.5	17.4	12.2	-
Working Capital CAC	1.0%		-	1.1	1.7	1.7	1.2	-
Fixed Asset CAC	2.0%		-	2.1	3.3	3.5	2.4	-
Excess Earnings			-	45.4	71.5	75.1	52.6	-
Present Value Factor	20%		0.83	0.69	0.58	0.48	0.40	0.33
Present Value - Technology		130	0.00	31.54	41.39	36.22	21.13	0.00
Implied Royalty Rate - % of Revenues		43%						
		130						

Existing Technology Sold to Existing Customers - Quadrant I			**Year 1**	**Year 2**	**Year 3**	**Year 4**	**Year 5**	**Year 6**
Revenue			1,000	735	496	289	122	-
COGS	15.0%		150	110	74	43	18	-
R&D	8.8%		88	64	43	25	11	-
S&M	10.0%		100	74	50	29	12	-
G&A	10.0%		100	74	50	29	12	-
Working Capital CAC	1.0%		10	7	5	3	1	-
Fixed Asset CAC	2.0%		20	15	10	6	2	-
Excess Earnings			533	391	264	154	65	-
Present Value Factor	20%		0.83	0.69	0.58	0.48	0.40	0.33
Present Value - Quadrant I		969	444	272	153	74	26	0.00
Less: Technology Royalty	43%		430	316	213	124	52	-
Present Value Factor	20%		0.83	0.69	0.58	0.48	0.40	0.33
Present Value - Technology (Quadrant I)		782	358	219	123	60	21	0.00
Present Value - Customers (Quadrant I)		186						

New Technology Sold to Existing Customers - Quadrant II			**Year 1**	**Year 2**	**Year 3**	**Year 4**	**Year 5**	**Year 6**
Revenue			-	184	331	434	486	479
COGS	15.0%		-	28	50	65	73	72
R&D	35.0%		-	64	116	152	170	168
S&M	10.0%		-	18	33	43	49	48
G&A	10.0%		-	18	33	43	49	48
Working Capital CAC	1.0%		-	2	3	4	5	5
Fixed Asset CAC	2.0%		-	4	7	9	10	10
Excess Earnings			-	50	89	117	131	129.2
Present Value Factor	20%		0.83	0.69	0.58	0.48	0.40	0.33
Present Value - Customers (Quadrant II)		239	-	34	52	57	53	43.28

Intangible Asset Values	
Technology Value	
Quadrant III	130
Quadrant I	782
Total Technology Value	913
Quadrant I	186
Quadrant III	239
Total Customer Relationship Value	425
Total Intangible Asset Value	1,338

2. Marketplace Evidence: It is not uncommon for businesses that sell technology to outsource the sales function to third-party resellers rather than employing an internal salesforce. In such an arrangement, businesses generally offer a discount to the reseller from the list price of the saleable technology. These discounts range from 25 per cent to 75 per cent, depending on the services provided by the reseller, the industry, the nature of the customer, and the technical expertise required. The reseller may be responsible not only for sourcing customers but also for providing varying levels of customer

service, technology support, and professional services such as training and installation.

Depending on the responsibilities and functions performed by these resellers, such arrangements may serve as a proxy to bifurcate Quadrant I. For example, let us assume a discount of 30 per cent on the selling price of the technology to third-party resellers in ABC Company's marketplace as compensation for originating sales and providing customer service. Using 30 per cent as a proxy for Quadrant I, we reach the following valuations of technology and customer relationships:

Existing Technology Sold to New Customers			Year 1	Year 2	Year 3	Year 4	Year 5	Year 6
Revenue			-	105	165	174	122	-
COGS	15.0%		-	15.8	24.8	26.0	18.2	-
R&D	8.8%		-	9.2	14.5	15.2	10.6	-
S&M	20.0%		-	21.0	33.1	34.7	24.3	-
G&A	10.0%		-	10.5	16.5	17.4	12.2	-
Working Capital CAC	1.0%		-	1.1	1.7	1.7	1.2	-
Fixed Asset CAC	2.0%		-	2.1	3.3	3.5	2.4	-
Excess Earnings			-	45.4	71.5	75.1	52.6	-
Present Value Factor	20%		0.83	0.69	0.58	0.48	0.40	0.33
Present Value		130	0.00	31.54	41.39	36.22	21.13	0.00

Existing Technology Sold to Existing Customers			Year 1	Year 2	Year 3	Year 4	Year 5	Year 6
Revenue			1,000	735	496	289	122	-
Less: Reseller Discount	30%		300	221	149	87	36	-
Adjusted Revenue - Technology			700	515	347	203	85	-
COGS	15.0%		105	77	52	30	13	-
R&D	8.8%		88	64	43	25	11	-
S&M			-	-	-	-	-	-
G&A	10.0%		70	51	35	20	9	-
Working Capital CAC	1.0%		7	5	3	2	1	-
Fixed Asset CAC	2.0%		14	10	7	4	2	-
Excess Earnings			417	306	207	121	51	-
Present Value Factor	20%		0.83	0.69	0.58	0.48	0.40	0.33
Present Value			347	213	120	58	20	0.00
Present Value - Technology in Quadrant I		758						

			Year 1	Year 2	Year 3	Year 4	Year 5	Year 6
Revenue			1,000	735	496	289	122	-
Less: Reseller Discount	70%		700	515	347	203	85	-
Adjusted Revenue - Customers			300	221	149	87	36	-
COGS	15.0%		45	33	22	13	5	-
R&D			-	-	-	-	-	-
S&M	10.0%		100	74	50	29	12	-
G&A	10.0%		30	22	15	9	4	-
Working Capital CAC	1.0%		3	2	1	1	0	-
Fixed Asset CAC	2.0%		6	4	3	2	1	-
Excess Earnings			116	85	58	34	14	-
Present Value Factor	20%		0.83	0.69	0.58	0.48	0.40	0.33
Present Value			97	59	33	16	6	0.00
Present Value - Customers in Quadrant I		211						

New Technology Sold to Existing Customers			Year 1	Year 2	Year 3	Year 4	Year 5	Year 6
Revenue			-	184	331	434	486	479
COGS	15.0%		-	28	50	65	73	72
R&D	35.0%		-	64	116	152	170	168
S&M	10.0%		-	18	33	43	49	48
G&A	10.0%		-	18	33	43	49	48
Working Capital CAC	1.0%		-	2	3	4	5	5
Fixed Asset CAC	2.0%		-	4	7	9	10	10
Excess Earnings			-	50	89	117	131	129.2
Present Value Factor	20%		0.83	0.69	0.58	0.48	0.40	0.33
Present Value - Quadrant II		239	-	34	52	57	53	43.28

Intangible Asset Values	
Technology Value	
Quadrant III	130
Quadrant I	758
Total Technology Value	888
Quadrant I	211
Quadrant III	239
Total Customer Relationship Value	450
Total Intangible Asset Value	1,338

Based on this analysis, the quadrant approach, using either implied royalty or marketplace evidence, produces a value for technology of approximately \$900; customer relationships, \$435; and total intangible value, \$1,335. This contrasts with a dual excess earnings approach that values technology at $400, customer relationships at $1,050, and total intangible value at $1,450.

Conclusion

In this chapter, we have presented the primary methodologies used in valuing a business and dealing with intangible asset issues most typically encountered. Even in volatile times, established valuation principles do not change. The valuation approach may suggest a specific value but, based on your experience, does it make sense? Test your conclusions against that derived from other approaches. Would an informed party pay this price or are there investment alternatives with similar returns but a lower price? Are there strategic buyers competing to acquire similar companies or assets or are there few buyers for assets in general given market malaise? Any asset or business can be valued. The question is what degree of precision can be brought to the final conclusion via the methodology being utilized?

APPENDIX A

References

Aswath Damodaran, *Damodaran on Valuation: Security Analysis for Investment and Corporate Finance*, 2nd ed. (Hoboken, New Jersey: John Wiley & Sons, Inc., 2006).

Aswath Damodaran, "Equity Risk Premium: Determinants, Estimations and Implications," Working Paper, www.damodaran.com (September/October 2008).

Aswath Damodaran, *Investment Valuation: Tools and Techniques for Determining the Value of Any Asset*, 2nd ed. (Hoboken, New Jersey: John Wiley & Sons, Inc., 2002).

James L. Horvath & Tim Dunham, "Valuation Methodologies: The Current Art and Science" in *Taxation and Valuation of Technology: Theory, Practice, and the Law*, James L. Horvath and David W. Chodikoff, eds. (Toronto: Irwin Law, 2008).

Roger G. Ibbotson & Peng Chen, "Stock Market Returns in the Long Run: Participating in the Real Economy," Yale ICF Working Paper No. 00-44 (March 2002).

Tim Koller, Mark Goedhart and David Wessels, *Valuation: Measuring and Managing the Value of Companies*, 4th ed. (Hoboken, New Jersey: John Wiley & Sons, Inc., 2005).

Russell L. Parr, *Investing in Intangible Assets: Finding and Profiting from Hidden Corporate Value* (Hoboken, New Jersey: John Wiley & Sons, Inc., 1991).

Shannon P. Pratt & Roger J. Grabowski, "Cost of Capital in Valuation of Stock by the Income Approach: Updated for an Economy in Crisis." *The Value Examiner, January/February 2009.*

Shannon P. Pratt & Roger J. Grabowski, *The Cost of Capital: Applications and Examples*, 3rd ed. (Hoboken, New Jersey: John Wiley & Sons, Inc., 2008).

Shannon P. Pratt & Alina V. Niculita, *Valuing a Business: The Analysis and Appraisal of Closely Held Companies*, 5th ed. (New York: The McGraw-Hill Companies, Inc., 2008).

Robert F. Reilly & Robert P. Schweihs, *Valuing Intangible Assets* (New York: McGraw-Hill, 1999).

Gary R. Trugman, *Understanding Business Valuation: A Practical Guide to Valuing Small to Medium-Sized Businesses*, 3rd ed. (AICPA, 2008).

The Use of the Market Approach to Valuation in Volatile Markets

Carl Leung & Jeff Horvath

Introduction

Many readers have witnessed several periods of elevated market volatility in their lifetimes, such as the lead-up to the technology bubble during the late 1990s and its bursting in March 2000, and the global financial and credit crisis in late 2008 and 2009. Such volatile market conditions create challenges for valuators in arriving at reasonable valuations for private (and even public) companies. For instance, in late 2008 and 2009, the volatile markets, the global financial crisis, and the global recession that followed soon after created a perfect storm for valuators and private equity investment funds when it came to applying fair value accounting to value companies. The economic factors significantly affected almost every business and, therefore, more scrutiny is required in assessing the reasonableness of a company's financial forecast. Many financial experts see the crisis as having the potential of being the worst since the Depression. In the valuation world, many experts have expressed their concerns that the nature and number of valuation issues encountered during the current global financial crisis have been unprecedented, and significant professional judgment is required in applying the valuation principles to all valuations.[1] For example, it may no longer

---

1 Based on discussions with certain valuation experts of the leading national valuation practices in Canada, many valuation issues encountered were not anticipated until the outbreak of the financial crisis. They indicated that there is currently no consensus on certain valuation issues (*e.g.*, the use of market versus fair value of debt in valuations, although the majority of the leading valuation and audit firms support the use of fair value). The experts also indicated that the industry (valuators and the investing community) should gather and derive a unified approach. This situation also mirrors the current fact that both accounting regulatory boards and security regulators are currently developing guidance to measure fair value of assets and liabilities in a volatile market environment. Such guidance would

be reasonable to use the general assumption that the book value of non-publicly traded debt approximates fair value in the valuation of private companies, as evidenced by many publicly traded debt issues that have a market value significantly lower than their book value.[2] To reach a reasonable conclusion, a significant amount of additional valuation analysis is required.

Another significant challenge facing valuation analysts during the global financial crisis is the use of value multiples of volatile comparable public companies when applying the market approach to private business valuations. We have witnessed a significant decline in the fund values of many private equity investment funds that mainly use the market approach to arrive at the fair value of their investments as a result of the sharp decline in the comparable multiples used, even when the subject company appears to be performing well fundamentally (*e.g.*, has the ability to maintain or even increase revenues and EBITDA). The decline in value multiples observed can be attributed to the re-pricing of all asset classes and/or reflective of the uncertainty of the companies' future performance because of the global financial crisis. This highlights the impact of applying the market approach to a valuation and the importance of being prudent in its use.

This chapter will examine the market approach and the impact of using public company comparable multiples on private company valuations. It also discusses certain specific issues surrounding the use of comparable companies' multiples in a volatile market and provides suggested approaches to deal with these issues.

---

be relevant to valuators for consideration in their valuation engagements, some of which we will discuss later in this chapter.

2 According to the May 2009 Exposure Draft of the *International Private Equity and Venture Capital Valuation Guidelines* (p. 27), the expected repayment amount at the debt settlement should be used for the valuation (typically, this is the par value since the debt is repayable at the disposal and the enterprise value is to be estimated on the basis of disposal - exit price basis per the definition of fair value - at the reporting date). However, according to the May 2009 the International Financial Reporting Standards (IFRS) Exposure Draft (pp. 19-21), the fair value of a liability reflects the effect of non-performance risk, which is the risk that the company will not fulfil an obligation. Non-performance risk includes, but may not be limited to, the company's credit risk (credit standing) and other risks. In addition, the valuation methodology applied for the measurement of the fair value of a liability by the company should be the same as the one applied by the counterparty of the corresponding asset. The IFRS Exposure Draft indicates that, if there is an active market for transactions for the subject debt security, the observed price in that market would represent the fair value of the issuer's liability.

Significance of the Market Approach

To arrive at a reasonable value conclusion, one generally needs to triangulate the value derived from the three main valuation approaches: the income approach (such as discounted cash flow and capitalization of earnings/EBITDA/cash flow), the public guideline companies' multiples, and the precedent transactions approach. The values derived from the various approaches should be relatively consistent with each other and the valuator should be able to explain or reconcile any significant differences. If there are significant differences, this may indicate that certain assumptions were incorrect in one valuation approach and inconsistent with the assumptions used in the other valuation approaches. This is especially relevant when most of the input variables for both the income approach and the market approach (using public guideline companies) are market based, such as the inputs under the income approach for the capital asset pricing model (CAPM) - risk-free rates, equity risk premiums, betas, *etc.* - and weighted-average cost of capital (WACC) method - weighting of the market values of debt and equity - and the trading values of debt and equity under the market approach.

More importantly, public companies' trades are probably the best fundamental barometers of general market conditions. Since a particular company's valuation reflects its value at a specific point of time and should reflect the general economic outlook and the condition and outlook of the specific industry in particular, a valuation that does not consider and incorporate market evidence into the analysis is not a reasonable valuation, especially since the common standard of fair market value and fair value (for financial reporting) requires the valuator to examine market transactions and the intentions of market participants.[3]

The Impact of Using Volatile Public Company Multiples on Private Company Valuations

Using comparable public companies' multiples can have a significant impact on a private company's valuation, especially when the comparable multiple approach is the main or only approach used.[4] In a volatile market, when trading multiples also fluctuate greatly, the impact of using comparable

---

[3] R. Schlegel, "Wrestling with Guideline Public Market Evidence: What You Need to Know," *BVUpdate,* March 2009.

[4] It should be noted that the comparable multiple approach should not be the only or main approach used in a formal business valuation because no two businesses are truly comparable and, therefore, not all of the value attributes of the subject company would be properly reflected by using the comparable companies' multiple.

multiples in a company's valuation is magnified. For example, given the market volatility experienced in late 2008 to mid-2009, the trading multiples have significantly declined as equity and debt values of the comparable public companies declined, reflecting the uncertainty surrounding the future economy and the companies' future performance. Many private equity investment funds that use a comparable multiple approach as the main or sole valuation approach in determining the fair value of the underlying investments have seen the fund values decline using mark to market (for fair value reporting purposes),[5] even when the underlying investments appeared to have performed well fundamentally. The value decline reflects the re-pricing across all asset classes that has taken place during the global financial crisis. For valuations used for other purposes, such as acquisitions or divestures, one needs to consider whether applying public comparable multiples during volatile market conditions properly reflects the long-term value of the business. (However, be careful not to abandon the market when it does not suit you. Otherwise, you are implicitly assuming the market is not efficient. This could be a form of smoothing.) Nevertheless, considering that the calculated value using the comparable approach is very sensitive to the two main input variables (*i.e.*, the economic income-based measurement and the value multiple), not using a careful selection of comparable companies and time periods of results for measurement and making the necessary adjustments would lead to an incorrect value conclusion, especially in a volatile market environment.

Issues in Applying the Market Approach in a Volatile Market

Having established the importance of including a market approach in performing valuations and the need of prudence in applying the approach, the following is a discussion of certain specific valuation issues that could arise in a volatile market, based on the recent experience:

- market value/fair value of debt;
- comparability;
- time period of operating results;
- Inactive market; and
- marketability discounts.

---

[5] The performance of a private equity fund is generally measured by the internal rate of return (IRR) it is able to generate, which is driven mainly by the realization of the investment (*i.e.*, the value of the investment at the divesture).

Market Value/Fair Value of Debt

The enterprise value (EV)/EBITDA multiple,[6] like the price-earnings ratio (P/E), is one of the most commonly used multiples in valuations. It has been the general practice of many valuators to assume that the book value of debt approximates the market value of debt in determining the comparable company's EV/EBITDA multiple. However, given the recent financial crisis, such assumptions may not be reasonable as evidenced by the credit quality deterioration of many corporate debt instruments, which reflects the increased credit risk that has stemmed from the business challenges in an economic downturn and/or leveraged financial positions. As a result, many publicly traded secured debentures and senior credit instruments are trading at lower values relative to the issuance or book values. For non-investment-grade or significantly leveraged companies, debt securities have been trading at a fraction of the face amount. Consequently, the value multiple would be overstated if the EV was based on the book value of debt which, in turn, would overstate the value of the subject company. This is particularly important when using the comparable approach in analyzing a reasonable purchase price for a particular company.

In determining the market value/fair value of debt of a comparable company, the valuator can first determine whether the debt of the comparable company is publicly traded in a market where values can be used for the estimation. If the debt is not publicly traded, the value of the debt can be estimated based on an estimated debt rating and related current yields of a comparable companies' debt with the same rating.

Comparability

The application of the public comparable multiples approach is only meaningful if the public guideline companies selected are reasonably comparable to the subject company in most business aspects. Note that no two businesses are identical in all respects, especially in a volatile market where each company is affected differently by internal and external factors. Therefore, care must be exercised in selecting relevant comparable companies for the val-

---

6 Other common enterprise value-based pricing multiples include EV/Revenues and EV/EBIT. EV-based multiples are often used because each company's capital structure is different and, therefore, the EV-based measure removes the effect of the financial leverage and reflects the market value of all invested capital of the company as a common basis for better value comparative analysis. Furthermore, in a private company valuation situation, where control interest is often the subject for the valuation, a purchaser for control is more interested in the value of the business (enterprise value) as the purchaser ultimately determines the capital structure of the company.

uation analysis. The following are some quantitative and qualitative factors that should be considered in the selection of comparable companies.

Industry and Products (or Services) Offered

In order to be comparable, public guideline companies should operate in the same or similar industry segment as the subject company because they are generally affected by the same economic and industry forces. Furthermore, the valuator must consider the differences and similarities of the products or services offered by each company as there may be differences in the market forces, product/service lifecycles, operating characteristics, pricing, and other factors that affect a company's value. For instance, Company A and Company B both operate in the medical-device industry (which may be considered as defensive investments in a volatile market); however, Company A focuses on orthopaedics, which has low expected industry volume growth in the near term, and Company B focuses on wound care, an industry with relatively higher growth expectations. Using public value metrics without adjustments could result in overvaluing Company A and undervaluing Company B.

Potential comparable companies will have the same Standard Industrialization Classification (SIC) code, which can be searched using Capital IQ, *www.sec.gov* or other online financial information services. Another source of information for determining whether a company is comparable is the competition section of its Form 10-K or through discussion with management of the company to be valued, who can identify similar publicly traded companies.

Diversification

Many companies offer different products or services in similar or different industry segments. Therefore, it is important that either the comparable company's product (or service) mix, measured by revenue or other relevant income measure, is comparable to the subject company's, or the comparable product (or service) offered by the comparable company represents a principal portion of the comparable company's business. Such comparative information, although often insufficient, is generally available in the segment information section of the public comparable company's financial statements.

Company Size

Size, which can be measured by revenue, assets or other meaningful measures, is an important selection criterion as it implicitly reflects the degree of operating leverage, economies of scale, market position, financial stability, diversification and so forth of a company. These factors influence operating performance and, importantly, investment risk and expected rates of return required by market participants. As a result, companies of significantly different sizes are unlikely to be meaningful comparables.[7]

Geographic Markets

Attention should be paid to understand the comparability of the geographic markets where the comparable companies and the subject company operate. Different geographic markets may have different customer demographics; market maturities; taxation and legal regulations; political risks; and degrees of local competition, all of which would have an impact on a company's operations, thus resulting in value differences. For instance, the risk profile of a company operating in an emerging market would be very different from one operating in the same industry but in a developed market. Since many companies nowadays have international sales or operations, it is necessary to review and compare the geographic mix of revenue and operations of the comparable companies and of the subject company in the selection process.

Profitability and Growth

Intuitively speaking, a company with higher profitability and/or growth would demand a higher multiple than a company with the same characteristics but with lower profitability and growth. Therefore, it is important to analyze the profitability and growth differences of the comparable companies and the subject company in order to enhance the analysis. The analysis is straightforward because it involves pure quantification analysis. Profitability ratios (*e.g.*, gross margins and operating/EBITDA margins) and historical growth rates can be calculated easily and compared. Future expected profitability and growth ratios can be estimated by using the comparable public companies' consensus estimate data and the subject company's forecast. Other operating ratios, such as current ratios and turnover ratios (accounts receivable, payable, inventory, *etc.*), can also be computed to enhance the comparative analysis.

---

7 I.R. Campbell & H.E. Johnson, *The Valuation of Business Interests* (Canadian Institute of Chartered Accountants, 2001), p. 331.

Net Tangible Assets

In relation to the fifth valuation principle mentioned in Chapter 2, a company would have a higher value if it has a higher value of net tangible assets (and therefore commands a higher multiple) compared with an identical company with lower net tangible assets. In the comparative analysis, therefore, the valuator should review the details of the underlying net tangible assets, including the value, asset mix, quality/liquidity of the assets (*e.g.*, current accounts receivable and inventory), remaining useful life of fixed assets (which can be estimated based on the gross cost recorded and accumulated depreciation) and other relevant analysis. This factor, in conjunction with the level of financial leverage of the company, is of particular significance in a market downturn as evidenced in the global financial crisis, where credit market conditions are tight and de-leveraging has been the focus of many corporations.

Time Period of Operating Results

Another significant factor for a valuator to consider when applying the multiple approach in a volatile market is the selection of the time period of operating results used in the calculation of the comparable multiple that will be applied when estimating the subject company's value. Note that the multiple comprises two main variables: price or market value of the equity/invested capital (the numerator) and an economic income-based measurement (the denominator). Therefore, the multiple and the resultant value are very sensitive to these variables. In practice, the common time periods used for operating results include the following:

- trailing/latest 12 months;
- last fiscal year;
- next fiscal year forecast;
- *pro forma* period; and
- average or weighted average of several relevant historical periods.

The time period selected is a subjective decision but should reflect the expected outcome in the future (and, assuming this is a going concern, you should account for future events and normalize across the cycle). Based on the foregoing, it appears that future forecast amounts are probably the most relevant base to use. However, this is subject to 1) the availability of a forecast[8] and 2) management's ability to prepare reasonable forecasts. The

---

8 A forecast may not be available for various reasons. For instance, senior personnel who were responsible for the preparation of the forecast are no longer with the company (this

latter factor is of particular importance in a market downturn such as the one in late 2008, when a significant amount of uncertainty was embedded in many companies' near-term forecasts because of the difficulty of estimating the extent of the impact of the global economic and financial crisis on their operating results. For instance, as a result of the sharp economic downturn in the U.S. economy and the unpredictable significant corporate and economic events that surfaced on an almost daily basis in late 2008 and early 2009, we have witnessed situations where a private company has revised its near-term forecast several times, with significant adjustments, within a three-month period before and after its year-end valuation (December 31, 2008). In such situations, the best information base may be the actual recent results, such as trailing 12 months data.

Inactive Market

Once a set of reasonably comparable public guideline companies has been selected, the valuator then needs to examine whether the comparable companies were actively traded in the period before and at the valuation date. This is to support the requirement of the fair market value standard that the transaction was undertaken "between a hypothetical willing and able buyer and a hypothetical willing and able seller, acting at arm's length in an open and unrestricted market, when neither is under compulsion to buy or sell and when both have reasonable knowledge of the relevant facts." Active trading and market efficiency are essential if the market forces are to interact in the manner necessary to reach the equilibrium point in the market known as fair market value. Greater market activity increases the possibility that fair market value will be achieved because many of the personal motivations of particular buyers and sellers would have been eliminated by offsetting their unique situations in arriving at the equilibrium point.[9]

This is also consistent with the requirement of fair value definition that the amount reflects "the price that would be received to sell an asset or paid to transfer a liability in an orderly transaction between market participants at the measurement date." An orderly transaction is a transaction that assumes exposure to the market for a period prior to the measurement date to allow for marketing activities that are usual and customary for transactions involving such assets or liabilities; it is not a forced transaction (*e.g.*, a forced

---

has been witnessed often in the financial crisis in late 2008) or a minor shareholder may not have access to management.

9 G.R. Trugman, *Understanding Business Valuation: A Practical Guide to Valuing Small to Medium-Sized Businesses*, 3rd ed. (American Institute of Certified Public Accountants [AICPA], 2008), p. 215.

liquidation or distress sale). The notion being that a transaction resulting from a forced liquidation or distressed sale does not represent fair value.[10]

In a volatile market, like that resulting from the onset of the global financial crisis in 2008, there may be fewer transactions for certain assets due to fewer sellers willing to transact at low prices that do not meet their required returns, in addition to the lack of financing available. At the same time, there could be situations where it is a seller's market and prices transacted are reflective of distressed prices as investors are willing to transact at unreasonably low prices in order to preserve liquidity. In these situations, the prices observed may not be applicable for the comparable multiple approach as these transactions do not reflect normal (orderly) market conditions.

The U.S. Federal Accounting Standards Board (FASB) recently provided certain guidance to determine whether the market is inactive, which is relevant for valuators to consider in their valuations and market assessments:[11]

- There are few recent transactions.
- Price quotations are not based on current information.
- Price quotations vary substantially either over time or among market makers (*e.g.*, some brokered markets).
- Indexes that previously were highly correlated with the fair values of the asset or liability are demonstrably uncorrelated with recent indications of fair value for that asset or liability.
- There is a significant increase in implied liquidity risk premiums, yields, or performance indicators (such as delinquency rates or loss severities) for observed transactions or quoted prices compared with the reporting entity's estimate of expected cash flows, considering all available market data about credit and other nonperformance risk for the asset or liability.
- There is a wide bid-ask spread or significant increase in the bid-ask spread.
- There is a significant decline or absence of a market for new issuances (*i.e.*, a primary market) for the asset or liability or similar assets or liabilities.
- Little information is released publicly (*e.g.*, a principal-to-principal market).

---

10 "Determining Fair Value When the Volume and Level of Activity for the Asset or Liability Have Significantly Decreased and Identifying Transactions That Are Not Orderly," Federal Accounting Standards Board (FASB) Staff Position FAS 157-4, April 9, 2009.

11 *Ibid.*

The FASB guidance indicated that, if there has been a significant decrease in the volume and level of activity for the asset or liability, a change in valuation technique or the use of multiple valuation techniques may be appropriate (*e.g.*, the use of a market approach and a present value technique). In other words, the value derived from the comparable approach may be less relevant.[12]

Marketability Discounts

In normal market conditions, a marketability discount is generally applied to account for the illiquidity resulting from the lack of an immediately available market in which an equity interest could be sold in the short term at a predictable price. However, in volatile market conditions, such a discount may not be applicable as the comparable public companies' market prices may have included an illiquidity discount. As mentioned previously, there are situations where it is a seller's market and prices transacted are reflective of distressed prices as investors are concerned by market uncertainty and are willing to transact at unreasonably low prices in order to preserve liquidity. Such situations could be evidenced by wide bid-ask spreads. Valuators, therefore, need to assess the market conditions and the underlying market data of the comparable companies in order to determine whether a marketability discount is applicable.

Conclusion

Applying the public comparable multiple approach is definitely a challenge for valuators in a volatile market or a non-market, where the market has stopped trading (*i.e.*, there is no or very little volume), as significant judgment is required. Underlying facts and circumstances of the subject company and market conditions that must be taken into consideration, along with prudence in selecting public guideline companies that are reasonably comparable to the subject company, are paramount in order to arrive at a reasonable value for the subject company.

---

[12] It is noted that the guidance provided by the May 2009 IFRS Exposure Draft (pp. 39-42) on this subject is consistent with the FASB guidance.

APPENDIX A

References

Ian R. Campbell & Howard E. Johnson, *et al.* "Comparative Value Analysis." *Business Valuation Commentary*, March 2000.

Ian R. Campbell & Howard E. Johnson, *The Valuation of Business Interests* (Canadian Institute of Chartered Accountants, 2001).

Stanley J. Feldman, *Principles of Private Firm Valuation* (Hoboken, New Jersey: John Wiley & Sons, Inc., 2005).

Shannon P. Pratt & Alina V. Niculita, *Valuing a Business: The Analysis and Appraisal of Closely Held Companies*, 5th ed. (McGraw-Hill Library of Investment and Finance, 2008).

Robert Schlegel, "Wrestling with Guideline Public Market Evidence: What You Need to Know," *BVUpdate*, March 2009.

Gary R. Trugman, *Understanding Business Valuation: A Practical Guide to Valuing Small to Medium-Sized Businesses*, 3rd ed. (American Institute of Certified Public Accountants (AICPA), 2008).

Richard M. Wise, "Caveats When Using Guideline Transactional Data in Valuing a Business" (2003) *Business Valuation Review* 40-43.

Valuation of Intellectual Property in a Distressed Economy

Robert F. Reilly

Introduction

In 2008, intangible asset values accounted for over 80 per cent of the total market value of the S&P 500 index companies. In 1975, the percentage of intangible asset values as a percentage of the total S&P 500 index companies market value was closer to 17 per cent. Intellectual property is one of the four categories of intangible assets. First, this discussion summarizes the procedures related to the identification of intellectual property. Second, this discussion summarizes the procedures related to the valuation of intellectual property as one of the four intangible asset categories. Third, this discussion summarizes the characteristics or elements that affect the valuation of an intellectual property in a distressed economy. And fourth, this discussion presents simplified illustrative examples of the valuation of intellectual property within the context of a distressed economic environment.

Business Enterprise Assets

From a valuation perspective, an asset is anything that (1) can be owned and (2) has value. If the subject business owner/operator cannot own a subject economic phenomenon, then it is not an asset. If the subject economic phenomenon exists and can be owned–but it has no value, then it is not an asset. For an intangible asset to meet this first threshold test of existence (*i.e.*, in order for an intangible to be an asset), it should (1) be subject to private ownership and (2) have value.

For a variety of reasons, valuation analysts often group all business enterprise assets into the following four asset categories:

1. tangible real estate;
2. intangible real property;
3. tangible personal property;
4. intangible personal property.

One way to identify any type of business enterprise asset (tangible or intangible) is to locate that asset in one of the four boxes presented in Figure 1.

Figure 1
The Four Categories of Business Enterprise Assets

	Realty Assets	Personalty Assets
Tangible Assets	Tangible Real Estate	Tangible Personal Property
Intangible Assets	Intangible Real Property	Intangible Personal Property

This discussion focuses on the intangible personal property category of business assets. In particular, this discussion focuses on the intellectual property category of intangible personal property.

Intangible Personal Property Assets

Valuation analysts are familiar with intangible personal property. Less experienced observers automatically think of the intangible personal property category as being synonymous with the term intangible assets. The definition of intangible asset as intangible personal property only is too limited from a valuation perspective. This is because that definition excludes the intangible real property category of intangible assets. However, it does not invalidate this explanation of intangible assets to limit this discussion to intangible personal property.

The value of intangible personal property comes from the legal rights, the intellectual property content, and/or the expected economic benefits that are associated with that intangible asset. Nonetheless, like all assets (both tangible and intangible), intangible personal property (1) can be owned and (2) has value.

Business Enterprise Intangible Assets

Valuation analysts often group all intangible personal property assets into four categories. Sometimes, this intangible personal property categorization process may have accounting, taxation, regulatory, or legal significance. This is because the four different categories of intangible personal property assets (although fundamentally similar) have different economic attributes. These four categories of intangible personal property assets are: (1) financial assets, (2) general intangible assets, (3) intellectual property, and (4) intangible value in the nature of goodwill

Financial Assets

All valuation analysts are familiar with the financial assets category. Common examples of financial assets include: cash, accounts and notes receivable, stocks and bonds, and other negotiable investment securities. When the financial assets owner is a business enterprise, these intangible assets are recorded as "current assets" for financial statement purposes.

General Intangible Assets

The second category of intangible personal property assets includes most other intangible assets. Because this category is quite broad, most intangible personal property assets are classified as general intangible assets.

Intellectual Property

The third category of intangible personal property assets is intellectual property. Intellectual property intangible assets are distinguished by their special legal recognition and, therefore, their specific legal rights. There are four types of intellectual property in this category:

1. trademarks and trade names;
2. patents;
3. copyrights;
4. trade secrets.

Intangible Value in the Nature of Goodwill

The fourth category of intangible personal property assets includes intangible value in the nature of goodwill. Valuation analysts typically consider intangible value in the nature of goodwill to be a separate (or fourth) category of intangible assets for various accounting, taxation, and other financial reporting purposes.

Intangible value in the nature of goodwill is often considered to be a residual intangible asset. That is, for valuation purposes, goodwill is often quantified as the intangible value component of a business enterprise (of whatever legal form) that cannot be specifically assigned to (or identified with) any of the other above-mentioned three types of intangible assets. Nonetheless, like each of the other three categories of intangible personal property, goodwill (1) can be owned and (2) can have value. While goodwill is an intangible asset, goodwill is not as easy to identify or to analyze as the other three categories of intangible personal property.

Each of these four categories of business enterprise assets can be further divided into several subcategories. Figure 2 expands the listing and relationships of the four categories of the business enterprise assets that were introduced in Figure 1.

Figure 2
The Four Categories of
Business Enterprise Assets

	Realty Assets	Personalty Assets
Tangible Assets	land building components building structures	machinery and equipment trucks and autos computers office equipment
Intangible Assets	leaseholds easements and rights of way mining and mineral rights	financial assets general intangible assets intellectual property goodwill intangible value

Reasons to Analyze Intellectual Property

Regardless of the state of the general economic environment, there are numerous individual reasons why valuation analysts are asked to value intellectual property. These individual reasons may be grouped in the following categories:

1. transaction pricing and structuring;
2. intercompany use and ownership transfers;
3. financial accounting and reporting;
4. state and local *ad valorem* property taxation planning and compliance;
5. financing collateralization and securitization;

6. litigation claims and dispute resolution;
7. management information and strategic planning;
8. corporate governance and regulatory/contractual compliance;
9. bankruptcy and reorganization analysis;
10. license, joint venture, and other development or commercialization opportunities

When conducting an intellectual property analysis, the valuation analyst may consider one or more of the following related (but subtly different) quantitative objectives:

1. Estimate a defined value associated with the specified ownership interest in the intellectual property.
2. Measure the appropriate royalty rate or intercompany transfer price associated with the use of the intellectual property.
3. Quantify the expected remaining useful life (RUL) of the ownership or operation (or associated rate of change in the value of) the intellectual property.
4. Determine the amount of lost profits or other economic damages associated with a damages event suffered by the intellectual property.

Corporate management is usually most interested in the first type of intellectual property analysis–*i.e.*, to estimate a defined value for the subject intellectual property. Nonetheless, there are numerous similarities in the generally accepted approaches, methods, and procedures that the valuation analyst may use in all four categories of intellectual property analyses.

Intellectual Property

An intellectual property is an intangible asset that enjoys special legal recognition and protection. The special legal status of an intellectual property is usually the result of specific statutory authority, either federal or state. General commercial intangible assets are typically created in the normal course of business operations. Common examples of general commercial intangible assets include customer contracts and relationships, supplier contracts and relationships, employee relations (as represented by a trained and assembled workforce), licenses and permits, operating systems and procedures, company books and records, *etc.*

Such general commercial intangible assets are typically created over time in almost every successful going concern business. Business executives do not have to make a special effort to create such general commercial intangible assets. Such general intangible assets develop naturally as the business executives manage the day-to-day operations of the subject business enterprise.

On the other hand, an intellectual property is typically created by the specific and conscious intellectual activity of the developer. The creativity involved in developing an intellectual property can be identified and attributed to a specific individual. When created, an intellectual property is a new and unique invention that can be either (1) artistic, like a book or photographic image, or (2) technological, like a chemical process or computer software code.

There are four types of intellectual property: (1) patents, (2) trademarks, (3) copyrights, and (4) trade secrets. Each of the four intellectual property types is summarized below.

Patents grant the subject patent holder the right to exclude others from making, using, or selling the patented invention or product for a specified duration of time. For example, a company that manufactures pharmaceutical drugs will register a patent on each new drug compound formula that it discovers. While the subject patent is in effect, no other company can manufacture a drug product using that particular chemical compound formula. Once the subject patent expires, other pharmaceutical manufactures can produce identical drug products, generally in the form of generic brands.

A trademark identifies goods as coming from a particular manufacturer. A trademark can be a product brand name, like Versace or Nikon. A trademark could also be a logo, like the red target logo for Target stores. Related to trademarks, service marks identify services as coming from a particular service provider. The "golden arches" of McDonald's is an example of a well-known and recognizable service mark. A trademark also grants the subject intellectual property owner the ability of preventing anyone else from using the trademark.

A copyright is an exclusive right to reproduce, publish, or sell an original work of authorship. As with a patent, the legal protection related to a copyright lasts for a limited period of time. An author of any original work of authorship owns a copyright on that original work the moment it is completed. However, to have assurance of the intellectual property legal protection, the author will typically register the copyright. Copyright law covers many forms of an author's expression, including books, movies, paintings, and songs.

A trade secret can be any commercial information that has value due to the fact that it is kept confidential and is not known to the public. In order to qualify as a trade secret, the commercial information must meet two criteria: (1) it must be kept secret from the public, and (2) it must provide a commercial advantage to the owner/operator. A trade secret is frequently a secret process, method, or formula for producing a product or service, such as the "secret formula" for the *Coca-Cola* soft drink syrup.

Patents

A patent grants the inventor of an invention the right to exclude others from making, using, or selling the patented invention for a statutorily determined period of time. A patent represents a property interest for the patent holder. There are three kinds of patents: (1) utility patents, (2) design patents, and (3) plant patents.

A utility patent may be issued with regard to an invention that has some type of usefulness or utility. An example of a patentable invention that has usefulness would be a new pharmaceutical product to control high blood-pressure.

A design patent may be issued for "any new, original, and ornamental design for an article of manufacture." A design does not need to meet the usefulness standard in order to qualify for a design patent. In order to qualify for a design patent (instead of for a utility patent), the design must be purely ornamental and not functional. However, two patents may be issued for the same device: (1) a design patent for the product design; and (2) a utility patent for the product useful characteristics.

A plant patent may be issued for an asexually reproduced "distinct and new variety of plant." A plant also does not need to meet a usefulness standard in order to qualify for a plant patent.

In order to qualify for a patent, an invention must meet certain specific requirements. For example, an invention must have "utility" and "novelty." Utility refers to usefulness, and this criterion is only required for utility patents. Novelty, required for all three types of patents, means the invention, design, or plant must be unique from all prior inventions, designs, or plants. However, an idea can not be patented.

There are many types of inventions that qualify for patent protection. However, not all inventions qualify for patent protection. Many creative works that are protected by copyright laws are not patentable. For example, movies, books, artwork, and songs cannot obtain patent protection. However, the design and functional elements of the camera used to film movies, the printer used to print a book, or the device used to record songs may receive patent protection. In addition, formulas (*e.g.*, chemical, cosmetic, or food) and computer software may receive patent protection.

Trademarks

A trademark is used to identify a brand or a company. A trademark lets a consumer know that a good is produced by a specific producer. A service mark is a closely related intangible asset to the trademark intellectual property. A service mark lets the consumer know that a service is coming from a specific service provider. A company that has developed a branded product and invested in the production of a quality product wants consumers to identify the product trademark with quality. The trademark associated with the subject product allows the intellectual property owner to achieve that objective.

A trademark can be licensed. Restaurant franchises often function using the license of the franchisor's trademark. For example, restaurant franchisor Burger King licenses out its name and logo to individual franchisees. These franchisees independently operate their own Burger King restaurants. When a consumer sees the restaurant with the Burger King name and logo, the consumer has established expectations as to what food products will be on the menu and how those food products will taste.

Burger King has built a reputation as being a certain kind of restaurant with a specific menu. It is important to Burger King that, if a franchisee uses its trademark, the franchisee must meet specific presentation requirements. If any part of the Burger King experience is subpar to the consumer, the Burger King trademark may lose some of its value.

A trade name is a different intangible asset from a trademark intellectual property. A trade name is the name of a business entity. A trademark identifies products and a service mark identifies services that are produced by that entity.

Trade dress refers to the way a product or service is displayed and promoted. For a product, the trade dress could be represented by the product packaging. For a service, the trade dress may be the décor that the service is provided in.

There are restrictions on what names or logos qualify for protection under trademark law. Trademarks are only protected if they are continually used. A mark that is too generic will also not be protected by trademark law. For example, a company could not trademark the brand name "Cola." This is because the name cola is a generic term that describes an entire class of beverages. A company could, however, have a brand name that combines a trademark and a generic term, such as Pepsi Cola.

Copyrights

Copyright law protects "original works of authorship." To qualify for copyright protection, an original work must display at least some creativity and must be fixed in a tangible medium of expression. There are several types of original works of authorship that may qualify for copyright protection:

1. literary works,
2. musical works, including any accompanying words,
3. dramatic works, including any accompanying music,
4. pantomimes and choreographic works,
5. pictorial, graphic, and sculptural works,
6. motion pictures and other audiovisual works,
7. sound recordings, and
8. architectural works.

An author is (1) the person who created the work, (2) a business that pays someone to create the work in an employment context, or (3) a business that commissions the work under contract. The author is the owner of the copyright except in two cases: (1) the author assigns away the rights before completing the work; or (2) the author is an employee who made the work as part of the author's employment.

Trade Secrets

A trade secret is any information that has (1) economic value and (2) it is not generally known by the public. The owner of a trade secret can ensure that the information is generally unknown to the public by taking reasonable measures to maintain the confidentiality of the information. An example of such reasonable measures would be to have a nondisclosure agreement signed by all company employees, consultants, and visitors with access to the secret business information.

The term "trade secret" covers a wide spectrum of information. The type of business information that is typically considered to be a trade secret includes: (1) information about customers, such as customer order and credit characteristics, customer lists and mailing lists, (2) information about personnel, suppliers, or distributors, such as sources of supply, (3) information on the costs and pricing of goods, as well as books and records of the business, (4) information concerning new business opportunities and current methods of doing business, and (5) some databases and know-how.

Unlike patents, trademarks, and copyrights, trade secrets cannot be registered with any governmental agency. For copyrights, patents, and trademarks, the registration process involves producing documentation of the invention or work that registration is sought for. If the trade secret owner had to register that intellectual property with a government agency, the "secret" would immediately be lost.

Since trade secrets are not registered, they do not have a statutory legal protection life. That is, a trade secret can exist so long as it remains unknown to the general public. This is the second reason why trade secrets are not registered. Patents and copyrights have a limited legally protected life. Once either a patent or a copyright expires, competitors are free to use the inventions and works that were formerly protected.

Even though a trade secret is not registered with a government agency, it still enjoys many elements of legal protection. If someone obtains a trade secret in an improper way, a court will usually grant the trade secret owner (1) economic damages and (2) an injunction to prevent further dissemination of the trade secret material. There are limits as to what information can be considered a trade secret. Clearly, generally known information cannot be a trade secret. In addition, information that others could easily acquire or duplicate will most likely not qualify as a trade secret.

Intellectual Property Intangible Assets

The main difference between intellectual property and general commercial intangible assets is that intellectual property is consciously and creatively produced. General commercial intangible assets tend to develop naturally in the regular course of business. For example, an intellectual property may be a logo designed for a company. That company logo would qualify as a trademark. That same company may also own general commercial intangible assets, such as supplier relationships and supplier contracts related to purchased goods and services.

Customer relationships, customer contracts, and general goodwill are examples of commercial intangible assets that do not qualify as intellectual property. No specific design or artistic creativity went into creating such general commercial intangible assets. On the other hand, a patent on a production process, a trademark on a new product, a copyright on a design, and secret knowledge of the formula recipe for a food product are all examples of intellectual property. Of course, these illustrative intellectual property examples also qualify as intangible assets.

Generally Accepted Intellectual Property Approaches and Methods

There are many methods and procedures that are appropriate for the valuation of intellectual property. Because these methods and procedures have fundamental similarities, they are typically categorized into three generally accepted valuation approaches. These three valuation approaches are based on fundamental economic principles. The three generally accepted intellectual property valuation approaches are: (1) the cost approach, (2) the market approach, and (3) the income approach.

These intellectual property valuation approaches encompass a broad spectrum of microeconomic principles and property investment dynamics. Each of the three generally accepted valuation approaches has the same objective: to arrive at a reasonable indication of a defined value for the intellectual property. Accordingly, analytical methods and procedures based on the same economic principles are grouped into the same valuation approach.

The valuation analyst typically attempts to value an intellectual property using all three generally accepted valuation approaches so that a multidimensional perspective of value is obtained. However, individual methods and procedures associated with one of the three valuation approaches may or may not be applicable to the valuation of a particular intellectual property. Consequently, the selection of value methods and procedures used to value an intellectual property will depend on:

1. the unique characteristics of the subject intellectual property,
2. the quantity and quality of available data,
3. the purpose and objective of the analysis, and
4. the experience and judgment of the valuation analyst.

The objective of using more than one valuation approach is to develop mutually supporting evidence for the value conclusion. The valuation analyst's value conclusion is typically based on a synthesis of the value indications derived from each applicable valuation approach and method.

Market Approach Valuation Methods

The market approach is based on the economics principles of competition and equilibrium. These economics principles indicate that, in a free and unrestricted market, supply and demand factors will drive the price of an intellectual property to a point of equilibrium. The principle of substitution also influences the market approach. This is because the identification and analysis of equilibrium prices for substitute intangible assets will provide pricing evidence with regard to the intellectual property value.

Market Approach Valuation Principles

The valuation analyst will often attempt to apply market approach methods first in the valuation process. This is because "the market"–that is, the economic environment where arm's-length transactions between unrelated parties occur–is often the best indicator of value.

However, the market approach may not be appropriate for the valuation of certain intellectual property. This is particularly the case if the condition of the subject intellectual property is not sufficiently similar to the intellectual property that are transacting in the marketplace. In that case, the transactional prices may not indicate the expected price for the subject intellectual property.

The price of an intellectual property is not necessarily equal to its value. Value is often defined as an expected price. That is, value is the price that an intellectual property would expect to fetch in its appropriate marketplace. In contrast, price represents what one particular buyer paid to one particular seller for one particular intellectual property.

In any particular intellectual property sale transaction, either participant may have been influenced by nonmarket, participant-specific influences. If such influences did occur, and if such influences are not general to the marketplace, then a particular intellectual property transactional price may not be indicative of the expected price of the subject intellectual property.

Even if the subject intellectual property was itself bought or licensed, that subject transactional price should not be naïvely relied on to indicate an expected future price. This is because this transactional price may have been influenced by nonmarket, participant-specific influences.

The Market Approach Valuation Process

Within the market approach, there are somewhat fewer valuation methods available as compared to either the cost approach or the income approach. Nonetheless, the practical application of the market approach involves a complex and rigorous analytical process. There is a general systematic process–or framework–to the application of market approach methods. The principal procedures of this systematic process are summarized as follows:

1. Research the appropriate exchange market to obtain information about sale or license transactions, involving "guideline" (*i.e.*, generally similar) or "comparable" (*i.e.*, almost identical) intellectual property that may be compared to the subject intellectual property–in terms of characteristics such as intellectual property type, intellectual

property use, industry in which the intellectual property operates, date of sale, *etc.*

2. Verify the information by confirming (a) that the data obtained are factually accurate and (b) that the sale or license exchange transactions reflect arm's-length market considerations. If the guideline sale or license transaction was not at arm's-length market conditions, then adjustments to the transactional data may be necessary. This verification procedure may also elicit additional information about the current market conditions for the sale or license of the subject intellectual property.
3. Select relevant units of comparison (*e.g.*, income multipliers or dollars per unit–units such as "per drawing," "per customer," "per line of code") and develop a comparative analysis for each selected unit of comparison.
4. Compare "guideline" intellectual property sale or license transactions with the subject intellectual property using the selected elements of comparison; and adjust the sale or license price of each guideline transaction appropriately to the intellectual property. If such adjustments cannot be measured, then eliminate the sale or license transaction as a guideline for future valuation analysis consideration.
5. Reconcile the various value indications produced from the analysis of the guideline sale and/or license transactions into either (a) a single value indication or (b) a range of values.

The reconciliation procedure is the last procedure of any market approach valuation analysis in which two or more value indications are derived from guideline market data. In the reconciliation procedure, the valuation analyst (1) summarizes and reviews the data and (2) analyses that resulted in each value indication. The valuation analyst then resolves these intangible asset value indications into either a range of values or into a single value indication. The valuation analyst should consider the strengths and weaknesses of each value indication derived, examining the reliability and appropriateness of (1) of the market data compiled and (2) the analytical procedures applied.

Cost Approach Valuation Methods

The cost approach is based on the economics principles of substitution and price equilibrium. These economics principles indicate that a willing buyer will pay no more for a fungible intellectual property than the cost to obtain (*i.e.*, either to purchase or to construct) an intellectual property of equal utility.

In other words, a willing buyer will pay no more for a fungible intellectual property than the price of an intellectual property of comparable utility. For purposes of this economics principle, utility can be measured in many ways, including functionality, desirability, and so on. Accordingly, an efficient market will adjust the price of all properties in equilibrium so that the price the market will pay is a function of the comparative utility of each property.

Within the cost approach, cost is influenced by the marketplace. That is, the relevant cost is often the greatest amount that the marketplace is willing to pay for the fungible intellectual property. This value is not necessarily the actual historical cost of creating the commercial intellectual property, and it is not necessarily the sum of the historical costs for which the willing seller would like to be compensated. This is because value is not equal to cost, at least not to cost as measured in the historical accounting sense.

The conceptual foundation of all cost approach valuation methods relate to the following economics principles:

- The substitution principle indicates that no prudent buyer would pay more for a fungible intellectual property than the total cost to construct a new intellectual property of equal desirability and utility.
- The supply and demand principle indicates that shifts in supply and demand (1) cause costs to increase and decrease and (2) cause changes in the supply of different intellectual property types.
- The externalities principle indicates that gains or losses from external factors may affect the value of an intellectual property. For this reason, external conditions may cause a newly constructed intellectual property to be worth more or less than its cost.

Definition of Intellectual Property Cost

There are several generally accepted cost approach valuation methods. Each of these valuation methods uses a particular definition of cost. The two most common definitions of cost are:

1. reproduction cost new, and
2. replacement cost new.

There are subtle, but important, differences in these two different definitions of cost.

Reproduction cost new is the total cost, at current prices, to construct an exact duplicate or replica of the subject intellectual property. This duplicate intellectual property would be created using the same materials, standards, design, layout, and quality of workmanship used to create the original intellectual property.

Replacement cost new is the total cost to create, at current prices, an asset having equal functionality or utility of the subject intellectual property. Functionality is an engineering concept that means the ability of the intellectual property to perform the task for which it was designed. Utility is an economics concept that means the ability of the intellectual property to provide an equivalent amount of satisfaction.

The replacement intellectual property would be (1) created with modern methods and (2) constructed according to current standards, state-of-the-art design and layout, and the highest available quality of workmanship. Accordingly, the replacement intellectual property may have greater utility than the subject intellectual property. If this is the case, the valuation analyst should adjust for this factor in the obsolescence analysis of the replacement cost new less depreciation method.

Moreover, while the replacement intellectual property performs the same task as the subject intellectual property, the replacement asset is often "better" (in some way) than the subject intellectual property. The replacement intellectual property may yield more satisfaction than the subject intellectual property. If this is the case, the valuation analyst should adjust for this factor in the obsolescence estimation of the replacement cost analysis.

There are several other definitions of cost that may be applicable to a cost approach analysis. For example, some valuation analysts consider a measure of cost avoidance as a cost approach method. This method quantifies either historical or prospective costs that are avoided (*i.e.*, not incurred) by the intellectual property owner due to the intellectual property ownership.

In addition, some valuation analysts consider trended historical costs as an indication of value. In this method, actual historical asset development costs are identified and quantified and, then, "trended" to the valuation date by an appropriate inflation-based index factor. Regardless of the specific definition of cost used in the analysis, all cost approach valuation methods typically include a comprehensive and all-inclusive definition of cost.

Intellectual Property Cost Components

The intellectual property cost measurement (whether replacement cost, reproduction cost, or some other measure of cost) should include direct costs (*e.g.*, materials) and indirect costs (*e.g.*, engineering and design labor).

The intellectual property cost measurement should also consider the intangible asset developer's profit (on the direct cost and indirect cost investment) and an opportunity cost/entrepreneurial incentive (to economically motivate the intangible asset development process). And, the intellectual property cost measurement should be reduced by all relevant forms of obsolescence–including economic obsolescence.

The developer's profit is a cost component that is sometimes overlooked in the cost approach analysis. From the perspective of the intellectual property developer, first, the developer expects a return of all of the material, labor, and overhead costs related to the development process. And, second, the developer expects a return on all of the material, labor, and overhead costs related to the development process. For example, a building contractor expects to earn a reasonable profit on the construction of any residential, commercial, or industrial building. Likewise, an intellectual property developer expects to earn a reasonable profit on the intellectual property development.

The developer's profit can be estimated using several procedures. It can be estimated as a percentage return on the developer's investment in material, labor, and overhead. It can be estimated as a percentage markup–or as a fixed dollar markup–to the amount of time involved in the development process. It can also be estimated as a fixed dollar amount.

The valuation analyst sometimes disaggregates the developer's investment into two subcomponents: (1) the amount financed by external financing sources (*e.g.*, banks and other financial institutions) and (2) the amount financed by the intangible asset owner directly. The developer's profit associated with the costs financed by external sources is analogous to construction period interest accrued in the construction of a tangible asset.

Some valuation analysts include this construction period interest in the developer's profit cost category, and some valuation analysts include it in the overhead cost category. Usually, a higher rate of return is assigned to the cost amount financed by the intellectual property owner directly, as compared to the cost amount financed by external financing sources.

The opportunity cost is another cost component that is sometimes overlooked in the cost approach valuation analysis. Nonetheless, the opportunity cost component should be considered in each cost approach analysis. The opportunity cost is the amount of economic benefit required to motivate the intellectual property owner to enter into the development process.

With regard to the cost approach, intellectual property developers are sometimes compared to real estate developers (*e.g.*, the developer of a shopping mall or a residential apartment complex). There is an opportunity cost associated with the development process for both the intangible asset developer and the real estate developer. The time (and resources) they devote to the subject project is time (and resources) they are diverting from another development project.

Likewise, both the intellectual property developer and the real estate developer expect to be compensated for the conceptual, planning, and administrative efforts associated with putting the entire project together. They both expect to be compensated for the period of time between (1) when they initially begin production of the project and (2) when they realize the full commercial potential of the project.

Perhaps this opportunity cost concept is easier to understand with regard to the real estate developer. From the time the real estate developer first begins to construct the shopping mall until the time all of the retail stores are leased and occupied, the developer is likely to experience negative cash flow. Let's assume that this time period is two years. A real estate developer who purchased an already leased shopping mall two years earlier would likely experience positive cash flow during that same two-year period. The foregone cash flow during the two-year development period is one indication of the opportunity cost required to motivate the real estate developer to build a new shopping mall (instead of buying an existing shopping mall).

The same type of opportunity cost is necessary to motivate the intellectual property developer to produce a new patent, trademark, computer program, chemical formulation, food recipe, or other intellectual property. The intellectual property owner should be compensated for the risk of the new development process compared to the relatively low risk of using the last generation of technology, consumer brands, computer software, and so on.

Obsolescence Adjustments

Whether the valuation analyst uses the replacement cost new method or the reproduction cost new method to value an intellectual property, the intellectual property cost (however measured) should be adjusted for any losses in value due to:

1. physical deterioration,
2. functional obsolescence,
3. technological obsolescence (a form of functional obsolescence), and
4. economic obsolescence (a form of external obsolescence).

Physical deterioration is the reduction in the value of an intellectual property due to physical wear and tear resulting from continued use. It is unlikely an intellectual property will experience physical deterioration. However, the valuation analyst should consider this concept in a cost approach analysis.

Functional obsolescence is the reduction in the value of an intangible asset due to its inability to perform the function (or yield the periodic utility) for which it was originally designed. Technological obsolescence is a decrease in the value of an intellectual property due to improvements in technology that make an asset less than the ideal replacement for itself. Technological obsolescence occurs when, due to improvements in design or engineering technology, a replacement intellectual property produces a greater standardized measure of utility production than the actual intellectual property.

Technological obsolescence is typically considered to be a specific form of functional obsolescence. Accordingly, valuation analyst may capture all of the value influences due to both design flaws and changing technology in one category–and call that functional obsolescence.

Economic obsolescence (*i.e.*, a specific form of external obsolescence) is a reduction in the value of an intellectual property from the effects, events, or conditions that are external to–and not controlled by–the intellectual property current use or condition. The impact of economic obsolescence is typically beyond the control of the owner/operator. For that reason, economic obsolescence is typically considered incurable.

In any cost approach analysis, the valuation analyst will estimate the amounts (if any) of physical deterioration, functional obsolescence, technological obsolescence, and economic obsolescence related to the intellectual property. In this estimation, the valuation analyst may consider the intellectual property actual age–and its expected remaining useful life (RUL). Such an age/RUL consideration may be an important component of the cost approach.

In the cost approach, the typical formula for quantifying intellectual property replacement cost new is:

Reproduction cost new
− Curable functional and technological obsolescence
= Replacement cost new

The following cost approach formula is often used to estimate intellectual property value:

Replacement cost new
− Physical deterioration
− Economic obsolescence
− Incurable functional and technological obsolescence
= Value

Income Approach Valuation Methods

The income approach is based on the economics principle of anticipation (also called the principle of expectation). In this approach, the value of the intellectual property is the present value of the expected economic income to be earned from the ownership/operation of the intellectual property. As the name of this economics principle implies, the willing buyer "anticipates" the "expected" economic income to be earned from the intellectual property.

This expectation of prospective economic income is converted to a present worth–that is, the indicated intellectual property value. This conversion requires the valuation analyst to estimate the investor's required rate of return on the intellectual property generating the prospective economic income. This required rate of return will be a function of many economic variables, including the risk–or the uncertainty–of the expected economic income.

Measures of Intellectual Property Income

There are numerous alternative measures of economic income that may be relevant to an intellectual property valuation. If properly applied, many different measures of economic income can be used in the income approach to provide a reasonable indication of value. Some common alternative measures of economic income include:

1. gross or net revenues,
2. gross income (or gross profit),
3. net operating income,
4. net income before tax,
5. net income after tax,
6. operating cash flow,
7. net cash flow, and
8. several other types of income (such as incremental income).

Since many different measures of economic income can be used in this valuation approach, the valuation analyst should ensure that the discount rate of the direct capitalization rate used is derived on a basis consistent with the measure of economic income chosen.

Types of Income Approach Valuation Methods

These are at least as many income approach valuation methods as there are alternative measures of intellectual property income. All of these different income approach valuation methods can be classified into two groups: (1) direct capitalization methods and (2) yield capitalization methods. In addition, most of these methods can be grouped into five categories of income approach valuation methods summarized below:

1. Valuation methods that quantify the incremental level of intellectual property economic income—that is, the intellectual property owner/operator will expect a greater level of economic income (however measured) by owning/operating the intellectual property as compared to not owning/operating the intellectual property.
2. Valuation methods that quantify a decremental level of intellectual property economic costs—that is, the intellectual property owner/operator will expect a lower level of economic costs—such as other required levels of capital costs or operating costs—by owning/operating the intellectual property as compared to not owning/operating the intellectual property.
3. Valuation methods that estimate a relief from a hypothetical royalty payment—that is, the amount of a royalty payment that a hypothetical third party intangible asset license would be willing to pay to a hypothetical third-party intellectual property licensor in order to obtain the use of—and the rights to—the intellectual property.
4. Valuation methods that quantify the difference in the value of the owner/operator overall business enterprise—or similar economic unit—as a result of owning the intellectual property (and using it in the owner/operator business enterprise)—as compared to not owning the intellectual property (and not using it in the owner/operator business enterprise).
5. Valuation methods that estimate the value of the intellectual property as a residual from the value of the owner/operator overall business enterprise (or of a similar economic unit), or as a residual from the value of an overall estimation of the total intangible value of the owner/operator business enterprise (or of a similar economic unit).

Direct Capitalization Methods

In a direct capitalization analysis, the valuation analyst (1) estimates a normalized measure of economic income for one period (*i.e.*, one period future to the valuation date) and (2) divides that measure by an appropriate investment rate of return. The appropriate investment rate of return is called the direct capitalization rate.

The direct capitalization rate may be derived for a perpetuity period of time, or the direct capitalization rate may be derived for a specified finite period of time. This decision will depend on the valuation analyst's expectation of the duration of the economic income stream.

Yield Capitalization Methods

In a yield capitalization analysis, the valuation analyst projects the appropriate measure of economic income for several discrete time periods into the future. This projection of prospective economic income is converted into a present value by the use of a present value discount rate. The present value discount rate is the investor's required rate or return–or yield capitalization rate–over the expected term of the economic income projection.

The duration of the discrete projection period–and whether a residual or terminal value should be considered at the conclusion of the discrete projection period–will depend on the valuation analyst's expectation of the duration of the economic income stream.

Intellectual Property Valuation in a Distressed Economic Environment

The valuation analyst should consider the state of the national and regional economy during the intellectual property valuation process. Likewise, the valuation analyst should consider the competitive structure of the industry in which the intellectual property owner/operator operates. In particular, the state of the general economy will affect the valuation variables that the analyst selects in each of the three generally accepted valuation approaches.

Cost Approach Valuation Variables

In the cost approach, both the reproduction cost new and the replacement cost new may be lower in a recessionary economy than in an expansionary economy. The intellectual property reproduction cost new may be lower because the inflation-based trend factors that are applied to the historical cost components would be lower than in an expansionary economy. Likewise, the market-derived replacement cost indicators may be lower in a recessionary economy. This is because the market-derived influences of decreased demand and increased supply have driven down the current replacement costs for the intellectual property cost components.

In fact, all of the following intellectual property cost components typically would be lower in a recessionary economy than in an expansionary economy:

1. Direct costs – due to the market influences on direct materials prices;
2. Indirect costs – due to the market influences on labor costs of developer employees and of outside contract employees;
3. Overhead costs – due to the market influences on the costs of development supervisory and support personnel and to the fact that many owner/operator organizations cut back on employee bonuses, benefits, pension contributions, *etc.*;
4. Developer's profit – the market may indicate that independent intellectual property development companies typically add a much lower (if any) profit margin to their development costs in a distressed economy;
5. Entrepreneurial incentive – empirical data may indicate that interest rates and the corresponding time valuation of many is lower in a recessionary economy; in addition, the developer's opportunity cost may be much lower in a distressed economy due to the reduced operating profit of the intellectual property owner/operator.

In addition to influences on the development cost factors, that state of the economy will influence the cost approach obsolescence factors. These factors may be influenced as follows:

1. Functional obsolescence – this factor may be influenced by changes (increases or decreases) in the (a) excess operating costs and (b) excess capital costs related to ownership/operation of the subject intellectual property (compared to the replacement intellectual property).
2. Technological obsolescence – competitors may introduce intellectual property more quickly in a depressed economy, in order to stay competitive in the marketplace; likewise, competitors may also introduce intellectual property less quickly in a depressed economy, due to their reductions in R&D and other intellectual property development expenditures.
3. Economic obsolescence – this form of obsolescence will typically increase in a recessionary economy; this is because it is more likely that the owner/operator will experience an income shortfall; for cost approach valuation purposes, and income shortfall occurs when the owner/operator cannot earn a fair rate o return (typically measured as a cost of capital) on the intellectual property replacement or reproduction cost new (less other forms of obsolescence).

Accordingly, the market will typically adjust the cost approach valuation variables to produce a lower intellectual property value indication in a recessionary economy than in an expansionary economy.

Market Approach Valuation Variables

The market will also adjust the intellectual property market approach valuation variables in a recessionary economy. For example, current guideline intellectual property sale or license transactions may indicate (1) lower sale pricing metrics and (2) lower license agreement royalty rates.

In a valuation performed in a recessionary economy, the valuation analyst should be careful to select timely guideline sale or license transactions. To the extent that the only available transactional data are stale (*i.e.*, pre-recessionary economy), then the analyst will have to make what are called market adjustments (or training adjustments) to the transactional data. The objective of the market adjustments is to adjust the stale transactional pricing metrics to what the corresponding license metrics would be in the current recessionary economy.

In a recessionary economy, the valuation analyst will typically rely more on guideline license transactional data than guideline sale transactional data. As summarized below, there are several reasons for this increased reliance on the guideline license transactional data–and the use of the market approach relief from royalty valuation method.

First, there are more intellectual property license transactions than sale transactions in the commercial marketplace. Therefore, the available guideline transactional license data may be more timely than the available guideline transactional sale data.

Second, in the relief from royalty (RFR) method, the market-derived license royalty rate is multiplied by the owner/operator operating revenue. The product of that multiplication is the intellectual property license fee that the owner/operator is "relieved" from having to pay (because the owner/operator, in fact, owns the subject intellectual property). In a depressed economy, the intellectual property-related operating revenue will be less than in an expansionary economy. Therefore, the market approach value indication will also be less than in a robust economy.

Third, in the RFR method, the "relieved" intellectual property license fee is capitalized by the difference of (1) the present value discount rate minus (2) the expected long-term growth rate. In the typical recessionary economy, the present value discount rate is lower than it would be otherwise. This increased present value discount rate is due to the increased risk associated with the increased owner/operator business risk in a distressed economy. Also, in the typical recessionary economy, the expected long-term growth rate (in the owner/operator projected revenue) is lower than it would be in an expansionary economy. An increase in the present value discount rate and a decrease in the expected long-term growth rate will cause the intellectual property market approach value indication to be lower than it would be in a robust economy.

Income Approach Valuation Variables

Virtually all of the valuation variables in the intellectual property income approach analysis will be affected by the state of the economy. Accordingly, in a depressed economy, the income approach value indication should automatically reflect a lower value for the intellectual property. This conclusion is correct regardless of whether the yield capitalization method or the direct capitalization method is used in the income approach valuation analysis.

In addition, the income approach should conclude a lower intellectual property value indication regardless of which of the following measures of economic income are considered in the valuation analysis:

1. owner/operator residual income
2. owner/operator excess income
3. owner/operator differential income
4. owner/operator incremental income
5. owner/operator profit split income

The reasons why the depressed economy will cause the income approach to reflect a decreased value indication are severalfold. First, the owner/operator revenue will typically be reduced in a recessionary economy. And, all intellectual property income approach valuation methods start with a revenue projection. Second, the owner/operator selling expense, R&D expense, and other expense will be increased in a recessionary economy. This is because the owner/operator is attempting to increase (or maintain) sales in an increasingly competitive environment. Third, the owner/operator investment in capital expenditures and not working capital may increase in a recessionary economy. Again, this is because the owner/operator is attempting to remain competitive in a decreased overall market. Fourth, all of these factors contribute to a projection of decreased economic income (however defined) for the intellectual property owner/operator.

Accordingly, whatever method is used to allocate a portion of the owner/operator income to the intellectual property, that allocated income will, typically, be lower in a recessionary economy than in an expansionary economy. Therefore, the intellectual property income approach value indication will be lower in a depressed economy than in a robust economy. And, that value affect is only magnified if the intellectual property RUL is reduced due to the increased industry competition that occurs in a depressed economy.

Valuation Synthesis and Conclusion

As explained above, the intellectual property values indicated by all three generally accepted valuation approaches should be lower in a recessionary economy than in an expansionary economy. This is due to the fact that the valuation variables used in each of the three generally accepted valuation approaches should automatically adjust to reflect the current conditions of the depressed economy.

The following discussion presents three simplified illustrative examples with regard to intellectual property valuation. Each simplified example will illustrate one of the three generally accepted valuation approaches. First, each example will illustrate the valuation of the indicated intellectual property in an expansionary economy. Second, each example will change to reflect the valuation variables that would be appropriate to the same intellectual property–but in a recessionary economy. The difference between the analysis scenarios (and the value indications) should reflect how the valuation approaches will automatically adapt to changing economic conditions. And, the difference between the analysis scenarios (and the value indications) should reflect how the use of the appropriate valuation variables should result in an appropriate intellectual property value–even in a depressed economy.

Illustrative Example of the Application of the Cost Approach and the Income Approach

Exhibits 1 through 5 present a simplified illustrative example of the valuation of a trade secret intellectual property. This illustrative intellectual property relates to the manufacture of compressed meal replacement bar (MRB) products by Healthy Morning, Inc. ("Healthy Morning"). For the last year or so, Healthy Morning has produced a popular MRB product that has a good taste, crunchy texture, high protein, and nutritional balance. The subject intellectual property includes the trade secret proprietary process by which these MRB products are manufactured.

The subject trade secret is the compress and form manufacturing process of the MRB product recipe and formulation. This trade secret is documented in a set of engineering drawings and in a process flow chart notebook. Healthy Morning management has elected not to patent this proprietary process for competitive reasons. However, both the Healthy Morning process engineers and the Healthy Morning intellectual property legal counsel believe that the manufacturing process would be patentable. Nonetheless, if the trade secret became public knowledge through the patent procedure, Healthy Morning management is concerned that the company's competitors could reverse engineer an equally effective manufacturing process that would not violate the patent.

Healthy Morning management treats this proprietary technology as a trade secret. All of the engineering and other documentation related to this manufacturing process is protected in a locked cabinet in the process engineering department. Only a select number of Healthy Morning engineering and production managers have access to that information. And, all of those Healthy Morning employees have signed nondisclosure agreements.

Healthy Morning management also believes that this proprietary process gives the company's MRB product a distinct competitive advantage. Healthy Morning marketing personnel stress this product differentiation feature in all of the company marketing materials and presentations.

In summary, the subject intellectual property is the trade secret (including the technical documentation) related to the "compress and form" manufacturing proprietary process (hereinafter referred to as "the MRB trade secret").

For illustrative purposes only, first, the valuation analyst will value the MRB trade secret assuming an expansionary economy. Second, the valuation analyst will value the MRB trade secret assuming a depressed economy. In both economic environment scenarios, the valuation analyst will use the income approach and the cost approach to value the subject intellectual property.

Illustrative Example Fact Set and Analysis Assumptions

The objective of this valuation is to estimate the fair market value of the MRB trade secret intangible asset as of December 31, 2009. The purpose of this valuation is for management information, strategic planning, and corporate governance.

The MRB trade secret is used in the manufacture of a health food product line that is projected to generate $147 million in net revenue next year.

The Healthy Morning process engineers have developed a unique modification to the standard compression process. The Healthy Mornings trade secret produces an MRB product that has a crunchy texture and a "snappy" break. In addition, the final product maintains a good taste and a high nutritional value. Also, a lower moisture content of the final product increases the retail shelf life of the MRB product. The company's trade secret produces an MRB product with much greater consumer appeal than competitive products. And, the Healthy Morning MRB product can be produced at the same cost of sales than the lower quality competitor MRB products.

Selection of Valuation Approaches and Methods

In this analysis, the appropriate standard of value is fair market value. In this analysis, the appropriate premise of value is value in continued use. This premise of value is consistent with (1) the valuation analyst's assignment and (2) the valuation analyst's assessment of the highest and best use of the technology intangible asset.

Based on the quality and quantity of available data and the purpose and objective of the subject analysis, the valuation analyst decided to use two generally accepted valuation approaches: (1) the cost approach and, specifically, the reproduction cost new less depreciation method, and (2) the income approach and, specifically, the differential income method.

Cost Approach Analysis

The valuation analyst decided to use the reproduction cost new less depreciation (RCNLD) method to value the MRB trade secret. In this case, the valuation analyst had access to the actual historical development costs related to the MRB trade secret. This type of historical cost information is not always available to a valuation analyst. However, because this trade secret was so important to the company, Healthy Morning management tracked the original cost of its proprietary process development efforts. Therefore, the valuation analyst was able to restate the historical development costs of the trade secret in current (*i.e.*, valuation date) dollars. This trended historical cost analysis provides the valuation analyst with an estimate of the cost that would be incurred by a hypothetical willing buyer to reproduce the MRB trade secret.

Cost Approach Valuation Variables—Expansionary Economy Environment

Healthy Morning management provided the valuation analyst with the historical accounting information regarding the number of hours spent by Healthy Morning food engineers and scientists on the various aspects of the trade secret development. In applying the RCNLD method, the valuation analyst estimated a full absorption cost related to the Healthy Morning employees who developed the trade secret. This full absorption cost included all employee salaries, employee benefits, employment-related taxes, and related company overhead. This full absorption cost also included a component for development period interest related to the direct costs.

The valuation analyst calculated each of these full absorption cost components as of the valuation date. Accordingly, the full absorption cost represents the reproduction cost for the subject intellectual property. The valuation analyst concluded the current cost per person-hour for all of the company employee hours actually spent on the development, testing, and implementation of the MRB trade secret.

The product of (1) the total number of person-hours actually spent to develop the trade secret and (2) the estimated full absorption cost per person-hour results in an estimate of the reproduction cost new for the MRB trade secret.

The valuation analyst considered adjustments to the reproduction cost new estimate for losses in value due to functional, technological, and economic obsolescence. In particular, the valuation analyst considered: (1) the age and expected RUL of this trade secret, (2) the intellectual property position within its technology life cycle, and (3) the owner/operator's return on investment related to the use of the trade secret.

Exhibit 1 summarizes the RCNLD analysis. The total reproduction cost includes (1) direct costs, (2) indirect costs, (3) developer's profit, and (4) entrepreneurial incentive. The direct costs include the direct salary costs of the Healthy Morning process development team. The indirect costs include the related employee benefit costs, employment taxes, overhead allocation, and development period interest expense. The developer's profit includes an estimate of the profit margin that an independent engineering firm would charge to Healthy Morning if that engineering firm was retained to develop the trade secret. And, the entrepreneurial incentive is the opportunity cost related to the intellectual property development process. The valuation analyst quantified this opportunity cost as the difference in the amount of cash flow that Healthy Morning would earn with versus without the trade secret. The valuation analyst estimated that incremental cash flow during the period of elapsed time required to develop (*i.e.*, reproduce) the trade secret. Healthy Morning engineers estimated that the trade secret development period would be 24 months.

As indicated in Exhibit 1, the reproduction cost new (RCN) for the MRB trade secret is $10,784,000. Based on the current age (*i.e.*, one year) and RUL (*i.e.*, five years) of the MRB trade secret, the valuation analyst concluded that a 15 per cent functional obsolescence allowance was appropriate for this particular intellectual property. That 15 per cent functional obsolescence allowance results in $1,618,000 of "depreciation." The indicated RCNLD estimate is $9,166,000. And, this RCNLD estimate is rounded to a fair market value indication of the MRB trade secret in an expansionary economy of $9,200,000.

Income Approach Analysis

Using the differential income method, the valuation analyst first projected the prospective cash flow generated by Healthy Morning associated with the use of the MRB trade secret in its current operation. Second, the valuation analyst projected the prospective cash flow that would be generated by Health Morning without the use of the MRB trade secret. The trade secret value indication is based on the difference between the present value indications from the two different operating scenarios–*i.e.*, (1) with the MRB trade secret in current operation, and (2) without the MRB trade secret in current operation.

Valuation Variables—Expansionary Economy Environment

Healthy Morning marketing management provided the valuation analyst with projections of the MRB product unit selling price, unit volume, and market share for the five years after the valuation date. Healthy Morning management also projected the cost of goods sold and the capital expenditure data related to the production of the MRB food product. In addition, Healthy Morning management prepared a five-year projection of the selling, general, and administrative expenses related to the MRB food product line. After a due diligence review of the Healthy Morning financial projections, the valuation analyst concluded that these product line financial projections were reasonable.

This valuation method measures the difference in the economic income potential of Healthy Morning both with and without the operation of the MRB trade secret. The economic income potential represents the amount of economic income that is available to the business after consideration of a required level of reinvestment for continued operations and for expected growth. The valuation analyst selected net cash flow as the appropriate measure of economic income.

For purposes of this analysis, the valuation analyst defined net cash flow as follows:

Net Sales

Less:	Cost of sales
Less:	Operating expenses
Equals:	Net income before taxes
Less:	Income taxes
Plus:	Depreciation and amortization expense
Less:	Capital expenditures
Less:	Additions to net working capital

Less:	Capital charge on contributory assets
Equals:	Net cash flow

In this analysis, the product line net cash flow is projected over the expected RUL of the subject trade secret. The net cash flow projection is discounted at an appropriate discount rate in order to conclude a present value.

Based on industry experience, Healthy Morning management expects that it will develop a replacement trade secret in about five years. Both Healthy Mornings and all of its competitors continuously develop improved MRB products. The Healthy Morning process engineering staff is already working on the development of a new and improved compression process. Management expects that the new and improved process will be developed, tested, and implemented within five years. At that time, the current MRB trade secret will be obsolete.

This five-year expected RUL is consistent with the company's historical experience regarding its trade secret technology life cycle. And, this five-year expected RUL is consistent with the industry's historical experience regarding a trade secret technology life cycle. Therefore, the valuation analyst selected five years as the appropriate measure of the MRB trade secret RUL.

The valuation analyst selected the following valuation variables:

Scenario I: With the MRB trade secret in place

- Net sales growth rate: 10 per cent per year
- Gross margin percentage: 26 per cent of net sales
- Other operating expenses: 11 per cent of net sales
- Effective income tax rate: 36 per cent of pretax income
- Depreciation expense: 1 per cent of net sales
- Net capital expenditures: equal to depreciation expense
- Capital charge on all contributory assets: $2.2 million per year
- Incremental net working capital: 5 per cent of net sales
- Present value discount rate: 15 per cent
- Remaining useful life estimate: 5 years

Scenario II: Without the MRB trade secret in operation

- Expected sales decrement: −10 per cent per year
- Other operating expenses: 11.5 per cent of net sales
- Incremental net working capital: 7 per cent of net sales
- All other valuation variables remain unchanged for Scenario I

The capital charge is included to account for the fair return of the investment of all the contributory assets that are used with the MRB trade secret. The contributory assets include net working capital, tangible operating assets, and the Healthy Morning trade name.

The projected decrease in product line sales without the MRB trade secret in operation is based on valuation analyst discussions with Healthy Morning management. This projected sales decrease indicates management's estimate of the consumer response to the decrease in taste, crunchiness, and retail shelf life of the MRB product without the trade secret. The negative sales growth rate reflects management's projection of the combined effects of (1) decreased unit selling price and (2) decreased unit volume sales.

Without the product differentiation provided by the MRB trade secret, management estimates that it will have to increase its marketing expense. This marketing expense increase accounts for the one-half of one per cent projected increase in other operating expenses.

In addition, management projects that it will have to liberalize its customer credit policy in order to stimulate sales of the less desirable MRB product. Management estimates that it will have to give 60-day credit terms instead of 30-day credit terms. This change in credit policy will affect the company's accounts receivable balances. This change in credit policy will result in an expected change in the company's net working capital investment.

The 15 per cent present value discount rate is based on the valuation analyst's estimate of the Healthy Morning weighted average cost of capital.

Income Approach Valuation Analysis in an Expansionary Economy

As presented in Exhibit 2 (following at the end of the chapter), the sum of the product line discounted cash flow with the MRB trade secret in operation is \$49,500,000. As presented in Exhibit 3, the sum of the product line discounted cash flow without the MRB trade secret in operation is \$40,900,000. The difference of these two income projections indicates a differential related to the MRB trade secret of \$8,600,000. As summarized in Exhibit 4, the income approach indicates a fair market value of the MRB trade secret, in an expansionary economy, of \$8,600,000.

Value Conclusion—Expansionary Economy Environment

The valuation analyst decided to assign equal weight to the value indications provided by the two valuation approaches. Based on the analyses presented in Exhibits 1 through 4, the fair market value of the Healthy Morning trade secret, assuming an expansionary economic environment, is \$8.9 million (rounded). Exhibit 5 presents the valuation synthesis and conclusion for this illustrative valuation—assuming an expansionary economic environment.

Cost Approach Valuation Variables—Recessionary Economy Environment

Let's assume that the valuation analyst performs the same cost approach valuation analysis of the MRB trade secret, but during a depressed economic environment. In this continuing example, the historical costs of the research and development expenditures required to develop the MRB trade secret are still restated at current (*i.e.*, valuation date) costs. This trended historical cost analysis is used to estimate a reproduction cost new. The valuation analyst will also make adjustments to the reproduction cost new estimate to account for any losses in value due to functional, technological, and economic obsolescence.

Again, Healthy Morning management provided the valuation analyst with accounting information regarding the number of hours spent by Healthy Morning food engineers and scientists on the various aspects of the trade secret development. The valuation analyst estimated a full absorption cost related to the Healthy Morning employees who developed the subject proprietary process. This full absorption cost included all employee salaries, employee benefits, employment-related taxes, and related company overhead. This full absorption cost also included a component for development period interest. This full absorption cost reflects the costs and overhead experienced by Healthy Morning in a depressed economy.

The full absorption cost represents the reproduction cost for the subject intellectual property, assuming depressed economic conditions. Based on this full absorption cost analysis, the valuation analyst concluded the current cost per person-hour for all of the company employee hours actually spent on the development, testing, and implementation of the MRB trade secret.

The product of (1) the total number of person-hours actually spent to develop the MRB trade secret and (2) the estimated full absorption cost per person-hour results in the MRB trade secret reproduction cost new.

The valuation analyst again considered adjustments to the reproduction cost new estimate for losses in value due to functional, technological, and economic obsolescence. In particular, the valuation analyst considered: (1) the trade secret age and expected RUL, (2) the trade secret position within its technology life cycle, and (3) the owner/operator's return on investment related to the trade secret.

Exhibit 6 summarizes the RCNLD analysis, assuming depressed economic conditions. The total reproduction cost includes (1) direct costs, (2) indirect costs, (3) developer's profit, and (4) entrepreneurial incentive. The direct costs include the direct salary costs of the Healthy Morning trade secret development team. The indirect costs include the related employee benefit costs, employment taxes, overhead allocation, and development period interest expense. The developer's profit includes the valuation analyst's estimate of the profit margin that an independent engineering firm would charge to Healthy Morning assuming depressed economic conditions. And, the entrepreneurial incentive is the opportunity cost related to the trade secret development process. In this analysis, the valuation analyst quantified this opportunity cost as the difference in the amount of cash flow that Healthy Morning would earn with versus without the trade secret. The valuation analyst estimated that incremental cash flow during the period of elapsed time was required to reproduce the trade secret in a recessionary economy. Healthy Morning engineers estimated that the trade secret development period would be 24 months.

As indicated in Exhibit 6, the total reproduction cost new (RCN) for the MRB trade secret is $9,556,000. The valuation analyst concluded a 15 per cent functional obsolescence allowance. That 15 per cent functional obsolescence allowance results in $1,433,000 of "depreciation." Accordingly, the indicated RCNLD for this trade secret is $8,123,000. And, based on valuation variables appropriate to a depressed economy, this RCNLD estimate is rounded to a fair market value indication for the MRB intellectual property of $8,100,000.

Income Approach Valuation Variables—Recessionary Economy Environment

Healthy Morning marketing management provided the valuation analyst with depressed economy financial projections of the MRB product unit selling price, unit volume, and market share for the five years after the valuation date. Healthy Morning management also projected the cost of goods sold and the capital expenditure data within a recessionary environment. Healthy Morning management prepared a five-year projection of the selling, general, and administrative expenses related to the MRB food product line. After a due diligence review of the financial projections, the valuation analyst concluded that these product line financial projections were reasonable within the context of a depressed economy.

This income approach valuation method measures the difference in the economic income potential of Healthy Morning both with and without the operation of the MRB trade secret. The economic income potential represents the amount of economic income that is available to the business after consideration of a required level of reinvestment for continued operations and for expected growth. Based on the prospective financial data available, the valuation analyst selected net cash flow as the appropriate measure of economic income.

The product line net cash flow is projected over the expected RUL of the subject trade secret. The net cash flow projection is discounted at an appropriate discount rate in order to conclude a present value. The difference between (1) the present value of the product line net cash flow with the MRB trade secret in operation and (2) the present value of the product line net cash flow without the MRB trade secret in operation equals (3) the indicated value of the intellectual proprietary.

Management expects that it will develop a replacement trade secret in about five years. The Healthy Morning process engineering staff is already working on the development of a new trade secret. Management expects that the new and improved process will be developed, tested, and implemented within five years. At that time, the current trade secret will be obsolete. Therefore, the valuation analyst selected five years as the appropriate measure of the MRB trade secret RUL for purposes of this recessionary economy valuation analysis.

The valuation analyst selected the following valuation variables with respect to this depressed economy valuation analysis:

Scenario I: With the MRB trade secret in place

- Net sales growth rate: 10 per cent per year
- Gross margin percentage: 26 per cent of net sales
- Other operating expenses: 12 per cent of net sales
- Effective income tax rate: 36 per cent of pretax income
- Depreciation expense: 1 per cent of net sales
- Net capital expenditures: equal to depreciation expense
- Capital charge on all contributory assets: $2.2 million per year
- Incremental net working capital: 10 per cent of net sales
- Present value discount rate: 15 per cent
- Remaining useful life estimate: 5 years

Scenario II: Without the MRB trade secret in operation

- Expected sales decrement: -10 per cent per year
- Other operating expenses: 13 per cent of net sales
- Incremental net working capital: 10 per cent of net sales
- All other valuation variables remain unchanged for Scenario I

The capital charge is included to account for the fair return of the investment of all the contributory assets that are used or used up in the production of the income associated with the MRB trade secret. The contributory assets include net working capital, tangible operating assets, and the Healthy Morning trade name.

The projected decrease in product line sales without the MRB trade secret in operation is based on valuation analyst discussions with Healthy Morning management. This projected sales decrease indicates management estimate of the consumer response to the decrease in taste, crunchiness, and retail shelf life of the company's product without the MRB trade secret. The negative sales growth rate reflects management's projection of the combined effects of (1) decreased unit selling price and (2) decreased unit volume sales.

Without the product differentiation provided by the MRB trade secret, management estimates that it will have to increase its marketing expense. This marketing expense increase accounts for the one per cent projected increase in other operating expenses.

In addition, management projects that it will have to liberalize its customer credit policy in order to stimulate sales of the less desirable MRB product. Management estimates that it will have to give 60-day credit terms instead of 30-day credit terms. This expected change in credit policy will affect the company's accounts receivable balances. And, this change in credit policy will result in an expected change in the company's net working capital investment.

The 15 per cent present value discount rate is based on the valuation analyst's estimate of the Healthy Morning weighted average cost of capital.

Income Approach Valuation Analysis—in a Recessionary Economy

As presented in Exhibit 7, the sum of the product line discounted cash flow with the MRB trade secret in operation is $42,500,000. As presented in Exhibit 8, the sum of the product line discounted cash flow without the MRB trade secret in operation is $34,000,000. The difference of these two limited life income projections indicates a discounted cash flow differential related to the MRB trade secret of $8,500,000. As indicated in Exhibit 9, the income approach indicates a fair market value of the MRB trade secret, assuming a recessionary economy, of $8,500,000.

Value Conclusion—Recessionary Economy Environment

The valuation analyst decided to assign equal weight to the value indications provided by the two valuation approaches. Based on the analyses presented in Exhibits 6 through 10, the fair market value of the Health Morning trade secret, assuming a recessionary economic environment, is $8.3 million (rounded).

Summary

This simplified illustrative example indicates how the cost approach and the income approach automatically adjust to reflect an intellectual property value decrease in a recessionary economy. This Healthy Morning trade secret valuation analysis concludes a higher value for the subject intellectual property in an expansionary economy than in a depressed economy.

Illustrative Example of the Application of the Market Approach

Let's also consider a simplified illustrative example of the application of the income approach to an intellectual property valuation. Let's assume that Charitable Taxpayer Corporation (CTC) is a pharmaceutical products company.

CTC management has developed a new pharmaceutical drug compound. CTC management expects that the new drug product will enjoy considerable commercial success. CTC management has decided to donate the patent rights for the new drug compound to a medical school and to claim a charitable contribution deduction for federal income tax purposes.

Let's assume that CTC management retains the valuation analyst to perform a charitable contribution valuation of its donated intellectual property. Let's assume that the valuation date for this charitable contribution valuation is January 1, 2009 (the date of the donation).

Let's assume that the valuation analyst decides to use the income approach and the relief from royalty (RFR) valuation method to value the donated drug compound patent related to one specific CTC drug product–a product commonly called Vigor. The Vigor drug product treats the medical condition called erectile dysfunction (or "ED").

Illustrative Example Fact Set and Analysis Assumptions

The Vigor drug compound was patented, passed its clinical trials, and received all FDA approvals. In fact, Vigor has just been introduced on the market. CTC management expects that Vigor will generate about $400 million in first year (*i.e.*, 2008) product revenue for CTC.

Let's assume that the valuation analyst concludes a nine-year economic RUL for the Vigor patented drug product. This valuation analyst intellectual property RUL conclusion is based on the following:

1. the consensus of CTC management
2. the life cycle of the previous generations of ED drugs
3. the current research stage of potential replacement drugs
4. the expected impact of generic pharmaceutical products
5. published product life estimates from taxpayer industry analysts
6. CTC management plans for developing its own replacement (*i.e.*, more effective) pharmaceutical compound

Market Approach Valuation Variables—Expansionary Economy Environment

The valuation analyst concludes the following Vigor product expected revenue growth rates, assuming a robust economic environment:

1. 10 per cent expected product revenue increase for the first 3 years
2. 0 per cent expected product revenue increase for the next 3 years
3. 12 per cent expected product revenue decrease for the last 3 years

The valuation analyst concluded that there will be no residual revenue from the Vigor product after the nine-year RUL. That is, CTC management indicated to the valuation analyst that it will discontinue the manufacture of Vigor and, instead, manufacture a replacement drug product after year nine.

Based on discussions with CTC management, the valuation analyst learned that CTC is expected to incur an expense of approximately $10,000,000 a year related to the legal defense, marketing, and administration of the Vigor patented drug product. CTC management projects that this level of expense will increase at the rate of three per cent per year, regardless of the level of the Vigor product sales revenue.

CTC management believes that any owner of the Vigor drug compound patent would incur such an annual expense. CTC management also informed the valuation analyst that CTC would continue to incur this type of expense if it was the licensee of the patent (and another corporate taxpayer was the licensor of the patent).

The valuation analyst also concludes that a 20 per cent pretax present value discount rate is appropriate for this patent valuation analysis, given the risk of the Vigor drug product.

Guideline Intellectual Property License Search Procedures

The valuation analyst researched all four of the following online intellectual property license royalty rate data sources:

1. Financial Valuation Group intellectual property transactions database
2. Recombinant Capital rDNA biotech intellectual property transactions database
3. AUS Consultants Royalty Source intellectual property transactions database
4. RoyaltyStat intellectual property transactions database

The valuation analyst searched each database (1) for the pharmaceutical industry SIC code and (2) for pharmaceutical compound or product patent license agreements. The valuation analyst searched for pharmaceutical compound patent licenses entered into within three years of the subject valuation date.

The valuation analyst searched for patent licenses where the royalty payment was expressed primarily as a percentage of revenue. And, the valuation analyst scanned all of the identified patent license agreement descriptions for a similar disease (*i.e.*, vascular) and a similar therapy (*i.e.*, a pill type drug) to the subject Vigor drug product.

Guideline Patent License Agreement Royalty Rates

Based on the above-described patent license search criteria, the valuation analyst selected comparable uncontrolled transactions–or CUTs. These CUT hypothetical drug compound patent license agreements are presented in Exhibit 10.

Illustrative Example of a Royalty Rate Adjustment Grid

Based on the comparability factors that the valuation analyst considered to be the most relevant to the subject analysis, the valuation analyst adjusted the hypothetical guideline intellectual property license transactional data as presented in Exhibit 11.

Market Approach Valuation Analysis—in an Expansionary Economy

Based on the uneven expected revenue growth rate and the RUL analyses summarized above, the valuation analyst decided to use a yield capitalization method model (instead of a simple direct capitalization model). This RFR method yield capitalization model is simply an expanded format of the RFR method direct capitalization formula mentioned earlier. The Vigor drug patent yield capitalization analysis is presented in Exhibit 12.

In this simplified illustrative example, and based on the application of the RFR valuation method, the valuation analyst concluded that the fair market value of the CTC Vigor pharmaceutical compound patent is $90 million, as of the January 1, 2009, valuation date. This $90 million market approach value conclusion is appropriate assuming an expansionary economic environment.

Market Approach Valuation Variables—Recessionary Economic Environment

The assumption of a recessionary economy does not affect the valuation analyst's conclusion with regard to the Vigor patent RUL. However, the valuation analyst concludes the following Vigor product expected revenue growth rates, assuming a depressed economic environment:

1. 0 per cent expected product revenue increase for the first 3 years
2. 2 per cent expected product revenue decrease for the next 3 years
3. 4 per cent expected product revenue decrease for the last 3 years

The valuation analyst also concluded that there will be no residual revenue from the Vigor product after the nine-year RUL under the recessionary economy assumption.

Based on discussions with CTC management related to the recessionary economy scenario, the valuation analyst learned that CTC is expected to incur an expense of approximately $12,000,000 a year related to the legal defense, marketing, and administration of the Vigor patented drug product. CTC management projects that this recessionary economy level of expense will increase at the rate of three per cent per year, regardless of the level of the Vigor product sales revenue.

The valuation analyst concludes that a 20 per cent pre-tax discount rate is still appropriate for this patent valuation, even in a recessionary economy.

Guideline Patent License Agreement Royalty Rates

The valuation analyst used the same guideline intellectual property license search procedures that were summarized above. Based on the above-described patent license search criteria, the valuation analyst selected as CUTs the same drug compound patent license agreements presented in

Exhibit 11. Based on the comparability factors that the valuation analyst considered most relevant, the valuation analyst again adjusted the hypothetical guideline intellectual property license transactional data as previously presented in Exhibit 12.

Market Approach Valuation Analysis in a Recessionary Economy

Based on the uneven expected revenue growth rate and the RUL analyses summarized above, the valuation analyst decided to use a yield capitalization method model in the depressed economy valuation analysis. The recessionary economy Vigor drug patent yield capitalization analysis is presented in Exhibit 14. Assuming a recessionary economic environment, and based on the application of the RFR valuation method, the valuation analyst concluded that the fair market value of the CTC Vigor pharmaceutical compound patent is $50 million, as of the January 1, 2009, valuation date.

Summary

This simplified illustrative example indicates how the market approach valuation variables can automatically adjust to reflect an intellectual property value decrease in a recessionary economy. This CTC patent valuation analysis concludes a higher value for the subject intellectual property in an expansionary economy and a lower value for the subject intellectual property in a recessionary economy.

Summary and Conclusion

This discussion summarized the procedures related to the identification and valuation of intellectual property in a depressed economy. First, this discussion summarized the procedures a valuation analyst may use (and the factors a valuation analyst may consider) to identify the existence of intellectual property. Second, this discussion summarized the generally accepted valuation approaches, methods, and procedures that a valuation analyst may use to estimate the value of an intellectual property in a depressed economic environment.

There are numerous economic and legal attributes that a valuation analyst should consider in the identification of intellectual property. For the valuation of intellectual property, there are three generally accepted approaches–the cost approach, the market approach, and the income approach. Each of these valuation approaches has the same objective: to arrive at a reasonable value indication for the intellectual property. Within each of the three valuation approaches, there are several generally accepted methods and procedures that may be appropriate for the intellectual property valuation.

The selection of the appropriate valuation methods and procedures is based on (1) the characteristics of the subject intellectual property, (2) the quantity and quality of available data, (3) the purpose and objective of the analysis and (4) the experience and judgment of the valuation analyst. The intellectual property final value conclusion is typically based on a synthesis of the value indications derived from each applicable valuation approach and method.

These generally accepted valuation approaches and methods are relevant whether (1) the economic environment is robust or (2) the economic environment is depressed. This is because the selected valuation variables should adjust to the economic conditions in which the intellectual property owner/operator functions. When the appropriate economy-dependent valuation variables are used in the appropriate valuation methods, these methods will provide reliable value indications, given the current state of the economy.

Finally, this discussion presented simplified illustrative examples of the application of the cost approach, the income approach, and the market approach to value an intellectual property. Each simplified example illustrated (1) valuation variables related to a robust economy and (2) valuation variables related to a depressed economy. The examples indicate that each valuation approach can provide a credible intellectual property value indication for both (1) expansionary economic environment assumptions and (2) recessionary economic environment assumptions.

EXHIBIT 1
HEALTHY MORNING, INC
MRB TRADE SECRET
COST APPROACH
REPRODUCTION COST NEW LESS DEPRECIATION METHOD
ASSUMING AN EXPANSIONARY ECONOMY
AS OF DECEMBER 31, 2009

Intellectual Property Development Procedures: Type of Laboratory Research & Testing	Total Person-Hours to Reproduce the Development Procedures	Average Base Cost per Person-Hour ($)	Employee Benefits and Overhead Cost Allocation Factor	Full Absorption Cost per Person-Hour ($)	Reproduction Cost New ($)
Compression Process Analysis	15,000	75	1.85	139	2,085,000
Food Ingredient Mixtures	8,000	75	1.85	139	1,112,000
Manufacturing Process Testing	10,000	85	1.85	157	1,570,000
Manufacturing Process Drawings and Documentation	8,500	90	1.85	167	1,420,000
			Total Direct and Indirect Costs [a]		6,187,000
			Plus: Developer's Profit at 15% [b]		928,050
			Plus: Entrepreneurial Incentive [c]		3,690,000
			Indicated Reproduction Cost New (rounded) [d]		10,805,000
			Less: Functional Obsolescence (at 15% of RCN) [e]		1,621,000
			Equals: Reproduction Cost New Less Depreciation		9,184,000
			Indicated Fair Market Value (rounded)		9,200,000

Footnotes:

[a] The full absorption cost allocation factor includes a component for development period interest.

[b] The developer's profit represents a fair profit margin that an independent food engineering company would charge to a client to develop a manufacturing process like the MRB trade secret.

[c] The entrepreneurial incentive indicates the incremental amount of net cash flow than the owner/operator of the MRB trade secret will earn during the 24 month process development period--compared to the amount of net cash flow the same owner/operator would earn from using an alternative trade secret. See exhibits 2 and 3 for years 1 and 2.

[d] This reproduction cost new (RCN) estimate includes all related direct costs, indirect costs, developer's profits, and entrepreneurial incentive.

[e] The valuation analyst concluded that a 15 percent functional obsolescence allowance was appropriate. Management expects to develop and implement an improved compression process in a few years. The curren trade secret has been in use for approximately one year. Therefore, the total expected lifeof this trade secret is approximately 6 years (i.e., one year age plus five years RUL) Therefore, this intellectual property is approximately 15% (i.e., on year divided by 6 years) from an age/life perspective. Since this intellectual property is earning a fair return on investment, the valuation analyst concluded that no allowance for economic obsolescnece is needed.

EXHIBIT 2
HEALTHY MORNING, INC
MRB TRADE SECRET
INCOME APPROACH
DIFFERENTIAL INCOME METHOD
ASSUMING AN EXPANSIONARY ECONOMY
SCENARIO I: WITH THE SUBJECT TRADE SECRET IN OPERATION

MRB Product Line Projection Variables ($ in 000s):	Year 1	Year 2	Year 3	Year 4	Year 5
Net Sales	$ 146,912	$ 161,603	$ 177,764	$ 195,540	$ 215,094
Gross margin	38,197	42,017	46,219	50,840	55,924
Operating expenses	(16,160)	(17,776)	(19,554)	(21,509)	(23,660)
Earnings before interest and taxes	22,037	24,240	26,665	29,331	32,264
Income tax expense	(7,933)	(8,727)	(9,599)	(10,559)	(11,615)
Operating income	14,104	15,514	17,065	18,772	20,649
Depreciation expense	1,469	1,616	1,778	1,955	2,151
Capital expenditures	(1,469)	(1,616)	(1,778)	(1,955)	(2,151)
Capital charge on contributory assets	(2,200)	(2,200)	(2,200)	(2,200)	(2,200)
Incremental net working capital investment	(696)	(735)	(808)	(889)	(978)
Net cash flow	11,208	12,579	14,057	15,683	17,471
Present value discount factor [a]	0.9325	0.8109	0.7051	0.6131	0.5332
Discounted net cash flow	10,451	10,200	9,912	9,616	9,315
Sum of product line discounted net cash flow (rounded)	49,500				

Footnote:
[a] Assumes a mid-year discounting convention

EXHIBIT 3
HEALTHY MORNING, INC
MRB TRADE SECRET
INCOME APPROACH
DIFFERENTIAL INCOME METHOD
ASSUMING AN EXPANSINARY ECONOMY
SCENARIO II: WITHOUT THE SUBJECT TRADE SECRET IN OPERATION

MRB Product Line Projection Variables ($ in 000s):	Year 1	Year 2	Year 3	Year 4	Year 5
Net Sales	$ 146,912	$ 161,603	$ 177,764	$ 195,540	$ 215,094
Expected sales decrement without MRB process	(14,691)	(16,160)	(17,776)	(19,554)	(21,509)
Net Sales without proprietary process in operation	$ 132,221	$ 145,443	$ 159,987	$ 175,986	$ 193,584
Gross margin	34,377	37,815	41,597	45,756	50,332
Operating expenses	(15,205)	(16,726)	(18,399)	(20,238)	(22,262)
Earnings before interest and taxes	19,172	21,089	23,198	25,518	28,070
Income tax expense	(6,902)	(7,592)	(8,351)	(9,186)	(10,105)
Operating income	12,270	13,497	14,847	16,331	17,965
Depreciation expense	1,322	1,454	1,600	1,760	1,936
Capital expenditures	(1,322)	(1,454)	(1,600)	(1,760)	(1,936)
Capital charge on contributory assets	(2,200)	(2,200)	(2,200)	(2,200)	(2,200)
Incremental net working capital investment	(876)	(926)	(1,018)	(1,120)	(1,232)
Net cash flow	9,194	10,372	11,629	13,012	14,533
Present value discount factor [a]	0.9325	0.8109	0.7051	0.6131	0.5332
Discounted net cash flow	8,573	8,410	8,199	7,978	7,748
Sum of product line discounted net cash flow (rounded)	40,900				

Footnote:
[a] Assumes a mid-year discounting convention

EXHIBIT 4
HEALTHY MORNING, INC
MRB TRADE SECRET
INCOME APPROACH
DIFFERENTIAL INCOME METHOD
ASSUMING AN EXPANSIONARY ECONOMY
AS OF DECEMBER 31, 2009

Sum of the Product Line Discounted Net Cash Flow:	Exhibit Reference		$ in (000s)
Scenario I: With Trade Secret	2	$	49,500
Scenario II: Without Trade Secret	3		40,900
Indicated Fair Market Value of the Trade Secret (rounded)		$	8,600

EXHIBIT 5
HEALTHY MORNING, INC
MRB TRADE SECRET
VALUATION SYNTHESIS AND CONCLUSION
ASSUMING AN EXPANSIONARY ECONOMY ENVIRONMENT
AS OF DECEMBER 31, 2009

Valuation Approach:	Valuation Method:	Value Indication ($ in 000s)	Value Indication Emphasis	Value Conclusion ($ in 000s)
Cost	Reproduction Cost New Less Depreciation Method	9,200	50%	4,600
Income	Differential Income Method	8,600	50%	4,300
	Fair Market Value of the Trade Secret (rounded)			8,900

EXHIBIT 6
HEALTHY MORNING, INC
MRB TRADE SECRET
COST APPROACH
REPRODUCTION COST NEW LESS DEPRECIATION METHOD
ASSUMING A RECESSIONARY ECONOMY
AS OF DECEMBER 31, 2009

Intellectual Property Development Procedures: Type of Laboratory Research & Testing	Total Person-Hours to Reproduce the Development Procedures	Average Base Cost per Person-Hour ($)	Employee Benefits and Overhead Cost Allocation Factor	Full Absorption Cost per Person-Hour ($)	Reproduction Cost New ($)
Compression Process Analysis	15,000	70	1.70	119	1,785,000
Food Ingredient Mixtures	8,000	70	1.70	119	952,000
Manufacturing Process Testing	10,000	80	1.70	136	1,360,000
Manufacturing Process Drawings and Documentation	8,500	85	1.70	145	1,233,000
			Total Direct and Indirect Costs [a]		5,330,000
			Plus: Developer's Profit at 10% [b]		533,000
			Plus: Entrepreneurial Incentive [c]		3,693,000
			Indicated Reproduction Cost New (rounded) [d]		9,556,000
			Less: Functional Obsolescence (at 15% of RCN) [e]		1,433,000
			Equals: Reproduction Cost New Less Depreciation		8,123,000
			Indicated Fair Market Value (rounded)		8,100,000

Footnotes:

[a] The full absorption cost allocation factor includes a component for development period interest.

[b] The developer's profit represents a fair profit margin that an independent food engineering company would charge to a client to develop a manufacturing process like the MRB trade secret.

[c] The entrepreneurial incentive indicates the incremental amount of net cash flow than the owner/operator of the MRB trade secret will earn during the 24 month process development period--compared to the amount of net cash flow the same owner/operator would earn from using an alternative trade secret. See exhibits 7 and 8 for years 1 and 2.

[d] This reproduction cost new (RCN) estimate includes all related direct costs, indirect costs, developer's profits, and entrepreneurial incentive.

[e] The valuation analyst concluded that a 15 percent functional obsolescence allowance was appropriate. Management expects to develop and implement an improved compression process in a few years. The curren trade secret has been in use for approximately one year. Therefore, the total expected lifeof this trade secret is approximately 6 years (i.e., one year age plus five years RUL) Therefore, this intellectual property is approximately 15% (i.e., on year divided by 6 years) from an age/life perspective. Since this intellectual property is earning a fair return on investment, the valuation analyst concluded that no allowance for economic obsolescnece is needed.

EXHIBIT 7
HEALTHY MORNING, INC
MRB TRADE SECRET
INCOME APPROACH
DIFFERENTIAL INCOME METHOD
ASSUMING A RECESSIONARY ECONOMY
SCENARIO I: WITH THE TRADE SECRET IN OPERATION

MRB Product Line Projection Variables ($ in 000s):	Year 1	Year 2	Year 3	Year 4	Year 5
Net Sales	$ 146,912	$ 161,603	$ 177,764	$ 195,540	$ 215,094
Gross margin	38,197	42,017	46,219	50,840	55,924
Operating expenses	(17,629)	(19,392)	(21,332)	(23,465)	(25,811)
Earnings before interest and taxes	20,568	22,625	24,887	27,375	30,113
Income tax expense	(7,405)	(8,145)	(8,959)	(9,855)	(10,841)
Operating income	13,164	14,480	15,927	17,520	19,273
Depreciation expense	1,469	1,616	1,778	1,955	2,151
Capital expenditures	(1,469)	(1,616)	(1,778)	(1,955)	(2,151)
Capital charge on contributory assets	(2,200)	(2,200)	(2,200)	(2,200)	(2,200)
Incremental net working capital investment	(1,469)	(1,469)	(1,616)	(1,778)	(1,955)
Net cash flow	9,495	10,811	12,111	13,542	15,118
Present value discount factor [a]	0.9325	0.8109	0.7051	0.6131	0.5332
Discounted net cash flow	8,854	8,766	8,540	8,303	8,060
Sum of product line discounted net cash flow (rounded)	42,500				

Footnote:
[a] Assumes a mid-year discounting convention

EXHIBIT 8
HEALTHY MORNING, INC
MRB TRADE SECRET
INCOME APPROACH
DIFFERENTIAL INCOME METHOD
ASSUMING A RECESSIONARY ECONOMY
SCENARIO II: WITHOUT THE TRADE SECRET IN OPERATION

MRB Product Line Projection Variables ($ in 000s):	Year 1	Year 2	Year 3	Year 4	Year 5
Net Sales	$ 146,912	$ 161,603	$ 177,764	$ 195,540	$ 215,094
Expected sales decrement without MRB process	(14,691)	(16,160)	(17,776)	(19,554)	(21,509)
Net Sales without proprietary process in operation	$ 132,221	$ 145,443	$ 159,987	$ 175,986	$ 193,584
Gross margin	34,377	37,815	41,597	45,756	50,332
Operating expenses	(17,189)	(18,908)	(20,798)	(22,878)	(25,166)
Earnings before interest and taxes	17,188	18,907	20,799	22,878	25,166
Income tax expense	(6,188)	(6,807)	(7,488)	(8,236)	(8,808)
Operating income	11,001	12,101	13,311	14,642	16,358
Depreciation expense	1,322	1,454	1,600	1,760	1,936
Capital expenditures	(1,322)	(1,454)	(1,600)	(1,760)	(1,936)
Capital charge on contributory assets	(2,200)	(2,200)	(2,200)	(2,200)	(2,200)
Incremental net working capital investment	(1,322)	(1,322)	(1,454)	(1,600)	(1,710)
Net cash flow	7,479	8,579	9,657	10,842	12,448
Present value discount factor [a]	0.9325	0.8109	0.7051	0.6131	0.5332
Discounted net cash flow	6,974	6,956	6,809	6,648	6,637
Sum of product line discounted net cash flow (rounded)	34,000				

Footnote:
[a] Assumes a mid-year discounting convention

EXHIBIT 9
HEALTHY MORNING, INC
MRB TRADE SECRET
INCOME APPROACH
DIFFERENTIAL INCOME METHOD
ASSUMING A RECESSIONARY ECONOMY
AS OF DECEMBER 31, 2009

Sum of the Product Line Discounted Net Cash Flow:	Exhibit Reference	$ in (000s)
Scenario I: With Trade Secret	7	$ 42,500
Scenario II: Without Trade Secret	8	34,000
Indicated Fair Market Value of the Trade Secret (rounded)		$ 8,500

EXHIBIT 10
HEALTHY MORNING, INC
MRB TRADE SECRET
VALUATION SYNTHESIS AND CONCLUSION
ASSUMING A RECESSIONARY ECONOMY ENVIRONMENT
AS OF DECEMBER 31, 2009

Valuation Approach:	Valuation Method:	Value Indication ($ in 000s)	Value Indication Emphasis	Value Conclusion ($ in 000s)
Cost	Reproduction Cost New Less Depreciation Method	8,100	50%	4,050
Income	Differential Income Method	8,500	50%	4,250
	Fair Market Value of the Trade Secret (rounded)			8,300

EXHIBIT 11
CHARITABLE TAXPAYER CORPORATION
VIGOR PHARMACEUTICAL COMPOUND PATENT VALUATION
SELECTED HYPOTHETICAL GUIDELINE INTELLECTUAL PROPERTY LICENSE AGREEMENTS
AS OF JANUARY 1, 2009

Guideline Drug Patent License	Guideline Drug Patent Licensee	Guideline Drug Patent Licensor	Guideline License Start Date	Guideline License Term Years	Guideline License Royalty Rate %	Other Consideration Paid to the Licensor	Type of Licensed Drug Product
1	Pfizer, Inc.	Columbia U.	2008	15	6	$4m [a]	ED
2	Glaxo Smith Kline	Autogen	2005	10	5	$10m [b]	cardiovascular
3	Johnson & Johnson	Nobel N.V.	2006	12	10	[c]	anti-obesity
4	Merck & Co.	All Saints Hospital	2006	10	4.5	[d]	vascular
5	Pharmacia & Upjohn	MIT	2007	15	5.5	[e]	pulmonary hypertension
6	Wyeth-Ayerst	MD, LP	2007	20	8-10 [f]	[f]	botanical ED

Footnotes:
[a] represents an upfront (i.e., development financing) license payment.
[b] represents a milestone payment after the 5th year of the license.
[c] the license agreement also settles a pending $50 million litigation between the various license parties.
[d] the physician owners/employees also receive research grants from Merck.
[e] there are also numerous other relationships between the licensor/licensee parties.
[f] the royalty rate range is based on the level of the drug product annual sales volume.

EXHIBIT 12
CHARITABLE TAXPAYER CORPORATION
VIGOR PHARMACEUTICAL COMOUND PATENT VALUATION
GUIDELINE ROYALTY RATE ADJUSTMENT GRID AND SELECTED SUBJECT-SPECIFIC ROYALTY RATE
AS OF JANUARY 1, 2009

Guideline Drug Patent License	Guideline Patent Royalty Rate %	Guideline Patent Comparable to the Subject Patent [a]	Size of the Guideline Product Market [b]	Growth Rate of Guideline Product Market [b]	Guideline Product Market Share Relative to the Subject Product [b]	Affect of Other Consideration Paid to the Licensor	Adjusted Guideline Patent Royalty Rate
1	6	3	0	0	--	+.5% [c]	6%
2	5	2	++	++	0	+1% [c]	7%
3	10	2	+	0	0	-2% [c]	8%
4	4.5	3	+	0	-	- [c]	4%
5	5.5	2	+	+	0	- [c]	6%
6	8-10	3	++	-	-	-2% [d]	7%
				License Royalty Rate Mean			6.3%
				License Royalty Rate Trimmed Mean			6.5%
				License Royalty Rate Median			6.5%
				License Royalty Rate Mode			6.5%
				Selected Subject Patent Royalty Rate Conclusion			6.5%

Footnotes:

[a] based on a scale of 0 to 3; where 0 means that the guideline patent is less comparable to the subject patent; and 3 means that the guidelien patent is more comparable to the subject patent.

[b] based on a scale of --, -, 0, +, ++; where -- is the smallest in size relative to the subject patented product; and ++ is the largest in size relative to the subject patented product.

[c] valuation analyst adjustment, based on an assessment o fother factors (1) in the guideline intellectual property license agreement or (2) between the guideline intellectual property licensor and the licenseee.

[d] valuation analyst adjustment, due to the different nature of a botanical drug product versus a pharmaceutical drug product.

EXHIBIT 13
CHARITABLE TAXPAYER CORPORATION
VIGOR PHARMACEUTICAL COMPOUND PATENT VALUATION
RELIEF FROM ROYALTY METHOD VALUATION
ASSUMING AN EXPANSIONARY ECONOMY
AS OF JANUARY 1, 2009
(in $ millions)

	Projection Period								
Patent Valuation Analysis:	Year 1	Year 2	Year 3	Year 4	Year 5	Year 6	Year 7	Year 8	Year 9
Patented product revenue expected growth rate	10%	10%	10%	0%	0%	0%	-12%	12%	12%
Patented product revenue amount (year 0 revenue = 400)	44	484	532	532	532	532	469	412	363
Selected patent license royalty rate	6.5%	6.5%	6.5%	6.5%	6.5%	6.5%	6.5%	6.5%	6.5%
Projected "relief from royalty" license expense (rounded)	29	31	35	35	35	35	30	27	24
Projected patent maintenance expense (year 0 expense = 10)	10	11	11	11	12	12	12	13	13
Projected net "relief from royalty" license expense (rounded)	19	20	24	24	23	23	18	14	11
Present value discount factor (at 20%, mid-year convention)	0.91	0.76	0.63	0.53	0.44	0.37	0.3	0.25	0.21
Present value of "relief from royalty" net license expense	17	15	15	13	10	9	5	4	2
Total present value of "relief from royalty" net license expense	90								
Indicated fair market value of the Vigor pharmaceutical compound patent (rounded)	90								

EXHIBIT 14
CHARITABLE TAXPAYER CORPORATION
VIGOR PHARMACEUTICAL COMPOUND PATENT VALUATION
RELIEF FROM ROYALTY METHOD VALUATION
ASSUMING AN RECESSIONARY ECONOMY
AS OF JANUARY 1, 2009
(in $ millions)

	Projection Period								
Patent Valuation Analysis:	Year 1	Year 2	Year 3	Year 4	Year 5	Year 6	Year 7	Year 8	Year 9
Patented product revenue expected growth rate	0%	0%	0%	-2%	-2%	-2%	-4%	-4%	-4%
Patented product revenue amount (year 0 revenue = 400)	400	400	400	392	384	376	361	347	333
Selected patent license royalty rate	6.5%	6.5%	6.5%	6.5%	6.5%	6.5%	6.5%	6.5%	6.5%
Projected "relief from royalty" license expense (rounded)	26	26	26	25	25	24	24	23	22
Projected patent maintenance expense (year 0 expense = 12)	12	13	13	14	14	14	15	15	16
Projected net "relief from royalty" license expense (rounded)	14	13	13	11	11	10	9	8	6
Present value discount factor (at 20%, mid-year convention)	0.91	0.76	0.63	0.53	0.44	0.37	0.3	0.25	0.21
Present value of "relief from royalty" net license expense	13	10	8	6	5	4	3	2	1
Total present value of "relief from royalty" net license expense	52								
Indicated fair market value of the Vigor pharmaceutical compound patent (rounded)	50								

Finding the Invisible Trail: The Valuation of Technology

James L. Horvath & Paul Gill

Introduction

The success of any business in the world today is tied to technology. Defined as "the practical application of knowledge," technology contributes to the well-being and, ultimately, the overall value of the company that owns it. But as technology develops at an ever-increasing pace, it can be challenging to value a technology asset, whether for strategic and/or operational reasons, for the purpose of financial reporting, or from the point of view of tax planning, and in determining its contribution to the company. The technology valuator has to take into consideration a number of factors in order to appropriately determine the technology's value, including examining what drives the technology's value, then applying accepted methods of analysis to assess and quantify that value. In the process, the valuator must determine whether the technology will succeed or fail and, if it succeeds, how long it will last before becoming obsolete.

Over the years, we have valued many different technologies and reviewed many more technology-related valuation reports prepared by others. In some cases, we concluded that the technology could not deliver its intended benefits or was merely a modification of an existing technology, designed to cash in on an overzealous marketplace. In others, we concluded that the technology was a successful modification of a previous version. Only in a very few instances did we confirm that the technology was a truly innovative, game-changing advance.

We have also found that the development of new technology generally costs more money and requires more time and resources than its inventors anticipate. In addition, most inventors do not possess all of the technological, financial, management, and marketing expertise required to commercialize (*i.e.*, bring to market) a new technology. Even the most innovative and desirable technology, developed by competent and talented inventors, may not make it in the marketplace without a number of factors working together in its favor, such as the following:

- adequate financial and human resources to complete a prototype and develop a market;
- sound strategic and operational planning;
- lack of competitors who can readily imitate or duplicate the technology;
- adequate feasibility evaluations;
- a convincing business plan;
- adequate patent protection;
- sufficient production facilities;
- the ability to overcome unexpected obstacles in a timely fashion;
- appropriate industrial and economic conditions to successfully commercialize the technology and achieve market acceptance; and
- sufficient market demand for the technology.

While all of these factors do not necessarily have to be present at the same time to create an innovative and desirable technology that has value, in the rare case when they all work together, the valuator will recognize a truly innovative technological advance.

In the following sections, we look at some of the considerations and methods employed in valuing technology and technology-based companies.

Practice Tip

Superior technology alone is rarely enough upon which to build competitive advantage.

David J. Teece[1]

Technology Valuation Contexts

The valuation of technology can be examined within the following contexts:

- strategic and operational;
- financial reporting; and

1 D.J. Teece, *Managing Intellectual Capital: Organizational, Strategic, and Policy Dimensions* (Oxford: Oxford University Press, 2000), p. 8.

- tax planning.

Strategic and Operational

Mergers and acquisitions and divestitures – many companies derive a significant component of their value from technology. A valuator must understand the value of a company's technology and any of its other significant tangible and/or intangible assets to make an informed determination of the company's most likely selling price – its value to the marketplace. In addition, the value of the underlying technology will often be a function of the overall value of the related company. As a result, the valuator must also understand, among other factors, the potential of the technology asset relative to its current stage of development.

Licensing – a fair licensing royalty rate depends on a technology's market value. This value is often determined before the technology developer engages in licensing negotiations.

Portfolio mining – companies make significant investments in intangibles such as technology and other related assets. To protect these most valuable assets – often through the legal measure of patents – and to fully exploit all potential benefits, companies must continuously monitor their portfolio of technology assets and track any changes in value.

Revenue enhancement and/or cost reduction – many businesses depend on technology assets for their success. A valuator must understand how these crucial intangible assets drive a business's value. Based on this understanding, a company can enhance net cash flows by making additional investments in similar assets, by improving the utility of existing assets, by increasing its service potential, and/or by improving its value-added capabilities. This information can also help determine which business model is most appropriate (*e.g.*, the decision to sell software licences versus the provision of software as a service) in order to monetize the technology and to maximize the net cash flows and the value and use of the technology itself.

Resource allocation – a company can allocate its resources most effectively if it identifies its technology assets and estimates their contributions to the company's future cash flow. It can then direct its capital resources toward those investments offering the greatest returns, which also helps maximize the potential growth and success of the technology.

Financial Reporting

Many businesses acquire significant intangible assets in the process of merging with or acquiring other businesses. As a result, financial reporting requirements have increasingly focused on determining the value of these acquired intangible assets and the post-acquisition allocation of the purchase price among them.

According to Canadian Institute of Chartered Accountants (CICA) Handbook Section 1581,[2] an intangible asset should be recognized apart from goodwill at its estimated or appraised value under the following conditions:

i) The asset results from contractual or other legal rights (regardless of whether those rights are transferable or separable from the acquired enterprise or from other rights and obligations) or
ii) The asset is capable of being separated or divided from the acquired enterprise and sold, transferred, licensed, rented, or exchanged (regardless of whether there is an intent to do so).

In the United States, the Financial Accounting Standards Board (FASB) provides guidance for recognizing intangible assets in financial statements. In 2001, the adoption of Statement of Financial Accounting Standards (SFAS) 141 eliminated the pooling of interests as a method of recognizing acquired assets in business combinations, leaving the purchase method as the acceptable alternative for companies governed by FASB. As part of a joint project with the International Accounting Standards Board (IASB) to converge U.S. and international accounting standards, SFAS 141 was replaced by SFAS 141R for fiscal years beginning after December 15, 2008. The criteria set out in SFAS 141R for recognition of intangible assets apart from goodwill, are similar to the Canadian criteria described above. SFAS 141R establishes the following five broad categories for recognizing intangible assets (these same categories are also specified in CICA Handbook Section 1581):

i) Customer-related intangible assets (*e.g.*, customer lists; order or production backlog; customer contracts and related customer relationships; and non-contractual customer relationships);
ii) Artistic-related intangible assets (*e.g.*, plays, operas, and ballets; books, magazines, newspapers, and other literary works; musical works such as compositions, song lyrics, and advertising jingles; pictures and photographs; and video and audiovisual material, including motion pictures, music videos, and TV programs);
iii) Contract-based intangible assets (*e.g.*, licensing, royalty, and standstill agreements; advertising, construction, management, service, or supply contracts; lease agreements; construction permits; franchise agreements; operating and broadcast rights; serv-

2 CICA Handbook Section 1581 will be superseded by CICA Handbook Section 1582 for business combinations that have an acquisition date on or after the beginning of the first annual reporting period beginning on or after January 1, 2011.

icing contracts such as mortgage-servicing contracts; employment contracts; and use rights, such as drilling, water, air, mineral, timber cutting, and route authorities);

iv) Technology-based intangible assets (*e.g.*, patented technology; computer software and mask works (such as a two- or three-dimensional layout of an integrated circuit); unpatented technology; databases, including title plants; and trade secrets such as formulas, processes, and recipes); and

v) Marketing-based intangible assets (*e.g.*, trademarks and trade names; service marks and collective marks, certification marks; trade dress [unique colour, shape, or package design]; newspaper mastheads; Internet domain names; and non-competition agreements).

In January 2009, the International Valuation Standards Council (IVSC) issued separate exposure drafts for each of the following topics: (i) the valuation of intangible assets and (ii) the valuation of intangible assets under International Financial Reporting Standards (IFRS). The criteria for the recognition of intangible assets apart from goodwill in both of these exposure drafts are similar to the Canadian and U.S. criteria described above, and the five broad categories established for recognizing intangible assets are similar to the categories outlined in CICA Handbook Section 1581, CICA Handbook Section 1582, SFAS 141, and SFAS 141R. The IVSC exposure drafts also indicate that the valuation assumptions, regardless of which valuation approach is adopted, should reflect assumptions that would be made by market participants, which is also relatively consistent with current Canadian and U.S. financial reporting standards.

Accordingly, as a result of merger and acquisition activities, technology-based intangible assets, and intangible assets in general, are now significant components of the corporate balance sheet. As a consequence, an increased degree of valuation analysis is required to establish post-acquisition values, which can also affect the amount of annual amortization (if any) of these intangible assets, and to help quantify impairment (if any) in subsequent reporting periods.

As noted by Robert F. Reilly in Chapter 4, in 2008, intangible asset values accounted for more than 80 per cent of the total market value of the S&P 500 index companies. In 1975, intangible asset values as a percentage of the total market value of the S&P 500 was closer to 17 per cent. Since technology is one of the categories of identifiable intangible assets, Table 1 illustrates the percentage of value of technology-related and other intangible assets in selected recent transactions.

Table 1

Allocation of Identifiable Intangible Value in Recent Transactions US D Millions

Allocation of Identifiable Intangible Value In Recent Transactions
USD Millions

Buyer	Target	Year of Transaction	Technology-Related Intangibles	Customer-Related Intangibles	Licenses, Trade Name, Brands, Trademarks, and Other	Total Identifiable Intangible Value	Perecntage of Identifiable Intangible Value Related to Technology
Cisco Systems Inc.	Navin Networks Inc.	2008	95	6	7	108	88.0%
Dell Inc.	EqualLogic, Inc.	2008	499	46	16	561	88.9%
Electronic Arts Inc.	VG Holding Corp.	2008	189	-	63	252	75.0%
eBay Inc.	Bill Me Later, Inc.	2008	38	138	24	200	19.0%
Hewlett-Packard Company	Electronic Data Systems Corp.	2008	1,379	3,199	-	4,578	30.1%
Google Inc.	Click Holding Corp.	2008	143	630	28	801	17.9%
IBM Corporation	Cognos, Inc.	2008	534	512	78	1,124	47.5%
Sun Microsystems Inc.	MySQL, Inc.	2008	110	71	32	213	51.6%
Oracle Corp.	BEA Systems, Inc.	2008	2,768	530	62	3,360	82.4%
Yahoo! Inc.	Maven Networks Inc.	2008	57	7	1	65	87.3%
Cisco Systems, Inc.	Webex Communications, Inc.	2007	310	152	79	541	57.3%
Dell Inc.	ASAP Software Express, Inc.	2007	18	144	9	171	10.5%
Oracle Corp.	Hyperion Solutions Corp.	2007	788	682	46	1,516	52.0%
Research in Motion Limited	Various Acquisitions	2007	1,995	-	-	1,995	100.0%
RF Micro Devices Inc.	Sirenza Microdevices Inc.	2007	141	85	-	226	62.5%

Note: Technology-related intangible assets included developed technology, patents, technology licenses, and in-process research and development.

In addition to the recognition of intangible assets acquired from merger and acquisition activities, certain internally developed intangible assets can be recognized under CICA Handbook Section 3064,[3] which states that developed intangible assets should only be recognized when all of the following criteria can be demonstrated by the company (assuming that the intangible asset has met the criteria to be classified as being in the "development phase" as stipulated in the related guidance):[4]

---

3 CICA Handbook Section 3064 applies to annual and interim financial statements relating to fiscal years beginning on or after October 1, 2008.

4 CICA Handbook Section 3064 stipulates that the creation of internally generated intangibles may be split into the following two separate phases: (i) the research phase refers to activities of an investigating nature for the purpose of gaining new knowledge. Costs incurred with this intention cannot be separated or controlled by the entity and therefore do not meet the criteria for capitalization and should be expensed; (ii) the development phase refers to the application of information (*i.e.*, research) to create new materials, products, processes, *etc.*, prior to commercial production and/or use. The criteria for classification as a development activity are consistent with the superseded CICA Handbook Section 3450, Research and Development. Costs classified as development costs may be capitalized. "Other" activities are often carried out by the entity with the intention that they will provide future economic benefits to the entity. These activities include start-up costs, training, advertising, promotional, and relocating and/or reorganizing part or all of the entity. These types of costs do not meet the recognition criteria and should be expensed. As a result, CICA Handbook Section 3064 prohibits the common deferral of start-up and/or pre-operating expenditures under Canadian generally accepted accounting principles (GAAP), bringing it more in line with IFRS and U.S. GAAP, although some differences still exist.

i) The technical feasibility of completing the intangible asset so that it will be available for use or sale;
ii) The intention to complete the intangible asset and use or sell it;
iii) The ability to use or sell the intangible asset;
iv) How the intangible asset will generate probable future economic benefits. Among other things, the entity can demonstrate the existence of a market for the output of the intangible asset or the intangible asset itself or, if it is to be used internally, the usefulness of the intangible asset;
v) The availability of adequate technical, financial, and other resources to complete the development and use or sell the intangible asset; and
vi) The ability to measure reliably the expenditures attributable to the intangible asset during its development.

For companies whose financial disclosure is reported in accordance with IFRS, both acquired and internally generated intangible assets can be recognized if the recognition criteria are met. We note that the aforementioned CICA standards are relatively similar to the standards set out by IFRS.[5]

Tax Planning

Many tax-related scenarios require the valuation of technology assets to determine their fair market value. Such scenarios include the following, among others:

- transfer pricing activities and/or transactions involving non-arm's-length parties;
- migration of assets to tax-beneficial jurisdictions;
- charitable donations involving technology; and
- estate planning.

5 The main difference observed (as it relates to identifiable intangible assets) between IFRS standards (IAS 38) and CICA standards is that under IFRS, an entity may choose either the cost model or the revaluation model as its accounting policy. If the revaluation model is used, an identifiable intangible asset, after its initial recognition, shall be carried at a revalued amount, being the fair value at the date of revaluation less any subsequent accumulated amortization and any subsequent accumulated impairment losses. However, the revalued amount cannot be greater than its original recorded fair value. Revaluations shall be made with such regularity that at the balance sheet date, the carrying amount of the asset does not differ materially from its fair value. If an identifiable intangible asset's carrying amount is increased (*i.e.*, up to, but not greater than, its original recorded fair value) as a result of a revaluation, the increase shall be credited directly to equity under the heading of revaluation surplus. CICA standards, on the other hand, do not allow for the recognition of any subsequent increases in value.

Information

Key Sources of Information

The valuation of technology requires obtaining, reviewing, and/or assessing relevant information from various sources, including the following:

- *Historical and prospective financial information* – historical and interim financial statements, budgets, projections, forecasts, business plans, and previous valuation reports may be useful;
- *Motivations* – the valuator's understanding of the strategic and operational, financial, and tax-related motivations of the valuation stakeholders is critical (*e.g.*, the acquirer, seller, and/or management's motivations with respect to the valuation). This understanding can also help identify potential synergies and whether such synergies are available to others in the marketplace (*e.g.*, market participants) or if they are entity-specific (*e.g.*, buyer-specific) in nature;
- *Discussions with management* – these discussions should (where possible) involve key financial, operational, and strategic management personnel, including the chief executive officer, chief financial officer, chief operating officer, and chief technology officer, as well as key research and development and sales and marketing personnel, to help obtain a clear understanding of the technology, the industry, the markets, competitive factors, the product life cycle, relationships with customers and suppliers, and the short-, medium-, and long-term strategy and/or vision with respect to the technology;
- *Research and development budgets* – these budgets often provide details with respect to the costs to complete and/or commercialize the technology and help provide a sense of the research and development life cycle associated with the technology and the release of new versions;
- *Planning documents and technology research and development road maps* – these can often provide detailed descriptions of the company, plans for the technologies and the sub-technologies, key development milestones, expected release dates, and the budgeted use and/or allocation of resources;
- *Presentations made to the board of directors or senior management* – presentations outlining key benefits, risk factors, and/or functionalities of the technology can provide insight into the business model, growth expectations, key success factors, product development, synergies, expected dates for the completion of specific milestones, *etc.*;

- *Prospectus documents (relevant for initial public offering [IPO] transactions) and other regulatory filings* – descriptions of the business and/or the industry will often supply useful information with respect to the key drivers of the business, which may provide insight into the technology;
- *Purchase and sale agreement* – where a transaction has occurred, particularly for those transactions structured as an asset purchase, the purchase and sale agreement will often include a complete listing of the technology assets acquired, among others;
- *Due diligence reports* – financial, technological, and legal due diligence reports prepared for the acquirer will typically provide insight into the key technology assets and their characteristics;
- *Acquisition valuation models* – where an acquisition has occurred, the acquisition pricing model (prepared by the purchaser and/or the seller) can often provide valuable insight into the future outlook and expected costs and benefits of the technology, as well as the overall business;
- *Corporate websites, press releases, and/or promotional materials* – publicly available information disclosing and/or discussing the technology can help explain (usually in plain English) the key benefits, functionality, business model, and/or intended purpose of the technology;
- *Newspapers and industry trade magazines* – these media resources may provide articles discussing the technology (or similar technology) and the related key benefits and/or risk factors;
- *Industry and analyst reports and credit rating agency reports* – these reports may also refer to the technology assets of a given company or other players in the same industry; and
- *Past experience of the valuator* – previous experience of the valuator in valuing similar businesses and/or technologies can provide significant insight into identifying key value and risk drivers of the technology.

Prospective Financial Information[6]

The valuation of technology and technology-related companies most often involves the consideration of the prospective financial information (PFI) in

6 Based on information obtained from, among other sources, (i) American Institute of Certified Public Accountants (AICPA) in-process research and development (IPR&D) Practice Aid and (ii) the IVSC January 2009 *Exposure Draft of Revised International Valuation Guidance Note No. 4: Valuation of Intangible Assets* and *Exposure Draft of Proposed New International Valuation Guidance Note No. 16: Valuation of Intangible Assets for IFRS Reporting Purposes.*

the application of either the market approach or the income approach (or in determining whether a cost approach is most appropriate). Accordingly, the valuator must understand the key assumptions in the PFI and how they relate to the technology, which can include the following, among others:

- expected sales of the technology and the projected share of the market, including expected sales volumes and product pricing;
- historical profit margins and any variations thereof in relation to current and future market expectations;
- likelihood of completion of products and/or technologies in development, including estimates of the stage, time, costs, and probabilities associated with each stage of completion;
- product life cycle and technology-development strategies;
- potential for the introduction of new technologies that may lead to reduced selling prices or obsolescence of the technology;
- commercialization, production, marketing, and other costs;
- growth rates after the explicit projection period that are appropriate for the technology's expected life, reflecting the industry and economies involved, and market expectations;
- competitors' expected market responses;
- amount of contributory assets required relative to the other tangible and intangible assets of the company, as well as to the overall business operations;
- taxes on income generated by the technology asset;
- working capital and capital expenditure requirements of the technology asset;
- taxes on income generated by the technology asset;
- market-participant versus buyer-specific synergies; and
- discount rates used to value the projected cash flows.[7]

In addition, the projection period should be compared with the useful life of the technology to ensure consistency (*e.g.*, as the life of the technology may be finite or assumed to be infinite, projected cash flows may be for a finite period or may run into perpetuity).

---

7 There is typically a strong relationship between the basis under which the PFI is prepared and the basis under which an appropriate discount rate is determined. Under the traditional, or implicit, approach, the projected cash flows reflect the current cash flows and are discounted at a rate that is consistent with the risk of the underlying technology. As a result, when developing the PFI, it is important to clearly understand which approach is being used so that risks are not double-counted or missed. Under the expected, or explicit, approach, express assumptions are factored into the projected cash flows to reflect the performance risk of the technology; therefore, these are discounted at a rate that reflects the time value of money only. The determination of such a discount rate should, at the very least, also include the consideration of non-performance risk (*i.e.*, credit risk), uncertainty risk (*i.e.*, default risk and collateral value risk); and liquidity risks.

The PFI obtained from different sources may also need to be benchmarked by the valuator to assess the appropriateness of the PFI for use in the valuation. Benchmarking is the process of performing consistency checks on the PFI assumptions. When performing a market approach valuations (see Section 4, Valuation Approaches, for detailed descriptions of the different approaches), benchmarking includes comparing the assumptions with data derived from the market to assess and improve their accuracy and reliability (*e.g.*, the PFI being used to determine the market value of intangible assets, growth rates, margins, tax rates, working capital, and capital expenditures can be benchmarked to corresponding data from market participants to ensure appropriateness and/or reasonableness).

When the PFI is used in the application of the income approach, the valuator should also ensure all projected annual operating costs and capital expenditure requirements are appropriately matched with the projected annual revenues, including the revenues and costs for each of the technologies (and sub-technologies, where applicable) of the company. The PFI can also be used in the application of the market approach as valuation multiples are frequently applied to prospective financial parameters as well as to historical financial parameters.

Other factors affecting PFI assumptions may include the current and expected economic and political outlook and related government policies. Matters such as currency exchange rates, inflation, and interest rates may also affect technology assets that operate in different jurisdictions. As a result, consideration should be given to how such factors affect the specific market and industry in which the technology asset is being valued.

When cash flows are projected into perpetuity, specific consideration should be given to the growth rates used. These growth rates should not exceed the long-term average growth rates for the technology being valued and the industries and jurisdictions involved unless a higher growth rate can be reasonably justified.

When using the PFI to determine the value of a technology, a sensitivity analysis of the resultant value can also be useful in assessing the impact of possible variations in the underlying assumptions. The elements of the PFI to which the resultant value is most sensitive should be assessed to ensure that the assumptions underlying them are reasonable. The extent of the valuator's work will likely be affected by the type of valuation being performed. Methods for testing the reasonableness of the PFI include, but are not necessarily limited to, the following:

- calculate the internal rate of return (IRR) implied by the PFI in reference to the purchase price paid (if applicable);
- understand significant differences between the implied IRR (if

relevant and/or available) and/or the calculated weighted-average cost of capital (WACC) for the business and/or the industry;
- review the PFI in conjunction with the historical results of the business;
- understand differences between the projected trends in growth and earnings and the related historical trends;
- understand differences between the operating results of industry peers and historical and projected operating results of the company; and
- compare projected growth rates, margins, *etc.*, with the expectations for the industry as a whole as estimated by industry analysts and/or studies.

Because of the complex nature of technology assets, the valuator must also assess the technical strengths and weaknesses of the asset. An expert familiar with the technology can help the valuator assess its market potential, technical merits, quality, manufacturing viability, and other critical factors.

Technology companies often operate in particular niches or sub-sectors of the overall industry and experts in the niche market can help the valuator understand the nuances of the particular niche and the key elements driving the business's value. It is important to know that broad industry expertise, although helpful, is not necessarily sufficient when examining a technology and/or a technology-related company in a specific niche. In addition to industry or technology experts, company management, company employees (engineers), and trade associations and publications can also prove to be useful sources of information to gain further insights.

Use of Market-Participant Assumptions

When estimating the value of technology assets, the valuator generally incorporates assumptions that market participants would use in their determination of value whenever the information is available without undue cost and effort. SFAS 157 indicates that unobservable inputs should be used to the extent that observable inputs are not available, allowing for situations in which there might be little, if any, market activity for the asset or liability at the measurement date.

Unobservable inputs should reflect the reporting entity's own assumptions about the assumptions market participants would use in pricing the asset or liability. If such information is not easily obtainable, the company may use its own assumptions. This concept is best described through an example where market participant assumptions may differ from the assumptions employed by companies in arriving at business enterprise value. CICA Handbook Section 1581 suggests the following:

- The enterprise's managers might intend a different use for the asset than what others would intend or might have uses different from what others would not have.
- The enterprise's managers may prefer to accept risk of a liability and manage it internally rather than transferring that liability to another enterprise.
- The enterprise might hold special preferences, such as tax or zoning variances, not available to others.
- The enterprise might hold information, trade secrets, or processes that allow it to realize (or avoid paying) cash flows that differ from others' expectations.
- The enterprise might be able to realize or pay amounts through the use of internal resources. For example, an enterprise that manufactures materials used in particular processes may acquire those materials at cost rather than at the market price charged to others; an enterprise that satisfies a liability with internal resources may avoid the markup or anticipated profit charged by outside contractors.

In order to apply this concept of market participants, the valuator must understand who the likely market participants are.[8] In general, market participants include all potential buyers (other than financial buyers and investors, who would not intend to take an active role in managing the subject company) whether or not the potential buyers are engaged in discussions with the seller of the business. In considering which potential buyers may be market participants, the valuator would consider only those potential buyers that appear to have the ability to acquire the assets being valued. Ability should be evaluated in the context of financial wherewithal or the ability to obtain it, as well as a plausible post-combination operating strategy for the assets being valued. Market participants would include competitors in the same line of business as the technology and/or technology-related company being valued. Market participants would also obtain information from public sources and would perform other due diligence efforts.

A key issue that must be addressed when determining appropriate market participant assumptions is the concept of synergies. Buyers may be willing to pay more for a technology asset if it will provide a synergistic benefit to their organizations. If the buyer pays the seller any significant consideration for strategic or synergistic benefits in excess of those expected to be realized by market participants, the valuator would identify those excess benefits and remove them from the valuation. In other words, buyer-specific synergies are not included in the valuation of technology assets under a market-

---

8 SFAS 157 defines market participants as being (i) knowledgeable; (ii) able to transact; (iii) willing to transact; and (iv) independent.

participant scenario. In these instances, buyer-specific synergies must be removed from the PFI being used to determine the value of the technology on a market-participant basis.

Figure 1 below illustrates the continuum of value as it relates to synergies and strategic value, among other components.

Figure 1

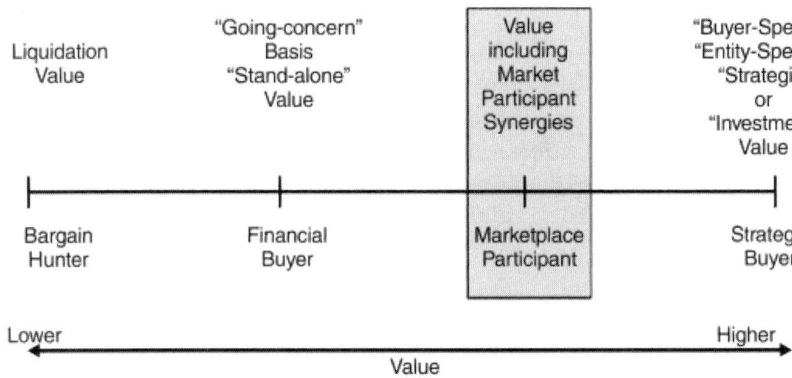

We note that with the introduction of SFAS 157, the level of effort required to use market-based measures has increased substantially. This is directly due to the new fair-value definition, which explicitly includes references to market participants, as well as to the fair-value hierarchy, which places greater emphasis on market-based data rather than entity-specific data. Moreover, factors that are specific to a company and not available to market participants should be excluded from the assumptions used in market-based valuations. Examples of entity-specific factors that generally may not be available to market participants include the following:

- additional value derived from the existence or creation of a portfolio of similar technology assets;
- synergies between the technology and other assets owned by the company;
- legal rights or restrictions;
- tax benefits or tax burdens;
- the ability to use the technology asset globally rather than in a specific geographic area;
- the ability to sell the technology in certain markets (***e.g.***, the business-to-business market as opposed to the business-to-consumer market); and
- specific cost and revenue synergies.

Whether factors such as these are specific to the company or would be available to others in the market generally needs to be determined on a case-by-case basis.

Valuation Approaches[9]

Section 7, Examples of Technology Asset Valuations, provides a detailed discussion on common valuation approaches and associated methodologies. Valuators can use some of these in the valuation of technology assets. The approach and method used will depend on the factors and information available in the given circumstances. Below, we discuss some general and specific issues relevant to the valuation approaches commonly used to value technology assets.

General

Understanding the Technology

In addition to the various sources of information discussed in Section 3, Information, the valuator should obtain and review the following information in detail for each technology (and sub-technology) in order to understand the technology better:

- a listing and description for each, including patents registered (if any);
- term of each registered patent (origination date to expiration date);
- jurisdiction (country);
- groupings;
- management's knowledge of licensing agreements for the use of the technology;
- management's knowledge of the licence fee the company would expect as a percentage of sales, if management were to license the technology; and
- the valuation premise (*e.g.*, going-concern value, liquidation value, value in exchange, value in use, and market-participant

9 This section includes information obtained from, among other sources, (i) AICPA IPR&D Practice Aid and (ii) the IVSC January 2009 *Exposure Draft of Revised International Valuation Guidance Note No. 4: Valuation of Intangible Assets* and *Exposure Draft of Proposed New International Valuation Guidance Note No. 16: Valuation of Intangible Assets for IFRS Reporting Purposes.*

versus buyer-specific synergies) and how it relates to and/or affects the technology.[10]

Using the Premise of Value to Determine the Valuation Approach

Depending on the definition of value and the given facts and circumstances (including consideration of the valuation premise and the purpose of the valuation), a technology asset should in general be valued based on the greater of its value in exchange (*i.e.*, based on a market approach), its value in use (*i.e.*, based on an income approach), or its value under a cost approach. It might be appropriate to consider more than one approach, and within each approach there may be different methods available. When performing a valuation where the objective is to determine the market value of a technology asset, the valuator should adopt the approach(es) and method(s) that would be used by the parties to the hypothetical transaction, which would generally include market participants. Understanding the nature of the market for the technology asset being valued is critical to determining the most appropriate valuation approach.

Technology Asset Valuations without Historical and/or Current Cash Flows

The valuation of technology can be challenging if historical and/or current cash flows are not indicative of the future cash flow–generating ability of the technology asset. In this regard, a significant portion of the value of the technology asset might be generated in the long term, while short-term cash flows are either nominal and/or negative. In such instances, a greater degree of reliance should be placed on the PFI in order to project the future benefits (*i.e.*, value) of the technology asset, a large proportion of which are dependent on future growth opportunities.

As mentioned in footnote 7, there is a strong link between the basis under which the PFI is prepared and the basis under which an appropriate discount rate is determined.

Aggregation and/or Grouping of Technology Assets

In some cases, it may be appropriate and/or possible to value a technology asset on a stand-alone basis; in other instances, it may either be impossible

---

10 We note that a valuation for financial reporting purposes may require a different valuation premise and/or assumptions than a valuation for tax purposes.

or impractical to value a technology asset other than in conjunction with the company's other tangible and/or intangible asset(s). Furthermore, the valuator should know whether a technology asset has been valued on a stand-alone basis or in conjunction with other asset(s). If the technology asset has been valued with other asset(s), the valuator should clearly be aware of the rationale as to why it was necessary to aggregate the subject technology asset with other asset(s).

More specifically, in valuing a technology asset, the valuator must identify the key technology and sub-technologies related to the subject technology asset, which will often assist the valuator in determining whether each of the key technologies and/or sub-technologies needs to be considered separately for valuation purposes because of differences in risk, growth, and/or remaining useful life. The nature and extent of the groupings can also depend on the ultimate purpose of the valuation (*e.g.*, for financial reporting purposes, each of the key technologies and/or sub-technologies may need to be valued separately because of differences in amortization and disclosure requirements, while the tax authorities may only be concerned with the value of the company's technology on a combined basis). Below we discuss the typical technology-related groupings seen in practice, which can be further grouped, classified, and/or separated into various technologies and/or sub-technologies based on the given facts and circumstances.

- *Existing technology (core or base technology)* – technical processes, intellectual property, and institutional understanding that exist within an organization with respect to products or processes that have been completed and that will aid in the development of future products, services, or processes designed to incorporate similar technologies. The terms base technology and core technology are often used synonymously. The basic definition reflects the existence of underlying technology that has value through its continued use (or re-use) in a number of products and/or generations of a single product (*i.e.*, a product family). This base (or core) technology of a company may be represented by, for example, a portfolio of patents, a library of potential candidates for therapeutic drugs, or a superior manufacturing capability. The existence of base (or core) technology is dependent on facts and circumstances. In some cases, companies in-license technology that serves as a base (or core) for their product development efforts. In other cases, base (or core) technology may not exist at all, as each new product is developed from a new or novel technology platform;
- *Existing technology (developed technology)* – technology as it exists in a current product(s) offering. Current developed technology may result in future base (or core) technology. In a valuation

model that apportions revenues or profits, developed product technology and base (or core) technology may be combined into one category of existing technology. From the perspective of GAAP, base (or core) technology and developed technology should be identified separately if they have different useful lives for amortization purposes. Often, base (or core) technology and developed technology are grouped into a single existing technology for valuation purposes as they are most often inextricably linked to each another, having relatively similar useful lives, as well as the same levels of risk;

- *In-process research and development (IPR&D) technology* – a technology asset related to a research and development project that has not been completed (*i.e.*, IPR&D technology is a subset of an intangible asset to be used in research and development activities). From the perspective of GAAP, existing technology (*i.e.*, base (or core) technology and/or developed technology) and IPR&D technology should be identified separately if they have different useful lives for amortization purposes. IPR&D technology is also often grouped with base (or core) technology and developed technology into a single existing technology for valuation purposes;[11] and
- *Internally developed software* – through its contribution to a company's efficient operation, a critical intangible asset, even if it only indirectly affects the design and production of technology. Companies may apply proprietary software in managing their finances, for example, or scheduling purchases of critical supplies or for use in managing relationships with customers. A valuator must look beyond the obvious locations in a company's operations to uncover and identify internally developed software.

Market Approach

Valuation methods that use the market approach determine the value of a technology asset and/or technology-related company by reference to market activity (*e.g.*, transaction bids and/or offers involving identical or similar assets). The valuation process under the market approach involves a comparison and correlation between the subject technology asset and other

---

11 Under SFAS 141R and CICA Handbook Section 1582, IPR&D is separately identified and valued and booked as an asset and subject to annual impairment testing until the project is complete (*i.e.*, IPR&D will not be amortized until the project is complete). Once an IPR&D project is complete, the IPR&D will be amortized over its useful life. Subsequent research and development costs related to the IPR&D project will be expensed as incurred.

similar assets. In other words, based on observable transaction values, multiples of financial, operational, or other relevant data are typically inferred and then applied to the subject technology asset. When using the market approach, the valuator gathers information on comparable technology assets and makes adjustments to reflect observed prices in the determination of value for the subject technology asset. An example of the market approach is the market-transaction method, which determines the value of a technology asset by reference to transaction prices or valuation multiples implicit in the transaction prices of identical and/or similar assets.

A valuation multiple is a multiple determined by dividing the transaction price of an asset by a financial parameter, such as historical or prospective sales or profit at a given level. Some of the valuation multiples that are used in practice in the valuation of technology assets are calculated based on the transaction price divided by the following:

- sales generated by the technology asset;
- profit contribution of the technology asset after deducting certain costs, such as research and development and/or sales and marketing; and
- earnings before interest and tax (EBIT) or earnings before interest, tax, depreciation, and amortization (EBITDA) generated by the technology asset.

Valuation multiples are applied to the corresponding financial parameters of the subject technology asset in order to value it. For instance, if a valuation multiple of 1.5 times historical sales is identified from a market transaction and the subject technology asset had historical sales of $100,000, the value indicated by use of the valuation multiple would be 1.5 * $100,000 = $150,000.

The required assumptions for the market-transaction method are the following:

- prices and/or valuation multiples with respect to identical and/or similar intangible technology assets; and
- Adjustments, as required, to such transaction prices and/or valuation multiples to reflect the differentiating characteristics of the subject technology asset and the technology assets involved in the transaction(s).

There are practical difficulties that restrict the use of the market approach for the valuation of technology assets. There are often either very few or no transactions involving identical and/or similar assets for which price information is available (typically, technology assets are transferred as part of the sale of a business and not in piecemeal transactions). In those select instances where the sale prices of technology assets are available, the valuator must ensure the technology assets are comparable. Even where transactions can be identified and information regarding prices paid is available, it can be difficult to determine the appropriate adjustments either to the prices or the valuation multiples necessary to reflect the differentiating characteristics of the subject technology asset and the technology assets involved in the transactions (*e.g.*, assuming stand-alone transactional data is available, the availability of that data is often limited, making meaningful comparisons with the subject technology asset difficult). In practice, such adjustments may only be determined on a qualitative, rather than quantitative, basis. For example:

- the technology asset being valued may command a more dominant position in the market than those technology assets involved in the transaction(s);
- the technology asset being valued may have a much higher likelihood of receiving regulatory approval, achieving market acceptance, and/or being commercialized than the technology assets involved in the transaction(s); or
- the technology asset being valued may have a much longer useful life, regulatory protection, and/or fewer competitive pressures than the technology assets involved in the transaction(s).

The valuator must also consider the timing of when the comparable transaction(s) occurred. The timing of the transaction(s) may limit comparability, given that the market and/or economy may have changed to such an extent as to render the historical transaction(s) less relevant.

As such, the difficulties described above may restrict the reliability of the market-transaction method in the valuation of technology assets. Consequently, in practice the market-transaction method is often only used to support the overall reasonableness of the valuation of a technology asset as determined through the application of another valuation method.

The market approach also typically increases in applicability and feasibility as a company progresses through the middle stages and enters the later stages of its development (see Section 5, Technology Value Drivers, for more details). It is highly unlikely that comparable companies with readily determinable values for either their operations or their intangible assets will be identified during the earlier stages of their development (sometimes early-stage companies are acquired by academic institutions, which can provide some useful information; however, relevant comparable transactions are otherwise rare).

Moreover, investments by non-arm's-length parties in the company, which typically occur during earlier stages, are unlikely to be reliable indicators of value for the company and/or its technology assets. In this regard, all investments in the technology company should also be assessed to determine any buyer-specific synergistic value that may be associated with those investments (which may need to be excluded from the value determination, depending on the definition and/or premise of value).

In order to obtain a general understanding of the factors that may affect the value of the technology under the market approach, the valuator should also request and/or review the following information:

- details of any significant technology that has either been purchased outright or the rights to use it have been acquired and is currently or expected to be used in the operations of the business;
- whether management is aware of any comparable transactions in the industry that may be relevant to the valuation of the technology asset; and
- whether the company typically sells the technology asset on an exclusive basis and/or whether customers have the ability to resell the technology asset.

Income Approach

Valuation methods that use the income approach determine the value of a technology asset by reference to the present value of income, cash flows, and/or cost savings that could actually or hypothetically be achieved by a market participant owning the technology asset. Thus, any income approach is heavily reliant on the PFI, which, in the context of a technology asset, should generally include the following components:

- sales;
- gross profit, operating profit, and net profit;
- profits before and after tax;
- cash flows before and after interest and/or tax; and
- length of the remaining useful life of the technology asset.

The income approach is typically applied to later-stage companies (see Section 5, Technology Value Drivers, for more details) as opposed to early-stage companies because there is a greater likelihood at later stages of there being a financial history on which to base the PFI to be used to value the technology asset and/or the technology-related company.

The principal valuation methods that use the income approach in valuing technology assets are the following:

- *Relief-from-royalty method (sometimes known as the royalty savings method)* – given that the owner enjoys the right to manufacture and sell products that incorporate the technology asset(s) without having to pay a royalty fee to the inventor, the relief-from-royalty method provides a cash flow savings that is discounted to present value. Alternatively, the right to the technology asset may afford its owner a cost savings over the next best alternative available (*i.e.*, a reduced or eliminated cash outflow). These cost savings also represent a measure of the benefits enjoyed by the owner of the technology asset. The present value of the cost savings would be included in determining the value of the technology asset provided that the cost savings would be available to market participants if they owned the technology asset; and

- *Multi-period excess earnings method* – in cases where the technology asset results in a unique product (*e.g.*, proprietary chemicals) or the technology asset is necessary to compete in an industry (*e.g.*, complex computer-assisted design software), a multi-period excess earnings method may be the best indicator of value. This method requires a projection of cash inflows, cash outflows, and *pro forma* charges for an economic "return of" and "return on" tangible and intangible assets employed (*e.g.*, working capital, property, plant and equipment, trademarks, distribution channels, work force, and other technologies). Cash outflows include expenses related to direct and indirect costs to complete, manufacturing, sales, marketing, routine technical maintenance, general and administrative, and taxes. The net cash inflows (or multi-period excess earnings) are ascribable to the technology asset and, when discounted to present value, provide a determination of its value.

Each of these methods involves the present value of projected cash flows using either discounted cash flow techniques or, in simple cases, the application of a valuation multiple. In addition to the present value of income, cash flows, or cost savings that may be derived from use of the technology asset, it might be appropriate to increase the technology asset value with respect to any tax relief available on the amortization of the technology asset for tax purposes. Such an adjustment, commonly known as the tax amortization benefit, reflects the fact that the income generated by the technology asset includes not only the income directly attributable to its use, but also the reduction in income taxes payable by a business using the technology asset. If estimating the market value, an adjustment to the cash flows for tax amortization should be made only if this benefit would generally be available to market participants (*i.e.*, if the technology asset is being valued on a market-participant basis rather than on an entity-specific basis). When performing a valuation under a basis other than market value, a tax amortization benefit adjustment should be made if the availability of amortization is consistent with the basis of the valuation. Thus, if an entity-specific valuation is being performed, a tax amortization benefit adjustment should be included only if tax amortization would be available to the specific entity concerned.

Relief-from-Royalty Method

The relief-from-royalty method determines the value of a technology asset by reference to the present value of the hypothetical royalty payments that would be saved through owning the technology asset as opposed to licensing the technology asset from a third party. The relief-from-royalty method involves estimating the total royalty payments that would need to be made over the technology asset's life by a hypothetical licensee to a hypothetical licensor. The hypothetical royalty payments over the life of the technology asset are adjusted for tax and discounted to present value. Royalty rates are typically applied as a percentage of the sales expected to be generated when using the technology asset. In some cases, royalty payments may include an upfront (lump-sum) payment, in addition to periodic amounts based on sales or some other financial parameter.

Relief-from-Royalty Valuation Assumptions – Technology Assets

The following valuation assumptions are typically required to apply the relief-from-royalty method as it relates to technology assets:

- the royalty rate and corresponding financial parameter(s), such as a percentage of sales, that would hypothetically be paid in an arm's-length transaction by a willing licensee to a willing licensor for the rights to use the subject technology;
- PFI for the financial parameter, such as sales, to which the royalty rate would be applied over the life of the technology asset together with an estimate of the life of the technology asset;
- rate at which tax relief would be obtainable on the hypothetical royalty payments;
- costs that would be borne by a licensee in using the technology asset (*e.g.*, marketing costs and/or research and development costs to switch the value of the technology);
- discount rate to enable estimated periodic royalty payments to be brought to a single capital value; and/or
- in simple cases, a capitalization multiple to apply to constant cash flows.

Important Considerations in Selecting Appropriate Royalty Rates – Technology Assets

Royalty rates can often vary significantly in the market for apparently similar technology assets. As a result, we suggest that a valuator should perform a cross-check of the selected royalty rate by reference to the operating margin that a typical operator would require from sales generated from the use of the technology asset (in Section 7, Examples of Technology Asset Valuations, we discuss in further detail various other considerations in applying the relief-from-royalty method in valuing a technology asset).

Moreover, the valuator should also review royalty rates related to (i) current agreements in place for the use of the technology asset, which we note may not be entirely indicative of the technology asset's value since the terms of the agreement may include differing factors as discussed later; (ii) third-party agreements for the licensing of similar technology assets; and (iii) similar technology-related intangibles and licensing agreements from the valuator's past experience in applying the relief-from-royalty approach. Accordingly, the valuator should consider the following factors, among others:

- large upfront fee (*e.g.*, a large upfront fee can result in a relatively lower royalty rate than would otherwise have been the case);
- large fixed-fee component (*e.g.*, a large fixed-fee component can result in a relatively lower royalty rate than would otherwise have been the case);
- escalating royalty (*e.g.*, the royalty rate can be small initially but can increase as sales increase, so judgment would be required as to which rate to use);
- exclusivity (*e.g.*, with all things being equal, exclusivity would require a relatively higher royalty rate compared with an agreement with non-exclusivity);
- territory covered as sales may be concentrated in one region (with all things being equal, the larger the territory covered by the agreement, the higher the royalty rate);
- expected sales volume (*e.g.*, if significant sales are expected, the royalty rate might be relatively lower because of the large amount of absolute dollars to be generated by the royalty);
- length of the stated term and any limitations on the term (*e.g.*, with all things being equal, the longer the term, the larger the royalty);
- non-arm's length versus arm's length agreement (*e.g.*, transactions between non-arm's length parties may not be representative of market value);
- differences in the financial condition of the parties and/or their negotiating abilities and/or positions (*e.g.*, the relative financial

deal experience and/or strength of the parties may affect the amount of the agreed-upon royalty than would otherwise have been the case);

- industry (*e.g.*, some industries may command higher and/or lower royalties depending on general factors such as industry-wide growth expectations, profitability, and ability to obtain financing);
- international transactions (*e.g.*, with all things being equal, a lower royalty rate would be required in countries where protection is weak);
- economic life of the underlying process and/or technology (*e.g.*, a technology asset with a short life span may require a higher royalty rate than a technology asset with a longer life span);
- other forms of compensation included in the agreement that may affect the agreed-upon royalty rate (*e.g.*, cash, shares, convertible bonds, and contingent consideration);
- required investment in complementary assets and/or capital expenditures (*e.g.*, the greater the investment in complementary assets and/or capital expenditures, the higher the required royalty rate, with all other things being equal);
- the competitive environment for alternative technologies and the relative strength of the technology asset among competitors (*e.g.*, the lower the number of technology alternatives and competition, the higher the required royalty rate, with all other things being equal);
- the proportion of the main driver of the operating margin the technology asset represents relative to other intangible assets (*e.g.*, the more critical the technology asset is to the operating margin in comparison with other intangible assets, the higher the required royalty rate, with all other things being equal);
- obligations of each party to the agreement (*e.g.*, the functions to be performed by each party, such as continued research and development, marketing, administration, technical assistance, and ancillary services, that may affect the royalty-rate negotiations);
- history, heritage, recognition, awareness, and quality of the technology (*e.g.*, the stronger the history, heritage, recognition, awareness, and quality of the technology asset, the higher the required royalty rate, with all other things being equal);
- group of licences versus a single licence (*e.g.*, negotiating groups of licences may affect the royalty rate in comparison with agreements negotiated on a stand-alone basis);
- strategic alliances (*e.g.*, negotiating a licensing with a strategic partner might include synergistic benefits that may affect the

royalty rate in comparison with agreements negotiated with non-strategic partners);

- operational risks (*e.g.*, fixed- versus variable-cost structure, with the latter requiring a lower royalty rate, with all other things being equal);
- stage of development of the technology asset (*e.g.*, early-stage versus later-stage development, with the latter requiring a higher royalty rate, with all other things being equal);
- commercialization risks (*e.g.*, an early-stage technology versus a later-stage technology, with the latter requiring a higher royalty rate, with all other things being equal);
- development risks (*e.g.*, if significant incremental short-term investment is required, a higher royalty rate would be required); and
- various other components of the licensing agreements that may influence and/or directly affect the royalty rate. Where factors other than the technology asset have a significant impact on profitability, the incremental profit from using the technology asset is likely to be limited (*e.g.*, an assessment of the corporate strategy and/or any excess capacity related to the use of the technology may also affect the agreed-upon royalty rate).

The valuator should also consider assessing the operating margins of the company to see what a reasonable royalty rate should or could be and the amount of risk a licensee would be willing to accept to generate a reasonable economic return. According to a study conducted by Robert Goldscheider, John Jarosz and Carla Mulhern, entitled "Use of the 25 Per Cent Rule in Valuing IP,"[12] licensing negotiations for intangible assets typically begin with the application of one-third to one-quarter of long-term operating margins as a baseline, to be adjusted upward or downward based on the specific attributes of the technology and/or the specific attributes involved in the licensing agreement being used as a benchmark (*e.g.*, in consideration of the factors as noted earlier). In practice, the 25 Per Cent Rule is often used by valuators in assessing the reasonableness of the royalty rates selected in applying the relief-from-royalty method.

Multi-Period Excess Earnings Method

The excess earnings method determines the value of a technology asset based on the present value of the cash flows attributable to the technology asset, exclusive of the proportion of the cash flows attributable to other

---

12 R. Goldscheider, J. Jarosz & C. Mulhern, "Use of the 25 Per Cent Rule in Valuing IP" (2002) 37 *les Nouvelles* 123.

assets. As discussed earlier, the excess earnings method can be applied either using a single period of projected cash flows - the single-period excess earnings method - or using several periods of projected cash flows - the multi-period excess earnings method. In practice, since a technology asset normally brings monetary benefits over an extended period, the multi-period excess earnings method is more commonly used.

The multi-period excess earnings method involves projecting the cash flows expected to arise from the business or businesses that use the technology asset being valued. From these projected cash flows, a deduction is made with respect to the contributions to the cash flows that are made by assets, tangible and intangible, other than the technology asset itself.

The effects of goodwill should also be excluded from the technology asset value, which can be done by ensuring the following:

- The projected cash flows are only reflective of the benefits that are expected to arise from the technology that was in existence at the valuation date (*i.e.*, the projected cash flows should be representative of existing technology rather than future technology).
- The appropriate adjustments to the cash flows have been made for components of goodwill that contribute to value, such as assembled work force and other factors giving rise to future economic benefits that are not identifiable intangible assets.

The projected cash flows attributable to the technology asset are capitalized by the application of present value techniques and an appropriate discount rate or, in simple cases, a capitalization factor. The contributions to cash flows made by assets other than the technology asset being valued are known as contributory asset charges or economic rents. These contributory assets support the technology asset that is being valued in generating cash flows and should be excluded from the projected cash flows attributable to the technology asset that are being capitalized.

Considerations in Using the Multi-Period Excess Earnings Method – Technology Assets

There are several important considerations that may be relevant in valuing technology assets using the multi-period excess earnings method (in Section 7, Examples of Technology Asset Valuations, we discuss in further detail various other considerations in the applying the multi-period excess earnings method in valuing a technology asset):

- Where various technology revenue streams can be separately identified as having different levels of gross and/or operating margins, each of these revenue streams may need to be valued and/or considered separately (*e.g.*, if they represent different groups of technologies with different risk profiles and/or different remaining useful lives).

- The valuator may also need to separate the company's revenues into technology versus customer revenues (*e.g.*, a portion of the company's revenues may be attributable to customer relationships, rather than technology).
- The valuator should identify and understand the nature of all one-time implementation, and/or service revenues that are not associated with the sale and/or use of the technology and should be excluded from the valuation of the existing technology asset.
- Annual sales and marketing costs in the early stages of a technology-related company or those related to an existing technology release may not be reflective of ongoing sales and marketing costs of the existing technology in the later stages of a company's development.
- Annual research and development costs should be reasonable in terms of required growth and sustaining research and development efforts for the existing technology relative to a future technology.
- Cost structures should be matched with the related revenues on an annual basis and the valuator should ensure that the projected costs are not based solely on historical results, which may not always be indicative of future requirements.
- The valuator should ensure market participant and/or buyer-specific synergies have been identified and appropriately included and/or excluded from the valuation.
- Later-stage and/or mature technologies may require different levels of sales and marketing relative to early-stage technologies.
- Each group of technologies (or sub-technologies) may have a different risk profile, may require different technology migration curves (see Section 7, Examples of Technology Asset Valuations, for further detail), and may have different estimated useful lives.
- Rates of return used in the valuation analysis should be appropriate relative to the risks and rewards of the technology asset being valued. In this regard, when market evidence is available, it should be used. In other cases, rates of return should be reasonable when compared with the rates of return of the other assets of the company.
- Tax losses incurred by the overall business are not considered in the valuation of a specific technology asset as these losses are either captured by the accounting for income taxes and booked to the balance sheet or constitute part of goodwill. However,

losses generated by the technology asset itself over the life of the technology asset's cash flows should be considered.

Cost Approach

Historically, the cost approach (using depreciated replacement cost of the technology asset) has been applied primarily to early-stage companies with low barriers to entry. The cost approach is typically applied when there is a limited (or no) basis for using the income or market approaches. That is, there are no comparable market transactions and the company has virtually no financial history and, consequently, is unable to use past results to reasonably support the development of the PFI. The cost approach may also be appropriate in situations where comparable technology assets can be developed in-house or purchased from a third party and/or when future expected cash flows from the subject technology asset have not been developed.

More specifically, the cost approach, often known as the depreciated replacement cost (or replacement cost new less depreciation [RCNLD]) method, determines the value of a technology asset by calculating the cost of replacing it with an asset with similar or identical service capacity (see Section 7, Examples of Technology Asset Valuations, for further detail). In such cases, the replacement cost provides a ceiling, or maximum, for the value of the technology asset as a rational purchaser would not pay more for an asset than for something to replace its service capacity. Adjustments, including depreciation, may be required to reflect differences between the cost of replacing the asset with one with similar service capacity and the cost of replacing it with one with the depreciated service capacity of the technology asset.

In practice, there are only a few types of technology assets for which the depreciated replacement cost method is typically used to determine value, such as the following:

- The method can be applied to value software since the price of software with (the same or) similar service capacity can often be obtained in the market. These assets demonstrate substance, but they are still in the development stage and are not far enough along the development path for expected future cash flow projections to exist.
- The method is sometimes applied to value internally developed software (*e.g.*, websites) because it may be possible to determine the relevant costs (*e.g.*, the costs of constructing the website). There are many situations where companies that develop sup-

porting or contributing software assets do not have directly identifiable revenues and/or cash flows associated with these software assets. In these situations, cost may be the only approximation of value. In this regard, the constructive cost model (COCOMO), used to value software applications, determines value in reference to the lines of code contained in the underlying software. While the COCOMO may be useful for high-level calculations, its accuracy is limited because of its lack of factors to account for differences in hardware constraints, quality of personnel, and experience, among other things.

The use of the cost approach is generally less appropriate once a company has generated significant intangibles and internal goodwill. The generation of these intangibles often starts to gain momentum in the middle stages of a technology-related company's development and continues to build through the later stages.

Considerations in Using the Cost Approach (Depreciated Replacement Cost Method) – Technology Assets

In valuing technology assets using the depreciated replacement cost method, some or all of the following factors should be considered (Section 7, Examples of Technology Asset Valuations, for further detail):

- the cost of developing or purchasing an identical technology asset with the same production or service potential;
- the cost of developing or purchasing a similar technology asset with the same or similar production or service potential;
- in the case of the cost of a similar, rather than identical, technology asset with the same or similar production or service potential, the adjustments required, including amortization (if appropriate), to that cost in order to reflect the specific characteristics of the technology asset being valued; and
- the expected difference between the cost price of the replacement technology asset and the exchange price of the technology asset being valued since value is a measure of the amount that could be obtained in an exchange transaction.

The valuator should also consider the relevance of opportunity costs and/or lost profits during the reproduction phase that a purchaser may have to incur by purchasing the ready-made technology. In many cases, too narrow a definition of cost is applied in determining value using the cost approach, whereby opportunity costs and/or lost profits, which (if relevant) are an important element of the benefit obtained (or cost avoided) by an actual and/or hypothetical purchaser, are not appropriately included in the valuation of the technology asset.

Technology-Related Company and Asset Value Drivers

General

In our view, throughout the entire valuation process, the valuator should continuously apply (or at least be cognizant of) Michael Porter's Five Forces Model (Porter, 1985) to the technology asset and/or technology-related company being valued as it will help highlight various key issues that should be considered in the valuation. Figure 2 illustrates Porter's Five Forces Model.

Figure 2

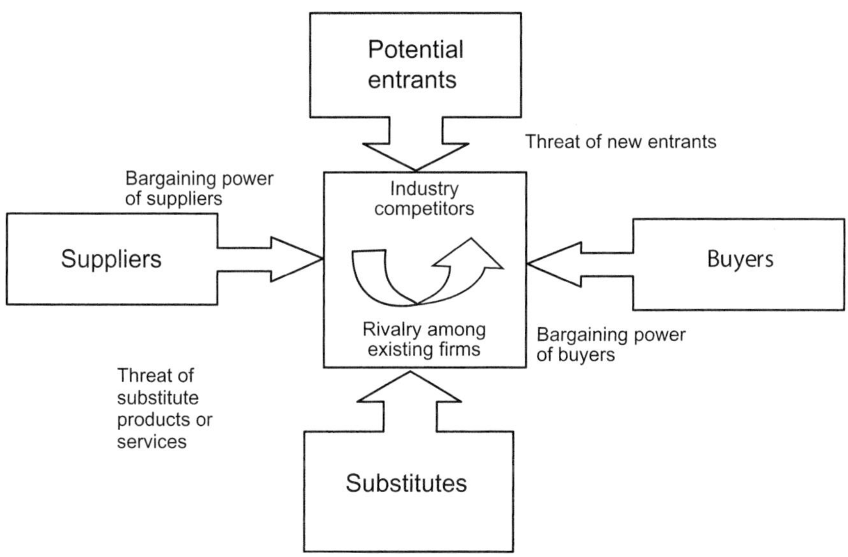

According to the model, the fundamental value of any investment is a function of the future cash flows it is expected to generate, the so-called value drivers, and the return investors require from their investments. In general, the value of a growth company is highly sensitive to changes in these value drivers. It is therefore not surprising that prices of growth companies are so volatile. Technology assets can be directly linked to sales or indirectly linked to profitability when they are used as enablers to enhance efficiency or increase effectiveness.

We also note that traditional valuation approaches are somewhat limited in that they do not capture all of the future potential and/or benefits of a given technology. In this regard, key factors that may not always be appropriately reflected in projected cash flows include the following, among others:

- *Business model and margins* – the nature of the selected business model (*e.g.*, the software-as-a-service business model) may be a critical differentiating factor and a key competitive advantage that allows a technology-related company to obtain market share and achieve significant growth relative to its competitors. While there are many business models for technology-related companies, those technology companies with operations that deliver relatively higher margins will be more highly valued than those generating larger revenues at relatively lower margins;
- *Flexibility and quality of management* – the ability of management to assess the market, the competition, and the requirements of customers and to adjust the business and the operations to capitalize on these opportunities is essential in achieving growth;
- *Growth* – the speed at which a technology-related company can grow its business is critical. Investors have an ever-shortening time horizon over which they will tolerate the time between the inception of a technology-related company and the period of time it requires to achieve critical mass. Investors often simplistically look to revenue, profit, and cash flow growth;
- *Quality of growth* – a higher quality of growth should attract higher valuation levels. Technology companies that can grow with value addition – and that can sustain that value addition – will attract the highest valuation levels over time;
- *Customers and marketing* – the likely behavior of the customers of technology businesses is not well understood (*e.g.*, loyalty, effectiveness of marketing spend, and first-mover and size advantages); however, these factors are key drivers of both growth and margins;
- *Capital intensity* – in the early stages of development, technology-related companies require a large amount of cash. This cash is primarily used to market their businesses and to develop new applications and services. The greater the amount of cash required to generate business development, the greater the degree of risk the investment holds; and
- *Premium return on investment* – technology companies include the value of the growth and profitability of the ongoing business as part of their total valuation. Typically, investors allocate a sub-

stantial amount of value to the ability of technology companies to generate additional growth from the success that they are expected to experience. The value related to the ability to continue to find new investment opportunities that can deliver high levels of return, which are measured by their excess over the cost of capital, is the premium return on investment.

Below, we discuss additional key considerations and/or value drivers the valuator should assess when valuing technology assets and/or technology-related companies.

Stage of Development and/or Technology Product Life Cycle

General Methodologies

A key consideration when determining the appropriate valuation methodology for a technology asset and/or technology-related company is its stage[13] of development and/or the product life cycle of the technology asset. For a mature technology-related company, the traditional income- and market-based methodologies would be relevant. However, for early-stage technologies and/or companies with no record of profitability or no record of sales or those that have large expected growth rates, the valuator should consider alternative methodologies. In these situations, there is often a significant amount of uncertainty involved with respect to the future prospects of the business. Consequently, sensitivity and scenario analysis are useful analytical tools to help evaluate the variability of value as the assumptions regarding overall business conditions change. Monte Carlo simulations, real options methodologies, multi-period discounted cash flow techniques (*e.g.*, multi-period excess earning and/or relief-from-royalty methods, as discussed earlier), and/or probability-weighted discounted cash flows can be useful in capturing the associated uncertainty and/or variability. Further to the above, managers of a technology-related project may require, at various points (or gates) during the life cycle, an evaluation of the probability of success and the potential economic results. At each gate, a decision must be made about whether to continue funding the project.

13 The Private Equity Industry Guidelines Group describes privately held venture investments as being classified as either seed, early stage, expansion, or later stage with respect to its position in its life cycle (Source: Reporting and Performance Measurement Guidelines, March 1, 2005, p. 12).

As per the AICPA IPR&D Practice Aid, the product and/or service life cycle of a technology asset can be illustrated as shown in Figure 3.[14]

Figure 3

Conceptualization		Applied Research			
Idea	Development Concept	Product Definition	Product Feasibility	Development	Pre-Production

A future product, service, or process is defined and its potential economic benefits are identified at some point within the life cycle after the project's conceptualization. Once a future product, service, or process has been defined and its potential economic benefits have been identified, a specific technology-related project begins to demonstrate substance. This generally occurs when more than insignificant research and development efforts have been expended after the characteristics of the future product, service, or process have been defined and management has approved continued project funding. In addition, at this stage, management can reasonably determine the project's completion date, has considered the impact of potential competition, and can reasonably project costs to complete, sales volumes, average selling prices, and other related costs over the anticipated economic life of the technology asset.

At some point before commercialization (*i.e.*, before earning revenue) and possibly before the end of the development or preproduction stage, the research and development project is no longer considered incomplete (*i.e.*, ultimate completion of the project has occurred) and a developed technology asset resulting from research and development emerges from what was previously an asset used in research and development.

Further to the above, a clear understanding of the subject technology and/or technology-related company's stage of development and/or product life cycle can also provide the valuator with key information with respect to the expected prospective growth rates of the company and the general risk profile of the subject technology asset. Figure 4 below illustrates typical valuation issues that arise during the stages of development and/or product life cycle of a technology asset and/or technology-related company.[15]

---

14 The section is based on information obtained from, among other sources, the AICPA IPR&D Practice Aid.

15 Based on information obtained from A. Damodaran, *The Dark Side of Valuation: Valuing Old Tech, New Tech, and New Economy Companies* (Upper Saddle River, New Jersey: Prentice Hall PTR, 2001).

Figure 4

Valuation Issues across the Product Life Cycle

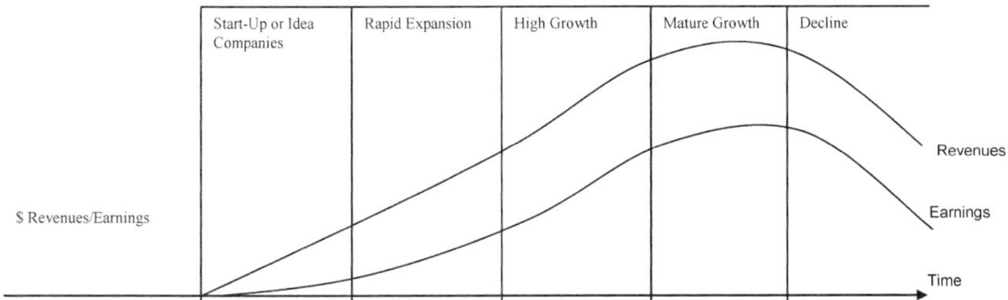

	Start-Up or Idea Companies	Rapid Expansion	High Growth	Mature Growth	Decline
Revenues Current Operations	Non-existent or low revenues/Negative operating income	Revenues increasing/Income still low or negative	Revenues in high growth/Operating income also growing	Revenue growth slows/Operating income still growing	Revenues and Operating income growth drops off
Operating History	None	Very limited	Some operating history	Operating history can be used in valuation	Substantial operating history
Comparable firms	None	Some, but in same stage of growth	More comparable, at different stages	Large number of comparables, at different stages	Declining number of comparables, mostly mature
Source of Value	Entirely future growth	Mostly future growth	Portion from existing assets/Growth still dominates	More from existing assets than growth	Entirely from existing assets

Each of the stages of development and/or product life cycle of a technology asset and/or technology-related company is discussed in further detail below[16] (the terms technology assets and/or technology-related company are used synonymously).

- *Start-up* – this represents the initial stage after a business has been formed. The technology is generally still untested and does not have an established market. The company has little in terms of current operations, no operating history, and no comparable companies. The value of the company rests entirely on its future growth potential. Valuation poses the most challenges at this stage, since there is little useful information to go on. The assumptions have to be determined and are likely to have considerable errors associated with them. Projections of future growth are often based on assessments of the competence of existing managers and their capacity to convert a promising idea into commercial success. This is often the reason why companies in this phase try to hire managers with a successful track record in converting ideas into dollars, because it gives them credibility in the eyes of financial backers.

16 *Ibid.*

- *Expansion* – once a company succeeds in attracting customers and establishing a presence in the market, its revenues increase rapidly, although it still might be reporting losses. The current operations of the company provide useful clues on pricing, margins, and expected growth, but current margins cannot be projected into the future. The operating history of the company is still limited and shows large changes from period to period. Other companies generally are in operation, but they are usually at the same stage of growth as the company being valued. Most of the value for this company comes from its expected growth. Valuation becomes a little simpler at this stage, but the information is still limited and unreliable, and the inputs to the valuation model are likely to shift substantially over time.
- *High growth* – while the company's revenues are growing rapidly at this stage, earnings are likely to lag behind revenues. Both the current operations and operation history of the company contain information that can be used in valuing the company. The number of comparable companies is generally the highest at this stage, and these companies are more diverse in where they are in the life cycle, ranging from small, high-growth competitors to larger, lower-growth competitors. The existing assets of this company have significant value, but the larger proportion of value still comes from future growth. There is more information available at this stage, and the estimation of assumptions becomes more straightforward.
- *Mature growth* – as growth starts levelling off, companies generally find two phenomena occurring. The earnings and cash flows continue to increase rapidly, reflecting past investments, and the need to invest in new projects declines. At this stage in the process, the company has current operations that are reflective of the future, an operating history that provides substantial information about the company's markets, and a large number of comparable companies at the same stage in the life cycle. Existing assets contribute to the company's value as much as or more than expected growth, and the assumptions to the valuation are likely to be stable.
- *Decline* – the last stage in this life cycle is decline. Companies in this stage find both revenues and earnings starting to decline as their businesses mature and new competitors overtake them. Existing investments are likely to continue to produce cash flows, albeit at a declining pace, and the company has little need of new investments. Thus, the value of the company depends entirely on existing assets. While the number of comparable companies tends to become smaller at this stage, they are all likely to be

either in mature growth or decline as well. In general, valuation is easiest at this stage.

Based on the above, valuation is clearly more of a challenge in the early stages of a company's development and/or product life cycle. Furthermore, in valuing the technology asset and/or technology-related company, the valuator should also clearly understand the following factors as they relate to the stages of development and/or product life cycle:

- the stage of development as indicated by the development milestones attained for the company as a whole, as well as for each of the key technologies and the related sub-technologies owned by the company;
- probability of successful completion at each stage of development;
- remaining technological, engineering, or regulatory risks to overcome;
- production and related costs;
- time and costs to complete, including capital requirements (if incomplete);
- time and costs to commercialize, including capital requirements (if incomplete);
- revenues during the time to complete and commercialize (if incomplete);
- share of the market and market growth; and
- growth potential of the company with respect to each of its key technologies and sub-technologies.

The stage of development also depends directly on the level of resources and general effort allocated to research and development. By increasing the resources allocated to research and development, a company increases the likelihood that the technology will materialize, and the company will successfully advance at each stage of development throughout the product life cycle where sufficient resources are allocated.

We note that rates of return become relatively lower as the relevant stages of development are completed. The valuator should also understand the potential and timing with respect to a potential IPO and/or liquidity event, which can have a significant impact on projected growth, risk, access to capital, and, ultimately, value.

Venture Capital Valuation Guidelines

Two sources of venture capital valuation guidelines include the U.S. Private Equity Valuation Guidelines and the International Private Equity and Venture Capital Valuation Guidelines (the International Guidelines). Significant overlap exists between these two guidelines. Canada's Venture Capital and Private Equity Association (CVCA) endorses the International Guidelines.

According to the International Guidelines, for ventures with minimal revenues, no significant profits, or no significant positive cash flow, the price involved in a recent investment would be the most appropriate valuation methodology. Such companies would generally include seed or early-stage companies whose future profitability cannot be reliably projected. The price of a recent investment would include the cost of the recent round of financing and would be considered increasingly relevant the closer the date of the actual investment is to the valuation date. The relevance of this measure of value will diminish as company-specific circumstances and/or the environment changes.

Even for ventures with expected recurring revenue, profits, or positive cash flow, the price of a recent investment provides a good indication of value for a certain period of time. After that time, an earnings multiple or discounted cash flow methodology would typically be more appropriate.

Seed and Early-Stage Company Considerations

Some important considerations relevant to seed or early-stage companies include the following:

- *Amount of capital requirements* – start-up ventures require capital in order to translate their ideas into an end product. The magnitude of capital required and a comparison of this amount to the relative availability of such levels of capital in the market are important considerations to determine whether the venture has the possibility of obtaining capital sufficient to even attempt a successful launch.
- *Milestones* – those providing funding to ventures often provide financing depending on certain milestones being achieved by the venture. The nature and breadth of the required milestones need to be assessed to determine if they are feasible.
- *Time until next financing* – if the amount of time until the next milestone funding or next round of financing extends beyond the time that the funds are required by the venture, the success of the venture is compromised.
- *Time to liquidity event* – those funding a venture are ultimately interested in the amount of time it will take to realize their expected return on investment. The longer the time to the liquidity event – most frequently an IPO or third-party acquisition – the more risk to the financier and the increased return required.

Understanding the Big Picture: The Development of Technology Markets

The value of any technology asset is fundamentally driven by the cash flows generated by it and the expected timing of this cash generation, in addition to the associated risks and growth profile. In any valuation, the assessment of risk and growth of the cash flows are the most sensitive inputs to the value conclusion; thus, it is critical to understand the dynamics of the specific situation in order to make an informed judgment regarding these inputs. When dealing with technology, understanding how high-tech markets develop is critical for the valuator in order to be in a position to understand the risk and growth profiles of the subject of the valuation.

The first step in obtaining this understanding is to gain an appreciation of the distinction between continuous innovation and discontinuous innovation. The concept of discontinuous innovation leads to a discussion of the technology-adoption life cycle, based on the work of Everett Rogers and his Harvard colleagues, which is a good starting point for understanding how high-tech markets develop. Finally, the link between the technology-adoption life cycle and the product-category life cycle needs to be understood.

- *Continuous versus discontinuous innovations* – continuous innovations, which are relatively more common, leverage off from established standards and infrastructure. For example, an improved cell phone, a new computer monitor, or an enhanced printer are continuous as they simply build upon existing infrastructure. The customer only needs to purchase them and start enjoying their benefits. Discontinuous innovations, on the other hand, bring forth a new type of offering. The first cell phone, computer monitor, or printer would have been a discontinuous innovation since it introduced a completely new offering. In order to start using discontinuous innovations, someone had to create new infrastructure because the existing infrastructure could not support them. In such situations, society must wait for both the infrastructure and the associated products and services that make up the overall system to be set up (*e.g.*, a car without highways or a printer without software) – that is, without the infrastructure, the idea or product has little, if any, value. Faced with the novel nature of a discontinuous innovation, stakeholders can react in several ways and the technology-adoption life cycle tries to model the typical reactions.
- *Responses to discontinuous innovation (the technology-adoption life-cycle model)* – the technology-adoption life cycle, as identified in *The Gorilla Game: An Investor's Guide to Picking Winners in High Technology,* by Geoffrey A. Moore, Paul Johnson and Tom Kip-

pola, illustrates the five major customer reactions when faced with a discontinuous innovation based on their differing attitudes about new technology adoption. In effect, they are the basic strategies various constituents can use to respond to the potential benefits of the discontinuous innovation. Individuals may choose different strategies depending on their perception of the given technology (*i.e.*, different reactions to different technology) as illustrated in Figure 5.

Figure 5

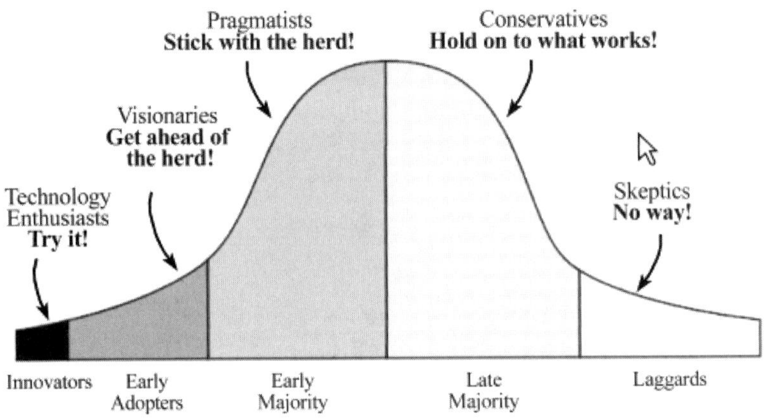

- Technology enthusiasts (innovators) – the technology enthusiast experiments with discontinuous innovations and believes in the innate value of technology. These could include those in research and development departments, independent developers, and general gadget lovers. This group helps a new technology obtain its initial visibility and credibility; however, they are not representative of the general market, and their enthusiasm is therefore not highly correlated with general market acceptance.

- Visionaries (early adopters) – visionaries want to build significant competitive advantages in order to obtain leadership in their industries. These are generally high-ranking executives who push through the development of the discontinuous innovation in order to differentiate their organizations from competitors or revolutionize an entire industry and obtain the associated advantages. Visionaries help the innovation gain visibility (especially in the business press);

however, their support for a new technology is not highly correlated with general market acceptance (as with technology enthusiasts). In many cases, the technology that they support becomes obsolete by the time it is mature enough to roll out to the market.

- Pragmatists (early majority) – pragmatists are referred to as the "herd" in that they recognize the value of the discontinuous innovation, but only after the standards and infrastructure are firmly established. Consequently, they adopt the new technology once "everyone else does." Once the pragmatists decide to adopt, they adopt simultaneously, creating a surge in growth – what is termed the "tornado".
- Conservatives (late majority) – conservatives are content with the status quo, irrespective of the superior benefits of the new technology. They adopt after the pragmatists and, therefore, are in a position to take advantage of the relative maturity of the "new" technology and negotiate more favorable terms and prices.
- Skeptics (laggards) – skeptics are part of the total population of potential customers who never adopt the new technology as they do not consider investments in new technology worthwhile from a cost-benefit perspective. The significance of this group is that they hinder adoption of new technology.
- The result – the interaction among the groups identified above leads to the development (or lack of development) of the market of a discontinuous technology.

- *Tying it all together – high-tech market development* – The development of high-tech markets can be represented by Figure 6, below.

Figure 6

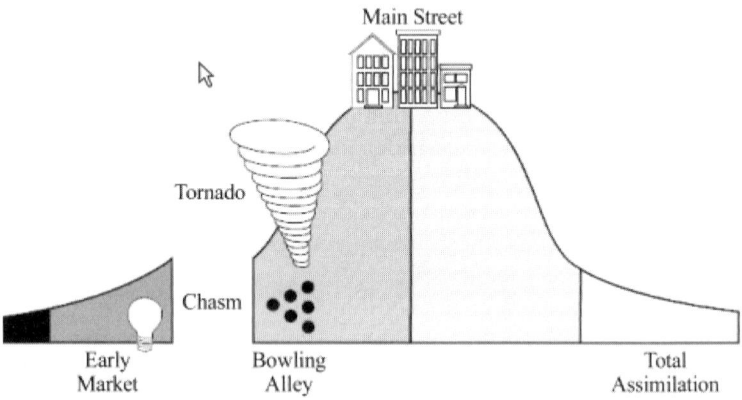

- The early market – the early market refers to the first commercial activities that occur in relation to the discontinuous innovation. Visionary customers, with the aid of technology enthusiasts, are the key champions in this stage as they seek to create a competitive advantage for their organizations. The visionaries, as mentioned earlier, are high-ranking executives – a requirement in order to drive the idea throughout the organization and gather the required corporate resources. In this phase of market development, the offering is built around individual customers rather than entire market segments; therefore, the customer list for these initiatives would typically not have more than one customer per market segment. The early market creates a spike in demand for professional services firms that have expertise in process re-engineering and systems integration. Thus, in the early market, professional services firms obtain the bulk of the profits. In this stage, the company introducing the new technology does not earn a significant amount of revenue or profit as it is generally a phase to test feasibility. Consequently, these companies want to move on to the mainstream market as soon as feasibility has been established. The chasm (see below) stands in the way of moving into the mainstream market.

- The chasm – due to the resistance between the visionaries and the pragmatists, there is a point in market development where no customer exists. This gap represents the chasm in market development when the visionaries are bringing out new ideas, but there is a lack of customers due to the pragmatists' not wanting to go against the norm. The longer it takes for the visionaries' idea to be adopted by the main market, the greater the risk that the visionaries will start losing interest in continuing to push forward as they start feeling the possible competitive advantage dwindling. If the ideas are too discontinuous for customers, they will never adopt the new technology. Consequently, these ideas never move across the chasm.

- The bowling alley – the bowling alley is made up of groups of pragmatist customers who are the first to adopt the discontinuous technology. These initial groups adopt ahead of the rest of the "herd" because they are facing fundamental issues in their operations and need a revolutionary solution to help them urgently overcome and fix them. Thus, they are effectively forced to turn to discontinuous innovations. However, these customers will only adopt the technology if the provider of the product can deliver a comprehensive solution to their problems. Consequently, the provider of the discontinuous innovation needs to provide an entire package of services to the specific customer. This will cause the provider to partner with other companies to obtain competencies not possessed in-house, which in turn creates a new value chain – a new marketplace that facilitates the discontinuous innovation. The reason why this stage is called the "bowling alley" is because the growth in this phase is through small groups or niches and not from mainstream acceptance. Some markets never make the leap out of the bowling alley into the mass market. Instead, they eventually run out of new niches and gravitate toward Main Street. In other cases, the technology transforms from a niche market to the mass market, which creates the tornado.

- The tornado – this represents a stage of hyper-growth, where there is mass market acceptance of the discontinuous technology. The result is a significant spike in demand and a resultant imbalance between supply and demand. The herd mentality that worked against the technology in the chasm is now working in its favor. As such, this increase in demand creates the tornado, or hyper-growth. Suppliers of the technology turn to building capacity to satisfy the demand. The firm that is first to market typically sets the standards for the new product category and thus reaps rewards from the established competitive advantage. The tornado typically lasts up to five years as the demand will continue until the supply-and-demand dynamics equalize and there is more competition among established firms. This leads to a phase termed Main Street.

- Main Street - Main Street is the assimilation and variation phase of the technology-adoption process. In this phase, the technology acts like other sectors in the economy. The focus in this phase is on creating small variations on established standards to enhance utility. The core activity in this phase is not innovation and creation but instead marketing. A relatively minor enhancement on the core technology for a specific market segment creates enhanced value. The focus for the players is on serving existing customers instead of acquiring new customers. Although incremental customers will add to the success, the majority of the profits are generated from the customers gained in the hyper-growth phase.

- Total assimilation - this is the end of the technology-adoption life cycle. However, it is important to keep in mind that this does not represent the end of the *product category*. Consequently, the illustration below on the product category life cycle is important to understand. The Main Street phase starts in the technology-adoption life cycle and extends into the rest of the product category's life. The tornado phase, therefore, takes on particular significance since it sets the foundation in terms of important factors such as market share that extend for the remaining period of the product category's life. At the end of the product category's life, there is often something else that takes its place (a displacing technology), which enters its own tornado, thus creating a new product-category life cycle based on a new discontinuous technology.

Figure 7

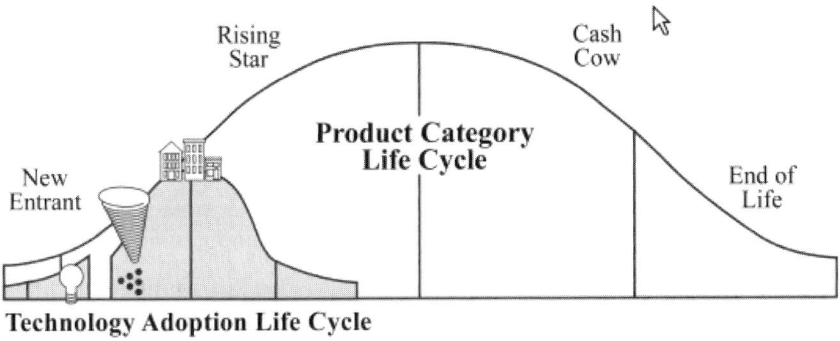

- *Practical uses in valuation* – understanding the concept of discontinuous innovation, typical responses to these innovations, the technology-adoption life cycle, high-tech market development overall, and the product-category life cycle provides important context during the valuation of any technology. As mentioned earlier, a critical task for the valuator is the assessment of risk and growth for the subject of the valuation. By understanding the type of technology that is being valued, where it fits in terms of the adoption process and product-category life cycle, the valuator can better estimate these important inputs. A company that has introduced a technology that has crossed the chasm and gained market acceptance has likely created a strong source of competitive advantage that would influence the future prospects of cash flows. If a technology has not achieved mass market acceptance, then there are very different growth prospects that can be expected for the company than for one that has technology with mass market acceptance. Each stage of market development has a fundamentally different risk and growth profile. As such, it is critical to understand the above topics in order to make risk and growth assessments.

Work Force

Technological advances in both research and development require significant creativity and insight. The quality of the research and development work force directly influences the stage of technological development. The better the work force, the better the chances of advancing to the next stage of development. Since creative workers generally thrive in a more open, unrestricted work environment that cultivates their creativity, they need to be managed in a special way. In addition, unrestrictive organizational culture and a high level of education, expertise, and competence of the work force improve the chances of the technology and/or technology-related company of advancing to the next stage of development.

Technology Attributes and Differentiating Factors

Accounting-based attributes often do not identify all of the future potential and/or benefits of a technology asset. Accordingly, an understanding of the key attributes and differentiating factors of a technology asset and/or technology-related company can help the valuator assess future benefits, growth potential, and risk. Below, we list a number of attributes, among others, that a valuator should consider in assessing the risk and/or growth potential of a technology asset and/or technology-related company:

- historical cost;
- product throughput;
- product quality, usefulness, robustness, and competitive advantage;
- complementary and new products;
- technological partnerships and strategic alliances;
- external technologies required for the subject technology to function effectively and the speed at which these technologies evolve;
- strategic options for the use and future development of the technology;
- ability to leverage the technology for use in other products;
- availability and extent of distribution channels;
- degree of reliance on the technology by customers;
- how often customers change technologies;
- customer satisfaction;
- environmental impact; and
- growth of the industries served by the technology, including the speed of innovation in these industries and the speed of innovation required by both customers and suppliers of technologies that are complementary to the subject.

Customer Base[17]

A company's customer base is one of the key determinants of long-term success. A growing customer base indicates successful scalability of the technology. Moreover, it is many times more expensive to attract a new customer

---

17 *Ibid.*

than it is to keep an existing one, so attracting and maintaining a large customer base is clearly a strong indicator for expanding sales of a given technology and/or technology-related company.

In terms of valuation, high-quality customers that generate a large number of transactions at relatively higher margins are more valuable than those that are less profitable or more costly to serve. Dividing the value of transactions by the number of transactions (average transaction value) allows an estimate of how much money a technology asset and/or technology-related company can potentially earn per transaction. In addition to growing the overall customer base, retaining key customers and selling them more services are important to every line of business (penetration). We note that losing a key customer can be devastating. As a result, a higher value is placed on companies that are able to secure positions with strategic customers or on companies that have a relatively small individual-customer risk because they have numerous customers.

Suppliers

With respect to supplier power, we would place more value on industry leaders that have a large number of weak suppliers because they can take advantage of opportunities to secure better terms from these suppliers, thereby enhancing profitability. Also, as mentioned earlier, the speed of innovation of suppliers of complementary technologies and/or products can have a direct impact on the timing and amount of the investment and research and development requirements of the subject technology asset and/or technology-related company.

Business Model

A thorough understanding of the business model is central in determining the potential value of a technology asset and/or technology-related company. Such an understanding assists the valuator in assessing the PFI for reasonableness and in determining the comparability of the subject with the companies, products, technologies, transactions, *etc.*, in the marketplace. The key factors associated with a successful business model include the following, among others:

- easy to understand and implement;
- scalable;
- ability to handle a large number of transactions;
- market share and/or market position;
- first-mover advantage; and
- adaptable to sectors with high-value transactions.

Perpetuity Assumption

In capitalized cash flow methodologies or the terminal value component of a discounted cash flow analysis, there is an implicit assumption that the cash flows will continue in perpetuity. This assumption may not hold in many cases for a technology asset and/or technology-related company. For example, if the company has one technology asset and the useful life of that asset is five years, the value analysis should only encompass the five years. The valuator must ensure that the perpetuity assumption, if used, is reasonably supported. On the other hand, a limited explicit projection period fails to capture the high growth often associated with early-stage technology companies. Many growth companies have traditionally been priced on the assumption that a premium growth rate can be maintained for longer than, say, a five-year explicit projection. This means that the growth rate in the terminal value calculation has to be a quasi-average of continuing high growth for a limited period plus the real long-term growth; in other words, it is almost impossible to estimate. For technology companies, it is not uncommon for more than 100 per cent of its value to be in the terminal value (*i.e.*, the cash flows in the explicit projection period are nominal and/or negative).

Intellectual Property Protection

Legal protection of the technology asset is also imperative to the differentiating factors of a technology asset and in preventing competitors from creating an alternative that will drive down the technology asset's value in the long term. As such, the perpetuity assumption should also be assessed in the context of a technology asset's strength of preservation and/or legal protection (*e.g.*, patents, copyrights, and trademarks), which help determine the likelihood that a company can preserve its competitive advantage and prevent competitors from adopting the technology's differentiating, unique factors over time.

Growth Rates[18]

While historical growth rates are often used as benchmarks for future growth rates in many businesses, they should be used with caution in valuations of high-growth technology-related companies. In these cases, significant growth in the earlier years is not indicative of long-term levels of growth. In such instances, it may be useful to use multi-period valuation models that

18 *Ibid.*

incorporate different levels of growth during the various stages of development and/or product life cycle.

The valuator should also focus on revenue growth rather than earnings growth to get a measure of both the pace of growth and the momentum that can be carried forward into future years. Revenue growth is less volatile than earnings growth and is much less likely to be swayed by accounting adjustments and choices.

Rather than looking at average growth over the last few years, the valuator should also look at growth in each year, which can provide information on how the growth is changing as the company becomes larger and can help in developing the PFI. In addition, the valuator should use historical growth rates as the basis for the PFI only in the near future (the next year or two), since technologies can change rapidly and can become inconsistent with the PFI. The valuator should also consider historical growth in the overall market and in other companies that are serving it. This information can be useful in deciding what the growth rates of the company being valued will converge on over time.

Growth is also determined by a number of subjective factors: the quality of management, the strength of a company's marketing, its capacity to form partnerships with other firms, and management's strategic vision, among many others.

Market Indications

It is often difficult to find truly comparable companies or transactions since the technology asset being valued often serves a distinct niche or may be in a breakthrough market. Consequently, care should be taken to understand the similarities and differences between any companies or transactions being considered as comparables in order to make the appropriate assumptions. Although this is important in situations when adopting a market approach, it is particularly important with technology companies as the underlying technology asset (in most cases a significant value driver) is often very unique and thus broad industry comparables are not necessarily meaningful for comparative purposes. Furthermore, the valuator should consider the market potential and market dynamics associated with the technology asset and/or the technology-related company as follows:

- *Market potential* – if the purpose of a technology asset is to generate sales, then the total market potential serves as a gauge of the maximum level of sales that the technology asset can generate. An innovative technology demanded by only a few customers is relatively less valuable than a technology with the same profitability but demanded by a larger customer base.

- *Market dynamics* – the fundamental attributes of the market in which the technology asset is intended to be sold is critical in determining its value. A technology that will be useful to a high-growth market will be in much greater demand than in a lower-growth market. The higher the level of competition, the lower the potential to realize first-to-market price premiums.

Financial Analysis and Related Considerations

In general, the trends of the subject business must be analyzed with respect to key measures. The key measures can be linked directly to those that provide insight into the key value driver areas for the specific company of interest. When analyzing the historical financial statements and the PFI of a technology-related company, specific considerations that are often useful include the following:[19]

- *Revenue* – the valuator should perform an assessment of the key assumptions related to revenue from current products and revenue that is expected to result from both existing technology assets and future technology projects, including the projected number of units expected to be sold, projected selling prices throughout the selling period, projected market penetration, and projected market share. Year-over-year unit growth (or decline) rates over the product(s) life cycle(s) (*i.e.*, the period of years over which revenue is expected to be received for a given technology) and the reasonableness of average per-unit selling prices during the period should be considered by the valuator, giving due consideration to expected competitors' reactions, anticipated technological developments, and historical trends. Once these key assumptions relating to revenue are understood by the valuator, the valuator should obtain an appropriate amount of support for material assumptions.
- *Costs of sales* – the valuator should understand the difference between company-wide costs of sales and specific product-by-product costs of sales, which may change over a product's life cycle and will likely differ from product to product. The valuator should also compare the trend of costs of sales for prior product offerings with those contained in the PFI.

---

19 Based on information obtained from, among other sources, (i) AICPA IPR&D Practice Aid; and (ii) IVSC January 2009 exposure drafts on the valuation of intangible assets and the valuation of intangible assets for IFRS reporting purposes.

- *Research and development expenditures* – the level of these expenditures relative to sales or on an absolute basis (*i.e.*, if there are no sales) is an important indicator for companies that need to innovate in order to remain competitive. In addition, there are research and development costs that can be viewed as capital investments and, for some, as sustaining in nature; therefore, when valuing existing technology, the valuator must ensure that only sustaining costs are included in cash flows if the revenues exclude future technology revenues.
- *Sales and marketing expenditures* – sales and marketing is an important factor in gaining adoption of a new technology or in increasing market share. Sales and marketing effectiveness can be assessed by measuring sales and marketing expenses relative to new sales. Product-launch costs should be included in the PFI if product development activities are expected to lead to the introduction of new product offerings. Product-launch costs are commonly incurred during the introduction of new product offerings and can differ dramatically from routine sales and marketing expenses. Objective information can often be obtained from the results of previously launched product offerings or from industry and market participant data.
- *General and administrative expenses* – historical financial data of the technology and/or technology-related company is a common source of objective information to support the assumptions in the PFI regarding general and administrative expenses (as well as to support the other assumptions in the PFI). Industry data, data from public filings of market participants, and reports generated by market research firms and industry analysts may also be sources of objective information to support general and administrative expense assumptions in the PFI (again, as well as to support the other assumptions in the PFI).
- *Cash burn rate* – this is the amount of cash the company consumes on a periodic basis. This can be compared with the level of anticipated cash flow generation and/or financing in order to determine if the company will be facing liquidity problems in the future.

In addition to the above, for an asset to possess value, it must generate attractive profit margins. Assets that generate negative or low returns (*i.e.*, returns below the cost of capital) will have no value when future cash flows are present-valued.

Economic Useful Life and Technical Obsolescence

Technology advances at a very fast pace in many industries, with today's promising technology often becoming obsolete tomorrow. In 1965, Gordon Moore, co-founder of Intel Corporation, forecast that computing power would double every 18 months to two years. With this in mind, a technology asset's value will depend to a large extent on the amount of time required to displace it with improved or alternative technologies. If a valuator uses an income approach to valuation, the period covered by the PFI will reflect this amount of time. Consequently, technological obsolescence drives the period over which the technology asset's profitability can be maintained.

The valuator should also consider the following in assessing the economic useful life (*i.e.*, the technology migration curve) of a technology asset:

- management and/or the company's history of innovation; and
- degree of competition and speed of innovation in the industry.

Furthermore, the economic useful life should be determined for every technology and sub-technology that needs to be valued to help ensure that the relevant attributes are appropriately captured in the valuation (*e.g.*, technology migration, growth, and risk).

Practice Tip

To simplify complications is, in all branches of knowledge, the first essential of success.

H.T. Buckle

Technology Value Risk Factors

Assessing value drivers forms part of the overall qualitative assessment of value. Another qualitative consideration is the evaluation of the key risk factors facing the technology asset and/or technology-related company of interest (*i.e.*, in the context of certain key risk considerations).

Stage of Development[20]

In considering the stages of development, which were discussed in detail in Section 5, Technology-Related Company and Asset Value Drivers, two stud-

20 The section includes information obtained from, among other sources, the AICPA IPR&D Practice Aid.

ies, also referenced in the AICPA IPR&D Practice Aid, provide guidance related to the rates of return commanded by venture capital investors at various stages of an entity's development. A summary of these rates of return is set forth in Table 2.

Table 2

Stage of Development	Plummer[1]	Scherlis and Sahlman[2]
Start-up	50%-70%	50%-70%
First Stage (Early Development)	40%-60%	40%-60%
Second Stage (Expansion)	35%-50%	30%-50%
Bridge/IPO	25%-35%	20%-35%

[1] J.L. Plummer, *QED Report on Venture Capital Financial Analysis* (Palo Alto: QED Research, Inc., 1987).

[2] W.A. Sahlman & D.R. Scherlis, *A Method for Valuing High-Risk, Long Term Investments: The "Venture Capital Method"* (Boston: Harvard Business School Publishing, 1987).

Furthermore, start-up stage investments are typically made in companies that are less than one year old. The venture funding is used primarily for product development, prototype testing, and test marketing. Early-development investments are made in companies that have developed prototypes that appear viable and for which further technical risk is deemed minimal, although commercial risk may be significant. Companies in the expansion stage have usually shipped some product to customers (including beta versions). Bridge/IPO financing covers such activities as pilot plant construction, production design and testing, and bridge financing in anticipation of a later IPO.

In developing a range of discount rates to be used in valuing an early-stage technology or under the traditional approach (see footnote 7), the rate of return expected for start-up investments could be used as the upper boundary for the selection of a discount rate. Once an early-stage technology is complete, a premium over the WACC observable for young, single-product companies in the industry segment of the early-stage technology being valued could be used to approximate a market discount rate for technologies with similar risks. For practical purposes, the use of the WACC without the premium may be a reasonable approach. These rates would serve as the lower boundary for discount rates used for completed technologies (*i.e.*, existing technology). However, young, single-product companies in the same industry segment are more likely to exhibit risk characteristics similar to completed technologies. Moreover, early-stage technologies should be thought of as an early-stage technology-related company, even if it is actually being conducted by an established or diversified entity.

Therefore, the best way to determine an appropriate discount rate for assets to be used in early-stage technology-related activities, including specific technology projects, would be to determine the WACC of several early-stage entities that intend to provide the same or similar products or services. In our view, it may be inappropriate to use the WACC of a large or diversified company in valuing early-stage technologies because the goal of valuation is to approximate the rates of returns required by market participants on the early-stage technology asset being valued. Entities whose value is based partially on such items as established brand names, significant financial resources, or diversified (and, therefore, less risky) product lines will generally have a lower WACC, reflecting these relatively less risky operations.

Furthermore, the expected behavior of discount rates over the life of an early-stage technology and the presumed lower boundary from which discount rates may be selected for young, single-product companies are illustrated in Figure 8.

Figure 8

Discount Rates Used to Value Early-Stage Technology

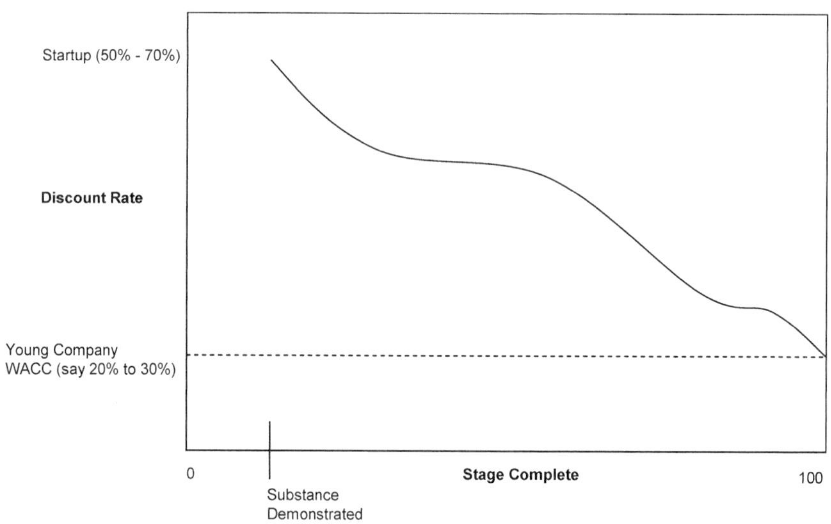

As progress toward completion is made, we would expect discount rates to behave in a step fashion, reflecting the reduction of risk as progress is achieved. That is, even though development activities may be taking place, technological or engineering risk may not be reduced until a particular hurdle has been accomplished. A study referenced by Richard Razgaitis of the approximate values of risk-adjusted hurdle rates used in licence negotiations, based on various other characterizations of risk, is summarized in Table 3.

Table 3

Approximate Values of Risk-Adjusted Hurdle Rate Used in License Negotiations	
Characterization of Risk	**Approximate Rate Adjusted Hurdle Rate (RAHR)**
Risk-free, such as building a duplicate plant to make more of a currently made and sold product in response to presently high demand	Approximates the corporate rate of borrowing, which can be in the range of 10% to 18%
Very low risk, such as incorporating a new but well-understood technology into making a product presently made and sold in response to existing demand	15% to 20%; discernibly above the corporation's goals for return on investment to its shareholders
Low risk, such as making a product with new features using well-understood technology for a presently served and understood customer segment with evidence of demand for such features	20% to 30%
Moderate risk, such as making a new product using well-understood technology for a customer segment presently served by other products made by the corporation and with evidence of demand for such a new product	25% to 35%
High risk, such as making a new product using a not well-understood technology and marketing it to an existing segment or a well-understood technology to a new market segment	30% to 40%

Approximate Values of Risk-Adjusted Hurdle Rate Used in License Negotiations	
Characterization of Risk	**Approximate Rate Adjusted Hurdle Rate (RAHR)**
Very high risk, such as making a new product with new technology to a new segment	35 to 45%
Extremely high risk (sometimes known as "wildcatting," borrowing an expression from the oil exploration industry), such as creating a start-up company to go into the business of making a product not presently sold or even known to exist using unproven technologies	50% to 70%, or even higher
Source: R. Razgaitis, *Valuation and Pricing of Technology-Based Intellectual Property* (New Jersey: John Wiley & Sons, Inc., 2003).	

Based on the rates of return observed for the various characterizations of risk above, as well as for the various stages of development and/or the product life cycle, we found that the use of appropriate rates of return based on the relevant stage(s) of completion and/or stage(s) of the product life cycle is critical. We also note that where the PFI has been probability-adjusted and/or the cash flow risks are explicitly reflected in the cash flow model, the required rates of return should also be adjusted to ensure consistency (*e.g.*, it may be appropriate to use a risk-free discount rate, such as government bonds with maturity dates reflecting the life of the technology asset and/or technology-related company in such instances). However, it would be rare for all risks to be eliminated in the PFI, and, therefore, most investors in a technology asset would expect a return above that of risk-free government bonds.[21]

Early-stage technologies can also be viewed as progressing through two distinct phases (*i.e.*, the use-of-funds phase and the generation-of-funds phase), with each having its own risks (see Figure 9, below).

21 The determination of such a discount rate should, at the very least, include the consideration of non-performance risk (*i.e.*, credit risk), uncertainty risk (*i.e.*, default risk and collateral value risk), and any necessary liquidity premiums.

Figure 9

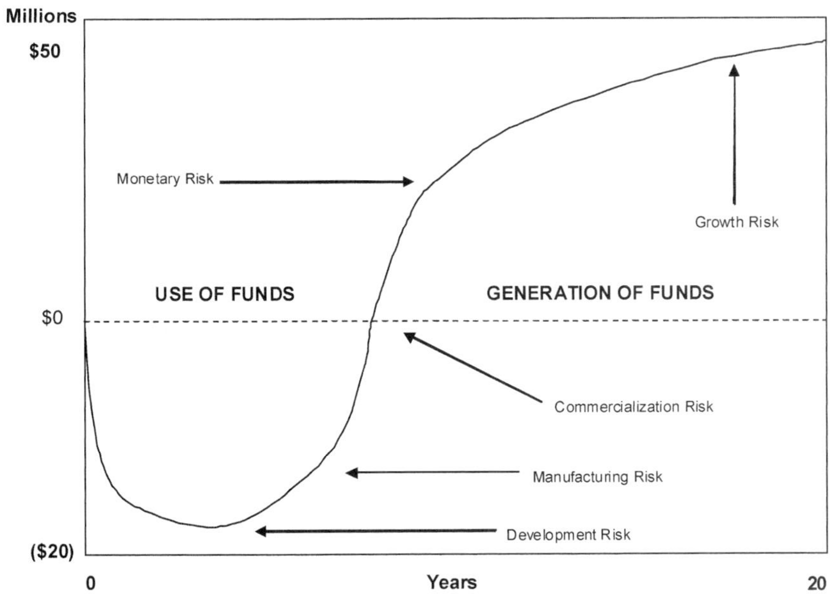

The use-of-funds phase includes development, manufacturing, and marketing risks before eventually reaching commercialization, which typically results in an initial deficit position. While the generation-of-funds phase generally includes monetary and growth risk, this is where the real profits from the technology are generated. These risks must individually and collectively be assessed in arriving at the appropriate probability and/or discount rate adjustments discussed earlier.

Other considerations in selecting rates of return for technology assets and/or for technology-related companies include the following, among others:

- probability of successful completion at each stage of development for each of the company's technologies and/or sub-technologies;
- length of time to complete each stage of development for each of the company's technologies and/or sub-technologies;
- remaining technological, engineering, or regulatory risks to be overcome;
- share of the market and market growth;
- nature of products, processes, and/or services offered;
- growth potential of the company and each of the key technologies and/or sub-technologies;
- industry segment (growth and trends);

- history of the company and/or experience of management in completing successful projects, technology and future enhancements, longevity of products, and retention of competitive advantage; and
- competitive position (current and required to make the technology successful).

Research and Development Risks

As mentioned earlier, the stage of development is a key driver of the value of a technology asset, and research and development activities are a key influence in determining the stage of development. The following are important considerations associated with the assessment of research and development risks:

- *Sufficiency* – there is a risk that the research and development conducted is not sufficient. This will lead to problems once commercialization or use (*i.e.*, for enabler-related technology) begins and end users find problems with the product. Developing a technology that will meet the end user's functionality requirements is essential. The research and development should also incorporate features that anticipate and address manufacturing issues.
- *Cost of completion* – the research and development may require so much time and money that the cost does not justify completing the technology development.
- *Time required to complete* – if remaining development requires too much time, competitors may produce and bring to market an alternative technology first.

As discussed earlier, we also note that rates of return become lower as a technology asset and/or technology-related company progresses through the stages of development (*i.e.*, throughout the product life cycle).

Manufacturing Risks

The following risks are applicable to technology assets and/or technology-related companies that involve manufacturing:

- *Quality control* – technology assets are often critical to the end use. If quality control falls short in manufacturing the asset, even the best-designed technology will ultimately fail in its end use.
- *Efficiency* – without an efficient manufacturing process, the best-

designed technology will be too expensive for the end user's purposes.

- *Effectiveness* – to satisfy demand, the manufacturing process must execute the design specifications effectively and in the required volumes.
- *Environmental issues* – if by-products of the manufacturing process cannot be recycled or disposed of cost-efficiently, the manufacturing costs will be prohibitively expensive to the end user.
- *Suppliers* – as mentioned earlier, industry leaders that have a large number of weak suppliers have a lower level of risk because they can take advantage of opportunities to secure better terms from these suppliers, thereby enhancing profitability.

To make a meaningful relative assessment, the valuator should measure these risks in relation to the competition. We also note that insufficient demand for the manufactured technology will compromise the ultimate value of the asset. The company must take effective marketing steps to develop interest in the target market and to gauge demand for the purposes of planning manufacturing procedures. Since marketing often distinguishes one manufacturer from another, the valuator should also assess marketing effectiveness relative to the competition.

Legal Risks

The following risks are applicable to technology assets in relation to legal issues:

- *Restrictions* – government laws and regulations may restrict the use of certain technologies, thus impeding the commercialization of a given technology. The valuator should assess the risk of negative government sentiment (if any) toward the subject technology.
- *Intellectual property* – the enforceability of the patents used to protect the technology's competitive advantage influences competitive risk.

Competitive

The valuator should assess all qualitative factors relative to similar technologies from current or potential competitors. If these factors fall short of the level achieved by competitors, the technology's maximum value cannot exceed that of the competing technology and will likely be less.

Management

The ability of management to execute and manage the above risks is an overarching risk. If management is incapable of dealing with the above risks, the venture will be unsuccessful. Investor perception of management's vision, effectiveness, competence, credibility, and ability to execute are also important factors to consider when valuing technology assets and technology-related companies.

Examples of Technology Asset Valuations[22]

Common Technology Asset Categories

As discussed earlier, the general technology asset categories include the following:

- existing technology (*i.e.*, core technology and/or developed technology);
- in-process research and development technology (*i.e.*, IPR&D technology); and
- internally developed software.

In the following pages, we present examples of common valuation methodologies used to value each of the above technology asset categories. It is important to note that the methodologies used in the examples represent only one of a number of potential ways of valuing the given technology assets. The selection of the most appropriate methodology depends on a number of factors such as the specific asset in question, the particular situation, and the quality of information available.

Relief-from-Royalty Method

Example: Valuation of Existing Technology

A number of income-based approaches are available to establish existing technology value conclusions, which include the relief-from-royalty method and various profitability-based methods. Using income-based approaches, the valuator projects the expected economic benefits associated with asset ownership to determine the value of the existing technology. In these ap-

22 Based on information obtained from, among other sources, (i) AICPA IPR&D Practice Aid; (ii) IVSC January 2009 exposure drafts on the valuation of intangible assets and the valuation of intangible assets for IFRS reporting purposes; and (iii) CICBV Valuation for Financial Reporting course.

proaches, the valuator considers the duration and timing of the economic benefits attributable to the existing technology, as well as the associated risk characteristics.

The relief-from-royalty method is a form of the income-based approach. It has gained wide acceptance in the valuation of existing technology such as patents, proprietary technology, licences, trade names, and other intellectual property, but it is generally considered to be inappropriate for the valuation of IPR&D technology.

The relief-from-royalty method, which is a form of discounted cash flow analysis, is based on the premise that a technology asset is worth the net present value of the future expected foregone royalties paid due to the ownership of the underlying IPR&D technology asset. Application of this method involves a few key assumptions, which are extremely subjective. Being direct, it is an ideal approach to avoid the possible double-counting that might otherwise exist in other valuation approaches (*e.g.*, the simultaneous valuation of customer contracts and technology using the multi-period excess earnings method, without making the appropriate adjustments and/or considerations).

Based on the factors noted above, we have provided in Schedule 1 an example of the relief-from-royalty method. In this example, existing technology is being valued, which was assumed to be used to provide software as a service to the company's customers, helping the company generate revenues. Each of the key factors we considered is discussed in further detail below.

Revenues

In applying the relief-from-royalty method, similar to the multi-period excess earnings method, the valuator must determine an appropriate revenue or earnings stream to the royalty to be applied. As discussed earlier, the valuator must have a thorough understanding of the technology asset being valued and be able to relate this understanding to the future revenues expected to be generated by the technology asset. Often, the overall business cash flows, separated into principal product and/or technology groupings, are used as the starting point.

Technology Migration (Remaining Useful Life)

In our example, we have assumed that the existing technology will have a remaining useful life of 10 years and will have an annual technology migration rate of 10 per cent (the first year of the example includes an adjustment for mid-year technology migration), and, therefore, the after-tax royalty streams end after 10 years of the discrete cash flow period. The tax amortization benefit is added to the net present value calculation to arrive at an indication of value.

Selection of the Royalty Rate

We then assumed an arm's-length royalty rate to apply to the above-noted revenues in order to calculate royalty cash flows. The selection of the royalty rate is not unlike determining an appropriate discount rate in the sense that several factors are often considered in this exercise, many requiring judgment. Various database resources exist to benchmark and collect data on licensing transactions. In reviewing this data, the valuator must be aware of the comparability of the underlying data and give consideration to various factors (a number of relevant factors to consider in the selection of royalty rates were discussed in Section 4, Valuation Approaches). Moreover, the royalty rate represents the technology asset's contribution to cash flows or, in other words, the importance of the technology asset to the revenue- and earnings-generating ability of the business. In this regard, the more important these factors are to the technology asset, the greater one would expect the royalty rate to be. When performing royalty cash flow calculations, maintenance and/or other support costs must be treated consistently. Thus, if the licensor is responsible for maintenance costs (*e.g.*, advertising or maintenance research and development), the royalty rate, as well as the royalty rate cash flows, should reflect this. Alternatively, if maintenance costs are not included (or assumed) in the royalty rate, maintenance costs should be excluded from the royalty cash flows. Similarly, tax must be treated consistently in the royalty cash flows.

Reasonableness checks should also be performed with respect to the selected royalty rate (*e.g.*, the total profit at a particular level, such as gross or operating profit, and how much of that profit would accrue to each of the licensee and licensor if a selected royalty rate was used in the determination of the licence fee). The reasonableness of such a profit split can then be reviewed for reasonableness (see the Section 7, Examples of Technology Asset Valuations, for more on the 25 Per Cent Rule).

Once the net pre-tax royalties have been determined, income taxes should be deducted at rates consistent with those for other market participants.

In our example, revenues for the overall business have been used as the basis upon which we applied the royalty. A pre-tax royalty rate of eight per cent was then applied to the revenues of the overall business. Taxes were then deducted (we assumed an after-tax royalty rate of 4.8 per cent to account for taxes at a rate of 40 per cent) to arrive at after-tax royalty cash flows.

Selection of the Discount Rate

The net present value of the after-tax royalties was determined using a discount rate that we assumed was commensurate with the risk of achieving those cash flows. Below we discuss some additional considerations in selecting a reasonable discount rate.

With respect to individual assets, the risk level generally increases from low for monetary assets of a current nature (*e.g.*, cash and cash equivalents, accounts receivable, and inventory) to moderate for long-term tangible assets (*e.g.*, capital assets) and high for intangible assets (*e.g.*, technology, brands, and customers). See Figure 10, below, for an illustration of these relationships.

Figure 10

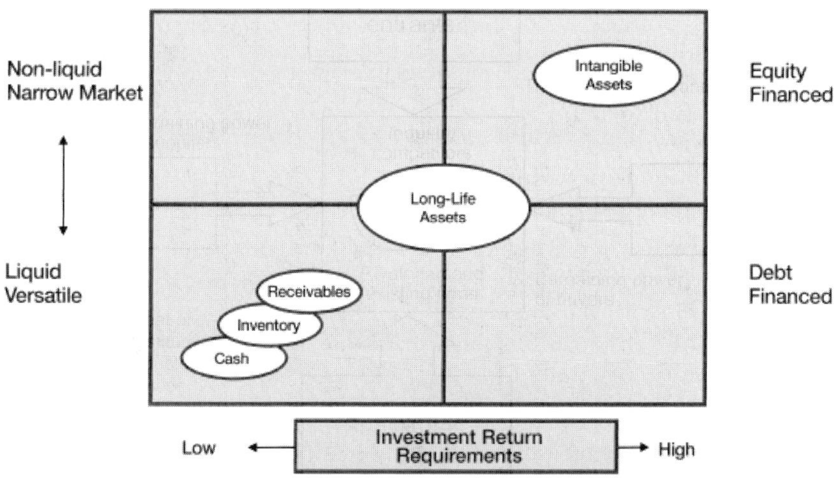

As an example of the risk/reward relationship, consider the required returns on three types of assets:

- working capital;
- existing technology; and
- goodwill.

All other things being equal, one would expect that given the liquid nature of working capital, its required returns would be lower than for existing technology and goodwill. For existing technology, these returns (also known as discount rates) would typically be lower than for goodwill given their identifiable nature, whereas goodwill represents assets that inherently cannot be specifically identified.

Potential Tax Amortization Benefit

The last step in the relief-from-royalty method is the consideration of the potential tax benefits associated with the amortization of the existing technology asset for income tax purposes. This benefit is added on the premise that a potential purchaser acquiring the technology asset on a stand-alone basis would be willing to pay an additional amount that reflects the net present value of the tax amortization benefit of the asset over its tax life (TL). In cases where there is a business combination, the tax amortization benefit is included regardless of the form of the transaction (*i.e.*, irrespective of whether it was an asset deal or a share deal). In addition, the tax amortization benefit is typically determined using the income tax regulations in the jurisdiction in which the technology asset is domiciled.

Our discounted cash flow analysis indicates a \$2.715 million value before the consideration of the tax amortization benefit. The existing technology asset value of \$2.715 million before amortization considerations was based on a 25 per cent discount rate, a 40 per cent tax rate, and a tax amortization life of 15 years. The calculation of asset value (AV) begins with the calculation of the mid-period annuity discount factor (ADF).

$$\begin{aligned} \text{ADF} &= \frac{((1-(1+r)^{-TL})(1+r)^{0.5})}{r} \\ &= \frac{((1-(1.25)^{-15})(1.25)^{0.5})}{0.25} \\ &= 4.31 \end{aligned}$$

After the annuity discount factor is calculated, the asset value is determined according to the previously derived mathematical relationship as follows:

$$\text{AV} = \text{PAV}/(1 - t(\text{ADF})/\text{TL})$$

If the amortization factor (AM Factor) is defined according to the following relationship:

$$\text{AM Factor} = (1/(1 - t(\text{ADF})/\text{TL}))$$

then the asset value is calculated as follows:

$$\begin{aligned} \text{AV} &= \text{PAV} * \text{AM Factor} \\ &= \$2{,}715{,}000*(1.130) \\ &= \$3{,}069{,}000 \end{aligned}$$

With the tax amortization benefit, the existing technology asset value is indicated to be $3.069 million. The tax amortization benefit in our example thus reflects an approximately 13 per cent increase beyond the pre-amortization value for the existing technology asset value. Ignoring the tax amortization benefit in applying the income approach will understate the intangible asset value.

Potential Issues

The valuator must ensure that any market-based data used in the royalty rate selection is in fact comparable. In practice, finding such data can be difficult and placing undue reliance on this data will lead to unreasonable results. As discussed earlier, a clear understanding of, among other factors, the industry, the company, and the technology will assist the valuator in assessing the reasonableness of the royalty rate and the value conclusion.

While a commonly used tool is the 25 Per Cent Rule, as well as other high-level criteria, not all technology assets for which royalties can be assessed will fall into general ranges of operating margins. Blindly using the 25 Per Cent Rule and other high-level criteria to value a technology asset may cause the valuator to completely ignore the fundamentals of the asset and business in question.

Also relevant to technology assets is that they will have a finite life in their current state. In other words, if a technology is not constantly upgraded and/or refreshed, it will quickly lose relevance in the marketplace and revenues will decline. As a result, the application of the relief-from-royalty method must also consider the economic life of the technology asset.

Multi-Period Excess Earnings Method

Example: Valuation of In-Process Research and Development Technology

It is common for technology assets, including IPR&D technology, to be valued using the multi-period excess earnings method.[23] As discussed earlier, the multi-period excess earnings method involves several steps. The

---

23 The multi-period excess earnings approach is often suitable in the following situations: (i) the intangible in question is a key driver of the business's cash flow; (ii) the contribution of the intangible asset to the business value cannot be directly measured in other ways (*e.g.*, a key piece of intellectual property with no comparables with which to perform a relief-from-royalty analysis); (iii) information with respect to existing market conditions is available; and (iv) historical and projected operating results are available and that information can be used to analyze and/or develop the project cash flows in a reasonable manner.

first is to prepare projected future cash flows attributable to the IPR&D technology. In many instances, the PFI for the IPR&D technology will be a by-product of (or at least directly related to) the PFI of the overall business operations. Ideally, the PFI for the overall business operations will have been prepared either in the normal course of business or by an acquiring company (*i.e.*, where an acquisition has occurred).

In using the PFI for the overall business operations as the starting point for the derivation of the PFI for the IPR&D technology, the valuator may need to adjust the cash flows for some or all of the following:

- The valuator should ensure that the duration of the revenue and cash flow projections is consistent with the time frame over which the IPR&D technology that existed at the valuation date is expected to contribute to the projected cash flows of the business. For example, assumptions with respect to costs to complete and technology migration may need to be factored into the valuation. In addition, for IPR&D technology, the future cash flows may need to be adjusted for the increasing and/or declining contribution that the IPR&D technology will have over time. It is also possible that the appropriate cash flow duration will extend beyond the discrete cash flow period contained in the PFI obtained and/or developed during the information-gathering process. In these instances, the PFI must be extended using assumptions that are appropriate based on the given facts and circumstances.
- Include only those projected revenues that are generated directly from the use of the IPR&D technology. For example, if valuing an IPR&D technology, all of the products and services sold by the company may not contain the IPR&D technology, nor would ownership of the IPR&D technology be required to generate all revenues.
- Operating expenses should either be increased or decreased to reflect their use in deriving cash flows from the IPR&D technology (*e.g.*, costs to complete the IPR&D project, appropriate levels of research and development costs allocated to the IPR&D technology, new product development costs, and sales and marketing costs to help achieve the projected level of IPR&D technology revenues).
- Determine taxes on income generated by the IPR&D technology.
- Apply contributory asset charges for the use of other assets that assist in the generation of the IPR&D technology's cash flows.
- Determine the present value of the IPR&D technology excess earnings (*i.e.*, the after-tax cash flows attributable to the IPR&D technology) using an appropriate discount rate.
- Include a tax amortization benefit, which represents the income

shield attributable to the amortization of the IPR&D technology's value over its tax life. When combined with the present value of the cash flows, it forms part of the technology asset value.

- Evaluate the overall reasonableness of the IPR&D technology's value relative to the other operating net assets of the company and the overall value of the business operations.

Based on the factors above, we have provided an example of a valuation of an IPR&D technology asset using the multi-period excess earnings method in Schedules 2a and 2b. The key factors we considered are discussed in further detail below.

Technology Migration

As future versions of technology are released, the revenue generated by the future technology will also be attributable to the research and development that is undertaken in the future (referred to as future research and development or future technology). Since projected future revenues are based on the sale of technology, there is often a direct correlation between a technology project and a new technology offering. When the subcomponents of a company's technology are used by many product offerings or when the subcomponents will be used over numerous generations of technology offerings, the valuator should go through a process of assigning a portion of the revenue stream from each technology offering to the subcomponents. The allocation of the cash flows to the subcomponents should also consider the relative contribution of existing technology, IPR&D technology (*i.e.*, existing IPR&D projects), and future technology over successive releases of the technology that incorporate these subcomponents (the process of allocating the cash flows is referred to as technology migration). The contribution of each subcomponent of technology will be based on the specific facts and circumstances.

In Schedule 2a, we allocated the PFI for total technology revenues to the various subcomponents of the company's technology (*i.e.*, existing technology, IPR&D technology, and future technology) and, as such, a migration curve was effectively applied to the prospective revenue streams. The concept of technology migration also assumes the re-use of existing technology and/or IPR&D technology from one generation of a product to the next, where it is assumed some components of the existing technology and/or IPR&D technology will be used in future versions of the company's technology, the use of which, in most instances, will gradually decline over time (*i.e.*, over time, existing technology and/or IPR&D technology will be replaced and/or diluted by future technology and/or obsolescence).

We note that the key factors that influence technology migration include the following, among others (each of these factors should be considered for each of the company's technologies, sub-technologies, and their respective subcomponents):

- historical cost;
- date the development began and/or will be completed;
- number of lines of code added and/or changed (or planned to be added and/or changed);
- the functionality of the products that were added and/or changed (or planned to be added and/or changed);
- uniqueness of the technology and whether alternative solutions are available in the marketplace (or will be available);
- relative complexity of technical issues addressed and resolved by the technology;
- whether the technology is (or could be) protected by patents;
- difficulty of designing around the patented technology;
- whether the technology allows the company to charge premium prices for the product;
- economic useful life;
- the company's track record in developing new technology;
- strategic plans, research and development road maps, and allocation of resources (*i.e.*, management commitment);
- required speed of innovation in the industry;
- complementary technologies and their speed of innovation;
- experience of research and development and ability to create innovative products and designs;
- research and development tax incentives that influence the degree of expenditures in this area;
- percentage of success at each stage of development;
- degree of competition in the industry;
- customer requirements and demands;
- economic conditions;
- political influences; and
- professional judgment.

The valuator should also obtain support for the allocations assumed in determining the technology migration assumptions based on interviews with management from various departments of the company, including personnel from research and development, sales and marketing, finance, and operations. External verification can be obtained through the review of industry data and the valuator's experience in valuing similar companies and/or technologies.

Schedules 2a and 2b illustrate the contribution of the IPR&D technology to the projected revenues included in the PFI (in other words, the technology mitigation over the projection period). In year 1, all revenues were attributed to existing technology since the IPR&D technology was assumed to be incomplete, whereas in year 2, the year in which the IPR&D technology was assumed to be completed and available for sale, a portion of the projected revenues was attributed to the IPR&D technology. In year 3, the contribution of the IPR&D technology as a percentage of total revenues increased as the IPR&D was commercialized, and then the contribution decreased from year 4 to year 6 as existing technology and IPR&D technology revenues were gradually replaced by future technology revenues.

We note that the technology mitigation discussion above can be applied to the valuation of existing technology under both the relief-from-royalty method and the multi-period excess earnings method.

IPR&D Technology Revenues and Costs

Based on the technology migration assumptions discussed earlier, Figure 11 illustrates the allocation and/or contribution of the technology subcomponents to projected revenues included in the PFI. A typical migration curve results in an allocation (or transition) of revenue over time from existing and/or IPR&D technology revenues to future technology revenues as new technologies are created and/or as existing and/or IPR&D technologies are diluted over time due to ongoing changes, additions, deletions, new innovations, and/or obsolescence.

Figure 11

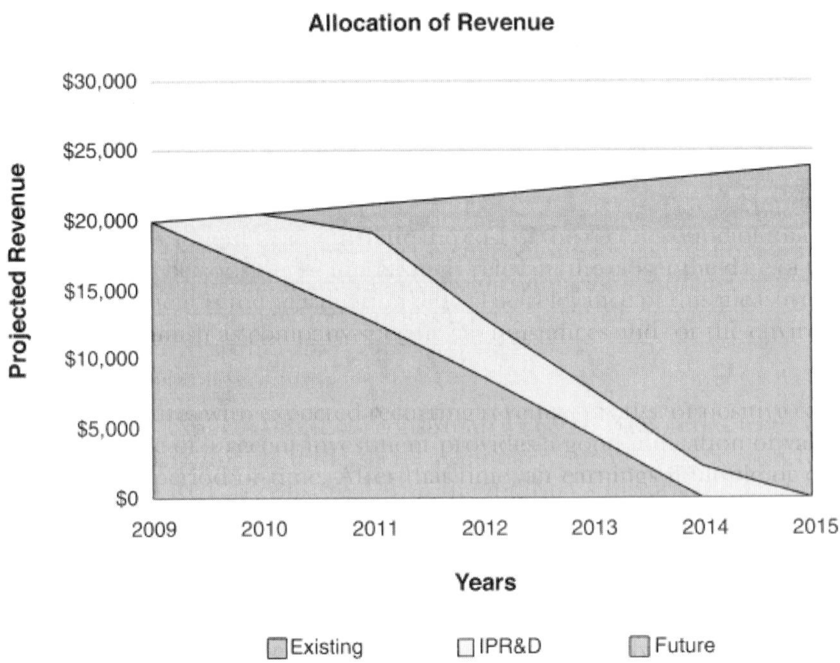

The allocation of revenue to the subcomponents (***i.e.***, technology migration) may be reflected in the PFI as follows:

- adjustments to revenues and costs to eliminate everything but revenues and costs associated with existing technology, IPR&D technology, and future technology (sometimes referred to as revenue splitting); or
- contributory asset charges related to existing technology (charges that decrease over time) and future technology (charges that increase over time); or
- a combination of the above.

It is important to note that, in a valuation model that apportions revenues or profits, care must be taken to ensure that proper consideration is given to all existing technology and IPR&D technology. In addition, the valuator may need to ensure that the total revenue stream is appropriately separated between technology and other identifiable intangibles, such as customer relationships. In this regard, while we have assumed that all of the revenues in our example are attributable to technology, in practice, customer relationships (if they exist) must also be identified and valued, which may require a further separation of the total revenue stream. We note that the valuation of customer relationships is beyond the scope of this chapter; however, irrespective of how a particular transaction may be structured (*e.g.*, a transaction may have been structured as an asset deal to specifically acquire technology), customer relationships may exist within the total revenue stream that is being valued and, as such, the valuator may need to value both the technology and customer relationship intangibles to ensure that the conclusions are both appropriate and reasonable.

Expenses to be attributed to the IPR&D technology should include costs of sales, selling and marketing expenses, general and administrative expenses, maintenance research and development costs (including ongoing charges to debug and/or maintain technology, once completed), costs to complete the IPR&D technology, any one-time rollout or launch costs, contributory asset charges, and income taxes. Unrelated expenses, including costs of financing, should not be deducted in arriving at after-tax cash flows. All levels of expenses should be reflective of what would be experienced by market participants.

In many industries, technical support is provided as part of product sales or in exchange for product maintenance fees. To the extent that such fee revenues are appropriately excluded from the projected cash flows attributable to the IPR&D technology, it would be inappropriate for the associated expense to be included in the projected cash flows. If, however, such technical services are incapable of being unbundled from the sale of a product employing the IPR&D technology, the appropriate level of expenses should be reflected in the PFI.

Research and development expenses attributable to the IPR&D technology typically include significant up-front expenses related to costs to complete, as well as ongoing expenses that may be incurred by the research and development staff subsequent to project completion that may relate to maintenance, debugging, post-market approval surveillance, and/or other activities. The product road map of the subject company, combined with research and development budgeting documents, will often serve as a primary source of information supporting the appropriate required levels of costs to complete and ongoing expenditures. A useful cross-check is to add up all project costs to complete and ongoing expenditures per year and compare the total with the research and development budget or with research and development expenses as a percentage of sales either historically for the subject company (or the acquiring company, if applicable) or in comparison to market participants, when relevant data is available.

Tax expenses attributable to IPR&D technology should exclude specific tax circumstances of the subject company (or the acquiring company, if applicable). More specifically, net operating loss carry-forwards, penalties, and special tax payments should be excluded from the valuation of the IPR&D technology. Industry data demonstrating the effective tax rate experienced by market participants should also be considered and compared with company-specific data and statutory rates (see Section 7, Examples of Technology Asset Valuations, for more on the impact of income taxes on the determination of value).

Contributory Asset Charges

Contributory asset charges are applied in situations where the value of contributory assets can be determined separately. Once future after-tax earnings have been determined, the PFI must be adjusted for contributory asset charges in every year of the projection for which those contributory assets are required in generating cash flows. See Schedule 2b for an example of the valuation of IPR&D technology, which includes the application of contributory asset charges for the return on net working capital, fixed assets, assembled work force, existing technology (which was discussed earlier and valued using the relief-from-royalty method in our previous example), and internally developed software (discussed later and valued using the cost approach in our next example). It was assumed that the return of charges related to fixed assets was facilitated through deductions for depreciation, and the return of charges related to the other contributory assets (where applicable) was facilitated through appropriate costs included in the projected operating expenses.

Selection of the Discount Rate

As illustrated earlier, we note the required rate of return on identifiable intangible assets (such as IPR&D technology) may be determined through the assessment of the relative levels of risk of the intangible assets compared with the entity's overall WACC (or the IRR of the transaction, if applicable). Typically, technology assets (such as IPR&D technology) necessitate a higher rate of return than the WACC, due to their riskier and less liquid nature relative to working capital and tangible assets, as illustrated in Figure 12, below.

Figure 12

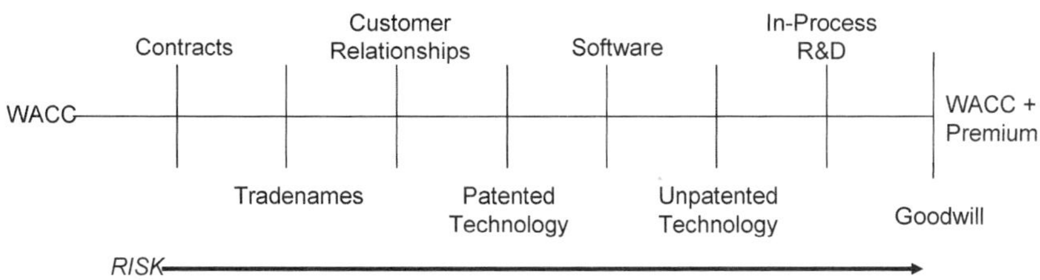

Since IPR&D technology assets are not typically financed with debt but with equity, the required rate of return is often highly correlated with equity rates of return.

For IPR&D technology, asset returns need to be determined based on the stage of completion of the IPR&D project, and in certain industries, this will approximate venture capital returns for early-stage development companies (to the extent that a discount rate adjustment technique is being used). The valuator should consider the risk of the project and the typical returns in the industry as not all development projects would yield high venture capital–like returns (as discussed in Section 5, Technology-Related Company and Asset Value Drivers).

As discussed earlier, there is typically a link between the basis under which the PFI is prepared and the basis under which an appropriate discount rate is determined (*i.e.*, the traditional, or implicit, approach versus the expected, or explicit, approach and the differences in risk thereof). Based on our assumption that the WACC of the subject company was 25 per cent, consideration of the 20 per cent discount rate selected in valuing the relatively less risky existing technology, and the range of the various early-stage discount rates we discussed earlier, we selected a discount rate of 30 per cent in valuing the IPR&D technology in our example.

Potential Tax Amortization Benefit

The last step in the multi-period excess earnings method is the consideration of the potential tax benefits associated with the amortization of the IPR&D technology asset for income tax purposes.

Our multi-period excess earnings analysis indicates a $5.486 million value before consideration of the tax amortization benefit. The IPR&D technology value of $5.486 million before amortization considerations was based on a

30 per cent discount rate, a 40 per cent tax rate, and a tax amortization life of 15 years. The calculation of AV begins with the calculation of the mid-period ADF.

$$\begin{aligned} ADF &= \frac{((1 + (1 + r)^{-TL})(1 + r)^{0.5})}{r} \\ &= \frac{((1 - (1.30)^{-15})(1.30)^{0.5})}{0.30} \\ &= 3.73 \end{aligned}$$

After the annuity discount factor is calculated, the asset value is determined according to the previously derived mathematical relationship as follows:

$$AV = PAV/(1 - t(ADF)/TL)$$

If the amortization factor (AM Factor) is defined according to the following relationship:

$$\text{AM Factor} = (1/(1 - t(ADF)/TL))$$

then the asset value is calculated as follows:

$$\begin{aligned} AV &= PAV * \text{AM Factor} \\ &= \$5,486,000*(1.110) \\ &= \$6,091,000 \end{aligned}$$

With the tax amortization benefit, the IPR&D technology value is indicated to be $6.091 million. The tax amortization benefit in our example thus reflects an approximately 11 per cent increase beyond the pre-amortization value for the IPR&D technology value. Ignoring the tax amortization benefit in applying the income approach will understate the intangible asset value.

Potential Issues

The valuator should be cognizant of various challenges and potential issues that can arise when using the multi-period excess earnings method. For example, the multi-period excess earnings method may not be relevant for intangible assets with an indefinite useful life as the value of any business goodwill may end up intertwined with the intangible asset.

Given the residual nature of this approach, once the cash flows allocable to all of the other enabling net assets have been deducted (to the extent that business goodwill exists in the company), the excess cash flow being analyzed, if assumed to continue into perpetuity, would inherently include those cash flows attributable to the intangible asset plus goodwill.

To mitigate this issue, one would have to estimate the stand-alone value of the goodwill and deduct a fair return on it prior to calculating the intangible value. However, the elements of goodwill are often difficult, if not impossible, to value directly and may comprise ambiguous items such as location, market presence, geographic presence, customer service capability, and distribution channels.

In addition, this approach is predicated on the assumption that all significant intangible assets have been identified, reasonably measured, and deducted in deriving the excess cash flows assigned to the intangible asset. If any relevant supporting contributory assets are omitted from the analysis, the result is a likely overstatement in the determination of value.

Furthermore, the possibility of double-counting cash flows exists with the multi-period excess earnings method because once it has been used to value an intangible asset, depending on the revenues and cash flows used, if those same cash flows or a portion thereof are used to value another intangible asset, double counting results.

Accordingly, the valuator must clearly understand the relationship between intangible assets and their respective cash flows to avoid such situations. The best way to avoid double counting is to use alternative techniques to arrive at value, if possible, or to segregate cash flows through cash flow splitting. We acknowledge, however, that the latter technique may involve subjective elements that are difficult to substantiate. The valuator is cautioned that the use of counter-reciprocal contributory asset charges, while potentially reducing the impact of double counting, creates circularity in the valuation model and does not entirely eliminate the issue.

Cost Approach

Example: Valuation of Internally Developed Software

In valuing internally developed software (*e.g.*, computer software), it is frequently difficult to apply either the market approach or the income approach because of informational deficiencies that may limit their usefulness. For example, in many instances, a valuator cannot use the market approach because relevant market transactions involving internally developed software are unavailable (*i.e.*, the valuator is unable to develop a market-derived indication of value). When internally developed software is used to provide a service (*e.g.*, in the software-as-a-service [SaaS] model) or is only used internally and is not sold to customers in the marketplace, a specific revenue stream cannot be attributed to the computer software, so an income approach cannot be applied. As a result, with internally developed software, the cost approach is generally used to determine its value.

More specifically, implementing the cost approach, the valuator must ensure that it is the most appropriate method for valuing the internally developed software. There are various factors that must be considered in making this determination, including the following:

- assessing whether the cost approach approximates value, including whether the cost approach will result in a value that reflects the asset's highest and best use; and
- understanding the underlying characteristics of the asset, including age, level of establishment, whether it is a wasting asset, uniqueness, and obsolescence.

Following this assessment, one of the three cost methods (*i.e.*, reproduction cost new, replacement cost new, and depreciated replacement cost) is selected. Depreciated replacement cost is often the valuation premise, particularly if the internally developed software in question is a technology asset with a finite life and at the time of the valuation was at least partway through the product life cycle. For example, in the case of internally developed software that was developed fairly close to the valuation date, reproduction cost may be an accurate reflection of what would be required to create a similar asset with substantially the same economic life. If, however, the asset was developed many years prior to the valuation date, a significant portion of the software could be technologically obsolete and not used, and creating a product with the equivalent level of functionality using more recent development tools and system platforms would require considerably less time. In this type of scenario, replacement cost new would be more appropriate. Using either of these two amounts and taking appropriate amounts of depreciation (*i.e.*, obsolescence), which would obviously vary across the two starting points, the valuator can determine the depreciated replacement cost. The valuator should also consider whether there are any opportunity costs, lost profits, and/or other costs that are attributable to the internally developed software (*i.e.*, costs over and above the depreciated replacement cost) with respect to already owning the ready-made software and/or avoiding the time to market, which may also need to be added to the determination of value under the cost approach.

Based on the factors noted above, we have provided in Schedule 3 an example of the valuation of an internally developed software using the cost approach. Each of the key factors we considered is discussed in further detail below.

Replacement Costs

Once the cost approach is selected, the components of cost must be addressed. The cost approach typically includes a comprehensive and all-inclusive definition of cost. To apply the cost approach, the replacement cost of a similar asset or one with similar service potential must be determined. This may be done in one of two ways:

- identifying the price of a replacement asset in the market; or
- determining the cost of developing or building a similar asset.

More specifically, the valuator must determine the replacement cost for the internally developed software to replicate its current level of functionality. The cost approach considers the amount of labor expended to develop and, more importantly, to re-create each of the functional aspects of the software. The valuator determines the cost of the effort to replace the software functionality based on the cost of programming and operations required to initially develop the software. The valuator considers, among other factors, the number of programmers, their rate of pay (including benefits), and the total amount of time spent on developing the software.

To determine the cost of the effort to replace the internally developed software's functionality, the valuator assesses the development phases of the internally developed software project. The valuator specifies the percentage of original cost or effort associated with each phase based on current cost models, which can include assumptions related to off-shore resources and third-party consultants involved. See Schedule 3 for a summary of the Phase 1 to Phase 4 costs that we assumed were required to redevelop the software that we valued.

When applied to internally developed software, the cost approach involves estimating the typical investment required to develop computer software with capabilities equivalent to the subject software. This involves the examination of the specifications for the particular application. Since the value of internally developed software is established by estimating the current expenditures necessary to re-create the functionality of the existing software, the costs should include the purchase of any software packages from vendors along with the salary, benefits, and overhead associated with programmers performing enhancements to the computer software. The development of costs requires knowledge pertaining to the modeling techniques, design standards, and current state of technology for the software.

Costs should also incorporate the materials and services used to develop a computer software application. These development costs include software design, software configuration, software interfaces, coding, and hardware installation. Development costs also include fees to specify interfaces and configuration along with the cost of any required software purchased from third parties. Payroll costs include fringe benefits and allowances for contractor expenses, including markup. Testing is an additional cost associated with computer software development. For large software projects, capitalized interest is also a cost element relating to the financing of the project. Computer software costs include the total expenditures necessary to assemble the computer software and place it in a ready position for commercial operation.

With the accumulation of these historical costs, the valuator adjusts the aggregate amount for inflation (*i.e.*, inflation between the time the expenses were incurred and the valuation date). Typically, the valuator's biggest challenge with the cost approach is gaining access to sufficiently detailed historical development records. Another issue emerges if the cost to simply replace the software is lower than the amount to redevelop the software. If this is the case, the replacement cost represents the value of the software (see Section 4, Valuation Approaches, for further detail).

Examples of specific costs to consider include the following, among others:

- research and development (labor, material, overhead, *etc.*);
- testing and regulatory approval costs;
- fees for contracted outside services;
- patent protection costs;
- equipment and other capital investments;
- opportunity costs of diverted resources;
- allowance for risk that technology cannot be independently developed or patent(s) avoided; and
- sub-optimal final product and/or process value because of patent work-around constraints.

Once the replacement cost new has been determined, for the purposes of this example, an adjustment for obsolescence (*i.e.*, depreciation) is deducted based on its remaining economic life to determine the depreciated replacement cost of internally developed software.

Adjustment for Obsolescence

Based on the factors noted above, the reproduction or replacement cost new of the internally developed software is based on current prices and labor. As a result, when using reproduction cost as the starting point, depreciated replacement cost is determined by making appropriate adjustments for physical deterioration (depreciation) and functional, technological (a form of functional obsolescence), and economic obsolescence (a form of external obsolescence). However, when replacement cost is used as the basis for depreciated replacement cost, the valuator must make adjustments for physical depreciation and economic obsolescence to arrive at the depreciated replacement cost (*i.e.*, functional and technological obsolescence are not required in this scenario).

Examples of the various forms of obsolescence are summarized below:

- *Physical deterioration* – the reduction in the value of an intellectual property due to physical wear and tear resulting from continued use. It is unlikely for an intellectual property to experience physical deterioration. However, the valuation analyst should consider this concept in a cost approach analysis. The result of age and wear and tear, this form of depreciation can be divided into two components: curable and incurable. Curable physical deterioration is a loss in value that can be recovered or offset by repairing or replacing defective items causing the loss, provided that the resulting value increase equals or exceeds the cost of the work. Incurable physical deterioration, on the other hand, is a loss in value that cannot be offset or that would involve a greater cost to correct than the resulting increase in value. This is not typically a relevant factor for technology asset valuations.
- *Functional obsolescence* – the reduction in the value of a technology asset due to its inability to perform the function (or yield the periodic utility) for which it was originally designed. Technological obsolescence is a decrease in the value of an intellectual property due to improvements in technology that make an asset less than the ideal replacement for itself. Technological obsolescence occurs when, as a result of improvements in design or engineering technology, a replacement intellectual property produces a greater standardized measure of utility production than the actual intellectual property. This could be any loss in value resulting from inappropriate architectural design, inefficient process flow, or poor construction or layout for the intended use. As with physical depreciation, functional obsolescence may be either curable or incurable.
- *Technological obsolescence* – typically considered to be a specific form of functional obsolescence. Accordingly, the valuation analyst may capture all of the value influences due to both design flaws and changing technology in one category and call that functional obsolescence. This represents the loss in value due to improvements in technology.
- *Economic obsolescence (i.e., a specific form of external obsolescence)* – a reduction in the value of an intellectual property from the effects, events, or conditions that are external to – and not controlled by – the intellectual property's current use or condition. The impact of economic obsolescence is typically beyond the control of the owner/operator. For that reason, economic obsolescence is typically considered incurable. This reflects the reduction in value

> due to the effects of events or conditions that are not controlled by the current use or condition of the asset.

We note that functional and technological obsolescence are already factored into the calculation of replacement cost new, as the basis of this method is to create an asset of a similar utility. For example, for internally developed software, replacement cost new may be lower than reproduction cost due to more efficient ways of achieving similar functionality. However, a quantification of additional functionalities of the replacement asset versus the asset to be valued must be addressed. In our sample in Schedule 3, we assumed an obsolescence factor of 15 per cent based on our assessment of the factors noted above. In addition, relevant income taxes are deducted from the depreciated replacement cost to arrive at after-tax depreciated replacement cost.

Asset Developer's Profit and/or Entrepreneurial Incentive

Relevant opportunity costs, lost profits, and/or other costs related to an otherwise delayed market entry, which are avoided by the owner (or acquirer, if appropriate) due to owning the ready-made software (*i.e.*, to reflect the asset developer's profit and/or the entrepreneurial incentive), are added to the after-tax depreciated replacement cost before the consideration of the potential tax amortization benefit.

In our example in Schedule 3, we assumed that, due to the opportunity costs related to the delayed market entry, the asset developer's profit and/or entrepreneurial incentive was approximately $50,000.

Potential Tax Amortization Benefit

The last step in the cost approach is the consideration of the potential tax benefits associated with the amortization of the internally developed software asset for income tax purposes.

Our cost approach analysis indicates a $253,337 value before the consideration of the tax amortization benefit. The internally developed software value of $253,337 before amortization considerations was based on a 20 per cent discount rate, a 40 per cent tax rate, and a tax amortization life of 15 years. The calculation of AV begins with the calculation of the mid-period ADF:

$$\text{ADF} = \frac{((1-(1+r)^{-TL})(1+r)^{0.5})}{r}$$

$$= \frac{((1-(1.20)^{-15})(1.20)^{0.5})}{0.20}$$

$$= 5.12$$

After the annuity discount factor is calculated, the asset value is determined according to the previously derived mathematical relationship as follows:

$$\text{AV} = \text{PAV}/(1 - t(\text{ADF})/\text{TL})$$

If the amortization factor (AM Factor) is defined according to the following relationship:

$$\text{AM Factor} = (1/(1 - t(\text{ADF})/\text{TL}))$$

then the asset value is calculated as follows:

$$\begin{aligned} \text{AV} &= \text{PAV} * \text{AM Factor} \\ &= \$253{,}337*(1.158) \\ &= \$293{,}411 \end{aligned}$$

With the tax amortization benefit, the internally developed software value is indicated to be $293,411. The tax amortization benefit for our example thus reflects an approximately 16 per cent increase beyond the pre-amortization value for the intangible asset value. Ignoring the tax amortization benefit in applying the income approach will understate the intangible asset value.

Potential Issues

There are several potential challenges to implementing the cost approach. The first is that the cost approach may not reflect the underlying economic value of the asset. For example, it is possible to have a technology development effort that goes on for years at great expense without ever producing a commercially viable product. The converse may also be true in that great discoveries may be made and commercially developed for relatively little cost.

In addition, the valuator must accurately consider all of the effects of depreciation and obsolescence. More specifically, in order to appropriately determine value, various forms of obsolescence have to be identified, quantified, and subtracted from the estimated replacement or reproduction cost new. Each form of obsolescence is indicative of a decrease in value of the subject intangible asset relative to a new intangible asset for specific reasons. Quantifying these issues is often extremely subjective.

Often, too narrow a definition of cost is applied in determining value using the cost approach. For example, the valuator must consider whether the asset developer's profit and/or an entrepreneurial incentive is an important element to the analysis. As mentioned earlier, such an adjustment should include the relevant opportunity costs, lost profits, and/or other costs related to an otherwise delayed market entry, which are avoided due to owning the ready-made software.

Assessing Reasonableness[24]

PFI

Before the reasonableness of the PFI can be assessed, the valuator must ensure the appropriate PFI has been obtained. For example, in the case of an acquisition, the acquiring company will often have prepared several types of PFIs as part of the due diligence and/or price-setting process. In such instances, the valuator should select the PFI that best represents the information that was used in negotiating the final purchase price and, therefore, is most representative for the purposes of determining the value of the technology and/or the technology-related company.

As with any valuation exercise, the PFI should be reviewed to a sufficient level so the valuator can understand the key risks and assess the overall reasonableness of the PFI. Valuators must consider assumptions such as revenue growth, operating margins, and net cash flows in light of recent historical results and future expectations for other companies in the same industry. This may include a review of analysts' forecasts for the industry participants. As part of this exercise, the valuator should understand the process by which the PFI was prepared, as well as the key factors and assumptions used in its preparation.

As best practice, significant differences between the PFI used in the valuation and any PFI presented to the board of directors of the company (or the acquiring company, if applicable and/or appropriate) and/or senior management (as appropriate), financial advisors, financial lenders, *etc.*, should be documented and reconciled, including the underlying reasons.

---

24 Based on information obtained from, among other sources: (i) AICPA IPR&D Practice Aid; (ii) IVSC January 2009 exposure drafts on the valuation of intangible assets and the valuation of intangible assets for IFRS reporting purposes; and (iii) CICBV Valuation for Financial Reporting course.

Selection of Discount Rates

The discount rate used to determine the value of a technology asset and/or technology-related company should reflect the risk profile of the subject, as well as the risks of achieving the related cash flows. There are two common tools, in addition to professional judgment, to establish a benchmark for the selection of discount rates related to technology assets and/or technology-related companies:

- the WACC and
- the IRR.

The WACC is the overall required rate of return for the business in question and takes into account the required rate of return on all forms of invested capital (*i.e.*, cost of debt and cost of equity capital). It is the rate of return indicative of the investment risk inherent in the ownership of the asset. For additional guidance on the WACC, see Section 6, Technology Value Risk Factors.

The IRR is the discount rate that equates the projected cash flows of a business (typically in an acquisition scenario) to the purchase price. The IRR is often used as an important reasonableness check, along with the WACC, in order to aid in the selection of the discount rate. A caution is that the IRR is only relevant if the purchase price paid was reasonable in light of the economic benefits expected and the risks of achieving them. If this is calculated to be extremely low relative to the WACC, this may give the valuator the impression that the future cash flows are of low risk, which may not be an appropriate rate of return if the acquirer overpaid for the business. Conversely, if the calculated IRR is particularly high, it would suggest that either the cash flows are relatively risky or the acquirer obtained a bargain purchase. Accordingly, these factors may cause the IRR to differ significantly from the WACC and the valuator should understand the key factors that reconcile the two sets of discount rates.

Weighted-Average Return on Assets Analysis

The weighted-average return for the portfolio of assets (including tangible and intangible net assets) should theoretically approximate the weighted cost of all forms of capital employed to finance the business (*i.e.*, the IRR and/or the WACC). An analysis of the weighted-average return on assets (WARA) allows the valuator to review the value and required returns of the overall business enterprise, including the various tangible and intangible net assets of a subject company, in order to determine the resultant levels of implied residual goodwill and its implied required rate of return (*i.e.*, the WARA allows the valuator to assess the reasonableness of the asset-specific returns for identified intangible assets and the implied [or calculated] return on goodwill). In particular, the WARA analysis is based on the sum of the required rates of return for all operating net working capital (normalized), fixed assets (normalized), and identifiable intangible assets, weighted by each of these assets' proportionate share of the total value of the company (*i.e.*, the total value of debt and equity investment required in the subject entity).

While a WARA analysis is considered best practice in purchase-price allocations, we recommend that a WARA analysis be prepared (where possible) when valuing technology assets. Moreover, irrespective of whether the valuation of a technology asset is a component of a larger valuation (*e.g.*, the valuation of various tangible and intangible net assets of a company acquired as part of an acquisition) or if the technology is being valued on a stand-alone basis, in valuing a technology asset, the valuator should value (even at a relatively high level) the other identifiable tangible and intangible net assets of the company. Such an analysis is useful as it allows the valuator to assess the reasonableness of the value attributed to the technology relative to the value of other identifiable tangible and intangible net assets, as discussed above. In Schedule 4, we have provided an example of a WARA analysis based on our examples for the valuation of existing technology, IPR&D technology, and internally developed software (all of which were discussed earlier) and an assumed business enterprise value of $45 million for the company as a whole. Based on this analysis, the return on the assumed operating assets of the company illustrates the increasing required rate of return as the level of liquidity decreases and the level of equity investment increases (*i.e.*, as assets become more and more intangible in nature, with goodwill requiring the highest rate of return). In this example, the overall rate of return for the company is 25 per cent, which is the rate of return to which the WARA analysis reconciles.

In assessing the WARA analysis for reasonableness, the valuator should also consider whether the residual balance allocated to goodwill is reasonable based on the valuator's understanding of the business. The components of goodwill may include the following, among others:

- location;
- monopoly;
- buyer-specific synergies;
- high profitability;
- market presence;
- market potential;
- geographic presence;
- distribution channels;
- future growth prospects;

- effective advertising programs;
- fund-raising capabilities;
- customer-service capability and product or service support;
- customer base (*e.g.*, population in which customers are known or a group of customers that is not known or identifiable to the company);
- assembled work force;
- training expertise;
- technical expertise;
- training and recruiting programs;
- outstanding credit ratings and access to capital markets;
- non-union status or strong labor relations; and
- favorable government relations.

CICA Handbook Section 1581 also sets out examples of goodwill-like assets that may exist in business combinations. The valuator must consider both the qualitative and quantitative factors in order to conclude on the reasonableness of the resulting goodwill balance. However, we note that it may not be possible to perform a quantitative goodwill analysis that completely reconciles the goodwill balance. By definition, some elements will be unquantifiable. In addition, there is no predefined range of goodwill return that implies the overall results of the intangible assets and goodwill are reasonable. However, such an analysis can be illustrative of results that may require further review.

Cross-Checks

Further to the various reasonableness checks discussed earlier, the results obtained using a primary method should be cross-checked for reasonableness against another (perhaps secondary) valuation method. More specifically, the valuation methodologies chosen depend on situation-specific factors (*e.g.*, the key value drivers, the nature of the technology, information availability, the context of the valuation, and the manner in which the technology contributes to the company's overall cash flows). No matter which primary valuation methodology is chosen, it is prudent to perform an analysis involving several methodologies, where applicable, to gather as many data points as possible. In this way, the valuator can ensure that a reasonable determination of value emerges.

In additional to the above, if a technology asset is valued using multi-period excess earnings or depreciated replacement cost as the primary method, implied royalty rates can be calculated that would be required had the relief-from-royalty method been used instead. Such rates could then be considered for reasonableness.

Practice Tip

To endure uncertainty is difficult, but so are most of the other virtues.

Bertrand Russell

Conclusion

The improvements and advances of technology companies and their related assets generate innovations that can potentially change the world. In this context, technology assets have become significant contributors to the value of many companies and represent valuable investments. Considering the complexities surrounding technology assets, valuators need to use a reasoned analytical process to understand and gauge the value of these assets. At the same time, the valuator should be cognizant of the fact that more than 66 per cent of new technology-based firms fail. Many of these same failures were previously analyzed by venture capitalists and other professionals and deemed to have a reasonable chance of success.

Regardless of the context in which the technology-related valuation is taking place, it is imperative to identify and thoroughly understand the appropriate valuation approaches, the underlying key value drivers, and the many risk factors. Only with this perspective can one hope to perform a reasoned and informed valuation analysis of a technology asset and/or a technology-related company.

APPENDIX A

References

Assets Acquired in a Business Combination to the Be Used in Research and Development Activities: A Focus on Software, Electronic Devices, and Pharmaceutical Industries (American Institute of Certified Public Accountants (AICPA) Practice Aid Service, 2001).

F. Peter Boer, *The Valuation of Technology: Business and Financial Issues in R&D* (New York: John Wiley & Sons, Inc., 1999).

Canadian Institute of Chartered Business Valuators (CICBV), Advanced Business and Securities Valuation course and Valuation for Financial Reporting course.

Aswath Damodaran, *The Dark Side of Valuation: Valuing Old Tech, New Tech, and New Economy Companies* (Upper Saddle River, New Jersey: Prentice Hall PTR, 2001).

R.K. Ellsworth, "Identifying the Economic Value of Trade Marks" (1998) *Trade Mark Yearbook* 16–20 (London: Managing Intellectual Property, 1998).

Exposure Draft of Proposed New International Valuation Guidance Note No. 16: Valuation of Intangible Assets for IFRS Reporting Purposes (London: International Valuation Standards Council, January 2009).

Exposure Draft of Revised International Guidance Note No. 4: Valuation of Intangible Assets (London: International Valuation Standards Council, January 2009).

Robert Goldscheider, John Jarosz & Carla Mulhern, "Use of the 25 Per Cent Rule in Valuing IP" (2002) 37 *les Nouvelles* 123.

Roger Heller, "An Introduction to Function Point Analysis," *CrossTalk – The Journal of Defense Software Engineering,* November/December 1995.

James L. Horvath & P.J. Canham, "Bits and Bytes and Bucks," *CA Magazine*, August 1988, pp. 65–68.

James L. Horvath & Richard Ellsworth, "The Invisible Path: Valuing Technology," *Taxation and Valuation of Technology: Theory, Practice, and the Law* (Toronto: Irwin Law, 2008), pp. 533–575.

James L. Horvath, "Strategies for Valuing Intellectual Property for Tax Purposes," Infonex, 4th Annual Taxation of Intellectual Property, pp. 7.1–7.42.

James L. Horvath & S. Hacker, "Valuing Computer Software, Brands, and other Intellectual Property: Concepts, Complexities, and Controversies," *Advocacy & Taxation in Canada* (Toronto: Irwin Law, 2004), pp. 346–395.

Brian Kettell, *Valuation of Internet and Technology Stocks: Implications for Investment Analysis* (Oxford: Butterworth-Heinemann, 2002).

Geoffrey A. Moore, Paul Johnson & Tom Kippola, *The Gorilla Game: An Investor's Guide to Picking Winners in High Technology, Revised Edition* (New York: HarperBusiness, 1999).

James L. Plummer, *QED Report on Venture Capital Financial Analysis* (Palo Alto: QED Research, Inc., 1987).

Richard Razgaitis, *Valuation and Pricing of Technology-Based Intellectual Property* (Hoboken, New Jersey: John Wiley & Sons, Inc., 2003).

Robert F. Reilly & Pamela J. Garland, "The Valuation of Data Processing Intangible Assets," *Valuation of Intangible Assets in Global Operations* (Westport, Connecticut: Greenwood Publishing Group, 2001).

Robert F. Reilly & Robert P. Schweihs, *Valuing Intangible Assets* (New York: McGraw-Hill, 1999).

William A. Sahlman & Daniel R. Scherlis, *A Method for Valuing High-Risk, Long Term Investments: The "Venture Capital Method"* (Boston: Harvard Business School Publishing, 1987).

Mohan Sawhrey, Ranjay Gulati, Anthony Paoni & the Kellogg Techventure Team, *TechVenture: New Rules on Value and Profit from Silicon Valley* (New York: John Wiley & Sons, Inc., 2001).

David J. Teece, *Managing Intellectual Capital: Organizational, Strategic, and Policy Dimensions* (Oxford: Oxford University Press, 2000).

Valuation of Privately-Held-Company Equity Securities Issued as Compensation (American Institute of Certified Public Accountants (AICPA) Practice Aid Service, 2004).

Dr. M. Werner, "Real Option Valuation" (2001) 137 *Journal of Business Valuation*.

The Invisable Path: Valuing Technology

Valuation of Existing Technology (Relief-from-Royalty Method)

As of December 31, 2008

Schedule 1

	Projected									
	31-Dec-09	31-Dec-10	31-Dec-11	31-Dec-12	31-Dec-13	31-Dec-14	31-Dec-15	31-Dec-16	31-Dec-17	31-Dec-18
Revenue	**20,000**	**20,600**	**21,218**	**21,855**	**22,510**	**23,185**	**23,881**	**24,597**	**25,335**	**26,095**
Revenue Growth %	*N/A*	*3.0%*	*3.0%*	*3.0%*	*3.0%*	*3.0%*	*3.0%*	*3.0%*	*3.0%*	*3.0%*
After-Tax Relief-from-Royalty @ 4.8%	**960**	**989**	**1,018**	**1,049**	**1,080**	**1,113**	**1,146**	**1,181**	**1,216**	**1,253**
Technology Migration Factor	95.0%	85.0%	75.0%	65.0%	55.0%	45.0%	35.0%	25.0%	15.0%	5.0%
Net After-Tax Revenues	**912**	**840**	**764**	**682**	**594**	**501**	**401**	**295**	**182**	**63**
Net After-Tax Revenues Growth %	*N/A*	*(7.8%)*	*(9.1%)*	*(10.7%)*	*(12.8%)*	*(15.7%)*	*(19.9%)*	*(26.4%)*	*(38.2%)*	*(65.7%)*
Terminal Value										
Partial Period	1.0000	1.0000	1.0000	1.0000	1.0000	1.0000	1.0000	1.0000	1.0000	1.0000
Discount Period	0.5000	1.5000	2.5000	3.5000	4.5000	5.5000	6.5000	7.5000	8.5000	9.5000
Discount Factor @ 25.0%	0.8944	0.7155	0.5724	0.4579	0.3664	0.2931	0.2345	0.1876	0.1501	0.1200
Present Value of Cash Flows	**816**	**601**	**437**	**312**	**218**	**147**	**94**	**55**	**27**	**8**

Schedule 2a

The Invisable Path: Valuing Technology

Valuation of IPR&D Technology (Excess Earnings Method)

As of December 31, 2008

Migration of Technology					Projected				
	31-Dec-09	31-Dec-10	31-Dec-11	31-Dec-12	31-Dec-13	31-Dec-14	31-Dec-15	31-Dec-16	31-Dec-17
Migration of Invisable Path Technology:									
Existing	100%	80%	60%	40%	20%	0%	0%	0%	0%
IPR&D	0%	20%	30%	20%	15%	10%	0%	0%	0%
Future	0%	0%	10%	40%	65%	90%	100%	100%	100%
Total	**100%**	**100%**	**100%**	**100%**	**100%**	**100%**	**100%**	**100%**	**100%**

Revenue Detail by Technology					Projected				
	31-Dec-09	31-Dec-10	31-Dec-11	31-Dec-12	31-Dec-13	31-Dec-14	31-Dec-15	31-Dec-16	31-Dec-17
Technology Revenue Summary:									
Existing	20,000	16,480	12,731	8,742	4,502	-	-	-	-
IPR&D	-	4,120	6,365	4,371	3,377	2,319	-	-	-
Future	-	-	2,122	8,742	14,632	20,867	23,881	24,597	25,335
Total	**20,000**	**20,600**	**21,218**	**21,855**	**22,510**	**23,185**	**23,881**	**24,597**	**25,335**

The Invisable Path: Valuing Technology
Valuation of IPR&D Technology (Excess Earnings Method)
As of December 31, 2008

Schedule 2b

	Projected								
	31-Dec-09	31-Dec-10	31-Dec-11	31-Dec-12	31-Dec-13	31-Dec-14	31-Dec-15	31-Dec-16	31-Dec-17
Revenue	**20,000**	**16,480**	**12,731**	**8,742**	**4,502**	-	-	-	-
Revenue Growth %	*N/A*	*(17.6%)*	*(22.8%)*	*(31.3%)*	*(48.5%)*	*N/A*	*N/A*	*N/A*	*N/A*
Cost of Sales	2,000	1,648	1,273	874	450	-	-	-	-
Gross Margin	**18,000**	**14,832**	**11,458**	**7,868**	**4,052**	-	-	-	-
Gross Margin %	*90.0%*	*90.0%*	*90.0%*	*90.0%*	*90.0%*	*N/A*	*N/A*	*N/A*	*N/A*
Operating Expenses:									
Selling	4,000	3,296	2,546	1,748	900	-	-	-	-
Marketing	2,000	1,648	1,273	874	450	-	-	-	-
General and Administrative	1,600	1,318	1,018	699	360	-	-	-	-
Research and Development (Maintenance)	3,200	2,637	2,037	1,399	720	-	-	-	-
Depreciation	200	165	127	87	45	-	-	-	-
Cost Adjustment	(200)	(165)	(127)	(87)	(45)	-	-	-	-
Operating Expenses	**10,800**	**8,899**	**6,875**	**4,721**	**2,431**	-	-	-	-
Operating Expenses %	*54.0%*	*54.0%*	*54.0%*	*54.0%*	*54.0%*	*N/A*	*N/A*	*N/A*	*N/A*
Operating Income	**7,200**	**5,933**	**4,583**	**3,147**	**1,621**	-	-	-	-
Operating Income %	*36.0%*	*36.0%*	*36.0%*	*36.0%*	*36.0%*	*N/A*	*N/A*	*N/A*	*N/A*
Less: Taxes @ 40.0%	2,880	2,373	1,833	1,259	648	-	-	-	-
Net Operating Income	**4,320**	**3,560**	**2,750**	**1,888**	**972**	-	-	-	-
Net Operating Income %	*21.6%*	*21.6%*	*21.6%*	*21.6%*	*21.6%*	*N/A*	*N/A*	*N/A*	*N/A*
Contributory Asset Charges:									
Net Working Capital	215	44	33	23	11	-	-	-	-
Return-On Fixed Assets	54	48	41	30	16	-	-	-	-
Assembled Workforce	254	209	162	111	57	-	-	-	-
Existing Technology (Relief-from-Royalty Method) @ 4.8	960	791	611	420	216	-	-	-	-
Internally-Developed Software	360	49	38	26	13	-	-	-	-
Contributory Asset Charges	**1,842**	**1,142**	**884**	**609**	**314**	-	-	-	-
Contributory Asset Charges %	*9.2%*	*6.9%*	*6.9%*	*7.0%*	*7.0%*	*N/A*	*N/A*	*N/A*	*N/A*
Excess Earnings	**2,478**	**2,418**	**1,865**	**1,279**	**658**	-	-	-	-
Excess Earnings %	*12.4%*	*14.7%*	*14.7%*	*14.6%*	*14.6%*	*N/A*	*N/A*	*N/A*	*N/A*
Partial Period	1.0000	1.0000	1.0000	1.0000	1.0000	1.0000	1.0000	1.0000	1.0000
Discount Period	0.5000	1.5000	2.5000	3.5000	4.5000	5.5000	6.5000	7.5000	8.5000
Discount Factor @ 30.0%	0.8771	0.6747	0.5190	0.3992	0.3071	0.2362	0.1817	0.1398	0.1075
Present Value of Cash Flows	**2,173**	**1,631**	**968**	**511**	**202**	-	-	-	-
Cumulative Present Value %	*39.6%*	*69.4%*	*87.0%*	*96.3%*	*100.0%*	*100.0%*	*100.0%*	*100.0%*	*100.0%*
Sum of Present Value	**5,486**								
Tax Amortization Benefit	605								
Fair Value	**6,091**								

The Invisable Path: Valuing Technology

Valuation of Internally-Developed Software Technology (Cost Approach)

As of December 31, 2008

Schedule 3

Phases	Number of Hours per Staff	Number of Staff	Total Hours	Average Hourly Rate	Professional Fees	Overhead	Total Professional Fees
Phase 1	200	10	2,000	80	160,000	32,000	192,000
Phase 2	80	8	640	100	64,000	12,800	76,800
Phase 3	75	6	450	150	67,500	13,500	81,000
Phase 4	30	3	90	175	15,750	3,150	18,900
						Total Professional Fees	**368,700**
						Total Expenses	**30,000**
						Replacement Cost New	**398,700**
						Less: Adjustment for Obsolescence @ 15.0%	(59,805)
						Depreciated Replacement Cost	**338,895**
						Less: Taxes @ 40.0%	(135,558)
						After-Tax Depreciated Replacement Cost	**203,337**
						Add: Asset Developor's Profit / Entrepreneurial Incentive	**50,000**
							253,337
						Add: Tax Amortization Benefit	40,074
						Fair Value	**293,411**
						Fair Value ($000's)	**293**

5.121724

Schedule 4

The Invisable Path: Valuing Technology
Valuation of Identifiable Intangible and Tangible Assets
Valuation Summary (Weighted-Average Return on Assets)
As of December 31, 2008

	Fair Value	% of Total Fair Value	% of Total Premium	Required Return	Weighted Return
Business Enterprise Value	**35,000**				
Reconciliation of Net Assets:					
Net Working Capital	7,500	21.4%		5.0%	1.1%
Depreciable Fixed Assets	5,000	14.3%		10.0%	1.4%
Total Net Tangible Assets	**12,500**	**35.7%**			
Existing Technology (Relief-from-Royalty Method)	3,069	8.8%	13.6%	25.0%	2.2%
In-Process Research and Development (Excess Earnings Method)	6,091	17.4%	27.1%	30.0%	5.2%
Internally-Developed Software Technology (Cost Approach)	293	0.8%	1.3%	20.0%	0.2%
Total Identifiable Intangible Assets	**9,453**	**27.0%**	**42.0%**		
Assembled Workforce	1,000	2.9%	4.4%	25.0%	0.7%
Implied Goodwill (excluding Assembled Workforce)	12,047	34.4%	53.5%	41.3%	14.2%
Total Implied Goodwill	**13,047**	**37.3%**	**58.0%**		
Total Premium	**22,500**	**64.3%**	**100.0%**		
Business Enterprise Value	**35,000**	**100.0%**	**N/A**	**N/A**	**25.0%**

Equity Risk Premium and Volatility: A European Perspective

Péter Harbula

Introduction

The determination of the equity risk premium is without discussion one of the most interesting, challenging, and debated topics in corporate finance. It is a critical item in developing discount rates and a tremendous amount of literature has developed over the last decades on the subject. Yet, it does not seem that there is a consensus among practitioners or academics on what is the best way to assess the equity risk premium and what its level should be, even in "normal times", let alone in a volatile business environment.

The importance of the equity risk premium relies in the fact that its use goes way beyond simple business valuation: implicitly or explicitly, it is used in many fields of finance, such as asset management and asset allocation, corporate investment decisions, *etc.*

As will be explained in this chapter, most methods used to develop the equity risk premium come with an associated volatility. As such, the underlying question that needs to be addressed is how the economy's volatility should be reflected in the determination approach and what figure should be selected. Since there is no clear cut consensus on the equity risk premium itself, this remains a critical and difficult task. In volatile times, this already complicated task is increasingly becoming difficult.

The aim of this analysis *is to provide the necessary framework and tools that hopefully give the right factors to consider*. . . so that everyone can make his own judgment on the topic. Most suggestions and discussions are valid whether applied in volatile or in more "normal" times.

For the purpose of the following pages, focus will be directed as much as possible on the European data, perspectives, knowledge, and experience.

Equity Risk Premium: Concepts and Definitions

Why is equity risk premium important for almost any investment decision? Its importance relies on the nature of how business decisions are made. Most textbooks on finance agree that the best tool to evaluate any project remains the NPV method. The NPV method requires the computation of the required cost of capital by investors. Investors have a wide variety of investment opportunities in different forms of assets. Most *risk averse and prudent investors* will assume that *investing in equities* (directly or indirectly) *requires an additional remuneration* for taking risk. The concept of risks/rewards for evaluating investment opportunities goes beyond most popular business and financial theories; it is simply common sense.

In general, thus, the "equity risk premium" can be defined as the additional remuneration required by a rational investor in order to invest in equity instead of preferring lower risk fixed and certain obligation security investments.

The concept became popular and widely used after the development and spreading of the CAPM[1] and its widely accepted use to estimate the required rate of return for investing in equities. The equity risk premium appears in the original CAPM as well as in the expanded/extended version used by practitioners (adjusted with specific risk premium), the intertemporal CAPM by Merton *etc.*[2] Alternatives to the CAPM, such as the different multi-factor or APT models[3] also rely on the equity risk premium as a general concept, through a different estimated method.

---

1 Capital Asset Pricing Model, developed in the 1950s and 1960s by, among others, H. Markowitz, W. Sharpe, J. Lintner, J. Treynor & J. Tobin, *et al.*

2 The textbook CAPM draws on Sharpe and Linter while Merton's intertemporal CAPM is an extension of the textbook CAPM. The main difference between the intertemporal CAPM and standard CAPM is that the former considers stable variables that acknowledge the fact that investors hedge against shortfalls in consumption or against changes in the future investment opportunity set.

3 Multi-factor or APT (Arbitrage Price Theory) cost of equity models generalize the CAPM by estimating that return is function of more than one explanatory variable. They are mostly used in asset management and asset allocation strategies (and advocated by many academics) and are less common in business valuation. If S. Ross is one of the key academics behind the concept, the most famous model is probably the Fama-French 3 factor model (Fama-French (1992)). Many academics have tackled the field of finance developing similar models and related theories. For instance, the Hamon-Jacquillat (2001) model uses liquidity as an additional variable to explain the required return of equity. For more details on the alternative models and the APT, please refer to Brealy-Myers-Allen Chapter 8.4 or other finance textbooks.

Although the definition of the *equity risk premium* seems simple, as often in finance one must be cautious to be sure to match what stands behind a definition and what people understand when quoting a term. Yet, one of the key items that needs to be emphasized is that the *equity risk premium can vary on how it is derived* (historic, prospective . . .) *and* in general *for what purposes it is applied* (valuation, fairness opinion, asset management, investment decision in the stockmarket, corporate investment decision *etc.* . . .). Thus, in order to discuss the different techniques for estimating the equity risk premium, one needs to remember the components of the CAPM model.

The components of the CAPM model are presented in basic form here.[4] The CAPM theorizes that the required return of equity is the sum of the yield on securities representing the systematic risk (the risk-free rate) and the remuneration corresponding to the non-diversified risk assumed by investors, as presented in the equation below:

$$r = r_{f1} + \text{ß}(r_m - r_{f2})^5$$

In the equation above, the equity risk premium is the term, *i.e.*, the difference between the expected market return and the risk-free security yield. Corporate finance theory in general and business valuation in particular is forward looking. Thus, the market risk premium in the CAPM model (or the alternative models) should be the expected (*ex ante*) equity risk premium. The equity risk premium is a forward looking concept which, in itself, is a prohibition to use historic data as a predictor of the future.

Determinants of the Equity Risk Premium

The equity risk premium (independently whether applied within the CAPM or not) is determined by a number of factors. First of all, there is *fundamental judgment* on how much risk one sees in *the market, the economy* and how we judge the level of uncertainties in the economy in general. The equity risk premium reflects, therefore, the price of risk and is as dependent on individuals as on the "market" in general. As such, one could argue that there is *no single expected equity risk premium for the market as a whole, nor* is there *a single expected risk premium for all investors.*[6]

---

4 For a more detailed presentation of the CAPM, the reader is invited to refer to most mainstream corporate finance textbooks, such as the Brealy-Myers-Allen (2008) which is my personal favorite.

5 In the formula, r is the required rate of return of investors, r_{f1} is the yield of risk-free assets as at the estimation date, r_m is the market return (historic or expected), r_{f2} is the risk-free rate that is determined consistently with market return while ß captures the sensitivity of the given assets towards the market in general. For more details, see Vernimmen Chapter 25 Section 1 and 2, Brealy-Myers-Allen Chapter 8.2 or Pratt-Grabowski Chapter 8.

6 Fernandez (2007).

There are *many determinants* for the equity risk premium. We present here a summary review of the main components as identified by academic research. The understanding of the key explanatory factors is just as necessary when making a judgment on the level of the equity risk premium as it is for a financial analyst to understand the key simplifying assumptions lying behind CAPM. Damodaran (2008) and Siegel (1999) provide an excellent overview of the main determinants of the equity risk premium. The equity risk premium is determined by, among others, the following:

1. The *risk aversion* of investors: the more risk averse people are, the higher the equity risk premium should rise. A perfect example of this is the evolution of equity risk premiums during market downturns; economic turmoil, *etc.*

2. *Economic risk*: the more predictable an economy is (inflation, growth, *etc.*), the lower the equity risk premium should be. As such, predictability is the key word on the subject.

3. *Consumption patterns* (current versus future) and indebtedness of households: these are key factors influencing the equity risk premiums. In economies where people have a high net saving rate and lower indebtedness (such as Western Europe was for many years), the equity risk premium should be lower as opposed to an economy that prefers current consumption (*i.e.*, people are net consumers) and uses indebtedness to fund such consumptions (such as the U.S. has been over the last few decades).[7]

4. *Corporate governance*: the better the corporate governance system is, the more investors can rely on earnings as an aggregate and the less uncertainty investors will face and thus include in their pricing of the risks. Clearly, factor is directly related to market regulations and the enforcement of such regulations over time. As accounting and earnings become less and less meaningful to investors (accounting scandals, weakening oversight authorities, collusion in the oversight function of auditors, distortion to accounting earnings because of new accounting standards, *etc.* . . .), this is something that investors will directly include in their pricing of the market risk.[8] In addition, economic scandals also have an impact on the equity risk premium:

7 Damodaran (2008).

8 See a detailed explanation in Harbula (2004) on how corporate governance has an impact on market and macroeconomic data.

as trust decreases in the market and the system, equity risk premiums measured instantly will most certainly be overshot.[9]

5. *Liquidity*: many studies have explained and detailed why investors cherish liquidity more than many other items.[10]

6. *Economic crisis*: the risk that economies will turn down abruptly, causing a great loss in corporate (equity) value is a key item in the pricing of risks.[11]

7. *Irrationality*: there are phenomenons whereby investors do not behave as rationally as economic theory or model would predict it. The money illusion effect (investors are using historical inflation rates to forecast earning growth but current inflation rates for determining the appropriate discount rate) may result in low asset values and high equity risk premiums, such as in the 1970s.[12]

Determining the correct *expected equity risk premium* requires the analyst to form an assumption on each and every one of these factors. Selecting different methods or sources for the equity risk premium implies a judgment (or a choice) on every one of these items, as none of the available methods can be applied correctly without understanding and interpreting the underlying relevant assumptions.

Investors do not always behave rationally and there is a risk that the equity risk premium is distorted upwards or downwards by such behavior. The role of the analyst is thus not only to make a judgment on the impact of the above-mentioned items, but also to look and screen such irrational items out of its estimate. As when making a fundamental analysis of the company and adjusting for non-recurring and extraordinary items, the same *care and analysis is required* for the purpose of determining the equity risk premium.

---

9 An example of the evolution of the forward looking equity risk premium, as measured by the implied market equity risk premium in period of crisis or scandals, can be observed in the later sections.

10 See the Hamon-Jacquillat (2001) as an example.

11 Barro (2006) uses this argument to justify a substantial portion of the equity risk premium.

12 Damodaran (2008).

Approaches to Compute the Equity Risk Premium

In general, there are three main approaches for assessing the equity risk premium, depending on whether one looks into history, asks others, or scrutinizes the future to predict the future:[13]

- the *historical approach*, based on the observation of historic stocks return on the long run;
- the *prospective approach*, which will try to measure the anticipations of investors based upon current asset prices. This method will either try to estimate the implied risk premium based upon share prices or will be based upon predictive forward looking models in order to forecast the equity risk premium based upon exogenous and endogenous parameters of the companies;
- the *survey approach*, which is based on summarizing the different views existing in financial markets at one point of time.

The advantages and pitfalls of each of these methods will be reviewed in details in the following pages.

Historic Equity Risk Premium

The approach using historic stock market returns is based upon the assumptions that *the study of ex post return may reveal* what investors should consider as *the ex ante anticipated equity risk premium*. As such, this represents the average historical return of the market risk portfolio over the risk-free debt security. A number of studies have addressed and analyzed the question of market return over time and history. Some studies go back to the beginning of the nineteenth century to trace back data and estimate the historic equity risk premium.[14]

There are a number of studies that have already looked into the different historical analyses possible. Damodaran (2008), Fernandez (2007), or Chapter 9 of Grabowski-Pratt (2008) can provide the details for those wishing to read more about the state of the academic research.

The most cited and thorough study performed on the U.S. is, in my opinion, that of Roger Ibbotson *et al.*, which also represents one of the most cited and examined sources for the equity risk premium in the U.S. The data used by Ibbotson goes back to 1926.[15]

---

13 Regardless of the approach, equity risk premium is and should be a forward looking concept.

14 Siegel (1999, 2002).

15 Ibbotson Associates/MorningStar (2007).

However, a broader and more detailed look on the world is provided by LSE professors E. Dimson, P. Marsh and S. Staunton, who have done extensive research on the worldwide equity risk premiums. They analyzed data from 17 major countries (including the U.S.), using data that begins in 1900. Their work has gained much resonance in the finance world and it has the advantage of going beyond merely U.S. data. Their evidence on long-run risk premium is derived from a unique database, compiled with the support of the Dutch bank ABN AMRO.[16] The database comprises annual returns on stocks, bonds, bills, inflation, and currencies for 16 countries from 1900-2001. Together, these countries make up 95 per cent of the free float market capitalization of all world equities at start–2002, and they comprise over 90 per cent by value at the start of our period in 1900.

The following Table summarizes the findings of these two main studies:

Table 1: Historic equity risk premium according to Dimson *et al.* and Ibbotson *et al.*

	Dimson-Marsh-Staunton 1900 - 2005		Ibbotson Associates / Morningstar 1928 – 2007 US, 1970 – 2005 Europe	
	Arithmetic Mean	Geometric Mean	Arithmetic Mean	Geometric Mean
France	6.03%	3.86%	6.3%	N/A
Germany	8.25%	5.28%	9.2%	N/A
Great Britain	5.29%	4.26%	5.4%	N/A
Canada	5.67%	4.15%		
USA	6.49%	5.42%	6.4%	4.8%
World ex-US	5.18%	4.10%		
World	5.15%	4.04%	N/A	N/A
Euro zone (1)	5.53%	4.34%	5.8%	N/A

(1) *GDP weighted average based upon the author's own estimates*

Source: Damodaran (2008), Fernandez (2007), Dimson et al. (2006), Morningstar/Ibbotson SBBI Valuation Edition 2008/Ibbotson International Equity Risk Premium report.

Despite the acknowledgement of the enormous workload performed by these academics, one cannot escape noticing the growing number of critics on the historic approach. *There are a number of problems with the historic data,* as underlined by many studies criticizing the methodology of estimating the equity risk premium.

16 ABN AMRO has since been taken over by, among others, Royal Bank of Scotland.

First of all, what is the point of looking so far back in the past (over 100 years in some cases)? This would mean that we expect that investors' risk expectations and the market portfolio have not changed over the years and, moreover, that they will remain the same for future years. Do we really think that the investment behavior of our parents and grandparents was the same as ours (and that it will be the same as our children's)? Although there may be strong arguments to support that historical trends can predict future outcome, clearly there must be a link between what we see in the past and what we expect in the future (and why it is explained by past experiences).[17]

In addition, there are a number of *events and items that have occurred in the past that may not occur again in the future*. Much has been written on the difference between the realized risk premiums and the expected equity risk premiums by investors at the same time. Dimson *et al.*, although observing the realized equity returns, also states that equity returns in the second half of the twentieth century were higher than in the first half, because of, (1) falling transaction costs, (2) declining inflation rates (specially in the 1980s and 1990s, see Figure (1)), and (3) higher corporate cash flow growths as opposed to declining business environment risks.[18] Ibbotson-Peng report that the realized risk premiums are higher than those that would have been expected given the underlying economics of the 1926-2007 period.[19] *Ex post* returns are affected by the difference between realized and expected inflation. Although the difference is neutral to inflation, whether estimated in real or nominal terms, this assumes to some extent that the *average inflation expectations over a long period are a correct proxy for the inflation expectations of economic agents.*

---

17 Fernandez (2007), Damodaran (2008).

18 Dimson *et al.* (2003, 2006).

19 Ibbotson-Peng (2002).

Figure 1: U.K. and U.S. inflation over the last decade[20]

Also, several analyses have proved that the *serial correlation of the historic equity risk premium is very low or even negative*, thereby strongly undermining the credibility of the historic studies.[21]

In addition, one can also observe that the historic premium in the U.S. is well above other countries (except Germany, where the data is biased with the effects World War I and World War II). This phenomenon was referred to as the "*bias survivorship*". The U.S. equity market has been, over the past decades, the most successful equity market, earning the highest returns and premiums while investments in other markets would have earned smaller premiums. Thus, the survivor bias will result in *historical premiums that are overestimated versus the expected risk premium*, even if they factor risk correctly into asset prices.[22]

Finally, there remains the problem of the method of estimating the equity risk premium historically: arithmetic or geometric mean? While many studies have been written about the subject, a few comments on the question can be examined. If there is indeed a low serial correlation between the annual historic equity risk premiums over time, then the arithmetic average will overestimate the premium. As such, the use of an *arithmetic historical average relies on the assumptions that the distribution of market returns does not vary* (much) over time and that market returns are uncorrelated over time. Though not directly opposed to that, *geometric premiums will measure the*

20 Source: Federal Reserve, Bank of England data and Dimson *et al.* (2006).
21 See Fama-French (1988).
22 Damodaran (2008).

changes over many periods by using the buy and hold strategy (dividends being reinvested). There is probably no right or wrong answer to this question, just as it is difficult to tell whether averages or medians are more appropriate in general on a specific data subset. It depends on the data subset itself, the intended use *etc.* On the debate above, the average holding period of the investment is probably one of the key concepts that needs to be understood by any analyst choosing to apply historical equity risk premiums.

Most authors concede that the *equity risk premium has significantly declined in the last decades* versus the overall period. *This decline is structural indeed and not conjunctural* and this can be verified by analyzing the decomposition of most explanatory factors behind the level of historical equity risk premiums.[23]

Prospective Equity Risk Premium

The *prospective approach* will be based on looking into *future expectations of investors* as opposed to analyzing past occurrences. There are two methods of estimating the prospective equity risk premium:

- the *fundamental (bottom-up) method*, which models the implied equity risk premium imbedded in market prices; and
- the *predictive (top-down) method*, which models, based upon endogenous and exogenous economic and market factors, how the market portfolio is expected to develop (and thus the equity risk premium).

In the fundamental method, the implied equity risk premium is constructed by using an implied DCF approach (free cash flows to equity, alternatively dividends or some form of residual income stream) in order to solve for each component of the portfolio, the following equation:

$$0 = -P + \sum_{t=1}^{n} \frac{CF_t}{(1+r)^t}$$ [24]

Solving the above equation for each "market portfolio" company yields a *market return* which can, by subtracting the risk-free rate, yield the "*implied*" *market premium*. Some academics also consider the option pricing method to derive the bottom-up or implied equity risk premium.

23 One of the best analyses on this topic is provided by Dimson *et al.* (2006).

24 *P* denotes the current market price and *r* the discount rate (implied return) for which the equation is solved. CF is the appropriate metric (free cash flow to equity or dividends) to measure the return from a shareholder's perspective.

There are a number of commercial sources that use such an approach to estimate an equity risk premium: Bloomberg, Reuters, Value Line Institutional Brokers' Estimate System (IBES), Associés en Finance (Euro-zone, 350 companies) or Fairness Finance (France, CAC40 index), *etc.* Some of them will use a market consensus and make the computation based upon the average expectations of investors. Others, who perform the analysis more accurately, will make their own estimates for each market portfolio and compute the implied risk premium through it.

Table 2: Evolution of the Bloomberg equity risk premium over recent years

	Bloomberg Equity risk premium - vs LT government bonds						
	Dec-05	June-06	Dec-06	June-07	Dec-07	June-08	Dec-08
Bloomberg - Euro-zone	6,4%	6,5%	6,7%	6,7%	6,8%	5,6%	6,0%
Bloomberg US	4,8%	5,0%	5,3%	5,3%	5,2%	5,0%	6,5%

Associés en Finance[25] *runs a bottom-up model* (Trival©) on 300 European corporations that builds upon 25-year operating free cash flow forecasts for all companies plotted against the share price. The implied market return is computed using an adjusted CAPM where, besides the "classic" measures of risk and return, the expected illiquidity is also featured in the regression analysis: the results of the implied market risk premium are "netted" from any potential illiquidity phenomenon. The model runs since 1986 in its current form. The implied equity risk premium is considered by many as applicable in a CAPM model, although derived through a multi-factor approach. The 10-year average of the equity risk premium computed by them lies at 5 per cent, with a range of 3.8 per cent to 6.2 per cent if we consider a standard deviation at a 95 per cent confidence level.

25 *Associés en Finance* is an independent financial consultant firm founded by French economics professor Bertrand Jacquillat.

Figure 2: European Equity risk premium according to Associés en Finance since 1986[26]

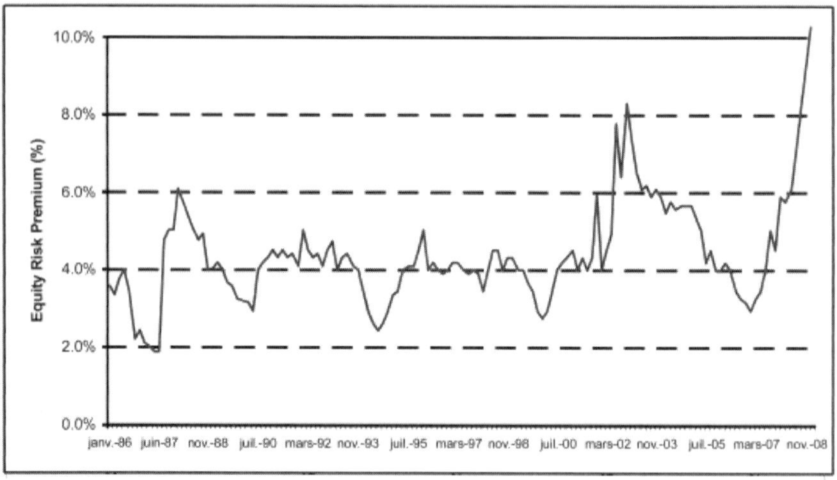

Fairness Finance[27] uses a similar model on the 40 largest French firms also operating free cash flows plotted against shares. The implied risk premium is adjusted for bias in analysts' forecasts but the implied premium is considered directly applicable in any CAPM model. The computation is available since mid-2008 and yields between 8 per cent and 9 per cent in the current market environment. Détroyat & Associés[28] also runs a free cash flow based model to compute the implied equity risk premium since the 1990s. Their model provides a monthly estimate on 21 different European indices (country and industry specific).

In the field of academic research, there were some efforts to tackle the issue similarly to the U.S. studies performed since the 1980s. In a similar approach to what Associés en Finance or Fairness Finance use, Schröder (2005) used a *dividend discount model* ("DDM") *and a residual income model on the Eurostoxx 50* and FTSE 100 index, using among others Bloomberg data inputs.[29] Gameiro (2008) analyzed with *a three stage DDM the return of 20 different countries worldwide over the 1995–2008* period using IBES analysts' consensus to build market portfolios. She finds that, among others, expected risk premiums tend to vary depending on the risk aversion of investors towards a particular market, *i.e.*, systemic changes in investor risk appetite towards a specific

[26] Excerpt of the Lettre Vernimen no. 71, December 2008.
[27] An independent financial consultancy company based in Paris.
[28] An independent financial consultancy company based in Paris.
[29] Schröder (2005).

country.[30] *Both academics estimate a median implied equity risk premium in the region of 4 per cent.*

It is rather interesting to rerun a similar model for the whole Western European region in order to see the evolution of the equity risk premium from a different source. For the purpose of this book, I have rebuilt a *Western European market portfolio composed of the 250 largest French, German, U.K., Spanish, and Dutch stocks* to simulate the evolution of the implied prospective equity risk premium since 1998 (the date from which I had an extensive database on analyst forecast information available for each and every year). The average equity risk premiums lies at 5.0 per cent during that period, with the lagged two-year average giving a 10-year average of 4.9 per cent. The range of the equity risk premium with a confidence level of 95 per cent lies between 3.6 per cent and 6.1 per cent. Results are presented in Figure 3.

Figure 3: European Equity risk premium since 1998[31]

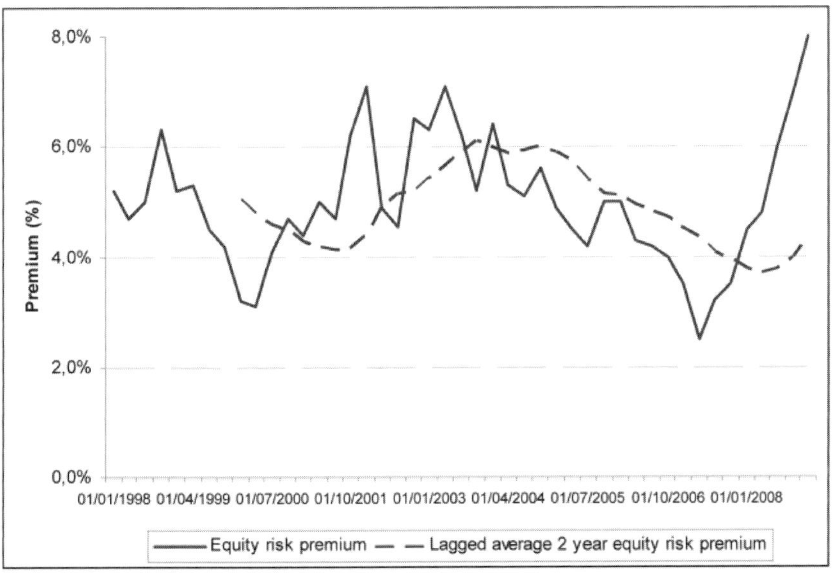

Source: the author

As observed, the equity risk premium did remain in a 2 per cent to 8 per cent tunnel over the last decade according to my computations. External shocks and economic

[30] Gameiro (2008).

[31] Based upon the author's own research and computations. Using analyst forecasts (Deutsche Bank, Exane, Bloomberg and Reuters), the implied prospective premium is re-computed at the beginning of every quarter during a given year. The model uses an un-levered free cash flow based DCF model. Explicit cash flows are taken from the analysts

turmoil naturally causes the equity risk premium to overshoot its long term or trailing average, just as periods of high economic growth and prosperity make it decrease very significantly.

The main weakness is also apparent in this same respect. The number yielded by this approach is rather volatile and tends to over-reflect market trends, because of the stock market volatility. On one hand, this is the reflection of market investors' expectations at one point in time, on the other, is this really meaningful for a long-term fair market value perspective? More on that subject in a later section.

In the *predictive (top-down) method*, independent lagged predictors are used on the equity risk premium using regression techniques:

$$ERP_t = \alpha + [\beta_1 ... \beta_n][X_1 ... X_n] + \varepsilon_t$$ [32]

Used and tested predictors include the dividend yield, short term interest rates, inflation, earnings ratios, defaults spreads *etc. However, recent research has been rather dubious about the efficacy and accuracy of any of these models on the long term.*[33] Also, these models rely on historical observations to fuel the predictive model, creating potential room for disconnect and misappreciation.

This approach is also often used by macroeconomic analysts and bank strategists when they aim to predict market movements.

In an extension of the historical studies, Ibbotson-Peng (2003) estimate a forecast of the equity risk premium based upon the earnings growth, price to earnings ("P/E") growth, and GDP growth per capita (supply side model). Since the expansion of P/E ratios is not expected to continue forever, it should be restated to estimate the expected equity returns.[34]

A comparison between the first and second half of the 102-year period analyzed by Dimson *et al.* makes an interesting point. Over the first half of the century, the arithmetic average world equity risk premium relative to risk-free securities was 4.1 per cent, whereas, it was 7.7 per cent over the period 1950-2001. Why this difference? As Dimson *et al.* (2002, 2006) explains it, there was unprecedented growth in productivity and efficiency as well as a fall in the required rate of return due to diminished business and

---

forecasts for 3 years, the extrapolated through 2 stages of super growth (2 year then 5 years) and then faded towards ROCE = WACC over a period of 10 years. Terminal value is computed after the 20th year.

32 These models can use a large number of factors, starting from one or two explanatory variables (X) up until a dozen variables.

33 Goyal-Welch (2006).

34 Ibbotson-Peng (2003).

investment risk. Factors such as these, which led to a reduction in the required risk premium, have contributed to further move upward stock prices. While there are obviously differences in risk between markets, they are more likely attributable to country-specific events that will not reoccur. *When making future projections,* there is a strong case, particularly *given the increasingly international nature of capital markets, for taking a global* rather than a country-by-country *approach* to *determining the prospective equity risk premium.* Based on the above understanding and modeling dividend growth, inflation, exchange rates, and equity returns, Dimson *et al.* (2006, 2007) infer a global worldwide equity risk premium of 4 per cent.

Siegel studies the relationship between real equity returns, P/E, and the value of capital (replacement cost/market value) and infers a long-term equity risk premium estimate based upon a range of P/E ratios and real average equity returns of 2 per cent on a geometric basis.[35] Cornell uses growth in GDP and earnings/dividends to estimate a 3 per cent equity risk premium on the long run (geometric).[36]

On a slightly different approach, French economist P. Artus developed a multi-factor macroeconomic model within the French bank Natixis whereby the equity risk premium is driven by the market's P/E ratio; the expected evolution of earnings and default swaps interest rates (see the evolution in Figure 4).

Figure 4: European Equity risk premium as per Natixis research since 1995[37]

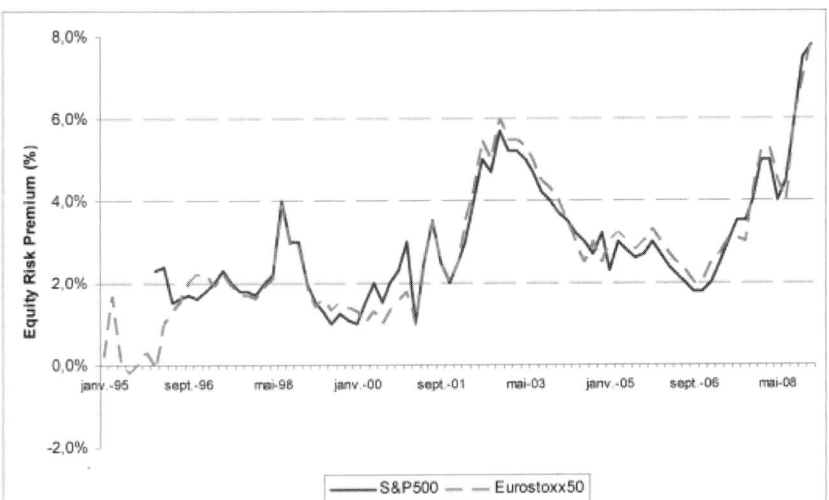

35 Siegel (2001).

36 Cornell (2001).

37 Natixis Special Report no. 13 : comment juger la prime de risque ? January 2009.

However, there are critics and pitfalls to this approach as well. First of all, *the ability to reproduce portfolios that recreate the whole* market *is not* an *easy* task. The equity risk premium is not the risk premium of the leading stock market index but that of the whole market. Furthermore, given the opportunities to cross-hedge and arbitrage between different markets, one could also question whether a world index is not more appropriate.

Second, the current *market prices* may or *may not be a correct reflection of asset prices*. In particular, in periods of crisis, there can be disconnect between market prices and consensus or analyst estimates. The *implied equity risk premium requires* accepting that the *market is rational and efficient*. If this assumption does not hold, any bottom-up prospective approach leads to erroneous results.

Third, but this is related to the previous points, *the prospective approach yields* a very *volatile equity risk premium*, that can change significantly between months. Is this reasonable from the perspective of a business valuation exercise?

Also, Goyal-Welch (2006) have *tested* a number of variables that have been held to predict the equity risk premium such as dividend yields, P/E ratios, interest rates, inflation rates, *etc. and found that most models are unstable to predict the resulting equity risk premium* over the *long term* as and soon as one tries to extrapolate over a period outside the sample data.[38]

In addition, *bias between actual and expected equity risk premiums* estimates are *overstated on the average*. Also, risk evaluation is based on a subjective "pain of loss" (this reinforces the argument that there is not a single equity risk premium equal for each investor) which varies with initial wealth. If linked to the possibility of market bubbles, this means that returns can vary markedly over time between runs of high expected returns with runs of low ones.[39]

Finally, *equity risk premiums* may *follow a random walk phenomenon*, just as equity prices and interest rates do. If one assumes that this is the case, then even though the equity risk premium is supposed to follow a long-term investment pattern, the *expected equity risk premium will match the current / actual implied equity risk premium*.[40]

Survey Equity Risk Premium

Another way to estimate the required equity risk premium is to make a survey on market practices and market expectations. Such survey will typi-

38 Damodaran (2008).

39 Barberis-Huang-Santos (2001).

40 Lungu-Minford (2006).

cally include finance professionals and academics, from various fields and horizons. A *survey of the recent textbooks*, as proposed by Fernandez in a recent work paper, is also an alternative to this approach, but it is preferable to survey market professionals, as they are probably closer to investment trends and are more up-to-date than books, finance professors, or academics. Table 3 summarizes the review of recently published finance textbooks on the subject.

Table 3: Textbooks and the equity risk premium

Book	Position	Range used
Bodie-Kane-Marcus (2003)	Expected risk premium = arithmetic historic risk premium	5% to 8%
Brealy-Myers-Allen (2005)	No official position	5% to 8%
Copeland-Koller-Murrin (2005)	Expected risk premium = historic risk premium - 1 to 2%	3.5% - 4.5%
Arzac (2005)	Expected risk premium = arithmetic historic risk premium	5%
Damodaran (2006)	Expected risk premium =geometric historic risk premium	4%
Fernandez (2006)	Investors have different expected equity risk premiums	4%
Vernimmen (2008)	Prospective equity risk premium	3% to 6%
Pratt-Grabowski (2008)	Consensus for unconditional equity risk premium	3.5% to 6.0%

Source: Fernandez (2007) and the author's additions

Table 4 is an overview of recent surveys done by Ivo Welch and Pablo Fernandez on the *views of finance professors throughout the world.*

Table 4: Finance professor's consensus on the equity risk premium

	Fernandez		Welch (2007) (1) (2)		Welch (2009) (2)	
	Equity risk premium	Resp.	Equity risk premium	Resp.	Equity risk premium	Resp.
USA	6,5%	351	5,0%	369	6,2%	143
Euro-zone	5,3%	220				
UK	5,6%	52				
Canada	5,4%	29				
Australia	5,9%	23				
Other	8,0%	66	4,5%	219		

(1) other means non US participants surveyed
(2) geometric 30 year forward looking

Source: Fernandez (2007), Welch (2007, 2009)

Analyst or market consensus surveys are not necessary more reliable than the views of finance professors, though it is difficult to deny that the former are more close to the market and its evolution, while the latter may have more broad perspective on the subject. *Analysts* tend to be influenced or *biased with the investment recommendations* they are making and as such, their opinion on "technical subjects" may not be representative of an underlying perception of the subject.

Many studies have already underlined the *tendency of market analysts to overreact in their earnings forecasts* (upwards in good recession and downward in bad recession) and thus the predictive power of such survey may prove to be very low indeed. Table 5 illustrates an overview of a more market-oriented survey (investments banks and CFOs), including a much cited study done by Graham and Harvey on a large panel of CFOs in the US.[41]

Table 5: Equity risk premium survey: investment bank and CFO consensus

	Equity risk premium						
	Dec-05	June-06	Dec-06	June-07	Dec-07	June-08	Dec-08
Consensus Eu-Zone (1)	4,5%	4,7%	4,5%	4,4%	4,6%	5,2%	5,6%
standard error	1,2%	1,5%	2,0%	1,8%	2,0%	1,7%	1,5%
Consensus France (1)	4,5%	4,4%	4,5%	4,3%	4,5%	5,3%	5,5%
standard error	1,3%	1,4%	2,0%	1,8%	2,1%	2,0%	2,0%
Consensus US (2)	4,8%	4,9%	5,1%	5,4%	5,5%	6,0%	6,0%
standard error	2,0%	2,2%	2,2%	2,0%	2,5%	1,5%	2,3%
Graham - Harvey CFO Study	2,8%	2,5%	2,8%	3,6%	4,0%		
standard error	2,2%	2,0%	2,0%	2,1%	2,2%		

(1) consensus based upon 12 banks surveyed
(2) consensus based upon 10 US banks surveyed

Source: Graham-Harvey (2008), the author

The problem with surveys is that they represent the average opinion of people. Those opinions may be influenced by short-term considerations, the context in which the survey has been performed, and may be misled by the manner that the question was addressed. To make a crude comparison, people may jump out of windows for some (maybe legitimate) reasons but you will not jump out before giving thought to it, right?

Equity Risk Premium and Volatility

Is a historical approach more secure versus the volatility problem? While it may seem a superficial observation that historical equity risk premiums are more reliable in highly volatile periods, this is only partially true. If you believe *that markets,* in the aggregate, can be *significantly overvalued or undervalued,* the *historical risk premium* becomes a *good choice.* However, as explained in a later section and as proved by several other studies, historical risk premiums perform even worse than forecasts of actual risk premiums in the future.

Historic equity risk premiums are not subject to *less volatility* in the data than the implied equity risk premium! If we analyze the average standard error of most historical studies, we will find that there is about a +/- 200 basis points margin of error in the estimated equity risk premium, if we are contemplating the very long term (over 80 years). This same margin of error

[41] Fernandez (2007), Damodaran (2008).

goes up to 400 basis points if we analyze only the last 25 years! The shorter the period selected, the larger this standard error becomes, thereby offsetting the advantage of using more recent data. This means that using a standard statistical confidence level and relying on historical data, you are almost as sure not to find the correct future equity risk premium than to find the correct number.

However, in a similar level, just because a prospective implied equity risk premium is indicating a 10 per cent premium at one point of time, there is no reason to rely blindly on that number as an input for a business valuation.

It is interesting also to turn and examine the alleged large volatility of the implied equity risk premium and volatility. The analysis of the 2008 situation may give a lot of perspective in this respect.

The lagged equity risk premium may represent a solution to that problem. But as it has been observed end of 2008, *the implied equity risk premium may overshoot* to such excess levels that would render its use completely inadequate or inappropriate for some.

As illustrated in Figure 3, this was the case end of 2008 and early 2009, when the implied equity risk premium in Western Europe went up to 8 per cent according to my estimates and even 10 per cent according to other sources. Does this *discredit the implied equity risk premium* and its applicability? To answer this issue, we must take a closer look at the fundamental reasons that explain the high level of equity risk premiums experienced in the current market.

Since mid-2008, corporate issuing of debt (event AAA- or AA-rated debt) has seen enormously high spread rates applied. This is linked to the degrading environment and the low confidence in the debt markets today. It is therefore logical to consider that investors *arbitrage between equity and corporate bonds as a surrogate to risk-free assets.*

I have, therefore, restated my initial computation in Figure 3 to replace the risk-free rate with the credit default swaps on the secondary markets for issuers having a rating of at least A.[42] The results are provided in Figure 5.

---

42 Default rate on A or superior graded companies has been around 0.3% over the last 15 years in Western Europe.

Figure 5: European Equity risk premium since 1998 – adjusted for credit default swap rates[43]

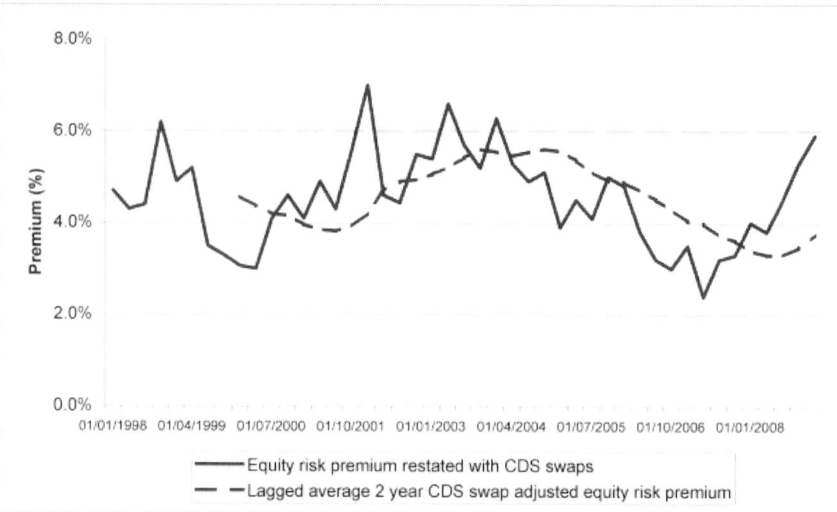

The implied equity risk premium adjusted for the CDS spread shows that the reasons of the enormous equity risk premium end 2008 is related to the low confidence in the financial markets in general and the aggravated default risk perceived by the investors. Corrected for the increase in the systematic (non-diversified risk), the equity risk premiums seem to remain at "normal" levels. So it is a dramatic *change in the consumption/investment pattern* that causes the huge shift and the large equity premiums in the model, not only the decrease of equity prices versus a relative stability in medium term earnings forecasts, as some may argue. In this case, the fundamental *change is in the risk aversion* of the investors and the validity of the underlying CAPM assumptions is broken (more seriously than usual) by having risk-free assets that are not so risk-free anymore. *This is something that an analyst (valuation professional) must adjust for.*

It is not necessarily the method itself that is wrong, but the economic situation is such that it generates results that may be considered not relevant. So yes, the implied equity risk premium cannot be applied blindly in any case and in any market situation, despite its many advantages and strong predictive powers. In case of extreme volatility, analysts' judgment must

---

43 Same methodology as Figure 3, but the risk-free rate is adjusted with the CDS swaps on corporate emissions instead of risk-free interest rates.

prevail over automatism. But only time will tell whether the risk aversion returns to its historic level or whether a fundamental change has occurred that will remain valid for long term. The unknown answer to this question (to date) is also a key to understanding whether implied equity risk premiums are indicators for the future.

Analysis of the Equity Risk Premium's Determinants with European Data

Historical equity risk premiums do not seem the best way to determine the expected equity risk premium. But how to overcome the natural volatility of implied equity risk premiums, especially in volatile business environments and conditions? Analysis of the European market data sheds some light on a couple of interesting observations that can help shape an opinion. The analysis will focus on some determinants of the equity risk premium deemed important for the understanding of its nature, predictive power, and whether historic or implied (current) equity risk premium is best.

Equity Risk Premium and Interest Rates: A Correlation

Many studies have suggested that the *forward looking expected equity risk premium seems correlated to the evolution of interest rates* (though some studies seem rather contradictory on the issue. See, as an example, the debate between Welch-Goyal (2007) and Campbell-Thompson (2008)).

It is therefore interesting to run a *regression between the equity risk premium and the level of interest rates* (both long-term interest rates, short-term interest rates, and a proxy for the shape of the yield curve):

$$ERP_t = \alpha_t + \beta_1 LT_t(i) + \beta_2 ST_t(i) + \beta_3 Y_t(i)$$ [44]

The results of the analysis are presented in Table 6. Long-term interest rates are representative of the price of risk-free assets, while the short-term interest rates are a proxy for the current inflation expectation and the yield curve variable for the medium-term inflation expectations.

[44] LT means the current level of long-term interest rates minus their average over the observed period, ST means short-term interest rates minus their average over the observed period and Y means the shape of the yield curve, proxied by the convexity/concavity of interest rates (3 months, 6 months, 1 year, 3 year, 5 year and 10 year) versus a linear average line.

It is interesting to observe that there is a strong correlation between the implied equity risk premium and the level of interest rates; the best correlation being observed on the lagged implied equity risk premium.

Table 6: Correlation between the equity risk premium and interest rates[45]

	Historical Equity risk premium (1)	Implied Equity risk premium (2)	Implied Lagged 2 year Equity risk premium (2)	Average of Implied Lagged 2 year / Historic Equity risk premium
Intercept	1,80%	1,75%	1,68%	1,71%
Long term interest rate (3)	0,132	0,232	-0,321	-0,211
statistical signifcance (t-stat)	++	++	+++	++++
Short term interest rate (4)	-0,012	0,023	0,039	0,015
statistical signifcance (t-stat)	+	*	++	++
Yield curve (5)	0,056	-0,112	-0,158	-0,252
statistical signifcance (t-stat)	++	*	+++	++++
Ajd. R^2	35%	48%	57%	45%
overall statistical signifcance	++	++	+++	+++

(1) Historic equity risk premium recomputed from the Dimson et al. and Ibbotson data from a period of 1950 to 1998 / 2008, for a combined Euro-zone index
(2) as per author estimates for the 1998 - 2008 period (see previous section)
(3) / (4) Composite long term (10 - 20 year) and short term (6 month) interest rate index with GDP based weighting, excerpt of Simons et al. and Ibbotson data
(5) Difference between the long term and short termin interest rate

Surprisingly, the level of long-term interest rates (versus their long-term average) is negatively correlated to the equity risk premium. This would imply that *equity risk premium goes at its highest level when interest rates are rather low.* However, short-term interest rates (versus their long-term counterpart) are mildly positively correlated with the equity risk premium.

These observations are not necessary incompatible. The positive correlation with the short-term interest rates (which is often representative of monetary intervention for the economy in general) is explained by the fact that central banks often drive short-term interest rates down in order to re-boost the economy.

The negative correlation with the yield curve is also explained by the same logic, as short-term interest rates are often low in periods of economic downturn but the medium-term outlook often indicates a return to a "normalized" level of interest rates.

To the contrary of what may have been indicated in some previous research, this means that there is *an inverse movement between the forward looking implied equity risk premium and the long-term interest rates.* This inverse movement is not a precise figure, nor does it mean that if interest rates drop by 1 per cent then the equity risk premium increases by 1 per cent, it is more of a trend analysis. The further implications of this analysis are that there is *no*

45 The analysis is performed for the years 1950 to 2007 for the historic equity risk premium and the years 1998 to 2008 for the measurements involving the implied equity risk premium. In the latter case, the analysis is extended to be on a quarterly basis to have as much data point as possible.

single level of equity risk premium but that it is rather *a range of premiums that make sense,* adjusted periodically, given the economic context.

Predictive Power of the Different Equity Risk Premium Measures

In finance, what we ultimately care about is the predictive power of the different explanatory variables. It is therefore also important to analyze the predictive power of the different measures of equity risk premium, *i.e.*, to establish a link between expectations and actual occurrences (see Table 7). Considering five predictors of this premium, it is interesting to see that the lagged implied equity risk premium and the survey premium seem the best predictors of short-term future.[46]

Table 7: Significance analysis of the equity risk premiums' predictive power

Correlation matrix	Next Year's Actual Implied Equity Risk Premium (4)	Actual Equity Risk Premium - 5 year rolling average (4)
Historical Equity risk premium (1)	0,235	0,221
statistical signifcance	+++	+
Implied Equity risk premium (2)	0,321	0,365
statistical signifcance	++	+
Implied Lagged 2 year Equity risk premium (2)	0,564	0,443
statistical signifcance	+++	+++
Average of Implied Lagged 2 year / Historic Equity risk premium	0,452	0,625
statistical signifcance	++++	++++
Survey Premium (3)	0,323	0,331
statistical signifcance	+	+

(1) Historic equity risk premium recomputed from the Dimson et al. and Ibbotson data from a period of 1950 to 1998 / 2008; for a combined Euro-zone index.

(2) as per author estimates for the 1998 - 2008 period (see previous section); computed on a quarterly basis.

(3) As per the investment bank consensus average on a quarterly basis.

(4) Rolling average on a quartely basis.

The results in Table 7 mean that over the analyzed period, *the implied equity risk premium at the end of the prior period was the best predictor of the implied equity risk premium in the next period,* whereas *historical risk premiums did worst.* Extending the analysis to include some medium-term vision as well, the *lagged implied equity risk premium seems to perform the best,* together with the

[46] See a similar analysis in Damodaran (2008).

average lagged-implied/historical equity risk premiums. In all cases, historical equity risk premium alone offers the worst perspectives.

This means that the *best indication of the ex ante equity risk premium* (as a looking forward concept in general) is neither the pure implied current equity risk premium, nor the historic equity risk premium, but probably the *lagged implied equity risk premium.*

In general, this sheds some additional doubt on the relevance of selecting a pure historical equity risk premium as an indicator of the expected required equity risk premium. Because of the underlying volatility of the implied premium, which may not be applicable in certain situations, the use of implied premiums alone seems also problematic.

What Equity Risk Premium Should Then Be Selected?

Recommendation for the Equity Risk Premium, Especially in Volatile Times

If the previous pages are not clear enough, then it is not too late to make an important point: there is no consensus that every professional would abide to on the equity risk premiums, let alone in volatile times. Like for the equity risk premium in "normal" times, every analyst has to make his own judgment on the subject.

What routes would be advisable on the different subjects to be considered in making a personal opinion?

Fernandez (2007) makes an interesting point: while the historic equity risk premium is the same for all market participants, there probably is no single *ex ante* equity risk premium for all market participants. If an *ex ante* market premium does exist, it is impossible to observe it, as it is different for all investors. Having said that, being one of those participants, there are two key concepts to consider and revise for such purposes. *First of all,* one needs to assess its evaluation of the underlying economics and determinants of the equity risk premium and *take a stance* on the *key aspects.* As such,

1. *Do you believe that markets are efficient?* The implied equity risk premium requires that you believe at least in a semi-strong market efficiency. If markets are overvalued or undervalued, then the implied equity risk premium may yield to erroneous results.[47]

---

47 Damodaran (2008).

2. *What is the predictive power of the different models?* In corporate finance, we care ultimately about the future equity risk premium. This question remains rather uncertain and is still a subject of academic debate. The historic equity risk premium comes under serious challenges as its explanatory power for the future implied equity risk premium is definitely very low as seen before.

Second, the *context of the use of the equity risk premium* is also a key determinant of what methodology one should retain for the purposes of such analysis. If the equity risk premium is used for *asset allocation, asset management*, and other short- and medium-term needs, the *implied equity risk premium is a must*. If you are looking at the valuation of a stock in the public market or a fairness opinion, it would be difficult to disregard the implied equity risk premium, as it is based on share prices which form the public market.

However, if you wish to do a "market neutral" valuation for a *long-term investment*, an M&A (non-public) deal, my suggestion would be to disregard the use of the implied equity risk premium, whether it be in low growth or in high growth times. For the purpose of a business or asset valuation, the lagged implied equity risk premium or a range of premiums based upon a consensus and adjusted for interest rates seems to make more sense.

In this respect, and for clarity's sake, it is my opinion that there are two different equity risk premium concepts that should be distinguished. The **short-term equity risk premium**, as assessed by the Security Market Line of the CAPM model, represent the current expected required return in excess of risk-free assets. It is conditional on current market expectations.

The **long-term equity risk premium** represents a normalized vision equity risk premium. It may incorporate economic cycles and changes of risk aversion as exposed by economic agents. This concept is the one that is applicable to the CAPM in the perspective of developing discount rates that shall be used to value long investments, businesses, *etc.* It thus represents the expected required return for investors over the long term. This is the concept that should be selected for business valuation purposes.

The best proxy for the long-term equity risk premium is, in my opinion, the lagged implied equity risk premium. Alternatively, the other solution would be the definition of a range of premium, and the choice of the equity risk premium within that range would be regularly adjusted based on the evolution of interest rates.

How to determine the equity risk premium range? It could be the **long-term equity risk premium** for most private valuation cases, determined by reference to the lagged implied risk premium over the last years, combined with the historical returns over the recent years for those that remain attached to actual performances as well.

In troubled times, the volatility generated because of uncertainties should be placed, as much as possible, in the future cash flow estimates rather than in a discount rate. In most business valuation cases, the company is being valued on a going concern basis with cash flows that are estimated (implicitly) until perpetuity. Therefore, having a very volatile number as a cornerstone of a valuation exercise may not be representative of such long-term vision and, as such, the use of a simple implied equity risk premium is not recommended in my opinion.

Should the equity risk premium be an absolute and invariable number? The recommendation would be no. As Damodaran (2008) summarizes it, equity risk premiums reflect both fundamental and economic expectations as well as the risk aversion of investors. These do change over time. Not to recognize it would be a failure in my opinion. External shocks to a system may cause abnormal and abrupt changes in the equity risk premium. This should be realized and integrated into a valuation by any business analyst.

A Cookbook Recipe for Those Who Would Still Like to Have One

My proposal for a cookbook recipe, for those who prefer to have one, would be the following. Since there is probably no single equity risk premium valid for all times, one should rather consider a range of equity risk premiums. The correct number within that range should be applied by correlating the evolution of risk-free rates with the estimated market return and adjusting the equity risk premium accordingly. As we have seen in Table 6, there is a correlation between interest rates and the equity risk premium and that correlation needs to be reflected. As an example, if the risk-free rate is 5 per cent and the market return is 9 per cent, the equity risk premium should be 4 per cent. If the risk-free rate falls to 4 per cent but market return is estimated at 10 per cent, then the equity risk premium should be 6 per cent. If the risk-free rate remains at 4 per cent but the market return goes down to 9 per cent, the equity risk premium should be 5 per cent.

The key to adjusting the equity risk premium estimate is to consider the market return instead of the equity risk premium directly. If one can estimate a long-term range for the market return, then it is easier to adjust for the evolution of the interest rates. The computation of Figure 3 for the last 10 years indicated, for instance, that the European market return (as approximated by the portfolio constructed) remained in a tunnel between 8.5 per cent and 10 per cent.

Conclusion

A few reminders based on the previous discussions:

- The *equity risk premium is not a single number* and certainly *not an invariable number*. There is probably no single equity risk premium equal to all investors.
- The *historical equity risk premium* may be a surrogate for the equity risk premium, but *not* necessarily a *good* one. In addition, it is not less subject to the volatility phenomenon, it is just not explicit but only implied in the determination method.
- For *business valuation purposes*, it is rather the **long-term equity risk premium** that should apply and not the *short-term (implied market) equity risk premium*.
- The equity risk premium should be assessed using the *lagged implied equity risk premium*, possibly adjusted for recent historical returns but, most importantly, the current level of interest rates versus the estimated overall market return.
- Western European data seems to indicate that, regardless of the economic cycle situation, the *equity risk premium* should be somewhere in a tunnel *between 4 per cent and 6 per cent.* Be sure to adjust the number within that tunnel by *correlating it* to the evolution of the *interest rates* so as to keep *the market return* in an acceptable tunnel (*8.5 per cent to 10 per cent*).
- The estimate of the equity risk premium needs to be *reassessed regularly*.
- Do *not rely* automatically on *any source of* data or *determination methodology*.

Finally, two closing remarks:

1. The computation of the opportunity cost of capital is a complex mechanism that requires the consistent application of several parameters (appreciation of the diversifiable and non-diversifiable risk, the industry and business risk, the impact of leverage, *etc.*).

2. The equity risk premium is but one component of the puzzle. The opportunity cost of capital cannot be assessed without knowing the underlying cash flows to which it will be applied. The cost of capital is a function of the risk and rewards of the asset and has to reflect both accordingly. It is, therefore, not sufficient to assess individually all the relevant parameters for the opportunity cost of capital, but also to make sure that it reflects the risk assumed by the investor.

APPENDIX A

References

P. Artus, Natixis Special Report no. 13 : comment juger la prime de risque ? January 2009.

N. Barberis, M. Huang & T. Santos, "Prospect Theory and Asset Prices" (2001) *Quarterly Journal of Economics* 116, 1-53.

R. Barro, "Rare Disasters and Asset Markets in the Twentieth Century" (2006) *Quarterly Journal of Economics* 823-866.

R. Brealy, S. Myers & F. Allen, *Corporate Finance*, 8th ed. (New York: McGraw Hill/Irwin, 2006).

J. Campbell & S. Thompson, "Predicting the Equity Risk Premium out of sample" (2005) HIER discussion Paper No. 2084.

J. Claus & J. Thomas, "Equity Premia as low as 3 percent?" (2001) *Journal of Finance* 56(5).

B. Cornell, *Equity Risk Premium: the long run future of the stock market* (New York: John Wiley & Sons, 1999).

B. Cornell, Historical Results: Discussion. Equity Risk Premium Forum, AIMR, 2001.

A. Damodaran, *Damodaran on Valuation*, 2nd ed. (New York: John Wiley & Sons, 2006).

A. Damodaran, "Equity Risk Premium: Determinants, Estimations and Implications", Working Paper, September/October 2008, www.damodaran.com

A. Damodaran, *Investment Valuation: Tools and Techniques to determine the Value of any asset*, 2nd ed. (Hoboken, N.J., John Wiley & Sons, 2002).

E. Dimson, P. Marsh & M. Staunton, "Global Evidence on the Equity Premium" (2003) *Journal of Applied Corporate Finance.*

E. Dimson, P. Marsh & M. Staunton, *Global Investment Return Yearbook* (ABN AMRO/London Business School, 2006).

E. Dimson, P. Marsh & M. Staunton, *The Triumph of the Optimists: 101 years of Global Investment Returns* (New Jersey: Princeton University Press, 2002).

E. Dimson, P. Marsh & M. Staunton, "Worldwide Equity Premium: a smaller puzzle", EFA 2006 Zurich meeting paper, AFA 2008 New Orleans Meeting Paper; SSRN.

E. Fama & K. French, "Dividend yields and expected returns" (1988) *Journal of Financial Economics* 3-27.

E. Fama & K. French, "The Cross-Section of Expected Stock Returns" (1992), 47 *Journal of Finance* 427-465.

E. Fama & K. French, "The Equity Premium" (2002), 57 *Journal of Finance* 637-659.

P. Fernandez, "The Equity Risk Premium in finance and valuation text-books", Ed. CIIF - International Center for Financial Research, 04/2008.

P. Fernandez, "Equity Risk Premium: Historical, Expected, Required and Implied", Working Paper IESE Business School, SSRN, 2007.

I. Gameiro, "Equity Risk premia across major international markets" (2008) *Banco de Portgual Economic Bulletin*.

J. Goyal & I. Welch, "A comprehensive look at the empirical performance of equity premium predictions", Working Paper, January 2006.

J. Graham & C. Harvey, "Expectations of Equity Risk Premia, Volatility and Asymmetry from a Corporate Finance perspective", NBER Working Paper, 2003.

J. Graham & C. Harvey, "The Equity Risk Premium in 2008: Evidence from the Global CFO Outlook Survey", Working Paper, SSRN, 2008.

J. Hamon & B. Jacquillat, "Is there value added information in liquidity and risk premiums?", Working Paper, 1998.

J. Hamon & B. Jacquillat, "Is There Value-Added Information in Liquidity and Risk Premiums?" (2001) *European Financial Management*.

R. Ibbotson & G. Brinson, *Global Investing: The professional's guide to the World Capital markets* (New York: McGraw-Hill, 1993).

R. Ibbotson & W. Goetzmann, "History and the Equity Risk Premium", Yale ICF Working Paper No. 05-04, April, 2005.

R. Ibbotson & C. Peng, "Long Run Stock Market returns; participating in the real economy" (2003) *Financial Analysts Journal*.

Ibbotson Associates/Morningstar, *Stocks, Bills, Bonds and Inflation 2007*, Valuation Edition (New York: McGrawHill, 2007).

Ibbotson Associates/Morningstar, *Cost of Capital Yearbook 2007*, Valuation Edition (New York: McGrawHill, 2007).

Y. Le Fur, P. Quiry, Lettre Vernimmen.net no. 71, December 2008 (*www.vernimmen.net*).

A. Lo & C. McKinlay, "Stock markets do not follow random walk" (1998) *Review of Financial Studies* 1, 41-46.

L. Lungu & P. Minford, "Explaining the Equity Risk Premium" (2002) 74 *Manchester School* 670-700.

Natixis Special Report no. 13: Comment juger la prime de risque ? January 2009.

S. Pratt & R. Grabowski, *The Cost of Capital* (New York: John Wiley & Sons, 2008).

D. Schröder, "The implied equity risk premium", An evaluation of empirical methods; Bonn Econ Discussion Paper 13/2005.

J. Siegel, "Historical Results: Discussion", Equity Risk Premium Forum, AIMR, 2001.

J. Siegel, "Sinking Equity Risk Premium" (1999) *Journal of Portfolio Management* 10-17.

J. Siegel, *Stocks for the Long Run*, 3rd ed. (New York: Irwin, 2002).

P. Vernimmen, Y. Le Fur & P. Quiry, *Finance d'entreprises*, 7ième éd. (Paris: Dalloz, 2008).

I. Welch, "The Consensus Estimate for the Equity Premium by Academic Financial Economists in December 2007", Brown University/NBER Working Paper, 2007.

I. Welch, "The Equity Risk Premium Consensus Forecast Revisited", Cowles Foundation Discussion paper no. 1325, September 2001.

I. Welch, "Views of Financial Economists On The Equity Premium And Other Issues" (2000) *The Journal of Business* 73-4, 501-537, with 2009 update. The 2009 update is available at http://welch.econ.brown.edu/academics/equpdate-results2009.html

Valuation During Periods of High Volatility

John Barton

Between August of 2008 and March of 2009, the S&P 500 stock index declined by 40 pe rcent. Much has been written about the economic causes of the crash and, with the exception of the Great Depression, its unprecedented damage to global wealth. To the layperson the recession could be summed up easily: excessive debt, lack of regulation, and simple greed all combined into a perfect storm which dramatically reduced retirement plans and college funds in a matter of months. To the valuation practitioner, though, the recession has had a potentially confusing impact, especially if the economic forces which drive valuation variables are not clearly understood.

This essay provides an overview of what happened to the macroeconomic variables that drive our assessment of a cost of equity, why those metrics sometimes drifted in the opposite direction of where we assumed they'd go, and some suggested methodologies to address what is hopefully a short-term problem. Numerous academic and professional articles have appeared that address this issue; this research is distilled here into a practical guide for valuation practitioners. Specifically, we will look at the risk-free rate, the equity risk premium (ERP), and beta measurements to assess the effects of market volatility.

A practitioner assessing the value of a closely-held company on a repeat basis, say for an ESOP or for an annual gifting program, would *a priori* expect that the valuation as of December 31, 2008 would be below the valuation as of December 31, 2007, all else being equal. Most of the value drivers that we count on to grow a company had been decimated by the end of 2008. Debt financing had dried up for everything from long-term investment to short-term working capital needs. Input prices, though helped by the declining price of oil, could not drop far or fast enough to justify investment. Customer lists suddenly became riskier since even the most solid relationships became subject to cost cutting and illiquidity. Under the specter of these developments, the first four sections of most valuation reports (*i.e.*, the company profile, macroeconomic analysis, industry profile, and subject company financial analysis) painted a very pessimistic picture. Before even beginning a DCF analysis or market approach, we already were trying to figure how to articulate to the client that they had suffered a material setback in value.

The derivation of a cost of equity, however, if done mechanically, yielded a counterintuitive result. Table 1 below reflects the change between 2007 and 2008 in the risk-free rate and the equity risk premium:

Table 1

	12/31/2007	12/31/2008
1-Year Treasury YTM	3.34%	0.04%
20-Year Treasury YTM	4.50%	3.05%
Equity Risk Premium (1)	4.85%	3.84%

(1) As measured in Duff & Phelps' Risk Premium Report (arithmetic average)

A rote calculation of a cost of equity in a build-up model would result in a *reduction* to the cost of equity of 2.5 per cent based on the above, and, all else being equal, an *increase* in value. If a CAPM is applied, the results could be more aggravated due to anomalies with the beta calculation, which will be discussed later. Table 2 reflects a company which earned $10,000,000 in 2007 and is being valued using a simple capitalization model at the end of 2007 and 2008.

Table 2

	12/31/2007	12/31/2008
Net Equity Cash Flow, Yr. 0	$ 10,000,000	$ 10,400,000
Risk-Free rate	*4.5%*	*3.1%*
ERP	*4.9%*	*3.8%*
Specific Risk	*7.5%*	*7.5%*
Equity Discount Rate	16.9%	14.4%
Long-Term Growth	4.0%	4.0%
Indicated Value	$ 80,933,852	$ 104,100,096
Change in Value		28.6%

A first cut analysis, in which no other variables are changed except cash flow growth in 2008, yields a 28.6 per cent increase in value given the parameters selected. This increase in value is directly attributable to the decline in the equity discount rate from 16.9 per cent to 14.4 per cent. Given the economic, industrial, and specific company events, most practitioners would have revisited this analysis unless there were specific reasons why the company would increase in value while much of the rest of the market was declining. Unfortunately, the typical fix that many analysts apply is to change those subjective variables that are derived from the practitioner's analysis rather than a macroeconomic source. Table 3 reflects an analysis with some of these fixes:

Table 3

	12/31/2007	12/31/2008
Net Equity Cash Flow, Yr. 0	$ 10,000,000	$ 10,400,000
Risk-Free rate	*4.5%*	*3.1%*
ERP	*4.9%*	*3.8%*
Specific Risk	*7.5%*	*12.5%*
Equity Discount Rate	16.9%	19.4%
Long-Term Growth	4.0%	2.0%
Indicated Value	$ 80,933,852	$ 61,000,575
Change in Value		-24.6%

In Table 3, the analyst reaches for two fixes that make intuitive sense. First, the growth rate is lowered since expectations for lower sales and higher expenses would be likely during a difficult recession. Second, it is not unreasonable to expect specific company risk would increase, although that would depend on the subject company's position in the economic quagmire at the end of 2008; not all companies suffered equally. Still, the practitioner may satisfy him or herself that an increased cost of equity from 16.9 per cent to 19.4 per cent and a resultant 24.6 per cent decline in value better satisfies his *a priori* position.

Any change in value, however, needs to be verifiable at each step in the analysis. Of course, the practitioner cannot just increase specific risk in Table 3 by 5.0 per cent because the original valuation result offends his sensibilities. Specific changes in risk between 2007 and 2008 must be identified in the company. Likewise, to reduce expected long-term growth by 2.0 per cent, the practitioner must be able to point to market opportunities that existed in 2007 that were lost in 2008. If this cannot be done, then the analysis is invalid.

More importantly, the components of the cost of capital need to be analyzed independently of the two variables changed in Table 3. The scenario in Table 2, albeit unlikely, shows a company which increased in value simply because of a decline in risk-free rate and equity risk premium. This begs the question, is it reasonable that a company that experienced no change in any operational or financial risk factor would see a material increase in value during one of the worst recessions in U.S. history? To answer that question, the variables that comprise the cost of equity need to be reviewed with the following questions in mind: 1) why did these variables change?; 2) what makes the variable valid for use in the cost of equity in the first place?

Risk-Free Rate

As shown in Table 1, the yield on the Long Term Treasury Bond declined by nearly 1.50 per cent over the twelve months preceding December 31, 2008. Since bond prices equal the bond coupon times the bond yield, and since most bond coupons are fixed, a decline in bond yield usually indicates an increase in bond prices. The two most common causes of a decline in bond yields (as is seen in Table 1), are: 1) the market perceives that the underlying risk of the bond issuer has declined relative to alternate investments; and/or 2) the market expects lower inflation and interest rates. The latter is intuitive when one considers the alternative: increasing inflation damages any investment that pays a fixed return. Each successive payment is worth less as inflation consumes value.

In his article "Problems With Cost of Capital Estimation in the Current Environment,"[1] Roger Grabowski discusses the factors that drove Treasury Bond yields lower during 2008. First, there was a "flight to quality", especially during the 3rd and 4th quarters as investors, seeing the increasing risk in the equities market, shifted cash out of equities and into bonds. The increased demand in the bond market helped to drive bond prices up. Second, even though inflation was high during the first half of 2008, the market decline drove the price of oil down, and inflation rates followed the price of oil.

---

1 R. Grabowski, "Problems With Cost of Capital Estimation in the Current Environment - Update" (2008) *Business Valuation Review* 209-220.

Graph 1
Annualized Inflation, July 2008 – March 2009

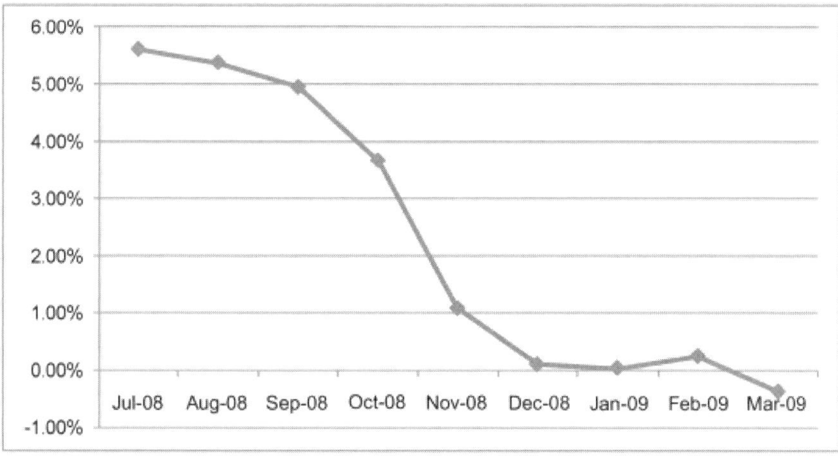

Source: Inflationdata.com

This flight to quality was taking place as early as April, 2008 as we see in a Reuters article from that month:

> U.S. Treasury debt prices rallied on Monday as renewed worries about the banking sector hammered Wall Street and spurred the appetite for bonds and other low-risk investments ...'The theme contributing to the bid into government securities is the concern over the banking sector,' said Eric Lascelles, chief economics and rates strategist with TD Securities in Toronto. *(Reuters, April 20, 2008).*

As Grabowski points out, though, the risk-free rate is relevant to the cost of equity if it reflects the market's expectations for *long-term* inflation. Consequently, it behooves the practitioner, when faced with such a dramatic short-term change in the risk-free rate, to ensure that it reflects long-term expectations and not a short-term anomaly. Grabowski shows that expectations for long-term inflation did not change during the latter half of 2008.[2] In fact, long-term inflation was actually expected to increase which, all else being equal, would lead to higher yields on government bonds. According to the Livingston Survey as of 2008, the 10-Year T-Note yield was expected to increase to 4.0 per cent by December 31, 2009 and 4.70 per cent by December 31, 2010. Table 4 reflects the 10-Year yield at the calendar year end between 2005 and projected 2010:

[2] Grabowski, *ibid.* p. 210.

Table 4

2005	**4.39%**
2006	**4.71%**
2007	**4.11%**
2008	**3.07%**
2009p *	**4.00%**
2010p	**4.70%**

* 2009 and 2010 projected years taken from the Fed's Livingston Survey

Table 4 shows that the 2008 yield is an exception over the recent past, as well as an exception to the expectations for the future. The expectations for long-term yields indicate that the decline in the Treasury Yield is more a function of the flight out of the equities market into safe investments. This is not a valid reason for using the 3.07 per cent yield as a proxy for the risk-free rate.

We cannot use hindsight in valuation due to the "known or knowable" restriction, but actual rates had increased significantly by July of 2009, which supports Grabowski's thesis. The 10-year yield increased from 2.25 per cent on December 31, 2008 to 3.72 per cent by July 31, 2009 and the 20-year yield increased from 3.05 per cent to 4.49 per cent. Grabowski suggests two ways to deal with the risk-free rate problem as of the end of 2008. One is to use an average of the long-term bond yields with an explanation that the current rate did not reflect long-term expectations. Another potential solution is to use a forward rate based on options on exchange traded funds on 20-year bonds.

Equity Risk Premium

The equity risk premium in Table 1, sourced from the Duff & Phelps' Risk Premium Report,[3] dropped by just short of 1.0 per cent in 2008. This poses a similar problem as the risk-free rate. A higher rate would satisfy our expectations for increased risk; instead, a lower ERP as of the end of 2008 sends the cost of equity in the opposite direction of expectations.

The Business Valuation Standards of the American Society of Appraisers define the equity risk premium as "a rate of return added to the risk-free rate to reflect the additional risk of equity instruments over risk-free instruments (a component of the cost of equity or equity discount rate)." It is important to remember that the ERP represents the market's ***expectation*** of

[3] Duff & Phelps' LLC Risk Premium Report 2008. Duff & Phelps measures the ERP by looking at large-cap returns between 1963 and the present.

future returns. The theoretical expected ERP is not an arithmetic or geometric measurement of historical premiums earned above the risk-free rate over some time period. Valuation practice merely got used to using historical measurements as a proxy for the expected rate.

Aswath Damodaran discusses the "implied ERP" which is the internal rate of return that equates a stock market index value with the expected dividends and stock buybacks from the equities on that market.[4] In this context, the ERP should certainly be expected to increase when the market declines. The historical arithmetic average ERP did not increase however in 2008, regardless of the time period used to measure those returns.

The valuation industry commonly used the arithmetic average returns on large-cap stocks over the income-only return on government bonds since 1926 as a proxy for the expected risk premium. Over the past five years, we learned that this measurement is actually one of the least appropriate proxies for the expected return. The many reasons for this are beyond the scope of this essay, but suffice to say, the 1926 to present measurement significantly overstated the ERP. Sourcing the ERP today has changed as a result of numerous articles that discuss the overstatement of the ERP in the 1926-present arithmetic average. One common source is the Duff & Phelps' Report, which looks at the 1963-present arithmetic mean. Another source is the Ibbotson's supply-side premium, found in *Stocks, Bonds, Bills, and Inflation* (SBBI).

Pratt and Grabowski[5] further our education on the ERP by distinguishing between the *unconditional* and *conditional* ERP. The *unconditional* ERP represents a long-term average premium that could be expected over an entire business cycle. Since most academics and practitioners agree that this long-term range is approximately 3.5 per cent to 6.0 per cent, it is not unusual for practitioners to apply a midpoint ERP, say somewhere in the 4.75 per cent range. The ERP that so many practitioners rely on as a proxy for the expected return (such as the return measured between 1963 and current) is usually an *unconditional* ERP. However, since the ERP is cyclical over a business cycle, the *conditional* ERP would measure the premium over risk-free that reflects current market conditions at a specific point in time. Pratt and Grabowski indicate that it is inappropriate to assume a midpoint in the ERP range over a business cycle, especially at an extreme market low like was seen in 2008 and early 2009. Given the market conditions at the end of 2008, they advocate using the conditional ERP.

---

4 A. Damadoran, Equity Risk Premiums (ERP): Determinants, Estimation and Implications, September 2008, adamodar@stern.nyu.edu

5 R. Grabowski & S. Pratt, *Cost of Capital, Applications and Examples* (New York: Wiley, 2008), p. 112.

At a market peak, it is intuitively pleasing that the expected ERP should be at the low end of the range above, as implied by Damodaran; this would indicate an ERP somewhere in the 3.0 per cent to 4.0 per cent range. Conversely, when the market is in a trough, the higher end of the range would be appropriate, probably in the 6.0 per cent range. According to Damodaran's analysis, the implied ERP as of January, 2009 was actually 7.0 per cent.[6] Since December 2008 was so clearly a downmarket, some adjustment to the unconditional ERP would seem appropriate. Given these analyses, a rote reliance on the historical arithmetic ERP of 3.84 per cent shown above, or even a midpoint of 4.75 per cent, with a valuation as of December 2008 would yield skewed results.

This distinction between the unconditional and conditional ERP poses several problems for the valuation practitioner. First, the practitioner must make a subjective decision as to whether the economy is in a trough, at a peak, or somewhere in between. While a macroeconomic analysis is required for all valuations, there were still plenty of economists at the end of 2008 who predicted that significant market declines lay ahead. It is probably even more difficult for the practitioner to know that a market peak has been reached. Further, explaining varying ERPs to a client or judge who is looking for consistency in measurement is a prospect that many would rather do without.

Having said that, relying on an ERP of 3.84 per cent at the end of 2008, when the real metric is likely somewhere between 6.0 per cent and 7.0 per cent, would yield a material overstatement of value of over 10 per cent.

Table 5

	12/31/2007	12/31/2008
Net Equity Cash Flow, Yr. 0	$ 10,000,000	$ 10,400,000
Risk-Free rate	*4.5%*	*4.5%*
ERP	*4.9%*	*6.0%*
Specific Risk	*7.5%*	*10.0%*
Equity Discount Rate	16.9%	20.5%
Long-Term Growth	4.0%	3.0%
Indicated Value	$ 80,933,852	$ 61,211,429
Change in Value		-24.4%

Table 5 contains what may be a more appropriate valuation, given the above discussion. Compared with Table 3, Table 5 keeps a 4.5 per cent long-term

6 Damodaran, above note 4.

risk-free rate and, instead of using the unconditional ERP, uses a conditional ERP, estimated at 6.0 per cent. A more modest and, perhaps, more realistic specific risk of 10.0 per cent is added and a long-term growth of 3.0 per cent is applied, instead of 2.0 per cent. The specific risk and long-term growth variables are moderated since it is unlikely that these variables would change so dramatically in one year without a significant change inside the company. The result is a similar decline in value as was seen in Table 3, but a decline that is probably more theoretically supportable. Clearly, the growth rate and subject company risk premium, which are contrived for these examples, in practice require extensive thought, judgment, and support.

Beta

The valuation examples in Tables 1 to 3 assume that the cost of capital is derived using a build-up model in which both the systematic and unsystematic risk is combined in the specific risk factor. The Capital Asset Pricing Model (CAPM) is used by most practitioners, especially if a sophisticated analysis of capital structure is required. The modified CAPM is shown as follows:

$$K_e = R_{f1} + \beta(ERP) + Alpha$$

Where:

Ke =	Cost of Equity
R_{f1} =	Risk Free Rate
β =	Beta
ERP =	Equity Risk Premium
Alpha =	Premium for size and specific risk

In the CAPM, the unsystematic, or diversifiable risk, is captured in the Alpha premium which may contain a company risk premium for size and specific risks. This is a necessary modification to the original CAPM since the modified CAPM is used to value a company in isolation instead of a well-diversified portfolio.

The beta captures the systematic, or non-diversifiable risk. In practice, volatility is used as a proxy for this risk and the beta is measured by regressing changes in the subject company's stock against changes in the market, often represented as the NYSE or the S&P 500. A beta of 1.0 indicates that the subject stock moves in equilibrium with the market; a beta above 1.0 indicates that the stock is more volatile than the market. Hence, a change in a company's beta is a function of two factors: 1) change in the company's stock price; and 2) change in market volatility.

During periods of extreme market volatility, the analyst must consider the extent to which the beta has changed because the company became more volatile or, in the alternative, the extent to which the market has become more volatile. During periods of hyper-volatility in the market, any single company's beta could decline even if the company experiences no change in volatility. A company's business risk will not change simply because the market has become more volatile. Grabowski points out that market volatility in late 2008 was initially caused by the precipitous decline in the financial sector.[7] The betas of companies outside the financial sector would be skewed even if measured against the broad market, such as the S&P 500. Optimally, the beta should be measured when the company is in equilibrium with the market.

If the analyst is using the CAPM to derive a cost of equity for a closely-held company, it is common practice to derive a beta from guideline companies or from an industry measurement. If guideline companies are used during a volatile period such as was seen in 2008-09, then the guideline companies' returns should be compared to the market returns to ensure that the companies were in equilibrium with the market before a beta is used.

In Graph 2 below, the compound returns for the S&P 500 and General Mills Corporation were calculated with December 2005 as the starting point. General Mills and the market are in equilibrium until the spring of 2008. As the market declines during the year, General Mills continues to increase until October when it sees a marginal decline in compound returns. As is suggested by Grabowski, the bear market began with financial stocks which dragged the market indices down starting in late spring 2008. General Mills was purposely chosen for this illustration since the company is a manufacturer of processed foods and would be recession resistant. In this case, General Mills tracks the market almost exactly until the start of the recession; the Company is not in equilibrium with the market during the third and fourth quarters of 2008. General Mills' stock continued to increase throughout the third and fourth quarter from \$57.00 to a peak above \$68.00 at the end of September, before settling back just under \$60.00 by year end.[8] It was not until the second market collapse at the end of the first quarter 2009 that General Mills stock yielded to the recession and declined to \$46.45.

---

7 Grabowski, above note 5, p. 212.

8 Stock prices shown are adjusted for splits and dividends.

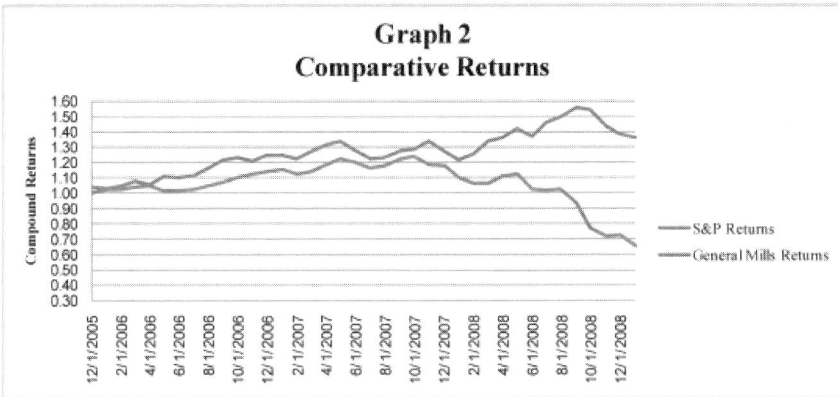

Grabowski suggests that an average of month-end beta estimates for the observed equilibrium period be taken. If the valuation date is December 31, 2008, the observed period of equilibrium might be April 2006 through April of 2008. It is this beta that the market would expect going forward.

Clearly, there are practical problems with this type of analysis. First, not all guideline companies will have a clear distinguishable pattern of equilibrium as is seen above with General Mills. Second, the process of charting returns against the S&P 500 for each guideline company can get cumbersome and beyond the budget for some smaller valuation engagements. Still, like the risk-free rate and the ERP, the beta used should reflect the expected relationship between the subject company and the market. A beta measurement that is skewed by the extreme conditions that were seen at the end of 2008 would be understated, leading to an overstatement of value.

Summary

The suggestion that we temporarily alter the method for deriving a cost of equity will not sit well with some analysts, especially those who work in adversarial environments. Many litigation experts stress in court testimony that we need consistency in our methods to avoid the appearance of advocacy. To return to these same courts, which are sensitive to valuations that change the rules, and testify that the derivation of the cost of equity must change during a period of extreme volatility puts the expert in a precarious situation.

Still, the immutable rule in valuation is that all historical-based analysis, whether it is qualitative research into an industry or a quantitative analysis of the cost of capital components, is only relevant to the extent that it reflects investors' expectations of the future. The stock market declined by 40 per cent during the 2008-09 recession. This highly unusual event affected valuation variables in a very profound way that was particular to that time period only. We cannot treat such a volatile time period as business as usual and assume that the market expects the events to repeat themselves in the future.

Critical Changes in the Playing Field Affecting Valuation

Richard M. Wise

The turbulence in the economy and the markets, and the concomitant effect on businesses, has caused business valuators to "retrofit" their procedures in developing appraisals. A valuator's scope of work, application of techniques, requirements as to the quality of the input data, level of assurance required, and extent of the analysis performed are now very different from those that they have been used to in the past. The classic valuation approaches now require more in-depth analysis and corroboration. To sum it up: the playing field is totally different.

This chapter highlights some of the major areas in which the so-called traditional valuation approaches, methodologies, procedures, and techniques require a "retrofit" involving significantly more analysis, insight, judgment and caution, whether the standard of value is "fair market value", "fair value" for financial reporting (in business combinations, the annual goodwill impairment test or fresh-start accounting), "fair value" in the context of a dissent or oppression remedy, or pricing a business interest for M&A purposes.

Much has appeared in the financial press regarding some of the industries that have been materially affected by the current economic crisis, such as (to name a few):

- advertising;
- airlines;
- automobiles;
- casinos;
- construction/housing;
- entertainment;
- forest products;
- newspapers;
- restaurants;
- retailers;
- transport; and
- travel, tour operators, hotels.

Anyone who studied "Investment Analysis", or who attended a securities or business valuation course, can no longer confidently play on what had been the "traditional" field, or apply the "rules" that had been taught over the past number of years. Investment counsel have their hands full these days in advising pension plans, charitable organizations, trustees, and private clients concerning their investment portfolios.

Business Valuation

Business valuators typically adopt one or more of the following approaches in performing a valuation: Income Approach, Market Approach, and Asset Approach. Within the Income Approach are the Capitalization of Earnings (or Cash Flow) Method and the Discounted Future Benefits Method, the latter which includes the Discounted Cash Flow (DCF) and the Discounted Future Earnings (DFE) Methods. The Market Approach includes the Guideline Public Company Method and the Guideline Transactions Method. Within the Asset-Based Approach is the Adjusted Balance Sheet Method (or Adjusted Shareholders' Equity Method), which is applied either under a going-concern premise or a liquidation premise.[1]

Income Approach

Level of Income

"Maintainable", or "representative", earnings for valuation purposes no longer provide the same comfort level under current market conditions. Projected cash flow and projected future earnings are not considered with the same degree of confidence (inasmuch as projections can provide confidence) in a valuation using a discounted future benefits model.

Can valuators still use, in a meaningful manner, the past three- to five-years' earnings, or the last twelve months' earnings, to arrive at a representative level of indicated future earnings? What guidance can a valuator obtain from such earnings in reviewing management's projections for purposes of applying the DCF Method?

Considering the lack of reliable data and the overall uncertainties regarding the economy and relevant industries in conducting a valuation engagement, business valuators should also consider the comments and guidance of the

---

1 For a description of these valuation approaches and methods, see R.M. Wise, J.E. Fishman & S.P. Pratt, *Guide to Canadian Business Valuations* (3 volumes) (Toronto: Thomson Carswell, (loose-leaf service)).

various accounting bodies concerning auditing challenges in light of the credit crisis and the economic climate.

AASB Risk Alert

A basic starting point in valuation is a review of the subject's financial statements. It is noteworthy that in January 2009 the Auditing and Assurance Standards Board (AASB) of the Canadian Institute of Chartered Accountants (CICA) issued a (non-authoritative) *Risk Alert*,[2] addressing matters of interest to public accountants who perform audit or review engagements. The *Risk Alert* refers to the degree to which a particular entity and its financial statements would be affected by the current environment, depending on such matters as:

- the industry in which the entity operates;
- the entity's financing or credit arrangements, including its ability to continue to obtain financing from financial institutions and other creditors, including suppliers; and
- the extent to which an entity has invested in financial instruments, the market for which has been severely affected by the credit crisis or other aspects of the serious economic downturn.

In performing a business valuation, the valuator must be satisfied with an entity's ability to continue as a going concern, unless it is clear that the liquidation method under the Asset-Based Approach is appropriate. For *financial reporting* purposes, this is the responsibility of management:[3] when assessing whether the going-concern assumption is appropriate, the entity's management takes into account all available information regarding the future, which is at least (but not limited to) 12 months from the balance sheet date. The *Risk Alert* notes that in today's environment, the reduced availability of credit and illiquidity in short-term funding may create conditions indicating a potential problem or jeopardize the continuation of the enterprise as a going concern. Issues surrounding credit risk and liquidity may create new uncertainties, or may exacerbate those already existing. Reference is also made to various conditions that may impact an entity's ability to continue as a going concern. Likewise, business valuators should have

---

2 In November 2008, the staff of the AASB issued a *Risk Alert*, "Auditing Considerations Regarding Fair Value of Financial Assets in a Credit Crisis". The January 2009 *Risk Alert* was prepared "in an environment when the breadth and depth of the current economic crisis will impact all audited entities to some degree", referring to "Global Financial Crisis" on the CICA website at *www.cica.ca*, "Responses to financial turmoil" on the Accounting Standards Board's website at *www.acsbcanada.org*, and the "Credit Crisis and Auditing" web page at *www.cica.ca/crisisandauditing* on the CICA's Implementation Support Gateway.

3 CICA Handbook, *General Standards of Financial Statement Preparation*, para. 1400.08A (January 2008).

similar going concern-related discussions with management (unlike in the past when such an issue was not a primary consideration).

Business valuators should also consider the following observation, as expressed in the *Risk Alert*:

> An important overall consideration in the current environment is the increased risk of material misstatement resulting from management bias. With or without fraudulent intent, there may be a natural temptation for management to bias judgments underlying estimates and disclosure towards the most favourable end of what may be a wide spectrum of possible decisions. On the other hand, management may bias judgments towards the least favourable end of the spectrum, taking the opportunity of the economic downturn to overestimate, for example, the write-down of assets. The incentive in doing this would be for management to manage earnings or smooth earnings trends.

The *Risk Alert* suggests that auditors consider making enquiries of the entity's *valuation experts* that the entity may have used, or review reports by financial analysts, banks, or rating agencies to obtain information about the entity.

The *Risk Alert* states that due to the economic environment, a primary area for increased risk of material misstatement relates to fair value measurements and accounting estimates, particularly those involving management judgment. Examples include fair value measurements of certain financial assets and impairment calculations for assets such as long-lived assets, accounts or loans receivable, goodwill, and other intangible assets not subject to amortization. In this regard, the evaluation of assumptions and data used by management in the fair value measurements or other accounting estimates is critical. The *Risk Alert* makes specific reference to the relevant paragraphs of CICA Handbook Section 5306, *Auditing Fair Value Measurements and Disclosures*.

The *Risk Alert* also refers to CICA Handbook Section 3063, *Impairment of Long-Lived Assets*, in the context of an audit, as well as CICA Handbook Section 3064, *Goodwill and Intangible Assets*, and provides certain commentary that is relevant in this regard.

CSA Staff Notice

In January 2009, Canadian Securities Administrators (CSA) *Staff Notice* 51-328[4] emphasized the importance for investors to be provided with critical

---

4 Continuous Disclosure Considerations Related to Current Economic Conditions, January 8, 2009.

information that would enable them to understand an issuer's current and prospective financial position as well as its operating results.

Appendix A to the *Staff Notice* contains an illustrative continuous disclosure letter to Chief Financial Officers of issuers, providing examples of the accounting and disclosure areas the CSA are focusing on when reviewing continuous disclosure filings, in light of "the current economic uncertainty and financial market volatility". They require the issuer to clearly disclose the current and anticipated impacts of market conditions on the company's operations, financial condition, liquidity, and future prospects. Such areas would include, for example, qualitative and quantitative discussion of how market conditions have affected the following:

- the demand for products and services, including any changes or expected changes to volume, selling prices, or other revenue drivers;
- costs, including changes in prices or constraints on supply, volume discounts, inventory adjustments or other factors that alter the relationship between costs and revenues;
- revenue and expenses, due to changes in interest rates, borrowing costs, foreign exchange rates and commodity prices;
- financial results due to unusual transactions or events including charges, gains, or losses that have not been typically reflected in historical results;
- the company's overall strategy or changes to strategies, including cost saving measures, restructuring initiatives, or a realignment of operational and financial resources; and
- any other relevant factors not referred to above.

Detailed disclosure and quantification must be made regarding the company's ability to generate sufficient cash and to access financial resources to meet operating needs in the current market environment.

The CSA requires the Management Discussion & Analysis (MD&A)[5] to discuss the specific impact of current market conditions on critical accounting estimates such as allowance for credit losses, fair value of financial instruments, inventory, revenue recognition, contingencies, goodwill and asset impairments, pensions, future income tax assets, and stock-based compensation.

Disclosure under the MD&A[6] requires "insightful information" on:

- the company's assessment of trends, events, or uncertainties that

---

5 National Instrument 51-102, *Continuous Disclosure Obligations*.

6 Item 1.12, *Critical Accounting Estimates*.

may affect the methods and assumptions used to determine critical accounting estimates;
- how sensitive the estimate is to a change in assumptions;
- the likelihood that estimates might change with evolving economic conditions; and
- the impact of a rationale for changes made to critical accounting estimates during the period.

The CSA also notes that recent economic and market events will cause actual results for many issuers to differ significantly from previously-disclosed forward-looking information. With respect to the issue of "going concern", it suggests that consideration be given to the recent amendments to CICA Handbook 1400.08A-08C, *General Standards of Financial Statement Presentation*, requiring a company to carefully assess and disclose in the financial statements the material uncertainties that may put into question its ability to continue as a going concern. Examples include continued and expected operating losses, negative operating cash flows, failure to obtain or renew financing, a significant decline in the demand for a company's products, declining prices, substantial refinancing requirements, and an inability to make scheduled payments on debt.[7]

Needless to say, Appendix A to the CSA *Staff Notice* makes specific reference to accounting guidance for impairment testing of goodwill, intangible assets and long-lived assets, pursuant to the standards promulgated in CICA Handbook Section 3064, *Goodwill and Intangible Assets*,[8] and Handbook Section 3063, *Impairment of Long-lived Assets.*

As the MD&A provides the users of financial statements with information to properly interpret and make reasoned judgment and decisions with respect thereto, a business valuator should scrutinize these types of areas in much greater detail than in the past.

IAASB Audit Considerations

In January 2009, the International Auditing and Assurance Standards Board (IAASB) issued *Audit Considerations in Respect of Going Concern in the Current Economic Environment.*[9]

It is instructive to note the IAASB's introductory comments. While they are specifically directed to the auditing profession, business valuators must

---

7 Appendix A, p. 5.

8 Replacing Handbook Section 3062, *Goodwill and Other Intangible Assets*, for annual and interim financial statements relating to fiscal years beginning on or after October 1, 2008.

9 The IAASB is an independent standard-setting board of the International Federation of Accountants.

similarly be aware of, and delve into, a number of the issues identified and commented on:

> This alert is issued by staff of the International Auditing and Assurance Standards Board (IAASB) to raise auditors' awareness about matters relevant to the consideration of the use of the going concern assumption in the preparation of the financial statements in the current environment. In particular, management, those charged with governance and auditors alike will be faced with the challenge of evaluating the effect of the credit crisis and economic downturn on an entity's ability to continue as a going concern and whether these effects on the entity ought to be described, or otherwise reflected, in the financial statements.
>
> While the Staff Audit Practice Alert, "Challenges in Auditing Fair Value Accounting Estimates in the Current Market Environment [October 2008]," refers to going concern in the context of the effects of valuation in illiquid markets, this alert addresses wider issues that are likely to be relevant to auditors of entities in all industries and of all sizes. While this alert refers principally to ISA 570, other ISAs contain requirements and guidance to assist the auditor in dealing with other issues that may also require particular attention in the current environment, such as inventory valuation and allowances for doubtful receivables.
>
> This alert does not take account of matters specific to industries or jurisdictions, both of which will be relevant to the issues discussed below. Government responses to the crises have been substantial, but varied. Thus in some jurisdictions certain aspects of credit availability may have been resolved while others continue to cause difficulties; and the particular matters tackled by governments may differ as between jurisdictions. Similarly, governments have been considering assistance to certain industries, the nature of which may have a material effect on the matters discussed in this alert. Further, the effect of the credit crisis and economic downturn varies both as to its severity and timing depending on the industry and the jurisdiction.

The IAASB discusses auditing requirements regarding:

- management's assessment of the entity's ability to continue as a going concern;
- the degree of consideration of the Going Concern Assumption;
- the period of time considered in making a going concern assessment; and
- factors in the current environment that may affect the going concern assessment, including availability of credit and forecasts and budgets.

The last factor, forecasts and budgets, requiring particular attention by auditors, is no less relevant for business valuators:

Forecasts and Budgets

An important component of the going concern assessment relates to an entity's ongoing forecasts and budgeting. In evaluating management's assessment, the auditor considers the process management followed to make its assessment, the assumptions on which the assessment is based and management's plans for future actions.[10] In considering alternative strategies that management may have to overcome any adverse factors, considerations include their effectiveness and the ability of management to execute them.

Analysis of cash flow may be a significant factor in considering the future outcome of events or conditions in the evaluation of management's plans for future action. Assumptions that have been used in prior years may no longer be relevant and may need to be adjusted to account for the pressures of the current environment. Factors that may be relevant in evaluating forecasts prepared by management include:

- Whether senior management and those charged with governance have been appropriately involved and have given appropriate attention to forecasts;
- Whether the assumptions used in the forecasts are consistent with assumptions that have been used in asset valuations and models for impairment;
- Whether the forecasts have been prepared on a monthly basis and, if so, how the forecasts reflect expected payment patterns (e.g., quarterly cash outflows such as tax installments, and variable cash inflows such as expected proceeds from the sale of assets);
- Whether the forecasts indicate months of insufficient cash and, if so, management's plans to deal with any shortfalls;
- Whether forecasts reflect an inappropriate management bias, in particular as broadly compared to others in a particular industry;
- How management's budget for the current period compares with results achieved to date;
- Whether the forecasts consider potential losses of revenue, including whether an inability of an entity to obtain letters of credit affects its international trade;
- Whether increases in the cost of borrowing have been factored into management's analysis, including potential increases in margin sought by banks and the effect of alternative sources of financing;
- Whether the forecasts account for trends typically noted in recessionary periods, such as reduced revenues, increased bad debts (because of trading conditions or the withdrawal of credit insurance), and extended credit terms to customers;
- Whether management has performed an appropriate sensitivity analysis, such as considering the effect of the loss of key customers or key suppliers due to bankruptcies;
- How the forecast deals with asset realizations, including whether these realizations are practicable and realistic in amount; and

10 ISA 570, para. 20.

- Whether the forecasts imply any future concerns over the entity's ability to meet debt covenant requirements.

Cost of Capital

For a business valuator, developing discount and capitalization rates are challenging enough under "normal" conditions. However, in these volatile and turbulent economic times, the standard procedures by which cost of capital is calculated are now being "retrofitted" and expanded by analysts, accounting professionals, regulators and others. While traditional methodologies such as the Capital Asset Pricing Model (CAPM), Modified CAPM and Build-Up Method are, of course, still applied, their inputs – both at the economic-benefits level (above) and the cost-of-capital level – now require additional (perhaps microscopic) analysis, reasoning and support.

As discussed below, the following factors require particular consideration and analysis:

- identifying and obtaining data that are the most relevant and meaningful for the current assignment;
- the impact on the validity of beta co-efficients caused by the turmoil in the public markets;
- the evaluation of the "risk-free" benchmark component in the CAPM and Build-Up Method;
    - the validity of the "risk-free" component;
    - recent experience regarding liquidity and its impact on the cost of capital;
    - the application of WACC when balance sheets reflect increased debt; and
    - weighing the economic benefit stream on a going-forward basis when past results and future projections cannot be very "reliable" in the valuation analysis.

The equity risk premium (ERP) can no longer – certainly in the short term – be that which would have normally been used "pre-economic turbulence". Many valuators are now adding, say, two percentage points to the ERP that would otherwise be used, and would then reduce it back to the ERP in "normal" economic times.

The Value Line Investment Survey commented as follows in its First Quarter 2009 Stock Market Review:

> Overall, the first period left few investors cheering, as household names *Alcoa, Bank of America, Dow Chemical,* and *International Paper*, to name a few, and blue chips *Boeing, Johnson & Johnson*, and *Procter & Gamble* dotted the new lows list–at

> times frequently—during the quarter. Even two of last year's few notable winners, *McDonald's* and *Wal-Mart Stores*, were unable to sustain their momentum. The few gainers, such as *IBM*, were up just modestly for the most part. All told, the losses were still rather sizable, with the Dow Jones Industrial Average shedding 13.3%, the Standard and Poor's 500 Index falling 11.7%, the NASDAQ edging down 3.1%, and the small-cap Russell 2000 Composite giving back 15.4% in the quarter. Such losses came on top of declines of a third, or more, for this quarter last year.[11]

Financial analysts and business valuators in the U.S. generally have three estimation approaches with respect to equity risk premiums:[12]

1. Survey Premiums
   - Investors (individual investors and institutional investors/investment professionals)
   - Managers
   - Academics

2. (a) Historical Premiums
   - Estimation questions and consequences
     - ➪ Time period
     - ➪ Risk-free security and market index
     - ➪ Averaging approach
   - Estimates for the U.S.
   - Global estimates
   - Survivor bias

2. (b) Historical Premiums Plus
   - Small cap and other risk premiums
   - Country risk premiums

3. Implied Equity Premiums
   - DCF Model-based premiums
   - Default spread-based equity risk premiums
   - Option pricing model-based equity risk premiums

Value Line also provides the following comparative statistics for March 31, 2008 and March 31, 2009:

---

11 "The Stock Market Review: First Quarter, 2009", Value Line Selection & Opinion, *The Value Line Investment Survey*, Value Line Publishing Inc., April 10, 2009, p. 3594.

12 A. Damodaran, *Equity Risk Premiums (ERP): Determinants, Estimation and Implications*, September 2008 (with an October update reflecting the market crisis), Stern School of Business, http://pages.stern.nyu.edu/~adamodar.

	Twelve Months		
Index	**3/31/08**	**3/31/09**	**% Change**
Dow Jones Industrial Average	12262.89	7608.92	−38.0
Dow Jones Transportation Average	4783.88	2684.08	−43.9
Dow Jones Utility Average	479.00	329.37	−31.2
Standard & Poor's 500 Index	1322.70	797.87	−39.7
NASDAQ Composite	2279.10	1528.59	−32.9
NASDAQ 100	1781.93	1237.01	−30.6
New York Stock Exchange Composite	8797.29	4978.98	−43.4
American Stock Exchange Composite	2231.83	1359.33	−39.1
Russell 2000	687.97	422.75	−38.6
Value Line (Arithmetic) Average	2050.82	1296.92	−36.8
Value Line (Geometric) Average	390.44	193.74	−50.4
Value Line Industrials	323.69	155.24	−52.0
Value Line Rails	2872.72	1573.57	−45.2
Value Line Utilities	265.13	182.40	−31.2
London (FT-SE 100)	5702.10	3926.14	−31.1
Tokyo (Nikkei)	12525.54	8109.53	−35.3
Toronto (TSE 300)	13350.13	8720.39	−34.7

In developing capitalization and discount rates for privately-owned businesses, more in-depth analysis is now required with respect to company-specific factors as they relate to the level and quality of the sales and, hence, profits of the business as well as the industries that the businesses serve. For example, if the subject business is a computer company serving the steel industry, the valuator must not only analyze the latter industry, but must also consider that many companies in the steel industry are affected by the auto manufacturing industry, construction, and other industries that consume steel. With so many industries adversely affected by the recession, the "typical" valuation analyses and techniques business valuators had applied until recently may no longer be appropriate or responsive to current realities.

Apart from the challenges that valuators must now face in developing equity capitalization rates, there are additional issues regarding the calculation of the weighted average cost of capital ("WACC"). Debt/equity ratios have been changing as a result of the economic turmoil; these changes are affecting many valuations. The debt/equity ratio that would have otherwise been considered "normal" for a particular industry, or "normal" *vis-à-vis* a specific company, may no longer be appropriate on a going-forward basis. For example, the equity component, which is stated at fair market value, will likely have decreased substantially more than its debt counterpart. As a result, the weighting of the equity component might now be so low as to render "meaningless" the relative weights in the WACC calculation.

Factors such as market volatility (which increases the equity risk premium), cyclicality, risk tolerance, marketplace liquidity, access to equity capital and debt capital, growth prospects of the business, leverage ratios and others must be analyzed in substantially more detail. That is, while these considerations are relevant in any valuation, they now require further in-depth analysis because of the changed playing field.

DCF Analysis

Another important change relates to the multi-period discounting model applying the DCF or DFE Method. This method typically involves the use of projections by management – often for a five-year period – and the estimation of a residual, or terminal, value at the end of the projection period. During the past number of years, when economic conditions were generally "normal", valuators would analyze management's projections, paying particular attention to the underlying assumptions.[13]

Considering the current economic crisis, what degree of reasonableness can the business valuator attach to the assumptions on which management's projections are based? How does the business valuator challenge or test these assumptions? Is there a benchmark or a reasonableness test that can be applied? In a DCF analysis, when the terminal value of the subject business is being estimated – say, five years from the valuation date – what capitalization rate should be used? Under "normal" conditions, the capitalization rate used for determining terminal value generally approximates the discount rate used in present-valuing the cash flows during the discrete projection period. However, in a five-year projection, is it assumed that the economic conditions being experienced would be "normalized" by the end of year 5? Or, should only a three-year projection period be used, considering that as projections are made further into the future, there is less certainty with respect to each year, going forward? Similarly, in reviewing the past five (or three) years' financial results for valuation purposes, how much reliance can be placed on these results to serve as an indicator of future

[13] See IAASB Audit Considerations, above. Also, The Canadian Institute of Chartered Accountants has promulgated an auditing standard on fair value measurement in Section 5306 of the CICA Handbook, requiring CA auditors to perform stringent assurance-related procedures in particular with respect to management's underlying assumptions.

earnings, when the subject company, itself, is carrying on its business on a different "playing field"?

Guideline Transactions Method

Can prices paid in recent prior years provide meaningful *indicia* of value? To the extent that prices include special-purchaser or strategic-buyer premiums, would these be relevant under current conditions? Public company shares are often priced having regard to dividends, their historical track record of payments and future expectations of dividend payments. However, a number of blue-chip and other public companies are re-evaluating their dividend policies. General Electric, with its very large and diversified operations (which include the NBC broadcasting group and GE Capital), announced that it would "evaluate" its planned dividend for the second half of the year "in light of the growing uncertainty in the economy".

Investment Holding Companies

Because of the economic turmoil and uncertainty, investment holding companies also incur greater portfolio discounts.

Similarly, undivided co-ownership interests in real estate (fractional interests) will suffer greater discounts from the size of discount experienced during the past several years. This is due to – as with other types of investments – reduced liquidity in the marketplace and the possible tendency for periodic (often monthly or quarterly) distributions to be decreased or suspended because of economic conditions.

Distributions during the holding period are, of course, important value drivers (as they are with real estate investment trusts and income trusts).

Valuation of Retractable Preferred Shares

Retractable preferred shares issued in conjunction with an estate freeze or corporate reorganization are intended to have a fair market value, at the time of issue, equal to their stated "retraction amount". At that point in time, they generally do. However, problems may arise at a future date, when a retraction demand is made by the holder of the shares, because the retraction amount might not equal the fair market value of the shares at the retraction date. This can be so irrespective of whether the shares are held by a controlling shareholder or by a minority shareholder.

The current economic conditions are requiring estate planners and other professionals to review the values now attaching to these types of shares that were issued in better economic times. Are they still worth their "retraction amount" as originally stipulated at the time of their issue, *i.e.*, at the time of the freeze?

Because fair market value is an objective standard and considers the price at which arm's length, informed, and uncompelled parties would transact, a valuation of retractable preferreds will consider:

- the rights and conditions attaching to the retractable shares (voting, dividends, *etc.*);
- whether the corporation has sufficient liquidity to pay the retraction amount at the holder's request, and then continue to be solvent thereafter;
- the tax liability to the issuer resulting from a disposition of assets to provide the liquidity to satisfy the retraction payment;
- the personal taxes of the preferred shareholder if there is a deemed dividend on retraction;
- whether the corporation has a capital dividend account and the likelihood of its making an election *vis-à-vis* such deemed dividend (which could favor the holder of the retractable shares);
- the legal rights and the reasonable and legitimate expectations of the other shareholders; and
- the principle that a notional purchaser would require an appropriate rate of return, and not pay $1 simply to receive $1 in return.

In the current economic environment, a notional purchaser of retractable preferred shares (and who does not control the company), must consider potential risks and impediments associated with his/her future exercise of the retraction right. In *Itak International Corp. v. CPI Plastics Group Ltd.*,[14] the Ontario Superior Court of Justice considered whether a refusal by CPI to honour Itak's retraction request was a valid business decision or whether it was oppressive to the retracting shareholder. In deciding not to redeem the preferreds held by Itak, CPI's board considered the impact that a redemption might have on CPI's banking covenants and on the other shareholders in light of potential adverse market conditions, including the rising cost of raw materials, exchange rate fluctuations, and the seasonality of its business. This was in 2006, well before the current credit/economic crisis.

The court concluded that there was no reasonable basis for imposing more stringent conditions than those implied by the relevant solvency provisions because CPI would not be in financial distress following payment of the retraction amount. Furthermore, the reasonable expectations of the shareholder, as reflected in the share conditions, should prevail. Although the

---

14 2006 CanLII 22117 (Ont. S.C.J.).

shareholder's retraction right was vindicated by the court, the case illustrates that an informed and uncompelled *non-controlling* holder of retractable shares, who might face delays and heavy legal costs in enforcing the retraction right, would consider this in pricing such shares.

Under current economic conditions, there may be valid reasons why a corporation might not honour a retraction request.

Fair Value Measurement

The U.S. Financial Accounting Standards Board ("FASB") Standard 157 establishes a three-level hierarchy with respect to market inputs used in fair value measurement. Level 1 and Level 2 inputs are defined as follows:

> ***Level 1 inputs***
>
> 24. Level 1 inputs are quoted prices (unadjusted) in active markets for identical assets or liabilities that the reporting entity has the ability to access at the measurement date. An active market for the asset or liability is a market in which transactions for the asset or liability occur with sufficient frequency and volume to provide pricing information on an ongoing basis. A quoted price in an active market provides the most reliable evidence of fair value and shall be used to measure fair value whenever available [with some exceptions]... .
>
> . . .
>
> ***Level 2 inputs***
>
> 28. Level 2 inputs are inputs other than quoted prices included within Level 1 that are observable for the asset or liability, either directly or indirectly. ... Level 2 inputs include the following:
>
> a. Quoted prices for similar assets or liabilities in active markets
> b. Quoted prices for identical or similar assets or liabilities in markets that are not active...
> c. Inputs other than quoted prices that are observable for the asset or liability (for example, interest rates and yield curves observable at commonly quoted intervals, volatilities, prepayment speeds, loss severities, credit risks, and default rates)
> d. Inputs that are derived principally from or corroborated by observable market data by correlation or other means (market-corroborated inputs).

How meaningful are such inputs when the observations, or market inputs, relate to transactions at the time that industry and economic conditions (say, 12 to 18 months immediately preceding the fair value measurement date) were substantially different? And, if we consider Level 3 inputs (which include, *inter alia*, the results using the DCF Method), the valuator must consider the types of issues noted earlier in this chapter regarding income/cash flow and cost of capital.

Preparers of financial statements, as well as auditors, recognize that the goodwill appearing on many balance sheets might now be impaired. Accounting for goodwill is addressed in CICA Handbook Section 3064[15] and SFAS 142 in the U.S., *Goodwill and Intangible Assets*. Step I of the two-step goodwill impairment test involves a comparison of the reporting unit's fair value with its carrying value. If the fair value of the reporting unit is less than its carrying value, then Step II must be performed, quantifying the amount of the impairment. This requires a calculation of the fair value of the reporting unit's goodwill. In some cases, an interim impairment test must be performed upon the occurrence of an event or change in circumstances that would, more likely than not, reduce the fair value of reporting unit below its carrying amount on the balance sheet.

Business valuators will be playing an increasing, and more frequent, role in assisting management with fair value measurement.

Contingencies and Guarantees

In performing a valuation in this economy, particular scrutiny must also be given to "off-balance-sheet" items. Apart from the impairment of intangibles, the valuator should determine whether there is increased risk of undisclosed or unidentified contingencies relating to matters such as, among others:

- actual, pending or threatened litigation;
- guarantees (product, performance, debt); and
- contractual commitments to acquire goods or services in excess of market values.

Estate Freezing

Business valuators now have a great opportunity to develop their practices in the area of income tax and estate planning. With values being so low, it is an opportune time for taxpayers to freeze their businesses and other growth assets. There exists an abundance of empirical data and other objective support from public sources to provide the appropriate backup for valuing family businesses and other closely-held equity investments. Numerous articles, analyses and reports, financial and economic data, market surveys, and government statistics can provide objective empirical supporting data.

---

15 Above note 8.

Other

Valuations are also affected by the economic crisis when valuation disputes arise. Examples include matrimonial, shareholder dissent, shareholder oppression, expropriation, business interruption, insurance claims and the quantification of economic loss. Valuation experts must be prepared to support and defend in court the many contentious valuation issues over and above, or in much more depth than, those typically encountered.

Conclusion

The business valuation profession has never faced such challenges. More analysis, realism, and "scepticism" are required. As suggested earlier, valuators should try to benefit from the professional guidance that could be readily obtained from pronouncements of the accounting, auditing, and regulatory bodies. Working papers should be documented with as many objective authorities, benchmarks, and statistical data as appropriate in the circumstances. This may also help in the event that reference to the valuator's opinion is made, for whatever purpose, several years hence.

Valuing Distressed Companies

James L. Horvath & Farouk Mohamed

Introduction

The number of entities in distress usually increases significantly during a downturn in the economic environment. Economic downturns and volatile markets often create invaluable opportunities for astute investors to capitalize on the inherent intrinsic value and reorganization potential of some distressed companies.

Often entities get into trouble because they forget their business purpose. They tend to lose sight of the factors that contributed to the firm's prosperity. A level of complacency that may have resulted from prior successes during times of economic prosperity can define the culture of these organizations. Distress tends to occur when organizations pay inadequate attention to a multitude of early warning signals as performance declines. As the level of distress cultivates in an organization, resolution efforts become more difficult and expensive which results in a narrower set of available options. A successful turnaround generally requires a sound understanding of the root causes of distress, its severity, and the viability of the reorganization plan for the entity. A successful reorganization plan also identifies the major value drivers. Thus, it builds on those business functions which create significant amounts of business value and eliminates efforts spent on activities which result in an unacceptable return on capital expenditures and expenses.

An equally important consideration when planning a turnaround strategy is how the restructuring is likely to affect the post-reorganization value of the entity. The valuation of distressed companies can be one of the more complex areas of valuation, which is why uncovering and quantifying the value inherent in such an entity presents a unique set of challenges that requires a valuator to modify traditional valuation methods.

For the purposes of the reading, distressed companies are defined to include entities that are struggling to make debt payments and meet their contractual obligations. At the further end of the distress continuum are companies that are nearing bankruptcy, and have either filed reorganization proposals to undertake significant restructuring plans, or are in immediate danger of doing so. Companies that have already filed for bankruptcy fall outside the scope of this definition.

Causes of Distress

In times of market prosperity and under positive economic conditions, the likelihood of distress is not as prevalent. Stakeholders tend not to fully scrutinize sub-optimal management decisions so long as growth and profitability targets are met. Issues, such as a poor strategic focus, inadequate leadership, an inability to innovate, hefty operating structures, and a lack of market awareness are usually masked when times are good. However, it is these very same factors that rise to the forefront during an economic downturn. Downturns can stem from a number of factors such as shifts in economic cycles, changing market conditions, and increased competition. Intangible value created over numerous years, including brands and customer relationships, can quickly disappear. Surviving during times of distress can be one of the most critical and challenging tasks that an organization can encounter. However, entities can better prepare themselves for volatile times by implementing systems to detect the warning signals of distress before they become unmanageable and beyond repair. Determining the severity of distress can help identify root causes and appropriate remedies.

Stages of Distress

There are three stages of distress that companies generally experience as performance declines. These stages along with specific responses, level of urgency, and overall goals of the response are illustrated in the graphic below:

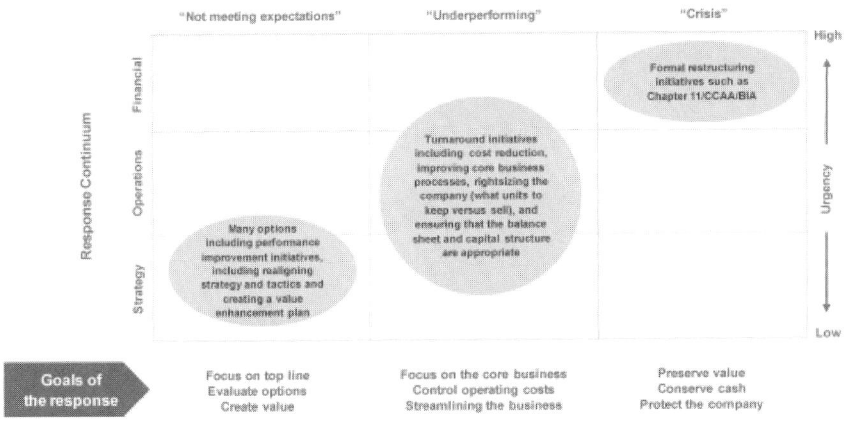

Source: CMA Management, October 2008

Note that with each progressive state of distress, there are fewer options to control and consequently enhance sub-par performance. Companies in the crisis stage can only survive by actively identifying and addressing performance glitches relatively early enough to ensure the damage can be rectified. By avoiding organizational distress in the first place, a company positions itself to take advantage of volatile markets and drive ongoing growth.

The three stages of distress as described by Ramesh Swamy are as follows:[1,2]

a. Not meeting expectations

In this initial stage of distress, companies generally exhibit lagging performance compared to expectations. Early warning signs include eroding market share due to inadequate responses to market conditions, softening top- and bottom-line performance, cost growth trends above industry average, and a slowdown in acquisition of new business.

These companies do not face immediate crisis; therefore, the level of urgency is relatively low and there is usually ample time to turn things around.

Note, however, that distress can multiply if root causes are not fixed, and related reorganization costs and risks may increase significantly. The focus of these companies should be geared towards top line and value creation or enhancement. Some organizations might pursue new markets for existing products and services while others may aim to serve existing markets more efficiently. Some may even seek to divest of certain non-growth business

1 R. Swamy, "Market turbulence challenges Canadian companies, Part 1 of 2: Know the warning signs of distress", CMA Management, August 2008.

2 R. Swamy, "Surviving and thriving in times of turbulence", CMA Management, October 2008.

units. The key is to create additional options as nothing is worse than running out of options. By tightly focusing on strategic business drivers and fixing issues before it is too late, an entity can successfully avoid a potentially dangerous scenario.

b. Underperforming

As performance continues to deviate from expectations, the symptoms become more frequent and pronounced. Symptoms of the underperforming stage of distress include increased concern from lenders, bankers and investors, reduced customer satisfaction and increased levels of customer discounts, rapid increases in cost structure, pressure on cash flows, and instability from sudden reversals in top- and bottom-line performance.

Underperforming companies face a medium level of urgency. These entities must focus on improving operational performance. However, similar to initial stages of distress, the situation can quickly deteriorate if not attended to by management. A two-phased approach should be utilized to rectify the underperformance: first stabilize the organization, and then fix the critical issues. Successful companies become more agile and competitive and are also particularly adept at refocusing on their core business.

c. Crisis

During the third and final stage, the damage is severe and often irreversible. Resolutions to crises may often be drastic or otherwise unfavorable to business leaders, investors, and other stakeholders. Key crisis symptoms include breaches of bank covenants, the inability to meet debt obligations, insolvency, high management and board turnover, and difficulty in finding new investment dollars.

At this stage, organizations face the most critical level of urgency. Because core operations have now been compromised, options are often few and painful. Leaders don't have the time, or the patience to assess strategies and measure results. They only want to preserve value and cash and protect the company. Financial aspects override all as the organization does everything in its power to survive.

Left without any viable options and an inability to discharge existing obligations, entities may be forced into an out-of-court settlement with its creditors or a more formal reorganization proposal[3] filed with the courts under the relevant country legislation. These include Chapter 11 in the United States and the *Companies' Creditors Arrangement Act* ("CCAA") and *Bank-*

---

[3] A proposal or plan of arrangement is an offer to creditors to settle debts under conditions other than the existing terms.

ruptcy and Insolvency Act ("BIA") in Canada. It is important to note that a company's ability to avert itself of these restructuring provisions is directly related to the support and/or co-operation it gets from its senior secured lenders. If each of the aforementioned options has been unsuccessfully exhausted, the entity may be forced into liquidation.

Determining the stage of distress an entity finds itself in is a critical step towards establishing the level or urgency and importance of planning and executing a viable reorganization strategy.

Considerations For a Successful Reorganization Strategy

A successful reorganization strategy should address the changes that have to be made to the business in order to bring its profitability to an acceptable level, while simultaneously considering the associated risks and costs. An appropriate turnaround remedy must define the key issues, address the underlying root causes as opposed to the symptoms, and be broad enough in scope to resolve the key issues. Note that strategies aimed at rectifying each and every problem, including non-mission critical issues, will generally divert limited resources away from critical issues and prove unsuccessful.

The seven key factors that need to be addressed in any successful reorganization strategy can be briefly described as follows:[4]

a. <u>Crisis stabilization</u>

This involves taking control of the crisis before it spirals out of control. Determining the stage of distress using the tools mentioned above is a prerequisite to the stabilization process. Cash preservation and generation in the short term is of extreme importance in order to enable the entity to develop a turnaround plan and agree to a financial restructuring. A sense of predictability of the operations' related cash flow needs to be evident. Therefore, rolling short-term cash flow generating forecasts should be prepared and communicated to stakeholders and, more importantly, must be achieved in order to rebuild stakeholder confidence by demonstrating that senior management has taken control of the situation.

b. <u>New leadership</u>

Distress can be frequently attributed to poor decisions and guidance of senior management or the departure of key management; which is why

---

4 S. Slatter *et al.*, "Leading Corporate Turnaround – How Leaders Fix Troubled Companies", (England: John Wiley & Sons, 2006).

most reorganizations require new leadership. Proponents of a change in senior management argue that those that led the company into failure would not likely be part of the solution. In line with the foregoing, note the leadership changes in the spring of 2009 at many of the major U.S. financial institutions and automotive manufacturers. A change in leadership also sends a strong message to stakeholders that the entity is serious about improving performance. A contrary view is that incumbent senior management usually has the most experience and knowledge of the company and possesses industry skills that may prove vital to the recovery process. Irrespective of what decision is made, a careful analysis of current leadership should be performed to determine whether management has the requisite abilities to turn around the business.

c. Stakeholder management

Companies in distress usually suffer from deteriorating relationships with key stakeholders. Each stakeholder can command varying degrees of influence and importance and are mostly concerned with mitigating their own risk exposure to the troubled company. They could possess minimal confidence in the company as a result of disagreeing with management decisions, poor communication, unpleasant surprises, and so forth. This is why a successful reorganization plan should address the key stakeholders in terms of priority. Additionally, the differing objectives of each stakeholder should be outlined and only mission-critical objectives should be addressed. Ultimately, stakeholder confidence must be regained.

d. Strategic focus

A well-defined strategy must clearly define the company's purpose and sense of direction, include realistic long-term goals based on genuine commercial opportunity, incorporate a feasible plan to achieve these long-term goals, and outline how the company intends to gain a competitive advantage over other players in the market. Corporations in decline tend to stray away from their stated strategies or do not have a well-defined strategy in the first place. Often, formal strategies are not clearly articulated or communicated to the organization. In addition, goals may lack commercial sense or be unrealistic because the organization simply does not have the skills or the resources to achieve them or to gain an advantage over the competition. A robust reorganization strategy must overcome these strategic shortcomings and receive buy-in from the entity's stakeholders.

e. Critical process improvements

Troubled companies tend to have many issues related to their core and support processes. These processes tend to be costly, time-consuming, and lack quality and flexibility. Compounding the problem is that these companies usually do not have the necessary financial resources to replace outdated IT systems, aging capital assets and machinery, and other infrastructure. Although a complete overhaul of the infrastructure may not be feasible, the tools and techniques of re-engineering business processes can be applied. The goals of these critical process improvements should be to make the organization more responsive by reducing manufacturing or service delivery times, increasing efficiency, thereby cutting both fixed and variable costs, and improving quality by including preventative and detective controls in processes.

f. Organizational change

People challenges tend to be at the forefront of troubled organizations. Employee turnover is likely high as staff may be demoralized, overworked and/or lack the requisite skills as others have left, and resistant to change. Company objectives may not be aligned with those of the employees, causing staff not to perform to their capabilities or act in the company's best interests. Potential remedies may include organization structural changes, key employee changes, improved communications, increased accountability and performance management, and better aligned remuneration and incentive compensation systems.

g. Financial restructuring

Distressed companies tend to be burdened by cash flow problems, inappropriate capital structures, and poor balance sheets. The objectives of a financial restructuring are to restore the business to solvency, align the capital structure with the level of projected operating cash flow, and to ensure that sufficient funds in the form of existing and new financing are available to fund the implementation of the turnaround plan. Capital restructuring generally involves co-operating with the company's creditors to reschedule or sometime convert debt payments to other forms of financial instruments, including equity. With respect to new financing, a company will often need an equity injection, if debt financing cannot be readily obtained at a fair price on fair terms and conditions.

Successful turnaround situations are characterized by significant actions in each of the seven areas, albeit to varying degrees. Failure to address any one of these may endanger the successful outcome of the turnaround.

An equally important consideration when planning a reorganization strategy is how the restructuring is likely to affect the value of the company. Note that any changes in firm value and strategic direction will likely affect many of its stakeholders and consequently determine the level of acceptance of the ultimate reorganization plan. Valuation considerations are addressed in the discussion that follows.

Valuation Considerations

In valuing a distressed company following the execution of a turnaround strategy, there are a number of key valuation issues that must be considered. The ultimate objective is to determine how the restructuring is likely to affect the value of the company; its post-reorganization value. Conventional valuation techniques tend to overvalue companies in distress as they tend to assume that any distress is temporary. Consequently, insufficient emphasis is placed on expected cash flows and the associated level of risk attached thereto, discount rates, and multiples in these models. Traditional methods to valuation are described below along with unique issues that must be considered in a reorganization setting.

Liquidation or Going Concern

The first key consideration is to determine whether a company or certain of its business units is worth more as a going concern than if its operations were to cease and its assets were to be disposed under a liquidation basis.

The valuator initially determines whether the subject business is a going concern by asking the following questions regarding the company and/or business unit:

- Is there a history of consistent positive operating cash flow?
- Is there an expectation of positive net cash flow in the future?
- Is the industry outlook positive?

If the valuator concludes that the business will continue for the foreseeable future, a going-concern approach to valuation is appropriate; otherwise, a hypothetical liquidation approach could be applicable. Note that this analysis can be applied on an entity-wide basis, or to specific underperforming business units that could be divested as part of the reorganization.

The responses to the questions noted above are not as obvious in a distressed company situation. Distressed companies normally do not have a history of consistent operating cash flows and may have very bleak outlooks. Depending on the level of distress, the possibility of bankruptcy may be imminent, which could warrant a liquidation approach. In most situations, however, the distressed company will choose, or may be forced, to restructure its operations by its creditors in hopes of achieving profitability in order to discharge its obligations.

Where a business has put together a reorganization plan for approval from its stakeholders, including the courts in certain instances, a liquidation approach may or may not be appropriate. The premise behind a stakeholder accepting a company's reorganization plan is that the party anticipates recovering a greater portion of the monies owed to them by allowing the business to continue to operate, rather than be liquidated. Thus, a going-concern valuation approach would be used in this instance as the reorganized value of the business as a going concern would presumably be higher than its liquation value. In some cases due to the many continuing and some new risks, the going concern value might only be marginally greater than the orderly liquidation value. In most cases, the differential in perceived value gain will be significant.

However, a valuator needs to be cognizant of unique instances where the net present worth of an entity or business unit as a going concern may be less than the combined net realizable value of its net assets on orderly liquidation.

Classic examples of such situations include:[5]

- retail stores with an outdated format that requires significant capital expenditures to "upgrade" and target new customers, yet the current inventory can be quickly realized;
- sub-prime finance companies that generate an insufficient return for the risks taken, yet hold liquid assets; and
- technology companies that exist solely as a result of their ability to raise money in capital markets.

For these reasons, a best practice is to calculate liquidation value of the entity and include a comparison to its going-concern value to determine which approach yields the highest proceeds to the stakeholders.

Liquidation

Liquidation value can be determined under an orderly or a forced scenario.

Orderly Liquidation

An orderly liquidation will result in higher net proceeds as compared to a forced liquidation. Given the time value of money and the risk of deteriorating market conditions for the assets being sold, an orderly liquidation is often perceived as an immediate one. However, the duration of a liquidation period depends on several factors, including:

---

[5] J.B. Cleveland, "Valuation in Bankruptcy and a Financial Restructuring Context", October 24, 2002.

- the conditions of the company's books and records;
- the nature and condition of the underlying assets;
- the ability to salvage a viable operating segment;
- the party initiating the liquidation process;
- the level of cooperation from owners and management;
- market conditions; and
- market supply and demand.

Forced Liquidation

Where a forced liquidation occurs, the company's assets are sold as quickly as possible – at an auction, for example. Such circumstances do not allow adequate time to solicit all prospective bids or expose the assets to the marketplace for an extended period.

In an orderly scenario, the company's shareholders often control the liquidation process and aim to maximize their after-tax proceeds, whereas a forced scenario is likely the result of a business being forced into receivership by its creditors. The determination of one scenario over the other should weigh the benefits and costs such as expected disposition costs, overhead, liquidation period costs, income taxes, and the time value of money.

For companies operating in distress, there is often a substantial disconnect between what is recorded on the balance sheet (*i.e.*, book value) and its net realizable or market value. As it is often a challenge to determine orderly and forced liquidation value, a viable option is to utilize multiple scenarios (*i.e.*, high, expected, and low) to gauge a possible range of value. Appraisers and auctioneers with relevant current experience can often assist in providing assistance in estimating the liquidation values.

Going Concern

Where the reorganized value of business is deemed to be greater than its liquidation value, a going-concern approach should be utilized. Going-concern value may be much greater than liquidation value because a continuing business with an organization in place, established customers, a knowledgeable workforce, and so forth, may well bring a higher price as a unit than would the sale of each asset separately. Going-concern valuation approaches, as opposed to liquidation approaches, are much better at capturing intangible value, such as brand name, customer relationships, workforce, and goodwill, which is why many distressed companies will seek to reorganize quickly in order to preserve this value.

The main going-concern valuation approaches include:[6]

- Income approach – discounted cash flow ("DCF")
- Comparable company method
- Comparable transactions method

Note that many of the key inputs and assumptions may need to be adjusted in a distressed company scenario.

Discounted Cash Flow Issues

The DCF approach is based on the premise that a company's value is equal to the present value of all the after-tax cash flows that a company can generate for its investors. The analysis can be varied by returns to each of the company's debtholders and equityholders. The projection and discounting of a series of annual cash flows is a complex undertaking on its own, and becomes increasingly difficult when valuing distressed companies. There are many special considerations to include in determining the post-reorganization value of an entity under the DCF approach. The post-reorganization value of the enterprise is of significant importance as stakeholders negotiate their stake in the distressed company.

The unique considerations pertain to cash flow estimation issues and required rate of return issues. Post-reorganization value also requires an estimate of the reorganization costs, which, as experience indicates, are often underestimated due mainly to unforeseen costs. Cash flows are typically projected on a debt-free basis and are discounted at the weighted average cost of capital ("WACC").[7]

---

6 A fourth going-concern valuation approach, the capitalized cash flow approach (income approach) is not advisable in a distressed scenario. This approach involves determining the estimated future maintainable after-tax cash flows from operations and capitalizing them by a multiple, which serves as a measure of the rate of return required by a prospective purchaser of the business reflecting, among other factors, the risk inherent in achieving the determined level of maintainable cash flow. The selection of an appropriate maintainable cash flow level must consider not only the company's actual performance to date but also the on-going revenue and cash flow generating potential. Given the relative volatility of historic earnings, combined with the unpredictability of cash flows in the interim period as the company restructures its operations, determining a maintainable state can be a challenging task. Consequently, this approach is often utilized in conjunction with the DCF approach in determining the residual value of a company once it is expected to complete its reorganization and thus reach a maintainable state.

7 An investment that is expected to generate a return equal to the WACC would be capable of covering interest costs to the company's debtholders and providing an acceptable rate of return to the company's equityholders. Accordingly, the WACC is the overall return on investment required by the company.

Cash Flow Estimation Issues

- *Credibility of forecast* – a significant amount of due diligence must be performed on the company's forecast given management's incentives to either depress or inflate projections. Considerations should also be made regarding management's history of meeting targets in the past. The valuation could consider pre-distress cash flows of the company as a benchmark for cash flows following the reorganization.
- *Timing of cash flows* – note that projections must take into account a reasonable time period and necessary costs to restore the business to a competitive balance. In addition, certain restructuring mechanisms[8] may impact the length of proceedings and time that an investor must wait for future cash payments. Cyclicality of the industry can also be an important consideration. For instance, determining whether an industry is in a downturn or in an uptick can have a dramatic effect on the timing and magnitude of cash flows if a correlation exists between the two.
- *Catch-up payments* – certain necessary expenditures may have been deferred due to a lack of financial resources and will need to be incurred in order to retain or gain market share. Examples include capital expenditures, marketing costs, and research and development.
- *Reorganization costs* – certain expenditures, including severance and facility closure costs, may need to be incurred at the onset of the projection period in order to restructure the entity. However, if key employee turnover is prevalent, significant costs could be incurred to recruit, re-train, and retain existing staff.
- *Working capital adjustments* – working capital deficits are not uncommon to distressed companies. Stretched payables and accelerated receivables will eventually need to be corrected in order to regain optimal levels. A determination should be made as to whether a one-time cash adjustment should be made up front (if financing exists) or whether a gradual adjustment should be made over the reorganization period in order to reach normalized levels.
- *Other considerations* – additional cash flow considerations include professional fees (legal, accounting, trustee/monitor fees), any outstanding or potential litigation matters, pending environmental claims, and contributions to underfunded pension plans.

[8] Examples include an in-court versus out-of-court restructuring. An in-court restructuring may be time consuming and costly which may be offset by certain benefits including smaller payouts to creditors.

WACC Estimation Issues

- *Optimal capital structure* – there are two methods for determining the optimal capital structure:[9]
    - the first alternative is to use the optimal capital structure of comparable companies in the industry. An important caveat with the use of this method is that the entire industry in which the company operates may be distressed, which will render such comparisons less effective; and
    - the second alternative, in a formal restructuring setting, is to use the actual debt level of the distressed company that has filed a reorganization plan with the courts. The theory behind this approach is that the capital structure was determined on an arm's length basis under the supervision of the court and a trustee/monitor. Note that where a company is over-leveraged at the onset of the reorganization plan and is expected to reduce its relative level of debt to equity over time in order to obtain an optimal capital structure, the use of a single period WACC is not appropriate. Instead, the capital structure, cost of equity, and cost of debt should be re-calculated over the reorganization period until the desired capital structure is achieved.
- *Restructuring risk*[10] – the WACC needs to reflect the incremental risk encountered by the company in the midst of restructuring. Restructuring risk accounts for the likelihood that the reorganization may not be successful and thus force liquidation or in some cases go through a second or even third formal restructuring. When aiming to quantify the level of restructuring risk, the source of distress should be analyzed. Consider the difference between the following situations:
    - Financial distress – a company in this scenario may be operationally sound, have good products, margins, customers, and so forth, but be inundated by debt and be cash flow insolvent. This company faces financial restructuring risk only.
    - Operational and financial distress – a company in this scenario not only has a poor balance sheet but faces significant operational issues. This company faces financial and operational restructuring risk.

---

[9] J.M. Risius, "Business Valuation Issues in Bankruptcy", December 4, 2007.

[10] *Ibid.*

The company facing financial distress faces a lower risk of liquidation due to an unsuccessful reorganization as compared to the company facing operational and financial distress. There is additional uncertainty related to the latter company as it may have to implement a new strategy, fire bad management, and so on, in order to restructure its operations. Therefore, there is an additional level of uncertainty related to the success of these actions.

- *Company-specific risk* – in addition, and closely related to restructuring risk, an incremental level of company-specific or unsystematic risk may need to be incorporated to account for unique operational challenges relative to the industry that have led to the company's distress.
- *Cost of debt* – there are a few nuances that need to be taken into account when arriving at an appropriate cost of debt including:[11]
    - when estimating the post-reorganization value of a company, the cost of debt *following* the restructuring should be considered; and
    - the cost of debt included in WACC is on an after-tax basis as it incorporates the deductibility of interest for tax purposes. To the extent that the distressed entity has significant historic or projected non-capital tax losses, the advantage of interest tax shields may be reduced. The valuator may consider excluding the interest tax shield in the WACC calculation over these periods.
- *Revisions* – note that the WACC calculated is not a static measure and needs to be revised over time to factor changes in circumstances over the reorganization period. Depending on the challenges or success of the restructuring plan, the WACC may need to be increased or decreased, respectively.

Comparable Company Issues

The comparable company valuation method involves applying valuation metrics implied by public company trading prices of comparable companies to the subject company being valued. Popular valuation metrics include enterprise value ("EV") /EBITDA,[12] EV/revenue, EV/EBIT, and price/earnings ("P/E") multiples.

Comparisons to comparable distressed companies are considered sufficient when determining the *pre*-reorganization value of the company. However, in determining the value of an entity *post*-reorganization, comparisons to

---

11 *Ibid.*

12 Earnings before interest, taxes, depreciation, and amortization.

healthy peer companies should be sought. Comparisons to distressed peer companies could result in overly conservative reorganization value conclusions. Distressed entities generally have higher risk profiles and lower profitability levels compared to their healthy competitors, and a proper discount for distress, usually at least 20 per cent of enterprise value, is typically factored into the valuation.[13]

Another common issue is the appropriate or "normalized" earnings or cash flow level for the subject company to which the comparable multiple can be applied. The subject company will likely have a history of negative earnings or might be undergoing significant changes in operating earnings due to various restructuring charges. Therefore an analysis of historic earnings in itself may be insufficient.

In addition to adjusting historic results to remove such non-operating and non-recurring items in order to obtain normalized earnings, other alternatives include:[14]

- utilizing comparable revenue multiples under the assumption that the subject company will achieve industry average margins;
- calculating forward multiples for public companies and applying to projected earnings of the company, assuming forward earnings are positive; or
- applying a historic multiple to forward and/or normalized expected future earnings of the subject company and then discounting this value back to present value.

When considering an appropriate valuation metric, the use of "debt-free" multiples such as EV/EBITDA or EV/EBIT are recommended in order to isolate the impact of differences in capital structures of comparable companies.

Lastly, when obtaining multiples for comparable distressed companies or those operating in distressed industries, it is important to adjust debt to market value when calculating the numerator in multiples. Debt is typically quoted at book value and market value can differ materially from book value in distressed and even in many normal market situations.

Comparable Transactions Issues

The comparable transaction valuation method involves applying valuation metrics implied by comparable transactions to the subject company being valued. Although acquisition multiples implied by purchase prices can serve

---

13 D. Lurvey *et al.*, "Hidden Treasures: Techniques for Valuing Distressed Enterprises", October 3, 2008.

14 J.M. Risius, "Business Valuation Issues in Bankruptcy", December 4, 2007.

as a good reference point, a valuator should keep in mind the following issues related to distressed companies:[15]

- To the extent that financial distress in a particular industry has been caused by acquirers overpaying for target companies, leading to inflated multiples, caution should be exercised in relying on this data.
- On the other hand, purchase prices from distressed sales incorporate significant risk premiums related to execution, restructuring, and timing risk, which may or may not be relevant to the valuation of the subject company.
- Acquisition premiums related to synergies that are inherent in transaction multiples may need to be normalized.

Consistent with the comparable company analysis mentioned previously, issues related to the use of debt-free multiples and calculating normalized cash flows also apply when utilizing this valuation method.

Additional Valuation Issues

In addition to the valuation issues related to the three going-concern valuation methods mentioned above, the valuator should also consider the following unique valuation issues that could have a significant impact on overall valuation conclusions:

- *Non-capital tax losses* – the analysis of non-capital tax losses can be an important component when valuing a distressed company. The ability to utilize historic non-capital losses to offset the payment of future cash income taxes can add significant value to the entity. In instances where there has been a change in control of the entity following a reorganization or acquisition, the availability of non-capital losses may be reduced or even eliminated. The relevant income tax guidelines applicable in the specific tax jurisdiction of the entity should be consulted.
- *Debt forgiveness* – as a consequence of reorganization, certain of the company's creditors may agree to amounts less than what is owed to them. In situations where a debt is absolved without any payment, or is settled at an amount less than the amount owed, the gain on settlement to the debtor could be subject to a series of complex rules, which can also affect the company's tax loss carry-forwards. Once again, the relevant income tax guidelines applicable in the specific tax jurisdiction of the entity should be consulted.
- *Non-operating assets* – any non-operating or redundant assets

---

15 *Ibid.*

should be identified and segregated as they may not contribute to the operating cash flows of the business or may contribute cash flows at a different risk than the cash flow generated by the operating assets of the business. A few examples of such assets include extraneous real estate or land, marketable securities, or underperforming business units that may be divested.

- *On-going valuations* – turnaround strategies typically take a relatively long time to play out. The outcome depends heavily on the extent of distress, reorganization measures taken, skill of management, and industry specific and general economic conditions. The resulting intrinsic value of an entity can vary dramatically depending of the success of a number of such elements or lack thereof. Therefore, regular valuations might be required to assess the relative contribution of such measures to the value of the entity.
- *Opposing interests* – opposing interests of the different classes of investors can lead to valuation uncertainty and biases on overall value conclusions. Investors holding senior claims have an incentive to undervalue the company's business whereas junior claimants have an incentive to overvalue it.[16] A valuator should be mindful and seek to avoid such biases when preparing a valuation or reviewing another party's valuation.

Conclusion

There is no shortage of distressed companies in times of market turbulence. Distress can destroy a company if the early warning signs are not identified and addressed promptly. The appropriate remedy will depend on the stage of distress identified and will drive the reorganization strategy. A successful reorganization strategy that addresses all seven considerations previously mentioned in some form or another will increase the likelihood of survival, and ultimately, the post-reorganization value of the entity. The valuation of a distressed company can be a challenging task when traditional valuation

---

16 Refer to the following example cited in M. Crystal, QC & R.J. Mokal, "The Valuation of Distressed Companies – a Conceptual Framework" 2006: "Consider the situation where the reorganization of company X, under with its business would be transferred to company Y, a new company, and in which debt claims against X would be swapped for equity claims in Y. Suppose that there are two types of debt claims against X: Senior and Junior. Note that if the present value of X's business (call this "v") is found to be higher than X's Senior liability, then both Senior and Junior claimants would have valuable claims against it, which means that both classes would have to be offered shares in Y. By contrast, if v is less than X's Senior liability, then Senior claimants would get the entirety of Y's equity, with Junior claimants being shut out altogether in recognition of the fact that they have no economic interest in X."

methodologies are utilized. In order to arrive at a reliable conclusion of value, adjustments to conventional valuation methods to account for the unique intricacies of distressed companies must be considered.

Valuation Issues Under IFRS

George Gadkowski & Christophe Bergeron[1]

Accounting Standards

Comparing accounting standards has always been challenging but often necessary in valuing a business in an international context. The introduction of International Financial Reporting Standards (IFRS) was designed to increase reporting homogeneity and consistency around the world and alleviate the requirement for reconciliation. However, with a large number of companies across a wide range of industries continuing to be at various stages of transition to such standards, it is conceivable that differences in application and interpretation may lead to increased earnings variation in an already volatile market. This latest evolution of accounting standards may lead to earnings distortions that a business valuator should recognise and may potentially have to adjust. This topic is explored further in this chapter and has particular relevance for valuations based on net profit after-tax multiples.

Previously adopted accounting standards, including U.S. GAAP (SFAS 141/142), have shaped business valuation in many ways by changing significantly the structure of the balance sheet, earnings profile, and earnings volatility of companies subject to significant merger and acquisition activity. More specifically, with the introduction of SFAS 141/142 and similar accounting standards in other countries, goodwill has no longer been amortised and the identification and valuation of intangible assets has become considerably more widespread and robust. In general, identifiable intangible assets (IIAs) and goodwill have become material balance sheet items for many entities.

With many companies reporting material IIAs and goodwill on their balance sheet, the determination of the fair value of such assets has become espe-

1 The authors wish to thank their colleague, Steven Ferris, for his editorial and content suggestions.

cially topical and subject to significant scrutiny in the current economic environment. In this regard, there is an increasing focus by valuation professionals to understand the differences between impairment testing procedures under existing and new or revised accounting standards. This heightened degree of scrutiny has also emphasised the need to understand the differences between existing and new or revised business combinations standards, as such standards could have a significant impact on a company's balance sheet, future earnings, and subsequent impairment analysis. Further, the transition to different accounting standards will have a direct impact on the application of the market valuation approach in certain instances. In particular, the use of a market approach may require adjustments to the subject company financial results, as well as financial results of guideline comparable companies used to determine an appropriate valuation benchmark.

It is widely anticipated that differences between existing accounting standards and IFRS will continue to have an impact on financial statement analysis, as companies become more familiar with the new standards, further improvements are drafted, and common interpretation and generally accepted practices emerge. In addition to impairment testing and business combinations, IFRS will require greater valuation expert involvement in the reporting of property, plant and equipment (IAS 16), financial instruments (IAS 39) and investment property (IAS 40).

Impairment testing

Introduction

Under previous accounting standards, testing for impairment of goodwill required a two-step approach whereby the book value of the net assets of a particular reporting unit was first compared to the fair value of the reporting unit. The fair value of the reporting unit was typically determined using a post-tax discounted cash flow analysis. If the book value of the net assets of the reporting unit exceeded the fair value, a step two analysis was required. A step two analysis necessitated the valuation of all individual assets and liabilities of the reporting unit, as would be the case in a purchase price allocation under a business combination scenario. The fair value of the goodwill was determined as a residual, by deducting the fair value of identifiable assets and liabilities from the fair value of the reporting unit.

Similar to the goodwill impairment framework, under previous accounting standards, including SFAS 144, long-lived assets with a finite life were subject to a recoverability test. The sum of the undiscounted cash flows of the asset was first compared to the carrying amount. If the carrying amount exceeded the sum of the undiscounted cash flows, a step two analysis was undertaken. Under a step two analysis, the fair value of the asset was determined by reference to a common valuation approach appropriate for the specific circumstances. An impairment loss was measured as the excess of the carrying amount over the fair value.

Under IFRS, the two-step analysis has been replaced by a single step approach that requires a comparison of the carrying amount of an asset to its recoverable amount. The transition to a single step approach represents a significant departure from previous standards in a broad sense and presents a number of seemingly immaterial nuances that may in fact have a significant impact on the valuation analysis. The differences should be considered by a business valuator.

Summary of IFRS Impairment Requirements

IFRS requires entities to make an assessment at each reporting date to determine whether there is an indication that an asset may be impaired. If an indication of impairment exists, the entity is required to estimate the recoverable amount of the asset. The recoverable amount is defined as the higher of the amounts determined under a fair value less costs to sell approach and a value in use approach. Where the carrying amount of the asset exceeds its recoverable amount, the asset is required to be written-down to its recoverable amount. In contrast to previous accounting standards, impairment losses recognised in prior periods for assets other than goodwill may be reversed when there has been a change in estimate. When analysing earnings, a valuator should be aware of such reversals and the volatility they may have created.

The impairment analysis is to be performed at the individual asset level or at the cash-generating unit (CGU) level, if cash flows directly attributable to a particular asset cannot be identified. A CGU is the smallest identifiable group of assets that generates cash flows that are largely independent of other assets. As the CGU testing level may be smaller than a reporting unit, a valuator should be prepared for a potentially higher incidence of impairment.

Should impairment exist, the loss is required to be allocated to goodwill and to the extent the loss exceeds the book value of goodwill, on a *pro rata* basis to the other assets of the CGU. This is a departure from previous accounting standards, in which the loss was first allocated to the tangible and identifiable intangible assets. Depending on the size of the impairment, a valuator may no longer be required to determine the fair value of tangible and identifiable intangible assets, as was previously required under a step two analysis. Moreover, the impairment loss recognised under IFRS may be larger and therefore have a greater impact on earnings, as previous goodwill impairment standards did not require an allocation of losses beyond the book value of goodwill.

Fair Value Less Cost to Sell Approach

Fair value less cost to sell (FVLCS) is defined as "the amount obtainable from the sale of an asset or CGU in an arm's length transaction between knowledgeable, willing parties, less the costs of disposal". The best evidence of an asset's FVLCS is a price in a binding sale agreement in an arm's length transaction, adjusted for incremental costs that would be directly attributable to the disposal of the asset. If there is no binding sale agreement but an asset is traded in an active market, the best evidence of FVLCS is considered to be the asset's market price less the costs of disposal. The appropriate market price is usually the current bid price.

If a binding sale agreement or an active market for an asset does not exist, FVLCS is based on the best information available to reflect the amount that an entity could obtain from the disposal of the asset in an arm's length transaction between knowledgeable, willing parties, after deducting the costs of disposal. As noted later in this chapter, a practical solution to this circumstance is to use a traditional post-tax discounted cash flow analysis to determine the fair value (FV) part of the equation and deduct a brokerage style charge (normally a few per cent) to estimate the cost to sell (CS), thereby deriving the FVLCS.

Value in Use Approach

Value in use (VIU) is defined as the present value of the future cash flows expected to be derived from an asset or CGU. It is determined using present value techniques based on estimates of future cash flows from continued use and subsequent disposal of the asset. Estimates of future cash flows are to exclude cash inflows or outflows from financing activities, future restructuring (if not committed) or any income tax receipts or payments. The discount rate used in the analysis is based on a market assessment of the risk associated with the amount and timing of the future cash flows. As the future cash flows exclude income tax receipts or payments, the discount rate is to be determined on a pre-tax basis.

As a consequence of the current global financial crisis, it is widely believed that comparable transactions or trading multiples no longer provide the highest recoverable amount and companies are increasingly relying on VIU for impairment testing purposes. This, in turn, leads to an increasing use of pre-tax discount rates.

Determining a Pre-Tax Discount Rate

Discount rates are commonly derived using a Capital Asset Pricing Model, which is based on post-tax market observations. As pre-tax discount rates cannot be observed directly in the market place, a generally accepted methodology is to calculate a pre-tax rate from a post-tax rate. Although there is no standard method for performing this calculation, there is a widespread belief that the formula referred to as the "gross-up" approach provides a suitable approximation:

Pre-tax discount rate = Post-tax discount rate / (1 − effective tax rate)

The pre-tax discount rate obtained using this approach is then applied to pre-tax cash flows to arrive at a VIU.

Why the Gross-up Approach Can Lead to Material Errors

All else constant, a pre-tax discount rate applied to pre-tax cash flows should be equal to a post-tax discount rate applied to post-tax cash flows. The gross-up approach rarely approximates the correct pre-tax discount rate because it adjusts the discount factor in a "compound" or "geometric" fashion, while cash flows are adjusted in a "linear" fashion when tax is removed. The difference can be significant.

The following example of an impairment of an indefinite life asset illustrates the margin of error by using a gross-up approach. The scenario compares the VIU determined on a post-tax basis to the VIU determined on a pre-tax basis. Using a hypothetical 10 per cent post-tax discount rate, the gross-up approach indicates that the pre-tax equivalent rate is 14.3 per cent [10.0% / (1 - 30%)].

Post-tax cash flows - Indefinite life assets	
Post-tax discount rate	**10.0%**
Tax rate	30%
Perpetual growth rate	3.0%

(000'S)	2009	2010	2011	TV
EBIT	**20.0**	**21.0**	**22.1**	**22.7**
EBIT growth		*5.0%*	*5.0%*	*3.0%*
Less: tax	-6.0	-6.3	-6.6	-6.8
EBIT after tax	**14.0**	**14.7**	**15.4**	**15.9**
Plus: depreciation	2.0	2.0	2.0	2.0
Minus: capex	-2.0	-2.0	-2.0	-2.0
Change in working capital	-1.0	-1.0	-1.0	-0.6
Post-tax FCF	**13.0**	**13.7**	**14.4**	**15.3**
Discount period	0.5	1.5	2.5	2.5
Discount factor	1.0	0.9	0.8	0.8
Discounted post-tax FCF	**12.4**	**11.9**	**11.4**	**12.1**

Sum of discounted post-tax FCF	35.6
Terminal value	172.2
Fair value	**207.9**

Pre-tax cash flows - Indefinite life assets	
Pre-tax discount rate (grossed-up)	**14.3%**
Tax rate	n/a
Perpetual growth rate	3.0%

(000's)	2009	2010	2011	TV
EBIT	**20.0**	**21.0**	**22.1**	**22.7**
EBIT growth		*5.0%*	*5.0%*	*3.0%*
Less: tax	n/a	n/a	n/a	n/a
EBIT after tax	**n/a**	**n/a**	**n/a**	**n/a**
Plus: depreciation	2.0	2.0	2.0	2.0
Minus: capex	-2.0	-2.0	-2.0	-2.0
Change in working capital	-1.0	-1.0	-1.0	-0.6
Pre-tax FCF	**19.0**	**20.0**	**21.1**	**22.1**
Discount period	0.5	1.5	2.5	2.5
Discount factor	0.9	0.8	0.7	0.7
Discounted pre-tax FCF	**17.8**	**16.4**	**15.1**	**15.8**

Sum of discounted pre-tax FCF	49.2
Terminal value	140.3
Fair value	**189.5**

Difference between Pre-tax and Post-tax	-8.8%

As illustrated in this simple case, the implications of using a gross-up approach can be significant and the difference in value may be material to the financial statements. The potential for error is even more significant for assets with a shorter life.

Post-tax cash flows - Finite life assets (4 year)	
Post-tax discount rate	**10.0%**
Tax rate	30%
Perpetual growth rate	3.0%

(000'S)	2009	2010	2011	2012
EBIT	**20.0**	**21.0**	**22.1**	**22.7**
EBIT growth		*5.0%*	*5.0%*	*3.0%*
Less: tax	-6.0	-6.3	-6.6	-6.8
EBIT after tax	**14.0**	**14.7**	**15.4**	**15.9**
Plus: depreciation	2.0	2.0	2.0	2.0
Minus: capex	-2.0	-2.0	-2.0	-2.0
Change in working capital	-1.0	-1.0	-1.0	-0.6
Post-tax FCF	**13.0**	**13.7**	**14.4**	**15.3**
Discount period	0.5	1.5	2.5	3.5
Discount factor	1.0	0.9	0.8	0.7
Discounted post-tax FCF	**12.4**	**11.9**	**11.4**	**11.0**

Sum of discounted post-tax FCF	46.6

Pre-tax cash flows - Finite life assets (4 year)	
Pre-tax discount rate (grossed-up)	**14.3%**
Tax rate	n/a
Perpetual growth rate	3.0%

(000's)	2009	2010	2011	2012
EBIT	**20.0**	**21.0**	**22.1**	**22.7**
EBIT growth		*5.0%*	*5.0%*	*3.0%*
Less: tax	n/a	n/a	n/a	n/a
EBIT after tax	n/a	n/a	n/a	n/a
Plus: depreciation	2.0	2.0	2.0	2.0
Minus: capex	-2.0	-2.0	-2.0	-2.0
Change in working capital	-1.0	-1.0	-1.0	-0.6
Pre-tax FCF	**19.0**	**20.0**	**21.1**	**22.1**
Discount period	0.5	1.5	2.5	3.5
Discount factor	0.9	0.8	0.7	0.6
Discounted pre-tax FCF	**17.8**	**16.4**	**15.1**	**13.9**

Sum of discounted pre-tax FCF	63.1

Difference between Pre-tax and Post-tax	35.3%

In addition to the time horizon, the margin of error is particularly sensitive to the profile of the forecast cash flows (*i.e.*, increasing, constant and/or declining) and the post-tax discount rate used as the basis. As illustrated below, the margin of error can be significant depending on the growth rate and discount rate assumptions.

		Discount rate		
		7.0%	**10.0%**	**13.0%**
Perpetual Growth Rate	**0.0%**	1.1%	1.6%	2.1%
	2.0%	-9.0%	-4.7%	-2.4%
	3.0%	-16.4%	-8.8%	-5.1%
	4.0%	-26.5%	-13.8%	-8.3%

Adjusting the post-tax rate using the gross-up approach will generate the same VIU conclusion as that determined on a post-tax basis only in the unusual situation where an asset or CGU with an indefinite life will generate the same cash flows each year into perpetuity. In such circumstances, the VIU can be determined by applying a capitalised cash flow valuation methodology. The capitalised cash flow valuation methodology is based on the perpetuity growth formula (Gordon Shapiro):

$$\textbf{Fair value} = \frac{\text{Post-tax CF x (1+PGR)}}{\text{(Post-tax WACC - PGR)}}$$

Where:

PGR = perpetual growth rate   t = tax

WACC = discount rate   CF = cash flows

When the perpetual growth rate is nil, the formula can be re-written as follows:

$$\textbf{Fair value} = \frac{\textbf{Post-tax CF}}{\textbf{Post-tax WACC}} = \frac{\text{Pre-tax CF x (1-t)}}{\text{Pre-tax WACC x (1-t)}} = \frac{\textbf{Pre-tax CF}}{\textbf{Pre-tax WACC}}$$

Conclusion

In most cases, the gross-up approach will lead to over-valuation or under-valuation which may be material in the determination of the VIU and hence may ignore or create potential impairment. The gross-up approach should be particularly avoided in industries with finite life assets and low discount rates such as the energy, infrastructure, and resources sectors.

A relatively simple way to correct the problem is to perform the VIU calculation on a post-tax basis and solve for the pre-tax discount rate required to equate the value using pre-tax tax flows to the value using post-tax cash flows. This methodology is commonly referred to as the "iterative" approach and is recommended in Section 5 of the Basis for Conclusions on IAS 36 Impairment of Assets.

A way to avoid the problem entirely is to consider FVLCS instead of the VIU approach. The FVLCS approach allows the use of, and facilitates the reconciliation to, generally accepted valuation techniques which incorporate broader commercial assumptions, such as a post-tax discount rate, reasonable expansionary capital expenditures and unrestricted use of projections in excess of five years. In addition to issues associated with the gross-up approach, the VIU methodology precludes the consideration of costs and benefits associated with future restructuring (unless committed) or expansion. Consideration of such future costs and benefits can often be fundamental to the fair value of an investment and would typically be included in the FVLCS determination. The restrictions of the VIU in relation to capital expenditures and cash flow projections are likely to reduce the recoverable amount and may in fact not meet management's intended objective.

Moreover, it would be reasonable to assume that in a number of cases the FVLCS will be higher than the VIU. In most instances, lacking a signed purchase and sale agreement, it would be difficult to determine the FVLCS to meet its definition. However, in the event a binding sale agreement or an active market for an asset does not exist, the accounting standards permit the determination of the FVLCS based on a theoretical value supported by the best information available. This would be premised on a value at which the asset would change hands between a knowledgeable willing buyer and a knowledgeable willing seller under no compulsion to act. A rational and knowledgeable willing seller would not normally sell an asset for less than its (economic) value in use. In the absence of better information, the FVLCS may be based on a traditional discounted cash flow analysis. This, in turn, would dispel a general interpretation that the FVLCS approach is to be based on comparable transactions or trading multiples only.

Limiting the impairment analysis to a VIU approach can also be counter-intuitive to the general fair value definition, which contemplates the intentions of a potential acquirer and how an asset may be used by a broader set of market participants. A potential acquirer may not use certain of the assets or may use them in a capacity that represents a higher and better commercial use. As such, the conclusion reached under a VIU approach may be different than that reached under a broader market participant approach.

Business Combinations – New Rules, New Outcomes, New Challenges

Introduction

Market volatility can often bring opportunity, as companies with sufficient capital may be able to revisit mergers and acquisitions previously contemplated but abandoned because of lofty valuations during peak economic times. Now, companies may be in a position to acquire certain assets that are fundamentally sound but have been subject to what could be an overly pessimistic economic outlook and an environment of repriced risk in the medium term only. While the current economic environment lends itself to a value investment strategy that is often premised on a long-term horizon, the short-term valuation implications should not be overlooked, as assumptions are changing quickly and the window of opportunity may not be open for long during this heightened level of market uncertainty. Deals may now be more promptly consummated and require greater involvement by valuation experts.

Amidst this time of uncertainty, one of the many challenges for the business valuator is to understand how previous merger and acquisition activity has impacted the comparability of financial statements and to assess how the transition to IFRS business combinations requirements will impact the comparability of financial statements on an ongoing basis. Not only do such requirements have a direct impact on the purchase price allocation process in which the valuator is often involved, they also have an impact on valuation metrics derived from financial and market information of comparable listed companies when applying the market approach. This becomes especially important when comparing companies that have chosen an organic growth strategy versus companies that have grown by way of acquisitions. Companies that have been acquisitive will likely have a significantly higher proportion of IIAs and goodwill on their balance sheet and earnings that will include a higher amortisation component. Understanding the impact of the new accounting requirements and the challenges and opportunities they present can have significant implications.

Valuation Considerations

Business combinations accounting standards are increasingly relying on fair value measurements and have become increasingly more complex. The IFRS requirements include a number of changes from previous accounting conventions and certain of the requirements are characterised by uncertainty that will involve a significant amount of judgement in determining the appropriate valuation assumptions. The changes will have an impact on both the balance sheet and income statement and may even lead to modifications in the way transactions are structured.

The analysis below aims at illustrating the distortions that new accounting standards can create on financial statements and what adjustments are necessary to income statement and/or balance sheet items if market valuation multiples are to be computed on a consistent basis.

Accounting Item	"Old GAAP"	"New GAAP" *	Impact
Measurement date for securities issued	A reasonable period of time before and after terms are agreed to and announced	At acquisition date	B
Contingent consideration (e.g. earn-out)	Record when determinable; subsequent changes reflected in purchase price	Record fair value at acquisition date; subsequent changes in liabilities hit P&L	E / V
Acquisition costs	Capitalise	Expense as incurred	E
Acquisitions of <100%	Record minority interest at historical cost	Record using either "full goodwill" method (record 100% of goodwill) or "purchased goodwill" method (exclude goodwill attributable to non-controlling interest)	B
Pre-acquisition contingencies	Fair value during allocation period, or follow contingency accounting; no re-measurement	Fair value at acquisition date if determinable	E / V
Restructuring costs	Accrued as cost of business combination	Expense as incurred	E / V
In-process R&D	Allocate in purchase price then immediate expense (for U.S. GAAP purposes)	Allocate in purchase price and amortise (immediate expense not required)	E
Negative goodwill	Pro-rata reduction of certain non-current assets (extraordinary gain)	No reduction of assets, record as gain	E

* based on requirements of IFRS 3
E - normalised earnings impact
V - potential future earnings volatility
B - balance sheet (future impairment risk)

Valuation Implications

Under IFRS, the expensing of acquisition costs, such as advisers' fees, will have an immediate impact on earnings. Such costs will no longer be included in the measurement of goodwill and could impact post-combination impairment testing. Similarly, the general requirement to expense restructuring costs as incurred may result in more volatile post-combination operating results. Determining a normalised or maintainable level of earnings for acquisitive companies may now be more challenging.

Conversely, the capitalisation of in-process research and development (IPR&D) acquired in a transaction is directly opposite to U.S. GAAP, which required the amount to be expensed. Recording IPR&D as an asset will result in higher earnings in the first post-combination period but will lead to greater amortisation expense in subsequent periods and may impact future impairment analysis. This may be of particular importance in transactions involving technology companies, as the motivation behind such transactions can be a company's IPR&D assets and activities to which a significant amount of value is attributed.

In a transaction involving an issue of securities as consideration, the ability to adjust goodwill has been reduced under IFRS. In determining the fair value of the securities issued, a valuator no longer has the flexibility of analysing share prices within a reasonable period of time before and after the terms of the transaction are agreed to and announced. Instead, the fair value must be determined at the acquisition date. Depending on the volatility between the date of announcement and date of acquisition, this may have a significant impact on the purchase price and could impact future impairment testing. Closing transactions closer to the announcement date could mitigate the impact but means that valuation issues will be required to be analysed at an earlier stage, most likely during the due diligence process.

Another area of particular interest to valuators is contingent consideration. Under IFRS, the fair value of contingent consideration, such as an earn-out, is required to be determined at the acquisition date. The fair value is included in the determination of the purchase price and therefore increases the amount of goodwill recorded as part of the transaction. This creates a valuation challenge in the initial assessment of the fair value and in the re-measurement of the fair value on an ongoing basis. To form the basis of the fair value assessment, the valuator will need to understand the contractual terms of the contingent consideration. The assessment will require a determination of the probability of payment, an appropriate risk-adjusted discount rate and an analysis to ensure consistency with the forecast used to price the acquisition. Possible valuation approaches may include a probability weighted discounted cash flow analysis or even option theory. On an ongoing basis, re-measurement of the fair value of the contingent consideration may lead to increased earnings volatility. A failure to achieve targeted results required for the contingent consideration to be paid out may result in increased earnings but may also indicate that goodwill is impaired.

In acquisitions of less than a 100 per cent interest, the business valuator must be aware of the IFRS implications in assessing the value of a non-controlling interest. If it is decided that the non-controlling interest be measured at fair value (referred to as the "full goodwill" method), the fair value of the non-controlling interest will not necessarily be proportionate to the price paid by the acquirer, as a minority discount will be applied to the non-controlling portion. Application of IFRS will result in higher post-combination net asset values and higher post-combination depreciation and amortisation. This in turn, may require a reconciliation of net asset and earnings valuation multiples when comparing companies that have an organic growth strategy versus companies that choose to grow by acquisitions.

Valuation of Businesses in Central and Eastern Europe

Tomasz Ochrymowicz & Malgorzata Stambrowska

Introduction

Today's unstable economy and volatile markets present serious challenges to anybody who values business enterprises, intangible assets, or real estate. It is even more difficult to put a reasonable value on a business in an economy that had been dynamically changing long before the recent financial crisis took place. This is especially visible in Central and Eastern Europe (CEE), which has been dramatically changing over the past 20 years as a result of a political system reform, the accession of several countries[1] to the European Union, as well as a dynamic growth driven by exports, strong internal consumption, and investments. The GDP growth rates of the "European Tigers" (as the region was often referred to) ranged from 5.4 per cent to 10.8 per cent between 2004 and 2008, which was substantially higher than the "Old Europe"[2] countries where the overall GDP growth ranged from 0.8 per cent to 2.9 per cent over the same period. Foreign investors were flocking to the region at any cost in search for either a quick deal or to secure a local foothold in hope of building a strategic presence.

Central European banks had a very limited exposure to toxic assets and one would expect that the impact of the recent credit squeeze should be limited. However, the Emerging Europe's economies have not been as immune as some analysts and local politicians claimed they would be. It is now quite clear that the financial sector will be affected by appreciating foreign cur-

1 Bulgaria, the Czech Republic, Estonia, Latvia, Lithuania, Hungary, Poland, Romania, Slovakia and Slovenia.

2 The "Old Europe" (EU16): Austria, Belgium, Cyprus, Denmark, Germany, Ireland, Greece, Spain, Finland, France, Italy, Luxemburg, Malta, the Netherlands, Portugal, and the United Kingdom.

rencies and higher loan loss provisions, which, combined with low liquidity, is likely to limit the amount of loans extended to local businesses. Ironically, despite limited exposure to toxic assets it appears that the perception and hence pricing of the risk related to both economies and businesses in Central and Eastern Europe have generally increased as investors fled to traditionally more secure assets, currencies, and countries. The impact of the crisis has been delayed compared to Western European markets but there appears to be a stronger impact on the fragile economies that cannot afford to inject the same amount of funds as their Western counterparts. At the same time, depreciation of most of the CEE currencies combined with reduction of salary levels and taxes increased the competitiveness of the CEE-based firms.

It is also unclear what measures the CEE governments will undertake and how those steps will influence the long-term reforms, the success of which is crucial for short- and long-term perspectives and values of businesses. All those and many other factors need to be considered in a valuation. As a result, valuation has generally, and particularly in CEE, become more difficult and more than ever, rather art than science.

How CEE Differs from Western Europe

Central Europe has made enormous progress since the early 1990s when democratic changes and market reforms started to come in. Until 2008, it has been one of the world's fastest growing regions. The economies of the "New Europe", which were once behind the "Iron Curtain", are quickly integrating with the "Old Europe" and gradually preparing to convert their currencies to the euro.

The CEE countries have been the motors of growth in the EU, especially during the early stages of the recent crisis in financial markets and the slow down in the eurozone. Until 2008, growth in Central Europe was helping to counter the slowdown in the eurozone. However, the GDP growth forecasts started to deteriorate as the world faced recession.

Eurozone GDP forecast

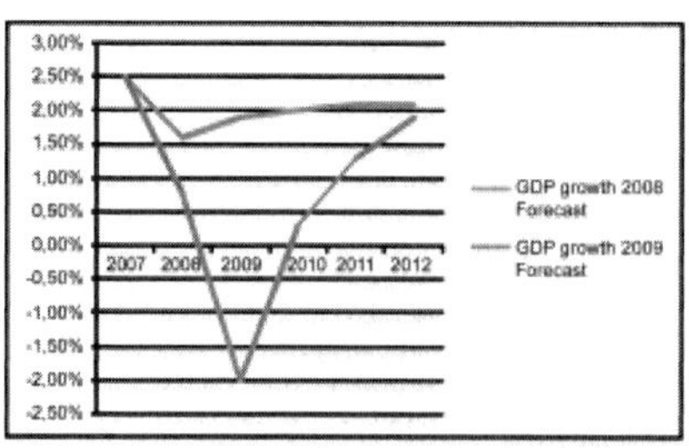

EU 27[3] GDP Growth Forecast

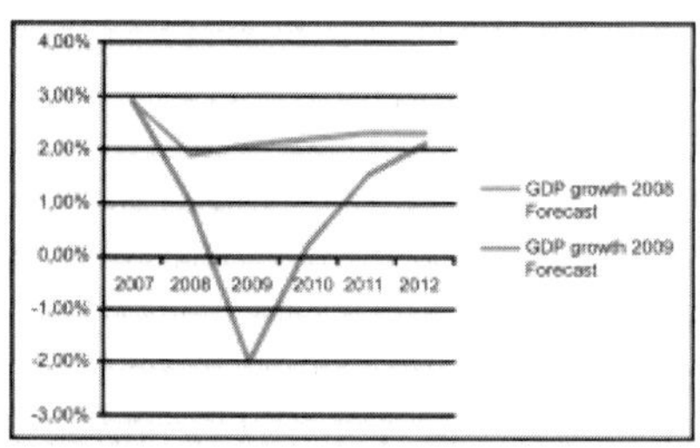

[3] The EU 27 includes Austria, Belgium, Bulgaria, the Czech Republic, Cyprus, Denmark,

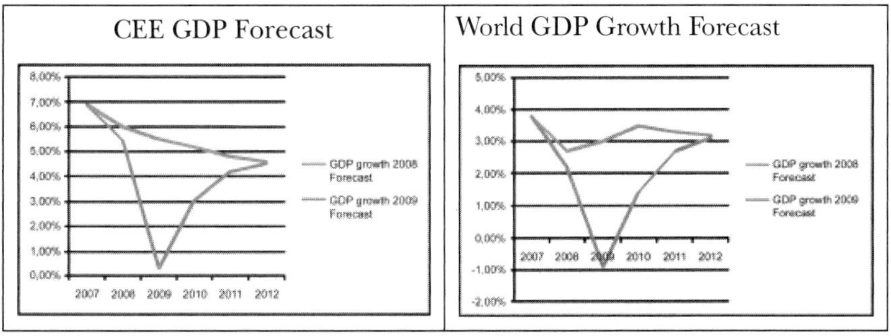

Source: EIU January 2009

The GDP forecasts have deteriorated since 2008, and it appears that CEE will be affected stronger than it was forecasted in 2008. The real impact of the crisis on the CEE economies will only be seen in 2009 and thereafter.

The chart below presents the actual data on the GDP growth in the fourth quarter of 2008 and the first quarter of 2009.

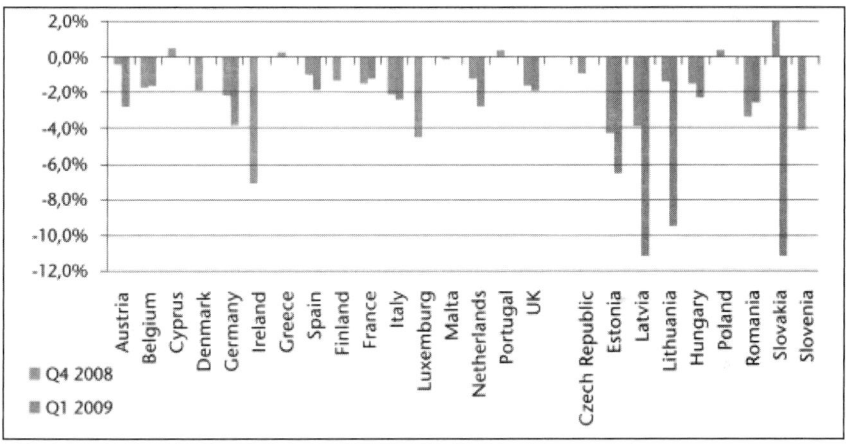

Source: Eurostat

As a result of a decreasing or mostly negative gross domestic product, many Central European countries, especially the Baltic states (Latvia, Estonia, and Lithuania), have been recording significant current account and budget imbalances. In the "good old times", those deficits were financed to a great

---

Germany, Estonia, Ireland, Greece, Spain, Finland, France, Italy, Latvia, Lithuania, Luxemburg, Hungary, Malta, the Netherlands, Poland, Portugal, Romania, Slovakia, Slovenia, and the United Kingdom. Source: Economist Intelligence Unit

extent by FDI[4] inflows or public debt and were not perceived as a major cause for concern. The imports of raw materials and advanced machinery, used to modernize or extend the existing production capacity, were offset by a dynamic growth of exports or a massive inflow of foreign direct investments. This fact, among others, has triggered an appreciation of local currencies and local exporters were forced to compete with Western companies not only on production costs, but also on quality and innovation. The strengthening of local currencies caused a major shock to local exporters in 2007 and until mid-2008. But once the financial crisis spread across the globe and investors fled to traditionally secure currencies, most of the CEE currencies depreciated significantly, making life easier for export-dependant companies and limiting imports. Several countries have announced plans to join the eurozone and replace their currencies with euro. Slovenia and Slovakia joined the eurozone in 2008 and 2009, respectively. Others realized that the adoption of the single currency could help stabilize their economies and shield them from abrupt changes, which may have little to do with the economic fundamentals. This, however, may become difficult now, as the current economic situation can make it impossible to meet the Maastrich eurozone[5] accession criteria.

Having joined the EU, most of the countries in the region reported substantial increases in foreign direct investments. Investors realized that the risk of investing in CEE had decreased and the growth prospects were to remain attractive compared to the old EU countries. As a result, Central Europe has been the prime FDI location during the past few years. Investors perceived the region as a strong and stable economy with a market of more than 120 million people.

It has to be noted that the pattern of FDI inflows is changing in many of the CEE countries. Low costs, especially low labor costs, are still the major factor attracting foreign capital. However, other factors are becoming increasingly important. In the case of such countries as Poland, the Czech Republic, Slovakia, Slovenia, and Hungary, significant number of high-profile invest-

---

4 Foreign direct investment.

5 Euro convergence criteria (Maastricht criteria) set to secure price stability in Eurozone after inclusion of new applicant. Maastricht criteria include:

1. Inflation rate: no more than 1.5 percentage points higher than the average of the three best performing (lowest inflation) member states of the EU,
2. Deficit: annual government deficit/gdp must not exceed 3%, government debt/gdp lower than 60%, ERM II participation of minimum 2 years,
3. Exchange rate: applicant countries should have joined the exchange-rate mechanism (ERM II) under the European Monetary System (EMS) for 2 consecutive years and should not have devaluated its currency during the period, long-term interest rates.
4. Long-term interest rates: the nominal long-term interest rate must not be more than two percentage points higher than in the three lowest inflation member states.

ments were made mainly in automotive, electronics, and IT sectors. The region's substantive number of well-educated, foreign language speaking graduates, positions CEE as an outsourcing hotspot. Foreign investors are interested not only in simple Business Process Outsourcing (BPO) investments, but also in opening far more advanced research and development operations.

Unemployment has been a serious problem in transition economies. Poland, where unemployment exceeded 20 per cent in the beginning of the decade, saw this indicator fall to approximately 8 per cent in 2008. After several Western European labor markets were opened to the ex-communist countries, many well-qualified and traditionally cheap workers have either left their home countries or become more expensive. This has badly affected several workforce-dependant services such as hotels, restaurants, construction or even banking as qualified and experienced employees left to work in Western Europe. As a result, Central European companies had to improve their skills at hiring, training, and retaining employees, something they had never considered so crucial before.

Recently, the whole CEE region has been suffering from a decreased economic activity. However, each country's problems are specific and so will be their recovery patterns, most likely. While CEE seems to have more chance for a mild recovery than the EU, economists expect that this recovery will be slow due to the lack of both external and internal financing for the growth.

Value is in the Eye of Beholder

How Investors Perceive CEE

As mentioned before, one of the fallouts of the crisis impacting the Central European economies was the rapid depreciation of their currencies. In all of the CEE countries, currencies had depreciated by 20-30 per cent over a relatively short time, except those that were pegged to euro.[6]

The depreciation of local currencies was caused by a massive withdrawal of funds by foreign investors, who feared that the economic crises in Hungary and Ukraine would have a negative impact on other large CEE economies such as Poland and the Czech Republic. This has proved how much the emerging economies, even the largest ones, are dependent on global investment flow and foreign investor sentiment towards the region. As a result, the yields on euro or dollar denominated government bonds of the CEE countries (indicator of a risk-free rate) increased in 2008, especially in the

[6] Estonia, Bulgaria, Latvia, Lithuania.

third quarter of the year. The effects on pricing the risk can be seen on the charts below. They depict yields on euro or dollar denominated long-term bonds issued by Poland, the Czech Republic, Hungary, and Slovakia.

Poland – USD bond (maturity 2024)

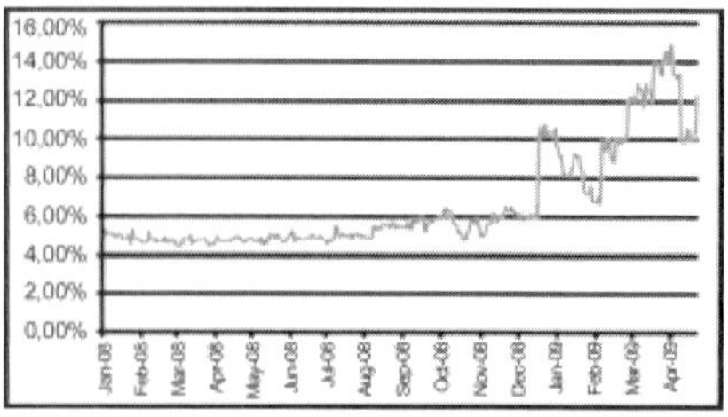

Hungary–Eurobond (maturity: 2017)

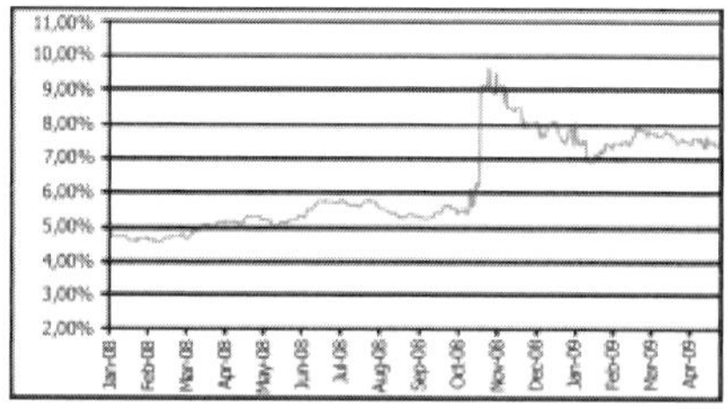

Czech Republic – Eurobond (maturity: 2020)

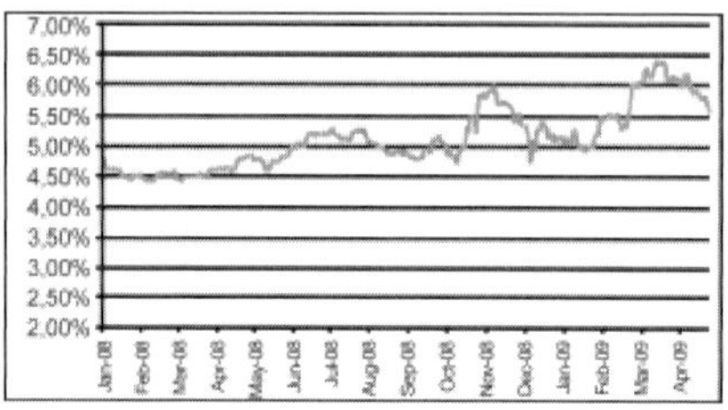

Slovak Republic – Eurobond (maturity: 2014)

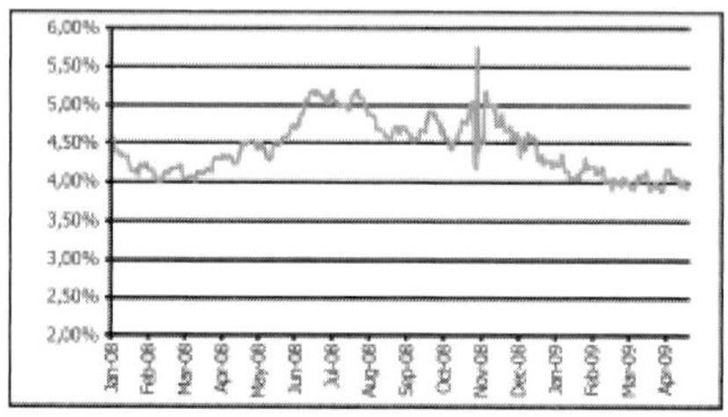

Source: Bloomberg

It remains debatable to what extent this was a result of the expected deterioration of the macroeconomic environment of the region or rather the change in pricing the risk.

As we know, the value is in the eye of a beholder. What makes the Central European region unique, compared to the developed economies, is the variety of investors. As everywhere else, each investor has his specific expectations as to the risk and reward profile of a potential investment. These in turn depend not only on the type of the investor (financial vs. strategic) but quite often on his origin. This crisis has revealed particularly that local and international investors have quite different perceptions of risk of operations in CEE. For example, a local investor is already familiar with the local business environment and the depreciation of the local currency does not affect the investment.

Although most of GDP in the CEE countries is already generated by a private sector, in 2007 almost 24 per cent of the largest CEE companies had state as their controlling shareholder, according to the research performed by Deloitte Central Europe. The revenues of the state-owned companies accounted for nearly 20 per cent of the revenues of 500 largest CEE companies and, despite the fact that privatisation policies are being pursued, this share is not falling. This is, above all, the effect of a failure to pursue the privatization process in energy and infrastructure sectors, which retained their special status granted in the times of the planned economy. This can be seen especially well in Poland where the state treasury tries to privatise its "crown jewels" through public offers, which enables it to retain control or merely, leaves some companies on the privatisation "shelf".

Foreign investors have been widely present in the region and the FDI continued to flow to Central Europe. But, whilst in the beginning of the market reform and privatisation in CEE, transactions involved primarily foreign purchasers from Western Europe, over the years CEE and Russian companies and their shareholders have more aggressively started using acquisitions as an expansion mechanism. Western companies generally perceive CEE as a more risky business environment compared to their home markets. This is caused by the variable progress of ongoing market reforms and the resulting high degree of uncertainty, frequent changes to regulations, and lower efficiency of the judiciary systems. In addition, CEE has been and still is exposed to the fluctuation of local currencies of some of the countries, insufficient capitalisation of the banking system, and generally smaller size of its companies when compared to their Western European or North American peers. These risks were often incorporated in foreign valuations of the CEE companies but appeared to be perceived as less relevant in view of local investors.

In addition to the above-mentioned differences in perception of risks, there is, generally, a different approach to forecasting future results.

Specific Issues Related to Valuation in CEE

As we mentioned earlier, the CEE countries have been in the process of developing their market economies over the last 20 years. Naturally, that period has been volatile in many aspects, as new rules had to be created at a pace allowing the region to catch up with the Western world as much and as soon as possible.

Mergers and acquisitions have been amongst the most dynamically developing areas. Businesses were established, privatised, bought, sold and merged, with the intensity typical for an emerging economy. After many years of centrally planned economies and almost exclusive state ownership of businesses, new managers and potential buyers were keen to know the value of their companies.

This called for a prompt development of the valuation profession. With several international professional firms (at that stage mostly offering only audit services) and numerous local experts active in the market, the process has been dynamic but also chaotic. At the beginning, market participants attempted to value businesses using their own resources. The lack of either appropriate experience or familiarity with any valuation standards whatsoever often resulted in transaction parties having to negotiate on the basis of two completely different valuations of the same company. The need for an independent valuation opinion was recognised.

Many issues faced by valuators in Central Europe are similar to the ones widely discussed in developed economies. Nevertheless, performing a valuation in any of the CEE countries still gives rise to numerous additional issues specific to the region and the country. Major reasons are still relatively immature financial markets as well as certain problems with applying the valuation standards generally accepted in the developed countries. The immaturity of the markets results in such common issues with the income and market approaches, as:

- inadequate quality of financial forecasts;
- difficulty in forecasting the long-term growth and profitability;
- problems with cost of capital estimation; and
- lack of comparability of local companies to the Western peers.

These specific issues will be discussed in more detail further in this chapter.

Financial Forecasts

In the early stages of a market economy in the CEE, valuation of a business was usually hampered by the lack of reliable management forecasts. Many companies were used to preparing only their annual budgets – as was required by law – and were unwilling to try and predict future beyond that period. Heirs of the planned economy, the managers feared being held responsible, should their companies fail to achieve the forecasted results. The majority of them also lacked the necessary education and experience in financial management. A general uncertainty as to the future development of the country's economy did not help in preparing forecasts that could be used as a basis for a sensible DCF analysis.

Preparation of a reliable DCF analysis for a local company often required a valuation practitioner to put additional effort into certain steps of the process. In many cases, his role entailed educating the management in the art of financial forecasting.

The most difficult part of the process was challenging and discussing the frequently unrealistic assumptions made by the management. Typically, managers would tend to either optimistically overestimate their future performance or too cautiously underestimate it. Convincing them to take a more objective and realistic look at their company's potential was hard and even harder when there was corporate politics involved in the forecasting process.

Even after each assumption had been discussed and agreed, management boards of state-owned companies (which constituted the majority of businesses at the beginning of the region's transformation) were often very reluctant to formally take ownership of the finalised forecast. This part of the whole process could consume most of an appraiser's time and effort.

Fortunately, nowadays availability and quality of management forecasts have significantly improved, together with their willingness to acknowledge their responsibility in that area. Many CEOs and CFOs combine modern education with experience gained in international companies. They are able to prepare forecasts that form a reliable basis for valuation, providing necessary assistance in the valuation process and taking full ownership of the presented information.

In the present time, we observe several region-specific issues while preparing forecasts for a Central European company. For instance, profitability of a business is often overstated because managers assume low cost of labor for the whole forecast period. Historically, workforce used to be significantly cheaper in CEE than in the rest of the European Union, thus giving the companies from the region a certain competitive edge. This situation has been changing for some time already (as was discussed earlier). Wages have reached levels comparable to the Western standards, especially in case of skilled professionals. An appraiser should take this into account when analysing the forecasted long-term profitability of the valued business.

Similarly to the above, the appraiser should reflect properly the growth perspectives of the valued company. Typically, forecasts are performed for the next couple to a maximum of five years as it is often argued that any longer term forecasts are not reliable. After say a five-year discrete forecast period, an appraiser assumes a steady growth rate of cash flow. While this makes perfect sense in mature industries and countries, this is often not applicable to many CEE companies that are still in their development phase and forecast a "moderate" 15-20 per cent growth rate in the last year of the five-year forecast. As a result, the forecast period needs to be extended beyond the customary three- to five-year period until a company reaches a stable growth and the capitalization formula can be applied.

As mentioned earlier, there are certain differences in how foreign and local investors see future growth of the CEE businesses. This applies to both the long-term and the short-term perspective. For example, local or CEE-based strategic investors would typically have a better, compared to a new entrant from Western Europe, understanding of the operating costs or minimum capital expenditures necessary to maintain or extend production capacity. Local investors would be more optimistic as to growth of the company given their typically positive experience in increasing revenues. On the other hand, a typical Western investor would assume benefits of lower operating costs or long-term economic, social, and technological trends affecting an industry.

Discount Rate

Derivation of a discount rate in the market economy that is practically only two decades old has to be a subject of endless doubts and discussions. In developed economies, major elements of a discount rate are usually derived from significant amounts of historical data researched over long periods of time. This is simply not possible in an emerging economy.

Estimation of a risk-free rate is particularly troublesome in transition economies, where financial markets are still developing and are traditionally perceived as extremely risky by international investors. The major problem for an appraiser is finding an appropriate example of a risk-free asset as well as a sufficient amount of reliable historical data on its performance. Even though most of the Central European governments issue bonds that may serve as a good proxy for a risk-free asset, there are at least two issues:

- Foreign investors would still apply additional premium to reflect their cautious perception of the local investment risk. The resulting risk-free rate of return may differ significantly from the yield on the local government bonds.
- Many government bonds are so thinly traded that any analysis of their yields is practically unusable in a valuation. This is usually the problem in the smaller countries but each case requires special attention while analysing historical trading of bonds in the whole region.

Therefore, it is sometimes more sensible to base an estimate of a risk-free rate on financial instruments issued by governments of developed countries. In general, practitioners choose one of two approaches:

- Using yields on local government bonds in countries where government bond markets are sufficiently liquid and the characteristics of traded instruments make them reliable proxies of a risk-free rate of return.
- Using Western European or American government bonds and applying an element of a country risk reflecting investors' per-

ception of an investment risk related in a subject country. This approach is common in the markets without sufficient liquidity or when it is more reasonable to approach the valuation from the international investor's perspective. Some practitioners argue this is in fact the only sensible approach since even the largest financial markets in the region are not liquid enough to provide sufficient data on risk-free returns.

The specifics of Central Europe also affect the estimation of a market risk premium and a beta factor. As was discussed earlier, Central European stock exchanges are very young compared to their American and Western European counterparts, with lower numbers of shares traded and lower trading volumes. Their volatility usually follows the behavior of the older and larger exchanges, as illustrated in the chart below.

Performance of major CEE exchanges and the S&P500

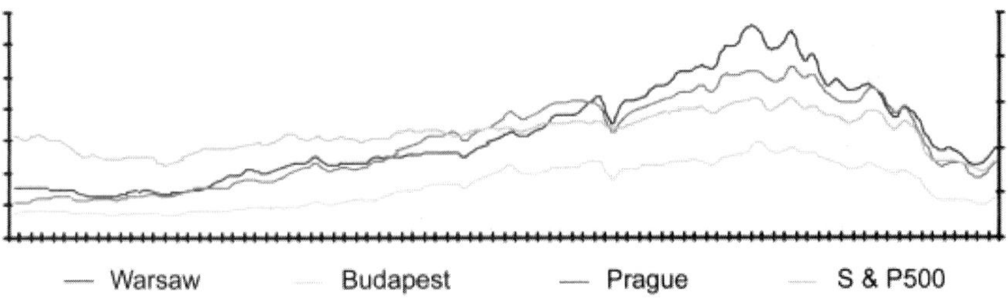

Source: Bloomberg

Stock exchanges in the region do not have a long enough history and cannot provide a sufficient amount of underlying data to facilitate an appropriate research and help us estimate trends and investor behavior. Any such analysis will bear the risk of being heavily influenced by short-term tendencies or one-time events.

As with the risk-free rate of return, various approaches are adopted to overcome those shortcomings and, in case of a market risk premium, the number of concepts is significant.

Some practitioners base their estimation on the data from the U.S. or sometimes European markets. They would choose from the available research on the equity market risk premium observed in the U.S. and apply the results to their discount rate estimation. Adjustments will be made (or not), depending on what an appraiser thinks of investors' perspective: are all investors similar and their required return on equity investments over the risk-free rate will be the same in the U.S. and in Central Europe? Or is the region so unique in the eyes of investors that the applied equity market risk premium should differ significantly from the U.S. experience?

Those appraisers, who acknowledge the uniqueness of the regional markets, try to find reliable ways to estimate specific market risk premium required by investors in those markets. Various types of research are suggested and applied, including a survey which analyses the market risk premium expected by the major market participants, like investment banks or market analysts.

Use of Market Methods

Applicability of market methods for appraising Central European companies has often been questioned. Practitioners are aware that the market, preferably the local one, is the best source of benchmarks for a valuation of a business. On the other hand, the quality of estimates made with the use of these methods has been severely affected by the relative immaturity of local capital markets. This immaturity is reflected mostly in two areas crucial for an appraiser:

- Lack of market depth: low trading volumes on stock exchange and small number of comparable private transactions.
- Lack of information: difficulty in finding data on private transactions and unlisted companies.

Let's look at the Polish stock exchange, currently the largest and the busiest exchange in the region. It was established in 1991, with only five companies listed. Even though it has been growing quickly (see the chart below), it still cannot be treated as a developed, mature market and can hardly provide sufficient amount of historical data to derive reliable pricing multiples or trend estimates. That is why professionals prefer to use data from more developed equity markets to, for example, determine certain elements of discount rates (as described before).

The Development of the Warsaw Stock Exchange

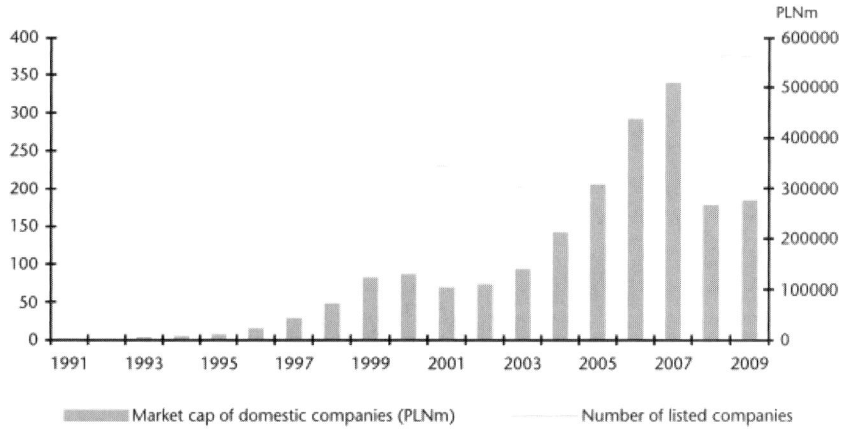

Source: Warsaw Stock Exchange

Another problem with the Warsaw Stock Exchange is that many industry sectors are practically not represented there. The current sector structure of the WSE enables a valuator to find a satisfactory sample of peers only when appraising a bank, an IT, or construction company. Applying the market multiples method to value *e.g.*, a coalmine, is much more complicated, as the first coalmine was only listed in Warsaw in June 2009 (for comparison: there are 13 companies from the coal mining sector currently listed on the New York Stock Exchange).[7] We could refer to other markets and find coalmines listed as close as in Prague, but in this particular case the specifics of the industry call for peers located physically in the same market as our valuation subject. This has been a significant problem for valuation practitioners in the region, due to a large number of heavy industry businesses being privatised or prepared for sale by governments in the last period. Such high-profile valuations required the use of multiple methodologies and one of the most obvious choices – the market multiples method – was practically inapplicable.

Unlike coalmines, many businesses can be compared to their counterparts abroad. But valuing a Central European company using the guideline company method on the basis of data from foreign markets creates another issue – how many will turn out to be even remotely comparable? Major characteristics that are taken into account as part of this method are typical for all markets, including size, diversification, profitability, accounting rules,

---

7 Source: nyse.com, as at 28 June 2009.

maturity/life cycle. But in the case of the CEE region, the differences seem to be much more noticeable.

Central European companies are, in general, significantly smaller than their Western peers and rarely are in the same stage of their life cycle as guideline companies from developed economies. Their current and forecast profitability is often not sustainable (as described earlier) and, due to their size, they are almost never as diversified or developed. At the same time, the CEE companies are generally perceived to have better growth prospects than their Western counterparts.

All this raises the need to apply numerous adjustments that are meant to make the multiples derived from the developed market more applicable for a valuation of a Central European company. This, in turn, increases the subjectivity of such valuation, making it more difficult to explain and defend.

Summary

Valuation of businesses in Central Europe has never been a straightforward exercise. The recent financial crisis has, in fact, made it more difficult. Mostly, this results from international investors' perceptions of the region's investment risk.

Even in the prosperous times, the CEE economies were perceived as less predictable albeit potentially more profitable. This perception of higher risk was gradually changing while the region's countries were developing their market economies and acquisitions generated hefty returns. In turbulent times, however, investors are disinclined to put their money in the economies traditionally seen as more risky, even if this perception is not supported by actual performance. This raises a threat that a period of bridging the economic gap between CEE and the developed markets might be followed by a – hopefully short – period of widening that gap. This, in turn, would affect the way businesses are valued and leave the issues we discussed above "region-specific" and unsolved for some more time.

Valuation Issues During Argentina's 2002 Financial Crisis

Miguel A. Molfino & Guido Dalla Bona

Argentina's Crisis

Argentina was under the worst economic crisis in its history during December 2001 and during 2002. The purpose of these introductory paragraphs is not to dig into the reasons that produced the crisis but to show its effects and how they changed the local business environment.

The huge currency devaluation and other decisions made by the government changed all the rules including legal and private agreements. Uncertainty affected all kind of companies: private, state-owned, local, foreign, *etc.*

After almost 11 years of convertibility as AR$1=US$1 (including currency stability and no inflation), citizens returned to their old myths:

- a terrible fear for inflation, that produced actions to try to cover from inflation effects;
- a desperate desire to buy U.S. dollars, as the citizens did not trust in the local peso anymore.

However, the desire to buy U.S. dollars was partly restricted because of the famous "corralito" (the restriction to withdraw deposits from the banks). Banks were nearly in bankruptcy due to the withdrawal of deposits (nearly 30 per cent of total deposits were lost in average) prior to the "corralito" and the difficulty to recover loans (including loans made to federal, provincial and municipal governments).

We are going to describe the actions taken by the government, prior to describing the impact in valuation:

- In response to increasing withdrawals from local bank accounts, the

Argentine government announced restrictions on banking and foreign exchange activities on December 1, 2001. Decree No. 1570 announced limitations to banking operations for 90 days and imposed restrictions on individuals and companies' access to their accounts by limiting cash. That decision caused anger in the population and riots were spread almost everywhere in the country.

- Following the collapse of the government of President de la Rua in late December and the short-lived tenure of President Adolfo Rodriguez Saa, Mr. Duhalde was appointed President by Congress on January 1, 2002. In the meantime, the government decided not to pay foreign debt, entering Argentina's federal bonds in default.
- In January 9, 2002, the Presidential Decree 71/2002 implemented the exchange rate provisions of Law 25,561 (the Public Emergency and Exchange Rate Reform Law). After 10 years of a fixed exchange rate, the government abandoned the Convertibility Plan that pegged the peso to the U.S. dollar at parity. On January 6, the government announced a 29 per cent devaluation of the official peso and the introduction of a dual exchange-rate system. The official rate was set at AR$1.4=US$1 and it was applicable for all trade and financial transactions. A free-floating foreign exchange rate would be used for all other transactions (the non-official rate was almost AR$4=US$1). The partial freeze of banking deposits imposed on December 1, 2001 remained in effect and it was strengthened.
- The Argentine government announced a new set of economic measures on February 3, 2002 (Decree 214/02):
    - All deposits in U.S. dollars were converted to pesos at a rate of 1.4 pesos per dollar. They were also indexed at a rate based on the consumer price index (CPI). Interest rates were left to the free determination of the market. Up to US$30,000 of every deposit (per person and per bank) could be exchanged for dollar denominated public bonds, guaranteed by the Treasury, in case there were savers that did not wish to "pesify" their deposits.
    - Certificates of deposits were rescheduled in their maturities.
    - The government announced some mechanisms to use certificates of deposits as legal tender, in order to provide people with additional means of payment.
    - Loans in U.S. dollars were converted to pesos at a rate of one peso per dollar. The principal was subject to indexation. After being "pesified", the current stock of loans and deposits had a regulated interest rate and an adjustment by CPI. To compensate

the currency mismatch in the bank's balance sheets produced by the "pesification" of dollar deposits at a higher rate than dollar loans, the government issued a peso denominated bond that was given to the banks.

- Adjustment of Deposits and Loans: After being "pesified", the current stock of loans and deposits in the economy had a regulated interest rate and were adjusted by the Reference Stabilization Coefficient (CER – "Coeficiente de Estabilización de Referencia") which varied according to the local CPI.
- New loans and deposits were freely arranged. New deposits entering the system had no restrictions for withdrawal, were not adjusted by the CER, and savers could collect in cash the interests on a monthly basis.
- Private contracts denominated in dollars were transformed into pesos at a rate of one peso per dollar.
- All legal actions against deposit restrictions were suspended for 180 days.
- Negotiations were announced with privatized public service companies (mainly utilities) to determine whether rate adjustment clauses, previously subject to variations in the U.S. dollar or U.S. price indices, were to be subject to new adjustment clauses in pesos.
- The unemployment rate had hit an historic high of 22 per cent and the GDP decreased nearly 11 per cent during year 2002.

So, with an economy in which the federal government was in default, the banks were nearly in bankruptcy, the contracts clauses were subject to changes, and there were restrictions in the cash available for citizens, a crisis hit the business and the political environment.

In those days, two sets of scenarios were usually construed: a pessimistic one assuming that the new government would be unable to govern for long and consequently the 2003 elections would be anticipated, and an optimistic one, assuming that the government would gather enough local and international support to manage the present crisis and to continue through 2003.

The pessimistic scenario was clearly one of rampant inflation, continuous peso devaluation, no credit available in the economy, GDP would not recover, *etc.*

The optimistic scenario was based on the assumption that politicians had learned the lessons, that consistent fiscal and monetary policies were to be implemented, and that finally the economy would start its recuperation.

Valuation in Times of Crisis

Considering the crisis, many analysts' concern was whether private companies could be valued (Argentina had a very small number of public companies). During crisis, foundational principles, historical trends, and commonly accepted valuation models might not be applicable. So, was it possible to value a firm competing in a market with new rules, with limited and changing data? The answer was yes, but the analysis of firms' key variables of value was required.

Approaches to Valuation

In our experience, after considering the three generally accepted approaches to valuation, commonly referred to as the income approach, market approach, and cost approach, the methodologies within the income approach were deemed most appropriate during Argentina's crisis, to value firms on a going-concern basis.

During the crisis, the lack of reliable and applicable market information about comparable companies and similar transactions discouraged analysts from the use of methodologies within the market approach. Although this was (and is) an issue in all of South America when compared to developed countries, it was a much deeper problem during those years.

Additionally, if importing multiples from foreign non-crisis markets, the adjustments required to control the differences on fundamentals in the firm subject to valuation were so material that the analysis relied on highly subjective assumptions.

Valuation rules of thumb were no longer useful. For instance, prior to the crisis there was a popular market approach rule that valued the equities at 5x EBITDA less financial debt. This rule of thumb was used in several industries. After the crisis, the rule changed to 3x EBITDA less financial debt. But, that was a mistake, because some industries were better situated than others (*e.g.*, companies with incomes originated in exports), so it was not the same for an export manufacturer compared to a manufacturer that only sold its products in the domestic market.

Regarding the cost approach, the lack of marketability showed by most of the firms' individual tangible assets, as well as the limits of these methodologies in capturing the intangible assets values during the crisis, resulted in considering this approach as not relevant for most of the cases.

Within the income approach, in the Discounted Cash Flow methodology, the cash flows anticipated over several periods, plus a terminal value at the end of that time frame, are discounted to their present value using an appropriate required rate of return to obtain the value of a firm's operations. Once the value of the firm's operations is calculated, the value of the firm's debt is subtracted so as to obtain the value of its operating equity. Upon arriving at the firm's operating equity value, any non-operating assets or liabilities owned by the firm are added or subtracted in order to arrive at the firm's total equity value. All of the steps of the exposed methodology were impacted by the crisis context and business environment.

Although in those days, it was more challenging from a technical view to try to calculate a discount rate for a company located in Argentina, in our opinion it was more difficult to project estimated cash flows at least for the following five years.

Examples of common valuation issues that analysts were required to deal with during the crisis included the following:

- Cash flow in local or foreign currency? Argentina devaluated its currency from AR1=US$1 to almost AR$4=US$1 between January 2002 and May 2002. Considering local currency instability, the use of a stable foreign currency was required. During the crisis, most of the valuation analyses were expressed in U.S. dollars. But, as to carefully attend to the overall trends in the local economic environment was key for the estimations, it was used to forecast nominal cash flow in local currency, including local inflation expectations, converting the resulting cash flow to U.S. dollars, by using projected FX rates on a year-by-year basis.
- History was not a useful tool to predict the short-term future level of activities. During the crisis, the significant changes in market rules resulted in completely new business scenarios for companies. Financial statements up to calendar year 2001 showed no inflation, no crisis, a steady foreign exchange rate, *etc.* In terms of valuation, it meant that historical financial statements were not going to be useful in forecasting cash flows, at least for the following two or three years.
- New earnings scenarios for the different industries appeared with the crisis, but the crisis did not hit all industries at the same level.
    - Industries competing in domestic markets suffered sensible revenue constraint as a consequence of the effects of the economic slowdown.
    - However, for those industries with incomes originated in exports, the devaluation of the currency produced an increase in revenues in local currency not correlated with the inflation that affected local costs. So, in those industries linked to exports (like food and grains) the EBITDA margins increased above historical

ratios, while in industries linked to imports (*i.e.*, technology) EBITDA margins decreased below historical ratios.

- Labor costs adjusted at lower rates than general inflation, improving margins of labor intensive businesses.
- Utilities tariffs were frozen by the federal government through new regulations. So, this was a cost that remained at historical levels at least for the first few years after the crisis.

To understand how each firm's value drivers would perform during and after the crisis was critical. How would revenues grow? How would margins perform? What would be the new level of normalized earnings? How long would it take the company to leave the crisis behind? These were the kind of questions that we tried to answer after evaluating each firm's position, considering both the context and the industry characteristics under the crisis. Detailed projection of each value driver was required for an explicit projected period that should be long enough so that the company would be able to reach normalized earnings by the end of that period. In some cases, the earnings of a specific historical year, or an average of the firm's earnings over certain prior periods, were helpful to estimate the new level of normalized earnings.

- Taxes. When companies are losing money they carry these losses forward in time and apply them to earnings in future periods. In Argentina, companies can apply those net operating losses ("NOL") to earnings of the next five years. These NOLs were considered in companies' projections only if sufficient positive earnings were expected for the next five years.
- Working capital was a crucial driver to calculate. Working capital behavior was very difficult to project. As there was no credit available in the economy, transactions were made basically in cash. Accounts receivables and payables balances were unusually low. On the other hand, several industrial stocks grew in order to prevent inputs shortage or to optimize strategic purchases. So, in many industries, there was a positive cash flow generated by the payment of account receivables and no further relevant account receivables balances were expected at least in the upcoming years. But the question was how long it would take to reach historical working capital requirements.

- Minimum capital expenditures were expected due to the crisis. In many industries, capital expenditures were reduced to a minimal assets' maintenance investment during the crisis. In other cases, they were suspended, and did not even match the financial statements' amortization. The question was how long a company could wait to begin with new capital expenditures.

- Terminal Value calculation was another crucial driver. During the crisis, almost a relevant degree of the value of many companies was attributed to the terminal value calculation. This was the case of companies that showed deteriorated earnings during the crisis, but reached better normalized earnings after a while.

- Regulatory new regimes changed the business environment. As was described in the introduction, a number of regulations changed in 2002 and affected domestic and foreign trade of goods and services, as well as financial markets. Examples of regulations included: commodities export taxes, energy and utilities price controls, "double indemnification" (in an effort to avoid massive layoffs, severance payments were doubled), and transfer and currency conversion restrictions. As the regulatory regime impacted each industry and company differently, it was used to handle regulatory risk by adjusting expected cash flow, weighting it by the probability of various scenarios.

- Discount rate calculation was difficult. During the crisis, traditional methods typically employed in estimating WACC were subject to significant data input problems:

    - *Cost of equity*. During the crisis, as most relevant data and information required for estimating cost of capital in Argentina was not available, we estimated a US-based cost of capital as a starting point for an Argentinean' company cost of capital, and to apply "adjustments" to the U.S.-based cost of capital for perceived differences in risk.

    - *Country Risk Premium*. The methodology applied was the Country Spread Model ("CSM"): The country spread model adds a country-specific spread to "internationalize" a cost of equity determined using U.S. data. Ideally, the spread is the difference between the yield on dollar-denominated international bonds and the yield on U.S. Treasury bonds. The proxy widely used between valuation practitioners as the country risk premium is JP Morgan Emerging Markets Index (EMBI).

    As it was explained before, Argentine sovereign debt default was formally declared in December 2001. During nearly four years, most of the sovereign debt payments were suspended and subject to a complex restructuring process. With sovereign bonds in default, if using EMBI as proxy of the country risk premium, discount rates ranging around 60 per cent to 70 per cent were obtained. So, the EMBI was no longer the best estimation of the country risk premium, as no evidence of using a 70 per cent discount rate was found in the local market for mature companies. Neither other practitioners, nor Private Equity Funds, nor corporations used such a high rate. With sovereign bonds in default and their IRR higher than 50 per cent, the hypothesis that sovereign risk set a minimum for country risk turned doubtful. Many local companies presented better risk conditions than the government itself. Considering this situation, we developed three alternative methodologies to estimate the spread required to use the Country Spread Model:

1. Historical Average Spread: one scenario was calculated on the basis of the historical average spread over the last three years before Argentina defaulted its debt. Sovereign bonds were expected to be restructured, and the assumption that their rates would decrease up to historical values could be done. Under this alternative, we assumed historical pre-default country spreads. The spread obtained with this alternative methodology was similar to the spread of a country rated B2 according to Moody's rate scale. And, in our opinion, it was reasonable to consider Argentina as a B2 risk country in average. Local history showed a cyclical country with frequent crisis and recoveries.
2. Corporate Bonds Spread: another scenario was to calculate the spreads between rates of Argentine and U.S. Corporate Bonds.
3. New Sovereign Debt Spread: another scenario was to analyze spreads between rates of Argentine New Sovereign Debt and U.S. Yield Curve. After the sovereign debt default declaration, in December 2001, Argentina issued three dollar denominated New Sovereign Debt: BODEN 2012, BODEN 2013, and BODEN 2005. These new bonds were expected to be paid without delays when most of the sovereign debt payments were suspended, and subject to the restructuring process. The assumption was that, during the restructuring process period, the debtor was in default although these new debts were not.

- Many country risks do not impact equally to all companies in a given country. Applying the same risk premium to all companies in the country would overstate the risk for some and understate it for others. Therefore, in some cases, an additional company risk-adjustment was considered.

- As we mentioned before, we understood that the effects of the regulatory risks were better handled by adjusting the cash flows. However, if regulatory risks were not considered in the cash flow estimation, to adjust the cost of capital in those companies with operations, products or services regulated by the government was also appropriate. In the case of Argentina, for industries such as utilities and banks (which were highly regulated) a premium risk should be added due to regulatory risk.
- *After-tax Cost of Debt.* During the crisis, long-term financing was simply not available for local companies. So, to obtain reference debt prices from comparable market debt issues was a very difficult exercise. The Performing Argentina's Corporate Current Debt yield curve was used as a best base for local companies' debt rates estimation. It must be considered that the corporate bond market in Argentina was limited to several big corporations, so additional risk premium adjustments were required for most of the cases.
- *Capital Structure.* The lack of credit from banks was a typical output of the crisis in Argentina. As corporate funding in Argentina used to be through bank loans, a significant reduction in companies' leverage ratios was considered for the short term. For the long term, the debt ratio was adjusted to the expected industry averages.

- *Liabilities.* Most interest-bearing debts were subject to renegotiation, mainly with banks. So their fair value was not clear due to the renegotiation process. It was a funny experience to negotiate debts with banks in those days. Banks and debtors were equally in bad financial shape, so they understood each other and they tried to renegotiate debts as serious as possible in the uncertain environment. Additionally, after Decree 214, loan holders were able to cancel their loans with banks in US$ dollars at a fixed exchange rate of AR$1=US$1. During the crisis, the fair value of most liabilities decreased significantly and one thing was certain: the current amount of a debt was no longer a proxy for its fair value.
- *Non-Operating Assets.* The values of many of the firm's financial assets, real estates, and other non-operating assets, for instance, were strongly deteriorated during the crisis due to the effect of currency devaluation, regulations, and lack of marketability.

- *Scenarios.* In order to capture the uncertainty about future performance, the company's growth potential, and its ability to generate future earnings, different probability-weighted scenarios were needed to be calculated. In some cases, evaluating the possibility of the firm going bankrupt if earnings did not improve was required.

A Final Thought

It was crucial during the crisis to understand the local macroeconomic context, the different industries' situation, the business environment and its risks, and the future expected behavior of local companies' value drivers. Foreign valuation practitioners that tried to value assets or companies in Argentina during those years were not able to fully understand some or all of the issues that we had described. It was recommended to involve local valuation practitioners to identify the crisis scenario and challenges for the subject company being valued.

Business Valuation: Practices and Challenges in China

Jiang Wei

Introduction

Since the reform and opening-up, China's economy has gained great momentum in its development. Within the valuation profession in China, the appraisal discipline has had the greatest level of growth and change or adaptation for the past twenty years. In fact, the first formal organizations of professionals involved in property valuation in China were those that participated in a business valuation project in 1988, in which the equity of Dalian Iron Mill was evaluated for the purpose of establishing a Sino-U.S. joint venture, marking the development prelude of the appraisal profession in China.

Being one of the most important market intermediary service providers in China, the valuation profession has been contributing greatly to the restructuring of China's State-Owned Enterprises (SOEs), IPOs, M&A, and other related market activities, *etc.* In practice, the valuer's involvement in those activities has become a legal requirement by the Chinese government and Valuers' Report is regarded as one of the legal documents used to safeguard the national interests and protect the benefits of relevent parties. According to a document released by the China's State Assets Management Committee, sales should be adjourned if the selling price of SOE assets (including equity transfer) is 10 per cent lower than the valuer's estimated value, which highlights the role of valuation and contributes an annual growth rate of over 30 per cent for the business valuation sector.

The course of professional development over the past 20 years has proved that appraisal practice in China is faced with a developing and changing environment. The changes in the economic development have exerted direct impacts on appraisal practice in China which, in turn, continuously set new demands on the formulation of valuation standards, facilitating the upgrading of Chinese valuation standards and constant improvement of the service quality of practitioners and their conduct.

Review of Business Valuation in China

Business valuation is a commonly used term among appraisal and valuation practioners worldwide, but there is no universally agreed upon definition of the term. As China is undergoing a transition from a planned economy to a market economy, its valuation professionals are learning it the hard way. Apart from the dilemma of attempting to understand the term "business valuation", people tend to agree upon such a notion that business valuation might refer to the aggregate value of a certain business, the summation of asset values of the business or both, sometimes, depending on various end users.

It is true that nowadays a business valuation usually focuses on earnings and cash flow derived from use of all underlying tangible and intangible assets. Such a valuation does not usually value a company by placing an amount on individual assets directly (but could – a real estate holding company, for instance), but may allocate the aggregate value of the business to several asset categories for specific reporting and/or management requirements. Thus, the summation of asset values will be equivalent to the aggregate value of the business enterprise, which is the economically justified and supportable basis for underlying asset values.

As a matter of fact, the Chinese appraisal profession, from the outset of its establishment, was supposed or expected to have such consensus in doing business valuation. However, owing to various reasons, their understanding of its essence and connotation remained at the level for a long time that "business equity value was nothing but the summation of asset value of each of the components of the enterprises". The approach so adopted in such appraisal practice is called the cost approach or China's Asset Value Summation Method, which looks similar to the assets-based valuation approach of their counterparts abroad, but is different in how it is used. The concept that revenues and equity value represent the business value is not regarded as an independent cognition.

According to James Horvath (2006),[1] asset-based valuation methods generally use the current value of a company's tangible net assets as the prime determinant of value. The approach is used where the business is not viable as a going concern, where the business is not earning an adequate return

1 J. Horvath, "The Practice of Business Valuation in Canada", (2006) 11 The Chinese Appraisal Journal 38-39.

on investment or, in the case of a real estate holding company, for example, where the going-concern value is closely related to the value that can be realized on a disposition of the underlying assets.

There are preconditions for the use of the asset-based valuation methods. But when this approach is used in China, it turns out to be China's Asset Value Summation Method, which means that it could be used under all circumstances, regardless of whether the company to be valued is profitable. And it is the sole approach that has been used for business valuation in China for more than ten years. The possible explanation for such an occurrence might be that it is easy for valuers to do the valuation with this method and it is easy for the government supervisors to check the valuation results, because of the lack of an efficient capital market in China and the lack of financial projections knowledge and techniques. In 2007, China's State Assets Management Committee released a document requiring those who undertake a business valuation project for SOEs to use at least two approaches (the income approach is a must) to make value estimates and China's Asset Value Summation Method could be used only when circumstances are appropriate, officially ending the era of using the sole approach (China's Asset Value Summation Method) in business valuation practice and integrating China's business valuation with its world counterparts.

China started to introduce appraisal concepts and methodologies from abroad in the late 1980s and early 1990s, and all of the disciplines were introduced and developed at the same time. Such a development pattern of valuation profession is quite different from that in other countries, which usually starts with physical assets appraisal discipline, real estate appraisal discipline, and then proceeds to business valuation discipline. The reason for this is that business valuation is regarded as an intermediary method to help restructure China's SOEs, and help set up Sino joint ventures. In this case, business valuation became the number one valuation discipline. As China was busy with reforming and opening up at that time, a huge number of SOEs were undertaking restructuring, which provided a golden opportunity for the rapid development of the appraisal profession. Under those circumstances, strategic restructuring of SOEs and corporate system reform were a major source of business revenues for the appraisal firms. Although concepts like "business enterprise value is not simply equal to the summation of assets value of each of the physical component item of the enterprise" were introduced, they failed to be applied in practice, and business valuation was often mingled with physical assets appraisal without any differentiation. For about ten years, business valuation was segmented into physical assets appraisal for each and every component of the enterprise. Of course, when compared with conducting transactions based on book value of net assets of enterprises, the valuation approach of using the asset value summation method to appraise the value of enterprises was more effective and helped boost transactions. However, this inevitably led to a misunderstanding among the public, clients, and practitioners that business valuation is merely a re-valuation of the book value of the total assets of a certain business, and business valuation tends to be a kind of transformation and extension of accounting and auditing operations. A number of clients even held the opinion that the appraisal profession was no more than a business affiliated with auditing. Therefore, neither the service providers nor the service recipients of business valuation have a full understanding of business valuation's concept framework.

Such a situation is in great disaccord with the requirements set forth for the appraisal profession by the current economic trends and the capital market home and abroad. With the increase of economic globalization and integration, assets restructuring is being carried out with unprecedented scale and speed among enterprises in China. The appraisal profession is already being challenged by higher demands from the continuous expansion of the appraisal market, the constant increase of valuation sectors, and greater complexity of problems. As the Chinese capital market is also undergoing a transition from assets restructuring at its initial stage to equity transfers, the pursuit of business value and equity value has become the main theme of the securities market, especially at this time when the equity disposition reform is coming to an end. So, the appraisal profession is expected to shift its attention from theoretical research on physical assets appraisal to studies on appraisal for business value and equity value. With over 35,000 certified public valuers and over 3500 appraisal firms, the valuation profession has a bigger role in the market economy in China.

Practice of Business Valuation in China

The appraisal profession is an indispensable key component of the Chinese socialist market economy, which plays a unique role in ensuring the safety of State-Owned Assets, protecting the rights and interests of investors, managing financial risks, and safeguarding fair dealings, *etc.* Under the circumstances of economic globalization and integration, the appraisal profession in China has already made enthusiastic efforts to meet the challenges and speed up its process of launching various valuation standards in order to cater to the development of the appraisal profession in the new era.

In February 2004, the Ministry of Finance issued *General Standards of Valuation* and *General Code of Conduct*, laying a solid foundation for the Chinese Valuation Standards (CVS). Over the years, a series of valuation standards were developed, such as *Valuation Standards–Intangibles*, *Guidelines for Gems and Jewelry*, and *Guidelines for Non-performing Loans (Pilot)*. The launch of *Guidelines for Business Valuation (Pilot)* by the China Appraisal Society (CAS) further embodied the concept that business valuation should meet the requirements of the capital market. The *Guidelines for Business Valuation* have drawn upon theoretical achievements and practical experiences of business valuation home and abroad, made references to the International Valuation Standards (IVS), and valuation standards of business valuation in the United States, European countries and other regions and, in the meantime, incorporated the international conventions in the field of business valuation. While drafting the *Guidelines*, CAS used its guiding philosophy of "[p]lanning with moderate far-sight, and [p]aying attention to practice", making bold breakthroughs in some key aspects in the *Guidelines*. For better understanding of the latest development of valuation standards in China, the following is a brief introduction of some breakthroughs in the valuation standards made by the appraisal profession over the years to meet the requirements of the capital market development.

- *Getting integrated into the international conventions and focusing on the professional characteristics of assets appraisal.* For the first time, the appraisal profession has defined what business valuation is. Business valuation is a conduct and process in which appraisers analyze and assess the aggregate value of enterprises as well as the total equity or partial equity value of the stakeholders on the designated date for special purposes, and express their opinions in the capacity of the professionals.

- *Drawing upon common practice of the international appraisal community.* In the course of assets appraisal and business valuation, appropriate types of value should be selected in accordance with relevant conditions like appraisal purposes, *etc.* This requirement is conducive to better serving the appraisal purposes by changing the usual practice of the appraisal profession in the past decade, which involved no discussions on the definition of value and no offering of qualitative definition and analysis of appraisal results.

- It is explicitly required that appraisers, when choosing appraisal approaches, should give full consideration to such relevant conditions as appraisal objects, value types and data-gathering, analyze the adaptability of the three basic approaches of assets appraisal, namely, the income approach, the market approach, and the cost approach, and adopt different appraisal approaches on proper occasions. It is also required that when business valuation is conducted with a going concern as the premise, the cost approach should not be considered as the sole appraisal approach to use. This key breakthrough is a good remedy for the old bad practices and welcomed by the practitioners and relevant authorities.

- In recent years, some problems arose when the income approach was used. In view of this situation, valuation standards have provided positive guidance and indicated that both the appraisal profession and others should not negate or evade the income approach on account of the problems existing in the process of its application. Instead, they should promote standardization of the application of the income approach and prevent the abuse of this approach on the basis of full affirmation that the income approach is able to effectively reflect the overall profit-making capacity of business enterprises. With reference to the international conventions, valuation standards have incorporated the income approach as one of the basic approaches to conduct business valuation. In the meantime, a multitude of provisions and stipulations put forward corresponding requirements concerning application of the income approach, such as analyzing the adaptability of the income approach, judging the rationality of expected earnings, determining the scheduled time of earnings, and choosing the capitalization rate or discount rate in a reasonable way.
- Emphasis has been placed on analyzing and disclosing factors that affect business value, such as majority holding right and minority interest. Modern business value theory believes stakeholders with majority holding right, compared with those with minority interest, have a louder voice in management strategies, patterns of administration, and marketing strategies. This is likely to influence the development direction of the enterprise and, consequently, leads to extra premium for stakeholders with majority holding right and discount for stockholders with minority interest. In China's business valuation practices, in most cases, valuation results are reached by the adoption of the method to multiply the overall equity value of enterprises by the equity holding ratio, without considering the effects on value caused by majority holding right and minority interest. Since both the theory and practice concerning premium for majority holding right and discount for minority interest are still at the primary stage of development in China, it will take some time for the domestic appraisal professionals, appraisal report users, and the economic circle to adapt to and accept these theories. The *Guidelines*, in principle, call for the appraisers to consider premium or discount brought about by majority holding rights and minority interests under practical and feasible circumstances, and make proper disclosers. This step reflects a vigorous attitude of the appraisal profession, which emphasizes the sig-

nificance of factors like majority holding right in theory, and the obligation of appraisers to remind report users of a better understanding and use of appraisal conclusions by means of asking the appraisers to disclose whether they have considered factors like majority holding right in their appraisal reports.

- Emphasis has been placed on the appraisers conducting business valuation who should pay close attention to the allocation of business assets as well as the condition of utilization, as well as to such key factors as non-productive assets, liabilities, and premium surplus that might affect business value. This requirement not only complies with international conventions, but also bears significant meaning to the practice of China's appraisal profession. For some historical reasons, the management of business assets in China leaves much room for improvement, and irrational allocation of assets exists in many enterprises. Valuation standards encourage the use of the income approach and, meanwhile, call for attention to proceedings like premium surplus when there is an imbalance between input and output. This step ensures that the value of those assets which are not put into operation or do not generate cash flows should not be left out when they are appraised by using the income approach.

Challenges of Business Valuation in China

The timely launch of the *Guidelines for Business Valuation* by CAS has brought about positive effects for the Chinese appraisal profession in upgrading its business valuation discipline, and greatly satisfied the need to expand the business scope of business valuation. This step fully embodies a sense of responsibility and sensitivity as well as far-sightedness of CAS in compliance with the requirements of capital market development. It has triggered strong repercussions in the appraisal profession and in society as well. However, the release of the *Guidelines* is merely one step forward for business valuation in China in the long run. There is still a long way to go before the *Guidelines* are implemented in an all-around way. Challenges and tasks facing the Chinese business valuation profession are as follows:

First, more work to do and more difficulties. Under the financial crisis, more companies may seek valuations for regulatory or financial report purposes, or management may want information to aid decision making or to have better internal control. Professional valuation advice can provide assurance in a variety of situations,which means business valuers might have more clients and more revenues. But finding a solution to the issues related to revenue recognition is more difficult for the local Chinese valuers. More training sessions are needed for valuers to gain competence and be prepared.

Second, the existence of diversified or multiple practicing qualifications and regulatory bodies is detrimental to the overall development of the appraisal profession, including the business valuation discipline. Currently, seven appraisal qualifications are recognized by relevant Chinese authorities, six for valuers and one for organizations engaged in valuing public companies, see the following Table:

Table 1
Appraisal Qualification and their Jurisdiction Body

	Name of appraisal qualification	**Name of the jurisdiction body**
1.	Certified Public Valuer	Ministry of Finance
2.	Securities Business Valuation Certificate	China Securities Regulatory Commission (CSRC)
3.	Real Estate Valuer	Ministry of Construction
4.	Land Valuer	Ministry of Land and Resources
5.	Valuer for Mining Rights	Ministry of Land and Resources
6.	Valuer for Second-hand Vehicles	Ministry of Commerce
7.	Insurance Assessor	China Insurance Regulatory Commission

Furthermore, the China Securities Regulatory Commission (CSRC) provides credentials to special valuation firms for valuing listed companies. Only the valuation firms that bear "Securities Business Valuation Certificate" issued by CSRC have the qualification to provide valuation service to listed companies, which is another obstacle towards fair competition. The existence of such a diversified system led to a complete segregation of the appraisal businesses, which not only increased the costs of regulatory supervision but also add burdens to business enterprises. To a certain extent, it may cause adverse impact on the reasonableness of the valuation conclusions and it is not conducive to a healthy development of the appraisal profession.

Third, legal responsibilities in the appraisal practice need to be further clarified. The prescription of current legal responsibilities with respect to appraisal is far from perfect and is scattered in different laws and regulations, but not in a comprehensive and systematic manner. Accordingly, there is no administrative measure which can impose an effective penalty on the irregularities of appraisal activities. In addition, the rights and obligations of the valuers are not compatible with those of the appraisal firms. This makes it difficult for the laws to effectively protect the legitimate rights and interests of valuers.

Fourth, the working environment of the appraisal profession needs to be further improved so as to facilitate the proper regulatory supervision or standardization of the valuation practices. Some government bodies may take no notice of the natural law of appraisal, and intervene at their own discretion in the appraisal process, valuation results, time to complete an appraisal, and related fee charges. Some companies subject to valuation refused to cooperate with appraisal firms, and deliberately provided partial or false information of financial or other testimonial documents, which severely affected the overall reliability and quality of the appraisal.

Conclusion

The world is now experiencing one of its worst economic recessions, but the valuation profession seems to be recession proof. Business valuation in China continues to be a vibrant and growing sector. At the moment, government regulatory reasons and more M&A are driving forces for the growth of the business valuation profession. The catalysts for such growth can also be attributed to increased globalization, improvements in data availability, and increased information processing capabilities.

This article aims to provide an overview of the latest developments of business valuation in China following its reform and opening up in 1978, and highlights potential challenges and problems that exist in the profession. Analysis is made on the breakthroughs in the *Guidelines for Business Valuation,* which are deemed a beacon of guidance that can win trust from clients, make the public feel assured, and can enhance the confidence of investors, thus further boosting the development of the business valuation profession.

APPENDIX A

References

James L. Horvath, "The Practice of Business Valuation in Canada" (2006) 11 The Chinese Appraisal Journal 38-39.

Jing Chenglian & Yuan Ziping, *Business Valuation* (Beijing University Publishing House, 2006).

Alfred M. King, *Valuation: What Assets Are Really Worth* (John Wiley & Sons, Inc., 2002).

Liu Ping, "Chinese Valuation Standards: On Its Way to Maturity", Kunming International Valuation Forum, 2006.

Wang Chengjun, "International Development and National Application of Business Valuation in China" (2006) 11 The Chinese Appraisal Journal 46-49.

Wang Haisu, *Business Valuation* (Fudan University Publishing House, 2005).

International Valuation Standards, 7th ed., International Valuation Standards Committee, 2007.

Valuing Businesses in Emerging Markets: Opportunities and Challenges

James L. Horvath & Monty Bhardwaj*

Introduction

With the globalization of the business environment and the mobilization of capital, emerging markets have grown rapidly in significance. This has increased the demand for valuations of emerging-market companies.

In this chapter, we address many of the factors and issues that business valuators, investors, and multinational corporations have to address when entering or valuing a business in an emerging market. These include the challenges of getting reliable company-specific and market data, political risk, country risk, macroeconomic uncertainty, possible significant cultural differences, accounting differences, and tax issues/opportunities and minimization through the migration of specific assets or business units.

The term emerging market describes a nation in the process of rapid industrialization. Through their political, social, and business activities, these countries are opening up their markets and restructuring their economies along market-oriented lines, emerging to become significant players in the global market.

According to the measures applied on a country-by-country basis by debt-rating agencies to 181 sovereign nations in the world, about 145 countries can be described as emerging market nations. To companies in developed markets, emerging markets provide significant opportunities in trade, technology transfers, and foreign direct investment.

---

* The authors would like to thank Kimberly Horvath, CA for her research, assistance and suggestions.

In particular, the economies of Asia and South America continue to expand. China and India now rank among the world's largest economies. For 2007, EconomyWatch listed the Top 10 economies, by Purchasing Power Parity (PPP) and Gross Domestic Product (GDP), as follows:

Ranking	Country	Approximate GDP-Purchasing Power Parity
1	United States of America	$13,860,000,000,000
2	China	$7,043,000,000,000
3	Japan	$4,305,000,000,000
4	India	$2,965,000,000,000
5	Germany	$2,833,000,000,000
6	United Kingdom	$2,147,000,000,000
7	Russia	$2,076,000,000,000
8	France	$2,067,000,000,000
9	Brazil	$1,838,000,000,000
10	Italy	$1,800,000,000,000

According to the World Bank, the five biggest emerging market nations are Brazil, Russia, India, China (often described by the acronym BRIC), and Indonesia. The four BRIC countries account for about 40 per cent of the world's population and 25 per cent of the land area.

On December 12, 2005, Goldman Sachs identified eleven countries that, along with the BRICs, could potentially become the world's largest economies in the 21st century:

Bangladesh;
Egypt;
Indonesia;
Iran;
Mexico;
Nigeria;
Pakistan;
Philippines;
South Korea;
Turkey; and
Vietnam.

Described as the Next Eleven (N-11), these countries could potentially have a BRIC-like impact on the global economy rivaling the G7.

Growth in Emerging Markets

In a paper published in 2001, Goldman Sachs provided GDP projections for the BRICs and estimated the year when each country would surpass the current G7 nations. Six years later, Goldman Sachs revised its projections and said the BRICs as a group would grow even more rapidly. For example, China would surpass the U.S. in 2027 vs 2035. Goldman Sachs stated that China's economy would be 84 per cent larger by 2050. India's economy would catch up to the U.S. by that year, as well. The BRICs would surpass the G7 in 2032.

The N-11, meanwhile, will also grow strongly over the next several decades. For example, many analysts project that by 2050:

- both Mexico and Indonesia may surpass most of the G7 countries except for the U.S.;
- Nigeria, Korea, Turkey, and Vietnam are all projected to overtake some of the current G7 members, with Nigeria potentially the largest of this next group; and
- Philippines, Iran, Egypt, Pakistan, and Bangladesh are all projected to catch up to the smaller of the current G7 members.

Within these emerging markets, many companies are growing fast, globalizing aggressively, and reshaping global industries. Of the 100 top companies in these markets identified by The Boston Consulting Group (BCG), 41 are from China, 20 from India, and 13 from Brazil. These companies operate in a wide range of industrial sectors including consumer durables, resources, food and beverage, mobile communication, IT services, and even wind energy.

According to the BCG report, their combined revenues will reach US$3.3 trillion by 2010 and US$11.8 trillion by 2015. Their revenues are growing faster than the S&P 500, and they are earning a higher average return on sales than many of the current industry leaders in the developed world. Increasingly, these companies are looking for acquisitions abroad. In 2007, they made 88 outbound M&A deals, a significant increase from 19 deals in 2000.

Companies based in India and Russia look for acquisitions primarily in Europe. Companies in Mexico and Brazil make acquisitions primarily in Latin America and the U.S. But Chinese companies look throughout the world.

Likewise, emerging markets often seek investment from foreign companies. Between 1985 and 2005, for example, the United States, Canada, Japan, and the European Union accounted for 25 per cent of the cumulative foreign direct investment in China. In the high-technology sector, 88 per cent of

China's exports originate from companies in which foreign investors own at least a minority share.

Opportunities and Challenges for Companies in Developed Markets

According to the common perception, the sole advantage of emerging market companies over companies in the developed world is their lower cost base. This may be true for some companies, but the ones identified in the BCG report that are expanding globally and challenging incumbent developed-world market leaders have many other competitive advantages. In addition to lower costs, these include: ambitious leadership, increasingly appealing products, and modern facilities. Without a strategy to counter the threat presented by these emerging-market competitors, an incumbent company will have difficulty weathering their broad-based, multi-pronged assault.

Emerging market companies have rapidly gained a strong global presence in several low-technology sectors and in a few high-tech niches, as well. At the moment, they lag behind the incumbents in their capacity to deliver high-tech products, and they face a major challenge to catch up. But they will do it over time and, when they do, emerging multinationals will likely challenge the incumbents head-on.

Already, many emerging market companies are expanding to gain access to production and new technology while maximizing the advantages of their low cost structure, broadening their customer base and increasing market share in developed countries. India's Tata Motors, for example, has so far produced only simple, cheap compact cars, but it is now trying to expand into Western markets by pursuing the established but recently suffering British brands Jaguar and Land Rover. With the successful acquisition of these brands, Tata hopes to gain access to leading-edge production technology and established distribution channels.

In Brazil, many businesses have taken advantage of economic liberalization to expand beyond their domestic market. Firms such as Embraer, the aerospace company, have successfully penetrated export markets in the developed world, demonstrating their capacity to compete in the global marketplace.

According to the BCG report, companies in emerging markets have developed six globalization models to expand:

1. taking their brands global;
2. turning their engineering into global innovation;
3. assuming global category leadership;

4. monetizing available resources in the emerging markets;
5. rolling out new business models; and
6. acquiring natural resources.

More than half of the companies in the BCG report have expanded by following the second model, turning their engineering into global innovations.

To meet the challenge presented by these rising emerging market businesses, incumbents must set their priorities and position themselves strategically in the competitive arena. According to the authors of the BCG Report, the "incumbents will need to learn how to compete head on, partner and/or create their own challenger via a subsidiary." Joint ventures, for example, provide incumbents with a strategy for dealing with acquisitive foreign firms. The emerging market businesses, because of the attractiveness of their markets generally have more bargaining power in forming partnerships with incumbents. Notwithstanding, the emerging market companies located in rapidly growing markets, can become valuable partners and customers.

Many global companies in developed markets are already investing actively in emerging markets to compete with their global challengers and profit from projected market growth. These companies usually enter emerging markets to cut costs and create growth opportunities. In the process, they strengthen their competitive positions against the growing threat posed by their emerging rivals. Prior to the recent meltdown, for example, General Motors was the leading auto company in China and a major presence in the automotive industries of Europe, Asia, and Australia. GM had located most of its production and derived most of its profits from outside the U.S.

Since multinational corporations (MNCs) from developed countries operate throughout the world, they have often countered the challenge of globalization and the threat of emerging market companies by aggressively moving production to offshore markets where they already conduct business. This trend is occurring not just in the manufacturing sector but in the technology sector, as well. Just a decade ago, for example, GM produced two-thirds of its output in the U.S., while Toyota located most of its production in Japan. Today, Toyota produces most of its vehicles in the U.S. and elsewhere.

On the consumer side, markets around the world are becoming more homogeneous. Although significant differences still prevail in income levels, culture, geography, and language, a middle-class consumer in India, for example, wants many of the same things as a middle-class British or American consumer.

With this in mind, companies such as Nestlé have positioned themselves to compete with their emerging market competitors by setting up subsidiaries and acquiring local companies throughout the world. Within its global operations, Nestlé uses common technology to produce the same products tailored to different consumer needs in different countries such as India, Germany, or the U.S.

Incumbents are also competing through specialization, focusing on a relatively small number of fields and developing their own unique structures involving human resources, infrastructure, and other factors.

In the next few years, for example, emerging countries could spend as much as US$6.6 trillion on infrastructure, according to Merrill Lynch, creating opportunities for engineering and capital goods companies. China alone plans to construct more than 100 new airports, 186,000 miles of new roads, and 75,000 miles of new railroad track and plans to expand port capacity by 85 per cent between 2010 and 2020. India plans to invest as much as US$460 billion in infrastructure in the next five years. By 2012, infrastructure spending in India could increase to 9 per cent from 5 per cent of GDP. Russia and Brazil also plan to make significant investments in infrastructure.

Similar opportunities will appear among consumer markets in emerging nations. Until recently, most people in BRIC countries and other emerging markets could barely afford the necessities of life: food, clothing, and housing. But, as their incomes have grown, they now spend almost one-third of their income on brand-name electronics, appliances, personal-care, and household products. To meet increasing demand, companies in specialty sectors like clothing, consumer durables, books, music, and luxury items will grow rapidly.

More than 1.3 billion people currently live in China, 1.1 billion in India, 190 million in Brazil, 140 million in Russia, 85 million in Vietnam, 71 million in Turkey and hundreds of millions more in other emerging markets. Within each country, a new middle class is emerging from poverty. By 2030, according to the World Bank, the global middle class will likely grow to 1.15 billion from 430 million in 2000, providing enormous promise for consumer products companies in the developed world.

At the turn of the 21st century, 56 per cent of the global middle class lived in developing nations. By 2030, analysts say that figure could reach 93 per cent. The McKinsey Global Institute say India's middle class will grow in the next two decades from 50 million people today to 583 million people. China's middle class will increase from 43 per cent of the population today to 76 per cent by 2025. To take advantage of this growth, companies in the developed world must learn how to operate in markets where consumers earn much lower incomes. Like Nestlé and other successful multinationals, they can counter the threat of globally expanding, emerging market companies not by trying to stop them but by entering the same emerging markets to acquire or forge alliances with local companies.

This presents a company with a strategic choice. Should it expand its existing businesses in the emerging market through a new operation, a joint venture or alliance, or an acquisition? All three present extremely complex challenges and companies should never assume that they can follow one of these paths without conducting extensive due diligence.

What to Expect

Regardless of the strategy that incumbents choose to compete in an emerging market, they will encounter a number of particular problems. Many of them will arise from differences in cultures. The more clearly an incumbent can identify and appreciate the nuances of a different culture, the more successfully it can establish itself in an emerging market.

Some of these differences include:

Language

A foreign language presents perhaps the most common obstacle to a successful foreign assignment. When negotiations cross language barriers, the potential for misunderstanding is enormous. It is therefore important to proceed slowly and to take nothing for granted.

Many people assume that India is a nation of English-speakers, for example, but in fact, only about 11 per cent of the population speaks the language, including a majority of business and political leaders. In fact, despite its history as a former British colony, a far higher proportion of people speak English in other Asian countries than they do in India. In the Philippines, for example, about 65 per cent of the 90 million people speak English proficiently.

In China, meanwhile, 20 million people a year are learning to speak English (with Jim's son, Michael Horvath, being one of the many English teachers in China), and the country will soon overtake the U.S. as the home of the most English speakers in the world.

Even when companies can conduct their business in the same language, interpretations of the same text may differ from one country to another and have different cultural, social, or religious connotations. These differences become even more pronounced when companies have to rely on translators and interpreters and the English-language capabilities, often imperfect, of the staff of a business that they're assessing.

Cultural Differences

In many countries, cultural differences exacerbate language difficulties. A foreign country's social attitudes, gender roles, and even body language may all differ significantly from North American conventions. A foreign country may pay more attention to religion and religious observance in everyday life. The accepted standards of hospitality may differ, as well, and play a greater role in successful business interactions. In many Latin American countries, for example, punctuality is not of great importance. Business meetings may begin late, and when they do, participants spend much of their time discussing other topics besides the business at hand. Business people strive to get to know each other first, before they get down to business.

In China, personal contact determines the relationships between individuals that provide the basis for any business deal. Participants depend on personal contact to measure each other's compatibility and trustworthiness.

In India, participants in a contract negotiation may often re-open their discussions many times before they reach a resolution. Many Indian businesspeople enjoy the thrust and parry of the argument at least as much as the agreement that they ultimately reach.

In a global supply chain that depends on large numbers of contracting and subcontracting arrangements, companies must pay close attention to the cultural context in which they manage their relationships. Not only do foreign cultures bring different values to the business environment, they may also have different attitudes toward knowledge transfer, management styles, even internal morale. Businesses entering emerging markets must take the time to learn about the culture, history, and business practices of a foreign country before business negotiations begin.

Fortunately, there are many websites that provide information about common differences between cultures in foreign countries. Among them is *www.cyborlink.com*

Sources and Quality of Information

Language may not only impede inter-personal relations, it may also affect a company's ability to collect information about local and industry conditions and other issues needed to negotiate a successful expansion, joint venture, or acquisition.

In some foreign countries, information such as employment, trade, and export data can be obtained from government documents. Quarterly or annual publications about a country's global trade are sometimes available, and boards of trade, chambers of commerce, and their equivalents can also provide useful data. Information may be available from local stock exchanges and institutes of directors and other local organizations, as well.

In emerging markets, however, these traditional sources of information may not exist. If they do, they may not allow access to foreign businesses. Most emerging markets have either rudimentary stock exchanges or none at all, for example, which makes it difficult to obtain market-related information. Some countries do not publish business data and do not support a publishing industry that focuses on individual companies or industries. Even if it's available, information may be written in a foreign language.

Use of Local Personnel

Reliable local personnel can sometimes provide relevant data and the names of individuals who can give further advice. These individuals include:

- personnel at reputable merchant banks;
- local officers of major international banks;
- senior staff of the domestic stock market, if one exists. These individuals can supply local investment advice and the names of portfolio managers and major investors;
- senior personnel of public accounting and law firms with expertise in local matters such as corporate income tax;
- local mergers-and-acquisitions consultants; and
- Canadian and U.S. embassy and trade consulate staff, who can advise on local practices and customs and offer references to helpful local contacts.

Businesses should prepare in advance a strategy for gathering and analyzing information, even if the information is less comprehensive or thorough than similar information collected in more developed countries.

Due Diligence Before Entering the Market

Cultural differences and inadequate or incomplete information can contribute to the impediments facing a company in establishing itself in a developing economy. These impediments include:

- a lack of market awareness of the product or service;
- failure to develop a distinct brand;
- failure to develop a local team in the emerging market as an integral extension of a company's global operations; and
- supply chain mismanagement.

A company can take steps, however, to overcome these obstacles.

As an essential first step, a company must research the target market thoroughly, using local personnel if necessary and other sources of information, as described. The company should identify and understand, for example, the relevant political, economic, social, technological, environmental, and legal issues that can make or break a successful entry into an emerging economy.

Managers should also understand their company's competitive advantage and the direction in which they intend to lead the company within the emerging marketplace. To this end, they must conduct extensive research into the commercial, political, and economic environment before expansion begins into an emerging market.

They should begin by developing a clear corporate strategy and a well-defined business plan. The business plan should clarify how an investment in the emerging market will provide the company with a competitive advantage and enhance its prospects for achieving its long-term corporate objectives. At the very least, the company must address the following basic questions in assessing an emerging market:

- How large and wealthy is the market?
- What is the history of local consumption of the product/service?
- Is there unsatisfied demand for the product/service? (Conduct market research to determine customers' wants and needs.)
- How important are parallel or grey imports (smuggled or counterfeit)?
- What has traditionally driven local consumption of the product/service?
- What are the current and likely future drivers of local consumption?
- How is local consumption likely to evolve in the next 5 to10 years?
- Who are the consumers/customers? What are their characteristics?
- What do consumers/customers want? (Interview buyers and dealers/distributors for preferences.)
- Where are they in the country in question? Where are the clusters or pockets of purchasing power?
- How do consumers/customers make their decisions?
- What are their spending patterns?
- How much money do they have to spend?
- How do other companies in the sector see the customer/consumer base and how much are they able to sell to them in reality?
- How difficult/easy is it to reach potential consumers/customers?
- Who are the potential local selling partners who need to be engaged?
- How do competitors and non-competitors reach their customers?
- Who can help with contacting potential partners?

- Which competitors already operate in the market (both international and local)?
- Are other competitors entering or planning to enter the market?
- What do customers/consumers think about competitors and their products/services?

With detailed answers to these questions, a company can create a business model and go-to-market strategy. The business model should have the flexibility to withstand unanticipated competitive pressures. After all, an emerging economy, by definition, will eventually attract new domestic and international competitors.

Entering the Market

Once the company develops a business plan, it has to find a reliable local partner who can assist the company in entering the market. The local partnership may take the form of a joint venture with a local company, the acquisition of a local company, or the commissioning of consulting services from investment banks, law firms, public accountants, or consulting firms. The quality and capabilities of the local partner can determine a company's emerging market success.

Joint Ventures

Joint ventures often raise particular difficulties. Companies should ensure that a joint-venture partner shares their strategies and objectives. Different styles of management and culture can present a particular problem. Companies should conduct frank and open discussions with a potential joint-venture partner about strategies, expansion plans, expectations, and tactics to achieve their mutual objectives before they proceed with a deal.

Acquisition in Emerging Markets

Acquisitions in emerging markets make sense, if they provide access to a significant brand or new market segment. An acquisition may also limit the threat posed by an emerging competitor.

An acquisition within the same industry stands a better chance of success than an acquisition within an unfamiliar industry. Acquiring a firm in a familiar industry, the investor can use the firm's experience and expertise to integrate it into the investor's worldwide operations. Without this familiarity, integration becomes more difficult.

Before acquiring a local company in an emerging market, an investor should become familiar with the target company and its business. The investor should assess the background of the company's clients, for example, as well as its business partners, distributors, agents, and consultants before committing to an acquisition.

Accurate information is essential. Without it, the investor is at a huge disadvantage. The information should cover four critical areas: macroeconomics, labor availability, legislation/regulation, and details about the local company itself such as its customers, competitors, technologies, *etc.*

For example, as emerging markets grow, they may impose restrictions on capital inflows. In recent years, Colombia, Argentina, and Thailand imposed such controls to keep their currencies from appreciating too quickly. Other countries such as Brazil, Russia, and China, used different procedures to manage foreign capital inflows that did not have such a direct affect on potential investors. Companies should investigate such potential developments before they proceed with an intended acquisition.

In a developed economy, companies can easily locate economic, legislative, labor, and corporate information through government reports, inflation data, labour reports, 10-K filings, and other publicly accessible sources. They can also readily obtain information on a target company's financial performance, employee demographics, compensation programs, and other personnel data. With some exceptions, the same information in emerging markets is much less accessible and much less reliable. Depending on the country, data may be incomplete, outdated, misleading, contradictory, or non-existent. As a result, an investor should be prepared to invest time, money, and human resources in conducting thorough due diligence prior to an acquisition in an emerging market.

From the outset, a company should set up a global acquisition team with knowledge of the emerging market. The team should include a local presence in the market or an intermediary with expertise in the market.

Intermediary services may include:

- public accounting firms;
- investment banks;
- corporate finance boutique firms; and
- business brokers.

In emerging markets, many investment banks and large accounting firms are structured to service global investors from outside the country. These intermediaries may assist in performing the following functions:

- identifying acquisition targets;
- initiating contact with potential acquisition targets and managing the flow of communications;
- preparing marketing literature;
- assisting in preparing pricing analysis;
- providing fairness opinions; and
- assisting in negotiations.

Steps Toward Acquisition

A company that decides to acquire another company in an emerging market rather than growing organically should:

- establish acquisition criteria;
- identify candidates;
- perform due diligence and valuation;
- negotiate the purchase; and
- restructure and integrate.

Establishing Acquisition Criteria

A company makes an acquisition in an emerging market primarily to take advantage of the acquired firm's low-cost structure, to broaden its own customer base, increase market share in developed countries, and penetrate additional markets.

After the buyer signs a confidentiality agreement, intermediaries will follow a buyer's due diligence checklist to ask for documents from the target company.

The due diligence checklist in emerging markets is particularly long and needs to be tailored to the specific emerging market. Many items on the checklist may be difficult to investigate and understand. It will include a few additional questions to the standard ones outlined earlier, including:

- Does the political risk, including business-related corruption, meet or exceed our level of tolerance?
- Does economic risk seem insurmountable?
- Is the emerging market business similar to ours or does it enable our company to diversify?
- Does the target company generate higher sales volume with lower margins or lower sales volume with higher margins?
- Where are the suppliers located in the emerging market?
- Will the government enable us to compete fairly and without interference?

- Can we rely on free-trade agreements in place?
- Will it be possible to ship goods out of the country efficiently and at a reasonable minimum cost?
- Is there a particular segment of the emerging market that interests our company?
- How will our company create value after the acquisition?
- What is our price range? How will we fund it?

Identifying Acquisition Targets

In emerging markets, it is difficult to find relevant and accurate financial information and competitive intelligence about a domestic industry. Instead, an investor must rely on direct local contacts to identify acquisition targets. A local public accounting firm, investment banker, or specialist firm of M&A advisers can carry out an industry search to identify companies that meet the established acquisition criteria. These individuals not only have experience in their domestic market, they can also conduct the search and evaluation process with objectivity.

Companies in developed markets may also identify targets through international trade shows and exhibitions, industry associations, trade directories, independent industry research, trade publications, and the personal market knowledge of senior management and industry contacts.

Performing Due Diligence and Valuation

Thorough due diligence is crucial to the success of any acquisition in emerging markets. As described earlier, due diligence involves developing an understanding of the business, collecting information, assessing risks related to the acquisition, and clarifying the opportunities. It may be tempting to let local advisers take the lead but, inevitably, the acquisition team and senior management have to make the final decision and should always be closely involved. These individuals understand the acquisition strategy, have participated in the business planning prior to entering an emerging market, and have first-hand contact with the deal.

In performing due diligence, one should talk to customers, distributors, industry experts, suppliers, trade unions, management, workers, and competitors prior to making a decision.

This is the general framework for conducting the due diligence:

Before the Deal

- agree on an information exchange protocol with the target;
- manage authorities and utilize local resources, leveraging relationships;
- don't overpay;
- avoid relying solely on documents and verify information by cross-checking;
- involve a local intermediary such as a reputable public accounting firm or investment banker with knowledge of the market;
- determine where the information is located, evaluate the quality of available information, and plan for extra effort to bridge information gaps.

As the Closing Approaches

- anticipate delays;
- assess ownership of assets, scope and validity of licences, supply contracts, and tax compliance;
- sign earn-out agreements;
- always have a plan B.

After Closing the Deal

- identify key employees and develop a retention plan;
- bring key functions such as finance and marketing under control;
- install head-office personnel in the emerging-market operation to act as a bridge between the two entities;
- develop a strategy to protect intellectual property rights.

In the process of integrating a company acquired in an emerging market, a conflict between business cultures can pose one of the major impediments. Some companies may have a top-down culture, for example, while others are more democratic and collegial. Bringing two different business cultures together can create friction among people, pitting one side against the other unnecessarily and to the detriment of the combined business. This problem becomes exacerbated when differences in national and regional customs and language are added to the mix.

While this issue is not unique to emerging markets, it can seem more challenging when combined with poor data or preparation at the due-diligence stage.

Valuation in Emerging Markets

Valuing a business in an emerging market environment becomes more complicated as a result of unsettled macroeconomic factors but the basic valuation principles apply in any marketplace. Price depends on supply and demand, which influences value. Value of any asset is a function of two components: the quantum of future cash flows and risk associated with those cash flows. Yet, distinctive economic, political, cultural, and social conditions may create many differences between an emerging marketplace and the domestic marketplace of a company in a developed country. In particular, government regulation in emerging markets and the local business environment have significant impact on the value of a business. Valuation analysis has to be done without full information and in an uncertain political and economic climate. Having said that, the financial crisis of late 2008-2009, brought about in large part by U.S. financial institutions and investment dealers, has added a whole new level of risk to investments in developed and emerging markets alike.

In general, there are three different approaches to **valuation of a business or asset in the developed and emerging markets**. The first, discounted cash flow **valuation approach (the DCF approach)**, relates the value of an asset to the present value of expected future cash flows on that asset after taking into consideration the risk associated with those cash flows. The second, relative **valuation approach**, estimates the value of an asset by looking at the pricing of "comparable" assets in the market relative to a common variable like earnings, cash flows, book value, or sales. The third, real option pricing **valuation approach**, uses option pricing models to measure the value of assets that share option characteristics. Even when using the same approach from one country to another, valuation terms may take on different meanings in different countries. Accounting standards, methods, and principles also vary significantly between one country and another.

In our own experience, the DCF approach is the most often used valuation approach in the global marketplace. The relative valuation approach is often used in conjunction with the DCF approach. The contingent claim valuation approach is not commonly understood and therefore is rarely used in valuing companies in the emerging markets.

When using the DCF approach in an emerging market, the projection and discounting of a series of annual future cash flows presents unique challenges to the valuator. When projecting cash flows, the reliability of the future cash flows diminishes with the forecast of each additional annual cash flow. In an emerging market, the forecasting process becomes even more unwieldy as a result of the impact of additional variables on the projections that are specific to the emerging market. This increases the risk of investing in the emerging markets.

In the DCF approach, at some point in the future, typically between five and 10 years, the valuator generally assumes that fluctuations in revenue growth and operating cash flow level off, or cannot be forecast with sufficient confidence. For simplicity, it is assumed that after the projection period the cash flows generated by the business become maintainable for the purposes of the valuation. When cash flows reach this maintainable level, they can be capitalized. This capitalized cash flow calculation represents the residual or *terminal value*. It captures the future benefits from the post-cash flow projection period at the point when future cash flow growth is assumed to be constant.

The terminal value in year "n" of the forecast is "present valued" together with the cash flows projected for the final year of the forecast period. The present value formula is amended as follows:

$$V_0 = \frac{CF_1}{1+r} + \frac{CF_2}{(1+r)^2} + \frac{CF_3}{(1+r)^3} + \ldots + \frac{CF_n + V_{n(Terminal)}}{(1+r)^n}$$

Where,

$$V_n = \frac{CF_1}{r - g_{Constant}}$$

V_n = Terminal value at year "n"

'g'$_{Constant}$ = Constant growth rate

As part of the discounting process, the valuator computes a terminal value at the point when growth slows to its expected long-term sustainable rate. Since a valuation often derives a significant portion of a business valuation from cash flows attributable to the terminal value, the firm's potential long-term growth must be accurately reflected. The longer the period from the present valuation date to the date of terminal valuation, the more difficult it becomes to estimate accurately the required numeric inputs. This makes it challenging to estimate a terminal value. In an emerging market, it is even more challenging to estimate the terminal value because additional consideration needs to be given in selecting the numerical inputs such as growth rate, inflation, and government regulations to calculate the terminal value.

The mechanics of the terminal-value calculation are identical to those of the *capitalized* cash flow valuation approach in the developed markets as well as the emerging markets. By capitalizing an estimate of the *maintainable* discretionary cash flow, the valuator determines the terminal value at period "n" in the future. In the emerging markets, as a result of increased uncertainty and lack of availability of valuation database, it is more difficult to make assumptions about the rate at which growth will stabilize, as well as net capital expenditures, working capital requirements, and all other variables necessary to perform a discounted cash flow analysis. In emerging markets, the resources and facilities that we take for granted in Canada or the United States, such as daily market data, may not be readily available.

The valuator often discounts the terminal value using the same risk rate as applied to the annual cash flow projections. Alternatively, the valuator may present the terminal value component distinctly from the annual cash flow forecasts, because the greater uncertainty of the distant time horizon and timing of changes in growth expectations may warrant a higher risk rate in calculating the present value.

Capitalized Cash Flow Approach

This approach assumes a level of maintainable cash flow and a constant growth rate into perpetuity. Majority of the companies in emerging markets that the investors would be interested in would likely be young and fast growing. The assumption of constant rapid growth rate into perpetuity may not apply to these companies. There may be some mature companies in certain sectors of the economy with stable growth rates where an investor from developed markets may be interested for strategic reasons such as market entry or shutting doors in the emerging market for a global competitor of the incumbent.

Since the capitalized cash flow approach captures more than dividend-paying common shares in its calculation, the valuator can use it to determine either enterprise value or equity value, depending on the specific cash flow used in the numerator.

$$V_n = \frac{CF_1}{r - g_{Constant}}$$

V_n = Value at period 'n'

CF_1 = Next year's cash flow

$'g'_{Constant}$ = Constant growth rate

In fact, the capitalized cash flow technique is a simplification of the discounted cash flow technique, but with several key distinctions:

1. Future cash flow growth is accounted for in the capitalization rate ($r - g_{Constant}$) rather than by specific annual forecast. The valuator assumes that after-tax discretionary cash flows have an infinite duration and are less susceptible to year-over-year variations than investments customarily valued using a discounted cash flow approach.
2. The valuator calculates the sustaining capital reinvestment required to maintain existing operations separately from after-tax operating cash flow. He offsets tax savings in the form of future capital-cost-allowance deductions against the gross amount to determine *net* sustaining capital reinvestment. By comparison, the discounted cash flow approach reflects the tax shield effect of sustaining capital cash outflows over the entire forecast period.
3. The capitalized cash flow approach requires a present-value calculation of the tax shield relating to the existing capital asset balances at the valuation date. This represents the aggregate present value of the anticipated future reduction in tax payment outflows.

The valuator combines the discretionary operating cash flow, after-tax, and the net sustaining capital reinvestment required to maintain that level of operating cash flow to arrive at the total discretionary cash flow, after-tax, for the business. The valuator determines the applicable capitalization rate ($r - g_{Constant}$) with reference to risk (r) and maintainable growth rate ($g_{Constant}$) to arrive at the present value of the business. He then adds the value of the existing tax shield to this amount.

When capitalizing the capital-cost allowance at the valuation date to determine the present value of the existing tax shield, the valuator sometimes uses a risk rate below that used to capitalize after-tax operating cash flows. The valuator uses different risk rates because the risk of the business earning enough to utilize its available capital cost allowance is significantly lower than the risk associated with the overall business operation.

Valuators face challenges similar to the DCF approach when estimating maintainable cash flows and appropriate discount rates in emerging markets due to the volatile nature of these markets, lack of reliable database, and the impact of variables specific to the emerging market.

Capitalization of Earnings

Valuators calculate capitalization of net earnings using a similar approach to capitalization of cash flows. Both require the valuator to adjust or normalize earnings reported in financial statements for non-recurring and unusual items. The valuator then multiplies normalized after-tax earnings from operations by the appropriate capitalization rate to produce the overall value of the business.

The earnings approach is appropriate when after-tax cash flow reasonably approximates accounting net income. Under these conditions, no further adjustments are required to reflect the difference between accounting and economic reality. This typically occurs in service-oriented businesses in which accounting depreciation approximates cash outflows for capital acquisitions, and working capital requirements remain relatively constant.

As a proxy for cash flow from operations, valuators also measure earnings before interest, taxes, depreciation, and amortization (EBITDA). EBITDA is an approximation of a company's future sustainable cash flow from ongoing operations. It ignores other non-cash items beyond depreciation and amortization. Further, it ignores changes in working capital accounts such as accounts receivable, inventory, and accounts payable.

Market-Based Approaches

Using a market-based approach, the valuator compares a company directly to other companies to estimate the fair market value of its common shares. Also called relative or comparable valuation, it involves the comparison of several key ratios. These comparable multiples are determined using traditional valuation methodologies such as earnings and cash flow analysis. The most commonly used ratios or price multiples include price-to-earnings, price-to-cash flow, price-to-book value, and price-to-sales. This approach becomes difficult in emerging markets with fewer publicly listed comparable companies. It is mainly used to corroborate value already arrived at using other primary valuation approaches such as the DCF approach or the capitalized cash flow approach.

Comparative – or relative – valuation techniques are intuitive, easy to compute, and quickly understood. They show how investments are currently valued in the broader marketplace. Unlike discounted cash flow models, they do not require the valuator to estimate multiple input variables.

However, the relevance of a comparable analysis depends on certain factors:

- The comparison must be appropriate in terms of industry, company size, historical growth rates, profitability margins, total assets, and risk characteristics.
- Open-market transactions may contain a synergistic component. The valuator will have difficulty segregating these perceived transaction-specific strategic advantages from the overall price.
- The valuator should understand how price multiples relate to the company's underlying fundamentals.
- The valuator should confirm that the industry group from which

the multiples are derived is not in the midst of extreme, broad-based fluctuations in valuation.

- A company's accounting choices will affect price multiples to varying degrees. The valuator may have to make normalization adjustments to improve comparability.
- Many open-market transactions include non-cash components such as share exchanges, vendor take-back notes at non-market interest rates, earn-outs, management contracts, and non-competition payments. The valuator must convert these alternative forms of payment into a cash-equivalent value.

All of these factors are equally applicable in the emerging markets and the valuator must analyze them with increased caution in emerging data due to lack of availability of comparable data.

Real Option Pricing Models

Using a traditional discounted cash flow analysis, the valuator will often consider only the most likely values for any input variables in a specific valuation model. He does not usually include possible but improbable variables such as natural disasters, regulatory changes, and sovereign risk. The valuator can best capture the impact of such variables on a business or investment valuation using alternative forms of analysis such as real-option pricing models.

A discounted cash flow analysis reflects the value at the current date of all options and their cash flow consequences. In applying a discounted cash flow technique to development-stage companies, however, the valuator does not fully capture all potential growth or risk-mitigating opportunities inherent in the development process. These may include, for example, the option to pause or abandon a project or strategic partnership.

Real option valuation approaches assign values to contingent decisions. They capture value most effectively in smaller firms whose potential value resembles an option-type outcome. These approaches depend on the application of fundamental financial option pricing theory to real assets.

We have rarely seen this approach used to value companies in emerging markets since the managers are more accustomed to the traditional methodologies such as the DCF approach and capitalized cash flow (earnings) approach.

Discount Rate

In the DCF approach and the capitalized cash flow (earnings) approach, the expected cash flows are discounted at a risk-adjusted rate that represents investors' expectations with respect to the time value of money and risk. This risk-adjusted discount rate is typically estimated using a model such as the build-up method or Capital Asset Pricing Model (CAPM). Regardless of the method used, the risk-adjusted discount rate for a given company is the same. To apply CAPM, however, betas must be developed from information available from public companies. Since few public companies operate in emerging markets, beta becomes difficult to estimate. Nor does CAPM capture unsystematic risk. Instead it assumes that systematic risk is relevant, and that unsystematic risk can be diversified as the financial portfolio grows. In practice, however, it is not practical to diversify all unsystematic risks. Even an investor with a diversified global portfolio may be unsuccessful in eliminating country risk. As such, many analysts use an adjusted CAPM by including unsystematic risk in the model.

In spite of these criticisms and limitations, CAPM in one form or another is still one of the most widely used models for estimating the discount rate.

CAPM

In CAPM, the required rate of return for a given security is composed of three factors:

1. the risk-free rate;
2. the market's general equity risk premium (expected market return); and
3. the stock's volatility to the market, commonly referred to as the beta.

It is represented by the following formula:

$$\bar{r}_a = r_f + \beta_a(\bar{r}_m - r_f)$$

Where:

r_f = Risk free rate

β_a = Beta of the security

$\bar{r}_m$ = Expected market return

CAPM assumes that investors need to be compensated in two ways: time value of money and risk. The time value of money is represented by the risk-free (Rf) rate in the formula. It is the compensation paid to investors for placing money in an investment over a period of time.

Market risk is measured by a factor called beta, which measures the sensitivity of returns of the company's shares to the market return. CAPM assumes that the risk premium of a security's expected return is a function of that security's market risk or systematic risk. CAPM assumes that all unsystematic risk can be eliminated by holding a perfectly diversified portfolio of risky assets.

Systematic or undiversifiable risk arises from the uncertainty of future returns and their sensitivity to variations in the returns of a composite measure of marketable investments. Unsystematic or diversifiable risk (also known as unique, residual, or specific risk) reflects the characteristics of the industry, the individual company, and the type of investment interest and is unrelated to variations in returns in the market as a whole. The valuator needs to adjust the unsystematic risk to capture the specific risk related to emerging markets.

Build-Up Method

The build-up method is a variation of the CAPM method. In the build-up method, the rate of return for a risk-free security (RF) is increased for the following factors:

- the market equity risk premium (RP_{Market});
- the risk premium for small size (RP_{Size});
- the industry risk premium ($RP_{Industry}$); and
- the specific company's risk premium ($RP_{Specific}$).

$$r_{CE} = R_F + RP_{Market} + RP_{Size} + RP_{Industry} + RP_{Specific}$$

Where,

R_F = Rate of return on risk free securities as of the valuation date.

RP_{Market} = Equity risk premium, which is the difference between the expected return on market portfolio and the risk-free rate.

RP_{Size} = Size-risk premium, added in case of small and closely-held companies.

$RP_{Industry}$ = Industry risk premium, which is a function of the specific industry in which the subject company operates.

$RP_{Specific}$ = Company specific risk, reflects the operational and financial risk specific to the subject company

The mechanics of calculating the discount rate are the same in developed markets and the emerging markets, however, in the emerging markets the valuator more often needs to use professional judgment and adjust the discount rate after considering the factors that may be specific to the particular emerging market. The risk-free rate and foreign equity risk premium should incorporate the foreign country specific risk premium, including any currency-related risk. In most cases, it may not be appropriate to use the U.S. risk-free rate in determining foreign country cost of capital. There may also be a need to include a country-specific premium, in the build-up formula to reflect uncertainties owing to economic and political instability in the particular country. The adjustment to the build-up and the CAPM model related to country risk is reflected in the unsystematic risk.

Factors Affecting Valuations in Emerging Markets

Company Risk

As we've discussed, many factors affect the value of a business, and these factors can have a different effect on a business in an emerging market than a similar business in a developed market.

Valuators use models such as CAPM and arbitrage-pricing theory to assess the required return of publicly-traded securities within a larger diversified portfolio. They use a company-specific risk premium to calculate the return required by investors for risks that cannot be tempered by diversification. There are no generally accepted models, formulae, equations, or methods to measure company-specific risk premiums. Either directly, in determining the cost of equity capital, or indirectly, in deriving pricing multiples from comparable company transactions, the valuator must use his professional judgment to measure and quantify the financial, operational, and strategic factors of the subject company.

Risk factors typical to company-specific analysis include:

- historic volatility of revenue and earnings;
- management depth and ability;
- key-person dependency;
- technology reliance and obsolescence risk;
- access to capital resources;
- geographical diversification;
- purchasing power and economies of scale;
- customer diversification;
- reliance on key suppliers;
- key contracts;
- owning intellectual property, such as patents, trademarks, and copyrights;
- forecast risk;
- unique product, proprietary products or market niche; and
- quality of financial reporting and controls.

When reviewing and quantifying the risk factors specific to the valuation of an individual company, the valuator must guard against double counting. Company-specific risk factors are difficult to segregate from the overall analysis of the subject company's return projections and its required return. In calculating company-specific risk and incorporating it into the valuation exercise, valuators most commonly make errors such as:

i. adjusting for the same company-specific risk factors in both the discount rate and the projection of future cash flows;
ii. making a company-specific risk adjustment that's already captured in the industry analysis and small-company risk premium; and
iii. making *en bloc* adjustments for company-specific risk for key person dependency, supplier dependency, and customer concentration that are already included in the discount rate to capitalize cash flows.

Other Risk Factors

Many of the risk factors discussed above apply equally to companies in the emerging markets. However, valuing a business in an emerging market can be more complex because of the higher risk and larger impediments raised by the combination of factors. While different businesses respond differently to different factors, some factors to consider include:

- **Investor Protection and Corporate Governance**

  Countries with sound investor protection and strong corporate governance tend to nurture a more active market for mergers and acquisitions, and the premiums paid for businesses in these countries are significantly higher.

  A balance must be maintained, however, between governance of the marketplace and its capacity to adapt readily to changing conditions. In the U.S., for example, foreign companies are beginning to reconsider the domestic marketplace because of its cumbersome regulations and the proliferation of class-action lawsuits.

- **Government Regulation and Controls**

  Most countries place some restrictions on foreign ownership, in emerging and developed markets alike, especially in sensitive areas such as banking and telecommunications. They also restrict the use or leasing of real property by foreigners.

  Some governments impose restrictions on the scope of a firm's management decisions, through legislation involving trusts, tariffs, and labor, for example. Countries extend different degrees of recognition to the rights of minority shareholders, as well, and differences may arise from one jurisdictional area to the next within the same country.

  The extent of these limitations will ultimately influence a company's value.

- **Infrastructure and Communications**

  North Americans may take for granted the adequacy of local infrastructure such as water, electricity, and sewage. But in emerging markets, these services may not measure up to the standards of the developed world. The cost and reliability of supply of electricity, gasoline, and other fuels, for example, can affect a company's value. Likewise, a business that delivers goods or services within or beyond the country requires adequate air, sea, road, and rail transportation, while businesses that depend on timely communication will need adequate local and international telephone and other communication systems. The availability of computers and other office machines, adequate service facilities, secure facilities for data storage, web hosting and other critical functions, and access to local personnel trained to maintain and administer them will influence the value of a business. Also, the availability and quality of office, warehouse, and manufacturing facilities in the local area will play a role.

The sophistication of infrastructure and communications facilities can differ widely between one emerging nation and another. China's road-haulage and air freight infrastructure is many times more extensive than India's, for example, and China spends three times the percentage of its GDP on infrastructure as India's 3.5 per cent.

- **Currency Risk**

  Even when a company's value remains stable in its local currency, an overseas purchaser can gain or lose money if the currency's value fluctuates relative to the purchaser's currency. Currency values fluctuate according to many different influences, but domestic inflation is a major contributor. Governments can also play a role if they interfere in currency exchange to control inflation, gain export advantage, or protect domestic production.

  The value of companies in emerging markets should be determined in inflation-adjusted local currency at the conversion rate prevailing at the valuation date. The value can then be converted to the desired currency. Otherwise, earning trends may be distorted by changes in the relative values of the foreign currencies. If a parent company translates the statements of a foreign subsidiary into its own currency, however, for consolidation within the parent's accounts, this may not be possible.

  Companies making long-term investments in emerging markets should also consider long-term risk measurements, such as normalized yield spreads. Yield spreads in emerging markets can range over hundreds of basis points in very short periods, especially in times of crisis. The risk evaluation should be based on a long-term credit-rating model that accommodates such wild fluctuations and distinguishes between systematic and non-systematic risk.

- **Business Environment**

  As global markets become more integrated, sector considerations have become at least as important in assessing risk as the attributes of a country. But in emerging markets, local developments within a particular business or industry can still influence a company's value.

  Factors such as the general standard of living, disposable income, and wealth distribution through the population affect a firm's potential for success. Likewise, the prospects of a business in any industry can differ dramatically from one country to another. A company's product may have reached the end of its life cycle in one country before it has even begun to gain popularity in another. While demand falls in the first, it may increase in the second. The nature of the competition may differ from one country to another. The value of a company in an emerging market may also be influenced by the availability and cost of skilled personnel, labor, supplies, and capital.

A company's value may depend as well on the people who assess it. In some cases, local investors may see more value in a particular business than foreign investors, because they understand the nuances of doing business in their own country, they build in less country risk than foreign investors, or because they wish to invest in businesses as a hedge against inflation.

- **Financing**

  Depending on the nature of the business, a company's value can depend on the availability of local debt and equity financing. If interest rates are volatile in an emerging market, as they often tend to be, they will influence the cost of domestic financing. An emerging-market business that has ready access to lease, short-term or long-term financing may offer an advantage over its competitors, as well.

  Banks in emerging markets may demand different types of security and coverage, which will influence the cost of local financing. The regulation, stability, and liquidity of an emerging market's stock exchange may also be a factor in determining a company's value.

- **Labor**

  The strength of the local labor market, the proportion of skilled to unskilled personnel, their level of literacy and numeracy, their motivation, and their physical health may vary considerably from one emerging market to another. The relative cost of labor may vary as well, providing a competitive advantage to a company seeking to establish a foreign subsidiary, particularly if the company manufactures labor-intensive products. A company's value will depend as well on local laws governing labor relations and employment. Local laws may restrict a firm's ability to dismiss workers, for example, or make pay increases mandatory.

- **Managerial Skills**

  The quality and depth of management influences the fair market value of a business in any country, especially during an economic downturn, which demands a strong capacity to cope with change.

  BRIC countries like China and Russia, for example, have only recently begun to follow capitalist practices, and inexperienced management can affect the value of a business in these locations.

- **Social Conditions**

  A country's social conditions can also affect the value of a business. Population growth or contraction, age distribution, and immigration trends, for example, contribute to a company's value. Value also depends on such social conditions as:

  - the degree of urbanization;
  - the distribution of the workforce among sectors such as agriculture, natural resources, and industry;
  - life expectancy;
  - mortality rates;
  - disease patterns;
  - access to health care;
  - religious traditions and practices;
  - cultural values; and
  - gender roles to the extent that they have an impact on business.

- **Linguistic Differences**

  As discussed earlier, misunderstandings can arise easily in an emerging market where English is not the predominant language. Misinterpretations, especially involving numbers and quantities, can lead to costly errors.

  Even if a company relies for its information on local personnel who speak fluent English, these individuals may not understand the particular business, its history, or financial performance, and they seldom have the authorization to make decisions on the company's behalf. Information gathered from these sources should be regarded with some skepticism.

- **Legal Environment**

  An emerging market's legal environment can significantly affect a company's value, and this environment changes from one country to another. Property rights, for example, may be stronger in one country than another. Governments may more easily expropriate property in one country than another, with or without compensation. Laws governing patents, trademarks, and copyright protection can also influence the value of a business. Can the business transfer licences and permits under current laws? How does the law affect licensing requirements and practices? Some countries require individuals rather than a corporate entity to hold licences. Different countries also impose different laws governing labor, competition, product liability, and the environment. Privacy issues have also become a significant issue in many countries and may affect a potential purchaser's access to critical information.

In some emerging markets, governments may or may not honor commitments made under earlier regimes and may or may not enforce contracts negotiated under previous administrations.

- **Accounting & Reporting Standards**

  As of 2005, most major countries in Europe and Asia adopted International Financial Reporting Standards (IFRS) and harmonized their accounting practices in the process. It is expected that most other countries will adopt either IFRS or U.S. GAAP, allowing for international comparisons and greater transparency for investors and valuators.

  In addition, IFRS and U.S. GAAP are now by far the two most common sets of accounting standards. Over recent years, they have converged. Standard-setting bodies have agreed on new standards in recent years to make the sets of guidelines under each authority more comparable.

  Even as globalization proceeds, however, in accounting and reporting standards, relationships between businesses and the state still vary from country to country.

  In addition, differences between IFRS and U.S. GAAP can affect the analysis and comparison of longer-term historical performance, since companies have only in the last few years started to report from country to country using similar accounting principles.

  Finally, reliable financial data may not exist at all and, if they do, they may not contribute much to a valuation analysis if they're based on different accounting practices and standards.

- **Articles of Incorporation**

  A company's articles of incorporation, bylaws, and charter amendments define shareholders' rights and determine restrictions, if any, on the company to a particular industry. In Canada or the United States, a company is usually incorporated under the laws of the country where it locates its head office. In an emerging market, this may not be the case. A privately held multinational corporation may operate from a head office in one country, conduct extensive operations in another, but be incorporated in a third country. A purchaser must determine which country's laws govern a minority interest in such a company.

- **Market Comparables**

  Unlike most industrialized countries, where organized stock exchanges provide information on the trading multiples of public companies, many emerging markets do not have organized stock exchanges. If they do, information such as comparable price/earnings and EBITDA multiples may be questionable.

  Some emerging markets are striving to create an investment environment in which subsidiaries and partners of foreign companies can operate with relative confidence. In India, for example, the securities market operates under a world-class regulator, the Securities and Exchange Board of India, while leading-edge market surveillance and safeguard mechanisms contribute to the safety and integrity of the markets.

- **Environmental Liabilities**

  Depending on an emerging market's environmental laws, potential environmental problems may arise, which will affect the value of a company's net tangible assets. Care must be taken to recognize and quantify all environmental liabilities.

- **Marketability**

  A company's value will be affected if a country requires investors to comply with stiff investment regulations, and a liquidity discount may be applied. In some countries, foreign investors must comply with residency restrictions, for example, which may limit the marketability of an investment in an emerging market.

- **Income Taxes**

  Since the tax ramifications of international mergers and acquisitions can often make or break a deal, an emerging market's income-tax legislation must be considered to determine a company's value. Critical points include:

  - relevant tax rates and taxable income;
  - cross-border taxation issues; and
  - the impact of taxation on shareholders in different countries.

  Tax rates: Governments may provide temporary tax relief for critical industries that they want to cultivate. Governments may also apply tax policies differently to domestically-owned companies and foreign affiliates.

  Foreign purchasers should also investigate the amount and nature of withholding taxes and the legal mechanism available to obtain relief from taxes paid in the emerging market in assessing the value of a potential acquisition in that country.

Cross-border tax issues: Tax policies in emerging markets may or may not lead to the taxing of profits more than once through cross-border taxation. Global companies should determine whether they can achieve consolidated tax status for entities within emerging markets and investigate applicable tax exemptions, credits, and treaties. Some treaty signatories prohibit member states from taxing profits distributed by a subsidiary from another member state. In other cases, countries provide tax credits to avoid double taxation.

Taxation of foreign shareholders: Double taxation on shareholder dividends may be eliminated through an integrated corporate and personal tax system. The value of an emerging-market company may be affected by such tax arrangements.

Tax policies differ from one country to another. Even when a treaty is in place, future income tax rates or tax disposition costs will be influenced by a country's income-tax legislation. For example, some countries apply capital-gains tax to the disposition of real property while others may not tax gains from the disposition of corporate real estate under certain conditions.

- **Transfer Pricing**

  Transfer pricing is applied to the exchange between related entities of services, tangible property, and intangible property such as software, medical and other patents, copyrights, trademarks, and business know-how across international borders.

  Different countries apply different criteria to determining the appropriate transfer price for property and services. An emerging market's policies on transfer pricing could affect the profitability of a business.

- **Value-Added Tax Recovery**

  About 140 countries, including many emerging-market countries, have adopted a value-added or similar tax. Global VAT rates range from 5 per cent to 25 per cent and are generally increasing, while corporate and personal income tax rates are generally falling.

  In most countries, businesses can recover eligible VAT costs, but in some countries VAT is not fully recoverable, which adds an additional input cost for businesses in those countries. In China, for example, the general VAT rate is 13 per cent. But China allows a business to recover only 9 per cent of that amount on inputs into products intended for sale into the Chinese market. On inputs into sales destined for export, however, China permits full recovery.

Other countries such as India apply different rules. In some cases VAT systems differ from state to state.

- **Capital and Profit Repatriation**

  The rate of return of an acquisition in an emerging market will be influenced by the nation's laws governing the ability and cost of repatriating an investor's capital and profits. India, for example, applies strict controls to the movement of funds by domestic entities to offshore jurisdictions. This will influence the value placed by a potential foreign purchaser on a target company, unless such controls can be mitigated.

  Even in a country that restricts the repatriation of capital or earnings by foreign investors, other allowances may such as interest, royalty, licence fee, commission, and dividend payments may mitigate the effect. Tax treaties may trigger withholding taxes in these situations, usually at a rate of 10 per cent to 25 per cent, and will affect the value of a company to the extent that they impede a foreign purchaser's ability to recover income from the acquisition. If tax treaties reduce the tax impact, however, the value may not be affected.

  Some emerging markets delay or restrict the repatriation of capital or income earned by foreign investors, which will also affect a company's value. Examples of such restrictions include:

  - A minimum waiting period of three years is required in Argentina before capital can be withdrawn.
  - In the event of a serious imbalance in the national balance of payments, the Brazilian government can restrict foreign capital remittances.
  - Foreign investors can repatriate a maximum of $3 million a year in payments from Taiwan.

  Some high-inflation countries apply inflation-indexation provisions to protect the value of foreign capital investments and retained earnings. In countries where inflation ranges from 500 per cent to 7,000 per cent per annum, the absence of such provisions makes even tax-free repatriation inconsequential.

- **Relationship of Business with its International Parent Company**

  The relationship between an emerging-market subsidiary and its parent company can affect the subsidiary's value substantially. The parent company may run the subsidiary through its own management team, for example, or market the subsidiary's products to its own multinational customers. The foreign subsidiary in such cases would have little intangible value since the purchaser would acquire neither operational expertise nor customers. A subsidiary that manages itself internally, develops its own expertise, cultivates its own domestic supply chain and creates its own markets would have a much higher value.

Parent companies may overcharge a subsidiary for supplies to reduce taxes, so transfer pricing and licensing agreements between parent and subsidiary should be examined to see if the subsidiary's value is higher than its books indicate. Alternatively, its value may be lower if essential licensing agreements with the parent will terminate when the subsidiary changes hands.

- **eBusiness Challenges**

eBusinesses seek and apply the tools that enable them to transcend local differences and achieve seamless worldwide coordination and rationalization. Nevertheless, eBusinesses still have to locate their bricks-and-mortar facilities in a specific location and will encounter the same challenges in and from this location as all other businesses.

In assessing an emerging-market company as part of a global e-business expansion, a purchaser must consider the challenges presented by local infrastructure and technology. These challenges include:

- variations in infrastructure from one country to another;
- system compatibility;
- language;
- common standards of measurement;
- cultural differences;
- organizational differences such as attitudes toward management, control, reporting;
- social barriers; and
- legal issues, including rules and regulations.

- **Country Risk**

Country risks arise from national differences in economic structures, policies, socio-political institutions, geography, and currencies. Using country-risk analysis, a potential purchaser can try to identify the potential for these risks to decrease the anticipated return of an emerging-market investment.

A country's political stability, for example, affects the value of domestic businesses. In a democracy with changing governments, one government may have a different attitude toward business than another and may take steps to undermine or even expropriate the value of a business. Depending on its ideology, a government may encourage, prohibit, or restrict business development. Some emerging-market governments are sensitive to the needs of business, providing significant support in the form of a central bank, ministry of trade, or export-assistance department. Others provide none of these facilities. While some governments actively pursue international relationships, others isolate themselves from the world. Such attitudes influence the value of businesses in these countries.

The prevailing economic climate also influences value. Instability, imbalance, and excessive inflation, for example, may deter investment. Capital outlay and the type of investment involved also play a role in the evaluation of country risk since some industries attract political intervention more readily than others, especially if the business is politically significant or sensitive in the domestic context.

What is Country Risk Premium?

It has been argued that country risk is diversifiable. In fact, it is not feasible to diversify a portfolio so perfectly that it eliminates all unsystematic risk, including unsystematic risk specific to a particular country.

Among other things, the risk associated with two similar investments, one in an emerging market and the other in a developed market, is vastly different. A real-estate project in Pakistan involves a higher level of risk than a similar project in Canada. The risk may involve such factors as levels of inflation, political instability, volatility, capital flow, government regulation, accounting rules, and corruption. As compensation for the higher risk, a potential investor would require a higher return for an investment in Pakistan than one in Canada. This premium reflects country risk.

Country-risk is not fiction. Several empirical studies have shown clearly that its effect on stock returns is frequently more sizable than the industry effect. In other words, a company's stock performance seems much more tightly linked to the volatility of the local economy than to the fluctuations and trends of the company's industry at the international level.

Factoring Country Risk in Valuation Methodology

There are three primary methods for measuring country risk when valuing investments in emerging markets:

1. adjust the cash flows;
2. adjust the discount rate; and

3. evaluate the project's DCF-NPV as if there were no country risk, quantify the country risk separately, and then subtract the quantified country risk from the project's net present value of cash flows.

Adjusted Cash Flows Approach

This method incorporates the country risk into the discounted cash flow instead of the discount rate when valuing a security. The country risk incorporated into the DCF may include such factors as high levels of inflation, volatility, political unrest, lax legal and accounting controls, and corruption and other factors discussed previously.

Some valuation practitioners and investors believe that probability-weighted scenarios provide a more accurate view of a company's value. These scenarios should be developed based on macroeconomic factors such as inflation rates, growth in gross domestic product, and foreign-exchange rate. They should also take into account the variables affecting the industry and the specific company.

This method is, theoretically, more sound since it allows the discount rate to reflect only the systematic or non-diversifiable risk, while the cash flows reflect the diversifiable risk. This not only contributes to a more accurate valuation of a company but also provides managers with better insight into the specific or diversifiable risks facing it. In turn, this will help in assessing alternative investments and developing better risk-mitigation strategies. For example, a fertilizer manufacturer contemplating construction of a fertilizer plant in an emerging market may identify a threat of power shortages. As a mitigation strategy, the manufacturer may build its own power-generation facility or relocate its plant to a more suitable location.

The strongest argument in favor of the adjusted cash flows method is that it tailors the risk to the specific industry or even the specific investment under analysis. By comparison, if the additional risk is incorporated into the discount rate, we implicitly assume that the same country risk would apply to every investment in a particular country. In the context of our current global economy, one size does not fit all. Some emerging markets have a better reputation in some business sectors than in others. For example, the technology sector in India has a better reputation than the agricultural sector. In some cases, a particular investment within a particular industry may have more to recommend it than the struggling industry as a whole.

Adjusted Discount Rate

The second way to address country risk in the valuation is to adjust the discount rate to reflect the incremental risk associated with investing in a particular emerging market. In our previous discussion of the CAPM and the build-up model, it was assumed that the country risk would be included in the discount rate and not reflected in the cash flows. Analysts use the adjusted discount rate more often than adjusted cash flow, because it is more difficult to calculate the effects of country risk on a company's expected cash flow.

Using the credit risk of a country to represent the risk faced by corporations can be misleading, however. Equity investments in a company can often be less risky than investments in government bonds. "The bonds of YPF, an Argentine oil company, for example, carry lower yields than Argentine government debt," say McKinsey consultants Mimi James and Timothy M. Koller. "A company's financial rating can be higher than that of a government."

Country risk is sometimes quantified as the difference between the yield of a risk-free rate in the domestic country of the investor and the emerging market. For example, if an investor in Canada invests in Pakistan, the following information will determine the country risk:

- a risk-free rate in Canada such as a Government of Canada five-year bond; and
- a similar risk-free rate in Pakistan.

If a country's government debt does not trade in international financial markets, rating agencies such as Moody's and Standard & Poor's offer an alternative for assessing a country's risk. These rating agencies rate long-term debt issued by countries based on default risk. For example, Standard & Poor's applies ratings of AAA, AA, A, and BBB to indicate low risk of default and B, CCC, CC, C, *etc.* to indicate a higher default risk. These ratings have an embedded yield in the financial markets. The country risk is calculated as the difference between this embedded yield and the risk-free rate of the investor country.

The Human Touch

Although technology has made it easier to communicate throughout the global marketplace, email, phone calls, and teleconferencing do not contribute much to strong relationships. International business requires an international presence. Relationships with contractors and subcontractors are critical for organizations that operate globally, and the trust that underlies such relationships can be nurtured only through face-to-face meetings.

Companies also need to educate managers about business practices in emerging markets where their organizations operate, and they must become familiar with regulations and trends, as well, most effectively by visiting these emerging markets regularly.

The miscommunication, mistakes, and misunderstandings that arise between the constituents of a multinational organization can be minimized if a company maintains strong and personal links throughout its global supply chain. Effective communication with strategic partners, consultants, customers, and clients in emerging markets and in developed markets alike will reinforce the organization's common purpose and ensure that all participants work together effectively.

Summary

Despite the potential risks, companies continue to pursue even greater rewards through mergers and acquisitions in emerging markets. The investment returns in these markets are projected to be higher than those for most businesses located in more developed countries, and these returns cannot be ignored. As a result, companies and business valuators have to address the complexities involved in global expansion, including:

- legal issues involved in acquiring businesses in unfamiliar markets;
- tax-related issues related to M&A and joint-venture transactions;
- the role of local government in M&A and joint-venture transactions;
- accounting principles of global M&A;
- managing risk across borders; and
- conducting thorough due diligence despite limitations on corporate and market data.

These complexities present a challenge to North American companies and valuators accustomed to working with domestic businesses. In addition to the business-related issues mentioned earlier, obstacles also arise from language, culture, and social practices. Working in a foreign country, companies and valuators may also find inadequate sources of information and accounting and reporting practices that fall below North American standards. They may also encounter inexperienced management and undefined and undocumented business procedures and practices. While investors, companies, and valuators may take it for granted in North America that governments are stable and infrastructure is dependable, they cannot make such assumptions in all parts of the world.

Fortunately, as global markets develop, standards of accounting, measurement, governance, and reporting are being harmonized. This will enable companies and valuators to work with much more certainty over time. Also, many professional services firms have established business valuation practices in the major emerging markets.

Even now, companies and valuators who take a disciplined approach to synergy identification and who place a strong emphasis on capturing the knowledge and lessons learned from each transaction will increase their likelihood of success. Structure, discipline, and the prowess to capture new learning and skills can vastly increase the success of an emerging market acquisition.

On a personal level, identifying merger and acquisition opportunities in foreign environments presents a combination of challenges and rewards. Travel exposes individuals to the everyday risks of in-flight fatigue, jetlag, long check-in times, frequent flight delays, cancelled flights, lost luggage, and tedious procedures at airport security checkpoints/passport control. But these foreign assignments offer great rewards, and many of these rewards far outweigh the hassles and risks.

APPENDIX A

References

Michael Backman, *Asia Future Shock* (Palgrave-Macmillan, 2008).

Boston Consulting Group, *The 2009 BCG 100 New Global Challengers: How Top Companies from Rapidly Developing Economies are Contending for Global Leadership* (BCG, 2009).

Bernardo Carvalho & Marcio Garcia, "Ineffective Controls on Capital Inflows under Sophisticated Financial Markets", in Sebastian Edwards & Marcio Garcia, eds., *Financial Markets Volatility and Performance in Emerging Markets.*

James L. Horvath, "Valuing Businesses in the Ever-changing Global Marketplace" in James L. Horvath & David W. Chodikoff, eds., *Taxation and Valuation of Technology: Theory, Practice, and the Law* (Toronto: Irwin Law, 2008).

Mimi James & Timothy M. Koller, "Valuation in Emerging Markets" The McKinsey Quarterly, 2000 Number 4: Asia Revalued.

Alan R. Kanuk, *Capital Markets of India: An Investor's Guide* (Wiley, 2007).

Thomas Lawton & Steven McGuire, "Supranational Rules on Strategy Context: Embraer and Brazil's Aerospace Program", in S. Benjamin Presad & Pervez Ghauri, eds., *Global Firms and Emerging Markets in an Age of Anxiety* (Praeger Publishers, 2004).

D.H. Meldrum, "Country Risk and Foreign Direct Investment" (2000), *Business Economics*

Terri Morrison & Wayne A. Conaway, *Kiss, Bow or Shake Hands: How to do Business in 12 Asian Countries (*Adams Media, 2007).

Barry Naughton, *The Chinese Economy: Transitions and Growth* (The MIT Press, 2007).

Pacek Nenad & Danny Thomily, *Emerging Markets – Lessons for Business Success & The Outlook for Different Markets* (2004).

Luis E. Pereiro, *Valuation of Companies in Emerging Markets: A Practical Approach* (John Wiley & Sons, 2002).

Richard Scase, *Global Remix: The Fight for Competitive Advantage* (Kogan Page, 2007).

Tom Travis, *Doing Business Anywhere: The Essential Guide to Going Global* (Wiley, 2007).

The IVSC: The Challenge of Developing Global Valuation Standards

Carlos Arenillas Lorente[1]

Introduction

Observation of the global financial crisis that unfolded during 2008 gives rise to the following question: if there had been robust valuation standards and if they had been applied globally in recent years, would the crisis have been so intense?

It could be argued that the effect of the crisis could have been less extreme. This does not mean that the existence of internationally accepted and uniformly applied valuation standards can be an antidote to economic crises. Crises are inherent to economic evolution: the existence of economic cycles of varying length and severity is well-known. However, the extent and seriousness of the latest crisis, whose origin should be traced to malfunction in the financial system, poses many questions related to financial stability and how it should be maintained. It is in this context that the urgent need arises to make up for the lack of quality in the valuation process of a whole range of assets and liabilities.

There are various reasons justifying the need to put into place quality valuation standards that are rigorously and universally applied.

In a global world with increasingly open markets for goods, services, and capital, financial information must be rigorous, understandable, and universal if markets are to function properly and if the economy is to be given

---

* Carlos Arenillas is an economist, a trustee of the International Valuation Standards Council (IVSC) and former vice-chairman of the Comisión Nacional del Mercado de Valores (CNMV).

the conditions in which to grow. If the contrary is true, *i.e.*, if the information is scarce, inexact, or asymmetrical, the participating agents make decisions that may have results contrary to their own interests. As a result, the markets become less efficient and economic resources – whether physical, human, or financial – are badly allocated. In the best of cases, this affects economic growth by reducing its potential; in general, it undermines the confidence of economic agents: this is in fact what happened at the start of this century with scandals such as Enron, Worldcom, and Parmalat. But, in the worst case scenario, defective financial information may combine with other factors to lead to periods of financial instability and economic recession. The current economic crisis is, unfortunately, a good example of this.

The need to use a common financial language in a global world has led to a wide variety of initiatives in recent years. Among the most notable are the development of International Financial Reporting Standards (IFRS) in the accounting field and bank solvency standards, known as Basel II, in prudential supervision. Nevertheless, the market and regulatory flaws that have surfaced in the recent financial and economic crisis demonstrate that there are still aspects on which reforms should be undertaken. In particular, there is the area of valuation.

There are numerous examples of the lack of a solid framework for valuation: problems and debates relating to the concept and application of fair value; the discussion on how to value multiple financial assets when the markets collapse; problems that have arisen in various countries relating to granting mortgage loans; conflicts concerning the valuations of companies that are initially admitted to trading, *etc.* In this context, globally applied IFRS will be of little use if there is no clear and universally applied set of valuation rules on which to rely. Accounting standards and valuation standards are two different (though in many ways complimentary) sets that interconnect in various aspects.

Valuations also have multiple applications in the economy. The following are just some of these:

- financial reporting of all kinds of companies and mutual funds;
- real estate transactions;
- investment in a wide variety of financial assets;
- company transactions;
- securitization operations;
- payment of taxes and duties;
- financial regulation and supervision;
- settlement of inheritance or other disputes covering a variety of goods; and
- measurement of the level of collateral in public and private loan transactions.

Valuations are the basis of important economic decisions taken in developed countries, where more weight is given to the concept of value than cost when making investment decisions or when measuring risk or determining solvency requirements.

This article deals with the importance of valuation and is divided into two sections. The first explains the benefits of having international valuations standards; the second deals with the role of the International Valuation Standards Council (IVSC) and its organization. Finally, by way of conclusion, it sets out the future challenges faced by the IVSC.

The Benefits of International Valuation Standards

The existence of globally-accepted valuation standards would provide multiple benefits for all the world's economies. Among them are the following:

1. Investment risks would be reduced. Currently, investors are obliged to make decisions in a world with many different sets of regulations. Sometimes these are inconsistent or overlap, which can generate significant costs in terms of time and effort. Applying international valuation standards would reduce this uncertainty and minimize the risks incurred by investors.
2. It would increase the reliability and trustworthiness of financial information. Standards can help increase confidence in financial information to the extent that they increase confidence in the estimated value of assets and liabilities. Fair value estimates are critical in many aspects of market transactions, such as the acquisition of companies or the lending used to finance it. They even have effects on financial stability. The application of independent valuations based on a set of common and internationally-accepted standards is essential for constructing a reliable body of financial information that reflects corporate reality.
3. The third benefit of applying common standards is that they would improve the trustworthiness and straightforwardness of audits carried out under IFRS. A valuation that has not been carried out in accordance with recognised standards and procedures may complicate the work of auditing or end up being rejected. This increases auditing costs and may mean that the financial report is insufficiently precise.
4. The standards would provide a more consistent analysis of portfolios and of asset valuations. In our globalized economy, there are an increasing number of actors who are active in different markets. Multinational companies need international valuation standards that provide them with an ordered process for valuing

their portfolios and assets. In addition, the increasing use of complex financial instruments backed by real-estate assets (shares and securitizations) increases the need for uniform and transparent valuation standards.

5. The application of common international standards would help minimize risk to the banking system. Efficient supervision of banking activity and its capital needs calls for robust valuation standards. The banking system is a basic provider of finance for economic activity around the world, particularly to large financial institutions. Thus, its capacity to measure risk is critical and should be based on valuations which may be applied consistently at an international level. Basel II needs international valuation standards if it is to avoid regulatory inconsistencies that could eliminate or reduce the advantages of harmonized global banking legislation.
6. The quality of valuation services provided by valuation, auditing, and consultancy firms would improve. This would reduce costs by minimizing duplication, conversion, and reconciliation. It would also allow more comprehensive services to be provided for clients.
7. The standards would enable markets and supervisors to operate properly. Securities markets need issuers of securities to provide clear and comparable financial information if they are to act efficiently. Thus, the standards would contribute to achieving the basic objectives of any financial market supervisor: market transparency, correct price formation, and investor protection. Obviously, the tasks of prudential supervision and solvency would also be enhanced.

In short, international valuation standards are a desirable goal for all the agents participating in economic activity and an essential part of a solid financial system that is capable of tackling the challenges presented by our global economy.

Now, the next question is: who will develop these standards? Will they be compulsory and what degree of international harmonization can be achieved? The answer to the first question is the IVSC; in answer to the second, it would be desirable for them to be compulsory, but there is some way to go to achieve this, and this is not something that the IVSC can achieve alone. The challenge for IVSC is to ensure that its standards are developed and written in a way that makes them capable of adoption and enforcement by others.

The IVSC Project

The origins of the International Valuation Standards Council (IVSC) date from 1981 when The International Asset Valuation Standards Committee (TIAVSC) was founded. The IVSC is now incorporated as a not-for-profit organization in Chicago, Illinois, although its operating headquarters are in London. In 2008, the IVSC underwent a major restructuring. Prior to that date, membership had been restricted to "not for profit" professional valuation bodies. To be eligible for membership, the bodies had to represent a significant element of the valuation profession in a particular country and provide education and/or qualifications to individual members. However, although the organisation was required by its constitution to act in the public interest, to regulators and the markets at large a body consisting only of professional organisations was seen as representing only the views of those organisations. It was necessary to create a more open and transparent organisation if the standards produced by IVSC were to gain wider credibility.

Also, the original TIAVSC had been solely concerned with real estate valuation. Although over the years the organisation had grown to include organisations involved in valuing businesses, plants and equipment, and intangibles, the old structure was not conducive to involving the diversity of valuation interests around the world.

The new IVSC that came into existence in 2008 has moved away from the "organisation of organisations" model, and membership is open not only to professional institutions but also to users and providers of valuation services as well as academia. The overall strategy and management of the organisation is the responsibility of a board of trustees, appointed by the membership. There are two operational boards, whose members are appointed by the trustees. These boards are independent and responsible for setting their own agendas within the strategic limits set by the trustees.

The International Valuation Standards Board is responsible for the development of the current international valuation standards, following a transparent and open process of consultation with all stakeholders in the valuation process.

The International Valuation Professional Board has a remit to represent the interests of and develop the valuation profession generally on the global stage, for providing supplementary guidance and educational material on the standards, and developing recognised benchmarks for professional qualification.

The IVSC does not have individual members and can be neither an educator, qualifier, nor a regulator of valuers. Like IFRS, the authority of the International Valuation Standards comes from their acceptance and adoption by others, for example, through being required by state law for certain regulated activities, through incorporation into the rules of professional bodies, or through acceptance by custom and practice.

The new structure of the IVSC is illustrated in this diagram:

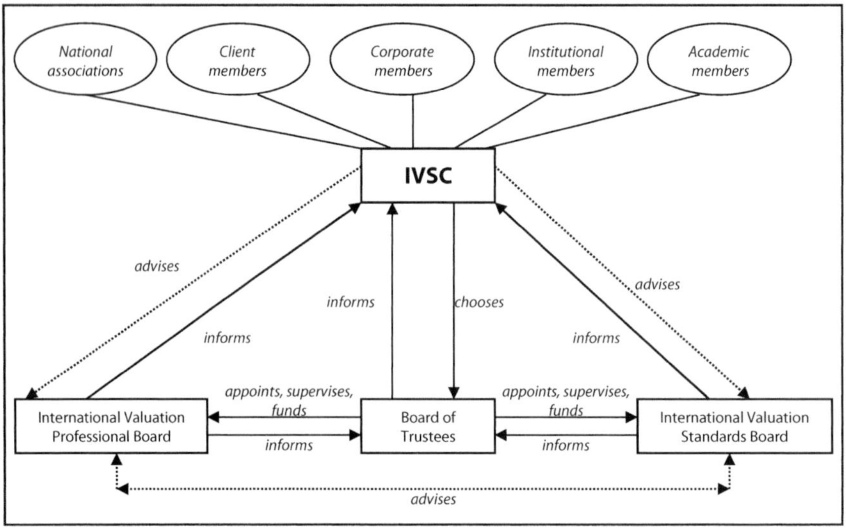

The International Valuation Standards (IVS)

Since its foundation in 1981, the IVSC has published eight editions of its International Valuation Standards (IVS). The continuing development of the IVS reflects the commitment of the IVSC to ensure that the basic definitions and approaches in the valuation field are always up-to-date in our changing world.

The latest publication, IVS 2007, retains the basic structure of earlier editions. It is divided into seven sections, with a glossary and analytical index. The seven sections are as follows:

1. General introduction on the background to the IVSC and the IVS
2. General Valuation Principles
3. Code of Conduct
4. The bases for valuation of the different property types, *i.e.*:
   a. real property
   b. personal property
   c. businesses
   d. financial interests
5. Standards

6. Applications
7. Guidance notes

In 2006-2007, the IVSC appointed a Critical Review Group to look at ways in which the standards could be improved. Its report coincided with the restructuring of the organisation and it is for the new IVSB to consider the recommendations and the detailed impact that these will have on future editions. However, since it is now the role of the IVPB to develop educational and guidance material, and also to set benchmarks for professional conduct, it is probable that the Code of Conduct and the content that is concerned with valuation theory and methodology will be removed from the standards and developed separately in the future.

One of the recommendations of the Critical Review Group was that future editions should remove the real estate bias of much of the material. Although there have been guidance notes on plants and equipment, intangible assets, personal property, and business for a number of years, much of the original core material has been written from a real estate perspective, reflecting the origins of the organisation. Although real estate is a major asset class, and one where valuation is often regulated at state level, it is important to ensure that the standards are seen as relevant to the valuation of all asset types.

Apart from the need to rewrite the IVS to reflect these principles, the IVSB also has the following current projects:

- improving the current guidance on Intangible Assets, particularly in the light of IFRS 3;
- developing new guidance on the valuation of investment property in the course of construction; and
- following the G20 summit in April 2009, the development of valuation standards for financial instruments has become a political priority. An expert group has been established to make recommendations for the development of standards and guidance for the valuation of financial assets and liabilities

Longer term projects include revising the standards for valuations in the extractive industries, forestry, and also for identifying and reporting valuation certainty.

Harmonisation

In a similar way to the agreement between the International Accounting Standards Board (IASB) and the Financial Accounting Standards Board (FASB) to converge accounting standards, the IVSC also has a Memorandum of Understanding with The Appraisal Foundation (TAF) in the U.S., which is the federally mandated standard setter for real estate valuation. This commits both organisations to work towards convergence of IVS and TAF's Uniform Standards of Professional Appraisal Practice (USPAP).

This is not just of relevance to the real estate sector. TAF has expanded its activities beyond its statutory responsibilities and also produces best practice guides for unregulated valuation activity, including for financial statements. In the field of business valuation, it is currently developing guides for identifying and valuing contributory assets and for the valuation of customer relationships; discussions are taking place as to how IVSC can develop these papers for the international market and valuations under IFRS.

The IVSC already has established working relationships with the IASB and the FASB and is developing a relationship with the International Federation of Accountants, which is responsible for the international audit standards.

If it is to succeed in its objectives, the IVSC needs to reinforce and expand its contacts with other international bodies. One of the principle drivers for the reorganisation of IVSC was to create a structure that was credible and acceptable to international institutions and regulators such as the Organisation for Economic Co-operation and Development (OECD), the World Bank, the International Monetary Fund (IMF), the Financial Stability Board, the Bank for International Settlements (BIS), International Organisation of Securities Commissions (IOSCO) and the European Commission. Active discussions are planned or in progress for building relationships with bodies such as these.

Conclusion

The aim of this article has been to show the importance of valuations in the modern world and the urgent need to have a set of robust and internationally-accepted valuation standards. At the same time, it has been a presentation of the IVSC, which is best placed to carry out this task, having led the development of valuation standards around the world for more than 25 years.

Having successfully completed its restructuring, there are a number of challenges faced by the IVSC if it is to meet its objectives. It has to extend its mission, vision, and activities. Obviously, the way ahead for the IVSC is dependent on the available financial and human resources. However, the benefits to be gained by all from achieving these objectives are worth the effort, especially at a time when regulators around the world have given the matter pride of place in their agendas. With the support of all those with a stake in establishing robust valuation standards across all sectors including valuation professionals, their clients, and public bodies, IVSC will surely succeed in its goals.

APPENDIX A

References

International Valuation Standards (IVSC), 8th ed. (2007) (ISBN 978-0-922154-94-4).

The Value of an Idea

James L. Horvath & Jennifer Lee

Introduction

While idea generation lies at the core of every company's future, determining the value of an idea is exceptionally challenging, especially in a market that still struggles to effectively value established operating assets that possess a proven performance history. Yet, placing a value on ideas has become critically important in today's knowledge-driven economy where companies are challenged not only to come up with great ideas, but also to choose the best of the best, develop them to the point of viability, monetize them, and protect them in the broader marketplace.

With this in mind, valuation professionals need to know how to determine the value of an asset in its preliminary stages. Beyond placing the idea in its industry-specific context and anticipating its potential market and participants, how does one arrive at the value of an idea.

This chapter addresses many of the major considerations valuators and businesses face when trying to place a value on an idea. While it does not detail valuation methodologies, you can find those details in Chapters 2, 4, and 5. Similarly, many of the methodologies that apply to the valuation of technology (discussed in Chapter 5) also apply to the valuing of an idea. This chapter lays out a framework for idea valuation that hinges on the concept that the pipeline of ideas, and the organizational culture that builds, maintains, and evolves it, is more instrumental to value creation and valuation than any single idea. It is the development process itself that forms the very basis of valuation.

As evidence, consider the vast number of one-hit-wonder organizations that failed to follow up successful products or services. Absent internal processes that consistently encourage idea creation, evolution, release, and support, ideas arguably lack inherent value. This concept is crucial for business valuators, as they do not have measurable tools to determine whether a specific idea – such as Facebook or the iPod – has intrinsic value. Rather, they look at the organizational structure and the hurdles that ideas and their sponsors must clear before seeing the light of day. Their ability to assess the process by which ideas move through the pipeline is fundamental to the valuation process.

Google – arguably the most influential technology-driven organization in existence – is a perfect example of this. While ideas lie at the core of Google's vaunted culture, it is the process by which the organization facilitates their evolution that sets this environment apart. Employees are given a day a week to pursue whatever projects they wish. What they come up with is not subject to the same checks and balances that would normally kill other ideas at their earliest stages. When these great ideas evolve further into nascent projects, Google's rapid-fire development process keeps them from becoming caught in the organizational inertia that often stymies idea and product evolution in more conventional environments.

As ideas take on the form of working products – Google Mail is an excellent example – the company rarely waits to complete a traditional product development cycle before releasing it to the world. Instead, it makes it available in beta – or larger-scale experimental – form and prompts the broader end-user community for real-time feedback. As Google integrates community response into product development, promising ideas evolve into promising deliverables. Google's pipeline is completely idea-based, and carries an intrinsic value that largely explains why the company has become such a powerhouse over the past decade.

The lessons inherent in how Google facilitates idea creation and then shepherds the best ones to a revenue- or value-producing stage apply beyond this one company or even this one sector. The Google experience serves as a lesson in value creation and measurement. The value of any one of its ideas does not lie solely in the idea itself – indeed, any idea can be a million-dollar winner once it is hastily scribbled down on the back of a napkin before dessert arrives. As brilliant as it may be, most business valuators would argue that an idea is technically worthless until it begins to pay its own way.

Truly quantifiable value, then, rests in the environment that's been built around the idea generation, evolution, and production process. When trying to determine the value of something, that "something" is often the last thing that matters before calculating a bottom-line figure. Broader culture matters more than any single idea in helping identify and quantify value. Ideally, such value-creating organizations will be built around a culture that motivates people to take the time to generate ideas, to winnow out the losers and identify the potential winners, to access resources from inside and outside the organization that will help evolve ideas from intangible thoughts to working prototypes, to take steps to protect them at an appropriate stage of their evolution, and to remove organizational obstacles that would normally kill them before they see the light of day.

To be successful in this changing landscape, organizations must recognize the power of ideas. They must also capture and disseminate knowledge through a network that facilitates the cross-pollination of ideas and innovation on a continuous basis.

What Not to Do

For every success story in idea incubation, there are also plenty of negative examples. The North American auto industry stands out in today's economy for its failure to develop ideas that would generate value, and for squelching those that could have laid the foundation for a more competitive future.

The industry's response to the sport utility vehicle craze of the 1990s serves as an excellent example of how great ideas can be permanently frozen in place if organizational culture gets in the way. When the automakers took the basic pickup truck – a relatively inexpensive product to design and produce – and created the fully enclosed SUV, they set the stage for a decade of significant profitability. Although SUVs were based on humble underpinnings, they were considerably more upmarket than the vehicles from which they were derived and could command higher transaction prices in a market driven by inexpensive fuel and strong economic growth. Profit margins per unit were greater than the smaller sedans that had previously dominated the market, and automakers rapidly threw everything they had into meeting burgeoning demand.

Years of hefty profits were reinvested in creating newer generations of ever-larger, feature-laden SUVs. Single-purpose factories were not upgraded to the new standard of flexible production lines that could easily switch between products to meet rapidly changing market demand. Internally, ideas that would have brought more efficient designs to market were de-emphasized in favor of high-margin SUVs. In many respects, the automakers, addicted to these easy-to-build cash cows, failed to prepare for the day when fuel prices would rise and demand for inefficient SUVs would fall.

As long as global energy prices remained inexpensive and stable, the incentive to invest in both near- and long-term, next generation propulsion technologies was relatively muted. Although it was inevitable that cheap gas would not last forever, and the resulting shift would render conventional gasoline-powered internal combustion engines obsolete, automakers varied in their level of preparation for this change. Toyota, which invested billions in its hybrid program a decade before global energy prices spiked, stands in stark contrast to General Motors and Chrysler.

When the inevitable happened and the global energy situation became more volatile, manufacturers that had nurtured their idea generation pipelines and invested in longer-term technologies such as hybrids, alternative fuels and lighter, stronger materials were better positioned to adapt to the new market reality and bring smaller, more efficient designs to market. Their early investments in flexible production lines began to bear fruit as they transitioned production away from heavier SUVs toward car-based crossovers and other suddenly-in-demand designs. North American automakers, on the other hand, have had a difficult time transitioning away from their inflexible infrastructure, a direct result of their failure to devote sufficient resources to an idea-driven culture. As a result, they find themselves playing catch-up with a lineup perceived as outdated, while Toyota's Prius gains stature as the *de facto* hybrid brand.

In many ways, the failure of General Motors to maintain market focus lies at the root of its long decline. While it may be tempting to view GM's fate in the same context as the other major North American automakers, its trajectory is unique among this group, and serves as an example of what happens when internal structures become more critical to operations than meeting market needs.

Market focus is little more than an organization's ability to devote resources only to activities that generate long-term, positive cash flows. Its corollary, namely rapidly exiting market segments that do not support this end goal, is equally notable, as GM's long-term maintenance of an untenably large brand portfolio virtually guaranteed a complete loss of market focus. So intent was GM on having a vehicle for every need that it ended up squandering enormous amounts of capital in areas where it could never compete, much less make money.

Its strategic goals, consistently focused on growing market share to the detriment of net cash flow, left it with few options when the economy turned sour. Competing automakers – namely Toyota – that carried a more focused array of brands and were cash flow positive as a result were better able to withstand the turbulence. GM, unfortunately, had spent decades as a slave to an overly broad brand strategy that consumed engineering and marketing resources.

Examples of what not to do can be found in any sector, even telecommunications. It is fair to say that traditional phone companies, long dominant in providing conventional voice service to businesses and consumers, were slow off the mark in understanding the potential impact of Internet-based voice and data technologies on their core business. Decades of consistent –

and lucrative – revenue streams from conventional sources created a culture where new ideas were forced to overcome significant internal hurdles before seeing the light of day. In many cases, they never did, and organizational agility suffered as upstart competitors – mostly cable-based operators whose culture was not constrained by legacy – brought next-generation voice and data technologies to market. Early delivery of Internet service via conventional coaxial infrastructure is an excellent example of cable company creativity. They have since used their first mover advantage over flat-footed incumbents – who stuck with inferior and more expensive DSL-based solutions – to bring faster speeds to market and maintain their qualitative edge over the traditional telcos.

As these emerging competitors outflanked the incumbent telcos on all sides – faster Internet, cheaper phone, bundled services, *etc.* – the formerly dominant players were hampered by an internal culture that failed to provide the agility required to fight back.

Looking for Value in All the Right Places

To avoid these missteps, it is important to know what to look for when valuing an idea or an organization. Business valuators use a number of approaches to determine whether a potential acquisition target, for example, is worth the asking price. When independence and a high level of accuracy are required, they use commercial due diligence (CDD), a comprehensive process of analysis that looks at market factors to identify potential opportunities and overall feasibility for a particular idea, as a framework for assessing value. Developing competency in this area – or engaging third party resources – is essential not only to the valuation process, but to long-term organizational performance as well. Of the 3,700 companies studied by the Corporate Strategy Board, only 3.3 per cent showed consistent growth in top- and bottom-line performance and shareholder returns. Fewer than 1 per cent sustained this growth over the past 20 years.[1] The lesson is clear: innovation drives long-term growth, which is closely tied to bottom-line success.

Against that context, CDD is an important component of determining value and using it to drive long-term growth. Using CDD to assess the idea pipeline and determine its potential to drive revenue involves a number of factors, including:

---

1 R.B. Tucker, "Driving Growth Through Innovation."

Assessment Depth

A company can have all the ideas it wants in the pipeline, but if it cannot deliver the ideas to either trial or launch, then the idea, ultimately, has little value to the organization. Due diligence is a critical part of the idea valuation process, and valuators who dig deep enough to understand the viability of a given idea do a better job of assessing value than those who don't.

A typical case involves valuators meeting with the client, reviewing the cash flow projections, and doing some market research to come up with a discount rate to apply to the cash flow projections. The end result is a value determination for what the valuator believes is a working product. Closer scrutiny sometimes reveals that the product has not yet been developed, and that the client is waiting for investment to be in place before proceeding with development and production. What was originally valued as a tangible or intangible asset is, in fact, little more than a potential idea.

Equal depth of investigation must also be applied to emerging market trends. Over time, market shifts can rewrite the context within which companies operate. In many cases, entire market sectors are restructured – or even replaced – by these enormous forces of change. Companies that fail to plan for these evolutions are less likely to withstand their force, resulting in a severe erosion of the value of their ideas.

To have commercial value, an idea, product or service must have utility to someone, be transferable, and have someone willing to pay for it. Regardless of the type of idea, commercial value is based on the quantum, timing, and risks associated with future returns generated by a particular asset or asset group.

In fact, the valuation process works best when the risks that stand between its current and target states are factored in. For this reason, valuators should pay close attention to the factors that can hold innovation back and hinder long-term competitiveness. Some key factors include:

- historical revenue/income volatility;
- inadequate management skills;
- overdependence on existing/older technology;
- lack of patent protection;
- dominance of key suppliers;
- insufficient R&D investment;
- below-par marketing maturity;
- inadequate financial and operational reporting.

Today's best valuators spend more time kicking the tires to better understand what they are valuing, determine its ability to withstand changing market conditions, and measure the risk factors that may impede the idea's movement towards product development or commercialization.

Stage of Development

CDD is becoming increasingly important because it allows valuators to determine, at the very minimum, that the client has put thought into market segmentation, market penetration, and the size of the market opportunity. It also allows them to confirm if the idea is properly timed to capitalize on prevailing market conditions. For instance, a product or service that is introduced to market either too early or too late will fail to generate expected revenues and should be valued within this reduced context.

Ford's EcoBoost technology can be characterized as too little, too late in light of how the parent company chose to target it, and when it decided to bring it to market. EcoBoost uses a range of technologies, including direct injection and turbo-charging, to raise output levels in otherwise conventional internal combustion engines. At a time when other vendors are pursuing more radical hybrid and alternative fuel programs, Ford has targeted EcoBoost to provide V8-level power in a more efficient, 6-cylinder-based package. While this is laudable, and reflects the reality that a certain market for larger-output trucks and other vehicles will continue to exist, it positions Ford out of step with the rest of the market as it rapidly realigns around smaller, more fuel efficient offerings. Five years ago, EcoBoost would have been a market-changing revelation. Today, it's viewed as yesterday's solution to a problem that no one much cares about. While Ford envisions introducing EcoBoost on increasingly small and efficient platforms, its initial market introduction, in larger crossovers, luxury vehicles, and trucks, is significantly out of step with market trends. Commercial due diligence, conducted after the conceptual stage, might have uncovered this misalignment by better testing the rigor and the business case supporting the idea.

Framework for Evaluating An Idea Through Commercial Due Diligence

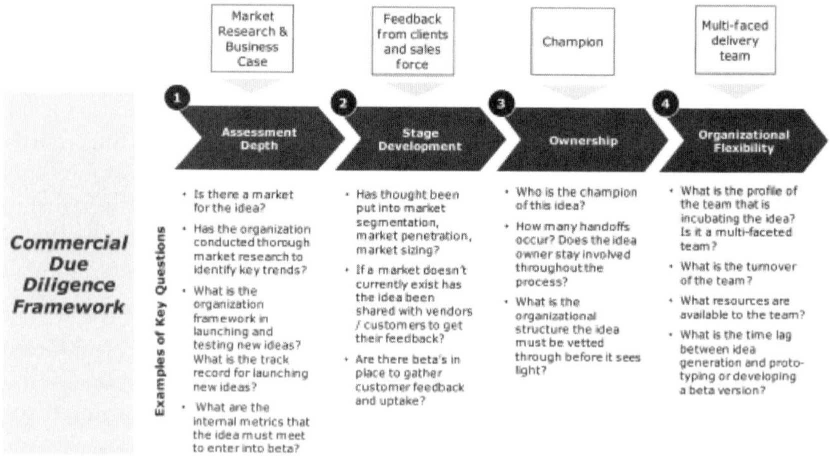

While some may argue that CDD tends to stifle truly innovative initiatives – who, after all, would have bet on social networking as the communication tool of the future? – failure for ideas to take root does not lie in CDD itself. Properly leveraged, CDD-based primary and secondary analysis can help organizations discover marketplace and consumer behavior shifts and trends. This can bring additional clarity and legitimacy to a specific business case.

More importantly, CDD helps solidify an idea's opportunity, and helps sell the idea both internally – for example, through marketing and sales channels – and externally through private equity and venture capital funding. It demonstrates to both these groups that the idea's owner has put thought into how the product can be executed and delivered. It helps generate support from potential stakeholders and helps frame the story in a way that maximizes the potential for buy-in.

Stages of Commercial Due Diligence

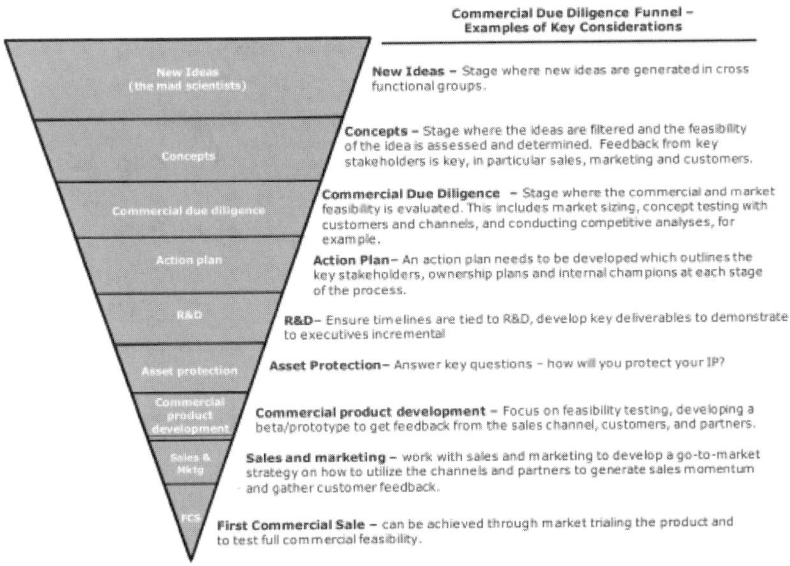

It is for these reasons that CDD is increasingly leveraged in the nascent stages of an idea's existence to better assess value at a stage previously ignored by conventional valuation methods.

Ownership

An idea stands a greater chance of succeeding when a champion stays with it through all phases of its development life cycle. Multiple handoffs between individuals and teams minimize the amount of personal stake in a given idea. As handoffs rise, value often drops. Individual passion for an idea cannot be underestimated, and organizational infrastructure that supports staff member movement through the hierarchy to reduce handoffs increases the potential for ideas to survive to the point that they can add bottom line value. Due diligence processes must evaluate the number of people who remain attached to an idea through its development, as this is a key indicator of value.

The flip side of this is key person syndrome, where knowledge locked within a specific individual is not transferable elsewhere within the organization. This situation can minimize the fair market value of an idea, especially if said individual exits and leaves the idea stranded. Organizations that implement knowledge sharing infrastructures are better positioned to minimize this risk and leverage knowledge beyond the individual – while ensuring that multiple handoffs don't erode the value-creating core.

In many cases, this hybridized approach has structural and operational implications. Some organizations create so-called expertise teams to evaluate ideas and move them forward. These teams, composed of experts from a range of fields, including finance, engineering, technical, production, marketing and sales, help address traditional weaknesses of end-to-end reliance on a single champion. Because champions can come from virtually anywhere within the organization, they may not have the skills required to clearly articulate the value proposition of their idea. Expertise teams support the idea champion with cross-functional capabilities – while at the same time maintaining the individual stake in the idea's evolution.

Continuity is key, also. Turnover rates provide insight into how intellectual capital is managed within an organization. High turnover rates, with little evidence of knowledge transfer and collaboration, are warning signs. A culture that encourages information sharing and exemplifies continuity following staff departures is seen as a value-enhancer.

Flexibility

To effectively assign value to a specific idea, valuation experts often need to look beyond the idea itself and focus on the flexibility of the company's infrastructure. Relatively inflexible organizations can place significant hurdles in an idea's path. This persistent form of corporate inertia can kill ideas that should otherwise be successful. Ultimately, it devalues the company. Improved flexibility enables viable ideas to move more rapidly to market, a key driver of competitiveness. This applies externally as well, as in many cases, full value cannot be realized until external infrastructure – for example, an airport and air traffic control capability to serve an aircraft manufacturer's market – is fully in place and market acceptance is realized.

Organizational infrastructure flexibility can accomplish three key tasks in streamlining and facilitating the evolutionary process:

- determine the feasibility of the business case;
- give valuators a sense of how fast a company can deliver and test an idea;
- help assess the timing for external infrastructure maturity and market acceptance.

The idea-centric approach to managing flexibility underscores a significant change in how organizations are managed. Twenty years ago, large corporations managed their business on an issue-by-issue basis. As issues arose, collaborative work groups were formed to identify and evaluate potential options. Then, analysts studied financial reports and projections and identified additional risks and related issues. Finally, task forces or committees would be formed to explore and evaluate options, develop recommendations, and present their findings to senior leadership for approval.

This top heavy, process-oriented, and bureaucratic approach is no longer feasible in today's accelerated business environment. Today's market leaders form teams to quickly identify issues, develop and evaluate possible solutions, and rapidly implement the selected solution.

These flexible teams deliberately narrow their focus to minimize the noise that often clouds effective decision-making and problem solving. They ask focused questions, pull in resources and skills as needed and restructure themselves if business conditions evolve over the life of the project. It is an organizational core competency that's increasingly seen in companies of all sizes, and it requires a fundamental re-thinking of how resources are deployed and managed.

Case Study

A U.K.-based software developer serves as an ideal example of ownership. To ensure the right ideas were selected for development, and that they subsequently survived from conception to production, the organization structured itself to allow staff members sufficient flexibility to drive the initiative from end-to-end. It developed a pipeline that encompassed the following key elements:

1. A submission process for capturing new ideas.
2. A committee/innovation team to evaluate ideas and develop a short-list.
3. Staff resourcing to develop the business case for short-listed ideas.
4. Prototype development.
5. Production.

In all cases, the employee who had come up with the idea stayed with it throughout its life cycle. The organization identified consistent ownership as a critical success factor and allowed flexibility in its human resources management processes to accommodate this. Whereas conventionally managed organizations would hand off business case creation to a separate individual or team, this firm allocated 20 per cent to 30 per cent of the employee's time to this task and made appropriate resources available to assist in the process.

Its innovation team tied specific sales objectives to the idea development process, ensuring ROI remained consistently visible through the evaluation and development life cycle.

The bottom line for this firm was highly positive. Of the hundreds of ideas submitted, two were granted patents. Largely on the strength of its market-leading pipeline, the company, initially backed by VCs, was eventually sold to a large software vendor.

Idea-Centric Culture

Given the key components of value creation, how then can organizations go about strengthening their idea-generating processes? In many cases, the answer lies in building an idea-centric culture.

Ideas are in and of themselves essentially worthless. Virtually anyone in a free market economy is eminently capable of coming up with an idea. And just because an idea has been created and shared doesn't necessarily mean it has some sort of inherent value.

Until it actually becomes something tangible – a product or service that generates (or has a very high likelihood of being able to generate) sustainable, material levels of revenue and profits – the basic idea is little more than paper-thin potential. Like any child, an idea demands investment to see it through the nascent stages of evolution. Like all children, the outcomes will vary. Unlike children, corporate parents have the option of abandoning ideas long before it becomes apparent that they won't fly on their own. With this thinking in mind, it is the pipeline within which ideas are generated and evolved that dictates organizational value more than the ideas themselves.

Depending on the nature of a given idea and the capabilities of the organizational environment within which it is developed, the experience can vary from relatively straightforward to somewhat difficult. In some cases, products and services can evolve from baseline ideas in a fairly linear manner, without requiring significant investments in new or evolved systems or processes. In other cases, the transition isn't quite so straightforward. Generally, ideas with the potential to seriously disrupt the market are more difficult to quantify, but the degree to which this is true is not universal. All of these variances can make it difficult to calculate the return on investment for initiatives designed to enhance an organization's ability to generate and evaluate ideas.

Just as damaging as missing an opportunity through undervaluing is wasting resources by overvaluing something. In 2001, Nortel wrote off $12.3 billion in goodwill in one disastrous quarter. Its late 1990s acquisition spree, fuelled by the Internet bubble and underpinned by little more than optimistic expectations of continued growth, was not based on fundamental principles of value. Ideas to which large dollar figures were attached were in many cases little more than possible future intangibles, with no development pipeline in place and no surrounding infrastructure to bring them to market. Had the process focused beyond the ideas themselves, the damage would likely not have been as severe.

Find the Right People

The need to more effectively evaluate ideas will only increase with time. Businesses must develop best practices in moving ideas through the pipeline with greater efficiency - because if they don't, it's a virtual certainty that their competitors will. Today's ideas could potentially become tomorrow's value-producing tangible and intangible assets. Knowing which ones will drive long-term value and which ones won't isn't something that happens by chance. It requires the right people, processes, and tools to weed out the underperformers, direct resources to the ones that merit it and develop them to the point where they create differential value. It is far from a random process and it won't move forward without the right person at the helm. The process often plays out as follows:

a. *Identify a champion.* This isn't so much a process of identifying a specific individual as it is understanding the kind of skills required to get an idea through the obstacles that most organizations place in the path of progress. It requires an appreciation of the capabilities needed to quarterback the process and pursue alternatives when the most direct route is not available.
b. *Determine champion's location.* An idea champion may exist within the organization. If the individual is external, the costs of engagement must be factored against the potential returns of any initiatives that result. If the individual is internal, the opportunity costs of not having this resource allocated elsewhere should also be considered.
c. *Sell it.* No one signs on to anything unless there's a glimmer of hope. Although it's too early to calculate detailed, long-term value streams, an idea champion still needs some high-level, mostly plausible numbers to understand potential value and assess the personal risks and opportunities of signing on.
d. *Present the idea.* Schedule a quick meeting to pitch the idea to the individual and determine next steps.

Ideas aren't created in a vacuum, nor are they moved through the pipeline without significant investment of individuals who have a material stake in their eventual success. Engaging these individuals early in the process is critical to separating the stars from the underperformers and to creating a culture that allows the greatest-value ideas to avoid premature death at the hands of an organizational culture and process that is inherently designed to squelch even the most successful ideas long before they can see the light of day.

Create an Appropriate Organizational Context

Organizations increase their chances of having the right people available by creating the kind of environment that encourages the right behaviors. The following elements can help drive staff creativity and create a culture conducive not only to generating ideas in the first place, but to assessing them consistently and moving them through the various stages of evolution to the point where they can add bottom-line value.[2]

1. *Alignment* – to focus employees' interests and activities toward the organization's goals.
2. *Self-initiated activity* – where employees step forward to work on solutions because they have a personal interest in finding the solution.
3. *Unofficial activity* – which occurs without specific organizational support.
4. *Serendipity* – where unexpected discoveries happen by accident.
5. *Diverse stimuli* – sanctioned support that provides fresh insight into a given initiative or helps the employee pursue a different approach.
6. *Within-company communication* – to connect individuals with diverse experience and capabilities to resolve issues and drive progress.

If a company has a huge internal systems infrastructure, the business case for the idea may never fly because of the capital expenditures (CAPEX) required. In many large organizations, ideas are forced to exceed specific hurdle rates or internal rates of return (IRR). The resulting capital requirements make it extremely difficult for smaller innovations to make it past the CAPEX or IRR requirements, meaning many ideas die on the vine simply because they couldn't meet inflexible organizational selection and resourcing criteria.

Build a Culture of Innovation

Organizations that extend their perspective beyond specific breakthrough ideas stand a better chance of building sustainable capabilities than those that don't. While one or two successfully produced and marketed ideas can vault an organization into market leadership, only a consistent pipeline of innovation will keep it there. Even the most successful products have a

---

[2] A.G. Robinson & S. Stern, "Corporate Creativity: How Innovation & Improvement Actually Happen".

limited shelf life, and failure to plan for their evolution and eventual replacement will hamper organizational capability and long-term value creation.

Apple's iPod is an ideal case-in-point. As successful as the iconic media player has been in establishing the parent company's leadership in high-end consumer-focused electronics, the window of opportunity for media players in general is already starting to close as buyers shift their attention toward smartphones and other all-in-one devices. Apple's decision to leverage its earlier investment in the iPod into extended platform devices – the iPhone and the iPod touch – exemplifies the kind of evolved thinking that has kept it at the forefront of mass market demand for over a decade. The firm's internal flexibility in enabling and rewarding innovative design and engineering has become a key differentiator, and one its competitors have thus far had difficulty replicating.

The following questions can help leaders identify the cultural current state within an organization – an important first step in determining what changes may be required to loosen the reins and facilitate improved internal agility:[3]

- What is the organization's current innovation effectiveness?
- What is its risk tolerance profile?
- Can the organization's culture accept ideas from the outside?
- Can its teams effectively assimilate dynamic information and act upon it?

Case Study – Google

It's easy to look at today's world-beating ideas – Google's search algorithms, Research In Motion's BlackBerry, Apple's iPod and iPhone, Toyota's Prius – and examine their evolution and ultimate success through the lens of 20/20 hindsight. Somewhat more difficult is looking ahead from the point where such massive successes take root and separating them out from the countless other ideas that are also taking root around them. Google was not the first Internet search engine and, for much of its early existence, critics doggedly predicted its demise, claiming it couldn't possibly make enough money to interest investors. Perhaps using the lens of the late 1990s, Google would have and should have been a failure. In retrospect, however, things turned out quite nicely for a radical idea to monetize search by leveraging technology to deliver the right form of advertising at the right time to the right individual.

At the same time, Yahoo, which defined the space in the three-year span before Google was founded, was at one time the most highly valued Internet

---

[3] Innovation.net. "Five Key Strategies for Making Open Innovation Work for You".

company in existence. The process by which Yahoo ended up an also-ran and Google an Internet-era powerhouse reinforces the stunning importance of ideas – and the value they contain – in today's information-based economy.

Case Study – BMW[4]

To protect its reputation as the creator of the "Ultimate Driving Machine" and ensure its future products remain not just relevant but groundbreaking in an increasingly competitive global auto market, BMW established a Central Innovation Organization at its headquarters in Munich. The CIO manages six innovation "fields", which are teams of engineers and managers around the world charged with early identification of trends in emerging technologies, industry developments, and regulatory changes.

These teams, dispersed throughout the world to ensure local input from all of BMW's key markets, are accountable for shepherding their discoveries and getting them integrated into future products. The company measures their success by the number of innovations that make it into production. Continuity is encouraged by rotating staff from the remote teams back to Munich.

A Valuation Toolkit

The process by which valuators derive the value of an idea is essential to leaders focused on operational planning and value-creation, as well as to those interested in pursuing an acquisition-based strategy. In all cases, standing still is not an option in an increasingly competitive market economy. By building – or engaging third parties that already possess – competency in this area, organizations improve their potential for understanding the value of an idea and leveraging that knowledge for future growth.

Establishing the Basis

Business valuation is complex enough when dealing with established assets, whether tangible or intangible. Ideas present their own challenges, as there is often little or no basis for applying an income valuation approach in the absence of historic earnings and reliable cash flow forecasts. The AICPA Audit and Accounting Practice Aid, "Valuation of Privately-Held-Company Equity Securities Issued as Compensation," outlines the six stages of enter-

---

4 Above note 1.

prise development. These six stages equally apply to an idea's life cycle, which helps inform the process by which the valuator can begin to calculate and assign value to the idea in question. Those stages are as follows:

1. *No revenue realized*, and financing, if any, is provided by the inventor/founder, family and friends. Usually at this stage, projected cash flows do not exist, are not reliable, or are very speculative. Generally, the value will be speculative too, a function of the likelihood of achieving the required milestones and the likely development costs. Analyzing the first round of financing could shed some light on the fair market value of the idea, especially if it was obtained from financially astute investors. A cost or cost plus valuation approach is often used.
2. *No revenue yet*, but substantial product development costs have been incurred. An indication of value may be obtained if additional funding, such as a second round of financing, was obtained from venture capital firms. Once again, a cost-related valuation approach is often the best indicator of value.
3. *Significant product development milestones have been realized* and, if applicable, alpha and beta testing has been completed. Financial forecasts are typically more reliable but still fairly speculative. If a discounted cash flow approach is used, a high discount rate will likely be warranted. As in stages one and two, valuators should also take into account value indications given by any additional rounds of financing and analyze the cost incurred to date and any value enhancement which might have resulted.
4. *There is a saleable product supported by minimal product revenue*, such as first customer orders. Value indications obtained from analyzing any mezzanine financing and income based approaches will likely be the prime factors driving the fair market value.
5. *Product revenues are being achieved*, together with operating profitability or positive cash flows. The prime value indications will come from a discounted cash flow income approach and, if comparables or semi-comparables exist, the market comparison approach.
6. *Operations have reached a sustainable level.* The prime valuation approaches will be income and market-based.

Of these stages, the first, and to some degree the second, stage best describe the likely valuation scenario applicable when determining what an "idea" is worth in the marketplace. Stages two and three address the combined value of an idea and the related in-process research and development (IPR&D). Assuming the IPR&D was completed in stage three, in stages four through six, one addresses the combined value of the idea and the business opportunity/business.

Traditional Valuation Approaches

When deciding on an appropriate valuation methodology to apply to a business and its ideas, it helps to understand the various approaches available. Valuation approaches are usually classified as market, income, or asset approaches, or a combination thereof, and include the following:

The Asset-based Approach

The asset-based approach uses the current value of a company's net assets as the prime determinant of value. This approach is generally used where a business is not viable as a going concern and is therefore suitable only for liquidation; where a company is properly valued as a going concern but where the going concern value is closely related to the value of its underlying net assets; or where it is used as an aid in establishing fair market value on a going concern basis.

The Income Approach

The income approach to value ascribes value to a company based on its ability to generate future discretionary cash flow and earn a reasonable return on investment after consideration of related risks. Examples of income approaches to value include the capitalized earnings/cash flow and the discounted cash flow methods.

The Market Approach

The empirical or market approach involves estimating the fair market value of a company based on value relationships and/or activity ratios derived or implied from the analysis of other market transactions that can be applied to the company in question. This approach has inherent limitations given the difficulty associated with identifying comparable companies or transactions on which to base value.

In addition, there are many generally accepted valuation methods which fall under the foregoing three approaches. The selection of the appropriate valuation method is a function of the stage of development of the idea or enterprise, and the existence and strength of the information required to perform the valuation. In most cases, valuators use more than one valuation method and, in some cases, combine market, income, and asset approach valuation methods.

Establishing Risks and Measuring Costs

In the context of a larger corporate entity, the value of a specific idea in isolation requires considerable judgment. Without meaningful financial ratios, traditional comparative and risk analyses will not work effectively. As such, it is critical to frame the value question in the proper context at an early stage of development. Much of this framing exercise requires an understanding of the industry within which the idea is expected to compete.

Framing the Value Environment

To a large extent, any value assigned to an "idea" involves a degree of comparative analysis. As mentioned above, this approach has inherent limitations given the unique nature of the asset being valued. However, analyzing the following variables assists in placing the idea in the proper context within the broader targeted market:

1. Market Growth – What is the targeted market's projected future rate of growth? Is the idea expected to penetrate this existing market and take market share or is it an advancement that might succeed in expanding the total market size?
2. Rate of Change – What is the historic rate of change in the market? How long is the expected market cycle and how quickly in the near term must the subject idea establish itself before the opportunity is lost to the next generation of ideas?
3. Legal Restrictions – Are there any rules, regulations, or standards that might slow the progression or development of the idea or impose an additional costs burden at completion?
4. Market Participants – What is the composition of the market? Are innovations typically initiated by established market dominant companies or is the market a collection of new entrants and upstarts where market shifting ideas are the norm?
5. Market Acceptance – How well does the idea fit into existing protocols? If the idea requires significant training for optimal use or is dependent on other products or systems, it materially increases risks.
6. Ownership – How easily is ownership of a new idea patented and secured? An environment where patent protection is challenging and infringement is common may make it difficult to establish value. This is especially the case if the owners of the idea do not have the market presence and legal resources to protect the asset.
7. Acquisitions – Is there an active market in the industry for acquiring and integrating new ideas? This variable matters regardless of whether the idea being valued is held by an established

company or a small entrepreneurial entity. A large company may have limited concerns relating to financing the idea and be well-positioned to meet competitive threats, but an active acquisition environment increases potential staff mobility. As a result, the loss of key idea generating human resources impacts both costs and risks. To the entrepreneurial entity, strategic value to an acquisitive company means potential liquidity if financing or competitive pressures become an issue.

8. Financing – How easily available is early-stage financing in the subject industry? Are there expected financial impediments around securing the necessary investment required for staffing, testing and development, legal costs, *etc.*?
9. Special Interest Buyers – With the globalization of business and the number of players in the global marketplace, it becomes increasingly difficult to determine if there are any special interest buyers who, for their own reasons, would pay a price substantially higher than other financial buyers or industry participants.

Quantifying Sunk Costs

All present value is prospective by definition and relates to future earnings and risks. Past capital investments do not dictate the basis of the asset's current value. Sunk costs are an accounting measurement and represent the condition of a business at a fixed point in time. However, a review of the historic capital invested in a very early stage asset, such as an idea, is an important step in ascertaining the overall project risks and the reliance that the valuator can place on the analysis and business plan surrounding the idea. An idea's historic sunk costs should be viewed in light of the following parameters:

1. Actual vs. Budgeted Costs – Has development stalled or incurred unforeseen costs? The viability of the idea may be indicated in the ability to stay on plan without unforeseen revisions and cost overruns.
2. Staffing Costs – Are there indications of high staff turnover or erratic human resource costs? Ideas with firm market viability typically attract enthusiastic champions and committed teams. Volatility in project staffing costs and personnel may indicate limited viability going forward and an inability to reach the market-ready stage necessary to generate significant cash flows.
3. Committed Parties – How have past costs been financed? Does the idea have the backing of multiple companies or individuals, and who else considers the idea attractive and potentially viable? A greater number of committed parties may increase the risk of

the idea being pre-empted by commercial espionage, although it primarily ensures the idea is less likely to be orphaned due to a lack of funds or strategic oversight.

4. Recouping Expenses – Does the investment have any potential alternative uses? If there are alternative uses for existing development costs or strategic investors can identify potential benefits, the idea will have established a minimum value.

Human Resource Assets

Practice Tip

I invest in people, not ideas.

Arthur Rock
Famed venture capitalist
who backed Intel and Apple Computer

Although it may be difficult to consider the nature of an investment in an "idea", it is often more conceptually friendly to consider an investment in "people". In reality, the two are closely linked. An accurate measurement of committed human resource assets, future budgeted personnel, and the opportunity costs of deploying these resources to development of the idea assists in establishing what returns the idea is expected to generate. Ask these questions:

1. What resources are committed to the idea and are they expanding or declining? Quantifying all personnel costs and the premium for lost opportunities going forward sets a base for the idea's tangible assets AND the level of investment return typical to such assets.
2. How specialized are the people developing the idea and what is their market value? Establishing the market value of the idea's key persons provides an additional basis for value. What would it cost to secure the key personnel in exclusive employment contracts or non-competition agreements? This provides a market-based measurement of a key component of the idea's value to its current owner.

The people responsible for developing the idea ultimately determine its success, and its profitability.

Concluding Notes on Methodology

When quantifying the value of an idea, both a technical understanding of the risks and specific industry experience are required. Given the lack of historic financial performance and the absence of prospective cash flow projections, specific expertise is more critical than when valuing an established tangible or intangible asset.

Of the available approaches to valuing any asset, the idea's current environment – as established by the risks delineated above – should provide some indication into the most suitable methodology. For example, an early-stage asset being developed outside of an established idea pipeline and involving unproven products within a rapidly changing market environment that requires specific support and training prior to implementation, may be most accurately valued based on historic costs and anticipated developmental expenditures going forward. In cases where the idea is being developed by an entity with a history of introducing innovations, able to acquire all necessary experience and marshal adequate human resources, and in possession of abundant financing, an income approach based on a scenario analysis may be possible. The specific risks of the idea and the ability to accurately identify them is central to any such effort. Income measurement tools such as Monte Carlo Simulations and Real Option Valuations often have a high degree of utility. When the certainty required to forecast a single future cash flow and associated risks is remote, these approaches allow for a wide range of scenarios under changing circumstances, better reflecting all developmental hurdles and potential market risks.

Appraisal in Delaware: Recent Cases and Considerations

Richard De Rose

Introduction

Overview

Section 262 of the Delaware General Corporation Law (the "DGCL") sets forth a procedure for the judicial determination of the "fair value" of shares owned by a stockholder of a Delaware corporation who dissents from a transaction contemplated by the statute (*e.g.*, a cash-out merger).

Appraisal cases decided under Section 262 provide valuable insights as to the Delaware judiciary's perspective on issues of valuation methodology. In particular, these cases suggest the approach to valuation that the Delaware courts might apply in other contexts (*e.g.*, the "fair price" component of the "entire fairness" standard).

In the years prior to the 1983 landmark case of *Weinberger v. UOP, Inc.*,[1] ("*Weinberger*"), the "fair value" of a share of stock was measured using the so-called "Delaware Block Method" pursuant to which the Court would (i) determine a company's earnings value, market value, and asset value, (ii) assign a particular weight to each component that varied with the circumstances of the case, and (iii) take the sum of weighted components as the fair value of the stock.

In *Weinberger*, the Delaware Supreme Court held that the Delaware Block Method would no longer control appraisal proceedings. Instead, in the Court's view, a proper valuation approach "must include proof of value by any techniques or methods which are generally considered acceptable in the financial community and otherwise admissible in court ..."

---

[1] 457 A.2d 701 (Del. 1982).

In the 25 years since *Weinberger*, 43 appraisal cases have gone to judgment in Delaware.[2] Of these, only seven cases have resulted in judicial appraisal values at or below the merger price. On average, the appraisal value has exceeded the merger price by a multiple of approximately 3.30x, with a median multiple of 1.55x.

As a consequence of the generally stockholder favorable trend of appraisal decisions, the appraisal process has garnered the attention of hedge funds, who have tried to exploit the remedy to their advantage. Examples of situations where hedge funds were successful in gaining a significant premium to the merger price through appraisal include:

- Greenlight Capital/Emerging Communications Inc. (270 per cent premium over the transaction price).
- Gabelli Asset Management/Carter Wallace (40 per cent premium over the transaction price).
- Prescott Group/The Coleman Company Inc. (455 per cent premium over the transaction price).

Hedge funds have also successfully used the threat of an appraisal proceeding in order to extract increased consideration from a prospective acquiror (*e.g.*, Ramius/Elkcorp; Healthcor Management LP/ICOS Corp.; Lawndale Capital/National Home Health Care Corp.).

In some cases, however, hedge funds seeking appraisal have received less than the merger price. For example, Highfields Capital ("Highfields") dissented from the merger between AXA Financial, Inc. ("AXA") and The MONY Group Inc. ("MONY") and received an appraisal award that reflected an approximate 20 per cent discount).

The following discussion highlights the judicial approach to a variety of valuation issues as exemplified by recent appraisal cases decided by the Delaware Chancery Court (the "Court").

The Continuing Battle of the Experts

The Delaware Supreme Court has characterized the appraisal process as a "battle of experts," who proffer widely divergent valuation opinions in the hope that the Court will "split the baby."[3]

In the past, the Court explored two procedural mechanisms to address the problem of "dueling experts." In *Gonsalves v. Straight Arrow Publishers, Inc.*,[4]

---

2 See Wolfe & Piltenger, "*Corporate and Commercial Practice in the Delaware Court of Chancery*," at §8.10[d].

3 *Rapid-American Corp. v. Harris*, 603 A.2d 796, 802 (Del. 1992).

4 CA 8474, 2002 Del. Ch. LEXIS 105 (Sept. 10, 2002).

the Court indicated that it would decide which expert was the more credible and would accept that expert's valuation in its entirety. A different approach, explored in *Kleinwort Benson Ltd. v. Silgan Corp.*,[5] involved the appointment by the Court of a neutral valuation expert. Ultimately, both approaches were abandoned because they were deemed to have impermissibly shifted the Court's statutory responsibility to conduct the appraisal.

Each party in an appraisal proceeding has the burden of proof to support its valuation by a preponderance of the evidence. The Court has recently observed that:

> This Court may not adopt at the outset an "either-or" approach, thereby accepting uncritically the valuation of one party, as it is the Court's duty to determine the core issue of fair value on the appraisal date. Nevertheless, having considered the parties' legal arguments and the respective experts' reports and testimony supporting their valuation conclusions, the Court has broad discretion either to select one of the parties' valuation models or to fashion its own.[6]

The appraisal cases decided by the Court over the last several years highlight that the Court is sophisticated in its understanding of valuation theory and is confident in its ability to undertake its own valuations. While the judges are somewhat influenced by the litigants' experts, the Court tends to use expert reports and testimony as a point of departure for its own independent assessment.

"Operative Reality"

The Statutory Mandate – Fair Value

Section 262(h) of the DGCL requires the Court to "determine the fair value of the shares [subject to the appraisal], exclusive of any element of value arising from the accomplishment or expectation of the merger ... [taking into account] all relevant factors."

In construing this statutory mandate, the Delaware Supreme Court has stated that:

> [T]he basic concept of value under the appraisal statute is that the stockholder is entitled to be paid for that which has been taken away from him, namely, his proportionate interest in a going concern.[7]

---

5 CA 11107, 1995 Del. Ch. LEXIS 75 (June 15, 1995).

6 *In re: Appraisal of Metromedia International Group, Inc.*, CA 3351 (Del. Ch. 2009).

7 *Tri-Continental Corp. v. Battye*, 74 A.2d 71 (Del. 1950).

The "proportionate interest in a going concern" premise precludes application of any stockholder level discounts in an appraisal proceeding. In this regard, the Delaware Supreme Court has concluded that:

> to fail to accord to a minority shareholder the full proportionate value of his shares imposes a penalty for lack of control, and unfairly enriches the majority shareholders who may reap a windfall from the appraisal process by cashing out a dissenting shareholder, a clearly undesirable result.[8]

Although Section 262 is silent as to the details of how fair value should be determined, the Court has held a company must be valued as a going concern based on its "operative reality" at the effective date of the merger. And while the statute precludes consideration of merger benefits, the Court can consider "elements of future value ... which are known or susceptible of proof as of the effective date and not the product of speculation ..." [*Weinberger*.] Indeed, the Court has said that:

> [A] valuation ... that does not take into consideration the non-speculative possibilities of developing [a] cornfield into something other than a cornfield is not a realistic valuation ... [M]inority shareholders ... are entitled to a valuation that reflects the value of ... a cornfield that can be developed into a major office center.[9]

Operative Reality – Representative Cases

In Re United States Cellular Operating Co., 2005 Del. Ch. LEXIS 1 (Jan. 6, 2005) ("U.S. Cellular")

In valuing two rural cellular phone companies, the petitioner's expert did not consider capital expenditures required to implement emerging cellular technologies because the timing of such implementation was "speculative". The Court held that the conversion to the emerging technologies and the resulting costs were not speculative and were part of the company's "operative reality".

Delaware Open MRI Radiology Assocs., P.A. v. Kessler, 898 A.2d 290 (Del. Ch. 2006) ("Delaware Open MRI")

In this case, minority stockholders were squeezed out of a company formed by a group of radiologists to open MRI scanning centers. The Company operated three centers as of the effective date, but had plans to open future centers.

---

8 *Cavalier Oil Corp. v. Harnett*, 564 A.2d 1137.

9 *Onti Inc. v. Integra Bank*, 751 A.2d 904 (Del. Ch. 1999).

The expert for the majority stockholder group excluded the new centers from his valuation. In criticizing the expert's omission of the new centers, the Court indicated that it was "abundantly clear" that the company's "operative reality" included plans to add additional MRI centers. In supporting its decision to include the new centers in its own valuation, the Court observed that new entities had been formed to own the new centers, leases had been fully negotiated, if not signed, and projections for the three entities had been prepared by a financial advisor to the majority group.

Cede & Co. v. MedPointe Healthcare, Inc., CA 19354-NC, 2004 Del. Ch. LEXIS 124 (Aug. 16, 2004) ("Medpointe")

In 2000, Carter-Wallace Inc. ("CW") sold itself in a two-step process. In the first transaction, CW sold the assets of its consumer product division to two private equity firms. Subsequently, CW merged its remaining healthcare division into MedPointe. In the time between the asset sale and the merger, CW stock lost $6.00 per share in value due to taxes on, and costs related to, the initial asset sale.

The petitioner argued that such taxes and expenses should not be deducted from the value of the remaining business because the sale and the merger were connected. The Court, however, disagreed, indicating that the asset sale was an "operating reality" of CW and that the Court's mandate was to value the remaining company that was merged into Medpointe.

Ng v. Heng Sang Realty Corp., CA 18462, 2004 Del. Ch. LEXIS 69 (Apr. 22, 2004), aff'd 2005 Del. LEXIS 45 (Jan. 27, 2005).

Two of the three stockholders of Heng Sang Realty wanted to convert the company from a Subchapter "C" corporation to a Subchapter "S" corporation for federal tax purposes. The third stockholder opposed the conversion and was squeezed-out of the company through a cash merger.

The expert for the dissenting stockholder urged the Court to value the company – more favorably – as an S Corp. However, because the petitioners' veto had prevented pre-merger conversion to S Corp. status, such status was held not to be part of the company's "operative reality" at the effective date of the merger. Any gain attributable to S Corp. status arose by virtue of the merger and should therefore be excluded from fair value.

Market Indicia of Value

Overview

Despite the statutory command to consider "all relevant factors," the Court has historically accorded a relatively limited role to third-party sale value in the appraisal process. Part of the reason for this was a judicial concern that adverting to third-party sales would violate the statutory exclusion of "value arising from the accomplishment or expectation of the merger." A second, and more practical approach, was that the transaction price would become a floor on fair value, thereby encouraging appraisal proceedings.

Recent cases reflect judicial acceptance of third-party sale and other market indicia of value. The cases appear to suggest that when a company is sold after a widespread sales effort and a full and fair auction, it will be difficult to achieve a higher price in a Delaware appraisal proceeding on the basis of theoretical valuation techniques. The cases also make it clear that by adjusting for the synergies inherent in a transaction, the Court is able, at once, to eschew its concerns regarding the statutory exclusion of value arising from the accomplishment of the transaction and the practical concern about setting a floor price. Indeed, the cases demonstrate that, after adjustment for synergies, a petitioner may receive an appraised value that is materially less than the transaction price.

The Court's acceptance of market indicia of value is dampened when there is a basis for impugning the effectiveness of the process (*e.g.*, presence of controlling shareholder or inadequate information provided), and a petitioner's chances for success are much improved.

Market Indicia – Representative Cases

Union Illinois 1995 Investment Lt. P'ship v. Union Financial Group, Ltd., 847 A.2d 340 (Del. Ch. 2004) ("Union Financial")

Union Financial ("UF"), a distressed bank holding company, was "shopped" by its investment banker to 36 parties. After several rounds of bidding by three potential acquirors, UF agreed to merge with First Bank. Dissenting stockholders sought appraisal.

As a threshold matter, the Court determined it had discretion to consider the price paid for UF in the merger. The Court took note of the fact that UF had been effectively marketed, with an "active auction following the provision of full information to an array of logical bidders." The process undertaken by UF was distinguished from a squeeze-out merger in which the parent company is the only available buyer.

In light of the robust auction process and the full disclosure of information to prospective buyers, the Court disregarded valuations prepared by both parties and, found that the fair value of a UF share was equal to the merger price less the value of synergies (as estimated in connection with the transaction by UF's investment banker).

Highfields Capital Ltd. v. AXA Fin., Inc., CA 804-VCL (2007), 939 A.2d 34 ("Highfields")

In September 2003, AXA agreed to acquire MONY for $31 per share in cash. Highfields - a large hedge fund - attempted to block the transaction and, ultimately, filed for appraisal claiming that the fair value of MONY was between $37 and $47 per share.

Taking its lead from *Union Financial*, AXA argued that merger price less synergies was the best indicator of going-concern value. AXA argued that there had been an arm's length negotiation between the parties and that there had been a lack of material impediments to a topping bid during the five-month period that the transaction was subject to regulatory approval.

The Court agreed with AXA and used the price paid in the transaction as the primary indicator of value. The Court noted that, with eight months between announcement and stockholder vote, "the only logical explanation for why no bidder ever emerged was that MONY was not worth more than $31 per share." After backing out the value of synergies embedded in AXA's $31 price, petitioners were awarded $24.97.

Market Indicia Deemed Inadequate – Representative Cases

Gholl v. eMachines, Inc., CA 19444-NC, 2004 Del. Ch. LEXIS 171 (Nov. 24, 2004), aff'd 2005 Del. LEXIS 200 (June 14, 2005) ("Emachines")

A financially distressed distributor of foreign-made computers sought indications of interest from 55 prospective purchasers. Of the parties contacted, only one party submitted a bid, which bid was rejected as inadequate and was not publicly disclosed.

Following a change in management, the company began a significant turnaround in its operations and financial performance. During the course of the turnaround, a member of the company's board of directors submitted an offer to acquire the company at a price lower than the bid received in the auction and rejected by the board.

The new bid was publicly disclosed and two prior bidders were re-contacted. The bidder whose original bid had been rejected submitted a new bid at a price higher that exceeded the bid by the director of eMachines. Without a second round of bidding, a slightly increased offer from the director was accepted.

In a subsequent appraisal proceeding, the respondents urged the Court to consider various market indicators of value. Such indicia included the fact that the merger price represented a 96 per cent premium over the pre-merger trading price of eMachine stock and that certain sophisticated stockholders had accepted the merger price. The respondents also claimed that a "thorough and fair auction" had taken place.

The Court rejected the respondents' approach, finding the market indicia to be inadequate. The Court found that the "auction" after the director's bid did not include all potential bidders and was conducted hastily without successive rounds of bidding. Moreover, no evidence was presented that the outside bidder had the same level of information regarding the company's turnaround as the bidding director. Lastly, the Court noted that the sophisticated investors who had accepted the merger price were, in fact, former strategic partners of eMachines, both of whom were anxious for a liquidity event.

Crescent/Mach 1 P'ship, L.P. v. Turner, CA 17455-VCN, 17711-VCN ("Crescent/Mach 1")

A sale of Dr. Pepper Bottling Holding was initiated by its controlling stockholder as a result of such stockholder's concerns about competitive challenges posed by Pepsi and Coke.

From the outset, the company faced a difficult situation. Although they were the most likely buyers, Coke and Pepsi were precluded from owning Dr. Pepper Bottling due to potential antitrust issues. On the other hand, Cadbury Schweppes, a key Dr. Pepper Bottling franchisor, "made it clear ... that it would not likely consent to a private equity transaction." Despite its threatened refusal to consent to a private equity transaction, a partnership of Cadbury and a private equity firm (Carlyle Group) acquired the company for $25 per share.

In a subsequent appraisal proceeding, the Court was unwilling to rely on the transaction price as the best indication of value. Noting the limited universe of potential buyers, the Court observed that "[the CEO] obtained the best price that he could from Cadbury/Carlyle, but how often will the only buyer pay full price?"

Discounted Cash Flow Analyses

Overview

Since *Weinberger*, the discounted cash flow methodology ("DCF") has become the theoretical approach to valuation most relied on by the Court. The Court has recently stated that "although it is appropriate to consider all accepted methodologies, the Court tends to favor the [DCF] method." [*Crescent/Mach 1*]. Moreover, the Court is willing to rely exclusively on a DCF; especially where the company has a long and stable financial history, making the projections for a cash flow analysis reasonable. [See *JR Cigar* and *Andaloro*.]

The fundamental premise underlying DCF is that the value of a company is equal to the present value of its projected future cash flows. A DCF analysis is comprised of three basic components. The first is a set of cash flow projections (typically, over a five-year period). The second component is a terminal value which represents the future value, as of the end of the projection period, of the company's cash flows beyond the projection period. The last component of a DCF is a discount rate by which the projected cash flows and the terminal value are discounted to a present value.

Each of the basic components of a DCF is subject to a host of variables and the Court has observed that within the basic DCF structure:

> ... the details of the analysis may be quite different. That is, not only will assumptions about the future differ, but different methods may be used within the model to generate inputs.[10]

Projections

The starting point in any DCF is an estimate of free cash flow over a specified forecast period. The Court has consistently stressed its strong preference for contemporaneous management projections created in the ordinary course of business. In the Court's view, a company's management is the most knowledgeable party regarding the company's future prospects. The Court finds such projections especially credible when they have been provided to third party business counterparties, such as a lending institution. The Court has generally expressed "healthy skepticism" for post-merger adjustments to management projections, or the creation of new projections.

Experts who ignore management projections risk having their entire analysis disregarded by the Court. Similarly, an expert's "professional opinion" as

---

[10] See *Cede & Co. v. Technicolor, Inc.* (Del. Ch. 1990).

to why an assumption or input should differ from those underlying management projections is likely to carry little weight. However, the Court will recognize when specific factors are present that may render a set of projections unreliable for a DCF analysis. Such factors might include, among other things:

- an erratic earnings history;
- recent performance that is inconsistent with the projections;
- a history of failing to achieve stated projection targets; or
- after-the-fact management disavowal of the projections.

Where contemporaneous management prepared projections are unavailable, experts must use extreme caution in crafting their own projections for the purpose of conducting a DCF analysis. Any such projections need to have the underpinning of substantial evidential support from authoritative and disinterested industry experts and/or other objective data sources (*e.g.*, governmental agencies).

Management Projections Available – Representative Cases

Union Financial

The petitioner's expert significantly deviated from management projections regarding growth and profitability of UF. The expert's revisions, which were not discussed with UF management, resulted in returns 80 per cent higher than management's expectations. The Court disregarded the entire analysis, finding the expert's departure from management projections "untenable".

In Re Emerging Communications Inc. Shareholders Litig., CA 16415, 2004 Del. Ch. LEXIS 70 (May 3, 2004) ("Emerging Communications")

In response to a proposal by the controlling stockholder of Emerging Communications, Inc. ("ECM") to take ECM private, a special committee of independent directors was formed. In connection with its deliberations, the special committee received projections for ECM that were developed in March 1998. Significantly, the special committee and its financial advisor were not provided with an updated set of projections that had been prepared in June 1998 for ECM's lender and that forecasted substantially higher cash flows.

The petitioner relied on the June 1998 projections without adjustment. In contrast, ECM's expert used the March projections, adjusted by the expert to increase working capital and capital expenditures (resulting in negative cash flow).

The Court found that the unmodified June projections were the appropriate basis for a DCF because they reflected ECM's then latest performance and were contemporaneously provided to third-party financing sources.

Prescott Group Small Cap. L.P. v. Coleman Co., 2004 Del. Ch. LEXIS 131 (Sept. 8, 2004) ("Coleman")

Sunbeam bought 79 per cent of the Coleman Company ("Coleman") from MacAndrews & Forbes in March 1998 for $32 in cash and stock. A contemplated squeeze-out merger of the remaining 21 per cent of Coleman was delayed for 22 months and was ultimately consummated at a price of only $9.31.

In a subsequent appraisal proceeding, Sunbeam's expert used projections for Coleman that were materially lower than those furnished to Sunbeam's lenders at the time of the merger and used lower EBITDA margins than those in Sunbeam's projections at that time. The Court was critical of the adjustments and rejected the Sunbeam expert's valuation in full.

Management Projections Unavailable – Representative Cases

Dobler v. Montgomery Cellular Holding Co., CA 19211, 2004 Del. Ch. LEXIS 139 (Sept. 30, 2004) ("Montgomery Cellular")

Although "after-the-fact, litigation-driven, forecasts" have an "untenably high probability of hindsight bias and other cognitive distortions," absent other reasonable analyses, the Court will countenance reliance on *de novo* projections.

In the absence of contemporaneous management projections for Montgomery Cellular ("MC"), both experts prepared their own projections. The petitioners expert prepared his projections in reliance on historical MC financial statements, data from an acknowledged industry expert source, and a valuation prepared by a third-party expert on behalf of a potential acquiror of MC. The Court approved of this approach and gave it a 30 per cent weighting in its overall valuation.

By contrast, MC's expert fashioned his own forecasts without outside input. The Court was highly critical of the fact that the expert did not rely on historical company trends or industry-based sources of information, and completely disregarded the analysis. In particular, the expert used a constant rate of growth beginning in year one. The Court highlighted that this approach caused the analysis to be "... nothing more than an extension of year one's financial results."

Delaware Open MRI

In valuing as yet unopened MRI centers for which there were no projections, the petitioner's witness created his own projections, utilizing management's projections for existing centers as a starting point for his analysis. The Court found the approach to be "reasonable and conservative".

In contrast, the respondent's witness claimed that it was impossible to value businesses that were not yet open using a DCF. The Court was highly critical of this contention, noting:

> That position would come as a revelation to finance professors, owners of franchisable retail establishments, and business persons of all kinds. Put simply, this did not instill confidence in me and seemed to be a posture designed simply to advance the [Respondent's] interest in not according the [petitioner's] any share of the value of [the new centers.]

Terminal Value

The second step in a DCF analysis is to determine a terminal value, which represents the present value of future free cash flows beginning at the end of the projection period. The terminal value, which can represent a significant portion of the value derived in a DCF, is generally calculated by one of two acceptable methodologies. The perpetuity growth rate methodology applies a constant growth rate after the forecast period into perpetuity. The second methodology applies a so-called "exit multiple" to the terminal year's earnings levels, often before interest, tax, and depreciation and amortization ("EBITDA"). The exit multiple is typically derived from multiples observed in comparable companies or transactions involving comparable companies.

Although both approaches have been approved by the Court (see *JRC Acquisition*, *Andaloro*, and *Crescent/Mach 1*), there is a judicial preference for the perpetuity growth rate methodology. In either case, however, the exit multiple or growth rate, as the case may be, should reflect long-term growth expectations for the company beyond the projection period and should be applied to a normalized level of EBITDA or cash flow, respectively. Adjustments may be necessary to terminal year depreciation, capital expenditures, and working capital changes. The Court has often rejected DCFs where the choice of terminal value was not adequately defended or where a substantial portion of the overall value depended on the terminal value.

When using an exit multiple approach, it is important to ensure that the comparable companies or transactions being used are, in fact, comparable. In particular, in several cases the Court observed that, when using an exit multiple based on comparable transactions, it is necessary, albeit difficult, to "back out" any implicit value attributable to merger synergies. [See *Highfields*, *Montgomery Cellular*, and *Andaloro*.]

Terminal Value – Representative Cases

Union Financial

The court severely criticized the petitioner's DCF because 97 per cent of the value was derived from the terminal value.

eMachines

The petitioner's exit multiple implied a 14 per cent perpetuity growth rate and the resulting terminal value constituted 70 per cent of the total value estimated by the DCF. The Court noted that such a large terminal value "raises a red flag in the Court's mind and suggests that the exit multiple approach is not appropriate in this case." The Court calculated and used a terminal value based on a perpetuity growth rate that reflected the average growth rate in management's projections.

Cede & Co. v. JRC Acquisition Corp., CA 19648-NC, 2004 Del. Ch. LEXIS 12 (Feb. 10, 2004) ("JRC Acquisition")

The fact that the terminal value represented half the company's overall DCF value did not impugn the analysis.

In Re PNB Holding Co. Shareholders Litig., 2006 Del. Ch. LEXIS 158 (Aug. 18, 2006) ("PNB Holding")

The respondent's witness derived an exit multiple based on an analysis of purportedly comparable companies. The Court found the companies in the analysis to be of "dubious" comparability. The Court also indicated that the use of an exit multiple to determine a terminal value raises questions about whether a minority discount is implicit in the exit multiple chosen. Instead, the Court approved of the petitioner's use of a 5 per cent perpetuity growth rate.

MedPointe

The Court rejected an exit multiple approach because the proponent's report concerning the comparable companies was not sufficiently developed to determine the growth inherent in the research pipelines of those companies. The Court reverted to a perpetuity growth rate.

Coleman

Where the use of an exit multiple resulted in the terminal value constituting 75 per cent of the company's DCF value, the Court rejected the analysis as being a "comparable companies analysis packaged in a different form."

Weighted Average Cost of Capital

The next step in a DCF analysis is to calculate a discount rate which will determine the present value of (i) the free cash flows during the projection period and (ii) the terminal value. Typically, the discount rate is based on the weighted average of the company's cost of capital (including debt, common equity, and preferred equity, preferably weighted by the relative market value of each (the "WACC").

A company's WACC is calculated as follows:

$$WACC = K_E\,(E/V) + K_D\,(1\text{-}T)\,(D/V) + K_P\,(P/V)$$

Where:

K_E	=	cost of common equity capital
E/V	=	ratio of market value of common equity to total invested capital
K_D	=	cost of debt
D/V	=	ratio of value of outstanding debt to total invested capital
T	=	corporate tax rate
K_P	=	cost of preferred equity capital
P/V	=	ratio of market value of preferred equity to total invested capital
V	=	market value of debt plus market value of preferred equity plus market value of common equity

Determining the appropriate discount rate is usually one of the most contentious issues in an appraisal proceeding. The Court has characterized the situation as follows:

> Once the experts' techniques for coming up with their discount rates are closely analyzed, the Court finds itself in an intellectual position more religious than empirical in nature, insofar as the Court's decision to prefer one position over the other is more a matter of faith than reason. [See *Delaware Open MRI.*]

Cost of Equity – Capital Asset Pricing Model

A company's cost of equity is most often determined through the application of the capital asset pricing model ("CAPM"), which employs three inputs:

- a risk-free rate of return (based on a long-term U.S. treasury instrument);
- an equity risk premium (derived from standard sources such as Ibbotson (now owned by Morningstar)); and
- beta (the measure of a stock's volatility as compared with the stock market as a whole).

The CAPM formula is as follows:

$$E(R) = R_f + \beta * (R_m - R_f)$$

Where:

E(R) is the expected return

R_f is the risk-free rate of return (typically, 20-year U.S. treasury bond)

β is Beta

R_m is the return on the market

$(R_m - R_f)$ is the equity risk premium, or the return of the market in excess of the risk-free rate

The Court has generally approved the CAPM for estimating a company's cost of equity. However, in recent cases, the Court has taken note of the academic literature which suggests that the CAPM estimated cost of equity is not always validated by actual market returns. Accordingly, the Court has begun to sanction the use of multi-factor models, such as the Fama-French Model (which includes size and book-value-to-market-value ratios as factors) ("FFM"), for determining the cost of equity.

Cost of Equity – CAPM – Representative Cases

Union Financial

In calculating the cost of equity for a troubled bank, Vice Chancellor Strine used the FFM, noting:

> ... that formula ... attempts to better account for certain factors that explain equity return than does the original CAPM. These factors include the relationship of market returns to underlying book value, which ... helps capture the risk associated with possible insolvency and other problems in highly leveraged firms.

Medpointe

The petitioner's expert based his 4.5 per cent market risk premium on the more recent market data underlying the FFM, while the respondent's expert based his 7.3 per cent market risk premium on the Ibbotson data. The respondent's expert criticized the FFM as being subject to academic debate.

The Court held that the mere fact that the FFM was new did not render it unacceptable. Citing *Union Financial*, the Court observed that the FFM captures useful data that contributes to a more real world cost of capital.

PNB Holding

In determining the fair value of stock in a bank holding company, the Court computed the cost of equity giving equal weight to the result of CAPM and FFM.

Cost of Equity – Equity Risk Premium

The equity risk premium ("ERP") is the amount of "extra return" that investors demand in order to invest in equity securities rather than riskless U.S. treasury securities.

Although it is a forward-looking concept that is used to develop an estimate of the expected return of a risky security over time, the general practice has been to estimate ERP based on historical returns (most often, from 1926 to the present, as compiled by Ibbotson). The Court has explicitly approved of the use of the historical Ibbotson data in cases such as *Delaware Open MRI* and *MedPointe*.

Some academics, however, have argued that the size of the equity risk premium has decreased over time and that a time frame shorter than 1926 to the present should be used. The Court has taken notice of the academic literature and, based on an academic study, appeared sympathetic, in *PNB Holdings*, to the use of a lower equity risk premium (5.75 per cent) than the premium of 7 per cent implied by Ibbotson data.

Cost of Equity – Beta

Beta is the component of CAPM which represents the systematic (non-diversifiable) risk of a security versus the systematic risk of the market as a whole. Generally, if beta value of a security is 1.0, the systematic risk of that security is equivalent to the beta of the market as a whole. A beta of less than 1.0 indicates that the security carries less risk than the market and a beta in excess of 1.0 suggests greater risk.

Published several sources of information regarding betas include:

- Morningstar

- CapitalIQ
- Bloomberg
- Value Line

Each of these sources calculates beta somewhat differently in terms of, among other things, (i) length of time for observation of returns and (ii) the frequency of return measures.

Time Period

Betas are often calculated using pricing data over a two- or five-year period. The Court has shown itself to be sensitive to the impact that differences in the period of observation can have. Accordingly, in choosing a time period, it is important to consider the events that have affected the company being valued during that time interval.

Andaloro v. PFPC Worldwide, Inc., 2005 Del. Ch. LEXIS 125 (Aug. 19, 2005) ("Andaloro")

The petitioners' expert measured beta for a financial institution over five years, whereas the respondent's witness used two-year data. Noting that "both methods find support in the literature as responsible methods, the Court observed that:

> The longer five-year period might be thought to provide an estimate that includes price movements in both bull and bear markets and that smoothes out any short-term anomalies.
>
> The two-year period might be thought to provide information that is more current and that provides a better insight into the current beta, especially where some seismic market or industry shift is thought to have occurred.

Frequency

The frequency of observation can significantly impact a security's beta. Typically frequency rates include daily, weekly, and monthly intervals. Although the Court has not expressed a preference for one frequency period over another, considerations similar to those relevant to time period should apply. Thus, in a volatile industry, like technology, a shorter period with daily betas may be more appropriate.

"Raw" versus "Adjusted" Beta

Certain published sources of beta information make adjustments to a company's historical "raw" beta. Such adjustments are predicated on academic studies which suggest that, over time, a company's beta will tend towards the average beta of its industry group. For example, Bloomberg produces an "adjusted" beta which assumes that betas regress toward 1.0 over time.

In *JRC Acquisition*, the Court indicated that "betas based on observed historical data are more representative of future expectations when they are adjusted."

Leverage

In determining a company's beta, an adjustment for leverage is necessary to remove the impact that differences in capital structure have on betas and allow for the re-levering of the beta for the capital structure of the company being valued.

Betas can be adjusted for leverage by de-leveraging the betas of the comparable companies by using their respective capital structures to produced un-levered betas. The selected un-levered beta from the comparable company universe is then re-levered using a capital structure that is assumed for the company. The capital structure assumption used to re-lever beta should be the same as used to determine the WACC.

PNB Holding

The petitioner's expert determined an un-levered beta of 0.5 by multiplying the peer group beta of 0.69 by 65 per cent, based on his belief that debt-free bank holding companies tended to have betas 35 per cent lower than the peer group's levered beta.

Although the Court rejected the analysis because no support was provided for the 35 per cent discount; the Court was not critical of the concept of de-levering the peer group beta.

Cost of Equity – Adjustments

Proponents of CAPM argue that only systematic risk, as measured by beta, is relevant to the cost of capital, and that company specific risks should be addressed by appropriate revisions to the cash flow estimates. In contrast, expert witnesses will often adjust the cost of equity to reflect company-specific risk factors.

The Court has declared that it is "understandably ... suspicious of expert valuations offered at trial that incorporate subjective measures of company-specific risk premium, as subjective measures may easily be employed as a means to smuggle improper risk assumptions into the discount rate so as to affect dramatically the expert's ultimate opinion on value." The cases demonstrate that the Court will not apply a company-specific premium without (i) a basis firmly grounded in valuation theory and (ii) fact-based evidence produced at trial.

Cost of Equity – Adjustments – Representative Cases

Emerging Communications

One adjustment to a cost of equity calculation that has received judicial acceptance is the so-called "small company premium". The application of such a premium is predicated on academic studies that have demonstrated that CAPM generally underestimates the required equity return of small companies.

In *Emerging Communications*, the Court affirmed that "[o]ur case law recognizes the propriety of a small firm/small stock premium in appropriate cases."

The respondent's expert added premiums totaling 4.1 per cent, to his calculated cost of equity. Such premiums included:

- a small company stock premium of 1.7 per cent;
- a super-small company stock premium of 1.0–1.5 per cent; and
- a "hurricane risk" premium of 0.9–1.4 per cent (EC operated in the Caribbean and had experienced hurricane losses).

After assessing the evidence proffered to support the suggested premiums, the Court (i) accepted the small company stock premium based on Ibbotson data, (ii) rejected the super-small company premium because no evidence was presented to support the thesis that the risk profile of ECM (a regulated telco) was akin to a micro-cap company and (iii) rejected the hurricane risk premium owing to the absence of theoretical or evidentiary support.

JRC Acquisition

The petitioner's expert used a small cap premium of 1.1 per cent because the JRC stock price was depressed due to its illiquidity. In contrast, the respondent's expert used a 2.6 per cent (micro-cap) premium based on the market capitalization of JRC prior to announcement of the squeeze-out transaction.

The Court rejected the petitioner's position, noting that even if JRC's price was affected by its illiquidity, the "petitioner cannot justify categorizing JRC as a low-cap, rather than micro-cap company (for purposes of CAPM) based on that fact." The Court also rejected the petitioner's attempt to categorize JRC as low-cap based on the fact that its beta was lower than other companies in the micro-cap category. The Court observed that size premium is not dependent on beta, and it is precisely because beta does not capture all the systematic risk that a size premium is added.

Gesoff v. IIC Industries, Inc., 902 A.2d 1130 (Del. Ch. 2006)

The Court rejected the application of a small size premium to the subject company's African subsidiary. The Court determined that any risks associated with operating a business in Africa were captured by the very high country-specific risk premium which was applicable.

Cost of Debt

The cost of debt in a WACC calculation should generally be based on the Company's actual cost of debt. The current cost of borrowing for each tranche of a company's debt (*i.e.*, revolver, senior term, subordinated) should be used to determine a weighted average cost of debt.

eMachines

Without credible support, the petitioner's witness used a 7 per cent cost of debt, whereas the respondent's witness based his 8 per cent cost of debt on an actual financing that took place before the merger in question.

The Court accepted the respondent's cost of debt, but tax-effected it (notwithstanding the fact that eMachines had large tax-loss carry-forwards). The Court noted that the "deductions for interest would allow the company to save its NOLs for subsequent years."

Emerging Communications

As a regulated telephone company, ECM historically had access to debt financing from the Rural Telephone Finance Cooperative (the "RTFC") at below-market rates. Accordingly, the plaintiff's expert used ECM's historical 6.3 per cent average cost of long-term debt.

In contrast, the respondent's expert assigned ECM an 8 per cent cost of long-term debt, based on his judgment that ECM would not be able to borrow indefinitely from the RTFC at below market rates. The Court rejected the respondent's position, highlighting that nothing in the record suggested, as of the merger date, that ECM would not be able to continue to borrow from the RTFC at below market rates.

U.S. Cellular

The petitioner's expert used U.S. Cellular's cost of debt to calculate the cost of debt of its subsidiary, U.S. Cellular Operating Company ("USCOC"). The record indicated that USCOC historically borrowed from its corporate parent at a rate of prime plus 1.0 per cent. The Court concluded that USCOC's actual cost of borrowing from U.S. Cellular was the appropriate cost of debt.

Capital Structure

Once the cost of debt and cost of equity have been calculated, a weighted average is computed, based on the Company's actual capital structure or a "target" capital structure. Valuation practitioners often use a target capital structure based on industry comparables for valuations of a controlling interest and the company's existing capital structure for valuation of minority interests. The Court, however, appears to favor the use of a company's actual capital structure.

Use of the existing capital structure should be supported by evidence as to why management plans to maintain the existing capital structure and the appropriateness of such plans (if different from industry norms).

On occasion, the Court has sanctioned the use of a target capital structure. However, the use of such a capital structure must be backed up by evidence such as the actual stated goals of management to seek a different capitalization structure over time, or evidence that a current debt level cannot be maintained over the long run, *etc.*

Capital Structure – Representative Cases

JRC Acquisition

The petitioner argued for a 25 per cent debt level based on, among other things:

- similar
- debt levels for comparable companies;
- the need for additional capital for expansion;
- the fact that JRC borrowed $55 million to complete the going-private transaction.

The respondent argued that a 10 per cent debt level was appropriate because JRC had no debt before the transaction and did not anticipate any large capital expenditures.

The Court accepted the 10 per cent rate, finding that (i) the comparable companies relied on by the petitioner were manufacturers rather than distributors like JRC, (ii) JRC had sufficient cash on hand to fund future expansion, and (iii) inclusion of the merger debt violated the statutory command to appraise shares "exclusive of any element of value arising from the accomplishment or expectation of the merger."

The Court dismissed the notion that JRC's debt-to-equity ratio should mimic the overall industry's debt-to-equity ratio, stating that "an appraisal proceeding does not attempt to determine the potential maximum value of the company" and that the goal is to "value [JRC], not some theoretical company."

Emerging Communications

The respondent's witness used a 30 per cent debt-to-equity ratio based on the assumption that the company's management would be able to reduce the existing amount of debt in the capital structure.

The Court was troubled by the use of a "target" debt-to-equity ratio that assumed that ECM would pay down 50 per cent of its debt in the future – an assumption that had no support in the record. Instead, the Court used the debt-to-equity ratio contemplated by the financing arranged to complete the going-private transaction.

MedPointe

The petitioner's expert used an 80 per cent equity/20 per cent debt capital structure, despite the fact that CW had always operated with a very low level of debt. The expert argued that the structure was realistic because CW's healthcare division had never operated as a stand-alone business. In contrast, the respondent's expert assumed an all equity structure because it was more consistent with CW's historical structure, which was all equity.

The Court accepted the respondent's analysis noting that "it must be assumed that [the company's historically all equity capital structure] would have continued into the future had the entity continued as a going concern.

Andaloro

In an appraisal relating to the squeeze-out of stockholders of a subsidiary ("PFPC") of a large bank, the petitioner's witness argued that PFPC's parent would continue to roll over $1.2 billion of inter-company debt (which was otherwise due in three years) in perpetuity at a favorable rate.

The Court sided with the respondent's witness who used an all equity target capital structure for PFPC because PFPC's projections showed that its goal was to become relatively debt-free.

PNB Holding

The petitioners dissented from a squeeze-out merger of a bank by its holding company parent ("PNB"). Because PNB was then in excess of its required capital levels, the petitioner's witness built in a one-time special dividend into his DCF. His model showed that, after payment of the special dividend, PNB would remain well-capitalized.

The Court accepted the premise that going forward PNB would maintain a target capital ratio that would allow it to distribute as much cash as would allow it to remain well-capitalized.

Henke v. Trilithic, Inc., 2005 Del. Ch. LEXIS 170 (Oct. 18, 2005), modified, 2005 Del. Ch. LEXIS 204 (Dec. 20, 2005) ("Trilithic")

The Court permitted an assumed capital structure of 100 per cent equity in light of the company's inability to obtain alternative debt financing and an existing breach with respect to outstanding debt.

Comparable Company Analyses

Overview

Notwithstanding the Court's expressed preference for valuations based on DCFs, the Court has been willing to accept comparable company analyses as a valuation methodology. This approach "involves reviewing publicly traded competitors or participants in the same market or industry, generating relevant multiples from public pricing data of the comparable companies and applying those multiples to [the company being valued] in order to arrive at a value."[11]

---

11 *Taylor v. American Specialty Retailing Group, Inc.*, 2003 WL 21753252 (Del. Ch. 2003).

The utility of the comparable company methodology is directly dependent on degree of similarity between the company being valued and the comparable companies being used for comparison. In this regard, the proposing party carries the burden of proving that the comparable companies are truly comparable.

Criteria for determining comparability may include, among other things:

- capital structure;
- earnings
- growth prospects;
- markets
- maturity of business;
- products;
- risk;
- size of business.

Once a universe of comparable companies is identified, financial metrics are calculated for the comps that can be used to value the company (adjusting for non-recurring items). The most common of such metrics are revenue, earnings before interest and taxes ("EBIT") and earnings before interest, taxes, depreciation, and amortization ("EBITDA") and earnings per share ("EPS"). An enterprise value ("EV") is then calculated for each of the comparable companies based on their respective equity market value plus the market value of their debt less the cash on the balance sheet. The EV of each comp is then divided by the chosen financial metric to derive a ratio that indicates each company's value as a multiple of the financial metric.

Based on a comparison of the subject company's financial performance, profitability, leverage, and business trends relative to the comparable companies, a range of multiples for the subject company is chosen from the range derived from the comparable companies. The company's financial metric is then capitalized using the range of multiples to determine the company's EV.

Interestingly, the Court believes that a comparable company analysis includes a built-in minority discount because individual shares of publicly traded stocks represent minority positions. Accordingly, the Court routinely permits the addition of a premium (of up to 30 per cent) to compensate for the minority discount. The Court's approach in this regard seems inconsistent with its treatment of the exit multiple approach to determine terminal value where no premium is allowed.

Representative Cases

Doft v. Travelocity.Com, Inc., CA 19734, 2004 Del. Ch. LEXIS 75 (May 20, 2004), on reargument, 2004 Del. Ch. LEXIS 84 (June 10, 2004)

The petitioners dissented from a transaction in which the corporate parent of Travelocity.com acquired the minority interest. A special committee was formed and Salomon Brothers was retained by the committee as its financial advisor. Given that the on-line travel industry was in its infancy at the time, no reliable projections were available for the company. Consequently, Salomon Brothers used a single comparable company, Expedia.com, in connection with its fairness opinion analysis.

In the subsequent appraisal proceeding, the Court concluded the only reliable metric for valuation was the sole comparable company, namely, Expedia.com. However, the opposing experts disagreed as to the appropriate discounts to be applied to Expedia.com's multiple. The respondent's expert argued for a 40 per cent discount, while the petitioner's witness argued for 10 per cent discount. Salomon Brothers had used a range of 20–30 per cent in its analysis.

In its analysis, the Court noted Travelocity.com's higher cost of capital, lower growth rate, lesser cash flow, and less attractive business model and, accordingly, applied a 35 per cent discount to Expedia.com's EBITDA multiple (2/3 weighting) and EPS multiple (1/3 weighting).

On its own initiative, the Court also noted that Delaware law recognizes the minority discount inherent in a comparable company analysis and the need to correct for this through the addition of a premium. In this regard, Salomon Brothers had used a 50 per cent premium based on a survey of a large number of transactions. The Court felt that the study included too many non-comparable transactions and instead pointed to other recent Delaware appraisal cases and used a 30 per cent premium.

eMachines

The petitioners used Gateway as their only comparable company, taking a 25 per cent discount to reflect differences between the two companies. In rejecting the analysis, the Court noted that Gateway had a different business model (manufacturing vs. outsourcing), was a well-known brand, had a broad product offering and was 12x larger in revenue.

Andaloro

The respondent's comparable company analysis applied EBITDA multiples using estimated 2004 results derived from analysts' reports. The Court approved of the approach and approved of using the median multiples, rejecting the argument that the subject company was a superior company.

PNB Holding

The Court rejected both experts' comparable company analyses because they were not "backed up by sufficiently reliable testimonial and record evidence." At trial, the experts evidenced little familiarity with the actual details of their comps. Both experts' comps were considerably larger than, and were geographically distant from, PNB.

Comparable Transaction Analyses

Overview

In the past, the Court eschewed comparable transaction analyses because "[t]he merger and acquisition data undoubtedly contains post-merger value, such as synergies with the acquirer that must be excluded from appraisal value." [See *Kleinwort Benson*.] Nevertheless, in the absence of reliable projections upon which to base a DCF, or as an additional valuation technique, the Court will consider comparable transactions if they are, indeed, sufficiently comparable. The Court will closely evaluate whether a party who relies on a comparable transactions analysis has met its burden of persuasion.

Representative Cases

Trilithic

Trilithic's expert based his analysis on the price Trilithic had paid to acquire one of its divisions. The Court found that use of a single transaction that occurred four years before the valuation date was unreasonable.

> Trilithic was a different company in 1993 than it was in 1989. It had developed new products and new lines of business. Further, the Texscan instruments division only became the Trilithic instruments line of business, not 100% of Trilithic ...

The Court afforded no weight to the analysis.

JRC Acquisition

The petitioner's expert relied on a list of "comparable" transactions compiled by the special committee's financial advisor, Merrill Lynch. The Court observed that the list of transactions included mainly change-of-control transactions rather than minority interest acquisitions.

Of the transactions in its analysis, Merrill identified and relied upon one transaction (Swisher International) as the most comparable because it was a minority acquisition in the same industry as JRC.

The Court dismissed the petitioner's analysis because it relied on a synergistic merger (Swedish Matchbox/General Cigar) that Merrill had determined was not comparable. In addition, the Court was critical of the fact that the expert had adjusted the multiples of the General Cigar transaction to reflect the results for the quarter after announcement of the transaction (thereby inflating the multiple).

Montgomery Cellular

MC was 94.3 per cent owned by, and was one of 16 subsidiaries of, Price Communications Wireless, Inc. ("PCI"). PCI had agreed to be acquired by Verizon Wireless ("VW") for $2.06 billion, contingent on VW's pending IPO. The IPO did not take place and the purchase price for PCI was reduced to $1.7 billion. Minority MC shareholders were squeezed out as a pre-condition to the VW merger.

In the appraisal proceeding, the petitioner's expert used the initial VW bid as one of his comparable transactions. The Court noted that the initial VW bid was problematic because it was never consummated, was contingent on VW's IPO, consisted of a cluster of companies (*i.e.*, PCI), and reflected synergies with VW. However, despite the problems, the Court was persuaded that the initial VW agreement was a valid comparable transaction because PCI had canvassed the market to find buyers and had negotiated with VW at arm's length.

Conclusion

The recent appraisal cases offer investment bankers and lawyers a valuable perspective as to the manner in which the Delaware judiciary approaches valuation issues. In addition to revealing how the Court views specific aspects of analyzing the value of a business enterprise (such as determining the cost of equity or a terminal value), the cases offer lessons in how best to approach valuation litigation.

One message that resonates through all the cases is that the Court will deal harshly with experts that take extreme positions or rely on their "professional judgment" as an explanation for a particular input in their valuation analysis. In scrutinizing an expert's valuation, the Court will look for well-articulated, fact-driven rationales for each of the inputs and assumptions underlying the valuation. Accordingly, a valuation expert should try to remain an independent and objective analyst rather than a partisan proponent. "Falling on one's sword" to advance a client's position is more likely than not to result in the rejection of the expert's testimony, in whole or in part.

Dealing With the Lost Tax Shield

Steve Z. Ranot

Introduction

Valuation of privately owned businesses is often tax driven. That is, it may be required for tax purposes, such as for corporate reorganizations or non-arm's length transfers. Or, if income tax requirements are not the reason for the valuation, the value of the company is affected by tax issues. These issues include the appropriate tax rate to apply when using the earnings approach and knowing how to value tax accounts, such as refundable dividend tax on hand ("RDTOH"), or the capital dividend account ("CDA") when valuing on an asset approach or calculating tangible asset backing.

It has been this writer's experience that valuators may not seek the input of qualified tax experts when preparing a valuation and, instead, rely on their own tax knowledge, most likely obtained from two years of audit experience and one six-month tax course from the Canadian Institute of Chartered Business Valuators.

Valuation is not an exact science and there is seldom one right answer. However, when it comes to matters of taxation, there is usually only one right answer and valuators should eliminate possible errors by using qualified tax personnel. In a nutshell, this writer has seen many valuation reports containing tax errors. In order for tax personnel to assist valuators, valuators must understand that tax personnel are there to assist them. Similarly, tax personnel must understand the purpose and effects of the tax aspects of valuation. One of these issues is the lost tax shield which, generally, occurs on the purchase of a business structured as an acquisition of shares.

In volatile times, more businesses are sold using an asset approach because the expectation of earnings has diminished. This paper looks at considerations of the sale of assets versus shares and one issue in particular, that is the present value of the lost tax shield when assets with low undepreciated capital cost are sold as part of a share sale.

Purchase of Assets Versus Purchase of Shares

A business carried on by a corporation may be acquired either by the purchase of the assets or by the purchase of the shares of the corporation. In comparing the advantages and disadvantages of a share purchase and an asset purchase, it is apparent that most of the issues relate to personal and corporate income tax. It is these tax issues that will likely influence the final determination of how the purchase is structured, the purchase price itself, the allocation of the purchase price among the assets purchased, and the terms of payment.

Purchase and Sale of a Business Assets Versus Shares

Advantages of a Share Purchase/Sale:

- availability of the capital gains exemption (or relatively high ACB of shares)
- availability of the capital gains reserve
- maintainability of non-capital losses, R&D credits and investment tax credits
- no PST, GST, or HST issues and no land transfer tax on real estate
- no loss of RDTOH if purchaser is also a CCPC

Advantages of an Asset Purchase/Sale:

- buyer does not assume liability for past transactions
- ability to allocate purchase price
- higher cost base for capital cost allowance
- ability to continue deferral of personal tax

Advantages of a Sale of Shares

1. Frequently, where the lifetime capital gains exemption forms a significant portion of the purchase price, the vendor has a strong incentive to sell shares, not assets. The same applies to a vendor who owns shares with an adjusted cost base ("ACB") that is significantly in excess of paid-up capital. If these vendors cause their corporations to sell assets and then withdraw the proceeds of disposition by way of salary or dividends, they will lose the benefit of the high ACB they paid earlier using after-tax money.

2. The capital gains reserve allows the capital gain on the sale of shares to be taken into income over five years if the purchase price is spread over such a period or longer. Where the sale of a business includes a significant portion for goodwill, the sale of assets would not permit a reserve to be taken on the gain on disposition of goodwill, no matter how the purchase price and period of payments is structured.

3. Non-capital losses can be carried forward to be applied against a corporation's future taxable income. Where a change of control has occurred, these unused losses may only be applied against future income from a same or similar business. Capital losses cannot be transferred. Research and development credits and investment tax credits can be transferred. A continuing business with unused non-capital losses or tax credits will likely lose these on a sale of assets while a sale of shares will permit the vendor to get something in return for them.

4. Unless you are a commodity tax specialist, no one likes PST, GST, or HST issues and a share sale eliminates these. A share sale also avoids payment of land transfer tax if real estate is owned by the corporation.

5. The vendor may have an RDTOH balance but, without cash, the necessary dividends to trigger the refund make it unavailable. If the proceeds of disposition must be used to repay debt, the RDTOH may remain unrealizable and of no value to the vendor. If the shares are sold to another Canadian-controlled private corporation ("CCPC"), the RDTOH may be of value and thus generate additional proceeds of disposition in a share sale.

Advantages of an Asset Sale

1. The most important non-tax issue is the assumption of legal liability. When you purchase a company's hard assets and goodwill, you start anew. When you purchase their shares, you assume liability for any lawsuits, tax reassessments, *etc.* that may have arisen prior to your ownership.

2. The *Income Tax Act* requires that the total purchase price be allocated on a reasonable basis. The amount allocated becomes the purchase price to the buyer and the proceeds of disposition to the vendor. Generally, Revenue Canada will accept the price allocation where it was negotiated between two arm's length parties as long as it is not grossly different from economic reality. In general, the buyer prefers to allocate proceeds to assets with a high depreciation rate. The vendor may be indifferent, in which case the difference between

allocation to an asset in a 30 per cent class for capital cost allowance ("CCA") versus allocation to goodwill (of which only 75 per cent can be deducted at only 7 per cent) can represent significant tax savings.

3. The formula we will discuss later shows that on $100,000, the difference between a 30 per cent CCA class and goodwill amounts to a present value of over $18,000, assuming a 10 per cent after-tax rate of return in the business. Obviously, an 18 per cent tax saving will be a significant factor in the purchase decision.

4. Personal taxes are triggered in the share sale if the shares are held personally. If the capital gains exemption is utilized, then, by definition, the shares must be held personally. A sale of assets by a corporation will not trigger personal tax unless the proceeds of disposition are subsequently paid to the individual as salary or dividends. Accordingly, if the individual will leave the proceeds in the corporation for a long period, this deferral will be a factor in the assets versus shares decision.

The third advantage of an asset purchase to the purchaser is the higher cost base for CCA. The loss of this is known as the "lost tax shield", that is, the loss of the higher CCA deduction each year resulting from the inheritance of an undepreciated capital cost ("UCC") that is lower than the fair market value of the depreciable assets. It has been our experience that CCA rates tend to be generous in the case of manufacturing equipment and that, in most cases, fair market value of equipment does exceed the UCC.

Calculation of the Lost Tax Shield

Let's examine a simple example of company X that wishes to acquire the operations of company Y, which has the following balance sheet:

	Book Value	FMV
Current Assets	$100,000	$100,000
Machinery (@ UCC)	200,000	500,000
Current Liabilities	(80,000)	(80,000)
Net Assets	$220,000	$520,000)

If X purchased net assets, it would pay $520,000 based on fair market value. If X purchased shares instead, it would acquire the exact same net assets, with one difference for income tax purposes, that is, the lower UCC on the machinery. Under an asset purchase, X would acquire the equipment with the right to depreciate $500,000. Under a share purchase the UCC is only $200,000. What is the present value of this extra $300,000 of UCC? If the

CCA rate is 25 per cent, the difference in the first year (ignoring the half-year rule) is $125,000 of CCA versus $50,000. At a 40 per cent tax rate, the $75,000 of extra CCA is worth $30,000 to X in the first year alone! Over the life of the asset, we calculate overall savings of $85,714 using the formula below and assuming a 10 per cent hurdle rate, or after-tax rate of return, in the company.

$$\text{Tax Savings of Asset Purchase} = \frac{\text{UCC} \times \text{CCA rate} \times \text{tax rate}}{\text{CCA rate x hurdle rate}}$$

$$= \frac{\$500{,}00 \times 25\% \times 40\%}{25\% + 10\%}$$

$$= \underline{\underline{\$142{,}857}}$$

$$\text{Tax Savings of Share Purchase} = \frac{\$200{,}000 \times 25\% \times 40\%}{25\% + 10\%}$$

$$= \underline{\underline{\$57{,}143}}$$

$$\text{Difference} = \$142{,}857 - \$57{,}143$$

$$= \underline{\underline{\$85{,}714}}$$

Based on the foregoing, if the asset purchase is worth $520,000, the share value must be $434,286 ($520,000 - $85,714).

The previous example was an oversimplification for a number of reasons:

- only one CCA class was used — most business operations would have more;
- the half-year rule was ignored — no half-year rule applies to inherited UCC on a share purchase, but it does apply on an asset purchase. The formula which considers the half-year rule is indicated below; and
- one single hurdle rate was used.

The formula which incorporates the half-year rule is as follows:

$$\frac{\text{UCC} \times \text{CCA rate} \times \text{tax rate}}{\text{CCA rate} + \text{hurdle rate}} \times 1 - \frac{\text{hurdle rate}}{2 \times (1 + \text{hurdle rate})}$$

In calculating the present value of the lost tax shield, we multiply the CCA claimable on the asset by the tax rate to determine each year's tax savings. You will note that the taxpayer's income is not a factor in the equation.

What happens if a company with accumulated losses acquires business assets as opposed to shares or if the acquiring company anticipates losses in the first few years of operations? The formula is no longer appropriate as CCA will not save any current taxes but will only serve to increase the loss carry-forwards. Accordingly, the purchaser in this situation should not be too eager to pay the premium for an asset purchase. In fact, this will likely be structured as a share purchase as the vendor generally prefers it as such and the purchaser has no income tax disadvantages but will pay a lower purchase price.

Hurdle Rate Issues

If we eliminate the issue of a company with accumulated losses, we know we should use the tax shield formula, but let's examine the issue of the hurdle rate. This rate is expected to be the measure of risk of a loss. Since risk and return are related, the greater the risk of a company's business, the higher its hurdle rate must be. A high-risk business such as a diamond mine has a higher hurdle rate and a greater risk of not making enough taxable income to utilize the CCA. If you look at the formula, you will see that as the hurdle rate increases, *ceteris paribus*, the present value of the lost tax shield decreases. This makes intuitive sense. Does this mean we should look at an industry's capitalization of earnings rate as the measure of its hurdle rate for the purposes of this calculation?

Let's say that in the widget manufacturing industry, companies trade at four times their earnings for a capitalization rate of 25 per cent. Should this be the hurdle rate we use in our calculations? Let's look at one specific taxpayer. It may have some long-term contracts with customers which accounts for 50 per cent of its productive capacity. This is enough to guarantee a small operating profit. How the company does each year varies with its ability to utilize the other 50 per cent of its capacity. But with enough guaranteed sales to earn a small profit each year, there is virtual certainty that the CCA can be utilized each year to reduce taxes. In this situation, the hurdle rate should be much lower since we know we will have use of the CCA. Using a numerical example, let's examine the impact of this adjustment.

1. Present Value of Tax Shield ("PVTS") based on:
   (a) $100,000 of equipment;
   (b) 30% CCA rate;
   (c) 40% tax rate; and
   (d) 25% hurdle rate
   PVTS = $21,818

2. PVTS using all else the same but 5% hurdle rate to reflect low risk of not being able to utilize full CCA in the future

   PVTS = $34,286

On $100,000 of equipment in a high-risk business, the recognition of a low risk of not being able to fully claim CCA, correctly results in a much higher PVTS. In this case, it is $12,468 higher or 12.5 per cent of original cost!

Comparison with Deferred Tax Credits or Future Income Taxes

When acquiring shares of an operating corporation, the PVTS represents a reduction of share value. Another deduction from value is sometimes reflected on the balance sheet in the form of deferred tax credits or future income taxes. It may be that this amount approximates the tax shield. If so, it is likely coincidental. The deferred tax credit balance represents the past differences between UCC and net book value based on the current tax rate with no present value adjustment. Where CCA exceeds the depreciation rate for accounting purposes, and where the depreciation rate for accounting purposes more closely approximates the decline in the market value of the asset, the deferred tax credit balance will approximate the PVTS where the asset is in a relatively high CCA rate class. If not, the time value factor in the present value calculation will keep the PVTS below the deferred tax credit amount. Where the asset's fair market value is not approximated by its net book value, there will be no correlation between the deferred tax credit balance and PVTS. Accordingly, there will be no correlation in the case of an appreciating asset, such as a building.

Adjusted Book Value and Accrued Capital Gains

The calculation of the lost tax shield is needed when valuing an operating business. It may also be appropriate when valuing a holding corporation with a portfolio of rental properties. Similar to the operating company Y example earlier, a buyer would have to be compensated for purchasing a portfolio of real property with a fair market value in excess of its cost for income tax purposes. This would be the appropriate approach to use where the real estate portfolio is expected to be retained in the long term, that is, it is not expected to be sold in the next 20 years or so. This is akin to an operating company situation where there is no expectation of the operating assets (such as machinery and equipment) being sold at a profit.

When an investment holding corporation is being valued, an adjustment is made for the present value of the accrued recapture and capital gains tax liability. This calculation must consider the lower UCC in a share purchase as compared to an asset purchase and the lower ACB of non-depreciable assets, such as land. Once the present value of this income tax liability is factored into the value of the shares, there is no requirement to calculate lost tax shield as the cost to the shareholder of the lower UCC and ACB has already been considered.

It should be noted that the present value of accrued capital gains on non-depreciable property such as land should still be considered in an operating company. Even if there is no expectation of selling the operating assets of the operating company, the present value of the income tax liability on the accrued capital gains is factored in the calculation of the company's tangible asset backing.

Conclusion

As stated above, valuation is an art, not a science. When valuing business interests in volatile times, asset-based approaches are used more often. Accordingly, a proper understanding of calculating the lost tax shield and utilizing the expertise of tax personnel may go a long way to achieving consistency among valuators.

Transfer Pricing in Times of Volatility

Jennifer Boundy & Dr. Muris Dujsic

It is almost a certainty that, in these economic times, all companies are facing unique challenges. These recessionary times can lead to a range of business issues including operating losses, reduction in work force and plant/operation closures, cash flow and debt service constraints, excess/obsolete inventory, "credit crunch", *etc.*

These business issues also impact a company's tax and treasury objectives. A multinational enterprise (MNE) may now be experiencing losses in some jurisdictions and be cash-taxable in others, or be realizing a build up of cash in some jurisdictions without an efficient way to move the cash to the entities that are cash short. A large determinant of whether a company will face these issues is dependent on their transfer pricing policy. In short, transfer pricing is the price charged for goods, services, and assets between legal entities that are part of the same MNE.

This chapter discusses some of the specific transfer pricing issues facing companies given the current economic environment. We will start by outlining some of the issues faced by companies using a central entrepreneur transfer pricing model. Then we will detail the challenges in supporting interest rates charged on intercompany loans given the credit crunch and lack of reliable third party transactions. Lastly, we will discuss the issues and considerations that are relevant in the context of dealing with capacity rationalization.

Central Entrepreneur Model

Over the last decade, in order to be consistent with globalization trends, many companies have centralized certain aspects of the business model in order to achieve synergies and remain competitive. This normally includes shifting their transfer pricing model to one of a central entrepreneur. A central entrepreneur model essentially argues that one entity in the MNE is the entrepreneur and responsible for the value derived by the company. Each of the remaining entities are characterized as low-risk entities *e.g.*, toll or contract manufacturer, commission agent, procurement agent, *etc.* The idea is that these low-risk entities have minimal functions and limited risks and therefore earn a limited return for their activities. The remaining profits earned by the consolidated company then belong to the central entrepreneur.

For instance, assume we have a MNE that manufactures and distributes highly-specialized and unique widgets. These specialized widgets have proven very profitable for the company and it earns 15 per cent operating margin on a consolidated basis. Let's further assume that this MNE relies on a central entrepreneur transfer pricing model. The manufacturing entities in the MNE are contract manufacturers bearing no risk related to selling its end products, price fluctuations on inputs, *etc.* The contract manufacturers earn a 5 per cent operating margin through the company's transfer pricing model. The distribution entities also bear limited risk and are provided a 3 per cent operating margin on their sales. This leaves 7 per cent operating margin to be earned by the central entrepreneur. If the central entrepreneur is located in a low tax jurisdiction, this can create a huge favorable impact on the company's effective tax rate.

In the current recessionary times, it is likely the consolidated company is facing any number of challenges: potential decrease in demand for its products, customers taking longer to pay all reduce the overall profitability of the company. If we assume that the overall operating margin of the company is now 8 per cent and there have been no changes in the company's transfer pricing policies and benchmarks, the contract manufacturer would still earn a 5 per cent operating margin as its return is somewhat isolated from risk. The same is true of the distribution entities. The result is that the central entrepreneur is earning a 0 per cent operating margin and potentially incurring a loss for tax purposes.

At first glance, the potential for the central entrepreneur entity to earn a loss, while still providing a guaranteed return to the low-risk entities, is counter-intuitive. The entity that owns the valuable intangibles, which enable the company to be successful on a consolidated basis, receives a negligible or negative return in a down economy. However, economically it does make sense when one looks at the transfer pricing profiles of the individual entities – their return is correlated to their risk (the higher the potential upside, the higher the risk). For instance, it is difficult to support a conclusion wherein the low-risk entities receive a lower return to allow the central entrepreneur to also earn a profit given the characterization of the low-risk entities in the central entrepreneur model. The characterization as a low-risk entity likely means that the entity has been left with a very limited market risk, hence the low-risk initial return. Unfortunately, it means that changes in the economy may not be sufficient as an argument to lower the entities' return. That being said, the adverse economic conditions faced by the low-risk entities are also likely to impact the comparable companies that are used to benchmark the low margin return, and may shift the entire range of arm's length returns downward which may result in a lower return to the limited risk entity.

This issue is even further exaggerated for a company in liquidation. For instance, let's continue with our example of the widget manufacturer. Let's assume that the company is now in bankruptcy and has found a purchaser willing to the buy the company. The company and its creditors now need to determine which legal entity (and therefore which creditors and tax authorities) will receive the proceeds. One suggestion would be to value each entity as a stand-alone entity to determine the relative contribution of value. Common valuation methodologies rely on discounting earnings or cash flow. In this case, the entities with earnings and positive cash flow are the low-risk manufacturing entities and the low-risk distribution entities. The central entrepreneur that owns the valuable intangible property (in this case the know-how behind the highly-specialized widgets), that is likely what a potential purchaser is buying will have little, or potentially negative, value. Again, the result may appear counter-intuitive and one needs to consider the nature of the business and corresponding transfer pricing model over the entire market-driven business cycle in order to arrive at the right pricing/valuation conclusion.

Financial Transactions

The credit markets have also undergone a significant contraction. This has led a number of MNEs to rely more heavily on intragroup financing as opposed to external financing. The interest paid from one group member to another on the lending of funds is caught by most country's transfer pricing regimes. As such, the MNE should undertake a transfer pricing analysis to ensure the rate, and the terms of the loan, are consistent with the arm's length principle.

Conducting an interest rate determination analysis involves searching for comparable debt instruments to observe the interest rate, and then making adjustments for differences in term, credit rating, *etc.* The illiquidity in the market is causing challenges in finding comparable debt instruments that become the starting point in a transfer pricing analysis. The graphic below highlights the decline in LBO/ MBO deals in the six-month period December 31, 2007 versus the six-month period ended March 31, 2009. The decrease is significant.

Exhibit 1: LBO/ MBO Deals in North America

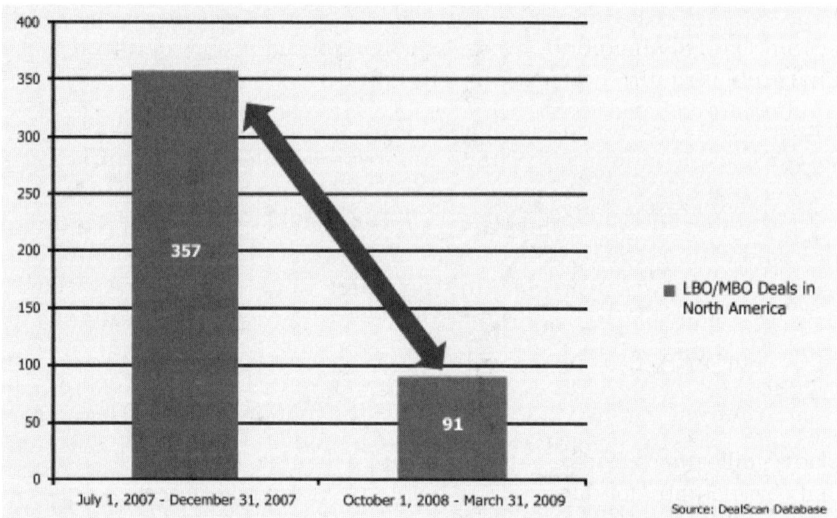

Another challenge is that the interest rate being reported on third party loans as disclosed by Loan Pricing Corporation (LPC) no longer represents the true cost of the debt. Lenders are now requiring commitment fees on new debt; these commitments fees are sometimes as high as 200-300 basis points annually. Generally, commitment fees or upfront costs are not disclosed by LPC but any company relying on LPC as its source of third party pricing information may be missing a significant cost of borrowing.

Historically, it is difficult to find arm's length loans perfectly comparable to the related party loan for which we are trying to determine an interest rate. One of the adjustments made commonly by practitioners is a credit risk adjustment (if the borrower does not have the same creditworthiness profile). Given what is being observed in the market and the significant widening of credit spreads, this adjustment is being increasingly more difficult to make in terms of the precision of the analysis that is required. As illustrated in Exhibit 2, the credit spread between the 30-year B- and the 3-month AAA has increased from 4.3 per cent in August 2007 to 15.3 per cent in March 2009.

Exhibit 2: US Industrial Curves Fair Market Yield Spreads

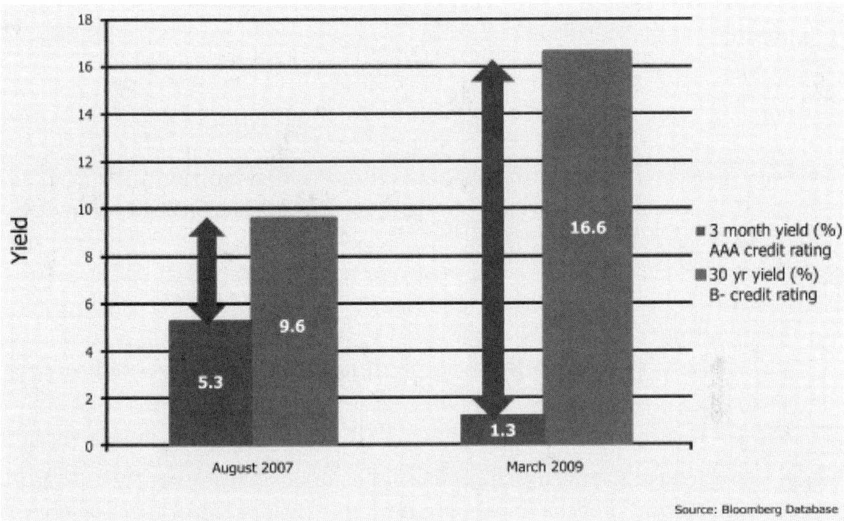

Last, practitioners in the current environment have to consider whether a transaction that would likely not have been entered into between arm's length parties would be consistent with the arm's length principle.

Although it is viewed as unlikely that the CRA would not respect the intercompany loan as debt, it does place a greater emphasis on ensuring the terms and conditions of the loan are reasonable given the current lending environment. For instance, in the current environment certain segments of the capital markets lost the most if not all of its supply (the arm's length lenders are either reluctant to land or have temporarely ceased the lending activity) which may be interpreted by the tax authorities as the lack of liquidity for any intercompany loans and, in extreme situations, even lead them to consider the recharacterization.

Capacity Rationalization

In recessionary economies, it is not uncommon for companies to face difficult decisions regarding under-utilized facilities. A couple of factors may lead to under utilization, general downward pressure on demand for the companies' products or specific product lines facing extreme lower demand.

Either way, the result facing the company is too much capacity for their current sales levels.

Plant closures present interesting transfer pricing considerations given the standard of the arm's length principle. Objectively, the decision of an MNE to shut down one of its plants, especially if another plant that is currently under-utilized can pick up the additional production is different than an independent entity deciding to shut its doors.

Commonly, companies are of the view that the largest transfer pricing decision to be made is which entity within the multinational should bear the costs associated with a plant closure? Should it be the parent who ultimately decided to close the plant or the local entity that is shutting its doors? In fact, even this postulation of the transfer pricing issue in and of itself is somewhat misleading, since most often it is not about who is to bear the costs of the closure. The most appropriate postulation of the issue would be whether the commercial arrangement in place would require a compensation payment (for instance, is a contract being terminated prematurely), or whether there was a transfer of something of value which would require the receiving entity to make a "compensating payment"? This analysis is very fact specific.

Given that the arm's length principle applies on a separate entity basis and not on a consolidated basis, one would have to consider the options available to the entity had it been a standalone entity. If any of the options available were more attractive than restructuring (taking into account any compensation received as part of the restructuring) then one might not be able to argue that an arm's length party would have entered into a similar restructuring.

As previously mentioned, an analysis of what will become of the entity being closed or restructured will also have to be conducted; specifically, in the context of determining whether there were any transfers of valuable rights or assets to other entities. These transfers could include:

- tangible assets;
- intangible assets;
- contractual rights; or
- human capital.

It is intuitive why the transfer of any of these items would be a benefit to the recipient and would likely indicate a need for a compensating payment. For example, in the arm's length world, an entity would require compensation to transfer an intangible asset to another party. Considering both the valuation and transfer pricing methodologies would be useful in determining the value of any of the above items for the purposes of complying with the arm's length principle.

Another possibility is the transfer of ongoing activity, *e.g.*, the transfer of the operations of one entity to another. Generally, it could be described as a bundle of the items listed above, but would also need to consider the goodwill and profit potential of the activity as an ongoing activity. This is an important consideration especially if relying on traditional valuation methodologies to assess the value of the transferred items. Valuing each of the assets separately would likely lead to a different value determination than valuing the transfer of going concern operations.

Table 1, below, summarizes a couple of possible scenarios that may be encountered and the considerations that should be contemplated based on the discussion above. The authors would like to note that the Table is for illustrative purposes only and that each analysis should be fact specific and the result should be consistent with the arm's length standard and the local transfer pricing regulations of the entities involved.

Table 1: Considerations for Various Restructuring Scenarios

Scenario	Considerations
Plant closing due to production cessation	What other options existed for the entity? And how do they compare to shutting down operations? Will there be a transfer of any items of value (*e.g.*, valuable supplier contract, local marketing intangibles)? Do the terms and conditions of the intercompany arrangement call for a termination or another similar compensating payment?
Plant closing, transferring production to another facility	Would this be considered the transfer of a going-concern business? What is the impact on the recipient's profitability? Would they be willing to pay to "buy" this business? What other options existed for each of the entities?

Scenario	Considerations
Full-fledged operation being restructured into a service provider, all tangible and intangible assets redundant to this role to be disposed of, any remaining customers to be served by another entity.	What is the value of the restructured service provider relative to the old full-fledged entity? What is the value of the transferred rights/ assets? What is the value to the recipient?

Conclusion

The transfer pricing issues raised during these recessionary times are more complicated than ever. The results of taxpayers who rely on the central entrepreneur model is one example where, at first blush, the results now seem counter-intuitive and are leading some taxpayers to want to adjust their transfer pricing policies. However, the results are consistent with the economic theory that led to the original transfer pricing *i.e.*, that risk drives potential reward. Entities that bear little to no risk should receive a low, but stable, return and entities that bear a significant amount of risk will see more volatility in their profitability.

For some transactions, the issues are being exaggerated by the lack of comparable market data and are potentially even raising issues as to whether the intercompany transactions would even occur between arm's length parties. The result is that practitioners, more than ever, need to be focused on the comparability of the transactions and resulting impact on pricing.

Last, recessionary times produce different types of transactions to be considered by taxpayers, specifically those transactions undertaken by companies to allow them to remain competitive in their markets. These restructuring type transactions create a whole new set of transfer pricing issues for companies to have to consider but, given the right approach to the analysis, may represent an opportunity to preserve cash and achieve the optimal distribution of profits and capital within the corporation.

Migrating Intangibles in Troubled Economic Times

Jamal Hejazi, Dale Hill & Mark Kirkey

I. Introduction

Transfer pricing involves the price that one member of a multinational group charges another for the transfer of goods, services, or intangibles. Though the current downturn in the global economy has had a dramatic impact on several industry sectors, the reeling technology sector has suffered disproportionately. Economies throughout the G7 which are dependent on high technology are struggling during the current economic turmoil. The rise of Asian economies such as China and India as "hubs" for technology-based corporations has put tremendous cost pressure on North American technology companies to compete along cost lines.

This new economic environment makes it understandably difficult for companies to contemplate the implementation of long-term tax strategies, when the focus is strictly on meeting profitability targets. Given that a corporation must function as a going concern, corporations owe it to their shareholders and other stakeholders to engage strategies that maximize short-term operations and long-term value. One such relatively inexpensive strategy, which serves to minimize the level of global taxes a corporation must pay, involves intangible migration including technology transfers between related parties.

The chapter is organized as follows: section II, details the current state of the world economy; section III provides an overview of the tax implications and the legislative guidance surrounding intangible transfers; section IV provides a discussion as to the process involved in transferring intangibles between related parties; section V provides a description of the complexities of intangible transfers and cites a particular case within the business community; and section VI concludes.

II. Economic Overview

In terms of overall growth, the world economy is projected to shrink in 2009. This outlook is corroborated by the forecast for world trade growth, which is expected to be -1.3 per cent, down from 3.2 per cent in 2008 and 5.2 per cent in 2007. Economic projections indicate that the slowdown will continue to significantly affect world growth going forward, which will have a substantial effect on subsequent company valuations, as much of these are based on projected future forecasts.

While Western economies are projecting economic growth rates as low as -2.8 per cent, China and India are helping to lift the global economy with their rapid economic expansions; China is forecast to experience a surprising 6.5 per cent growth rate, while India is expected to experience 4.5 per cent growth. The IMF has revised downwards its forecast of U.S. growth in 2009 to -2.8 per cent (with an estimated 1.5 per cent Q4-to-Q4 performance). Japan is expected to experience -6.2 per cent growth in 2009, illustrating its reliance on the weakened U.S. economy. It is likely these disappointing forecasts will reduce growth rates in East-Asian economies, which derive much of their income from exports to the U.S. and Japan.

Pessimism over euro-zone economic prospects remains high, as is illustrated by recent data releases. In 2007, GDP growth in the euro-zone hit a year-on-year rate of 2.7 per cent; however, the estimated 2008 and projected 2009 growth numbers are 0.9 per cent and -4.2 per cent, respectively.

Despite the slowdown in the overall world economy, these are times of expansion for emerging markets and the growth trend of these markets is projected to continue into 2009. This growth is in part reflective of the supportive global environment. Though world trade growth has experienced a considerable slowdown, the world average will be bolstered by the projections for developing economies (as noted above with China and India).

The outlook remains relatively favorable for other developing and emerging economies over the next 13 months. Economic growth is estimated at 2.0 per cent in Africa in 2009, rather than the 5.2 per cent seen in 2008. Central and Eastern Europe are benefiting from euro-zone exports, but will slow down to -3.7 per cent in 2009 from 2.9 per cent in 2008.

North America[1]

As a result of being "at the center of the intensifying global financial storm", the U.S. economy weakened significantly in the final quarters of 2008. The IMF currently expects the U.S. economy to shrink by -2.8 per cent in 2009, down from 1.1 per cent in 2008 and 2.0 per cent in 2007.

The dramatic downturn in the housing market has led to a significant overall decline in residential investment, and its spread throughout the markets has had a negative impact on the availability of credit and investment capital. Declining residential investment has in fact "been a major drag on output" since 2007, the culmination of which is currently evidenced in the dismal state of the U.S. economy.

The nature and extent of the U.S. recession will depend to some extent on what steps governments will take to rectify the economic crisis and the reactions of U.S. households in the face of inflation and rising market stress. It is likely that this uncertainty will put added pressure on world economies as customers and businesses become more reluctant to spend on goods and services.

In Canada, there has been a sharp decline in economic activity beginning in mid-2007, with growth forecasted to declined by -2.5 per cent in 2009. The U.S. slowdown, as well as the effect of past real appreciation of the Canadian dollar, has affected the manufacturing sector negatively. Throughout 2008 the Bank of Canada decreased interest rates to the lowest point in many years, which have been maintained into 2009 to combat a weakening economy. Fortunately, inflation has remained static due, at least in part, to reduced demand in the Canadian economy. Despite the dire predicaments of many banks south of the border, banks in Canada continue to effectively weather the economic crisis. While there are still risks given the strong economic and financial ties between Canada and the U.S, Canada's conservative regulatory regime has helped bolster the resilience of Canadian banks.

Asia[2]

Growth in the economies of developing Asian markets (including China and India) is forecast to average an impressive 3.3 per cent in 2009. These markets are expected to grow despite the decrease in demand from the region's main export markets of the West, particularly the U.S. and Europe, which are not expected to experience any significant growth.

---

1 Information cited from, or based on information provided within: World Economic Outlook, April 2009 "*Crisis and Recovery*," published by the International Monetary Fund.

2 *Ibid.*

Having learned lessons from the regional crisis of 1997-98, most Asian economies are characterized by current-account surpluses, large foreign-exchange reserves, high rates of domestic savings, and economic policies that are generally prudent. These improved economic fundamentals will serve the region well over the next few years as a higher level of investor risk aversion prevails and the global economy slows.

In China, the economy is expanding at a feverish pace and growth is estimated at 6.5 per cent in 2009. The booming trade surplus in China, will lead to intensified trade tensions with the U.S., and will exert added pressure on China to allow a faster appreciation of its currency. China's account surplus continues to exceed 10 per cent of GDP with "strong capital inflows despite a tightening of controls". Regardless of this positive growth, the IMF has concluded that "the renminbi" remains substantially undervalued relative to medium-term fundamentals."

The Association of South-East Asian Nations (ASEAN) is not expected to grow in 2009. While ASEAN grew buy 1.5 per cent in 2008, no growth is forecasted in 2009. Thailand and Vietnam responded to the growing inflation through a tightening of monetary policy, *inter alia*, by raising interest rates, while Cambodia chose to tighten reserve requirements. Singapore responded to the rising inflation by creating more scope for appreciation in the exchange rate band.

III. Tax Implication and Legislative Guidance

There are several benefits of migrating intangibles during these difficult times including lower valuations of the property being transferred and the potential offset of capital gains, on the sale of the intangibles, with current operating losses. Then, when the economy improves and profits return, the revenues derived from the intangibles will be reported offshore at a much lower tax rate. Consideration should be given to the capital gain that will be created versus the losses carried forward, and those expected for the current year, to ensure they are sufficiently high to offset capital gains that will result from the sale of intangible assets.

Many countries, including Canada and the U.S., require that intangible transfers, along with most intercompany transactions, occur at arm's length prices. Generally speaking, approaches to valuing intangibles include the comparable uncontrolled price (or market approach), the cost approach, residual profit split method, and the income approach.

CUP Market Approach

A common approach to valuing intangible assets is to apply the CUP methodology. This approach endeavors to find comparables that exhibit a high degree of similarity relative to the intangible being examined. A CUP would exist if a high degree of asset similarity, as well as similarities, in economic conditions and contractual terms exist. CUPs can be found internally by reviewing existing licensing agreements with unrelated parties or externally by searching proprietary databases such as RoyaltyStat. The attraction of using the CUP is that it provides a simple application when appropriate comparable data exists. The primary limitation associated with this approach is the limited availability of comparable transactions and data upon which to establish fair value. CUPs by their very nature are often difficult to find and, in many cases, material differences exist between the comparable and the actual transaction that preclude the application of the CUP.

Income Approach or NPV Approach

The income approach attempts to place a value of the future cash flow that a particular asset will generate over its useful life.[3] The first step involves a projection of the cash flow, which the intangible is expected to generate. This involves an analysis of financial information and discussions with marketing, operations, and financial personnel to develop the future income stream attributable to the asset.

The second step involves converting these cash flows into a present value equivalent through discounting. This discounting process uses a rate of return that discounts for the relevant risk associated with the asset and the time value of money.

Cost Approach

The cost approach determines the fair value of an asset as an estimate of the current cost to purchase or replace the asset. This is based upon the principle of substitution. An investor would pay no more for an asset than the amount necessary to replace the asset. The difficulty in applying this

---

[3] This can be illustrated mathematically using the following Net Present Value (NPV) equation:

$$NPV = \sum_{t-1}^{T} \frac{C_t}{(1+r)^t} - C_o$$

where $-C_0$ is the upfront costs of investing, C_t is the after tax cash flow, r is the discount factor (or measure of risk) and t is the number of periods the investment project is to last.

approach involves determining which factors present within a multinational are driving intangible value and placing a monetary value on such factors.

Residual Profit Approach

The residual profit split methodology is recommended by the OECD for use in cases where other methods (discussed above) cannot be applied. For a residual profit split method to be applied, each group in a related party setting is assigned routine profits for their functions, based on a set of comparables. The profits that remain are those attributable to the intangible assets (*e.g.*, the trademarks or patents). A discounting of these atypical profit streams forms the basis of valuing the intangible under question.

Technology companies must illustrate what the fair market value of such intangibles are in order to justify what the related party in the lower tax jurisdiction will pay for such intangibles. Valuation is generally performed by commissioning an expert report, and by reference to industry comparables.

IV. Migrating Intangibles: What Do They Entail?

Many Canadian technology firms have incurred or will incur this coming year business losses that can be carried forward 20 years or back 3 years. Such losses, if not utilized, eventually expire and can serve no future benefit and, if carried forward, the company may need to wait several years to see the refund. One strategy that Canadian corporations should consider when such losses exist, and where valuable intangibles (such as patents, copyrights, trade marks, and trade names) are present, is migrating such intangibles to low tax jurisdictions such as Barbados.[4] Table 1 shows jurisdictions that have favorable situations for migrating intangibles.

[4] Barbados is particularly appealing for Canadian companies due to the existence of a tax treaty, low tax rates on profits, of approximately 2.5%, and the ability to repatriate most of the after-tax profits without additional taxation.

Table 1: Common Countries to Migrate Intangibles

	Ireland	Madeira	Barbados
Tax Rate	12.5%	0% until 2011 22% thereafter	1% - 2.5%
W/H Tax on Dividends paid to:	Canada = 0%	Canada = 0%	Canada = 0%

While many considerations are relevant when deciding to which country intangibles should be migrated, the key benefit to consider is that profits generated from such intangibles will be taxed at a lower rate. In addition, during difficult economic times, valuations should be lower and you may be able to offset any capital gains with losses. This is not likely to be the case in better economic times where losses are less likely to be incurred and when the value of the intangible transferred will have more economic value. This is where we turn our attention next.

Capital Gains and Losses

The sale of an intangible asset from one tax jurisdiction to another will result in exposure to capital gains taxes. To calculate any capital gain or loss, you need to know the following three amounts:

A - the proceeds of disposition;
B - the adjusted cost base (ACB); and
C - the outlays and expenses incurred to sell your property.

To calculate capital gains or losses, you subtract the total of your property's ACB, and any outlays and expenses incurred to sell this property, from the proceeds of disposition.

You have a capital gain when you sell, or are considered to have sold, a capital property for more than the total of its ACB and the outlays and expenses incurred to sell the property.

It is important to examine whether the capital gain, resulting from the sale of the intangible, can be offset by losses either in the current year or carried forward from prior years. When migrating intangibles, it is preferable to minimize the "gap" between the capital gain achieved and the available losses. This gap can be described with the equation:

Gap = Capital Gain (CG) – Operating Losses (OL)

The elimination of this gap is achieved when all of the capital gain is offset by available losses. The optimum is reached when the capital gain is less than or equal to the operating losses (*i.e.*, CG OL). As the economy struggles, this optimum condition is more likely to be reached. Cash flows are likely to be lower in slow economic times relative to expansionary periods suggesting that the NPV of the future income stream that the intangibles generate is smaller, indicating such intangibles are less valuable.

V. Migrating Intangibles and the Canada Revenue Agency

If a multinational corporation had the luxury of perfect hindsight, it would optimize its global positioning and operational efficiencies by migrating intangible assets prior to those assets proving valuable. Most companies, however, do not have such luxury, and the decision to migrate assets often comes well after their value is realized. In light of this, it comes as little surprise that discussions regarding government crackdowns on tax havens have occurred recently, as more and more multinational organizations move profits offshore to low tax jurisdictions.

The CRA and other tax authorities have stepped up their enforcement activities related to various industries that employ valuable intellectual property, including pharmaceuticals. The CRA announced in 2005 that it set up 11 centres of expertise to deal with aggressive international tax planning. These centres are located in regional Tax Services Offices across Canada, and they bring together international tax auditors and tax avoidance officers. One of the priorities of the centres is to develop new ways to address aggressive international transactions. It seems as if transfer pricing transactions and, specifically, the migration of intellectual property, are a major target in CRA's audit compliance reviews.

With increased resources available to it, the CRA is combining both its rapidly improving knowledge of transfer pricing disciplines, with improved legislative powers, to raise transfer pricing adjustments.

From a tax perspective, any financial planning that involves moving profits offshore by multinational organizations can be justifiable if the corresponding functions, assets, and risks borne to earn these profits are also shifted offshore, and where the appropriate buy-in payments have been made. The world economy has become increasingly globalized, and the need to minimize after-tax profits is not only advantageous to improving corporate profits, but is also necessary in order to remain competitive. While implementing such a framework is a long and complex process, it can result in material tax savings.

While there are many clear benefits to migrating intangibles, such a strategy poses risks, including the potential for significant transfer pricing adjustments and penalties. Ideally, intangibles should be migrated when they do not possess considerable economic value. However, as stated earlier, companies do not often have the benefit of hindsight and often decide to migrate after the intangibles prove valuable.

During transfer pricing audits, government authorities have used existing legislation (*i.e.*, section 247(2)(b) of the *Canada Income Tax Act*) to re-characterize related party transactions after settlement negotiations have broken down, resulting in transfer pricing adjustments.

An application of the government's power to re-characterize a particular transaction has been seen in the recent transfer pricing dispute between the CRA and Merck Frosst Canada ("Merck"). The CRA examined the tax returns of Merck from 1998 through 2004, and reassessed Merck for "adjustments related to certain intercompany pricing matters". On October 10, 2006, the CRA issued a notice of reassessment related to various intercompany transactions totaling US$1.4 billion plus, US$360 million in interest. While all details of the case are not known, it has been disclosed in various media sources that the adjustments relate to Merck's patent for its asthma drug *Singular*. The drug, developed in Quebec, generated sales of US$950 million in the second quarter of 2006. The patent was later transferred to Barbados. Subsequently, the CRA used its ability to apply existing legislation to re-characterize the transaction as if the transaction did not occur, thus raising the corresponding adjustment. Merck recently reported that an agreement had been reached for C$786 million.

VI. Conclusion

In these tough economic times, technology companies should consider migrating intangibles to lower tax-rate jurisdictions, as future profits that such intangibles generate would then be taxed at a significantly lower tax rate. The usually contentious issue of valuation is reduced given the lower outlook for profits and the possible availability of losses which can allow the transferor to be conservative towards the source country in valuing the intangibles. Also, the objective of reducing or minimizing the gap in the CG Losses equation is more likely to be attained in recessionary, rather than expansionary times. It is important to note, however, that intangible transfer prices must represent arm's length consideration.

Transfer Pricing and Valuations in Asia

Steven Tseng*

Most major Asia-Pacific countries are moving towards, or have already adopted, the International Financial Reporting Standards (IFRS) or equivalent standards. Such standards have already been implemented in Australia, New Zealand, Hong Kong, the Philippines, Malaysia, Kazakhstan, Uzbekistan, Russia, Singapore, Bangladesh, Nepal, Papua New Guinea, and Sri Lanka,[1] while India, Japan, and Korea aim to implement IFRS standards by 2011, Taiwan by 2015 (or earlier for some countries), and Thailand is moving towards greater conformity.[2] Additionally, the Chinese Accounting Standards (CAS), which have been implemented for listed companies since January 1, 2007 are, with a few exceptions, "substantially in line with IFRSs."[3]

As IFRS becomes the international standard, consistency both within and between regions becomes important for many reasons. Besides reduced costs and time associated with conversion between different standards, consistency will also make it easier for the investment community to compare potential investments in Asia and elsewhere using similar standards. In fact, this is a purpose of the International Accounting Standards Board (IASB) itself, which created IFRS, and states that a "single set of high quality, uni-

* The views and opinions are those of the author and do not necessarily represent the view and opinions of KPMG in China. The author would like th thank Clark Chandler of KPMG's Washington National Tax Practice and George Brandt of KPMG China for their help.

1 KPMG's International Standards Group (internal list) December 2009.

2 "Implementing International Financial Reporting Standards in Asia: Bringing Greater Transparency and Comparability to Asian Banks' Financial Statements," Country Analysis Unit of the Federal Reserve Bank of San Francisco's "Asia Focus," March 2008; Deloitte and Touche's IAS Plus (www.iasplus.com) as of December 2009.

3 IAS Plus's November 2009 Jurisdictional Update for China (http://www.iasplus.com/country/china.htm#0902).

form, globally-applied, and enforced accounting [standards] is essential for both domestic and cross-border investment and financing decisions."[4]

Given what the investment community has recently learned about the consequences of inappropriate valuations, job displacement, loss of savings and so on, this issue has gained a larger prominence in the global agenda; however, for this article we will direct our focus mainly to the transfer pricing aspects of valuation.

The key issue is that under IFRS 3, the fair value of acquired assets and liabilities must be calculated by the acquiring company, rather than simply recognizing all excess value over acquired book value as goodwill. This is because purchase price allocation (PPA) forces the acquiring company to recognize and measure at fair value all such excess value, including intangible assets and contingent liabilities.

From a transfer pricing perspective, this standard comes into play in relation to intra-group restructuring and linking PPA to post-merger transfer pricing policy. The allocations required under IFRS 3, and the tax implications of these allocations, in many cases, will be highly dependent upon transfer pricing policies and, of course, the reverse may also be true, that transfer pricing policies may be formed differently depending on considerations relating to the valuation of intangibles and liabilities.

Post-merger Intra-group Restructuring

Many mergers involve a multinational that is operating in a number of different countries, taking control over another group with primary operations in the same countries. Once this occurs, IFRS 3 requires that all liabilities and assets, including intangible assets, be recorded at fair value, and that goodwill be allocated to cash generating units (CGUs). A CGU is defined as the smallest identifiable group of assets which generates cash inflows that are largely independent of the cash inflows from other assets or groups of assets. As multinationals often manage their operations on a business-unit basis, CGUs are often defined as the business units.

However, for some multinationals, CGUs are defined as legal entities. Impairment testing will require developing detailed financial forecasts of CGUs, resulting in more business-unit CGUs than legal entity CGUs, due to the availability of information on forecasts.

Using the individual subsidiaries as CGUs implies that the valuation of liabilities and assets, and the amount of goodwill allocated to the individual subsidiary, reflects the fair value of the individual subsidiary's shares at the

---

[4] Federal Reserve Bank's "Asia Focus", as above note 2.

time of acquisition. However, the allocation of goodwill also assumes that certain post-merger integration takes place and is often driven by the expected profits of the post-integration legal entity. As this income is greatly dependent on the transfer pricing policies that will be in effect post-merger, the allocation of the goodwill to the CGUs will be based on transfer pricing mechanisms. Accordingly, it could be argued that the accounting treatment also reflects the value for tax purposes at which the respective shares may be traded intra-group in connection with the integration process. This is relevant, as the two merging groups often have subsidiaries in the same country that will need to be merged. This can take the form of either:

- taxable sale of the subsidiary's shares so that the enterprises to be merged will constitute either a parent company subsidiary relationship or be affiliated enterprises with the same parent company; or
- tax-exempt merger of the two enterprises for consideration in shares (which is usually a requirement for tax exemption), which leads to a cross-ownership of the continuing enterprise after the merger, as the shareholder in the discontinuing enterprise will receive shares in the continuing enterprise. (Cross-ownership is often avoided as it leads to problems in relation to withholding tax and capital gains tax, potential negative effects on local joint taxation rules, and a complex group structure.)

In either case, an accurate allocation of intangible asset values and goodwill is important. For example, a taxable gain will arise on the share transfer in cases in which a low value is allocated to one of the subsidiaries. If, on the other hand, an excessively high value has been allocated to the other subsidiary, there is the risk that the subsidiary will not be able to generate enough cash flows to support the allocated value. As a result, the subsidiary faces an increased risk of having to write down the allocated value.

A similar problem arises when an acquired group has carried out any intragroup share transfers before the acquisition. In the eyes of tax authorities, the value fixed in prior transfers could be undermined in the case of taxable transfers if a higher value is subsequently determined for the transferred shares.

Analogous issues exist in cases in which CGUs are determined to be individual divisions of an enterprise. In these cases, the cost of the acquired group (the sum of the value of the individual divisions) must be consistent with the value allocated to the individual enterprises as part of the integration process. The subsequent allocation to individual enterprises is often particularly difficult to carry out and document for tax purposes, as the underlying documentation is limited to that required for the consolidated financial statements. In this case, it is important to take the additional step of developing the underlying documentation for legal entities, so that values can be supported in audits by the tax authorities.

So, the allocation of intangible assets and goodwill for accounting purposes should take into account tax considerations. An effective integration process considers any tax consequences and the resulting need to prepare the documentation that will be expected by tax authorities.

Linking the PPA to Transfer Pricing Policy

Transfer pricing policies are driven by the performance of functions, the assumptions of risks, and the employment of assets of the counterparties in related-party transactions. Intangible assets and components of goodwill often play big roles in defining the functional and risk profile of legal entities under transfer pricing analysis.

IFRS 3 requires the recognition and measurement of acquired assets and liabilities, including intangible assets. It also requires allocation of residual goodwill to the CGUs and subsequent annual impairment tests for each CGU that carries goodwill on its balance sheet. Accordingly, several transfer pricing issues arise.

IFRS 3 sets strict rules for which intangible assets can be separately recognised and measured. However, the tax and transfer pricing definition of an intangible asset is often much broader and less specific than the respective definitions under IFRS and U.S. GAAP. For example, customer lists, brand names, customer relationships, and backlogs are often recognised and measured separately under IFRS 3. Transfer pricing analysis often lumps all of these intangible assets together as marketing-related intangibles, which might include value that is classified as acquired goodwill under IFRS 3. So it is important to understand the scope of the intangible assets covered under each definition, and which intangible assets exist for transfer pricing purposes but not for IFRS purposes. Although accounting and tax definitions might not be consistent, their valuations should at least not contradict each other. If the fair value of a brand is determined under IFRS 3 to be 100, marketing intangibles should not fall below 100 for transfer pricing purposes if it includes customer lists, customer relationships, and the brand. Similarly, assumptions about discount rates for forecast cash flow and brand royalty rates under IFRS 3 should be consistent with those used in transfer-pricing analysis when the same basket of intangible assets is valued.

Also, IFRS 3 requires multinationals to divide themselves into CGUs so that acquired residual goodwill can be allocated. Although transfer pricing follows legal entities and not CGUs, transfer pricing policies often will affect the cash flows of each CGU and will even affect the allocation of goodwill to these CGUs. For example, a toll manufacturer will have different cash flows from a full-fledged manufacturer. The former is likely to have marginal but steady cash flow while the latter could experience fluctuation in cash flow with a much higher average profitability. These assumptions about expected future income will have a big impact on the allocation of goodwill.

Last, the intangible values developed under the PPA have to be examined each year for impairment. If the PPA assigns valuable intangibles to a CGU, while the transfer pricing analysis limits risk and profits achieved within this CGU, the income earned by the CGU might suggest that asset impairment has occurred even when an analysis of consolidated results suggests that there has been no impairment.

The determination of which intangible assets will be recognised separately will depend entirely on the characteristics of the individual enterprise. Figure 1 shows examples of intangible assets that can be recognised separately in the balance sheet.

Figure 1 – IFRS 3 illustrative examples of intangible assets

Contract-based intangible assets

- Licences, royalty and standstill agreements
- Advertising, construction, management, service or supply contracts
- Lease agreements
- Construction permits
- Franchise agreements
- Operating and broadcasting rights
- Use rights (drilling and extraction, water etc.)
- Servicing contracts
- Employment contracts

Technology-based intangible assets

- Patented technology
- Internet domain names
- Unpatented technology
- Databases
- Trade secrets such as secret formulae, processes and recipes

Marketing-related intangible assets

- Trademarks and trade names
- Service marks, collective marks, certification marks
- Trade dress
- Newspaper mastheads
- Non-competitive agreements

Customer-related intangible assets

- Customer lists
- Order or production backlog
- Customer contracts and the related customer relationships
- Non-contractual customer relationships

Artistic-related intangible assets

- Plays, operas and ballets
- Books, magazines, newspapers and other literary works
- Musical works, song lyrics and advertising jingles
- Pictures and photographs
- Video and audiovisual material

Fundamentally, under IFRS, the PPA is not influenced by how the buyer will use the acquired intangible assets. Instead, it is only dependent on how goodwill is allocated and subsequently impairment-tested. Buyer-specific assumptions and synergies should be ignored, with only market participant assumptions being taken into account.

However, in reality, post-merger intentions might affect recognition of intellectual property in the PPA process. If the buyer is acquiring a target with a brand, but intends to abandon this brand in favor of its own after the merger, the buyer is unlikely to assume a high value for the target's brand in the PPA process (or even pay anything for it). CFOs might be tempted to avoid recognition of certain intellectual property by stating their deal logic to auditors and valuation advisers. However, regardless of recognition, the total cost of the target will remain constant to the buyer, because the buyer will have taken its own deal logic into consideration in the negotiation. Whatever is not recognised from net tangible assets as intellectual property will instead be subsumed into goodwill.

Once the assets are valued and recognised on the balance sheet under IFRS 3, they might have implications on subsequent transfer pricing analyses. For example, take the case in which Group A acquires one of its competitors, Group B, in a share trade. The value of Group B could be illustrated as in Figure 2, according to the PPA.

Figure 2 – Example of purchase price allocation

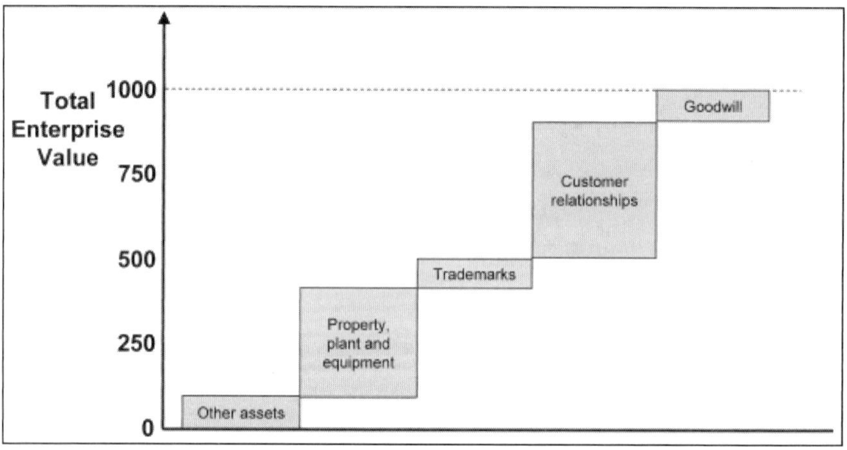

In the example, intangible assets, property, plant and equipment, and other assets have been identified and valued. The residual value is defined as goodwill. In this example, we assume that most of the purchase price has been allocated to customer relationships.

In Group A, transfer pricing policies have been developed under the assumption that the manufacturing companies carry out any non-routine activities and the activities performed by the sales companies qualify them as routine limited-risk distributors. The transfer prices for the transactions between the production facility companies and the sales companies are determined based on a resale minus method (RSM) and tested using the transactional net margin method (TNMM). Now, consider that Group A wants to apply the same structure to Group B.

The PPA performed during the merger leads us to conclude that the main driver for the acquisition is the value connected to the customer relationships within Group B. The customer relationships are built up and maintained for the account of the sales companies. So the PPA assigned a large portion of the intangible value to the sales function.

However, valuation and transfer pricing will result in very different treatments. Valuation assigns a value that is based on the simple expectation of repeat business, while transfer pricing examines which of two parties has the legal/economic rights needed to capture that value. For example, there may be a customer relationship value of 100 in the U.S. However, if a Canadian manufacturing company supplying the U.S. can terminate the contract with penalty and find another distributor, the manufacturing companies can effectively capture the residual profits that give rise to the customer relationship intangible. However, if there is a 20-year contract or if the U.S. distributor has a unique aspect such as its own trademark, then the distributor may be able to capture the customer relationship value.

Given this, and given a large PPA value for customer relationships, there are two issues. First, while the tax authorities auditing Group B's sales affiliates are likely to expect a payment for the customer relationship, the OECD Guidelines indicate that you have to look at the terms of the intercompany contracts to see whether an exit payment is needed. Depending on the customer contracts, Group A may or may not need to continue to leave the high profits in the sales subsidiaries or make an exit payment.

Second, if Group A is able to move the profits from Group B's sales subsidiaries without a high exit payment is it "planning into" an impairment charge? If the sales subsidiaries form a CGU and they have been assigned a high value of customer relationships based on Group B's historic pricing, shifting the transfer model of Group A's will lead to lower profits and, therefore, make impairment charges likely. The only way to avoid this is to use the expected going forward transfer pricing policies in the PPA allocation.

There are obvious issues with respect to the development and implementation of a consistent transfer pricing policy going forward. Group A wants to apply its transfer pricing policies to all transactions, and so wants to apply the transfer pricing rules that were in effect for Group A to the combined

Group A and Group B transactions after the merger. However, the allocation of intangible assets under the PPA suggests that Group B's sales affiliates have significant intangibles, and the transfer pricing policy should reflect that. In this case, a routine payment does not appear to apply for the sales companies, as the activities cannot be characterised as routine (unless, before implementing this routine payment, a buy-in payment is made to the subsidiaries for the transfer of non-routine intangible assets (that is, customer lists, relationships) and inter-company contracts are adjusted to shift risks).

Instead, a transfer pricing policy should be developed that reflects the fact that the sales companies create value along the supply chain, that is, where the sales activities are at least partly remunerated based on excess earnings. This will pose a challenge if Group A has planned to charge royalties for the use of the subsidiaries' trademarks, particularly if the free cash flow associated with the trademarks would result in a value for the trademarks that exceeds the value estimated for accounting purposes.

A group can be easily locked up in its considerations when determining its transfer pricing policies, despite the fact that this was never the intention. Also, functional analysis related to intangible assets must be aligned and consistent.

Integrating the Groups' Transfer Pricing Policies

When a group is acquired and the two groups' transfer pricing policies are to be integrated, it is important to establish a coherent and thoroughly documented future policy, as well as to address transition issues created in the implementation of this policy. The above example illustrates the complications that can arise in determining transfer prices. In particular, it demonstrates the tension between the need for policies that are applied to Group A and Group B transactions (for example, Group A's desire to extend its transfer pricing policies to all transactions) and the need to know whether policies are consistent with the allocation of intangibles under IFRS 3.

Moreover, any changes to the previous policy could lead to new risks. For example, if Group B from the above example has a history of not making separate payments for the use of trademarks, the capitalised value of the trademarks could constitute a historical risk.

This risk will increase if the acquiring Group A prospectively decides on a separate contributory charge for the use of the trademarks.

One way of reconciling the disparity between the application of historical policies and the considerations for intangible assets implied by the PPA is the introduction of a contributory charge for certain intangible assets. The example given above dealt with a transfer pricing structure in which no direct separate payment takes place for the use of the underlying intangible assets. Taxpayers can also use intercompany transfers to shift assets that have been identified under a PPA, and use these transfers to support a shift in transfer pricing method, although the contributory charges are likely to draw attention to transfer pricing issues. Moreover, the introduction of a new separate contributory charge could lead tax authorities to other issues. For example, the historical pattern might have been to include the payment for intangibles in product pricing, where it does not attract withholding and other taxes.

However, once the value of the relevant intangible assets has been identified and at least partially valued, certain local tax authorities might be encouraged to assess withholding taxes even for prior years. This will be most relevant when intra-group trade takes place between countries that levy tax on such payments and when the effect of this taxation has not been eliminated by a double tax treaty.

Implications for Transfer Pricing Audits

With transfer pricing issues receiving more attention in the Asia Pacific region, and many regional authorities looking for ways to increase their tax revenues, multinationals will want to know more about the implications of IFRS on transfer pricing audits.

The new IFRS requirements, particularly the requirements for separate recognition of intangible assets, have given the tax authorities a new tool for tax and transfer pricing audits. IFRS creates a much higher degree of transparency between the recognised carrying amounts and the related tax considerations and consequences. In addition the tax authorities now have other new tools at their disposal with Vietnam and Sri Lanka issuing their first transfer pricing laws, while China, Hong Kong, Singapore, Korea, and Malaysia release major new rules or requirements. This is in addition to increased audit activity in Australia, Thailand, Korea, and Japan.

For this reason, companies have strong incentives to establish enough thorough documentation to ensure the necessary link between the fair values of assets (in particular, intangible assets) determined for accounting purposes, the planned integration process, and the future transfer pricing policy.

Value Alignment Essential

Transfer pricing and PPA are interconnected, and PPAs give an indication of the value of intangible assets for transfer pricing purposes. In-house tax directors should be involved in the PPA process to ensure that the fair values are calculated properly and that any tax impacts are considered up front. In particular, if the values for IFRS 3 purposes are different from those calculated for transfer pricing purposes, reconciliation is needed.

At the same time, companies are now starting to face the reality of impairment testing under IAS 36. CGUs and reporting units are often defined in such a way that transfer prices affect revenue or cost, so the transfer pricing policy will affect cash flows, and also risk impairment.

Business Valuation Experts On Trial: A Canadian Perspective

David W. Chodikoff & Tarsem Basraon

Introduction

Perhaps it is a reflection of the complexity of the modern world. But, over the last several decades, there has been an ever increasing use of expert witnesses at trials in Canada. Experts are called upon to offer opinions on subject matters of which they have special knowledge in order to help a judge and/or judge and jury correctly understand and fully appreciate the facts put before them at trial.

The Tax Court of Canada is one legal arena that has truly seen a marked increase in the use of opinion evidence by the litigants. In many respects, it is fair to say that the Tax Court of Canada is a business court as the issues primarily involve the taxpayer challenging the state's assessment of tax. And since this assessment can take numerous forms, it is easy to understand why an expert would be called to testify in a tax court.

The subjects of business valuation experts in the Tax Court of Canada cover a broad spectrum from accounting, valuation, appraisal, business profitability and operations, highest and best use, and even native rights.

The subject areas keep developing as experts in the tax realm are permitted to testify in new and previously unexplored areas of expertise. Some questions we intend to address in this chapter are as follows: What is the general criteria for the acceptance of opinion evidence? What is the Court's role in respect of expert evidence? What is privilege and how does it impact the disclosure of the expert's working papers? We briefly examine the way to challenge a valuation expert and also consider the costs of such experts. Finally, we examine some of the specific rules regarding expert witnesses in the Tax Court of Canada.

Mohan Criteria

A common practice of litigation counsel is to suggest to the court that the expert's evidence should be admissible and any potential concerns with the expert's evidence can be dealt with as a matter of how much weight is given to this evidence. However, in *R. v. J. (J.-L.)*,[1] the Supreme Court of Canada warned that judges must take into account that they are to serve as "gatekeepers" when confronted with this precise argument. The Supreme Court of Canada specifically stated that:

> The admissibility of expert evidence should be scrutinized at the time it is proffered, and not allowed too easy an entry on the basis that all the frailties could go at the end of the day to weight rather than admissibility.[2]

To assist judges in adhering to this "gatekeeper" role, the Supreme Court of Canada in *R. v. Mohan*[3] established four criteria to determine whether the expert's evidence is admissible. Though subsequent cases have addressed the issue of whether expert evidence should be admissible, *Mohan* remains the seminal case on the subject.[4] The Supreme Court decision in *Mohan* establishes a case-by-case approach. There are four fundamental factors to consider and these are as follows:

- relevance;
- necessity in assisting the trier of fact;
- the absence of any exclusionary rule; and
- a properly qualified expert.

Relevance

Similar to any other evidence introduced before the court, relevance is a requirement for the admission of expert evidence. Relevance is a requirement that should be decided by the judge as a question of law. The expert evidence must be logically relevant such that the expert evidence is so related to a fact in issue that it tends to establish it.[5] However, the judicial inquiry does not end there. The judge must then move on to decide whether the probative value of the expert evidence exceeds its prejudicial effect. The judge has to determine whether the expert evidence's "value is worth what it costs".[6] In other words, the judge performs, in effect, a cost-benefit analysis. In *Mohan*, the Supreme Court of Canada stated that:

---

1 [2000] 2 S.C.R. 600 [*R. v. J.*].

2 *Ibid.* at para. 28.

3 [1994] 2 S.C.R. 9 [*Mohan*].

4 G.R. Anderson, *Expert Evidence*, 2nd ed. (Canada: LexisNexis Canada Inc., 2009) at 115.

5 *Mohan*, above note 3 at 20.

6 *Ibid.* at 21.

> Evidence that is otherwise logically relevant may be excluded ... if its probative value is overborne by its prejudicial effect, if it involves an inordinate amount of time which is not commensurate with its value or if it is misleading in the sense that its effect on the trier of fact, particularly a jury, is out of proportion to its reliability.[7]

Whether this analysis is undertaken within the relevance criteria or treated as an exclusionary rule, the effect is the same. An example of this analysis is the determination of whether the expert evidence distorts the fact-finding process, such that the expert evidence has the effect of having more weight than it deserves. Further, the expert evidence should be reliable and essential.

Necessity

The Supreme Court of Canada in *Mohan* stated that the word "helpful" was not the appropriate threshold and set too low a standard to determine whether the expert evidence in question is necessary to assist the trier of fact.[8] The court also warned against setting too strict a standard. In order for expert evidence to be necessary to assist the trier of fact, it must be outside the experience and knowledge of a judge and/or judge and jury. The evidence must be necessary to enable the judge and/or judge and jury to appreciate the matters in issue due to their technical nature. In most cases, due to the complexity of business valuation, the Tax Court will likely find that a business valuation expert's evidence is outside the experience and knowledge of the court. Therefore, business valuation experts are likely to be qualified as experts and heard by the Tax Court.

Even so, as is the case with the relevance factor, the evidence must be assessed in light of its potential to distort the fact finding process. So, for example, expert evidence should not be permitted to usurp the functions of the trier of fact. The closer the expert's testimony goes to the ultimate issue at hand, the stricter will be the courts' application of the requirements of reliability and necessity before admitting the evidence.[9] In addition, the expert cannot be used to determine matters of law that should be left to the judge such as the interpretation of a particular provision in the *Income Tax Act*. Simply put, the Supreme Court of Canada warned that too liberal an approach could result in trials becoming nothing more than a contest of experts with the judge serving as the referee.[10]

---

7 *Ibid.*

8 *Ibid.* at 23.

9 J. Sopinka, S.N. Lederman & A.W. Bryant, *The Law of Evidence in Canada*, 2nd ed. (Markham: Butterworths, 1999) at 641.

10 *Mohan*, above note 3 at 24.

Absence of Any Exclusionary Rule

The admissibility of an expert cannot violate a general exclusionary rule of evidence.[11] For example, allowing expert evidence cannot infringe on the rule against oath-helping, privilege, or the exclusionary character rule. However, most of the general exclusionary rules of evidence deal with criminal cases and do not apply to business valuation experts testifying in the Tax Court of Canada.

Properly Qualified Expert

The expert must have "acquired special or peculiar knowledge through study or experience in respect of the matters on which he or she undertakes to testify".[12] Once it is established that an expert is properly qualified in a particular area, he or she may only provide evidence directly related to that area of expertise.

Business valuation experts are a unique subset of experts. While not absolutely essential, a professional designation is unquestionably an advantage. For example, in *Trepanier v. M.N.R.*,[13] the court stated that:

> With rare exceptions, anyone who represents himself as an expert in valuation should be a member of a professional corporation of valuators. If an exception is to be made, it must be shown, for example, that the individual not only has a great deal of experience but has also worked in the property field for a number of years.[14]

The Canadian Institute of Chartered Business Valuators ("CICBV") was formed in 1971 to further the educational and professional standards of business valuators. The CICBV regulates Chartered Business Valuators ("CBV"). CBVs are specifically equipped to value businesses and being a CBV is essential to being qualified as a business valuation expert in court. In addition, the valuation expert should have significant experience in valuing the type of business in question. For example, a CBV that exclusively has experience valuing forestry and mining companies may be unqualified to value a software company due to the fact that the two industries have their own distinctive characteristics.

---

11 *Ibid.* at 25.

12 *Ibid.*

13 [1979] C.T.C. 3164, 79 D.T.C. 924 (T.R.B.) [*Trepanier*].

14 *Ibid.* at 926 [D.T.C.].

The Importance of Analyzing the *Mohan* Criteria

Depending on the size and complexity of a business, the costs associated with hiring a business expert can be considerable. Therefore, counsel should be fairly confident that the expert's appearance at court and testimony are essential to the success of the case. Counsel should study the *Mohan* factors carefully before making a decision on whether to retain a valuation expert. In particular, counsel should be certain that the probative value of the expert evidence exceeds its prejudicial effect.

Court's Function with Respect to Experts

Even if the expert's evidence is admissible, the trier of fact must still ultimately make the decision as to the actual valuation. This view has been upheld by the Federal Court of Appeal in *Connor v. R.*,[15] where a trial judge accepted some of the evidence presented by the two opposing experts but rejected some of the methods used by the experts:

> As noted earlier, the Trial Judge did, in fact, refuse to accept the valuations of the experts, including Thompson, and made his own calculations to arrive at a valuation of $625 per share as at December 31, 1971. It is trite to say that the Trial Judge is the trier of fact and he is thus entitled to accept or reject, in whole or in part, any of the evidence adduced before him. In this case, he accepted some of the evidence but he rejected in all cases the methods, at least in part, whereby the experts arrived at their valuations. *He was entitled to do so and unless it can be said that thereafter he proceeded on a wrong principle or that he made a palpable error in reaching his own conclusions as to value, we ought not to interfere with his findings.* We have not been persuaded by the arguments of counsel that he proceeded on a wrong principle or made any such error. Certainly he appears to have adopted parts of the methods used by the witnesses in making their calculations but in using only parts and not the whole of their respective methods we do not believe that he erred in law.[16] [Emphasis added.]

As stated in *Hallatt v. The Queen*,[17] a business valuation expert's role is to assist the court in arriving at its own conclusions:

> From the foregoing it is clear that the court is not bound to accept any expert opinion. Indeed, since the function of the expert is to assist the court in arriving at its own conclusion, the expert's conclusion is frequently of less importance than the reasoning that lies behind the conclusion.[18]

---

15 [1979] C.T.C. 365, 79 D.T.C. 5256 (Fed. C.A.) [*Connor*].

16 *Ibid.* at 5257 [D.T.C.].

17 (2000), [2001] 1 C.T.C. 2626, 2001 D.T.C. 128 (T.C.C.), appeal dismissed [2004] 2 C.T.C. 313, 2004 D.T.C. 6176 (F.C.A.) [*Hallatt*].

18 *Ibid.* at para. 44.

Objectivity

Due to the expert's primary role being to assist the judge or jury, expert witnesses in Canada must provide an objective, unbiased opinion. Business valuation involves many subjective factors such as "goodwill" calculations and, therefore, the objectivity of the business valuation expert is essential to the functioning of a fair judicial system. The case that is used by most Canadian courts to evaluate objectivity is the English decision of *The Ikarian Reefer*.[19] The *Ikarian Reefer* establishes various duties and responsibilities for an expert witness. The expert evidence should be the independent product of the expert and the expert should provide independent assistance to the court by way of an objective, unbiased opinion. In other words, the expert witness should never be an advocate for one side of the dispute. In addition, the expert must state the facts and assumptions on which his or her opinion is based and should not omit any material facts. The expert should also make it clear as to why a particular question or issue falls outside the expert's knowledge and must state if there was insufficient data to arrive at an appropriate valuation. If after the exchange of reports, an expert witness changes his or her valuation conclusions after reading the other side's expert report, he or she must inform the opposing party of the change of view. Finally, if the expert evidence refers to calculations, analyses, or other similar documents, the expert must provide these documents to the other party at the time the reports are exchanged.

Business valuation experts need to ensure that their report is as objective as possible as expert evidence is usually given more weight if it appears that it is an impartial and balanced opinion. For example, in the family law case of *Debora v. Debora*,[20] the court concluded that the husband's business valuation expert did not meet the level of objectivity and neutrality required of an expert. Each party hired an expert to value a marketing company owned by the husband. However, the husband's expert relied solely on the financial statements of the company and failed to take into account obvious other factors that were taken into account by the wife's expert such as a reassessment of the company prepared by the Canada Revenue Agency ("CRA").

Sometimes an expert's objectivity is challenged because the expert is paid for his or her services. For example, many times the expert called by the Minister of National Revenue (the "MNR") is actually a CRA employee. However, the courts have generally taken the following approach as stated in *Hallatt*:

---

19 *National Justice Compania Naviera SA v. Prudential Assurance Co.*, [1993] 2 Lloyd's Rep. 68 (Eng. Q.B.) [*The "Ikarian Reefer"*].

20 [2004] O.J. No. 4826 (S.C.J.), appeal dismissed [2006] O.J. No. 4826 (C.A.) [*Debora*].

> Mr. Gamble took the position that since Mr. Eagle and Mr. Jones were employees of CCRA their testimony as experts should not be accepted, because of the apparent lack of independence. I did not accept this contention. *If a person who is otherwise qualified as an expert happens to be employed by the party who calls him or her, this is not a basis for excluding that person's evidence.* If there is any ground for believing that their evidence may be tainted by bias or lack of independence, this is something that can be explored on cross-examination. Essentially I agree with the observations on this point of Bowie J. in *Gilvesy Enterprises Inc. v. R.* (1996), 97 D.T.C. 811 (T.C.C.), at 815.[21] [Emphasis added.]

In addition, the CICBV has a Code of Ethics that specifically addresses independence. It requires experts who are providing professional services where there is an expectation of independence to hold themselves free of any influence or interest in respect of the client's affairs. If the valuator is easily influenced by the client, it could impair his or her professional judgment or objectivity.

Use of Hearsay Information

In the course of arriving at a valuation, business valuators will often have discussions with third parties such as competitors or industry regulators of the business in question. Due to the complexity and plethora of factors involved in valuing a business, this practice is permissible and sometimes even necessary. Therefore, experts sometimes rely on information that is technically "hearsay". In other words, the experts may rely on information that the expert does not know of personally. According to the Supreme Court of Canada in *R. v. Lavallee*,[22] expert opinion is admissible even if it is based on second-hand evidence.[23] However, the second-hand evidence is only admissible to show the facts on which the expert's opinion is based and not as evidence going to the existence of those facts. The Supreme Court of Canada also stated that even if the facts are based in part upon "suspect" information, the matter is dealt with as one of weight.[24] This exception to the general rule against hearsay evidence also extends to the ability of expert witnesses to answer hypothetical questions.[25]

---

21 *Hallatt*, above note 17 at para. 8.

22 [1990] 1 S.C.R. 852 [*Lavallee*].

23 *Ibid.* at 898.

24 *Ibid.* at 900.

25 A.M. Schwartz & E.T. Yanoshita, "The Use of Expert Witnesses in Tax Litigation" in *Advocacy & Taxation in Canada* (Toronto: Irwin Law Inc., 2004) at 238-240.

Third Party Experts

Even though hearsay evidence is admissible, the use of a third party expert to assist with arriving at an expert opinion raises several issues. The reputation and qualifications of the third party expert must be evaluated by the court and the third party expert should be available to testify in court if necessary.[26] If the third party expert is not available, the opposing party is at an unfair disadvantage as there would be no opportunity to evaluate the abilities of the third party or subject them to cross-examination.

Another issue arising out of the use of third party experts occurs when the author of an expert report leaves the firm they were working for and another expert takes his or her place and testifies in court on behalf of the expert that authored the report. In *McCoy v. The Queen*,[27] the judge concluded that one expert cannot put in another expert's report and submit it as evidence. In *McCoy*, the replacement expert's testimony was not given "the sort of evidentiary weight or value necessary to establish ... the conclusions expressed in the report".

Privilege of the Expert's Working Papers

With a task as involved as valuing a business, there will be a large quantity of notes, calculations, draft reports, and other working papers accumulated by the business valuation expert throughout the valuation process. Working papers could also comprise of the expert's communications with the lawyer, other experts or with the client. A critical issue is whether these working papers have to be disclosed to the opposing party or whether these working papers are covered by the legal concept of litigation privilege. Litigation privilege, as opposed to solicitor-client privilege, protects a litigant's interest in being able to "prepare his or her case thoroughly without fear that he or she will be required to disclose findings made at each stage of the litigation process."[28]

As expected, litigation privilege is narrower than solicitor-client privilege but the issue is how much narrower? Unfortunately, the case law in Canada does not provide a precise answer and the decisions do appear to conflict when the issue concerns the subjects of disclosure versus privilege and the working papers of the expert.[29] For example, in *Bell Canada v. Olympia &*

---

26 J.L. Horvath & S.A. Hacker, "Reflections on the Expert's Role in the Tax Court of Canada" in *Advocacy & Taxation in Canada* (Toronto: Irwin Law Inc., 2004) at 274.

27 [2003] 4 C.T.C. 2607, 2003 D.T.C. 660 (T.C.C.) [*McCoy*].

28 M.J. Freiman & M.L. Berenblut, *The Litigator's Guide to Expert Witnesses* (Aurora: Canada Law Book Inc., 1997) at 23.

29 Above note 25 at 245-249.

York Developments Ltd.,[30] the court found that there was no waiver of privilege by having the witness testify at trial but, in the case of *Vancouver Community College v. Phillips, Barratt*,[31] the court found that, by having the witness testify, there was a waiver of privilege. The authors of the *Law of Evidence in Canada* took the middle ground and concluded that confidential information that is not part of the foundation of the expert's opinion is not automatically waived by having the expert witness testify.[32] *Piché v. Lecours Lumber Co.*[33] is an insightful Ontario case that reaches a similar conclusion to that of the authors in the *Law of Evidence in Canada*. *Piché* also provides some general guidelines for whether privilege applies to the working papers of an expert such as:

a) The privilege claims for documents in an expert's file are not waived simply by calling the expert as a witness.
b) Privilege may be waived in respect of those facts or premises in the expert's file which have been used to base the expert's opinion and which came to the expert's knowledge from documents supplied to that expert.
c) Whether there is privilege can be ascertained in one of two ways. The judge can examine the documents or materials for which the privilege is claimed. Alternatively, the judge may cross-examine the expert to determine whether all or part of the file is privileged.
d) As a general rule, if facts are supplied that are not found in other evidence, or if certain assumptions are asked to be made in the instructing documents, privilege should be waived for those facts or assumptions.

A strategy that is occasionally used by counsel to minimize disclosure is to limit the information provided to the expert in order to minimize the provision of information. However, this approach could backfire as the expert may not have enough information to provide a reliable and worthwhile valuation. By providing the expert with limited information, counsel may be providing ammunition for the opposing party's cross-examination of the expert witness. The opposing party could raise the argument that the report is missing various material facts or key documents and, therefore, the reliability of the report is restricted and/or of little value to the court.

Of particular concern to counsel are draft reports. Draft reports may contain contradictory conclusions to that of the final report, which may raise questions regarding the reliability and objectivity of the expert witness. One

---

30 (1989), 68 O.R. (2d) 103 (H.C.) [*Bell Canada*].
31 (1987), 20 B.C.L.R. (2d) 289 (S.C.) [*Vancouver Community College*].
32 Above note 9 at 762.
33 (1993), 13 O.R. (3d) 193 (Gen. Div.) [*Piché*].

strategy that lawyers have been known to use in order to protect the possibility of draft reports having to be produced at trial is to have the expert destroy all of the draft reports. However, this will likely throw into question the expert's objectivity. Another strategy employed by counsel is to instruct the expert to write his or her final report only after oral consultation with counsel so that there is only one written expert's report. However, this may also result in the judge drawing a negative inference in relation to the expert's objectivity. Furthermore, the disclosure obligations would apply to oral and written communications.

According to the guidelines set out in *Piché*, it should be noted that it is questionable whether a draft report even needs to be produced. There is an argument that the draft report itself does not form the basis for the expert's opinion and, therefore, privilege should not be waived.

Challenging a Valuation Expert

If the judge concludes that the *Mohan* criteria have been met and allows the expert to testify, counsel must explore options to challenge the valuation expert's conclusions. The most obvious strategy is to hire a business valuation expert to prepare a rebuttal report. However, another less costly strategy may be to hire a valuation expert that does not produce his or her own expert report but assists in interpreting the opposing party's expert report and assists in constructing cross-examination questions.

An often overlooked strategy to challenging a valuation expert is to hire a litigation consultant before the opposing party's valuation expert even begins their work. Using a litigation consultant well versed in business valuation experts while the opposing party's expert is valuing the business in question provides counsel with a head start. For example, the litigation consultant can inform counsel as to why the opposing party's expert is demanding a certain type of document or a certain financial statement. In addition, having knowledge of what documents were produced and given to the opposing party's expert may provide a basis for challenging the valuation by proving that the expert ignored vital documents that were in his or her possession. The litigation consultant will also be able to provide advice throughout discovery and even at trial by preparing cross-examination questions for the opposing party's expert.

One of the most vital options to challenging an opposing expert's valuation conclusions is to cross-examine the expert. A source for potential cross-examination questions may come from earlier published works by the opposing expert. It is critical for counsel to read all of the published material by the opposing expert as an article authored by the expert may contain contradictory theories or methods than the ones used by the expert in his or her expert report.

Counsel should also read case law in which the expert provided evidence to determine the credibility of the expert. Another option is for counsel to review the CICBV Practice Standards to ensure that the expert adhered to these standards. For example, Standard No. 110 provides valuation report standards and recommendations.

Ensuring that there are no errors or contradictions in the expert's evidence is also critical. The presence of any errors or contradictions will likely result in the expert's evidence as a whole being viewed as questionable and lacking reliability. For example, in *Taylor Estate v. M.N.R.*,[34] the court found that the Minister's expert's evidence contained contradictions and concluded that the appellant's valuation was much more realistic. The court further stated that:

> Nor do I express an opinion on the correctness of the data of the appellant's expert witness, but I could not find any fundamental errors in their presentation that might seriously have distorted the results of his valuation and the opinions he expressed.[35]

There are also several other specific areas that can be addressed during a cross-examination of a business valuation expert that may put into question the reliability or objectivity of the expert's evidence. Examples of these other specific areas are as follows:

- Does the expert have appropriate credentials to offer a quality valuation?
- Has the expert ever been denied qualification as an expert in another trial?
- What valuation methods did the expert use?
- Are these valuation methods commonly used in the industry?
- What information or documents did the expert rely on or ignore?
- Did the expert visit the premises of the business?
- Did the expert interview individuals that could have provided insight into valuation such as customers and competitors?
- Did the expert take into account the specific characteristics of the industry in question?
- Is there a relationship between opposing counsel and the expert or the opposing party and the expert that questions the objectivity of the report?
- Does the expert's compensation depend on the outcome of the case?

---

34 [1990] 2 C.T.C. 2304, 90 D.T.C. 1777 (T.C.C.) [*Taylor Estate*].

35 *Ibid.* at 1785 [D.T.C.].

- Do the expert's standards, methods, theories, and calculations match those of earlier reports by the expert, *i.e.*, is he or she consistent?
- What assumptions did the business valuation expert use and are they unreasonable and challengeable?
- Did the expert take into account special purchasers, discounts, or premiums?

Cost of Business Valuation Experts

Due to the complexity of some business valuations, the cost of hiring an expert to prepare an expert report, assist in interpreting the opposing party's expert report, and to testify at trial, may be significant. As we discussed in this chapter, counsel should be relatively certain that an expert will be accepted by the court and is necessary to assist in determining a critical issue before the court. The cost consequences of hiring a valuation expert also raise concerns related to access to justice. For example, in a family law dispute, if one spouse has a valuable business and uses a "hired gun" to undervalue it, the cost to the other spouse to obtain a business valuation expert on top of legal fees may be overwhelming. Also, if a taxpayer is appealing a tax ruling, the taxpayer's resources may be limited whereas the Minister may have the resources to hire multiple business valuation experts. Not only are the costs to the parties noteworthy but judicial resources may be misused and abused. As stated by Major J. in *R. v. D. (D.)*:[36]

> Finally, expert evidence is time-consuming and expensive. Modern litigation has introduced a proliferation of expert opinions of questionable value. The significance of the costs to the parties and the resulting strain upon judicial resources cannot be overstated. When the door to the admission of expert evidence is opened too widely, a trial has the tendency to degenerate into "a contest of experts with the trier of fact acting as referee in deciding which expert to accept".[37]

One option to combat the costs of an expert is for the successful party to ask the court to recover the fees it paid to hire an expert. For example, the successful party under the General Procedure in the Tax Court of Canada may recover costs incurred for an expert under Rule 147 of the *Tax Court of Canada Rules*. Whether the costs are recoverable and the quantum of the costs is ultimately in the discretion of the court. It must be shown that the business valuation expert's fees were necessary and a proper expenditure

---

36 [2000] 2 S.C.R. 275 [*R. v. D.*].

37 *Ibid.* at 301.

of the party's case.[38] In exercising its discretionary power, the Tax Court of Canada may consider, among other factors:

- the result of the proceeding;
- the importance of the issues;
- the complexity of the issues; or
- the conduct of any party that tended to shorten or to lengthen unnecessarily the duration of the proceeding.

Statutory Rules Related to Expert Witnesses

Most courts in Canada have their own specific rules in relation to the use of expert witnesses and these must be addressed before hiring an expert. For example, in General Procedure tax cases, Rule 145 of the *Tax Court of Canada Rules (General Procedure)* governs expert witnesses. Section 53.03 of the *Rules of Civil Procedure* governs expert witnesses for civil cases. In addition, experts and expert evidence also fall within the general rules of evidence.

The rules of a particular court deal with a variety of issues related to the use of an expert witness. For example, paragraph 145(2)(c) of the *Tax Court of Canada Rules (General Procedure)* requires that the expert witness be available at the hearing for cross-examination. Additionally, for the purposes of disclosure and giving the opposing party the opportunity to prepare for trial, the expert usually needs to file an expert's report that sets out his or her calculations, assumptions, and conclusions. Some courts mandate specific requirements for the expert's report. For example, subsection 53.03(2.1) of the *Rules of Civil Procedure* lists requirements for an expert's report such as:

- the instructions provided to the expert in relation to the proceeding; and
- the expert's reasons for his or her opinion, including,
    - a description of the factual assumptions on which the opinion is based,
    - a description of any research conducted by the expert that led him or her to form the opinion, and
    - a list of every document, if any, relied on by the expert in forming the opinion.

---

38 R.W. McMechan, "The Valuator as an Expert Witness and Managing the Tax Dispute Resolution Process", 1995 Corporate Management Tax Conference 18:1.

Conclusion

Business valuation experts are now commonplace in the Tax Court of Canada. The challenge for the litigants and, specifically, for the counsel for the taxpayer and for the government is the selection of an expert that has the appropriate skills to properly assist their respective party put forward the best possible case before the judge of the Tax Court. This is not an easy task. In fact, the retention of an expert is quite complicated because it often involves the balancing of multiple interests between the lawyer, client, and expert and this further involves the balancing of experience, skills, personalities, and costs. Sometimes counsel may find one expert cheaper but not necessarily more experienced than a second expert. Possibly a third expert is great to work with but he/she is too expensive or the client does not want to work with that expert because of a clash of personalities. The selection of the business valuation expert may be time consuming and difficult. In the end however, the selection is critical.

The product that both sides want is a clear and understandable expert report that can be backed up by oral testimony. If the business valuation expert prepares a clear and relevant report, more often than not the Tax Court judge will allow him/her to testify. The business valuator's testimony and report can play a pivotal role in the ultimate disposition of a tax case. It seems clear that in the years to come there will be an ever-expanding need for certified business valuators to appear on behalf of litigants in the Tax Court of Canada.

Tips, Thoughts, and Observations

James L. Horvath & Robert Low

In valuing a business or investment by mechanically applying methodologies, a valuator can easily – and sometimes conveniently – overlook the practical reality. A comprehensive and well-founded valuation analysis will appear reasonable, both from the perspective of the input-output of valuation methods and equations as well as a common sense viewpoint. The value conclusion should result from a progression of logical thought that makes sense to valuation professionals and non-practitioners alike. The following tips, thoughts, and observations are a collection of first-person accounts, third-party observations, and suggestions on the sensible application of valuation theory and practice.

General Valuation Process

The process of completing a valuation assignment can run the gamut from very ordinary and familiar to incredibly intricate and arduous. It is important to not get lost in either the detail or the lack thereof.

Make the Complex Simple

Practice Tip

> Make everything as simple as possible, but not simpler.
>
> **Albert Einstein**

Valuations are becoming ever more complex with ever changing market conditions and rules, numerous valuation methodologies, the ever-increasing amount of market information that has to be analyzed and complex issues of fact. The valuator's job is to shift through and analyze all the data and issues and then crystallize his findings into a simple, easily comprehendible report which draws the reader to the desired conclusion on value.

The Day After the Day Before

What a difference a day can make. Value is at a point in time. In some cases, a day can have a very significant impact on fair market value. Take, for example, some of the more extreme global stock market value change dates: Black Tuesday, October 29, 1929, Black Monday, October 19, 1987, and the attacks of September 11, 2001.

Confirm Existence of the Asset

It is important to "kick the tires" when completing any valuation. In one case, we were asked for an opinion on the value of a company's software. The company had just obtained two valuations. One valued the software at $140 million, the other valued it at $40 million. Both valuations depended on a discounted cash flow approach. Management believed that the fair market value of the software was likely $140 million or more and wanted a third, supporting opinion.

As part of our valuation analysis, we asked for a copy of the software so that we could verify its functionality and richness and estimate its replacement cost using function-point analysis. We learned that the company had not yet developed the software. The executives of the company said they planned to use the proceeds from the sale of partial interests in the software to finance its development.

The previous two valuators apparently had blindly applied a discounted cash flow approach to value non-existing software, or at best, an idea.

Verify Key Information

We were involved in the valuation and merger of two companies. The purchaser paid $6 million for Target A. The transaction price was incorrectly reported in the financial section of a major newspaper as $24 million. A few months later, we were asked to review a valuation report prepared by a valuator from another firm on a company competing in the same industry. We concluded initially that the valuation was unusually high. When we looked at the benchmark comparables, we discovered the valuator had relied heavily on the $24 million incorrectly reported as having being paid for Target A.

In addition to confirming the actual amount of a comparable transaction, the underlying attributes and substance of the transaction must also be reviewed. Unusual features and motivations can affect a transaction price. Unless you were involved in the transaction, this information is frequently not available. In some cases, valuators can obtain or verify transaction details through discussions with the seller and buyer and their representatives.

Internet Research

The Internet is a powerful and easily accessible information source but be wary of credibility.

Site Visits and Management Discussions

Early in my valuations career, I was scheduled to appear as an expert witness. As the trial began, the judge spoke to the solicitors who had hired me and suggested that they should settle, in part, because he would place little weight on the opposing expert's report. The opposing expert had not visited the business, conducted a site inspection, or interviewed management.

A simple tour of the business can easily sway a valuator's views on value. In some extreme cases, such as: when a business presents badly, appears like a place waiting for a major accident or catastrophe to happen, or indicates the potential for extraordinary environmental liabilities, the valuator could conclude that prudent investors would potentially avoid such a business altogether.

Unrealistic Cash Flow Projections (the Hockey Stick Forecast)

Over my career, I've seen many unrealistic cash flow projections. In certain cases, we have walked away from prospective valuation assignments if we could not account for the inherent risk contained in management's operational forecasts. In other cases, we applied probabilities with "normal" discount rates, or a very high discount rate to account for the additional risk that the company would ever realize management's projections.

Unrealistic Discount Rates

From time to time, a client will argue for an unrealistically low discount rate. The client usually argues that these lower rates are industry norms. The client will occasionally support his argument with a survey of rates from analyst reports. Unfortunately, discount rates do not exist in isolation. They depend on the specific company and on factors such as operational risks, market competition, anticipated growth opportunities, *etc.* Conversely, a very high discount rate may indicate that the valuator should not have used a discounted cash flow or an earnings approach to reach his conclusions. Instead, he should have used a replacement-cost or multiple-of-cost approach.

Rules of Thumb

Rules of thumb, generally known, simple formulae for valuing a business (for example, 1 x revenue or 10 x EBIT), may exist in an industry. Examples of industries where rules of thumb are believed to exist are radio and television stations, cable television operators, and funeral homes. Frequently they suggest values that appear high. A valuator should ignore them at his peril.

A valuator needs to assess the existence of rules of thumb in an industry, why they exist, what they represent in the nature of a transaction, and how to rationalize them with standard valuation methodologies. For example, some rules of thumb are representative of larger companies simply buying a "book of business", say for an insurance agency, with a realization of significant economies of scale.

Major Assumptions and Limiting Conditions

To minimize costs while providing the reader/user with a reasonable estimate of value, the client and valuator will often make simplifying assumptions or estimates. In assessing the market value of the company's real-estate holdings, for example, they may rely on a management representation. Or a solicitor who wants to present to the court a value based on a certain specific scenario may ask the valuator for a calculation based on that specific hypothetical situation. Clearly state these assumptions and ensure that the parameters that have confined the valuation analysis are known and quantify how they have impacted the valuator's conclusion.

Isolate Key Value Drivers

Practice Tip

When you are in the middle of the trees, you don't see the forest.

The most renowned and efficient valuators are able to use their professional judgment in order to focus on the major value drivers, colloquially-speaking they will "separate the forest from the trees". For example, using a market approach, they focus on a company's major strengths and weaknesses compared to the selected set of comparable companies. In performing a discounted cash flow analysis, they do not incorporate excessive detail but regard the valuation as an estimate and focus on the company in the same way as a buyer, looking mainly at the critical value drivers. The valuator acquires this ability from his/her prior experience in valuing similar companies and a knowledge of how businesses are typically bought or sold.

Mid-year Discounting

A standard present value table or cash flow discounting exercise will assume that the cash flows occur entirely at the end of each specific fiscal period. In practice, a business's operating cash flows are generated over the entire course of the year, often following a seasonal pattern. In these cases, reducing the length of the forecast time-unit to quarterly or monthly will improve the accuracy of the valuation conclusion. More commonly, valuation practitioners will apply a mid-year discounting adjustment, assuming operating cash flows occur at a constant rate over the forecast period. A valuation conclusion arrived at using end-of-year cash flows is *multiplied by* $(1+r)^{1/2}$ to reflect mid-year discounting.

Fairness Opinions in a Market Consolidation Transaction

A market consolidator sets out to amalgamate a number of participants in a fragmented market. The consolidator acquires incremental value for investors relative to its standalone targets because of its accumulated leading market position, anticipated operating efficiencies, and economies of scale. But how do the acquirer and vendor share this increment in value, if at all? Why would the acquiror pay for what he brings to the transaction?

The buyer and seller in a market consolidation transaction must understand their options to determine the fair treatment of their respective interests. An independent valuator would assess the following:

- consolidation rationale and suitability;
- stage of market consolidation achieved through the acquisition;
- quantification and timing of synergies;
- implementation and integration strategy.

Several issues influence this assessment: knowledge of, or speculation with respect to, what the buyer may be able to do after the acquisition, and the degree of negotiating leverage held by the vendor in the transaction negotiation and the likelihood of another liquidity event occurring for the vendor.

Prior Purchase Offers

Valuators review *completed transactions* of a company's shares using several criteria such as arm's length basis, time proximity, transaction size, and contractual caveats. They must apply a much higher threshold of scrutiny to an *offer to purchase* before giving it any evidentiary value. Prior offers must be *bona fide* and freely negotiated, for example. The party making the offer should have had the financial capacity to consummate the transaction and sufficient detail should be available to compute the cash equivalent value of the offer.

Ultimately, the valuator must identify the practical reasons for the transaction's failure and somehow reconcile these with comparable completed transactions before he can use a prior offer to help in measuring a company's market value.

Disaggregated Analysis

In many cases, a business includes several divisions or operating lines. For example, a retail company may operate a credit card division in association with its branded retail outlets. The valuator must identify these different lines of business and assess the material differences, if any, in their associated risks and prospects. If they have different risks and prospects, then key inputs such as discount rates, growth assumptions, and operating margins will also differ across the various lines of business. Assessed together, an aggregate analysis of the lines of business may lead to distorted value conclusions. Instead, the valuator should value each distinct business operation separately, then aggregate the individual values to determine the value of the business in its entirety.

Verify Ownership Terms of Intangibles

An analysis of the value of technology-related intangibles such as patents, copyrights, and trade-secrets begins with a review of the terms and security of ownership. The valuator must:

- identify the intangible by name, date granted, and registration number;

- review all copies of application documents and identify limitations;
- determine the intangible's expected life and the ability to extend protection beyond the statutory life; and
- establish the potential for new spin-off patents, copyrights, or trade-secrets that can be filed from the original technology.

Don't Overlook Electronic Evidence

Practice Tip

Remember that financial and other relevant information often exists both in paper form and electronically. Analysis by computer forensics experts of a party's electronic data, such as email, may uncover undisclosed side agreements, liabilities, etc.

Gary Moulton, CA•IFA

A valuation of a business or an investment is only as credible as the information upon which it is based. In a dispute valuation, it is vital that the valuator critically assess the evidence upon which the valuation is to be based.

It is important to remember that much information today is maintained in electronic form. Most organizations store huge amounts of vital information, including email, electronically rather than the traditional method of paper and microfiche. Much data is sitting on networks and hard drives without the user ever being aware it exists – often even partially destroyed information can be recovered by forensic experts.

How can this information be of value? Consider the scenario where a party to a dispute has represented that his company has entered into a lucrative long-term contract with a customer and has produced a signed contract from that customer as evidence. The valuator must be wary of the possibility of altered documents, undisclosed side agreements, and other misrepresentations. Having access to the party's electronic data might show that related email traffic between the party and customer sheds a different light on the true intent and force of the contract.

Using Technology in a Valuation

In recent years, technology has increasingly influenced the valuation process itself. Valuators now have access to Internet-based comparable transactions and risk-analysis databases. They can use valuation software to select an appropriate methodology and calculate the value conclusion. Although such tools may provide some assistance in reaching a value conclusion, they do not provide definitive answers. As always, a valuation conclusion involves both art *and* science. The input-output nature of a software program or website cannot replace the nuanced judgment of the valuator.

When using valuation software, valuators should consider several factors, including:

- underlying mechanics of the software;
- key variables that drive the value output;
- potential for embedded errors;
- dated or unrealistic assumptions;
- reasonableness of the conclusion compared to industry norms;
- sensitivity analysis.

Industry Multiple Valuations

Business valuations which utilize industry multiples are reducing more complex cash flow and discount rate variables to simple linear relationships. When selecting optimal proportional relationships – for the purpose of performing relative valuations – the appraiser should be wary of several key considerations:

- isolating key value drivers for the subject company and industry is critical in determining the most suitable multiple;
- the best multiples are those industry "constants" or comparables that, when plotted on a simple graph, offer the tightest distribution;
- the tighter the distribution, the greater the expectation that any specific subject company will be near the industry average;
- public company data – although abundant – must be analyzed for suitability when used to value a closely-held company. Public companies often have different risk variables, investment time horizons, and liquidity risks.

The Price/Sales Multiples' Method

The use of the price/sales multiples' method (or, the P/S ratio as it is commonly referred to) in valuing a business implicitly assumes that revenue generates an appropriate level of bottom-line profit/earnings in a given industry. This assumption is consistent with one of the principles of valuation which is that (with one exception) the value of an asset is based on, or directly linked to, what it can *earn* (as opposed to what it can generate by way of sales). The exception is where the asset is worth less on an earnings basis than if it is liquidated.

The use of price/sales multiples in valuing a closely-held entity is actually a variation of what business valuators refer to as the Guideline Public Company method. In valuing private companies' shares, the Guideline Public Company method is typically used to derive stock market trading value parameters (*e.g.*, sales, earnings, book value, EBITDA multiples, *etc.*) from somewhat comparable public companies. These value parameters are then adjusted (generally downwards) to reflect the relative size differences and lack of marketability inherent in the shares of a private company vis-à-vis the selected public companies.

The application of the P/S ratio to value private companies has intuitive appeal, since private companies, if they publicly disclose any financial information at all, are less averse to disclosing sales/revenues than earnings. The danger in a cursory application of the multiple of sales method, however, is that one may tend to overvalue the subject (assuming the latter has little or no earnings) by simply extracting revenue multiples from the market place. Simply put, it is always easier to generate a dollar of revenue than a dollar of earnings. The tendency during the dot.com craze of 1999/early-2000 to use revenue multiples (some as high as 80 times!) on *prospective* sales, when such fledgling companies had yet to generate a dollar of current revenue, let alone earnings, underscores the abuse to which this method was subject.

Although, price/sales is an accepted term to describe this method, the numerator "P" should realistically be "EV" (enterprise value). Enterprise value reflects the total capitalization of the company, *i.e.*, market capitalization plus interest-bearing debt less cash and near-cash equivalents (*e.g.*, marketable securities). The concept is that a dollar of sales/revenue generated has to cover not only corporate costs and expenses, but also the cost of servicing the debt (interest costs), before providing a return to the stockholder(s). Moreover, the use of the EV/S multiple (as opposed to the P/S multiple), in effect, eliminates differences in the way in which the subject company is financed vis-à-vis comparable public companies.

Even if industry convention (such as, for those operating as professional practices, travel agencies, insurance agencies, and other service businesses) dictates the use of the P/S method (or, EV/S as some prefer to call it), it should not be applied in isolation and without corroboration using other valuation methods. Apply the "smell-test". Does the result obtained when applying this method support a capitalized earnings value? If not, then an attempt at reconciliation may be useful since it may lead to a finding of a positive or negative element of value previously ignored.

Purchased Goodwill and Non-compete Agreements

When purchasing a business with goodwill, if the buyer pays the vendor an *additional* amount (*i.e.*, over and above the fair market value of the business) for a limited-period management/consulting contract and/or a non-compete agreement, it would be likely tantamount to overpaying for that business.

For example, let's assume that the fair market value of a business is $1,000,000, comprising $400,000 of net tangible assets and $600,000 of "goodwill". To emphasize the point we are trying to make, let's also assume that the bulk of the goodwill is attributed to the vendor being a key (though not entirely indispensable) person in this business. The concept of fair market value ("the highest price" being one of the principal tenets in its definition) implies that the vendor will take all reasonable, prudent steps to maximize value on disposition of his/her interest. These steps may include entering into a consulting contract (assumed value $250,000) and/or a non-competition agreement (assumed value $200,000) for a reasonable pre-determined period, both of which are meant to assist in the smooth transference or commercialization of goodwill primarily created by the vendor. From the buyer's perspective, the agreements afford continuity (through the consulting contract) and a degree of protection from goodwill erosion (by virtue of a non-compete agreement). Absent these agreements, there would be no economic justification for the buyer to pay the full amount (*i.e.*, $600,000) for the indicated goodwill. From a valuation perspective, therefore, the business's value can be broken down into the following components:

Net tangible assets	$400,000
Consulting contract	250,000
Non-compete	200,000
Indicated goodwill	150,000
Fair market value	$1,000,000

If the above example was an open market "real-life" transaction, there is no implied assumption that these agreements will have been entered into contemporaneous with the closing of the transaction. The buyer, with the help of his advisor(s) during the negotiation process, would be well-advised to have these agreements in place in order to justify the $1,000,000 price tag for the business as a whole. If, for any reason, the vendor refuses to enter into such agreements, the buyer has the option to pay a lower amount for the goodwill, say, $150,000 [$600,000 minus ($250,000 + $200,000) based on the above example], or simply walk away from the deal.

Understanding and Identifying Potential Accounting Abuses

As recent corporate frauds demonstrate, abusive or improper financial reporting can take many forms; transactions can be recorded so that profits or losses appear in one accounting period rather than another; transaction prices can be inflated; revenues can be recognized before they're fully earned, cost of goods sold can be manipulated; expenses can be capitalized to understate operation expenses, an asset's useful life can be misstated impacting depreciation expense, and off-balance-sheet financing can be used to avoid reporting debt obligations. These and many other mechanisms can be used to manipulate earnings in order to achieve financial projections.

Improper accounting is often difficult to spot. The valuator should thoroughly analyze all financial information, especially if the valuation will affect the price paid in an arm's length transaction. As financial statements and corporate disclosure presentation become increasingly complex, the valuator may consider consulting complex-accounting specialists in some cases.

Quasi-Equity Debt

The securities that comprise a company's capital structure such as convertible bonds, preferred stock, warrants, and options must be analyzed and deconstructed based on their restrictive attributes. Typically, all components can be assigned to either straight debt or straight equity. When valuing the various capital components, remember that it is the specific attributes that are important, not the classification provided on the balance sheet.

Accounting for Uncertainty

The valuator should strive for the most precise conclusion possible given the available facts. But the more complex and intricate the subject company, the more difficult it becomes to determine an exact conclusion of value. With technology-based businesses in particular, the final conclusion of value and the corresponding value range will reflect the increased uncertainty in estimating all of the relevant variables. These variables will include:

- future economic conditions;
- relevant company-specific risks;
- tax-law complexities and interpretations;
- technological change;
- competitors' strategic decisions;
- industry consolidation and merger activity.

Generally, the greater the level of uncertainty in the forecast variables, the more acceptable it becomes to provide a wide range in the final conclusion of value. However, it should be recognized that too wide a range of value conclusion will be of no "value" to the user of the report.

Diversity of Opinion

In combining both art and science, a valuation can be controversial and subjective. Most valuators strive to be unbiased and fair. But each valuator is different, with a different level of education, work and other experiences, different ideas, concerns and perceptions, different knowledge about the specific business and industry, a different understanding of the prices that industry and special-interest buyers might pay for the company, different access to valuation models and other tools, and different sources of relevant information - including that which may be confidential. Even though valuators operate with integrity and apply high standards of expert analysis and professionalism, they commonly form different opinions on the value of a business or asset. At times, these differences, expressed as both percentages and dollar amounts, can vary substantially. In some cases, additional analysis or focused discussion and debate can serve to reduce the gap. Other cases may require the intervention of a mediator or judge.

Valuation differences often result from different instructions by clients to their valuators. This may become evident after a review of the sections in their reports on the "Purpose" and "Major Assumptions" of their valuations. The major assumptions are particularly critical. The valuator relies on them to reach a valuation opinion, and one valuator may use different assumptions than the other.

Elastic Values: Uncertain Information and Specific Values

Business valuators are often asked to analyze and interpret uncertain information and risk factors, and to conclude on specific values. The degree of uncertainty attaching to the uncertain information often varies for the valuators acting for the seller and the buyer, with the advantage going to the seller's valuator. However, the synergistic value benefit, if any, is generally best quantified by the buyer's valuator. Due to these uncertainties, values are generally expressed in a most likely range, or probability ranges based on different scenarios.

The Value of an Idea

Practice Tip

The value of an idea lies in the using of it.

Thomas A. Edison

Arriving at a Value Conclusion

Valuators usually derive different estimates of value from different valuation methods. In some cases, they will change some of their basic assumptions to estimate the value under different scenarios. In the end, valuators determine the required standard of value and express a conclusion most typically in the form of a value range.

When valuators arrive at their value conclusion by applying their professional judgment, as supported by market data rather than a mathematical formula, the value estimate itself carries greater weight.

In firms with more than one valuation practitioner, a value opinion is usually arrived at through discussion and debate. In some firms, the number of concurring partners required reflects the perceived risk level. For example, in a normal risk engagement, two senior practitioners must agree on the valuation conclusion. Engagements involving greater than normal risk requires concurrence among three senior practitioners. Given the complexities and global nature of today's business environment, these diverse views - both expressed and considered - usually contribute to the strength of the final value conclusion.

The Art of Writing

It's both what you say, and how you say it. Clearly and concisely expressing your thoughts and conclusions in writing is usually the last major step in a valuation assignment. A valuation specialist should have a good knowledge of accounting principles, superior skills in financial analysis, the ability to assess all relevant information, awareness of key value drivers, and the ability to write a valuation report in a structured and persuasive way.

A valuator may apply his skills and careful reasoning to arrive at a valuation conclusion, but the report will be of little use if it does not convince the reader that the final opinion of value is supportable, fair, and reasonable.

At least one or two other valuators should review your draft report before you present it to the client. I recall several instances when the second quality-assurance reader identified a point of confusion. The writer and first quality-assurance reader interpreted a sentence in the same way, but after reviewing the second quality-assurance adviser's editorial comments and re-reading the sentence, they reconsidered when they realized that most readers would give the sentence an entirely different meaning than they had intended.

Write Reader Friendly

If you are the only person who understands your work, it does not matter who's right and who's wrong, you'll unavoidably lose.

Beware the "Cash" Business

Known cash businesses and those that would not normally be considered to be (but there is evidence of cash transactions), present additional difficulties to valuators. How can the valuator be certain that all cash transactions have been recorded and therefore accorded proper consideration in the value of the business? And where it is known that cash has been diverted and unrecorded by the owners, what affect should there be, or what consideration of the cash transactions should be considered by the valuator?

Where the valuation is required for a transaction between shareholders that are all aware of the cash diversions, it may be appropriate to include consideration of these transactions in the valuation.

Where the issue arises in the context of an expropriation, for example, the client may have to face the consequence of not realizing full "value" for his business, since admitting to cash diversion may lead to other adverse consequences, such as a CRA/IRS audit.

How does the valuator assess the validity and quantum of cash diverted except through reliance on the person perpetrating the fraudulent act?

How do you "satisfy" an acquirer of the business that the cash transactions exist and that he should pay something for them?

Last, in an open market transaction, evidence or suspicion of fraudulent cash transactions should be a key determinant in a decision to acquire assets and not shares so as to avoid the "acquisition" of latent liability for taxes and penalties related to the fraud.

Appropriate Comparables

It is almost trite to say that comparables used in a valuation exercise should in fact be comparable. However, we reviewed a report that was presented in a shareholder dispute trial, that compared a relatively small, owner managed, fruit juice processing business to the multiples and other factors derived from a world class, publicly traded, alcoholic beverage business that happened to include a fruit juice business as well. Not only was the comparison totally rejected by the court, but the entire report was rejected as useful.

Tendencies in Methodology

> *Practice Tip*
>
> Valuation methodologies often vary based on specific circumstances and individual practitioner preferences.

Methodologies Used in Corporate Purchase

Our domestic and international experience indicates that the discounted cash flow approach is the most used and preferred *primary method* of corporate purchasers. Often these purchasers use more than one method to arrive at their purchase price. The methods used can vary between industries, jurisdictions, and company-specific conditions.

a) The discounted cash flow approach is used as the primary valuation method 65 per cent to 75 per cent of the time in North America, increasing to upwards of 85 per cent internationally;
b) A "cash flow" or "quasi-cash flow" approach based on multiples such as EBITDA, EBIT, or Free Cash Flow less Capex is used 40 per cent to 50 per cent of the time;
(c) Capitalization of earnings (net income) is used 30 per cent to 40 per cent of the time;
(d) Adjusted net tangible value is utilized 25 per cent to 35 per cent of the time;
(e) Industry rules-of-thumb are used 10 per cent of the time; and
(f) Various other methods or somewhat obscure pricing/bidding strategies are used less than 10 per cent of the time, including:
    - Revenue Multiples
    - Net Book Value Multiples
    - Current Bid +5% ('Strategic Premium')

- Intrinsic Value + up to 50% of estimated synergies ('Special Buyer Premium')

Emerging High Growth Companies and DCF Alternatives

Practice Tip

The preferred valuation method for emerging high growth companies is the present value of future cash flows from the business, less the present value of capital investments required to be injected first in order to generate those cash flows. In some cases it may be appropriate to discount the first stream of cash flows at an appropriate risk-adjusted rate, while the capital injection is discounted at rates applicable to relatively risk-free investments.

Zareer Pavri, CA, CBV

A valuation analysis that discounts future cash flows or earnings or that capitalizes point-in-time earnings depends on the variables of expected future earnings and required capital re-investment. An established business with a profitable history and retained earnings can usually meet its capital requirements from internal sources of funds or prudent borrowings. It does not need to surrender a portion of ownership to obtain external equity financing. A valuation model that focuses solely on expected earnings will deliver an adequate valuation for such an established business.

Emerging high-growth companies, however, often need considerable capital for developmental purposes, expansion, or new-product introductions. The availability of financing for these companies at the valuation date is far from certain. In such cases, the valuation analysis has to capture the importance of such a capital investment to support a level of sales sufficient to produce the expected profit. An emerging high-growth or fledgling business with little or no past history of sustainable profit has to meet its capital needs by selling equity to external sources. Bank borrowing is usually not an option.

The valuator properly assesses emerging high-growth companies therefore by calculating the present value of future cash flow from the business, less the present value of capital investment required to generate those cash flows. This resembles a calculation typical of net present value processes often more commonly associated with capital budgeting exercises.

Valuing Software and Its Associated Implementation Costs

> ***Practice Tip***
>
> In the face of complex and rapidly changing business requirements, today's successful companies need to be agile and responsive. Technology plays a significant role in determining how quickly new challenges can be met.
>
> Thus the valuation of software applications must consider not only the dollars spent but also the utility it provides, both now and in the future.
>
> **Roger Tait, BA, CMA**

The first step in determining the actual software costs will be to separate out infrastructure costs including both actual physical acquisitions and labor costs associated with installing them. Given that large software implementations are complex and costly, a formal cost tracking mechanism is the norm. This enables a means of accounting for total funds spent on the implementation project - including both software and infrastructure costs. If this information is not available then an estimate can be determined using the same techniques employed in bidding for new implementation work.

There are two main costs associated with software. The first is software license fees that are paid to the software vendor. The software license fee itself requires no particular analysis. It is simply what has been negotiated and paid to the software vendor to acquire usage of the software. The second cost, and most significant, is the cost of actually implementing the software. Be wary of implementation inefficiencies as an inefficient implementation will overstate the cost of the installed system. Annual maintenance costs must also be paid to the vendor but these are not part of the initial acquisition cost. Once the initial cost of implementing the software has been determined, there are a number of factors which can be considered to determine the current value.

Age of the System

The age of the software - if updates are not available - will impact its functionality and value. Less utility is provided to the organization and workaround spreadsheets must be used to cover this shortfall.

Platform

The age and type of platform may eventually force a change of software and thus its current value. The current value of the software must be reduced if there is a finite life due to technology constraints.

Scalability

Software which is capable of growing along with the company is less likely to require replacement in the short term and thus may have a higher value.

Integration

The degree to which the system is integrated or can be integrated with other systems in the company will impact its value. Lack of integration causes additional work and extends the time requirement for key activities such as month-end closing and report generation.

System Audit Capability

Current regulatory requirements mandate that a company be able to provide clear evidence of controls and to have an ability to provide senior management with all pertinent information. Systems which are deficient in this area will be less valuable.

Specialization

Some systems have been developed to support a very specialized, industry-specific requirement. A replacement cannot be purchased and development of a replacement would be an expensive undertaking. Software existing in such circumstances is valued at a premium.

Valuation Models

Valuation Models vs. Reality

Valuation models assume rational behavior, but in the real world you often don't have rational behavior.

Check the Valuation Model for Errors

Mistakes are inevitable. The valuation model should be evaluated for errors, reliability, and reasonability. Such evaluations are generally best performed by modeling specialists in conjunction with valuation specialists who test the output(s) for reasonableness. At times there are even errors in relatively simple valuation models within a valuation report, the identification of which in an opposing party's report gives you the easy points to win and diminishes the other party's credibility.

Many models are built using spreadsheets and, specifically, Microsoft Excel, due to its widespread use and understanding and its high degree of flexibility for making changes. This ease of use and change can also lead to an increased risk of error. Even the simplest models typically contain hundreds of separate calculations. Studies have shown that the typical human error rate in any complex task, such as building a financial spreadsheet model, is about one per cent. In other words, one out of every hundred calculations in a model could contain an error. Interestingly, these studies also show that error rates do not improve significantly with the experience of the developer, although more experienced users may make different types of mistakes.

Human errors can be classified in the following manner:

1. Mechanical errors: *e.g.*, using a plus sign instead of minus.
2. Logical errors: *e.g.*, inappropriate algorithm applied.
3. Omission errors: *e.g.*, leaving something out.
4. Data errors: *e.g.*, use of inappropriate data or inconsistent data sets.
5. Interpretation error: *e.g.*, an underlying assumption is incorrectly understood or the outputs of the model are misinterpreted.

Logic errors can be further subdivided into Eureka errors and Cassandra errors. Eureka errors are easy to spot, or prove to be incorrect, whereas Cassandra errors are difficult to prove that they are incorrect.

When testing a spreadsheet for errors or omissions you should consider the following types of testing procedures:

(1) Specification test – comparing the model against the detailed specification to determine whether the model contains all the elements and functionality originally planned and that algorithms have been implemented as documented.

(2) Analytical review – analyzing the outputs of the model under one or more data sets to check whether these are in line with expectations and the users' wider knowledge of the business. If not, this is often an indication of an error in the model.

(3) Logical review – close inspection of the logic of a model, calculation by calculation, checking the logic and links to data and other calculations.

(4) Parallel modeling – creating a "parallel" model independently of the forecast model and comparing outputs and investigating discrepancies. This approach is particularly useful for testing for mechanical, logical, and omission errors as separate developers are unlikely to make the same errors and may interpret logic and content slightly different if it is not clearly understood.

(5) Map test – producing a "map" of the calculations within a model and their relationships to one another either manually or more accurately and efficiently by using spreadsheet analysis software looking for inconsistencies in calculations where none is intended. The opposite, where calculations are consistent but should not be is also a risk and therefore consideration should be given to any key change over points in the projection time period, such as when construction ends in a real estate model or in the terminal year of the projection period.

(6) Flow Test – analysis of the flow of data and results throughout a model to highlight branching problems related to conditional logic.

(7) Redundancy Test – searching for redundant inputs or intermediate calculations that could be removed to make the model simpler and easier to understand.

(8) Consistency Test – where a model has template or repeated elements, comparing these to check whether repeated elements that should logically be identical are identical.

(9) Dummy Data Test – populating every input with a random number between -n and +n followed by inspection of model outputs and checks to identify errors that may only relate to certain input values.

(10) Real Data Test – populating with real data followed by inspection of outputs and checks to see if it meets expectations.

(11) Stress Test – varying values of input data, often to extreme values, and examining outputs and checks to test the functionality of the model under different input data.

(12) Sensitivity Test – varying the values of input data and measuring the sensitivity of key outputs to the variation in the inputs to see if they have the expected impact on outputs (note: this is different from just running sensitivities of various data sets and is designed to analyze the relationships between inputs and outputs).

(13) Reconciliation Test - comparing outputs against input data or other sources to check the methodology has been applied correctly and that the output matches the inputs where such comparisons can be made.

(14) Sense checks - checks on key outputs to make sure they make sense given specific rules (*e.g.*, does the balance sheet balance).

Fair Value Measurement

Contributory Value

A business enterprise can be regarded as a portfolio of assets that must provide a return to the investors of debt and equity financing. Accordingly, a company's total cash flows must satisfy the risk-adjusted-returns required by both debt and equity security holders from each of the firm's tangible and intangible assets, also called the weighted average cost of capital (WACC). A company's WACC represents the weighted average return of all the assets utilized in a company's operations and may be attributed according to the relative risk associated with each asset.

This concept is particularly relevant with respect to the valuation of intangible assets using an income approach based on excess earnings. Using an excess-earnings method the valuator assumes that the value of an intangible asset equals the present value of its net attributable earnings. A business generates earnings from tangible and intangible assets. To isolate the net earnings attributable to a particular intangible, the valuator must reduce total earnings by the fair returns on all the other assets classes, typically referred to as contributory asset charges. By reducing the return requirement for the entire firm to the level of individual assets, the valuator can establish asset charges based upon an asset's relative risk and discrete return capability.

Initial Interview (for Fair Value Measurement assignments)

Five opening questions to ask of the buyer:

1. Why did you buy the company?
2. How much did you pay?
3. How did you arrive at the purchase price?
4. Did you get a bargain? If so, why?
5. What is the materiality limit for purchase price allocation valuation purposes?

Common Audit Review Questions (Asked and Received)

General

1. Were you engaged to do a PPA or a valuation of the intangible assets?
2. In this case, what is the appropriate level of valuation assurance?
3. What procedures were carried out around identification of intangible assets that were valued? Why were these assets valued?

Information

1. Please provide:
   - The contributory asset charge worksheet
   - WARA (weighted average return on assets) reconciliation
   - WACC calculations
   - TAB (tangible asset backing) calculations
   - Sensitivity analysis based on a WACC range of x% to y% (or some other variable)

Market-participant assumptions

1. How have entity-specific and market-participant synergies been dealt with in the valuation? And why?
   - Revenue synergies
   - Cost synergies
2. Who is in the set of likely market participants?

Support/sufficient appropriate audit evidence

1. What analysis was done to get comfort over the forecast?
2. What support exists for:
   - Customer attrition rates
   - Technology economic obsolescence curve
3. What analysis was performed to get comfort over the terminal growth rate?

Intangible assets return

1. Why was the goodwill return associated with the workforce and not the IRR or WACC?
2. Why did the WARA not consider deferred taxes/present value of foregone tax shield/asset vs. share deal?

3. How did you differentiate among the discount rates between the various intangible assets? What factors were considered?

Cost of capital

1. What data and deciles within data such as Ibbotson is appropriate for application in the circumstances?
2. Should U.S. data (risk-free rate, ERP, country risk adjustment) be used to determine the WACC for a non-U.S. company where the market participants are likely also non-U.S.?

Contributory asset charges

1. Why did you/didn't you cross-charge certain other intangibles in the excess earnings approach?
2. In the context of a PPA engagement should the "with and with-out approach" have contributory asset charges?
3. Was accounting depreciation or fair value depreciation used in calculating the fixed asset contributory asset charges?
4. Should the workforce contributory asset charge be a constant % or a decreasing % (since revenues are growing)?
5. Should a core-technology contributory asset charge be applied?

Taxes

1. Why was workforce tax-effected?
2. Should announced but not enacted tax rates be used?
3. Should the taxable amortization benefit be circular?

Non-compete agreements (NCA)

1. Is there any residual value to the NCA beyond their contract life?
2. Does the NCA have any value?
3. Why are there/aren't there contributory asset charges when valuing the non-compete agreement?

Accounting-related

1. How is the forecast used to value the intangible assets consistent with client's expected useful life of intangible for depreciation purposes?
2. To what does the goodwill relate? Is the goodwill amount reasonable? What cash flows are attributable to the goodwill value?

3. How were contingent considerations and options accounted for and considered in the valuation?

Common audit review questions – Key messages

1. Fair value of intangible assets and goodwill impairment is an accounting exercise so the measure of "correctness" will usually be the rules, with some leeway for professional judgment.
2. Consult, consult, consult.
3. Review other office and reports of other firms.

Identification of Assets to be Fair Valued

To assess the reasonableness of management's identification and classification of the assets to be fair valued, the valuator's investigation and analysis should include reviewing:

- Board of Director minutes of the purchaser and the target, and any presentations made to the boards.
- The CIM (Confidential Information Memorandum) and the other information in the Dataroom, if any.
- Due diligence reports.
- Information available on the target, including on its website.
- Analyst and industry reports.
- Press releases.

Financial Instruments

Consider Counterparty Risk

Adjusting for creditworthiness is something that happens daily in financial markets and is a central component of valuation discovery. Debt markets are constantly measuring the likelihood of default on corporate names through credit spreads and debt valuations are continually adjusted to reflect changing opinions of issuer solvency and required rates of return. When calculating the fair value of financial assets and liabilities, credit quality is a relevant consideration not only for fixed-income securities but also for over-the-counter ("OTC") derivative instruments as well.

Conventionally, counterparty risk was ignored for OTC derivatives when reporting fair values. However, this has changed as a result of recent modifications to accounting rules for financial instruments. Credit Valuation Adjustment or "CVA" is a methodology of adjusting the value of OTC derivative securities beyond their theoretical fair value to account for the risk that either counterparty to the contract may default on its obligations. For example, two interest rate swaps with identical terms, positive fair valuation to the holder, but transacted with two different counterparties (one rated AA and the other BB-), are not of equal value. A CVA is required to adjust the theoretical value to reflect such differences.

To determine the level of the adjustment, it is necessary to measure the future exposure of a derivative and consider the following factors, among others: the type of derivative, maturity of the contract, netting and collateral agreements, credit quality of counterparty, and the size of the obligation in relation to the counterparty's capitalization.

Reliance on Dealer Quotes

We often see users of derivatives relying on dealer quotes for an indication of pricing. Although dealers are familiar with the markets in which they trade and have access to pricing information not easily available to the public, dealers typically provide quotes for free and do not have an obligation to ensure their accuracy or appropriateness. It is prudent to corroborate dealer quotes and make any necessary adjustments. For example, the fair values provided by bank counterparties for most derivatives do not include adjustments for counterparty risk.

It is better to use dealer quotes as part of an overall pricing process when observable, independent pricing sources are not available. If possible, obtain several quotes from different dealers. At a minimum, perform a reasonability check.

Be Cautious of Model Risks

Valuation models are theoretical frameworks that try to estimate the price of an asset. They are limited in their ability to do this based on the quality of the model selected and the assumptions they contain. Practitioners should be wary of the following:

- The choice of the model being used: It is important to know which valuation model is appropriate for a particular instrument. For example, valuing an American-style option would require using a binomial pricing model rather than using the Black-Scholes model, which is better suited for pricing European-style options.
- The reliability of your inputs: The inputs and assumptions to valuation models can have a significant impact on your conclu-

sions. Models based on simple, observable inputs typically produce reliable and readily verifiable results. Valuations for currency forwards or interest rate swaps are based on observable forward curves in liquid markets hence the value estimated by the model is fairly reliable. In contrast, valuation models for complex instruments like Collateralized Debt Obligations require non-market inputs (*e.g.*, expected base correlation) and a higher level of diligence is warranted when selecting or verifying the inputs.

- The reliability of the model: The more complex the model, the greater the risk that there will be errors in the valuation calculation. When creating models in-house, have the math calculations checked by others familiar with the model. Conduct rigorous testing and reasonability checks to ensure that the model stands up in all conditions and that the results make sense.

Verify Key Information

Financial instruments are highly flexible tools that are frequently tailored to meet the needs of a specific party. Such instruments are not based on standard contracts and there is typically considerable documentation outlining the terms and conditions that govern future cash flows. It is imperative to undertake a detailed review of the contract and understand all terms and nuances of the instrument that may impact the valuation. Using a debt instrument as an example, there may be embedded optionality, such as a prepayment option, that could impact future cash flows, required rates of return, and value.

Dirty Price vs. Clean Price

Financial instrument pricing can be quoted as either a "dirty price" or a "clean price". The dirty price is the full fair value while the clean price excludes any accrued amounts (*i.e.*, the dirty price less accrued interest). For example, the quoted price for a debt instrument is usually the clean price while the fair value of a derivative instrument provided by a dealer is the dirty price. It is important to know which price has been received to avoid either omitting accrued amounts or double counting them.

Volatility

When valuing options using a theoretical option-pricing model, be cautious of the underlying volatility input used in the calculation. The value of an option is highly sensitive to the selected volatility, especially when the option is at the money, and the estimation of volatility can be subjective.

Option-pricing models require an estimate of volatility that reflects expected price fluctuations over the term of the option. Accordingly, the most appropriate volatility estimate is one that is forward looking and considers potential share returns (in the case of a stock option) over the life of the option. While there is a tendency to rely on observed historical volatility, one must also consider that future volatility may differ from the past.

An observable forward looking volatility may be available if there are traded options on the same underlying stock (referred to as implied volatility). However, when the implied volatility is not available, understand that selecting an appropriate measure is crucial to arriving at a price that is reasonable and defendable.

The next best choice after the implied is the historical volatility. Some practitioners prefer to match the term to maturity of the option with the period used to calculate the historical volatility. For example, if you have two years remaining until expiry on your option you may use the two-year historical value. Others feel that more recent historical volatility numbers, say 30 or 90 days, is a better reflection of recent volatility environments. Whichever measure you choose, the best practice is to use the same methodology consistently.

If the option you are valuing is on a private company, you may not be able to calculate the historical volatility. In this case, the volatility of similar, publicly-traded companies may be a relevant benchmark.

Fixed Assets

With the advent of fair value accounting triggered by mergers and acquisitions, the demand for fixed asset appraisal services has increased dramatically. For many large manufacturing firms, the resultant professional service hours associated with such appraisals often exceeds the total hours associated with valuing the intangibles and other assets of the business. In addition, fair value accounting often requires the estimation of the dark value of a property (usually replacement cost new less depreciation), which can take longer to estimate than going-concern value of the same fixed assets derived through the application of an income approach.

Location and Management

The value of real estate is set by location, management, and location – not by location, location, and location.

The Appraisal Should Interpret the Market – Never Establish It

This is an important concept and an underlying principal of valuation practice. Although appraisals should have regard to the most current information available, the interpretation and use of this information should always reflect the attitude of the local marketplace. For instance, discounted cash flow analysis may not always be appropriate in less sophisticated markets where sale prices, lease rents, and capitalization rates may be established through calculations undertaken "on the back of an envelope". Also, in certain developing countries the concept of market value is still strongly interpreted as being the value of the land plus the value of the buildings – in other words a "bricks and mortar valuation".

It is not the function of an appraiser to dictate the basis on which value should be determined. This is a function of the marketplace. The appraiser's job is to research, analyze, and interpret information and then apply it in a way that is understood and accepted by the marketplace.

Cost and Value – Are They the Same?

There are several definitions of value – for example, replacement, liquidation, or going concern value. However, from the perspective of establishing market value, the answer to the question of what is value, is that, generally, in *an established and organized market, cost and value often diverge*. The sole determinants of market value are the forces of supply and demand. If there is no demand there can be no value, regardless of cost.

Nevertheless, there is a relationship between cost and value. In a stable or gradually expanding market, cost is often used to estimate market value. A buyer will measure the value of an existing home by gauging the cost of building a similar but new home. Also, new home builders establish their selling prices with reference to the cost of building the homes. However, in these examples the relationship between cost and value has more to do with economics rather than the principles of valuation.

So, although there are times when the value of an asset may appear to equate the cost of replacing it, this relationship is normally short-lived and limited to new construction projects. Over time, influences such as location, the type and quality of development, physical condition, and other general economic forces play a far greater role in establishing value.

Building Appraisals - Note the Obvious

Always make note of the obvious. For example, every office building has a floor finish, a ceiling, and lighting. When you are inspecting this type of building, specifically note the type of ceiling, "[a] suspended ceiling with 2 ft x 4 ft fiberboard panels and that the lighting is recessed with four fluorescent tubes". It is easy to overlook these types of items because they seem to be obvious in all offices. When it comes to pricing the ceiling and lighting you need to know the specifics. It makes your write-up of the description more credible and shows the reviewer that your inspection was thorough.

Building Appraisals - Use Published Cost Data Resources

When using a published cost data resource make sure that the definitions in the resource match the building that you are appraising. Carefully study the specifications for the type of building, occupancy, and features. In nearly every case, the model in the cost resource must be adjusted either for height, size, or a specific component of construction and location. Most published resources make provisions for these and other matters. In every case, become familiar with your cost resource and its intended use before applying it.

Appraising Special Purpose and Unique Properties

The manufacturing facilities of many hi-tech businesses are located in special purpose or unique buildings. When estimating the value-in-use of a special purpose building you must take into consideration many of the physical requirements that are necessary to make the building functional for the business. For example, telecommunications buildings must be located near fiber-optic carriers and must be able to accommodate the operation of many computers with special emphasis on security, power supply, and extensive cabling. Security often includes mantrap doors and bulletproof glass. Power supply is critical for the many computers and the air conditioning capacity is often four or more times that needed in a typical office building. Power must be uninterruptible and reliable, and the building should be located as close to a substation as possible. The building also often needs to accommodate diesel-powered backup generators, battery farms, and provisions for onsite diesel fuel storage. The provision for cabling is generally extensive and can be accommodated through raised floors or by high ceilings, as well as cable risers and shafts. Fire suppression equipment is generally sophisticated and includes zoned dry sprinkler systems and sophisticated smoke and heat monitoring systems. Fire doors, building materials, and shaft regulations are somewhat unique to these buildings and are generally governed by local fire codes.

Work Closely with the Client

Always communicate and work very closely with your client or management of the business whose assets are being appraised. You cannot ask too many questions – remember he knows his business better than anyone else. Don't hesitate to ask him about relevant cost studies, the cost of equipment recently purchased, past appraisal reports, the condition of assets, and future business plans that may have an effect on the assets being valued. At the very onset, explain the methodologies and approaches you will be using and inform him of findings as you proceed. By following this policy you can address any plant equipment valuation issues immediately. A client who understands appraisal methodology and the approach used in valuing his property, in almost all cases, is a satisfied client.

Establish and Maintain Supportable Data Files

One of the most beneficial procedures to a valuator is to establish and maintain supportable data files. Good data files are organized and arranged by industry. For example, construction equipment, paper mills, steel mills, all the way to office furniture. When performing most appraisals you must obtain specific industry data, this should be maintained for reference as it is often beneficial in future unrelated appraisals. File data examples might include items such as: "a six-year-old piece of construction equipment, in good condition, would sell for a certain percent of replacement cost new"; "construction cost per megawatt for a coal powered electric generating plant"; or "office furnishing costs based on costs per work station".

Three Basic Appraisal Segments

An appraisal should consist of three basic segments:

1. Identify the assets to be valued.
2. Gather data pertaining to these assets.
3. Based on the data, arrive at a supportable and realistic conclusion.

Using the engineering approach to value as an example: identify all assets that are relevant to the plant and should be included within its battery limit, establish the replacement cost of the plant either by producing an inventory of the assets or the unit of production, address depreciation of assets including both physical and functional aspects, consider future business plans, *etc.*

The conclusion of value is based only on *facts as recorded* in the appraisal and the past experience of the appraiser *interpreting those facts*.

Functional Depreciation

Don't overlook functional depreciation when valuing an asset or group of assets. Functional depreciation can take many forms. For example, the difference in cost to maintain a plant where reproduction cost is greater than replacement cost; cost savings associated with technology; excess labor cost; and more efficient utilization of raw materials. Another example is the depreciation associated with a warehousing facility having a ceiling height of 15' to 20' relative to a new or more modern warehouse facility that would have a ceiling height of 40' to 80'. This higher height would reduce the building "foot print" size, provide greater volume capacity, and also allow for automated order picking systems. Functional depreciation would address the height of the building in conjunction with required storage height, and excess operating cost associated with storage location and product flow.

Pitfalls of Indexing Valuation Approach

We are personally skeptical about the use of an indexing approach for the valuation of equipment and other fixed assets, other than for those rare occasions where the facilities have been recently constructed, where a high margin of error is acceptable, or for the purposes of developing a preliminary value. In the few cases where one might use the indexing approach, it must be ensured that the basic costs are accurate, that they include all costs associated with the development process, and there is no undue influence by issues such as labor strikes, shortages of materials, or equipment delays.

Based on our experience, it is those appraisers who are unfamiliar with an industry or are restricted by the cost of an engagement that are most likely to use an indexing approach since it requires less time and knowledge. Where used, it is our contention that it should always include an appropriate description of the assets, supported by a return on investment analysis that is comparable to a justification study found in a financial forecast and preconstruction budget often required before a new plant is constructed.

Our own experience, as well as that of other equipment appraisers that we consulted on this matter, supports that the indexing approach to valuation is not nearly as accurate as other traditional approaches such as the inventory cost approach or unit cost approach – nor is it as supportable. The appraisal profession's jargon for this approach is "*trend and bend*" which sums up the professional thinking behind the methodology (the American Society of Appraiser's language for "trend and bend" is an indirect cost approach; an inventory or unit cost approach is referred to as a direct cost approach). A common comment made in support of this approach is that the methodology is defensible as long as the data used is supplied by the client and that a recognized trend is applied to it. Should problems arise thereafter, the fall back position would then be that the client supplied the basic data and other analyses associated with it.

Unfortunately, more and more equipment appraisers today are less likely to base their conclusions on an inventory approach or concern themselves with the issues of methodology, choosing instead to adopt an indexing approach that is easier to undertake and which can be prepared relatively quickly and inexpensively by less experienced staff – often by accountants [many of whom on a plant inspection could not recognize the difference between a blast furnace (which makes iron), an electric arc furnace (EAF), and a basic oxygen furnace (BOF) – the latter two employ different technologies for producing steel] rather than professional machinery and equipment appraisers. In these situations, it is not unusual for the appraiser to add to his report words similar to "our conclusion will be adjusted to reflect the value concluded by the income approach". If this is the case, how much reliance and weight should be placed on the indexing cost approach, or a variation thereof, for financial reporting purposes?

Some of the issues that concern us with regards to an indexed approach include the following:

The Accuracy of Records

Without an accurate base from which to work, it is unlikely that the appraiser can ever arrive at the true value of the assets. Accuracy extends beyond recording the correct information in the asset ledger and making amendments from time to time to reflect additions, deletions, and transfers. It also encompasses an understanding of accounting policy so that an appraiser should be aware of assets that may have been fully depreciated and routinely removed from the asset register but which still have significant value. Alternatively, in the case of new projects and where perhaps a company has its own engineering personnel, it must be determined whether the costs recorded on the books include all engineering costs and/or construction financing charges. As mentioned, it is also important to ensure the in-service date of the asset is accurate to make sure the proper index value is used and to determine physical depreciation on an age-life analysis.

Original Cost versus Actual Cost

The original cost recorded in the asset ledger may not always be a true representation of the asset's actual cost, so that unless adjustments are made, a valuation prepared on an indexed basis will simply carry forward these inaccuracies. Examples of this are varied but may include:

- leased assets that are subsequently acquired and booked at a cost that is only equivalent to the last lease payment;
- plant expansions that may have required the demolition of some existing equipment from which the cost of this demolition has not been deducted;
- equipment purchased at a discounted price from liquidated stock;
- equipment based on manufacturers' rebates or promotions that excludes taxes, freight, installation, equipment rental during time of construction, engineering, appropriate overheads, and startup costs;
- costs incorrectly allocated – such as plant foundations – where they may also have been allocated to the cost of the building;
- used equipment purchases; and
- allocated costs from a previous valuation (in the case where the company acquired other companies or facilities).

Company's Capitalization, Expense, and Replacement Policies

These may also complicate the ability of an appraiser to correctly identify the true cost of an asset. For example, a company may capitalize the cost of a replacement machine without deducting the original cost of the machine now replaced. Alternatively, it may be company policy to expense the cost of all items under a particular amount – say $100,000, thereby understating original costs. In the case of pooled assets it may not be possible to identify the original cost for a piece of equipment that is now abandoned. Also, rebuilds or repairs may or may not be included as asset line items.

Indexing

Indexing or trending is a method of pricing whereby an index factor is applied to the original cost of an asset in order to estimate its current reproduction cost. It is very complicated, even impossible at times, to make adjustments when using the trending approach to determine functional depreciation for specific areas of a plant. Original cost records are often pooled and not specific to an area of the plant.

The majority of indices are developed using a standard mix of assets within a particular industry. It is important, therefore, for the appraiser to reassure himself that the assets being valued reflect the asset mix of the index being referenced – if they are not consistent, the valuation will be flawed.

Depreciation used in the trending approach generally reflects plant averages. Plants, generally, are unique, having their own specific conditions and, therefore, will an average or ballpark value estimate result be an appropriate value conclusion? Often assets in the category of machinery and equipment have a wide range of useful lives that should be recognized in the analysis. A critical aspect of trending is that the appraiser must verify the base to which the trends are applied and which base should reflect the original cost of the equipment rather than allocated costs or the costs of used equipment.

Summary

Once a facility becomes mature at a certain number of years or has gone through several upgrades and modifications, many companies will no longer use indexed or trended original costs to establish the insurable values for their fixed assets. Instead they will authorize a full insurance appraisal – yet in similar circumstances, many appraisers are still willing to use the original cost base to develop their conclusion of reproduction cost. In these situations, one must consider whether the appraiser is giving the client accurate advice and value for money when using an approach that examines the client's own asset ledger, makes adjustments where possible and trends and then depreciates the data base, before returning it to the client as an appraisal. Can the resulting conclusion be considered an independent appraisal and should such a valuation be used for fair value accounting purposes?

In our view, fixed asset appraisals that are based solely on indexed original costs are more likely to be criticized and are less easily defended than those based on the more traditional appraisal approaches such as the inventory or unit cost approach, which establish a replacement cost of the assets as opposed to reproduction cost. However, if the shortcomings of this approach are fully understood, and it is used with caution, there may be some situations – most frequently in conjunction with other approaches – where it can be used effectively.

Valuation of Environmental Assets and Liabilities

Although the regulatory environment is becoming more stringent and complex, compliance with environmental regulations does not replace good business conduct or knowledge of past environmental practices. As valuators, we need to be diligent in assessing environmental liabilities through supporting scientific and engineering reports to maintain standards of accuracy.

Practice Tip

Increased understanding of environmental matters and the associated civil and regulatory liabilities has required greater attention in the assessment of environmental liabilities and assets in business valuation. Although difficult to quantify with any degree of certainty, there is a growing consensus that environmental matters are materially significant and will play an increasingly important role in business valuation.

Andrew Craig, MBA, MSc

Compliance Doesn't Equal "Clean"

Through the normal course of business activities, it is reasonable to expect that some level of property contamination has occurred at most industrial sites across North America. Consideration must be given to historical contamination issues, as they represent a liability that may materially affect the fair market value of shares or net assets of the company subject to the valuation.

Review Phase I, II and III Environmental Site Assessments

As a key component of the due diligence and valuation process, these documents provide third party support of the existence of environmental liabilities and provide details as to the magnitude of the liability in financial terms.

Legacy Issues can be Significant

Site vintage, number of previous owners, and variety of previous industrial operations conducted on-site are flags for environmental liabilities. Often these problems are difficult to identify, such as soil and groundwater contamination, and hazardous materials – such as asbestos, mercury, and PCBs – contained in buildings, machinery, and other assets.

Assess Environmental Reputation

Regulators and NGOs can often shed light on the environmental reputation of a company or property and help provide clues as to historic areas of concern or cultures of positive environmental management and conduct.

There is No Substitute for a Site Visit

Site tours, visual inspections, and on-site discussion with site personnel are important components of measuring environmental liabilities in the valuation process.

Permitting Framework

During an acquisition, the buyer inherits Company X's environmental permits, accreditations and certificates of authorization or collectively the "Permitting Framework". The "Permitting Framework" is a requirement to operate a business in almost all business sectors and jurisdictions in Canada and the U.S. and will often have value as an intangible asset. By acquiring Company X along with this existing framework, a buyer would be able to avoid the costs associated with acquiring such permits. As regulations and the permitting approval process becomes more stringent and complex, the level of effort, time, and costs required to successfully achieve all necessary permits will increase materially.

Subject Matter Experts Know Best

Due to the complexity of the permitting and approval processes, numerous engineering and environmental consulting firms have developed expertise in assisting industrial clients' as they navigate the permitting process. Our experience shows these subject matter experts typically have a greater and more up-to-date understanding of the regulatory environment and can provide more accurate estimations of the effort, time, and costs associated with achieving compliance.

Working in Unfamiliar Jurisdictions

When working in unfamiliar jurisdictions, use local knowledge. The differences in permitting processes across regulatory jurisdictions can be significant. Our experience has been to draw on local knowledge to support estimations of levels of effort, time, and costs. This includes consulting local subject matter experts, regulatory agencies, and experts within the practice.

Assess Regulatory Compliance

The acquisition of properties and facilities that are in a state of regulatory non-compliance is not uncommon, especially during the acquisition of older facilities that may not abide by the latest permitting requirements. For a number of reasons, these non-compliant facilities have been overlooked by enforcement branches of the local regulator. New ownership will often trigger costly reassessment processes by regulators. The acquirer may be subjected to greater scrutiny, including environmental audits and inspections, especially if the company acquired had a record of poor or dated regulatory compliance.

Watch for Emerging Regulatory Issues

An emerging area of risk in North America is carbon regulatory exposure. Currently, regulatory frameworks with financial incentives are being established at the provincial and federal levels across Canada, most notably the Alberta Specified Gas Emitters Regulations commonly referred to as Bill 3. Energy intensive sectors such as oil & gas, metals, and other resource-based companies may need to operate under carbon restrained markets where financial incentives are available to innovative, energy efficient companies and financial penalties are applied to those that lag expected emission standards.

Creating Value Through Restructuring Distressed Companies

Valuing Assets of Distressed Companies

For companies bordering on the line of becoming distressed, there is a fine line between going-concern value and orderly liquidation value. Thus, it is important for owners and managers of distressed companies to recognize when restructuring is required. Frequently, the need to restructure is realized when it is too late for pre-emptive restructuring and by which time restructuring and asset sale options are limited.

Open Communications to Ensure Transparency

For a successful restructuring there must be open communications to ensure transparency so that all stakeholder groups come to the same level of knowledge. A restructuring cannot even move into the critical stage of negotiating and settlement until all the stakeholder groups are brought to a common level of knowledge. It is for this reason that restructurings often take far longer than what many believe to be a reasonable timeframe.

Exiting and/or Restructuring a Business is Complex

Exiting and/or restructuring a business is similar to marriage and divorce. It's easy to get into and very expensive to get out of. It's easy for one to start a business. One can incorporate and commence a start-up or buy an already established entity. If the business underperforms, some initial stages of the restructuring process are typical and these are: 1) a company will drift along underperforming; 2) management becomes aware of the underperformance; and 3) generally management enters a stage of denial. Consequently, an external party will usually force a change in direction.

The Courts and Expert Witness Testimony

Providing a valuation opinion for court purposes, and presenting expert witness testimony, introduces variables entirely distinct from those factors that underlie decisions related to valuation analysis. The admissibility of experts, rules of evidence, and constructing effective case presentation all introduce additional complexities into how "value" is determined.

Practice Tip

> There is only one invariable rule in litigation and that is to expect the unexpected and be ready to change your course at a moment's notice.
>
> **The Honourable Mr. Justice Donald G.H. Bowman,**
> **Associate Chief Justice of the Tax Court of Canada**

Judicial Judgments on Value

The courts are often asked to make judgments on value. The reasons are many and typically acknowledge the diverging views on value that the interested parties and their valuation experts put forward. These diverging views often arise in defined categories of cases: shareholder disputes, commercial and international arbitrations, corporate restructuring – as mandated under Chapter 11 in U.S. and CCAA in Canada – when the corporation's abiding value must be divided between the various equity and debt holders, and income tax disputes, which may require the value of an estate to be appraised on a shareholder's death. Any particular judgment on value reflects multiple considerations: the governing statutes, regulations and other legally effective prescriptions in the jurisdiction where the action proceeds, the pertinent statutes, regulations and other legally effective prescriptions in any other related jurisdiction, any persuasive judicial precedents, any discernible changes in the direction of the law, the kinds, quality, and strength of the evidence submitted, the credibility of the expert witnesses, the lawyering skills of the parties' counsel, and the interests and proclivities of particular judges.

Preparation is Everything

The single largest factor in successful expert testimony is preparation. The expert must be thoroughly familiar with his/her report, the underlying data and information, and the opposing expert's report, theory, and information.

Admit when Appropriate

An expert's credibility diminishes when he refuses to admit an error or "fights" an obvious conclusion. Be prepared to admit an error or mistake, they do happen occasionally, even to the best expert. When opposing counsel puts a hypothesis to an expert that is different than that used by the expert and effectively proves a point in the opposing case, be prepared to admit the point, *then* either point out the problem with the hypothesis or that the hypothesis is something for the court to determine.

Growth Rates Versus Discount Rates – Reconciliation is a Necessity

When applying a discount rate to a forecast cash flow in a discounted cash flow approach, careful consideration should be given to the growth rate inherent in the forecast cash flow. I saw a situation where the growth rate selected by a valuator was significantly larger than the discount rate applied to the resulting cash flows. Every year that the cash flow analysis was extended resulted in a higher value conclusion. No consideration had been given to the fact that the high growth rate in itself represented a significant risk that had to be reflected in the discount rate selection.

Less is More

When preparing a report for a trial, think about whether less is more. Keep the report content to the required facts and assumptions, and minimize extraneous content. Not only is there less chance for error in the report material, but readability and comprehension is likely enhanced.

Review your Testimony with Counsel

Prior to providing expert witness evidence it is a good idea to conduct a thorough review with counsel. However, there is a fine line between being prepared and sounding rehearsed. One beneficial tactic is to compartmentalize the testimony along various topics or *lines of questioning*. Have counsel mix them up when conducting a review of the case as this will help facilitate a more natural discussion across topics and throughout the entire testimony.

Faulty Evidence

In some cases, opposing valuators will present selective and faulty evidence. Upon further due diligence and review, you may discover that the information in its entirety does not support the opposition's point and may even damage its position.

In one situation, the valuator for a defendant presented to the court 28 pages of a 30-page article. Fortunately, the valuator for the prosecution had a copy of the entire article. The missing two pages contained information damaging to the other side's case. Upon reading these two pages, the presiding judge raised his eyebrows, likely indicating that he now had cause to question the defending valuator's credibility and entire expert testimony.

Get the Necessary Facts into Evidence

The judgment will be based on only the facts introduced at trial. Ensure those facts required to support your opinion of value have been introduced during the course of your testimony. Counsel's closing argument will be drawn from your evidence as presented to the court. If it's not in evidence, it won't be in the final argument regardless of its relevance, necessity, or accuracy.

In the Witness Box – Be Prepared for Credibility Challenge

Be fully prepared to have your suitability as an expert witness challenged by opposing counsel. Undermining credibility is a core cross-examination tactic - be it related to qualifications, previous court testimony, publications, public presentations, or any other participation in your field of professional expertise. Adequate steps should be taken to prepare for those likely challenges, review what you have said previously and be prepared to explain any inconsistencies relating to the present case.

In the Witness Box – Listen Carefully

Carefully listen to the question and only answer what has been asked. Do not anticipate questions and, particularly during cross-examination, do not volunteer information that has not been asked for. It is important not to guess where opposing counsel is trying to go in a line of questioning, or to disrupt your counsel's line of questioning by jumping ahead.

In the Witness Box – Take Your Time

Take your time. Think about what is being asked, and how you will respond, before you actually respond. Do not risk providing an incorrect response by rushing into an answer. It should be remembered that in the transcripts that will undoubtedly be reviewed by the judge, no matter how long you take to develop a response, your reply will appear on the very next line of the transcript, as though the response was given immediately. A rushed response may unwittingly result in an answer that is inconsistent with your report or examination in chief. If you are asked to refer to a specific document or passage, do not hesitate to take the necessary time to re-read or re-acquaint yourself with it.

In the Witness Box – Maintain a Thick Skin

Practice Tip

> People are always much easier to take advantage of when they are upset.

Maintain a thick skin in the face of courtroom antics. Although you are supposedly giving evidence as a friend of the court, it is not unusual for opposing counsel to insult or seriously challenge your reputation. To our surprise, judges seem largely to lend a deaf ear to such courtroom tactics; seldom will they come to the assistance of the expert. Often the weaker the case, the more likely opposing counsel is to deliberately utilize accusations and misrepresentations. A valuator accepted by the court as an expert valuation witness has succeeded in establishing a considerable amount of professional credibility. Attempt to maintain a professional composure in what is, by definition, a hostile witness environment.

In the Witness Box – Become "Synchronized" with Counsel

Successful expert witness testimony and, in turn, successful litigation outcomes, are dependent on a symbiotic relationship between counsel and expert. The witness needs to understand the cadence and direction of examination in chief, the level of detail required and, ultimately, how to respond to hostile cross-examination. In turn, counsel needs to recognize the expert's strengths and weaknesses – from qualifications to reporting style – and to prepare the witness accordingly. The courtroom is a litigator's home turf and to get the most from his expert, counsel must attempt to fully prepare the expert to become familiar and comfortable in that setting.

In the Witness Box – Speak Clearly

Speak clearly, slowly, confidently, and with sufficient volume. In addition to helping the judge, this will assist the court reporter and avoid disruptive transcribing delays. Avoid lengthy sentences, jargon, and provide organized responses. Do not read the report. Explain complex, technical issues in layman terms without sounding patronizing or professorial.

The Court's Expert Witness Perspective

In *Daubert v. Merrell Dow Pharmaceuticals, Inc.*, the United States Supreme Court discussed the following four non-exclusive factors that trial judges may consider in ruling on the reliability of an expert's testimony:

1. Has the theory or technique been tested or can it be tested?
2. Has the theory or technique been subjected to peer review and publication?
3. What is the method's known or potential rate of error?
4. Is the theory or technique generally accepted within the relevant specialist community?

Although Daubert is often cited regarding expert witnesses, it is not a hard and fast rule. Ultimately, the decision on any "expert" and their testimony will be made on a *case-by-case basis*. The trial judge will determine what weight or reliance to place on the evidence offered by those parties presenting themselves as experts before the court.

Measuring the Quality of the Valuation Expert

Ancillary or non-case-specific factors can often provide the foundation of the expert's standing before the court. This will contribute to the court's assessment of *its risk* when considering the more company-specific analysis contained in the valuator's report and presented as expert witness testimony. In measuring the quality of the valuation expert, consider:

- Is there an aspect of the business's products or services that requires specialized valuation knowledge and is it evident that the valuator has this previous experience?
- Is the methodology applied in the valuation of the business unique or atypical of standard valuation approaches and does the valuator have experience in previously utilizing the methodology?
- Was material, relevant data that should have been revealed during discovery left undiscovered and omitted from the analysis contained in the expert report?
- Was there a failure to reconcile or deal with any inconsistent facts or premises, or any use of unsupported assumptions or outright conjecture?
- Are transcription errors, inaccurate quotes, grammatical, and mathematical mistakes abundant?

These factors represent mistakes or elections made by the valuation expert and comprise the environment within which the company-specific value was concluded. They will often impact how the court views the valuator's analysis of the risk/return profile of the subject company.

Cross-examination and the Valuator's File

It is common practice now to have to produce the entire file supporting a valuation report prior to or during trial to the opposing counsel and expert. This has also been extended to all e-mail communications between the counsel, client, and the expert (except where these are actually held to be privileged). Accordingly, in litigation circumstances, e-mail communication should be avoided in favour of face to face or telephone communication. In a recent case, an expert was disqualified after examination of e-mail correspondence between the expert and the client indicated that the expert was solely the mouthpiece for the client's opinion, a classic example of "oath helping".

Measuring the Quality of the Expert's Valuation Opinion

Generally, the expert enjoys considerable discretion in selecting the data that will form the basis of their opinion of value. Through training and experience, a good expert can locate available resources and assess their reliability. Outdated, inappropriate, or immaterial information will compromise the expert's ultimate opinion. Before accepting an expert's opinion, the client should review the underlying data and information. The most common failures and lapses – including some of those previously cited – typically include the following:

- lack of documentation to support the conclusion and poor document retention;
- valuation conclusions obtained through oblique methodologies and untested theories;
- lack of company-specific analysis and over-reliance on general market data, industry averages, and rules of thumb;
- improper calculation of the weighted-average cost of capital, such as utilizing rates from different periods;
- failure to visit the company being valued and properly interview management;
- double counting, a common example being the recognized expected future growth in both the selected level of maintainable cash flow and the capitalization rate;
- applying inappropriate capitalization rates, such as an after-tax cap rate to a pre-tax level of maintainable earnings;
- mixing or misapplying discount rates and capitalization rates;
- improperly accounting for company size and company risk;
- improperly calculating the tax shield;
- improperly calculating cash flow by failing to account for the increased working capital required by the projected revenue levels;
- improperly calculating maintainable earnings or cash flows by failing to make appropriate normalization adjustments;
- failure to adjust for seasonal variances;
- an unrealistic residual value, often resulting from an unrealistically high growth rate in perpetuity;
- failure to subject the draft report to review by another senior valuation specialist;
- using the wrong beta or improperly levering and unlevering the beta;
- relying too heavily on management representations without performing the appropriate level of due diligence.

Check Valuator's Credentials

To qualify as an expert in business valuation, the valuator must have sufficient training or experience. Preferably, the expert will be certified by one of the relevant accrediting bodies. Certification acknowledges the expert's qualifications to render an opinion on valuation issues.

Before hiring an expert, a potential client must understand the expert's special experience, training, education, and abilities. As with any profession, clients can make a huge mistake if they hire the wrong expert to deliver a professional opinion. In preparing for the deposition of an expert, clients should carefully review the expert's written reports and preliminary drafts to assess the thoroughness and reliability of the raw data and identify misstatements, misrepresentations, and major assumptions.

To meet the minimum threshold of a business valuation expert, the individual must demonstrate four qualities:

An Expert Must be Qualified by Knowledge, Skill, Expertise, Training, or Education

The best-known organizations are detailed below in Table 1. These organizations confer designations and credentials on individuals who successfully complete their accreditation programs.

Table 1

BUSINESS VALUATION PROFESSIONAL DESIGNATIONS SUMMARY	
AIBA, FIBA, CBA, MCBA, BVAL	Accredited by Institute of Business Appraisers (IBA), Fellow of the IBA, Certified Business Appraiser, Master Certified Business Appraiser, and Business Valuator Accredited for Litigation
ASA, AM, FASA	Accredited Senior Appraiser, Accredited Member, and Fellow of the American Society of Appraisers (ASA)
CVA, AVA	Certified Valuation Analyst, and Accredited Valuation Analyst (National Association of Certified Business Appraisers)
CBV, FCBV CA.CBV	Chartered Business Valuator, and Fellow of The Canadian Institute of Chartered Business Valuators (CICBV) Chartered Accountant with a specialty in business valuation
CFA	Chartered Financial Analyst (Chartered Financial Analyst Institute)
CPA/ABV	Certified Public Accountant Accredited in Business Valuation (American Institute of Certified Public Accountants)

The Experts Must Have Credibility and be Believable

In addition to checking an expert's professional qualifications, a potential client may consult the expert's professional references. The client may also investigate previous court cases in which the expert participated to assess the expert's perspective in these cases and the court's reaction to the expert.

Individuals achieve credibility when their conduct over time earns them a reputation for sincerity, integrity, and honesty. Judges use their own experience to determine the credibility of experts and will disregard the testimony of experts whose credibility they dismiss. Before retaining an expert, the potential client should research the expert's published writings to see if the expert's views contradict their comments concerning value.

An Expert Must be Unbiased and Independent

Valuation experts should not be mirror images of the lawyers or clients who hire them. They should use their best judgment in forming their opinions, based on data, knowledge, and experience. Experts who advocate the position of one side in a controversy do not contribute to the examination of fact and actually do a disservice to their clients and the court.

An Expert Assists and Educates the Client in Understanding the Evidence

As part of their job, the most helpful and persuasive experts explain in comprehensible terms the components of business-valuation approaches and the mysteries of capitalization rates. They do not assume an understanding of underlying data or analyses, and they carefully and meticulously support their conclusions. Most importantly, the best experts explain clearly the analyses they used to arrive at their ultimate opinions. Without an explanation of the underlying data and facts, a client should not accept the expert's conclusions.

Pick Your Battles

When negotiating a settlement, be selective. Don't sweat the small stuff, carefully pick your battles.

Bits and Tidbits

Valuing a Gold Mining Company

Practice Tip

We have gold because we cannot trust governments ... Paper money is a great aid to politicians: it makes it possible for them to confiscate the savings of the people by manipulation of inflation and deflation.

President Herbert Hoover

Gold is not an official currency, but it has significant purchasing power, is a form of permanent, natural money and behaves differently than other commodities/precious metals.

You Can't Predict the Unpredictable

Whenever new information comes into the marketplace, prices change. You can't predict the unpredictable.

Working with People You Dislike

In business, as in life, there will be people you like and people you dislike ... so learn how to get along with people you dislike.

Valuing Expansion Plans

One rarely puts a lot of value on or pays for expansion plans, in large part because the majority never realize the projected levels of return.

Reliance on Computers vs. The Eye of Judgment and Sentient Knowledge

Computers may be precise and minimize human error ... but are they a replacement for and more reliable than experience and sentient knowledge?

Shades of Grey

A business valuator should have an effective client acceptance and risk management policy. Clients sometimes have to be rejected because of actual or perceived conflicts of interest, but more importantly the valuator must be able to identify the *fabricated* story teller, dishonest client who stretches the truth, or skilled con artist who fabricates the information given to the valuator in an attempt to influence the valuator's view on value.

Bear Market

In a bear market, investors rush for quality.

Be Realistic and Fair

Your valuation analysis should be objective, balanced and even-handed ... or risk losing all credibility for the rest of your career. Don't omit, ignore, or rationalize away bad news.

Goodwill: Pay Now or Pay More

There are advantages of purchasing a business with an established cash flow. Buyers of businesses are often hesitant to pay for goodwill and other intangible assets, thinking that they can more easily build a similar business from scratch without paying for intangible assets. However, most startups fail due to the many hurdles that have to be overcome, and the past experience of many suggests that the best and least risky path to success is to purchase an existing business with an established cash flow.

Impact of Globalization

In today's era of globalization, the potential buyer or transaction price influencer can come from almost anyplace, thus making it more difficult to opine on the fair market value of many businesses.

Ask Key Questions of Multiple People

To minimize the chance of asking questions of people who are motivated to give you the wrong answer, ask other knowledgeable people the same key questions.

Ask Well-timed, Well-phrased Critical Questions

The order in which you ask your critical questions can influence the answers you get. And know when to ask follow-up questions.

Unfair but Reasonable

Fairness is determined primarily by quantitative issues, and reasonableness by qualitative factors. Thus, it might be unfair to squeeze out a minority shareholder at less than ratable value per share, but reasonable in light of all the disadvantages associated with holding a minority position.

Everybody Has an Opinion

Everybody has an opinion ... that's what makes a market ... and that's what makes it rise and fall.

Tips from the Lighter Side

Being on a Good Footing

You may not be right, but if you cannot easily be proven wrong, then at least you are on a good footing.

Valuing Trade Secrets

Client says: "It's a trade secret, so I can't tell you about it."

Valuator responds: "Okay, then I can't value it, because I don't know what you are talking about".

(In such a case you would look at alternative value indicators. Basically, perform an analysis of margins realized by comparable companies who do not have trade secrets. If the margins being realized by the company with the trade secrets are similar, then there is likely little or no value to the trade secrets.)

Differing Opinions

The worlds of valuations, mergers, and acquisitions would be a dull place if everybody agreed on everything.

Round to the Nearest Error

An opposing expert had submitted a report that was "awesome" in its length and detail. It was intimidating at first glance. Through extensive review, it was found to be fraught with errors in calculation, cross referencing of conclusions building on one another, *etc.* Our counsel carefully led the expert through these errors, with the expert responding "oh, that is just rounding, or that it was not material to his conclusion". After one more of these responses from the expert, counsel said, in a tone of wonderment, "I finally get it, you rounded to the nearest error." Even the judge had to stifle a laugh. The expert's credibility was finished.

Valuation Insights

This chapter contains a mix of practice tips and short essays on valuation methodologies and issues by senior and renowned professors and business valuators. The essays generally address potential issues faced in volatile markets.

* * * * *

Valuing Businesses in Volatile Markets*

Stamos Nicholas & Carla Iavarone

Recently, the market environment has presented numerous challenges to valuation practitioners. There are many things to consider when valuing companies in these changing and volatile times, as market-based inputs may be skewed due to market anomalies. Additional due diligence and review is required in assessing certain assumptions in estimating the value of a business, including the selection of an appropriate discount rate, selection of market multiples, and consideration of implied control premiums for pub-

* This publication contains general information only and Deloitte Financial Advisory Services LLP is not, by means of this publication, rendering accounting, business, financial, investment, legal, tax, or other professional advice or services. This publication is not a substitute for such professional advice or services, nor should it be used as a basis for any decision or action that may affect your business. Before making any decision or taking any action that may affect your business, you should consult a qualified professional advisor. Deloitte Financial Advisory Services LLP, its affiliates and related entities shall not be responsible for any loss sustained by any person who relies on this publication.

licly traded companies. Provided below are specific items to consider and suggested leading practices for performing business valuations in volatile environments.

Rates of Return

Given significant declines in debt and equity markets, valuation practitioners may consider making adjustments to the standard CAPM model in order to appropriately reflect market risk. Valuation specialists may then also carefully consider each of the discount rate inputs and make adjustments, where appropriate. During times of stock market turmoil, discount rates may be skewed due to anomalies in current market data and, therefore, careful consideration is given to the key discount rate inputs, including optimal capital structure, beta, and equity risk premium.

In depressed equity markets, current capital structures may not be reflective of a company's optimal or normal capital structure. A possible alternative to adjust for this is to consider each guideline company's debt to capital ratio as of the valuation date, as well as an average over some historical period. Analyzing each guideline company's capital structure over time could assist in identifying a normalized debt to capital ratio. Given that beta measures the volatility of stock returns over a prior period, the volatility would also capture the characteristics of the capital structure during that same time period. Therefore, instead of using a point estimate of capital structure as of the valuation date, un-levering the beta using an average capital structure matched to the duration of the beta estimation period can yield more accurate results.

In addition, as a result of the credit market crisis, the default risk premium on corporate bonds has significantly widened. Since the price of a bond moves inversely to its yield, this would suggest that the current fair value of the debt is significantly below its face value. Considering that a WACC analysis assumes a market value weighting of debt and equity, using the face value of debt may yield inaccurate results during a market crisis, as it could skew the company's capital structure. A possible solution for this issue is to estimate each guideline company's market value of debt by using observable market prices, to the extent available, and adjust the capital structure accordingly.

A common methodology used by appraisers in estimating the equity risk premium to be applied in the WACC calculation is to consider the historical equity risk premium as a basis for the forward looking rate. However, considering that market-based inputs may deviate from the norm in periods of market volatility, history may be an inadequate proxy in estimating the equity risk premium. Therefore, appraisers need to carefully consider using current inputs to derive the implied equity risk premium in order to predict a forward looking estimate. Another possible solution to appropriately compensate for the additional market risk is to consider increasing the equity risk premium to take into account the significant decrease in risk-free rates and the implied return in equity markets. Furthermore, assessing the reliability and reasonableness of the forecasted cash flows is also a key consideration in estimating an appropriate rate of return. This can be particularly challenging in an unstable market.

Market Multiples

Under efficient market conditions, trading multiples based on guideline public companies typically provide reasonable estimates of the marketable, minority value of the company. In order to estimate the controlling interest value, a control premium may be applied to the marketable, minority value and is generally expected to fall within the historically observed range of control premiums evidenced in the subject company's sector or industry. In periods of market volatility, practitioners closely evaluate each comparable company used in the market approach analysis and consider whether the market inputs are representative of the operations of the company as of the valuation date, or if there are company-specific factors that may be impacting the guideline company or potentially the other companies operating in that industry.

Practitioners ordinarily perform a thorough comparative analysis of the subject company's growth, profitability, and risk profile relative to the selected peer companies and adjust the multiples accordingly. In periods of volatility, market data may be especially probative and, therefore, it is not prudently ignored in the fair value analysis simply due to the volatility. Facts and circumstances used to support applying a lower weighting or exclusion of a guideline company, or the overall market approach analysis, are not best attributed to general conditions in the capital markets but to specific unique facts. To the extent no weighting is applied to the market approach, appraisers need to sufficiently document the reasons for this decision and reconcile to the values estimated under the other methodologies utilized in the analysis.

Implied Control Premium

Another leading practice is performing a reconciliation of the sum of the overall value of a company's reporting units to its public market capitalization as a test of the reasonableness of the fair value conclusions. In depressed market conditions, this analysis deserves even more emphasis, and a reporting entity's management is well-advised to thoroughly understand the factors that impact the implied control premium relative to the prevailing public market capitalization. Solely relying on general, weak macroeconomic conditions is often a poor justification for higher implied control premium. Steady declines in stock prices may be indicative of factors that are important considerations in estimating the fair value of the company. Such factors are not typically ignored simply due to volatile market conditions. The reasonableness of the implied control premium is also best based on the specific facts related to the subject company. For example, if the subject company has not yet disclosed to the investor community information regarding future financial plans, such as a major acquisition or restructuring, the stock price may not be reflective of fair value. With this additional information, a higher control premium may be justified. In addition, if the stock price of a company is negatively impacted by a major investor selling a large number of shares due to extraneous factors such as margin calls, the stock price may be distorted and the market capitalization may not be indicative of the fair value of the business. To the extent supported by the applicable facts, appraisers may adjust for any temporary declines in stock prices due to company specific factors in the reconciliation process.

Summary

Volatile times present numerous challenges to valuation professionals when determining the fair value of a business enterprise. Additional analysis is necessary in assessing the business and valuation assumptions utilized. Determining appropriate discount rates and market multiples where market information is limited or possibly significantly distorted are major challenges for valuation professionals. During these periods, it is especially important that valuation professionals carefully evaluate all of the inputs and perform a more rigorous analysis to test the reasonableness of the assumptions and resulting valuation conclusions so that the results of their analyses reflect current reality.

* * * * *

New Risks Emerge During Economic Downturns

Russell L. Parr

Actually, there aren't really any new risks, just those that become enhanced during economic downturns. While recently valuing an early-stage medical technology, I realized that two risks I would have previously ignored had a powerful impact on the assignment. The assignment involved valuing a new implantable medical technology. The enhanced risks related to funding and clinical trials.

Valuing embryonic technology requires addressing concerns not typically associated with established technologies and products. Some include:

1. proving the efficacy and safety of the technology;
2. gaining market acceptance;
3. obtaining approval from the Food & Drug Administration; and
4. obtaining insurance reimbursement approvals.

At the time of the valuation, the technology had proven itself in laboratory and animal studies. The medical community was aware of the success and eager to adopt the new therapy. The new therapy was sure to be a success once it got to the marketplace. Large scale human clinical trials were the next step.

A significant risk for early-stage medical therapies is found in clinical trials. Failure of the technology may come in the form of failure to provide benefits to patients, side effects, and even patient death. The risks associated with clinical trials are nothing new but the unique risk regarding clinical trials for this assignment went beyond the typical. In this case, the hospitals that had been recruited to participate in the studies were experiencing financial stress and withdrew from the program. Alternate hospitals, also experiencing the same financial pressures, were proving difficult to recruit. Normally, a technology that had proven itself to the extent of the technology being valued would not have difficulty finding a place to conduct clinical trials. In fact, there might have even been competition among the hospitals. Not now. A risk that would never receive any consideration in the past was now threatening to kill the technology. Even if new hospitals were recruited, the path to commercialization would be delayed by at least two years. This delay impacted the value conclusion dramatically and hopefully delay would be the best case scenario.

The other risk was funding. Once again, finding funds for the clinical trials would never have been difficult given the proven success of the technology at the time of the valuation. In fact, there would likely have been competition among venture capitalists in any other environment. Not now.

An example of funding scarcity is the market for Initial Public Offerings (IPO).[1] A *Fortune* article dated August 26, 2008 indicated that "2008 has been one for the record books in the sheer paucity of companies that have made it out the door – 43 so far, down a stunning 75% compared to the same time last year". It stated further that 2008 had been a disaster in terms of both the number of companies able to go public and also in terms of the amount proceeds they were able to obtain.[2]

A *Business Week* article dated July 1, 2008 echoed the *Fortune* report. In its article, *Business Week* stated "[t]he market for initial public offerings is on ice. In the second quarter of 2008, there were no IPOs for companies with venture capital financing, according to the National Venture Capital Association. (NVCA). That's the first time a quarter has passed without an initial public offering since 1978. This dismal performance follows an unusually slow first quarter during which only five venture-backed companies went public. The situation is so dire that representatives from the NVCA are making a press tour and calling it a "capital market crisis" for the startup community. The article also reported that venture capitalists don't see the climate improving anytime soon.[3]

A poor market for IPOs makes venture capitalists worry. If they invest in new companies and technologies, where is their exit strategy if IPOs are stalled? Venture capital has dried up.[4]

---

1 Initial public offering (IPO), also referred to simply as a "public offering", is when a company issues common stock or shares to the public for the first time. They are often issued by smaller, younger companies seeking capital to expand, but can also be done by large privately-owned companies looking to become publicly traded.

2 M.V. Copeland, "Will the IPO season end with a whimper?", *Fortune*, August 26, 2008.

3 S.E. Ante, "The Worst IPO Market on Record?", *Business Week*, July 1, 2008.

4 Venture capital (also known as VC or Venture) is a type of private equity capital typically provided to early-stage, high-potential, growth companies. Venture capital is most attractive for new companies with limited operating history that are too small to raise capital in the public markets and are too immature to secure a bank loan or complete a debt offering.

The *Wall Street Journal* reported on January 5, 2009 that "[i]t's now taking VCs an average 6.5 years to see returns on their investments, compared with just two years in 2001 ... Many insiders project 2009 will continue to be a very rough year for VC-backed companies and those looking to attract VC money. The IPO climate shows no signs of improvement, giving investment companies little leverage to negotiate better acquisition prices with potential buyers ... A new survey by the National Venture Capital Association shows that a hefty 96% of VCs think it will be harder for companies to get funding this year, and 72% don't think the IPO markets will open up until 2010 or beyond. That means start-ups looking for private equity will be hard-pressed to find it."

So, the value of the early-stage medical therapy I was valuing faced new, or more accurately, enhanced risks not typically worth noting for such a successful technology. Funding to complete clinical trials was nowhere to be found and even if funding was obtained, there was no place to conduct the trials. Sadly, the best assumptions that could be made required delayed commercialization. This meant delayed cash flows and, when high discount rates are used, the present value of even a short delay dramatically impacts value. Another real possibility was that continued development might never happen. The lack of funding could easily cause the team of development experts to seek opportunities elsewhere abandoning the project and killing the technology outright.

This economic environment has lessons to teach us. It forces us to question long-held assumptions. It also forces us to consider that just when you finally think you know what you are doing, it's time to embrace humility.

* * * * *

Personal vs. Enterprise Goodwill: Four Examples From My Recent Practice

Shannon Pratt

Two Contexts in Which it is Useful to Separate Personal from Institutional Goodwill

Divorce

In most states personal goodwill is not a marital asset subject to division. In these states, it is necessary to separate personal from institutional goodwill.

Sale of Company or Practice

In the sale of a company or practice, any part of the proceeds that is for personal goodwill is taxable at long-term capital gains rate to the individual (assuming that the taxpayer has held the goodwill for 12 months or more). From the buyer's perspective, it is amortizable over 15 years, same as enterprise goodwill.

I've had four experiences in separating personal vs. institutional goodwill in the last two years, two in the context of divorce and two in the context of company sales.

General Characteristics of Personal vs. Enterprise Goodwill

Personal Goodwill Characteristics:

- Small entrepreneurial business highly dependent on shareholder's personal skills and relationships.
- No pre-existing non-compete agreement between selling company and shareholder.
- Personal service provided by the shareholder is an important feature in the company's product or services.
- Sales largely depend on the shareholder's personal relationships with customers.
- Product and/or services know-how, supplier relationships, and client relationships rest primarily with the shareholder.
- Excellent industry reputation.

Enterprise Goodwill Characteristics:

- Large business which has formalized organizational structure, systems, and controls.
- Employees have pre-existing non-compete agreements with selling company.
- The business is not heavily dependent on personal services performed by the shareholder.
- Company sales result from name recognition, sales force, and sales contracts.
- Company has formalized production methods and business systems.
- Company owns contracts with major customers.
- Company owns contracts and/or non-compete agreements with key personnel.
- The Company's name does not include the shareholder's name.

Case #1 – Divorce

- 60-person neuropsychiatric practice
- Owned by 1 doctor
- Represented wife
- Husband's expert claiming 100% of goodwill personal
- Over 20 years of operations, the doctor had institutionalized most of the goodwill
- Non-compete contracts with key employees
- Most of the professionals had built their own relationships with clients

- Organizational structure requiring little involvement with leading doctor
- Controversy over amount of time doctor spent on institute affairs, which had been increasing during year or two preceding divorce
- SP's conclusion: personal goodwill 25 to 40% of total goodwill, which the court accepted

Case #2 – Divorce

- I reviewed reports of both husband's and wife's experts on value of a wholesale insurance agency
- I represented husband
- Wife's expert had highly inflated conclusion as to goodwill, all of which she attributed to practice goodwill
- One of the reasons for wife's expert's highly inflated conclusion as to value of goodwill was a huge reduction in reasonable compensation to the owner
- I approved husband's conclusion
- We held a settlement conference, which the Judge attended
- Case settled a little over husband's expert's value

Case #3 – Taxes

- Wholesale insurance agency (different specialty than case #2)
- In business 25 years
- Owner was responsible for hiring and training 90% of all agents and for relationships with all underwriters
- Owner was active and highly regarded nationally in the agency's specialty

Intangible Assets Owned by the Company

- The ——— firm name
- The ——— distribution agreement, which has no real value to the company in a sale because it is cancellable by ——— immediately in case of a change of ownership
- Trained workforce, but all are loyal to ——— and none have employment agreements with the company
- Policy language developed by ———, but over which no copyright protection has been sought
- Business records

Intangible Asset of Goodwill Owned by ———

- Mr. ——— was the founder of the business over 25 years ago and has been responsible for attracting over 90% of the company's current agents, on whom the company depends for its revenues. He tells us, and other company employees concur, that if he left ——— and focused on another company, most or all of the agents would follow him.
- Mr. ——— has recruited and trained most or all of the company's workforce, most of whom he has known for a long time, some long before coming to work for ———. If he formed another company, most or all would go with ———.
- The company has had a number of underwriters over the years, with all of whom ——— has been responsible for the relationships.
- ——— is known nationally as a leader in the niche field of insuring non-profit organizations. This is because, for over a quarter of a century, Mr. ——— has spoken at most national industry meetings and has served as a committee member, committee chair, officer or director of every organization associated with the niche market served.

For the above reasons, it is our opinion that 65% of the intangible value in ——— is attributable to ———'s personal goodwill, and 35% to the enterprise goodwill.

Case #4 – Taxes

- Seller same as Case #3 – different company and different buyer
- Same attributes as Case #3

Intangible Assets Owned by the Company

- The ——— firm name
- An assembled and well-trained workforce, who are loyal but none of whom have employment agreements with the company
- Business records

Intangible Asset of Goodwill Owned by ———

- Mr. ——— was the founder of the business over 25 years ago and has been responsible for attracting many of the company's current agents, on whom the company depends for its revenues.
- Mr. ——— has recruited and trained most or all of the company's workforce, most of whom he has known for a long time, some long

before coming to work for ——. If he formed another company, most or all would go with ——.

- The company has had a number of underwriters over the years, with all of whom —— has been responsible for the relationships.
- The ability to negotiate and effect results with suppliers because of his personal relationships with them.
- —— is known nationally within the industry. Mr. —— has spoken at most national industry meetings and has served as a committed member, committee chair, officer or director of every organization associated with the niche markets served.

For the above reasons, it is our opinion that 65% of the intangible value in —— is attributable to ——'s goodwill, and 35% to the enterprise intangibles.

A representative of KPMG, the buyer's auditor, called me to further explain the allocation between enterprise and personal goodwill. She thought that I should have work papers leading up to the 65/35 allocation. I told her that any mathematical support would be bogus, and it was based on professional judgment. After two or three phone conversations, she accepted this.

Bibliography

The *Martin Ice Cream* case (110 T.C. 189, U.S. Tax Ct. LEXIS 17 100 T.C. No. 18) is the seminal tax case quoted by everyone.

The next most quoted case is *Norwalk v. Comm* (T.C. Memo 1998-279; 1998 Tax Ct. Memo LEXIS 281; T.C.M. (CCH) 208).

BVR's Guide to Personal vs. Enterprise Goodwill, 2009 Edition, is a comprehensive set of articles and cases on the subject. It contains case abstracts and comes with a disc with the full texts of cases.

* * * * *

Fair Market Value Definition: Canada vs. USA

Zareer N. Pavri

The definition of fair market value generally accepted in Canadian valuation practice differs in one important aspect from that adopted in the United States. In my view, this difference has important implications affecting the value of capital property between the two countries.

The two generally-accepted definitions of fair market value are stated below:

Canada

> The **highest** price, expressed in terms of money or money's worth, obtainable in an open and unrestricted market between informed prudent parties, acting at arm's length and under no compulsion to transact. (Emphasis added.)

United States

> The price at which the property would change hands between a willing buyer and a seller when the former is not under any compulsion to buy and the latter is not under any compulsion to sell, both parties having reasonable knowledge of relevant facts.

The Canadian definition implies that in the finding of value, both financial purchasers and special-interest purchasers (or, strategic purchasers) are to be included in the total population of possible purchasers for the subject property. The operative word is the "**highest**" price.

On the other hand, the U.S. definition of fair market value implies that a willing buyer is a **financial buyer** rather than a strategic buyer. Under the U.S. interpretation of value standards, synergistic value represents value to a particular buyer, *i.e.*, *investment value* rather than fair market value.

Special-interest purchasers are those who can, or believe they can, enjoy post-acquisition economies of scale (or synergies), diversification of business risk, or strategic advantages by combining the acquired business with their own. Financial buyers are typically not in a position to do this. That is why, all things being equal, special-interest purchasers would be prepared to pay, and often do pay, more for a subject property than the financial buyer.

In Canada, this fact also underscores one of the basic principles of valuation. Where there is only one special-interest purchaser, that purchaser will pay only a nominal amount more than all ordinary (read financial) purchasers; also known as the "one-tick up" theory. Where, however, there are two or more special-interest purchasers, a special purchaser market exists from which ordinary purchasers are excluded.

When using the Merger and Acquisition Method (*i.e.*, comparable M&A transactions) in valuing a controlling interest, valuators have to be particularly cognizant of data on control premiums (over the price of marketable minority shares) because most acquisition transactions combine pure control premiums with premiums for synergies specific to particular buyers. These transactions would be irrelevant in the context of a hypothetical "willing buyer" under the U.S. fair market value standard. The word "pure" in the phrase "pure control premiums" is meant to signify premiums devoid of any perceived synergistic benefits that may accrue to a purchaser. It does not signify a premium over the ratable or *pro rata* value of a company's shares.

You may ask what a consensus range for pure control premiums is and upon what sources of information are they typically based? My discussions with U.S. practitioners revealed that there are no dedicated studies done on this topic and no known established sources for such information. They did indicate that, in their view, a reasonable range would be 10 per cent to 20 per cent, with exceptions falling on either side. An analysis of publicly available information on going-private transactions, MBOs (management buy-outs), and buy-outs (*i.e.*, acquisitions) by privately pooled investor funds within a specific industry would, I believe, be good sources of such information ... if you can readily get it!

* * * * *

Challenges of Valuation Using the Market Approach in China

Duncan McPherson

Business valuation in China is evolving and there has been increased use of the income approach more recently compared to the predominant use of asset-based valuation methods previously.[5] Here I discuss some of the challenges of using the market approach when valuing Chinese companies, in particular the use of the guideline company method.

Using the guideline company valuation method under the market approach to value the equity interests of a business enterprise, the analysis may include consideration of the financial condition and operating performance of the company being valued relative to those of publicly traded that: (1) operate in the same or similar lines of business; (2) are potentially subject to corresponding economic, environmental, and political factors; and (3) could be considered reasonable investment alternatives. When adopting the market approach for the valuation of a Chinese company, one would therefore expect to derive an appropriate valuation multiple with reference to publicly-traded Chinese companies operating in the same industry. In China, as is often the case elsewhere, it may be difficult to identify sufficient directly comparable businesses. In addition, the use of the market approach in China is not as straightforward as it may be in some other countries due to unique characteristics of the Chinese markets.

There are two major stock exchanges in China, the Shanghai Stock Exchange and the Shenzhen Stock Exchange. Companies incorporated in mainland China are traded in these mainland A-share markets. 'A' shares are denominated in Renminbi, and currently only domestic investors and qualified

5 Prof. Jiang Wei, Business Valuation: Practices and Challenges in China", in J.L. Horvath & D.W. Chodikoff, eds., *Valuing a Business in Volatile Markets*, Shenyang University, China. See ch. 13 of this book.

foreign institutional investors are allowed to trade in 'A' shares. Several companies whose 'A' Shares are trading on the Shanghai and Shenzhen markets have a dual listing in Hong Kong where their 'H' shares are traded. 'H' shares are Hong Kong Dollar denominated shares of a company incorporated in the Chinese mainland that is listed on the Hong Kong Stock Exchange.

In recent years, 'A' shares in China have typically traded at a significant premium to the same company's 'H' shares in Hong Kong. According to the Hang Seng China AH Premium Index, which tracks the relative share prices of the largest and most liquid stocks with this dual listing, this premium peaked in January 2008 when 'A' shares were trading at 2.13x their 'H' share counterparts. Although the sharp falls in the PRC markets since have reduced the difference, at 30 June 2009 'A' shares were still trading at a 37 per cent premium to 'H' shares.[6] Some examples are set out below.[7]

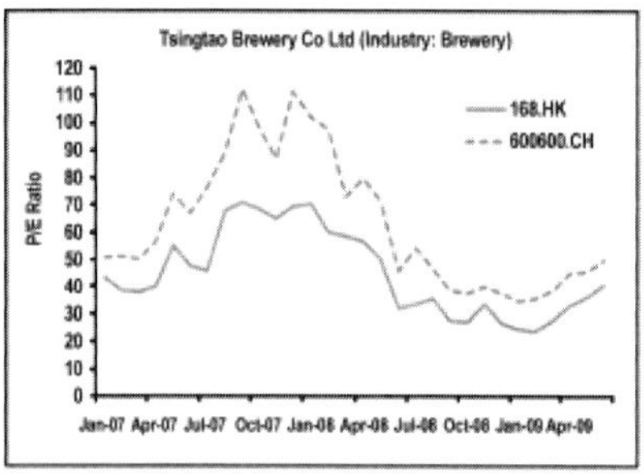

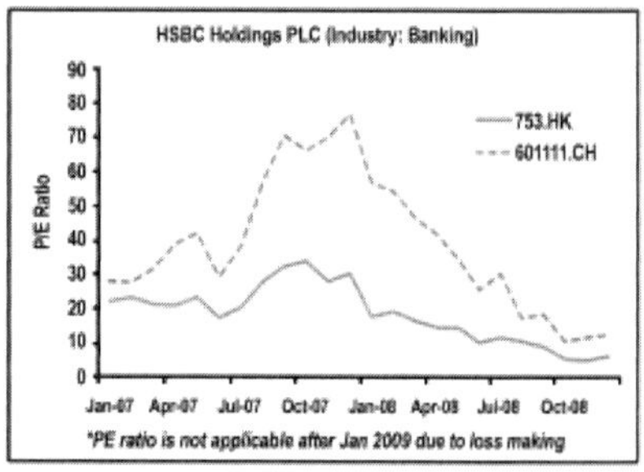

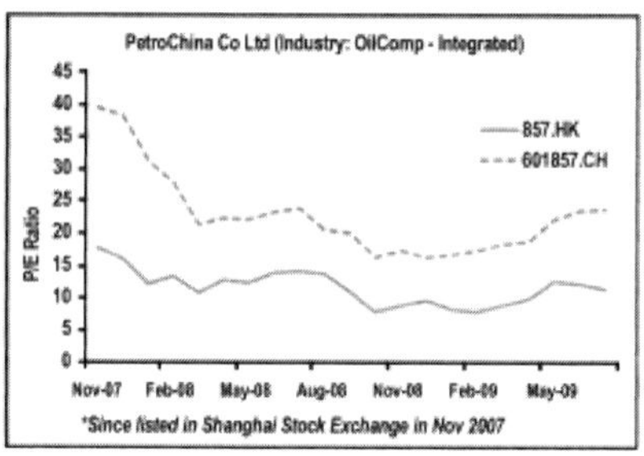

There are a number of reasons which may explain this difference:

- capital controls in China, which create two separate markets and eliminate the opportunity to arbitrage the difference between the two markets. When it was rumoured in 2007 that Chinese

6 Hang Seng China AH Premium Index; Bloomberg.
7 Bloomberg.

investors would be allowed to invest in the Hong Kong stock market, anticipation of a flood of money coming into Hong Kong to buy cheaper 'H' shares was a major factor in the Hang Seng Index increasing by 55 per cent to a peak of 31,638 between August 17, 2007 and October 30, 2007;

- limited supply of shares in China, where the actual free float is typically very low and around 60 per cent of tradeable market capitalization remains in the hands of the government;
- limited institutional investor base in China, where retail investors, who may behave less rationally, account for 50 per cent to 60 per cent of market activities (compared to around 20 per cent in Hong Kong).

In contrast, if we analyse HSBC, which trades in both London and Hong Kong, both among the leading financial services centres with open markets, we see a very different picture as the two share prices track very closely as illustrated below.[8]

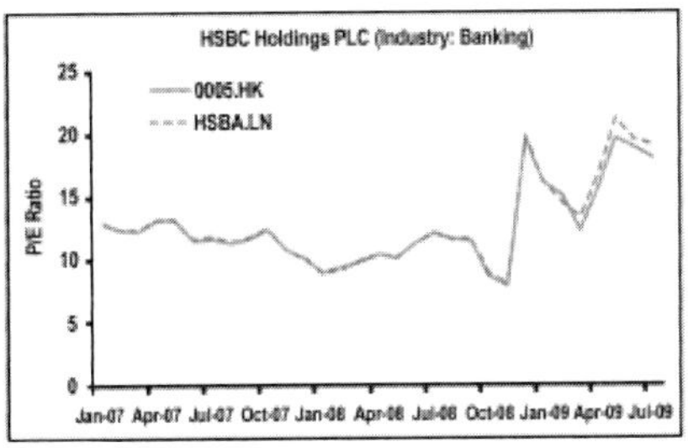

Clearly, the existence of such a premium and two "values" creates significant difficulties if a valuer is trying to apply the market approach to value a Chinese company. This is also the case when many of the comparable companies identified may trade in the 'A' Share market only – the earnings multiples of these companies will likely be much higher than if they traded on a different international exchange.

If we look at the trading multiples of Chinese companies more closely, we see that the Shanghai Composite Index peaked at an average 49 times historical earnings in November 2007 and the Shenzhen Index peaked at an average of 68.8 times earnings in May 2006.[9]

These multiples are much higher than are typically seen in more mature markets. For example, when the Dow Jones Index reached 14,198 on October 11, 2007, the index was trading at 16.9 times historical earnings.[10] The

8 *Ibid.*

9 *Ibid.*

10 *Ibid.*

NASDAQ Index, whose constituents may be expected to exhibit higher growth and commend higher valuation multiples, was trading at 35.9 times historical earnings when it hit a high of 2,589 on October 31, 2007.[11]

With the benefit of hindsight, it is easy to say that the China markets were overvalued in 2007 – with the impact of the global financial/economic crisis the Shanghai and Shenzhen indices had fallen by 70 per cent and 65 per cent respectively from their peaks by December 31, 2008 (though they have since rebounded in 2009). However, it is worth considering the following factors:

- The price-earnings multiples of a company should reflect the expected growth in that company's earnings. For example, if Company A and Company B both earned $10 in profits last year, but Company A expects 20 per cent growth in earnings in the future and Company B only expects 10 per cent earnings growth, then one would expect Company A to trade at a premium to Company B.
- Taking a simple analysis, we can estimate the level of earnings growth required to support an earnings multiple of 69 times (equivalent to the Shenzhen Composite Index valuation peak) by doing a cross-check using an indicative discounted cash flow analysis (a capitalized earnings approach cannot be used due to the high level of earnings growth).

P/E 69 times		**Terminal Growth Rate**				
		3%	**4%**	**5%**	**6%**	**7%**
Discount Rate	**12%**	43.4%	40.4%	37.2%	33.5%	29.2%
	14%	47.9%	45.5%	42.9%	40.0%	36.8%
	16%	51.6%	49.6%	47.4%	45.1%	42.5%
	18%	54.7%	53.0%	51.2%	49.2%	47.0%
	20%	57.4%	55.9%	54.3%	52.6%	50.7%

- This indicative analysis assumes :
  - five years of discrete cash flows until stable earnings growth is achieved and a terminal growth rate is applied;
  - free cash flows are equal to 75 per cent of earnings (since significant investment in fixed assets and working capital is likely to

[11] *Ibid.*

be required to achieve significant levels of growth as shown above).

According to EIU, the long-term GDP growth rate from 2009 to 2030 for China is expected to be 5.6 per cent.[12]

Although China has achieved spectacular growth in recent years, GDP growing by an average of 9.4 per cent from 1999 to 2008,[13] the above analysis illustrates that significantly higher average growth rates would need to be achieved over a sustained period to support these levels of earnings multiples. While certain companies may be able to demonstrate such performance, it is doubtful whether such a high average growth rate could be attained.

Conclusion

Factors such as capital controls and limited investment opportunities, which result in China 'A' shares trading at a substantial premium to the equivalent 'H' shares in Hong Kong, have historically created challenges to the use of the market approach for valuing Chinese companies. Although the premium of 'A' share values to 'H' shares has dropped significantly since peaking in early 2008, a substantial premium of 37 per cent still existed in June 2009.

With the asset approach only appropriate for certain companies, and the limitations of the market approach described above, adopting the income approach as the primary valuation method for Chinese companies is often the best way to proceed. Use of the market approach may be limited to a sanity check of the implied multiples of the income approach result.

As with any valuation, the purpose of the valuation is of primary importance. If for example, a private equity fund is looking to exit an investment through an 'A' share IPO in China, then the earnings multiples of comparable listed companies' 'A' shares may be the most relevant valuation metric to the investor.

The situation may change in time, as currency restrictions are relaxed and as more large overseas companies seek listings in the Chinese market as is widely expected, when the market approach may be more widely adopted.

* * * * *

---

12 Economist Intelligence Unit, Country Forecast April 2009.

13 Economist Intelligence Unit, Country Report June 2004; July 2009.

Valuation Standards in China

Minghai Chen & Edwina Tam

Business valuation is the process of estimating the economic value of a business interest. It is an art, not an exact science. Professional technical and ethical standards, judgment, and experience are integral parts of the process. In an emerging market such as China, particular attention should be paid to valuation standards to guide the valuer through the additional complexities of such a market.

Purpose of Valuation Standards

In China, due to the globalization of businesses and the shift from a socialist market economy to a capital market economy, valuation has become a focal point in business transactions. The Chinese government has made it a legal requirement for a professional valuer to be involved in market related activities such as restructuring of State Owned Enterprises, initial public offerings and mergers and acquisitions to protect the national interest and provide assurance to all parties involved that the transaction was reasonable.

In the absence of a set framework guiding the valuation process, the value of a business interest can vary tremendously, even within a short time period. This is especially true during volatile times. In the absence of ethical and technical guidance, a valuer can choose a certain valuation methodology, a different valuation date, or a different definition of value to bias towards a certain outcome in each instance. Valuation standards promote consistency in defining valuation terms, the application of valuation methodologies, and the use of uniform principles in the valuation process to ensure objectivity and to provide assurance as to the valuation conclusion.

China Appraisal Society ("CAS") was created by the Ministry of Finance ("MOF") first and foremost to set valuation and ethical standards for the profession and to regulate its members according to these standards. These valuation and ethics standards were created with the view of elevating the valuation industry in China on par with global standards and to provide a common platform for better understanding with defined terms, theoretically sound methodologies, and ethical standards to ensure objectivity.

Two of CAS's objectives are to promote the research and development of valuation theories and to regulate the profession ensuring compliance to the standards set by the organization. The continual improvement of valuation theories ensures compliance with global standards and regulation of the profession protects the reputation of objectivity and credibility of the profession.

Main Objectives of the Valuation Standards

Maintain and Enhance the Technical Standards of the Profession

The valuation standards set by CAS are being continually monitored and revised to ensure relevance of standards to the marketplace. Further, one of CAS objectives is to upgrade professional expertise, promote ethical accomplishments, and to uphold public confidence in the profession through coordinated efforts with valuation professionals at home and abroad.

Maintain Transparency of the Valuation Process

The valuation standards set by CAS provide transparency in the valuation process. These standards allow for uniform assessment of technical criteria in the application of valuation methodologies, processes, and practices.

Maintain Independence and Objectivity

The risk of a valuer's ability to manipulate the valuation conclusion is high without ethical standards and monitoring of such standards. A precise and specific code of conduct enforced by CAS will preserve and maintain the credibility and respect of the profession and ensure the protection of public interests.

Chinese Valuation Standards

The system of Chinese Valuation Standards ("CVS") encompasses professional standards and code of ethics. CAS has developed four levels of professional standards: the first level is general valuation standards; the second level relates to specific valuation issues or industries; the third level relates to the application of the valuation standards for specific purposes; and the fourth level is guidance notes on specific types of valuations.

Since 2001, CAS, under the guidance of MOF, has issued seventeen valuation standards, including:

- Valuation Standards–General;
- Code of Ethics–General;
- Valuation Standards–Intangibles;
- Valuation Standards–machinery;
- Valuation Standards–real property;
- Valuation Standards–valuation report;
- Valuation Standards–valuation procedures;
- Valuation Standards–work paper;
- Valuation Standards–engagement;
- valuation application for financial report purpose;
- valuation application for state-own-assets report;
- guidance notes for Concerning Legal Title of Subject Property;
- guidance notes for Gems and Jewelry;
- guidance notes for Business Valuation (pilot);
- guidance notes for Non-performing Loans (pilot);
- guidance notes for value type; and
- guidance notes for patents.

The three main objectives that CAS wanted to convey to their Chinese valuation professionals through the development of the CVS are:

Principle-based Standards

In terms of content, CVS are principle-based. The standards set minimum procedures that valuers must perform but the intent is not to mandate how the procedures are performed.

Consistent Quality

The CVS is developed to ensure a minimum level of quality preserving and enhancing the credibility of the profession. The "Valuation Standards –General" sets out eight procedures that must be included in a valuation engagement:

- identify valuation matters;
- define the engagement;
- adopt an appropriate valuation methodology;

- perform industry, economic and company research;
- collect valuation materials;
- perform valuation analysis;
- prepare a written report documenting the analysis; and
- documentation of work in a working paper file.

Credibility and objectivity

"Code of Ethics–General" became effective in 2004. It provides a set of guidelines and values that governs the business behavior of the profession and encompasses the interaction among professionals, and interaction between professionals and the general public. These standards are designed to deter wrong doers and promote honest and ethical conduct, including ethical handling of actual and apparent conflicts of interest, fair and objective valuation analysis, and compliance with applicable laws, rules, and regulations.

* * * * *

Market Efficiency in the Middle East?

Ben Moore & Fahad Khan

Valuers always look to the market, where possible, when valuing an asset. When using more developed markets such as the United States of America, United Kingdom, and Japan its is likely that valuers will take for granted that markets are sufficiently efficient and, as such, security prices can be regarded as a good starting point when valuing a company. However, when looking at companies in emerging markets, such as the Middle East, the degree to which the market is efficient and, therefore, prices a reliable benchmark, is not so clear.

The region in general, and the Gulf Cooperation Council (GCC) Countries (which comprise Oman, the Kingdom of Saudi Arabia, Qatar, Kuwait, the United Arab Emirates and the Kingdom of Bahrain), in particular, have enjoyed strong growth in the recent past. However, it could be argued that the securities market has lagged behind and has a long way to go in some aspects, in particular in the transparency relating to historical performance and plans for the future.

Several factors make one question: just how efficient is the market in the region? While the strong form of efficiency is sometimes questionable even in mature markets like the United States of America, the United Kingdom, and Japan; there are several factors that make GCC markets different.

One such factor is the relatively low "free float" in the majority of listed securities compared to other markets. The Dubai Financial Market (DFM) and the Abu Dhabi Securities Exchange (ADX), the two major exchanges in the United Arab Emirates (UAE), have a minimum 55 per cent free float requirement for initial listings. The third, and newest, local exchange, NASDAQ Dubai (previously known as Dubai International Financial Exchange or DIFX) requires this to be only 25 per cent.

This low "free float" requirement along with the fact that there are "lock in" periods applicable to founding shareholders (which are about two years for companies listed on the DFM and ADX) substantially reduces the total value of shares available for trading in the market. The size of the "free float" alone does not indicate whether quoted prices are truly reflective of the market's views. However, when combined with other factors such as ownership restrictions, lock in periods, limited corporate communications and media coverage, and infant regulatory bodies, the bigger picture on market efficiency looks less clear.

One major factor that impacts market efficiency is the ownership structure that is in place in the region. In UAE and most GCC countries, there are restrictions on the proportion of foreign ownership of companies. For example all public joint stock companies (PJSCs) listed on DFM and ADX have to be 51 per cent owned by UAE nationals. The remaining 49 per cent ownership, which is the maximum foreign ownership, is further subdivided into non-GCC Arabs, GCC Arabs, and non-Arabs. As a result of such restrictions, 49 of the total 68 companies listed on the ADX have average foreign ownership of only 19 per cent. The remaining 19 companies do not have any foreign ownership at all. Considering that the population of the UAE is approximately 4.8 million as of the end of 2008, of which at least 80 per cent is made up of non-UAE nationals, the prices quoted for a sizeable percentage of the stocks are therefore only impacted by the investment decisions of only a small population of people.

Another important factor that is prevalent in the GCC markets, and one that is common to emerging markets, is the lack of detailed information. Quality information available in an efficient and timely manner is essential for the functioning of financial markets as it provides investors the basis to form their views. A recent study by The National Investor (TNI), a UAE-based merchant bank, in Q408, found that about 90 per cent of companies in the GCC do not pre-announce the date of releasing annual reports. Moreover, only one quarter of the companies make public their AGM dates and almost one third of the companies in GCC do not publish annual reports in English, which is the functional business language of most of the GCC countries and the international business language.

One reason for this lack of information is the nature of the regulatory environment. The Securities and Commodities Authority (SCA), which regulates the DFM and ADX, was formed in January 2000 while the Dubai Financial Services Authority (DFSA), which supervises the NASDAQ Dubai, was formed only in 2004. These regulatory bodies are still trying to cope with the rapid pace of development of the economy and, therefore, the limited requirements. For example the SCA passed a law only in December 2008 to allow "book building" as an alternative method to price an Initial

Public Offering. Further, listed companies only have to release their financials within a stipulated timeframe to comply with the regulations. Management discussion and analysis or segmental reporting are not provided by many companies.

While the local media has evolved substantially over the years, it still has a long way to go in terms of providing good coverage and analysis on the various market players in a timely manner. Also, limited analyst coverage of a majority of listed stocks exacerbates the problem of quality information. This is evident by the fact that only 1 in 50 companies in the GCC hold analyst meetings or conference calls (as per the TNI report) and very few stocks on the DFM and ADX have any analyst coverage.

A direct consequence of the above factors is the low trading volumes observed in the majority of the listed securities. For example almost 80 per cent of the total traded value on the DFM in 2008 came from less than 15 per cent of the stocks. Further, around 60 per cent of companies in the GCC do not trade everyday, leading to "stale prices". While the aforementioned structural reasons play a major role in determining prices, another interesting characteristic of the GCC market that contributes to lower trading volume is the population breakdown. As mentioned above, more than 80 per cent of the population of the UAE consists of expatriates, who, regardless of their stay in the country, do not have the right to apply for citizenship. This "temporary" stay in the country leads to what behavioral finance terms as "home country bias", wherein people are more comfortable investing in securities with which they are familiar and comfortable. This coupled with the infant, albeit strongly growing, regional asset management industry makes non-UAE nationals more comfortable investing in their home countries, further impacting the trading volumes.

To conclude, if the basic tenet of efficient markets is that prices are the result of the market's view of the company's risk and prospects based on all available information, then there are several factors that lead one to question whether such argument currently applies to the Middle East. Structural factors like ownership restrictions, lock in periods, and low float factors coupled with qualitative factors like limited information and coverage and population mix prompts one to use the market multiple approach with caution.

For example, if you are valuing a mineral water bottling company in the GCC, Bloomberg would quickly show three DFM listed companies, namely, Dubai Refreshments, Gulfa Mineral water, and Jeema mineral water. Their financial performance as seen by EBITDA margins, net margins, and ROIC may suggest a fair degree of similarity. However, for example only 200,000 shares of Jeema, out of a total of 30 million, were traded in 2008 and trading in Gulfa was limited. So, can one use the efficient market argument and compare the market price to the value estimated under the DCF approach? While the DCF has its limitations in terms of estimating the relevant inputs, the estimated value might not reconcile with the quoted price due to market imperfections. Further, other valuation inputs like "Beta" can also be impacted as simple regression of the stock returns to the DFM index would provide skewed results as the stock would be quite illiquid and the index is dominated by few companies. Also, around 15 per cent to 20 per cent of the market capitalisation of the market is attributable to one company, Emaar, which is in the real estate sector. Valuers must, therefore, be cognizant of these factors in the GCC and apply greater degree of subjectivity in dealing with market multiples and data.

* * * * *

Valuation Insights – Indonesia

B. Sridhar Rao

The primary methodology used in business valuations is generally dominated by the Discounted Cash Flow method. Having said this, the secondary methodology is often the relative/comparable company method. This I have found to be the least reliable method in Indonesia. A few factors drive this hypothesis. First, the number of truly comparable companies in a particular sector often comes down to being only one or two comparable companies. This, I believe, is not sufficient to justify using the relative/comparable company method in valuations. Based on this, we have proposed that the valuation standards demand that at least five comparable companies should be available for this valuation method to be applied. Second, one has to study the correlation of share trading volumes to that of the share price. It is often observed that share trading volumes keep tumbling but, unusually, the share price on the other hand keeps going up. This is because we have a situation where the share often is a "controlled share". Yes, this is illegal, but difficult to prove and hence this anomaly continues to exist in the market place. This is primarily due to the Indonesian SEC's absolute disinterest for monitoring and tackling the issue.

I have randomly selected shares that are traded in the Indonesian Capital Market to read the correlation between share trading volumes to share price and compared them to similar companies in the sector across the region. The objective of this exercise is to prove that during certain periods these "controlled" shares see share trading volumes going down while share prices on the other hand go up significantly. Shares in the same sector in the region, indicate reasonably good correlation between share trading volumes and share price. So, once again, my point here is that shares that are traded with reducing share trading volumes but experience significant increases in share price **may not** truly reflect market value; hence, not appropriate to be considered as market comparable companies for the purpose of valuations. One could look further into analyzing bid and offer data to further justify this point. This I have not done in this insight. Let us look at the cases illustrated below:

Here is AALI, a company which is in the agribusiness sector and one can see how the share price has shown significant increases over the years. The share trading volumes on the other hand have shown a consistent disinterest from investors on the share. This is very unlikely. A share price performance of this nature should attract significant attention from investors and lead to high share trading volumes.

Description
AALI operates rubber plantations and manufactures cooking oil. Through its subsidiaries, the company also operates a variety of other plantations such as palm oil, tea, and cocoa plantations.

Country
Indonesia

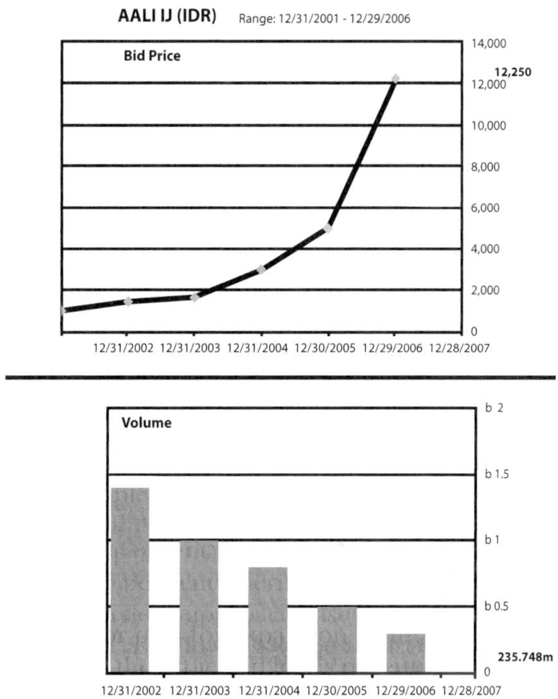

Source: Deloitte Research

Let us look at similar companies in the sector of agribusiness in other countries. We have Kuala Lumpur Kepong Berhad in Malaysia and Heilongjiang Agriculture Co. in China. Both shares indicate some correlation to share price movement to share trading volumes. These share prices are more reliable and justifiably mentionable as market price.

Agribusiness Companies in the Region

Description

Kuala Lumpur Kepong Berhad produces and processes palm products, natural rubber, and cocoa on its plantations. Through its subsidiaries, the company mills and refines oil palm products, cultivates ramie, and manufactures oleochemicals, soap, esters, latex gloves, toiletries, and parquet flooring products. Kuala Lumpur Kepong also develops properties and operates holiday bungalows.

Country

Malaysia

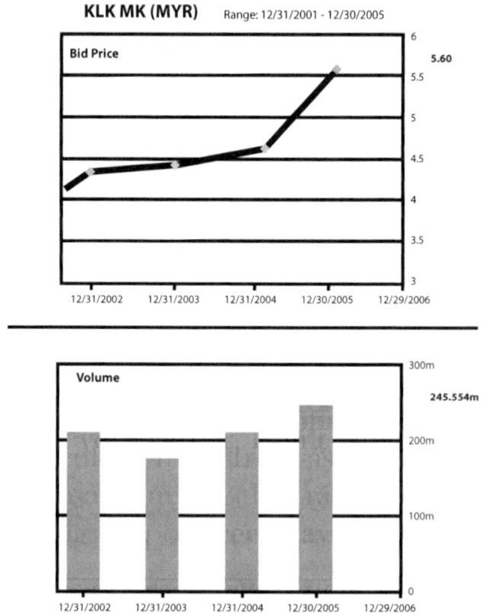

Source: Deloitte Research

Description

Heilongjiang Agriculture Co., Ltd. plants, processes, and sells rice, soy-bean, wheat, corn, and other grain products. The company also produces fertilizers and sells paper products.

Country

China

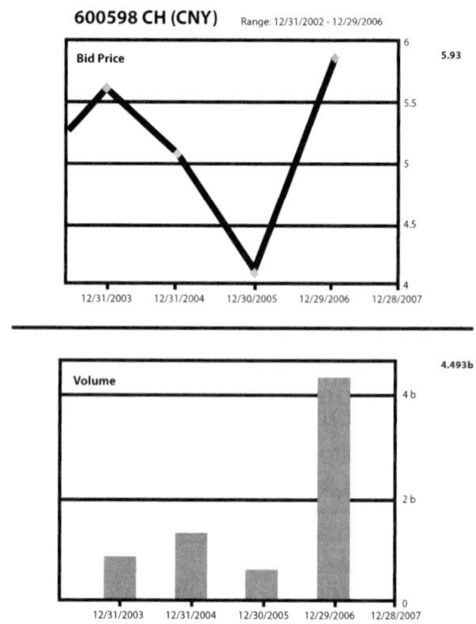

Source: Deloitte Research

Here, below is ASII, a company which is primarily driven by investments in the automotive sector. One can see how the share price has shown significant increases over the years. The share trading volumes on the other hand have shown a steep downward trend. This is very unusual. A share price performance of this nature should attract significant attention from investors and this being a share with a large market capitalization should logically lead to high share trading volumes.

Description

ASII assembles and distributes automobiles, motorcycles, and their related spare parts. Through its subsidiaries, the company also operates in the mining, development of plantations, financial and information technology.

Country

Indonesia

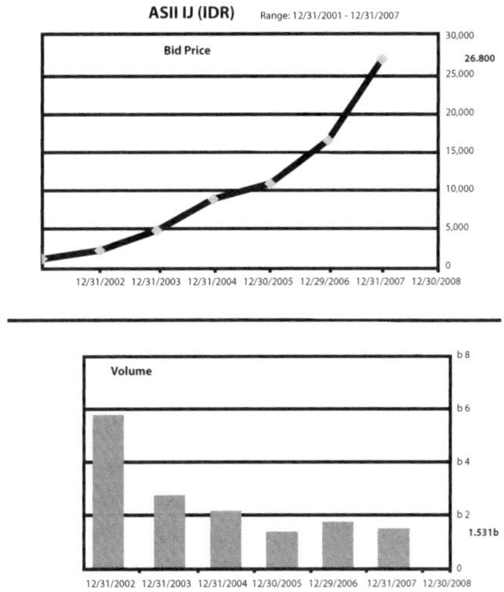

Source: Deloitte Research

Let us look at similar companies in the sector of automotives in other countries. We have SAIC Motor Corporation Ltd. in China, Oriental Holdings Berhad in Malaysia, Hyundai Motor Company in Korea, Dongfeng Motor Group Company Limited in China and Indus Motor Company Limited in Pakistan. All these shares indicate some correlation to share price movement to share trading volumes. These share prices are more reliable and justifiably mentionable as market price.

Comparable Companies

Description

SAIC Motor Corporation Ltd. manufactures and markets automobiles and related parts and accessories.

Country

China

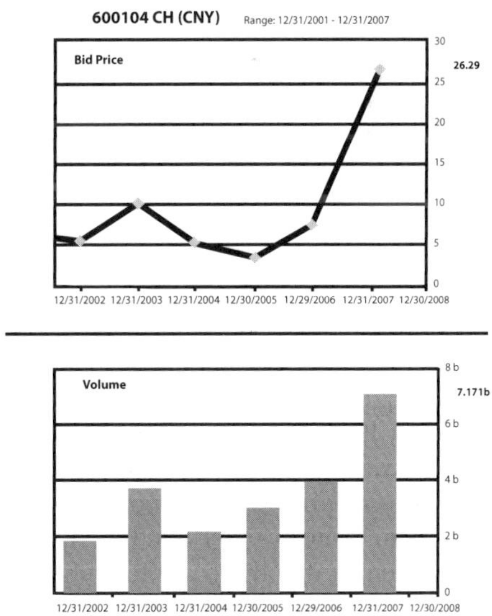

Source: Deloitte Research

Description
Oriental Holdings Berhad is an investment holding company whose subsidiaries distribute and assemble motor vehicles, manufacture motorcycles and bicycle components. The company also develops properties, processes rubber and oil palm, sells concrete products, electrical components, and motor parts. Oriental provides money lending and leasing services.

Country
Malaysia

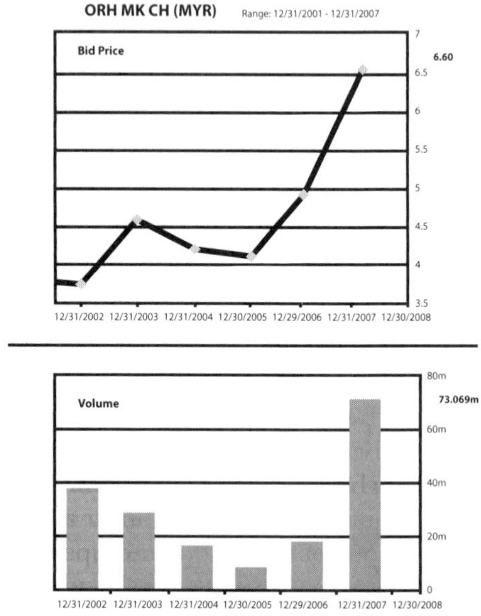

Source: Deloitte Research

Description
Hyundai Motor Company manufactures, sells, and exports passenger cars, trucks, and commercial vehicles. The company also sells various auto parts and operates auto repair service centers throughout South Korea. Hyundai Motor provides financial services through its subsidiaries.

Country
South Korea

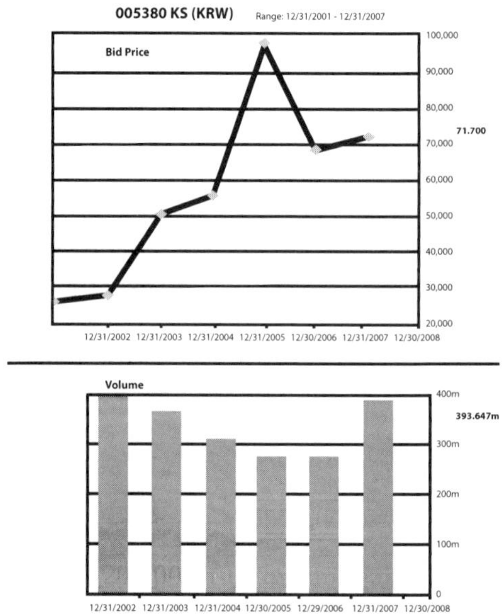

Source: Deloitte Research

Description
Dongfeng Motor Group Company Limited designs, manufactures, and markets diesel engines, light trucks, automobiles, castings, and related spare parts.

Country
China

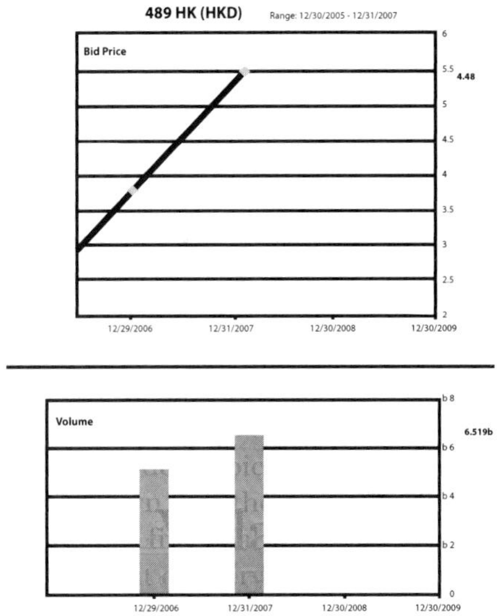

Source: Deloitte Research

Description
Indus Motor Company Limited was created through a joint venture agreement between the House of Habib, the Toyota Motor Corporation, and the Toyota Tsusho Corporation, in order to assemble, manufacture, and market Toyota vehicles. The company is also the sole distributor of Toyota vehicles in Pakistan.

Country
Pakistan

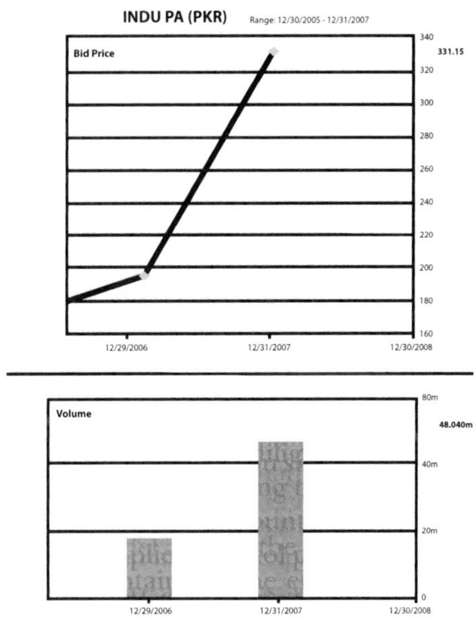

Source: Deloitte Research

Here below is AUTO, a company that manufactures and distributes a comprehensive range of automotive and motorcycle parts. The price has shown significant increases over the years. The share trading volumes on the other hand have shown a steep downward trend. This is very unusual. A share price performance of this nature should attract significant attention from investors and lead to high share trading volumes.

Description
PT AUTO manufactures and distributes a comprehensive range of automotive and motorcycle parts. The company produces a wide range of forged, cast, electrical, rubber, and plastic automotive parts, and (OEM) original equipment manufacturing.

Country
Indonesia

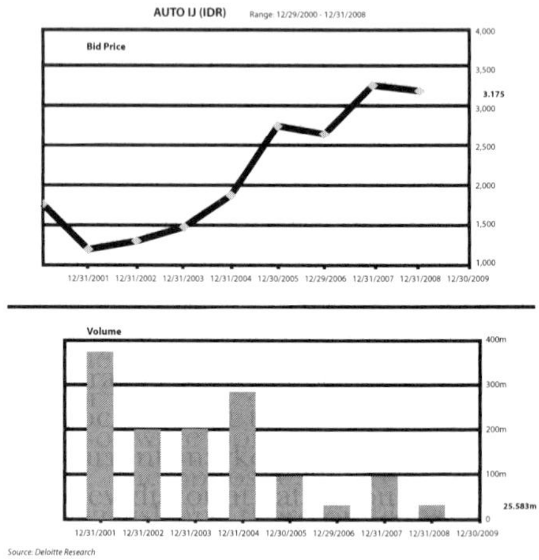

Let us look at similar companies in the sector of automotive parts manufacturing in other countries. We have Jiangnan Mould & Plastic Technology Co., Ltd. in China, Global & Yuasa Battery Co., Ltd. in Korea, Thai Stanley Electric Public Company Limited in Thailand, Zhejiang Glass Company Limited in China, and Tube Investments of India Limited in India. All these shares indicate some correlation to share price movement to share trading volumes. These share prices are more reliable and justifiably mentionable as market price.

Comparable Companies

Description
Jiangnan Mould & Plastic Technology Co., Ltd. manufactures and markets automobile bumpers, plastic products, moulds, plastics injection machines, and other related products.

Country
China

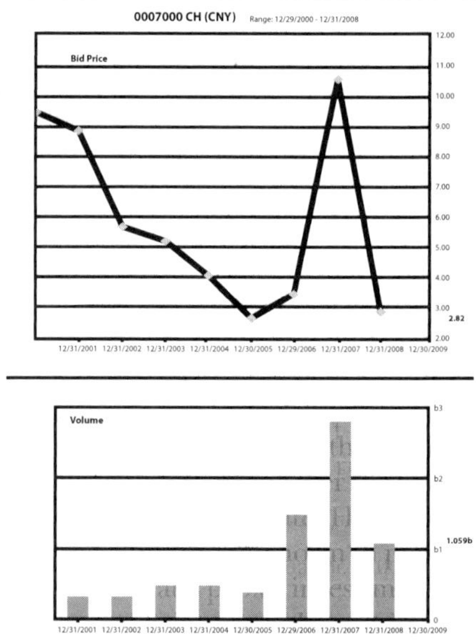

Description
Global & Yuasa Battery Co., Ltd. specializes in manufacturingstorage batteries used in automobiles, motorcycles, electric vehicles, and industrial machinery such as exca-vators and bulldozers. The company provides its products to do-mestic and overseas markets.

Country
South Korea

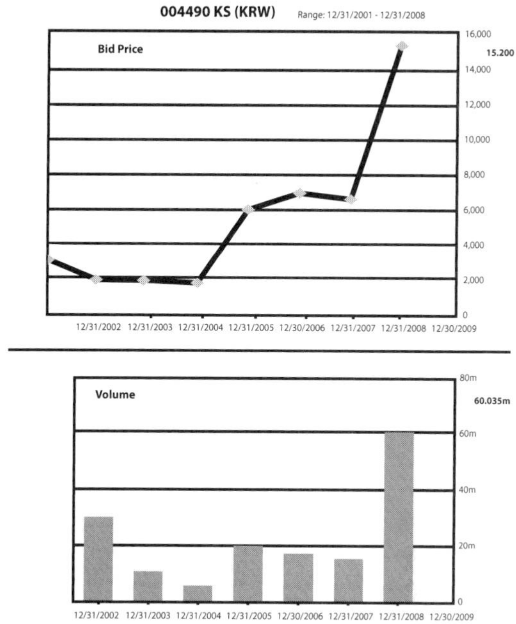

Source: Deloitte Research

Description
Thai Stanley Electric Public Company Limited manufactures automotive bulbs including headlight bulbs, taillight bulbs, stop taillight bulbs, and meter bulbs. The company also manufactures lighting equipment, as well as molds and dies for automobile and home appliance parts.

Country
Thailand

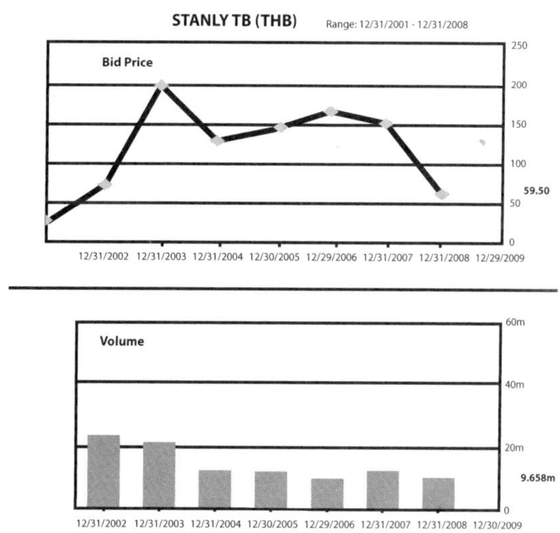

Source: Deloitte Research

Description
Zhejiang Glass Company Limited manufactures float flat glass in China. The products are mainly used in construction and automotive industries.

Country
China

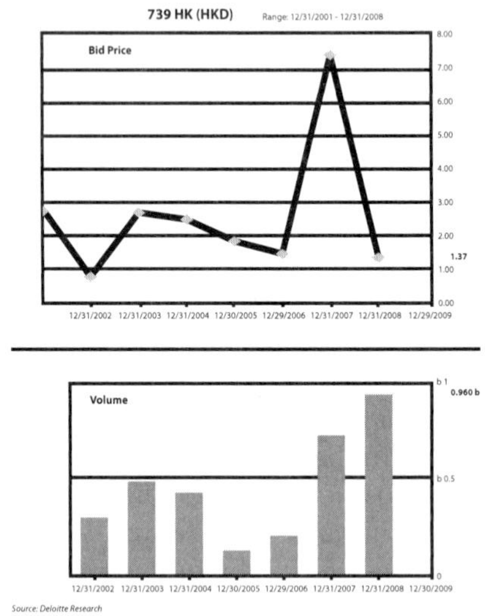

Description
Tube Investments of India Limited is a diversified manufacturing company with a special focus on steel and steel products. The company produces steel tubes, cold rolled steel strips and metal sections, as well as bicycles and all critical bicycle components. The company also has a subsidiary that sells insurance.

Country
India

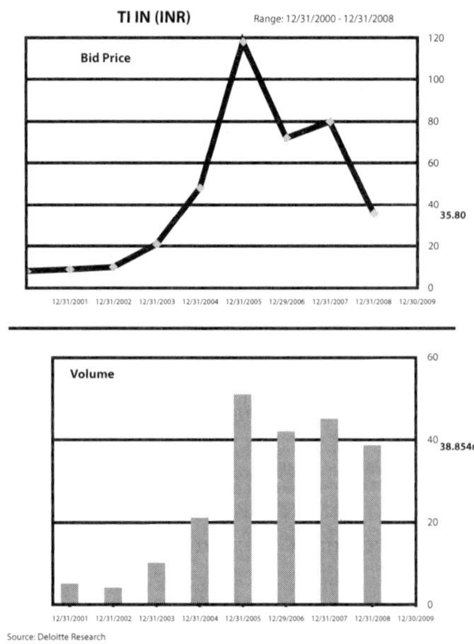

MPPA is in the department store business. The share price has shown significant increases over the years. The share trading volumes on the other hand have shown a steep downward trend. This is very unusual. A share price performance of this nature should attract significant attention from investors and lead to high share trading volumes.

Description
MPPA and its subsidiary operate department stores. The company's stores sell items such as clothes, accessories, bags, shoes, cosmetics, electronics, toys, stationery, books, and daily needs.

Country
Indonesia

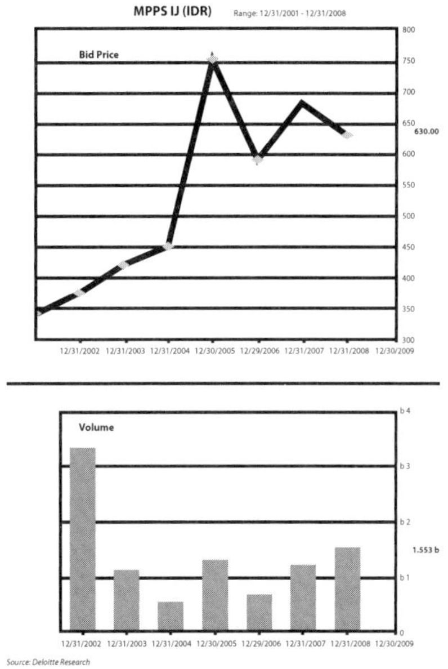

We have Zhongxing Shenyang Commercial Building Group Co., Ltd. in China, Parkson Holdings Berhad in Malaysia, Trent Limited in India, and Robinson Department Store in Thailand. All these shares indicate some correlation to share price movement to share trading volumes. These share prices are more reliable and justifiably mentionable as market price.

Comparable Companies

Description
Zhongxing Shenyang Commercial Building Group Co., Ltd. owns and operates department stores in Shenyang, Liaoning. Through its subsidiaries, the company also provides building decoration services.

Country
China

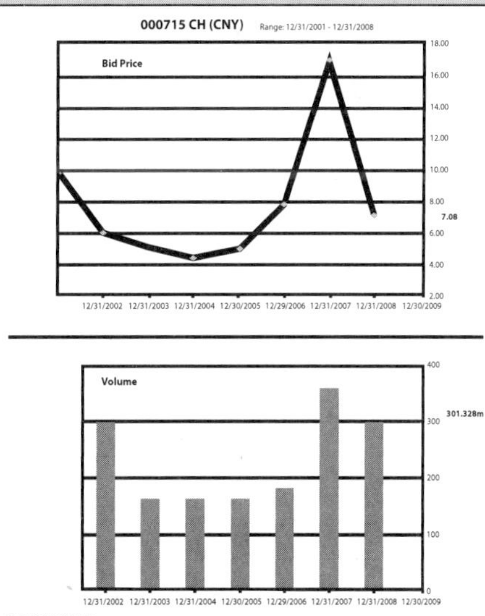

Description
Parkson Holdings Berhad is an investment holding company. The company, through its subsidiaries, operates a chain of department stores in Malaysia, China, and Vietnam.

Country
Malaysia

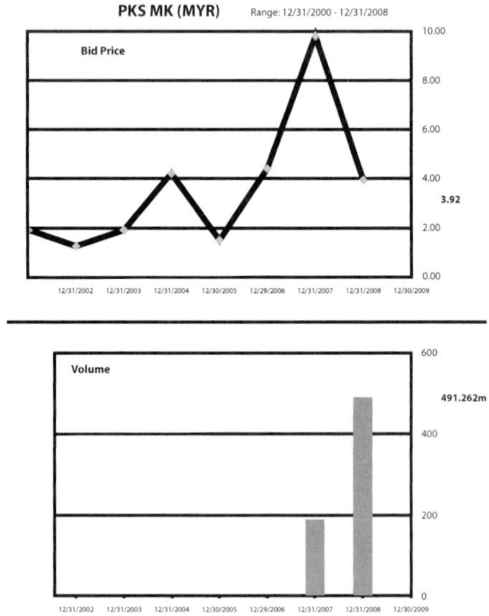

Source: Deloitte Research

Description
Trent Limited operates a chain of retail stores that sell fashion apparel, cosmetics, perfumery products, and toiletry items. The company sells apparel for men, women, and children. Trent sells its cosmetics products under the "Westside" and "Trent" brand names.

Country
India

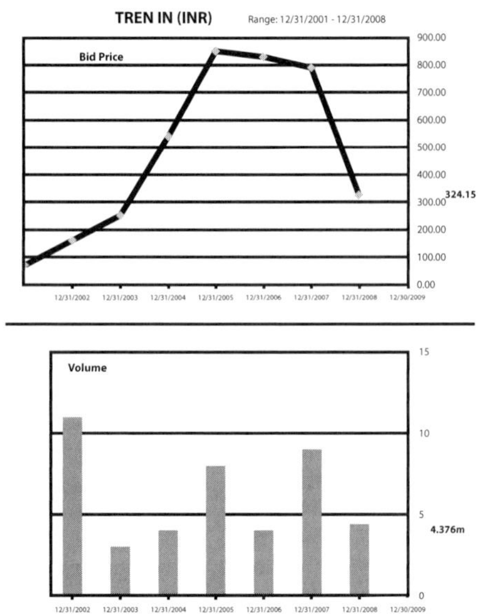

Source: Deloitte Research

Description
Robinson Department Store Public Company Limited owns and operates Robinson department store chain.

Country
Thailand

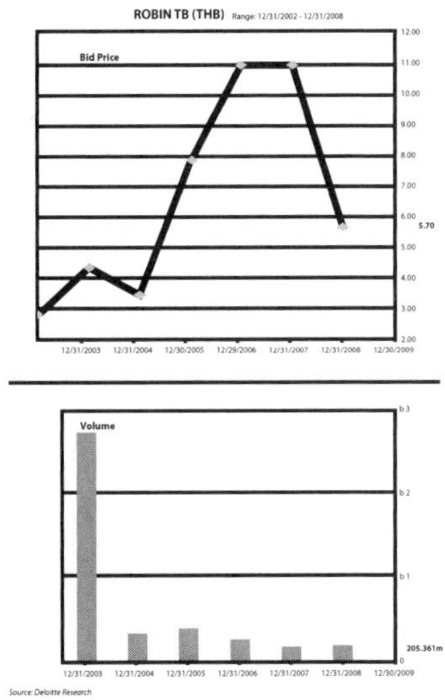

NISP is in the banking business. The share price has shown significant increases over the years. The share trading volumes on the other hand have shown a steep downward trend. This is very unusual. A share price performance of this nature should attract significant attention from investors and lead to high share trading volumes.

Description
NISP provides general commercial banking services. The bank has branch offices located throughout Indonesia.

Country
Indonesia

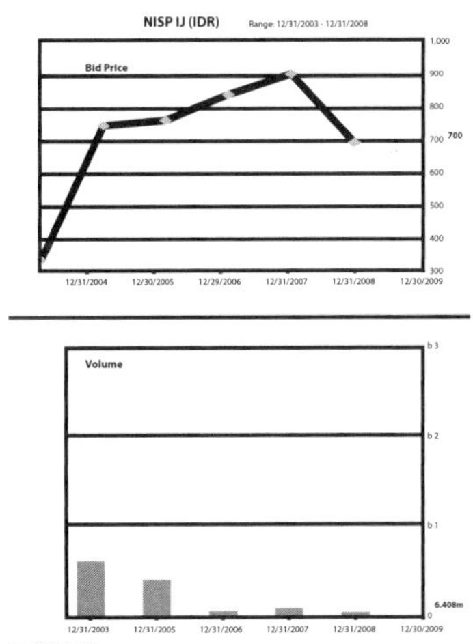

We have ING Vysya Bank Limited in India, UBG Berhad in Malaysia, and the Union Bank of Taiwan in Taiwan. All these shares indicate some correlation to share price movement to share trading volumes. These share prices are more reliable and justifiably mentionable as market price.

Comparable Companies

Description
ING Vysya Bank Limited is a full service bank. The bank offers a wide range of banking services and financial products, including corporate and commercial banking services, treasury management, retail banking, private banking, as well as mutual funds, Demat, and credit cards.

Country
India

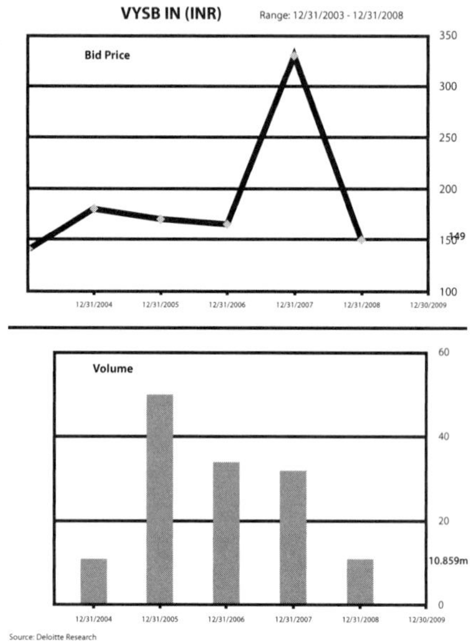

Description
UBG Berhad, through its subsidiaries, provides building construction and civil engineering works, mechanical and electrical engineering related activities. The company also invests in land, and develops residential and commercial properties.

Country
Malaysia

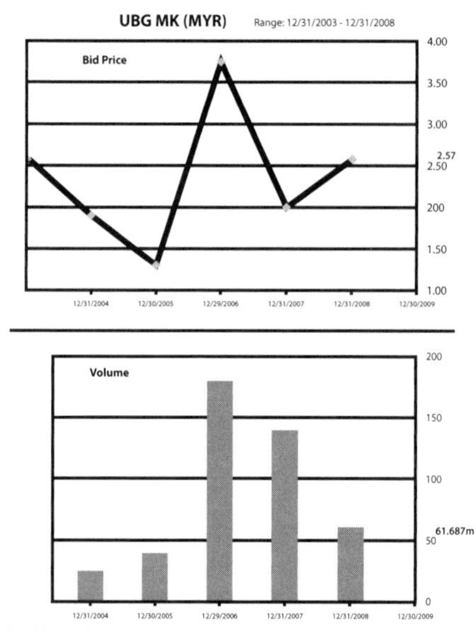

Description

Union Bank of Taiwan accepts various deposits and provides short- and medium-term loans. The bank issues discount notes, invests in government bonds, short-term bills, corporate bonds and financial debentures, issues domestic letter of credit, and conduct.

Country

Taiwan

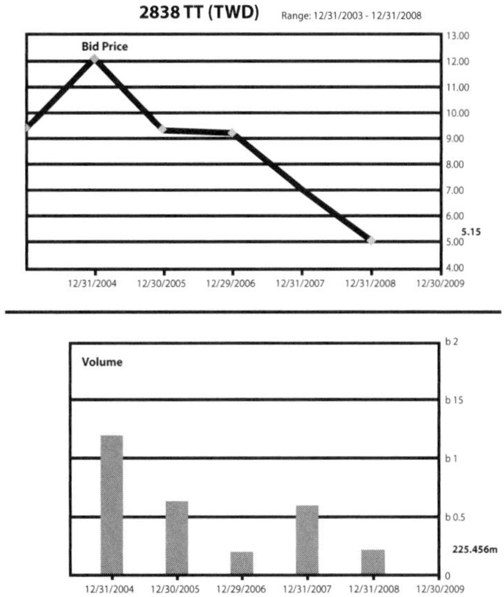

Source: Deloitte Research

In conclusion, it is not recommended that we use the relative/comparable company method for business valuations in Indonesia unless first and foremost a thorough analysis is done on the historical bid and offer data of the share price of comparable companies. Second, a study on comparable companies is made on the share price movement and its correlation to that of share trading volumes. If the results of the steps mentioned above are acceptable, only then can the particular company analyzed be categorized as acceptable to be used as a comparable company. Further, a minimum of five such comparable companies should be available before using the relative/comparable company method for valuations. Hence, a revision of the valuation standards to incorporate the hypothesis of this valuation insight is recommended.

The Valuation of Infrastructure Assets in Volatile Markets[1]

Richard K. Ellsworth

Infrastructure assets have emerged as a separate asset class that offers portfolio diversification opportunities for investors seeking to expand into alternative investment categories. The perceived stability of the cash flows associated with infrastructure assets has enhanced the investment attractiveness as an asset class. The emergence of infrastructure funds, public-private partnerships, and tax ownership arrangements provide investors with the opportunity to invest in the infrastructure asset class with its perception as a low risk investment offering attractive risk return characteristics. Historically, infrastructure funds have rewarded their investors and have been viewed favorably from a risk return tradeoff perspective.

Traditionally, infrastructure assets have been deployed in regulated industries where increases in the cost structure associated with these assets is transferred to the users of the infrastructure asset. Infrastructure assets are frequently operated by government agencies that are mandated to provide specific services and are responsible for the operation of the infrastructure

---

1 This publication contains general information only and Deloitte Financial Advisory Services LLP is not, by means of this publication, rendering accounting, business, financial, investment, legal, tax, or other professional advice or services. This publication is not a substitute for such professional advice or services, nor should it be used as a basis for any decision or action that may affect your business. Before making any decision or taking any action that may affect your business, you should consult a qualified professional advisor. Deloitte Financial Advisory Services LLP, its affiliates and related entities shall not be responsible for any loss sustained by any person who relies on this publication. Deloitte refers to one or more of Deloitte Touche Tohmatsu, a Swiss Verein, and its network of member firms, each of which is a legally separate and independent entity. Please see www.deloitte.com/about for a detailed description of the legal structure of Deloitte Touche Tohmatsu and its member firms. Please see www.deloitte.com/us/about for a detailed description of the legal structure of Deloitte LLP and its subsidiaries.

asset. As operators of infrastructure assets, government agencies are increasingly receptive to the sale or lease of these assets to solve short-term maintenance and budgetary problems, which have become increasingly difficult from an economic perspective. The sale of infrastructure assets provides government entities with a capital infusion to fund activities, such as the retirement of debt obligations, investment in new capital projects, or the pursuit of social programs, without the need to raise taxes.

Recent dramatic declines in global equity markets and increased volatility in the capital markets provide an impetus to evaluate the risk return characteristics of infrastructure assets and infrastructure funds. Because of the regulated nature of many infrastructure assets, transaction activity from which to gauge the price movement and value of these assets is limited, potentially producing disparate value indications for infrastructure assets. The valuation process for infrastructure assets in volatile markets is particularly challenging due to the frequent paucity of transaction activity related to these assets along with the effect of tax structures and financing mechanisms.

Infrastructure Assets

Infrastructure assets commonly operate on a monopolistic or oligopolistic basis where there is limited competition for the product or service provided. Infrastructure assets serve a variety of specialized functions and are commonly employed in commercial applications as well as historically regulated industries, including transportation, electricity, water, and waste management. Transportation assets include: highways, bridges, and tunnels; regional and national airports comprised of runways, terminals, parking structures, miscellaneous office buildings, and land improvements; and rail infrastructure with private and municipal rail systems as well as rail maintenance facilities. Thus, infrastructure assets are generally focused on industry sectors that are relatively stable and predictable rather than being driven by the vagaries of economic cycles.

Infrastructure assets in traditionally regulated industries, such as electricity and water, include generation assets, such as coal, gas, nuclear, and hydroelectric facilities, along with transmission and distribution assets. Water treatment facilities are also considered to be infrastructure assets including wastewater treatment projects that convert raw sewage into a water product that is acceptable for final discharge, such as effluent, along with fresh water facility assets that treat raw water to create potable water. Infrastructure assets play an important part in the continued operation of an efficient economy and fulfil a necessary role through the provision of a variety of societal services.

With the possible exception of public utility power assets, most infrastructure assets have historically tended to be inactively traded in the marketplace and generally used until their retirement. Infrastructure assets generally operate on a monopolistic or near monopolistic basis with significant barriers to entry for new entrants and, despite the diversity surrounding infrastructure assets, they have a number of common characteristics, the foremost being a relatively stable demand for the service delivered by the infrastructure asset.

Infrastructure assets share a number of additional common characteristics including:

1. long service life;
2. large capital requirements;
3. reliance upon proven technology;
4. stable demand for the product or service.

Infrastructure assets possess long service lives and can be operated for a significant period of time to maximize the returns associated with a financing transaction. Being long-lived assets, they are expected to experience minimal obsolescence to provide relatively predictable returns that can be indexed to rising price levels making them particularly well-suited for investors that desire to match the long-term horizons of their obligations with a trackable long-term investment.

Infrastructure assets require the deployment of significant capital resources for their construction projects, many in excess of a billion dollars and, as such, are infrequently replaced. Since these assets require significant initial capital investment and are unlikely to be replaced frequently, they possess the expectation of a long service life.

Infrastructure asset performance capability analysis also considers the proven or unproven nature of the technology employed along with the individual equipment components and technological stability. Proven technology has resolved design and operational idiosyncrasies to ensure consistent performance. Unproven technology, on the other hand, carries the risk of forced outages to correct unanticipated or unforeseen technical and operational deficiencies, which disrupt business operations and have a negative influence on facility economic performance.

To ensure a long service life, infrastructure assets generally utilize well-developed proven technology that is changing on an evolutionary rather than a revolutionary basis. The technology utilized in infrastructure assets has evolved over a long period of time so that any additional technology changes would be expected to occur on an incremental basis.

The demand for the product or service delivered by the asset is relatively stable and predictable. The treatment of wastewater and the disposal of municipal solid waste are strongly correlated to the underlying population and level of commercial activity within a service region. Electricity demand is more strongly related to the level of economic activity, since large industrial electricity users generally comprise a larger percentage of the demand base and are more influenced by the swings in the business cycle. In general though, the demand for these products or services provided by the aforementioned industries is going to be less affected by changes in economic activity.

Capital Structure Composition

Capital structure composition influences the cost of capital for creating and maintaining infrastructure assets, so it is important to understand the dynamics surrounding the endemic capital structure components. Infrastructure assets are typically financed with a capital structure comprised of debt and equity, with the overall return providing sufficient funds to pay debt obligations as well as providing an adequate return to equity holders. Financial leverage provides the ability to magnify the returns associated with an investment under the assumption that debt associated with the infrastructure asset enables the equity investors to increase their returns from the asset. The desire to maximize the returns associated with infrastructure assets generally results in their being financed through a highly leveraged capital structure.

Infrastructure asset rate-of-return expectations are based on the risk profile of the income stream generated by the asset. Rate of return expectations for the capital structure components are correlated to the perceived risk associated with the financing source. The risk and return trade-off correlates to less risk being associated with a lower expected return, while greater risk is associated with a higher expected return. The risk and return relationship implies that investors are risk-averse and consequently demand compensation in the form of higher anticipated returns when assuming additional risk. Debt financing rates are dependent on the current interest rate environment, credit quality, and the expected ability to repay the assumed debt obligation. The cost of equity capital reflects an additional risk premium above the risk-free rate that investors demand in the form of higher expected returns for investing in an infrastructure asset with risky attributes.

Many infrastructure asset investors are willing to significantly leverage their infrastructure asset investments to enhance the potential returns. The use of debt to leverage the capital structure for the infrastructure asset increases the returns available to equity holders, which is consistent with their objective of maximizing the returns associated with the infrastructure asset. Except in extreme circumstances, debt financing is less expensive than equity financing such that the cost of capital for the asset can be reduced through the leveraging associated with debt financing rather than relying exclusively on equity financing.

A highly leveraged capital structure, however, does have consequences since excessive amounts of debt can actually both increase the risk as well as the cost of capital for the infrastructure asset. Significant leverage may also lead to financial difficulties during an economic downturn, where the ability to meet interest and principle payment obligations associated with debt financing becomes limited. The capital allocation process between debt and equity correspondingly represents a balancing act with the desire to maximize leverage being weighed against a capital structure that maintains the ability to secure the repayment of the debt.

Infrastructure projects in the power, roads, transportation, telecommunications, waste/water, and gas sectors generally exhibit a leveraged capital structure with debt comprising more than 60 per cent of project capital and the mean leverage ratios varying between 61 to 78 per cent for each sector.[2] Unregulated electric generation facilities are generally financed with a highly leveraged capital structure that is comprised of up to 80 per cent debt, with the remaining capital comprised of equity.[3] Solid waste management facilities, such as waste-to-energy projects, have been financed with capital structures in which the equity financing component is 10 to 20 per cent of the facility cost.[4] These examples of capital structures for infrastructure projects support the leveraged capital structure concept for the financing of large infrastructure asset projects. As evidenced by the aforementioned practiced financing alternatives, infrastructure assets are typically found to be financed with a highly leveraged capital structure.

Infrastructure Investment Characteristics

Infrastructure investments provide the potential to produce long-term inflation adjusted income returns with the added benefit of matching the long-term nature of pension liabilities or other obligations. The infrastructure assets provide services that are based on or share characteristics with traditional regulated utilities where the services are considered to be essential for the continued functioning of the economy. Infrastructure assets

2 M. Dailami & D. Leipziger, "Infrastructure Project Finance and Capital Flows: A New Perspective" (September 1997), World Bank Policy Research Working Paper No. 1861.

3 Market-Based Advanced Coal Power Systems, U.S. Department of Energy, May 1999, pp. 9-11.

4 F. Kreith, *Handbook of Solid Waste Management* (McGraw-Hill, 1994), p. 14.2.

share investment characteristics with traditionally regulated public utilities in terms of expected price volatility.

Publicly traded utility stocks are expected to be less volatile than the overall stock market as measured relative to S&P 500 and evidenced by the betas associated with these equity securities. The betas for public utility stocks are generally less than one indicating less volatility in comparison with the broader stock market, however, recent history has exhibited dramatic declines in the values of some listed infrastructure assets funds. A closer examination of the listed infrastructure funds does indicate issues relating to the magnitude of leverage used to finance these funds and the substantial dividend yields offered by these investments.

The recent dramatic declines in listed infrastructure asset funds have raised questions as to the attractiveness of infrastructure investments. The value of infrastructure funds is dependent on the underlying infrastructure assets that comprise the investments held by the fund. Since most infrastructure assets transact infrequently, the importance of a formal valuation process, particularly given today's volatile markets, cannot be underestimated when assessing the value of the assets held in the infrastructure fund.

Infrastructure Asset Valuation

Infrastructure asset value indications are developed through the identification and compilation of the facts and circumstances relating to the cost, market, and income approaches. Value indications derived from the individual approaches are compared and weighted based on an examination of the information presented and the propriety of the underlying evidence involved in each valuation approach. Insights gained through the individual valuation approaches, as discussed below, are examined collectively and reconciled to reach an indication of value for the infrastructure asset.

The Cost Approach. The cost approach considers the value of an asset in terms of the investment in current labor and materials required to assemble an asset possessing comparable utility to the asset subject to the appraisal. The underlying principle with the cost approach is the principle of substitution as an indicator of value. Comparable utility implies similar functionality and economic satisfaction, but does not necessarily require that the comparable asset be an exact duplicate of the subject asset. A comparable asset is perceived as equivalent to the subject asset if it possesses similar utility.

The Market Approach. The market approach is based upon the observation of actual market transactions involving similar assets between buyers and sellers to establish a value for an asset. After gathering market transactions concerning similar assets, adjustments are made to the transaction information to reflect differences, such as market conditions, transaction terms, size, location, transaction date, and physical characteristics, between the subject asset and the observed comparable asset transactions. The market price of the comparable transactions can then be converted to a common unit of measure, such as price per output capacity or price per unit. An indication of asset value can then be developed by considering the productive capacity of the asset and the price per unit of productive capacity derived from the market transactions. The market approach thus provides a relatively straightforward characterization of how potential asset purchasers perceive value with the reliability of this approach dependent on a reasonably active market for the asset type.

The Income Approach. The income approach in the form of a discounted cash flow analysis measures the present worth of the expected future economic benefits in the form of cash flows associated with asset ownership. The expected future cash flows are projected over the remaining life of the asset and then converted to present value using a discount rate. The rate used to discount the future cash flows should consider the risks inherent in ownership of the asset and adequately compensate the investor for the risks assumed. The sum of the discounted cash flows generated by the asset provides an indication of asset value.

The Cost Approach

The cost approach relies upon the development of cost estimates as a method to establish an indication of infrastructure asset value. After developing an asset cost estimate, depreciation influences on the asset are considered in the form of physical deterioration along with functional and economic obsolescence. The impact of appraisal depreciation is quantified through an analysis of the reduction in value that occurs as an asset performs its intended purpose and its available service is consumed. Appraisal depreciation reflects the physical deterioration as well as the functional and economic obsolescence influencing the value of an infrastructure asset.

Physical Deterioration. Assets experience physical deterioration as they age with a consequential lowering of utility and a reduction in value. Physical deterioration is the reduction in asset value from the physical factors that reduce asset life and serviceability. The physical deterioration process is caused by wear and tear, action of the elements, and use in service. An important consideration when establishing physical deterioration is the maintenance policies and procedures applied to the asset, since good maintenance slows the physical deterioration process, while poor maintenance hastens it. Cracked and peeling paint, metal fatigue, worn machine parts, corrosion, and water damage are illustrations of physical deterioration.

Functional Obsolescence. Functional obsolescence is caused by internal asset characteristics such as inefficient layout, improvements in construction techniques, inadequate mechanical equipment, and functional inadequacies or superadequacies that diminish asset value. Assets normally become less than perfect replacements for themselves as piecemeal changes over time result in inefficient layout or less than optimal space utilization. Older assets are susceptible to obsolescence from new technologies and improved manufacturing processes available with newer assets. Functional obsolescence in the form of excess capital cost is eliminated by using replacement cost as the starting point thus eliminating the excess capital costs. Further functional obsolescence adjustments, if necessary, are made by estimating the excess annual operating expenses for the asset relative to the operation of a modern substitute asset over the remaining life of the asset.

Economic Obsolescence. Economic obsolescence is the loss in value caused by factors unrelated to the asset itself. Unlike physical deterioration and functional obsolescence that are intrinsic to the asset, economic obsolescence is caused by forces external to the asset. Economic obsolescence is thus referred to as external obsolescence, since it is beyond the control of the asset owner. Common causes of economic obsolescence include changes in market supply and demand, legislative enactments requiring stricter environmental standards, and changes in general economic conditions. The quantification of economic obsolescence is usually performed based on examination of the financial impact attributable to the external forces acting on the asset.

Infrastructure asset construction costs are commonly segregated into the direct and indirect costs related to project construction. AACE International (formerly the American Association of Cost Engineers) defines direct costs as the cost of installed equipment; material and labor directly associated with the physical construction of the permanent asset.[5] Direct costs are comprised of the equipment, materials, and labor costs connected with project construction. Direct equipment costs encompass the vendor costs for various equipment components comprising the asset, while labor costs include project labor costs, including fringe benefits and allowances for contractor expenses plus markup. Direct installation costs are comprised of the expenditures for physical foundations, equipment supports, and field erection along with items such as electrical work, piping, insulation, and painting.

Often overlooked in construction project estimates, indirect costs include the services and activities that support the construction process, but are not considered an integral part of direct contract project construction. AACE

---

5 *Skills and Knowledge of Cost Engineering*, 5th ed., AACE International, p. A.5.

International defines indirect costs as the costs which are not incorporated as a part of the final installation but that are required for the orderly completion of the asset. These may include, but are not limited to, field administration, direct supervision, capital tools, startup costs, contractors fees, financing costs and interest, insurance, taxes, and *etc.*[6] Indirect expenses are broadly categorized as the field expenses, corporate administrative allocations, startup costs, financing fees, and professional fees attributable to infrastructure asset construction.

Field expenses reflect the expenditures for construction supervisory personnel, temporary offices, and construction water supply, sanitary facilities, construction power, and site cleanup. Corporate administrative expenditures consist of the salaries and benefits for home office personnel, along with corporate cost allocations for office rent, insurance, utilities, legal, travel, and advertising expenditures. Startup costs include the performance tests to ready the asset for commercial operation and confirm that it satisfies performance specifications. Professional fees include the development fees, permits, and consultant and advisor fees that support the construction of the infrastructure asset. Financing fees reflect the financing burden associated with facility construction and incorporate the cost of carrying the facility investment during project construction otherwise known as capitalized interest.[7] The total investment to construct the infrastructure asset and place it in readiness for commercial operation is reflected in the sum of its direct and indirect costs.

Many infrastructure asset transactions involve recently constructed or unique assets where the cost approach is a particularly useful method to estimate asset value. In the instances where infrastructure asset costs are well-documented because actual construction costs are available, the cost approach represents an attractive method to estimate asset value. The cost approach is particularly useful when establishing the value for assets that have recently been placed-in-service, since a record of the actual construction costs is well-documented, and the facility has experienced minimal physical deterioration and is likely to be relatively unaffected by functional and economic obsolescence.

Infrastructure Asset Construction Costs

Infrastructure asset construction costs are influenced by factors such as design capacity, process specification, and equipment redundancy, along with geographic location and construction complexity. Infrastructure asset

---

6 *Ibid.*, p. A.7.

7 *The Appraisal of Real Estate*, 12th ed. (The Appraisal Institute, 2001), p. 359.

construction costs are comprised of the equipment, material, and labor directed to project construction. Construction costs vary for each infrastructure asset and are influenced by a multitude of individual factors, including location and labor factors as well as technical specifications. Site conditions, such as geographic location, space availability and transportation access, influence construction costs as does labor availability and workforce productivity. Equipment specification variability can also create sizeable cost differentials for infrastructure asset projects, with higher quality components generally resulting in greater costs in comparison with equipment of lesser quality. In addition, equipment redundancy influences the magnitude of infrastructure asset costs, with increased redundancy leading to increased construction costs.

Construction costs for many facilities are expressed on a cost per productive capacity basis to provide a common scale from which to study cost information. Consideration on a cost per capacity basis facilitates cost comparisons between individual assets when individual projects vary significantly in size, depending on market service requirements. Consequently, when expressed on a cost per capacity basis, infrastructure asset construction costs provide a method to examine the reasonableness of construction costs through the comparison with the experience from similar facilities.

Due to an increase in the regulatory requirements associated with infrastructure asset construction, costs have escalated as the steps involved to obtain approvals for the permits necessary to construct and operate an infrastructure asset have become more extensive in comparison with historical requirements. A variety of studies are needed to examine the community and environmental impact of the new infrastructure asset, along with state and federal regulatory agency approvals relating to any discharges as part of its operation. With the stricter regulatory environment, infrastructure asset projects typically necessitate increased administrative involvement during the planning and design phases of construction. The role of project administration has escalated with a corresponding increase in the time investment and participation by professional advisors and consultants, leading to higher expenditures for these activities relative to the overall infrastructure asset costs.

Development of Infrastructure Asset Cost Estimates

Many cost estimating techniques establish construction cost estimates based on the insights from historical experience with similar facilities. Construction cost estimates are frequently prepared by comparing the cost to build similar facilities – for which actual experience is available – and a record of the actual construction costs available for comparison purposes. Infrastructure asset construction cost estimates are then developed from an examination of construction cost information along with the associated productive capacity from the completed infrastructure asset projects. The construction cost estimating techniques typically rely on the scaling and indexing of prior construction cost experience from similar facilities to formulate the cost estimates. In addition to the compilation of direct and indirect costs and additional adjustments to convert these costs into a value estimate, a premium is generally considered to reflect the development risk.

Cost Indexing

Cost indexing is a method of estimating current infrastructure asset construction costs from the historical construction cost experience of previously constructed facilities. Cost indexing converts historical infrastructure asset construction costs to current cost levels and permits the preparation of infrastructure asset cost estimates from available construction cost information. Construction cost information is frequently available in many industries on a cost per unit of productive capacity basis from which to form a foundation for developing infrastructure asset cost estimates. Cost estimates with indexing rely on adjustments that use changes in cost levels from the time of original construction to the current estimation date. Many cost indexes are published for specific industries to track the composite price changes within that industry and consequently represent a useful tool to estimate infrastructure asset construction costs.

The construction cost information attributable to previously constructed waste to energy facilities is typically referenced to form the basis for formulating an estimate of current waste to energy facility construction costs. Since waste to energy technology is well developed, technological advances are progressing on an evolutionary, rather than a revolutionary basis, so that cost indexing is well-suited for estimating the cost of waste to energy facilities. The cost information for waste to energy facilities usually includes historical construction costs for major facility components along with their placed-in-service dates. When historical construction cost information is modified by a cost index factor, the result provides an approximation of current facility construction cost and is considered to be reflective of price movements over time.

Public utility construction costs for the utility industry in the United States have been published in *The Handy-Whitman Index of Public Utility Construction Costs* ("Handy-Whitman Index") by Whitman, Requardt and Associates.[8] The cost trend information for electric utility construction presented in the

---

8 Whitman, Requardt and Associates.

Handy-Whitman Index recognizes the change in construction costs over time and is used to modify historic facility construction cost information when preparing construction cost estimates for waste to energy facilities. This index has been further categorized to reflect the construction cost trends for six geographical regions within the United States.

Cost Approach Example – Waste-to-Energy Facility

Numerous waste-to-energy facilities have been constructed in the United States to satisfy the need for waste disposal capacity. Construction cost information for these facilities provides an informational database from which to estimate the construction cost of waste to energy facilities. With the construction costs for previously constructed waste to energy facilities and the Handy-Whitman Index, the historical construction costs are indexed to provide a method to establish waste to energy facility construction cost estimates. The indexing of historical construction costs considers the changes in prices from the facility placed-in-service date to an evaluation date, and yields an estimate of waste to energy facility construction costs. Exhibit 1 presents construction cost information indexed to 2008 dollars along with processing capacity in tons per day (TPD) for a representative sample of waste to energy facilities.[9]

Exhibit 1
Waste to Energy Facilities
Cost and Capacity Metrics

Facility	Capacity in TPD	Cost in 2008 Dollars
Warren County	400	100,383,000
Greater Portland/Portland, ME	500	94,342,000
Wheelabrator/W. Depford Township, NJ	575	116,735,000
Preston, CT	600	172,096,000
Bristol, CT	650	127,593,000
Spokane, WA	800	170,332,000
Onondaga, NY	990	256,816,000
Lancaster County/Marietta, PA	1,200	203,561,000
Lee County/Ft. Myers, FL	1,200	285,931,000
Southeast/Long Beach, CA	1,380	219,785,000

9 Above note 4 at pp. 11.40-11.42.

Union County/ Rahway, NJ	1,440	291,837,000
Haverhill, MA	1,650	248,813,000
Montgomery County/ Dickerson, MD	1,800	558,794,000
Bridgeport, CT	2,250	457,858,000
Hempstead/ Westbury, NY	2,505	553,336,000
Fairfax County	3,000	396,465,000

The information contained in Exhibit 1 regarding the cost and capacity for waste to energy facilities is presented graphically in Exhibit 2.

Exhibit 2
Cost and Capacity Comparison

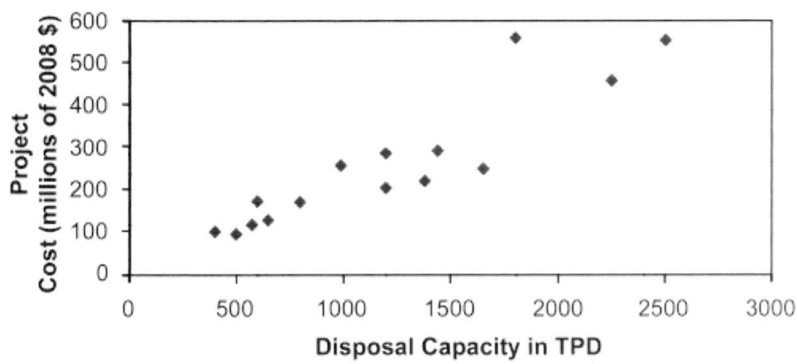

The information presented in Exhibit 2 illustrates the relationship between facility cost and generating capacity for the waste to energy facilities under consideration, with the general trend of facility costs increasing as generation capacity increases.

In many industries, including the waste management industry, construction cost information for facilities is expressed on a cost per unit of productive capacity basis. The conversion of construction cost information to a unit of capacity basis provides a common framework from which to examine facility costs and improves the ability to make cost comparisons between facilities. In the waste management industry, facility construction costs are expressed on a dollar per tons of daily capacity basis, since the size of waste to energy facilities varies significantly based upon the market served. After establishing the cost per daily ton of disposal capacity for waste to energy facilities, an estimate of facility construction cost is prepared. This is done by taking the proposed capacity in daily disposal capacity of the facility for which a cost estimate is desired to be prepared and then applying it to the cost per daily ton of capacity developed from the experience with prior construction of waste to energy facilities.

A cost per daily ton of disposal capacity analysis for waste to energy facilities suggests a linear relationship between the construction cost and megawatt capacity. Many assets exhibit economies of scale so that the performance of a cost to capacity analysis is used to test the linearity between construction cost and daily disposal capacity for the waste to energy facilities. In equation form, the cost to capacity relationship is stated as follows:

$$(C_b/C_a) = (S_b/S_a)^x$$

Where, C_b and C_a are the construction costs, S_b and S_a are the capacity sizes and x is the cost to capacity factor.

The cost to capacity factor x is calculated with linear regression techniques on transformed cost and capacity information, whereby cost information is transformed by calculating the natural logarithm of facility cost and capacity is transformed by calculating the natural logarithm of facility capacity. The linear regression analysis of the transformed cost and capacity information provides for the direct calculation of the cost to capacity factor, which is the slope of the regression line. The cost to capacity factor relationship indicates economies of scale when x is less than the value of 1, diseconomies of scale when x is greater than 1, and a linear relationship when x is equal to 1. The linear regression analysis for facility cost and capacity is presented graphically in Exhibit 3.

Exhibit 3
Cost/Capacity Regression Analysis

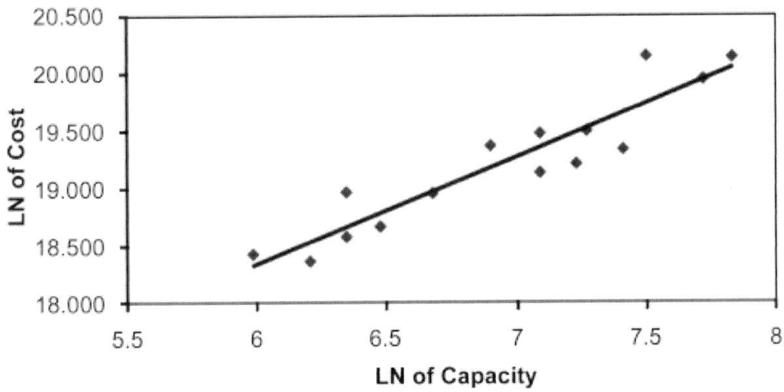

The regression analysis for the waste to energy facilities results in a regression line slope of 0.90, which indicates economies of scale, such that an increase in capacity results in a less than linear increase in cost. The adjusted R-squared for the regression analysis is 0.86, indicating a strong correlation of the observed data about the calculated regression line. Cost to capacity factors for facilities are typically less than 1 indicating some degree of economies of scale with a typical range between 0.5 and 0.9 based on the specific industry.[10] Earlier research with gas-fired and coal-fired generation facilities yielded a similar 0.9 cost to capacity factor for these facilities.[11]

To calculate the construction cost on a cost per daily ton of disposal capacity basis for waste to energy facilities, the historical construction cost experience and daily disposal capacity is identified for the individual facilities. The facility construction cost is then converted into a price per daily ton of disposal capacity by taking the indexed construction cost for the individual waste to energy facility and dividing that amount by its respective disposal capacity. A summary of the calculated cost per daily ton of disposal capacity for the individual waste to energy facilities is presented in Exhibit 4.

---

10 D.S. Remer & L.H. Chai, "Estimate Costs of Scaled-Up Process Plants", Chemical Engineering, April 1990.

11 R.K. Ellsworth, "Cost-to-Capacity Analysis for Estimating Project Costs", Construction Accounting and Taxation, September/ October 2005 and "Capacity Factor Cost Modeling for Gas-Fired Power Plants", Construction Accounting and Taxation, January/February 2009.

Exhibit 4
Waste to Energy Facilities
Cost per Daily TPD

Facility	Cost per TPD
Warren County	250,958
Greater Portland/Portland, ME	188,684
Wheelabrator/W. Depford Township, NJ	203,017
Preston, CT	286,827
Bristol, CT	196,297
Spokane, WA	212,915
Onondaga, NY	259,410
Lancaster County/Marietta, PA	169,634
Lee County/Ft. Myers, FL	238,276
Southeast/Long Beach, CA	159,264
Union County/Rahway, NJ	202,665
Haverhill, MA	150,796
Montgomery County/Dickerson, MD	310,441
Bridgeport, CT	203,492
Hempstead/Westbury, NY	220,893
Fairfax County	132,155

The identified facility construction costs expressed on a cost per daily ton of disposal capacity basis provide an estimate of the range of the construction costs to be expected when constructing a waste to energy facility. The construction cost in 2008 dollars for the facilities ranged from $132,000 to $310,000 per daily ton of disposal capacity with an average price of $212,000 per daily ton of disposal capacity. However, waste to energy facility construction occurs over a multi-year period and capitalized interest is usually excluded from construction cost estimates, but it is a capitalizable component of total cost. Capitalized interest is estimated through an examination of the disbursement pattern during an anticipated three-year construction period.

Based on the risk characteristics and the current interest rate environment, the interest rate for the calculation of capitalized interest is estimated to be 8 per cent. Waste to energy construction activity followed an expenditure pattern, whereby 15 per cent of costs were incurred in the first year of construction, 45 per cent in the second year, and 40 per cent in the third year. Using a linear expenditure pattern during each year of construction, the average amount financed for the first year is 7.5 per cent (15 per cent divided by 2). For the second year, the average amount financed is the 15 per cent from the first year, plus the average amount of 22.5 per cent (45 per cent divided by 2) from the second year, or a total of 37.5 per cent. For the third year, the average amount financed is 80 per cent calculated in a manner consistent with the second year. Capitalized interest is then calculated as the amount financed at the 8 per cent interest rate so that the interest cost for the first year is 0.6 per cent of facility costs, exclusive of capitalized interest considerations.

Exhibit 5
Waste to Energy Facility
Capitalized Interest Estimate

Construction Activity	Period Activity	Cumulative Activity	Amount Financed	Interest Cost
Year 1	15%	15%	7.5%	0.6%
Year 2	45%	60%	37.5%	3.0%
Year 3	40%	100%	80.0%	6.4%
Total				10.0%

Exhibit 5 presents the cost attributable to capitalized interest cost for a waste to energy facility expressed as a percentage of project cost. For a three-year construction period with a construction distribution as presented in Exhibit 1 and an 8 per cent interest rate, capitalized interest is calculated as 10 per cent of the direct and indirect costs, exclusive of capitalized interest considerations. Alternatively, when expressed as a percentage of total infrastructure asset capitalized costs inclusive of capitalized interest, capitalized interest is calculated as 9 per cent of total capitalized costs, representing a significant element of the indirect costs associated with facility construction. As previously discussed, an additional adjustment should be considered to account for the risk assumed by a project developer that is eliminated once a project is completed and accepted for commercial operation, sometimes referred to as a turnkey premium.

Based on the indexed facility construction cost information along with capitalized interest and turnkey considerations, an estimate of the total cost including capitalized interest using the average cost in 2008 dollars is approximately $250,000 per daily ton of disposal capacity for a waste to energy facility. The trended waste to energy facility construction cost information is comparable with current construction cost estimates for waste to energy facilities on a cost per ton of daily disposal capacity. Expanding the construction cost estimate range indicates a total cost estimate range for new waste to energy facilities from $230,000 to $270,000 per ton of daily disposal capacity.

The Market Approach

The market approach as a valuation benchmark has evolved into a cornerstone of the valuation process and has been discussed extensively in the literature by authors writing on valuation theory. Given the existence of an actively traded market, the market approach provides a value indication through the process of identifying actual transactions involving similar infrastructure assets, which establish guidelines for developing an indication of value. The search for similar infrastructure assets considers factors such as design characteristics, location, transaction date, and industry economics to minimize the differences between the market transactions and the subject infrastructure asset. Ideally, a transaction analysis identifies a sufficient number of similar infrastructure asset transactions to establish an indication of value.

Although the market approach has been accorded significant attention in appraisal literature, infrastructure assets require particular attention when considering the market approach. The market approach relies upon the existence and availability of sufficient information concerning transactions from which to develop a meaningful valuation opinion. The market approach is premised on the availability of comparable transactions along with specific performance information concerning the infrastructure asset. Because infrastructure assets are specialized projects, the number and general availability of truly comparable transactions usually are restricted. Consequently, robust markets and numerous transactions are not normally associated with the market approach for infrastructure assets and it is challenging to identify a sufficient number of truly comparable transactions from which to fully develop a market approach.

Infrastructure asset transactions provide information from which to develop insights into perceptions regarding asset value. Infrastructure assets are designed to meet specific performance requirements possessing varying performance capabilities depending upon the technical specifications and performance requirements of the owner. Since infrastructure assets generally possess varying performance capabilities, the search for infrastructure asset transactions considers factors, such as technology, design characteristics, age, location, transaction dates, and industry economics. The analysis of infrastructure asset transactions carries the implicit assumption of similar economics in terms of inputs and outputs to the production process.

The analysis of infrastructure asset transactions begins with the identification of observed transactions involving similar assets from which to establish valuation guidelines. Infrastructure asset transactions are first screened to ensure comparability with regard to asset type so that electric generating assets are compared with electric generating assets and not a completely different asset type such as wastewater treatment assets. After screening for asset type consistency, the operating mode of the electric generating facility is established to ensure conformity among facilities. The market approach establishes an indication of asset value through the identification and analysis of actual transactions involving similar facilities among buyers and sellers.

The valuation of infrastructure assets gives consideration to the nature of the industry served by the asset, the asset's revenue-generating capacity, and the asset's expense structure. The valuation process for an infrastructure asset must look beyond the macroeconomic health of an industry to examine the financial performance of the subject infrastructure asset and comparable infrastructure assets. Just because an overall industry is performing well does not mean that an individual asset in the industry is performing comparably. For instance, antiquated process technology and equipment can place an infrastructure asset at a competitive disadvantage relative to an asset with the latest technology.

Implicit within the market approach is the assumption that comparable infrastructure assets possess a similar ability to produce economic benefits. Infrastructure asset revenue and operating expenses are likely to vary and impact profitability depending on the individual capabilities of a particular infrastructure asset. Consequently, infrastructure asset transactions should be examined to ensure that the identified assets are similar in compensation, production expenses, and profitability for the product or service delivered. Values estimated through the market approach generally involve completed projects that have been accepted for commercial operation that inherently includes consideration of direct and indirect construction costs along with a turnkey element.

The economic analysis of an infrastructure asset also considers the expected economic benefits to be generated during its remaining life. Any residual value or financial obligation that may be generated when the facility is decommissioned at the end of its service life should be considered during the valuation process.

Many infrastructure assets transact as part of either a sale of a business or the sale of a portfolio of assets. In these instances, limited information is available with regard to the specific economics of individual facilities. The confidential nature of most infrastructure asset transactions also makes it difficult to obtain detailed purchase price information for use with the market approach. These factors make it challenging to develop meaningful information from which to derive transaction-based valuation indicators with the market approach.

Market Approach Example

Gas-fired facility transactions provide information from which to develop insights into perceptions regarding facility value. Since gas-fired facilities generally possess varying performance capabilities, the search for facility transactions considers factors such as technology, design characteristics, age, location, transaction date, and industry economics. The analysis of gas-fired facility transactions carries the implicit assumption of similar facility economics in terms of electricity price, capacity factor, and production costs.

Infrastructure asset transaction information is adjusted when possible to reflect differences in design characteristics, location, transaction dates, and asset economics between the subject infrastructure asset and the observed infrastructure asset transactions. With electric generating facilities, transactional data is expressed as a price per kilowatt of generating capacity to improve the ease of comparison between observed facility transactions. Facility transactions provide confirmation of the reasonableness of value indications through the process of identifying actual transactions involving similar electric generating facilities.

Electric generating facility transaction prices are impacted by location factors including economic forces such as the supply and demand influence on electricity prices, the facility operating mode (*i.e.*, base load, intermediate load, or peak load) and the facility technology. Additional facility transaction price influences include specific operating characteristics such as equipment efficiency, environmental regulations, and future capital expenditure programs along with any related contracts such as power or fuel purchase agreements. Ideally, the market approach identifies facility transactions that possess characteristics closely similar to the subject facility from which to develop an indication of value for the subject facility.

The market approach relies on the availability of observed gas-fired electric generating facility transactions from which to perform analysis leading to the development of a facility valuation estimate. Implicit with the market approach is the assumption that the comparable facilities possess a similar ability to produce economic benefits such that electricity is sold for similar prices and the fuel expense along with production expenses are similar for the facilities. However, gas-fired electric generating facilities are generally designed to meet the specific performance requirements of an individual owner such that gas-fired electric generating facilities possess varying performance characteristics depending upon design specifications and performance requirements. The transaction prices for facilities are impacted by location factors including market forces such as supply and demand balances or imbalances, raw material, and labor adequacy, as well as market accessibility. Additional influences on facility purchase price include specific operating influences such as equipment efficiency, environmental regulations, and future capital expenditure programs.

Facility assets are projects designed to meet the specific performance requirements of an individual owner. Consequently, facility assets generally possess varying performance capabilities depending upon design specifications and performance requirements of the owner. The market prices for facility assets are impacted by location factors such as electricity supply and demand balances or imbalance, raw material and labor adequacy, and market accessibility. Additional influences on facility market prices include asset specific operating practices regarding historic maintenance and repair expenses and capital expenditures. Furthermore, facility transaction prices are influenced by the purchaser's view of the contribution potential to its overall business strategy. Market incentives to divest generation assets maintain geographical and fuel diversification for risk management, and new plant construction strategy, and corporate liquidity needs also impact facility transaction prices.

The market approach examines sales or purchases of similar electric generating facilities as a basis for establishing value. The first step in utilizing the market approach is to identify transactions involving natural gas-fired combined cycle facilities. Publicly available power plant sales data is queried with regard to age, size, location, and technology. The market price is then converted into a price per kilowatt by taking the purchase price of the comparable transaction divided by its generating capacity. The comparable transactions identified in Exhibit 6 represented several transactions involving gas-fired combined cycle facilities.[12]

Exhibit 6
Comparable Transactions
Gas-Fired Combined Cycle Facilities

Announced Date	Facility	Location	Capacity (MW)	Price ($/kW)
10/1/2008	Auburndale Energy Center	FL	173.5	775
9/30/2008	Southaven Energy Center	MS	558.22	582

12 SNL Financial.

9/25/2008	Mint Farm Generation	WA	319	752
9/11/2008	Morris Power	IL	179	430
4/21/2008	Walter Higgins Generation	NV	645	775
4/18/2008	Whiting Clean Energy	IN	639.00	329
4/15/2008	Pittsfield Generating Station	MA	160.38	330
4/11/2008	Chehalis Generating Facility	WA	622.00	495
4/9/2008	Holland Energy	IL	702.10	523
4/3/2008	Channelview	TX	918.30	544
3/31/2008	Southaven Energy Center	MS	801.00	576
3/31/2008	Ravenswood CC	NY	2,625.00	1,067

Exhibit 6 indicates the range of values for gas-fired combined cycle facilities to be between approximately $329/kW to $1067/kW with a median of $560/kW and an average of $598/kW. The more recent transactions indicate an upward trend in the pricing associated with gas-fired combined cycle facilities in the range of $600 to $800 per kilowatt. Using the indicated range of value implies a value from $330,000,000 and $440,000,000 for the 550 MW gas-fired facility under consideration.

The Income Approach

The income approach measures the economic performance of infrastructure assets through the application of a discounted cash flow analysis. Infrastructure assets are characterized by diversity with respect to individual assets comprising industries such as electric generation, distribution and transmission; waste management; water; and transportation. Infrastructure assets in each industry employ a variety of methods to generate revenue and require an assortment of expense structures to provide the products and services associated with their operation.

Electric generating facilities use a variety of technologies to produce electricity that is sold to generate revenue. Waste-to-energy facilities charge a tipping fee for the disposal of municipal solid waste and sell electricity produced as a part of the combustion process. Wastewater treatment facilities charge a fee to clean water that is delivered to the facility. Airports and toll roads levy a service fee or toll for passengers to use the infrastructure asset. A discounted cash flow analysis begins with an examination of the future revenue and expenses associated with asset operation as well as any residual financial benefit or obligation associated with the infrastructure asset when it is retired at the end of its service life.

After developing a revenue forecast it is necessary to examine the operating expenses attributable to the infrastructure asset. Operating expenses include expenses such as operation and maintenance expense, general and administrative expense, insurance, and property taxes. Operations and maintenance expense consists of the materials and labor expenditures necessary to enable the asset to perform its function as well as to perform routine preventative maintenance. General and administrative expenses consist of the expenses incurred to manage and administer the infrastructure asset while insurance expense covers the expense of insurance usually associated with catastrophic breakdown of the asset. Capital expenditures include investments for improving and maintaining the productive capacity of the infrastructure asset. These expense elements are compared with industry norms from comparable assets to confirm the reasonableness of these elements in the economic projections. Future economic performance reflects these factors in a financial model that develops an estimate of the future available cash flows attributable to the infrastructure asset.

After considering the financial aspects relating to the operation of the infrastructure asset with the intent of estimating future cash flows, a discount rate is calculated to convert the future cash flows to present value. A discount rate is calculated utilizing the concept of a weighted average cost of capital with consideration given to the identification of an appropriate capital structure and the cost of the debt and equity capital components. Discount rate development identifies the typical range of capital structures used to finance the infrastructure asset and the cost of the individual capital components. The capital costs are then weighted according to the identified capital structure and summed to establish the discount rate. The projected cash flows are then discounted and summed to establish a value indication for the infrastructure asset.

Income Approach Example

With a proven technological track record and a plentiful supply to provide long-term fuel availability, coal-fired generation has historically been the dominant source of electricity generation in the United States. The discounted cash flow approach measures the value of the expected economic benefits associated with facility ownership over its anticipated remaining life. Revenue is projected based on facility generating capacity, facility capacity utilization, and the expectation for future electricity prices.

Facility revenue is dependent on the ability to generate electricity considering factors such as generating capacity, heat rate, capacity factor, design specifications, operation and maintenance history, and physical condition. Generating capacity is the maximum facility capacity sustainable over a specified time period, usually expressed in megawatts, while capacity factor incorporates the design specifications and availability along with operation and maintenance program for the facility. The forecast electricity price reflects the attitudes and expectations of market participants for the supply and demand for electricity. The product of the generating capacity, hours in a year, capacity factor and electricity price yields the annual revenue for the facility.

Revenue projections reflect current attitudes and market expectations regarding supply and demand along with future changes in electricity prices as presented in Exhibit 7. Facility expenses are comprised of fuel expense, operations and maintenance expense, depreciation expense, capital expenditures, and income taxes. Based on a comparison with expenses for similar coal-fired facilities, fuel expense is projected to be $19 per megawatt hour while operations and maintenance expense is $8 per megawatt hour for the first year of the discounted cash flow analysis. Fuel expense as well as operation and maintenance expense is then projected to increase at a rate consistent with inflation for the duration of the projection period. Depreciation expense is based on Modified Accelerated Cost Recovery System (MACRS) regulations applicable to the identified real and personal property allocation for the asset classifications of the facility. Capital expenditures to maintain the operational capability of the facility are based on expectations for capital requirements for the intended utilization of the facility. Income taxes applied to facility pretax income are calculated to be 40 per cent of pretax income.

Economic benefits in the form of future cash flows for each year of expected facility operation are converted to a present value using a discount rate that considers the risks inherent with facility operation and compensates an investor for the assumed ownership risks. The discount rate represents the cost of capital used to convert the projected facility cash flows to present value. The cost of capital provides a satisfactory return to debt and equity capital. The cost of debt is estimated by considering the current yield on corporate bonds, while the cost of equity is developed using the Capital Asset Pricing Model to develop an expected return for equity investors. The capital structure for the project is estimated by considering the capital structure of other coal-fired generating facilities. Considering the cost of debt, cost of equity, and the capital structure, a 9 per cent discount rate is estimated for the facility.

To develop the annual cash flows generated by the facility, an analysis of revenue, expenses, capital expenditures, and taxes is required to develop *pro forma* cash flows. Exhibit 7 illustrates the discounted cash flow analysis process for the first 10 years of facility operation using a mid-year discounting convention. Extrapolation of the discounted cash flow analysis for the remaining life of the facility indicates a value of $2,043,000,000.

Purchase Price Allocation Considerations

In some instances, infrastructure assets present unique valuation considerations whereby the assets necessary to operate the infrastructure asset encompass more than the underlying physical assets and include the rights associated with the operation of the asset. Infrastructure assets in these cases rely on other assets to fully realize the economic potential associated with the assemblage of the individual assets. Recently completed infrastructure transactions involving toll roads, including the $1.8 billion Chicago Skyway transaction and the $3.8 billion Indiana toll road transaction, illustrate the interaction between individual assets that makes the purchase price allocation process particularly challenging for infrastructure assets.

Toll road transactions involve a long-term lease of the physical assets comprising the toll road that is significantly longer than the expected life of the assets themselves. A long-term lease that extends well beyond the life of the toll road assets transfers tax ownership and is considered to be a purchase for tax purposes even though title to the toll road assets is not transferred as part of the transaction. For instance, the lease term for the Chicago Skyway was 99 years while the Indiana Toll Road was 75 years in both instances substantially beyond the life expected for toll road assets.

Another portion of the purchase price with a toll road transaction is attributable to the right to charge tolls for the use of the roadway. Tolling rights are generally not directly associated with the underlying property but separately awarded by a governmental agency or authority. Consequently, as part of the toll road transaction, a separate agreement is necessary that grants permission to collect tolls for the use of the toll road as the ownership of the underlying toll road assets does not include the right to collect tolls. In order to successfully operate a toll road, it is necessary to purchase the toll road assets as well as the right to toll. With most toll road transactions, the right to toll comprises a significant portion of the purchase price and is distinct from the underlying assets with the allocation between toll road assets and the right to toll having a significant impact on transaction economics. Consequently, the valuation process plays a critical role in the purchase price allocation of the acquired assets as part of toll road transactions and other infrastructure assets.

Conclusion

Infrastructure assets provide essential economic and societal services that have historically been offered by traditionally regulated industries and afford attractive risk return characteristics from an investment perspective. Infrastructure assets have been recognized as an attractive investment class with the ability to provide long-term income returns as well as a measure of inflation protection. Many infrastructure assets are regulated and exhibit limited transaction activity from which to measure price behavior and estimate the value of individual infrastructure assets. A robust analysis concerning an estimate of infrastructure asset value has assumed increased importance with the escalated levels of price volatility recently exhibited in the capital markets and the development of new investment mechanisms such as public-private partnerships, tax ownership structures, and structured sale-leaseback financings.

Adequate consideration of the factors influencing value during the valuation process for infrastructure assets in volatile markets is imperative and necessitates the examination of the industry competitive and economic circumstances along with asset specific technical factors. Infrastructure assets are complex operations necessitating careful analysis through the consideration of the cost, market, and income approaches from which to develop a value estimate for the asset. Valuation methodologies should reflect the competitive economic environment confronting infrastructure asset and its anticipated operation in light of the frequent paucity of transaction activity from which to measure value.

Valuing Real Estate in an Unstable Market

James L. Horvath & Ian Haigh*

The real estate market is affected by market forces, which can change at short notice. The changes can be brought about from global economic changes down to nearby influences. An appraisal report might be read years after its preparation and, therefore, the appraiser has a duty to explain the market environment as of the date of appraisal, especially if the market was unstable at the time of producing the report.

The valuation of real estate is based on general economic principles. Whether values are determined through the use of the cost, sales comparison, or income approaches, it is economic principles and particularly the forces of supply and demand that ultimately determine value. It is market forces that determine the capitalization rates, discount rates, and market values and other assumptions that are used in the income approach; it is market forces that determine the final selling price of properties, which are used as comparables in the sales comparison approach and it is the market that establishes the relevance of the cost approach.

It has often been said that cost and value are not necessarily the same. In volatile markets this is definitely the case. For example, in times of high inflation building costs may outpace the rate at which property values rise while in depressed markets the cost of building something may be far more than the market is prepared to pay.

The experiences of the 1930s severely downgraded the importance of the cost approach. Until then, cost had always been recognized as an indicator of value, the so called "bricks and mortar" approach, because the cost to create something was the first impression of value. However, economic

---

* The authors wish to thank Norm Height, FRICS, AACI for his reviews and suggestions for this chapter.

feasibility became the main consideration in the depression years. Although cost to build could be calculated readily, the existence of effective demand to transform cost to value was often in question. Considerable capital was available although at this time it was in the hands of a small group of investors whose confidence had been severely jarred by the recent securities market collapse. There was an overabundant supply of real estate facilities but many investors were unwilling to risk their money in new development. In volatile times, cost is no longer regarded as a predictable indicator of value for those types of real estate that are traded on a reasonably frequent basis.

When the market is in equilibrium and the forces of supply and demand are balanced, the cost approach as a means of valuation is a useful guide, since the value of the site plus the cost of constructing similar improvements less depreciation will more than likely approximate the market value, particularly where the buildings are relatively new. Also for certain types of property, particularly those designed for special purposes and for which there is little market demand, cost can be regarded as a predominant factor. Examples of these property types would be libraries, town halls, police stations, schools, and other public buildings, although it must be stated that the use of this method is not necessarily restricted to public buildings alone.

Being of specialized design they have limited utility for any other purpose and are rarely sold in the open market. Where this does occur, they generally need to be replaced by alternative premises so that the value of these properties to the seller is often related to the cost of providing equivalent alternative accommodation or the cost of acquiring an alternative site and erecting the necessary buildings. Alternatively, it would always be possible for a would-be user of these buildings to acquire an alternative site and construct a new building rather than purchase an existing property – unless of course the cost of doing so is significantly higher. In such circumstances, it is therefore reasonable to assume that for specialized properties cost and value are not unrelated.

In volatile times, cost is no longer regarded as a predicable indicator of value for those types of real estate that are traded on a reasonably frequent basis. On the other hand, when the market is in equilibrium and the forces of supply and demand are balanced, the value of the site and the cost of constructing similar improvements less depreciation will more than likely be close to market value.

As an alternative to the cost approach, the sales comparison approach has long been regarded as a reliable indicator of value, more so with regards to residential rather than commercial property simply because residential property tends to share many common characteristics that can be more easily compared.

Although by using the sales comparison approach, the aim of the appraiser is to provide an estimate of market value, it should not be assumed that the appraiser's estimate and the market price or market value will always be the same - particularly in volatile markets. In normal markets different appraisers could well place different values on a particular interest at a particular time because they are making estimates and there is normally room, within certain limits, for differences in opinion. Appraisers endeavor to assemble the most recent sales so as to reduce the time value adjustment to a minimum. This is because in times of stable market conditions, market prices result from estimates of value made by vendors and purchasers on the basis of prices previously paid for other similar interests. However in times of volatility, more serious differences may arise. In such unstable times the appraiser's estimate will be based on prices previously paid but these must be adjusted to allow for the changes since the previous stable time period, when transactions took place. The accuracy of his or her estimate will, therefore, depend on the appraiser's knowledge of the changes and skill in quantifying their effect.

In a stable market, appraisers will use comparable information from the immediate area and, if necessary, extend their search gradually outwards until sufficient data is found. However, in a depressed market, there may be periods when there are few or even no sales, making the application of this approach somewhat problematical. The only information available may be historic and, depending on the severity of the market decline, may be of little or no assistance. Transactions from a market that declines gradually over a long period of time would, for instance, be of greater use than one that collapses suddenly and where sales, sometimes only a few months old, are suddenly no longer relevant.

The current world financial crisis would be a case in point. Appraisals, particularly commercial appraisals, undertaken from the late spring of 2008 in Toronto onwards became an increasing difficult task towards the end of that year. As the effects of the credit squeeze spread quickly, fewer and fewer transactions occurred and the cascading effect of defaults, repossessions, and bankruptcies ultimately led to the destabilization of property values. Appraisers were faced with anecdotal evidence that pointed towards lower values but, in many cases, appraisers had difficulty referencing empirical evidence to support this conclusion.

Sales evidence from just a few months earlier was now redundant but even if it could be used, it clearly needed to be adjusted to take into account the changed environment - but how much of an adjustment was needed and what evidence was there to support any adjustment? Also, if sales evidence was available but it related to transactions that were the result of financial difficulties experienced by the sellers, could this be used as an indication of market value? To answer this we first need to examine the definition of market value. The Appraisal Institute of Canada defines market value as:

> the most probable price which a property should bring in a competitive and open market under all conditions requisite to a fair sale, the buyer and seller each acting prudently and knowledgeably, and assuming the price is not affected by undue stimulus.

Implicit in this definition is the consummation of a sale as of a specified date and the passing of title from seller to buyer under conditions whereby:

- buyer and seller are typically motivated;
- both parties are well-informed or well-advised and acting in their own best interests;
- a reasonable time is allowed for exposure in the market;
- payment is made in cash in Canadian dollars or in terms of financial arrangements comparable thereto; and
- the price represents the normal consideration for the property sold, unaffected by special or creative financing or sales concessions granted by anyone associated with the sale.

Apart from the sales process being open and well-advertised and both the buyer and seller acting responsibly, the most important requirement of this definition is that the sale must not be subject to any undue influence. Undue influence would include any action that requires a sale to take place under predetermined or specified conditions. For instance, it is unlikely that a forced liquidation sale would be considered to represent a property's fair market value, the definition of which is:

> the estimated gross amount expressed in terms of money that could be typically realized from a properly advertised and conducted public auction, with the seller being compelled to sell with a sense of immediacy on an as-is, where-is basis, as of a specific date.

On the other hand, an orderly liquidation sale shares several of the characteristics of a normal sale in that a reasonable period would be allowed for the disposal of the asset; that presumably the sale would be advertised openly and that both the buyer and seller would conduct themselves responsibly. However, the fact that the seller is not normally a willing party to the transaction and is forced to sell within a certain time frame clearly raises questions as to whether the price achieved would be equivalent to its market value. In some cases this may in fact be true but, in general, there is a perception that sales resulting from an orderly liquidation process are purchased at prices below their market value. A common definition of an orderly liquidation sale is:

> the estimated gross amount expressed in terms of money that could be typically realized from a liquidation sale, given a reasonable period to find a purchaser(s)

with the seller being compelled to sell on as as-is, where-is basis as of a specific date.

Similar to an orderly liquidation is a power of sale. This is the Canadian equivalent to the U.S. term disclosure and in the event of a default gives the mortgagee the right to force the sale of a property without judicial proceeding. Power of sale is the most frequently used method by which a mortgagee (usually a financial institution) will remedy a default by a mortgagor (the borrower/owner). The term, power of sale, indicates a sale under the power contained in the mortgage document or in the *Mortgages Act*.

The power of sale can often be the fairest, most inexpensive method to deal with an unpleasant financial circumstance. It allows the mortgagee/lending institution to retrieve only what it is entitled to and no more. If there is a surplus, then the owner/mortgagor will benefit. The power of sale does represent certain complexities, particularly in terms of gaining possession and the obligation of the mortgagee to obtain the best possible value.

If appraisers have difficulty in interpreting values in depressed times when sales evidence and/or market direction may be virtually non-existent, they also face challenges in times of extreme or excessive growth when it may be difficult to separate the fundamentals that drive solid sustained growth from those that create speculative and short-lived spikes in value. It is generally accepted that the current financial crisis that began in the United States had its roots firmly planted in the housing market. With easy access to loans at historically low rates and a government mandated program that enabled purchasers with questionable credit, no assets, no income and, sometimes, not even jobs to obtain mortgages for the purchase of homes, the foundations were laid for the “subprime mortgage” meltdown and the credit squeeze that now plagues the world. The major players in this tragedy have already been identified as investment dealers and other financial institutions, with supporting roles from Federal Governments, home builders, investors, real estate agents, borrowers, and other parties including appraisers who some would say helped to fuel the fire by not recognizing the warning signs thrown up by an over-heated market. For example, since August 2006 housing prices in Fairfax County, Virginia (like many other inner city and suburban communities throughout the U.S.) have grown 12 times faster than household income – so much so that the County’s median family had to spend 54 per cent of its income at that time to afford the County’s median home, compared with a figure of just 26 per cent in the year 2000 – a situation that was clearly unsustainable.

Of course, it could be argued that appraisers do not create value. They simply interpret the market based on transactional evidence and that, if excesses build up in a particular market, this is a result of the actions of others who either chose to ignore the warning signs or were prepared to take the risks in the interests of making a quick profit – so why shoot the messenger? The problem here is that appraisers do have a duty of care and by simply rubber stamping many of the transactions that occurred (even though these values might have been justified at the time by comparable transactions) without questioning the sustainability of these values, appraisers were, in fact, helping to perpetuate the notion that the spiral of ever-increasing values was likely to continue unabated. The above discussion has dealt with issues that arise out of the use of cost and direct comparison approaches which applied in times of volatility.

In the same way that appraisers use market data to arrive at a property's value through direct comparison, they use a similar process to arrive at a property's value using the income approach. The purpose of the income approach is to provide an opinion as to the value of a right to receive an annual stream of income. Although much of the information required for this process is readily available and can be found by analyzing existing lease agreements, income and expense statements, tax assessments, municipal zoning, and other planning issues, the translation of this information into a capital value requires reference to market data – in particular, market rentals, capitalization rates, and discount rates. In depressed or poorly performing markets, relevant current information is often in short supply and, depending on the severity and timing of an economic decline, can become out-dated very quickly. The use of such information clearly requires considerable caution on the part of the appraiser who must therefore make adjustments to reflect the changing economic climate – a task that requires considerable experience and judgment. For example, in volatile markets you can have many key value drivers change, such as occupancy rates, rental rates, defaults by tenants, availability of and the cost of financing, and restructuring segments of the economy. In an extreme situation it is possible that an otherwise well performing income producing property, because of sudden vacancies or other factors, could have a negative cash flow. It would be unreasonable to assume that such a property would have a negative value or no value at all. Clearly the Income Approach has difficulty in its application and sales of similar properties would be more indicative of value.

An appraiser has a duty to give the reader of an appraisal report reasoned opinions regarding the state of the market at the time of writing the report The appraiser should advise whether the market is still softening – leveling out, *etc.*

Thus in volatile times, in particular, the credentials of the appraiser plays a very important part and that in times like this there is no substitute for experience. Although an experienced appraiser is not going to invent a new valuation methodology that will compensate for the lack of meaningful information, he or she will, because of his experience, be better positioned to understand the issues that are critical to the valuation process.

Valuing Machinery in a Depressed Manufacturing Market

Greg Miocic

Introduction

When valuing machinery and equipment in a depressed market, it is important to understand how appraisals are typically performed and what considerations are employed under adverse market conditions. It is also necessary to recognize the conditions that indicate a depressed market for machinery and equipment in order to know what type of valuation should be performed. Conditions that indicate a depressed market include the following:

- economic recession;
- plant closings;
- shift in market demand;
- business experiencing continued losses with no projected turnaround;
- stock price less than carrying value of a company's assets;
- excess capacity within a company or entire industry;
- an inactive market *e.g.*, no buyers at any price;
- buyers limited to those in emerging markets.

Understanding the triggers of a depressed market will allow the buyers and users of machinery and equipment to make an informed request regarding the type of valuation. Is it necessary to know the fair market value, liquidation value, both, or some other value indication?

Regardless of the market conditions, generally accepted valuation practices still apply. A valuation of machinery and equipment will include the three commonly applied approaches which include the cost, market, and income approaches.

It is important to know the premise under which the assets are to be valued. To properly understand this, one must contemplate the future use of the asset or asset group. Is the asset going to be sold and moved to another location, or is this a sale of an entire facility where the asset(s) will continue to operate in the current configuration? Will the assets be used for their originally intended purpose? Is this sale some type of liquidation, either orderly or forced? This is when the concept of highest and best use needs to be considered.

The highest and best use refers to the use of an asset that would bring the most value. The highest and best use of the asset determines the appropriate premise of value. The two premises for establishing value are *in-use* and *in-exchange*.

- *In-use.* The highest and best use of the asset is *in-use* if the asset would provide maximum value to market participants principally through its use in combination with other assets as a group (as installed or otherwise configured for use). This might be the case for certain non-financial assets, for example. If the highest and best use of the asset is in-use, the fair value of the asset shall be measured using an in-use valuation premise. When using an in-use valuation premise, the fair value of the asset is determined based on the price that would be received in a current transaction to sell the asset, assuming that the asset would be used with other assets as a group and that those assets would be available to market participants. Generally, assumptions about the highest and best use of the asset should be consistent for all of the assets of the group within which it would be used.
- *In-exchange.* The highest and best use of the asset is *in-exchange* if the asset would provide maximum value to market participants principally on a standalone basis. This might be the case for a financial asset, for example. If the highest and best use of the asset is in-exchange, the fair value of the asset shall be measured using an in-exchange valuation premise. When using an in-exchange valuation premise, the fair value of the asset is determined based on the price that would be received in a current transaction to sell the asset standalone.[1]

Once the premise of value is understood, a decision can then be made on what type of value is required. This can range from fair market value, orderly liquidation value, forced liquidation value, salvage value, or scrap value. The

[1] Statement of Financial Accounting Standards No. 157, Fair Value Measurements, p. 5.

basic definitions of these per the American Society of Appraisers are provided below:[2]

Fair market value is the estimated amount, expressed in terms of money, which may reasonably be expected for a property in an exchange between a willing buyer and a willing seller, with equity to both, neither under any compulsion to buy or sell, and both fully aware of all relevant facts, as of a specific date.

Orderly liquidation value is the estimated gross amount, expressed in terms of money, that could be typically realized from a liquidation sale, given a reasonable period of time to find a purchaser (or purchasers), with the seller being compelled to sell on an as-is, where-is basis, as of a specific date.

Forced liquidation value is the estimated gross amount, expressed in terms of money, that could typically be realized from a properly advertised and conducted public auction,[3] with the seller being compelled to sell with a sense of immediacy on an as-is, where-is basis, as of a specific date.

Salvage value is the estimated amount expressed in terms of money that may be expected for the whole property or a component of the whole property that is retired from service for use elsewhere.

Scrap value is the estimated amount expressed in terms of money that could be realized for the property if it were sold for its material content, not for a productive use.

Understanding whether a depressed market exists, the various levels of value, the purpose and use of the valuation of, *e.g.*, fair value for accounting or tax purposes, property tax assessment, determining sales price for purchase allocation purposes, financing, *etc.*, one can begin to make an informed decision about the scope of a machinery valuation. In a depressed market it is important to understand both the requirements as well as the possible limitations in typical valuations.

Because a depressed market will often bring about conditions that will also depress the value of assets utilized by these businesses, it is usually necessary to understand the liquidation value. In a depressed market there may be little or no discernible difference between estimates of fair market value,

---

[2] American Society of Appraisers, *Valuing Machinery and Equipment: the Fundamentals of Appraising Machinery and Technical Assets*, 2nd ed., pp. 3, 4.

[3] The term auction usually refers to forced liquidation value, but there are exceptions to this general rule; for example, in certain industries, an auction is the standard industry method for disposing of assets, in which case it may be equal to orderly liquidation value, assuming a normal exposure time (and may be equal to fair market value under certain conditions). The essential difference between orderly liquidation value and forced liquidation value is one of exposure time. American Society of Appraisers, *Valuing Machinery and Equipment: the Fundamentals of Appraising Machinery and Technical Assets*, 2nd ed., pp. 4, 19.

fair value, or liquidation value. Liquidation value generally represents the minimum "floor" value. Understanding this floor value is vital when using an income approach as it is possible the income approach will indicate a value less than the liquidation value, or breakup value, of the machinery and equipment. In certain circumstances, the liquidation value may approximate salvage or scrap value. In an inactive market determining a liquidation value can present a significant challenge. Sources for liquidation values may include auction results or actual information that a company may have when disposing of an asset whether it be through an equipment liquidator or scrap dealer. Scrap values can also be depressed in a down market, which only reinforces the fact that using any "rules of thumb" regarding liquidation, salvage, or scrap values should be avoided.

Understanding of what type of value should be estimated will lend insight regarding which approach or approaches should be employed. If an active market for the subject machinery does not exist, or if information regarding comparable sales is not available, the market approach may have limited applicability. Also, while the income approach may be used when valuing an entire facility or a production line where identifiable cash flows related to the equipment are available, if specific items of machinery are to be valued where it is impossible to determine the cash flows related to an asset, the income approach may not be a practical approach. This may lead the appraiser to rely on the cost approach as the only reasonable valuation approach. Many times machinery appraisals are based on the cost approach which is certainly acceptable; however a depressed market can highlight the limitations of the cost approach. Machinery and equipment appraisers are effective in developing a cost approach which begins with estimating replacement costs of the assets. This is generally accomplished by applying cost indices either to historical costs of assets or finding evidence of current costs for new equipment. The appraiser then estimates physical depreciation by means of an age/life analysis. Functional and economic obsolescence is considered, however, if not obvious, it may be assumed that no adjustments are necessary. At this point some appraisers will opine on a value of the assets having performed these steps. This is commonly referred to as Replacement Cost New Less Depreciation (RCNLD).

In a strong and stable market RCNLD may provide an accurate picture of fair value. In a down market it becomes more critical to fully explore possible instances of functional and economic obsolescence to arrive at a reasonable estimate of value. If a cost approach is used, the Replacement Cost New is the starting point and getting this right is obviously critical to the overall analysis. Replacement cost can be calculated indirectly by applying cost indices to the historical cost of the asset. Over time this may not provide an accurate estimate of replacement cost due to changes in manufacturing and construction techniques or certain technological improvements. Having evidence of actual replacement costs for new equipment offering similar utility to the subject assets is preferable. This information may come from contacting equipment vendors or using actual cost invoices for new equipment. If the value of the assets is being performed under an in-exchange premise, the cost approach should only include the equipment being valued and exclude costs for installation, foundations, start up, building structure, *etc.*

Next an estimate of physical depreciation should be calculated. This is generally done using an age-life analysis where the normal useful life is estimated along with the remaining useful life of the asset.

When thinking about the physical condition of the asset/s, also consider if there are any deferred maintenance issues. If the industry and the company are in a down turn, one area that may be reduced is capital expenditures related to maintenance of the property plant and equipment. Consideration should be given to the extent to which maintenance expenditures were deferred and to the cost necessary to bring the equipment up to a normal operating condition.

Functional obsolescence is the next item to be considered in a cost approach. Functional obsolescence factors manifest themselves in items such as throughput and efficiency. New equipment may run at a greater capacity, require less space, or have lower operating costs. The older the equipment the more likely it is that functional obsolescence factors are present. It is always good to inquire about how the technology related to the equipment, process, or manufacturing may have changed.

Economic obsolescence is the final adjustment that should be considered in applying a cost approach to value machinery. This is where the effects of a depressed market can surface significantly. Economic obsolescence is external to the property. It can result from changes in market demand or government regulation, such as cost to comply with environmental regulation. One way to factor economic obsolescence into a cost approach is to consider the impact that a decrease in capacity utilization has on machinery and equipment. There are formulas that appraisers use to calculate what is known as an inutility penalty; however, the theory is that there is a penalty that should be applied to recognize that the asset is only required to produce an amount that is somewhat less than normal or design capacity. In some cases this adjustment could be made in the replacement cost by estimating the cost for an asset or group of assets that would have a lower capacity than the subject. This is referred to as the cost-of-capacity method. Either way, capacity utilization should be considered. When it is determined that a penalty should be applied, a decision needs to be made regarding what production level to use. The forecast for production for the current year should be viewed in context of what recent production levels have been;

however, more weight should be given to current and future projections and these estimates should be coordinated with actual projections for the business. If valuing an entire plant or group of plants where cash flows can reasonably be attributed to the tangible assets, an estimate of value can be determined by the income approach. Some appraisals will estimate economic obsolescence penalty by performing an income approach, *e.g.*, Discounted Cash Flow (DCF). The implied value of the tangible assets as measured by the income approach is compared to the RCNLD and adjusted downwards if the implied value is less than RCNLD. Generally, you would not reduce the RCNLD to a value that was less than the liquidation value of the assets as this would represent the breakup value of assets.

Applying the appropriate penalties for physical depreciation, functional obsolescence, and economic obsolescence to the RCN estimate will provide an estimate of value based on the cost approach.

The market approach, or sales comparison approach, will account for all forms of depreciation and obsolescence that exist but, as mentioned earlier, an active market must exist to be able to find comparable transactions that are similar to the subject equipment. There are many sources for market information on metalworking equipment, such as lathes, drill presses, machining centers, press equipment, injection molding equipment, air compressors, computer equipment, and construction equipment, to name a few. The more specialized the equipment, the less likely that meaningful market transactions will be found; however, this should always be investigated. New and used equipment dealers are obvious sources for market information, as well as published used equipment guides, internet searches, and sales information from equipment brokers and companies that have sold their own equipment directly. In a depressed market it is likely that there is more capacity in a given industry, such as the current automotive industry, which results in lower transaction prices for used equipment. In certain cases specialized equipment with limited or no alternative uses may only bring salvage or scrap value, or an owner may have to actually pay to have the equipment removed from a facility.

An indication of the value of machinery and equipment based on an income approach is extremely important in a depressed market. Many machinery and equipment appraisals will indicate that the income approach is not applicable as it is impossible to attribute accurately the income generated by an individual asset when the cash flows are actually generated by the subject asset working in concert with a group of assets in a business. This is true when trying to value assets on a piece-meal basis. If the assets in question are an entire production line or plant, where cash flows closely related to the assets can be identified, then the income approach may be utilized effectively. As mentioned earlier, applying the income approach usually involves a DCF analysis, such as would be included in a business valuation that would determine the total value of all of the underlying assets of a business. Once the underlying asset value is determined, the next step would be to subtract working capital and the value of any intangible assets to arrive at an indication of the total value of tangible assets. If this amount is less than the value of the machinery and equipment, and real estate as determined by the cost and/or market approaches, it is an indication that the earnings of the business cannot support the value determined. If there is insufficient earnings support for the tangible assets of the business, it is usually because a portion of economic obsolescence was not fully recognized in the other approaches.

As discussed earlier, this is why it is crucial to understand what the liquidation value of the machinery and equipment is on an in-exchange basis, as this is generally the minimum value at which the assets could be sold. If the cash flows of the business are negative or otherwise cannot support the liquidation value of the machinery, then the breakup value of the assets is greater than the value of the assets remaining in their current use. In a depressed market, if an appraiser indicates that they are assuming the earnings of the business are sufficient to support the value determined, there is a real possibility the assets could be overvalued, as economic obsolescence may not have been fully recognized.

Conclusion

It is imperative that one consider the many factors that bear upon the value of machinery, especially when market conditions are depressed. Understanding these factors allows for an informed decision regarding the appropriate premise of the valuation and application of the valuation principles.

Valuation Questionnaire

James L. Horvath & Alex Lourie*

A well-grounded value judgment is directly related to the quality of the information obtainable both on the business being assessed and on industry conditions. The valuator should therefore place considerable importance on amassing as much relevant material as possible in the time available for the assignment, which is frequently limited. To assist in this activity, it is useful to have a questionnaire or checklist in hand. Because no two businesses are identical, it is impossible to develop a single checklist that will apply in every case. It is, however, possible to produce a general guide to the valuation process. The questionnaires included in this chapter, which are applicable to businesses of various sizes and operating in a variety of industries, are intended as a guide and are not meant to be exhaustive. In some cases, it may not be necessary to pose all of the questions; in others, additional information may have to be procured on certain aspects of the business. Moreover, the information obtained in response to the questionnaire will often suggest further lines of enquiry that must be pursued if all the value-related factors are to be understood clearly.

There are generally two steps in the collection of data. In many cases, what is wanted initially is only some basic information that will bring to light the more significant valuation issues and allow a preliminary estimate of the appropriate value range to be made. The first checklist below is designed to assist in this early investigation and to help in the planning of further enquiry. The second questionnaire is more elaborate and is intended to address most of the issues that normally arise in the valuation of a business. Neither should be considered as providing anything more than a general overview of the valuation process, however. Keep in mind that posing these questions may lead to various answers, depending on the party responding and the potential presence of their respective bias. In that sense, a valuator

* The authors would like to thank Kimberly Horvath, CA for her research, assistance and suggestions.

must always exercise professional judgment throughout the valuation process.

It should be noted that the answers to many questions may already be known to the valuator or may become known through informal preliminary discussions with a potential client. As such, the questionnaire acts as a guide for what a valuator should consider during the valuation process; however, it is not suggested that all of the questions need to be answered in one formal interview session with the client.

Fact-finding interviews are an essential and important part of the valuation process. In some cases, you might tactfully ask your questions in a certain order so as to minimize the chance of influencing the answers you get. And with experience, you will learn when to probe with well-timed follow-up questions, and when to use open-ended questions to generate further discussion.

Many questions below can be presented to the client as a preliminary information request list. Depending on the relationship with the client and/or already established knowledge of the business and industry, each valuator can decide if the questions are better addressed through an interview process or an information request list format.

All those engaged in the valuing, buying, or selling of businesses should find the questionnaires helpful. No permission is required from the author or publisher to copy them, except where the object is republication.

SUMMARY BUSINESS VALUATION QUESTIONNAIRE

The following questionnaire, or, more precisely, checklist, may be used to review the basic facts that should be gathered and taken into account in the valuation of business enterprises. It can be used to determine appropriate follow-up questions for the client and/or allow you to select which questions are more relevant from the detailed questionnaire that is to follow. A guide only, it is not intended to be comprehensive, and users should make adjustments as necessary to meet the particulars of their valuation assignments.

1. Obtain copies of the financial statements of the enterprise being assessed for the five years preceding the date of valuation. Where available, provide copies of the financial statements for the appropriate period after the valuation date as well.

____

____

____

2. If relevant, the financial statements of related companies and/or other business entities should be sought out. The precise nature of the relationship between these entities and the enterprise being valued should be indicated both for the five-year period preceding the valuation date and, if necessary, for the appropriate period subsequent to it.

3. In the case of incorporated bodies, obtain a copy of the letters patent or articles of incorporation and of all subsequent adjustments to them.

4. Where the company operates from leased premises, summarize the key terms contained in the lease agreement. Obtain a copy of the lease in effect as of the valuation date.

5. Procure an outline of the nature and history of the enterprise and of its operations, including what products and services are provided by the company. If there is any sales literature, such as a brochure, request a copy.

6. Obtain a summary of the ownership and non-arm's-length relationships that exist between the company's shareholders, directors, and officers.

7. Request copies of all partnership and/or shareholder agreements in effect as of the valuation date.

8. Indicate the address from which the company operates.

9. If there have been previous valuations of, offers for, or sales of the equity interest(s) in question, obtain details of these transactions.

10. Indicate who the company's external public accountants are. Indicate the name of the accountant and/or partner in charge of the company's account.

11. Determine who acts as the company's solicitor.

12. Provide a listing of the company's principal shareholders (both common and preferred) and the percentage of their respective ownership share.

Name	*Type of Share*	*Per Cent Owned*

13. Provide a listing of the company's directors and officers.

Directors		*Officers*	
Name	Title	Name	Title

14. Obtain information on the company's strategic plans for the future, including a business plan, if available.

15. Obtain all correspondence to or from the security regulators (*i.e.*, OSC, SEC, *etc.*), tax authorities (*i.e.*, CRA, IRS, *etc.*), or other regulatory authorities regarding tax, accounting, or financial reporting for the last five years.

____

____

____

____

16. Obtain details of any other matters that might have a significant influence on the value of the enterprise.

____

____

____

____

____

____

DETAILED BUSINESS VALUATION QUESTIONNAIRE

Company Being Valued

____

Person(s) Interviewed	____________	Date __________
	____________	Date __________
	____________	Date __________
Questionnaire Completed By	____________	Date __________
Questionnaire Reviewed By	____________	Date __________

This questionnaire is designed to serve a wide range of valuation assignments. Accordingly, it is neither required nor is it intended that all of the information be obtained for every assignment.

Determining the information to be compiled will be a function of a number of factors, such as the history and value of the business being valued, the purpose of the valuation, the agreed scope of the investigation and analysis, materiality limits, and the content and timing of the valuation report.

In general, the inquiries mentioned in this questionnaire should be directed to company officials and others having responsibility for the operations, financial reporting, accounting, or other areas involved in the respective areas of the business.

In this questionnaire, the phrase "period under review" generally means five full fiscal years preceding the valuation date and includes whatever period remains between the last of these fiscal years and the valuation date. There may, of course, be circumstances in which the period under review will be less than five years. The phrase "report date" refers to the date when the valuation report is issued, which in certain instances may be significantly later than the valuation date.

This questionnaire is divided into the following sections:

A. General Information

- Administrative
- Valuation Basics
- Past Valuations
- Other

B. Ownership – Incorporated Business
C. Ownership – Unincorporated Business Supplement
D. General Information on the Business
E. Financial Information
F. Location/Fixed Assets
G. Management and Other Employees
H. Sales/Customer Profile
I. Purchasing
J. Industry Review
K. Research and Development
L. Contracts, Agreements, and Licences
M. Intangible Assets
N. Environmental Assets and Liabilities
O. Income Tax Considerations
P. Other Considerations

General Information

Administrative

A1. Client Information:

Client Name ______________________________
Address ______________________________
Phone Number ______________ Fax Number ______________
Contact Name ______________________________

Title ____________________
Office Phone Number ____________________
Mobile Phone Number ____________________
E-mail Address ____________________

A2. Company Being Valued:

Name of Entity ____________________
Head Office/ Other Offices ____________________
Address ____________________
____
Phone Number __________ Fax Number __________
Contact #1 Name ____________________
Title ____________________
Office Phone Number ____________________
Mobile Phone Number ____________________
Fax Number ____________________
E-mail Address ____________________

Contact #2 Name ____________________
Title ____________________
Office Phone Number ____________________
Mobile Phone Number ____________________
Fax Number ____________________
E-mail Address ____________________

A3. Indicate the name and title of the person(s) to whom the report is to be addressed.

____
____
____
____

A4. When is the report wanted?

Draft report ____________________ Final report ____________________

A5. How many copies are needed?
Draft report ____________________ Final report ____________________

A6. Identify the recipient(s) of the report and number of copies to be sent to each.

Valuation Basics

A7. Identify the business premises/plants to be inspected and the appropriate contact person(s).

A8. Indicate the valuation date(s).

A9. Outline the purpose of the valuation.

A10. If the valuation is required for the purpose of a proposed transaction, provide copies of the relevant agreements or preliminary drafts thereof.

A11. Identify any third party that may rely on our valuation.

A12. Indicate whether the valuation is likely to be litigated. Provide relevant legal documents/briefings/notes.

A13. What is being valued, the entire company or only a partial interest? In the second case, identify the particular interest in question.

A14. Specify the type of value to be determined (*e.g.*, fair market value, fair value, or *pro rata* fair market value) and relate back to the purpose of the valuation.

A15. Indicate the level of assurance and consequently the type of report required by the client (*e.g.*, comprehensive, estimate, or calculation).

A16. Identify your role in the engagement (*e.g.*, independent expert or advisor).

A17. Are all of the board members (if applicable) and shareholders/partners in agreement on the chosen course of action for which the valuation is requested (*e.g.*, are they all in favor of the sale of business)? If not, what impact could it have on the valuation?

Past Valuations

A18. If the company has been valued in the past, indicate who undertook the assignment. Where available, provide a copy of the report(s).

A19. Identify any share values that have been used in the five-year period preceding the valuation date for capital gains tax, income tax, gift tax, estate tax, family law (marital dissolution), obtaining financing or any other purpose.

A20. Provide the details for transactions involving the company or any of its subsidiaries.

A21. If the company acquired other business enterprises during the period under review or at any time after the valuation date, provide details of these transactions.

A22. In cases where the enterprise or any of its significant assets have been offered for sale either in the five-year period preceding the valuation date or in the period subsequent to it, provide the following information: the amount of the asking price, the identities of potential purchasers, the details of any offers made, and the reasons the transaction was not completed.

A23. If transfers of equity interests in the company have occurred during the period under review or subsequent to the valuation date, summarize the details of these transactions.

A24. Provide any other past indicators of value used for various purposes (*e.g.*, property tax assessments or insurance).

Other

A25. Have there been any major changes in the operation of the company for the fiscal year preceding the valuation date? If so, indicate the reason for the change(s).

A26. Provide a credit report on the company.

A27. If any change in external accountants has taken place during the period under review or subsequent to the valuation date, outline the reasons for the replacement.

A28. If possible, discuss the company and its activities with the external accountants and examine their working paper files on the business. Identify the contact person.

A29. Are the accountants willing to discuss the company's affairs and provide representations?

A30. Where management consulting or other studies (*e.g.*, engineering studies) have been conducted on the company or the industry it serves, provide copies or abstracts of the reports.

A31. Provide copies of any contracts, such as buy/sell or partnership/shareholder agreements, that may affect the transferability or value of the enterprise or of a partial interest therein.

Ownership - Incorporated Business

B1. When was the company incorporated?

B2. What are the applicable statutory laws?

B3. Provide the following for review: minutes of meetings of the board of directors, stockholders, audit committee (if applicable) and the by-laws of the company for the five-year period preceding the valuation date as well as for any relevant subsequent period. (Note that items that could affect the valuation in a significant way should be copied for future reference.)

B4. Provide a legal entity organization chart, with an explanation of the locations and activities of major entities.

B5. Provide a management organizational chart with salary, fringe benefits, head count, and turnover information.

B6. Provide copies of the letters patent or articles of incorporation and of any supplementary changes to them. Where applicable, provide copies of the articles of amalgamation.

B7. List all shareholders and outline their relationship to the company and to each other as follows:

Name of Shareholder	Position(s) Held	Number of Shares Owned by Class	Details of Non-Arm's Length Relationships	Key Share Class Characteristics

B8. List the directors and officers of the company, indicating their involvement with the enterprise according to the following headings.

Name of Director or Officer	Position(s) Held	Date of Appointment	Details of Non-Arm's Length Relationships

B9. Has the name of the company changed since incorporation? If so, indicate the various styles used, the dates on which each came into effect, and the reasons for the change(s).

B10. If there are any commitments to issue shares or any stock option agreements in existence at the valuation date, note the details of these undertakings.

B11. List all stock options or warrants outstanding with exercise price(s) and expiration date(s).

B12. Indicate whether the company is a public company and, if listed on a stock exchange, which one.

Ownership - Unincorporated Business (Proprietorship/Partnership)

C1. Has the proprietorship or partnership been registered?

C2. Provide details concerning the ownership of the company, including the name(s) and age(s) of the owner/partners as of the valuation date and particulars of all non-arm's length relationships.

C3. Summarize the details of the partnership agreement, if applicable, and provide copies.

C4. Where applicable, provide copies of the personal income tax returns of the proprietor/partners for the period under review as well as those available as of or subsequent to that date.

General Information on the Business

C5. Provide a two- or three-page narrative of the nature and history of the business. This summary should indicate when, where, and by whom the enterprise was established; outline the past and present business activities of the company; indicate the skills needed to conduct its operations; outline the competitive strength and weaknesses of the business; describe any seasonal fluctuations in operating results; account for trends in gross revenues, relevant expenses, and net earnings; and address any other significant matters.

Markets / Customers

D1. Describe the overall market of the company, including its definition (*e.g.*, products, territories, and customers), future prospects, market size, and anticipated growth.

D2. Describe the company's overall marketing strategy, including geographic objectives, pricing policy (*e.g.*, cost or demand based), and impact of pricing policies (*e.g.*, increase market share or profit potential).

D3. Describe target markets and customers. Please provide any marketing brochures of the company or its products.

Products/Services

D4. Provide a description of the company's primary products and services, including their history, target market, growth potential, advantages (*e.g.*, cheaper, better utility, and unique features), and any disadvantages.

D5. Describe the current status of the products or services, including the stage within their life cycles, overall expected remaining life span, and timing regarding introduction of any new products or services.

Industry/Competition

D6. Describe the current condition of the industry, including trends, demographic factors, technological developments, and growth potential.

D7. List and describe primary competitors' location, size and potential, market share, strengths and weaknesses, and basis of competition.

D8. Provide any relevant industry publications that would assist in understanding the factors described above.

General

D9. Were there any major changes in the products and services offered by the company during the period under review or after the valuation date? If so, provide details.

D10. Have the company's business prospects and its operations remained stable between the valuation date and the report date? If not, outline any significant changes.

D11. Provide current strategic, business and/or operating plans for the five years (or as available) subsequent to the valuation date.

D12. Describe any major changes in business operations in the past five years or anticipated in the future, such as discontinuation of a product line or business segment.

D13. Is the subject company related to other business entities? If so, describe the form of the relationship and give details of any transactions that have occurred between the related parties.

D14. If relevant articles on the company have appeared in newspapers, magazines, or other publications, provide such copies.

D15. Identify the relevant industry classification (*i.e.*, North American Industry Classification System codes) for the business.

D16. Identify key risk factors of the business.

Financial Information

E1. Provide copies of the financial statements and any annual reports or supplemental financial information of the company for each of the five years preceding the valuation date. It may also be necessary to provide any financial statements that may exist for periods after that date, if applicable.

E2. In cases where the valuation date does not coincide with the fiscal year-end, provide copies of the interim financial statements of the company.

E3. In cases where the valuation date is different from the most recent fiscal year-end or interim end date, provide a balance sheet as at the valuation date.

E4. If it is necessary to rely on interim or unaudited financial statements, provide responses to the following questions:

(a) How reliable is the company's internal financial reporting system?

(b) Roughly how many year-end adjustments are necessitated by the normal annual audits and how significant are they?

(c) Provide management comment letters prepared by the auditors and legal counsel responses to audit inquiries and correspondence to or from security regulators (*i.e.*, OSC, SEC, *etc.*), tax authorities, and/or other regulatory authorities regarding tax, accounting, or financial reporting for the last five years (applies primarily to public companies).

E5. Identify any past or expected unusual, non-operating, and non-recurring or extraordinary items.

E6. List significant inter-company and intra-company transactions including corporate overhead allocations.

E7. If the company has assets and liabilities that do not appear on its balance sheets for the period under review, provide a detailed listing and description of such assets and liabilities.

E8. List all the assets and liabilities for which, in the opinion of the company's management, fair market value differs from net book value. In each instance, management's estimate of the fair market value should be included.

E9. How is the allowance for doubtful accounts receivable estimated? How often is the collectability of the receivables reviewed? Provide an aged accounts receivable listing.

E10. How is inventory valued? If any changes in the manner of valuing inventory took place in the period under review, provide details.

E11. Was there uncompleted work-in-process as of the valuation date? If so, was the amount of unfinished work greater or less than usual?

E12. How is the allowance for obsolete or slow-moving inventory estimated?

E13. Is there any pledged inventory, consigned inventory, customer-owned inventory, or inventory not located at the company's facilities?

E14. Provide a listing of inventory, categorized by major groupings, including the relevant accounting policies for each inventory group.

E15. Provide a listing of major accrued liabilities included in accounts payable or otherwise. Which ones are considered to be part of normal business operations (to be included in the calculation of normal working capital levels)?

E16. Provide a listing of cash and short-term investment accounts, including information on the investments (*e.g.*, amount, investment horizon, estimated fair market value)

E17. Describe the terms of the company's short-term and long-term financings (*e.g.*, name of lender, duration, interest rate, repayment terms).

E18. In financial reporting, what rates were employed for depreciation and amortization? Given the expected remaining useful life of the subject assets, are the rates realistic?

E19. Provide both historical and forecast capital expenditures, broken down between maintenance versus growth, including information on individually significant projects and the basis for projected amounts.

E20. Is the company committed to any expenditures that are out of the ordinary either in terms of size or in terms of its normal business operations (*e.g.*, will there be substantial outlays for fixed assets)?

E21. Are there redundant assets in the company? If so, provide details, including any estimates of fair value.

E22. Does the company insure the lives of its key employees? If it does, the amount and type of insurance, as well as the beneficiary, should be indicated for each insured employee.

E23. Are there any legal claims against the company? If so, provide a complete account of them.

E24. Describe in detail all contingent liabilities or assets, including litigation pending and any liabilities with respect to guarantees, warranties, and past services.

E25. As at the valuation date, was the capital structure (*e.g.*, long-term debt, preferred shares, common shares) of the company appropriate and in line with that of its competitors?

E26. Provide a scheduled long-term indebtedness for each loan, indicating the lender; amount owing; interest rate; repayment terms, including any prepayment or conversion feature; the security; and any other significant rights.

E27. For each class of common shares outstanding as at the valuation date, provide a schedule indicating: the number of shares issued and outstanding, the issue price, the dividend rate, any cumulative rights, history of dividend payment, voting rights, and any other significant features.

E28. For each class of preferred shares outstanding as at the valuation date, provide a schedule indicating the number of shares issued and outstanding, the par value, whether they are redeemable or retractable and at what price, the dividend rate and any cumulative rights, the history of dividend payments, conversion features, voting rights, and any other significant features.

E29. As at the valuation date, who had voting control of the company? Was this likely to change in the near future? If so, identify the reason(s) for the change.

E30. Have accounting policies or the groupings presented in financial statements been adjusted in any way during the period under review? If so, provide particulars.

E31. If, between the valuation date and the report date, any significant changes occurred in the value of the company's assets or liabilities, whether tangible, intangible, or contingent, these changes should be outlined in detail.

E32. Where a forecast, as of or reasonably close to the valuation date(s), has been made of the company's operating results, obtain copies and solicit management's opinion on the degree of risk involved in achieving the budgeted results. If applicable, assumptions used in preparing the forecast should be detailed.

E33. What per cent of forecast sales is represented by an order backlog as at the valuation date? Provide historical backlog figures for the five years preceding the valuation date.

E34. During the period under review, how have the results achieved compared with forecast results? Explain significant differences.

E35. How are the company's revenues divided by type of business product or service line offered? Provide a breakdown for each fiscal year in the period under review.

E36. Explain any significant trends in revenues, expenses, and net earnings revealed in the operating results for the period under review and account for all non-recurring, unusual, or extraordinary revenues and expenses.

E37. Summarize the sales to and purchases from non-arm's length parties and competitors for the period of review. Are these transactions at arm's length rates? If not, indicate the reasons and the possible impact on the value of the company.

E38. Are any plants, divisions, or subsidiaries operating at a loss? If so, are losses expected to continue?

E39. Indicate how much of the company's sales, earnings, and assets stem from foreign countries? Are earnings from these areas likely to be maintained? Do the company's operations abroad involve any particular risks?

E40. Provide an account of the salaries and benefits the company provides to the five highest paid of its employees and to all non-arm's length employees, both by individual and for each of the five fiscal years preceding the valuation date.

E41. On average, how many hours did each of the non-arm's length employees work per week in each of the five fiscal years in the period under review?

E42. In the same period, what rates of interest were charged or paid on loans to or from non-arm's length parties?

E43. If the company was charged by non-arm's length parties for items unrelated to its business, provide details for each fiscal year of the five-year period preceding the valuation date.

E44. What sort of insurance coverage does the company have? Is it sufficient to protect its physical assets? Is there provision for interruption of business, errors and omissions, and other forms of liability?

E45. Enquire of the company's management whether they consider the insurance coverage to be adequate.

E46. Does the company guarantee its products? If so, on what terms? What has been the cost of warranties in the past?

E47. If the company has subsidiaries, are they reflected in the accounts on a cost, equity, or consolidated basis?

E48. What is the company's gross margin and break-even point by product line?

E49. If the historical operating results of the company for the five years preceding the valuation date do not reflect its maintainable earnings level as of the valuation date, can the discrepancy be explained? If so, provide details.

E50. As at the valuation date, what was management's estimate of the maintainable earnings level of the company? Indicate whether this is a pre- or after-tax level and describe how the figure was derived.

Location/Fixed Assets

F1. Describe fully and by individual location the company's land, buildings, machinery, equipment, and other facilities. (A tour of the facilities and the surrounding area is usually helpful in coming to a general assessment of the company and the efficiency of the office/plant layout.)

F2. Provide copies of any reports on the company's fixed assets (*i.e.*, land, buildings, equipment, *etc.*) that present estimates of value at any point in time from five years preceding the valuation date to the report date.

F3. For fixed assets that are leased (including land, buildings and/or equipment), provide details of the various assets in question, together with the terms of the lease(s) and any renewal options or options to purchase. Where appropriate, provide copies of lease agreements. In addition, discuss if any leases are in the process of being negotiated or terminated and what the effect would be of such a transaction.

F4. Provide details on any significant acquisitions and disposals of fixed assets during the three-year period preceding or the period subsequent to the valuation date.

F5. Has the company always operated from the present location(s)? If not, outline previous locations and the length of time spent at each.

F6. What is the approximate area (in square feet/metres) of each of the company's facilities? Does the space conform to the requirements of the company? Is there adequate room for expansion?

F7. Is the company operating at full capacity or less?

F8. Is the area in which the company is located considered "desirable"?

F9. Is the success of the company in any way dependent on its location?

F10. Is the status or the value of the location threatened or likely to be enhanced by any known or prospective future changes?

F11. Provide a listing of the major pieces of equipment. This listing should briefly describe each item and indicate its age, remaining useful life, historical cost, current undepreciated capital costs balance, going-concern market values and orderly liquidation value.

F12. Have other members of the industry acquired more technologically advanced methods of production than the company's? If so, what is the likely effect on the company's competitive position?

F13. Identify any idled property, including plant and equipment that has been reserved for, written off, or will require replacement earlier than originally thought.

F14. Identify any pledged property.

Management and Other Employees

G1. Provide a management organizational chart that shows how many individuals the company employs in each job classification.

G2. Who are the key employees? To what degree is the company's future earnings ability dependent on any of them?

G3. Have any changes in management or key personnel occurred during the period under review? If so, provide details. What were the number of employees and changes to the labor force during the five years preceding the valuation date?

G4. As of the valuation date, were any key employees expected to leave the company? If the business was sold, how many of the key employees would likely remain with the company?

G5. Assess the strengths and weaknesses of the company's management. Is there sufficient quality and depth? Provide curriculum vitae of all key employees.

G6. Describe management's compensation structure, specifying the split between salary and variable compensation (*i.e.*, bonus). Indicate what metrics are used to determine the amount of the bonus.

G7. What is the quality and depth of the company's other employees?

G8. Should any or all of the company's employees be unionized, provide the following:

(a) The name(s) of the union(s).

(b) A copy or abstract of the existing labor contract(s).

(c) The specifics of any labor negotiations pending as of the valuation date that may have a bearing on the valuation.

(d) Details of any relevant information concerning the history of labor relations at the company.

G9. Does the company enjoy amicable relations with its employees?

G10. Is there an adequate supply of qualified professionals, tradespeople, and other employees?

G11. Do employees receive market rates of remuneration for their work?

G12. Does the company have a good record with respect to industrial accidents?

G13. If the business is labor-intensive, can the selling prices of the company's goods and services be adjusted to reflect significant changes in labor costs?

G14. How is the business and management perceived by external stakeholders, such as local communities, environmental agencies, industry groups, and others?

Sales/Customer Profile

H1. List all customers who provide five per cent or more of the company's annual revenues.

H2. Has the company gained or lost any significant customers in the period under review? How does its experience compare with that of the industry generally? What is the average customer attrition over the past five years?

H3. Is the rate of customer turnover similar to that of the industry as a whole? If not, provide an explanation.

H4. Is the customer base capable of expansion?

H5. How much of the company's revenue is derived from recurring as opposed to non-recurring sources?

H6. If the company was sold, would it continue to be patronized? How many customers would likely be retained, expressed as a percentage both of total customers and of gross revenue?

H7. Does the company have any customers with whom it has a non-arm's length or some other form of special relationship? If so, what is the impact of the relationship on the value of the company?

H8. How does the company market its products? How important are advertising, distribution methods, and its skilled sales force in maintaining customers and markets?

H9. Are there any significant customer contracts that, if terminated, could have a material effect on the company?

H10. What is the geographical makeup of major customers (*e.g.*, multinational and local)?

Purchasing

I1. Provide a listing of all suppliers, subcontractors, or consultants who represent five per cent or more of the company's annual expenditures. Include the nature of the goods/services received from each.

I2. Are there any key suppliers, subcontractors, or consultants whose loss could affect the company's profitability? If so, provide details.

I3. Is the company generally able to change its selling prices to reflect changes in its material or other costs?

I4. As at the valuation date, did the company have any significant purchase commitments?

I5. What is the average attrition rate of suppliers over the past five years? Is attrition generally attributed to the company's decision to switch suppliers or is it due to circumstances outside of management's control?

I6. Does the company have any non-arm's length suppliers? If so, are goods and services supplied at market rates? What is the impact of this relationship on the value of the company?

Industry Review

J1. Which trade associations serve the industry? Provide copies of any industry studies prepared by these associations or any governmental or other bodies.

J2. Outline statistical and other relevant data, such as key business ratios, on the industry and the company's principal competitors. How do the company's ratios compare with those of its competitors?

J3. Does the industry have agreements with labor, customers, or suppliers that are unusual in any way? If so, provide details.

J4. What percentage of the market does the company have by product line?

J5. What percentage of the market by the company's product lines does each of its major competitors have?

J6. Does the competition provide products or services not offered by the company being valued? If so, what effect does this have on the value of the company?

J7. Describe, in general, the pricing policies adopted by the company's competitors.

J8. Is the company's line of business readily entered? Can the market area or customer base served be easily penetrated? Discuss the main barriers to entry in the industry.

J9. What steps does the company take to market its product lines and attract customers?

J10. How do the goods and services offered by the company compare in quality with those provided by its competitors?

J11. Has the company established a good reputation in the market area it serves?

J12. Provide copies of any significant financial or other information the company may have on its major competitors.

J13. Are there any seasonal patterns that affect the industry? Are all companies within the industry affected to the same degree by such patterns? If not, why?

J14. Have competitors introduced any changes in their methods of advertising or means of distribution that might work to the disadvantage of the company?

J15. Assess the state of the economy at the valuation date. How are the goods and services offered by the company expected to sell in the future?

J16. Discuss the market trends facing the industry.

J17. Discuss any precedent or potential takeovers of other companies in the industry or related industry.

J18. Are there any federal or provincial/state regulations affecting the industry?

J19. Identify key financial metrics of competitors that can be considered comparable with the subject company's (*i.e.*, total market capitalization, enterprise value, EBITDA, EBIT, total assets, net debt, *etc.*). This information can be used for cross-check analysis on the valuation of the subject company.

J20. Identify key recent transactions involving competitors or companies comparable with the subject company. Describe key metrics of the transaction, including consideration paid, net debt assumed, profitability of the company, and premium paid over a company's trading price. This information can be used for cross-check analysis on the valuation of the subject company.

Research and Development

K1. What research and development activities is the company engaged in?

K2. How much has the company spent on research and development, by fiscal year, for the five-year period preceding the valuation date?

K3. How are research and development expenditures reflected in the company's accounts?

K4. As of the valuation date, did the company envisage offering any new products or service lines or were any new markets being developed? If so, what was the anticipated result of these initiatives?

K5. Is the company competing in any markets where new and innovative products have a significant impact on market demand?

K6. Does the company have any products for which market demand is declining?

K7. Have any of the competitors introduced new products that could have a significant impact on the marketplace and on the future demand for the company's products? Can the company replicate such product or develop an adequate replacement for it within reasonable research and development costs?

Contracts, Agreements, and Licences

L1. Summarize and include copies or abstracts of all relevant contracts, agreements, and licences, such as the following:

(a) Debt-financing agreements

(b) Bank and other guarantees

(c) Collective labor agreements

(d) Employee pension plans (with specifics of any under- or over-funding)

____
____
____
____
____

(e) Employment contracts

____
____
____
____
____

(f) Employee-incentive plans/agreements

____
____
____
____
____

(g) Significant contracts with customers for products offered by the company

____
____
____
____
____

(h) Purchase/sale agreements, commitments, or options

____
____
____
____
____

(i) Government subsidy agreements

(j) Franchise and royalty agreements

(k) Agreements outside the usual course of business

(l) Licences and permits essential to the operations of the company

(m) Other contracts and agreements that may affect the value of the company

L2. At the valuation date, were any significant changes anticipated to result from any of the contracts noted in L1 above or from any contracts under negotiation or expected to be negotiated? Indicate the impact such changes would have on the future operations and earnings ability of the company.

Intangible Assets

M1. As of the valuation date, did the company own or otherwise have an interest in any patents, trademarks, licences, copyrights, or other identifiable intangible assets (computer software, non-patented proprietary technology, non-compete contracts, *etc.*)? If so, indicate where these were issued, applied for, or licensed.

M2. Indicate which products have historically been sold under the above-noted copyrights, patents, *etc.* Which products will be protected in the future? What would be the impact on the company of loosing copyright, patent, or other type of protection?

M3. To what degree is the value of the company related to identifiable intangibles? Indicate which intangibles are significant to the future success of the business and the reasons for their importance.

M4. What are the methods and rates of amortization used for recorded intangibles?

M5. In the company's view, what is the value of its various identifiable intangibles? Which valuation methods does the company believe to be most appropriate in valuing these assets?

M6. Have any intangible assets ever been licensed or sold? Is there a possibility that certain intangible assets could be licensed or sold if the company was willing to do so?

M7. To what extent is intellectual property documented?

M8. What procedures and safeguards does the company use to protect and manage intellectual property and intangible assets?

Environmental Assets and Liabilities

N1. As of the valuation date, did the company hold any identifiable environmental permits? If so, indicate under which regulatory body(s) these permits were issued and summarize the details and conditions of the permits (*e.g.*, permit to emit air pollutants and permit to discharge wastewater).

N2. To what degree is the value of the company related to identifiable environmental permits? Indicate which permits are significant to the future success of the business and the reasons for their importance.

N3. Is the company in a state of regulatory non-compliance regarding any of the identifiable environmental permits? If so, has the company been subject to any regulatory conditions or fines?

N4. What is the value of the company's environmental permits? Document the level of effort, costs, and time required to achieve a similar level of environmental permitting and regulatory compliance.

N5. To what extent are site environmental liabilities properly documented (examples of environmental liabilities include soil and groundwater contamination; hazardous materials contained in buildings such as asbestos, PCBs, mercury; site closure plans; and reclamation activities)?

N6. Are quantities, magnitudes, and costs associated with environmental liabilities supported by engineering/environmental consulting reports from third parties?

N7. Does the company have any outstanding legal issues associated with environmental contamination or health and safety prosecutions and/or fines?

N8. Is the company a large emitter of greenhouse gases? If so, has it been subject to any regulatory conditions or fines regarding greenhouse gas emissions?

N9. Provide any environmental filings the company may have, documenting compliance or confirming "non-applicability status" with respect to various environmental regulations.

N10. If performed, outline the findings of a preliminary assessment and site investigation that was completed by an appropriately qualified environmental expert.

Income Tax Considerations

O1. Provide copies of the provincial/state and federal income tax returns, complete with supporting schedules, for the three-year period preceding the valuation date.

O2. What have been the timing differences between financial statements and tax returns over the last three years? How have deferred income taxes been accounted for?

O3. As of the valuation date, what were the available carryovers (net operating losses, investment credits, foreign tax credits, *etc.*)? When will these carryovers expire?

O4. When did provincial/state and federal authorities conduct their latest corporate assessment or reassessment? Has such assessment ever required major changes in the corporation's tax returns?

O5. Will later subsequent examinations of tax returns likely result in further adjustments or in reassessment? If so, provide details.

O6. Is the company being valued associated with any other enterprises for income tax purposes? If so, obtain a list of these entities.

O7. Would a likely market-participant acquirer of the company or its assets be a tax-exempt entity such as pension fund?

O8. If the company is likely to have losses over the near term, to what extent can these be carried back?

Other Considerations

P1. What is the condition and appropriateness of the company's accounting and other records?

P2. Who is most likely to acquire the company?

P3. Could the most likely purchaser provide the same goods and services at an equal level of quality?

P4. Is the company attractive to special buyers? Can any individual special purchasers be identified?

P5. Quantify, if possible, the value of the company to the special purchaser(s).

P6. Do any brokers specialize in the sale of the particular type of business under consideration?

P7. Provide details of any sales of comparable businesses known to the owner(s)/management of the company.

P8. Are there any rules-of-thumb for valuing businesses in the industry?

P9. At the valuation date, what value was placed on the company by its owner(s)/management? How was the figure arrived at?

P10. Is there any legislation or jurisprudence that should be considered in arriving at the value estimate?

P11. If a partial equity interest is being valued, who controls the company and to what degree is group or family control relevant?

P12. Outline any matters not addressed in this questionnaire that might influence the value of the company.

M&A in Volatile Markets: Challenges and Solutions

Doug McDonald & Michael Morrow

Introduction

After many years of continued growth in mergers and acquisitions (M&A) activity leading up to the second half of 2008, the credit crisis caused a significant shift in the appetite for growth strategies including business combinations. At the peak of M&A activity in 2007, there were 2,000 deals closed as reported by Bloomberg representing nearly US$3.5 trillion in activity. Based on the first 19 weeks of 2009, 262 deals closed. Annualizing the year-to-date deals for 2009, 717 deals would close, which represents a significant drop in activity. The graph below illustrates the global M&A volume since 2001. This chapter outlines the M&A environment during an economic downturn, discusses the common issues and deal risks within a challenging economic environment, and outlines best practices and solutions for successful deals during uncertain and volatile times.

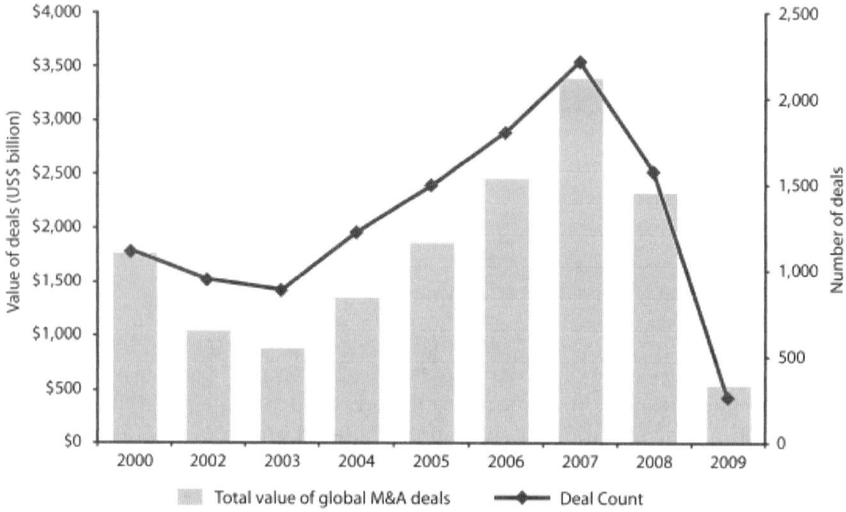

Source: Bloomberg. Note: 2009 includes the first 19 weeks of activity.

Market Overview

Acquisitions are typically funded, in part or in total, using debt financing. Debt financing is attractive given its low, after-tax cost versus other forms of capital. Equity holders, including private equity investors, can magnify or "leverage" equity returns given the relatively low after-tax cost of debt financing. The combination of stable economic growth, low interest rates, and availability of debt financing makes debt leveraged acquisitions very attractive, and will drive robust M&A activity.

Following the tragic events of September 11th, central banks made the cost of debt financing cheaper by lowering key overnight interest rates charged to banks, which allowed banks to lend at cheaper rates to its customers. Additionally, investment banks were creating innovative debt structures such as collaterized debt obligations (CDOs), whereby the value and payments are derived from an underlying portfolio of fixed-income assets such as mortgages, car loans, and other debt-related securities. CDOs allowed financial institutions to resell its loans to the investing public and greatly increased the amounts of funds available to lend. These combined forces encouraged borrowing, spending, and economic expansion. Loose borrowing standards allowed businesses to leverage their balance sheets to extreme levels to fund growth, including acquisitions. In 2008, when the economy slowed and the credit markets froze, those businesses with leveraged balance sheets were sent reeling, causing the house of cards to come crashing down and the most significant global economic downturn in decades. Following a period of record crashing M&A activity, frozen credit markets and a severe recession presented several challenges to the M&A market.

Buyers of companies are typically segregated into two types: strategic buyers and financial buyers. Strategic buyers are typically other businesses that are seeking transactions that are strategic in nature. Acquisitions for strategic buyers will typically include opportunities that will augment its offerings to customers or provide a competitive advantage. Strategic buyers will also seek similar types of business to increase market share and to create synergies including cost savings or revenue enhancement. Strategic buyers will often play an active role in managing the day-to-day activities of the acquired business. Conversely, financial buyers are investment firms such as private equity investment firms that engage in leveraged buyout (LBO) transactions. Financial buyers provide equity capital to fund a transaction and bring a combination of capital markets expertise, various important contacts, strategies for operational improvement and experience owning leveraged companies. Financial buyers rarely manage a company's day-to-day activities directly. Instead, financial buyers invest in the management team to run the operations of the business. Financial buyers are active in issues relating to the company's capital structure as well as strategic initiatives including mergers and acquisitions.

Strategic Buyers

The economic downturn was characterized with extreme uncertainty and caution. Businesses worldwide responded to the uncertainty by slashing all unnecessary spending. Companies prepared for the worst, including a possible depression. As a result, companies focused internally and trimmed expenses and conserved cash instead of considering expansion opportunities, including business acquisitions. Strategic buyers opted to keep "powder dry" or reserve cash to fund ongoing business expenses and liabilities. The lack of available credit hampered the ability of many strategic buyers to finance potential acquisitions. As a result of the economic uncertainty and lack of availability of financing, many businesses exited the M&A market, which significantly reduced the number of active strategic buyers in the market.

Financial Buyers

While several strategic buyers were forced out of the M&A market, investment firms including private equity firms and hedge funds were also encountering significant headwinds. The headwinds for investment firms originate from three primary sources: lack of highly leveraged credit availability, poor performance of portfolio companies, and decreased fund raising activities.

Financial buyers participate in LBO transactions where a significant percentage of the purchase price is financed through borrowed debt. The assets of the acquired company are used as collateral for the borrowed capital. The lack of highly leveraged credit at reasonable costs significantly hampered investment firms to achieve high internal rates of returns. Decreased debt leverage meant that the equity portion of the purchase price required was relatively higher, thereby forcing down the potential equity returns. The ability of investment firms to drive high rates of returns simply from financial engineering and highly leveraged capital structures ended with the credit crisis. Although there was some credit availability for smaller transactions, all multi-billion dollar leveraged buyout activity came to an abrupt end. For example, according to Standard and Poor's, U.S. LBO volume decreased from US$688.5 billion in 2007 to US$294.5 billion in 2008. Furthermore, 2009 is expected to record even lower activity. Even if investment firms were looking to deploy capital and had access to debt financing, they were faced with the challenge of competing for assets with businesses that could potentially pay cash, which represented an advantage in a volatile environment. The graph below illustrates the capital structure breakdown for acquisitions:

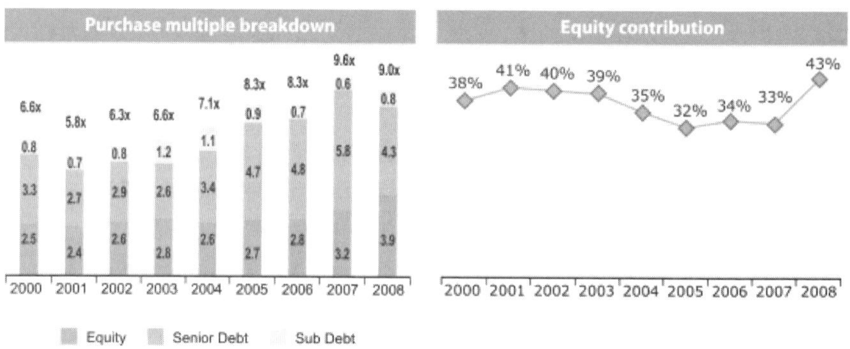

Source: Standard and Poor's

Portfolio companies owned by investment firms faced significant challenges during the economic downturn as business performance and operating cash flow deteriorated. Compounding the problem was the challenge of servicing the highly leveraged capital structures. Companies that were purchased with highly leveraged capital structures under the assumption that growth would continue into the future were often doomed for restructuring. Portfolio companies requiring refinancing were often faced with very few lending options. Lenders globally were faced with challenging regulatory bank capital adequacy ratios requirements, which stipulated the bank's capital used to cover the risk weighted amount of its credit exposures. Given the mounting credit related losses for the banks, capital adequacy ratios were being breached, forcing institutions to halt or limit lending activities. If a willing lender could be found, the costs associated with the new debt were very high and it included very strict terms. Increased interest costs and fees with shortened amortization periods meant that the operating cash flow required to service the debt also increased. Portfolio companies that broke lender covenants were not given much grace and many banks were aggressively pulling in capital to improve their balance sheets and liquidity. Deteriorating business performance combined with tight credit markets forced many economically sensitive portfolio companies to restructure or file for bankruptcy. The management of struggling portfolio companies was a huge distraction for investment firms. Their focus shifted from further acquisitions to assisting the survival of its current portfolio investments. Several investment firms were simply out of the M&A market unless there was a very compelling opportunity to add onto a current investment. Some investment firms also chose to sit on the sidelines and wait until there was evidence of an economic turnaround before deploying additional capital. The one subset of investment funds that encountered increase in activity during this period of economic uncertainty were restructuring investment funds. Restructuring investment funds seek opportunities where the underlying business is performing well or has the potential to perform well, but requires balance sheet restructuring due to the debt load or requires new management to cut costs and grow the company. Fundraising for restructuring funds also increased as investors rotated into defensive investments while seeking abnormal profits.

Investment firms manage investment funds, where they raise capital and deploy it until the fund is closed. Capital is raised well in advance of closing acquisitions. If a fund was raised before the credit crisis, then the investment fund would be well-positioned to take advantage of an eventual recovery. Conversely, some investment firms that didn't raise funds before the credit crisis were faced with depleting capital, which inhibited their ability to make further investments. Investment funds typically have a fixed term life of seven to ten years, which consists of a commitment period where managers seek new investments and a harvest period where managers exit positions. Given the illiquid nature of the investment fund's investments, it can be difficult for an investor to exit a fund before the fund's stated term. This illiquidity scared some investors away from this asset class, further eroding the ability to raise additional funds. Investment firms earn a percentage of capital deployed, which is highly geared to investment performance. Investment firms raise funds from limited partners. Limited partners typically include pension funds, insurance companies, and high net worth individuals and families. Pools of funds would typically have a limited life of seven to ten years until they were either reinvested or returned to the limited partners. Given the strong investment performance of private equity funds up until the credit crisis, money for new funds was available at increasing amounts. Investment firms that raised new funds prior to the credit crisis were positioned to continue business in normal course. However, those investment funds that aggressively deployed capital were faced with depleting capital resources, which inhibited their ability to continue to acquire businesses. Limited partners reduced allocations to private equity and hedge funds and the capital available to raise new funds dried up. Those investment firms with capital to deploy sought risk adjusted returns and often moved up the balance sheet in order to protect their capital. In an insolvency situation, the bankruptcy courts will liquidate the assets of a company in order to pay monies owed to the company's creditors. Depending on the jurisdiction, secured creditors such as banks that lend operating bank lines would be higher on the order of liquidation than unsecured lenders such as unsecured bondholders or subordinate debt holders. Equity holders would be very low on the order of liquidation and would be last to receive any monies before the other creditors were paid off in full. Typical common equity investors were now considering alternative structures such as convertible preferred shares and subordinate debt with warrants that would enable investment firms to achieve a desired level of return while offering some protection if business performance deteriorated and was forced to liquidate. The graph below illustrates the activity of private equity investors in Canada and the U.S.

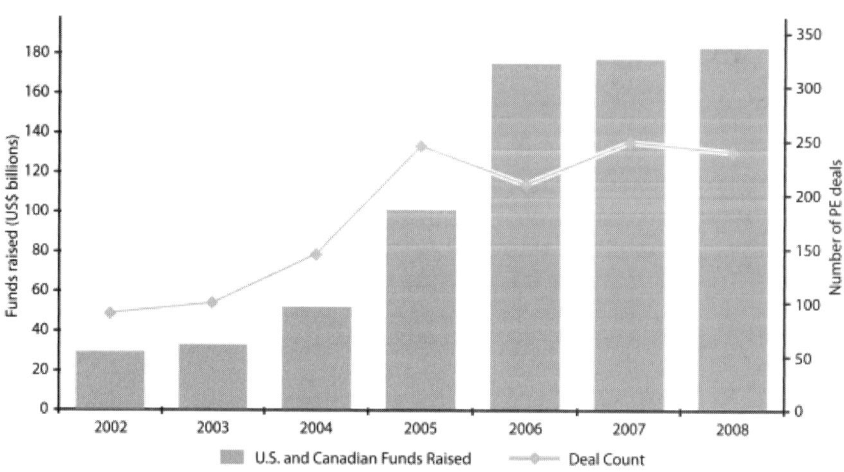

Note: Includes LBO, mezzanine, turnaround, and recapitalization focused funds; Source 2000-2004, National Venture Capital Association. 2005-2008, Thomson Financial, Buyouts

Fundraising Overview

Investment firms were increasingly active in the M&A market up to the credit crisis and would often comprise more than half of the potential buyer population during a deal process. As these buyers exited the market, so did a significant number of active buyers and capital for M&A transactions. With a reduced supply of funds available for M&A transactions, the cost of these funds increased. This, in turn, decreased valuations and caused a gap between buyer and seller valuation expectations, which increased the risk of a failed transaction.

Other Buyers

The changing economic environment did bring forward a new set of potential buyers that was seeking to be opportunistic given decreased valuations. Several small cap publicly-traded companies traded down to their cash value, particularly technology companies, and offered opportunities to purchase companies at bargain prices. Companies with excess cash were being opportunistic. Others seeking opportunities to build scale, cut costs, and gain market share were also active in an effort to become more competitive, squeeze out weaker competitors and position themselves for an economic turnaround. For example, Pfizer announced its US$66.8 billion acquisition of Wyeth on January 25, 2009 in an effort to bolster its pharmaceutical offerings and cut overhead and R&D rated costs between the two giants.

Vendors

The economic slowdown sent many vendors seeking to divest their businesses to the sidelines. Similar to buyers, many vendors, and particularly management teams, were forced to spend more attention operating businesses rather than selling them. Vendors that were looking for relatively high purchase price multiples were forced out of the market. Vendors that were currently in the market and seeking to divest a business witnessed buyers retracting due to the changing economic environment and lowered their valuations below the vendors' value expectations. Vendors often have "sticky" value expectations. Despite changes in the global economic environment, vendors maintained their value expectations during the credit crisis, in the face of deteriorating business performance and contracting multiples. Often vendors would reference multiples achieved in 2006 and 2007. With the hopes of maximizing value on exit, several vendors opted to wait for lofty times to return, even though there was no assurance as to when it would occur. Given the gap between vendors' expectations and what buyers were willing to pay in an uncertain economic environment, many deals weren't being driven to the finishing line and M&A activity stalled.

Certain deals were coming to a completion, but not on amicable terms for the vendor. Some transactions that were being completed in the market were those that were forced into a sale through bankruptcy proceedings. However, most of the sales transactions from bankruptcy often turned into liquidations as buyers were only interested in specific assets and not the entire business as a going concern. Once a business is suspected to be entering bankruptcy or has entered a bankruptcy process, customers will typically migrate to other suppliers to ensure continued supply of products and services. Once customers start switching to alternative suppliers, it is extremely difficult to win them back. One potential buyer of a business expected to enter into bankruptcy paralleled the situation to flushing a toilet and trying to get the water back. Other transactions being completed in the market included non-core asset divestitures, particularly from companies that were saddled with debt that required refinancing. An example was Canadian mining giant, Teck Cominco that used billions of dollars of debt to acquire a coal miner, Fording Coal. Teck Cominco's core mining activities include copper, coal, and zinc. Subsequently, Teck Cominco was forced to raise cash by selling non-core assets such as interests in gold mining operations including the sale of its Helmo gold operations to Barrick Gold and its sale of Kinross Gold shares.

Other deals being completed in the marketplace were from those companies that continued with their strategic, long-term plans. Driven by the trends of globalization and existing strategic plans, businesses seeking to expand into new, developing markets continued. For example, IBM's failed acquisition of Sun Microsystems paved the way for Oracle to make the acquisition and expanded its service offering into the server market in 2009.

Other Factors Affecting M&A

Another factor affecting M&A during the credit crisis was the change in the political administration in the U.S. Post-election regulatory change increased regulatory risk and put some buyers on the sidelines, particularly in healthcare and defense sectors. Concerns regarding U.S. spending on military efforts and regulatory changes to the U.S. medical system forced many potential deals to the sidelines as observers took a "wait and see" approach before making any strategic acquisitions.

The credit crisis caused dramatics swings in currencies as flows of money sought refuge from declining asset prices. Volatile currency markets made it difficult to determine the sustainability of profits for exporting businesses and also made it difficult for foreign acquirers to determine the level of profitability going forward when translated back into the acquirer's home currency. As such, cross-border M&A activity decreased during this period. The graph below illustrates the relative performance of major currencies versus the U.S. dollar.

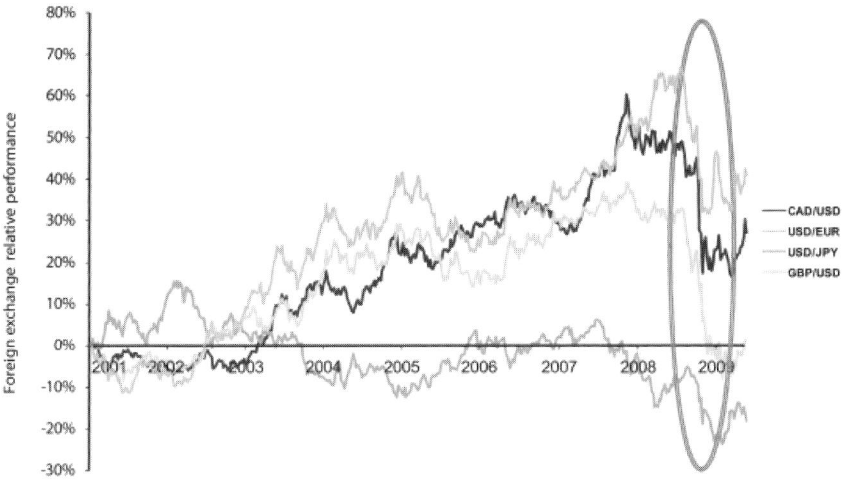

Source: Bloomberg

How Volatility Affects M&A

Deal Flow

Market volatility has a significant impact on deal flow as business owners and their advisors revisited their intent to divest. The economic downtown had a drastic impact on business operations and the market for business divestitures. Business owners seeking an optimal return on a sale transaction determined that the uncertainty in the markets and the depressed valuations was an inopportune time to divest a business. As a result, well-performing businesses that would have typically sought a market transaction during active markets were suddenly taken out of the market as shareholders opted to hold on to businesses through the downturn and then exit opportunity when the markets returned and optimal valuations could be achieved. Uncertainty in the market meant that business owners and their advisors were doubtful if acceptable valuations could be achieved and if the logical buyers, such as competitors with opportunities to drive synergies and pay relatively higher valuations, would even consider acquisitions. The economic downturn also forced management of businesses to focus on operating the business, whether it was focusing on cutting costs or being in front of customers to drive sales, management could not afford to be distracted during a sale process from the business operations. Furthermore, as several businesses encountered softening financial performance, so did the value of the business. At the onset of the credit crisis, it was generally expected that the duration of the downturn would be short. This is evidenced by the delay of the proposed BCE LBO by a consortium of Financial buyers, led by the Ontario Teachers' Pension Fund. The participants in the Bell Canada Enterprises (BCE) LBO, the largest LBO ever contemplated, mutually agreed to delay the closing of the BCE transaction from the summer of 2008 to December of 2008 when it failed to close. As the situation worsened through the fall of 2008, it prompted buyers to exit the market completely and the M&A market dynamics continued to sour. Uncertainly within M&A markets combined with challenging credit markets and poor financial performance resulted in many business owners to delay a sale transaction until market dynamics and business performance improved and deal flow dropped dramatically.

Setting Valuation Expectations

A significant decision criterion for business owners when deciding to sell a business is their value expectations. Value expectations can be critical to a successful transaction. If a business owner doesn't achieve their desired value expectations during a sale process, the owner could pull the business from the market and the transaction will fail or be delayed.

Often business owners will have some sense regarding the value of their business from benchmarks such as transactions in the public markets or from discussions with owners of similar businesses that have recently successfully sold the business. Whether accurate or inaccurate, once an owner has determined what the business is worth, it is very difficult to lower value expectations. Despite the credit crisis and a stock market crash that left public valuations down nearly 60 per cent from their recent record highs, some business owners continued to maintain the same valuation expectations prior to the economic downturn and were unable to adjust their expectations downward with the market. During discussions, business owners often quoted multiples achieved by similar businesses prior to the credit crisis and were unable to accept the fact that the world had changed drastically from 2007 to 2009. The "stickiness" of owners' value expectations caused many M&A deals to fail.

Financial advisors play a critical role in shaping the value expectations of business owners. When determining an appropriate range of value expectations, financial advisors will look to the market to determine benchmarks for value. Financial advisors can easily and quickly look to the valuations of comparable publicly traded companies and recent transactions to determine an appropriate benchmark for valuation. During stable economic times, an analysis of trailing publicly traded multiples and recent transaction multiples would provide a reasonable range of value expectations. However, the credit crisis changed the world. The lack of relevant or current multiples and uncertainly of future economic performance meant that using historical information such as publicly-traded multiples based on historic financial information and prior transactions was not applicable to the current environment and had become "stale".

Another alternative to determine valuation expectations is to analyze the public trading comparable multiples based on future expected earnings. The issue with this approach is that future analyst estimates of earnings were continuously being revised downward and their accuracy was questionable. Many public companies discontinued earnings guidance as not even management could provide accurate earnings estimates.

One possibility to determine value was the more labor intensive approach of using a discounted cash flow (DCF) model. Although the challenge again was to determine the forecast results for the business, the focus was on the long-term potential of the business. Knowing the economic downturn was severe and prolonged and an eventual economic recovery was likely to be slow, a return to normal economic conditions over a prolonged business cycle would be considered reasonable. Using a DCF model in volatile times presented many challenges. In a DCF model, projected cash flows from the business are discounted back to current value. Key inputs are forecasts of future performance and appropriate discount rate. Although risk-free interest rates were near zero, volatility and uncertainty in the markets caused equity risk premiums to rise dramatically. The volatility in the markets made it difficult to determine an appropriate risk premium to use in determining discount rates.

Valuation during volatile times becomes a critical part in a transaction. Setting value expectations for vendors and buyers is extremely difficult during uncertain economic times. For vendors, a best practice is to use a multiple of earnings as a basis for value expectations rather than an absolute number. If the business's financial performance deteriorates over the sales process, then the absolute value of the business will decline, but the multiple of earnings may remain the same. If the basis of a vendor's expectations is based on a multiple, then bids for the business would be considered reasonable irrespective of how the business performs. Advisors cannot control how a business performs but advisors can play a role in assisting in setting value expectations. Using a multiple approach, rather than an absolute number, can help to avoid disagreements in final values for the business, if financial performance has deteriorated. From the viewpoint of the shareholder, it was generally thought that the credit crisis would end and business performance would return and, if this happened, they would be selling their business at a depressed valuation.

Given the difficulties of forecasting future financial results, it is critical to provide potential purchasers with a defensible position evidencing the sales and gross margin achievable over the forecast period. It is important to provide potential purchasers with a detailed forecast of sales and gross margin by customer and/or project. Any long-term contracts or contracted backlog should be highlighted as this provides significant value in uncertain times. The length of customer relationships and trends in sales should be communicated to the buyer. Any support for continued sales and gross margin will come under considerable scrutiny during due diligence and this is a key building block for a defensible forecast and a successful transaction. Potential purchasers will be quick to discredit potential sales and gross margin in an effort to decrease the purchase price.

Negotiations

Once potential purchasers have expressed an interest in a potential acquisition opportunity, negotiations become a critical part of a successful transaction. There are several potential roadblocks that could scuttle a successful transaction. In addition, given the heightened level of potential risks for a potential purchaser, the length of time required for due diligence and negotiations increases.

Advisors will often sell a company through a structured auction process with stated deadlines for deliverables. A typical auction will include deadlines for an expression of interest and a letter of intent. All potential purchasers contacted will be asked to submit an expression of interest based on limited information provided. The advisor and the shareholders will select a number of the best potential expressions of interest considering the valuation, structure, and likelihood of closing. The shortlist of potential purchasers will be invited to meet management and perform due diligence in advance of submitting a letter of intent. Despite a structured process with stated deadlines, several potential purchasers will request extensions to deadlines or submit offers late. This is a result of the lack of urgency from potential buyers to acquire businesses during uncertain times and the ordinary businesses distractions for the management team.

Given the uncertain markets, potential purchasers know that it is a buyers' market as many potential purchasers are out of the market while management teams focus their efforts internally. Management teams also had a preference to reserve cash and "keep powder dry" during the economic downturn. As such, those companies considering acquisitions attempted to take advantage of the situation. Potential purchasers will often submit an expression of interest with a wide range with no intention of paying at the top end of the range. The purpose of this tactic is to ensure that they will be invited to the next phase of the auction, while limiting the acceptance of other credible potential purchasers with lower bids. These strategic bidders intend to then "grind-down" the valuation during due diligence and the valuation offered at the letter of intent will be materially lower than the valuation presented in their expression of interest. Advisors should consider allowing an increased number of parties invited to proceed to management meetings and due diligence in order to maintain healthy competition during negotiations in order to maximize valuation. Deal competition will also create some tension among potential purchasers to comply with stated deadlines and drive a deal to a close as most potential purchasers will lack urgency to close the deal.

Those companies and investment firms that were actively seeking M&A opportunities in the market used a very conservative and risk adverse approach. Potential purchasers will often increase the amount of due diligence performed during a transaction process due to the economic uncertainly. In particular, potential purchasers will be most concerned with the revenues and gross margins from the target's customers. Potential purchasers will seek opportunities that offer stability and some reasonable certainty of continued business performance during an economic downturn. Potential purchasers will look for long-term customers with long-term contracts or a stable history of sales. Potential purchasers will also be concerned with the stability of pricing and gross margins. The typical sale process may be lengthened by 50 per cent or more as buyers spend a considerable amount of time performing due diligence and stalling the transaction process in order to determine how actual business performance would be affected during the economic slowdown. Advisors should consider a realistic timeline for an auction process, knowing that potential purchasers will be distracted from the noise from the volatile economy and will require additional time for due diligence.

Indications or signals of sincere M&A interest from potential purchasers and sellers will become even more evident during volatile times. The willingness of potential purchasers and sellers to pay transaction related costs such as financial or legal advisors are strong indications of sincere interest. Given the level of economic uncertainty, potential purchasers and sellers are naturally more inclined to delay potential transaction costs as far as possible to ensure there is a high amount of certainty that a deal will occur. Resistance from sellers to pay work fees for financial advisors or legal fees is an indication that the seller may not be serious about selling. Indications of serious interest from potential purchasers could include the hiring of financial advisors to assist them during the transaction process (thus incurring legal costs), detailed questions during due diligence and the ability of the potential purchaser to meet the specified deadlines.

Financing

Up until the financial crisis, financing was readily available with low costs, loose covenants, and high leverage. The liquidity available to fund transaction was tremendous. The graph below illustrates the amount of global syndicated debt, which was a significant source of financing as financial institutions bundled debt and sold it off to the investing public through various structured products.

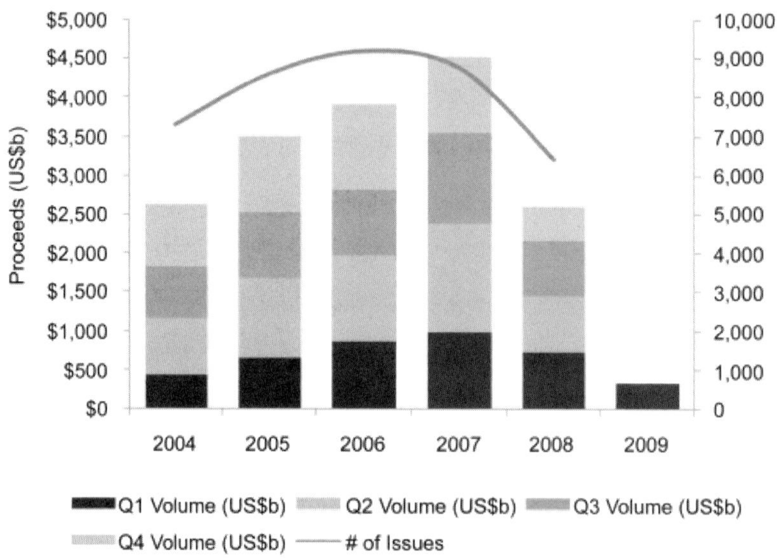

Source: Thomson Financial

During uncertain economic times, the availability of financing decreases as lending institutions become more risk adverse. In particular, higher risk lending for leveraged buyouts or acquisition lending in general becomes very difficult to obtain. Lenders will seek secure lending situations where business performance is stable or growing and there are assets available to cover loans. Lending based on a company's cash flows is very difficult to obtain. The availability of financing adds another element of uncertainty to a successful transaction. When evaluating offers for a potential target, the likelihood of financing should be a critical evaluation criterion. An offer that is contingent on financing should be viewed as very inferior to an offer that isn't contingent on financing. Often, vendors will accept a somewhat lower priced offer that is not contingent on financing. This puts financial or private equity buyers that require financing in order to complete transactions at a significant disadvantage compared to strategic buyers that are able to pay cash for transactions. In addition, the lack of financing or low leverage financing requires financial buyers to increase the amount of equity investment they would otherwise need to complete a transaction. This decreases the financial buyer's internal rate of return and will thereby affect the potential price to be offered. During the period leading up to the financial crisis when debt financing was readily available, financial buyers made up an increasing percentage of successful purchase transactions. During the financial crisis, strategic buyers made up an increasing percentage of the successful purchase transactions thus illustrating that "cash is king".

Although the overnight interest rate and other interest rates set by central banks decreased drastically during the credit crisis, interest rates available for corporate lending actually increased due to the increase in corporate spreads over government issued debt due to the economic uncertainty. As the economic uncertainty increased, so did the interest rate spread on corporate debt. In addition to interest rates, fees also increased.

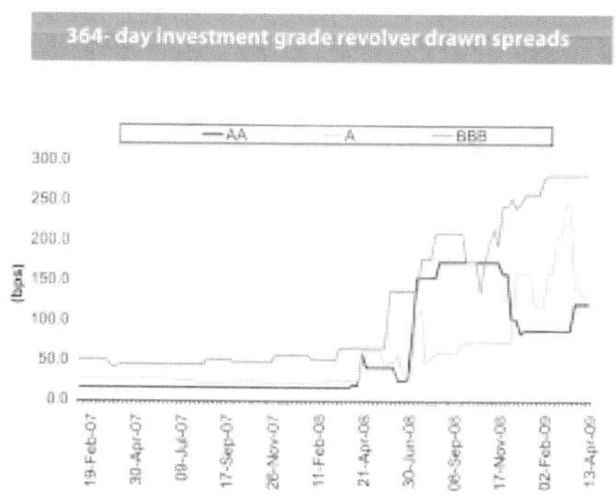

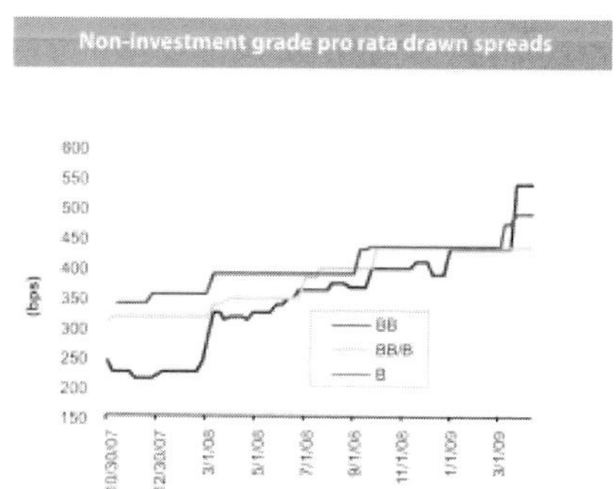

Source: Thomson Financial

Moreover, the general availability of debt was scarce during the credit crisis. Companies with good credit ratings were able to access credit markets, but at higher interest rates while those with poor credit ratings had few options. For example in April of 2009, Discovery Air, a distressed Canadian aviation company, replaced its secured operating line at an interest rate of 18 per cent with an unconventional lender. Meanwhile, a Government of Canada two-year bond yielded approximately 1.25 per cent. The credit crisis forced many lending institutions to not only restrict their new lending activities, but also to call-in existing loans, causing significant re-financing pains for several companies. Public outcry from restricted lending practices caused government lending agencies to help fill the gap left by traditional lenders. The Business Development Bank of Canada became very active in the lending environment, backed by additional government support. In certain circumstances, the government became the lender of last resort in the cases of General Motors Corporate and Chrysler Motors LLC.

Lending institutions drastically changed lending terms following the credit crisis. Not only did interest rates rise, but also the terms of the debt became more stringent which included stricter covenants and shortened amortization of loans. Prior to the economic crisis, amortization of senior debt was as high as 10 years and sometimes interest could be payment in kind (PIK), meaning that the interest could accumulate in arrears, thereby allowing a business's debt capacity to greatly increase. Conversely, during the credit crisis, high interest rates and shortened amortization (typically three years for senior debt) drastically lowered the amount of debt capacity that a business could carry. This subsequently caused several businesses to restructure its debt if it required refinancing during the credit crisis as the business was unable to sustain debt leverage used prior to the credit crisis while using the current terms available during the credit crisis. Increased interest and principle payments forced businesses to de-lever. As a result of the decreased financial leverage, the amount of debt an acquirer could obtain to finance a transaction greatly decreased. In order for investors and potential acquirers to obtain their desired rates of return, the purchase price paid would need to be lowered.

The active lenders remaining in the market approached new opportunities with significant risk. Not only was this risk reflected in the pricing of new loans, but the hold amount by a lending institution was significantly reduced. With the reluctance to hold loans or have the risk of syndicating the loans to other lenders, club deals became very prevalent for larger transactions. In a club deal, several lenders or investors pool their capital collectively to effect the transaction. Involvement of several lending instructions early in a process facilitates a smoother and more efficient transaction process.

Given the risk adverse nature of the investing environment during the credit crisis, private equity buyout firms who would typically provide buy-out equity for a transaction sometimes moved up the balance sheet to provide convertible preferred shares or subordinate debt. With the cost of money increasing and the uncertain economic environment, private equity investors were creatively seeking opportunities to earn their required IRRs while adjusting for risk. As such, several private equity investors were seeking opportunities to invest with cash yields of 12 to 18 per cent with an opportunity to sweeten returns with warrants. Private equity played a role in providing unsecured financing during the credit crisis.

Deal Structuring

Given all of the issues present in the M&A markets during volatile times, deal structuring becomes another critical piece in a successful transaction. One of the most significant deal challenges in economic downturns is valuation. Often there is a valuation gap between what bidders are willing to pay for a business and what the vendor is willing to accept. One structuring alternative available to bridge the gap in a privant transaction is an earn-out structure. An earn-out makes a portion of the purchase price contingent upon the future earnings of the target. Earn-outs typically have a period of two to five years and are usually based on a mix of sales, gross margin, and EBITDA targets. If the vendor is very confident of future financial performance, then an earn-out structure can be useful in bridging the valuation gap.

Although earn-outs seem to be a useful tool in bridging the valuation gap, they represent many challenges in negotiating, implementing, and monitoring. One significant issue with an earn-out structure is lack of control. Following the sale of the business, the vendor will typically have limited or no control over the business. This makes the vendor very nervous as changes to the business under the new ownership could significantly impact the likelihood of achieving the earn-out targets. Additionally, the monitoring and tracking of the business post-transaction is very difficult, particularly if the acquirer is merging the business and its operations into its current business. Given these difficulties, the use of earn-outs in practice are not overly common. Earn-outs have been frequently used in distressed situations where bidders see potential synergies or a turnaround, but require risk sharing with the vendor. During the credit crisis, acquisitions with a sizeable portion of the purchase structured in an earn-out could be found in distressed retailing and travel-related businesses with reputable brands. Given that the businesses were distressed, the vendors were highly motivated to complete a transaction or possibly face bankruptcy. Given that the businesses were challenged, an earn-out structure allowed some possible upside for the vendor while the buyer shared the downside risk with the vendor. In certain situations, an earn-out structure can be a key element in bringing a transaction to a successful close.

The lack of availability of acquisition financing can also be overcome through an appropriate deal structure. Vendor take back financing is one alternative whereby the vendor in effect, finances the transaction by opting for deferred compensation. The difference between a vendor take back note and an earn-out is that an earn-out is contingent whereas a vendor take back note is generally a guaranteed payment. A vendor take back note will also typically include a negotiated rate of interest. Lenders will treat the vendor take back note as very patient capital or even equity capital if payment is due several years out.

Given the lack of confidence in the ability of potential purchasers to close transactions, vendors increasingly sought break-up fee arrangements or requested a deposit as evidence that the potential buyer was serious and confident that it could close the deal. Although these arrangements were increasingly sought after during uncertain times, it was very difficult for potential buyers to agree to such conditions given the lack of vendor negotiating power.

Conclusion

Uncertainty and volatility in the marketplace presents several challenges to mergers and acquisitions. From forecasting financial performance to valuations to financing a deal – all of the fundamental pieces to a successful transaction become very difficult to align simultaneously. Prudence, preparedness, and foresight will afford the deal with greatest probability of a successful close. Human nature causes paralysis during uncertain times. However, the business leaders with long-term, strategic views can take advantage of opportunities presented during economic downturns and enhance the business positioning for an economic recovery.

Investment Strategies and Risk

Denis Kouroussis & Les Trojniak

The financial markets generally are unpredictable. So that one has to have different scenarios. The idea that you can actually predict what's going to happen contradicts my way of looking at the market.

– George Soros

In light of the recent economic turmoil, it is clear that something in the realm of investing and finance is amiss. The focus of this chapter is to provide a simple strategy that illustrates how an investment may be structured in order to minimize losses and maximize potential profits. The discussion is based on portfolio structuring, protection, and value at risk. Before we examine portfolio theory and asset allocation strategies, a quick overview will be cast in regards to the origins of money, fundamental investment vehicles, and various funds. All discussions on investment strategies do not include tax consequences and as such would require slight adjustments if implemented.

Introduction

A question that many people have difficulty answering is "What is money, and where does it come from?" An investor with a faint idea of how to answer this will yield insight into a successful, long-term portfolio. "What is money?" Well, the short answer is that money is an instrument of trade, a note that implies the holder is owed a certain amount of goods and services. In the past, people used to barter and trade with services, goods, and precious metals. Society progressed and gold became the instrument of choice due to its scarcity. Money, as we know it today, was developed as a derivative of the gold trading standard. The economy grew and as people accumulated more gold from their savings they began to entrust the local blacksmith with their gold, in exchange for a note. Each note was a promise from the blacksmith that the gold could be redeemed immediately. With the passing of time, it became common practice for individuals and businesses to exchange these notes for goods and services and thus the gold was rarely ever redeemed. Having noticed this, blacksmiths began to "print" more notes than what they had in reserves and this formed the basis of the modern banking system known as fractional reserve banking. These excess notes would in essence be lent out to individuals and businesses with compensation in the form of interest paid to the lender. Although this explanation is very abbreviated it does set the fundamental notions necessary in understanding credit and money supply and their effects on the economy. Today, money is the fundamental tool of the economy. Its speed of circulation and abundance are crucial to economic development. An overly simplified statement: the more money in circulation, *i.e.*, lower interest rates, the more stimulation the economy will have and, as interest rates increase, less money in circulation will yield a contracting economy. Of course there is a time delay associated with interest rate changes. These are the basic concepts for growth of any economy. In essence, the economic growth rate is controlled by one number and that is the interest rate!

The banking system has evolved to a high level of sophistication but the underlying goal is extremely simple: to lend money to businesses and individuals for use in a constructive manner that will produce further profits and thus the ability to pay interest on the money borrowed.

Note on Regulation

A topic of much debate is the regulation of banks and investment houses. For the most part, the banking and investment industry is self-regulating. This means that the banks and investment shops have set up independent organizations to ensure that all banks and brokerages adhere to good practices. Though this seemingly had worked in the past, with the recent events including the $50 billion Madoff scandal, failure of investment banks such as Lehman, and the possible nationalization of Bank of America and Citigroup, perhaps one can conclude that these self-regulating bodies need substantial restructuring and government intervention.

Investment Choices

For this discussion there are two types of *fundamental* investment vehicles in existence: fixed income securities and equities. Fixed income securities such as bonds and treasuries are investment loans made by an investor to a company or government. In this case, the investor becomes a creditor to the issuing entity and expects the return of capital with some predetermined interest to be paid as a reward for lending the money in the first place. Equities or shares issued by corporations to an investor represent partial ownership sold off to raise capital. The corporation may use this capital to fund day-to-day operations or expand business activities. As a partial owner of the corporation, the investor expects share appreciation or dividend payments as reward for investing in the company. On a newer front, derivatives have come into existence with the underlying notion to be used as hedging instruments for the protection of investment vehicles. Recently, however, we have seen an increasing number of hedge funds and investment banks use derivatives to generate income and substantial profits, all of which has in fact contributed to the financial crisis (*i.e.*, credit default swaps).

Today, investors have two very basic choices when allocating their capital. The investor who is more sophisticated and understands markets and financial products may decide to structure a portfolio of pure equities and fixed income. The investor who is less sophisticated and may have less capital may opt to participate in investing in a fund or pool. A fund is an abstracted investment vehicle by which a portfolio manager is paid a fee to structure the holdings of equities and fixed income according to the funds growth and risk profile. Typically, investors with portfolios of less than $500k use funds and investors with larger portfolios buy pure equities and fixed income. Of course, the threshold of portfolio value changes with investor sophistication and knowledge.

Funds

There are three general types of funds in existence today: mutual funds and segregated funds, which are highly regulated and available to most investors, tend to be simpler to understand due to the regulatory constraints placed on their investing and hedging positions. Hedge funds, though regulated, are not constrained in terms of the investments they hold and the derivatives that they can participate in. The simplified definition of a Canadian accredited investor, who is eligible to buy a hedge fund, is one who either has a net worth of $1M or has an annual salary in excess of $250,000.

Mutual Funds

Low cost professional money management, diversification, and choice are the main advantages of mutual funds. An investor with a small amount to invest, looking to diversify and structure a viable portfolio on their own will pay a substantial amount in brokerage fees that will surpass the fees associated with a mutual fund. Mutual fund fees, or the Management Expense Ratios (MERs) vary anywhere from less than 1% to 3%+ for specialty funds.

Mutual fund portfolio managers operate under specific guidelines that are imposed by the provincial securities commission, and in the fund's own charter and prospectus. Some restrictions include not being able to purchase more than 10 per cent of the total securities of an individual issuer, no leverage purposes, and no margin for buying or short selling. Subject to regulatory controls, fund managers are allowed to incorporate specific permitted derivatives as long as the maximum amount invested is not more than 10 per cent of the fund's assets.

There is a tremendous amount of selection for mutual fund investors. Mutual funds are distinguished by their basic investment policy or by the kind of investments that they hold. Canadian mutual funds are classified into 34 different categories within four broad groups:[1]

1. cash and equivalent funds;
2. fixed-income funds;
3. balances funds;
4. equity funds.

Within these categories the holdings are determined by the asset allocation models and investment styles of the portfolio manager.

Segregated Funds

Though similar in structure to mutual funds, segregated funds are offered only by life insurance companies and have unique features such as maturity protection, death benefits, and creditor protection. Unlike mutual funds, however, segregated funds are regulated by the provincial insurance regulators because they are insurance contracts and thus the contract holders do not own the fund's underlying assets. Due to the insurance benefits they offer, segregated funds are most often than not more expensive than their cousin counterpart mutual funds, hence end up with higher MERs.

Hedge Funds

A relatively new investment vehicle in the Canadian market, hedge funds have been growing in popularity since 2001. Even though several high profile funds have failed since their inceptions, hedge fund assets under management continue to grow rapidly.

The portfolio managers of hedge funds have great flexibility in their investment strategies, often referred to as alternative investment strategies. As

[1] Canadian Securities Course, 2007.

hedge funds are very lightly regulated, their managers are not constrained by rules that apply to mutual funds. Portfolio managers of hedge funds can take short positions, leverage assets, use derivatives without restriction for speculation, and invest in private equity, real estate, and commodities. This tremendous flexibility and the types of strategies that can be employed, lend to the fact that the manager's skill is the most advantageous and detrimental factor in the fund's performance.

Similar to any hedge fund, a sophisticated investor can structure a portfolio to be just as efficient and, at the same time, to minimize risk. The advantage that some hedge funds may offer, which would be very difficult for an individual investor to implement, is a quantitative trading strategy. Quantitative hedge funds use technology to find time-sensitive arbitrage opportunities and use back-tested algorithmic techniques for high frequency trading. Quantitative trading models work very well in minimizing downside risk and returning consistent performance. However, any investor looking to invest in a quantitative trading hedge fund should be wary of the fund's size. Historically, it has been shown that quantitative trading models work only for a certain level of assets. When using the quantitative model, if the trades begin to become too large, this will influence the price of the traded instrument negatively and lead to model failure.[2]

Introduction to Options

A derivative is defined as a financial instrument whose value depends on or is derived from the values of other more basic underlying variables. One type of derivative - a put option - is used to hedge against loss. There are two types of options. A call option gives the holder the right to buy the underlying equity by a certain date at a specified price. A put option gives the holder the right to sell the underlying equity by a certain date for a specified price. Options are, in essence, contracts. The price in the contract is known as the strike price or exercise price and the date in the contract is the expiration date. Most options traded on exchanges are "American style" options meaning that they can be exercised at any time up to the expiration date.

Table 31.1: An example of the prices on options on Feb 26, 2009 for IBM stock trading at $89.37 is shown (from Chicago Board Options Exchange, www.cboe.com)

---

2 E.P. Chan, *Quantitative Trading* (Hoboken, N.J.: John Wiley & Sons, 2009).

	Calls			Puts		
Strike Price	Apr.	Jul.	Jan.	Apr.	Jul.	Jan.
$	2009	2009	2010	2009	2009	2010
75.00	16.20	13.80	19.40	1.25	4.07	8.90
80.00	11.03	14.42	18.10	2.05	5.53	10.90
85.00	7.90	10.90	15.45	3.40	7.50	11.90
90.00	4.80	8.50	12.80	5.30	9.40	14.00
95.00	2.60	6.03	10.15	8.50	12.50	14.50
100.00	1.23	4.20	8.20	11.80	17.00	20.40

Table 31.1 gives the last transaction price for the American options trading on IBM taken during intraday trading on February 26, 2009 while the price of the stock was $89.37. The option strike prices are $75, $80, $85, $90, $95, and $100. The maturities are April 2009, July 2009, and January 2010. Options expire on the third Friday of their maturity month. Thus, the expiry dates are April 17, 2009, July 17, 2009, and January 15, 2010. The price quotes for call and put options are expressed on a per share basis. All exchanges trade option contracts in lots of 100.

From Table 31.1 we see that the price of a call option decreases as the strike price increases. Conversely, the price of the put increases as the strike price increases. Both calls and puts become more valuable as the time to maturity increases.

If an investor is interested in purchasing a $90 July 09 Call, the cost would be $8.50. As the expiration is approximately four months away, an investor doing this is speculating that the price at some point before expiration would be more than $98.50 and the investor can then exercise the option for a possible gain. What this means exactly is that if IBM stock is trading at $104 on or before July 17, 2009, the option holder would exercise the option, buying shares at $90, and then selling them immediately on the open market for a gain. The gain would be $104 - $90 - $8.50 = $5.50 per contract. That translates into 5.5 per cent gain. However, what usually happens is that the option itself is sold for a premium, perhaps a minimum price of $14 depending on the expiration date. The gain is again $14 - $8.50 = $5.50 but the calculated return based on the initial $8.50 is 64 per cent! This is one of the reasons why so many hedge funds speculate with options.

If an investor is bearish and believes that IBM stock will fall, the investor could buy an $85 July 09 Put for $5.53. In this case, the investor is speculating that within the expiration date the price of IBM stock will fall, and the put option will become more valuable. If the price of IBM stock falls to $75, the minimum value of the put will be $10 and the investor will profit $10 - $5.53 = $4.47 or an 80.1 per cent gain.

It is important to note that an investor does not have to exercise a purchased option. The option may just be left to expire worthless. The maximum amount that an option purchaser may lose is the amount paid for the contract. Therefore, the maximum loss on the call contract is $850 in this example. However, the maximum gain is unlimited with the unlimited gain of the share price. Figure 31.1 illustrates this with share price.

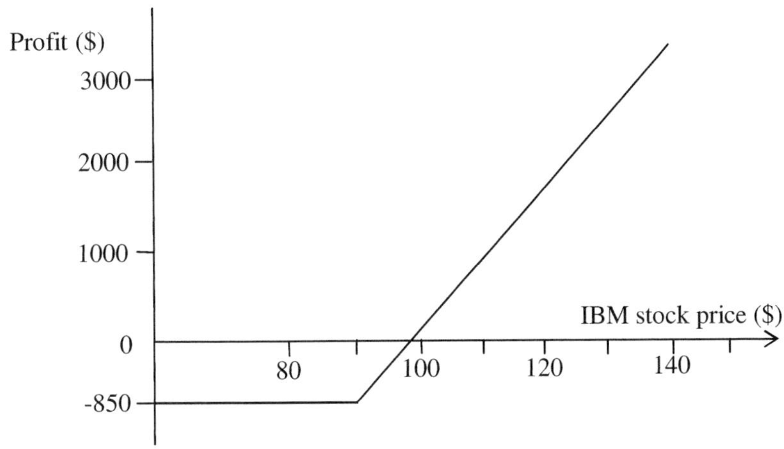

Figure 31.1: Net profit for purchasing 100 IBM $90 July 09 calls

An investor looking at the options markets may participate by being a:

1. buyer of calls;
2. seller/writer of calls;
3. buyer of puts;
4. seller/writer of puts.

Buyers are referred to as having long positions, while selling an option is also known as writing the option.

There are many strategies to using options. Their primary use is to hedge against losses and generate income on long positions. If an investor wishes to buy 1,000 shares of IBM at the current price of $89.37 this will cost $89,370. One way to minimize losses is to use a stop loss. The investor can set a stop loss for $80/share, meaning the position will be liquidated and sold when the stock price falls to $80. This will yield a loss of approximately $9,370, protecting from further downside. If the price of IBM continues to decline, then this protection mechanism performs well with the exception of some extreme circumstances. On the other hand, if the price of IBM dropped to $79 on one day alone and recovered to $84 within the same trading day, the stop loss mechanism liquidated the position and now the investor needs to repurchase higher. The other protection that a long investor can use is a put option. At this point, the investor would purchase 1,000 IBM $85 Jan 2010 put options for an additional cost of $11,900. The price of the stock can fluctuate and the maximum loss that the investor will see is $4,370 (on the stock purchase) plus the option cost of $11,900 for a total of approximately $16,720. There is a premium associated with this protection, however when compared to the frequency of getting stopped out using stop losses in a volatile market it would prove to be much more cost-efficient. Here, the investor has unlimited upside potential with limited downside up to the expiration date. Put strategies similar to this in the period of 2007-2008 have been shown to be very cost effective indeed and incredibly rewarding.

Micro-Speculation for Profit

The use of options has now opened the door for us in unlimited ways to structure portfolios. Assume that in a time of complete volatility we would like 100 per cent protection without the potential of losing the upside too much. What do we do? Well, on a $1M portfolio, assume a cash position, we can enter into the money markets and expect a return of 2 per cent. That will mean that in a year's time if we place $980,392 in the money markets we will have $1M back (not including tax consequences.) This can be done also with fixed income instruments including GICs, T-bills, and government bonds, depending on rates. An investor can then take $19,607 at the start of the year and purchase IBM call options as pure speculation. 1,400 IBM $95 Jan 2010 call options would cost $17,920. If the market continues to decline, and IBM along with it, the options expire worthless and the portfolio at the end of the year is back to the original $1M. However, say there is a market direction shift and markets roar with IBM approaching old highs of $130. The call option is worth a minimum of $56,000 and now the total return for the year to the portfolio is 5.6 per cent. This is a good reward return considering ZERO downside risk and plenty of opportunity. This small example clearly illustrates the power of using options within a portfolio to minimize the downside while maximizing the upside.

Further use of a strategy such as this would be to incorporate small cap stocks whose options are not priced too aggressively. The usage of small cap options may yield substantially higher returns with this ZERO risk downside, as small cap options move in larger proportions.

Conversely, if an investor is absolutely convinced that the market will continue on its downward spiral, the investor may speculate in purchasing put options. Let's assume that the investor in the previous example is absolutely convinced that continued doom and gloom will persist. The investor buys 2,100 IBM January 2010 put options for a total cost of $18,690 instead of a call option. If markets fall apart and IBM faces a similar fortune as Citigroup today, perhaps $2 per share stock price, then the option is worth $153,300. What a great return in a catastrophic marketplace!

Value at Risk

Institutional investors such as pension funds have access to groups of professionals that calculate the value at risk for their portfolios on a daily basis. Though such thorough risk analytic measures are not available to the individual investor, it is important to have a minimal understanding of risk measure. The example in the preceding section of micro-speculation with options is an example of a risk calculated portfolio tactical asset allocation strategy that minimizes downside to zero (in a year time) while having an upside possible potential of returning approximately 5.6 per cent.

Value at Risk calculations attempt to summarize as a single number the total risk in a portfolio of financial assets. Risk analysts are interested in making a statement such as:

> "I am X per cent certain there will not be a loss of more than 'Z' dollars in the next 'N' amount days."

The variable V is the Value at Risk (VaR) of the portfolio. V is dependent on two parameters: the time horizon (N days) and the confidence level (X %). Banks are required to calculate market risk for N=10 days and X=99% confidence level.[3]

There are two methods to calculate VaR, namely historical simulation and model building. Historical simulation involves using past data to determine what will happen in the future. This involves identifying all the market variables affecting the portfolio such as exchange rates, equity prices, interest rates, *etc.* and identifying how these variables have affected the portfolio over the last N days. This provides N possible scenarios of what may happen

---

[3] J.C. Hull, *Options, Futures and other Derivatives*, 7th ed. (Upper Saddle River, N.J.: Prentice Hall, 2008).

between today and tomorrow. The model building approach for volatility of a security or equity is considered on a per day basis by calculating the standard deviation for each, and then these standard deviations are correlated to one another to produce the VaR of the portfolio. VaR calculations are only as good as the data that is used to calculate them. Events that are outside the bounds of the data, for example 911 terrorist attacks, called "Black Swan" events, cannot be incorporated. So without going into further mathematical detail what does this mean for a retail investor?

Performing historical simulation and model building is a large undertaking for a retail investor; however, with the use of options, a VaR metric is not necessary as the downside may be limited to an absolute value for a specified time up to the option expiration date.

Portfolio Management

The tried and true investment principle of buy value and hold for the long term is one that does stand the test of time. However, being active within a portfolio, an investor can substantially protect gains and protect from short- and long-term losses if appropriate investment strategies are incorporated. Market timing and investment philosophy go hand in hand, and though market timing cannot be executed flawlessly there is a certain amount of value in appropriately and with due cause trying to somewhat "time the market" either for economic and/or technical reasoning. Market timing has different meanings depending on whether an investor is looking for a short-term or long-term horizon. Estimating the precise time associated with buying and selling particular securities is a form of short-term market timing and, if done in minutes and hours, is referred to as day trading. In the longer term, measured in quarters or years, market timing refers more to tactical asset allocation, which will be the focus of this discussion.

There are several steps in the investment management process including security selection, asset mix strategy, and portfolio management. We will work on the assumption that an investor has understanding of security selection using fundamental analysis.

Rule #1. It does not matter how good your investment is, if the market is sinking, your investment will, in all probability, follow!

The state of the market today and the effects of globalization have shown us how intertwined all investments throughout the world have become. The only way that a sophisticated investor can survive, minimize loses, and maximize returns is by having a general sense of market direction and preparedness. Awareness and decisiveness in the market place is crucial to becoming a successful investor, and tactical asset allocation is just the tool for this.

According to Investopedia, from the world wide web, the definition of Tactical Asset Allocation is:

> An active management portfolio strategy that rebalances the percentage of assets held in various categories in order to take advantage of market pricing anomalies or strong market sectors.

Amongst the numerous asset allocation techniques, tactical asset allocation is the one whereby the investor manages and chooses a rebalancing of their fixed income and equities according to market conditions and decisions.

Tactical Asset Allocation

In structuring a portfolio there are two very important decisions for an investor to make:

1. decision on market direction in one year's time;
2. acceptable risk reward metric.

The portfolio should be re-evaluated at minimum every six months and rebalancing of assets should take place if necessary.

Market Direction

A bull market is one where the economy is growing, money supply is plentiful, and speed of money circulation is high. This translates into an ascending market trend where equity values increase at a much higher rate than what fixed income products return. Savvy investors increase the asset allocation of their portfolios to much heavier weightings on the equity side in a bull market. In the bull market run of 2003-2007, "conservative" portfolios were considered to have 65 per cent fixed income and 35 per cent equities.

In bear markets, the growth rate of the economy begins to contract, as a consequence of shrinking money supply and reduced speed of circulation. This translates into a descent of the markets where equity values begin to have negative returns as investors sell equities and begin to flee to fixed income products for safety. In severe bear markets such as the one experienced in 2008/2009, some savvy investors have reverted to 90 per cent fixed income asset allocation.

Bull and bear markets occur in cycles. The long-term horizon in decades of the market has always been a bull and this will always prevail as long as there is population growth and economic activity. On shorter time frames however, bull and bear markets exist as a consequence of activity regulation to divert to a mean of economic growth. Historically, bull runs last for approximately five to seven years and bear markets follow, lasting between one and two years.

For an investor to make sound decisions about market direction it is important to have a clear mind and be able to filter the abundance of information that is available from the media and other sources. Further, having knowledgeable counsel that is in tune with the investor's goals and the market is also essential and of tremendous benefit.

Risk Reward Metric

What many investors fail to do is provide a risk reward metric for themselves. What is an acceptable loss (or VaR) for a potential reward? If a loss of 10 per cent is acceptable what should the potential reward be for such a loss? Many traders use a ratio of 2:1, meaning 2 times reward for every unit risk. Thus, a 10 per cent downside risk should provide potential for 20 per cent return. This is a very broad rule of thumb in the industry and the ratio can change depending on the strategy used. In the options example that we used, a 10 per cent downside could translate to $100,000 for IBM call options being purchased while the remainder of the funds stay in cash. This would allow the investor to purchase 9,800 IBM $95 January 2010 calls costing $99,470. If IBM stock returns to old highs of $130, the option would be worth $343,000. This translates to an overall portfolio return of about 24 per cent. This would provide an absolute risk reward investment minimizing downside to 10 per cent while expecting an opportunistic upside return of 24 per cent with further unlimited upside. This surpasses any type of stop-loss usage strategy which may be used on equities because the position is not affected by intraday fluctuations.

Investing on Opportunity

Just because the share prices of a company stock are down substantially does not mean that they cannot fall further. Many investors in bear markets get caught in "value traps" – companies that seem to be of exceptional value at an extremely discounted price, that continue to decline. In a bear market, "averaging down" is a good idea, but unsophisticated, and works on a long-term principal that should realistically be set out for decades. If an investor is genuinely interested in managing their portfolio when they buy value companies within a bear market, they should look to protect their holdings by paying the small premium associated with buying a put option. This small premium will prevent deep losses which can occur from continued market downward spiraling, and from Black Swan events. You would not drive a car without insurance, why should portfolios be driven differently?

Diversification Myth

Diversification is touted by many as the process of choice to minimize losses within a portfolio. Diversification only eliminates non-systematic risk. It leaves exposure to systematic risk which is the risk associated with inflation, the business cycle, and interest rates. It has been shown that for a fully "diversified" portfolio, only 20 equally-weighted stocks are required. Additional holdings do nothing to further reduce non-systematic risk and the portfolio begins to mirror indices. With the use of options for capital protection and absolute risk reward metrics, diversification becomes less urgent. In fact, it is much easier to manage a portfolio with a select few stocks that are protected since the investor can focus more time on due diligence for each.

Structuring the Portfolio

Once an investor has decided on market direction and a risk reward metric, the portfolio can be structured. If the decision on market direction is incorrect, the risk reward metric will keep losses to a minimum. In a volatile environment, fixed income securities should be kept to maturity assuming good credit on the issuers' behalf in order to avoid loss. *Short-term*, fixed income products should be used when interest rates are low. As interest rates rise, longer term to maturity bonds and T-bills may be considered as part of the Tactical Asset Allocation. In choosing equities, investors should consider companies with business activities that they understand. This makes the due diligence process easier and adds the possibility of the reward.

In a recession/depression or the current economic credit crisis, an investor may choose one of three possible market directions.

1. The recession is at its worst and markets will begin to recover very shortly.

   Based on the risk reward metric an investor should choose to buy equities long and protect with put options, or simply buy long-term call options/leaps with the risk amount, or participate with other strategies such as bull call spreads, *etc.*

2. The recession will continue or get worse and markets will decline.

   Based on the risk reward metric an investor should participate in buying put options on current holdings or look to implement a bear call spread with the risk amount. A bear call spread generates instant income while the risk amount should translate into the spread being covered in order to minimize losses to the risk metric.

3. The recession has hit bottom, it will be prolonged and markets will stay flat.

   Here an investor should be mostly invested in fixed income. In the current market conditions, there are many fixed income securities which have high yields. As a result of the lack of liquidity in the market place, many bonds are trading at highly discounted prices. When purchasing such bonds, it is imperative to ensure that the balance sheets of the issuers are in good standing and that they have sufficient funds at maturity of the bond to pay the debt holders.

Conclusion

There are many investment vehicles that an investor may use in order to profit. In the current turbulent times, the most important factor in attempting to profit is the ability to quantify risk and seek maximum reward for this risk. Structuring portfolios with this in mind, an investor can quantify what to expect in the worst of times. The use of options as a hedging tool against losses and even as a "micro-speculation" investment can protect and yield returns for most portfolios. Although the discussions did not include tax consequences or associated commissions, any such strategies would need to be modified slightly. When implementing any such strategy, it is important to understand all the consequences, including the time sensitivity associated with the plan, and to adhere to the investment plan as designed. Last, but not least, there are many other indicators which are far removed from this discussion such as the BDI which can help build an argument for a particular short- or long-term strategy.

Guarantees in Uncertain Times

Ronald Rodgers & John Kimpton

If stupidity got us into this mess, then why can't it get us out?

– Will Rogers

Introduction

At the time of writing this chapter, North America has just concluded one of the most challenging and devastating years that any financial advisor has ever witnessed. Without a doubt, 2008 could be described as *the annus horribilis.*

Here are some excerpts and comments from the BMO Nesbitt Burns Portfolio & Research Team Equity Market Recap Q4 2008:

- It is difficult to describe how extraordinary – and extraordinarily difficult – 2008 was for investors. In order to place 2008 in perspective, we will share some general domestic and global market statistics that will enlighten, and probably amaze, our readers just as they amazed us.
- In the fourth quarter 2008, in the wake of the failure of Lehman Brothers and the rescue of American International Group by the Federal Reserve, the equity bear market gained momentum and all equity indices sold off sharply.
- In Canada, the S&P/TSX Composite Index fell 23.5 per cent on a price basis, and 22.7 per cent on a total return basis (including dividends) in the quarter.
- In the U.S., the S&P 500 Index lost 22.6 per cent on a price basis and 22 per cent on a total return basis in the quarter. In Canadian dollar terms, the S&P 500 Index fell 10.7 per cent on a total return basis due to severe weakness in the Canadian dollar.

- Global equity markets as represented by the Morgan Stanley Capital International World Index fell 21.6 per cent in local currency terms on a total return basis. However, as was the case for U.S. equities, the loss was considerably more muted once translated into Canadian dollar terms – at -10.3 per cent.
- In Canada, the S&P/TSX Composite Index ended the year 35 per cent lower on a total return basis than at the end of 2007, and 40 per cent below its high made in June of 2008. For the full year, only about one in ten stocks in the Composite ended the year higher.
- South of the border, the S&P 500 Index fell 37 per cent in the year and ended 2008 42 per cent below its October 2007 record high. As was the case for the Canadian market, the bulk of the damage was done in the fourth quarter of 2008 when the S&P fell 22.6 per cent on a price basis and 22 per cent on a total return basis.
- At their worst levels made on November 20, 2008, both the S&P/TSX Composite Index and the S&P 500 Index were each more than 50 per cent below their highs, making this bear market considerably worse than average.
- In Canadian dollar terms, the performance for U.S. equities was considerably better due to weakness in the loonie. For the year, the S&P 500 Index fell 22.6 per cent in Canadian dollar terms.
- Global equity markets fared worse than North American equity markets in 2008. The Morgan Stanley Capital International World Index fell 40.3 per cent on a total return basis in local currency terms in the year.

To give a sense of just how unusual 2008 was for an individual investor, here are some statistics which offer perspective.

- According to the Wall Street Journal, the calendar year percentage loss for the Dow Jones Industrial Average, at -33.8 percent. This was the Dow's worst showing since 1931, and the third worst showing in its history.
- The average daily point range for the Dow was 280.8 points.
- Of the 30 constituent stocks in the Dow, 28 ended the year lower. Only two, McDonalds and Wal-Mart Stores, rose in the year.
- For the S&P 500 Index, only 15 constituent stocks finished 2008

in positive territory, according to Barron's. This is the worst market breadth for the S&P 500 since 1980.

- Despite the fact that 2008 saw the worst calendar year decline since 1937 for the S&P 500, there was exactly the same number of up days as down days - 126 each - according to Carpenter Analytix. Of course, the down days were considerably worse than the up days - the down days averaged at -1.92 per cent, compared to the 1.57 per cent average from up days.
- According to the Wall Street Journal, there were 18 days with a move of 5 per cent or more for the S&P 500 in 2008. There were only 17 days with a move of 5 per cent or more in the preceding 51 years.
- According to Morgan Keegan, the 10-year trailing returns for U.S. large capitalization stocks are at their worst level since 1827.
- The NASDAQ Composite Index fell 40.5 per cent in 2008, the worst calendar year in its history.

If it seems as though there was nowhere to hide in 2008, it is because there very nearly *was* nowhere to hide. Virtually, the only asset class that showed strong gains was government bonds with the strongest performance by U.S. Treasury bonds. For comparison, consider that in Canada, the DEX Long-Term Government of Canada Bond Index rose 12.95 per cent in 2008, while Barclay's (formerly Lehman Brothers) Long-Term Treasury Index gained 24.03 per cent, both in local currency terms.

Any "risky" security was likely to have performed very poorly in 2008. Moreover, it was not just the equity markets that suffered in the bear market of 2008. Investment grade corporate debt and high-yield debt markets also suffered mightily, as did the preferred share markets.

The National Bureau of Economic Research confirmed that the peak for U.S. economic activity was in December 2007. So, the U.S. economy has been in recession for over a year now. It appears as though economic activity slowed markedly in the wake of the failure of Lehman Brothers - there is a marked difference between the character of economic data pre- and post-Lehman Brothers.

All the important markers of economic activity now show the U.S. to be in a deep recession. Given the way that credit markets have seized up in the last 18 months, there is good reason to

> believe that this recession will exceed the length of the previous two longest recessions.
>
> The employment picture continues to darken. Purchasing managers' surveys for both the manufacturing sector and the services sector continue to show economic activity is receding.
>
> Here in Canada, the economy appears to be slowing rapidly as well.

So, what is an investor to do? This chapter presents two investment strategies: the Guaranteed Insured Annuity (GRA) and the Guaranteed Estate Multiplier (GEM). These vehicles provide low risk, reasonable return alternatives to the equity and bond markets. Moreover, these strategies provide the added benefit of preserving capital for an investor's estate.

You can't take it with you, so spend it while you can
and plan to leave behind what you can't.

In the investment world, the needs and wants of clients are as varied as the investment options available. While any client's investment desires are influenced by a unique set of factors or variables, there are consistent themes which reoccur. Generally, investors like security, consistent return, and tax-efficiency. Moreover, investors want a plan that effectively utilizes their capital both during their lifetime (lifestyle planning), and after their death.

No person can claim that they have properly planned their finances when they have not taken into account their annual taxation of income. We live in one of the most highly-taxed jurisdictions in the world; accordingly, it is imperative that investment planning revolve not just around yield, but net yield. It is one thing to make money, but an altogether different thing to keep it.

Swings in the equity markets become less tenable as investors age. Market fluctuations are less tolerable for older investors simply because there is usually less time for short-term losses to be recovered in an investor's lifetime. And once capital becomes the primary source of lifestyle income, investors are hesitant to risk their capital in any way. Given the unprecedented circumstances in the 2008 equity markets, clients are more than ever seeking guarantees in income and for legacy in their financial lives.

The definition of "retirement" means something very different to this generation than it did to our parents and grandparents. However, there remains a universal understanding that at some point in our lives we will want to be able to maintain a comfortable standard of living by our own means. In fact, financial success is often described as "the ability to live by one's own means".

For retirees who no longer work to generate income, there are investment choices which provide the stable income that they require. However, some form of risk comes with even the most guaranteed investment choices. For example, Government of Canada Bonds are probably the most guaranteed vehicles that exist – they are backed by the government's power of taxation. Still they hold an inflation risk *and* earn fully taxable interest each year. Further, the capital value of bonds can decline when interest rates rise. Thus, even the most guaranteed investment options can have costs or risks when they are providing income for estate planning.

Despite these costs and risks, the GRA strategy may be just the answer for retirees who want stable income with tax-preference and a guaranteed income that they cannot outlive. Additionally, a strategy often referred to as the GEM may be more appropriate for investors looking to quantify and guarantee their estate legacy plans. While these two vehicles are not applicable in all cases, these planning strategies can provide valuable guarantees for clients who employ these techniques.

Guaranteed Insured Annuity (GIA)

History

Until the 1970s, gaining market exposure for a portfolio was believed to be only part of the investment world of the affluent and sophisticated. Market exposure with stock and other securities was out of reach for the average Canadian, since it was thought to be too complicated and costly. Defined benefit pension plans and bank-issued Guaranteed Investment Certificates (GICs) were the mainstay of retirement savings for the majority of the population. While mutual funds were available in Canada since the 1930s, the proliferation of the equity-based mutual fund in the 1980s meant that markets around the world became available to average Canadians.

In the market rallies of the 1980s, 1990s, and 2000s, investors enjoyed unprecedented gains. Thus, investors came to believe that bear markets were something to be expected, endured, and too soon dismissed. Accordingly, there was a decline in the perceived need for guarantees and the use of guaranteed products. These investment vehicles were thought to be too conservative to provide an adequate hedge against inflation.

As the Baby Boomer generation now begins to retire, the recent devastation may cause this generation to question the cyclical nature of the equity markets. Specifically, the Baby Boomer investors may no longer have faith in a quick market rally that will provide the necessary capital for them to retire as expected. For the parents of the Boomers, who are now in their 70s and 80s, there may not be time for the markets to ever recover what has been lost in 2008. Thus, the return to guarantees, at least for the income portion of a portfolio, has finally come back in vogue.

Obstacles

The challenges with traditional guaranteed investments include:

1. They are only as sound as the institution or industry offering the guarantee.
2. Since we are anticipating a low-interest rate environment for many years, guaranteed investments pay very little income with no hedge against inflation.
3. The income they generate is usually fully-taxable at marginal tax rates and often result in a "claw back" of the Old Age Security (OAS) payments that investors would otherwise be entitled to receive. Essentially, this results in an additional 15 per cent tax added to the income generated.

Industry Strength

Canadian chartered banks and Canadian life insurance companies are among the most highly regulated in the world. Though nothing is as secure as the federal government's bond guarantees, the leading insurers and chartered banks have assets backing their guarantees. These assets provide investors with sufficient comfort to invest confidently in their guaranteed investment offerings. Reserves set aside to provide these guarantees are usually invested in pools of government bonds. Further, the banks have the Canada Deposit Insurance Corporation (CDIC) to protect deposits and the insurance industry has Assuris. Assuris is a not-for-profit organization supported by member insurance companies to ensure that, should a member insurer fail, there are guarantees on insurance and annuity contracts to protect depositors, insureds, and annuitants.

Low Interest and Inflation Erosion

Some investors are reliant upon a fixed income pool of capital – for instance, through bonds and GICs – to provide an adequate lifestyle. If an investor is reliant on these investments, then they have experienced continual decline in their income over the last 15 years. In the late 1980s and into the early 1990s, the guaranteed interest rates were approximately 12 per cent; however, in recent years, interest rates have been hovering below the 5 per cent mark. Indeed, at the time of writing, the current GIC rates are below 4 per cent. Essentially, this represents a 60 per cent pay cut for those who invested in the late 1980s. Moreover, the cost of living has surely doubled since the time of investment.

Income is Taxed at Marginal Tax Rates

Similar to bank-issued GICs, Canada Savings Bonds, or comparable investment vehicles, the interest earned on a government bond must be taxed annually. The tax on these investments must be paid regardless of whether the interest is received in hand. This annual taxation can easily reduce the yield by 40 per cent or more. Further, for every dollar of taxable income a retiree over the age of 65 earns in excess of an annually set limit, the Canada Revenue Agency (CRA) will "claw back" OAS benefits that would be otherwise payable. This effectively taxes retirees another 15 per cent if their total income is too high.

A Case Example

To illustrate the challenge facing so many retirees, consider a 72-year-old who has a total taxable income of $75,000. This income is comprised of:

- pensions (CPP and work),
- minimum RRIF payments, and,
- taxable interest in the amount of $10,000.

The interest is taxed at the marginal rate of 32 per cent,[1] which means that $3,200 is tax payable on the interest earned. Worse still, OAS benefits must be clawed-back at a rate of $0.15 per dollar of income. This means that another $1,500 in lost government benefits for 2009. Effectively, our retiree is losing $4,700 of the $10,000 in earned interest – she is taxed at 47 per cent! Clearly, our retiree either needs to earn a higher level of income, or

1 This percentage was the 2009 taxation rate in Ontario.

earn income that doesn't qualify as "taxable". Herein lays the beauty of the GRA strategy.

What Is It?

The strategy is really the marriage of two of Canada's oldest financial instruments: guaranteed life annuities and life insurance.

The *life annuity* is a return-of-capital instrument sold on a guaranteed basis by many of Canada's life insurance companies. The life annuity operates like a life insurance policy in reverse. The "annuitant", or the person upon whose life the contract is established, transfers a lump sum of capital as a deposit to the insurer. In return, the insurer guarantees a lifelong stream of payments to the annuitant. From the outset of the policy, the level of income is guaranteed for the life of the annuitant; it can be received monthly, quarterly, semi-annually, or annually, according to the needs of the individual. There is no variation for market return and no modification in income received based on changes in the bond rates. Once established, the payment stream is guaranteed for the balance of the life of the annuitant.

Depending upon the age of the annuitant, a significant portion of the payment stream is considered to be a *tax-free return of capital.* The older the annuitant is at the outset of the contract, the higher the level of income and the higher the proportion of the payment that is completely tax-free! Less "taxable" income means less tax and less OAS claw-back.

The "insured" aspect of the strategy is provided with tax-exempt *life insurance.* Many investors believe that they earned their money, so it is for them to enjoy during their life – whatever is left at the end should go to their kids. But, with an annuity purchase, the legacy left to children and grandchildren is minimal, since the annuity purchase actually transfers the capital to the insurer. There may be some minimum payment period guarantees provided to the annuitant regardless of whether the annuitant has deceased. However, beyond these guarantees in the policy, there is nothing left to heirs or charity. By owning a life insurance contract, the annuitant investor can replenish the estate with the tax-free death benefit.

With this estate-guarantee in place, the client can enjoy the rest of their life spending their capital without the risk of ever running out. Moreover, the investor may not yet be retired; so, purchasing the insurance coverage at a younger age will guarantee a low premium for life. Further, the pre-retirement investor can defer the purchase of the annuity to some time down the road when the income is needed. The delay of the annuity purchase can see an equivalent interest yield of well over 10 per cent.

As long as a beneficiary is named in the policy, the life insurance proceeds will generally by-pass provincial Estate Administration Tax (EAT). The investor can decide to replenish all or just a portion of the estate by owning an appropriate amount of life insurance. They can decide what portion of their estate they wish to spend on themselves and what portion to leave behind.

Benefits

When an individual has a traditional fixed income as their main income source, there is a long-term fear that the capital will have to be expended in order to provide a satisfactory standard of living. The concern is that ultimately the capital may run out; thus, there will be no further income and no estate left for the heirs. A life annuity combined with a life insurance contract:

- dramatically increases after-tax income to spend on lifestyle;
- guarantees an income that cannot be outlived;
- guarantees a quantifiable estate/legacy bequest that by-passes EAT;
- reduces taxable income which reduces tax payable and may increase OAS benefits received; and
- puts the client in control of when to start this higher income stream by allowing him/her to choose when to purchase the annuity.

Our Example

Let's revisit our 72-year-old retiree and the impact of this strategy on the take-home income from a $200,000 non-registered GIC that is earning 5 per cent. Let's assume she is a non-smoker of average health for her age, has a total taxable income of $75,000 from all sources, including $10,000 of interest.

Funds Invested in GIC	
Annual Interest Income	$10,000.00
Taxable Portion	$10,000.00
Tax Amount Payable	$3,200.00
Net Income	**$6,800.00**

Insured Annuity - T100	
Annual Annuity Income	$17,446.56
Taxable Portion	$3,058.09
Tax Amount Payable	$978.59
Insurance Premium	$7,456.00
OAS Savings	$1,041.29
Net Income	**$10,053.26**
* Equivalent GIC Rate	**7.39%**
* Increase over GIC yield	**47.84%**

* Annuity rates are subject to change until a purchase is finalized. Subject to satisfactory medical evidence life insurance premiums are guaranteed for life.

For this investor, a GRA strategy provides an after-tax income that is equivalent to a bond or GIC earning 7.34 per cent. If the investor is in a higher tax bracket, that equivalent rate is even higher. There may be a day when GICs are paying this sort of interest again; however, the interest would not be guaranteed for life. Rather, this interest rate would only last for the term of the GIC.

As discussed earlier, if our retiree doesn't need the income, she can delay the purchase of the annuity into the future, which could potentially increase her yield. If she does need the income now, she can start earning almost 50 per cent more income than using her GIC without the risk of running out of money.

Other Features

Additional assurances can be made with respect to the income stream:

- joint and survivor annuities can be purchased that pay based on the lives of two people;
- an annuitant can negotiate a minimum guarantee period. For example, the agreement may last for at least 10 years, or may pay out until the annuitant reaches 90;
- the payment to the annuitant can be indexed in order to keep pace with the yearly inflation; and
- a Refund of Deposit rider may be included so that if the annuitant dies prior to the commencement of income, the annuitant's deposit of capital would be returned.

Registered Accounts

It should be highlighted that the tax-preference on the income generated by the annuity is lost when Registered Retirement Savings Plans (RRSPs) or Registered Retirement Income Funds (RRIFs) provide the capital for the annuity purchase. The tax preference is lost because any income from these registered accounts is fully taxable. However, the use of annuities is still very popular where there is no need for a survivor income. The income stream from a registered annuity still surpasses the income that may be provided from a bond or GIC. Moreover, an annuity investment will protect against the ultimate capital depletion that is forced upon a RRIF by the government withdrawal formula.

The chart below details a RRIF earning 5 per cent and paying the minimum monthly amount. As the withdrawal requirements exceed the yield, the balance and the income steadily diminish.

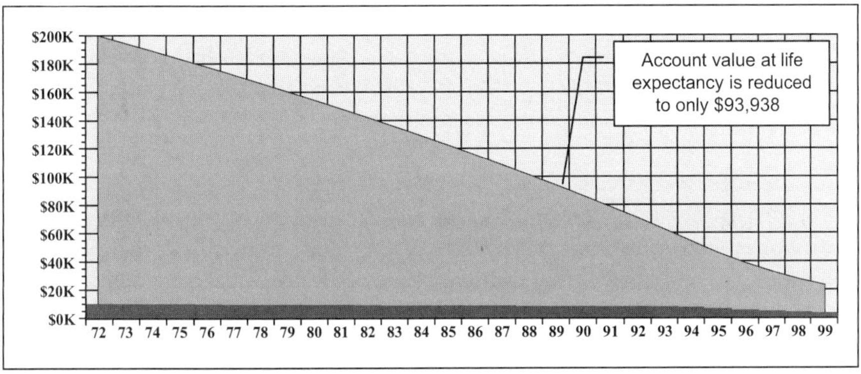

The traditional fixed income RRIF pays taxable income of $14,960, and will reduce to just $11,940 at life expectancy; however, the life annuity will pay $17,827 for life! This level of withdrawal from a 5 per cent GIC RRIF would deplete capital in 16 years. With the annuity, our investor can never run out of money.

Finally, if our investor is concerned about her legacy being lost, she could elect to own the life insurance policy for an amount equal to the estate value of her capital today. Assuming that her estate value is $100,000, the premium would be approximately $3,700 per year. This would leave her with the same after-tax income as the 5 per cent GIC. With the GRA, however, she cannot run out of capital *and* she guarantees her legacy.

Personal Versus Corporate Ownership

In 1995, CRA began an initiative to level the playing field between corporations and individuals. The result of this initiative is that the same total tax will have been paid regardless of whether the money was earned by a corporation or by an individual. Earning income through a corporation merely provides an opportunity for tax-deferral under the corporate tax rates and for income-splitting by paying taxable dividends to common shareholders of the corporation.

Many investors accumulated their fixed income wealth inside of investment corporations – commonly known as HoldCos. The benefits of an insured annuity strategy as an alternative to personally-held, interest-bearing investments are obvious. Moreover, when capital is held by a corporate entity, there is an added layer of benefit both to the investor who wants income and for the estate plan.

To earn income from corporate-held assets, investors must take taxable dividends each year from the company. These dividends help recover Refundable Dividend Taxes (RDTs) paid by the corporation. In effect, the investor pays the same tax as if the interest were earned personally. But, the major difference is to the estate of the investor when he/she dies.

For example, imagine that our 72-year-old female investor has her $200,000 GIC investment in a HoldCo. Let's assume she is in the top marginal tax bracket, since the owners of HoldCo often have other significant personal assets. This fact will eliminate any possible OAS claw-back reduction.

Her corporation earns the $10,000 of taxable interest. By the time the interest is paid to her as a dividend, her net income is about $5,300 (assuming that entire Refundable Divided Tax on Hand (RDTOH) balance is fully refunded each year by taxable dividend at a ratio of 3:1). The account balance remains essentially static at $200,000 with an after-tax estate value to her heirs of roughly $138,000.

Alternatively, the *corporate* GRA strategy pays her a net income of $7,185, net of insurance premiums – this is an increase of 36 per cent! Moreover, the corporate-owned annuity has a decreasing taxable component so that her annual after-tax dividend grows each year. By life expectancy, at age 89, her personal net income is almost $8,000.

Guaranteed Estate Multiplier (GEM)

Investors work their entire lives to accumulate the wealth necessary to achieve financial independence – indeed, some are successful. Investors that have successfully achieved financial independence soon realize that they will have excess capital toward the end of their life. For these individuals, proper investment planning may involve the deferral of income taxes on investments in order for the assets to grow more quickly. However, when an individual dies, income taxes will be due on all assets since the assets are deemed to have been sold immediately prior to death. Other individuals may want to leave a legacy but do not have sufficient resources to realize this dream.

Charitable bequests, family legacy to children or grandchildren, or offsetting the taxes due on a family's assets are all reasons that people need the GEM strategy. In fact, the GEM provides an immediate solution at a very low cost wherever there is a need for capital in the event of a death. The GEM strategy uses tax-exempt life insurance to create legacy values. These legacy values exceed what the deposits might otherwise be worth if they had simply been invested and left behind after death.

How Does It Work?

The tax-deferred accumulation of wealth is what essentially creates an estate problem. By investing these very assets into a tax-exempt life insurance contract, the assets which helped to create the problem can actually help to provide the solution.

Since investments in a tax-exempt life insurance policy are tax-exempt, the returns on the investments actually support the cost of insurance with pre-tax earnings. This investment account value of a policy – let's call this the Cash Surrender Value – can be structured any number of ways. It can either be invested with a hands-on approach or with a passive, professionally-managed approach. The specific needs and wants of a client determine how life insurance professionals structure these plans. To address mitigating estate taxes, it is usually preferable to use only guaranteed investment accounts and contractual minimum rates of return as the basis for the policy. Should the policy assume any variability, it would be improper to call this strategy "guaranteed".

Let's look at an example of a couple who, in their early 50s, have invested and planned well. With investment assets of over $500,000 and pensions that satisfy their income requirements, they want to:

- invest their money tax-effectively,
- have access to some supplementary income as needed,
- support their three adult children (and grandchildren) with the occasional gift, and,
- provide a legacy to the family when they are gone.

Not knowing when and how much the gifts to the children will be, they wish to have access to the cash. Moreover, they want to take a balanced approach to their investment. Using reasonable investment assumptions, with a 40/60 split of equities and bonds, the clients' $500,000 would be worth approximately $1,500,000 in 30 years if they do not end up needing the funds.

Using one of three approaches to an estate multiplier strategy, the client can:

- manage a portfolio of assets similar to the 40/60 balanced plan,
- allow an institutional money manager to handle the decisions, or,
- opt for a fully-guaranteed solution where there are never any decisions to make.

Each approach has pros and cons, and the structure will be dictated by the investment philosophy and comfort level of the investor. It is enlightening to compare the results of each approach, since in each case the estate value of the GEM is well over $3,000,000. That amount is more than double the traditional balanced plan invested in a non-exempt environment. In sum, the GEM is the most cost-effective strategy available for investors who are interested in making a specific estate bequest – individuals who want to ensure that each of their heirs receives a specific amount – or for investors who have specified estate liabilities for tax.

Personal Versus Corporate Ownership

Similar to the GRA strategy, adding layers of tax complexity through corporate ownership of the assets gives the GEM strategy even greater advantage.

Income from investments owned within a corporation face annual taxation of 48.67 per cent in Ontario. If capital that is ultimately bound for the estate can instead be parcelled into the tax-exempt accounts of a life insurance policy, the capital is allowed to grow without tax. Upon the death of the individual investor, what had been tax-deferred investment capital can be paid to the corporation by the insurer in the form of a tax-free death benefit. Because life insurance proceeds are paid tax-free, the years of accrual are never realized as a taxable disposition. Better still, the life insurance proceeds create a credit to the Capital Dividend Account (CDA) of the corporation (in excess of the policy ACB). This credit to the CDA allows shareholders to extract the money tax-free.

If it is tax-free accumulation, tax-free at death, and tax-free out of the company to shareholders after death, permanent life insurance is hard to surpass when planning for estate and legacy maximization – especially if the money is in a corporation.

Summary

Life insurance is a complicated investment tool with special tax-preference. As such, life insurance can perform particular tasks better than any other investment vehicle.

Permanent life insurance will often play a beneficial role for clients who seek security and guarantees in their life, or for those who require tax solutions for long-term objectives.

If anyone is planning their finances for their retirement, it is crucial to immediately consider the many benefits of this valuable tool. Policies can be issued on investors well into their 80s; however, health is an underlying requirement for the success of many strategies. Insurers don't expect anyone in retirement to run a marathon to qualify but basic health is important. Since health can change at any time, the best time to consider any insurance strategies is right now.

Real Estate: The Other Asset Class

Peter Jarman

Over the last decade, interest in real estate investment has grown dramatically in the Canadian market. No longer solely the domain of traditional investment managers at pension funds and banks, real estate has seen a significant increase in the number of middle-class investors, now participating in a wide array of private opportunities. Whether mortgages, mortgage pools, limited partnerships, or undivided interests, investors are becoming the source of capital for small- to medium-sized real estate projects. In view of the tumult and change in world markets, investors want to place capital in secure opportunities, isolated from the adverse impacts of volatility. In this chapter, we consider investment approaches to real estate investment and review the advantages and risks of including real estate in an investment portfolio.

The Demand for Alternatives

Ever since the technology bubble burst in 2001, investors have had a difficult time predicting market trends. Although there have been some significant growth periods in the stock market over the last 10 years, that growth has not come without a great deal of uncertainty. Unfortunately, watching the news through the fall of 2008 has given many an investor even more ulcers, in addition to the financial consequences. And while it would be a mistake to measure stock-based portfolios over this short timeline, it has created strong demand from middle-income Canadians for investments that are resistant to general market trends that can also produce strong returns.

Even prior to 2008, it is evident that average investors have good reasons to consider alternatives. Over the last eight years, the S&P Index has demonstrated strong trends, both down, and up, and then down again. Investors who placed capital close to the height of the index value at the turn of the millennium were exposed to the 2-1/2 year bear market which immediately followed. Following a buy-and-hold methodology is conventional wisdom and usually gives investors protection from volatility in the markets. However, it took all the way to 2008 for the S&P Index to reach the same value that it had attained eight years earlier. When one factors in the effect of inflation, the real value of capital placed in an index fund for this eight-year period actually decreased. Since late 2008, the index has presented investors with an even more uncertain picture. For many years, the standard line of reasoning could rely on the fact that in no single 10-year period had the S&P 500 Index ever delivered a negative return. As of March 9, 2009, even that threshold was crossed, with the S&P 500 Index reaching a value of 676.53, just over 100 points lower than the 776.76 recorded October 9, 2002. Going back 10 years from March 9, 2009, the S&P 500 Index stood at 1,279.84, a value almost double 2009's first quarter low.

Confining our review to select periods of market performance as a measurement of potential is certainly not the best way to decide on portfolio allocation. There have been notable successes in the market using a strategy of buying value and then holding through the long term. But it would be a mistake to ignore market behavior over the last 10 years, and the impact it has had on investors. It is precisely the short-term investment horizon that the average middle-class investor looks to, right or wrong, in determining his or her next investment decision. And although the short-term horizon provides only one frame of reference, many investors are now in the position that the time required to reach their investment goals is fixed, and the dramatic market downturns of late 2008 and early 2009 have forced them to reconsider their options.

Over and above the systematic risk of larger trends in the markets, one of the factors that has also contributed to negative performance is the cost structure of the financial system itself. While not always evident, systematic costs do influence investors to look for alternatives, particularly when they review the deductions of management fees, printed in black and white on current account statements. And it is not just management fees. The structure of the market is designed, of course, to pay brokers, financial advisors, and financial institutions, to provide services to the client. But, in the last two decades, a great deal of innovation has occurred in an entirely other area, in the field of financial product engineering. New products have been issued to investors, both individual and institutional, that rely on complex transactions to derive profit.

Often these products are designed with the assumption that market and economic trends will continue, more or less on the same track. And, as seen in the last few years, many products have embedded risk structures that are not easily understood by the investor. Risky assets have been accumulated into large portfolios, and re-categorized as "low risk", and then re-packaged and sold to financial institutions who, in turn, sold them to their investors. Collateralized Debt Obligations (CDOs), mortgage-backed securities, credit-default swaps, and other complex products allowed financial institutions to create products so complicated that many of our brightest minds could not predict their behavior. In an attempt to multiply the return potential in investment portfolios, financial institutions instead increased the risk to themselves and their investors. It was a combination of the following factors: leverage, risk management, and complexity that caused the collapse of Bear Stearns in March, 2008. With only 11.1 billion in equity, Bear Stearns had $395 billion in assets and a leverage ratio of more than 35:1.[1] Unwinding this collapsed portfolio, along with the financial restructuring in the U.S. economy of which Bear Stearns is only a minor example, has had wide-ranging implications across the investment marketplace.

John C. Bogle, founder of the Vanguard Mutual Fund Group, points out the impact of systematic deductions from investors' returns and, by extension, from the economy as a whole, in his recent book, *Enough. True Measures of Money, Business, and Life.* In a commencement speech given at Georgetown University in May 2007, well before the current market collapse, Mr. Bogle pointed out "that any endeavor that extracts value from its clients may, in times more troubled than these, find that it has been hoist[ed] by its own petard."[2] Unfortunately, his words were surprisingly prescient. Within the next six months, complicated financial products based on sub-prime mortgages in the U.S. housing market started a collapse of complex financial instruments within U.S. banks that has affected world markets, financial institutions, and the investors that depended on them.

Even without the larger market events, there are still the structural fees of our financial system to deal with. Financial products are designed by many of the largest financial institutions with transaction fees at every level. Brokerage commissions, deferred sales charges, management expense ratios, advisory fees, and administration fees provide ample opportunity for originating institutions to profit from a wide array of financial products. And this profit potential has grown dramatically in recent years. In Bogle's findings, he stated that "$215 billion of the $711 billion in earnings of the 500 companies that make up the S&P 500 Stock Index"[3] were attributed to the

---

1 R. Boyd, "The Last Days of Bear Stearns," Fortune Magazine [online] Available http://money.cnn.com/2008/03/28/magazines/fortune/boyd_bear.fortune/, March 31, 2008.

2 J.C. Bogle, *Enough. True Measures of Money, Business, and Life* (Hoboken, New Jersey: John Wiley & Sons, Inc., 2009), p. 32.

3 *Ibid.*, p. 34.

financial sector in 2006. In that year, financial institutions as a whole, who make their revenues from the creation, distribution, and management of financial products, accounted for approximately one third of the earnings of the S&P 500 Stock Index. This raises the obvious question, how can the economy be healthy if 30 per cent of the revenue reported by the S&P Index as a whole is derived from the business of finance, as opposed to actual feet-on-the-ground production and service?

Although structure and management are necessary for the efficient operation of financial markets, the fact that revenues in the financial sector represented such a significant proportion of the earnings of the S&P 500 makes it clear that the cost of the financial machinery required for investment represents a hidden tax on investors. Over time, these factors have a leaching effect on the potential return of a fund, and leaves investors with a significant chance of under-performance.

The costs of the system would not be of much issue, if we could depend on constant growth in our investment portfolios. However, investors in broad-based mutual funds have no guarantee that the management they are paying for will exceed market averages. In fact, the statistics point in the opposite direction. In an article for *Business Week Magazine*, Lauren Young points out the following: "During the five-year market cycle from 2004-2008, the S&P 500 outperformed 72% of actively managed large-cap funds, the S&P mid-cap 400 out performed 76% of mid-cap funds, and the S&P small cap 600 Pro performed 86% of small-cap funds."[4] If investors' retirement plans are riding on the performance of a management team that is taking significant fees while failing to beat the rate of return of a straightforward cross-section of the market, it is not surprising that many are now looking elsewhere for alternative investments to build their investment portfolios.

Hedge funds have fared no better. In a study released in March 2007, John Griffin and Jin Xu from the University of Texas examined the relative merits of hedge fund investing, as compared to mutual funds. The popular conception is that, if your mutual funds are not performing satisfactorily, hedge funds provide a more aggressive approach to building wealth. Hedge funds allow their managers much more leeway in deciding on the investment strategy required for particular market conditions. Managers trade much more frequently, using complex arbitrage and options strategies to protect returns. Often, these funds focus on smaller companies and smaller markets, placing capital in the short-term strategies. Managers also tend to look for

4 L. Young, "Active Mutual Fund Managers Still Can't Beat Indexes," BusinessWeek [online] Available http://www.businessweek.com/investing/insights/blog/archives/2009/04/where_have_all.html, April 20, 2009.

opportunities in international markets, or play off of trends in unique economic conditions, for example, shorting stocks on the New York Stock Exchange as one sector of the market falls, perhaps in response to new legislation, or a new tariff, or other market changes. Hedge funds appear to be a good alternative due to their ability to trade more quickly, and react more dynamically, to market events. Given that the amount of capital they allocate to a given trade is often much smaller than a mutual fund, hedge funds can move in or out of the market more easily.

Yet, despite the fact that hedge funds are often regarded as high-performance alternatives to more conventional market products, Griffin and Xu's study show that on average, hedge funds don't out-perform mutual funds in their selection of long-equity positions. In fact, the only recent time frame that demonstrated a noticeable performance advantage related directly to hedge funds taking profits from the boom in technology stocks in 1999 and 2000. In their words, "[t]he sector timing ability and average style choices of hedge funds are no better than that of mutual funds. Additionally, we fail to find differential ability between hedge funds."[5] In other words, on any given day, the average hedge fund doesn't beat the average mutual fund, when it comes to delivering profit to investors.

Whether or not investors understand the costs of the conventional markets, most have dealt with the consequences in the last 10 years, if not in the last 10 months. Perhaps never before has there been such necessity to protect capital while simultaneously generating positive return for investors. Recent market events, the underlying cost structures of managed investment products, the inability of many funds to beat the market average, and the lack of convincing alternatives in the global markets have raised the flag that diversification into other asset classes is necessary. Regardless of the education of the investor, our common experience is now motivating investors to look to real estate as an opportunity to build wealth in their investment portfolios.

Real Estate as an Asset Class

Real estate provides investors a distinctly different category for investment growth. In very significant ways, real estate differs from conventional market products. As an asset class, it gives investors the ability to put their capital into lower risk placements for the same return and it diversifies portfolios away from stock market risk. In many respects, investing in property fulfills capitalism's age-old dream. For centuries, one of the strongest anchors to

---

[5] J.M. Griffin & J. Xu, "How Smart are the Smart Guys? A Unique View from Stock Holdings," University of Texas. (2007), p. 2.

wealth has been the ability to own land. The historical growth of mortgage banking in many ways led to the rise of the middle class, providing the financing capability for average citizens to become landowners. For many of us, our home is our castle, both personally, and financially. Investing in a private residence allows us to build capital, and increase personal wealth. In both the U.S. and in Canada, citizens benefit from significant tax and estate laws which allow for the accumulation and preservation of family wealth through owning a home. Although laws differ in each jurisdiction, the result in both Canadian and U.S. economies has been much the same. For most people, their first goal upon leaving school is to achieve a mortgage on a personal residence. Some 25 to 30 years later, our paid-up mortgage becomes the financial freedom our parents and peers encouraged us to achieve.

However, there is much more that can be achieved through an organized approach to real estate investing. Real estate is a completely separate asset class, that often acts independently of the stock markets and allows investors to make money both in economic good times and declines. Real property is a real asset (as opposed to shares, and other certificates), and inasmuch as a property exists down the street, or in a new subdivision, or maybe even just outside of your current hometown, it may be reviewed, assessed, appraised, taxed and, of course, bought or sold. Investors in real estate like to use the term, "kicking the dirt", in reference to the ability of even the most minor investor in a larger group, to review all of the fundamental information about a specific property.

In many respects, investing in real estate also allows investors to step around some of the extensive and systematic costs that exist in the conventional stock and bond asset classes and return to the fundamentals of whether a particular property will show revenue. Although there is tremendous variability depending on the asset type in which the investor participates, real estate does allow outside analysis to quantify risk. Investors can step through the business model presented by a real estate investment company or general partner to determine its potential. Fees and costs can be reviewed, in advance of purchase, simply because transactions involving real estate typically follow well-established procedures in both law and commerce. Entry and exit points for investors' capital, whether private or public, are typically well-defined. In most real estate investments, the financial incentive behind the deal can be easily expressed. While there are risks and the potential for loss, real estate as an asset class provides investors with a more direct approach to information gathering.

This ability to review, and visit, if you like, not only the physical location, but also the financial and legal records of a property provides the fundamental information needed to decide on asset allocation within your portfolio. In fact, we can safely compare the research process to the type of thorough review a value-based investor will make when reviewing the balance sheet and cash flow of a profitable company. This accessibility to real information makes real estate an extremely strong alternative to stocks and bonds, let alone mutual funds and hedge funds.

Ironically, the financial crisis now assailing world markets in many respects was triggered by a real estate bubble of extreme proportions in the United States. While we do not lose sight of that fact, it is important to realize that investing in real estate in Canada as a single investor, or as part of a larger group, has very little to do with the phenomenon of the hugely-expanded sub-prime mortgage market in the U.S. The meteoric rise in property values in the U.S., and their subsequent collapse, have implications for real estate investment but we should not lose sight of the fact that in many markets these events have delivered the ideal conditions for acquisition, revenue generation, and capital appreciation that investors look for.

In Canada, the sub-prime phenomena did not occur, and our banking regulations have now been recognized as world-leading. In addition, we are very much a resource-based economy, and the trend projected by key economists is for continued gradual increases in demand for our commodities over the next 30 years. While there are some down-stream economic effects from the current economic upheaval, this leaves the Canadian market with stability and significant opportunity in the real property asset class. Today's investors need good information and an understanding of local and regional economies. So armed, investors will find that real estate as an asset class has the potential to provide ideal diversification in the next decade. In the following paragraphs, we will review a number of strategies that are available to investors through private and public companies in Canada.

Diversifying Into the Real Estate Asset Class

Investors and their advisers are always focused on achieving a balance between risk and performance. The science of portfolio management has made use of the tools of mathematics, psychology, economics, and geopolitical theory to try to pinpoint active markets with profit potential. Complex mathematical approaches are used to identify ways to invest in specific profit centers, while simultaneously addressing the probability of loss. For most investors the reflex response to the risk of loss is diversification. Investing in a basket of assets (in most cases, the typical discussion refers to stocks), provides investors some protection from specific risks inherent to each investment. While you could fill your library with books on diversification, mathematical theory, portfolio optimization and economics, many of them helpful on a theoretical basis, the root of today's understanding of diversification owes much to a single paper, published in 1952 in the *Journal of Finance*, by Harry Markowitz.[6] Considered the father of modern portfolio theory, Markowitz provided a framework for describing how portfolios could mitigate risks, when making specific investments in stocks.

In Markowitz's approach, risk was divided between systematic risk and unsystematic risk. Systematic risk of course refers to the market risks that affect every company, and the economy as a whole. This would include interest rates, tariff legislation, tax changes, recessions, and wars. Unsystematic risk, on the other hand, is risk that relates directly to the company being invested in. Management decisions, budget allocation, market penetration, sales and revenues are just some of the areas where companies show variance. Because each company is different, each company by definition has a different risk profile. This risk profile can be defined and understood through research, but it cannot be completely removed. To compensate for the unsystematic risks inherent in every company, Markowitz introduced the concept of co-variance. To his view, a portfolio could compensate for specific risk in any individual company stock by choosing a basket of stocks that did not move together in the market. In other words, individual companies that would be negatively impacted by a tariff legislation change could be offset in the portfolio by companies that would benefit from the same change. This ability to pair dissimilar stocks in an investment portfolio provides the investor the ability to protect return.

In the fall 2004 edition of *Real Estate Issues*, Professor Roy Black from Emory University illustrates the parallels between early descriptions of portfolio theory and its application more recently to real estate. In his view,

> Markowitz was the first researcher to prove the old adage "Don't put all your eggs in one basket." Essentially, he proved mathematically that by diversifying investments, the investor can lower the risk of the investment portfolio, or conversely, earn a higher return for the same amount of risk in an un-diversified portfolio. Perhaps more important than proving the common-sense adage, Markowitz gave us the tool by which we could measure the benefits of diversification. Put simply, the objective of the investor is either to minimize portfolio risk subject to a target rate of return or to maximize the return on the portfolio subject to the target level of risk.[7]

---

6 H. Markowitz, "Portfolio Selection" (1952) 7(1) The Journal of Finance 77-91.

7 R.T. Black, "Real Estate in the Investment Portfolio" (2004) Real Estate Issues 1. [Online] July 13, 2009. FindArticles.com. http://findarticles.com/p/articles/mi_qa3681/is_200410/ai_n11849580/

Markowitz's analytical approach makes it possible for investors to design portfolios that will give stable performance, with relatively constant rates of return in the stock markets. The important question for the investor stops being, "How much return will I make on this stock?", and instead becomes "How different are the companies that I invest in?" By creating a portfolio of stocks with low covariance and similar rates of growth, the investor's probability of achieving a specific target rate of return improves. Covariance, or correlation, is typically measured as a range, with values ranging from -1 to +1. If two companies' share prices move exactly the same amount under the same market forces, we would say their share prices are positively correlated. If, however, in a given market event, the price of one stock goes up one dollar, and the price of the second stock goes down one dollar, we would say their share prices are negatively correlated. The greater the magnitude of correlation, the more closely the correlation coefficient will be to one or -1. Stocks that move identically up and down would thus have a correlation factor (covariance) of +1. Stocks that move in exactly opposite directions, in equal magnitude, in a given market event would have a correlation factor (covariance) of -1.

Black gives the following example:

> Let's assume there are two different investments, A and B, both returning 10% over time. They're both volatile with high standard deviations of returns. However, whenever Investment A goes up by one dollar, Investment B goes down by one dollar. Conversely, whenever Investment B goes up by one dollar, Investment A goes down by one dollar. These two investments would be said to be perfectly negatively correlated; that is, their covariance is -1.[8]

While it is practically impossible to find two stocks with a perfect covariance of -1, this example demonstrates the ideal scenario. If you could include two stocks in your portfolio with this behavior, you would show a constant rate of return regardless of the variance of the individual stocks. This would represent the ultimate Markowitz portfolio.

The Big Advantage

The real estate investor uses this same essential economic idea to further strengthen his or her investment portfolio. However, real estate investors can apply the concept of covariance to a diversified basket of asset classes, with even greater effect. If we include real estate in a portfolio of stocks and bonds, we call the result a mixed-asset portfolio, since real estate is a completely different asset class from market-based securities. The advantage of

---

[8] *Ibid.*, p. 2.

mixed-asset portfolios is that including real estate allows investors to not only deal with diversification on the level of unsystematic risk, or, the risk of investing in individual companies, but to address systematic risk as well.

If diversification is only applied to a basket of stocks, then portfolio design is restricted to mitigating only unsystematic risk, or the risk of specific companies. Such an approach misses the significant advantage of reducing systematic risk across all asset classes. Adding real estate as an asset class to an investment portfolio magnifies the benefit of diversification by reducing the impact of systematic events. Cross-sector diversification aids investors in achieving their goal of protecting or increasing the portfolio return, since by definition we are adding an asset class that does not correlate directly with the stock market. This is perhaps the single most important advantage of real estate in investment portfolio design.

For many investors, this lack of correlation is something they have experienced first-hand. The first sign of this behavior is the very different volatility and price behavior of their own homes, compared to the price behavior of the stock market over a given period of time. Although at times the prices in these two very different asset classes may move together, very often they do not. For example, tax changes, recessions, and inflation may lead to dramatic volatility on the stock market. Depending on the local market, these economic forces create entirely different effects for the real estate investor. In fact, in periods of rapid economic change, often the real estate investor has more information at his fingertips to make profitable decisions than the investor or fund manager who must navigate the peaks and troughs of market turbulence.

A number of influential studies have examined the covariance of real estate with stock market indices worldwide. Low correlation between real estate investments and stocks can be found in comparisons of stock market indices with a number of real estate indices in the national U.S. market. Since investors participate in both private and public market real estate investments, it is essential to look for indices that demonstrate the behavior of both classes of real estate. The National Council of Real Estate Investment Fiduciaries (NCREIF), and the Frank Russel Company started the NCREIF Property Index (NPI) in the late 1970s.[9] This Index represents a broad spectrum of privately-held real estate assets across the United States. With a range of categories that include commercial, industrial, office, and retail properties, the NPI "is the most widely cited performance measure for the market in direct real estate investments."[10] According to Black, although

---

9 *Ibid.*

10 *Ibid.*

there are limitations in using this Index to track real estate performance, it remains a benchmark of real estate returns. Considering the parameters of the NPI illustrates the complexity of formulating a systematic approach to a very diverse asset class. However, even with the limitations (the Index relies on appraised values on investment-grade properties, and likely under-reports the volatility in local markets), the NPI Index provides a tool for assessing private real estate investment in comparison to stock portfolios.

The other index available for comparison is the National Association of Real Estate Investment Trusts Index (the NAREIT Index), which is based on share prices and dividends of all publicly-traded Real Estate Investment Trusts (REITs).[11] The securities that make up the NAREIT Index differ markedly from the NPI. The NAREIT Index ignores privately-held real estate altogether, and instead tracks publicly-traded REITs, which are large corporations or trusts that use the pooled capital of a large group of investors. These pools are invested in income-producing properties, such as hotels, commercial space, office space, or even residential apartments. The majority of earnings are passed on to investors, and as such, investors usually rate them by how much they yield per annum. In addition, REIT units are highly liquid, and trade daily on the major stock exchanges. This allows investors to trade REIT units, just as they would stocks. The NAREIT Index derives unit value statistics and broader market trends from daily reports of all REIT unit values in the U.S. markets.

Applying standard mathematical analysis, researchers have looked at the correlation between publicly-traded real estate (in REITs) and privately-held real estate, using the NPI. To assess the role of real estate in portfolio design, research has focused on how much correlation there is between REITs and the market, and how much correlation there is between private real estate and the market. In studies in the last 10 years,

> ... researchers found a high positive correlation (.722) between the NAREIT Index and the S&P 500, suggesting that publicly traded REITs do not provide much help in diversifying a stock portfolio. The correlation between the NAREIT Index and the Russell 2000 was even higher (.779). By comparison, there was a very low correlation between the NCREIF Index and the S&P 500 (.0523). The correlation between the NAREIT Index and the NCREIF Index was also very low (.0276), indicating no relationship between direct investments in real estate and investments in publicly traded REITs.[12]

Keeping in mind that the NCREIF index tracks the performance of privately-held real estate or direct investment in real estate, and that the NAREIT

---

11 *Ibid.*, p. 3.

12 *Ibid.*

Index pertains only to publicly-traded REITs, we can find two conclusions here. First, publicly-traded REITs are influenced by the public market and, in many respects, behave in some ways like a mutual fund, or a stock, rather than real estate. Second, direct investment in real estate, whether in limited partnerships, private REITs, or even individual landholding, does not correlate strongly with the stock market indices. Or, in other words, there is low covariance between private real estate investment and the stock markets. We should also note that the results published in Black's research also point out a low covariance, or a low correlation, between the NCREIF Index and the NAREIT Index. Given the principles of modern portfolio theory, this would indicate to investors that they should include both publicly-traded and private real estate to achieve a strong mixed-asset portfolio. By adding both types of asset to the mix, an investor would benefit in the same fundamental values in the underlying assets, but would eliminate unsystematic risk by maintaining a percentage in both types of real estate investment.

Given the low correlation with stocks and bonds, investors need to consider the argument that real estate should take a higher percentage of the portfolio than perhaps they realize. Many of the most recent research papers on portfolio efficiency and the inclusion of real estate utilized the concepts and approach first pioneered by Markowitz. Based on the principles of modern portfolio theory, researchers use mathematical models to represent the ideal portfolio mix needed to achieve a target rate of return. Perhaps one of the best discussions of mixed-asset portfolios comes from an article in the *Journal of Real Estate Portfolio Management*, by Andrew Mueller and Glenn Mueller, published in 2003.[13] In their study, they recognized the findings of Ziering and McIntosh (1997)[14] whose results showed that "core real estate had low correlations with stocks and bonds and lower volatility." Going further, Mueller and Mueller examined investment portfolios with an eye to achieving optimum performance for investors, using Modern Portfolio Theory analysis. They focused particularly on Markowitz risk-reward graphs, representing efficient portfolios. Their findings point out that investors can benefit significantly by adding private real estate to their other low risk investment options.

Dividing portfolios into low-risk and high-risk allocations, Mueller and Mueller showed the different behavior of directly-held and publicly-traded real estate. For the lower risk portions of the portfolio, they determined that including directly-held, or private investment in real estate, strongly

---

13 A.G. Mueller & G.R. Mueller, "Public and Private Real Estate in a Mixed-Asset Portfolio" (2003) 9(3) Journal of Real Estate Portfolio Management 193-203.

14 B. Ziering & W. McIntosh, "Revisiting the Case for Including Core Real Estate in a Mixed-Asset Portfolio" (1997) 13:4 Real Estate Finance 14-22.

reduced volatility in the portfolio. REITs and other public vehicles were not as effective, in the low risk region of the portfolio, probably due to their broader exposure to the market. However, the results were opposite in the higher risk portion of the portfolio. In higher-risk asset classes, such as stocks, volatility, and risk of loss could be mitigated more effectively by the inclusion of publicly-traded real estate, specifically REITs. In fact, including large allocations to REIT investment had a numerically greater impact in reducing volatility in the higher risk category, than the inclusion of private real estate had in the low risk category. Interestingly, this drives us to the same Markowitz-derived conclusion, that both publicly-traded and privately-held real estate investments should be held by investors, as they do not correlate with each other closely. Nor, as it turns out, does either category correlate strongly with stocks or bonds. Thus, to design the most effective portfolio, an investor should include all four classes of assets. The results of Mueller and Mueller's work represent some of the clearest evidence that the inclusion of REITs and private real estate investment adds tremendous efficiency and risk protection to a mixed-asset portfolio.

Perhaps even more interesting, but not surprising, Mueller and Mueller observe that most investment managers restrict the amount of real estate in large investment funds. Typically, institutional investors have to contend with the argument that real estate represents a relatively small market and that, as an asset class, it tends to be less liquid than other assets. This is certainly the case. In most economies, the securitization of real estate is really in its early stages, and there are no significant exchanges devoted exclusively to the trade of real estate-derived securities. It can be difficult to quantify real estate investment performance as there are few mechanisms that can be applied to bring a specific asset mark-to-market, nor would that necessarily make sense.

However, there is benefit in including real estate in both the low-risk and high-risk portions of an investment fund. Key studies in the area of portfolio analysis have shown the strong historic returns generated in the real estate sector. The low volatility of these assets, whether private- or publicly-traded, enables investors to maximize returns with a minimum of risk. Although past portfolio managers have been much more inclined to include bonds and stocks in portfolios, while minimizing real estate, Mueller and Mueller's study argues for the opposite. Their approach resulted in theoretical recommendations of over 50 per cent of subject portfolios being allocated to real estate. This represents a remarkable increase in capital placement, over and against what most portfolio managers would entertain. And Mueller and Mueller aren't the only ones to make this observation. Global Analytics LLC put forward a proposed model that "constructs an 'ideal' portfolio consisting of 46% publicly-traded REIT shares, 32% dedicated to an S&P

500 index fund and, and 22% devoted to bonds."[15] Keep in mind, the main reasons for including both public and private classes of real estate in a well-developed portfolio, are the different behavior and performance they exhibit. Private real estate is viewed as a stabilizing influence on a stock portfolio because it is unrelated to, and unimpacted by, the volatility of the markets.[16] REITs exhibit much more volatility – after all, they can be traded daily, and thus respond to rapid increases in demand, or lack thereof. As such they are not seen to stabilize portfolios as completely. They have, however, shown consistent, strong performance historically. Strong growth in real estate assets and downside protection from inflation are good arguments for a change in how we think of investment portfolio design.

Inflation and the Invitation to Real Assets

Martin Hoesli, in his study "Real Estate as a Hedge against Inflation - Learning from the Swiss Case", makes a strong case for protecting investment portfolios from inflation with real estate. His recent research develops this concept through a review of the performance of Swiss real estate mutual funds during stock market growth and decline. In his view,

> Two arguments are generally given to motivate the decision of including real estate in portfolios of financial assets (e.g. stocks and bonds). These arguments are: the diversification benefits stemming from the less-than-perfect correlation of real estate with the other assets included in the portfolio; and a better protection against inflation provided by real estate.[17]

Leaving the inflation hedge discussion for the moment, we find in Hoesli's examination of mixed-asset portfolio performance a good example of Markowitz's principal of diversification. Instead of using REITs or private real estate holdings for his comparison, Hoesli reviews the performance of Swiss real estate mutual funds. As compared to American REIT shares, "Swiss real estate mutual fund unit-holders can ask for redemption of their shares at the intrinsic value,"[18] at any time. Since Swiss investors have the option of either selling their shares on the market or asking for redemption, the share value tends to reflect the market value of the underlying properties. Where North American REITs have been observed to be influenced by larger

---

15 R.T. Black, "Real Estate in the Investment Portfolio" (2004) Real Estate Issues 1 [online] July 13, 2009. FindArticles.com. http://findarticles.com/p/articles/mi_qa3681/is_200410/ai_n11849580/

16 *Ibid.*, p. 6.

17 M. Hoesli, "Real Estate as a Hedge against Inflation – Learning from the Swiss Case," (1994) 12(3) Journal of Property Valuation & Investment 51-59.

18 *Ibid.*, p. 51.

market trends, Swiss real estate mutual funds tend to track the underlying values of the real property they hold more closely.

This gives an even better example of how real estate does not relate directly to the stock market. It also illustrates one of the other main advantages of real estate investment, the argument of intrinsic value. Real estate assets in the Swiss example are observed to "rise without any restriction" in a bullish market, and "in a bearish market they will be stopped by the intrinsic value".[19] Hoesli's research shows that Swiss real estate securities, although members of the publicly-traded family, behave very similarly to private real estate assets. In his words, "[A]s a result, they [Swiss real estate mutual funds] will be quite independent of stock market price fluctuations; for example, the October 1987 return on the BOPP Index of Swiss real estate mutual funds was -2.84%, as compared to -23.21% for the stock market." You might expect Swiss real estate mutual funds to be impacted significantly by the market crash in 1987 but, due to the intrinsic value of the underlying asset class, these real estate-based investments were resilient.

Although his research is focused on providing data for institutional investors and pension funds, the core rationale for including real estate in larger investment vehicles, Martin Hoesli's results are applicable to all investors. He found that

> ... [I]n the long run real estate seems to provide a better hedge against inflation than common stocks. When data for five year time increments are used the better coefficient for inflation is marginally positive in the case of real estate, whereas it is significantly negative for common stocks. Moreover, when the inflation rate is broken down into its expected and unexpected components, all coefficients are negative for stocks, whereas some coefficients are positive for real estate.[20]

Given the similar behavior of Swiss real estate mutual funds to privately-held real estate, whether in syndications, small pools, or individual ownership, the research demonstrates the inflation hedging ability of investments in the real estate asset class. Investors benefit in two ways: first, in the downside protection of investing in real assets with intrinsic value and, second, any anti-inflationary behavior of those same assets.

There is ample evidence that real estate functions as an inflation hedge, or protection, even in small-scale real estate investment. Real estate itself is an asset. As prices rise in the overall economy, real estate prices tend to rise as well. Where inflation begins to impact the economy, tangible assets rise in value against the falling price of the monetary unit, and thus conserve value.

---

19 *Ibid.*, p. 52.

20 *Ibid.*, p. 58.

In practical terms, it is hard to find a more tangible asset than real estate. And, in an inflationary market, real estate has another advantage. As the price of goods and services increases, rent (or the price of the use of property), also increases and tends to conserve its value in real terms. As rents and leases increase in monetary value in both residential and commercial properties, the revenue generation increases, and REITs and other pooled real estate investments benefit. By providing investors with consistent income, and the potential for increasing income, real estate provides an ideal asset for combatting the effects of inflation.

Barriers to Entry

However, for many decades, smaller investors have felt that participation in real estate represented too large a demand on available capital. The average investor often does not have enough funds to properly place the required proportion of their overall portfolio in real estate assets. Since the average investment in real estate represents a large dollar figure, the common perception is that there is a significant barrier to investment in real estate. One only needs to look at the price of the average home of a duplex, or an apartment building, to realize that this perception has merit.

However, given the availability of finance in the form of mortgages, investors often overestimate the amount of capital necessary to invest. Banks routinely provide investment capital in the form of mortgages to investors who are looking to diversify. In many respects, it is easier to make the bank your partner in an apartment building then it would be to convince the loan officer or your investment planner of the viability of borrowing several hundred thousand dollars to invest in a sizeable stock portfolio. On a day-to-day basis, banks and financial institutions public and private offer ready finance facilities to investors and owners across a wide spectrum of real estate categories.

But it's not just about finance facilities or educating investors of their availability. There is an even more dynamic change occurring in the Canadian investment marketplace, particularly in Western Canada. Investors are increasingly choosing opportunities in local property markets as an alternative to market-based funds. This is not really due to the availability of finance but rather due to innovative and creative structures that allow large groups of investors to participate in projects that would otherwise be the sole domain of high net worth individuals or larger institutions. By piecing investments out to individual investors with amounts as small as $10,000, it has become possible for significantly large projects to be developed. In keeping with the principles of diversification provided by Markowitz, investors now have the opportunity to include a wide array of real estate-based investment securities within their investment portfolios. This chapter does not permit us to review all of the possible investment structures but we can discuss how syndication provides investors with a number of ways to capture equity growth.

Real Estate Syndication

Syndication itself is not a new concept. Most people identify with the idea of owning a small piece of a larger asset in the context of a corporate entity. For example, if you buy shares in a public corporation, you are participating in a type of syndication. You do not own the whole corporation but you benefit from the profits that the company generates. Whether through share appreciation or dividend payout, the investor benefits from owning a small fraction of the company. In the same way, a large real estate investment can be financed through the participation of a large number of investors, each contributing a small amount of capital. This type of investment participation may take place through either a debt or equity investment structure. If equity, funds invested in the project may take the form of partnership units or shares. If debt, investor funds may be placed in the project through mortgages, bonds, debentures, or unsecured loans. From a portfolio design standpoint, it is important to review the parameters or requirements of the investor before selecting the investment opportunity. Careful review of the real estate investment will reveal whether funding will be long-term or short-term, and whether there will be any cash flow in the meantime. The expected liquidity, or exit point for the capital, is of prime importance for assessing the success of the investment and the expected return on investment.

Although many different types of syndication exist, in equity and debt structures, a singular advantage that real estate affords is the capability of offering security of capital. Real property can be appraised and/or compared to other properties with the same characteristics. This allows the investor to determine the value of the property without depending on the investment company. With this in hand, the investor can further analyze an investment offering to assess whether the collected investment capital matches the property value. If an investment offering is raising $10 million, and the appraisal for the property comes in at $5 million, it should lead the investor to question whether the investment is valid. What will be done to the property to increase its value by a factor of two? On the other hand, if an investment offering is raising $10 million, and the appraisal for the property comes in at $10 million, then there is an adequate asset to back the investor's capital. As long as the legal structure of the investment is sound, the investor can sleep at night, knowing that there is capital security based on the intrinsic value of the property.

Four Categories of Real Estate Investment

We can review real estate investments by organizing them into four main categories: property conversion, land banking, development, and cash flow investments.

The popularity of the TV show "Flip This House"[21] is an easy way to understand property conversion investments. In the show, a homeowner usually renovates or improves a run-down property, and then sells it for a profit. Required for this type of investment is an underperforming revenue property or a property that is undervalued in its local market. In Calgary and Edmonton, a large number of condo conversion project were completed from 2004 to 2008. Many of these were funded by private investors. Generally, an underperforming rental block would be optioned or purchased and the ownership group would make a number of improvements to the property. To realize the profit, the property was then sold. Often, the timeline for this type of investment is quite restrictive and is dependent on the type of financing secured from lending institutions. Investors provide the initial equity but a mortgage and/or a construction loan are required to complete improvements. If the market shifts in the time the project is under way, or if labor and material costs change significantly, the expected profit may be at risk. The advantage of this type of investment is that it can allow investors to generate a profit in a relatively short time. In addition, investment capital is secured by the property. This strategy usually increases the value of a property, and that increase, less cost, is passed on to the investors.

Land banking, on the other hand, requires a much more patient approach. In this type of investment structure, investors pool their funds to purchase large areas of land in or around a rapidly-growing municipality, town, or city. This type of investment is reliant on the continuous growth of an urban center and the resulting demand for more and more land for development. In rapidly growing regions, continuous growth can create significant profit potential. The land banking strategy usually involves a comprehensive review of the planning protocols of a town or city, with special attention to planned land use. In some cases, a municipality will already have approved an area structure plan, or zoning, which indicates that a property within this area will have a specific use. If investors purchase a property early enough, they may see the demand for a property increase dramatically. But the

---

[21] ©1996-2009, A&E Television Networks.

property has to be in the path of growth. Land banking may encounter economic risks, as the anticipated growth of a region fails to materialize. Political risks may be unforeseen over the longer term, as the planning priorities of a town or region may shift after an election to match a new development criteria. Environmental concerns may develop as a region considers its growth pattern.

Land banking is considered a longer-term investment strategy. Investors usually participate at a fairly low entry price and they may be recognized on the land title. But the risk is time. If there are any delays in the expected growth in the region, the land banking investment must wait until the demand is there to sell to a developer. By virtue of this dependence on a sale for exit, land thinking is often deemed to be speculative in nature. If an investment offering with a land banking strategy does not lay out the comparative value of land in the same area, or refer to an appraisal, an investor could be taking a greater risk than they might think. If, however, the initial value of the property is known, it can be relatively easy to assess the potential profit.

Real estate development is the third category we will consider. This type of investment play differs significantly from land banking in that a development typically adds value to an existing property. A development deal may be structured either as a debt investment, in the form of a mortgage or bond, or as an equity participation in the land and improvements. Development brings a specific set of advantages to the investor. Generally, the strategy relies on due diligence and market review to determine the best use of the subject property. Developers often speak of bringing a property to best use, and by that they mean fully developing the property's economic potential. As a property is built out, significant increases in value occur upon completion of each stage of development. For example, a given property may have an appraised value as raw land of $10 million. The value will, likely, increase upon completion of zoning. The value will likely increase further as the developer completes the approved planning for a development permit. As each stage is completed, the property is worth more, because it could be sold to a third party who would then be in a position to complete the project without having to go through zoning or development permit application processes. Values typically increase when infrastructure (such as utilities, water, and sewer) is completed, when the foundation is poured, when the building is completed to lock up and, finally, when construction is completed.

Developers have the additional advantage of carefully reviewing the opportunity before purchasing the property. Careful assessment of demographics in the region, market demand, and economic stability can assist the developer deciding on a specific plan for a given property. A development plan is usually completed in stages, further limiting the risk to the investor. If economic conditions change, it is usually possible to sell a development, or put it on hold. As long as there are no significant financing costs, a project may wait for the appropriate economic conditions without losing significant equity. However, development investments are vulnerable to volatility in local markets. If the price of housing units drops dramatically, developers can be caught between the cost of financing the development and the rapidly dropping sale price of the end product. If economic conditions are relatively stable, this risk can be mitigated by completing a development in phases, with only a select number of units released for sale at any given time.

Real estate developments require the partnership and support of lending institutions. Banks and construction lenders provide the financing necessary to build projects. Investors may participate in a development in either the equity or the debt side of the deal. Typically, the equity component is structured as a limited partnership, or as share ownership in a corporation that owns the project. As the project is initiated, the equity component may represent a relatively small piece of the required funds. This provides automatic leverage to the equity owner, as all additional funds are borrowed from a lender. If properly managed, this financial leverage can allow equity holders to experience gains of over 100 per cent return on investment. In addition, if the investment is held outside of a registered retirement savings plan, equity participation in a limited partnership allows payment of all profits as capital gains. Distributions to limited partners are then taxed at much more favorable rates, increasing the after-tax return. Investors who participate on the debt side of a development typically do not experience the same level of profit. They trade the potential upside for the security of a mortgage paying at approved lending rates. Typically, these returns are in the order of 8 to 15 per cent per annum. Although the return is less than that expected for equity, the investor has significantly more security in that their capital has first charge against the property.

The last category we will consider is cash flow real estate investments. These are private and public investment securities that allow investors to participate in the revenue generated by a property. in the public markets, REITs provide the main access to cash flow or revenue-based real estate investment. Backed by real property, REITs generally provide a steady return, year-on-year, due to the constant flow of revenue from properties that make up the portfolio. The revenue is generated from rent and lease payments made annually by tenants, whether the properties involved are multi-unit residential, such as apartment buildings and townhouse complexes, or commercial office space. REITs are sold in units that may rise in value depending on the perceived value of real estate in general and then specifically based on improvements to the properties, higher appraisals, increased rent, or increased occupancy. Good management is often crucial to developing significant returns for REIT investors. One of the significant advantages of the REIT structure is the tax efficiency allowed under CRA guidelines. The taxable portion of the revenue can be reduced, depending on the amount of costs that flow through the structure to the investors. The combined return of revenue, tax savings, and capital gains upon sale provides significant advantages for investors.

Another cash flow strategy that provides significant security to investors is the Mortgage Investment Corporation (MIC). A MIC takes funds from investors and invests them in a portfolio of mortgages to homeowners and developers. The advantage of this structure is that it has a relatively low risk profile, given that all investment capital is placed in mortgages with the underlying real estate as security. A MIC structure is, in many respects, similar to a REIT, in that it is a flow-through structure that typically distributes a large proportion of revenue generated from mortgage payments directly to the investor. This makes the structure highly-efficient, with low management costs and significant profit potential. Typical returns range from 6 to 10 per cent per annum. Another key advantage of this structure is that many MICs qualify as RRSP-eligible investments, and thus investors may defer any liability until funds are withdrawn from their RRSP accounts. Many private companies also offer private mortgage pools which function in much the same way. Large mortgages are syndicated into smaller investment units that allow investors to be secured against the property, and receive quarterly payments as cash flow, either into registered or non-registered accounts.

Each of the outlined categories has its own characteristics. With the broad array of real estate investment products that are now available to investors, an individual portfolio can significantly reduce correlation in asset classes. But, perhaps even more effective diversification can be achieved within the real estate component of the portfolio by participating in varying types of real estate securities. A well-developed mix of short-term and long-term opportunities, in both debt and equity investments, can create a stable, efficient, and profitable portfolio.

Advantages of the Fourth Asset Class

As an asset class, real estate will continue to function as an ideal diversification within investment portfolios for the next decade. Given the attention that is now shifting to real estate, investors need to treat real estate as the fourth asset class, and develop strategies for including it in their portfolios along with stocks, bonds, and cash. By combining public and private investment in real estate, investors have the capability to avoid systematic risks of overall market trends. Low correlation between market events and real estate investment strategies may be the best way to address the challenges of the volatile markets we expect to see over the next few years. Current studies point out that high proportions of real estate in a portfolio can normalize returns, add tax efficiency, and protect capital by securing it against real property. When you combine these advantages with the demonstrated capability of real estate to hedge against inflation, there are strong reasons to include a variety of real estate investments in a productive portfolio.

APPENDIX A

References

R.T. Black, "Real Estate in the Investment Portfolio" (2004) Real Estate Issues [online] July 13, 2009. FindArticles.com. http://findarticles.com/p/articles/mi_qa3681/is_200410/ai_n11849580/

J.C. Bogle, *Enough. True Measures of Money, Business, and Life* (Hoboken, New Jersey: John Wiley & Sons, Inc., 2009), p. 32.

R. Boyd, "The Last Days of Bear Stearns," *Fortune Magazine*, March 31, 2008 [online] http://money.cnn.com/2008/03/28/magazines/fortune/boyd_bear.fortune/

J.M. Griffin & J. Xu, "How Smart are the Smart Guys? A Unique View from Stock Holdings," University of Texas. (2007), p. 2.

M. Hoesli, "Real Estate as a Hedge against Inflation – Learning from the Swiss Case" (1994) 12(3) Journal of Property Valuation & Investment, 51-59.

H. Markowitz, "Portfolio Selection" (1952) 7(1) The Journal of Finance 77-91.

A.G. Mueller & G.R. Mueller, "Public and Private Real Estate in a Mixed-Asset Portfolio" (2003) 9(3) Journal of Real Estate Portfolio Management 193-203.

L. Young, "Active Mutual Fund Managers Still Can't Beat Indexes," BusinessWeek [online] April 20, 2009 http://www.businessweek.com/investing/insights/blog/archives/2009/04/where_have_all.html

B. Ziering & W. McIntosh, "Revisiting the Case for Including Core Real Estate in a Mixed-Asset Portfolio, (1997) 13:4 Real Estate Finance 14-22.

New Realities of Formal and Informal Restructuring

Ryan Brain & Huey Lee

Introduction

Restructuring - whether formal or informal - has never been a simple process. Under-performing companies are often guilty of ignoring the signs of financial crisis until it's too late. As management goes through stages of drifting and denial, financial performance continues to deteriorate, limiting the company's options for recovery. This tends to make restructuring both arduous and time-consuming for organizations working to stabilize their business operations and financial position.

In recent years, however, restructuring has become even more complex thanks to three key factors: globalization, increased capital structure sophistication (including creative, and often opaque, financial instruments), and organizational evolution. This chapter explores each of these factors in turn to explain how they contribute to the growing complexity of both formal and informal restructuring proceedings.

Due to these new realities, a greater number of less experienced stakeholders are involved in the restructuring process, resulting in less consensus among parties at the negotiating table. The recent credit crisis has also played a significant role, making it extremely hard for troubled companies to refinance with suitable terms. Add in the increased complexity of capital structures, which are difficult to unravel, and you have a recipe for more unsuccessful restructuring outcomes. These factors diminish a company's ability to recover from challenging times, heightening the prospects of business failure.

To respond effectively, under-performing companies must do more than act quickly to identify the root causes of their underperformance. They must also identify immediate stabilizing activities, address their debt-structuring and capital needs, take steps to protect their core competencies, and understand all available options.

Globalization

Eroding Boundaries

The liberalization of trade in countries around the world has created many benefits for corporations eager to reach new markets, reduce labor costs and partner with world-class organizations no matter where they're located. In addition to facilitating an easier flow of goods, trade liberalization allows people and capital to move around the globe more freely.[1] At the same time, this erosion of boundaries creates greater operational complexity for companies as they expand into increasingly remote locations that may lack familiar cultures, business structures, or economic transparency. It also creates greater restructuring complexity as companies work to meet the needs of divergent and geographically dispersed stakeholders.

International Investment

The instantaneous and massive flow of capital around the world also contributes to growing complexity – both for individual organizations and for markets in general. Consider: between 2006 and 2007, foreign direct investment (FDI) outflows from countries in the Organization of Economic Co-operation and Development (OECD) increased by over 50 per cent to a record US$1.82 trillion (see table). This was US$580 billion higher than the previous record outflows in 2000. Flows into OECD countries also grew in 2007, increasing 31 per cent to US$1.37 trillion – a new record for OECD inflows.[2]

---

1 "Managing Complexity in Global Organizations," IMD International, February, 2007.

2 Organization for Economic Co-operation and Development (OECD), "OECD Investment News", Issue 7, June 2008, http://www.oecd.org/dataoecd/18/28/40887916.pdf.

Foreign Direcct Investment, billion US$

	Inflows			Outflows		
	2006	2007	% change	2006	2007	% change
Australia	18.9	23.6	24.8	23.8	25.7	7.9
Austria	6.2	30.7	395.6	9.7	31.4	225.3
Belgium	63.9	39.1	-38.9	56.2	51.9	-7.7
Canada	69.0	107.4	55.6	45.2	49.5	9.3
Czech Republic	6.0	9.1	51.7	1.5	1.3	-9.1
Denmark	3.6	11.3	214.6	8.5	16.2	91.0
Finland	5.5	8.5	54.6	3.2	8.6	172.7
France	78.2	158.0	102.0	121.4	224.6	85.1
Germany	55.2	50.9	-7.7	94.8	167.5	76.7
Greece	5.4	1.9	-64.3	4.2	5.3	28.1
Hungary	6.8	5.6	-17.9	3.6	4.1	13.7
Iceland	4.0	3.8	-3.1	5.3	12.5	134.6
Ireland	-0.9	25.9	na	14.7	22.1	49.6
Italy	39.3	40.2	2.4	42.1	90.8	115.7
Japan	-6.5	22.5	na	50.2	73.5	46.4
Korea	3.6	1.6	-56.7	7.1	15.3	114.4
Luxembourg	125.0	118.8	-4.9	110.7	181.9	64.3
Mexico	19.2	23.2	20.8	5.8	8.3	43.4
Netherlands	8.0	99.5	1145.5	47.1	31.2	-33.9
New Zealand	8.0	2.9	-64.2	0.4	2.8	650.9
Norway	6.5	0.6	-90.7	21.1	11.2	-47.1
Poland	18.9	17.6	-7.1	8.9	3.2	-63.6
Portugal	11.3	5.6	-50.2	7.0	6.2	-10.8
Slovak Republic	4.2	2.9	-31.3	0.4	0.2	-44.7
Spain	26.9	53.4	98.5	100.3	119.6	19.3
Sweden	23.1	18.8	-18.6	22.0	36.7	66.4
Switzerland	26.3	40.4	53.7	69.9	51.0	-27.1
Turkey	19.9	22.0	10.3	0.9	2.1	127.4
United Kingdom	147.7	186.0	25.9	79.5	229.9	189.3
United States	242.0	237.5	-1.9	241.2	333.3	38.2
Total	**1045.1**	**1369.2**	**31.0**	**1206.6**	**1817.9**	**50.7**

Notes: data are converted to US dollars using average exchange rates.

Sources: OECD International Direct Investment Database and MEI.

Although international investment plays a positive role in encouraging global development, it also complicates the restructuring process by making it challenging to track the flow of corporate assets and capital around the world.

Outsourcing

A third contributor to business and restructuring complexity is the ongoing trend towards international outsourcing. According to a 2008 study by management consulting firm PRTM, 50 per cent of manufacturing will be globalized by 2010 (see chart).[3] As organizations across industries extend their supply chains to include a growing number of foreign partners, global events can disproportionately influence an organization's functioning, and potentially compromise its viability. When this happens, companies face added challenges in gaining consensus for a restructuring proposal from global suppliers.

GLOBALIZED FUNCTIONS 2008 AND PROJECTED INCREASE BY 2010

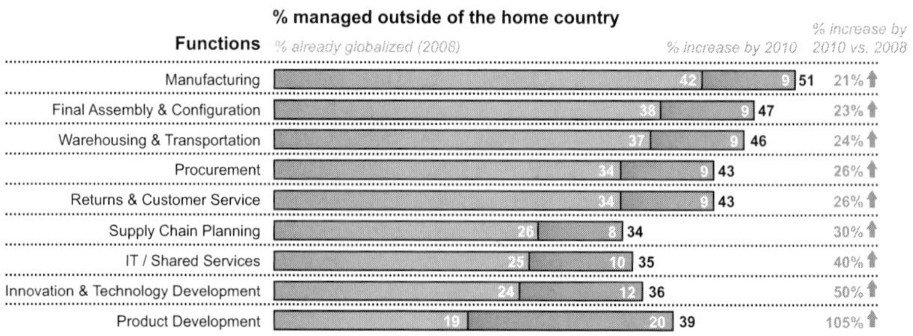

More than 50% of manufacturing will be globalized by 2010.

Economic Interdependence

One of the more subtle effects of increased globalization is the growing tendency for seemingly isolated events to influence world markets. In 1998, for instance, an earthquake in Taipei disrupted the world's supply of computer chips and shut down the production lines of several PC manufacturers in the U.S.4 More recently, the 2008 financial downturn that had its genesis in the U.S. sub-prime housing market rapidly infected central banks and economies across North America, Europe, and Asia.

As companies come to rely more on international sales, economic interdependence is only set to rise. This means companies will increasingly be affected by events outside of their control, and may find themselves facing unforeseen – and unplanned for – financial crises.

---

3 "Global Supply Chain Trends 2008 – 2010," PRTM, 2008.

4 "Globalization, localization and the cost of complexity – a network approach," International Society for Ecology and Culture, April, 2008.

Capital Structure Sophistication

Beyond globalization, a second factor making restructuring more complex is the rising sophistication of today's capital markets. In the not-so-distant past, companies generally relied on relatively simple debt and equity structures to finance their operations and expansion. In recent years, the introduction of increasingly complex and creative financing vehicles has complicated business structures, making it much more difficult for companies to easily restructure their operations. To understand the nature of this complexity, consider the types of financial instruments companies now rely on:

Debt

Asset-Backed Securities

Asset-backed securities (ABS) are a form of debt whose principle and interest payments are repaid from (or backed by) cash flows from a specified pool of underlying assets. In some cases, the assets underlying ABS are not sufficiently liquid to be sold individually. By pooling them, investors can reduce their risk by diversifying their holdings across an entire pool of assets with various investment grades. Different types of ABS include:

Term ABS

These securities are issued to third-party investors for a specified term.

Asset-based loans

Generally, asset-based loans are secured by inventory, accounts receivable and/or other balance sheet assets. They generally run for three to five years, to match the term of the underlying leases or retail loans. These loans typically help companies finance transactions such as cross-border expansion, debt restructuring, strategic acquisitions, or management buyouts.

Asset-Backed Commercial Paper (ABCP)

While similar to asset-based loans, ABCP is issued as short-term commercial paper, which means it typically matures in 30, 60, or 90 days. This type of structure has more inherent uncertainty than term ABS as it effectively funds longer-term assets (three- to five-year loans and leases) with short-term obligations. To further complicate matters, ABCP is often packaged into securities that are then sliced into different classes ranked by seniority of investors (a process called "tranching").[5] From there, it can be sold by one central sponsor or by multiple sellers.

Distressed securities

Distressed securities are either corporate or central bank securities that are already in default, under bankruptcy protection, or in distress and heading toward such a condition.[6] Examples of distressed securities can include underperforming bank loans, high yield bonds, convertible securities trading below their conversion value (also called busted convertible bonds), trade claims held by suppliers, public or private senior and junior debt, non-performing loans, and distressed real estate.

Collateralized Debt Obligations (CDOs)

CDOs are investment-grade securities backed by a pool of bonds, loans, and other assets. CDOs do not specialize in one type of debt, but are often non-mortgage loans or bonds.

Collateralized Loan Obligations (CLOs)

CLOs are special purpose vehicles (SPVs) backed by loan receivables. CLOs are frequently tranched (see explanation under Asset-Backed Commercial Paper, above) and sold to a variety of different investors.

Syndicated loans

These loans are offered by a group of lenders, called a syndicate, that works together to provide funds for a single borrower. The borrower can be a corporation, a large project, or a government entity. Thanks to a number of financial innovations that have led to the creation of new asset classes, the syndicated loan market has increased tremendously in the past 20 years. The secondary market alone grew by more than 1,600 per cent between 1991 and 2003, when it hit trading volumes of $135 billion.[7]

---

5 "The 2007/2008 Demise of the Non-Bank ABCP Market in Canada", McDowell & Bond.

6 "Distressed Securities", http://www.hedgefund-index.com/d_distressed.asp

7 "Growth of Syndicated Loan Market in U.S. Has Led a Quiet Revolution in Capital Market, Says New Milkin Institute Study", http://www.thefreelibrary.com/Growth+of+Syndicated+Loan+Market+in+U.S.+Has+Led+a+'Quiet+Revolution'...-a0124072728

Credit Default Swaps (CDS)

A CDS is a swap contract designed to transfer the credit exposure of fixed income products between parties. In essence, in exchange for paying the seller, the buyer of the contract receives a payout if a credit instrument (like a bond or loan) goes into default.

Mezzanine debt

A typical mezzanine investment consists of a debt or debt-like instrument, paired with an equity "sweetener". The equity component of the investment gives the mezzanine lender upside potential, while the debt component - which generates steady interest payments and ranks senior to the company's common stock - provides a measure of downside risk protection.

Equity

Debt markets are not the only areas showing increased sophistication in recent years. Equity markets have also evolved with the introduction of numerous new players, including:

Private Equity Firms

Private equity firms invest in companies at various stages of their development, and will typically specialize in defined industries or a specific growth stage. Although different types of investors offer different types of capital to investee companies, the characteristic they all share is that investee companies are private - which means they are not (yet) listed on any public exchange. In 2006, their peak year, private equity firms carried out more than US$664 billion worth of corporate buyouts, according to data firm Thomson Financial. Private equity funds' share of global mergers and acquisitions (M&As) also increased from 4 per cent in 2001 to more than 35 per cent in the first half of 2007.[8] However, private equity sales volume in 2008 dropped to U.S.$211 billion as tightened credit markets limited the amount of available financing.[9]

---

8 K. Singh, "Taking it Private - Consequences of the Global Growth of Private Equity," Sept. 2008.

9 Bloomberg, "Pimco's El-Erian Says Buyout, Hedge Funds May Shrink by Half," March 16, 2009.

Hedge Funds

Hedge funds typically pool capital from institutions and affluent individuals to make investments in both private and public companies. Because they are not governed by many of the regulations that apply to mutual funds, hedge funds can engage in aggressive investing strategies, short selling, leverage, program trading, swaps, arbitrage and derivatives.[10] The current economic crisis has caused severe suffering in the industry. Chicago-based Hedge Fund Research Inc. estimated that approximately 920 hedge funds, which represent 12 per cent of the industry, closed in 2008.[11]

Sovereign Wealth Funds

Sovereign Wealth Funds (SWFs) are large pools of assets and investment funds owned and managed by governments. The funding for SWFs typically comes from central bank reserves that accumulate as a result of budget and trade surpluses and from revenue generated from national exports.[12] While SWFs are not new, their number has grown significantly since the 1950s (see chart). Today, the top ten funds, which hail from the Middle East, Norway, Singapore, China and Russia, account for roughly 80 per cent of all SWF assets.[13]

10 "Hedge Fund", http://www.investorwords.com/2296/hedge_fund.html

11 Above note 9.

12 "Sovereign Wealth Fund", http://www.investopedia.com/terms/s/sovereign_wealth_fund.asp

13 K. Singh, "Frequently asked questions about sovereign wealth funds", October 2008.

Chart 1: Number of Sovereign Wealth Funds Since the 1950s

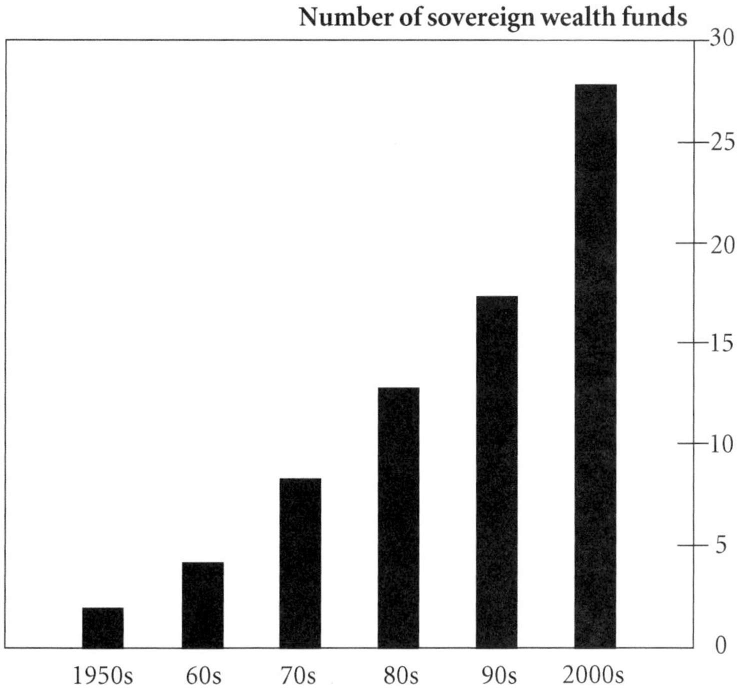

Source: Deutsche Bank and Morgan Stanley

Case Study

To gain an understanding of the way in which capital market complexity has altered the restructuring landscape, consider the case of Coventree Inc. Founded in 1998, Coventree created and administered various ABCP conduits, including Aurora Trust, Apollo Trust, Comet Trust, Planet Trust, and Rocket Trust. These trusts sold short-term investments backed by longer-term assets such as auto or credit card receivables, mortgages, and more complex instruments.[14]

At its height, Canada's ABCP market was valued at approximately C$35 billion, with Coventree responsible for arranging nearly half of this amount. Following the meltdown of the U.S. sub-prime market, however, Canadian investors became concerned about the assets underlying ABCP. This con-

14 "Coventree wind-down awaits ABCP restructuring plan", *Ottawa Citizen*, June 25, 2008.

cern quickly spiraled into a market seizure that left investors holding over $32 billion in instruments they couldn't sell.

On August 14, 2007, Coventree's shares plummeted 72 per cent to close at $2.37 on the Toronto Stock Exchange (TSX).[15] In the past, this type of corporate decline may have affected only direct shareholders. However, the interconnectedness of the capital markets meant that Coventree's losses could potentially threaten the stability of Canada's entire economy. As a result, the response had to include more stakeholders than ever before.

In September 2007, a group of Canada's ABCP participants formed the Pan-Canadian Investors Committee. Together, the committee hammered out the Montreal Accord, an agreement by ABCP stakeholders to refrain from trading ABCP, triggering default provisions or exercising security rights over the underlying assets. With the short-term threat at a standstill, the participants then took steps to formally restructure the ABCP market by implementing a plan of arrangement under the *Companies' Creditors Arrangement Act* (CCAA).

Ultimately, 96 per cent of noteholders agreed to the CCAA plan of arrangement in April 2008. For its part, in early 2008, Coventree announced its intention to seek an orderly wind-down of its business.[16]

Organizational Evolution

A final factor that cannot be discounted when considering rising restructuring complexity is the evolution of organizational structures. Gone are the days when companies focused predominantly on selling a small handful of targeted products and services to mostly local markets. In pursuit of growth, companies have extended their operations and supply chains around the globe, while vastly expanding the array of solutions they offer. This frequently results in the adoption of business systems that feature layers of specialization. In a restructuring setting, this means companies are faced with the almost insurmountable task of unwinding complex organizational and financial structures, while adhering to sometimes conflicting regulatory requirements in all the locations where they do business. Some of the ways in which organizations have evolved over time include:

---

15 McDowell & Bond, "The 2007/2008 Demise of the Non-bank ABCP Market in Canada," 2008.

16 "Debt restructuring hurts Coventree", *Toronto Star*, February 2, 2008.

Product, Market, and Channel Growth

In a bid to win a growing share of both domestic and international markets, companies today seek growth by rolling out new products and introducing brand extensions of existing products. Between the 1970s and the 2000s, this quest has resulted in ongoing product complexity (see chart). As companies work to tailor their offerings to ever-smaller niches, this complexity is bound to continue. Unfortunately, it also threatens to create greater market instability. As organizations adopt more competitive tactics to appeal to smaller market segments, they risk experiencing lower growth rates and decreasing profit margins. For companies that cannot survive this race, restructuring often begins by reducing superfluous or failed product offerings.

Examples of Product Complexity*

	1970's	2000's
Crest Toothpaste	**15 SKUs** (mint, original, one formula, tubes only)	**49 SKUs** (gel, paste, pumps, tartar control, whitening, baking soda)
Philadelphia Cream Cheese	**3 SKUs** (three sizes of one flavor, one style of packaging)	**30 SKUs** (block, soft, whipped, light, regular, flavors)
Coca-Cola	**6 SKUs** (Classic Coke, cans, bottles)	**25 SKUs** (cherry, diet, diet cherry, caffeine free, caffeine free diet, vanilla, diet vanilla, etc.)
The average supermarket	**8,000 items carried**	**35,000 items carried**

**For illustration only. Based on Deloitte Consulting observations of shelf sets in selected retail outlets. Not meant to be a comprehensive product line review for any manufacturer.* [17]

[17] "Achieving Profit Advantage via Business Simplification", Deloitte Consulting, Mid-Fall 2006 issue.

Growth Through Acquisition

Growth strategies that include strategic mergers and acquisitions also contribute to increasing organizational complexity. As companies acquire competitors or other market players, they are often faced with redundant product lines, unwieldy supply chains, disconnected systems and processes, divergent cultures, and conflicting customer demands. All of these factors increase the complexity of running a business, and, unless special care is taken, may eventually increase costs.[18] They also create greater challenges in a restructuring scenario as stakeholders attempt to salvage the most profitable parts of the business.

Global Expansion

As noted earlier, the trend towards globalization has created more complex business networks. The trend is expected to continue in sectors as diverse as financial services, manufacturing, power generation, and technology. Companies that operate in numerous different countries often face unanticipated management and strategic challenges. They also face the added complexity of complying with divergent national and local regulations. This does more than heighten the risk of financial underperformance; it also makes it difficult to effect a smooth restructuring process.

Supply Chain Complexity

As companies introduce new products, acquire new businesses and expand internationally, the complexity of their supply chain rapidly rises. Too frequently, this results in companies relying on a number of authorized vendors, many of whom may not be sufficiently qualified.[19] This creates significant challenges in the event of a formal restructuring, as organizations and their advisors work to identify the suppliers around the world that rank in priority during restructuring proceedings. It also heightens the prospect of legal action as suppliers take steps to protect their interests.

Case Study[20]

To get a sense of how organizational structure complexity complicates the restructuring process, consider the case of Delphi Corporation. Headquar-

[18] K. Jagersma, "Managing Business Complexity", 2004.

[19] Above note 17.

[20] "Restructuring at Delphi Corporation", Harvard Business School.

tered in Michigan, Delphi was one of the largest global suppliers of vehicle electronics, transportation components, integrated systems, and other electronic technology. It was founded in 1991 as a wholly-owned subsidiary of General Motors Corporation (GM) and served as GM's primary parts supplier. In 1998, GM was also Delphi's largest customer, accounting for 78 per cent of its annual revenues. At year end 1998, Delphi employed almost 200,000 people around the world. Its workers were largely represented by three unions.

In 1999, GM sold its Delphi holdings to investors as part of a public offering at $17 per share. From the outset, however, Delphi struggled to meet its financial goals. By 2005, the company and 38 of its subsidiaries filed for reorganization under Chapter 11 of the U.S. Bankruptcy Code. Its shares plummeted to $0.33.

Due to its unduly complicated operating structure (see chart), Delphi ultimately had to work out a deal with administrative claimants, in addition to eight additional classes of claimants, including secured claims, flow through claims, general unsecured claims, bondholders, GM, and common equity holders. It had to negotiate with three different labor unions to resolve issues with its unfunded pension programs, plant closures and the modification/termination of labor contracts. It also had to negotiate directly with GM to address the claims between the two companies.

Exhibit 4 Delphi's Corporate Structure

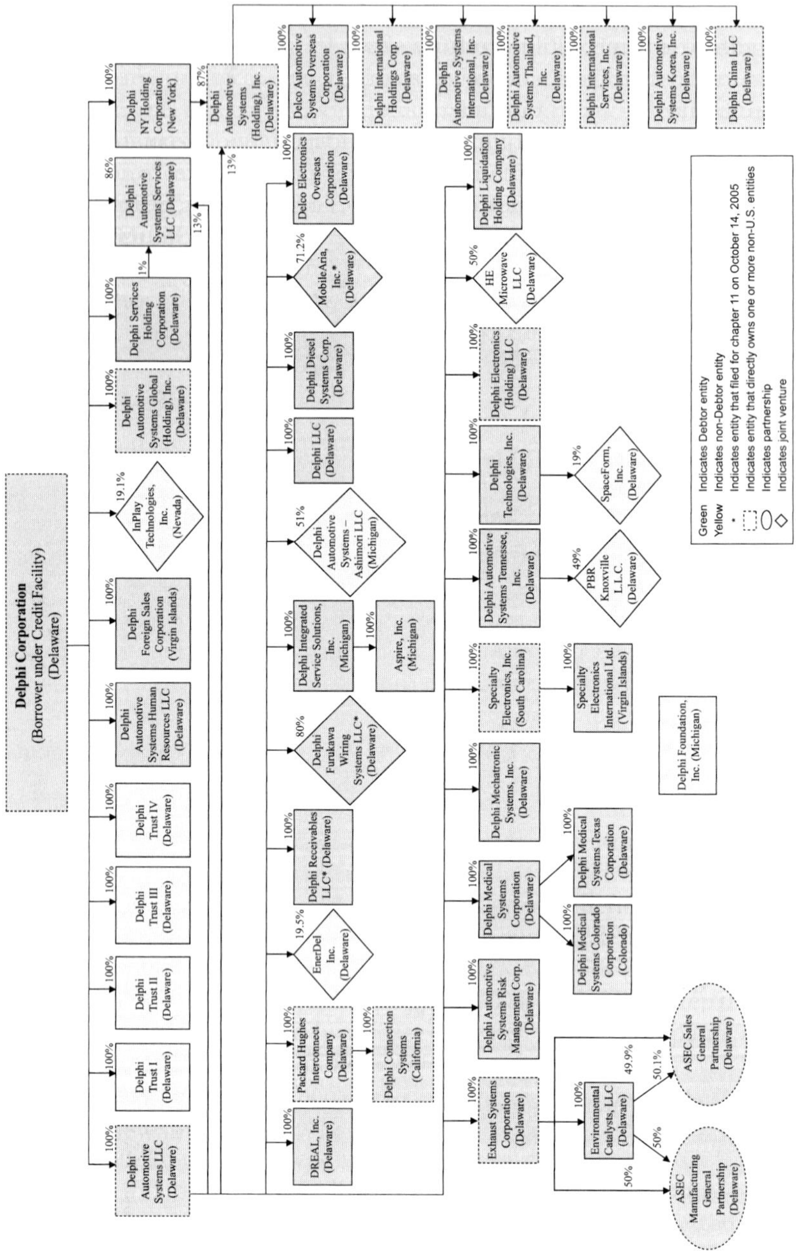

Source: Delphi Corporation, Disclosure Statement, p. DS-34.

Current and Future Realities in Restructuring

Restructuring Today

Canadian companies facing financial challenges have four primary options for restructuring their businesses.

- Informal restructuring includes various attempts to improve performance without court protection and allows organizations to negotiate with their creditors to arrive at a mutually agreed upon repayment arrangement.
- Formal restructuring under the *Companies' Creditors Arrangement Act* (CCAA) allows for a court-supervised process that is generally used for large corporate restructurings.
- Formal restructuring under Division 1 of the *Bankruptcy and Insolvency Act* (BIA) is a more detailed and less flexible process that is generally used for smaller restructurings.
- Formal restructuring under the *Canada Business Corporations Act* (CBCA) allows solvent corporations to make arrangements to try to preserve shareholder equity, as well as value for creditors.

Informal Restructuring

An informal restructuring is an out of court, non-statutory process that allows a troubled company to negotiate directly with its creditors. Informal restructuring offers a solution which is typically less expensive and can benefit stakeholders by speeding up the process. To succeed, companies generally must gain approval for the deal not only from their secured creditors, but also from their unsecured creditors and suppliers. For this reason, informal proposals work best for companies that have few creditors and relatively simple operations.

For organizations that can make them work, informal restructurings offer a number of additional advantages. First, they allow a company to develop a customized arrangement with the creditors of its choice. Second, they give companies greater control over the disclosure of information as they are negotiated behind closed doors. Finally, because they are consensual, informal restructurings signal that knowledgeable parties remain confident in the company's ongoing operating viability.[21]

Conversely, informal restructurings do not bind unsecured creditors who refuse the offer. This frees creditors to take action against the company

---

21 F. Spizzirri & N. Washington, "Restructuring and Associated Documents", Corporate Securities and IP Law Forum, Cassels Brock & Blackwell LLP, January 30, 2008.

despite the existence of an informal proposal. Companies (or creditors) that require a stay of proceedings consequently tend to prefer a more formal restructuring process.

Formal Restructuring

Companies unable to restructure informally can file for formal restructuring under the BIA or CCAA or, less commonly, under the CBCA. These processes are designed to allow companies to regain their financial footing under either statutory or court supervision. To succeed, management must develop a viable turnaround plan and gain access to the capital necessary to finance the turnaround.

Generally, formal restructuring under the CBCA is available only to solvent companies interested in taking pre-emptive steps to restructure their organizations in advance of a severe financial crisis. As such, a CBCA restructuring process tends to be more rapid, and less costly, than other formal restructuring options.

For their parts, formal restructuring under the BIA or CCAA can take months, or even years, to implement and can be very expensive. In addition to ongoing operating costs, companies must pay for numerous professional advisors, including monitors/trustees, accountants, financial advisors, lawyers and others.[22] As a result, companies often require additional financing during a restructuring. Typically, this capital is provided by Debtor in Possession (DIP) lenders who, in exchange for advancing funds, receive priority over other secured creditors. Companies that can't secure DIP financing must resort to other funding methods, including asset liquidation.

On the downside, formal proceedings under the BIA or CCAA diminish management's control over the company and frequently take a negative toll on the business. For instance, customers may refuse to deal with the company, key employees may leave, and the company's value will almost certainly fall. This is not the case with CBCA restructurings, as companies using this process do not have to acknowledge insolvency.

That said, companies filing under the BIA or CCAA do enjoy certain advantages. With an immediate stay of proceedings, they have the ability to maintain ongoing operations while they seek to reorganize. The stay provides stability and may also protect management and directors from actions by creditors or other stakeholders.

As the process governing formal restructurings differs, companies must also decide what process they prefer. In some cases, they may have no choice.

---

22 *Ibid.*

Insolvent corporations generally do not have access to CBCA proceedings. Companies with debt below $5 million do not have access to the protection that the CCAA affords. For its part, the BIA threshold is only $1,000 in debt.

CCAA Reorganization

The CCAA deals with reorganization of companies that have a minimum of $5 million in total debt, including the debt of their affiliates. Once a company applies for a protection order, the court grants a stay of proceedings prohibiting creditors from enforcing claims against the company. While this initial stay is valid for only 30 days, the court typically extends the stay as long as restructuring progress is being made and funding is available.

To help the company restructure, the court appoints a monitor (typically a trustee in bankruptcy) to work with management to reorganize the company. While companies retain control over the business during the restructuring, the monitor is responsible for reporting to the court on the company's restructuring progress.

To complete a restructuring, the company needs to file a plan of arrangement with the court. Unlike the BIA process, companies do not have a time limit for filing this plan. Additionally, CCAA plans tend to be more flexible than BIA plans. For instance, creditors of the same class do not need to be treated equally under the CCAA. That said, a majority representing two-thirds of the value of the claims of each class of creditors does have to approve the plan before the court will sanction it.

Division 1 Proposal

Under Division 1 of the BIA, companies file a proposal asking their creditors to accept a compromise on the amounts owed to them. The process begins when a debtor either files a notice of intention to make a proposal or submits a completed proposal. As soon as forms are filed, a stay of proceedings is automatically created. Unlike under the CCAA, the scope and content of the stay is fixed. The length of the initial stay is 30 days, and it can be extended for subsequent periods of 45 days each, to a maximum of six months.[23]

A trustee in bankruptcy is appointed to help the company restructure during that time period. In negotiating an arrangement under the BIA, companies must treat creditors in each class equally. To be binding, the proposal must be approved by a majority of creditors representing two-thirds of the value

23 "The Restructuring Review", Law Business Research, McMillan LLP.

of the claims of each class of creditors, as well as by the court. If the proposal is rejected, or is not filed before the end of the stay, the company is automatically assigned into bankruptcy.

CBCA Restructuring

Companies facing financial challenges that have not spiraled into insolvency often prefer to take pre-emptive action by initiating restructuring proceedings under the CBCA. By acting proactively, companies that qualify for CBCA restructuring can remain in control of the restructuring process without risking the stigma associated with insolvency. That's because the CBCA does not impose court-ordered restrictions on operations, nor does it empower creditors to monitor corporate response. As an added advantage, if the process fails, companies do not automatically become bankrupt.

CBCA proceedings are best suited to organizations that are having difficulty refinancing their loans or meeting onerous debt covenants. Using this process, companies can offer their creditors the opportunity to exchange their debt for equity. The legislation also allows debtors to impose an approved deal on dissenting creditors, if necessary. That said, the CBCA does not apply to private debt or trade creditors, which generally limits its utility to companies facing public debt challenges.

Restructuring Tomorrow

Although Canada's restructuring processes have remained essentially unchanged over the years, their application has shifted considerably due to the complexities outlined earlier in this chapter. Specifically, our new economic reality has resulted in the following restructuring implications:

Less Financing

Successful restructurings depend on access to DIP financing, particularly in CCAA proceedings, which tend to be quite costly. Oddly enough, DIP financing tends to dry up during challenging economic times. The result? At a time when companies most need access to these funds, lenders are less inclined to advance them.

Higher Prospect of Liquidation

Unable to raise capital to finance a restructuring, struggling corporations are more likely to face the prospect of liquidation than in the past. While rarely a first-choice solution, liquidation is particularly undesirable in an environment of declining multiples. As liquidations rise, traditional buyers also find themselves awash in an oversupply, driving asset values to exceptional lows.[24]

Difficulty Unravelling Layered Structures

Complex capital structures that include private loans, public debt instruments, and derivative hedging tools are making restructuring more legally complex and costly.[25] Because they are difficult to penetrate and understand, companies face greater challenges attracting new lenders, who are concerned about throwing their hats into an already Byzantine fray. Conversely, the very presence of layered structures can vastly complicate restructuring proceedings.

Second-lien financings are a case in point. While similar to high-yield bonds, these debt vehicles are secured against corporate assets. They are considered "second-lien" because lenders rank behind traditional senior secured lenders. Trouble spots occur when the various lenders begin to assign different values to the corporate assets. If one party thinks the loan is worth 98 cents, and others think it's worth 68 cents based on their valuations, the inter-creditor agreements that underpin second-lien loans begin to break down. These situations frequently result in a stalemate while the company stagnates.[26]

New Players, Less Experience

Yet another factor complicating restructuring proceedings is the proliferation of new industry players. In addition to the familiar group of asset-based lenders, companies undergoing restructuring must now negotiate with an expanding array of debt and equity holders. Hedge funds, in particular, have become a dominant force in restructurings. While some of these players are experienced, those that are completely new to the field have already begun to inject greater complexity into the restructuring process.[27]

---

24 A. Nackan, "A view from the precipice", Financier Worldwide, January 2009.

25 "Survey: Restructuring Industry To Benefit From Complexity As Credit Cycle Turns," S&P, October, 2007.

26 "DRAW YOUR SWORDS en garde: The Right Side of the Balance Sheet in a Time of Turmoil," The Secured Lender, November - December 2008.

27 "Bankruptcy Trends: What's Next in the Restructuring World?", Commercial Lending Review, November - December 2008.

More Stakeholders, Less Consensus

More stakeholders involved in the restructuring process also results in less consensus among parties to a deal. In some ways, this challenge can trace its genesis to rising capital market complexity. The proliferation of complex financial instruments in recent years has attracted a new group of sophisticated participants to the markets. Many of these players entered the market at its height and, consequently, lack experience handling the restructurings introduced by a downturn.

Uncertain of how to proceed, some of these stakeholders have shown themselves willing to adopt obstructionist positions – particularly where their management is incentivized to avoid defaults and write-offs.[28] In other cases, these funds are adopting a "loan to own" strategy. In essence, this sees them refusing to convert their debt to an equity position. Most problematic are scenarios where funds refuse to sign confidentiality agreements to gain access to the debtor's non-public information and restrict their trading. Despite their lack of information, these funds sometimes try to steer the company's reorganization in the direction most advantageous to their own trading books, without considering the debtor's business or its other creditors.[29]

This trend appears to hold true around the world. In a European survey by Standard & Poor's,[30] key market participants identified a range of factors contributing to restructuring complexity, including complex financial structures, highly leveraged deals, and a diverse and changing investor base stimulated by active secondary markets. Due to this complexity, survey participants agreed that they had seen a rise in non-alignment between creditors of various classes, as well as fickle voting behavior by lenders that lacked ongoing economic exposure to the company.

How Companies – and Their Advisors – Can Respond

Given prevailing realities, it seems fair to conclude that stakeholders across the value chain must adopt new strategies and tactics if they hope to successfully navigate today's evolving restructuring landscape. While there are no hard and fast rules, some best practices have already emerged. Here are some of the ways companies, and their advisors, can position themselves for an advantageous restructuring outcome:

---

28 Above note 26.

29 "Seminar Grapples with Hedge Funds' Influence", Bankruptcy Court Decisions, Kirkland & Ellis LLP, www.kirkland.com

30 "Survey: Restructuring Industry To Benefit From Complexity As Credit Cycle Turns," S&P, October, 2007.

Act Quickly

While precipitous action is never advised when companies are undergoing challenges, experience shows that options dwindle when companies fail to address underperformance in a timely manner. When a crisis threatens, an accelerated situational and financial analysis is the key to cost-effective results. In addition to internally reviewing corporate performance at regular intervals, companies should seek external restructuring advice as early as possible to maximize the number of available options.

Maintain Capital Investment Agility

By ensuring flexibility regarding capital investments, companies can prevent themselves from being tied down by fixed-cost decisions. It is critical to look forward to assess whether current capital investments could impair agility in a fluctuating environment. Investments that are thought to be wise today (*i.e.*, in plant and equipment) may prove less desirable in the future. While an economic downturn can change the game, proactively maintaining an agile investment structure can both lower the chances of a restructuring and simplify any potential formal or informal action.

Be Transparent with Stakeholders

Ignoring an issue or potential problem won't make it go away; chances are it will only get worse. Board members, lenders, suppliers, customers, and other stakeholders don't appreciate surprises, which is why it is important to keep them appropriately informed throughout a downturn. Active communication keeps all parties well-educated about their respective rights and company issues, minimizing conflicts during any potential restructuring.

Assess the Options

Although informal and formal restructuring remain options for troubled companies, they are rarely the avenue of first resort. Long before commencing restructuring proceedings, companies can take steps to shore up their operations by simplifying their organizational structures, changing management, and amending debt contracts. To gain access to necessary funding, companies can also divest non-core assets, engage in strategic mergers, sell excess inventory or even work with existing lenders to swap debt for equity. Working capital optimization also offers a powerful way for organizations to reduce costs and free up much-needed capital. Plus, restructuring always remains an option for companies that can no longer access financing or that require a stay of proceedings to freeze their creditors' claims.

Identify Opportunities to Strengthen the Balance Sheet

When a company faces near-term performance issues or liquidity pressures, a strong balance sheet is imperative. There are fewer options available during periods of poor performance, which is why it is important to act prudently to afford greater flexibility. Companies should exploit opportunities as a precaution while they remain in line with covenants. Specific actions include optimizing working capital, negotiating more lenient covenants, and setting up credit facilities after taking into consideration both short- and long-term requirements.

Over-Communicate

When companies face difficulties, their default response is often to underplay the severity of the situation. What management fails to realize is how quickly a bad situation can worsen absent a coordinated response. Rather than sweeping financial challenges aside, organizations should take active steps to enhance their communication with stakeholders during periods of difficulty. This means advising employees and key managers of the roles they must play to help sustain corporate operations. It also means communicating with the Board of Directors, lenders, suppliers, customers, and other stakeholders long before any defaults occur. By bringing these players on-side, companies may be able to forestall these parties from taking action in a worse case scenario. Often, they can even elicit assistance from these stakeholders in the form of concessions that allow the company to regain its footing.

Creating Value Through Management of Your Asset Mix

Shaun R. Darchiville

My Perspective

My objective in this chapter is to provide some background for perspective and to draw your attention towards the areas that most people overlook and to share with you some simple strategies that could work for you.

I started working in the investment industry just after the crash of October 1987. Back then, the business provided access to three principal products:

1. cash
2. bonds
3. stocks

Derivatives (puts and calls) were also offered to the more sophisticated clients.

Within the cash category, one could choose between myriad of short- and medium-term options. Twenty-two years on, to me the business still offers the same three options on their own or now through various of products and hybrid offerings.

Within the fixed income category we offered access to government, provincial, and corporate-issued bonds, while the equity group was divided into two primary categories:

- income earners
- speculative (with varied degrees of risk)

And volatility was always present. I remember one of my colleagues mentioned to me that October and November were typically volatile months, followed only by the remaining 10 months of the year. One should always manage their accounts based on this reality, despite periods of growth.

I remember another conversation that I had where a manager cautioned me never to buy a stock unless I was willing to lose the money. I countered, "but it's TransCanada Pipelines". He then deadpanned, "it doesn't matter which company".

These casual conversations would go a long way towards defining what I learned and what I experienced. And, ultimately, what I have seen that works.

When I started in the business, the market participants were many and varied. The Canadian investment dealer community consisted of well over 25 firms, most of which are no longer around today.

During the 1990s, there was a period of continued consolidation of the investment dealers. This period of consolidation saw several firms join into one, as the case with most of the bank-owned firms. During this time, we saw a dramatic growth spurt in the amount of investment/hybrid products and products providers. Hedge funds and conventional mutual funds were springing up everywhere.

As the menu of options grew so did the degree of market volatility. This growth spurt continued throughout other major capital markets – creating similar volatile markets.

These volatile market realities seem to get all the attention. From my experience, most investors do not address some key fundamentals towards achieving success. Choosing the right investment strategy is fourth on the list of priorities.

Before You Make an Investment Decision

One of the key components to managing your money in volatile markets is often one of the most overlooked areas – *service and process.*

In my experience, many people operate and make decisions based on behavioral patterns, personal views of money, fears, concerns, and their current circumstances. Yet most advisor/client relationships do not support this reality. I always remind my clients - I can tell you what I think, but I cannot tell you how to feel.

The primary job of an advisor is to understand how someone feels about a potential decision and the impact it will have on their lives, versus the most common mantra - provide a solution to address their current need for action.

The following processes/mechanicals must be in place *before* you and your advisor can make an informed decision(s):

1. **Service Approach**

    a. When does your advisor do their Brain Work?

    b. When does stuff get done? Early in the morning? After the market closes? During the day when calls and e-mails are constant? During lunchtime? When? Is the solution a customized versus shelf solution? How often is the account reviewed for rebalancing?

        If you are using Options/Futures - when does your advisor review risk exposure for their clients?

        The answers to these questions are more important than you may realize. When a recommendation is made, the time that went into making it is crucial towards determining how valid it is to you and your family.

    c. How often will you sit down or have a phone conversation? What time is made for addressing investment, estate, insurance, and tax planning realities?

    The absence of a clear service approach/process leaves the door open for problems well before decisions are made.

2. **Total Return and Asset Mix**

    The amount of income earned in a portfolio coupled with market growth/decline paints a realistic growth picture. Projection charts and tables are too subjective to use and too many tools assume a straight-line relationship between time and money. The reality is that earned income and a more realistic expectation for growth are necessary.

    In my experience, if an investor is contributing $20,000 to their RRSPs, and the natural income earned is $12,000 per year, and it's expected that the market could add an additional $10,000 in capital appreciation, then the contributor is the most important factor towards growing the account followed by earned income, then market performance.

In this case, the degree of market risk to which the account is exposed should reflect this chain of command.

Some key points to consider:

a. When looking at the growth of a portfolio – consider the chain of command:

    i. contributions
    ii. earned income (dividends and interest)
    iii. market growth/decline

b. Your total return expectation is very important in determining how much market risk you need to achieve your overall goals.

c. What is the natural cash flow from the proposal? Is the income generated 60 per cent dividends/distributions and 40 per cent interest income?

d. Your total return objective then leads towards the creation of your ideal asset mix. How much bonds, cash, and stock do you need to hold and how much risk exposure do you need to have?

    For example, if your total return objective in order to achieve your goals is 8 per cent, how much of that 8 per cent is dependent on market growth? If your natural cash flow is 5 per cent and your objective is 8 per cent, then you know how much you are depending on the market to add to the equation.

3. Costs

The quality of investment guidance and management is directly related to costs. Understanding how your advisor makes decisions is a critical step towards looking after your relationship with them.

Are they being paid a salary? If a mutual fund company were paying them, how would a sell recommendation impact their compensation? Is their advice biased towards keeping you invested? I would be cautious and prone to revisit the situation in the complete absence of this information.

The separation and understanding of compensation is critical towards long-term success. I look at it like rent – a good landlord wants to keep a nice place, charge a reasonable rent, keep people for a long time, and make their stay comfortable.

Some things to consider:

a. What are you paying? How many people are you paying?

b. Is your advisor paid a base salary, bonus, commission, or a combination of these?

c. What are your payment options?
Essentially there are three primary categories for costs:

- commissions
- annual fees (a percentage of total assets)
- mutual fund fees

I cannot emphasize enough the importance of understanding your costs and its impact towards your long-term investment success.

Understanding Your Investment Psychology

Another key consideration towards knowing how you and your advisor interact is understanding yourself. Do you get anxious when the stock markets are volatile? Or do you feel optimistic that everything will turn out fine? Both reactions – natural parts of your psychological makeup – can actually impede your progress towards your investment goals.

Think about it this way. If you hired a general contractor to look after your house, would you actively oversee their daily activities? Or do you wait for a weekly update? Your home is almost as important and emotional as your investment portfolio – understanding how you make and manage decisions would set you on the right track towards how you should be prepared to deal with your other investments.

The good news is that you can gain some control over your responses – unlike the financial markets. The following will help identify some key pitfalls of investing and how you can avoid them.

1. Optimism

People have a natural tendency to overestimate the likelihood of positive results on everything from the weather to investing. This largely explains why people are so often disappointed by their investment performance – they simply felt they would do better based on this psychological outlook.

Avoiding the feeling of disappointment is only one good reason why you should consciously compensate for this natural optimism. If you base your financial goals on unrealistically positive expectations, you could fall short of your goals. This can affect your anticipated retirement date, amount of retirement income, or the value of your estate.

2. Over-confidence

Another powerful psychological trait is over-confidence. Just as people tend to be overly optimistic about the probability of positive results, they also tend to be over-confident about their own talents. Some investors think that they can "outsmart the market" - and even control largely unpredictable events such as stock market volatility.

This leads to one of the most common pitfalls of investing - market timing. Many investors try to time the market so that they always buy low and sell high - despite the fact that not even the most accomplished professional investors can do this consistently. One of my mentors once told me, "It's time in the markets not timing the markets".

Recognizing this tendency towards over-confidence is the first step towards dealing with it. Be honest about your abilities and, if you find yourself falling into traps such as market timing, take a step back and rethink your approach.

3. Hindsight

Hindsight is the tendency to believe that after something has happened you knew all along that it would - even though you didn't. This tendency can lead you to believe that events are far more predictable than they really are, raising unrealistic expectations about how well your investments will perform and your advisor's ability to foretell the future, among other things.

If you find yourself confidently declaring that you "knew it all along", ask yourself whether you really did. As with optimism and over-confidence, you may have to consciously compensate for hindsight.

4. Obsession

Do you follow the performance of your investments minute-by-minute on TV or the Internet? Do you dwell on short-term changes in the market value of your investments?

Do you fixate on the negative performance of a single investment, even when your overall portfolio is doing well? These can all be signs of obsessive behavior commonly displayed by investors.

Take a step back and look at the big picture. Are you on track to achieving your long-term goals? Are you comfortable with the level of investment risk in your portfolio? If not, you may have to make adjustments to stop obsessing about short-term events.

5. Denial

When stock markets go down, investors can sometimes panic and sell what is still fundamentally a good investment. The flipside of this is denial – when investors continue to hold an investment that has gone bad, thinking it will eventually come back. When an investment has fundamentally deteriorated, it may be time to sell.

Having an investment discipline in place with specific criteria for buying and selling can help you overcome this tendency.

6. Greed

The desire to "profit quickly" compels many investors to take bigger risks than they should, such as investing too much in a single investment. When the risk doesn't pay off, it can jeopardize their financial security. That doesn't mean you should never take a risk – it's a normal part of investing.

The key is to take well-calculated risks within a properly diversified investment portfolio, which is designed with your personal risk tolerance in mind. That way, when the occasional risk doesn't pay off, the impact is mitigated by the other investments in your portfolio.

7. Herd Mentality

When we see other people doing something, we have a natural tendency to think that it must be a good thing and we should do it too. This "herd mentality" is often behind sharp ups and downs in the financial markets. When other people are buying, propelling the market upwards, we buy too, sending the market even higher. Similarly, when other people sell in a panic, sending the market downwards, we sell too, fueling the decline.

Unfortunately, this often results in buying at the height of the market euphoria, or selling close to the depths of the panic. Instead of following the herd, follow a disciplined investment strategy based on logic and reason.

Successful investing over the long term is less about how the markets are doing than how we react to what the markets are doing. Unfortunately, many of our natural psychological reactions – like denial, panic or greed – can impede our long-term success.

Weathering the Storm – Living With Your Decisions

Volatile markets bring with them tumultuous times for investors. When stock markets get volatile, investors often think there's nothing they can do except watch hopelessly. But while you can't control the markets, you can control how you react to them. Here are seven things you can do now to survive today's volatile markets.

Stay Calm

It can be extremely difficult to stay calm when you're watching your investments go down day after day with seemingly no end in sight. But, as history shows, the market volatility will eventually end and markets will resume their upward advance.

Unfortunately, many investors get caught up in the emotions of the moment when the markets go down. Fearing further losses, they sell their investments, which helps send the markets even lower. This, in turn, prompts other investors to sell, sending the markets lower still.

This self-reinforcing cycle of panic selling tends to be very indiscriminate, taking down both good and bad stocks. So if you decide to simply sell everything, you could be selling high quality stocks with solid fundamentals that will be among the leaders when the markets come back. Instead of simply dumping all your stocks, fearing the worst, it's better to stay calm, take a rational look at your investments, and then make any adjustments that may be appropriate.

Keep Your Sense of Perspective

When you're in the middle of a painful market correction, it can certainly feel like it's somehow different – and more serious – than previous corrections. Unquestionably, the current correction has been very sharp. It also has some serious underlying causes, particularly the credit crisis in the U.S. and Europe and its impact on global economies.

But while it may seem especially severe, the current correction is actually in line with previous corrections, including those in 1973/74 (-48.2%), 1980/81 (-27.1%), 1987 (-33.5%) and, most recently, 2000/2001 (-49.1%). In each case, there was a serious underlying cause, which helped stoke fears of a more serious economic collapse: the oil crisis in 1973/74, run-away inflation and interest rates in 1980/81, inadequate market controls in 1987, and a robust technology sector that helped create a massive equity bubble in 2000/2001.

Although each of these corrections were painful - and may have felt like the worst ever at the time - the economy didn't collapse and the markets went on to reach new highs, as they have always done.

Be Rational

Staying calm doesn't mean you shouldn't do anything about your investments. While you don't want to sell everything in a panic, you should take a rational look at your investments to determine if any changes should be made. Market corrections can expose weaknesses in certain stocks, which you may want to sell. They can also reveal compelling opportunities to purchase solid stocks at temporarily depressed prices.

Look for stocks with strong underlying fundamentals, including a strong management team, consistent profitability and history of rising dividends. Having solid, dividend-paying stocks in your portfolio helps take some of the sting out of declining share prices - they still pay a dividend while you wait for the market to recover. These high-quality stocks are also typically the leaders when the market recovers.

Avoid the Temptation of Market Timing

I mentioned this previously, but it is worth repeating. Some investors - thinking they can wait out the worst of the market storm - sell all their stocks, sit on cash until they feel the market has bottomed, and then buy back in. The problem with this strategy - as good as it sounds in theory - is that it is very difficult to turn a negative into a positive.

Stay Diversified

It's one of the fundamental laws of successful investing - but unfortunately it's one that's often forgotten during stormy markets. To help minimize the impact of market volatility, your investment portfolio should be diversified in several different ways: by individual investment, asset class, geographic area, and industry sector, to name a few. The basic idea is that when one investment goes down, another goes up, reducing your portfolio's volatility and smoothing out your returns.

Diversification is not a one-time thing: it must change as your needs change, attitudes towards risk change and, also, as the markets change. With the current volatility, it may make sense to rebalance your portfolio's diversification - possibly in favor of some more conservative income producing investments - but it most likely doesn't make sense to ignore it completely.

Revisit Your Comfort Level with Risk

Like many investors, you may have found your risk tolerance drifting upwards with the markets between 2002 and 2007. When the markets keep on going up for so long, it's easy to forget that risk is a normal part of investing, and that market corrections happen regularly. Now is a good time to review your risk tolerance and asset mix to ensure they remain appropriate, given your long-term goals.

During periods of intense stock market volatility, it can be very difficult to know what, if anything, you should do.

Taking Action in Volatile Markets

Once you understand how you will be treated/managed, where your returns are coming from, and what your costs are, then you can make some decisions.

When market turbulence increases, as it did dramatically over 2007 to 2008, the natural impulse for investors is to take action. But it's not just about taking *any* action. By working with your advisor, you can determine what actions or strategies would be the best for you and make the *right* decisions for your long-term success.

Three Courses of Action

There are three paths that investors can evaluate and pursue:

1. Reduce your risk.
2. Capitalize on opportunities.
3. Stay the course.

Reduce Your Risk

When entering a volatile market it is best to determine the current weight of equities, cash, and bonds that you have. Once you have a good picture of this, you can determine what level of risk exposure you are willing to take, or how much equity exposure you are willing to manage.

As an example:

In an up or stable market your asset mix could be:

10% cash
10% bonds
40% dividend paying equities
40% growth riskier equities

Entering into a volatile market you may feel more inclined to have a balance of:

30% cash
30% bonds
20% dividend paying equities
20% growth riskier equities

Once this mix is identified, you will know how much time you need to spend towards managing it and if it's worth hiring an advisor/broker, and what cost options make the most sense for you.

Capitalize on Opportunities

There are a number of ideas that could work in a volatile market. I consider that most volatile markets are periods where economic uncertainty and risk management are at their highest, where interest rates are trending down, and credit defaults become a concern.

Be Careful With These

There are derivatives tool available to take advantage of opportunities. I would caution you towards their use for the following reasons:

- The level of risk/potential liability associated with futures and (put and call) options has dramatically increased over the years. Few brokers are licensed to do this type of business. The larger investment firms have dedicated advisors that focus on this area for clients, while smaller firms would have resources in the major cities.

This is important for you to understand. If you have an advisor working for you in this area you must understand how they manage their time to manage your risk.

- I think this area makes sense and is deserving of careful exploration. Ensuring that value is added to a well functioning investment portfolio.
- The term "hedge funds" has become such an over-used and slightly abused term. Hedge funds are designed to short, long equity, and bond markets and commodities, while some hold private companies and mortgages. In addition to their operational risk, one should be cautious with their use of leverage and how they charge their fees.
- Index linked notes/index up and down strategies – another area where your due diligence is needed to uncover the hidden truths behind leverage and fees. In this segment when it works well it works well. When it does not work well, it turns very bad quickly, to the point where money may not be recoverable.

Some Comfortable Solutions

I like these strategies because I have seem them work with limited negative repercussions. And, from the standpoint of an investment advisor, they are simple to manage and to follow:

- Understand the technical aspects of the market: **Resistance and Support** levels. In a volatile market, the fundamentals come second to the technical picture.
    - Resistance determines the level of a market index where an upward trend would have to break out before another higher level can be reached.
    - For the North American market, the S&P 500 Index is one of the best measuring tools. If the Index sold off to 650 and then rallied to a level of 700, and if the technical Resistance were 750, then a rally to 775 would indicate the possibility of surpassing 775 and heading past 800.
    - Support levels work in the opposite. So, in a market sell-off, the support levels are very important. If the Index sold off to 600 and the next support is 550 or 500, in this case the

furtherance of bad news would provide a case for where the next down leg would be.

- Your understanding of where the levels are allows you to set your **limit buy and sell orders** appropriately:
    - If you like BCE shares and you feel the market has weakness – then set the buy order 5 per cent or 10 per cent below the last trade.
    - These orders have a 30-day live window and must be re-set at close of the last order day. Also, in a rapidly declining or rising market your limit order is not guaranteed to be filled. In most cases, for liquid companies, fills are usually not an issue.
    - Make your list and check it twice. You only need to be successful with the names on your plate. Don't get carried away with too many names/companies. Make a short, concise list of key companies/sectors and target them. You could miss some opportunities doing this. But you would reduce your chances of significant loss while increasing your chance of success with your chosen names.
- Index exposure to gold and precious metals, namely **silver and gold**. The markets options have improved and you have access to some good offering via the exchange where you have held physical gold through certificates. The New York and Toronto market have enough options to keep you satisfied.
- In a volatile market, **corporate bonds** from certain companies are worth buying. The caveat is that you want to stay with issuers that are not likely to default before their maturity date. They are an attractive option and their risk/reward profile is the best before and during volatile markets. Again, make sure you stay with B and above-rated bonds and from issuers that are not in jeopardy of running into problems.
- For a simple way to identify what corporate bonds make sense, just get the top holdings for some corporate bond mutual funds. They have already done the work for you. And if the inventory on the street is tight then go with the corporate bond fund that has the best potential.

Conclusion

Volatile markets are usually during times of fear and panic in the market; at best, before, during, and on the way out of a down cycle. Having a strategy that increases your chances of success is important. Focusing on how stuff gets done, who's doing it, at what cost they are doing it and how your risk is being managed are important areas that must come before a decision to buy. Then staying the course becomes the easy part.

Inside the Black Box: Clear Thinking About the Financial Crisis*

Maneesh Mehta

Summary

At a fundamental level, the current economic crisis is the result of a system that attempted to "manage" risk through manipulations that aimed to shift perceived risk.[1,2] This revealed a telling example of how greed, and its pursuit, by some, can infringe on the rights of others. Adam Smith noted that virtue and trust "lubricate the wheels of society", and thus play a crucial role in facilitating the work of the market. Economic transactions involving unethical or greedy behavior impose higher costs for monitoring and enforcing contracts. This article summarizes briefly the 2008-9 financial crisis. Since much can be read elsewhere, our interest is in providing an historical context and understanding of this crisis, and in looking to our learning from past crises and fundamental principles to provide some useful guidelines.

2008-9 Financial Crisis

> Things take longer to happen than you think they will and then they happen faster than you thought they could – Rudi Dornbusch [3]

Many experts believe that the global economic crisis was triggered by the U.S. housing market and general credit collapse. The main contributing factors were:[4,5]

- *Pervasive availability of credit*: Falling interest rates, which facilitated increased access to mortgage financing, lenders relaxing their standards and writing a large number of sub-prime loans,

* This chapter was written in early March 2009 when many were saying that most major stock markets were in a downward spiral with the bottom nowhere in sight.

and a ready market for securitization, enabled the originators of mortgages to substantially eliminate their risk. In combination, this spurred a growth in the number of mortgage seekers and, as house prices increased, further encouraged consumers to buy homes.

- *Inadequate regulations*: The invention and use of complex debt derivatives such as collateralized debt obligations (CDO) and credit default swaps (CDS) made it difficult to identify and contain credit problems. Regulators did not keep pace with innovations in U.S. financial products, which became too complex, had poor transparency and much greater, often unmanageable, risks.
- *Demand collapse*: The property boom led to an over-supply of housing and prices which could no longer be supported. As prices fell, foreclosures became more frequent, increasing the supply of homes on the market. Lenders started to tighten their standards and fewer consumers could qualify for mortgages to help absorb the supply. This triggered a ripple effect into other markets and countries as well as the stock market.

In addition, the following factors have likely contributed to an exacerbation of the problem:

- *Riskier investment decisions by banks*: Poor decision-making on the part of banks resulted in them keeping large amounts of mortgage-backed securities (MBS) on their balance sheets in spite of the sub-prime risk involved. They financed these and other risky assets with short-term market borrowings and, when the housing market started to decline, banks found it difficult to roll over short-term loans against these mortgage backed securities and hence were forced to sell the assets at a substantial loss. An international regulation (Basel I)[1] that came into effect in 1988 may have contributed to this behavior. This regulation mandated that banks hold more capital if they make riskier loans or investments. This encouraged banks to get rid of risky loans by turning them into securities to be sold to investors.
- *Unintended consequences of three pillars*: First, ratings agencies such as Moody's, Standard & Poor's, and DBRS granted AAA ratings to risky MBS. Almost all agencies follow an "issuer-pays" revenue

1 That is, the 1988 Basel Accord, focused primarily on credit risk. Assets of banks were classified and grouped in five categories according to credit risk, carrying risk weights of zero (for example home country sovereign debt), 10, 20, 50, and up to 100% (this category has, as an example, most corporate debt). Banks with an international presence are required to hold capital equal to 8% of the risk-weighted assets.

model, and this posed potential conflicts of interest,[2] which some experts contend led to inappropriately high ratings for risky MBS. [6] Second, financial regulation, such as mark-to-market accounting, stipulated that financial firms must treat potential losses as cash losses. Even though many financial instruments may still yield returns in the future, their current asset price is highly devalued. This results in the recognition of unrealized losses and the need to raise additional capital to meet solvency requirements. Third, government statistics (*e.g.*, GDP and unemployment rate) may have been revised over the years to show the best possible picture of the U.S. economy. Perhaps such revisions in economic statistics are misleading and were used by Wall Street to sell over-valued products.

The current financial crisis[3] in the U.S. has triggered a number of similar exposures in advanced and emerging economies, and has become the most severe global financial crisis since the Great Depression. [7,8] This development has highlighted a number of questions about the linkages between the financial sector and the rest of the economy during recessions: specifically, to use IMF parlance, how do macroeconomic and financial variables behave around recessions, credit crunches, and asset (house and equity) price busts? [9]

An Historical Perspective

> Government is the only institution that can take a valuable commodity like paper and make it worthless by applying ink. – Ludwig von Mises [8]

If inflation is defined as rising prices then it is reasonable to assume that private businesses are the cause of inflation. However, if inflation is defined as an increase in the supply of money and credit, with rising prices as a consequence, and it is reasonable to ask, "[who] increases the money supply?", rising prices are not the only consequence of monetary and credit expansion. Inflation also erodes savings and encourages debt. It undermines confidence, deters investment, and destabilizes the economy by fostering booms, busts, and credit crunches. Governments inflate because their appetite for revenue exceeds their willingness to tax and/or their ability to borrow.

---

2 Profits of ratings agencies grew rapidly over the last decade.

3 A timeline of major events related to the crisis and mapped to the Dow Jones Industrial average is shown in Figure A. [4].

Keynes wrote: "[by] a continuing process of inflation, governments can confiscate, secretly and unobserved, an important part of the wealth of their citizens."

A recession is a period of decline in total output, income, employment and trade, usually lasting six months to a year and marked by widespread contractions in many sectors of the economy. [10] Figure B provides a capsule history of recessions and depressions, and provides data on various aspects of each of the episodes for a number of countries. [11]

Are recessions that are associated with "credit crunches" and "asset price busts"[4] different than other recessions? [9] Findings from a major IMF study are shown in Figure C and can be highlighted as follows:

- The typical recession lasts almost 4 quarters and is associated with an output drop of roughly 2 per cent.
- Episodes of credit crunches, house price, and equity price busts last much longer than do recessions.
- In one out of six recessions, there is also a credit crunch underway and, in one out of four recessions, there is an associated house price bust.
- Most importantly, recessions associated with credit crunches and house price busts are deeper and last longer than other recessions.

According to the IMF [9], while recessions have been becoming shorter and milder over time, they have remained highly synchronized across countries. In addition, recessions often coincide with periods of contractions in domestic credit and declines in asset prices. A housing bust tends to persist even longer—four-and-a-half years, with a 30 per cent fall in real house prices. And an equity price bust lasts approximately ten quarters, ultimately halving the real value of equities. Recessions accompanied by credit crunches or house price busts, although not lasting much longer, result in output losses that are two to three times greater than recessions without these financial stresses. And the IMF has found that the extent of declines in house prices appears to influence the depth of recessions, even after accounting for changes in other financial variables, including credit and equity prices.

Broadly speaking, the aftermath of financial crises share three characteristics:

- Asset market collapses are deep and prolonged. Real housing price declines average 35 per cent extended over six years, while equity price collapses average 55 per cent over a downturn of about 3.5 years.

---

[4] IMF terminology.

- Profound declines in output and employment occur. The unemployment rate rises an average of 7 percentage points over the down phase of the cycle, which lasts on average four years. Output falls (from peak to trough) an average of over 9 per cent. However, the duration of the downturn, averaging roughly two years, is considerably shorter than the average four years for the unemployment cycle.
- The real value of government debt tends to explode, rising an average of 86 per cent in the major post WWII episodes. Interestingly, the main cause of debt explosions is not the widely cited costs of bailing out and re-capitalizing the banking system. Even upper bound estimates pale next to actual measured rises in public debt. In fact, the big drivers of debt increases are the inevitable collapse in tax revenues that governments suffer in the wake of deep and prolonged output contractions, as well as often-ambitious countercyclical fiscal policies aimed at mitigating the downturn (see Figure D). [4]

How relevant are historical benchmarks for assessing the trajectory of the current global financial crisis? Since the onset of the current crisis, asset prices have tumbled in the U.S. and elsewhere in a manner similar to that found in previous recessions. The analysis of the post-crises outcomes for unemployment, output, and government debt provide benchmark numbers for how this crisis may unfold. The global nature of this crisis will make it far more difficult for many countries to unilaterally overcome through higher exports, or to buffer their decline in consumption through foreign borrowing. In such circumstances, the recent lull in sovereign defaults is likely to come to an end. As Neil Reynolds [12] points out, defaults in emerging market economies tend to rise sharply when many countries are simultaneously experiencing domestic banking crises.

Policy Responses

> Yielding to political pressures to "do something" may frequently do more harm than good. There is a saying that the best is often the enemy of the good. ... The goal of an extremely high degree of economic stability is certainly a splendid one. Our ability to attain it, however, is limited; we can surely avoid extreme fluctuations; we do not know enough to avoid minor fluctuations; the attempt to do more than we can will itself be a disturbance that may increase rather than reduce instability. - Friedman [13]

The causal factors distilled from an historical analysis of recessions point to the need for three types of measures, to be implemented in parallel [14]:

Repair the financial system by recapitalizing banks and isolating bad assets. [15] Successful resolution of the financial crisis is a precondition for achieving sustained growth. As an example, consider Japan where fiscal actions following the bursting of its asset bubble failed to achieve sustained recovery because financial sector problems were allowed to fester. Delaying interventions, as was also done in the U.S. during the Hoover administration and during the savings and loans crisis, typically leads to higher fiscal costs later on. Assuring full transparency with respect to the valuation of assets and the recognition of losses and liabilities must be a top regulatory priority. The Japanese experience taught painful lessons about the dangers of government support and the encouragement of measures that seek to rearrange balance sheets so as to avoid facing painful realities. Regulatory policy needs to focus on assuring that financial institutions raise adequate amounts of capital to maintain their activities, even if this is dilutive for existing shareholders. Only when this is achieved can there be a sustained flow of credit and a lasting recovery.

Use monetary policy to increase demand. Currently, capacity for further monetary easing – at least in a traditional sense – is shrinking: in some countries, including the U.S. and Canada, policy interest rates are approaching zero. Policymakers should consider focusing attention not on their traditional policy rate but on targeting some more meaningful indicator of the cost of credit to households and businesses (such as the 3-month LIBOR) (see Figure E). [16]

Apply fiscal stimulus. In the short run, a fiscal stimulus, if designed correctly, can limit the decline in demand as well as output. Fiscal policy needs to have its impact in a *timely* manner. It has to be *targeted* to assure that increased government borrowing translates directly into increased spending and demand. And, critically, it must be *temporary* so that its effects are not offset by higher long-term interest rates. [3] The optimal package is one that raises spending and the deficit in the short run while reducing the deficit in the long run and thereby reducing long-term interest rates.

Governments (of major economies) should ensure that programs are not cut for lack of resources. Spending programs, from repair and maintenance to investment projects delayed, which are interrupted or rejected for lack of funding or macroeconomic considerations, need to be (re)started quickly. A few high profile programs, with good long-run justification and strong externalities (for example, for environmental purposes), can also help, directly and indirectly, through raising expectations. Given the higher degree of risk facing companies at the current juncture, the state could also take a larger share in private-public partnerships for valuable projects that would otherwise be suspended for lack of private capital.

Address consumption. Three specific factors are affecting current consumption [17]:

- Decreases in wealth, whether it be housing, financial, or human (*i.e.*, declines in current and expected disposable income), are leading consumers to cut consumption.
- Tighter credit constraints are becoming widespread, as lenders tighten underwriting practices and some consumers see their credit lines eliminated or they face much higher interest rates.
- High uncertainty is leading consumers to become more precautionary, and to take a wait and see attitude.

Government could target tax cuts or transfers to those consumers who are most likely to be credit constrained. Measures along these lines include augmenting unemployment benefits, increasing earned income tax credits, and expanding safety nets in countries where such nets are limited. Where relevant, support for homeowners facing foreclosures, including a write-down of mortgages using public resources, should be encouraged because it helps to not only support aggregate demand, but also improves conditions in the financial sector. Finally, we should recognize that those individuals who cannot meet their original mortgage obligations are nonetheless the highest value occupants of their homes.

- Even more than a fiscal stimulus, what is needed now is a commitment by governments to follow whatever policies are required to avoid a repeat of the Great Depression scenario. By making such a commitment, the fear that people and firms have today is more likely to dissipate, leading eventually to a reversal in the decline in aggregate demand.

- Beyond the current crisis, the main threat to the long-term viability of public finances in advanced countries comes from publicly funded pension and health entitlements. In net present value terms, the magnitude of these future fiscal costs far exceeds any fiscal stimulus package (see Figure F). Eventually, governments will have to tackle these large burdens on the public finances. Both the markets and the people need to be assured that their government is making a credible commitment to address these long-term issues. [13]

The Way Forward

"Just" risk should be justly rewarded. [1]

The Achilles heel of capitalism is the business cycle of boom and bust or, alternatively, greed and fear. [18] We have synthesized the manifestation of each emotion at specific instances of a recessionary cycle. Beyond this, however, the current crisis begs us to ask some more fundamental questions: how can a capitalist society be protected from being corrupted by the special interests that are an integral part of its political economy?[5] Here are some basic principles, adapted from Dieffenbach, which we propose for further discussion [13,19]:

- *Government should be trusted*: Government is an institution, a social contract *created* by the people for the purpose of enforcing the country's laws and constitution (based on justice principles). It is imperative that the people hold the government to account, so that its *actions* are consistent with that goal.
- *Government and markets are partners*: Markets are the game; the government should enforce the *fair* rules of the game. Special interests influence government away from its mission and undermine the people's trust in their government and markets. Once again, the people need to assert their responsibility and hold the government to account.
- *Government is the guarantor of last resort*: Government has always *implicitly* stepped in and *facilitated* the functioning of markets in the event of a major crisis. This role should be made *explicit* with an associated clarity of economic tradeoffs.
- *Behavioral insurance premium*: On the assumption that greed and fear will continue to manifest themselves, the following questions need to be explored: Should a portion of the federal tax collected be *regarded* as an "insurance premium" against economic crises and natural disasters? Should financial institutions operating outside commercial banking pay a direct *insurance premium* to the government? Some kind of insurance premium to protect against inevitable disastrous behaviors may make sense.
- *Cannot become too big to fail*: Size often confers a great deal of bargaining power to firms, similar to a *natural monopoly* argument. Large firms should, therefore, earn a fair (not monopoly-like) profit for participating in liquid markets, in exchange for the downside protection that inevitably will be provided by government.

[5] Shortcomings of Capitalism: Adam Smith Theory of Moral Sentiments (1759) vs. The Wealth of Nations (1776): How do you balance *self-interest* with *social responsibility*?

- *Executive insurance*: There is a distortion in effect today in corporations that leads to a magnification of behavior stemming from greed and fear. Executive overconfidence should therefore be viewed as a negative *externality* that leads to major disasters. Corporations should internalize the social cost of "bad" *persistent* executive decisions. This has implications for re-examining the paradigm in which current reward mechanisms operate.

Conclusion

The current crisis, which started in the U.S. housing and financial sectors, has now led to a strong fall in aggregate demand. This fall is larger than in any period since the Great Depression and is affecting multiple industries and exposing structural issues. [20] The causes of the current recession are being expounded on daily.

We have synthesized an historical review of recessions, so that we can distill how to appropriately respond in such circumstances. We have found that a successful policy package should address both the financial crisis and the fall in aggregate demand and, so, should have two components: one, aimed at getting the financial system back to health; the other, aimed at increasing aggregate demand. There are obvious interactions and synergies between the two. Financial measures, from recapitalization to asset purchases, have important implications for credit flows and aggregate demand. Measures to support aggregate demand, for example by helping homeowners and improving the housing market, have clear implications for the health of financial institutions.[6]

However, the current crisis is also causing us to reflect at a deeper level and ask some basic questions about the structural flaws in the current capitalist model. For the longer term, this presents some old[7] basic principles that should be considered as part of a revised design for capitalism.

---

6 As of February 2009, early indications are that a majority of executives (43%) believe that governments' actions overall have positively affected the global economic recession. [21]

7 From Barack Obama's inauguration speech: "Our challenges may be new, the instruments with which we meet them may be new, but those values upon which our success depends, honesty and hard work, courage and fair play, tolerance and curiosity, loyalty and patriotism–these things are old. ... What is demanded then is a return to these truths. What is required of us now is a new era of responsibility–a recognition, on the part of every American, that we have duties to ourselves, our nation and the world, duties that we do not grudgingly accept but rather seize gladly, firm in the knowledge that there is nothing so satisfying to the spirit, so defining of our character than giving our all to a difficult task."

APPENDIX A

References

1. Dr. Christophe Faugere, Associate Professor of Finance, *The 2008 Financial Crisis: Causes, Consequences and Solutions* (UAlbany School of Business, 2008).
2. Darryl Robert Schoon, *The Great Depression of the 2010s*, 2008.
3. Lawrence H. Summers, Charles Eliot University Professor, Harvard University, *The State of the US Economy* (The Brookings Institute, December 19, 2007).
4. Grail Research, *Global Financial Crisis*, January 24, 2009.
5. Mike Cragg, The Brattle Group, *Foundations of the Credit Crisis*, January 2009.
6. John Hull, *Derivatives and Risk Management, The Finance Crisis and Rescue* (University of Toronto Press, 2008).
7. J. Bradford De Long, University of California at Berkeley and NBER, *Fiscal Policy in the Shadow of the Great Depression*, January 1996.
8. Lawrence W. Reed, *Great Myths of the Great Depression*, Foundation for Economic Education, 2008.
9. Stijn Claessens, M. Ayhan Kose, & Marco Terrones, *What Happens During Recessions, Crunches and Busts?*, IMF Working Paper, December 2008.
10. Conference Board Magazine, *Across the Board* (Chapter 3: Recession or Depression), May 1982.
11. Carmen Reinhart, University of Maryland, NBER & CEPR & Kenneth Rogoff, Harvard University, NBER, *The Aftermath of Financial Crises*, January 3, 2009.
12. Neil Reynolds, "Stimulating our way into a crisis", *The Globe and Mail*, February 18, 2009.
13. Bruce Dieffenbach, Department of Economics, University of Albany, *Financial Crisis in the Great Depression*, 2008.
14. Antonio Spilimbergo, Steve Symansky, Olivier Blanchard & Carlo Cottarelli, *Fiscal Policy for the Crisis*, IMF Staff Position Note, December 29, 2008.
15. Grail Research, *Global Financial Crisis*, December 16, 2008.
16. Timothy Bruculere, Vice President, Members United Corporate Federal Credit Union, *The 2008 Financial Crisis*, September 2008.

17. Olivier Blanchard & Carlo Cottarelli, *IMF Spells Out Need for Global Fiscal Stimulus*, IMF Survey Magazine: Interview, December 29, 2008.

18. George M. Taber, "A Question Revisited: Is Capitalism Working?," Knowledge@Wharton, March 4, 2009.

19. Lawrence W. Reed, Mackinac Center for Public Policy, *Seven Principles of Sound Public Policy*, 2006.

20. *Industry Trends in the Downturn: A Snapshot*, McKinsey Quarterly, December 2008.

21. *Economic Conditions Snapshot*, McKinsey Global Survey Results, February 2009.

APPENDIX B

Figures

Figure A: Timeline of Recent Events

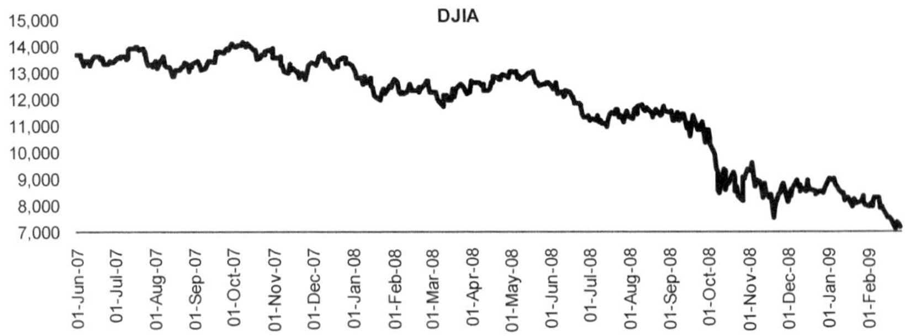

Jun '07 - Jul '07	Two Bear Sterns hedge funds forced to dump assets due to losses. Bear Sterns funds file for bankruptcy
Aug '07	Lehman Brothers and HSBC shut some of their offices
Sep '07	Federal Reserve reduces fed funds rate by half of a percentage point
Oct '07	Merrill Lynch reports loss on USD 8.4B write down
Nov '07	Morgan Stanley suffers USD 3.7B write down
Dec '07	Fed and other central banks share USD 40B in special loans to banks
Feb '08	US financial crisis affects UBS which confirms loss of USD 18.4B
Mar '08	JP Morgan and Federal Reserve take steps to rescue Bear Sterns
Jun '08	S&P cuts ratings of Morgan Stanley, Merrill Lynch and Lehman Brothers
Jul '08	Merrill has USD 5.7B in write downs; sells shares
Sep '08	Lehman Brothers files for bankruptcy Bank of America buys Merrill Lynch for USD 50B; Bank of China buys 20% stake in Rothschild Government rescues banks by nationalizing Fannie Mae and Freddie Mac and giving AIG an emergency loan of USD 85B

Oct '08	Russia, Romania and Ukraine close their stock exchanges for a few days due to crisis Governments of many countries announce bailouts for their financial institutions Iceland's financial crisis grows as all three of its major banks are nationalized
Nov '08	The U.S. Treasury Department purchases a total of $33.5 billion in preferred stock in 21 U.S. banks under the Capital Purchase Program. Citigroup issues preferred shares to the Treasury and FDIC in exchange for protection against losses on a $306 billion pool of commercial and residential securities
Dec '08	The SEC approves measures to increase transparency and accountability at credit rating agencies The U.S. Treasury Department purchases a total of $55 billion in preferred stock in over 50 U.S. banks under the Capital Purchase Program
Jan '09	President Bush submits to a request to Congress for the remaining USD 350B in TARP funding for use by incoming administration The Treasury and FDIC enter a loss sharing arrangement with Bank of America on a USD 118B portfolio
Feb '09	Fannie Mae reports loss of USD 25.2B in the fourth quarter of 2008, and a full year loss of USD 58.7B The FDIC announces that the number of "problem banks" increased from 171 institutions with $116 billion of assets at the end of the third quarter of 2008, to 252 insured institutions with $159 billion in assets at the end of fourth quarter of 2008

Source: Grail Research; The Black Box Institute

Figure B: A Capsule History of Recessions and Depressions

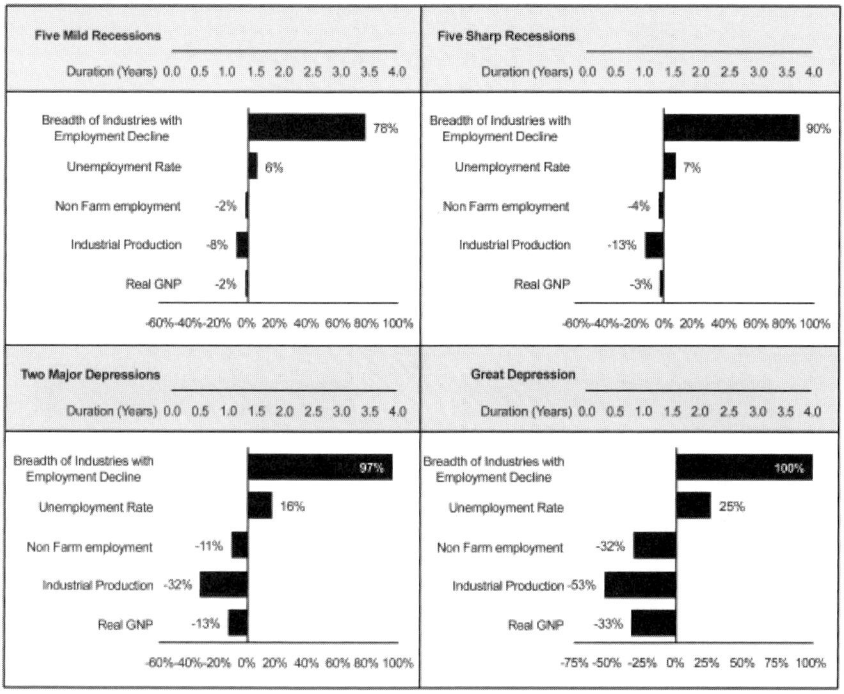

	House Prices		Equity Prices		Unemployment Increase		Real per Capita GDP		Real Public Debt
	% Decline	Duration (Yrs)	% Decline	Duration (Yrs)	% Increase	Duration (Yrs)	% Decline	Duration (Yrs)	% Increase
Argentina, 2001	25%	4	28%	3	6%	3	22%	4	-
Austria, 2008	5%	-	69%	-	-	-	-	-	-
Chile, 1980	-	-	-	-	-	-	-	-	260%
Columbia, 1998	51%	6	65%	3	13%	6	6%	2	280%
Finland, 1991	50%	6	63%	3	14%	4	12%	4	280%
Historical Average	36%	6	56%	3	7%	4.8	9%	1.9	186%
Hong Kong, 1997	54%	6	29%	2	4%	5	5%	1	-
Hungary, 2008	5%	-	56%	-	-	-	-	-	-
Iceland, 2007	14%	1	92%	1	-	-	-	-	-
Indonesia, 1997	41%	5	68%	2	3%	5	14%	2	220%
Ireland, 2007	21%	1	58%	1	-	-	-	-	-
Japan, 1992	36%	17	59%	3	3%	11	0%	1	142%
Korea, 1997	20%	4	69%	3	5%	2	7%	1	150%
Malaysia, 1997	15%	3	67%	5	2%	3	9%	1	140%
Mexico, 1994	-	-	-	-	-	-	-	-	141%
Norway, 1899	22%	7	-	-	-	-	-	-	-
Norway, 1987	40%	5	31%	2	4%	7	1%	1	143%
Philippines, 1997	52%	7	57%	4	3%	4	2%	1	146%
Spain, 1977	32%	4	66%	5	12%	7	-1%	-	210%
Spain, 2008	-	-	43%	-	-	-	-	-	-
Sweden, 1991	28%	4	39%	3	8%	5	5%	3	160%
Thailand, 1997	19%	4	84%	5	3%	1	13%	2	170%
UK, 2007	13%	1	40%	1	-	-	-	-	-
US, 1929	12%	8	64%	4	22%	4	28%	4	-
US, 2007	25%	1	42%	1	-	-	-	-	-

Source: Conference Board; Rogoff & Reinhart

Figure C: Association of Recessions with Credit Crunches and Asset Price Busts

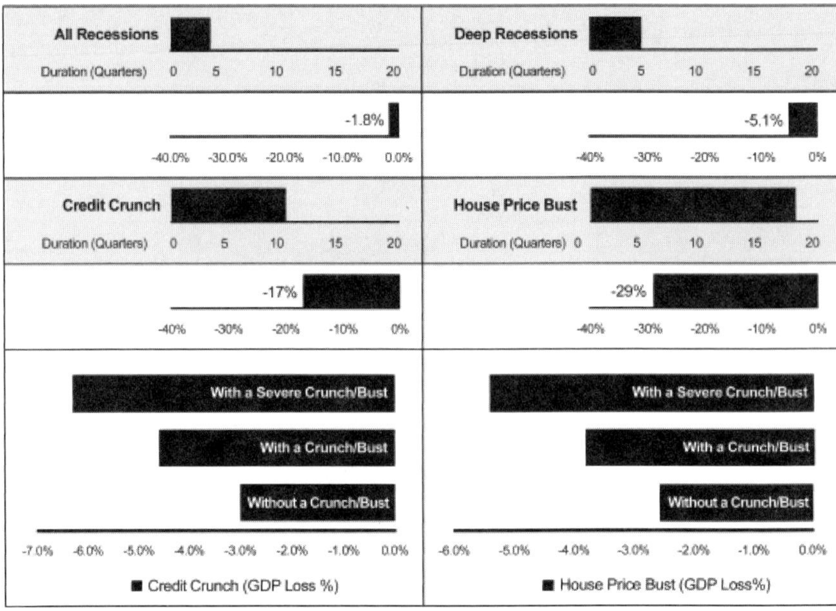

Source: IMF

Figure D: Announced Government & Company Bailouts (To February 2009)

	Government Bailout funds		Company Bailouts	
	USD Bn	%GDP	USD Bn	%GDP
Latvia	10.8	39.88%	1.3	-
Iceland	2.0	26.14%	0.7	-
UAE	32.6	25.13%	-	-
Hungary	31.9	23.11%	-	-
UK	511.2	18.74%	101.4	-
Russia	216.4	16.76%	23.5	-
Norway	-	12.81%	0.8	-
Qatar	5.3	12.48%	-	-
Ukraine	16.5	11.75%	1.3	-
Belarus	4.5	10.05%	-	-
Denmark	17.8	5.81%	0.9	-
Oman	2.0	5.60%	-	-
Austria	20.3	5.38%	4.7	-
Pakistan	7.6	5.29%	-	-
US	725.0	5.25%	646.6	-
Kazakhstan	5.0	4.82%	-	-
Spain	68.3	4.78%	-	-
South Korea	42.2	4.35%	-	-
Germany	136.6	4.14%	92.2	-
El Salvador	0.8	3.96%	-	-
France	54.1	2.11%	17.9	-
Canada	21.6	1.63%	3.3	-
Serbia	0.5	1.25%	-	-
Sweden	2.6	0.59%	-	-
Chile	0.9	0.52%	-	-
China	8.0	0.24%	1.5	-
Australia	1.3	0.16%	-	-
Switzerland	-	-	59.3	14.27%
Netherlands	-	-	54.2	12.50%
Luxembourg	-	-	4.2	8.76%
Belgium	-	-	24.6	4.92%
Ireland	-	-	7.7	3.02%
India	-	-	0.7	0.06%

Source: Grail Research; TBBI

Figure E: TED Spread (March 2008 – Feb 2009)

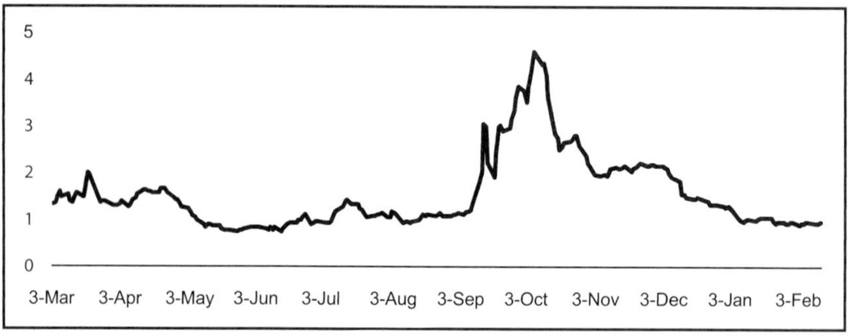

Source: British Bankers Association and the St. Louis Reserve Bank

Figure F: US Government Spending vs Revenue

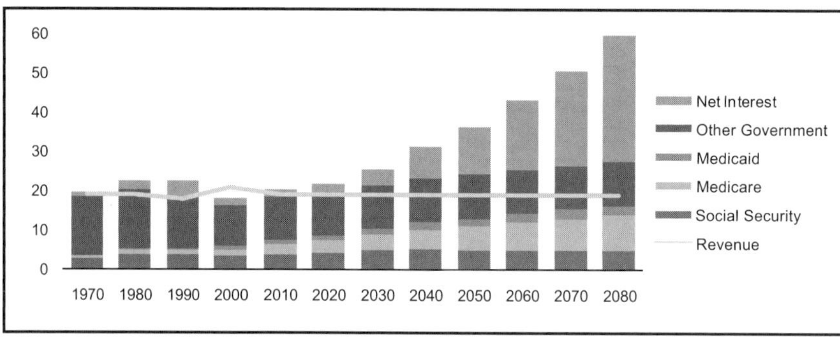

Source: GAO Citizen's Guide 2007; Dieffenbach

Psychological Diversity and Economic Health

Jacob B. Hirsh & Maneesh Mehta

The overall health of a natural or human economy is directly linked to the diversity of roles within it. What has not been appreciated historically is the importance of psychological diversity in ensuring economic health. Incomplete solutions result from applying a single psychological framework to a complex challenge, yet psychological diversity among top managers has become increasingly narrow over the past 30 years. This loss of diversity has constrained our thinking about business and damaged the health of the economy.

When evaluating any complex system, diversity is one of the best indicators of overall health and productivity. In natural ecosystems, biodiversity (the number of different functional roles, species, and genes within the system) predicts the stability and efficiency of the system (Loreau, Naeem, & Inchausti, 2002). A diverse system will be more robust against failures due to built-in redundancy; should one part of the system fail, another can compensate by assuming a similar role. Conversely, when biodiversity is threatened, the ecological balance becomes progressively delicate, increasing the vulnerability of those that depend upon the system's good health. The Irish potato blight of the mid 19th century is a good example of the consequences of lack of diversity. Although the blight spread throughout most of Europe, only Ireland depended so largely upon a single crop (Kinealy, 1994). This practice of monoculture increases short-term agricultural efficiency and productivity but it does so at the expense of increased risk and vulnerability should the emphasized crop fail.

Similar parallels can be drawn to economic and financial diversity. If a region's economy depends too strongly upon a particular sector, it becomes vulnerable to market fluctuations within that industry (Malizia & Ke, 1993). Take the case of Detroit, with its narrow focus on automobile production.

The region's health and economic performance, tied to that of the American automobile industry, grew immensely in the early- to mid-20th century, but has since deteriorated in tandem with the "Big Three" automakers. These same parallels can also be applied to financial diversification as a risk management technique. Indeed, a commonly held truism in the wealth management industry is that investing in a diverse array of industries, regions, and investment vehicles helps safeguard a portfolio against poor returns in any one domain.

The power of diversity is well-understood in the areas described above (and, in fact, codified in the idiom, "don't put all of your eggs into one basket"). What is less often appreciated, however, is the value of psychological diversity, which reflects the full range of cognitive and motivational strategies that can be brought to bear on the environment. The importance of psychological diversity for economic health is outlined below, drawing parallels to natural economies (ecosystems) and shedding some light on the current economic crisis by detailing the process by which this diversity has diminished over the past 30 years. This article offers some suggestions for rebuilding this diversity, in the interest of developing a sustainable and productive global marketplace.

Psychological Diversity

Psychological diversity refers to the natural breadth of psychological characteristics that comprise the human species. Philosophers have long noticed the relatively stable differences existing between individuals. Hippocrates, writing around 400 B.C., identified four personality types, each characterized by a unique pattern of emotional disposition. Contemporary personality psychologists recognize five broad dimensions of variation in human personality - Extraversion, Agreeableness, Conscientiousness, Emotional Stability, and Openness (see Table 1) (Goldberg, 1993). An individual's personality profile comprises a score on each of these dimensions, resulting in important implications for the workplace and other life domains (MacCoby, 2009; Ozer & Benet-Martinez, 2006). For instance, individuals who score highly in Conscientiousness tend to demonstrate better workplace performance and greater relationship integrity, whereas Openness is associated with enhanced creativity and innovation.

While an individual's personality is not set in stone, it is significantly rooted in genetic inheritance, showing an impressive degree of stability across the lifespan (McCrae & Costa Jr, 2008). As a result, an individual's psychological profile acts as a powerful constraint on the behavioral options ("affordances")[1] that are readily available. When navigating a social environment, for example, a highly extraverted individual is more likely to maximize gain from social networks, whereas an introvert will likely focus on solitary activities. From an evolutionary perspective, each psychological profile can be considered a strategy for succeeding amidst a complex and ever-changing environment (Buss, 1991).

By the same token, the continued diversity in personality traits reflects the fact that no single behavioral strategy is universally beneficial across all environmental contexts (Nettle, 2006). In times of plenty, an extraverted, reward-focused strategy is certainly the most beneficial, whereas a cautious, neurotic strategy is advisable in dangerous, tumultuous times. Each "psychological segment" of the population serves a unique social function coherent with their underlying cognitive and motivational preferences (*i.e.*, promoting innovation, justice, conservation, compassion, *etc.*). Because any given outlook encompasses a unique set of biases, strengths, and weaknesses, the overall health of society hinges upon the balanced integration of many different psychological frameworks.

Given the non-overlapping strengths and weaknesses of each psychological profile, the value of psychological diversity in organizational success is clear. Just as the loss of diversity in natural economies and financial markets promotes vulnerability, so does the loss of psychological diversity heighten an organization or society's exposure to risk.

Unfortunately, this is exactly what has occurred in the business world, and the consequences of this increased risk are emerging in view of the global economic crisis. Over the past 30 years, maximizing short-term rewards at the expense of long-term value, while simultaneously ignoring the hidden costs and negative externalities[2] associated with business actions, has prevailed as the dominant psychology. To examine how this outlook came to dominate the business world, it is again instructive to apply the principles of natural economies. In particular, we examine the role of parasitic strategies in natural economies and human societies.

Parasitism as an Evolutionary Strategy

Parasitic strategies rely on the exploitation of a host party's resources, with little given in return. In relatively benign cases, the parasite[3] is not too

1 The array of possible actions presented by an object or situation.

2 The costs that an economic transaction produces for uninvolved third parties (*e.g.*, pollution as a by-product of industrial production).

3 An entity that survives by consuming another's resources, without providing anything useful in return.

demanding or disruptive of the host, and so does not pose a major threat. In severe cases, however, the parasite exacts a large toll, substantially hindering its host's adaptive functioning. Because parasites are able to benefit from the work of others without having to expend their own energy, a population of parasitic agents are to be expected in any system. As long as the ratio of parasites to producers remains in check, parasitism can be considered an effective evolutionary strategy.

The same holds true for human economies, in which the parasitic strategy corresponds to the psychological profile of the narcissistic psychopath (Hare, 1999). Psychopathy does not reflect a qualitatively unique psychological composition, but instead reflects the extreme end of a set of continuously distributed psychological characteristics, including impulsivity, a grandiose sense of self-worth, and a callous lack of empathy (Edens, Marcus, Lilienfeld, & Poythress Jr., 2006). While only 0.6 per cent of the entire population can be considered psychopathic, many more individuals display less severe forms of this psychological profile. In terms of the elementary personality traits described above, the psychopath is characterized by high levels of Extraversion and Emotional Stability, and low levels of Agreeableness and Conscientiousness (Miller, Lyman, Widiger, & Leukefeld, 2001).

A psychopathic individual has a strong desire for power, and is not concerned about the people who may be hurt during his or her rise to the top. In addition, these individuals value instant rewards over long-term sustainable growth. In the business world, the strategic expression of this psychology manifests itself in deception, manipulation, and exploitation in the interest of enhancing immediate rewards (Babiak & Hare, 2006). Indeed, the short-term personal gains of such strategies can be substantial, but the long-term costs to the economy as a whole are enormous.

An example can be seen in the practice of emphasizing short-term profit and shareholder value at any cost. The easiest route to boost immediate shareholder value involves liquidating resources, whether monetary, in the case of capital investments; tangible, in the case of buildings and equipment; or social, by way of a company's reputation or human capital. Unfortunately, the negative long-term consequences on revenue-generating potential of such short-term gains will not be recognized for years to come. By then, those in power will have reaped the benefits and bonuses of short-term profits, and will often have departed the company. Indeed, the North American turnover rate for CEOs is 18 per cent per year, arguably facilitating the option of a "quick getaway" by decision-makers before the full extent of damage is recognized.

An additional characteristic of the psychopathic disposition is a dramatically heightened sensitivity to rewards versus risks. As a result, these individuals tend to vigorously pursue opportunities for profit, even when the associated risks are enormous. The 2008 sub-prime mortgage crisis is a good example of the focus on high returns despite the associated higher risk (Stulz, 2009). Again, such purely reward-focused strategies may pay off in the short-term, but they are almost guaranteed to fail in the long-term when previously ignored risks become manifest.

In the preceding examples, the exploitation is of one's own company but parasitic strategies also manifest themselves in the business world through reliance on negative externalities. In any balanced system of exchanges, all parties mutually benefit from an interaction. In the parasitic case, businesses grow their wealth by transferring their operating costs to other parties. Sometimes these displaced costs are clearly recognized, as in government subsidization of private industry, but in other cases negative externalities are hidden. A prime example of the latter is environmental damage resulting from industrial expansion. Although governments are beginning to regulate environmental impact and put these costs onto the balance sheet, they were traditionally not factored into an organization's financial accounting (or decision-making). Consequently, it has been easy to ignore the long-term costs of these actions (which again involve the extraction of near-term revenue at the expense of future value).

As in natural economies, parasitic strategies in business are only effective when a relatively small segment of the population engages in such practices. When the ratio of parasites to producers becomes too high, the entire system's stability is threatened and long-term productive potential jeopardized. How, then, has the parasitic mindset of exploitation and short-term reward come to dominate the business world?

Loss of Psychological Diversity

The disproportionate influence of the psychopathic psychological profile is the result of three key factors: emulation, selection, and retention. Emulation stems from the potential of the parasitic/psychopathic strategy to reap enormous short-term rewards, with the costs well-hidden or displaced. This leads others to regard this fundamentally unsustainable economic strategy as the most powerful and efficient method for increasing monetary gain. Accordingly, such strategies are emulated in order to gain a "competitive edge". This behavior is evident in the psychology of a market "bubble". During periods of rapid economic expansion (which often involve hidden or displaced costs), many companies mimic the strategies of the agents leading the growth. In the short term, before the bubble bursts, the profits are large and the risks are completely out of sight. Any attempt to voice concerns during such periods is met with the strongest form of disdain and groupthink, quickly silencing alternative frameworks. Because rapid growth is unsustainable, however, it eventually leads to a collapse of artificially-inflated asset values and, subsequently, shareholder value. Nonetheless, this rapid growth of revenue generation, regardless of sustainability, is codified as the capitalist ideal toward which all businesses should strive. Although future-oriented models are more flexible and adaptive (Mehta, 2005), they are often ignored in favor of the salient benefits of a short-term strategy.

While emulation describes the psychological pressure upon those already within the system, selection biases influence who enters the system to begin with. As argued by Mintzberg (2004), MBA programs do not attract individuals spanning the full breadth of psychological profiles. Rather, the promise of money and power associated with high-status leadership positions tend to attract individuals with narcissistic[4] personality traits. This is not to say that every manager is a narcissist, but rather that current MBA programs attract a disproportionate share of individuals with narcissistic characteristics. These individuals view the world of finance as an opportunity to fulfil their ambitions of power, reward, and self-interest. Thus, by funnelling this segment of the population into leadership positions, MBA programs have contributed to the loss of psychological diversity in the business world. It must be noted, however, that narcissistic personality traits in the general population have trended upward since the 1980s (Twenge, Konrath, Foster, Campbell, & Bushman, 2008). The increased prevalence of narcissistic tendencies in business students must, therefore, be regarded within the larger cultural context.

Finally, biased retention and advancement also limit psychological diversity within higher levels of organizational structure. Quite simply, individuals whose psychological constitutions conflict with dominant business practice are more likely to withdraw from the game. This is not because they are "unfit", but rather due to the fundamental incongruence between their psychological dispositions and the logic that defines the competitive parameters of contemporary business. Conversely, individuals with narcissistic and psychopathic personality characteristics have an inherent advantage in rapidly climbing organizational hierarchies because they are unconcerned with the negative social consequences of their actions. These individuals frequently emerge in leadership positions, despite their volatility and risk-insensitivity making them less-than-ideal decision-makers (Brunell, *et al.*, 2008). Furthermore, such individuals tend to surround themselves with a like-minded entourage, further suppressing alternative perspectives.

In combination, emulation, selection, and retention processes ensure that the psychological frameworks within the upper echelons of business do not encompass the full breadth of human abilities. As in natural economies, this

---

4 Characterized by self-preoccupation and lack of empathy.

loss of psychological diversity creates a tremendous vulnerability in the system, paving the way for economic downturns to occur when the dominance of short-term, parasitic strategies reaches a critical threshold. In natural economies, this is the point where the parasite kills the host, or excessive harvesting fully depletes a natural resource. No longer self-supporting, the system must then be dramatically restructured. It is worth noting that the reduced consumer confidence characterizing periods of economic turmoil is not merely irrational fear to be assuaged by stimulus packages. Rather, it is a rational psychological response toward decision-makers who have abused the trust of consumers. The same rationale applies when investors sell shares in a company after losing confidence in its integrity. Successful capitalist markets are founded on mutual trust, which acts as the basis for any effective system of exchange (Fukuyama, 1995). When this trust is broken by revelations of fraud, mismanagement, greed, or hubris, the foundation upon which the entire financial system stands is threatened.

Rebuilding Integrity

Although the loss of psychological diversity has weakened the integrity of the global economy, a number of steps can be taken to promote sustainable prosperity. The first, and perhaps most important, is recognizing the hidden costs involved in any endeavor. As long as these costs are kept off the official books, parasitic strategies which limit potential future revenue are able to flourish. Governmental regulation and improved Board of Director governance, however, can expose the potential consequences of a company's actions and explicitly incorporate them into the balance sheet. By way of example, the 2008 financial crisis could have been mitigated by astute government policies and robust governance that limited the extent to which high-risk options filled investment portfolios.

Second, a high-integrity financial system requires reward contingencies that do not emphasize quarterly profits and immediate return on investments but, rather, long-term sustainable growth, prosperity, and innovation (*cf.*, Mehta, 2006). Compensating CEOs for short-term profits earned at the expense of long-term profitability is the equivalent of rewarding self-destruction. As long as immediate gains are idealized above long-term value, individuals with psychopathic and narcissistic personality profiles will continue to make reckless decisions in the name of personal profit, culminating in immense organizational and economy-wide losses. Providing incentives for long-term growth supported by the promotion of a greater range of personalities and psychological profiles is a step toward economic balance (Ash, 2009). Because above-market executive compensation packages and reward structures that favor leaders further promote a sense of entitlement and narcissistic tendencies, reward structures should de-emphasize individual performance and lean toward a team-based approach. Indeed, any successful organization depends on the activities of a large number of talented individuals working together as a group.

Third, selection mechanisms for MBA programs must be refined to ensure a balance of bright and talented individuals of all personality profiles – not just those that have come to dominate the business world. This influx of individuals possessing a full spectrum of strategies would be of enormous value to organizations. It is essential that such individuals be encouraged to adopt leadership positions, as they would provide a stabilizing force in the global economy (in contrast to the inherent instability of the parasitic mindset). For generations, the North American economy was built on hard work, trust, and integrity. Stable growth requires that these principles not be exchanged for the sake of immediate profits.

Finally, it is important to promote diversity within existing organizations. Recognizing the limits of the dominant organizational paradigm requires the full utilization of human capital. This capital rests not only in the skills and abilities of an organization's employees, but also in the psychological diversity found within these individuals, as no single perspective is universally optimal. Agreeable people are needed to ensure a socially-conscious economy. Conscientious people are required to sustain high levels of industriousness and integrity. Open people are critical in ensuring continued progress and innovation. Just as biodiversity fosters a thriving ecosystem, a diverse set of perspectives improves decision-making processes for greater overall economic health. In harnessing the psychological diversity within an organization, greater flexibility and robustness can ultimately be obtained in the face of economic challenges.

APPENDIX A

References

T. G. Ash, "From the ashes, a new capitalism", *The Globe and Mail* (May 8, 2009).

P. Babiak & R. Hare, *Snakes in suits: When psychopaths go to work* (New York: HarperCollins, 2006).

A. Brunell *et al.*, "Leader Emergence: The Case of the Narcissistic Leader" (2008) 34(12) Personality and Social Psychology Bulletin 1663.

D. Buss, "Evolutionary personality psychology" (1991) 42(1) Annual Review of Psychology 459-491.

J.M. Digman, "Personality Structure: Emergence of the Five-Factor Model" (1990) 41(1) Annual Reviews in Psychology 417-440.

J. Edens *et al.*, "Psychopathic, not psychopath: taxometric evidence for the dimensional structure of psychopathy" (2006) 115(1) Journal of Abnormal Psychology 131.

F. Fukuyama, *Trust: The social virtues and the creation of prosperity* (New York: Free Press, 1995).

L.R. Goldberg, "The structure of phenotypic personality traits" (1993) 48(1) American Psychologist 26-34.

R. Hare, *Without conscience: The disturbing world of the psychopaths among us* (New York: The Guilford Press, 1999).

C. Kinealy, *This great calamity: the Irish famine, 1845-52* (Dublin: Gill & Macmillan, 1994).

M. Loreau, S. Naeem & P. Inchausti, *Biodiversity and ecosystem functioning: synthesis and perspectives* (Oxford, UK: Oxford University Press, 2002).

M. MacCoby, "To win the respect of followers, leaders need personality intelligence" (2009) 73(1) Ivey Business Journal.

E. Malizia & S. Ke, "The influence of economic diversity on unemployment and stability" (1993) 33(2) Journal of Regional Science 221-235.

R. McCrae & P. Costa Jr., "The stability of personality: Observations and evaluations" (2008) 3(6) Current Directions in Psychological Science 173-177.

M. Mehta, "Future signals: How successful growing companies stay on course" (2005) 70(2) Ivey Business Journal 1-7.

M. Mehta, "Growth by design: How good design drives company growth" (2006) 70(3) Ivey Business Journal 1-5.

J. Miller *et al.*, "Personality Disorders as Extreme Variants of Common Personality Dimensions: Can the Five Factor Model Adequately Represent Psychopathy?" (2001) 69(2) Journal of Personality 253-276.

H. Mintzberg, *Managers not MBAs: A hard look at the soft practice of managing and management development* (San Francisco: Berrett-Koehler Publishers 2004).

D. Nettle, "The evolution of personality variation in humans and other animals" (2006) 61(6) American Psychologist 622.

D.J. Ozer & V. Benet-Martinez, "Personality and the prediction of consequential outcomes" (2006) 57 Annual Review of Psychology 401-421.

R.M. Stulz, "6 ways companies mismanage risk" (2009) 87(3) Harvard Business Review 86-94.

J. Twenge *et al.*, "Egos inflating over time: A cross-temporal meta-analysis of the Narcissistic Personality Inventory" (2008) 76(4) Journal of Personality 875-902.

Table 1: The Five Dimensions of Personality

Personality Dimension	Description	Outcomes at Low End	Outcomes at High End
Extraversion	Variation in being outgoing, energetic, and focused on rewards.	Patience Detachment Independence	Reward Focus Impulsivity Excitement
Agreeableness	Variation in empathy, compassion, and politeness.	Defiance Selfishness Anti-Social Behavior	Citizenship Behavior Gratitude Compliance
Conscientiousness	Variation in self-discipline, industriousness, and organizational ability.	Carelessness Lack of Principles Organizational Chaos	Integrity Hard-Work Rigidity
Emotional Stability	Variation in stress tolerance and experience of negative emotions.	Vigilance Risk-Aversion Health Problems	Confidence Risk-Insensitivity Resilience
Openness	Variation in cognitive flexibility, breadth of thinking, and artistic sensibilities.	Closed-Mindedness Conventionality Pragmatism	Creativity Innovation Distractibility

Sources: Digman, 1990; Goldberg, 1993.

Effective Tax Strategies for the Individual Investor

Stanley M. Tepner[1]

A fool and his money are soon parted.
The rest of us wait until income tax time.

*****

No matter how successfully you navigate the complex investment world, at the end of the day you must face the gnarling teeth of the Canada Revenue Agency (CRA). You make, they take.

Yet there are numerous, easy-to-deploy tax strategies that you can use to keep more of what you earned. The key to successful investment tax planning is to follow the "three Ds": deducting, deferring, and decreasing.

- Deducting means that you should consider all the available tax deductions that you are entitled to claim to reduce your personal or family's taxable income.
- Deferring simply means that you structure your investment holdings so the tax bill you would have paid today will be paid tomorrow; as a result, your money works for you longer.
- Decreasing means seeking ways of paying less tax overall on your investment income.

---

[1] The views of Stanley Tepner are not necessarily those of CIBC World Markets Inc. These calculations and projections are for demonstration purposes only. They are based on a number of assumptions and, consequently, actual results may differ, possibly to a material degree. Readers are advised to seek advice regarding their particular circumstances from their personal tax and legal advisors. The information contained herein is considered accurate at the time of printing. CIBC and CIBC World Markets Inc. reserve the right to change any of it without prior notice. It is for general information purposes only. CIBC Wood Gundy is a division of CIBC World Markets Inc., a subsidiary of CIBC and member CIPF.

The Finance Minister to King Louis XIV of France, Jean-Baptiste Colbert, is attributed with a statement which the CRA and every tax department in the world probably have framed in their offices. He said "the art of taxation consists of plucking the goose so as to obtain the largest possible amount of feathers with the least possible amount of hissing." Let's take a look at some of the many ways that you can maximize the feathers in your own nest, and generate greater after-tax investment returns using the "three Ds."

Different Investment Incomes Have Different Tax Teeth – Beware of the Bite!

If you are going to use the tax rules to your benefit, it's best to first understand how different incomes are taxed. In Canada, not all investment income is treated equally. Chart A lists the top tax rates charged on different kinds of income for an Ontario resident taxpayer as of January 31, 2009, including surtaxes.

CHART A. Top marginal tax rates – Ontario 2009

	Marginal tax rate	Cash retained per $1,000 income
Employment income	46.41%	$535.90
Interest	46.41%	$535.90
Foreign dividends	46.41%	$535.90
Canadian dividends - eligible	23.06%	$769.40
Canadian dividends - ineligible*	31.34%	$686.60
Capital gains	23.20%	$768.00
Return of capital (deferred capital gains)	0.00%**	$1,000.00

* these are dividends that are received from Canadian-controlled private corporations that paid tax at the small business rate
** 23.20% when eventually realized ($768.00 after tax per $1,000 income)

Source: www.taxtips.ca

The chart suggests that all incomes being equal, it is better to generate income as return of capital, which defers the recognition of income into the future, at which time it will be subject to the lower capital gains rate. Alternatively, it is better to receive capital gains and eligible Canadian dividends for tax purposes than it is to earn interest and foreign dividends.

Note that this assumes equal amount of incomes. Take, for example, a Canadian dividend-paying stock appreciates by 12 per cent a year, on top of its dividend yield. As the pre-tax return from a lower-taxed vehicle increases, the total tax paid on the combination of growth when the stock is sold and the dividend may well exceed the total tax paid on an interest-generating investment.

Restructure Your Portfolio to Reduce the Potential Tax Bite

RRSPs and TFSAs

Canadians are fortunate to have access to Registered Retirement Savings Plans (RRSPs). RRSPs not only provide tax deductions for amounts contributed to the plans - they are also a haven in which all kinds of investment incomes earned are not taxed until they are withdrawn from the plan (and then taxed like ordinary income at the annuitant's marginal rate).

As of January 2009, Canadians have a new domestic tax haven, the Tax-Free Savings Account (TFSA). While the TFSA does not provide tax deductions for contributions, all incomes earned while inside the plan and all capital and incomes withdrawn from the plan are free of tax. Any Canadian resident aged 18 and over can contribute up to $5,000 annually to a TFSA. Note that contribution limits will be subject to indexation in the future.

You should carefully examine all the components of your investment portfolio for their growth, income, and income tax potential, and consider which components should be allocated for the potential tax deferral provided by RRSPs and TFSAs. We will look at strategies for both tax-preferred plans in the pages ahead.

Contributions May Be in Cash or "In Kind"

There are two ways to make contributions to a RRSP or a TFSA. The most common approach is to simply write a cheque. However, you may already own an investment that ought to be inside one of these registered plans for optimal tax sheltering purposes. You do not have to sell it, contribute the proceeds to the plan in cash, and re-buy the investment inside the plan. Instead, you may make a contribution of an existing investment "in kind" to the plan, subject to the prevailing contribution limits (be aware of the consequences of making an "in kind" contribution using an asset whose market value is less than its adjusted cost base - this is discussed below).

"Swapping" Investments

If you have already reached your contribution limit but still want to move that non-registered investment to your plan, consider executing a "swap" of investments of equal value. A "swap" is a transaction where investments of equal value are exchanged, say between one's open investment account and one's RRSP. When a swap occurs neither a RRSP contribution nor a RRSP withdrawal takes place. Rather, there has been a transaction where, for example, a $10,000 GIC is swapped to the RRSP in exchange for $10,000 worth of an equity mutual fund. The mutual fund begins its life in the taxable environment with a $10,000 adjusted cost base (ACB). The GIC will continue to live its life within the tax-deferred environs of the RRSP.

The only proviso about making contributions in kind to RRSPs and TFSAs is that when the contribution occurs, the investment is deemed to have been disposed of at its market value at the time. This may trigger a capital gain or a capital loss. If it is a gain, the taxpayer has to report the gain in their income for the year. If it is a loss, unfortunately, then the taxpayer cannot use the loss to offset their capital gains. As a result, you generally do not want to make contributions in kind for assets that have accrued losses.

RRSP Strategies

The Basic Rules

If you had earned income in a prior year, you may be entitled to make a tax deductible RRSP contribution. Contributions are deductible for a given year if you make the contribution within the calendar year or within 60 days after the calendar year-end. Your contribution limit is determined by three variables: i) a specific dollar maximum; ii) 18 per cent of your previous year's earned income; and iii) your pension adjustment, if any.

The formula is straightforward. Your current RRSP contribution limit equals 18 per cent of your earned income of the previous year, subject to a specific maximum, minus any pension adjustment.

i) The contribution maximum for 2009 is $21,000. Accordingly, the $21,000 contribution limit will be reached with 2008 earned income of $116,667. The contribution maximum for 2010 will be $22,000, and will be indexed annually thereafter.

ii) "Earned income" consists of your gross salary (before deductions), net business or professional income if you are self-employed or an active partner, net rental income from real estate, taxable spousal and child support, net research grants, CPP/QPP disability pension income, and royalties, less deductible employment-related expenses, net business losses, real estate rental losses, and deductible maintenance, alimony, and child support paid.

iii) The pension adjustment is reported by your employer and reflects the amount of benefits deemed to be earned by your pension plan in the previous year.

Age Considerations

The last time that you can make a contribution to your own RRSP is in the calendar year that you turn 71. You cannot make a contribution to your own RRSP in the 60-day period after that year since your RRSP will no longer exist. Its assets will likely have been transferred to a Registered Retirement Income Fund (RRIF) although there are other, less frequently used options available.

If you continue to have "earned income" after age 71 and have a spouse or common law partner who is at least one calendar year younger than you, you may be able to make a tax-deductible spousal RRSP contribution. The contributions may continue up to and including the year in which your spouse/partner turns 71.

Spousal RRSP Contributions

If you are married or living common law and are planning to make a RRSP contribution, consider whether it would be beneficial to make a spousal RRSP contribution. The mechanics of a spousal RRSP contribution are simple. You make a contribution in cash or in kind to a designated "spousal" RRSP in the name of your spouse or common law partner. You are entitled to the tax deduction, your spouse or common law partner is entitled to the investment asset.

There are several advantages to creating and building spousal RRSPs. It is one of the tools that can be used to equalize taxable incomes between spouses/partners in their retirement years. Spousal RRSP contributions can build an investment asset in your spouse/partner's name that may reduce your overall tax bill in retirement, when income is drawn from the RRSP and its successor, the RRIF. With two taxpayers to split this retirement income that is subject to graduated rates, there could be a shifting of income that would have been subject to a higher tax bracket into a lower tax bracket.

A higher-income spouse should not automatically make spousal RRSP contributions to a lower-income spouse. The lower-income spouse may have a smaller (or no) RRSP limit, but may be entitled to a large retirement income from the accumulation of other assets. Thus, when deciding whether a spousal contribution is appropriate for future income splitting, consider whether your spouse/partner's future taxable income may be affected by the existence of a pension plan, from the growth of an investment portfolio, or from the likelihood of a material inheritance.

Since 2007, Canadians have been entitled to transfer up to 50 per cent of their income that is eligible for the pension income credit to their spouse/partner (a RRIF withdrawal, from age 65 onwards, is one example of income eligible for the pension income credit). This certainly makes it easier for couples to income split in the future, but it doesn't negate the potential benefits of making spousal RRSP contributions today. Some of these benefits include:

- the ability to make tax-deductible contributions after you reach the age of 71, which may continue until the year in which your spouse/partner turns 71;
- younger spouses/partners may be able to double up on the assets to draw from if they choose to make withdrawals for the Home Buyer's Plan or the Lifelong Learning Plan. (Note: one should consider the potential forfeiture of RRSP growth when these plan withdrawals are made and decide whether the withdrawals are the best course of action.);
- if there is a significant age difference between the spouses/partners, building the younger spouse/partner's RRSP through spousal contributions means that you will be able to lengthen the time that these investment assets can grow before they need to be withdrawn from the younger spouse/partner's retirement plan, which further defers the taxation on these assets;
- when couples who are not entitled to pension plans at work plan to retire early, spousal RRSPs provide income-splitting options (splitting income before age 65 can only be done with superannuation pension income); and
- if a lower income spouse makes a spousal RRSP/RRIF withdrawal and invests this money, there will be no attribution to the higher income spouse of the income earned outside the registered plan. This is subject to the "three-year rule" outlined in the next paragraph.

There is one provision in place that is intended avoid the potential abuse of the spousal RRSP – the "three-year rule". The rule states that if you make a spousal contribution to *any* spousal RRSP in the year of a spousal plan withdrawal or the two preceding calendar years, you will be taxed for the withdrawal, not your spouse/partner. This rule was instituted to prevent a higher-income spouse from contributing to the spousal plan in one year and making a withdrawal at the lower spouse/partner's tax bracket immediately or within the following two calendar years.

The easiest way of tracking when withdrawals can be made from a spousal RRSP without attribution to the contributor is simply to look at when you made your last spousal contribution. Once three December 31sts have passed, spousal plan withdrawals can be made without attribution to you, the contributor.

Note that if spousal contributions were made to an RRSP that subsequently converted to a spousal RRIF, any withdrawals up to the amount of the annual RRIF minimum withdrawal limit will be taxed in the hands of the spouse. This is true even if they occur before the three calendar year-end deadline expires. Amounts withdrawn in excess of the minimum and within the deadline will be taxed in the hands of the contributing spouse.

If your spouse/partner has earned income in a previous year, she/he may be entitled to make her/his own personal contribution in the same year that you are making a spousal contribution. Some financial institutions permit both contributions to be made into the same spousal plan. They issue separate tax receipts that identify whether the contribution was your spousal contribution, or your spouse/partner's personal contribution.

The $2,000 RRSP Over-contribution Limit

If you have maximized your RRSP contribution and your TFSA contribution but still have assets whose income you would like to shelter, you should consider adding a one-time $2,000 over-contribution to your RRSP or to a spousal RRSP. The $2,000 is not immediately deductible but all the income it earns is tax-deferred. One oft-stated weakness of the $2,000 over-contribution strategy is that while you do not get to deduct the $2,000 when it goes into the RRSP, it is a taxable withdrawal when you withdraw it from the RRSP or RRIF.

The solution to this dilemma is to plan to use the $2,000 over-contribution as part of your RRSP deduction for the last year in which you are entitled to make an RRSP contribution. In that last contribution year, instead of making a full contribution in cash or in kind, reduce that contribution by $2,000. Your RRSP contribution receipt will be $2,000 below the maximum for the year, but there will be a friendly reminder of the previous year's tax assessment that you have "undeducted contributions" of $2,000. Then deduct the "undeducted contributions" and maximize your RRSP deduction for the year. Chart B depicts the sequence of this strategy.

Chart B. Deducting the $2,000 RRSP over-contribution

	Penultimate Contribution Year	Final Contribution Year
Over-contribution carryforward	$2,000	$2,000
RRSP limit, *e.g.*	25,500	25,500
Contribution in cash or in kind	(25,500)	(23,500)
Drawdown of over-contribution	-	(2,000)
Over-contribution, end of year	$2,000	$ 0

(Note: you are still entitled to deduct your RRSP over-contribution for yourself if you are over age 71 and continue to have "earned income".)

TFSA Strategies

Contribution Strategies

Should you maximize your RRSP before your TFSA, or should your TFSA take precedence over your RRSP? There is no really simple answer, since so much depends on variables such as:

- your current marginal tax rate;
- your expected marginal tax rate upon withdrawal;
- your expected taxable income level in retirement with respect to income-tested entitlements (*e.g.*, RRSP/RRIF withdrawals could affect your Old Age Security and the age credit, but TFSA withdrawals will not);
- how much you have available in cash or in kind to contribute to either plan or both;
- your need to maintain a level of liquidity for emergencies;
- existing liabilities that you have, such as a mortgage or personal line of credit.

The TFSA is far more flexible than an RRSP. It doesn't attract any tax at any time, amounts withdrawn can be replaced in a future year, and there are no minimum withdrawal requirements. The main drawback is that the annual contribution limit of $5,000 is far less than the RRSP contribution limit.

If you expect your marginal tax rate to be lower in retirement than it is currently, and you can not maximize both RRSP and TFSA contributions, you would probably benefit by making your RRSP contribution first. If you have maximized the RRSP contribution and still have available funds, then you may want to direct them to the TFSA. You may also wish to take any tax refund that will be generated by your RRSP contribution and apply up to $5,000 of that to your TFSA.

Alternatively, it may make more sense to take your tax refund and/or available cash and reduce your liabilities, especially where the interest is not tax-deductible.

If you keep a pool of money around for emergencies, it can sit in a TFSA, because it can be withdrawn quickly and without tax consequences. Any amount that is withdrawn from a TFSA can be replaced in the following calendar year, on top of amounts that are contributed to reach the $5,000 annual contribution limit. As with RRSP contribution limits, any unused contribution room carries forward indefinitely.

You are also entitled to give or lend your spouse/partner or an adult child the funds to make their own TFSA contributions. Any earnings in their plans will not be attributed to you while the funds are in the plans.

Investment Strategies

The beauty of a TFSA compared to a RRSP is that all the money withdrawn from the plan, no matter how profitable it had been, will be free of tax. I have often said that one doesn't want their RRSP to grow too large, relative to one's non-registered investment account, since the ultimate tax obligation grows in lockstep with the RRSP.

However, a TFSA cannot grow large enough compared to the non-registered investment account, because there are no taxes to pay when funds are withdrawn from the TFSA. The question then becomes what kind of investment is most appropriate to own in a TFSA?

Your immediate response might be the same answer given when asked what kind of investment is most appropriate for an RRSP: a fixed income investment, because in an unsheltered environment it attracts tax at the highest rate. For conservative investors, this may be the appropriate strategy.

However, I think that the best investment to hold in a TFSA is the one that would attract the most tax over its lifetime if it was owned in an unsheltered environment (subject to the amount of risk an investor is comfortable with). This means that if you expect the equity investments you own to generate enough capital gains and dividends that the taxes you would have paid on these unsheltered earnings would have exceeded the taxes you would have paid on other investments, then equity investments are the best choices for your TFSA. Of course we can't know what kind of returns any form of investment will provide in the future, but this is one way of allocating your investment assets between your taxable and non-taxable portfolios.

When it comes to deciding whether an investment should be allocated to a TFSA or a RRSP to maximize the tax sheltering potential of these structures, there is no difference for tax purposes whether the investment sits in one or the other (assuming a level marginal tax rate over your holding period). In the following chart, we assume that you have earned an incremental $1,000, and will always be taxed at the 40 per cent marginal level. You can contribute the full $1,000 to your RRSP, or you can pay $400 tax and contribute $600 to your TFSA. Assuming a 6 per cent annual growth rate, the after-tax results are identical.

After-tax result of 6% returns in TFSA vs. RRSP

Year	TFSA	RRSP	RRSP after 40% tax
1	$600	$1,000	$600
2	636	1,060	636
3	674	1,124	674
4	715	1,191	715
5	757	1,262	757
6	803	1,338	803
7	851	1,419	851
8	902	1,504	902
9	956	1,594	956
10	1,014	1,689	1,014
11	1,075	1,791	1,075
12	1,139	1,898	1,139
13	1,207	2,012	1,207
14	1,280	2,133	1,280
15	1,357	2,261	1,357
16	1,438	2,397	1,438
17	1,524	2,540	1,524
18	1,616	2,693	1,616
19	1,713	2,854	1,713
20	1,815	3,026	1,815

21	1,924	3,207	1,924
22	2,040	3,400	2,040
23	2,162	3,604	2,162
24	2,292	3,820	2,292
25	2,429	4,049	2,429
26	2,575	4,292	2,575
27	2,730	4,549	2,730
28	2,893	4,822	2,893
29	3,067	5,112	3,067
30	3,251	5,418	3,251
31	3,446	5,743	3,446

American and Other Foreign Dividends

Foreign dividends are taxed at the highest rates in Canada. You are entitled to claim a foreign tax credit against your Canadian tax liability for foreign taxes withheld on the dividend. If the foreign dividend is paid into your TFSA or RRSP/RRIF, you will receive the after-tax amount only, and you cannot claim the foreign tax credit against your Canadian tax liability. One exception exists: dividends from American companies paid to a RRSP/RRIF are paid without the reduction of tax withholding, thanks to the U.S.-Canada tax treaty. This treaty exception doesn't apply to TFSAs, so you may choose to allocate your American dividend-paying stocks to your RRSP/RRIF.

Capital Gains and Losses

Calculating Gains and Losses

When you dispose of an investment either by selling it outright or by a deemed disposition (for example, a contribution in kind to, or a swap with, a RRSP or a TFSA (see above) you must calculate the capital gain or loss on this transaction by deducting the adjusted cost base (ACB) of the investment from the proceeds of disposition. The ACB is frequently your original cost. However, your ACB may also be your original cost plus or minus certain adjustments. These adjustments may include re-invested mutual fund distributions that increase the ACB, and distributions of income treated as return of capital that decrease the ACB.

Over the course of a calendar year, all capital gains and losses are offset against each other to determine your overall capital gain or loss for the year. In 2009, one-half of the overall capital gain (the "taxable capital gain") is added into your taxable income.

If the overall result is a capital loss, one-half of the loss (which is called the net capital loss) is not deducted from your taxable income. Instead, the net capital loss may be carried back up to three calendar years to offset taxable capital gains that you previously reported. This will generate a tax refund for each year in which the net capital losses could be applied. Alternatively, the net capital loss can be carried forward indefinitely to offset taxable capital gains in the future.

As an attentive investor, you should be aware of your most recent three-year history of taxable capital gains or the amount of the net capital losses that you are carrying forward, in order to tax-manage your investment portfolio. The concept of tax-managing your investment portfolio means that you are continually looking for ways to use your less-successful investments to trigger capital losses and offset the capital gains taxes you may have paid, or will pay, on your more successful investments.

The "tax loss selling season" is an annual occurrence in November and December, as investors use the time near year-end to tax-manage their portfolios. In any tax-managed transaction you undertake for a specific year, you must ensure that the settlement date, which is the date you actually receive the proceeds of disposition, falls within that calendar year. The settlement date for stocks and most mutual funds in Canada is "T+3", or three days after the transaction date. Make sure you leave enough business days before the year runs out for your transaction to settle within the calendar year.

The Superficial Loss Rule

The superficial loss rule was instituted to prevent investors from triggering capital losses and immediately buying back the investment that was sold. The superficial loss rule disallows the capital loss if the same security was re-acquired directly or in an affiliated account (for example, in one's RRSP) within 30 days of the original transaction. If the security was re-acquired within the 30 days, the amount of the capital loss will be added to the ACB of the re-acquired investment.

When you are considering triggering a capital loss, you must consider whether it makes sense to keep an investment that you would otherwise not have sold out of your portfolio for 30 days, because you may miss an investment opportunity that could outweigh the benefits of having triggered a capital loss. There are some alternatives to consider as replacement investments. You could replace a single stock with a similar company for the 30-day period. Or you could replace the stock or a mutual fund with a correlating index fund for the same period. Always pay attention to transaction costs when tax-managing a portfolio.

Mutual fund investors may have a significant advantage in staying invested while they tax-manage their portfolios. That is discussed in the mutual fund section that follows.

How to Pay No Tax on Your Capital Gains: Donate Your Appreciated Investments to Charity

If you are planning to sell publicly-traded investments that have appreciated, STOP! Before selling them on the market, consider whether you ought to donate them, in kind, to one or more charities or foundations. The capital gains realized on this deemed disposition will be free of tax. And you get a full charitable receipt for the fair market value of the investment at the time of the donation.

This is a very powerful tax strategy for individuals with charitable intentions. The final paragraphs of this chapter outline a unique donation strategy using flow-through share partnerships that can dramatically reduce your after-tax cost of making charitable donations.

Mutual Fund Taxation – Don't Get Taxed Twice!

Mutual funds are widely-held instruments in investment portfolios in Canada. Unfortunately, many investors are over-paying taxes on their mutual fund earnings by not paying close enough attention to the history of their fund's investment income.

There are two ways you can be taxed when you own mutual funds:

a. From dispositions - when you sell all or part of your mutual fund holdings, and
b. From distributions - when a mutual fund distributes its income and capital gains, either in cash, or in the form of re-invested new fund units; you normally receive a T3 or T5 tax slip with your allocation of the income for tax purposes.

The double taxation problem often arises when an investor sells a mutual fund after having received distributions in the form of new fund units. The value of these units should be added to the ACB of the mutual fund, which increases its cost for tax purposes and reduces the future potential capital gain. Too many investors forget to bump their ACBs. They simply report their capital gain as the difference between their final proceeds and their original cost. So they end up paying tax twice on the income that had been distributed on the T3s and T5s.

Chart C details how to calculate a mutual fund's adjusted cost base (the same calculation can be done for stock investments with dividend re-investment programs (DRIPs) for example). Too many investors simply calculate the capital gains as $20,000 - $10,000 = $10,000. It actually amounts to $6,000.

CHART C. Avoid double taxation on your mutual funds

Example:

Original investment in growth fund	$10,000
Cumulative re-invested dividend income	$2,000
Cumulative re-invested capital gains	$2,000
Proceeds on complete redemption	$20,000

Solution:

Adjusted Cost Base (ACB) = $10,000 + $2,000 + 2,000 = $14,000

Capital gain =	Proceeds	$20,000
	Less ACB	14,000
		$6,000

Other Mutual Fund Tax Strategies

Track Your ACBs

Keep a chart to track your ACBs that you update annually. You can get the information directly from your T3 and T5 slips. When in doubt, call the client service desk at the mutual fund company for assistance.

Track Your Systematic Withdrawal Amounts

When a mutual fund unit has been redeemed, an investor must determine whether the transaction resulted in a capital gain or loss. Some investors take regular cash flow by systematically redeeming mutual fund units (monthly or quarterly, for example). It is important to remember that each withdrawal is a disposition for tax purposes, and triggers a capital gain or loss. If the investment has appreciated, the amount withdrawn is apportioned as part principal and part capital gain, in identical proportion to the underlying fund.

Consider the example of a $10,000 investment that has appreciated by 10 per cent and is worth $11,000. Assume there have been no re-invested distributions of income or capital gains. If an investor redeems $1,000 of the fund at that time, $909.09 is deemed to be principal ($10,000/$11,000 x $1000) and $90.91 is deemed to be a capital gain ($1,000/$11,000 x $1,000). For an investor with a systematic withdrawal plan in a steadily appreciating mutual fund, the portion allocated to capital gains will gradually rise, and the portion allocated to principal will gradually decrease. Make sure you include every disposition in your calculation of capital gains or losses for the year's tax return. This is particularly important when markets are significantly lower than they had been, since many dispositions may generate capital losses which can offset past, present, and future capital gains.

Beware of the "Year-end Fund-buyer's Blues"

Mutual fund companies usually make their largest distributions for their entire year's capital gains in one fell swoop in the last quarter of the calendar year (usually on December 15th or December 31st). If you acquire units in the fund just before the distribution record date, you will also receive the distribution. While this may sound appealing on the surface, it really is not. While it is true that you will receive a distribution in either cash or new mutual fund units right after acquiring your investment, the market value of your investment will drop by the value of the distribution received. As a result, you are no better off on your investment statement. However, you will probably take an economic hit for the income taxes that may be payable on the distribution you received. The solution is to inquire about the possibility of an upcoming material distribution before making your investment in the fund. If one is expected, it may make sense to defer your investment.

Note that if you do pay income taxes in this kind of situation, you are simply pre-paying taxes that you would likely have to remit at some future point. That is because the ACB of your mutual fund investment increases, which will decrease future capital gains or increase future capital losses. Therefore, this is really just a timing difference, not an absolute payment of taxes.

Beware of the "Built-in Tax Bite"

A mutual fund distributes income and capital gains based on the history and activity of its own portfolio, not based on your personal history with the fund. You may find that a fund that interests you has a portfolio whose cost base is dramatically less than its current market value. This could stem from the fund owning many holdings that appreciated over very long periods of time within the fund. It could also be due to some skillful short-term stock picking. In either event, the fund has a significant accrued, but unrealized, capital gain. If the fund managers should choose to unload these positions, the fund may distribute large capital gains to all unitholders at distribution record date. Consider this simple example:

Original cost of a stock to a mutual fund		$20
Value of the stock in the fund when individual purchased the fund		$50
Price of stock when sold by the fund		$75
Results:		
Economic benefit to investor:	$75 - $50 = $25	
Investor's tax liability based on:	$75 - $20 = $55	

If you are a recent investor, like the investor in the example above, you may experience a disproportionately large capital gains tax bite that stemmed from the "built-in" accrued capital gains. While many fund managers proactively manage their capital gains and losses, it may be hard to avoid the built-in tax bite from such legacy positions. One way to estimate the potential of such gains is to study a fund's annual or semi-annual financial statement, where the ACB and market value of every investment is disclosed. If you come across a fund that has large net unrealized gains, you should consider this in your investment decision. Once again, this is really just a timing difference, not an absolute payment of taxes.

Consider Corporate-structured Mutual Funds for the Benefit of Tax-free Switching Amongst Funds in its Family

Many mutual fund companies offer both the traditional trust structure and the newer corporate structure on their menus. The latter structure is growing in popularity, since it permits an investor to switch from fund to fund around the family without triggering a capital gain. It also permits the fund company to allocate some forms of investment income more efficiently.

Unfortunately, too many investors are under the impression that corporate-structured mutual funds do not attract any income tax, until they are sold outright. This is not the case. While corporate-structured mutual funds may manage income more efficiently than an equivalent mutual fund trust, both structures must ultimately distribute excess amounts in the form of interest, dividends, and capital gains.

Can You Avoid a Mutual Fund's Capital Gains Distribution?

It has recently become common practice for mutual fund trusts to announce their estimated annual capital gains distributions well in advance of the record date for these distributions. This practice aims to help potential investors avoid the "year-end fund buyer's blues" referred to above. These announcements also give existing unitholders time to consider making tax-effective portfolio adjustments with these funds.

As an example, imagine that in late November you learn that a Canadian equity fund that you own is planning to make a capital gains distribution equal to 16 per cent of the net asset value of the fund. You know that the distribution will be made to investors who own the fund on the distribution record date, which is December 15. As a prudent investor, you should analyze whether it makes financial sense to receive the distribution, or whether you should alter your holdings to avoid the distribution.

First, you have to determine what the tax impact of selling your mutual fund would be. By selling, would you trigger a capital gain as large as or larger than the distribution that you would receive by standing pat? It does not make much sense to do that, but it may make sense to trigger a smaller gain or a capital loss to avoid the expected distribution. The second consideration is what to do with the proceeds from a sales transaction. Should you sit in cash for a few days and re-buy the fund after the distribution date of record? How do you feel about the prospect of being out of the market for this period of time? Is there a similar investment that you can own in the interim? Are there any transaction costs to consider in executing these changes to your portfolio?

If you choose to sell a mutual fund to avoid the capital gains distribution, the amount of the capital gains distribution that would have been allocated to you will be spread among the remaining unitholders at the distribution record date.

Corporate-structured mutual funds are not likely to provide this type of early guidance of expected distributions for a very simple reason. As noted above, there are no tax consequences when a shareholder switches from one fund to another within the corporate structure. So there would be little incentive for any shareholders to stick around for the potential tax liability if there was no tax cost to avoiding it. A pre-announcement of a 16 per cent capital gains distribution in a corporate-structured fund would probably have investors running to switch to a fund with little or no distribution expected.

If the prospect of having to deal with potential capital gains distributions becomes too onerous, you may wish to investigate exchange-traded funds. These funds mimic the return of various stock market indices and sub-indices and they generally have measurably fewer capital gains distributions than actively managed funds.

Triggering Capital Losses with Mutual Funds

As discussed earlier, net capital losses can be carried back three years or carried forward indefinitely. The superficial loss rule deters investors from triggering capital losses and immediately buying back the same investment. However, mutual fund investors may have a way of purchasing back an investment after triggering a capital loss.

As noted above, mutual funds are structured as trusts or corporations. Frequently, a mutual fund family offers the same fund in both structures. The sister funds are rarely identical but tend to be fairly similar. If you own the trust version of a Canadian equity fund, for example, and its market value is sitting below its ACB, you may be able to trigger a capital loss by switching to the corporate-structured version of the same fund. Conversely, if you own the corporate-structured version and wish to trigger a capital loss, you may be able to accomplish this by switching your investment to the trust version. In both cases you will have maintained your market exposure, without triggering the superficial loss rule.

One caveat to be watchful of when employing this strategy: be aware of any potential capital gain distribution that may be planned for the fund you are acquiring. Just because the fund that you plan to switch is worth less than you paid for it doesn't preclude its sister fund from distributing capital gains that year.

Managing Your Tax Exposure

Consider managing your tax exposure with a new breed of mutual fund that empowers the investor to choose the tax treatment, regardless of the form of income received. As we can see from Chart A, different forms of investment incomes attract different rates of taxation. Investors seeking the safety of bonds and GICs are faced with having to pay the highest rate of tax on their earnings. Canadian equity investors can generally expect to earn a mix of more attractively taxed Canadian eligible dividends and capital gains.

There is a new breed of corporate-structured mutual fund that enables investors to decide in advance how they wish to have their investment earnings taxed, regardless of what kind of income the underlying investments ordinarily generate. With this new structure, investors can allocate their assets among four "classes" of funds, each with a different tax orientation. The classes are: i) the capital gains class, ii) the Canadian eligible dividends class, iii) the return of capital (ROC) class, and iv) the compound growth class. The first three classes are suitable for investors who wish to receive some form of tax-efficient income. The fourth class is designed for investors who prefer to let their investment return compound on a completely tax-free basis until they sell some or all of their holdings.

Using this structure, a bond investor could choose to receive his or her income in the form of lower-taxed capital gains, or could choose the compound growth class and defer the taxation of the earnings until the investment was sold. Investors seeking the most tax-efficient form of income can select the ROC option, where all the income received will be deferred until a) the adjusted cost base of the investment reaches zero, or b) some or all of the investment is sold.

In each case, the choice of the underlying investment is unrelated to the tax treatment of the income from the investment. The investment selection and its tax consequences are mutually exclusive. As a result, this structure provides Canadian investors with the ultimate control over their investment taxation destiny, and gives rise to myriad tax planning opportunities.

A simple example can illustrate the power of this mutual fund structure. A recently retired businessman named Levi, aged 60, had just realized an after-tax profit of $4,000,000 from the sale of his business. He wanted to invest this money to provide him with an annual after-tax income of $200,000. The $4,000,000 was in his personal account, not in a corporate account. He had unutilized tax losses of $15,000, and considered himself to be a conservative investor. He had absolutely no other income.

The challenge for Levi's financial advisor:

1. protect and conservatively grow Levi's capital; and
2. tax optimize the investment portfolio and the $200,000 income stream

Steps:

1. *Determine Levi's optimal investment mix for his risk profile.* Levi agreed that an asset mix of 60 per cent conservative equities (75 per cent Canadian, 25 per cent foreign), 30 per cent in Canadian bonds and 10 per cent in Canadian money market funds suited his investor risk profile. A mix of mutual funds in the fund family was selected to achieve this asset allocation.

2. *Create the $200,000 income stream.* This was created in two parts:

   a. Use the Canadian dividend class to generate $51,200 of eligible Canadian dividends. $853,000 of his $4,000,000 was allocated to the Canadian dividends class. At a pre-determined 6 per cent payout rate, the class would pay a $51,200 eligible dividend to Levi. An Ontario resident may receive $51,200 in Canadian dividends virtually tax-free if they have no other taxable income in that year.

   b. Generate $148,800 in tax-free distributions from the ROC class. $1,984,000 of his $4,000,000 was allocated to the ROC class. At a pre-determined 7.5 per cent payout rate, this class would pay $148,800 to Levi. The payouts from steps 2a and 2b combine to create Levi's desired after-tax income of $200,000.

3. *Clean up his $15,000 historical tax loss.* This was done by allocating $300,000 to the capital gains class. If the fund distributes $15,000 capital gains that first year, the tax loss will have been used up. The capital loss could otherwise have been carried forward indefinitely.

4. *Invest the remainder of the $4,000,000 ($863,000) in the tax deferred compound growth class.* Once the capital loss has been used up, the $300,000 from the capital gains class should be switched, on a tax-free basis, to the compound growth class.

Levi's initial portfolio thus consisted of:

$ 853,000	Canadian dividends class
$1,984,000	ROC class
$ 300,000	Capital gains class
$ 863,000	Compound growth class
$4,000,000	

It is designed to generate $200,000 of dividends and ROC annually to him virtually tax-free. While Ontario health tax and a small amount of refundable alternate minimum tax (AMT) would be due, the remainder of his portfolio is designed to enjoy potential long-term tax-deferred growth. It is worth noting that Levi's AMT credit only carries forward for seven years. In order to recover some of the refundable AMT, he will need to have taxes payable that exceed his AMT liability in this time frame.

Other Tax Deductions and Tax Credits for Investors

Flow-through Share Partnerships

Flow-through share partnerships provide investors with direct access to the Canadian natural resources sector, and offer generous tax incentives. The partnership usually invests in a portfolio of flow-through shares issued by Canadian resource companies. These common shares are similar to each company's other common shares, but there is one notable difference. The proceeds from their issuance must be spent on resource exploration, and the generous tax deductions generated by this exploration activity must be "flowed-through" to the partnership and, thus, its investors.

In general, an investment in a flow-through partnership is fully deductible against a taxpayer's other income. Most of the deduction is claimable in the year the investment is made. For example, if you are an Ontario investor at the top personal income tax bracket in 2009, your tax savings on a $10,000 flow-through investment would be $4,641. Your effective cost of ownership would be only $10,000 - $4,641 = $5,359 after taxes.

Once an investment is fully deducted for tax purposes, it is deemed to have an adjusted cost base (ACB) equal to zero. When the investment is ultimately disposed of, the entire proceeds received may be taxed as capital gains.

As a result, these investments may be quite profitable on an after-tax basis even without substantial capital appreciation. This is because of the different tax rates in effect when purchasing and deducting the investment (46.41 per cent) and when selling and treating the proceeds as capital gains (23.21 per cent).

For example, assume that you made a $10,000 investment in a flow-through share partnership which you eventually sold for proceeds equal to its original cost. The tax on your $10,000 capital gain would only be $2,321, which would net you $7,679 after taxes. On an after tax-basis, your overall profit from this investment would be $2,320 ($7,679 - $5,359), which amounts to a 43.3 per cent positive return.

The difference in tax rates also provides substantial downside protection to an investment on an after-tax basis. The value of a $10,000 investment can drop as low as $6,980 and still provide a positive after-tax return. The after-tax proceeds are $5,360 ($6,980 – ($6,980 x 23.21 per cent)), which is comparable to the after-tax cost of ownership of $5,359.

Most flow-through share partnerships are illiquid for up to two years, after which they will be rolled, on a tax-deferred basis, into a mutual fund. This mutual fund can be retained in an investor's portfolio, redeemed, or gifted to a charity. Each new partnership is typically offered for sale for a relatively short time period – anywhere from a few weeks up to two months – after which it is closed to new purchasers.

How to Reduce the Cost of Your Charitable Donations

Most higher-income individuals have significant charitable obligations to fulfil every year. Tax legislation recognizes this trend, and encourages charitable giving by providing generous tax credits for the donations we make.

If you make a gift of cash or property to registered charities and other qualified donees in 2009, you are entitled to claim an income tax credit equivalent to the bottom marginal tax rate on the first $200 donated. For the remainder of your charitable contributions, you may claim an income tax credit equivalent to the top marginal tax rate.

Does it make sense to make a gift of property, instead of writing a cheque? Consider this scenario: You have an investment that has appreciated in value, and are considering selling it this year to realize the capital gain. If you sell it on the open market, you will have to include one-half of the capital gain realized in your taxable income (assuming it is not offset by capital losses you realized in 2009).

If, for example, your investment has an ACB of $5,000 and you sell it for $10,000, the tax you will pay amounts to $5,000 (the gain) x 50 per cent x 46.41 per cent = $1,160. Note that this example assumes a top-tax bracket Ontario taxpayer.

If on the other hand, you *gift* the same qualifying publicly-traded property worth $10,000 (on an arm's length basis) to a public charity or public foundation, you are deemed to have disposed of it for the same $10,000 but the tax payable on the gain would be *zero.*

You can expect to receive a tax credit worth $4,641 for every $10,000 charitable donation above $200 made this calendar year, whether you write a cheque or make an "in kind" donation by gift of property. But if you have an investment you planned to sell for a profit, you can by-pass the capital gains taxes by gifting it instead of selling it and gifting the cash proceeds.

The Benefits of Gifting Your Flow-through Investments to Charity

Gifting your flow-through investments to a charity synergizes all of the aforementioned tax benefits. Let's see what happens when we consolidate flow-through investing with the donation of appreciated investments to charities or foundations:

STEPS	TAX CALCULATION	OUT-OF-POCKET CASH	
Invest $10,000 in flow-through		Expenditure	$10,000
Claim deduction	Deduction against income	Tax saving	(4,641)
Gift $10,000 worth of flow-through to charity	Donation tax credit	Tax saving	(4,641)
Calculate capital gain	Tax-free when asset donated	Tax cost	0
NET OUT-OF-POCKET COST FOR $10,000 CHARITABLE DONATION			$718

Compare the $718 net out-of-pocket cost of this donation in kind to the $5,359 after-tax cost of making a $10,000 cash donation ($10,000 - 46.41 per cent tax credit). It amounts to only about one-seventh the cost of a cash donation of the same amount. The corollary way of looking at this, which will be most attractive to charitable fundraisers, is that taxpayers could increase the amount they donate to charities by 600 per cent, without increasing the cost to themselves by gifting flow-through share partnerships.

The key variable in the above comparison is how much the flow-through investment will be worth in two years when an investor is ready to gift it. As with most investments, future values are unpredictable, so let's compare three possible outcomes: first, where a $10,000 initial investment declines to $7,500, which becomes the eventual amount of the donation; second, where it remains at $10,000 (as in our example above) and is gifted; and third, where it appreciates to $12,500 and is gifted.

Value of investment in two years	$7,500	$10,000	$12,500
Initial investment (cost of donation)	$10,000	$10,000	$10,000
Initial tax benefits	(4,641)	(4,641)	(4,641)
Donation tax credit	(3,481)	(4,641)	(5,801)
Capital gain tax payable	0	0	0
NET COST OR (PROFIT) OF DONATION	$1,878	$718	($442)

This chart indicates that the more profitable the investment becomes, the less costly the donation becomes.

Next Steps

Before embarking on this program, there are a number of items to take into consideration, including:

1. your marginal tax bracket for the year in which you make the contribution;
2. the possible effect of the Alternative Minimum Tax;
3. the selection and availability of the appropriate flow-through share partnership for your needs;
4. determining whether the charity you wish to gift the investment to is equipped and willing to accept this form of investment.

As an investor, you know how challenging it is to generate the level of pre-tax returns you need to meet your financial goals. The threshold becomes that much more difficult when your returns are diminished by income taxes.

This chapter was designed to give you some of the tools and techniques that can be used to keep some of the money that had been earmarked for the CRA in your own possession. Always keep the "three Ds" - deducting, deferring, and decreasing - at the forefront of your strategizing with every investment decision you face. Because it isn't just what you make ... it's what you manage to keep that counts.

Commercial Real Estate in Today's Environment – Surviving the Perfect Storm

Eli Swirsky

Introduction

To most, commercial real estate is an investment tool that is included in a larger portfolio, along with stocks, bonds, and commodities. However, if properly handled, commercial real estate can become a powerful investment tool on its own. Indeed, commercial real estate can actually be a much stronger single investment than a diversified portfolio. The current recession has the potential to become the most severe downturn in recent memory. Accordingly, the recession will present challenges and opportunities unimagined just a short time ago. In fact, the current downturn in the economy is presenting itself as a perfect storm in commercial real estate, combining falling real estate prices, economic slowdown, rising unemployment, and a liquidity crunch. When entering into the initial stages of a recession, there are several points to try to keep in mind:

> *Not every recession is the same.* Just because you have experienced a recession does not mean that you are any better prepared than those who have not. Each recession is a result of a unique set of economic, financial, and political circumstances. Therefore, the current economic downturn will have a varied and unpredictable impact on real estate values.
>
> *The lessons learned in the last recession are not as useful as you would like to believe.* In the last economic downturn, those involved in the commercial real estate industry learned painful lessons which will forever be ingrained in their psyche. However, since not every recession is the same, these lessons will not always be useful in the current economic downturn. The

> factors which were major contributors to one recession sometimes have little or no impact on the timing and occurrence of the next recession.
>
> *The timing of a recession is difficult, if not impossible to project.* Trying to predict the duration and timing of the next recession is about as easy as timing the top and bottom of the next bear or bull market. Your chances of success are unlikely.

So what are the best ways to prepare for the current recession? Looking back on my experiences, there are certain factors which contributed to the success and longevity of my real estate career. These considerations have not changed throughout my 30-year career. More importantly, these factors have not varied whether the market was booming or was experiencing recessionary pressures. Accordingly, in this chapter I present 17 key points which I believe are essential to a successful career in real estate.

(1) Always, always consider the long-term aspects of your real estate decisions.

There used to be a motto when purchasing commercial real estate: it's all about location, location, location. This motto was disregarded in the past real estate boom – location considerations were marginalized and replaced with other variables such as tenancy types, yield on investment, and other financial benchmarks. While these are important factors, location should still be the number one consideration in commercial real estate. Tenants come and go, interest rates change, and the market surely fluctuates. However, if you find the right location, you will always be ahead in the long run.

(2) Money is important, but your reputation is far more valuable.

What is more important: money in the bank or a solid reputation? The answer is, of course, both. But if you are in a position where you are forced to choose between the two, having a good track record and a solid reputation in the real estate industry is the more important and desirable quality. In commercial real estate, a strong reputation is essential for your relationship with potential lenders, business associates, and tenants. Moreover, the benefit you receive from building a good track record will far exceed the costs of establishing your reputation – once a good reputation is earned, it will pay back dividends in perpetuity. Furthermore, once a stellar reputation is lost, no money in the world can buy it back.

(3) In all business dealings, be tough, but fair.

When buying, selling, or leasing commercial real estate, the process of negotiation will always present unforeseeable twists and turns. Regardless of these unexpected developments, it is important to be consistent with your approach and always convey a position that is firm yet fair. You will not get every deal, since there are those who will look for short cuts and take advantage of someone's weakness. However, in the long run, people feel more comfortable in dealing with someone who is direct.

(4) Treat your tenants as your equal – never make them feel inferior.

There are three inevitable truths regarding tenant relationships: (1) there are more tenants than there are landlords; (2) tenants will always trust each other rather than the landlord; (3) the landlord/tenant relationship is not the relationship between the strong and the weak, but rather it is a relationship between two equal partners. In short, the success of your tenant is integral to your success; more importantly, his failure will inevitably contribute to your loss. Treat your tenants as your equals and keep in mind that some of them may be smarter, more experienced, more educated, and sometimes more successful than you. For you, the lease may be one of many. But for some tenants the lease is the single most important agreement they will enter into. Therefore, their concerns and desires should be considered carefully.

(5) Your staff is one of your most valuable assets.

Besides your family, the people who work for you are probably the most important contributors to your success. You probably spend more time with them than with your family and they certainly cost you less. Treat them like you wish you were treated by your first boss. Earn their respect. Allow them to feel like they are an important part of the team - because they are.

(6) Always protect your agents who refer the leads to you – being top on the list of real estate agents guarantees opportunities down the road.

Part of setting up a successful network of agents means exposing yourself to the marketplace. Accordingly, you should be on the "Hot List" of as many real estate agents as possible. Getting access to properties before they hit the market is key, since it allows you to look at deals and take advantage of new opportunities. Real estate agents prefer to deal directly with purchasers rather than going to the market, since going to the market increases the likelihood of having to share their commissions with other agents. However, at the end of the day, the agents want the deal to close; so, being on their "Hot List" also means that you should be responsive and capable of actually closing deals.

(7) Your relationship with your partners and investors must always take priority in considering business opportunities.

In contrast to public real estate corporations, private real estate companies typically rely on a network of investors and partners that they can call upon to take advantage of purchasing opportunities. If they are active in the market, most private real estate companies are typically fully invested in projects. To take advantage of new opportunities, these fully invested companies must have myriad new sources of investors available on short notice. Keeping your partners and investors engaged, happy, and informed is essential for the growth of your company.

(8) Your commitments, financial or contractual, must always be honored even if they are costly or other more attractive options present themselves.

Real estate companies that are actively engaged in the market inevitably encounter "bumps" on the road to prosperity. Mistakes are an unavoidable part of the learning process. Good faith business commitments sometimes have unforeseen and costly results, and making these mistakes is an integral part of making daily decisions. Dealing with your own mistakes is easy – you try to make good and attempt not to repeat the same mistake again. However, addressing ill-advised financial or legal commitments to third parties requires a much more disciplined approach. Not honoring these commitments may seem tempting; however, this decision may have disastrous long-term effects. In contrast, a decision to live up to a contract even though it is not financially prudent to do so will sometimes pay huge dividends in the long run precisely because you did not choose the easy way out.

(9) Be disciplined – some of the "best" deals are the ones to say no to.

Going through the different cycles of the economy requires the real estate investor to make decisions relating to participation in different ventures.

When prices are obviously inflated due to cyclical factors such as easy availability of credit or a low interest rate enviroment, it is tempting to want to participate. However, sometimes discipline is required to just say NO. Probably the most money that you will ever make will be the loss you avoided by saying no to a bad deal.

(10) Do not hesitate to be the first, if you have an idea that no one else has tried and you think would work – go for it!

Being the first in a new venture in commercial real estate is not that common. Most deals are cookie-cutter projects incorporating similar elements in a variety of designs. For example, most neighborhood shopping centers or regional malls have a similar mix of tenants that have evolved over time to serve the community around them. Similarly, downtown and suburban neighborhoods have a predictable pattern. Since a truly original concept and opportunity does not present itself often in commercial real estate, do not hesitate to go for it when one does! But before you invest, make sure that you have done your homework, done your due diligence, and analyzed your realistic upside and downside. It is also wise to have a "Plan B" in your pocket as an escape hatch.

(11) Cash flow is the most important aspect in ensuring the corporation's survival.

At the risk of stating the obvious, cash flow is king. The reality of real estate investment is that the value of your real estate portfolio will fluctuate markedly over time. This may be reassuring if the market tells you that you are worth 10 per cent more today than six months ago. Conversely, it may be incredibly distressing to discover that your portfolio is worth 30 per cent less today than last year. However, all this information is not relevant if you are not planning to liquidate your holdings. As long as your cash flow is relatively steady, you are under no pressure to participate in a selling process in a depressed environment. In fact, market downturns do not have to affect you negatively - you can even profit if you use these downturns as buying oppurtunities.

(12) Manage your own assets: no one knows your portfolio better than you, so you are the best manager to achieve that long-term appreciation of your assets.

Owning and holding real estate is not the same as putting your money in the bank or investing in the stock market. So when making the decision on whether you want to invest in residential, commercial, industrial, or other real estate ventures, you should think about how you want to manage your portfolio. Being able and willing to provide hands-on direct management is key to maximizing your real estate value. There are numerous capable management companies that can provide competent management of real estate assets. However, there are multiple factors that you must consider as a real estate investor (there are certain inherent limitations in hiring a management company for your real estate portfolio):

(i) Only you have a real vested interest in the long-term appreciation of your assets.

(ii) Individuals working for management companies may not be with the company forever. Therefore, simply because you have a competent manager today who knows all the ins and outs of your portfolio does not mean that he or she will be with the company in the future.

(iii) Compensation to property management companies is typically based on a flat fee with an additional payment per transaction. The bottom line profitability can not and does not come into the equation. Oftentimes this means that third-party management contracts are inflexible and too expensive.

In contrast to these drawbacks, managing your own portfolio has several important advantages. First, it guarantees continuity, since presumably you will not fire yourself. You also gain first-hand knowledge of the building and tenants. Moreover, by managing your own portfolio you are in a better position to deal with all issues immediately as they arise. Additionally, you can better respond to changing market conditions. You can also adjust your level of staffing as your portfolio expands or shrinks. Finally, and most pragmatically, managing your own portfolio is much more affordable. Your time is already spent in dealing with your investments, so why pay twice?

(13) Focus – find a market niche and become a specialist in that field.

Admittedly, finding a niche in commercial real estate is not easy – moreover, it is not an absolute requirement. However, one way to really excel in real estate is to specialize in a certain type of real estate product. You can gain a market advantage over your competitors simply by repeatedly doing the same type of development. For example, my first medical center development was the beginning of a long learning curve, but it formed the basis for developing better and more efficient projects. You will certainly make mistakes, but the repetitive problem-solving gives you the edge that only experience can provide. What's more, when you develop a rising market recognition that you are the person to go to for certain developments, you build a reputation that helps create positive momentum in your real estate growth.

(14) Differentiate yourself from the competition.

You need to find a way to differentiate yourself from the pack. Whether through size, geographical presence, specialized product or design, you need to be noticed and recognized. It helps to have your sign throughout the market that you operate in, but this alone is not enough. You need a unique concept, design, or product that sets you apart and provides immediate recognition. Do not hesitate to be creative and original – it does not matter whether people love it or hate it, as long as they remember it!

(15) Keep the portfolio manageable both in geographic proximity and project type.

As discussed in Point 12, being hands-on has its clear advantages and obvious limitations. It should be noted that if you choose to be truly hands-on, there are certain realities that will limit the size of your portfolio. Essentially, the choice is either to assemble a portfolio that can be managed hands-on or become part of a public vehicle. What does being hands-on mean? To me, it means knowing all your tenants, suppliers, and professionals personally. It also means having a portfolio that is concentrated geographically so that all the projects are within one to two hours from where you work. Finally, being hands-on means that part of your time should be spent viewing the projects on a regular basis. In my career, I have decided that the advantage of having your finger on the pulse of your portfolio far exceeds the limitations imposed by geographic proximity and project type.

(16) Sacrifice upside for stability and security of income. If the deal is too risky at the time you look at it, walk away.

Typically, the "risk and reward equation" is a major challenge for the commercial real estate investor, since it is always difficult to find the right balance. The problem is that depending on whether the economy is in a recession or a boom, the pendulum always seems to swing too far in either direction. The pendulum is clearly now at the risk-adverse extreme: government treasuries are trading at historic lows and banks are paying a mere pittance for savings accounts. What does this mean for a commercial real estate investor? Clearly, it is not an option to take no risk at all. Therefore, you must develop the ability to delicately balance the risks and rewards of any project. You need to take measured, calculated risk to grow. If this calculation of risk and reward is done responsibly, it will be rewarded handsomely. This is especially true when the market is so risk-adverse, since many players that would otherwise be participating choose to forego opportunities.

(17) Don't let success go to your head.

Just because you made money in the past boom does not make you smarter or less immune to failure than everyone else. Everybody made money. In fact, it would have required real talent to have lost money in the last boom! Your success was probably at least partially attributed to the overall market rise, not solely to your brilliant strategy. Therefore, you should not make business decisions based on lessons learned from the most recent expansionary business cycle.

Conclusion

Doom, gloom, and boom - how is a real estate investor to respond to these cycles? First, it is important to realize that predicting the start or end of these cycles is virtually impossible. Predicting the duration and severity of the recession is similarly useless. Finally, turning to the "experts" to guide you through these cycles is not just unhelpful – it is downright frustrating. These experts not only disagree amongst themselves but they also contradict their own predictions and change their outlook as time goes on.

The astute investor has to maintain his focus, implement his chosen strategy, and try to disregard the extraneous factors as much as possible. Having a disciplined approach to your real estate investment means never having to say "I should have" or "I could have". If you set realistic and achievable goals, you will certainly reap the benefits of your hard work.

* * * * *

Commercial Real Estate Development – A Profession or a Style of Activity?

Sam Cohen

During adolescence, youngsters often seek advice for their future. By and large, the question is always the same: should they pursue a professional career or simply follow their dreams? Many believe that our children should choose a future that makes them happy. But the fact is that what makes them happy today may not be satisfying for them tomorrow.

This is certainly true of my own career path in real estate.

I graduated as a Mechanical Engineer. That was my dream: I wanted to design machinery and equipment that would create and produce products. Essentially I wanted to make a career out of converting ideas into machinery. I would build a device and enjoy the creative and financial results.

My expertise was in designing and building equipment to automate the food manufacturing process. I eventually invested in a machinery manufacturing facility. During the years that I ran the plant, I had approximately 100 workers reporting to me. My staff consisted of engineers, sales people, and office staff. Even with all this help, I had to be physically everywhere. The main challenge was to continually obtain new orders while ensuring the timely deliveries of quality products. The pressures to secure enough orders for export were very high. I travelled internationally on an almost weekly basis to obtain new orders. I supervised the design and the manufacturing of product, and had to be present for deliveries and assembly at client facilities. Certainly, I had help from my professional staff; however, somehow my responsibilities forced me to be personally involved everywhere.

So, even with my success and achievement, I was very unhappy. Trying to provide enough new orders to keep 100 people employed wore me out. I could not even afford to get ill and my time devoted to my family was minimal. After years of what I felt to be slavery, I decided to quit. I sold my equity and the morning after had to decide what to do next.

While in this process of self-discovery, I knew, based on my past experience, exactly what I did and did not want to do:

I did not want:

1. To employ a large number of people.
2. To work in a field where I would need to employ experts that I would need to depend on and have difficulty replacing.
3. To be in a field where I had to continue to expand and develop in order to survive.
4. To be in a cash business where close monitoring and trust is needed.

On the other hand, I wanted:

1. To be in a field where I could plan, commit, and deliver my commitment.
2. To be in a field where I was not required to be physically present all the time – fax and e-mail would have to suffice.
3. To work in a field that challenged my imagination and creativity.
4. To create a business with a steady cash flow that did not depend on ordering.
5. To create a business that would provide independent positions for different family members and be challenging for the next generation.
6. To create a business that could be as large or as small as I wanted.

Since I had rented 80,000 sq. ft. for my previous factory and built my first home, I had some experience with real estate development. However, I never paid much attention to property development. I was curious to understand how the real estate market worked. After studying the many opportunities available, I concluded that a career in commercial real estate would be best suited to my goals.

When I was making this career switch at the end of 1983, the real estate market in greater Toronto was quite expensive. As a result, it was difficult to find an investment opportunity to start with in the Toronto region. Moreover, with my lack of experience I was uncomfortable investing a large amount in my first project.

In the end, I decided to invest in an opportunity in Ottawa. Shortly after, another investment opportunity arose in Ottawa. I felt comfortable with the price of the lands and the size of the buildings. I moved forward and executed the process of development while learning along the way.

While in Ottawa, I met my present partner. We had similar goals and we have been in business together ever since. We have seen both the good times and the bad times together.

In real estate development you can find professionals from all walks of life. There are lawyers, accountants, engineers, dentists, medical physicians, computer hardware/software entrepreneurs, industrial manufacturers, and other professionals. Many left their original professions for similar reasons to my own.

You feel a sense of excitement when you build a real estate structure from an idea. You have the opportunity to establish the shape, size, and colors of the overall project, as well as the details of the tenants' interior design. Since real estate projects are multi-disciplined, they require the skills of many different professionals that come together in a common purpose. Projects require design, construction, leasing, property management, accounting, bookkeeping, and legal input. Thus, real estate development is a natural vehicle for the employment of family members. Whatever their interest, a second generation of family members can find their niche in some aspect of real estate.

Entrepreneurial Spirit in the Face of Uncertainty

William (Bill) Zinger

I dedicate this chapter to my father who passed away on July 5, 2008 after a courageous battle with Alzheimer's disease. He is the greatest man I have ever known.

*****

I have worked for large, multi-national corporations. I have been an entrepreneur who turned failing companies into flourishing companies. I have successfully grown business in robust economies and in zero growth economies.

Over the years, I have learned that regardless of whether you are a company employee or its owner, regardless of whether the economy is strong, stagnant, or in recession, the secrets of success remain the same. I have also learned that the so-called "secrets" of success aren't necessarily secrets. Is hard work a secret? Or is treating staff with respect a secret? Or building your organization around customer needs? I suppose I will call them basic principles - the rules of business that have worked well for me over the years. When we face uncertain times, we should, more than ever, stay true to these fundamentals that made us successful in the first place.

There are five of these basic principles of entrepreneurial success outlined in this chapter. However, my principles of success are largely rooted in the early years of my work life. So, before outlining these basic principles, I first want to chronicle my personal experience as an entrepreneur. These observations I made and lessons I learned in my earlier years had a profound effect on the way I have run my business.

I was raised on a farm in rural Ontario by devoted parents who committed their lives to providing a solid foundation for our family. My father worked full time at Roxton Furniture and he also worked on our farm in the evenings and on weekends. The farming was necessary to supply food to the 10 hungry mouths that would descend on the kitchen table three times a day.

Driven by love for his family and a passion for excellence, my father worked tirelessly to provide us with more than creature comforts in our humble surroundings. I didn't know it at the time, but he was a role model who moulded my very being. He showed me that there is no replacement for hard work. My childhood taught me to appreciate what you have but also to constantly strive for improvement. Most importantly, I discovered something crucial about my own career aspirations: I never wanted to be put in a situation where I was simply looking to survive.

My father provided my first job at age 12. I had to sweep and clean three floors of a large factory for the majority of the weekend. At 14, I had a full-time summer job that started the very Monday after the school year ended. I worked until the return to school in the fall. The job was repetitive line work for unskilled laborers. I found it extremely difficult to return to work for yet another day and be passionate about the tasks at hand. However, the slowness of the day did allow me time to observe the behavior of management and co-workers. It also gave me the desire to continue my education. Essentially, it formed the basis of my dream to succeed.

Since I had a passion for mechanics from an early age, I entered college to study to become a mechanical engineering technician. Throughout my college years, I worked two 12-hour shifts each weekend. These time demands were exhausting, but the job allowed me to continue my education and earn a significant income. I worked as a maintenance mechanic, quickly learning the equipment and getting to know the staff operating the textile machines. Within a short period of time, I was appointed to shift manager and was responsible for over 20 staff. The prestige of a managerial position was very appealing and I enjoyed the added responsibility, the authority, and the positive impact my team could have toward corporate performance.

My part-time career while I was a working student was personally rewarding. However, for my co-workers, this was their permanent career. They were largely uneducated and labored at unskilled jobs. I was amazed that people could be satisfied with such an existence, toiling in jobs without any opportunity for growth or satisfaction. I concluded that the only reason why a person would perform such mundane tasks was out of necessity for required income. The more I had worked in substandard conditions, the more motivated I became. Also, I didn't realize it at the time, but my early observations in the workplace later became valuable lessons. These early observations helped me to develop my current management style and motivational techniques.

After graduating as a mechanical engineering technician, I thought I was set to take on the world. With my diploma in hand, I hit the job lines. However, I quickly discovered that the roles available to me were junior and the pay was meager. It was difficult to have managed people for years and then be placed in a position with limited responsibility. Unwilling to accept the prospect of a long, methodical journey, I took a different path.

One day, by chance, an insurance agent called to sell me life insurance. He ended up selling me on a sales career. He said selling life insurance is the highest paying hard-working job and the lowest paying lazy job. Knowing I was a hard worker, I signed on to a career I didn't have the faintest idea about. I became a life insurance sales representative. My parents thought I had lost my marbles.

The transition from plant to office was overwhelming. The atmosphere and attitudes brightened, the morale was high, and the motivation to succeed was beyond my imagination. I could not help but wonder why there was such a significant difference between the two workplaces. I quickly concluded, the difference was pay plan driven. Life insurance sales were based on commission, so success was rewarded.

After a few weeks of participating in the weekly sales meeting, it was evident that certain sales representatives were much more successful than others. Wanting to be the best, I began associating with the top producers. I questioned them and listened. I emulated their habits and practices – but with a couple of differences. First, I added creative prospecting ideas of my own invention and used sales approaches that were far from standard. Second, I had higher productivity. In the first eight months I qualified for the President's Club, which had a 12-month qualifying period. I also achieved Million Dollar Round Table status, an accomplishment that only about 5 per cent of all insurance agents worldwide achieve in a lifetime.

Although I was successful, I did not enjoy life insurance sales. One day while prospecting, I met a young Xerox salesman who earned double my income. A few weeks later, I was working for Xerox. I spent a year in life insurance, but I spent 15 years in the office automation industry with Xerox and Canon. My competitive spirit was formed while selling life insurance. With Xerox, my competitive edge was nurtured, fed, and strengthened to the point where I refused to lose.

At the time of my career change, Xerox and Canon were two organizations at the top of their game and fighting for supremacy in a crowded marketplace. Each company had a distinct business model: Xerox was a complete service company, manufacturer, seller, and distributor, whereas Canon focused on manufacturing and appointed privately owned distributors to sell and service the products. Both organizations spent tremendous energy and effort on sales and product training.

Xerox's famous sales training modules were sold at home and around the world, including to the U.S. army. The training was intense, with long days and even longer nights filled with assignments. My sales training module took place on a Xerox campus in Leesburg, Virginia. We were housed in a dorm and held captive with our classmates for three of the longest, most grueling weeks you could imagine. Most people are under the impression that a sales representative is a fast-talking smooth operator who will force you to buy something you do not need. In fact, Xerox training taught the opposite. To Xerox, the best sales people are great listeners, not talkers. The Xerox sales process breaks the sales call into a needs analysis concluding with a successful closed sale. Once you were given the skills, provided with quality product, and monitored for daily activity, failure to achieve budget was not an option. These organizations carefully design pay plans with marketing incentives to fuel the competitive spirit. They instill in the sales force that second place is no place to be, there is only one winner, and the runner up will never be remembered. Winning became a way of life.

I enjoyed my success at Xerox and Canon. But, after many years of watching, learning, questioning, and listening, I believed that I had a solid foundation to exercise the skills I had learned in my own business. I spent quite some time searching for a company with the right mix, but I finally found it. The company I acquired was a family-owned supplier and distributor of chemicals and salt products that had been in business since 1878. Kissner was well-established, underperforming, and had a large target market. Prior to my acquisition, the company had not kept up with the times and was nearly bankrupt. I acquired this small distribution company with the intention of growing the company and expanding market share.

I believed that the key to future growth at Kissner lay in developing an expanding group of team leaders. If I could build each department with the best possible leaders, they could relay the new corporate message throughout the organization. It is usually necessary to start a turnaround scenario in the sales department, since without sales revenue there is little else to manage. Also, having exposure to the sales training and management style of the office automation industry, the sales department was the natural place to start my recruiting process. My recruits used aggressive solicitation and direct customer contact; sales quickly grew. As sales strengthened, it became necessary to hire a professional purchaser who could secure products at or below market pricing. In many cases, purchasing can be a better profit centre than sales once the customer base has been acquired. The next department to require attention was logistics and distribution since transportation costs are one of the largest budget components of a distribution income statement. As the team grew, it became important to recruit a sales-minded General Manager to bring departmental cohesion and capitalize on the improvements. Most importantly, once this structure was in place, I still constantly looked for improvements that could take Kissner to the next level.

After 15 years of a collective team effort, I am proud to say that the Kissner Group is now a market leader in supplying salt and chemical products, offering food and industrial chemicals, ice melt products, water softener salt, food grade salt, and packaging wrap. It is a large-scale operation, sourcing products from thousands of manufacturers around the world and distributing to business, manufacturing, and residential markets across North America. From a company on the verge of bankruptcy, Kissner is now an ISO-certified organization with solid revenue and increasing market share virtually every year.

In building the company, I followed five basic business fundamentals. I truly believe that these principles remain constant, regardless of the state of the prevailing economy.

1. Leadership is a full-time job.

When you are a leader, you must always lead – never become complacent. You are the company and your actions determine the company's success.

You must establish a winning corporate culture. When I purchased Kissner, it was filled with employees completely comfortable with mediocrity, complacency, and failure. For example, in one of the first telephone conversations I overheard at the company, a receptionist told a customer that we could not guarantee a shipment at the appointed time. She said if the customer needed that assurance that the shipment would be received prior to the deadline, he would be better off buying from our competitor. My everyday life for 20 years prior to acquiring Kissner was one of working extended hours, being motivated to succeed, and having a focused desire to exceed the expectations of corporate objectives – so the passive environment at Kissner posed a real challenge. I was soon to learn that old habits die hard. But I led by example. I was first into the office and the last to leave.

I worked diligently and displayed a winning attitude all the time. The team slowly began to rally around the positive results. Those that could not make the transition were terminated and replaced with like-minded individuals. If you believe, you will achieve.

Leaders set goals with action plans. Each year, our corporate goals are established collectively by sales management after an in-depth review of the previous year's performance. The performance is assessed on a per customer basis. Together, we review our successes and failures, as well as look for opportunities for improvement. We discuss new product launches, marketing campaigns, and new horizons for growth. Once the goals are established, we formulate the action plan and implementation timelines. We review the required support and assign tasks to each manager as a sales support system. Note that this type of leadership involves a team effort.

Corporate success comes from the leaders, not the corporation. There is an army of self-declared business experts who can explain why businesses fail. These experts display thousands of PowerPoint slides providing elaborate strategic explanations for failure: poor customer service, underestimating the competition, bad acquisitions, too much debt. The failure is usually described as an abstract collective failure. "The company failed to innovate, the company ignored direction. The company did this. The company did not do that." Companies are artificial constructs. A *company* does not fail to do anything, individuals do. Businesses are simply a product and an extension of the personal attributes of its leaders. What is more, when you probe a bit, you usually find the failure lies not in a string of strategic mistakes; rather, the real fault lies in the leader of the company.

How does a leader fail to lead? Most importantly, if you are a leader of any enterprise that is achieving great sales and profit, you must be careful. When your company is profitable you are in danger of becoming comfortable. Once you are comfortable, failure is just around the corner. You should live uncomfortable, wake up broke every morning, and finish the day only after you have made your day's target. Also, you should make sure you take time to think. Not taking time to think is just plain foolish, even dangerous to the business. Time to think is not a luxury, it is a necessity: "Action is easy; thought is hard."

When I acquired Kissner, the company was a leader in certain markets for salt products but did not manufacture ice melt products. I added this capability and now we ship over 4 million bags annually throughout North America. Similarly, our manufacturing plants used significant quantities of stretch film, so I decided to create Kissner Plastics to supply our requirements as well as those of other end users. Today, we have a significant presence in the Ontario market. Food ingredients and industrial chemicals, sourced from North America, had been a limited offering when I took over the company. Today we source and import from around the world and stock over 200 products for most manufacturing needs. The lesson is simple: never become comfortable with your share in the market.

2. Treat your people like people.

When you recruit the right personnel and establish a positive work atmosphere, your people will be productive and your company will prosper.

When you take over a department or a company, your greatest resource is your staff. When I acquired Kissner, the first order of business was to assess what I had just purchased. However, even after in-depth due diligence, I could not fully understand the culture, the motivation, or team members. Therefore, it was important as a new leader to meet with all department heads and their subordinates in order to gain knowledge of what the company was doing right and search for opportunities for improvement.

I have been involved with several successful turnarounds and each starts with this necessary exercise. Be prepared, since you will learn more in a day from the staff than you would in a year trying to figure it out on your own. It must be in a relaxed environment with no fear of reprisal. Ask lots of questions related to the method of operation, how it could be improved, and why competitors do it better. An MBA could not provide you with the knowledge your employees have, so never underestimate their feedback.

Create an environment where people can grow responsibly. I have not been present in the company office on a daily basis for the past 12 years. Yet the business has grown significantly. I attribute this success to creating an atmosphere that responsibly allows individuals to grow and achieve their career goals.

My early years of observing employee behavior led me to conclude that if you are trained like a monkey, you will act like a monkey. In absence of independent thought, people may take comfort in repetitive tasks and never progress. Conversely, if employees are asked to identify any problems and propose the solution, people gain a tremendous feeling of self-worth and believe that they are a valuable part of the team. Assuming that you have recruited the appropriate personnel, their competitive spirit will drive larger and more rewarding challenges. Over the years, it has been evident that most people will be more critical of the decision they make on their own than if the decision was guided by their superior. Allow your staff to grow and flourish, and you will be amazed at the level of talent within your organization. Listen to their feedback. Note that a desk is a dangerous place from which to view your business. You must listen carefully to your staff's feedback, without creating a climate of fear. A positive work environment is often a rare thing, but you can achieve it if you try. Once a positive work environment is achieved, your staff and your company will reap the benefits every year.

Seek and trust others who can share leadership responsibilities. Some of the most successful and talented people I've known and worked with have the humble tendency to avoid the spotlight. Wisely, they are willing to share the stage. Whatever you do in life, you should surround yourself with people who will argue with you. That is one reason I am a strong believer in management teams. When a team of leaders complement and balance one another, one person's short-coming is often offset by another's strength. I have been very fortunate to have a strong executive team working with me that would not only tell me on occasion that I was wrong, but when I was *dead* wrong and that they would be proceeding as they saw fit.

3. Know your customers, know your market.

Entrepreneurs approach business as if their very livelihood depends on each customer; I suppose because it is true.

Find a market niche for upside gain and diversify for downside protection. It is critical to evaluate the market you are involved in and determine how your organization is best suited to handle market needs and competitive threats. The management team at Kissner has determined that we are not interested in competing at the commodity level. Rather, our products and services are value-added, premium-priced solutions that larger competitors cannot provide, either because of rigid systems, corporate bureaucracy, or simple complacency. For example, we don't just offer natural rock salt to melt ice; we offer 14 different ice-melt products to precisely suit every conceivable application. Taking such a position has reduced competition and established our organization as solution finders in the minds of the customer. Note that while finding a market niche, you should be certain the market is large enough to allow for achievement of your corporate goals.

More importantly, diversify. Do not allow your company to be tied to one specific market, since the ebb and flow of economic cycles is guaranteed. You can protect your downside through diversification of markets and products. Relying on one product or marketplace is the kiss of death when the market moves. It is not a matter of if the market will change, but when.

Customer focus starts by putting your executives in the field. At Kissner, our executive managers spend a significant portion of our selling season traveling 3 to 4 days per week for 6 to 10 weeks per year with a sales representative. The sales force appreciates the support as they are paid commission regardless of who may have convinced the customer to switch. The internal staff witnesses the support and appreciates the difficulty of attracting new customers in a competitive environment.

The practice of having executives in the field goes back to day one. My first task after purchasing Kissner was to visit the customer base to determine why our customers purchased from Kissner. In many cases I found it was out of necessity, complacency, or simple convenience. In an effort to grow the business I would inevitably ask: "Are there any other products you purchase that I may quote on?" The response was always yes. We soon began to sell ourselves as a one-stop shop that would supply all the customers' needs with one call. We offered the convenience of a single source, one purchase order, one invoice and one cheque. Not long into the ownership, Kraft/Nabisco tendered 18 commodities for 13 plants. Kissner was the only organization of 12 vendors that quoted on all products, so we won the tender.

Additionally, Kissner management makes it a priority to understand the customers' needs, competitive strengths and weaknesses, and potential market opportunities. My favorite customer question is: "Are there any products or services that you are having difficulty with?" Once, when our largest customer described being unable to outsource a particular requirement, I met the need by building a small production plant on a handshake for the order. That customer now calls us "the go-to guys." We make it easy to do business with us, and have great difficulty saying no to any customer.

In short, there is little that is left to chance – our environment is designed for success. Every single employee understands how valuable each customer and order is to our organization. Customer satisfaction is paramount.

Marketing matters at all times. The power of persuasion is a powerful tool. As much as we would like our sales force to do all the corporate selling and represent our firm at the customer level, it is impossible for them to have the necessary coverage without marketing. Not long after I acquired Kissner, I knew we had the capability to fill larger orders; however, we lacked the track record or image to be awarded these larger contracts. I wanted to portray our company as being larger than we were in the market. So I hired an advertising agency to develop a brochure and corporate website which created an illusion of size and depth. The image was quickly accepted by the market, and opened the doorway for larger contracts with national firms.

Strategic marketing will provide product features and benefits to a mass audience that a sales force cannot penetrate. For example, we have enjoyed considerable success via the Internet. Kissner goes to great lengths to be the first hit on as many search engines as possible. With countless potential viewers on a daily basis, it is imperative that your company, products, or services are found by buyers seeking your goods and services. Our efforts have yielded great returns from Central and South America, Europe, the Middle East and Africa, locations where we have no direct sales presence. Also, e-marketing is a very cost-effective method of keeping in touch with both prospects and existing customers.

In difficult times, the marketing budget is often the first to go. On the contrary, I believe that the marketing budget should increase during times of economic trouble. During a recession, you are usually inundated with images of doom and gloom. If you buy into these messages as a corporate leader, so will your team. Failure will become a self-fulfilling prophecy. Once your sales force collectively believes the company is no longer supporting their effort, there will be a paradigm shift. Sales will fall and this, in turn, will support the theory of economic collapse already established in your sales force. Regardless of the significance of the economic downturn, business will continue if you ensure your company succeeds at the customer level. That will only happen if a team believes that they deserve to win and that they have the support of the corporation behind them.

4. Operate with an entrepreneurial edge.

Know your business inside and out, always seek new opportunities, and trust your own judgment.

Analyze your business ... daily. When I took over Kissner, I broke down the financial statement one general ledger line at a time. I looked for any causes for concern. Any anomaly was drilled down to the source and action put in place to correct for the future.

Once the ratios for inventory turns, accounts payable, and accounts receivable are in order relative to the sales volume, it is necessary to focus on the margin. Gross margin is the single most important item to review on a daily basis. After 15 years of ownership, I still review our daily invoice journal for each customer and product to ensure every order meets our margin qualifiers. Look to your suppliers and marketplace for cost improvements. When there are cost increases, move them through to your customer base. Most executives and sales people will give you hundreds of reasons why you cannot increase the customer's price. I will give the one reason that you must – to stay in business. You owe it to your suppliers, your staff, and your competitors.

Take calculated risks. "He who is overcautious will accomplish little." Many things could happen when you take risks, and some of these things could be negative. However, I assure you, nothing good will materialize if you don't take the risks. It's reasonable to think that because you have achieved some level of success, you should quit taking risks. It is human nature – I've got something good, why risk it? But not taking risks is one of the major diseases of success. Regardless of your level of success, feel discontent and search for opportunities. The world belongs to the discontent, so don't become the company that died risk-free.

One of the most widely studied business stories of risks not taken is the Xerox story. In the early 1970s, Xerox had grown to over $1 billion in revenue in less than 10 years. This enormous profit was generated from taking a risk on a single technology to replace carbon paper. However, Xerox then lost its way because the company didn't take a risk on a product which they had invented. In 1973, Xerox developed the first personal computer and mouse. Xerox had at least a five-year head start over their competitors. But headquarters failed to take the risk of developing this product, since they were too comfortable with their new-found copier success. By the late 1990s, Xerox had lost its leadership in copiers and was posting losses and announcing large layoffs. They ignored the simple truth that creating profits in the long term requires innovation in the short term. If you are too comfortable, either remove yourself or the chair from your office. You become an impediment to the company's success. Be prepared for change. "For this is the tragedy of man – circumstances change, but he does not."

Another example: In 1980, IBM forecast revenues of $250 billion by 1995. In 1984, IBM posted nearly $6.6 billion in profits. This was the greatest after-tax profit of any company in history. Nine years later, IBM set another record: The company announced the greatest corporate loss in history, nearly $8 billion. What happened? IBM was too comfortable with their mainframe business and didn't take the risk on the PC. They had market dominance and believed that the computing power would remain at the mainframe level. The executives were too comfortable and inflexible. Now, PCs have more computing power than the mainframes of that time.

In contrast to these stories of missed opportunity, in 2003 I took a calculated risk that paid off handsomely. At that time, two manufacturers dominated the Canadian ice melt market – Kissner and Nu-Gro Fertilizers. At Kissner, we had gained significant market share over a four-year period. However, this success strained our production facility. Looking for additional capacity,

I approached Nu-Gro to determine their interest in selling a production plant and their industrial ice melt division. To my surprise, they agreed to put a proposal together – that focused on their consumer ice melt product. However, in conducting our due diligence, our VP Finance and two accountants concluded that the industrial ice melt profit would not justify the plant purchase, especially considering the plant was outmoded and in need of repair. They advised me not to proceed. But experience had taught me that advisors often guide from a conservative position. A great many times, I have encountered experts and consultants, often armed with flashy PowerPoint presentations, who tried to talk me into decisions that went against my better judgment and gut instinct. Remember: consultants, accountants, and lawyers are not generally entrepreneurs, so they are usually guiding from a cautious point of view. They do not want to deal with future lawsuits, so they may steer you toward the safest approach. Rarely do they look at the future opportunity and the positive "what ifs." In this case, they saw a division needing restructuring and equipment requiring automation. I saw that our sales force required production capacity to expand revenue, and I had an opportunity staring me in the face. I purchased the operation. We doubled our sales the first year after the acquisition and have continued to grow over 20 per cent in per year profitability since the purchase. Let people guide you, but also remain uncomfortable with the status quo of your company, and take calculated risks.

Embrace technology. Technology is third only to sales revenue and quality staff in terms of importance to a corporation. It is therefore essential to invest heavily in computerization systems and controls. Computerized controls are key in assessing the financial condition of the company, measuring corporate efficiencies and maintaining customer satisfaction.

I am always amazed when I observe that some companies lack control and have a limited amount of information available to access their financial condition. Far too many organizations judge their success based on the state of the company's bank account. These organizations usually only have financial reporting completed on an annual basis. But, if you cannot determine on a daily basis whether you have made money per shipment, by product, or by customer, then you are not equipped to survive tumultuous times. This data provides necessary daily tracking and is the basis of analysis for your go-forward plan. Through technology, you can track historic events so you can predict the future with a high degree of certainty. Growth requires cash and operational costs consume cash. So the only way you can determine if the money is well spent is by being able to analyze the profitability at the customer, territory and market level – through technology.

Technology must also be used to measure efficiencies. At Kissner we use GPS to track our delivery routing, plant line efficiencies, sales performance, and customer relationship communication.

Furthermore, customer satisfaction can only be assured if the appropriate financial tracking is present. The use of technology ensures you have access to appropriate inventory levels, on-time order tracking, and up-to-date invoicing and payables. With these statistics, technology will significantly improve customer satisfaction and communication with the sales representatives responsible for the account. Additionally, since instantaneous response time has become a market norm, anything less puts you in a very unfavorable position. You will be at risk of losing the business due to customer frustration if you do not have the technology to respond to customer needs immediately. Finally, customer profiles allow the sales person to take the opportunity to show the customer that they are special: contact, on special occasions like birthdays and anniversaries, goes a long way in showing that our company cares.

5. Approach life with a positive attitude.

There is no doubt in my mind that your chance to succeed increases greatly when you always view the glass as half full instead of half empty.

See the positive, not the negative. Given the nature of media today, being optimistic may seem like a challenge. Television is the greatest gift to pessimism since the invention of communication devices. With the Internet and cable churning out negative stories 24/7, we are inundated with reports of disaster from every corner of the globe. Since television is the lens through which we see the world, these negative stories shape your whole attitude toward life and the future. We are bombarded into a mood of extreme despair and pessimism over even the most inconsequential issues.

The most serious problem with pessimism is that it is absolutely paralyzing. People become so afraid of dire consequences that they throw their hands up in despair and do nothing. Fear of the future guarantees that the future will be a failure. Is trouble and turmoil the way we want to see life? As the story goes, two men looked out through prison bars. One saw mud and one saw stars. A tilt of a head, a different attitude, makes all the difference on how you shape your world. Helen Keller once said, “No pessimist ever discovered the secret of the stars, or sailed to an uncharted land, or opened a doorway for the human spirit.”

I am often asked, "When is a good time to start a new business? What are the preconditions that you look for?" If you believe those who fear monger, there is never a good time to start a business – something is always wrong. But if you believe in the essential creativity of entrepreneurs, then almost any time is a good time. Look at the preconditions and simply ask: Is there a market? If the answer is yes, then it is a good place and time to start a business. To aspire to any kind of leadership in business you simply have to be an optimist. If you want to fail, be afraid of the future. If you want to succeed, approach the future with optimism and passion.

Reach for your goals with passion. A major component of happiness in the business world is finding something you love doing and finding a way to do it. To have success you need a high level of desire to get up in the morning and go to work. You have to be passionate about the task at hand to get the best results possible. The easiest way to develop an inner passion in a business setting is to focus your mind on your customer, your staff, and your dream.

The same idea applies to staff. Rallying the troops is not telling the staff to have more fun. It's telling them to work harder because they have the capability of doing better. For their own satisfaction, they deserve to perform at a higher level. It is that passion to work as a team to strive for a common goal that must be rewarding.

Make an emotional connection with your dream, whatever it may be. Dreams do not come true by wishing, but if you internalize them and are determined to grow into them and visualize them coming true, then there is a greater chance they will be realized. I have had the pleasure of dreaming and living the dream most of my life. I owe gratitude to my parents for the teaching, to my wife for understanding the passion, to my children for caring, and to every single employee and customer for the many contributions to our corporate success.

Conclusion

When I look back at my business experience thus far, I likely owe most of my success to hard work and common sense. However, as the saying goes, common sense isn't all that common. I suppose hard work might be rarer these days as well.

I truly believe that focusing on business fundamentals (the same practices that brought me success over the years) will sustain and grow a business during uncertain times. I know that I will stay true to the principles that brought me here. I will resist complacency, continue to motivate my staff, keep customers satisfied, maintain my entrepreneurial edge, and stay positive.

Though I make the point that it should be business as usual regardless of the state of the economy, there are certain practices I have outlined that do become particularly important when the economy is struggling. For example, it becomes more critical to keep staff positive so they aren't dragged down by negativity in the marketplace. Be sure you are protecting your downside through diversification of markets and products or services. Look for ways to reduce costs. Maintain your marketing presence. Above all – keep your customers satisfied, or you'll work twice as hard to replace them.

The entrepreneurial spirit can really benefit anyone. I believe that if you apply your lessons learned, remain persistent, take calculated risks, and stay perpetually optimistic, you will be better positioned to profit during good times and to face challenges at all times.

Hedge Fund Investing: Success in any Market Environment

Greg Knudsen[1]

Is someone living in the United States more likely to die from (a) a shark attack or (b) debris falling from an airplane? More often than not, people answer (a) a shark attack; they are dead wrong. Statisticians have found that people living in the U.S. are 30 times more likely to die from falling airplane parts than shark attacks. So why do people so often answer (a)? Why this bias towards thinking that sharks are killers? Blame the media: people recall and retain sensational news like shark attacks more easily. Experts refer to this human tendency as the "ease-of-recall bias" (Michael Mauboussin, *Decision-Making for Investors*, May 2004).

Another important element of human nature is a fear of the unknown. People know very little about sharks - thus are very quick to believe the worst. This is very similar to the public perception of hedge funds. The hedge fund world is one most people know very little about, and so it is more likely that people may fear them. While I cannot ask readers to avoid this human tendency, I can only ask everyone I discuss the topic with to maintain an open mind. One crucial point I must stress is this: *unfamiliar, doesn't mean risky*. Even though some investors may use the terms interchangeably, these are two very distinct concepts.

These two biases in human nature are the Achilles' heel of the hedge fund industry. In 1999, there were 6,100 hedge funds in the U.S.: Long-Term

---

1 The views and opinions in this publication are that of the author and are not necessarily representative of those of Blackmont Capital Inc. (BCI). Commissions, trailing commissions, management fees/expenses may be associated with mutual/hedge fund investments. Read the prospectus before investing. Mutual/hedge funds are not guaranteed, their values will change and past performance may not be repeated. *Blackmont Capital Inc. is a member of CIPF and IIROC.*

Capital Management was just one of them. Unfortunately, when Long-Term Capital Management failed, the whole hedge fund industry was scarred by the fallout and media maelstrom surrounding this single company. Similarly, the media coverage in 2008 of Bernie Madoff's Ponzi scheme is another example of the damage done to the reputation of the hedge fund industry by one participant. I must emphasize that this one participant operated a scam – not a legitimate hedge fund.

This sensational and consistently negative media coverage deters investors. The investing public is done a crucial disservice by a media that reports seemingly only negative news surrounding hedge funds. Virtually no positive news is heard about the more reputable participants in an industry that is now more than 10,000 strong. This environment perpetuated by the media, has created a situation where people want to blame hedge funds, not invest in them. Hedge fund managers were the first group called to a congressional hearing surrounding the financial crisis of 2008. For those who watched, it was laughable. Congress quickly realized there was no wrongdoing, and that was it.

The very concept of hedge investing grew out of an effort to *lower* investment risk. The purpose of this chapter is to establish that this goal of minimizing risk has been achieved by the hedge fund industry. In a positive market environment, any investment strategy with equity exposure will be successful. However, it is important to diversify during strong markets, so that you are prepared when the tide shifts. Many people will make the mistake of noting that hedge funds don't add value during up markets. This observation is grossly incorrect. Moreover, this assumption proves detrimental every time the market turns down. To achieve success in any market environment, an investor must build their portfolio with the fundamental understanding that only one thing is certain: uncertainty!

Through this chapter I address the hedge fund industry as a whole. There are arguably 25 distinct and unrelated hedge fund strategies; however, in the interest of simplicity, I will address the asset class as a whole. I will focus on broad-based hedge fund indices, mainly the Hennessee Hedge Fund Index.[2] The data compiled in this Index will demonstrate the strength of the entire asset class, and the benefit to each investor. Unless otherwise stated, all the numbers shown in the chapter regarding return and statistical risk figures will be representative of the Hennessee Hedge Fund Index.

---

2 Each month over 1,000 hedge funds report their performance net of fees directly to Hennessee Group LLC to comprise this broad hedge fund index.

I firmly believe that hedge funds are an asset class that every single investor can benefit from owning because:

1. On a relative and absolute basis, hedge funds have offered strong performance in all markets.
2. Hedge funds have a better risk/reward profile than other asset classes. They have also experienced less risk by all common measures.
3. From an ideological perspective, hedge funds offer true alignment of manager and investor interest; therefore, they are a much better partnership for growth than the relationship between a mutual fund manager and investor.

Before I discuss these attributes, it is necessary to address the misconceptions commonly held by investors about hedge funds. Many investors have heard the attributes of the asset class; however, the evidence of these attributes is not enough to dispel these strongly held misconceptions. By addressing these misconceptions, I will demonstrate how these incorrect beliefs are true deterrents to successful investment. Further, I will discuss a few basic investing strategies which are the main competitors to hedge funds, and misconceptions regarding these more widely accepted investment approaches.

Misconceptions about Hedge Funds and Other Investment Strategies

Misconception #1: *Buy and hold is the best investment method*

In my experience, almost all retail investors believe that the market should return 10 per cent if you hold your investments for the long term. Most retail investors believe this is an investing reality, never to be questioned. But "buy and hold" is one of the great market clichés. Several other clichés are equally erroneous and almost as popular. For example, retail investors may claim "it's not a loss until you sell", "long term, the market looks undervalued", "you have to be invested because you don't know when the market will turn around" and, my personal favorite, "if you're a long-term investor, short-term volatility doesn't matter at all." I cannot emphasize enough that these are not facts. Rather, they are rationalizations made by people who are reared to step outside the box and think independently. They do not represent rational thinking, but rather support for an emotional decision. These people believe long-term investing is the only way despite any and all rational evidence. Investors who promote these beliefs have a range of names for their investment strategies: growth, value, GARP dividend investing, or similar. However, the basic approach of all these investment strategies is the same. They all involve buying stocks, and hoping that they go up if you hold them as long as possible.

In his article entitled "When Rome Burns", John Mauldin sums up the basic logical flaw in this investment approach. He writes:

> Let me be very candid. As the saying goes, if you only have a hammer, the whole world looks like a nail. Many investment professionals only have one tool. They live in a long-only world. If the markets don't go up, they don't make a profit. So, for them the markets are always ready to enter a new bull phase, or stocks are almost always under-valued. That is what they sell, and that's how they make their money. What mutual fund manager would keep his job if he said you should sell his fund? Frankly, it is a tough world.[3]

Mauldin takes the words right out of my mouth and phrases them much more eloquently than I could. Simply put, buy and hold is an investment tenet held up as superior by those who have no other options–namely the mutual fund companies. It is a "strategy" based on the hope that markets always go up over time.

Investors rarely question the belief that the markets will always go up over time - in fact, it is considered almost sacred. However, the reality is that there is only one market condition that we can be certain of: *we have no idea what the market's future will look like*. With that reality in mind, why don't we question our belief that markets always go up over time? Is it really true? And even if it were true historically, is it still logical to continue to invest that way without paying attention to the current economic climate?

Rationally speaking, there is absolutely no reason why the index of any developed country will repeat its performance from the previous century. Let's look at the situation. In developed countries around the world, governments seem committed to keeping long-term GDP at approximately 2 per cent. This usually equates to the risk-free rate of return around 4 per cent. In a perfect world, this rate of return would cause equities to trade at around 12 to 18 times forward earnings. Sounds rational, but what if earnings decline substantially and investor sentiment is destroyed - why then would investors automatically pay up for uncertain earnings? What if this balance can't be controlled by governments? What if governments dig too large a debt and have to raise taxes at a time of national despair? What if the world has a finite capacity in commerce? What if developed world population demographics prove far too top-heavy for our aging economies to overcome (i.e., Japan for the last 20 years)? These are all entirely possible scenarios and, if any of these events occurred, the market would do anything

---

[3] J. Mauldin, "When Rome Burns", weekly newsletter, February 20, 2009.

but go up. Given the likelihood of any of these events, why would you tie yourself to investing in a buy and hold strategy that will only help you make money if the markets rise?

Let's consider some historical evidence regarding the "superiority" of buy and hold strategies. In the article "Waiting for Growth",[4] Gavin Montgomery acknowledges that there have been periods during which equity markets have grown strongly, for example in 1945-1965. However, Montgomery points out that there have also been extensive and almost generational periods when the indices were range-bound, as was the case in 1965-1985. Moreover, he also states that there have been decades where the equity markets were in negative territory. He concludes that , "when looked at in the cold light of day, it is evident that returns for equity markets do not rise consistently, or in a completely explicable way and the expectation that they will do so is unreasonable and irrational."[5]

Montgomery goes on to note that there have been three significant booms in equity markets over the past 100 years: 1920-1929, 1945-1965, and 1982-2000. Montgomery argues that these booms were directly related to unusual and unprecedented circumstances. For example, the boom in the Roaring '20s can be directly linked of the end of WWI, mass urbanization, the economic benefits of the railway programs, and new technologies such as the automobile. These factors fueled an exuberant economy which seemed to defy gravity–until it didn't. Similarly, the most recent boom from 1982-2000 was driven largely by innovations in the mutual fund industry, savings tools like the 401-K and RRSPs, mass globalization, the emergence of new technologies like the personal computer, and the end of communism. Then, the technology bubble burst.

The point is that in recent history, long-term growth trends were *not* the norm - they were cyclical. Thus, it's naïve and unrealistic to assume that long-term growth will always occur. Montgomery notes that the crucial factor in each growth period is a fundamental shift in the national mood, and a birth of fundamental optimism. This fundamental optimism in turn causes stock prices to rise uncontrollably as evidenced by the rise in P/E multiples from 7 in 1982 to 42 in 2000. As I write this in early 2009, this birth of optimism has never seemed further away. Buy and hold could be more appropriately referred to as "buy and hope".

---

4 Mann Investments' Q3 2008 report. It should be noted that Montgomery's article is analyzing the performance of the Dow Jones Index.

5 *Ibid.*

In "When Rome Burns", Mauldin establishes (referencing work from Ed Easterling of Crestmount Research) that in difficult markets, a buy and hold strategy can actually be incredibly harmful to investors. Mauldin's work in this case postulates that markets go in cycles based on P/E ratios from low P/Es to high P/Es. This basically means that at the end or top of a bull market, investors are simply paying more for the same earnings.

As Mauldin explains with the use of his P/E ratio chart:

> For many, the "long run" is about 20 years. We work hard to accumulate assets during the formative years of our careers, yet the accumulation for the large majority of us seems to become meaningful somewhere after midlife. We seek to have a confident and comfortable nest egg in time for retirement. For many, this will represent roughly a 20-year period. We can divide the 20th century into 88 rolling twenty-year periods, from 1900-2002. **Though most periods generated positive returns before dividends and transaction costs, half produced compounded returns of less than 4%**! Less than 10% generated gains of more than 10%! The P/E ratio is the measure of valuation reflected in the relationship between the price paid per share and the earnings per share ("EPS"). The table below reflects that higher returns are associated with periods during which the P/E ratio increased, and lower or negative returns resulted from periods when the P/E declined.

BEGIN YEAR	ENDING YEAR	ANNUAL ROR	BEG P/E	END P/E
1975	1994	9.6%	10.9	20.5
1977	1996	9.7%	11.5	25.9
1942	1961	9.9%	12.2	20.5
1983	2002	10.9%	7.3	25.9
1978	1997	11.9%	10.4	31.0
1981	2000	12.8%	8.8	41.7
1979	1998	12.9%	9.4	36.0
1982	2001	13.0%	8.5	32.1
1980	1999	14.0%	8.9	42.1

> **Only nine of 88 twenty-year periods from 1900-2002 showed 20-year returns above 9.6%,** and this chart shows all nine. What you will notice is that eight out of the nine were associated with the stock market bubble of the late 1990s, and during all eight periods there was a doubling, tripling, or even quadrupling of P/E ratios. **Prior to the bubble, there was no 20-year period which delivered 10% annual returns.**

The bias of stronger returns at the end of the last century explains why the majority of investors today still believe that markets will always go up. Many investors still cling to this belief, despite the fact that some markets in Canada and the United States are now down 50 per cent from their peak. The majority of wealth in North America is held by baby boomers, many of whom flourished during the greatest bull market in history. During this period, both retail and institutional investors came to accept long-term growth in the market as a fact. To them, 10 per cent annual growth wasn't a goal: it was the norm. Moreover, this belief that the markets will continually grow was indoctrinated into the next generation through university lectures and marketing material produced by mutual fund companies. "Experts" were simply those who mined the data to support the belief system already in place.

In short, those who choose to stick with a buy and hold strategy during sideways markets are doing themselves a disservice. Look at the opportunity cost for those who held equities like zealots in 1929-1955 or 1965-1985, when the buy-and hold strategy was clearly not optimal. I don't believe many investors have the ability and discipline to stick with a strategy that isn't working for more than a few years – let alone 10 to 20 years. This can create major problems, as investors try to time the market or eventually get too distraught and retreat from equity markets for good. Buy and hold can be a losing and costly game. Moreover, despite what the mutual fund companies want you to believe, buy and hold is not your only investment option.

Hedge Funds vs. Equities: Which Would Have Yielded Higher Returns for Investors?

More than anything else, investors are interested in returns. Most investors turn down hedge funds in favor of some form of buy and hold strategy. So let's compare hedge funds and equities over the past 20+ years from a performance perspective.

Many skeptics point out that hedge fund indices have a short history. This observation is correct: equity indices have significantly longer histories, since hedge funds are a fairly new asset class. The Hennessee Hedge Fund Index is the longest index history I have come across. It dates back to 1987, when the index began with only about 100 funds.

In spite of the relative short history of hedge fund indices, the last 22 years will serve as a great proxy for any investment strategy. There has been a diversity of market environments over the past two decades. From 1987-2000 the market went straight up with little deviation. Over the last nine years, the market has been flat to down globally, with a very high degree of volatility. Certainly, hedge funds are a new asset class; thus unlike equities, we don't have more than 100 years of history to analyze. However, this is a poor reason to disregard hedge funds. The last 20 years have provided investors with a plethora of information about performance, volatility, and risk through vastly variant market conditions. There is more than enough information available to make an informed decision.

Simply put, hedge fund returns over the past two decades have been far superior to equity returns based on indices. *This is fact.* The performance data over recent decades shows that, on average, investors would have earned more money investing in hedge funds than in equities or mutual funds. Note that these findings are not unique to the Hennessee Index. I selected The Hennessee Index for this piece because of its extended history; however, other hedge fund indices will yield similar results.

Below is a graph and chart showing the year-by-year returns[6] for each $100 invested in: (1) The Hennessee Hedge Fund Index, (2) The Dow Jones Industrial Average[7] and (3) the S&P 500.[8]

	Hennessee Index		**S&P 500**		**DJIA**	
	% Return	$ Growth	% Return	$ Growth	% Return	$ Growth
1987	11.99%	$111.99	2.03%	$102.03	2.26%	$102.26
1988	20.16%	$134.57	12.40%	$114.68	11.85%	$114.38
1989	24.58%	$167.64	27.25%	$145.93	26.96%	$145.21
1990	11.97%	$187.71	-6.56%	$136.36	-4.34%	$138.91
1991	25.83%	$236.20	26.31%	$172.24	20.33%	$167.15
1992	15.57%	$272.97	4.46%	$179.92	4.15%	$174.09
1993	25.68%	$343.07	7.05%	$192.60	13.73%	$197.99
1994	18.00%	$404.82	-1.54%	$189.64	2.15%	$202.25
1995	17.70%	$476.48	34.11%	$254.32	33.46%	$269.92
1996	19.08%	$567.39	20.26%	$305.85	26.02%	$340.15
1997	18.79%	$674.00	31.01%	$400.69	22.65%	$417.20
1998	1.41%	$683.51	26.67%	$507.55	16.11%	$484.41

6 The numbers presented in the charts are rounded to two decimal places.

7 It should be noted that the Dow Jones Industrial Average operates more like a mutual fund than an index, since companies that don't meet minimum standards are often removed and replaced with better companies.

8 The S&P 500 is widely accepted as the best proxy for equities both in the United States and globally. I often hear that 45% of the revenue generated by S&P 500 companies is derived from global sources – however, I cannot verify this figure.

1999	30.78%	$893.89	19.53%	$606.68	25.19%	$606.43
2000	8.16%	$966.83	-10.14%	$545.16	-6.15%	$569.14
2001	8.36%	$1,047.66	-13.04%	$474.07	-7.10%	$528.73
2002	-2.88%	$1,017.49	-23.37%	$363.28	-16.76%	$440.11
2003	18.80%	$1,208.77	26.38%	$459.11	25.33%	$551.59
2004	8.24%	$1,308.38	8.99%	$500.39	3.15%	$568.97
2005	7.85%	$1,411.08	3.00%	$515.40	-0.63%	$565.39
2006	11.40%	$1,571.95	13.62%	$585.60	16.29%	$657.49
2007	11.64%	$1,754.92	3.56%	$606.44	6.42%	$699.70
2008	-19.83%	$1,406.92	-38.49%	$373.02	-33.84%	$462.92
Cumulative Return	1406.92%		373.02%		462.92%	
Annualized Return	12.81%		6.37%		7.46%	

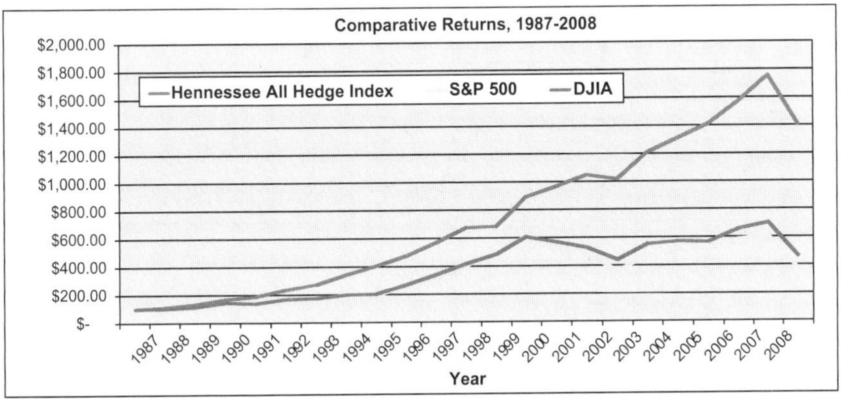

These graphics tell an obvious story over the last two decades. The most obvious difference in the performance of these three indices has occurred in the period since 2000. However, it is crucial to note that the Hedge Fund Index was also performing better than the other two indices during the bull market leading up to the tech bubble crash of 2000.

I also analyzed the above figures over shorter time-frames. Since many investors believe that 5 years is a very reasonable investment horizon, 5 year rolling periods is a time frame many portfolio managers try to think about. Therefore, it is appropriate to analyze the performance of these indices using that time frame. What I found was this: if you were to invest $100 in each index every year from 1987 through 2004 and hold for five full years, you only would have been better off investing in the S&P or the Dow Jones in three of the seventeen complete five-year periods. The three years in which you would have been better off were 1994, 1995, and 1996. In these three five-year time frames, the long-only indices out-performed the hedge fund index by a very narrow margin. This period also represented the strongest bull market over the last 100 years.

	Hennessee Index		**S&P 500**		**DJIA**	
	% Return	$ Growth	% Return	$ Growth	% Return	$ Growth
		$100.00		$100.00		$100.00
1994	18.00%	$118.00	-1.54%	$98.46	2.15%	$102.15
1995	17.70%	$138.89	34.11%	$132.04	33.46%	$136.33
1996	19.08%	$165.39	20.26%	$158.80	26.02%	$171.80
1997	18.79%	$196.46	31.01%	$208.04	22.65%	$210.72
1998	1.41%	$199.23	26.67%	$263.52	16.11%	$244.66
CAGR[9]	**14.78%**		**21.38%**		**19.60%**	
		$100.00		$100.00		$100.00
1995	17.70%	$117.70	34.11%	$134.11	33.46%	$133.46
1996	19.08%	$140.16	20.26%	$161.28	26.02%	$168.19
1997	18.79%	$166.49	31.01%	$211.29	22.65%	$206.28
1998	1.41%	$168.84	26.67%	$267.65	16.11%	$239.51
1999	30.78%	$220.81	19.53%	$319.92	25.19%	$299.85
CAGR	**17.17%**		**26.18%**		**24.56%**	
		$100.00		$100.00		$100.00
1996	19.08%	$119.08	20.26%	$120.26	26.02%	$126.02
1997	18.79%	$141.46	31.01%	$157.55	22.65%	$154.56
1998	1.41%	$143.45	26.67%	$199.57	16.11%	$179.46
1999	30.78%	$187.60	19.53%	$238.55	25.19%	$224.67
2000	8.16%	$202.91	-10.14%	$214.36	-6.15%	$210.85
CAGR	**15.20%**		**16.47%**		**16.09%**	

The charts above represent the three five-year time frames in which the long-only indices out-performed the Hedge Fund Index. It should be emphasized that in these periods the Hedge Fund Index also performed well – it just slightly lagged behind the long-only indices. It is worth noting that the Hedge Fund Index performance during this time was also negatively impacted by the attrition of Long-Term Capital Management, a large hedge fund which

---

[9] CAGR stands for compounded annual growth rate.

failed September 1998. The majority of hedge fund investors enjoyed returns that were easily as strong as equities through this time period as well.

In contrast, the Hennessee Hedge Fund Index returned higher in 14 out of the 17 five-year time frames since 1987. In the charts below, I've listed the three five-year time horizons in which markets were weakest. In these charts, we see the significant value a hedge fund adds. As I've mentioned, when markets are strong, any strategy that has equity market exposure should provide a good return on your capital. Instead, it is important to examine what has earned a return on your capital through the most difficult of market environments.

	Hennessee Index		**S&P 500**		**DJIA**	
	% Return	$ Growth	% Return	$ Growth	% Return	$ Growth
		$100.00		$100.00		$100.00
1999	30.78%	$130.78	19.53%	$119.53	25.19%	$125.19
2000	8.16%	$141.45	-10.14%	$107.41	-6.15%	$117.49
2001	8.36%	$153.28	-13.04%	$93.40	-7.10%	$109.15
2002	-2.88%	$148.86	-23.37%	$71.58	-16.76%	$90.86
2003	18.80%	$176.85	26.38%	$90.46	25.33%	$113.87
CAGR	**12.08%**		**-1.99%**		**2.63%**	
		$100.00		$100.00		$100.00
2000	8.16%	$108.16	-10.14%	$89.86	-6.15%	$93.85
2001	8.36%	$117.20	-13.04%	$78.14	-7.10%	$87.19
2002	-2.88%	$113.83	-23.37%	$59.88	-16.76%	$72.57
2003	18.80%	$135.23	26.38%	$75.68	25.33%	$90.96
2004	8.24%	$146.37	8.99%	$82.48	3.15%	$93.82
CAGR	**7.92%**		**-3.78%**		**-1.27%**	
		$100.00		$100.00		$100.00
2004	8.24%	$108.24	8.99%	$108.99	3.15%	$103.15
2005	7.85%	$116.74	3.00%	$112.26	-0.63%	$102.50
2006	11.40%	$130.04	13.62%	$127.55	16.29%	$119.20
2007	11.64%	$145.18	3.56%	$132.09	6.42%	$126.85
2008	-19.83%	$116.39	-38.49%	$81.25	-33.84%	$83.92
CAGR	**3.08%**		**-4.07%**		**-3.44%**	

During each of these five-year time frames, the long-only indices were negative while the Hennessee Hedge Fund Index was profiting. Keep in mind, the Hennessee Index was also positive during favorable markets.

It is useful to look at these numbers on a percentage basis; however, what has it meant in absolute dollar terms at the end of five years? For every $100 invested from 2004 to 2008, hedge funds were $35.14 dollars ahead of the S&P, and $32.47 dollars ahead of the DJIA. That is a *significant* gap. In order for the S&P to catch up to the hedge fund returns, the S&P would have to first recover a 43 per cent gap. The S&P would have to earn 43 per cent *while* the hedge fund index returned nothing in the same time frame. Is that likely? Let me make this very clear. Based on these averages, if you chose to invest in equities over hedge funds at the beginning of 2004, in absolute dollar terms you would likely *never* catch a friend who chose to invest in hedge funds! The differences are even more pronounced for a person who invested in S&P equities in 1999 or 2000.

I must mention again that the media has contributed hugely to this negative view of hedge funds. At the end of 2008, hedge funds were taking all the blame – they were accused of having lost more investors' capital than any other asset class. But in 2008, hedge funds actually succeeded in preserving capital better than their equity counterparts. The moral of the story is clear: be careful what you read in the paper. The facts and figures on hedge funds tell a much more accurate story.

Despite these statistics, trying to encourage investors to diversify using assets uncorrelated to the market direction in 2004 was like trying to get a 150-pound bull mastiff into the tub for a bath: nearly impossible. I can't stress this point enough to retail investors, "Noah built his ark before the storms came." It is crucial to your investing success that you select assets for your portfolio that can succeed in differing market conditions.

The ability to profit during a downward market is a trait that common equities will never be able to exhibit on aggregate. However, most investors will remain steadfast and only invest in equities. These investors place their faith in market direction over all rational evidence. I can only hope a few decide to consider hedge funds as an investment strategy. For those that do not consider hedge fund investments: know that you are taking a significant risk. Remember, what feels good when investing is all too often dead wrong. This could lead to a lengthy discussion or behavioral finance, however we don't have the chapter space; another time.

Misconception #2: *Hedge funds are high risk, speculative investments*

The conventional belief held by the public is that hedge funds are high-risk and speculative investment options. Like the first misconception outlined, this perception is largely incorrect. A report entitled *The Case for Hedge Funds*[10] sums it up well:

> There is a general perception that hedge funds are dangerously high-risk vehicles designed only for the elite. The majority of statistical and intellectual evidence suggests otherwise.

The notion that all hedge funds are risky is rooted in and perpetuated by fear of the unknown. It is important to re-emphasize that unfamiliar doesn't equal risky.

As noted earlier, hedge funds were actually created to *reduce* overall portfolio risk - moreover, they have done just that. As an asset class, hedge funds have significantly reduced volatility and largest draw-down figures compared to long-only equity investments. In fact, much of hedge fund outperformance is directly a result of hedge fund investments reducing losses during adverse markets. I'll examine this trend in detail later in the chapter.

So why this continued popular belief in the "inherent" risk of hedge funds? Ed Easterling of Crestmont Research explains it best:

> A misapplied concept of risk and return leads many people to assume that the higher returns from hedge funds must be driven by higher risk. The prior financial market models (e.g. Modern Portfolio Theory, etc.) assumed perfectly efficient markets and left no room for skill. Today we know better, that financial markets are an efficient process rather than a consistently efficient condition. Superior hedge fund performance is driven by the skills of execution and risk management in markets that present miss-pricings and inefficiencies.[11]

Misconception #3: *All hedge funds are blowing up*

Another commonly noted objection to investing in a hedge fund is that all hedge funds are "blowing up". However, it is simply *not true* that all hedge funds are failing. This notion has been perpetuated by our ease-of-recall bias.

Some investors have conducted research to support the premise that all hedge funds are failing. These investors have concluded that hedge fund

---

10 Issued by Tass Investment Research 1999.

11 April 10th, 2007 article, "Myths and Facts".

investments are blowing up based on the attrition of hedge funds from their indices. However, this is actually an example of a concept from the mutual fund world being misapplied to the hedge fund industry. When mutual funds leave a database, they do so for usually only one reason: they have gone out of business. However, hedge funds operate in a much different manner. Crestmount Research explains:

> Twice as many hedge funds stopped reporting after good performance compared to those that stopped reporting after poor performance. Hedge funds voluntarily report to these indices often times as an attempt to attract investors. Good performance leads to asset growth which in turn causes many hedge funds to stop reporting.[12]

Generally speaking, hedge funds do not want to be huge. They realize that the larger your fund, the further down your "best investment ideas" list you have to go to fill capacity. Smaller is generally better, since there is much more opportunity for the manager to grow your capital. In contrast, mutual fund investors rarely operate with an investment mandate cap, since they earn a fee based on total assets managed

This voluntary practice of hedge funds removing themselves from their indices dispels the survivorship bias which many say is inherent in hedge fund indices. This survivorship bias is just not true in the case of hedge funds - in fact, due to the above mentioned phenomenon, the survivorship bias could actually be more accurately termed as a survivorship hindrance. This is in direct contrast with the very obvious survivorship bias inherent in the Dow Jones Industrial average. The Dow Jones replaces underperforming companies that no longer meet minimal criteria with "better" companies nearly annually. Further, in most cases where there is bad hedge fund performance, this does not result in total loss of capital. Rather, bad hedge fund performance results in an erosion of capital, similar to countless mutual funds and long-only stock strategies through bear markets, which the investing public rarely, if ever, terms a blow-up.

Misconception #4: *There is no regulation of the hedge fund industry*

Many people believe that hedge funds are unregulated since hedge funds are not required to report their positions as often as mutual funds. It is true that hedge funds are not regulated in the same manner as mutual funds; however, it is incorrect to conclude that they operate in a space without regulatory oversight. Hedge funds are highly regulated and comply with all

12 *Ibid.*

rules and regulations that apply to investors participating in financial markets.

It is true that hedge funds do value their privacy more than mutual fund companies. However, the reason hedge funds value their privacy is that constantly disclosing short and long positions would negatively affect the success of these strategies – it would be like asking a company to publicly list their clientele and marketing plan. That said, some hedge funds do choose to report more frequently than others; moreover, all hedge funds are required to list their holdings within their annual reports. Therefore, while hedge funds do have a different disclosure strategy than mutual funds, it is incorrect to conclude that hedge funds are unregulated.

Misconception #5: *The fees are too high*

Many people know that hedge funds commonly charge a performance fee in addition to the management fee. However, most investors do not realize that this performance fee actually benefits them; managers *only* charge a performance fee when they have earned a return for you, often above a hurdle rate, or a high water mark that is a new high for your account.

There are really only two things a money manager can do for you that add value for the increase in fees over indexing:

1. Increase your return over a given index.
2. Reduce your volatility below that of a given index.

If either of these tasks were not accomplished, then one would have always been better off indexing.

Cost does matter when choosing an investment vehicle. However, cost only matters to the extent that all other variables remain the same. In long-only equity investing, the cheapest index fund should be sought, since the less you pay for the same return, the more your net return is. This basic premise led to the development of the Exchange Traded Fund (ETF). Investors realized that the mutual fund world has become obsolete. Very few funds have managed to beat the index over long periods of time, net of fees. This problem is directly related to their compensation scheme. So why not pay less and receive the benchmark performance? It makes perfect sense and I'd advise people to use ETFs everyday for the equity portion of their portfolio.

However, hedge funds are not the same as long-only equity mutual funds. They don't play by the same rules. Thus, unlike mutual funds, they are not highly correlated to traditional equity indices. Hedge funds take steps to actually control the amount of volatility and risk. They try to actively manage your exposure in situations that could cause a bubble or significant decline in equity markets. They are not paid to pick the best stocks in a horrible sector – unlike many mutual fund managers. It is a different strategy, and it has returned more money and been less volatile to investors over the past two decades *net of any and all fees*. Isn't that worth paying for? I certainly don't have a problem if I paid someone an extra $1, and received an extra $1.50 in return.

In my personal experience, over the past four years I've invested significant client assets into hedge funds. Without exception, the hedge fund investments have showed significantly less volatility. Moreover, in every case the funds I selected returned a higher rate of return than equity indices. This is after the standard fee structure (2% MER) and then 20 per cent of gross performance has been deducted. So the hedge fund fees might be higher; however, only when performance justifies it. Furthermore, all the performance figures that the investor sees are net of any and all fees which are charged.

One final important point: without the fees, the performance wouldn't be possible. One of the laws of capitalism is that talent follows capital. The best and the brightest gravitate to where they can earn the most money. You can earn the most money as a portfolio manager managing a hedge fund, which has attracted the brightest minds in the field. This is no different in other fields. The best athletes play in the major leagues of the United States, because that is where they earn the best living.

Taking issue with a hedge funds fee structure is a perfect example of finding evidence to back-up a viewpoint rather than conducting research and then framing a viewpoint. It seems that most people who criticize hedge funds for charging too much usually already have their minds made up. By criticizing a hedge fund's pricing, these individuals are simply searching for reasons to support their predisposed viewpoint. It is a natural human tendency to seek out information to support a predisposed idea, rather than to generally uncover information on a topic. However, given the obvious benefits of investing in a hedge fund, many sensible investors have concluded that the additional performance fee is worth it.

Hedge Fund Merits

Proper Alignment of Interest and Effort

> Alfred Winslow Jones started the world's first hedge fund in 1949. The genesis for his creation seems to be the research he did for an article published in the March 1949 issue of Fortune entitled, "Fashions in Forecasting." Jones was struck by the fact that nearly every Wall Street expert he interviewed said it was nearly impossible to predict the market's direction with any consistency. For Jones the light bulb went on.[13]

Very few fund managers are bold enough to boast a consistent ability to forecast the market's direction. Likewise, Alfred Jones was considered to be only an average predictor of market direction. Yet, as reported by Carol Loomis in a 1966 *Fortune Magazine* article in the decade prior to the article's publication, the fund which Jones created had out-distanced the top performing mutual fund by an astounding 87 per cent![14] It was in this article that the term "hedge fund" was first coined to describe the investment strategy used by Alfred Winslow Jones.

Nearly every Wall Street expert today agrees that no one can predict market direction with any consistency. This should be distressing news to the average retail investor, since most investors are invested almost exclusively on the long side of the market under the direction of these mutual fund managers or advisors. These investors have no choice but to constantly hope that the market will go up. Over periods of three and five years, direction can't be reasonably predicted; yet certain investors continually invest in only one direction.

Research from Barometer Capital Group has found that the return of any given stock from point A to point B is based on three factors:[15]

1. The company's fundamentals: such as the experience of the board members, market share, margins earned, brand recognition, and the earnings growth rate. These and others fundamentals affect approximately 20 per cent of the return on a share price.
2. Industry or Sector factors: Is the industry in growth or decline? What policy issues are affecting the industry? How cyclical is the industry? These and other industry factors affect approximately 30 per cent of the return on share price.
3. Most importantly, market forces: Where is the economy in its cycle?

---

13 J. Owens, *The Prudent Investor's Guide to Hedge Funds* (2000), p. 52.

14 C. Loomis, "The Jones nobody keeps up with," 1966 *Fortune Magazine.*

15 It should be noted that many studies exist which come to the same conclusions.

> What party is in government? What is the inflation picture? Likely the most important market factors are the emergence of any outlier or black swan events. (Events such as 9/11, war, or bursting bubbles, such as housing in 2008 or the tech bubble of 2000). Black swan events are market forces far beyond the control of any investor. These forces affect approximately 50 per cent of the return on share prices over any time frame.

Spelled out this way, it is easy to see that no matter how much effort goes into the analysis of a stock or its industry, these factors can only account for up to 50 per cent of your portfolio's overall performance. Moreover, in most mutual funds, all sectors have to be represented to a varying degree of the index weight. If representation of every industry sub-group is a criterion for a mutual fund, then the manager can only truly take into account the company fundamentals. Accordingly, in most cases the manager can actually only affect slightly more than 20 per cent of the performance. This is not the mutual fund manager's fault – it is the structure of the mutual fund industry. The largest factor affecting stock returns is something that not even the most astute professionals can control or even predict. Moreover, most investors have the majority of their financial net worth invested in long stocks and bonds, or long-only mutual funds and bonds – assets which are tied to market direction. In short, mutual fund managers are highly exposed to and dependant upon what is unknown and uncontrollable to make money. This is a misuse of time and effort, when 100 per cent of an investor's energy is spent affecting only approximately 20 per cent of returns.

As an individual who is admittedly addicted to golf, I can't stand days where I am hitting the ball well, only to have the wind begin howling. Accordingly, if I could play golf indoors with perfect weather conditions, I would. This is exactly what a classic hedge fund manager is trying to do with the market. They attempt to remove the market and sector factors, which they cannot control, from the investing equation. They are working to take your money, and make you more money. It makes ideological sense and places all the emphasis, alongside the effort, where it matters most!

How Do the Hybrid Managers Invest?

I watch professional golfers play the game every chance I get. At the end of watching the professionals play, I always leave knowing two things: 1) I have total respect and admiration for the golfer's professional skill level, and (2) I have just figured out a new method which will help me to become a better player. This is actually the dominant form of learning: emulation. To learn, we find those who are the best. We then try to emulate their habits, their methods and, ultimately, their performance. This is why every investor quotes Warren Buffet as often as possible.

With this human tendency in mind, it is necessary to ask: how do the best professionals invest their money? The vast majority of those entrusted to manage the wealth of others in both long-only mutual fund structures and hedge fund structures have their personal capital invested in the hedge fund. This is truly the best litmus test of all. I have yet to meet the portfolio manager who manages both hedge funds and mutual funds who has any significant percentage of their net worth invested in their mutual funds. Isn't that the most important question of all? Where does the person controlling your investments invest their own money? For my clients and me, this is crucial. I want my money to be cared for and cultivated as if it was the portfolio manager's own.

In an interview I conducted with Michael Mahoney of Picton Mahoney, he elaborated on why managers choose to invest in hedge funds:

> At Synergy, we only have so many tools available to control risk. If we do a great job in our long-only strategy this year (2008), we're down 35% vs. being down 40 or 45% with the market. This leaves me entirely exposed to the health of the bull market, I cannot control it at all. With the Market Neutral Fund, I can actively take steps to control the amount of risk experienced for both me and the investors.[16]

At Picton Mahoney, less than 15 per cent of the assets they manage are in hedge funds. However, the percentage is completely reversed for their own personal funds. The only financial assets they have in long-only mandates are their RRSPS. The vast majority of their personal financial assets are in their hedge funds.

It has been my experience that the most talented market participants are the portfolio managers. Thus, the fact that the majority of portfolio managers have their personal savings invested in their hedge funds when available is compelling evidence that individuals should expose themselves to hedge funds.

The Hedge Fund Mandate: A More Properly Aligned Goal

The entire investing world would benefit from a shift towards focusing on a positive return rather than beating the market. The world has brainwashed itself into believing that relative returns are the only thing that matters, and

---

16 Interview with Michael Mahoney, early 2009.

beating the market should be the sole goal. Sometimes, beating the market can still be extremely painful – like in 2008.

The mandate of an authentic hedge fund is to earn a return for investors of seven, nine, or 11 per cent annually, regardless of the prevailing market environment. An example of a good mandate statement comes from Altairis Long Short, "[t]he Altairis strategy seeks to produce positive absolute returns with low volatility and low correlation to equity markets through superior stock selection, both long and short."[17] This type of mandate is significantly more appealing than the average mutual fund mandate: to beat the stock market over the long term, net of fees.

In 2008, the markets declined 35 to 45 per cent. In this environment, some mutual funds could and did beat the market; these funds declined by 30 per cent, give or take. A decline of 30 per cent is very difficult to recover from. It requires a 43 per cent return to simply return to your previous capital level, not to mention lost years in your investment plan. For those mutual funds that did not beat the index, some went down as much as 50 per cent. These investors must see 100 per cent gain to return to their previous capital level. This isn't to say some hedge funds didn't do the same thing – one or two hedge funds did decline by 50 per cent. However, most didn't. Moreover, the media coverage of the few hedge funds that did decline means that the public thinks all hedge funds are blowing up. However, the public perspective is fundamentally skewed. A mutual fund declining by 50 per cent just doesn't make the news.

Mandates are not guarantees; however, in life you generally accomplish a variation of your stated goal. Absolute returns used to be the focus of investors and everyone could benefit from a re-visit to that approach. I personally find it more comfortable to be invested in a vehicle like a hedge fund, where the entire goal is to help investors preserve capital and provide absolute returns, regardless of the market environment. In contrast, it is of little comfort to be invested in a mutual fund, since these investment vehicles are considered successful even when they are drowning, provided that the fund is drowning less than the others.

Quantifying Risk: How Do Hedge Funds Stack Up?

If returns for two investments are the same, then the better portfolio is the investment which achieves that return with the least amount of risk. We've

---

17 Note: this mandate is noted both in the company prospectuses and updates and commentary at the end of each month.

looked at the returns for hedge funds in a previous section; let's now turn our attention to their risk characteristics.

For any risk assumed beyond the risk-free rate,[18] investors are trying to achieve a higher rate of return. Many retail investors unfortunately have no idea how to price or measure risk. Accordingly, the average investor sets return targets and does not pay much attention to risk or volatility. During bear markets, investors feel the pain of failing to manage their risk.

Standard Deviation

Investors should strive to control the volatility of an investment for two reasons.[19] First, a high degree of volatility increases the chance that an investment will be at a depressed level at the time of a liquidity event. Second, a high degree of volatility increases an investor's anxiety; therefore, with a high standard deviation, there is an increased chance that an investor will redeem a fund and lock-in a loss. Standard deviation is commonly used to measure the volatility of an investment's annual return; however, it can be used to measure volatility over any measurement period. When examining the standard deviation, investors need to remember that big is bad, since a large standard deviation represents a high degree of volatility.

	Hennessee Index	**S&P 500**	**DJIA**
Cumulative Return	1406.92%	373.02%	462.92%
Annualized Return	12.81%	6.37%	7.46%
Standard Deviation	11.01%	18.58%	16.33%

As you can see from the above chart, the annualized standard deviation of the Hennessee Index compares very favorably with that of the S&P and the Dow Jones. In fact, it is significantly lower. This has meant hedge funds have had a much smoother drive across a very bumpy investment road.

18 The risk-free rate is commonly measured by the 91-day government T-bill.

19 It should be noted that many investors believe that volatility isn't always a negative, since upside volatility means your capital is growing. However, too often high volatility has ended in huge losses. It has been my experience that high volatility acts as a remarkable red flag for impending disaster and de-valuation.

Largest Draw-down

I've read a lot of commentary from the most successful investors and traders from the past 50 years. Among all these success stories, the number one investment goal is consistent: each investor and trader wants capital preservation and to control losses. Without exception, these successful investors all state that keeping an eye on the downside is the most important factor in investing. They caution strongly against taking the *mother of all losses* that can't be recovered from. To preclude this type of loss, it is necessary to examine the largest draw-down figure.

Managing draw-downs is absolutely critical to the strength of a long-term strategy. If you are down 45 per cent on an investment, you need a return of 82 per cent to climb back to your previous high. This is astounding. Moreover, this is a fact most investors don't quite clearly comprehend. As your capital pool falls in value, much larger percentage returns are required to nominally equate the loss during recovery.

When looking at the risk equation, it is imperative to examine the largest draw-down figure for an investment. Hedge funds shine in this category: their largest draw-down figures are significantly less than standard long-only stock indices.

Over the 22-year stretch from 1987 to 2008, the largest draw-down of the Hennessee Index was during the crash of 2008. From peak to trough, this Index lost 23.66 per cent. A sub-set of this category, market neutral hedge funds,[20] experienced a maximum draw-down across this time frame of 8.32 per cent. As of the end of 2008, the S&P had a maximum draw-down of 53.05 per cent during the same period. Similarly, the Dow Jones experienced a maximum draw-down of 47.53 per cent. These are significant differences. Avoiding a huge loss is critical to your investing success. Hedge funds have proven that, as a group, unequivocally, they have done a better job of controlling losses than equities, their nearest asset class competitor.

The chart below contrasts the performance of hedge funds and S&P 500 during the worst 15 months of S&P 500 decline in this 20-year period. This is graphical evidence of how well hedge managers control draw-downs.

[20] Note that these are also commonly referred to as authentic hedge funds.

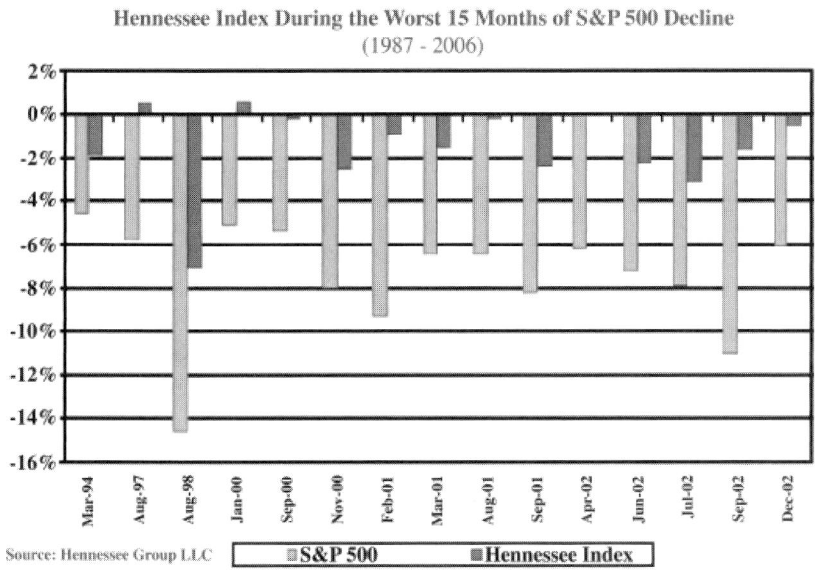

The Sharpe Ratio

After reading this chapter, the Sharpe Ratio should be the first metric you search for when evaluating fund investments. It is an all-encompassing, single point of data which you must address initially when conducting due diligence. It demonstrates, in no uncertain terms, exactly how much return you are gaining for each unit of risk your investment takes on. The Sharpe Ratio is calculated:

$$S(x) = \frac{R(x) - R(f)}{\text{Std. Dev.}}$$

Where

- x represents the investment strategy being evaluated
- S(x) represents the Sharpe ratio of x
- R(x) represents the investment's return over the given period
- R(f) represents the risk-free rate of return, in most cases the 91-day t-bill
- Std. Dev. represents the standard deviation of investment x

This ratio is the most telling initial indicator of the strength and efficiency of an investment strategy. A high Sharpe Ratio indicates better risk-adjusted returns.

You often hear investors using the phrase "risk-adjusted returns." However, investors toss about this term without knowing truly what it means – it has almost become a catch-phrase. When markets are strong, most investors are more worried about missing an investment opportunity than making sure they don't take on more risk. Without exception, investors need to focus less on historical returns and more on the amount of risk associated with each investment. Too often, investors see only the return numbers and do not focus enough on risk or the process used to achieve a given result. Thus, comparing Sharpe Ratios is imperative and not done enough by investors.

Below is the same chart I've used to display the standard deviation for volatility. This time I added a third row to include the Sharpe Ratio. It is clear based on this measure that hedge funds have been far more efficient on the aggregate than the major stock indices. This establishes that those who have invested in hedge funds over the last 22 years have been paid far better for the amount of risk they have assumed. Isn't a better return with less volatility what every investor is searching for in today's market environment?

	Hennessee Index	**S&P 500**	**DJIA**
Cumulative Return	1406.92%	373.02%	462.92%
Annualized Return	12.81%	6.37%	7.46%
Standard Deviation	11.01%	18.58%	16.33%
Sharpe Ratio	1.09	0.30	0.41

It should be noted that the Sharpe ratio does have its limitations and should not be used in isolation. Michael Mahoney, Portfolio Manager at Picton Mahoney Asset Management, explains the limitations of the Sharpe Ratio:

> The Sharpe ratio on its own isn't perfect. Investors need to look at process above all. The Sharpe ratio will not reveal tail risks (these are outlier events, often called black swan events). For example, in 2008, many fixed income products, or hedge funds concentrated in CDOs, mortgage-backed securities, or ABCP products would have exhibited consistent (but not high) Sharpe ratios; however, in 2008 several lost excessive amounts due to excessive leverage among other factors. The real key is diversification. If a strategy is controlling volatility using only one position, or a very narrow group of products, it likely has a high degree of concentration risk despite possibly exhibiting a smooth return. This is something there is no formula for, you must conduct thorough due diligence.[21]

[21] As stated in an interview in December, 2008.

The Sharpe ratio is a great place to start, but it isn't the only factor to consider. Results in the investment field can vary greatly over short periods of time. Therefore, it could be a huge trap to just consider results.

Hedge funds have proven to be superior to equity markets in assessments of standard deviation, largest draw-down, and the Sharpe ratio. They offer less volatility and more return for the risk they assume. This is clear from the scatter plot below, which plots return on the y axis and risk on the x axis. Obviously, the sweet spot is the upper left–precisely where the hedge funds appear.

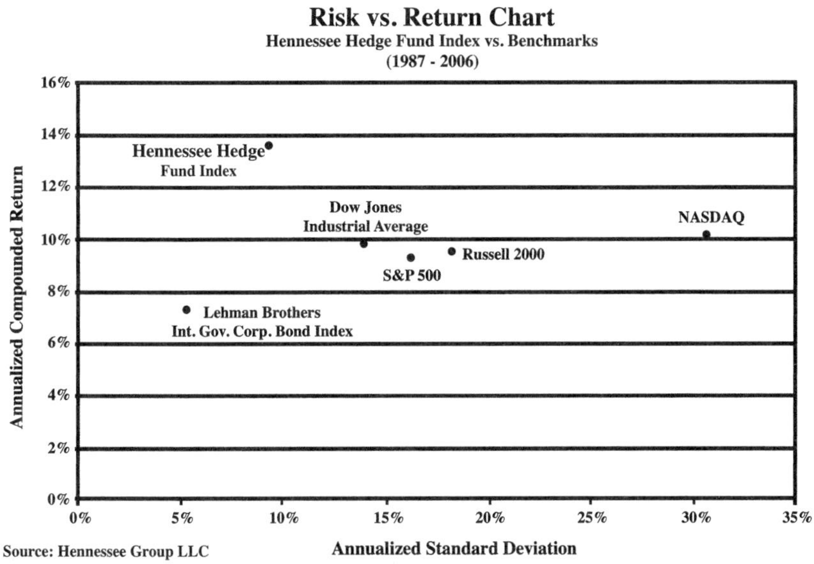

Brandes, Capital International, and countless other large fund companies have emphasized the importance of process, and marketed it very well over the past 30 years. However, even with this repeatable and consistent process, these companies base every investment theory on the assumption that markets will always go up. Their consistent process at best has afforded them performance of a few percentage points above the index net of fees over the long term. However, they are still tied to the anchor of market direction, and can't provide a cushion from large draw-downs and extreme volatility in the broad markets. Therefore, the largest decision an investor is making when purchasing from one of these large funds is whether to be in the market. If the market is up, they will be, too. If the market is down, guess what? Odds are that the investor is down, too.

A Point about Emotion: It is an Investor's #1 Enemy

Hedge funds have historically shown significantly less volatility than long-only equities. Controlling volatility means controlling to a much higher degree the emotional component of investing. When emotion can be controlled, your chances of investing success increase dramatically.

It never ceases to amaze me, how many people—even sophisticated investors— will quote a newspaper article which alleges that all hedge funds are crumbling. The reason for this is simple: hedge funds are similar to the CIA. To quote Al Pacino in *The Recruit*, "[t]heir successes are silent, yet their mistakes are made public embarrassments." In the past 20 years, public company insolvency has lost a far greater amount of money than hedge fund insolvency. In fact, I was once told that approximately ten times the amount of money has been lost in public company insolvency.[22] Also, it is necessary to note that most of the horrible and memorable cases of hedge fund losses are simply large losses; the losses experienced by investors in these cases are analogous to holding a stock that has gone down 65 per cent.[23] In contrast, if there are large losses in a mutual fund or stock holding, the media rarely refers to these losses as "blow-ups". The point is that there are very few cases like Long-Term Capital Management in hedge funds. Moreover, for each of these cases of hedge fund losses, there are plenty more Lehmann Brothers, Bear Stearns, Enrons, CitiGroups, Bre-Xs, or Oilexcos; the list goes on.

At the end of any presentation where I argue that hedge funds are the safer instruments for your investments, the question I most often receive is: "Why isn't everyone investing in hedge funds?" It's a great question. The answer boils down to one basic problem; when it comes to our money, we are emotionally-based decision makers. Many psychological tests over the past several decades confirm that we are emotionally-based decision-makers; moreover, these tests also confirm that emotion is the single greatest enemy of a successful investor. It is understandably easy to become emotional about money. The problem is, this attachment leads investors to make decisions that feel good, rather than those which make rational sense. Unfortunately for the average investor, what feels right and what makes rational sense are too often not the same.

---

22 Unfortunately, the exact data proved too difficult to pinpoint.

23 For example, see the losses of Amaranth in 2005, Epic Capital in 2008, or Lawrence Partners in 2008.

Ian Clark of CIBC Wood Gundy made a great observation on this point, comparing institutional investors to retail investors. He sent me the following e-mail in October, 2008:

> Individuals tend to make emotional decisions based on fear and greed. This is best viewed by examining mutual fund flows, an indicator of individual investor buy/sell decisions.

Here are some of the numbers surrounding the infamous tech bubble earlier in the decade.

Year 2000

- Net sales on equity funds in the U.S. were $+262 billion. Fixed income/money market funds were $-49 billion.
- This turned out to be terrible timing, as a vicious 3-year bear market followed.
- Greed-driven behavior led to aggressive equity buying at the top of a bull market, and the abandonment of fixed income/money market which outperformed the S&P500 by 60 per cent during the correction

Year 2002

- Net sales on equity funds in the U.S. were $-29 billion. Fixed Income/Money Market were $+140 billion.
- Fear-driven decision making led to aggressive selling of equity near the bottom of the bear market, and aggressive buying of fixed income and money market when rates were at multi-decade lows.
- Unfortunate timing again as a massive 5-year bull market followed that saw the S&P 500 Total Return deliver more than 80 per cent from 2003 to 2007, while fixed income and money market returns were a fraction of this.

The chart below shows this "buy the top, sell the bottom" behavior. Notice when the S&P has a few good months, investment spikes, then when the S&P has a few bad months, equity redemptions begin to come in. Unfortunately, it's like clockwork. As volatility picks up, the moves in and out of the market pick up as well. This strongly demonstrates the need to control volatility within an investment vehicle. This also serves to show that although investors often preach buy and hold, it has proven difficult for average retail investors to practise it. Instead, they try the even less successful strategy of timing the market.

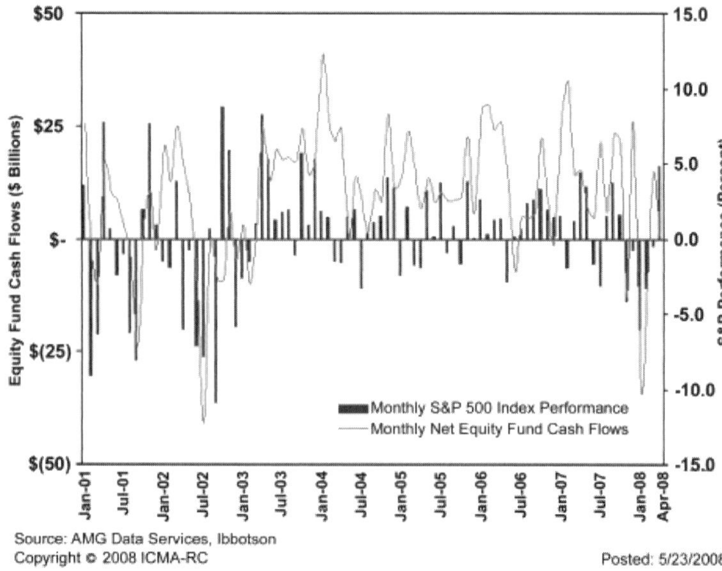

Average investors seek comfort in the numbers (whether they know it or not is irrelevant); these investors know that if they are down, so are their neighbors, colleagues, and friends. This same phenomenon leads them to slough off hedge funds, because most people they know don't employ these strategies. They are not publicly accepted and this means fear to average retail investors.

In 2009, I routinely asked prospective investors how they performed through 2008. Most have told me they lost at least 25 per cent. However they were quick to chime in with the emotionally reassuring statement, "[b]ut the market is down 35% so I guess I'm doing alright. Everyone is way down." This makes the average investor immediately feel OK about a million dollars being reduced to $750,000.

Mental Capital

One final aspect of risk must be addressed: *mental capital.* I have come to realize that mental capital is the least discussed, yet most substantial pleasure of owning a proper hedge fund. Volatile investments cost energy and thus consume valuable mental capital. It is obvious that most investors do not want to use this mental capital, since they hand their money to a third party manager in most cases. If you are a lawyer, doctor, architect or some other professional, you do not want to spend your time worrying that your money is going to depreciate in value. However, volatility increases your depreciation worries.

Over time, I've experienced and observed an increase in mental capital for those who invest in hedge funds. The hedge fund portion of my clients' portfolios has been the most-discussed asset class during the allocation process. However, it is consistently the least-discussed asset class during subsequent portfolio reviews. Clients rarely call in wondering if the Picton Mahoney Market Neutral Equity Fund is tanking because the market has tanked. They have gained peace of mind through their investing experience with Picton Mahoney, Altairis, or JC Clark Alternative Investments. These investors have learned that with these hedge funds the market environment isn't the driver of their portfolio; rather, the skill of the manager is the main driver. Isn't that why you placed your trust in their hands in the first place?

This increase in mental capital allows an individual to perform to the maximum of their ability. The less time you spend worrying about the safety of your money, the more time you can spend earning money in your chosen profession. Investors usually think this will work in the opposite direction, that a hedge fund will cause sleepless nights and constant fret. However, I have learned that with hedge funds, what people think is generally dead wrong.

Conclusion and Recommendations

Hedge funds were created in order to reduce market risk. Alfred Jones recognized this need to reduce risk; therefore, he initiated the world's first hedge fund in 1949. Since then, hedge funds have offered sophisticated investors a reliable way of reducing market risk in their portfolio. Furthermore, hedge funds have helped investors achieve investment returns that are based on skill, rather than on market movements.

Of course, there have been disasters in the hedge fund world that people will not soon forget. But these are no different than the disasters in public equity markets. These events are necessary in the growth and progress of any industry. Nothing grows without regulation. An investor shouldn't shy away from hedge funds because Bernie Madoff was caught managing a scam. At the end of 2008, there were more than 10,000 hedge funds in North America. His was just one – a fraudulent one, at that.

Hedge funds are on the leading edge of innovation in the investment world. They should be nurtured and accepted by the investing public. Yet, as is typical of human nature, investors are suspicious of what is new. We do not like change and we protect our beliefs and routines. Hedge funds are one of the few areas where portfolio managers are working very hard to earn money for investors in spite of the bad market. What is more, many hedge fund managers have succeeded in earning returns for their investors in 2008. Contrast this attitude with the mindset of others in the investing world. Investment managers in other areas will either throw their hands in the air and say, "What can we do? It's a terrible market." Conversely, they may assure investors: "Think long term and don't worry, everything will be OK." Quite frankly, I think we have all heard these lines too often lately.

The title of this book references investment strategies for difficult markets. It is precisely during these difficult markets that investors need an investment like a hedge fund to protect their capital. Most investors react to bear market by trying to implement reactionary strategy after their investments are already down 25 or 35 per cent. They will write covered calls, try to actively trade in and out, or put tight stop losses on their remaining holdings. These aren't bad strategies; however, they will only stop further losses. These strategies will not yield returns in a bad market. Unfortunately, by the time most people have stopped calling it a correction, and have accepted that it's much worse, they've likely already lost considerable capital. The only way to truly preserve your capital and perhaps succeed at earning a positive return in a bear market is to employ a strategy that doesn't correlate to the market at any stage of the cycle.

I want to caution readers that all hedge funds are not created equal. One of the major issues overhanging hedge funds as an asset class is a lack of a proper distinction and definition among different strategies. The hedge fund world is as diverse as the world of sports. Is it fair to compare golfers and hockey players regarding the danger of their profession to their physical health? Obviously it isn't. This isn't any different than comparing a market neutral hedge fund to an aggressive growth hedge fund. Consider Altairis Long Short, a conservative, low net exposure strategy, and Salida, an aggressive growth hedge fund, over the past four years.

Altairis Long Short

2008	0.73%	1.57%	(1.91)%	1.13%	3.86%	(2.23)%	0.14%	0.05%	(1.89)%	(0.67)%	0.07%	4.80%	5.55%
2007	1.37%	1.55%	1.44%	1.48%	1.93%	0.05%	0.40%	(0.11)%	1.25%	0.44%	(0.61)%	0.95%	10.63%
2006	1.35%	2.83%	1.48%	(0.37)%	0.72%	(1.99)%	1.78%	2.77%	0.76%	3.03%	1.57%	0.59%	15.38%
2005	(0.29)%	0.01%	2.60%	(0.63)%	2.56%	1.55%	0.42%	1.44%	0.10%	1.48%	1.45%	1.32%	12.64%

Salida

2008	-9.62%	15.79%	-3.44%	-4.55%	9.42%	4.26%	-28.26%	-5.00%	-24.74%	-34.18%	-12.79%	3.39%	-66.50%
2007	4.38%	5.12%	7.52%	9.43%	5.30%	0.55%	3.16%	-14.47%	9.08%	13.53%	-8.24%	-0.88%	35.84%
2006	22.08%	7.48%	10.59%	8.15%	-0.84%	-1.98%	2.39%	1.88%	-3.01%	7.29%	10.96%	2.00%	87.40%
2005	8.14%	11.93%	-5.86%	-6.02%	-2.35%	2.44%	1.72%	7.20%	10.13%	-8.86%	6.79%	7.22%	34.25%

I would consider Altairis a very strong absolute return, long-short fund. They have exhibited a modest amount of volatility, and little correlation to broad markets. Further, they have succeeded in providing returns to investors regardless of the overall market. Across this four-year stretch, their worst month is negative 2.23 per cent, and their best month was +4.8, making their monthly skew only 7.03! Compare this to Salida, whose worst month is -34.18 per cent and best month is +22.08 per cent, which makes for a monthly skew of 56.26! The difference should be clearly evident.

Obviously, these are two completely different strategies. I'm not saying there is anything wrong with Salida. However, there is need for greater definition in the industry going forward so investors can allocate funds based on their strategy, rather than solely relying on the fact that they are investing in a hedge fund.

The problem here is that both these mandates use the term "absolute return." This underlines the need for prospective investors to conduct their own due diligence. Do not assume that any fund which uses the term "hedge" in the title is a conservatively managed, risk reducing, absolute return-oriented fund.

Unfortunately, in most publications, there is only one category for either "hedge funds", or "alternative strategies". However, the same publication will list 20 to 25 types of mutual funds. The irony is that these 25 mutual fund categories are usually much more comparable to each other than the different hedge fund strategies. There are only two basic similarities between all hedge funds: the manager is paid a performance-based fee and investors have the luxury of having their capital beside the manager inside the fund.

For those interested in pursuing their own hedge fund research, I would advise you to consider funds referred to as "authentic," "market neutral," or "long short." I feel these strategies are both the simplest and the best. I recommend searching for funds which maintain a constant short book of significance,[24] and try to ensure that the fund is never more than 75 per cent net-long. Another factor to consider is what James Owen refers to as "The Owens Rule": seek out funds where the largest monthly draw-down is 1/4th or less than the annualized return. This should give you a good start on selecting a proper hedge fund to cultivate your wealth.

Below is a chart of the Market Neutral Index and Long Short Index from Hedge Fund Research Index (HFRI). The data measures net performance

---

[24] This short book should represent at least 25% of the gross investment at all times.

of two specific hedge fund strategies I've just endorsed since 1990, net of all fees.

<u>Market Neutral</u>

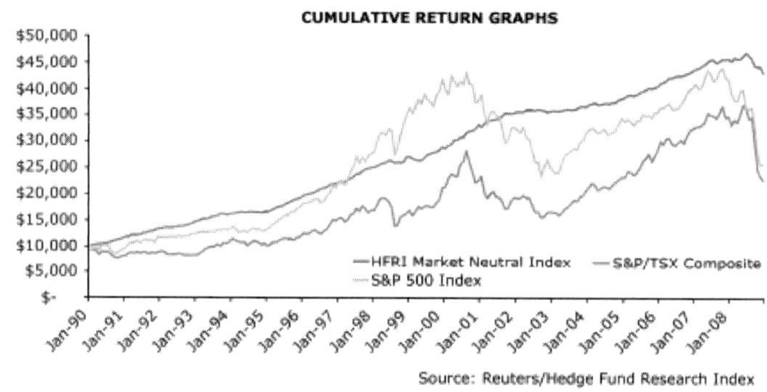

<u>Long Short</u>

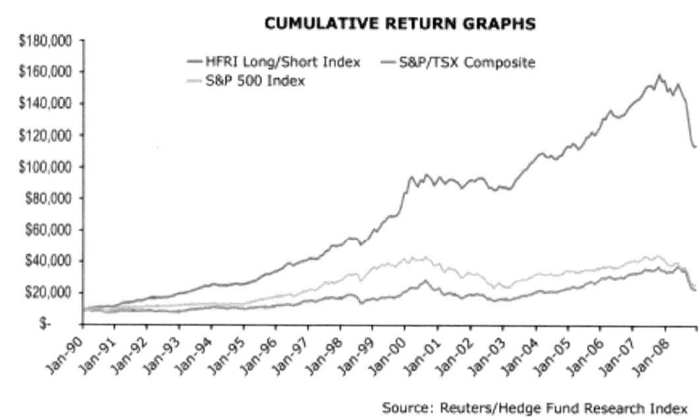

These two graphs break the market neutral and long-short strategies away from the broad hedge fund index I referenced throughout this chapter. Clearly it's been advantageous to invest in these strategies, both from an increased return perspective, and from a reduced volatility perspective.

Again, allow me to reiterate my firm belief that every investor can benefit from the addition of an authentic hedge fund to their portfolio. I realize I'm swimming upstream on this subject, and can only hope this chapter has opened your mind to a hedge fund investment. I'm an investment advisor who has looked at the evidence and advocates hedge funds as one of the best portfolio investments you can make. From an asset gathering perspective, I likely would've had more personal success selling the top 10 publicly-traded stocks each year. But when you examine what really matters, the preservation and cultivation of client wealth, I know unequivocally that I've made the right decision. Hedge funds are an asset class I'll always employ. I'm actually comforted knowing that these strategies aren't unanimously, publicly accepted. After all, the best investors in history have generally been contrarian.

Still Profitable: Strategies for Corporations With Excess Capital

Jordan Waldman

Like most Canadians, business owners are always searching for ways to reduce the amount of taxes that they pay. One of the main differences between a business owner and a regular employee is the various forms of income that they have, and the corresponding tax obligations that go with each income type. The income types are regular employment income, business income, and capital gains on the growth of the business. Owners of many successful businesses choose to maintain corporate profits within the corporation as retained earnings, rather than drawing them as personal income to reduce their personally-owed tax obligations. By using the corporation's lower tax rate, business owners realize savings on the corporation's excess cash. However why stop the tax efficiency there? Why not reduce or effectively eliminate the tax liability for the corporation? By implementing a corporate asset transfer strategy, businesses can reduce tax obligations, increase available cash on hand, and address succession planning and taxation issues. This chapter outlines some of the methods available and the advantages provided by the corporate asset transfer method in both expansion and contraction economic conditions in offsetting or eliminating tax obligations on both business income and capital gains.

Economic Cycles and Investment Vehicles

When deciding on an appropriate investment vehicle for your money, it is important to understand how the investment will behave in different environments. Additionally, any outside influences that can affect the performance of the investment should be reviewed. This chapter first examines the basic influences on typical investment portfolios created from equity and bond portfolios.

Different market conditions introduce the use of different economic factors to the financial world by government agencies. When economies grow, there is little economic action required from central banks to stimulate activity. With continued and sustained growth, the central banks can increase their overnight lending rates. This will decrease the affordability of borrowing and increase the rate of return on interest bearing investments, such as GICs and high interest savings accounts. Increases in overnight lending rates and prime banking rates occur in tandem with rising local and global stock markets. As the stock gains rise, central banks use their control over the lending and prime rates to influence the behavior of investors throughout the economy. The overnight lending rates can be increased to curb investing.

Market Behavior

Rising stock markets create several ripple effects to investors. The first and most obvious effects are the gains from the purchase and sale of individual shares and equities. The sale of any share creates a taxable capital gain for the shareholder. Fifty per cent of this realized gain is taxable to the individual or corporation selling these shares. In a rising market, this could create large tax obligations for any investor. Other effects are the yields from safe havens such as government and corporate bonds which decrease as the demand for low risk, low growth investments evaporates. The rule of thumb in the investment world is that when stock prices increase, bond yields decrease. This is good news from a tax liability perspective since the decreasing yields result in a lower tax implication.

Common alternatives to bonds during growth periods are interest-bearing investments such as high interest savings accounts and GICs that earn interest for their holders. Earned interest is 100 per cent taxable at either the individual's personal marginal tax rate or the appropriate provincial corporate tax rate as income. Because of the large tax obligation on relatively small yields, finding methods to shelter/defer the tax can create much better outcomes. This is what happens on the upswing of the economic cycle. Let us now look at the downswing in the market cycles.

The other half of the economic cycle occurs when economies reach their peaks and begin to turn into the negative territories. When this downturn occurs, it causes the central banks to decrease their overnight lending rates and prime banking rates in an attempt to help stimulate economies and overt major losses to stockholders and businesses. The decrease in rates reduces the cost of borrowing money, in turn allowing institutions to continue to access capital for spending projects or individuals to borrow for home mortgages and investment financing. At time of writing, central banks were cutting interest rates to all time record lows. The Bank of Canada has established an interest rate of 0.5 per cent, and has pledged that it will maintain that rate for at least the next 12 months. This eases the cost of borrowing funds but also minimizes the interest rates that investors are able to receive from interest-bearing products, for example, high interest savings accounts and GICs. Therefore, in an economic downturn, the security of interest-bearing products can be unparalleled but the returns are minimal. Moreover, the taxes payable on these investments are proportionally large, and usually eat away at most of the gain realized. 2008 and early 2009 have demonstrated what can occur in a prolonged declining market, where equities can suffer extreme losses. While these losses do produce possible realized losses and possible tax credits against past or future gains, the decrease in value hurts the bottom line and is an unfavorable scenario for any investor. For corporate earnings, losses are unacceptable to most business owners, no matter what the potential for gains, which is why GICs are so popular within holding companies. Using a bear market to invest added capital in anticipation of a recovery is a strategy often used. However, the short-term volatility of this strategy is not always suited to corporate investment accounts.

Investment Vehicles and the Their Corresponding Tax Obligations

How different investments are taxed plays a large factor when selecting an asset mix for corporate investments. As previously mentioned, 50 per cent of the realized capital gains are taxed at the personal or corporate marginal tax rates. Depending on the type of business paying out a dividend, and the province in which it is registered, dividends received by individuals are subjected to a gross up and tax credit. However, when a corporation receives a dividend there is no gross up (*ITA* ss. 112(1)). Dividends received by corporations can only be deducted when distributed from a Canadian corporation that is paying a tax already that is known as Part I tax. If these dividends are held within the receiving corporation they create a Part IV tax obligation with a tax rate of 33.3 per cent of the dividend (*ITA* ss. 186(1)). Any payable Part IV tax creates a separate notional credit to the Refundable Dividend Tax On Hand (RDTOH) account on the balance sheet. Once dividends have been paid to shareholders, the Canadian Controlled Private Corporation (CCPC) is credited $1 for every $3 paid (*ITA* ss. 129(1)). The RDTOH credit can be carried forward until the necessary or optimal time to be used. The RDTOH credit would be used to offset taxes owed on future dividend payouts to shareholders. Any interest income earned is fully taxable at the marginal tax rate. During the different economic stages of a market cycle, tax obligations from investments will follow the market cycle. During the growth years, taxes owed will be higher, and during contraction years taxes will be reduced. However, this corporate asset transfer will defer all of the taxes owed on these investments. The corporate asset transfer provides for secure, long-term growth and above average rates of return for low risk, fixed income investments.

Corporate Asset Transfer

The test to determine whether an individual should invest in tax-advantaged investments is whether the result will be a greater increase in wealth than with another type of investment.[1]

The goal for the business owner is generally to increase the value of their overall estate and minimize any taxes owed at the same time. The corporate asset transfer model takes the goals of each business owner into account, and then designs a customized plan that will benefit the corporation through various stages of its owner's life and beyond. The model uses life insurance, the most tax-efficient method of transferring wealth, to increase estate values while minimizing tax obligations. Life insurance can also be used to defer investment growth within the policy, based on limitations determined by the size of the policy and government regulations.

The Key Component – Life Insurance

Life insurance policies are able to serve as tax-deferred investment accounts as long as the policy stays within the limitations established by regulation 306 of the *ITA*. Insurance companies are required to test each and every policy on its anniversary date to make sure that the policy is still maintaining its tax-exempt status. If the growth and value of the policy is kept under the Maximum Tax Actuarial line (MTAR, which is calculated independently for each policy) the policies are non-taxable. The death benefits from these policies are then passed to the beneficiaries tax-free upon the insured's death. The MTAR limit is set so individuals and corporations cannot use life insurance policies as tax sheltered investment vehicles, to avoid paying taxes upon the disposition of the investments. Any growth that occurs within the policy limits is hidden from income tax. Furthermore, growth within the MTAR limits does not trigger any credits to the RDTOH account for corporate-owned policies. Policies that have been overfunded may lose their tax exempt status, and policyholders will be forced to bring them back to exempt status within 60 days. Generally, this will involve not only paying

[1] Contemporary Practices in Financial Planning, Advocis, 2008.

outstanding taxes owed but also withdrawing funds from the policy. This corporate asset transfer model utilizes participating life insurance to produce stable, tax-deferred investment returns over a long-term period, while increasing the overall estate value for business owners.

Benefits of Life Insurance

The use of participating insurance brings many variables to the table that work in the favor of the business owner. The volatility of the fund is minimal as the asset mix is strongly geared towards the conservative end of the spectrum. These performance rates are very respectable for a long-term fixed income investment, especially considering the fund's limited exposure to volatility and equity markets. In selecting a permanent life insurance policy, one must choose wisely and not simply go for the lowest premium. Since this policy is designed to be held as long as you live, you require the company to be in business for the same time frame and longer. Be sure to look at the financial strength of the company you select to carry your policy. You must also carefully examine the historical performance of the participating account in good times and in bad.

Every year, the returns of the participating account are held as an account surplus. This surplus is reviewed by the board of directors to determine how much should be paid back to policyholders. Three factors are considered by the fund directors on an annual basis in evaluating the returns to fund holders; 1) the mortality rates of the fund holders; 2) the investment performance; and 3) the fund expenses. Once these factors are considered by the directors, the fund will distribute to the policyholders dividends that are held within their respective policies. These distributed dividends are responsible for the growth of a participating policy. The dividends can be held in various forms, either as cash savings, or additional insurance used to offset the growth in the estate value of a policyholder, or to keep pace with the inflating cost of funerals over time.

The surplus not distributed to policyholders is held within the participating account to maintain the long-term strength and stability of the fund. Roughly 97.5 per cent of the participating account is paid back to policyholders yearly, while the remaining 2.5 per cent is paid to the shareholders, in accordance with s. 461 of the *Insurance Companies Act*. If the dividends are used to purchase additional insurance in the policy, the dividends also create a cash value within the policy. Once applied to the policyholder's account, the cash value is guaranteed to be in the investor's account. The amount will never be reduced; it will only increase every year with the new dividend pay-out. This security makes the investment choice parallel to a

GIC; however, it provides better returns and less maintenance than a standard five-year GIC. The surplus account and the income generated in it can also be used by the investment managers to smooth out any possible short-term fluctuations in the market, creating a better overall picture for policyholders.

The composition of these funds has changed over the years as equity markets were on long, positive runs. Most funds have increased their exposure to equity markets to roughly 15 to 20 per cent of holdings. The remaining holdings are fixed income investments, such as bonds, t-bills, and mortgages. Another benefit to policyholders of the participating fund is that overall mortality rates are decreasing. As the modern healthcare system improves, individuals live longer. This allows the par fund to hold onto policy premiums for extended periods of time, and increase the overall rate of return for all fund holders over what was possible 50 years ago. For example, the expected life span of a typical healthy woman born in 1952 was 71 years, whereas the average life expectancy of a woman born today is well into her 80s.

A major concern for business owners is also with the accessibility of their corporate dollars. Certain mutual funds and segregated funds are able to stop redemptions without notice to fund holders. This can mean that a business that has invested in those funds may have only one option of accessing cash, namely borrowing. Also, if the funds are needed during an economic downfall, the investments may be below their original purchase price and would not be optimal to redeem at that point. It is never optimal for any investor to redeem investment funds when they are in a loss position; however, there can be certain tax advantages that will not be discussed here in doing so. Business owners who are holding excess profits generally do not intend on using these funds, however, the intent is not to tie up funds so they are inaccessible either. The participating life insurance policy enables policyholders' access to up to 90 per cent of the cash value of the policy. There are various methods to accessing the cash value that has built up inside the tax-exempt policy and the most commonly used method is assigning the policy as collateral to a third-party lender. Once the policy is assigned, the third party will then issue a line of credit to the business or individual for the predetermined percentage of the cash value. The line of credit is only paid off when the insured has died. The life insurance policy will pay out the owed amount to the lender and the remainder will go to the original beneficiaries. In short, this strategy allows the policyholder to access the cash value without incurring any taxes owed on the growth over the previous years inside the policy. The lender does charge an interest rate on the outstanding balance; however, the interest paid on the line of credit is less than the growth of the policy. With the additional savings added by not paying tax on the growth within the policy, the overall benefit to the policyholder is substantial. Should the full cash value be needed by a policyholder, the strength of the liquidity for this participating fund is demonstrated by the speed at which it is able to pay out any mortality claims that are filed. In 2008, most par funds paid all claims within an eight day period.[2]

The Universal Life Alternative

This is another form of life insurance that is more commonly used by advisers trying to accomplish the same task as the corporate asset transfer model does. This technique uses a universal life insurance policy to defer the taxes owed on any investment returns. The universal life (UL) insurance is subjected to all of the same income tax reporting and insurance guidelines as set out earlier. The basis of a UL policy is to provide a client with a base amount of life insurance and a tax advantaged area for investing. The investment amounts are proportional to the insurance amounts since, otherwise, government regulations would distinguish the policy as strictly being used for investment purposes and tax evasion. The proportions are set by the MTAR limits and monitored annually. The investment mix under a UL policy is strictly controlled and monitored by the policyholder and their corresponding advisor. Because of this, there are greater investment choices for these policies as well as greater administration for all parties involved. However, it differs from the participating insurance in several ways. These types of policies are not involved in corporate investments, there is no dividend yield, the asset mix is controlled by the policyholder (and their adviser), insurance amounts can fluctuate, MTAR limits can fluctuate, and the investments are generally tied to market conditions. A typical UL policy will include the life insurance for a minimum premium amount and an additional pre-determined investment amount. The premium and investment amounts are deposited into an investment mix designed by the adviser. This investment mix should be established based on the client's investment risk tolerance for the given assets. Most corporate clients will keep their retained earnings invested in lower risk investments. Equity portfolios generally include index linked funds to certain North American and international stock indexes, as well as bond indexes. By including investment in equity portfolios linked to stock indexes, a UL policy allows for a well-diversified investment portfolio. However, since the UL policies are linked to equities, the main goal of sustained positive growth through sagging economic markets may not be achieved.

2 Participating life insurance financial facts December 2008 London Life (41-4031-5/09).

Secondary issues that arise from the UL policy stem from problems regarding the bigger estate picture. If you have a regular investment portfolio that is 80 per cent weighted in equities, and a UL policy that is also 80 per cent weighted in equities, you will not have many options during an economic downturn. Most of these investments will decrease during an economic recession, and any withdrawals during the downturn can leave a portfolio in a position where it would be unable to recover from the losses. This does not bode well for any individual or business owner who is looking to use their personal and/or corporate assets for their looming retirement. Alternatively, the UL investments can be made up of GICs or daily interest accounts. However, these are low interest-bearing investments. They do serve the purpose of eliminating volatility but do not provide you with ample long-term returns. This is especially true when global interest rates shrink because of a global recession.

The fluctuations in account value under a UL policy can also have implications should the insured die during an economic downturn. Since all investments in the UL policy are sold and transferred to the beneficiary as tax-free cash upon the death of the insured, shortfalls in the insurance coverage can be created if the policy has not been properly designed. For example, imagine a base UL policy purchased for $2 million to cover the corporate succession plan. An additional $1 million was invested within the policy. A total value of $3 million should be present plus or minus any investment fluctuations. If the markets took a turn for the worse at the time the insured died, and the investment portion was down 40 per cent, it would leave an account balance of $600,000 plus the additional insurance coverage of $2 million. The beneficiary would receive a cheque for the $2,600,000. If the estate planning obligations totalled more than the $2,600,000, then the beneficiary may not have the resources to deal with the remaining tax bill on the transfer of the estate to the next generation. This may lead to the beneficiaries having to sell certain assets to cover the tax liability, resulting in an unsuccessful attempt to properly plan for the estate transfer.

A UL policy will have greater administration requirements behind the scenes by the insurance provider and the adviser. Administration will arise from the investment component of the policy and the MTAR limit dedicated for it. The MTAR limits and actual insurance amount of a UL policy will fluctuate every year based on investment performance and the premiums deposited. The base amount of insurance will adjust within a range based on the amount of growth within the policy. During growth years, additional invested premium will be allocated towards purchasing additional life insurance in the policy. These purchases will ensure the tax-sheltered status of the policy. During negative growth years, the premiums paid will be allocated towards the investment account which will reduce the value of the insurance back to the initial coverage amount. Accordingly, the MTAR levels will also fluctuate based on the amount of premium deposited into the UL policy. If a policyholder buys a policy in which to invest corporate assets down the road, they will see significantly lower MTAR lines compared to a business owner that invests the retained earnings directly into the policy upon approval. By postponing the additional investment premiums, the MTAR line is lowered over the life of the entire policy, which will limit future growth within the policy.

Additional Benefits of Life Insurance

With both of these types of corporate-owned life insurance policies, a small business owner may choose to use the assets within the policy to help fund their retirement. Several techniques were briefly mentioned earlier on how a policyholder can access the funds within the policy, should the need arise. The best method will depend on specific circumstances of your scenario. The most common form of using the corporate asset transfer method for retirement is to use a third party lender to borrow funds equal to a high percentage (85 to 90 per cent) of the available cash value within the policy. In a typical collateral loan scenario, the life insurance policy is adequate security for the line of credit. However, because the policy is owned by the corporation, the shares of the business owner must be put up as collateral until the loan has been repaid. The business owner will then have access to a large amount of cash that is only subjected to a negotiated interest rate. The life insurance policy will still be able to grow at its full rate, since the large amount of cash value and premium has been deposited into the policyholder's account. Since policies tend to have greater growth towards the end of the policy, to disrupt this growth could have an adverse affect on the policy value and the ability to offset the tax obligation for the beneficiary. The growth of the cash value inside the life insurance policy will outperform the growing liability of the line of credit. When the business owner does finally die, the proceeds of the insurance policy will still be paid to the corporation as the sole beneficiary. However, the difference will be that the lending institution is now a shareholder of the CCPC, thus the dividend that will be paid out to shareholders will equal an amount for the outstanding line of credit to the lender. The remainder will be passed onto the beneficiary of the shares and the new business owner under the tax-free capital dividend account. This will still allow for the succession planning that was put in place earlier to take form, and allow for the continuation of the business going forward. Under the current tax laws, if the lending institution and insurer have an arm's length relationship, then no disposition occurs at the point when the policy is assigned collaterally. This allows the business owner to receive the financial resources from the lending institution in a non-taxable form.

If the loan has been set up with capitalized interest then the interest will be applied back to the total amount borrowed and only paid off once the life insurance policy has been claimed. When using this method, the total amount must never exceed the maximum ratio of loan to cash value, since the resources must be able to pay off the loan balance. Alternatively, the business owner could choose to pay off the interest on a monthly or annual basis. Some of the risks associated with this strategy include the loan obligation exceeding the value of the life insurance policy. Longevity to the individual's life can create a sustained debt obligation and would cause interest to accumulate and the total value to get out of control. The lender can also demand repayment of the loan in certain situations. It is very important that each client is aware of all of these risks, and knows when and how the lender can demand repayment of the loan. Should the loan be required to be repaid, it is possible that the life policy would have to be surrendered, and the estate and succession planning would be in ruins. As well, if the policy is surrendered, the corporation would be on the hook for the capital gains between the current value and the adjusted cost base (ACB) of the cash value in the policy. It is possible that at this point the business owner may not be insurable, and would be required to dispose of other assets to help offset the taxable gains incurred to the next generation.

The corporate asset transfer takes into consideration both the current capital available as well as possible taxes owed for the estate of the owner and corporation upon the death of the original owner. By reviewing and/or creating a succession plan simultaneously, a business owner can take care of multiple needs at the same time. By establishing a life policy, the eventual tax obligations caused by the transfer of shares to the next generation can be offset for the beneficiaries. While examining the eventual estate tax obligations, considerations such as market value of the corporation are key factors which should be taken into account.

During a recession, companies who want to implement a long-term strategy like the corporate asset transfer are not worried about the overall viability of the business. Rather, the companies are looking for techniques to capitalize on the situation. Many tax lawyers and accountants advise some of their clients to undergo an estate freeze during downward economic cycles. The estate freeze is a useful technique to minimize taxes owed by the estate. Valuations during growth periods can be substantially higher than during a market contraction or recession. By completing an estate freeze, the company shareholders may have to pay significantly less taxes upon their death than would be the case in normal economic periods. The new valuation would allow for a lower market value and would decrease the spread between the ACB and the market value of the business. Note that before implementing any kind of an estate freeze, the proper professionals should be consulted to determine the necessity and proper technique of completing any freezes.

The estate freeze enables the current owner to plan properly for the disposition of assets down the road, when the assets are passed onto the beneficiaries of choice. Once the freeze has been completed, any growth that occurs for the assets will be forwarded to the beneficiaries and only taxed once they have disposed of the assets. Business owners will often switch their common shares for preferred shares in the company after completing an estate freeze when the desired beneficiary is a family member. This allows the owner to maintain receipt of any dividends from the business, while foregoing the controlling voting common shares of the company. The common shares are then sold to the beneficiary of the business for a reasonable fee which will avoid and disposition being triggered until the original owner's death. This kind of method can also be performed with a holding company, however consult a tax professional before performing this technique. Once an estate freeze has been performed it does not have to be permanent. There is still an opportunity to unfreeze the estate should certain economic situations change. A revaluation of the assets can also be performed.

Business owners form corporations for various reasons, but one of the major reasons is to allow the business to continue operating after the original founder(s) has ceased participating in the business. Accordingly, a corporate-owned participating fund would be held by the holding company of the corporation; however, the life(s) to be insured is the business shareholder(s). As with all life insurance policies, once the insured life has passed away, all proceeds are paid to the designated beneficiary as a tax-free cash benefit. Any outstanding direct policy loans would be paid first, then the remainder issued to the beneficiary. In the corporate asset transfer model, the corporation would be the sole beneficiary. A one-time cash deposit into the corporation would be ineffective, since it would again result in too much cash being held within the corporation and no tax-efficient method to access it. However, instead of cash holdings, the proceeds of the policy, above the adjusted cost basis, are paid into the Capital Dividend Account (CDA) for the Canadian Controlled Private Corporation. The appropriate proceeds can then be distributed to the business owner's estate or to the new shareholders as a tax-free dividend payout. There is no urgent rush for the corporation to pay out the CDA in any specified timeline. The CDA payout limit is generally a one-time non-taxable payout of $750,000 per shareholder. It is up to the corporate directors or a previously established corporate policy to make the CDA payment when necessary. In certain cases, corporations have decided to pay out part of the policy proceeds to the shareholders, and used the remainder to pay down existing corporate debts or to finance new research or expansion initiatives. This technique can be useful if the corporation is having a difficult time raising capital for the new projects even after taking advantage of the Small Business Deduction limit of $300,000 (*ITA* s. 125). In these scenarios, the remaining tax-free dividends owed can be paid using the future earnings of the corporation. In the case of multiple business owners, a buy-sell agreement may be triggered upon the death of one partner. Since the proceeds have been paid out to the corporation in this scenario, they would normally be used by the company to buy back the shares of the deceased partner, allowing the remaining partner(s) to be the sole shareholders. The terms of the partnership agreement should have instructions for these kinds of scenarios and how they are to be settled.

Other planning techniques may be necessary, depending on the scenario and the individual's will. If the shares of the company are bestowed to a spouse there is no tax obligation owed. In many cases, the business owner has no desire to have their spouse involved in the business and, therefore, beneficiaries of the shares tend to be the children or grandchildren in family run businesses. When shares are passed on through to family members, the shares are usually intended as a gift, not a headache. If the shares are passed onto another generation, massive capital gains issues could be triggered for the receiving party. This is where having a proper estate and succession plan will make any business transition as smooth as possible. The tax-free dividend received by the estate should be used to offset the taxes owed on the capital gains for the new shareholder. The tax obligations owed on successful businesses can be well into six or seven figures which, without the proper estate and succession planning, could force the new shareholder to sell the company to fund the tax obligation.

Under the current income tax regulations there is no inclusion of tax obligations for collaterally assigned life insurance policies. Of course, it is possible that the Finance Minister may choose to tax collaterally-assigned life insurance policies in the future. It also must be noted that not all financial institutions will offer a line of credit with capitalized interest, or with a collaterally-assigned life insurance policy to secure it. There is no way of entering into a contract with an institution for a future collateral loan arrangement. It is up to each institution to determine the risks associated with the loans that they issue. A lender who does perform this type of loan cannot ignore the risks associated with the loan.

Another advantage to the corporate collateral loan is that the interest charge may be deductible, which allows access to the cash value in the policy at almost no cost. The benefit is dramatically increased if the interest can be deducted. However, consult with your tax professional to determine if it is suitable for your application. If the loan is used to fund retirement, then proper planning must be performed to avoid retirement compensation arrangements under the *ITA*. Again, it is important to stress that the purpose of the corporate-owned life insurance policy is not simply to shelter growth for the eventual use in retirement. While this may be the essence of why the policy is even looked at, the underlying impetus for the policy is to offset some sort of tax obligation or to protect the corporation upon the loss of a key person or the funding of a buy-sell agreement. The byproduct and additional benefit is the ability to use the participating fund as a method to enhance the retirement of the business owners. If it is determined by the CRA that the policy was originally purchased with the sole intent for funding of the retirement income, then a series of tax obligations can arise.

It should also be pointed out that CRA does have the ability to apply general anti-avoidance rules against these business owners. From a tax standpoint, there are two methods of accessing the cash value within the policy without physically pulling dollars out of the policy. The collateral loan option is one method, the second method being a policy loan from the insurer. This scenario would create a taxable scenario for the policyholder above the ACB of the policy. If the CRA determines that the policy loan method could be used instead of a collateral loan, taxes may be owed. Outside this determination, the client reserves the right to structure their financial matters within the boundaries of the law in the most tax-efficient method possible.

One consideration that must be taken into account when assessing the corporate asset transfer relates to the creditor protection that is usually applied to life insurance contracts and the cash value growing inside them. When a corporation owns a life insurance policy, it is considered to be an asset of the company. Should the company become insolvent for any reason, the cash value within the life insurance policy can be seized by potential creditors. To avoid seizure by potential creditors, various professionals need to be consulted. A good financial adviser will consult with a tax and estate planner, your company's accountant, and lawyers.

The overall mission of the corporate asset transfer is to provide a business owner with a long-term, stable, and tax-deferred investment growth. An additional goal is to provide benefits to the final estate of the business owner. As a bonus, once the strategy has been implemented, there is little to no administration that is required. By providing sustainable tax-efficient growth through positive and negative markets, fund holders are able to see both short- and long-term benefits. The long range plan can allow the fund holder advantages of accessing the cash value in the policy on a tax-free basis, followed by a tax-free death benefit paid to the beneficiary of the fund (the corporation). By coordinating with a legal and tax professional as well as an accountant, the estate of the owner can benefit from the proceeds of the participating fund to create a succession plan for the business itself.

Optimizing Human Capital

Jon G.E. Cooper

Negative economic reports, bank failures, plant closings, volatile stock markets, worldwide fluctuations in currency, high unemployment rates, hard to get credit: it seems as though we are constantly inundated with casualty reports which tabulate the global economic damage. Each of the issues listed above is a significant problem, so, the combination of all these developments is indicative of very difficult economic times.

In the 19th and 20th centuries, physical assets were the key assets that made most firms competitive. In 1928, 10 of the top 15 firms worldwide in market capitalization owed their success to ownership of natural physical assets, including minerals, oil, and land. Later on in the 20th century, the emphasis shifted towards ownership of plants and equipment.[1] Financial assets became a more important determinant of competitive advantage. On the basis of these assets, firms such as IBM, AT&T, GM, Eastman Kodak, and Sears Roebuck emerged as the world's most valuable firms by 1969.

However, by the late 20th century, the terms of competition had changed dramatically. Dominant physical and financial assets no longer determine success. Many of the firms currently listed in the top 15 firms in the world by market capitalization began recently with no significant physical or financial assets.[2] Rather, the vast majority of the firms on the list depend on superior *human assets* for their advantage. These human assets include great research scientists, inspired code writers, distribution geniuses, and product innovators. Additionally, these leaders in market capitalization – like Microsoft, Cisco, Intel, AOL, and Wal-Mart[3] – increasingly depend on *knowledge assets* like patents, brands, know-how and experience. Finally, the leading

1 www.hrpa.ca/HRPA/HRResource, Center/Growing Communities of Human Capital.

2 *Ibid.*

3 *Ibid.*

firms in the early 21st century firms depend on *network/social assets* for their competitive advantage. Network/social assets consist of relationships with suppliers, distributors and customers, alliance partnerships, and relationships with educational institutions.[4]

To sum up, in the emerging world of competition, successful companies will strive to attract the best *human capital*. By attracting the best human capital, the corporation will create an environment in which they create superior *knowledge assets*. These knowledge assets will, in turn, build and reinforce the *social capital* of the firm.

Re-conceptualization of Human Resources

Historically, Chief Financial Officers and Chief Executive Officers tended to think that their human resource department was a "cost center" within the organization. As a result, these corporate executives largely relegated non-strategic tasks to their human resource staff. For example, the HR Department was typically burdened with maintaining employee records, enrolling employees in healthcare plans, maintaining the employee handbook, ensuring legal compliance and assisting with the entry/exit process. Starkly absent from these tasks were any strategic development initiatives, such as linking compensation to performance, identifying, educating, and grooming future executives, or developing specific human resource strategies that support the organization's corporate goals and objectives.

However, with low unemployment rates, an acute skills shortage in certain occupational areas, and steady job growth, corporate executives have recently learned that the human resource department is a competitive differentiator which enables them to attract top-talent. Furthermore, executives have realized that the human resource department can also reduce employee turnover and control the high cost of benefit enrolment and utilization.

Industry consultants and academics were instrumental in crafting this new role for human resources. These experts have helped to make corporations aware that human resource development is a key component of a company's ongoing success. As part of this change, best-in-class organizations now recognize employees as valuable "assets" of a corporation. These organizations recognize that a corporation's staff produces "productivity", "customer service", and "expertise".

---

4 *Ibid.*

Building human capital is about an organization's ability to develop a strategy to not only retain, but further develop its skilled workforce. Regardless of how human capital is built, a company should not think that if they invest in their staff the employees will be headhunted or leave the company. Rather, whatever the strategy that is developed should be seen as a strategy to build a positive employee culture. If the values of the individual align with the values of the organization, there will be a good fit between the employee and the company. With the right opportunities, culture, values, and practices to support the individual with the principles of life-long learning, staff are more likely to stay. In turn, the organization is more likely to achieve its strategic goals.

Measuring Human Capital

One enormously important distinction between the current knowledge era and the preceding periods is that unlike physical capital and natural resources, human capital cannot be owned by employers. Consequently, an enormous premium now accrues for corporations that have developed a superior capacity for managing human capital. In fact, human capital management is the single most important predictor of an organization's ability to outperform its competition.

There are six key attributes of human capital measurement.[5] The system must be:

1. *Descriptive.* At a minimum, a measurement system should produce statistics that provide a clear and succinct summary for each issue of interest. For example, descriptive statistics can help an organization monitor the degree to which an important best practice is (or isn't) being implemented throughout the organization.
2. *Credible.* A measurement system must be designed to provide the credible and unbiased insights needed to improve business results. Any system designed primarily for the purpose of self-justification will be quickly seen as suspect. For example, many Return on Investment ("ROI") initiatives fall into this category.
3. *Predictive.* The system should produce statistics that help an organization predict where it is headed. Predictive measures are measures that have been linked to the organization's desired business results.
4. *Detailed.* The information provided in the measurement should be

[5] http://www.humanresourcesmagazine.com.au/articles/A7OC0267A7.asp?Type=60&Categ. . .2/26/2009.

sufficiently detailed to provide insight into where action should be taken. Information must be available across departments in order to allow for a possible intervention to be targeted to the appropriate areas.

5. *Actionable.* There should be a focus on the issues on which an organization can exert influence. Other items, however interesting they may be, are unhelpful in enabling action to drive business results.
6. *Cost-effective.* A powerful measurement system for human capital is important to any well-managed business; however, the system must be cost-effective in order for it to be sustainable.

There are six key elements in human capital measurement. Whoever undertakes an assessment of human capital within a company must measure these elements.

Leadership/managerial practices. These include communication, performance feedback, supervisory skills, demonstration of key organizational values, and the ability to instil confidence.

Workforce optimization. An organization's success in optimizing the performance of its workforce through the establishment of essential processes for getting work done, the provision of good working conditions, strong hiring decisions, and emphasis on accountability.

Learning capacity. An organization's overall ability to learn, innovate, and continually improve.

Knowledge accessibility. An organization's level of collaboration and its capacity for making knowledge and ideas widely available to employees.

Employee engagement. The organization's capacity to engage, retain, and optimize the value of its employees.[6]

The best way to measure all of these factors is to conduct a carefully constructed survey of employees. Be aware that this should not be a typical employee satisfaction survey. Each of the five capital categories and their specific components should be linked to a variety of alternative measurements of business outcomes. Such linkages provide executives with clear prioritization of human capital management initiatives that will generate the greatest improvement in business results.

---

[6] *Ibid.*

Human Capital Problems Facing Companies Today

It is clear that a measurement of human capital may be a key contributor to a company's success in the marketplace. However, when strategizing for long-term development, any successful long-term human capital approaches must also take into account certain market forces and impending demographic shifts. To some, these strategies may seem unimportant and trivial in the current climate of economic despair. However, it is crucial that companies consider these trends and develop their human resources accordingly. Indeed, given the importance of human capital in the 21st century, it would be foolhardy not to consider these trends.

Invest in Your Human Resource Development

We know that human capital is a key factor of business success. Therefore, one of the avenues that will allow a company to improve its performance in productivity and innovation is investment in human resources management practices.

According to the U.S. Small Business Administration, most small businesses who have less than 100 employees do not have a Human Resource professional on staff.[7] However, the human resource function can be a source of strategic capital for these companies as well. A company without the resources to hire full-time human resource staff should consider outsourcing professional development to a specialist company.

Generally, most companies attempt to constantly improve in four areas: develop innovations that increase revenue; keep clients loyal; protect and grow the company's market share; and increase efficiency to reduce costs. Based on these goals, a key concern for every employer is whether the corporation has the right people to get the company through the current economic climate. Accordingly, corporations must always be open to bringing on individuals with the special skills necessary to keep the company's competitive edge. Companies must always be willing to upgrade their staff – even under a no-hire edict. Selective hires may provide the human capital necessary to keep the company competitive during tough times; thus, companies must constantly be on the lookout for these key resources.

The economic slowdown has impacted virtually all manufacturers. Consequently, many progressive companies have begun to focus on upgrading technologies and hiring highly-skilled talent. It goes without saying that these

7 http://www.EmployHR.com/HR.Administrtion.

innovations will result in a reduced demand for certain types of labor; however, there will also be a corresponding demand for the right type of employee. These new technologies and upgrades will mean that employers will need people who can problem-solve, think on their feet and contribute beyond their assigned role.

Employers must look for employees that possess the ability to assemble and analyze information. Robert Reich calls these employees "symbolic analysts"; these workers manipulate symbols such as mathematical data and words to identify and solve problems.[8] Future leaders must have an intuitive ability to understand how different functional pieces of the business interact and interrelate. We operate in a complicated environment in which one seemingly isolated action can have an impact on an entire process in a company.

One of the most important skills for any employee is oral and written communication. The decline in literacy has enhanced the value of those who can write clearly, concisely, and grammatically. Additionally, individuals who have the ability to make effective presentations are incredibly beneficial to any corporation.

Plan for the Impending Demographic Upheaval

Corporations do not grow and develop in isolation – they are social organisms. As such, a company's structure will reflect the demographic composition of society. Currently, North American society is in the process of a huge demographic shift: the so-called baby boomer generation (born 1946-1964) is nearing retirement age. The retirement of baby boomers began to increase in 2005. The population of managers and operators has not been hugely impacted by the phenomenon of retiring boomers; however, the fallout should be felt in the next three to five years.[9] The retirement of the boomer population is therefore becoming a decisive element in business recruitment policies. Companies must develop strategic initiatives that ensure that they will have the right people with the right skills at the right time to continue to operate efficiently.

In the coming months and years, companies may be distracted by the economic slowdown. Accordingly, some corporations may lose sight of this impeding shortage of skilled workers. Yet the upcoming demographic shift is a crucial consideration that must be addressed. In fact, some demographic

---

8 Online: http://logisticsmagazine.ca/sustainableselection/vol_12/no_1.

9 www.logistics-mag.com/Trends in Recruitment of Logistics Personnel, January/February 2007 Vol. 10, No. 1.

studies have hypothesized that by approximately 2015 there will be a huge war for talent among employers in North America. This struggle for talented staff will be driven by a number of factors, including a declining birth rate, the mass retirement of the baby boom generation and employment growth.[10] Some studies estimate that there will be a shortfall in the United States of millions of workers.

Thus, one of the most significant issues facing business leaders today is the current demographic upheaval. Across North America, human resource professionals are wondering: What is to be done with the immense know-how developed over the years by an aging population of workers and managers? In short, the demographic upheaval poses a serious concern to employers. If this shift in demographics is not properly addressed, a company may face a serious disruption of continued operations.

If a company does not provide incentives to stay longer, the retiring boomer population will leave with invaluable knowledge, skills, and wisdom. It is becoming clear that there are simply not enough people out there with the high skill sets and business experience needed to meet growing demand. Demographics are a major contributor to the problem.[11] A large portion of current senior level managers are approaching retirement age and will take with them many years of hands-on expertise that will be hard to replace.

To remedy the boomer dearth, companies will be forced to hire and train new employees from a demographic pool with vastly different expectations about work-life balance, company loyalty, and job satisfaction. Recruiting the "millenials"[12] (born 1980-1995) will accordingly require companies to create a new image tailored to the characteristics of this younger generation. Companies will have to broaden their appeal as a flexible employer, offering opportunities for a wide range of experiences and skills development.

As another alternative to remedy the demographic shift, some innovative companies should reconsider the definition of retirement. Additionally, corporations should become more creative in recruiting and retaining the next generation of employees. By re-conceptualizing what retirement means and by implementing creative recruitment strategies, companies can ensure that they have the right workforce skills in place; in turn, the corporation can avoid any disruptions in productivity and customer service that negatively impact profits.

---

10 H. Dunn, "Talent War: A reality or just a myth" (Nov. 2007) *Mississauga Business Times*.

11 http://www.logistics-mag.com/leadership and development of managers/March/April (2008), Vol. 11, No. 2.

12 http://en.wikipedia.org/wiki/Millennial_generation.

To solve problems created by the aging population and the ensuing loss of know-how, organizations are also leaning increasingly towards policies of internal mobility. The use of internal promotions still remains an excellent means of defense against the retirement of boomers.

Younger employees often seek challenges that implement their skills and allow them to make a difference. If it is feasible, the creation of focus groups or special projects that draw on knowledge from newer employees will allow less experienced staff to contribute to the big picture. It is worth paying attention to these younger employees, since a new set of eyes and a different set of experiences may give the corporation a necessary edge. Additionally, the appointment of these staff into lateral positions can provide challenging work and job satisfaction for younger employees. Lateral transfers have the added bonus of creating depth in the organization – particularly when the move is across departmental lines. This move may create the opportunity for change in how information is shared, product or data is moved, and staff interacts.

A company will face myriad challenges that result from the retirement of the baby boomer population. However, if a company addresses some or all of these strategies, the "millennial" generation will develop strong skills that can be applied to the many different challenges they will face during their careers.

Retain Your Current Employees

A recent survey developed by Robert Half International found that even in the current economy, employers are most concerned about being able to keep their good employees. For example, 35 per cent of senior executives stated employee retention was the company's biggest staffing concern – only 23 per cent said staff morale.

Generally speaking, employees care about a corporation's well-being. Therefore, if a company gives employees the necessary tools, goals, and information, the staff will likely be motivated to make better decisions. Management's efforts at worker engagement should be ongoing. The company also needs to set aggressive targets and stress to employees the importance of reaching these goals. Furthermore, HR Departments should measure progress and communicate results to the employees. Strong performances should be rewarded through incentives programs. Finally, and most importantly, a company should always listen to suggestions from employees. A corporation's staff deals with the company's system and process more than anyone else. Accordingly, a company should solicit employee ideas for how to make things better. It has been my experience that the best ideas for change come from those doing the job, so make sure to take a serious look at what employees are proposing.

Employee Inclusion

Every day at work, employees should have a sense of purpose and mission. An employer should communicate to all workers that their role is important, since company results tend to mirror employee efforts. Moreover, each employee should understand how their particular effort affects departmental or divisional goals. The more employees know about the role they play in the company's objectives, the more meaningful their jobs will become.

Every employee in a corporation should have an opportunity to provide direction, goal-setting, and feedback. All employees are responsible for adding value and contributing to the company's objectives. No matter how cynical an employee may be about the importance of their role, the opportunity to contribute should be extended to all employees.

When things start to go poorly, a company should consider conducting "round table discussions". These discussions will improve the appearance of transparency between management and staff. By acting transparently, the company can create a strong sense of belonging among the staff and unite the team behind the needed action plan.

Accountability is crucial; therefore, establishing key objectives in each department allows staff to show progress, celebrate successes, and establish metrics. However, a company must be careful not to bury performers in objectives – six key goals are all anyone can effectively manage.

Management should also follow up with formal employee evaluations. These evaluations should clearly establish the progress made by the employee, as well as the further actions that will be necessary to meet the set goals. It is often helpful to let employees do a self-review. In many cases, employees tend to be much harder on themselves than an evaluator would be.

Lighten up during the evaluation process. You should create an atmosphere of trust, value, recognition, and praise – better to be a coach than a judge. The net result of adopting this attitude will be that the employee will be motivated to perform.

Incentives Programs

Employees that are motivated to challenge themselves will understand that today's success is the groundwork for tomorrow's achievements.

The majority of employers would not notice if an employee were to increase or decrease their workload by 15 per cent. This represents a 30 per cent range in discretionary effort that a company may or may not get from your employees. Consider for a moment that this 30 per cent range in effort could help your company outperform your competitors by 15 to 30 per cent. It is necessary to ask how your company can encourage this effort. Although not the only answer, recognition and rewards programs can play a key role in increasing employee workload.

Recognition and rewards programs are generally responsible for productivity improvements of 20 to 30 per cent. Accordingly, companies should strive to promote employee reward programs regardless of the market condition. While the most common rewards are financial, rewards must be tailored to specific circumstances. Many are all familiar with rewards programs; however, it is necessary to repeat and elaborate on them here.

- *Job Evaluation*: For the purpose of inter-job comparison, the job evaluation format needs to be consistent across disciplines. The factors that need to be considered when evaluating supervisors/managers are 1) both direct and indirect responsibility; 2) expertise; and 3) human relations.
- *Merit*: Merit is often used as an indicator of performance. Employees are usually rated under exceeds expectation, meets expectation, or needs improvement. Unfortunately, this ratings system can become mechanical and often carry a heavy bias in favor of the rater. This bias can usually be offset by having each rater present the rating to a group of his or her peers and comparing the employee to others in similarly responsible positions.
- *Profit Sharing*: Profit sharing initiatives can be applied on a large- or small-scale basis, targeting either the entire company or a particular group in the employee's direct scope of influence.

Any incentives system must boost employee morale to create a productive working culture. Celebrate success. Your celebration may be as simple as a pizza lunch for the group or a bonus tied to individual performance. Whatever celebration you decide on, remember to honor your employees' hard work and dedication!

Plato once stated, "What is honored is cultivated". Perhaps you can cultivate your employee's performance by honoring the performance you demand.

Continuing Education

Progressive corporations should explore continuing education as an alternative in the current economic climate. Continuing education programs guarantee that an employee is up-to-date in his or her industry. These programs also develop employee loyalty and allow employees to be promoted within the company. Although continuing education is a calculated risk, funding education for staff can be a win-win situation. Training creates a stronger workforce of more confident employees.

Certain findings support the proposition that continuing education for employees is a worthwhile investment for a company. A major study conducted by Harvard and Wharton business schools and the Center for Business Innovation found that companies that invest in work training are more profitable than those that do not.[13] "[This is] a landmark study demonstrating that a company's surest way to profits is to treat employees as assets," said Robert Reich, economist and a former U.S. Secretary of Labor.

At the end of the day, continuing education is a bottom line issue: can the company afford the costs associated with the education? However, professional development targeted at your industry, your culture, and your workers can be a very worthwhile decision. Not only is the company likely to be more profitable, but the programs also show your staff that the company believes in them and is willing to invest in them! The employees come away with a sense of confidence and assurance that they will be with the company for a while. Investing in your people is the most effective, enduring strategy for growth.

Focus on Customer Service

There is a good reason why customer service is so often raised as a crucial component of any business strategy. No matter what industry a company belongs to, at the end of the day all a corporation really offers is service. Thus, all employees have the opportunity to make a significant contribution to maintaining and improving their organization's customer service.

Good customer service is the lifeblood of any business. A corporation can offer endless promotions and slash prices to bring in new customers; how-

---

13 http://www.kltprc.net/books/choosing/chpt_19.htm.

ever, unless the company can get some of those customers to come back, the business cannot be profitable in the long run. Good customer service is really about two things: sending customers away happy and getting customers to return for business. If a customer leaves your business happy, it is likely that the customer will pass positive feedback along to others. These individuals may try the product or service you offer and in turn become repeat customers.

The essence of good customer service is forming a relationship that the individual customer feels he would like to pursue. How can a company form such a relationship? By remembering that the one true secret of good customer service: *You will be judged by what you do, not what you say.*

It is essential to make excellent customer service a top priority among your employees. Ask your customers what they want, communicate their expectations to your employees and then deliver upon those expectations. Any assumption that you know what a customer wants will put the relationship and business at risk.

Many years ago, I worked for a large multi-national company. A commitment to Total Quality was established within our group. This commitment, called A1-Service, was led by a visionary director, Ernie Barber. A1-Service was explained, taught, advertised, and reported on by each department head on a monthly basis. It became a way of life within our group of employees. The results were solid, consistent, dependable, do what we said we were going to do, client service, along with an expanded business portfolio!

For the record:

A1 – *Accountability* for attaining credibility with our clients rests with all of us. Our day-to-day attitudes will reflect a readiness and willingness to be of assistance.

S – *Service* to our clients will be reliable and predictable. Our clients will consider us dependable.

E – *Excellence* in the performance of every activity will be our goal. We will not knowingly provide less than our best in completing any job activity.

R – *Reliability* on data provided or commitments made by any member of our team will become a trademark with our clients. Our success will come from the mutual support of each team member.

V – *Value* for each dollar spent. We will optimize total costs while maintaining a high level of service.

I - *Integrity* with our clients will be fostered through relationships that are open and sincere and built on mutual trust and understanding.

C - *Communication* of our client's requirements to other members of the team and follow up in a timely manner so that our performance will ensure the provision of high quality service.

E - *Every* day, every way, everything we do will contribute to the provision of A1-Service.

The employees who were part of the Al-Service program had a sense of pride in their accomplishments. The program helped staff became part of the overall group's success; accordingly, morale was high and team spirit became a way of life in the company.

Technology: Friend and Foe to Business Development

When Japan was trying to compensate for labour shortages in the 1960s and 1970s, the country embraced labor-saving technology. Since then, technology has become an integral part of all western industry. This significant development in information and management systems means that, over the next decade, proficiency in information technologies will undoubtedly be the dominant competency in any area.

Technology continues to develop at a staggering pace. Driven by these advancements, "millennials" are using technology to network and expedite their job search. Top "millennial" job candidates may thus be less loyal about staying with a company than the baby boomer generation. Some amount of turnover is inevitable with these "millennials"; however, a first step toward avoiding employee attrition is to locate the candidates who best fit in a position. Since even happy "millennials" may shop for jobs, it is also necessary for a company to post available jobs to popular websites.

Another recent technological development is automated answering. I have always found it interesting that companies choose to make an automated voice their first impression with a potential client. What are these companies thinking? What happened to the receptionist? One receptionist can recognize who is calling, make the client feel important, and ensure the client is connected with the appropriate party. A company should always make sure that someone is picking up the phone when a client calls your business. Get call forwarding, or hire staff if necessary; but remember that clients will always want to talk to a live person.

Conclusion

Given the complexities of modern commerce, it is crucial that business owners have a plan in place to identify and defend against risks. Volume will be lost through attrition; clients will be lost through failure. If a business does not plan to grow in the current economic environment, by default, it is planning to shrink. This is a time for marketing initiatives which offer new and improved services. Moreover, there is the opportunity to grow your company's market share, since some weaker companies may be laying off good people, exiting markets, or reducing service levels.

These are challenging times that require excellent navigational tools to keep you on course. If your organization does not have a well thought out, properly resourced and controlled plan, it doesn't really matter how well you execute on a daily basis. You don't know where you're going to end up and you'll never know if you're there yet.

In short, in this time of economic duress it is more important than ever to optimize performance. The success of any company solely rests on the abilities of their collective employee workforce to improve, grow, and meet the challenges ahead. Therefore, it is crucial to optimize your corporation's human capital. You will find that employees who are quick to try new approaches, and take responsibility for new initiatives and improvement are your most valuable people.

No one goes into business to be an employer; yet being a good employer is the cornerstone of your success.

Conducting International Business in Volatile Markets: Corruption Risk and the Bottom Line[1]

James M. Klotz

Introduction

When recession occurs and sales decrease, businesses naturally do everything they can to turn around the situation. Companies that have not traditionally exported their goods and services look to international business opportunities outside of North America. Unfortunately, while it is easy for business people to maintain their ethical and moral code in good times, it may look more attractive to take short-cuts on these values when times are tough. This is exacerbated by the fact that the opportunities for corruption in volatile international markets are ever present and, more particularly, present in the markets that seem most tempting. What Canadian companies often do not realize is that the risk arising from corruption may be the most significant risk they will encounter in international business. This chapter discusses the ways in which Canadian companies participate in international corruption, the primary Canadian law which prohibits international corruption, and the consequences (both criminal and civil) for participating in corruption. The chapter also offers recommendations for minimizing international corruption risk for Canadian companies.

---

1 This chapter is adapted from a number of recent publications by the author, including *Power Tools for Negotiating International Deals*, 2nd ed. (New York: Kluwer Law International, 2008); "Canadian firms do pay bribes, they just aren't punished" *The Lawyers Weekly* (2 May 2008); "Facing Corruption in Overseas Procurement: Compliance, Due Diligence, or Prison" (paper presented at the Canadian Institute's 4th Annual Forum on Public Procurement, 17 January 2007); "Corruption legislation should not be overlooked for exporting companies" *The Lawyers Weekly* (13 October 2006); "Not seeing is no defence" *CA Magazine* (October 2006) at 49.

How Bribes Are Paid in International Business

In international business, corruption is extremely common, and the need to bribe is often considered merely as a fixed cost that all bidders must bear, rather than an opportunity for competitive advantage.[2] The pervasive nature of corruption is not restricted to those countries that are on the bottom of Transparency International's Corruption Perceptions Index.[3]

However, what is surprising about international corruption is how easily Canadian companies, who wouldn't dare consider flirting with domestic corruption, are caught in its web - often in a manner which is not immediately obvious to even the savviest in-house counsel. While in the past, companies could rely on their ethical value statements and codes of corporate conduct, times have changed and these structures are no longer sufficient to protect companies, officers, and directors from criminal and civil liability.

Most Canadian business executives are quite savvy to the fact that paying out cash gifts to foreign officials is against the law, and is not to be done. However, Canadians often see little wrong with providing perks to visiting officials, such as travel and entertainment expenses, schooling or job-training for children, or even making charitable donations to the official's favourite charity.[4] As will be discussed further, even these "non-cash" benefits can give rise to criminal liability.

---

2 G.T. Ware & G.P. Noone, "The Anatomy of Transnational Corruption" (Fall/Winter 2005) 14:2 International Affairs Review 29 at 33-34. "Kickback schemes are quite simple, even in their grandest form. A multinational company that wins a contract pays a large bribe to government officials, who influence the award of this contract. . . . Even in international competitive bidding involving multinational companies, contractors know the going "market rate" for bribes in specific regions and factor that percentage into the bidding process."

3 Those countries at the bottom of the Index being Haiti, Iraq, Myanmar, and Somalia. The Index ranks 180 countries. Each country's score relates to perceptions of the degree of corruption as seen by business people and country analysts. Canada is currently ranked 9. See http://www.transparency.org/policy_research/surveys_indices/cpi/2008 (as viewed February 16, 2009).

4 There are a number of instructive cases in the U.S. that address perks and donations. For example, see *SEC v. Schering-Plough Corporation*, Case No. 1:04CV00945 (D.D.C., June 9, 2004) (http://www.sec.gov/litigation/admin/34-49838.htm (as viewed, November 28, 2006): The SEC alleged that Schering-Plough's Polish subsidiary paid approximately $76,000 to the Chudow Castle Foundation, a charitable organization that restores castles and other historic cites in Poland. The president of the Foundation was also the director of a regional government health authority in Poland. The SEC alleged that although the payments by the subsidiary were made to a *bona fide* charity and recorded as such, they were made with the intention of inducing the Foundation's president to use his authority as director of the health authority to promote the purchase of Schering-Plough's pharmaceuticals. As a result of a civil complaint brought by the SEC, Schering-Plough consented to the entry of a final judgment that required it to pay a $500,000 penalty.

Canadians seem to be far less savvy, however, to the problems that lie with agents (and other intermediaries such as joint venture partners, distributors, and even foreign subsidiaries)[5 6] as it is common for Canadian exporters to pay monies to agents who are thereafter free to pay bribes to foreign officials on their own. The theory relied upon by exporters engaged in this practice is that the separation between the payment to the agent, and the subsequent payment by the agent of the bribe, is sufficient to avoid culpability. In this, they are wrong. Nevertheless, most Canadian companies maintain an "ask no questions" policy in regards to the retention of their foreign agents. They expect their agents to "do what they have to do" to win business. Agents ideally positioned to serve Canadians are usually the ones that have the most connections and, in most developing countries, those connections are typically to government officials. Thus, the top agents are often precisely those who are best positioned to pay bribes.

To combat the problems associated with agents, many countries have adopted rules to govern their public procurement processes. Either the supplier is prohibited from having an agent, agrees to the maximum commission the agent can be paid, or requires (at a minimum) the agent to be registered with the procuring agency. The purpose of these rules is to ensure that agents are either barred from the process, are not paid enough for them to pay a significant bribe to an official, or at least are put under a spotlight. These rules are often ignored by Canadian suppliers and flouted by agents. However, Canada's anti-bribery law, the federal *Corruption of Foreign Public Officials Act*,[7] prohibits payments to agents where the paying company is wilfully blind to subsequent bribe-paying by the agent.[8]

---

5 For example, see *United States v. ABB Vetco Gray, Inc. and ABB Vetco Gray (UK) Ltd.; SEC v. ABB Ltd.* Case No. CR H-04-279 (S.D. Tex. June 22, 2004): In 2004, the defendants pleaded guilty to offences of offering and making illicit payments to government officials relating to their U.S. and foreign-based subsidiaries doing business in Nigeria, Angola, and Kazakhstan. It was further alleged that the payments were made with the knowledge and approval of certain management level personnel of the relevant ABB subsidiaries. The payments were allegedly recorded as "payments for consulting services", "ordinary business expenses", per diem payments to "'future decision-makers' in 'key positions'" and "sham contracts for purportedly legitimate consulting services related to the maintenance of drilling equipment". ABB consented to an entry of a final judgment enjoining it from future FCPA violations, and requiring it to pay $5.9M in disgorgement and prejudgment interest and a $10.5M penalty.

6 The term "agent" is used throughout this chapter to include generally all intermediaries.

7 S.C. 1998, c. 34.

8 The *CFPOA* offences require *mens rea*. An accused's knowledge of a fact can be established through the doctrine of wilful blindness. "For wilful blindness to be established, the Crown need only prove that the failure to inquire was motivated or informed by a desire to avoid the truth, or knowledge on the part of the accused that avoiding an inquiry will shield his eyes and ears from the guilty truth:" *R. v. Morales* (2006), 81 O.R. (3d) 161 (C.A.), at para. 23.

The CFPOA

As a result of Canada's commitment to the Organisation for Economic Co-operation and Development ("OECD") (when it signed the *Convention on Combating Bribery of Foreign Public Officials in International Business Transactions* in 1997), Canada enacted the *Corruption of Foreign Public Officials Act* (the "*CFPOA*"), which came into force in early 1999. Shortly thereafter, Canada amended the *Criminal Code* to treat an offence under the *CFPOA* as a "designated offence" whereby the proceeds of crime are forfeited. There has been only one prosecution under the *CFPOA* in Canada, and that case, unfortunately, had atypical facts.[9]

The operative section of the *CFPOA* is ss. 3(1)(a) which reads as follows:

> 3. (1) Every person[10] commits an offence who, in order to obtain or retain an advantage in the course of business, directly or indirectly gives, offers or agrees to give or offer a loan, reward, advantage or benefit of any kind to a foreign public official or to any person for the benefit of a foreign public official
>
> (a) as consideration for an act or omission by the official in connection with the performance of the official's duties or functions; or
>
> (b) to induce the official to use his or her position to influence any acts or decisions of the foreign state or public international organization for which the official performs duties or functions.

This section is actually quite complex and the provisions are drafted very broadly. Fortunately, the *CFPOA* is quite similar to its U.S. cousin, the *Foreign*

---

9 In the sole known Canadian case, the President and assistant manager of Hydro Kleen Systems Inc. bribed a U.S. Customs agent to facilitate the entry of its employees into the U.S. and to delay the U.S entry of competitors' employees. In connection with this arrangement, the defendants paid him up to $2,000 a month to provide "immigration consulting services". All three were charged with violations of the *Corruption of Foreign Officials Act* and the *Criminal Code* of Canada. The Customs agent pleaded guilty and served a six-month jail sentence. Hydro Kleen entered a plea of guilty in the Court of Queen's Bench in Red Deer, Alberta on January 10, 2005. The company admitted to one count under s. 3(1)(a) of the *CFPOA* and was ordered to pay a fine of $25,000. Two other charges against a director and an officer of the company were stayed. See *R. v. Garcia*, 2002 ABPC 156 (Alta. Prov. Ct.), and also as reported at in the Sixth Report to Parliament (October 21, 2005) on the Implementation of the Convention on Combating Bribery of Foreign Public Officials in International Business Transactions, and the Enforcement of the *Corruption of Foreign Public Officials Act*.

10 Note that the *CFPOA* applies equally to individuals as to corporations. Canadian *Criminal Code*, s. 2 provides that "every one", "person", "owner" and similar expressions include Her Majesty and public bodies, bodies corporate, societies, companies and inhabitants of counties, parishes, municipalities or other districts in relation to the acts and things that they are capable of doing and owning respectively.

Corrupt Practices Act ("*FCPA*"),[11] under which there have been many prosecutions during its 30-plus year existence. For example, the definition of a foreign public official[12] is extremely wide and includes employees of state-owned corporations.[13] By way of example, in one U.S. case, doctors at a state-owned hospital were deemed to be public officials.[14]

The definition of a bribe is very broad and may include anything of benefit to a public official. This can include travel benefits that are customarily provided to foreign officials to travel to Canada to enable them to visit a Canadian company. It can even include donations made to an official's favorite charity. The actual payment does not even need to be made; for the offence to occur, there merely needs to be an offer to make the payment.

---

11 15 U.S.C. §§78(b), 78dd-1, 78dd-2. There is a story to the 1977 enactment of the *FCPA*. In 1975, a U.S. Senate Committee held hearings on illegal payments by the Lockheed Corporation to the Prime Minister of Japan. Senator Proxmire (one of the drafters of the *FCPA*) recounted the developments of that scandal in a speech on the Senate floor:

> "The Japanese discovered that the Lockheed Corporation had paid a $1.4 million bribe to their Prime Minister. The Prime Minister – the top elected official in Japan – was convicted. He was sent to jail. His life was ruined. His Government, friendly to the United States, fell ... No Lockheed official went to jail. No Lockheed official was fined. The corporation was actually rewarded big for paying the bribe. The bribe was a brilliant investment. For that $1.4 million bribe Lockheed paid the Prime Minister, the firm made tens of millions of dollars of profits in return for that bribe. This was a shocking, shameful development that sullied the reputation of our country."

See G.H. Mazzarantani, *Foreign Corrupt Practices Act* (1989) 26 American Criminal Law Review 855 excerpt from *Lockheed Bribery: Hearings before the Senate Comm. on Banking, Housing and Urban Affairs*, 94th Cong., 1st Sess. (1975).

12 *CFPOA*, s. 2: "foreign public official" means

(a) a person who holds a legislative, administrative or judicial position of a foreign state;

(b) a person who performs public duties or functions for a foreign state, including a person employed by a board, commission, corporation or other body or authority that is established to perform a duty or function on behalf of the foreign state, or is performing such a duty or function; and

(c) an official or agent of a public international organization that is formed by two or more states or governments, or by two or more such public international organizations.

13 *CFPOA*, s. 2: "foreign state" means a country other than Canada, and includes: . . . (*c*) any agency of that country or of a political subdivision of that country.

14 In *U.S. v. Syncor Taiwan, Inc.*, Cr. No. 02-1244 (C.D. Cal. Dec. 2002), Syncor Taiwan had sought to obtain business and patients for its medical imaging centres by making $457,000 in contractual "commissions" and referral payments to foreign doctors employed by state-owned hospitals in Taiwan. Syncor's subsidiaries in Taiwan, Mexico, Belgium, Luxembourg, and France made payments to state-employed doctors totalling at least $600,000. Cardinal Healthcare, a U.S. company negotiating an acquisition of Syncor, discovered the payments during its due diligence investigation, and they were disclosed soon thereafter. Syncor Taiwan eventually pleaded guilty to a one count FCPA anti-bribery offence and agreed to pay a $2M penalty.

There are three exceptions to the *CFPOA*. Of these, the exception for "facilitation payments" (more commonly known as "grease payments") is the most problematic. A payment will not be considered to be contrary to the Act if it is "made to expedite or secure the performance ... of any act of a routine nature[15] that is part of the ... officials duties or functions."[16] The Act gives a number of examples that include the processing of visas, issuances of licenses, or police protection. Regrettably, the Act does not provide any further detail about these exceptions and Canadian executives incorrectly rely on this escape clause to justify corrupt payments. It is likely that the intention of this exception was to permit those payments that are routinely requested by minor functionaries in developing countries, who rely on these payments for their wages. CIDA suggests in its publication "'Anti-Corruption Programming: A Primer', that facilitation payments are typically small payments to low-level government officials to speed up a process which is the official's job to do. The payments are intended to be relative to the bribee's income and to the briber's potential rewards."[17] Unfortunately, the Act does not give any guidance on the size of the payment, and it is at best a grey area as to whether a million dollar bribe to a Minister to speed up his approval process would be deemed a criminal act.

The second *CFPOA* exception permits the payment of a foreign official's reasonable expenses where the payments are made in good faith and are directly related to the promotion of the person's products or services, or the performance of a contract between the Canadian company and the

---

15 *CFPOA* ss. 3(5): For greater certainty, an "act of a routine nature" does not include a decision to award new business or to continue business with a particular party, including a decision on the terms of that business, or encouraging another person to make any such decision.

16 *CFPOA* ss. 3(4): For the purpose of subsection (1), a payment is not a loan, reward, advantage or benefit to obtain or retain an advantage in the course of business, if it is made to expedite or secure the performance by a foreign public official of any act of a routine nature that is part of the foreign public official's duties or functions, including

(a) the issuance of a permit, licence or other document to qualify a person to do business;

(b) the processing of official documents, such as visas and work permits;

(c) the provision of services normally offered to the public, such as mail pick-up and delivery, telecommunication services and power and water supply; and

(d) the provision of services normally provided as required, such as police protection, loading and unloading of cargo, the protection of perishable products or commodities from deterioration or the scheduling of inspections related to contract performance or transit of goods.

17 B. Bailey, "Anti-Corruption Programming: A Primer, June 2000", as published on CIDA's website www.acdi-cida.gc.ca/INET/IMAGES.NSF/vLUImages/HRDG2/$file/Eng-Primer.pdf (viewed February 16, 2009).

foreign state.[18] For example, it is possible to pay the expenses of a visiting official if the purpose of the visit is to permit the company to promote its products or services. Similarly, a Canadian exporter could pay the expenses of an official to visit Canada for the purposes of signing a contract or for an annual review of the contract. Indeed, it is becoming more frequent for *CFPOA*-savvy Canadian companies to suggest that their agreement include a mandatory meeting in Canada each year that the key foreign official must attend for purposes of "consultation and assessment" of the contract.

The third exception permits payments to be made to officials where such payments are permitted or required under the laws of the foreign state.[19] In most countries in the world, the payment of a bribe to an official is a criminal offence. However, there can be exceptional circumstances where the payment is permitted. In those cases, the *CFPOA* itself would not be violated.

Other Flaws in the Legislation

In addition to the difficulty with the exceptions to the *CFPOA*, there are a number of hurdles facing a prosecutor of a *CFPOA* case.

The first is the issue of "nationality jurisdiction". Canada was the only OECD country that did not accept the principle of assuming jurisdiction over the actions of nationals outside of their country. Canada prefers the "territorial principle" as set out over 30 years ago in *R. v. Libman*,[20] whereas the U.S. tends to apply the broader nationality principle. The defense will be that there is no "real and substantial connection" of the crime to Canada. While

---

18 *CFPOA* ss. 3(3): No person is guilty of an offence under subsection (1) if the loan, reward, advantage or benefit ...

- (b) was made to pay the reasonable expenses incurred in good faith by or on behalf of the foreign public official that are directly related to
  - (i) the promotion, demonstration or explanation of the person's products and services, or
  - (ii) the execution or performance of a contract between the person and the foreign state for which the official performs duties or functions.

19 *CFPOA* ss. 3(3): No person is guilty of an offence under subsection (1) if the loan, reward, advantage or benefit

- (a) is permitted or required under the laws of the foreign state or public international organization for which the foreign public official performs duties or functions;

20 *R. v. Libman* (1985), 21 D.L.R. (4th) 174 (S.C.C.). The defendant used a "boiler-room" telemarketing operation in Canada to convince U.S. residents into investing in a worthless Central American mining company. He was charged with both fraud and conspiracy to commit fraud. The Court set a test for finding territorial jurisdiction under Canadian criminal law – there must be a "real and substantial link" between the offence and Canada before criminal liability will be imposed in this country.

there is an excellent argument that Canada, by virtue of signing the various international conventions against bribery, intended to recognize nationality jurisdiction *de facto*, it remains to be seen if the courts will agree. If Canada had wanted to be explicit, it could have made (and can still make) the appropriate statutory change to the *CFPOA*.[21] But, this will likely not occur unless the Crown loses the first few cases.

The second hurdle will be to prove the necessary *mens rea* for the offence of bribery under the CFPOA. As bribery is an indictable offence, a high level of knowledge and intent is required for a conviction. As many of the cases will involve culpability through wilful blindness, it remains to be seen whether mere recklessness will be sufficient for a finding of guilt.

Finally, an education process will be required both at the prosecutorial level and the judicial level. At first blush, it is all too easy to excuse bribery of foreign officials as a victimless crime that allows Canadian companies to win contracts and create profits – "everyone does it". This defence was rejected by the Privy Council in 1621 when Sir Francis Bacon was convicted of accepting bribes in the Court of Chancery. It remains as unacceptable today, as bribery ultimately harms the poorest of people.

What's Changed?

When the *CFPOA* first became law in Canada in 1999, most significant Canadian companies paid attention to it. Many amended their codes of conduct to address the payments of bribes and grease payments, and some amended their contracts to insert the obligation to comply with anti-corruption laws. Thereafter, there was relative silence as to the application of the *CFPOA*, and most Canadian exporters currently believe that they are in full compliance with the law. When Canada enacted the *CFPOA*, the government failed to delegate real responsibility, within either the RCMP or the federal Justice Department, for pursuing allegations of illegal bribes made by Canadians to foreign officials. With no one responsible, there was little interest for anyone to divert valuable resources away from domestic commercial crime to pursue what appears to be a victimless non-violent crime. With no significant prosecutions yet in Canada, exporters were correct in believing that there was little risk that Canada's law would affect them.

However, the landscape in Canada is changing dramatically and quickly. A *CFPOA* offence is a designated offence under the *Criminal Code*. This means

---

[21] In 2009, the government tabled Bill C-31 which recognized nationality jurisdiction. It has not yet been passed into law.

that the proceeds of a contract obtained by a bribe – not just the profits – are forfeitable to the government. Even modest bribes can now have much greater significance. That in itself would not be particularly noteworthy but for the spate of recent cases coming out of the U.S.

Over the past four years, there have been a series of high-profile foreign bribery convictions in the U.S. A phenomenon common to these convictions is the manner in which the criminal evidence was found. In the past, the source of evidence was often a disgruntled employee or an irritated competitor. However, in these recent cases, the evidence was uncovered by U.S. lawyers doing routine due diligence in the course of business acquisitions.

In one case, Lockheed Martin was in the process of a billion-dollar takeover of Titan Corporation. During the due diligence process related to the acquisition, Lockheed's lawyers uncovered evidence of improper payments to Titan's foreign agents. A savvy potential buyer will not purchase a company in a situation like Titan's unless the authorities are notified and the matter is dealt with, as there can be successor corporate liability. Titan ultimately pled guilty to a *FCPA* offence, and the acquisition fell through.[22]

As a result of these cases, U.S. lawyers are now on the alert for evidence of out-of-the-ordinary agency agreements or payments to agents. Canadian lawyers have also been recently alerted to the need to perform due diligence for compliance with the CFPOA on any financing, acquisition, or sale as there is no statute of limitations on these offences, and the proceeds of the bribe are traceable and forfeitable.[23] It seems fair to assume that it is only a matter of time before a Canadian exporter finds itself in the unpleasant situation of being the first major case brought under Canada's anti-bribery law.

Given that Canada has recently been faulted by the OECD for not taking strong action to enforce its anti-bribery law,[24] Canada has an incentive to

---

22 *SEC v. The Titan Corp.*, Lit. Release No. 19107 (Mar. 1, 2005). The basic facts of this case were as follows: In 1998, Titan embarked on a joint project with Benin to build and operate a wireless telephone network in that country. To retain the business, Titan engaged the services of an agent who was a close associate of the then-President of Benin. Titan paid the agent for "consulting" services for the purpose of influencing Benin's upcoming presidential election. At Titan's request, agent submitted two million dollars of false invoices, and Benin increased Titan's fees fourfold. On March 1, 2005 Titan pleaded guilty to *FCPA* violations and settled parallel SEC civil claims, and agreed to pay $28.5M in criminal fines, disgorgement, and prejudgment interest.

23 For example, the author's recent article "Corruption Legislation Should not be Overlooked for Exporting Companies", *The Lawyers Weekly* (13 October 2006).

24 2008 G8 Progress Report: G8 falling short on keeping commitments to fight corruption.

pursue prosecutions. In fact, where prosecutors choose not to pursue a prosecution, the *Federal Prosecution Service Deskbook* advises them to record their reasons, as these may be relevant if allegations are made that improper political concerns influenced prosecutorial decision-making.[25] The *CFPOA* also contains a provision requiring senior ministers of the government to report each year on the implementation of the OECD Convention and on the enforcement of the *CFPOA*.[26] This report is to detail the nature and status of any prosecutions taken pursuant to the *CFPOA*, and attention is being paid to the fact that there are no cases.[27]

The federal government has tasked the RCMP with taking action to fulfil Canada's international obligations. In 2008, the RCMP created an "International Anti-Corruption Unit" with 14 full-time officers. It now appears that the task force has not been idle. In January, 2009, Niko Resources Ltd. (TSX:NKO) announced that it was being investigated by the RCMP in connection with allegations relating to possible improper payments to officials in Bangladesh by either Niko or its subsidiary in Bangladesh. The company has denied any wrongdoing.

Additional investigations are sure to materialize as those involved in international business know that there is no shortage of offenders. There is little

---

http://www.transparency.org/news_room/latest_news/press_releases/2008/2008_07_03_pre_g8 (as viewed February 16, 2009).

25 Part VI, chapter 33.4. http://www.justice.gc.ca/eng/dept-min/pub/fps-sfp/fpd/ch33.html (as viewed February 16, 2009).

26 *CFPOA*, s. 12: "Within four months of the end of each fiscal year, the Minister of Foreign Affairs, the Minister for International Trade and the Minister of Justice and Attorney General of Canada shall jointly prepare a report on the implementation of the Convention on Combating Bribery of Foreign Public Officials in International Business Transactions, and on the enforcement of this Act, and the Minister of Foreign Affairs shall cause a copy of the report to be laid before each House of Parliament on any of the first fifteen days on which that House is sitting after the report is completed."

27 From the *Federal Prosecution Service Deskbook*, Part VI, chapter 33.3: "On or before January 1 of each year, the Senior Regional Director in each region, and in Ottawa-Hull, the Prosecution Group Head, shall forward to the Senior General Counsel (Strategic Prosecution Policy Section) a report on activities with respect to the provisions of the *Corruption of Foreign Public Officials Act*. The report shall detail:

1. the nature and status of any prosecutions undertaken by the Attorney General of Canada pursuant to the provisions of the *Act*, or the *Criminal Code*;
2. the nature and status of any other proceedings taken pursuant to the *Act* or the *Criminal Code* to which the Attorney General is a party, such as seizure of assets.

The Senior General Counsel (Strategic Prosecution Policy Section) shall collate the information and provide it to the Senior General Counsel (Criminal Law Policy Section) to assist that section in preparing the Department's contribution to the final report."

doubt that charges under the *CFPOA* will follow if the evidence is sufficient, but conviction is not guaranteed as there are hurdles to surmount.

Senior management, directors, and shareholders of any Canadian company that has been involved in international business, and which anticipates the possibility of selling the company to a U.S. buyer at any time in the future, should take careful note of this potential scenario. They would be severely remiss to wait for such a third party action to materialize before commencing the process of introspection as to their company's past conduct, especially if they have failed to introduce a "gold standard" of corporate behavior as to their ongoing business relations with agents.[28]

Four Pillars of Action

How does a Canadian company avoid the risk of payoffs on its behalf to foreign government officials, and the ensuing civil and criminal liability and reputation damage? Four pillars of action are required. Companies must clean house, ensure a robust code of conduct, put proper systems in place, and exercise restraint.

Clean House

Canadian exporters of goods or services must realize that in any future refinancing, share sale, or divestiture, lawyers will now be asking the following six questions as part of their due diligence process:

1. Does the target company export goods or services?
2. Has the target company made any payments directly or indirectly to any foreign public official?
3. Have payments been made to intermediaries, such as sales agents, in connection with such sales?
4. Has regular due diligence been performed on the intermediaries, and on the payments that have been made, to ensure that no indirect bribes were paid?

---

28 *In SEC v. Triton Energy Corp.*, 3 FCPA Rep. 699.462-473 (D.D.C. 1997), the SEC alleged that in 1997, a subsidiary of Triton Energy Corporation, a U.S.-domiciled public company, acting through the officers at the subsidiary, Triton Indonesia, made approximately $450,000 in payments to an intermediary for the purpose of obtaining favorable treatment of a royalty agreement by Indonesian tax authorities. Triton's liability apparently was premised not on direct participation in the wrongdoing, but in the parent company's failure to take adequate steps to prevent illicit foreign payments after certain warning signs came to the attention of management.

5. Has the target company monitored its relationships with its intermediaries regarding bribery risks?
6. Has the target company trained its staff dealing with difficult regions on bribery and compliance risk?

Most due diligence processes will result in production of agency agreements which, in many cases, will pay the appropriate lip service to the *CFPOA* and contain a prohibition against the payment of bribes by the agent. However, due diligence cannot stop there. Notwithstanding detailed agreements, it has been the rare Canadian exporter that performs the requisite level of background investigation regarding the engagement of its agents. This investigation is necessary to ensure that the *CFPOA* is not being contravened through wilful blindness, that is, fault brought on by deliberately failing to inquire when one suspects there is reason for inquiry.[29] Not only must the investigation be performed before the agent is engaged, it should also be updated on an annual basis. This is the "gold standard" to which the most savvy companies are now striving to adhere. If a company performs the necessary inquiries, it will likely avoid the most obvious and egregious indicia of bribe-paying, such as engaging an agent who is, for example, the son of the president of the foreign country to which it has sold or intends to sell goods.

If the exporter has not itself undertaken a due diligence exercise, it would be wise to do so before a third party does on its behalf.[30] By so doing, where due diligence reveals payments that indicate that the *CFPOA* has been breached, the exporter will be able to retain control of the situation and see to its orderly resolution. Note that in many of the U.S. cases, the defendant companies have terminated the employment of all those connected to the making of the improper payments. Exporters should also be aware that a number of the accounting and forensic investigation firms have developed tools to assist them in spotting suspicious payments in an exporter's books.

---

29 *R. v. Sansregret*, [1985] 1 S.C.R. 570.

30 For example, *In the Matter of GE InVision, Inc.*, SEC Admin. Proc. Rel. No. 34-511 (Feb. 14, 2005). In June 2004, InVision employees, sales agents, and distributors pursued transactions to sell explosive detection machines to airports in China, the Philippines, and Thailand. According to the SEC, in each of these transactions, InVision was aware of a high probability that its foreign sales agents or distributors made or offered to make improper payments to foreign government officials. Despite this, InVision allowed the agents or distributors to proceed on its behalf, in violation of the *FCPA*. The SEC also charged that InVision improperly accounted for certain payments to agents or distributors as "cost of goods sold" or "sales commissions" and failed to have internal controls to detect and prevent violations of the *FCPA*. InVision paid total penalties of about $1,500,000. InVision voluntarily brought this matter to the attention of the SEC and DOJ.

For example, this can include "one-off" payments to agents[31] or payments to an agent's bank account located in an off-shore jurisdiction.[32]

If evidence of contraventions of the *CFPOA* are found, the exporter faces a dilemma. There is no obligation in Canada to self-report an offence, though the discovery will require them to restate their financial statements and tax returns as bribes are not a deductible expense. However, self-reporting is often perceived to be a better option than waiting for the offence to be discovered by others.[33] As there have been no meaningful prosecutions in Canada, the exporter should be rightly concerned about being the first in Canada to come forward. Additionally, there is currently no process for a voluntary disclosure of a *CFPOA* violation as there is for *Income Tax Act* or *Competition Act* violations. In part, this is due to the fact that a *CFPOA* violation requires two players - the Canadian violator, and the foreign official. Any process to give immunity from prosecution, prior to the disclosure to the public official's country, will give prosecutors some concern. As well, Canada has no process comparable to the U.S., where the U.S. Department of Justice participates in *FCPA* investigations. In Canada, investigations must be performed by law enforcement agencies such as the local police or the RCMP.

Nevertheless, the concept of voluntary disclosure can be a critical tool in the fight against international corruption. The World Bank is the leader in this regard having recently introduced a Voluntary Disclosure Program designed to give firms an opportunity to avoid being debarred from World Bank work. To take advantage of the program, companies make three commitments: (1) not to engage in misconduct in the future; (2) to disclose to the Bank the results of an internal investigation into past fraudulent, corrupt, collusive, or coercive acts in Bank-financed or supported projects or

---

31 For example, in *U.S. v. Rothrock*, 4 FCPA Rep. 699.818801 (W.D. Tex 2001), a sales commission to the Director General of Nestro, an entity owned by the Government of the Russian Republic (and thus an "instrumentality" of a foreign government), was paid to a new company via a phony invoice. The payment was labelled a "consultation fee and market study" in the books.

32 For example, in *U.S. v. Herbert K. Tannenbaum*, 98 Cr. 784 (S.D.N.Y., 1998), Tannenbaum was alleged to have committed a conspiracy to violate the *FCPA* by offering to make clandestine payments to an undercover agent posing as a procurement officer of the government of Argentina to induce the agent to purchase garbage incinerators on behalf of Argentina. To disguise the offered payments, Tannenbaum allegedly opened a bank account in the name of a fictitious entity. Tannenbaum eventually entered into a plea agreement with the DOJ.

33 Above note 5. Of particular note, in determining to accept ABB's settlement offer, the SEC considered the full cooperation that ABB provided to the SEC staff during its investigation and, as well, the fact that ABB brought the matter to the attention to the SEC and DOJ.

contracts; and (3) to implement a robust internal compliance program which is monitored by a World Bank-approved compliance monitor.[34] The World Bank promises that the disclosures are confidential and will not be identified to the exporter's national authorities. Needless to say, without a similar program in Canada, a Canadian exporter would be foolhardy to make such a disclosure to the World Bank, as the consequences from an accidental disclosure to Canadian authorities could be severe.[35]

Ensure a Robust Code of Conduct

Senior management needs to create a robust employee training program to properly educate employees about what is, or is not, a bribe. Although many Canadian companies have adopted codes of conduct and guidelines regarding improper payments, they rarely provide active training, monitoring, and auditing of the codes. Consequently, few employees have the tools and the confidence needed to ensure that bribes do not get paid.

Most employees (and uneducated management) are, without ample and specific training, relatively happy to either facilitate or to turn a blind eye to the indications of improper payments. "Our competitors do it" is the oft-relied upon mantra, which is regrettably, and likely, quite true. However, given the consequences of this sort of wilful blindness, a decision to allow this sort of conduct is one that only senior management should make. If they are prepared to make such a decision, it should only be on the basis that they are prepared to risk serving time in a Canadian prison for so doing.

For example, simply telling employees that they must comply with the *CFPOA* gives them very little true guidance, as most laypeople can apply the "grease payment" exception to almost any improper payment. Some companies take a hard line, prohibiting "grease payments" entirely. However, there are many circumstances, such as emergencies, where a "grease payment" will be made regardless of what is in the code of conduct. Thus, a

---

[34] The World Bank's Voluntary Disclosure Program is available at http://web.worldbank.org/WBSITE/EXTERNAL/EXTABOUTUS/ORGANIZATION/ORGUNITS/EXTDOII/EXTVOLDISPRO/0,,contentMDK:20996886~menuPK:2720524~pagePK:64168445~piPK:64168309~theSitePK:2720459,00.html (as viewed February 8, 2009).

[35] Despite the author's viewpoint, the author was recently informed by Acting Manager of the World Bank's Voluntary Disclosure Program (VDP) that many companies have made voluntary disclosures during the World Bank's four-year pilot VDP.

much more comprehensive understanding is required at all levels of the organization.[36]

Those Canadian export company employees who are already responsible for compliance should take note of *SEC v. Pillor*.[37] In that recent case, a director and former senior vice-president for sales at InVision Technologies[38] who was responsible for internal *FCPA* compliance, faced charges by the SEC for failure to establish adequate internal controls. It was alleged that he received emails from regional sales managers that indicated that improper payments were going to be made by the company's foreign agents. He neglected to take action to address the emails and approved payments to the agents without further inquiry. The case was settled by Pillor paying a civil penalty and agreeing to an injunction.

Put Proper Systems in Place

When engaging an agent in a foreign country, it is not enough to simply demand that the agent not pay bribes. While this demand can (and should) be entrenched in a company's standard agency agreement,[39] a company must put in place proper guidelines for the actual appointment of agents and anyone else who earns commissions or payments related to sales. These guidelines should commence with a formal procedure to question the rationale for appointing the agent, the purpose being to ensure that the agent has the requisite skills and background to legitimately make the sales. Thereafter, substantive due diligence must be performed to determine where the agent's business premises are located, who the agent's partners are, what the agent's history and track record is, and whether the agent is of good

---

36 For example, as found in General Electric's policy on Improper Payments: "**NEVER GIVE A GRATUITY** or other payment to government officials or employees to expedite a routine administrative action without fully disclosing it to the GE National Executive or GE legal counsel." (http://www.ge.com/files_citizenship/pdf/TheSpirit& TheLetter.pdf, viewed on February 16, 2009).

37 Case No. 06-4906 (N.D. Cal. Aug. 15, 2006) (Complaint); SEC Lit. Rel. 19803 (Aug. 14, 2006).

38 See the related case at note 29, above.

39 An example of a minimum clause is the following, which is required by CIDA to be inserted into all contracts with it:

> "No offer, gift or payment, consideration or benefit of any kind, which constitutes an illegal or corrupt practice, has or will be made to anyone, either directly or indirectly, as an inducement or reward for the award or execution of this contract/contribution agreement. Any such practice will be grounds for terminating this contract/contribution agreement or taking any other corrective action as required." See http://www.acdi-cida.gc.ca/CIDAWEB/acdicida.nsf/En/REN-218124737-P7R#sec5 (as viewed February 9, 2009). The author has developed a series of more detailed clauses.

repute.[40] The due diligence must also confirm that the agent does not employ government officials or individuals related to a government official. A company does not want to learn, too late, that its agent in a foreign country is, for example, the spouse of the country's Minister of Public Works.[41]

In addition to checking for evidence that the agent's background, references, and "connections" were regularly investigated and found to be satisfactory, the exporter must also look for tell-tale signs of corruption which include out-of-the-ordinary commissions or fees, and payments to unrelated off-shore accounts.[42] What may be deemed ordinary depends on the circumstances. For example, in some countries and industries, a 5 per cent com-

---

[40] For example, below is an excerpt of a due diligence checklist currently used by a U.S. defense contractor (as modified by the author):

- Analysis of business case for engaging intermediary, and selection criteria review;
- Compensation comparable analysis;
- List of all owners, directors, officers, partners, key employees;
- Past or current government employment;
- Family members in government employment or office (note: consider definition of "family");
- Political party officials or candidates;
- Public media search;
- Public record search;
- Financial and business references;
- Local law requirements: registrations, permits, commission disclosure, residency, and citizenship;
- Most anti-corruption practitioners have developed a very detailed initial questionnaire to consider a new intermediary.

[41] For example, see In *the Matter of BellSouth Corp.*, Exchange Act Release No. 45279 (Jan. 15, 2002). A Nicaraguan law prohibited foreign companies such as BellSouth from acquiring a majority interest in Nicaraguan telecommunications. BellSouth's Nicaraguan subsidiary, retained the services of the wife of the Nicaraguan legislator who was the chairman of the Nicaraguan legislative committee with oversight of Nicaraguan telecommunications. The wife lobbied for repeal of the foreign ownership restriction. During the lobbyist's retention, the legislator/husband drafted the text of the proposed repeal of the foreign ownership restriction and enlisted support for the proposed repeal from other committee members. They were successful. BellSouth settled with the SEC, and consented to a judgment directing it to pay a $150,000 penalty.

[42] From *EDC's Guide for Canadian Exporters*, http://www.edc.ca/english/docs/csr_anticorruption_e.pdf (as viewed February 15, 2009).

Warning Signs of Corruption

The following signs may indicate that your business has been exposed to corruption. These examples are only a few of the possible indications of commercial impropriety:

- unusually high profit margins;
- substantial and unjustified agent commissions;
- business arrangements with no obvious commercial purpose;
- requests for compensation for unspecified or questionable services such as introductions and special treatment.

mission is normal; in others, 15 per cent might not be unusual. Distribution agreements also need to be examined as these can effectively be agency agreements under a different guise.

What level of investigation is enough to be satisfactory? That depends on the circumstances. For agents working in countries that are ranked high on Transparency International's Corruption Perceptions Index, or in those industries which are known for having corruption issues, a more intense investigation will be required.[43] A good way to formalize the process is to create a due diligence checklist.

None of the required information is difficult to ascertain. For example, TRACE, a U.S. not-for-profit industry organization, provides a due diligence service as part of its membership fee although, in some cases, a more thorough level of due diligence may need to be performed. Surprisingly, while due diligence is relatively easy to perform, many Canadian companies still do not realize the need for doing it. Other companies conduct initial due diligence but are unaware that it must be updated on a regular basis. For example, if the agent is a corporation, changes in the shareholders and employees of the corporation may be important and relevant.

Even Canadian companies already cognizant of the need for due diligence still frequently encounter situations where their salespeople need to rush through a quick payment to an agent in order to facilitate an unexpected sale. The rationale for not undertaking the due diligence in advance is that companies may have a large number of agents who never make a sale, and do not wish to go through the process of due diligence until an agent actually produces a customer. This creates a strong momentum inside the company to process the payment and worry about the law afterwards. Before making payments to an agent, an exporter must have in place a control mechanism that is outside the influence of the company's sales personnel. Ideally, whenever a payment is to be made to an agent, a senior non-sales member of management should sign a confirmation that there is a valid agency agreement in place, due diligence has been undertaken on the agent within the previous year, the payment is being made to the agent's home country (or, if not, there is a valid reason for making the payment elsewhere), and that there are no other red flags.

---

43 For example, in *SEC v. Ashland Oil, Inc.*, 18 Sec. Reg. & L. Rep. (BNA) 1006 (July 11, 1986), the SEC alleged that Ashland Oil purchased a nearly worthless chromite mine owned by a foreign official for approximately $25M to obtain crude oil contracts with Oman Refining Company, and instrumentality of the Omani government.

A recent English case highlights the need for proper procedures. In early 2009, the British Financial Services Authority fined Aon Limited £5.25M for failing to take reasonable care to establish and maintain effective systems and controls to counter the risks of bribery associated with making payments to overseas firms and individuals.[44] In its Final Notice of Penalty, the FSA listed four failings of Aon in connection with its dealings with foreign agents, as follows:

1. Its payment procedures did not require adequate levels of due diligence to be carried out, before the relationship was commenced;
2. It failed to monitor its relationships with its agents in respect of specific bribery risks after the initial relationship was set up;
3. It did not provide its staff in business divisions which dealt with agents with sufficient guidance or training on the bribery and corruption risks involved in such dealings; and
4. It failed to ensure that the committees it appointed to oversee these risks received relevant management information or otherwise routinely assessed whether bribery and corruption risks were being managed effectively.[45]

Not surprisingly, most Canadian companies do not have these controls in place. As a consequence, by the time the company President learns the company has been making payments to offshore accounts in Cyprus, Bahamas, or any other jurisdiction unconnected to the agent, it will be too late. Even when such controls are in place, the sales employees of the company need to understand that it is very difficult, if not impossible, to conduct "on the spot" satisfactory due diligence of an agent.[46] Proposed sales should be summarily rejected unless the due diligence is in place.

Exercise Restraint

The fourth pillar is restraint. While there are many who believe that good business can be done in any country, it truly depends upon the industry, the nature of the goods, and whether the sale is vital to the foreign country, as to whether corruption can be truly be avoided. In the experience of many seasoned international businesspeople, there are many countries where business cannot be done without participating in corruption, either directly or blindly. Business with those countries should be avoided as the Canadian

---

44 Press release, January 8, 2009. http://www.fsa.gov.uk/pages/Library/Communication/PR/2009/004.shtml (viewed February 15, 2009).

45 Final Notice. http://www.fsa.gov.uk/pubs/final/aon.pdf (viewed February 15, 2009).

46 One major U.S. defense contractor's legal counsel has told the author that it takes their company about one year to approve a new agent.

anti-corruption legislation carries with it a criminal penalty of up to five years in jail.[47] In the U.S., business executives in breach of the *FCPA* are sent to prison on a fairly frequent basis.

There are also civil consequences to consider. Directors and officers may be liable to shareholders for failure to protect the company's assets. The company itself can be held accountable by the foreign government. Recently, Siemens AG, one of the world's largest engineering firms, pleaded guilty in the U.S. to paying over USD$1.4 billion in direct bribes to government officials around the world in return for business. It was fined approximately the same amount, the largest fine in U.S. history. What was interesting about this case is that the corruption by Siemens spanned several decades in multiple operating groups and regions. The most senior echelons of management in Siemens were revealed to have knowingly circumvented or failed to implement internal controls. The consequences to them and the company were severe. In addition to the fines, all senior management lost their jobs and several face criminal charges. Almost all of the board of directors of Siemens AG was replaced, and the company has sued the past directors for its loss.

Jail and fines are not the only penalties. A conviction could result in debarment of the company from government and World Bank procurement. Additionally, as bribes are not deductible,[48] the exporter will be required to restate its financial statements, pay the necessary tax, [49] and suffer the related consequences.

---

47 *CFPOA*, ss. 3(2): Every person who contravenes subsection (1) is guilty of an indictable offence and liable to imprisonment for a term not exceeding five years.

48 The *Income Tax Act* of Canada permitted bribes to be deducted until it was amended following an embarrassing question in the House of Commons in 1990 concerning the permissive deductibility of bribes. Until then, as provided for in Information Circular 76-4R2, dated January 31, 1986, Article 5, under the heading "Kickbacks, Bribes, Etc.," provided as follows:

> "An unvouchered expenditure that may be described as an "under-the-table" payment is not deductible unless the following conditions are met:
>
> (a) the recipient thereof is identified, and
>
> (b) the expenditure was made or incurred to earn income and the amount was reasonable in the circumstances."

49 *Income Tax Act* of Canada, ss. 67.5(1): "In computing income, no deduction shall be made in respect of an outlay made or expense incurred for the purpose of doing anything that is an offence under section 3 of the *Corruption of Foreign Public Officials Act* or under any of the sections 119 to 121, 123 to 125, 393 and 426 of the *Criminal Code*, or an offence under section 465 of the *Criminal Code* as it relates to an offence described in any of those sections.

Conclusion

Troubled times make for hard business decisions when it comes to ethical and moral conduct. However, when it comes to participating in corruption, the legal consequences in Canada leave little room for Canadian businesspeople to take chances. For those Canadian companies choosing to engage in international business, without taking care to ensure that the proper structures and processes are in place in Canada, the risk of corruption will remain a risk that may greatly outweigh the benefit.

Fraud Detection for Business Valuators in an Increasingly Complex World

Gary Moulton & Peter Dent

Introduction

Business valuators must be increasingly adept at both knowing, and spotting, the risks of fraud and that someone may be "cooking the books". If the risk of fraud is ignored, the valuator may find their analyses skewed by fraudulent financial reporting. Compounding the ever-present risk of financial statement fraud, a slowing economy may increase pressure on companies to meet, and even exceed, short-term performance goals or to demonstrate that shareholder value has improved due to management's leadership. Despite the stringent *Sarbanes-Oxley Act* ("SOX"), enacted to ensure publicly traded companies have robust fraud prevention and detection protocols, fraud and other business crime continues to be a major problem for business and it is likely on the increase because of the deteriorating economic environment.

Interestingly, SOX came into being after the last economic downturn, between 1999 and 2001, during which numerous financial reporting fraud scandals rocked public confidence in the financial markets. If past experience is any indicator, then we should expect a tumultuous next few years as similar schemes are laid bare, and desperate people engage in high-risk activities, during the current financial crisis. Given the risks noted above, the business valuator's effectiveness will increasingly depend on the efficacy of an entity's anti-fraud programs and controls, as well as the valuator's familiarity with the fraud schemes typically committed and the industry specific differences in those schemes.

Financial reporting scandals are still occurring and, in the past few months, a number of major Ponzi schemes have come to light, costing investors millions of dollars. Also, the number of foreign corruption investigations is increasing. Therefore, fraud will continue to be a costly risk of doing business and, like all risks, must be contained to the extent possible.

Types of Fraud and Why Fraud Happens

Fraud generally refers to deliberate misstatements in financial reporting, a misappropriation of assets that have a material impact on financial statements, or corruption schemes carried out by management. All of these types of fraud should be of concern to the business valuator.

Fraud occurs because of the presence of three factors; opportunity, motivating pressures and incentives, and rationalization on the part of the perpetrator. Many organizations have controls in place to minimize the opportunity for fraud to happen and to deter illegal activity. Fraud happens when these controls are ineffective, when they break down - a not uncommon occurrence - or when they are overridden by members of senior management and others in a position of trust. The fraudster often operates in an environment where they perceive a low likelihood of detection. Obviously, in smaller, privately-owned businesses, the opportunity for fraud to occur is exacerbated because of the control exerted by the owners, the lack of segregation of duties, and the likelihood that the financial reporting regime is relatively unsophisticated.

Motivating pressures and incentives includes situations where the perpetrator stands to gain financially from the fraud. The objective of a business owner requiring a valuation of their business is to achieve a result that is in their personal best interest. When selling to a third party, the business owner's motivation would be to obtain the highest valuation possible to increase the sales price. On the other hand, in a divorce proceeding, the business owner's motivation may be to understate the value of the business. In both scenarios, the business owner may resort to "cooking the books" to make it appear that the business is more or less valuable than it really is. This can present a major problem to the business valuator in evaluating the quality and accuracy of the financial information provided by the business. The valuator must be skeptical that the information provided may have been misstated or fraudulently represented by the owner in order to achieve the result desired by the owner.

Perpetrators of fraud have a tendency to rationalize their behavior as something other than criminal. They often make statements like:

"I needed to make my financial plan."

"If everybody takes something it's not fraud."

"I was going to pay it back."

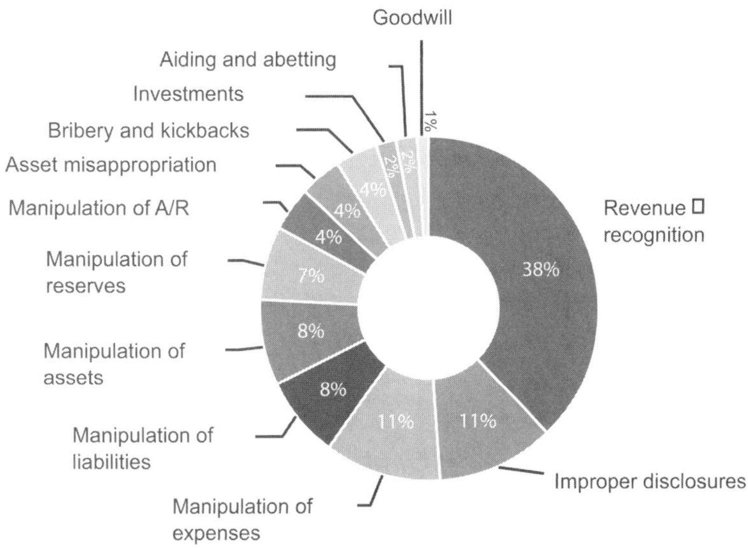

Financial Reporting Fraud

In the context of valuing a business, the business owner will have a very personal view as to the value of the business and may therefore rationalize his or her behavior when it comes to producing financial information concerning the business. This could cause the person to rationalize a wholly unrealistic value and, therefore, manipulate the financial results to achieve their objective.

Deloitte recently issued a study on fraud based on a review of data maintained by the U.S. Securities and Exchange Commission from January 2000 to December 2007.[1] The study found that revenue recognition fraud schemes continued to be the most common type of financial reporting fraud. Manipulation schemes involving accounts receivable, other assets, expenses, liabilities, and reserves, were also prevalent. While bribery and kickbacks accounted for a relatively small percentage of the schemes, this category saw an increase in the more recent years of the study. Improper

[1] "Ten things about financial statement fraud-second edition" © Deloitte & Touche LLP December 2008.

disclosures were also common. This often happens because of related party transactions which are not carried out at fair market value.

The study found that the most common types of revenue recognition fraud included:

- recording fictitious revenue
- recognizing inappropriate revenue from swaps, round-tripping, or barter arrangements
- recognizing revenue despite unresolved contingencies
- recognizing revenue from sales billed but not shipped ("bill and hold")
- recognizing revenue despite lack of delivery, incomplete delivery, or lack of customer acceptance
- accounting improperly for (or failure to reserve properly against) refunds, exchanges, cancellations, refusals, or returns

The study found that financial reporting fraud occurred in virtually all industries. The technology, media and telecommunications industries, and consumer business industry accounted for two-thirds of the fraud schemes identified, followed by manufacturing, life sciences and health care, financial services, energy and resources, real estate, aviation, and transportation.

In addition to frauds involving revenue recognition, expenditures of a business may also be fraudulently misstated by a business owner in order to skew a valuation of the business. The amount of compensation taken by the business owner might be over- or under-stated. Management compensation may be hidden in other accounts or funds may be removed from the business through lavish perks and expense accounts, meaning the business may actually be more or less profitable than the reported financial results would indicate. Personal expenses may be buried in the business accounts.

Intercompany transactions are often not transacted at fair market value. For example, real estate, operating machinery, and office equipment shared among various related businesses could mean that an inappropriate splitting of costs among the businesses, leading to an incorrect valuation of one or more components of the business. Undisclosed related party transactions could also lead to inappropriate valuations, for example, consulting contract arrangements between the business and related parties that are not carried out at market value. It is important that the business valuator be able to identify transactions with related parties, determine whether they were carried out at fair market value, and consider that, if they were not, was this deliberate on the part of the owner in order to fraudulently portray the financial requests of the business.

The deliberate use of inappropriate accounting policies can also lead to an incorrect business valuation. Examples could include revenue recognition policies that recognize revenue prematurely, expense policies that either write off the costs of assets too quickly or too slowly, and the non-segregation of unusual or non-recurring revenues and expenses from regular profit and loss calculations. There could also be assets and liabilities recorded in the business that really are personal in nature to the owners, for example, on the asset side, real estate, or works of art, or loans that were used by the owner to finance the acquisition of personal assets rather than business assets. Reserves, such as bad debt reserves, may be deliberately over- or under-stated to adjust the valuation.

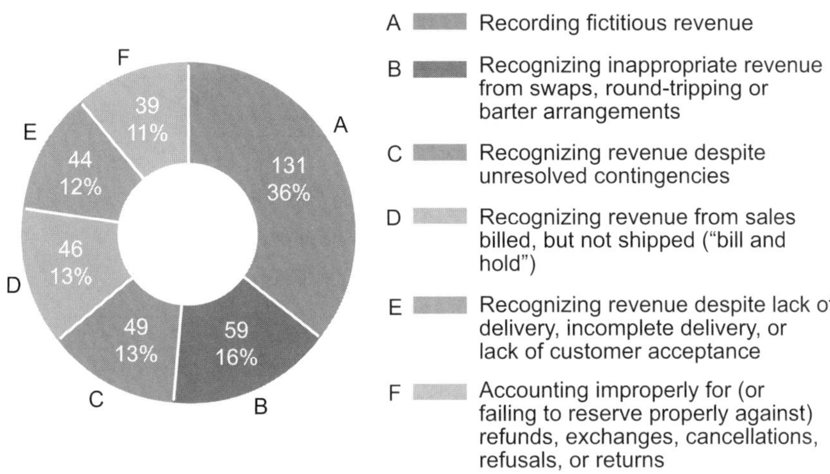

Bribery and Corruption Risks

If the business being purchased operates internationally, and especially if it sells goods or services to foreign governments, it is possible that illegal acts (foreign corruption) have occurred and that there could be expensive regulatory or enforcement investigation consequences down the road. Therefore, the business valuator should be aware of the types of business the company is involved with internationally, assess the risk of corruption, and investigate the books and records to identify possible illicit payments made by the company to obtain business in the foreign jurisdiction.

The True Cost of Fraud

The cost of fraudulent activities goes well beyond the actual dollars lost. Significant investigation and legal costs are often incurred by the company, especially if the nature of the fraud is such that regulators or law enforcement agencies are also investigating. This is especially true of financial reporting fraud engaged in by the company itself through its top management. In these cases, the victims can be public shareholders, lenders, and other creditors, prospective purchasers, in other words, those who relied on the financial disclosures made by the company. There can be serious damage done to the company's reputation and credibility and, in some cases, its ability to carry on.

On the other hand, frauds resulting from the misappropriation of assets victimize the company itself. These frauds are usually carried out by employees or outsiders in collusion with employees and often are the direct result of a breakdown in basic internal controls, such as a proper segregation of duties. As discussed above, of particular concern to the business valuator would be assets of a business that are misappropriated through related party transactions not carried out at fair market value or compensation paid to the owners that is excessive.

Anti-Fraud Regimes

Since fraud can take many shapes and forms, and materiality can be both quantitative and qualitative in nature, management of a business should consider all types when designing and implementing anti-fraud programs and controls, including:

- fraudulent financial reporting
  - improper revenue recognition
  - improper capitalization of expenses
  - improper asset valuation
  - related party transactions
- misappropriation of assets
- improper or unauthorized expenditures (including bribery and other improper payment schemes)
- self-dealings (including kickbacks)
- violations of laws and regulations (including those that expose the company or its agents to regulatory or criminal actions)

A company's anti-fraud efforts should be focused in the following areas:

- a Formal Fraud Risk Assessment program
- a Whistleblower program
- a Code of Conduct
- a process for reporting through the audit committee and the board of directors
- proactive fraud detection methodologies

1. *A formal fraud risk assessment*: There is no single, standard method that an organization should follow with regards to a fraud risk assessment. The goal of any formal, systematic fraud risk assessment is to evaluate risk factors, detect possible fraud schemes and scenarios, and prioritize identified fraud risks. With this information in hand, management can then evaluate whether existing controls will be effective or if new controls must be designed and implemented.

Management has the primary responsibility for performing fraud risk assessments. However, most material frauds have been directed by management – at least in part – and detected by employees and/or those responsible for corporate governance at other levels in the organization. It is therefore critical that employees outside of management are involved in the fraud risk assessment.

A fraud risk assessment should include business process owners or those who have significant knowledge, control, or influence over the activities within a significant business process or cycle. The fraud risk assessment should also involve IT management, as some fraud schemes are enabled by the disabling or circumventing of information system controls. Additionally, internal audit should have an active role in the development, monitoring, and ongoing evaluation of fraud risk assessments. Finally, the audit committee or the board of directors should evaluate management's identification of fraud risks, and should have an active role in the oversight of the fraud risk assessment process.

For companies operating in multiple jurisdictions, the fraud risk assessment must take into account additional threats and regulatory issues. Not only is the likelihood of victimization greater, these companies face a greater risk of unknowingly participating in fraudulent activity. The more geographically diverse a company's business activities – the greater the challenge and the risk. Organizations operating in foreign locations – especially in emerging economies – need to implement adequate programs and controls to prevent fraud, bribery, and corruption from the perspective of both victim and perpetrator. Given the sense of urgency felt within the international community, the level of scrutiny that companies face will continue to increase. If a company is operating in an environment where corruption is widespread, it may be embedded in the local business processes and thus extremely difficult to identify. Unfortunately, this makes it no less dangerous to a company's reputation and vitality.

2. *A "whistleblower" program*: Most fraud surveys indicate that the most common way for fraud to be uncovered is through whistleblowers. Public companies are required to implement whistleblowing mechanisms, and private and not-for-profit organizations are increasingly adopting them as well. These initiatives must be robust in nature – an information line

or answering machine will not suffice. Companies must be able to demonstrate the effectiveness of their whistleblower program in terms of education and training for employees, ease of use, monitoring, and follow-up.

The hotline, a method for accepting information on a confidential basis, should be accessible to all employees. Those companies looking to go beyond mere compliance with this requirement may opt to broaden access to vendors, customers, and agents, and encourage them to report inappropriate activity. The program must also include specific procedures to ensure that proper follow-up occurs for allegations received. Additionally, once the occurrence of unethical or inappropriate activity has been identified, a whistleblower program must ensure the evidence is collected and preserved in an appropriate and consistent manner suitable for further action.

3. *A code of conduct*: A company's code of conduct or ethics is often the first line of communication concerning its philosophy on fraud prevention and, therefore, considered obligatory for creating a strong internal control environment – and for preventing fraud. While a code of conduct outlining ethical behavior standards may seem to state the obvious, distinguishing black and white from grey – even for seasoned business executives – is more difficult today than ever before. Language barriers, cultural differences, and even observed precedence make the need for spelling out the difference between right and wrong a critically important exercise. As companies develop a code, they should consider the following suggestions:
   - Convene a team that draws from a cross-section of departments, titles, and locations.
   - Keep language simple and concise. Avoid jargon and "legalese".
   - Don't write the code in a "Thou Shalt Not" format; instead, state expected behavior.
   - Apply the code equally to all employees and board members across divisions and geographies.
   - Revise and update the code as needed to reflect changes to the business and regulatory changes.

Simply having a good code of conduct is not enough. It must be understood, accepted, and used. When introducing the code, a letter from management can set the tone by defining the importance of ethics and compliance for each and every employee and for the company as a whole. It should be described as a guide for helping employees make the right choices in the context of the company's mission statement, vision, and values.

To make the code of conduct even more proactive, it should be presented with a list of resources for obtaining guidance and for reporting suspected misconduct, such as:

- anonymous reporting mechanism; employee hotline; whistleblower line
- ethics and compliance officer/office
- reporting chain of command (*e.g.*, supervisor, department head)
- ethics and compliance intranet site

It should also explain enforcement and implementation mechanisms - details of disciplinary actions that will be applied to unethical behavior, and circumstances that would result in termination. Finally, the code of conduct should provide examples of acceptable and unacceptable behavior.

4. *Oversight by the audit committee and board of directors*: Understanding and assessing the effectiveness of anti-fraud programs and controls is a key component of the audit committee's responsibilities. To demonstrate their oversight of anti-fraud activities, the audit committee should go beyond mere review to challenge management on the identification of fraud risks and the effectiveness of control activities. As the occurrence of significant fraud can frequently be attributed to an override of internal controls by employees, the audit committee plays an important role in ensuring that internal controls address the appropriate risk areas and are functioning as designed. The audit committee should also ensure that the organization has implemented an effective ethics and compliance program, and that it is periodically tested.

5. *Proactive fraud detection methodologies*: Computerized processes in all sizes of organisations generate data that can be mined for many reasons, including searching for fraudulent transactions. Data mining is efficient and enables faster testing, reduces the risk of error, and enables repeat testing. Data mining enables 100 per cent testing of the population, rather than drawing conclusions based on a sample of items and allows the observation of patterns and trends that could not have been detected through sample testing. An example of where data mining for fraud can be helpful is in the area of procurement. A common fraud is the creation of a fictitious vendor by an employee which is used to extract funds from the company. The employee will keep the size of individual transactions below certain approval thresholds in order to avoid scrutiny. Data mining can help easily identify transactions with this type of characteristic for followup. Being proactive about detecting fraud in and of itself can act as a deterrent to others in the organization who may have been inclined to engage in this behavior.

An effective anti-fraud program will include the elements listed above, and strive for continuous improvement by reflecting information obtained through the monitoring process. The primary goal of anti-fraud activities is to prevent, deter, and detect fraudulent financial activity and the misappropriation of assets. However, a vibrant and effective anti-fraud program will not only provide a company with a robust foundation for continued economic viability, it will go a long way towards demonstrating to external parties that the company "did all it could". In today's zero-tolerance and highly complex business environment, that's the new cost of doing business.

Summary

In summary, the business valuator should always ask the following questions when considering the risk of fraud:

- What are the opportunities, motivation, and rationalizations of the owner of the business being valued that could lead to fraud?
- What are the typical methods used by fraudsters to misstate financial results or misappropriate assets from a business?
- If the business operates internationally, what is the risk that it has been involved in corruption?
- If the business is of a size that it has implemented an anti-fraud program, is the program effective?

Contributors

Dalton J. Albrecht, BBA (Hons.), LLB (Gold Medalist), LLM (Harvard), Dip. Inter. Law, (Hague) is a Partner and Chair of the Commodity Tax, Customs and International Trade Group of Miller Thomson LLP. Dalton specializes in all aspects of international trade law including anti-dumping, countervail and NAFTA and WTO/GATT related matters, including trade and investment and trade in services. His other areas of practice include customs law value for duty, origin of goods, tariff classification and duty relief matters, export and import controls, and goods and services tax (GST) and provincial sales tax planning and dispute resolution matters. Dalton appears regularly on behalf of clients before the Canadian International Trade Tribunal, the Tax Court of Canada, the Federal Court of Canada, and provincial courts. Dalton has been featured in the UK publication *Chambers* 2006-2009 *Global Guide to the World's Leading Lawyers* for WTO/International Trade. Dalton is also profiled in the 2008-2009 Lexpert/American *Lawyer Guide to the Leading 500 Lawyers in Canada* in the Commodity Tax and the International Trade practice areas and in the Who's Who of World's Leading Trade & Customs Lawyers, 2008-2009. Dalton has also been recently featured in *Best Lawyers in America*, Canada Edition, 2009-2010.

John J. Barton, ASA, CPA, is responsible for the analysis and valuation of closely-held equities and intangible assets. He also provides expert witness testimony in litigation matters. Since 1987, John has been involved in the valuation of over 500 business entities, ranging in size from small sole proprietorships to multinational corporations. He has provided valuation and litigation support services across a wide spectrum of manufacturing, retail, and service industries, including companies in the health care, insurance, construction, apparel, and automotive markets. John has been qualified as an expert valuation witness in courts in Pennsylvania, New Jersey, and Florida as well as in U.S. Federal District Court. In addition to litigation support, he has been involved in valuations for the purposes of sale, restructuring, goodwill impairment, and estate planning. Before starting BVC, John was Vice President at Murray, Devine & Company, a valuation firm providing financial and security services to corporate and individual clients. At Murray, Devine, John was responsible for providing both valuations as well as other financial consulting services. John holds a Masters in Business Administration from La Salle University as well as an M.A. from Fordham University. He is also a Certified Public Accountant and a senior member of the American Society of Appraisers (ASA). John currently serves as the Chairman of the ASA's Business Valuation Committee. He is a past member of the ASA's Education Committee where he was charge of course content and development for the ASA's business valuation educational program. John is an instructor of Finance in Villanova University's MBA Program and also teaches business valuation courses for the ASA.

Tarsem Basraon is an Associate in the Miller Thomson LLP tax group. Tarsem's practice focuses on tax litigation, commodity tax and international trade. Tarsem has assisted on cases heard before the Tax Court of Canada and dumping cases before the Canadian International Trade Tribunal. Tarsem has also been involved in various writing projects and has published articles in such newsletters as Mann's Technology Newsletter and the Miller Thomson LLP International Trade, Customs and Commodity Tax Bulletin. He obtained his Bachelor of Business Administration from Wilfrid Laurier University in 2005 and his LL.B. from the University of Western Ontario in 2008 and has also successfully completed the Canadian Securities Course. Prior to joining Miller Thomson for his articles in 2008, Tarsem worked as a junior financial analyst at a Fortune 500 Company. Tarsem has also been involved with the incorporation of a bio-diesel company in addition to creating its projected financial statements and investor packages.

Dominic C. Belley is a Partner with Ogilvy Renault LLP. He practises in the area of tax litigation as it relates to income tax and commodity taxes. He is generally involved for long periods of time in files that have entailed the representation of taxpayers before the Court of Québec, the Quebec Superior Court, the Quebec Court of Appeal, the Tax Court of Canada, the Federal Court of Appeal, and the Supreme Court of Canada. His expertise pertains more particularly to deductibility of business expenses and of interest, depreciation, amortization and pension costs, transfer of paid-up capital, lifting of the corporate veil, capital tax, rectification of commercial transactions and corporate records, cancellation of dividends, determination of worker status, liability of corporate directors, challenges to sample-based and net-worth assessments and application of the general anti-avoidance rule. Mr. Belley also represents taxpayers before the tax authorities in connection with requests for advance rulings, audits, objections to assessments, and voluntary disclosure. In addition, he represents tax and accounting professionals in actions for professional negligence.

Christophe Bergeron is a director in the corporate finance practice of Deloitte in Sydney, Australia. He has an Honours Bachelor of Commerce degree and a Master of Applied Finance. Christophe joined the Australian practice in 2007, after spending approximately five years in Deloitte's financial advisory group in Paris, France. Christophe has extensive valuation experience in providing services to both private and public companies in connection with mergers and acquisitions, corporate restructuring and financial reporting under IFRS and U.S. GAAP. He has provided valuation services across a number of industries, including mining and resources, financial services, media, technology, consumer business and manufacturing.

Monty Bhardwaj is a senior manager in Deloitte's valuations practice in the Greater Toronto Private Company Services group. He is qualified as a Chartered Business Valuator and a Chartered Accountant with a specialist in Investigative and Forensic Accounting. He has conducted litigation and valuation assignments involving the quantification of economic loss (under tort, breach of contract, product liability, patent infringement etc), valuation of shareholdings in minority oppression cases, purchase and sale of businesses, purchase price allocation and goodwill impairment. He has also been involved with numerous due diligence reviews, and intellectual property cases. Monty has over twelve years of industry experience, including the assurance and advisory of insurance, construction, manufacturing, not- for-profit organizations and real estate companies.

Guido Dalla Bona is a director in the Valuation Services practice of Deloitte in Argentina and LATCO organization. Guido has over thirteen years' experience in the valuation industry where he has performed more than 400 engagements in all Latin America. His experience includes business valuations, as well as tangible and intangible assets valuations, for clients from different industries. Guido is also a frequent speaker, and author on valuation topics.

Jennifer Boundy is a senior manager with Deloitte's National Transfer Pricing Group in Canada. Jennifer holds a Chartered Financial Analyst designation and a Master of Tax. Jennifer has extensive experience as a transfer pricing specialist with the international tax practice of Toronto office of Deloitte. Jennifer has assisted numerous multinational companies across various industries in establishing, implementing and defending their transfer pricing policies.

Ryan Brain is a Partner in Deloitte's Financial Advisory group, and he leads the firm's Performance Enhancement services across the Canada. Ryan has extensive and diverse project experience including Board and stakeholder advisory, informal restructuring and turn-arounds, commercial due diligence, 100 day planning, and a variety of cost reduction initiatives. Ryan has worked on a number of complex and high-profile projects across various industries, with a particular emphasis on Consumer Business industries. He had advised Boards of Directors, Private Equity, Commercial Banks, Provincial and Federal Governments, and a variety of Executives across a series of business and market challenges. Projects include work for the Board of Trustees for XS Cargo Income Fund, advising the Federal Government on Air Canada's restructuring and current government funding to the automotive industry, and turnaround and performance improvement initiatives with SC Johnson, Labatt, Coors, McCain Foods, West 49, Grand & Toy, ED Smith, Grocery Gateway, Hudson's Bay Company, and a series of other public and private organizations. Ryan is a Certified Management Consultant (CMC), and has his Masters of Management Science (MMSc) from the University of Waterloo.

Anil Chawla is a Partner with Deloitte based in Mississauga and specializing in Manufacturing and leads our Greater Toronto Area SR&ED tax practice. Anil has 24 years of experience including 10 years as a tax partner and 21 years as a tax specialist. He has experience in dealing with complex tax issues for corporations in the manufacturing and high tech areas, personal tax and financial planning with an emphasis on tax planning for professionals, Scientific Research and Experimental Development (SR&ED) Tax Incentives as well as Corporate tax compliance and planning.

Minghai Chen, PhD, deputy director, professional standards department, China Appraisal Society. Worked in the Chinese Institute of Certified Public Accountants for five years. In 2000,Minghai joined the China Appraisal Society to develop China Valuation Standards.

David W. Chodikoff, BA (Spec. Hons.), MA, LLB, is a Partner of Miller Thomson LLP specializing in tax litigation (civil and criminal) and international tax dispute resolution. David was a solicitor, a tax litigation lawyer, and Crown prosecutor with the Department of Justice (Canada) for over 15 years. He has conducted hundreds of court bases and has over 80 reported decisions. David is the conceptualizer, co-editor, and contributor to *Advocacy & Taxation in Canada* (Irwin Law, 2004); co-editor and contributor to *Taxation & Valuation of Technology* (Irwin Law, 2008); and the senior Canadian editor of *The Tax Advisor's Guide to the Canada-U.S. Tax Treaty* (Thomson Carswell, 2 volume, looseleaf, 2008-). David is a member of the Editorial Board of *It's Personal (Preserving Wealth for People and Private Companies)*. Since 2006, David has served on the Executive of the Tax Section of the Ontario Bar Association. David continues to work on a number of books scheduled to be published in 2011. He is the author of the forthcoming books entitled: *Tax Evasion and the Demise of Global Banking Secrecy: A Canadian Analysis* and *Canadian Tax Litigation: The Courts, The Law and Practice.*

Shlomo (Sam) Cohen was born in Israel. He studied mechanical engineering at the prestigious *Technion Institute* of technology, reaping numerous awards and scholarships. After his service in the army during the Six Day War, Shlomo married Rina, and accepted an engineering position designing equipment for bakeries. His contribution to the company was so valuable that they financed his MBA studies and offered him shares in the firm. He received worldwide recognition for his inventions, and was recruited by Canadian investors to help develop a new food machinery factory. Consequently, he moved his family to Canada, where he designed innovative automatic machines that are used today in the food industry throughout North America. Shlomo and Rina built a successful and rewarding life in Toronto, raising three cherished sons, Oz, Eyal, and Maor.

Vince Conte, CA, CFA, CBV, is a Senior Manager with Deloitte's Financial Advisory practice in Toronto. He specializes in the valuation of business interests and intangible assets for purposes of M&A, restructuring, litigation, taxation and financial reporting. He has also worked in the areas of dispute consulting and forensic investigation and has provided fairness opinions in support of public and private transactions. Industry specialization includes mining, financial services and technology.

Jon G.E. Cooper, MCIT, has been in the Logistics field, actively involved in Human Resources Management, for over 30 years. Jon has served as Director of The Private Motor Truck Council, the Trucking Advisory Council, and the Canadian Trucking Human Resources Council, leveraging his prior operating experience where he ran the Canadian business of a large staffing company.

Gerald D. Courage, B. Comm., LLB LLM (Harvard), is the Chair of Miller Thomson LLP. He has practiced tax law for over 25 years. Gerry's practice covers the full range of taxation and tax-related matters with a primary focus on corporate tax. Gerry has provided advice on domestic and international tax issues and on a number of significant public and private businesses – based in Canada and abroad –and across a wide range of industries. He has particular expertise in the tax aspects of mergers and acquisitions, corporate reorganizations, corporate finance, and business succession planning. Gerry has authored numerous papers and is a much sought after speaker on tax topics.

Shaun R. Darchiville is an Investment Advisor with TD Waterhouse –Private Investment Advice where he specializes in helping his clients manage their wealth and lifestyles. He spends time to ensure that his clients are knowledgeable and comfortable with their investment decisions. Since Shaun entered the investment industry in 1987 he has gained expertise in such areas as individual financial planning, fixed income & equity trading, mergers & acquisitions, corporate finance, and national sales management. He attended Humber College where he focused on management and marketing studies, in addition to obtaining other industry credentials such as Professional Financial Planning and his Life Insurance license. Shaun is also one of the few Investment Advisors in Canada that the *Globe and Mail* uses for their Financial Facelift case study articles. He strives to live a balanced lifestyle making time for his parish, family, and friends. Shaun and his wife Tamara have three children, Kyleigh, Hayden, and Sasha.

Peter Dent is a Partner and the National Leader of Forensic & Dispute Services of Deloitte & Touche LLP based in Toronto. Peter has 15 years of experience practicing in the areas of investigating and providing expert testimony regarding allegations of fraud and corruption with a focus in the global arena, in addition to providing anti-fraud and anti-money laundering management strategies in the public and private sectors. Between 2000 and 2004 Peter was the Team Leader of the Forensic Services Unit within the Department of Institutional Integrity of the World Bank Group in Washington, DC leading international fraud and corruption investigations into World Bank financed projects. Prior to joining Deloitte in 1992, Peter was a Police Constable with the York Regional Police Force. Peter has degrees in Sociology and Commerce from the University of Alberta, and a Law Enforcement Diploma from MacEwan College.

Richard De Rose is a Managing Director in the New York office of Houlihan Lokey Howard & Zukin, where his primary responsibilities providing investment banking, valuation and transactional opinion services. Mr. De Rose is a member of the Firm's Fairness, Solvency and Technical Standards Committees. Prior to joining Houlihan Lokey, Mr. De Rose served as managing director in the Mergers & Acquisitions and Financial Restructuring Groups of Bear, Stearns & Co. Inc. Mr. De Rose began his career as a corporate attorney at Wachtell, Lipton, Rosen & Katz. Mr. De Rose earned a B.A. in philosophy from the University of Pennsylvania, a Ph.D. in philosophy from Brown University and a J.D. from the New York University School of Law. He is a member of the Association of the Bar of the City of New York, the American Bar Association and American Bankruptcy Institute.

John Doma, BBA, CA, is a Partner with Bateman MacKay LLP, working with small and medium enterprises. Since 1987, he has worked with owner managers on various business issues including corporate/personal tax planning, succession planning, cash flow management, and financing. John was an executive member of the Golden Horseshoe Venture Forum, a forum for early stage companies seeking financial assistance. John is a co-founder of Innovation Night, a vehicle which provides access to the Halton Region's thought leaders in start-up strategy. He is also an Independent Review Committee member of the AIC and Copernican Group of Funds.

David A. Douglas, CA, MBA, CIRA, Associate Partner, SR&ED Tax has been with Deloitte for 15 years and is currently an Associate Partner in our SR&ED Tax Practice where he leads the practice's Manufacturing Costing team. David provides leadership in the full range of SR&ED tax and consulting services including opportunity assessments, R&D Industry consultation, claim preparation and review, system installation & training, and audit support expertise. He has financial advisory experience in the life sciences, automotive, food, and general manufacturing industries. To complement a CA designation, he holds an MBA from the Richard Ivey School of Business, and a Diploma in Taxation from the University of Waterloo.

Dr. Muris Dujsic is a Partner with Deloitte's National Transfer Pricing Practice. Muris has assisted numerous multinational companies across various industries in establishing, implementing, and defending their transfer pricing models and policies. He is a frequent speaker at major national and international events and has authored articles on transfer pricing, financial analysis, and economic policy in various Canadian and European scientific and professional publications. Muris was named as one of the World's Leading Transfer Pricing Advisors in the Biannual Euromoney Survey in 2003, 2005 and 2007. Muris is also a member of the Canadian Institute of Chartered Business Valuators.

Richard Ellsworth is a director in the Valuation Services practice of Deloitte Financial Advisory Services LLP in New York City. Rick has over twenty-five years experience in the valuation industry where he has supervised and performed both domestic and international engagements. Rick has authored over ninety articles on valuation topics that have been published in a variety of professional and trade journals. Mr. Ellsworth is a licensed Professional Engineer (PE), an Accredited Senior Appraiser (ASA), a Chartered Financial Analyst (CFA) and a Certified Cost Engineer (CCE). Mr. Ellsworth earned BS and MBA degrees from Lehigh University.

James A. Fraser, BA (Hons.), JD, is an Associate in the Toronto tax group of Miller Thomson LLP. James has a broad tax practice advising both corporations and individuals. James regularly assists clients with tax planning, cross-border tax matters, settlement structuring, and estate planning.

George Gadkowski is an associate director in the corporate finance practice of Deloitte in Perth, Australia. He has an Honours Bachelor of Accounting degree and is a Chartered Accountant and a Chartered Business Valuator. George joined the Australian practice in 2008, after spending approximately four years in Deloitte's financial advisory group in Toronto, Canada. He has extensive valuation experience in providing services to both private and public companies in connection with mergers and acquisitions, corporate restructuring, income tax planning and financial reporting under Canadian GAAP, U.S. GAAP and IFRS. He has provided valuation services across a number of industries, including mining and resources, financial services, real estate, technology, consumer business and manufacturing.

Paul Gill, CA, CPA, CBV, ASA, is a senior manager in the valuation services practice of KPMG in Toronto, Canada, where he specializes in public and private company valuations and financial modeling engagements. Paul has significant experience in the preparation of purchase price allocations, valuations of intangibles, testing for the impairment of goodwill and other intangibles/long-lived assets for financial reporting purposes, providing fairness opinions for publicly listed issuers in Canada and the US, valuations for employee share purchases, shareholder disputes, transfer pricing issues, and valuations for tax filings with the Canada Revenue Agency and the Internal Revenue Service. Paul is also a member of the Professional Practice Committee of the Canadian Institute of Chartered Business Valuators.

George H.R. Goldsmith, BSc, MBA, CA, is President of Rosmir Capital Corp., a private holding company involved in the medical products, mining and financial services sectors (insurance merchant banking and corporate finance advisory activities). An expert in sophisticated applications of insurance, George has pioneered the creative use of life insurance products in both corporate and individual scenarios. A published author on a broad range of financial topics, George consults with government and quasi-government entities on matters relating to fiduciary and pension liability management.

Ian Haigh is a Senior Manager at Deloitte and has over 37 years of international experience in the real estate industry, primarily in the fields of valuation and consultancy. In Canada, he has advised many government departments (including Transport Canada, Ontario Realty Corporation, Hydro One, Public Works and Government Services Canada and the Ontario Ministry of Natural Resources) major financial institutions, multi-national corporations and privately owned companies. Ian's area of expertise is the financial analysis and valuation of traditional real estate investments such as offices, retail buildings, industrial complexes, residential and recreational properties as well as a wide range of other special use properties such as hospitals, nursing homes, airports, transportation corridors, military bases, etc.. He is a Member of The Royal Institution of Chartered Surveyors (MRICS) and an Accredited Appraiser of the Canadian Institute (AACI).

Péter Harbula is Executive Director of Corporate Finance at Accor Services, a division of Accor Group. Péter is the Vice President of the Valuation Commission of the French Association of Financial Analysts and a member of the French Society of Appraisers. He holds a PhD degree from the Paris II University in Business Administration, a Master of Sciences degree in Business Administration from the Budapest University of Sciences and a Master in Banking and Financial Techniques from the Paris II Assas University. Péter is as Accredited Senior Appraiser (ASA) with the American Society of Appraisers. He is the author of various articles in the field of corporate finance and corporate governance and a lecturer at the HEC business school in France.

Dr. Jamal Hejazi is a senior member of the Gowlings Transfer Pricing and Competent Authority team. Working in conjunction with the Firm's National Tax Practice Group, Jamal helps organizations optimize their global tax position and reduce exposure to unfavorable audit assessments through proper tax planning and implementation strategies. He has been involved in work for a number of industries including automotive, pharmaceutical, energy, computer software and manufacturing. He also specializes in intangible valuation and has done work for both the technology and biochemical sectors. Prior to joining Gowlings, Jamal was a senior transfer pricing economist with the Canada Revenue Agency, where he participated in the resolution of a number of transfer pricing issues and was instrumental in the negotiation of Advanced Pricing Agreements between Canada and foreign tax authorities. Jamal has also held a faculty position at the University of Windsor and was a lecturer at Carleton University. He is currently a faculty member at the University of Phoenix where he teaches various courses in economics. Jamal is published widely in leading tax journals and is also a published author.

Dale Hill is the national leader of Gowling Lafleur Henderson LLP's Transfer Pricing and Competent Authority team. As a Partner in the Ottawa office, he works in conjunction with the Firm's National Tax Practice Group to help organizations optimize their global tax position and reduce exposure to unfavourable audit assessments through proper tax planning and implementation strategies. Since 1997 and before joining Gowlings in 2005, Dale was involved in international transfer pricing with the Canada Revenue Agency ("CRA") where he participated in more than 40 Advanced Pricing Agreements with numerous countries, as well as hundreds of Competent Authority requests relating to international transfer pricing adjustments involving a vast array of issues. Dale has dealt with virtually every contentious transfer pricing issue when dealing with various tax authorities around the world including consignment manufacturing, permanent establishment and business restructuring issues. His work has spanned a multitude of industries including automotive, pharmaceutical, energy, computer software, gaming, manufacturing and services. Dale has published widely in leading tax journals and has been invited to speak at numerous conferences and seminars around the world.

Jacob B. Hirsh is a Doctoral Researcher in Psychology at The University of Toronto. His research has examined the use of psychological measures in performance prediction and techniques for improving the validity of personnel selection procedures. He is also a Senior Fellow at The Black Box Institute, where he provides a psychological perspective on business issues.

James L. Horvath, FCBV, ASA, CA, MBA, is a Managing Director with ValuQuest Limited. Prior to joing ValuQuest, Jim was a Partner with Deloitte (1988 to 2009). Over the past thirty-five years Jim has specialized in business and securities valuations and related intellectual property. Having completed over three thousand valuation assignments, including the supervision of large, complex multidiscipline valuation engagements, he has worked in a wide variety of industries and given expert testimony on valuation matters on multiple engagements. Jim also has extensive international experience, having worked on valuations, mergers, and acquisitions in over 60 countries. He has authored several books and numerous articles on valuation and, both in Canada and internationally, is a frequent speaker on valuation methods and issues. His recent publications as editor and principal author: *Valuing a Business in Volatile Markets* (Thomson Carswell, 2010); and as co-editor (with David W. Chodikoff) and contributing author include: *Taxation & Valuation of Technology* (Irwin Law, 2008) and *Advocacy & Taxation in Canada* (Irwin Law, 2004). Jim is also the author of *Valuing Professional Practices* (CCH International, 1990) and principal author (with Stanley Strychaz) of *Saylor Commercial Square Foot Building Costs* (1991-2010 editions).

Jeff Horvath is a Senior Consultant in Valuations and Dispute Consulting/ Financial Advisory for Deloitte (Toronto). He is a Chartered Accountant, holds an Honours Bachelor of Business Administration degree from Wilfrid Laurier University, and is a candidate for the Chartered Business Valuator designation. He has completed valuations for acquisition, divestiture, tax, financing, fairness opinion, and financial reporting purposes. Jeff has performed both domestic and international engagements in the technology, media, manufacturing and consumer business industries.

James A. Hutchinson, BA (Hons.), LLB, is a Partner and the Co-Chair of the Miller Thomson LLP tax group in Toronto. Jim's practice covers a full range of complex tax issues including corporate reorganizations, business succession planning, loss utilization, structuring mergers and acquisitions, executive compensation, and cross-border transactions. Jim is an expert in both domestic and international tax law. As a problem solver, Jim regularly resolves disputes on behalf of clients with the Canada Revenue Agency and provincial tax authorities. Jim is a sought after speaker and frequently he contributes chapters and articles on domestic and international tax issues to various tax publications.

Carla B. Iavarone is a Senior Manager in the Valuation Services practice of Deloitte Financial Advisory Services LLP in New York City. Carla has over eight years of experience in the valuation profession, with a particular expertise in the valuations of business enterprises, including private and publicly traded equity, debt securities, and intangible corporate assets. Carla has performed valuations of businesses, both domestic and international, ranging in size from small, closely held businesses to divisions of Fortune 500 companies. She has performed these appraisals in connection with strategic planning, mergers and acquisitions, corporate restructurings, division spin-offs, estate planning and tax planning. Carla has experience in serving national and multinational clients in a broad range of industries, with a concentration in the media and entertainment industries. She is a Candidate of the American Society of Appraisers (ASA) and holds a Bachelor of Business Administration, Finance, from Loyola College.

Peter Jarman is the President of Stoneset Equity Development Corp., a real estate development and investment company based in Calgary, Alberta. An entrepreneur and business leader since 1996, Peter developed a financial services company in 2003 with a client base of 1,400 clients and an agent team of over 50 agents. He continues to work with this team and with other financial consultants across Canada to develop programs to educate clients about the opportunities in real estate based investments. In 2006, Peter and two other partners established Stoneset, a company with real estate projects in residential, commercial, and recreation properties. The company has since listed on the Canadian National Stock Exchange and is developing key properties in Alberta and B.C., with offices in Calgary, Saskatoon, Toronto, and Singapore. Peter's experience includes origination of private offerings in debt and equity, property acquisition, management of mortgage investments, review and implementation of financial products, and development of training materials. Peter continues to lecture at national conferences for continuing education for financial advisors and publishes a newsletter for interested investment professionals.

Fahad Khan is a Manager in the Financial Advisory Services division in the Deloitte Dubai Office. He has over 4 years of experience in business valuations and financial modeling. Fahad has advised numerous clients in the MENA region and has worked extensively in the valuation of financial services institutions (commercial and investment banks). Prior to joining Deloitte, Fahad was working for a brokerage company in New Jersey, USA. Fahad has an MBA –Finance, from Oklahoma State University, USA and is a CFA charter holder.

John Kimpton, CFP, CLU, TEP, began his career in financial services in 1990, shortly after graduating from McMaster University in Hamilton. First starting in sales and building a private practice of his own, John moved into a technical role with a major life insurer in 2000 where he eventually lead a team of insurance specialists supporting the advanced estate, insurance, and tax-planning of a sales force of over 500 advisors. John joined BMO Nesbitt Burns in 2007 and enjoys working to provide technical planning support for advisors and clients of Nesbitt Burns and Harris Private Bank.

Mark Kirkey is a Certified General Accountant and senior member of the Gowlings Transfer Pricing and Competent Authority team. Working in conjunction with the Firm's National Tax Practice Group, Mark helps organizations optimize their global tax position and reduce exposure to unfavourable audit assessments through proper tax planning and implementation strategies. Working with clients, Mark develops strategic and defensible transfer pricing policies to reduce their level of audit controversy and maximize tax positions. His transfer pricing experience encompasses a broad range of industries including automotive, oil & gas, financial services, computer services, etc. Mark was formerly a senior analyst for the Canada Revenue Agency's International Tax Directorate. During his tenure with the CRA, he worked on over 100 Competent Authority cases and numerous Advanced Pricing Agreements. During his time with the CRA, Mark also served as a senior tax advisor, responding to complex technical questions from the CRA's field offices across Canada.

James M. Klotz is a Partner and Co-Chair of the International Business Transactions Group of Miller Thomson LLP, and is currently President of Transparency International Canada Inc. James is recognized as a leading international lawyer by *Canada's Best Lawyers* (2010) in international finance and international trade. He is the author of several books for lawyers including *Power Tools for Negotiating International Deals*, 2nd ed. (New York: Kluwer Law International, 2008) and *International Sales Agreements: A Drafting and Negotiating Guide*, 2nd ed.) (New York: Kluwer Law International, 2008). James is Chair-elect of the Bar Issues Commission of the International Bar Association (IBA), and Chair of its Policy Committee. He was previously Co-Chair of the IBA's International Sales Committee. He has served as a Divisional Chair of the American Bar Association's International Law Section, as Chair of its Canada Law Committee, and as a Vice-Chair of its Anti-Corruption Committee. He has also served as Chair of the International Law Section of the Canadian Bar Association (CBA), and of the Ontario Bar Association, and as Chair of the CBA's International Development Committee. He teaches international business law as an adjunct professor of international law at Osgoode Hall Law School in Toronto, where he received his LLB in 1982. He is admitted to practice in Ontario, England, and Wales and speaks both French and Mandarin.

Greg Knudsen began his career at a boutique investment firm in Toronto. During the summer of 2009, Greg successfully transferred his business to CIBC Wood Gundy, to become a member of a larger team, "The Knudsen Brady Vaughan Advisory Group". He is a second generation investment advisor, operating a successful practice centered on alternative investment strategies. Historically, despite popular opinion, alternative investment strategies or "hedge funds" have reduced volatility, thus reducing the emotional strain associated with investing, preserving investors' "mental capital". As an advisor, Greg realized one thing above all else, control of emotion is paramount to investor success. When not in the office, Greg can be found spending time with family at the cottage, or playing golf.

Denis Kouroussis has a PhD in electrical and computer engineering. Denis's background not only spans the world of semi-conductors, EDA, and power electronics but also, on a personal level, that of automotive modifications and performance tuning. Denis has successfully designed and implemented solutions in low power design and developed algorithms for power grid verification with numerous publications in the subject in top conferences and journals. Denis's engineering career has spanned ATI/AMD, IBM Microelectronics and a few start-ups where he was responsible for managing the design of the companies' products. Denis's undergrad and Master's work was primarily focused on power electronics, motor control, and power distribution. Denis has followed the alternative energy market for the last 15 years and is looking forward to the future as governments and corporations are finally giving serious consideration to sustainable energy solutions. In 2006, Denis co-authored a peer reviewed paper in the Bulletin of Science, "Alternative Fuels in Transportation".

Huey Lee is a Vice President of the Reorganization Services group of Deloitte in Toronto. He leads consulting engagements, viability assessments, monitoring assignments and formal insolvency proceedings including bankruptcies, receiverships and court-appointed plans of arrangement. He advises lenders and investors on the performance of distressed companies and also assists management of underperforming companies to identify and resolve issues affecting financial performance. Huey is a Certified Management Accountant, Chartered Insolvency and Restructuring Professional and licensed Trustee in Bankruptcy. He also holds an MBA from Queen's University.

Jennifer Lee is a Senior Manager, Financial Advisory for Deloitte & Touche LLP. Previous to this role, Jennifer was a Senior Associate Director for a large Canadian Telecom company in Toronto, Canada; was an Associate within the Mergers & Acquisitions Group for a large US Telco in Hong Kong; and worked for a large US Consumer Electronics company in Stuttgart, Germany. She is also a key advisor to the Azerbaijan Microfinance Association where she has advised on the restructuring of the microfinance market in Azerbaijan and the Caucuses in Central Asia. She has authored an article in the Rotman School of Management entitled 'Restructuring the Azerbaijani Microfinance Market." Currently, Jennifer focuses on assisting clients on analyzing market trends through commercial due diligence. She advises clients on how to improve the overall performance of their organizations by understanding the impact of market trends on their business. Jennifer holds a BA from the University of Waterloo and a Masters of Business Administration from the University of Toronto's Rotman School of Business.

Carl Leung is a manager with the Ontario Teachers' Pension Plan (OTPP) where he is responsible for the valuations of the OTPP's private equity and venture capital investments. Carl is a past senior manager in the Valuation

Services practice of Deloitte LLP's Financial Advisory Services in Toronto, where he specializes in business and intangible asset valuations and dispute consulting services. Carl is a Chartered Accountant, Chartered Business Valuator, charterholder of Chartered Financial Analyst and Certified Management Accountant.

Carlos Arenillas Lorente is an economist who has developed his professional activity in the financial sector -both the public and private sectors - specifically in the securities and money markets over the last 28 years.Thus, he has been able to co-operate in and attend the transformation and modernization process of the financial markets during the last 28 years. Carlos worked for Citibank and SIAF and co-founded CIMD-Intermoney, a group with a range of financial service companies which gathers together a group of firms in the following industries: broker-dealer financial services, asset management funds, securitisation, valuation services and consulting as well as economic and financial analysis. He has also been Chairman of AMMI, the Spanish Association of Brokers in the Interbank Market and Chairman of SENAF, the Official Spanish Secondary National Debt Market. From 2004-2008 Carlos was Vice-Chairman of the Spanish Securities and Exchange Commission (CNMV). During that period, among other positions, he was Member of the Board of the Bank of Spain, Chairman of the Consulting Committee of the CNMV, Member of CESFI - the Spanish Committee for Financial Stability, Member of IOSCO's Technical and Executive Committees, Vice Chair of the European IOSCO Committee and Member of the Chairmen Committee of CESR, the Committee of European Securities Regulators. Carlos continues to collaborate with a variety of forums and publications as well, giving conferences and writing articles on financial market related matters.

Alexander Lourie is a Manager in the Valuation Services group of Deloitte's Financial Advisory practice (Toronto). Alex has been involved in several large-scale and complex valuation projects, including purchase price allocations, fairness opinions, litigation support and valuations for tax purposes. Clients served have included multinational corporations and small private companies in the real estate, manufacturing, mining, retail, new media and various other industries. Prior to joining the Valuation Services group in November 2006, Alex has served in Deloitte's Real Estate audit group, gaining real estate industry experience by serving companies involved in property ownership, management and development. Alex provided audit services to companies that reported under both Canadian and US GAAP. Alex obtained his Chartered Accountant designation in September 2006 and his Chartered Business Valuator designation in November 2008. He is a graduate of the Schulich School of Business at York University, Canada where he obtained a Bachelor of Business Administration in April 2003 and also studied a semester abroad at the Copenhagen Business School, Denmark.

Robert Low is a Partner in Deloitte's Financial Advisory practice, leading the Dispute Services practice in the GTA. A Chartered Accountant and Chartered Business Valuator, he has been involved exclusively in business valuations, financial litigation and related matters since 1978, acting on behalf of shareholders and other parties, including federal, provincial and municipal governments, regarding companies in diverse industries. Robert conducts business valuations for corporate reorganizations, fairness opinions, estate planning, expropriations, matrimonial disputes, mergers and acquisitions, shareholder agreements and disputes, and tax purposes. For litigation clients, he quantifies economic damages for cases involving disputes related to business operations, contract and commercial disputes, expropriation, intellectual property, international arbitration, professional and product liability and class actions. He has qualified as an expert witness in the Federal Court of Canada, various provincial superior courts and tribunals across Canada, and for international arbitration purposes. Robert has also acted as an arbitrator and mediator in commercial disputes.

Douglas McDonald is a Senior Partner with Deloitte (Toronto office). He is responsible for the management and execution of corporate finance engagements. Doug also leads Deloitte Canada's Consumer Business M&A team, and has executed numerous transactions in this market in Canada, the United States and Europe. Doug has specialized in providing corporate finance services for more than 20 years. His expertise includes structuring and executing merger and acquisition transactions, raising all forms of capital from both public and private capital markets, and assisting clients with the development of capital markets strategies. Doug has held senior positions in Canada and the United Kingdom during his career with major investment banking and professional services firms including Credit Suisse First Boston, Ernst & Young and CIBC. Doug graduated from the University of Western Ontario with an MBA in 1982 and received his Masters degree in Medical Physiology from the University of Manitoba in 1979.

Duncan McPherson is a principal at Deloitte and is the leader of the China valuation practice, having been with Deloitte in Hong Kong for fourteen years. He specializes in business and intangible asset valuation and has been involved in numerous projects across Asia in addition to Hong Kong and China. Duncan graduated with an M.A. (Hons) in Accountancy from the University of Aberdeen and is a member of the Institute of Chartered of Scotland and a Fellow of the Hong Kong Institute of Certified Public Accountants.

Maneesh Mehta co-founded The Black Box Institute last year, following a 19 year career at Deloitte. Maneesh has held a wide range of responsibilities, the most recent being M&A strategy and commercial due diligence, where he provided advisory services to private equity firms and strategic buyers. Prior to that he was the Deputy Managing Partner of Clients & Markets for Deloitte, including being the Chief Marketing Officer. Before that, Maneesh was Deputy Managing Partner of the Global Emerging Strategic Clients (ESC) program where he focused on growth organizations. Maneesh started his career with Deloitte in the Consulting division and was a founding member of the Toronto Braxton Associates strategy practice. Maneesh's expertise covers a range of functional areas, including strategy, marketing, and business operations. In particular, Maneesh has extensive experience in strategic analysis, market assessment, financial analysis, demand forecasting, and general business planning. A few of his clients are Ontera, Nortel, CCI Entertainment, IFC as well as various government agencies and regulators. Maneesh has recently completed his ICD DEP certification and sits on several not for profit Boards.

Craig Mills, BA (Hons.), LLB, is a Partner practicing commercial and insolvency litigation at Miller Thomson LLP. He acts for a broad range of clients including financial institutions, private corporations, insurance companies, and trustees in bankruptcy. Craig is involved in proceedings relating to debt collection, contract disputes, insurance defence, determining priorities between secured lenders, bankruptcy, insolvency, and debt restructuring. He has experience in insolvency and restructuring proceedings under the *Bankruptcy and Insolvency Act* and the *Companies' Creditors Arrangement Act* and has appeared in cases on the Commercial List and in Bankruptcy Court in connection with bankruptcies, receiverships, and proposals. Craig has appeared as counsel before the Ontario Superior Court of Justice, the Ontario Divisional Court, and the Ontario Court of Appeal. He has also been involved in numerous mediations and arbitrations. Craig strives to provide his clients with timely advice in order to ensure that they understand the legal process and the options available to them at each stage. He works proactively with his clients, working towards a just result.

Greg Miocic is a director in the Valuation Services practice of Deloitte Financial Advisory Services LLP (USA). He focuses on tangible asset valuation and fixed asset management for manufacturing and processing industries, with emphasis on the automotive and steel sectors. He also provides analyses of construction and fixed assets for construction litigation support, project planning and depreciation optimization through cost segregation services. Greg has extensive experience working in the engineering and construction industries, including four years of construction project field experience. He holds a B.S. degree in mechanical engineering from Point Park College and an M.B.A. from Robert Morris College.

Farouk Mohamed is a manager in Deloitte's valuations practice in the Greater Toronto Private Company Services group. During his time in the valuations practice, he has prepared valuation reports for clients in connection with mergers and acquisitions, fairness opinions, share capital reorganizations, goodwill and long-lived asset impairment testing, internal restructuring, tax and estate planning, and shareholder disputes. His primary industry experience includes technology, manufacturing, and alternative energy companies. He is a Chartered Accountant, CFA charter-holder, and is a candidate for the Chartered Business Valuator designation.

Miguel A. Molfino is a Partner with Deloitte in Argentina. He is the leader of the Valuation practice in Argentina and the LATCO organization and one of the members of the Global Valuation Executive Committee at Deloitte. He has specialized in business valuations for different purposes, and tangible and intangible assets valuations. Having completed over five hundred valuation assignments, including the supervision of large valuation engagements, he has worked in a wide variety of industries in all Latin America. He is a frequent speaker at different events and he is also leading Deloitte Corporate Finance office in Rosario.

Ben Moore is a Managing Director in the Financial Advisory Services of Deloitte in Dubai and leads the valuation practice of the MENA region. Over the last 12 years he has advised numerous clients in different sectors on valuation matters relating in a variety of contexts including: mergers and acquisitions, IPOs, corporate restructuring, regulatory compliance, fairness opinions, financial reporting, tax planning, expert determination and dispute resolution. Prior to moving to Dubai, Ben was with Deloitte in the U.K. Ben is an economics graduate from Exeter University and a qualified Chartered Accountant from the Institute of Chartered Accountants of England & Wales.

Michael Morrow is a Vice President and Director with Deloitte's Corporate Finance Advisory group in Toronto, Canada. Key roles and responsibilities include advising clients with respect to deal execution, and providing clients with innovative solutions and deal insight. Michael's experience includes acquisition and divestiture advisory, debt advisory, and complex financial modeling. Michael graduated from Wilfrid Laurier University with an Honours Bachelor of Business Administration. Michael holds a Chartered Accountant designation and a Chartered Financial Analyst designaton.

Gary Moulton is a Partner in the Financial Advisory group at Deloitte and leads the Forensic & Dispute Services practice in Toronto. He has over 25 years of experience as an investigative and forensic accountant and has led many high-profile financial investigations and litigation support assignments, both in Canada and abroad, in the corporate, public and not-for-profit sectors. He has been retained by police and prosecuting authorities and litigation lawyers on assignments involving employee fraud, management fraud, vendor fraud, fraudulent financial reporting, government grant abuse, bribery and corruption, tendering irregularities and other types of financial impropriety. He serves as the Immediate Past Chair of the Board of the Canadian Institute of Chartered Accountants' Alliance for Excellence in Investigative and Forensic Accounting which provides leadership to uphold the professional integrity, standards and pre-eminence of CA-designated specialists in forensic accounting. He has written extensively on forensic accounting and fraud detection, prevention and investigation issues, including a cover story in *CA Magazine* entitled *"Safe Disclosure"*, concerning whistle blowing and an article in *Canadian Government Executive* entitled *"Confronting Fraud and Unethical Behavior in Government"*. He was certified as a specialist in investigative and forensic accounting by the Canadian Institute of Chartered Accountants in 2000. He was elected as a Fellow of the Institute of Chartered Accountants of Ontario in 2009.

Mustafa Nazarali, CA, is a senior tax manager with Grant Thornton LLP, where he services owner-managed businesses, public corporations, partnerships, and individuals. Mustafa received his Bachelor of Commerce from Concordia University (1991) and Graduate Diploma in Public Accountancy (1997) from McGill University. Mustafa has completed his CICA In-Depth Tax Courses and is now a facilitator for the CICA tax courses. Mustafa has done a number of presentations, including presenting a paper at the Ontario Canadian Tax Foundation Conference (2007) on eligible dividends and tax planning for the owner-manager. Mustafa also seconded with the Canadian National Office of Grant Thornton LLP (2007 to 2009), providing support to the National Management Committee and to the National Clients Service Partners with respect to implementation of key firm initiatives, playing a key role in business planning, execution and monitoring, and planning and executing key firm meetings and events.

Krystle A. Ng-A-Mann, BA, LLB, is an Associate in the Tax Group at Miller Thomson LLP, where she is currently focusing on building a general tax practice in areas such as corporate tax, cross-border, and individual estate planning. Krystle's practice includes assisting in the structuring and implementing of various types of corporate and estate reorganizations, dispute resolution with the Canada Revenue Agency, advising on income tax matters associated with carrying on business in Canada, and other types of compliance under the Canadian *Income Tax Act*.

Stamos Nicholas is a Principal and the national leader of the Business Valuation practice of Deloitte Financial Advisory Services LLP (USA). He has more than 25 years of experience in providing valuation and financial valuation consulting services worldwide for the purposes of accounting, tax planning, financing, bankruptcy, litigation, mergers and acquisitions, and investment. Mr. Nicholas has particular experience in the valuation of intellectual property (i.e., patents, proprietary technology, trademarks, trade names, customer intangibles, copyrights, agreements,etc.). He has extensive experience serving national and multinational companies such as financial services, manufacturing, media/entertainment, natural resources, consumer businesses, technology and life sciences, among others. Additionally, Mr. Nicholas has supervised large, complex multidiscipline (real estate, machinery and equipment, and financial) valuation engagements and has performed several transfer pricing studies for multinational corporations. Stamos has been a formal speaker and presenter to many industry organizations and professional groups such as the American Society of Appraisers, Tax Executive Institute, Emerging Issues Task Force ("EITF") Advisor on Customer Relationships, Financial Executive Institute for Biosciences, Pharma Association, National Restaurant Association, New York State Society of CPAs, New Jersey State Society of CPAs, Deloitte Regional Bank Forum, Financial Executives International ("FEI") Committee Member on Business Combinations, and a Private Equity Valuation and Performance Reporting conference at Dartmouth Tuck School of Business.

Tomasz Ochrymowicz, CFA, ASA, Partner at Deloitte Central Europe with thirteen years of business valuation and transaction advisory experience. Tomasz leads the Deloitte's Central European valuation practice and has performed numerous valuations in various countries of Central and Eastern Europe. Tomasz experience includes 18 month secondment to the financial advisory group of Deloitte in Toronto.

Russell L. Parr, CFA, ASA, is President of IPRA, Inc. He is a consultant, lecturer, author and publisher focused on the valuation and management of intellectual property. Mr. Parr has completed complex consulting assignments involving the valuation and pricing of patents, trademarks, copyrights and other intangible assets. His opinions are used to accomplish licensing transactions, acquisitions, transfer pricing, litigation support, collateral-based financing, and joint ventures. Mr. Parr has also served as an expert witness regarding intellectual property infringement damages. Past assignments have included the valuation of the Dr. Seuss copyrights and the patent portfolio of AT&T. Mr. Parr has also conducted valuations and royalty rate studies for pharmaceuticals, semiconductor process and product technology, agricultural formulations, automotive battery technology, biotechnology, camera technology, chemical formulations, communications technology, computer software, cosmetics, consumer and corporate trademarks, drug delivery systems, flowers, incinerator feed systems, lasers, medical instrument technology, motivational book copyrights. Among Mr. Parr's many books are *Intellectual Property: Valuation, Exploitation and Infringement Damages*, *Royalty Rates for Licensing Intellectual Property*, and *Investing in Intangible Assets*, published by John Wiley & Sons. In addition, IPRA, Inc.

publishes three other books by Mr. Parr including *Royalty Rates for Technology, 4th edition, Royalty Rates for Pharmaceuticals & Biotechnology 6th edition* and *Royalty Rates for Trademarks & Copyrights, 3rd edition*. Mr. Parr holds a Bachelor of Science in Electrical Engineering and a Masters in Business Administration both from Rutgers University.

Zareer Pavri, President of Business Valuations & Strategy Inc. ("BVS Inc.") based in Toronto, is a Chartered Accountant (CA-Ont.) and a Chartered Business Valuator. He has specialized in business valuations since 1977, rendering opinions of value relating to mergers & acquisitions, corporate reorganizations, income tax and succession planning, shareholders' disputes and intellectual property, in a broad spectrum of industry. He has provided expert witness testimony with respect to value-related matters in the Ontario Court of Justice (General Division), authored several articles and spoken on topics relating to intellectual property and corporate share valuations.

Shannon P. Pratt, CFA, FASA, MCBA, MCBC, CM&AA, is a well-known authority in the field of business valuation and has written numerous books that articulate many of the concepts used in modern business valuation around the world. Shannon Pratt is Chairman and CEO of Shannon Pratt Valuations, Inc., a business valuation firm headquartered in Portland, Oregon. He is also a member of the board of directors of Paulson Capital Corporation, an investment banking firm that specializes in small cap IPOs. Over the last 35 years, he has performed valuation engagements for mergers and acquisitions, employee stock ownership plans (ESOPs), fairness opinions, gift and estate taxes, incentive stock options, buy-sell agreements, corporate and partnership dissolutions, dissenting stockholder actions, damages, marital dissolutions, and many other business valuation purposes. He has testified in a wide variety of federal and state courts across the country and frequently participates in arbitration and mediation proceedings. Dr. Pratt's professional recognitions include being designated a life member of the Business Valuation Committee of the American Society of Appraisers, a life member of the American Society of Appraisers, past chairman and a life member of the ESOP Association Advisory Committee on Valuation, a life member of the Institute of Business Appraisers, the Magna Cum Laude in Business Appraisal award from the National Association of Certified Valuation Analysts, and the distinguished service award of the Portland Society of Financial Analysts. He recently completed two three-year terms as trustee-at-large of the Appraisal Foundation. Dr. Pratt is the author of *Valuing a Business: The Analysis and Appraisal of Closely Held Companies,* 5th edition, available in 2007, and the co-author of *Valuing Small Businesses and Professional Practices,* 3rd edition, published by McGraw-Hill. He is the co-author with Roger Grabowski of the forthcoming *Cost of Capital: Applications and Examples,* available in 2008, the co-author with Jay Fishman and William Morrison of *Standards of Value,* author of *The Market Approach* *to Valuing Businesses,* 2nd edition, *Business Valuation Body of Knowledge, Business Valuation Discounts and Premiums,* and co-author with the Honorable David Laro of *Business Valuation and Taxes: Procedure, Law and Perspective,* all published by John Wiley & Sons, and *The Lawyer's Business Valuation Handbook,* published by the American Bar Association. He is also co-author of *Guide to Business Valuations,* 17th edition, published by Practitioners Publishing Company.

Steve Z. Ranot is a chartered accountant, chartered business valuator and a designated specialist in investigation and forensic accounting. He has a B. Comm. from the University of Toronto (1986), graduated from the Canadian Securities Course (1986), completed the Canadian Institute of Chartered Accountants 3-year In-Depth Income Tax course (1990) and won the bronze medal in the CBV membership entrance exam (1993). He was admitted to partnership at Marmer Penner Inc. in 1996. Mr. Ranot's practice consists of a wide range of litigation support, including income tax matters and business and securities valuation. Mr. Ranot has testified in court as an expert witness in matters of business valuation, quantification of pecuniary damages, quantification of income, and income tax.

B. Sridhar Rao is the Director of Corporate Finance at Deloitte Corporate Finance (Jakarta, Indonesia). He is qualified in Management and Finance from one of Asia'a premier business and management schools and is trained in business valuations from the New York Society of Security Analysts. Sridhar started his career in the real sector and graduated to be in senior management. Subsequently, he had a brief stint at the Capital Market Desk of Credit Suisse, Singapore and then became a senior corporate finance advisor at Arthur Andersen, Jakarta. He moved on to become an investment banker with a leading investment bank in Indonesia, where as the Head of Corporate Finance. He successfully placed numerous public offerings in the Indonesian capital market. His experience over the years has a proven track record in business valuations, corporate finance and other financial advisory services covering prominent Indonesian corporates, conglomerates and state owned enterprises in Indonesia. He has acclaimed success in corporate restructurings, mergers & acquisitions and deal structurings for placement in the capital market.

Robert F. Reilly is a managing director of Willamette Management Associates. Robert has been the principal analyst on over 2,000 valuations of businesses, business interests, and intellectual properties in virtually every industry and business sector. Robert holds an MBA in finance and a BA in economics, both from Columbia University. He is an Accredited Senior Appraiser in business valuation, a Certified Public Accountant/Accredited in Business Valuation, a Chartered Financial Analyst, a Certified Management Accountant, a Certified Business Appraiser, an Enrolled Agent, and an Accredited Tax Advisor. Robert has authored over 300 professional journal articles on valuation-related topics. He is the co-author or co-editor of numerous professional books, such as *Valuing a Business*, *Valuing Intangible Assets*, and *The Handbook of Business Valuation and Intellectual Property Analysis*. Robert has served as an editor and regular columnist for such publications as *Small Business Taxation*, *The Ohio CPA Journal*, *Business Valuation Review*, and *The Journal of Real Estate Accounting and Taxation*. He is currently an editor for the *ABI Journal* and he is the intellectual property editor for *Valuation Strategies*.

The Honourable Chief Justice Gerald J. Rip received a Bachelor of Arts in 1962 from Sir George Williams University (now Concordia University) in Montréal and a degree of license en droit "avec distinction" from the University of Montréal in 1965. He was admitted to the Bar of Québec in 1966 and to the Law Society of Upper Canada in 1973. In 1968, Chief Justice Rip started his career in tax litigation with the Department of Justice. In 1973, he joined the private sector with Soloway, Wright, Houston & Associates in Ottawa where he worked for 10 years. Chief Justice Rip has guest lectured on various aspects of tax law in law schools and universities across the country. He was appointed Judge of the Tax Court of Canada in July 1983 and Associate Chief Justice in September 2006. He was appointed Chief Justice on July 15, 2008.

Martin J. Rochwerg is a Tax Partner of Miller Thomson LLP. He specializes in estate planning and is the Co-chair of Miller Thomson's Tax Group. According to Euromoney's Best of the Best for 2010, Marty is one of the world's top 25 pre-eminent Trusts and Estates Practitioners. He is a member of the Board of Governors of the Canadian Tax Foundation. He is rated annually by L'expert as one of the most frequently recommended estate planning lawyers in Canada. Marty provides advice on personal tax planning, estate planning, and succession and family business. Marty also advises trustees and beneficiaries on estate, trust and charitable administration and dispute resolution, and corporate clients on tax minimization, reorganizations, and ownership regimes. Marty has particular expertise and extensive experience in multi-jurisdictional tax, trust, and estate issues. Marty is an adjunct professor at Osgoode Hall Law School York University, a post he has held since 1980 and he has also been the recipient of a distinguished teaching award. Marty is the Editor-in-Chief and co-author of *Miller Thomson on Estate Planning* (Toronto: Carswell, 2011).

Ronald Rodgers, BA LLB, FCSI, CIM, ChP Strategic Wealth, Vice-President, Investment Advisor, BMO Nesbitt Burns. Ron has been a successful investment advisor for the past 15 years. From 1979 until 1996, Ron was a practising lawyer specializing in securities and banking law. Ron was the former General Counsel, Citibank Canada and President, Citibank Canada

Securities. In his spare time, Ron can be seen skiing the major, world back-country peaks. He is also known to be a BBQ afficionado and a lover of fine Scotches and good cigars.

Nick Sauro, CA, CMA, CPA, MBA, Hons. BComm, is Chief Financial Officer for Valiant Machine & Tool Inc. He directs and supervises a staff of seven divisional and corporate controllers in a multinational reporting environment with operations in Austria, Germany, Belgium, India, United States, and Canada. Nick also manages and negotiates terms and conditions for the banking facilities in North America and in Europe. Prior to 2001, Nick was a financial consultant providing business advisory services and finance and investment banking advisory services in both Canada and the USA. His consulting services included profit enhancement, debt restructuring, alternative financing solutions, accounting assurance, and compilation of financial business plans. Nick began his career in 1983 as a CA articling student at Price Waterhouse.

Claudio R. Saverino, CA, is a senior manager with Grant Thornton LLP specialized in taxation. Claudio services a broad range of clients such as owner-managed businesses, public corporations, partnerships, and individuals. Claudio received his Bachelor of Commerce degree from the University of Toronto (1996) and completed the CICA In-Depth Tax Courses (2001). Claudio currently facilitates at the CICA In-Depth Tax Courses and has instructed at the ICAO School of Accountancy. Claudio has done numerous presentations on various tax topics and has been quoted in The Graphic Arts Magazine.

Malgorzata Stambrowska is Assistant Director in the Corporate Finance team of PricewaterhouseCoopers in Poland. She is a valuations specialist with ten years' experience in the corporate finance teams of PwC and Deloitte in Poland and the United Kingdom. Malgorzata has advised clients on various aspects of valuations, particularly with reference to business valuations for transaction purposes, purchase price allocations for business combinations as well as valuations for income tax purposes.

Eli Swirsky was born in Israel, and raised in Ramat Gan. Eli received his high-school education at *Carmel College* in England, where he excelled in both sports and academic studies. Carmel College reinforced the values of hard work, charity, and social responsibility which Eli first learned at home, and which he adheres to today. After his army service in Israel, Eli worked for one year in the computer department of the *Israeli Military Industries*, igniting his interest in computers. He then moved to Canada where his parents had resettled, and he studied computer science at York University. Eli joined his father's development company, *Torgan*, named for the two cities his family had resided in –Toronto and Ramat-Gan –and, in 1981, he married Joanne. In 1983, Eli joined forces with Shlomo Cohen, founding

The Torgan Group. Eli's excellent entrepreneurial skills and Shlomo's brilliant background in engineering were a winning combination, and their business flourished. Eli is the proud father of four children, Jonathan, Ben, Jack, and Liyana.

Edwina Tam, CBV, is an Associate Director, Valuation Services, with Deloitte China. She joined the Hong Kong in 2009 after working in the valuation group of Deloitte's Toronto office since 2006. Edwina specializes in business and intangible asset valuations and corporate reorganization for both public and privately held entities involving mergers and acquisitions, strategic planning, financial statement reporting, and tax reorganization. Edwina has worked on several significant valuation engagements in various industries including financial services, insurance, healthcare, retail food, alternative power, retail pharmacy, and newspaper publishing.

Stanley M. Tepner, MBA, CA, CFP, TEP, is First Vice President and has been an Investment Advisor at CIBC Wood Gundy (and predecessor companies) since 1991. Prior to that, he worked for over a decade at public accounting firms, primarily in the income tax practice. Stan heads a five-member team of financial professionals that provides tax-efficient investment, income, and estate planning solutions to affluent Canadian business owners, professionals, and their families. A longstanding member of his firm's prestigious Chairman's Council, Stan has also been a prolific contributor of financial knowledge to the Canadian public through countless articles, interviews, and broadcast appearances. He is the immediate past Chair of the Board of Directors of the Hearing Foundation of Canada.

Les Trojniak, CFP®, FMA, DMS, FCSI, specializes in Investment Management and Portfolio Risk Analysis. Les designs and implements investment strategies for clients with precise risk vs. reward measures. Les began his career over a decade ago managing private family funds and corporate accounts. His strong belief in providing unbiased advice along with access to the entire continuum of asset classes led him to partner with an independent IDA member firm where his sole focus is money management. Les's formal education includes a Bachelor of Science (specialization in Genetic Engineering) as well as both the CERTIFIED FINANCIAL PLANNER® (CFP®) professional and the Financial Management Advisor (FMA) designations. Most importantly, Les is a qualified Derivatives Market Specialist (DMS). Les is also a fellow of the Canadian Securities Institute. Les regularly conducts educational seminars for industry professionals on risk management with derivatives. Les serves his community as a member of the advisory board of CHIP CHARITY. In his free time, he spends time with his wife and three children, playing soccer, golf, fine woodworking and, of course, reading research reports and exciting company financials!

Steven Tseng is the Asia Pacific Leader of Global Transfer Pricing Services (GTPS) for KPMG's network of firms and Partner-in-Charge of GTPS for KPMG in China. He leads over 200 transfer pricing specialists in China and 450 in the Asia Pacific region. He holds both an AB and MBA from Dartmouth College. He has been actively advising multinational companies on transfer pricing issues since 1994. Steven's transfer pricing career included experience in the US, Japan, Nordic region and he has been working on transfer pricing in China since 2005. Steven is a frequent public speaker and contributor of articles on transfer pricing and related subjects. An Accredited Senior Appraiser (ASA) of the American Society of Appraisers, Steven is also an active member of the American Chamber of Commerce in Shanghai, and has conducted several technical trainings on transfer pricing for tax authorities in the region. International Tax Review has recommended Steven as a leading transfer pricing adviser in China.

Andrew D. Valentine, BA (Hons.), LLB, is an Associate in the Charities and Not-for-Profits Group in the Toronto office of Miller Thomson LLP. Andrew's practice focuses on providing advice to charities and non-profit organizations on a full range of issues, including gift planning, incorporation and registration, ongoing compliance matters, and audits. He has assisted in several litigation matters involving charity law issues, including at the Federal Court of Appeal and the Supreme Court of Canada. Andrew has authored and co-authored several articles in the area of charities law.

Jordan Waldman graduated from York University in June 2005 with an Honours Bachelor of Arts degree in Business and Society focusing on economics and sociology. After working in numerous capacities with various financial companies, he has built a successful financial services business with Freedom 55 Financial. The main focus of his business is to help assist business owners and individuals with tax efficient investing as well as implementing proper risk management instruments.

Jiang Wei, PhD, is now a professor and the head of the Department of Finance at the Economics College of Shenyang University in China. He studied finance in Liaoning University where he obtained his Master's degree and Doctor's degree. Apart from giving lectures on money and banking in his department, he actively engages in appraisal and investment projects for local SOEs' and transnationals. Being a liaison officer r the international affairs of the China Appraisal Society (CAS) and a member of the Standing Council of Liaoning Provincial Appraisal Association, Jiang Wei has helped translate many documents from English into Chinese, including International Valuation Standards (IVS). As a consultant to the local government, he is frequently featured on television and in print media?

Richard M. Wise, FCA, FCBV, FASA, CA•IFA, CVA, is Managing Partner, Wise, Blackman LLP. Richard, a graduate of McGill University, is Past President and Fellow of The Canadian Institute of Chartered Business Valuators, former member of Council and a Fellow of the Order of Chartered Accountants of Quebec, Fellow of the Institute of Chartered Accountants of Ontario, Fellow and former International Governor of the American Society of Appraisers (ASA) and Vice-Chair of the ASA Practice Standards Committee. Richard writes and lectures extensively in both Canada and the U.S., is a frequent speaker at professional conferences. He is principal co-author of the 3-volume *Guide to Canadian Business Valuations* (Thomson Carswell) and author of *Financial Litigation – Quantifying Business Damages and Values*. He has testified before courts, arbitration panels, securities regulators and disciplinary boards of law societies as an expert in Business Valuation and related areas in over 190 cases across Canada and in the U.S. and has been appointed by the courts and arbitration panels as their valuation expert. Richard is a recipient of the Governor General's *Canada 125* medal.

Bill Zinger is the Chairman of the Kissner Group, a network of companies primarily involved in the manufacture and distribution of chemicals, salt products, and packaging equipment throughout North America and internationally. Bill has over 15 years experience in global supply chain management and manufacturing. His endeavours reflect an education in mechanical engineering and an initial career in sales. Bill spent 15 years in sales and marketing, including sales management and training, mainly in the office automation equipment industry with Xerox and Canon. The involvement with Kissner began in 1994 when Bill sought an undervalued company with significant growth prospects and purchased Kissner Milling, located in southwestern Ontario. Through organic divisional growth and mergers and acquisitions, Kissner grew continuously to become one of the leading manufacturers and distributors of its product lines in North America. Bill continues to expand his operation by acquiring or investing in related companies that offer promising growth opportunities. Today, the Kissner Group includes Kissner Fine Ingredients, Kissner Salts, Kissner De-Icing, Kissner Plastics, Kimbil Distribution, Blendtech, Magco USA, and Hydrant Resources.

Topical Index

Supply chain, 618-619, 644, 648, 744, 1032, 1040
Supply chain mismanagement, 619
Survey equity risk premium, 502
Sustaining capital reinvestment, 278-279, 629

Numerical

Other Books by James L. Horvath and David W. Chodikoff

David W. Chodikoff and James L. Horvath (eds. and contributing authors), *Valuing a Business in Volatile Markets*, 850-page text (Toronto: Thomson Carswell, 2010).

James L. Horvath and David W. Chodikoff (eds. and contributing authors), *Taxation & Valuation of Technology*, 1,004-page text (Toronto: Irwin Law, 2008).

David W. Chodikoff and James L. Horvath (eds. and contributing authors), *Advocacy and Taxation in Canada*, 738-page text (Toronto: Irwin Law, 2004).

James L. Horvath, Stanley Strychaz & Ian Haigh, *Commercial Square Foot Building Costs*, 2001 to 2010 editions, 279-page manual (annual) (Chatsworth, California: Saylor Publications, Inc.).

James L. Horvath, *Valuing Professional Practices*, 329-page text (Don Mills, Ontario: CCH Canadian Limited, 1990).

David Kerzner, Vitaly Timokhov & David Chodikoff, *The Tax Advisor's Guide to the Canada-U.S. Tax Treaty* (Toronto: Thomson Carswell, 2008).